SURVEY OF ACCOUNTING

James D. Stice, PhD
Brigham Young University

Earl K. Stice, PhD
Brigham Young University

W. Steve Albrecht, PhD, CPA, CIA, CFE
Brigham Young University

K. Fred Skousen, PhD, CPA
Brigham Young University

Monte R. Swain, PhD, CPA, CMA
(Consulting Editor)
Brigham Young University

SOUTH-WESTERN College Publishing

An International Thomson Publishing Company

Accounting Team Director: Richard Lindgren
Acquisitions Editor: Sharon Oblinger
Marketing Manager: Dan Silverburg
Developmental Editor: Leslie Kauffman
Production Editor: Mike Busam
Production House: Litten Editing and Production
Composition: GGS Information Services
Cover and Internal Design: Michael H. Stratton
Internal Icons: Julie Baker
Cover Photo: PhotoDisc
Preface Copywriter: Steve Mott, Words and Occasional Wisdom
Preface Design: Krista Wilmink, Insignia Design

I(T)P®

International Thomson Publishing
South-Western College Publishing is an ITP Company.
The ITP trademark is used under license.

ISBN: 0-538-846178
3 4 5 6 7 8 KT 5 4 3 2 1 0
Printed in the United States of America

Library of Congress Cataloging-in-Publication Data

Survey of accounting / James D. Stice . . . [et al.].
p. cm.
Includes index.
ISBN 0-538-84617-8
1. Accounting. I. Stice, James D.
HF5625.S87 1998
657--dc21 98-43289
CIP

BRIEF CONTENTS

see HOW, know WHY.

PREFACE 1E

While Safeway has the third largest sales of major supermarket chains, its sales today are down ten percent since 1986. But its current net income is higher than that of Kroger and American stores, which have higher sales volumes.

What does the Safeway experience tell us? It tells us that to truly comprehend what is going on in a business, whether in the grocery store or in the corporate boardroom, one must understand accounting data—both how it is prepared, and why it is meaningful.

The Language of Business

Understanding the numbers—it's the essence of business. Understanding what the numbers reveal, and what they cannot reveal, allows business managers and investors to make every type of business decision: expand, merge, close, launch, subcontract, downsize, invest, reposition, lease, replace. As the basis for all these decisions, accounting is the universal language of business.

Take, for instance, the case of Safeway, a major supermarket chain, as examined in the opening vignette of **Chapter 2: Financial Statements: An Overview.** In the last twenty years, Safeway has experienced, at various times, falling market share, challenging union demands, high overhead, significant job cuts, an aggressive construction and remodeling program, a leveraged buyout, and reintroduction of the firm as a public company.

A Proven Approach

During the past few years, there have been many calls for improving accounting education. The central themes in all these calls for change have been (1) that the business world and accounting professions are changing rapidly, (2) that accountants of the past must become the premier information professionals of the future, and (3) that accounting and business graduates need new skills and knowledge if they are to effectively meet tomorrow's professional demands. These are significant changes. As one person said, "There is a bulldozer of change moving across America and

"Accounting is the universal language of business."

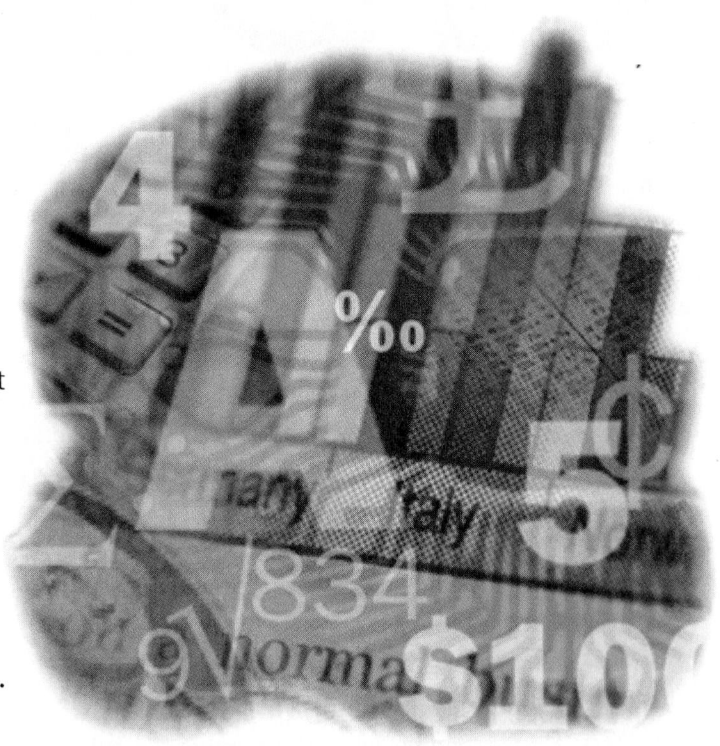

if you are not part of the bulldozer, you will be part of the road."

In creating this textbook, we were very sensitive to these calls for change. Much of our basis for writing this text has come through our experience developing and deploying the innovative accounting curriculum at Brigham Young University, an original grant recipient from the Accounting Education Change Commission (AECC). While constantly looking for ways to improve the program, we consider the BYU accounting program to be a success. Employers seem to agree, creating great demand for graduates.

Our purpose here is not to extol the strengths of BYU's program. Rather we wish to share what we learned in the process of improving that program. We learned a great deal about the needs of business, both within and beyond the accounting profession, about the way students prefer to learn, and about the way instructors prefer to teach. **Survey of Accounting** embodies the lessons we learned. It is written and organized in a manner that allows students and instructors at all institutions to capitalize on our positive curriculum development experience.

'How' Means Nothing Without 'Why'

Students taking their first accounting course need to understand the basics of accounting, regardless of their future career plans. Most will be users of accounting information rather than preparers, but even users need to understand the essentials of accounting. And those who plan to pursue the field as a career need a strong foundation upon which to build. Emphasis in **Survey of Accounting** is on the "why" as well as the "how." As such, it provides a proper balance between conceptual understanding and procedural training.

This text is intended to be the most innovative, interesting, and understandable introductory accounting text on the market. It provides an appropriate mix between financial and management accounting topics.

Our approach to this book is to introduce students to basic accounting concepts, excite them by using lots of real world examples (both U.S. and international), provide them with some basic accounting knowledge, and then show them how accounting is used and analyzed in actual case situations. This book does not take an encyclopedic approach to every possible nuance of financial statement preparation or alternative way to perform accounting functions. We know that the few students who desire that level of detail will find it in more advanced classes.

Focus on Business Activities–Financial Accounting

Every company, regardless of its industry or type, must manage its business to acquire and sell products or services, make financing decisions, and invest in assets that will help the company generate growth and income. In this book, we use an organizational format that is consistent with business activities and cycles (as opposed to the more traditional financial statement organization). Specifically, after introducing and explaining financial reporting and the accounting cycle in Part 1 (Chapters 1-3), we discuss the operating activities of a business in Chapters 4-5 and the investing and financing activities in Chapters 6-7. We conclude the financial portion of the text by discussing the statement of cash flows in Chapter 8. This focus on business activities helps students understand functions of business and see accounting as a tool to assist in making business decisions, not as an end in itself.

The Full Perspective–Management Accounting

In our discussion of management accounting, we emphasize both a process and a strategic issues view. The process view considers the **planning**, **controlling**, and **evaluating** that are contained in most management accounting texts.

The strategic issues view, in contrast, considers how organizations must compete on issues of **quality** and **timeliness**, not just on price (i.e., **cost**). The traditional focus on cost opens doors for competitors, especially international competitors, to distinguish their product in other ways, thereby earning market share. This creates a new challenge for accounting–*balancing* quality and time information with traditional cost measures. Simply appending chapters to the end of the text to address these issues is not sufficient.

This text reflects the reality that the traditional **manufacturing** view in accounting is inadequate today. The growing importance of **merchandising** and **service** markets requires students to be conversant in issues relevant to all three. Hence, this book contains extensive discussions of merchandising companies and service firms. In addition, all management accounting chapters have been revised to incorporate important issues common to all three or specific to each.

show HOW, explain WHY.

Consider the following features:

Special Margin Features

FYI features provide relevant information for students, drawing from real business events or situations.

STOP&THINK Students are encouraged to take a step back occasionally to consider thought-provoking issues.

CAUTIONS These reminders speak directly to students, helping them avoid common mistakes or misconceptions.

NET WORK exercises give students practice in seeking out information on the Internet.

LEARNING OBJECTIVES

SETTING THE STAGE

BUSINESS ENVIRONMENT ESSAYS

KEY TERMS

SUMMARIES

REVIEW PROBLEMS

FOCUS ON GLOBAL ECONOMY

FOCUS ON ETHICS

This text connects to business with the use of many insightful pedagogical features and real-world examples. As real companies and current events are examined, the focus is not only on how business managers collect and record data, but also why the information is important as the basis for decisions. Microsoft's annual report is provided at the end of the text and referenced throughout.

Each chapter begins with specific learning objectives to guide students in their study of the chapter.

An interesting, real-life scenario sets the stage for each chapter. These scenarios tie directly to materials covered in the chapter and help students relate chapter topics to actual business happenings.

The text contains numerous real-world vignettes, adapted from financial newspapers and business publications, that illustrate important concepts being discussed. These examples enable students to see how the accounting topics they are studying are applied and interpreted in real-world situations.

Throughout each chapter, key terms are defined in the margins. A list of key terms (with page references) is presented at the end of each chapter, and all key terms are defined in a comprehensive glossary at the end of the book.

Several concise summaries are presented within each chapter to help students remember the important points just discussed, and each chapter concludes with a comprehensive summary, organized by learning objectives.

A review problem is provided at the end of each chapter (where applicable). These review problems (with solutions) demonstrate the application of the major concepts and procedures covered in the chapter.

As mentioned, the focus in today's business world is on a global economy. To help students develop this global perspective, many international examples are provided throughout the text. In addition, there is at least one International Case provided at the end of each chapter.

Ethical considerations are increasingly important in all aspects of business. A section in Chapter 1 introduces the topic of ethics and emphasizes its importance in modern business. Each chapter contains an Ethics Case relating to the topics covered in the chapter. These cases present ethical dilemmas that require students to think about behavioral and moral issues in business and accounting. We believe these ethics cases will provide a basis for rich classroom discussions and more responsible business conduct by students exposed to them.

Practice How, Analyze Why: End-of-Chapter Material

Like most introductory texts, this book has all the traditional end-of-chapter assignments. Before describing the traditional material, however, we want you to understand our excitement for the "Competency Enhancement Opportunities" (CEO) that are included in the end-of-chapter material. Responding to well-justified calls for changes in accounting education, this new material is included to help students develop critical thinking, ethical perspectives, oral and written communication skills, experience with electronic research, and team skills.

In each chapter's assignments, the CEO section begins with **Analyzing Real Company Information** exercises, based on actual company annual reports and data. CEO also includes:

- **International cases**, focusing on businesses that operate across international borders
- **Ethics cases**, examining issues of personal and business responsibilities
- **Writing assignments**, to be completed individually or in groups
- **Debates**, requiring two teams to argue the opposing sides of an accounting issue
- **Internet search exercises**, requiring students to find specific information on the Net

We believe students will find these assignments very relevant, interesting, and beneficial in their business careers.

The discussion questions are intended to refine students' understanding of specific accounting terms and concepts. The discussion cases encourage classroom discussion of real-world business situations. Exercises deal with single concepts, and each can be completed fairly quickly. Problems probe for a deeper level of understanding. Those problems identified as "Unifying Concepts" and those with "Interpretive Questions" require students to analyze or interpret the computed results.

Modem Art

Technology is allowing—even forcing—business to be conducted in new and different ways. E-mail will soon be as ubiquitous as the phone and the fax. Millions of business transactions are conducted via the Internet each day. Web-based retailers such as bookseller Amazon.com and on-line financial service firms like E-trade have changed the entire customer contact model. Data stored in computer databases is often a firm's most valuable asset. In short, managers in every industry, from paving to publishing, must capitalize on the power of technology to keep pace with the expectations of their customers and the efforts of their competitors.

Technology's potential impact on accounting education is equally dramatic. Educators now have the opportunity to bring more information to students in more media than ever before. **Survey of Accounting** takes full advantage of these possibilities with a broad technology package:

- Comprehensive software supplements (see ancillaries section)
- NetWork and Internet Search Exercises in each chapter, directing students to various web resources to find solutions
- Virtual Community Web site at: **stice.swcollege.com**

Access Microsoft's Web site at microsoft.com. Identify the different kinds of information found on Microsoft's home page, e.g., marketing, product information, etc.

Can you find any financial information?

www.microsoft.com

FEATURING:

• **The Resource Source** – This is where you will find the tools to take your course to the next level. Organized by chapter and topic, this hyperlinked syllabus offers PowerPoint™ slides, the Instructor's Manual, the Solutions Manual, relevant *Inc.* articles and recaps, software resources, and much more. A quick and easy registration process opens the door to special restricted material for text adopters.

• **The Community Commons** – Consider this your own town square. This is the place to share information and exchange tips with other instructors. Compare notes through discussion forums, learn how other instructors make the most of the Internet, subscribe to accounting-oriented listservs, or contact the authors or editors directly.

• **The Reserve Room** – This student resource provides additional study tools, available 24 hours a day. Here students have free access to hyperlink demo problems, Frequently Asked Questions, downloadable spreadsheet templates, and an online study guide. Organized by chapter, this page is extremely student-friendly.

• **The Reference Room** – Students click links here to access academic tips, financial research, newspapers and business periodicals, accounting firm sites, tax information and tools, and a variety of career and job search resources. Check the Reference Room for *The Wall Street Journal*, CNNfn, *American Employment Weekly,* and much more.

• **The Bookstore** – Students visit this page to conveniently order supplements at substantial discounts.

SUPPLEMENTS

This textbook is part of a comprehensive and carefully prepared educational package that offers various forms of assistance to both instructors and students. Each of the supplementary items available for use with the text is described briefly on the following pages.

ancillary MATERIALS

AVAILABLE TO INSTRUCTORS

ITP is committed to providing you, our educational partners, with the finest educational resources available. Because we prepare our instructor resources with a variety of teaching environments in mind, it is likely that you will need only a portion of these for your course. Before you request an item, we ask that you please read thoroughly the description of each resource. If you still need more information about resources, we urge you to contact your local ITP sales representative or visit our Web site at stice.swcollege.com. Many teaching and learning resources can be downloaded directly from this site.

Solutions Manual (Prepared by Jim Stice and Kay Stice)
This manual contains independently verified answers to all end-of-chapter discussion questions, discussion cases, exercises, problems, and Competency Enhancement Opportunities (CEO). Suggested solutions to the Stop & Think questions are also included.

Instructor's Manual (Prepared by David Cottrell, Brigham Young University)
This manual contains learning objectives, chapter outlines, topical overviews of end-of-chapter materials, and assignment classifications with level of difficulty and estimated completion time. Transparency masters for each chapter are also provided.

Test Bank (Prepared by Leslie Turner, Northern Kentucky University)
The test bank contains a collection of examination problems, multiple-choice questions, true-false questions, and matching exercises, all accompanied by solutions.

Computerized Test Bank
A computerized version of the test bank is available in Windows format.

Solutions Transparencies
Acetate transparencies of solutions for all end-of-chapter exercises and problems are available to text adopters.

PowerPoint™ Slides (Prepared by David Cottrell, Brigham Young University)
Selected teaching transparency slides of key concepts and exhibits are available in PowerPoint presentation software, improving lecture organization and reducing preparation time.

Virtual Community: Online with South-Western stice.swcollege.com
Organized by chapter and topic, this hyperlinked syllabus includes text-specific and other accounting-related resources. We invite you to be part of this community by sampling what we've provided and by sharing your own material, ideas, and comments with your colleagues and students. Visit our discussion forum and exchange information on current developments in the profession, and share ideas on the course and curriculum.

BusinessLink Videos
Two videos, one for financial accounting and one for management accounting, feature segments of actual companies illustrating key accounting concepts. Instructor's Manuals are available to assist in the use of the videos and the optional student workbooks.

AVAILABLE TO STUDENTS

Study Guide (Prepared by Jim Stice and Kay Stice)
The study guide provides a means for students to re-examine the concepts and procedures in each chapter from several different perspectives. This publication includes learning objectives; detailed chapter summaries; discussions of topics that typically cause problems for students and suggestions for overcoming those problems; and tests for student self-assessment.

Working Papers
Forms for solving end-of-chapter exercises and problems are perforated for easy removal and use.

Homework Assistant and Tutor (HAT) Software (Prepared by Ray Meservy, Brigham Young University)
This user-friendly software for Windows visually teaches the relationships among journals, ledgers, and financial statements. A built-in tutor function offers numerous hints and help screens. The software can be used to solve selected end-of-chapter exercises and problems, identified with the HAT icon. It is also an ideal teaching aid.

Spreadsheet Templates (Prepared by Leslie Turner, Northern Kentucky University)
Lotus 1-2-3 and Excel templates are provided for solving selected end-of-chapter exercises and problems, which are identified with the spreadsheet icon. Unlike traditional templates, these spreadsheets are colorful, interactive, and intuitive, many with the capability of performing "what-if" analysis.

BusinessLink™ Video Workbooks
These workbooks enrich understanding of the BusinessLink videos through questions and related activities.

acknowledgements

Throughout the textbook, relevant publications of standard-setting and professional organizations are discussed, quoted, or paraphrased. We are indebted to the American Accounting Association, the American Institute of Certified Public Accountants, the Financial Accounting Standards Board, and the Institute of Management Accountants for material from their publications.

Survey of Accounting reflects many comments and suggestions from colleagues and students, all of which are deeply appreciated. In particular, we wish to thank the following accounting educators who have served as reviewers and focus group participants:

Sheila Ammons Austin Community College **Florence McGovern** Bergen Community College

Jill M. Bale Doane College **Susan B. Murphy** Aquinas College

Linda Brown St. Ambrose University **Gale E. Newell** Western Michigan University

Irel Clendenon Franklin University **Bill Potts** University of Wisconsin-Platteville

Sandra W. Easton Northern Kentucky University **Mike Ruble** Western Washington University

Vicky J. Eidson Culver-Stockton College **Paul Schloemer** Northern Kentucky University

Rob Faulkner St. Ambrose University **Bill Smith** Xavier University

Paquita Davis Friday University of Notre Dame **Sarah Smith** Cedarville College

Hubert W. Gill University of North Florida **Leonard Stokes** Siena College

Dell Ann Janney Culver-Stockton College **Leslie Turner** Northern Kentucky University

Cynthia Jeffrey Iowa State University **Dan Wyatt** Columbus State Community College

We would like to thank Sheila Ammons, Austin Community College, and Alice Sineath, Forsyth Technical Community College, who served as verifiers for the test bank and study guide, respectively. We would also like to thank Marisa Rollins Skousen, Brigham Young University, for help in manuscript preparation.

Jim Stice
Kay Stice
Steve Albrecht
Fred Skousen

about THE AUTHORS

The Right Team

Authors James D. Stice, W. Steve Albrecht, and K. Fred Skousen are all key players in the curriculum change process at BYU. Kay Stice, formerly a professor at Hong Kong University of Science and Technology, brings an international dimension to the book. Monte Swain, an outstanding young professor of management accounting, served as a consulting editor to bring currency and relevance to the rapidly changing management accounting chapters. Individually and as a team, we feel passionately about making this the most relevant and useful book you will ever use.

James D. Stice

James D. Stice is an Associate Professor in the School of Accountancy and Information Systems at Brigham Young University. He holds bachelor's and master's degrees from BYU and a Ph.D. from the University of Washington, all in accounting. Dr. Stice has been on the faculty at BYU since 1988. During that time, he has been selected by graduating accounting students as "Teacher of the Year" on numerous occasions, and he was selected by his peers in the Marriott School of Management at BYU to receive the "Outstanding Teaching Award" in 1995. In 1996, he was selected by BYU to receive a "University Young Scholar" fellowship. Dr. Stice has published articles in *The Accounting Review, Decision Sciences, Issues in Accounting Education, The CPA Journal*, and other academic and professional journals. He is also co-author on *Intermediate Accounting*, 13th edition, and *Accounting: Concepts and Applications*, 7th edition. Jim and his wife, Kaye, have seven children: Crystal, J.D., Ashley, Whitney, Kara, Skyler, and Cierra.

Earl K. Stice

Earl K. Stice is a Professor of Accounting in the School of Accountancy and Information Systems at Brigham Young University. He holds bachelor's and master's degrees from Brigham Young University and a Ph.D. from Cornell University. Dr. Stice has taught at Rice University, the University of Arizona, Cornell University, as well as a three-year term at the Hong Kong University of Science and Technology (HKUST). He won the Phi Beta Kappa teaching award at Rice University, and was twice selected at HKUST as one of the ten best lecturers on campus. He has published papers in the *Journal of Financial and Quantitative Analysis, The Accounting Review*, and *Issues in Accounting Education*, and his research on stock splits has been cited in *Business Week, Money*, and *Forbes*. Dr. Stice has presented his research results at seminars in the United States, Finland, Taiwan, Australia, and Hong Kong. He is co-author on *Intermediate Accounting*, 13th edition, and *Accounting: Concepts and Applications*, 7th edition. Kay and his wife, Ramona, are the parents of five children: Derrald, Han, Ryan Marie, Lorien, and Lily.

W. Steve Albrecht

W. Steve Albrecht is the Arthur Andersen & Co. Alumni Professor of Accountancy and the Associate Dean of the Marriott School of Management at Brigham Young University. He received a bachelor's degree in accounting from Brigham Young University and MBA and Ph.D. degrees from the University of Wisconsin

MORE about THE AUTHORS

at Madison. Dr. Albrecht, a certified public accountant, certified internal auditor, and certified fraud examiner, came to BYU in 1977 after teaching at Stanford and at the University of Illinois. Earlier in his career, he worked as a staff accountant for Deloitte & Touche. Dr. Albrecht has received numerous awards and honors, including the BYU School of Management's Outstanding Faculty Award, the BYU Outstanding Researcher Award, and was recognized, as part of Utah's Centennial Celebration, as one of 131 Utahians who have made outstanding contributions or brought unusual recognition to the state. Dr. Albrecht is Past-President of the American Accounting Association and has served as President of Administrators of Accounting Programs. Dr. Albrecht has done extensive research on white-collar crime and business fraud. His research has resulted in the publication of over eighty articles in professional journals. He is the author or co-author of 16 books or monographs, including *Intermediate Accounting,* 13th edition, and *Accounting: Concepts and Applications,* 7th edition. Dr. Albrecht is married and has six children and two grandchildren.

K. Fred Skousen

K. Fred Skousen is Advancement Vice President at Brigham Young University. Previously, he was Dean of the Marriott School of Management and Director of the School of Accountancy at BYU. He earned a bachelor's degree from BYU and master's and Ph.D. degrees from the University of Illinois. Dr. Skousen taught at the University of Illinois and the University of Minnesota prior to joining the faculty at Brigham Young University. In 1983, Dr. Skousen was awarded the Peat Marwick Professorship at BYU. In 1984, Dr. Skousen was elected to the AICPA Council, and in 1985, he received the UACPA Outstanding Faculty Award. Dr. Skousen has been a consultant to the Financial Executive Research Foundation, the Controller General of the United States, the Federal Trade Commission, and to several large companies. He currently serves on the Board of Directors of several corporations. Dr. Skousen is the author or co-author of more than 50 articles, research reports, and books, including *Intermediate Accounting,* 13th edition, and *Accounting: Concepts and Applications,* 7th edition. Fred and his wife, Julie, have five sons, one daughter, and nine grandchildren.

Monte R. Swain (Consulting Editor)

Monte R. Swain is an Associate Professor of management accounting and information systems at Brigham Young University. He received his undergraduate degree in accounting and his master's degree in management accounting from Brigham Young University and was distinguished as the School of Accountancy's Outstanding Graduate. In 1992, Dr. Swain received his Ph.D. in management accounting and information systems from Michigan State University and was honored with the department's Outstanding Doctoral Scholar award. At BYU, he has received the Teaching Excellence Award for Management Skills in 1994 and 1995. In addition, he was designated as the Price Waterhouse Research Fellow beginning in 1995. Dr. Swain has published papers in a number of journals, including *Decision Sciences, Internal Auditor,* the *Journal of Accounting Case Research,* the *International Journal of Applied Quality Management,* and *Accounting Education: A Journal of Theory, Practice and Research.* In addition, he served as Consulting Editor for *Accounting: Concepts and Applications,* 7th edition. He and his wife, Shannon, have six children: Nicole, Jessica, Jacob, Carly, Joseph, and Larkin.

CONTENTS

Appendices

Indexes

SURVEY OF ACCOUNTING

AN INTRODUCTION TO ACCOUNTING

PART 1

CHAPTERS

CHAPTER

1 ACCOUNTING INFORMATION: USERS AND USES

SETTING THE STAGE

In 1987, IBM was the most valuable company in the world, worth an estimated $105.8 billion. By the end of 1992, IBM had an estimated value of $28.8 billion. This decline in value can be traced to a strategic error made by IBM in the early 1980s. Prior to 1981, IBM was the major player in the computer market and was the primary provider of computers for government, universities, and businesses. At this time, believe it or not, there were virtually no computers available at an affordable price for individuals. But, in 1981, IBM introduced its personal computer (IBM PC), and it quickly established the standard by which other PCs would be measured. However, IBM elected to leave the software development for PCs to other companies. Instead of developing their own disk operating system (DOS), IBM elected to use a DOS developed by a small company located in Seattle—Microsoft.[1]

Microsoft was founded in 1975 by Bill Gates and Paul Allen. With the founding of Microsoft, Gates and Allen envisioned that computers would eventually find their way into everyday life (contrary to IBM's prediction in the 1950s when one IBM executive forecast the total worldwide demand for computers to be about five). While IBM's performance floundered in the mid- and late-1980s, Microsoft demonstrated an amazing ability to become a major player in practically every aspect of the computer software market—from operating systems to the Internet to networks to spreadsheets and word processors.

With Microsoft's many accomplishments comes the question: "Just how successful is the company?" The answer to that question depends on how you define the term "success." Measured in terms of number of employees, Microsoft has grown from a company employing 32 people when IBM elected to use Microsoft's DOS in 1981 to over 20,000 employees in 1997. In terms of social impact, Microsoft and its employees donate millions of dollars each year to such charitable causes as Special Olympics, Boys and Girls Clubs, and the United Negro College Fund. Microsoft

1. The decision to have another company develop the software for their personal computer was not IBM's only strategic error. At the same time, IBM decided to use another company's microprocessors—the "brains" of the computer. As a result, another successful company was born—Intel. IBM lost the opportunity to dominate the software market as well as the computer chip market. By mid-1997 Microsoft, Intel, and IBM each had market values exceeding $100 billion.

LEARNING OBJECTIVES

After studying this chapter, you should be able to:

1. *Describe the purpose of accounting and explain its role in business and society.*
2. *Identify the primary users of accounting information.*
3. *Describe the environment of accounting, including the effects of generally accepted accounting principles, international business, ethical considerations, and technology.*
4. *Analyze the reasons for studying accounting.*

also supports elementary and high schools throughout the country in their efforts to incorporate technology in the curriculum, and the company has established scholarship programs to encourage minorities and women to pursue careers in computer science and other related technical fields. In terms of stock price, Microsoft's per share stock price (adjusted for stock splits) has gone from $25 in 1986 to over $3,300 in 1997 (see Exhibit 1–1). On virtually every dimension you can think of, Microsoft has succeeded. But most of these dimensions are a by-product of Microsoft's ability to produce products that are valued by the market. If Microsoft was unable to produce and sell quality products, the company would be in no position to employ so many people, to give so much money to charities, or to experience such an incredible increase in stock price. And this is where accounting enters the picture.

EXHIBIT 1-1

History of Microsoft's Stock Price Per Share

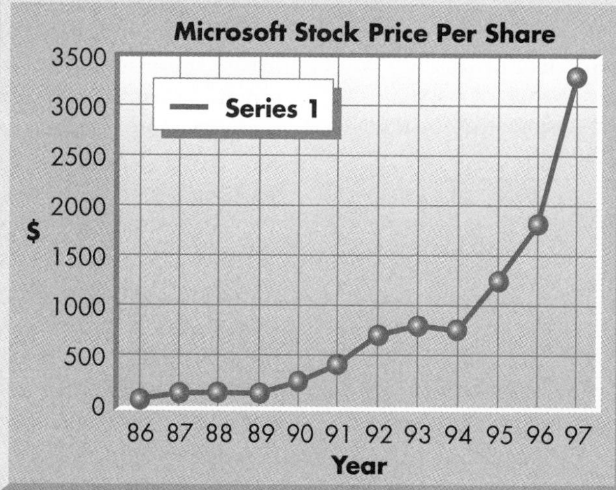

CAUTION

Don't be too concerned with all the new and unfamiliar terms you see in the first chapter of the book. Learning a "new language" takes time. Be patient. Before too long, you will be speaking the "language of business" (accounting) quite fluently.

In this textbook, you will begin your study of accounting. You will learn to speak and understand accounting, "the language of business." Without an understanding of accounting, business investments, taxes, and money management will be like a foreign language to you. In brief, an understanding of accounting facilitates the interpretation of financial information, which allows for better economic decisions.

The major objectives of this text are to provide you with a basic understanding of the language of accounting and with the ability to interpret and use financial information prepared using accounting techniques and procedures. With the knowledge you obtain from this exposure to accounting, you will be able to "read" the financial statements of companies such as Microsoft, understand the information that is being conveyed, and use accounting information to make good business decisions. Also, through discussion of the business environment in which accounting is used, you will increase your understanding of general business concepts such as corporations, leases, annuities, leverage, derivatives (the financial kind, not the calculus kind), and so forth.

You will become convinced that accounting is not "bean counting." Time after time you will see that accountants must exercise judgment about how to best summarize and report the results of business transactions. As a result, you will gain a respect for the complexity of accounting, and obtain a healthy skepticism about the precision of any financial reports you see.

Finally, you will see the power of accounting. Financial statements are not just paper reports that get filed away and forgotten. You will see that financial statement numbers, and, indirectly, the accountants who prepare them, determine who receives loans and who doesn't, which companies attract investors and which don't, which managers receive salary bonuses and which don't, and which companies are praised in the financial press and which aren't.

So, let's get started.

1 *Describe the purpose of accounting and explain its role in business and society.*

WHAT'S THE PURPOSE OF ACCOUNTING?

Imagine a long distance telephone company with no system in place to document who calls whom and how long they talk. Or a manager of a 300-unit apartment complex who has forgotten to write down which tenants have and have not paid this month's rent. Or an accounting professor who, the day before final grades are due, loses the only copy of the disk containing the spreadsheet of all the homework, quiz, and exam scores. Each of these settings illustrates a problem with bookkeeping, the least glamorous aspect of accounting. **Bookkeeping** is the preservation of a systematic, quantitative record of an activity. Bookkeeping systems can be very primitive—making marks in a stick to tally how many sheep you have or moving beads on a string to track the score in a billiards game. But the importance of routine bookkeeping cannot be overstated; without bookkeeping, business is impossible.

bookkeeping The preservation of a systematic, quantitative record of an activity.

To evaluate the importance of bookkeeping records, we'll use a thought experiment. Suppose that sometime during the night, every copy of every novel ever written were to disappear. Could life proceed normally the next day? While the cultural loss would be incalculable, the normal activities of the next day would not be noticeably affected. What if television were suddenly gone when we woke up? While we might wander around wondering what to do with our time, life would go on. But what if we woke up tomorrow morning to find the bookkeeping records of all businesses worldwide destroyed during the night? Businesses that rely on up-to-the-minute customer account information, such as banks, simply could not open their doors. Retailers would have to insist on cash purchases, since no credit records could be verified. Manufacturers would have to do a quick count of existing inventories of raw materials and components to find out whether they could keep their production lines running. Suppliers would have to call all their customers, if they could remember who they were, to renegotiate purchase orders. Attorneys would find themselves in endless arguments about their fees because they would have no record of billable hours. Routine and dry as it may seem, the world simply could not function for one day without bookkeeping.

Rudimentary bookkeeping is ancient, probably predating both language and money. The modern system of double-entry bookkeeping still in use today (described in Chapter 3) was developed in the 1300s–1400s in Italy by the merchants in the trading and banking centers of Florence, Venice, and Genoa. The key development in accounting in the last 500 years has been the use of the bookkeeping data, not just to keep track of things, but to evaluate the performance and health of a business.

This use of bookkeeping data as an evaluation tool may seem like an obvious step to you, but it is a step that is often not taken. Let's consider a bookkeeping system with which most of us are familiar—a checking account. Your checking account involves (or should involve) careful recording of the dates and amounts of all checks written and all deposits made, the maintenance of a running account total, and reconciliations with the monthly bank statement. Now, assume that you have a perfect checking account bookkeeping system—will the system answer the following questions?

- Are you spending more for groceries this year than you did last year?
- What proportion of your monthly expenditures are fixed, meaning that you can't change them except through a drastic change in lifestyle?
- You plan to study abroad next year; will you be able to save enough between now and then to pay for it?

In order to answer these kinds of evaluation questions, each check must be analyzed to determine the type of expenditure, your checks must then be coded by type of expenditure, the data must be boiled down into summary reports, and past data must be used to forecast future patterns. How many of us use our checking account data like this? Not many. We do the bookkeeping (usually), but we don't structure the information to be used for evaluation.

accounting system The procedures and processes used by a business to analyze transactions, handle routine bookkeeping tasks, and structure information so it can be used to evaluate the performance and health of the business.

In summary, an **accounting system** is used by a business to (1) analyze transactions, (2) handle routine bookkeeping tasks, and (3) structure information so it can be used to evaluate the performance and health of the business. Exhibit 1-2 illustrates the three functions of the accounting system.

EXHIBIT 1-2

Functions of an Accounting System

Analysis

Analyze business events to determine if information should be captured by the accounting system

Bookkeeping

Day-to-day keeping track of things

Evaluation

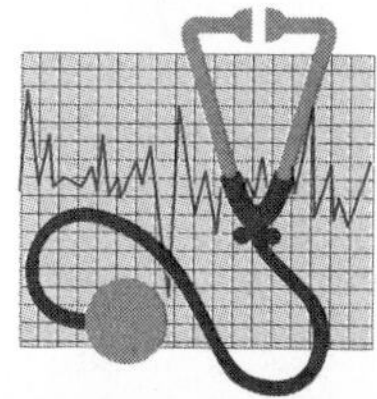

Use summary information to evaluate the financial health and performance of the business

accounting A system for providing quantitative, financial information about economic entities that is useful for making sound economic decisions. Accounting is often called the "language of business" because it provides the means of recording and communicating business activities and the results of those activities.

Accounting is formally defined as a system for providing "quantitative information, primarily financial in nature, about economic entities that is intended to be useful in making economic decisions."[2]

The key components of this definition are:

- *Quantitative.* Accounting relates to numbers. This is a strength because numbers can be easily tabulated and summarized. It is a weakness because some important business events, such as a toxic waste spill and the associated lawsuits and countersuits, cannot be easily described by one or two numbers.
- *Financial.* The health and performance of a business is affected by and reflected in many dimensions—financial, personal relationships, community and environmental impact, and public image. Accounting focuses on just the financial dimension.
- *Useful.* The practice of accounting is supported by a long tradition of theory. U.S. accounting rules have a theoretical conceptual framework. Some people actually make a living as accounting theorists. However, in spite of its theoretical beauty, accounting exists only because it is useful.
- *Decisions.* Although accounting is the structured reporting of what has already occurred, this past information can only be useful if it impacts decisions about the future.

Making good decisions is critical for success in any business enterprise. When an important decision must be made, it is essential to use a rational decision-making process. The process is basically the same no matter how complex the issue. First, the issue or question must be clearly identified. Next, the facts surrounding the situation must be gathered and analyzed. Then, several alternative courses of action should be identified and considered before a decision is finally reached. This decision-making process is summarized in Exhibit 1-3.

One must be careful to make a distinction between a good decision and a good outcome. Often, many factors outside the control of the decision maker affect the outcome of a decision. The decision-making process does not guarantee a certain result; it only ensures a good decision is made. To illustrate this process, let's consider an example. It's Friday afternoon, the sun is shining, your homework is done, and you have the rest of the afternoon and evening ahead of you. What to do? You check the movie listings in the newspaper to see if there are any new movies you haven't seen, you call several of your friends to see what they are doing, and you review

2. *Statement of the Accounting Principles Board No. 4,* "Basic Concepts and Accounting Principles Underlying Financial Statements of Business Enterprises," New York: American Institute of Certified Public Accountants, 1970, par. 40.

EXHIBIT 1-3

The Decision-Making Process

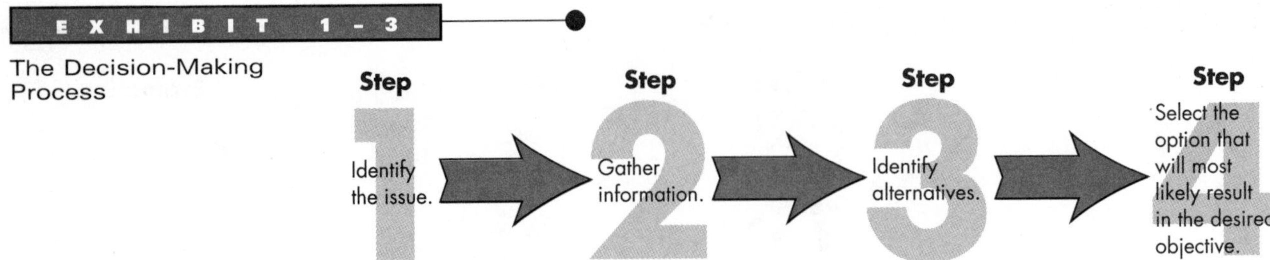
Step 1
Identify the issue.
Step 2
Gather information.
Step 3
Identify alternatives.
Step 4
Select the option that will most likely result in the desired objective.

your list of "things you always wanted to organize around your apartment but never had the time." With this information, you decide that you could either (1) go to the new Tom Hanks movie with a group of friends or (2) go over to your friend's house and watch TV. (Spending time at home organizing your sock drawer on a Friday night is out of the question.) You decide to go to the movies. You get to the movie theater, buy your tickets, your popcorn, and your drink, then select a seat. The lights dim, the movie starts, and the only empty seat left in the theater is right in front of you. It turns out you have the best seat in the house—until Shaquille O'Neal (7′2″, 300 pounds) comes in and sits in that seat. Good decision, bad outcome.

The four steps of the decision-making process lead to the best decision under the circumstances, but the outcome always has an element of chance. Part of business is learning how to protect yourself against bad outcomes. The first step in achieving a favorable outcome begins with making a good decision.

Accounting plays a vital role in the decision-making process. An accounting system provides information in a form that can be used to make knowledgeable financial decisions. The information supplied by accounting is in the form of quantitative data, primarily financial in nature, and relates to specific economic entities. An economic entity may be an individual, a business enterprise, or a nonprofit organization. A **business**, such as a grocery store or a car dealership, is operated with the objective of making a profit for its owners. The goal of a **nonprofit organization**, such as a city government or a university, is to provide services in an effective and efficient manner. Every entity, regardless of its size or purpose, must have a way to keep track of its economic activities and to measure how well it is accomplishing its goals. Accounting provides the means for tracking activities and measuring results.

business An organization operated with the objective of making a profit from the sale of goods or services.

nonprofit organization An entity without a profit objective, oriented toward providing services efficiently and effectively.

Without accounting information, many important financial decisions would be made blindly. Investors, for example, would have no way to distinguish between a profitable company and one that is on the verge of failure; bankers could not evaluate the riskiness of potential loans; corporate managers would have no basis for controlling costs, setting prices, or investing the company's resources; and governments would have no basis for taxing income. No list of examples could fully represent the pervasive use of accounting information throughout our economic, social, and political institutions. When accounting information is used effectively as a basis for making economic decisions, limited resources are more likely to be allocated efficiently. From a broad perspective, the result is a healthier economy and a higher standard of living.

The value of accounting information can also be illustrated on a personal level. Since very few of us will ever make more money than we can spend, we each will be making choices as to what to do with our limited incomes. For example, assume you have a job that results in take-home pay of $2,000 per month. What do you do with the money? If you are making monthly payments on a home and/or an automobile, you previously made choices to use part of your monthly income for these two items. How about a trip around the world, season tickets for your favorite basketball team, or a new home entertainment system? You could spend your money on these items, but that might not be the best use of your income. After all, you haven't eaten yet. Routine expenditures for food, clothing, and utilities must be made. How much money will you need for these and other everyday expenditures?

By collecting financial information relating to prior months' inflows and outflows of cash, you will be able to approximate how much money you will need for this month. This process—called *budgeting* (discussed later)—is often used by individuals (and businesses) to ensure that monthly income is used in the best manner possible. While it is true that budgeting is not necessary, budgeting is part of good decision making.

The Relationship of Accounting to Business

Business is the general term applied to the activities involved in the production and distribution of goods and services. Accounting is used to record and report the financial effects of business activities. Thus, as mentioned earlier, accounting is often called the "language of business." It provides the means of recording and communicating the successes and failures of business organizations.

All business enterprises have some activities in common. As shown in Exhibit 1-4, one common activity is the acquisition of monetary resources. These resources, often referred to as "capital," come from three sources: (1) investors (owners), (2) creditors (lenders), and (3) the business itself in the form of earnings that have been

EXHIBIT 1-4

Activities Common to Business Organizations

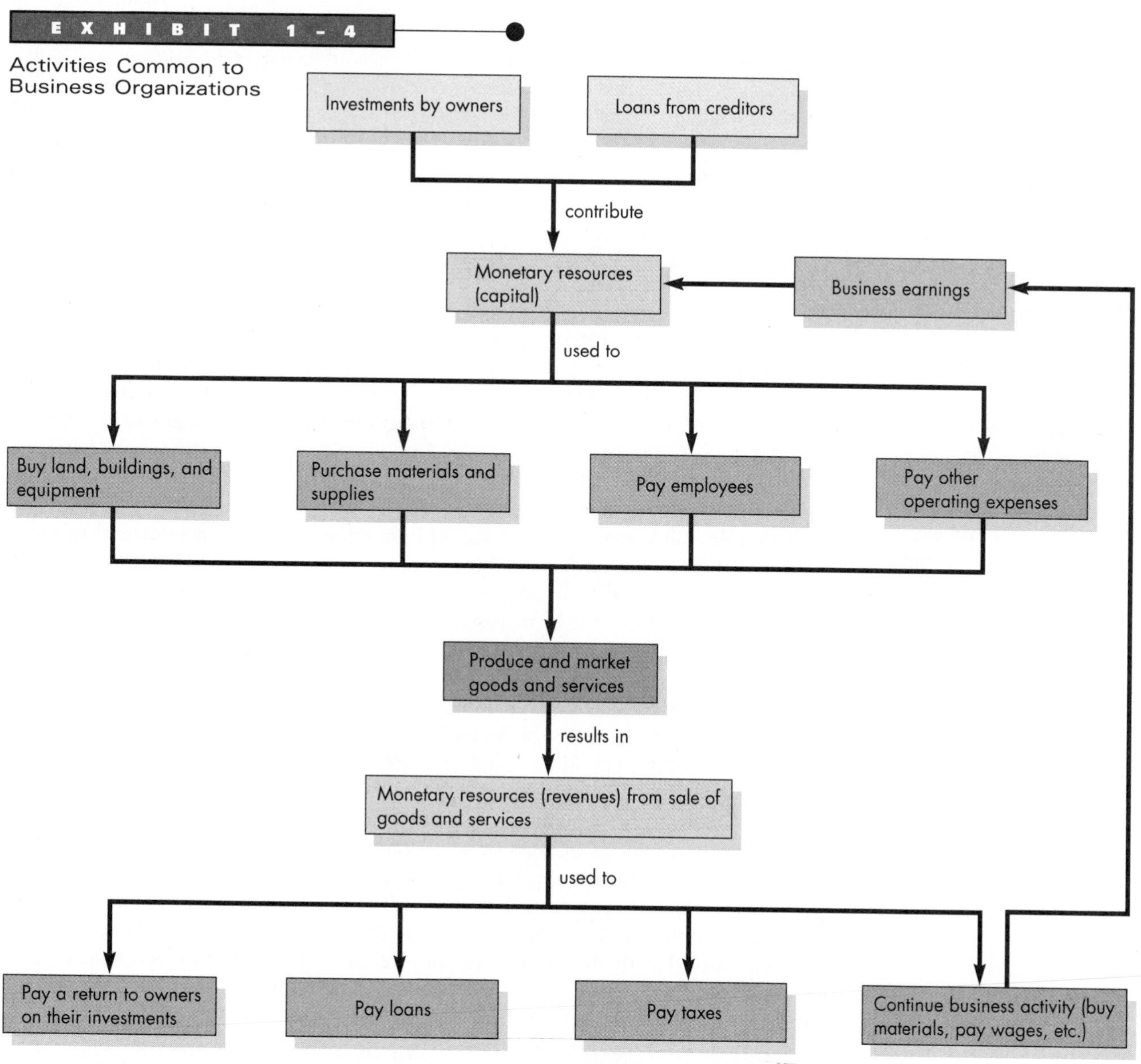

retained. Once resources are obtained, they are used to buy land, buildings, and equipment; to purchase materials and supplies; to pay employees; and to meet any other operating expenses involved in the production and marketing of goods or services. When the product or service is sold, additional monetary resources (revenues) are generated. These resources can be used to pay loans, to pay taxes, and to buy new materials, equipment, and other items needed to continue the operations of the business. In addition, some of the resources may be distributed to owners as a return on their investment.

accounting cycle The procedures for analyzing, recording, classifying, summarizing, and reporting the transactions of a business.

Accountants measure and communicate (report) the results of these activities. In order to measure these results as accurately as possible, accountants follow a fairly standard set of procedures, usually referred to as the **accounting cycle**. The cycle includes several steps, which involve analyzing, recording, classifying, summarizing, and reporting the transactions of a business. These steps are explained in detail in Chapter 3.

TO SUMMARIZE

Accounting is a service activity designed to accumulate, measure, and communicate financial information about economic entities—businesses and nonprofit organizations. Its purpose is to provide information used to make informed decisions about how to best use available resources. Accounting is often called the "language of business" because it provides the means of recording and communicating business activities and the results of those activities.

2 *Identify the primary users of accounting information.*

WHO USES ACCOUNTING INFORMATION?

management accounting The area of accounting concerned with providing internal financial reports to assist management in making decisions.

The accounting system generates output in the form of financial reports. As shown in Exhibit 1-5, there are two major categories of reports: internal and external. Internal reports are used by those who direct the day-to-day operations of a business enterprise. These individuals are collectively referred to as "management," and the related area of accounting is called **management accounting**. Management accounting focuses on the information needed for planning, implementing plans, and controlling costs. Managers and executives who work inside a company have access to specialized management accounting information that is not available to outsiders. For example, the management of **McDonald's Corporation** has detailed management accounting data on exactly how much it costs to produce each item on the menu. Further, if a local burger price war is started by **Burger King** or **Wendy's** in, say, Missouri, McDonald's managers can request daily sales summaries for each store in the area to measure the impact.

Other examples of decisions made using management accounting information are whether to produce a product internally or purchase it from an outside supplier, what prices to charge, and which costs seem excessive. Consider those companies that produce computers. Most computers are shipped with a disk operating system (DOS) already installed. Approximately 85% of computers have **Microsoft**'s version of DOS (Windows) pre-installed. The computer makers must decide whether to develop their own version of DOS or pay Microsoft a licensing fee to use Windows. Most computer manufacturers have determined it is cost effective to license from Microsoft. Companies such as **Sears** and **Radio Shack** often use products produced by outside suppliers rather than manufacture the products themselves. The products are then labeled with the "Kenmore" or "Realistic" brand names and sold to customers. These are just two examples of decisions that must be made by management given available financial information.

EXHIBIT 1-5 Output of the Accounting Cycle

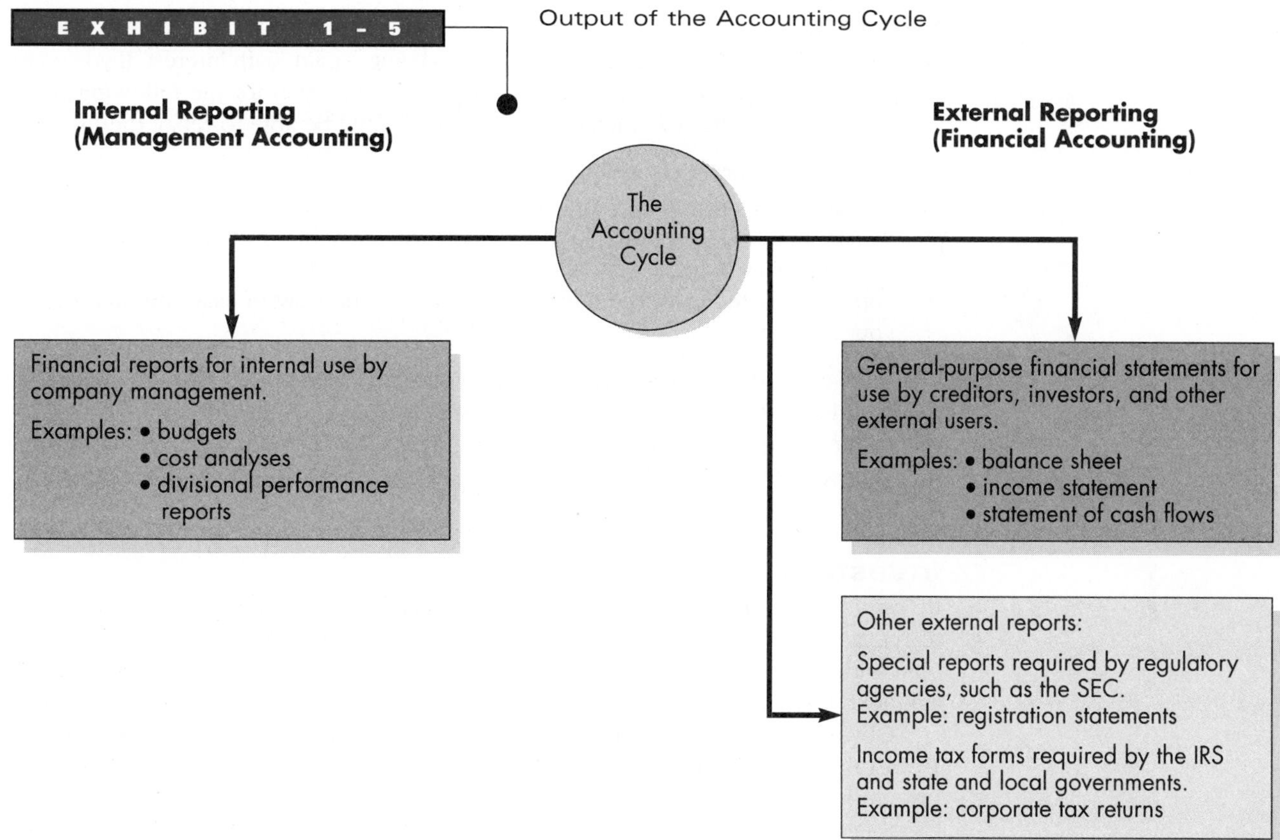
Internal Reporting
(Management Accounting)
External Reporting
(Financial Accounting)
The Accounting Cycle
Financial reports for internal use by company management.
Examples: • budgets
• cost analyses
• divisional performance reports
General-purpose financial statements for use by creditors, investors, and other external users.
Examples: • balance sheet
• income statement
• statement of cash flows
Other external reports:
Special reports required by regulatory agencies, such as the SEC.
Example: registration statements
Income tax forms required by the IRS and state and local governments.
Example: corporate tax returns

annual report A document that summarizes the results of operations and financial status of a company for the past year and outlines plans for the future.

financial statements Reports such as the balance sheet, income statement, and statement of cash flows, which summarize the financial status and results of operations of a business entity.

financial accounting The area of accounting concerned with reporting financial information to interested external parties.

External financial reports, included in the firm's **annual report**, are used by individuals and organizations who have an economic interest in the business but who are not part of its management. Information is provided to these "external users" in the form of general-purpose **financial statements** and special reports required by government agencies. The general-purpose information provided by **financial accounting** is summarized in the three primary financial statements: balance sheet, income statement, and statement of cash flows (more formally introduced in Chapter 2).

- The *balance sheet* reports the resources of a company (the assets), the company's obligations (the liabilities), and the owners' equity, which represents the difference between what is owned (assets) and what is owed (liabilities).
- The *income statement* reports the amount of net income earned by a company during a period, with annual and quarterly income statements being the most common. Net income is the excess of a company's revenues over its expenses; if the expenses are more than the revenues, then the company has suffered a loss for the period. The income statement represents the accountant's best effort at measuring the economic performance of a company.
- The *statement of cash flows* reports the amount of cash collected and paid out by a company in the following three types of activities: operating, investing, and financing. The types of activities in each of these three categories will be explained in Chapter 2. The statement of cash flows is the most objective of the financial statements since, as you will see in subsequent chapters, it involves a minimum of accounting estimates and judgments.

Examples of external users of the information contained in these three financial statements, along with other available information, are described in the following paragraphs.

Lenders

Lenders (creditors) are interested in one thing—being repaid, with interest. If you were to approach a bank for a large loan, the bank would ask you for the following types of information in order to evaluate whether you would be able to repay the loan:

- a listing of your assets and liabilities
- payroll stubs, tax returns, and other evidence of your income
- details about any monthly payments (car, rent, credit cards, etc.) you are obligated to make
- copies of recent bank statements to document the flow of cash into and out of your account

In essence, the bank would be asking you for a balance sheet, an income statement, and a statement of cash flows. Similarly, banks use companies' financial statements in making decisions about commercial loans. The financial statements are useful because they help the lender predict the future ability of the borrower to repay the loan.

Investors

Investors want information to help them estimate how much cash they can expect to receive in the future if they invest in a business now. Financial statements, coupled with a knowledge of business plans, market forecasts, and the character of management, can aid investors in assessing these future cash flows.

Obviously, millions of Americans invest in **McDonald's**, **Microsoft**, **Exxon**, and **General Electric** without ever seeing the financial statements of these companies. Investors can feel justifiably safe in doing this because large companies are followed by armies of financial analysts who would quickly blow the whistle if they found information suggesting that investors in these companies were at serious risk. But what about investing in a smaller company, one that the financial press doesn't follow, or in a local family business that is just seeking outside investors for the first time? In cases such as these, investing without looking at the financial statements is like jumping off the high dive without looking first to see if there is any water in the pool.

Management

In addition to using management accounting information available only to those within the firm, managers of a company can use the general financial accounting information that is also made available to outsiders. Company goals are often stated in terms of financial accounting numbers, such as a target of sales growth in excess of 5%. Also, reported "net income" is frequently used in calculating management bonuses. Finally, managers of a company can analyze the general-purpose financial statements (using the techniques introduced in Chapter 2) in order to pinpoint areas of weakness about which more detailed management accounting information can be sought.

Other Users of Financial Information

There are many other external users of financial information, including suppliers, customers, employees, competitors, government agencies, and the press. These are described below.

Suppliers and Customers

In some settings, suppliers and customers are interested in the long-run staying power of a company. On the supplier side, if **Boeing** receives an order from an airline for 30 new 747s over the next 10 years, Boeing wants to know whether the airline will be around in the future to take delivery of and pay for the planes. On the customer side, a homeowner who has foundation repair work done wants to know whether the company making the repairs will be around long enough to honor its 50-year guarantee. Financial statements provide information that suppliers and customers can use to assess the long-run prospects of a company.

Employees

Employees are interested in financial accounting information for a variety of reasons. As mentioned earlier, financial statement data are used in determining employee bonuses. In addition, financial accounting information can help an employee evaluate the likelihood of the employer being able to fulfill its long-run promises, such as pensions and retiree health-care benefits. Financial statements are also important in contract negotiations between labor and management.

Competitors

If you were a manager at **PepsiCo**, would you be interested in knowing the relative profitability of **Coca-Cola** operations in the United States, Brazil, Japan, and France? Of course you would, because that information could help you identify strategic opportunities for marketing pushes where potential profits are high or where your competitor is weak.

Government Agencies

Federal and state government agencies make frequent use of financial accounting information. For example, in order to make sure that investors have sufficient information to make informed investment decisions, the Securities and Exchange Commission monitors the financial accounting disclosures of companies (both U.S. and foreign) whose stocks trade on U.S. stock exchanges. The International Trade Commission uses financial accounting information to determine whether importation of Ecuadorian roses or Chinese textiles is harming U.S. companies through unfair trade practices. The Justice Department uses financial statement data to evaluate whether companies (such as **Microsoft**) are earning excess monopolistic profits.

The Press

Financial statements are a great place for a reporter to find background information to flesh out a story about a company. For example, a story about **Microsoft** can be enhanced using the sales data shown in its annual report. In addition, a surprising accounting announcement, such as a large drop in reported profits, is a trigger for an investigative reporter to write about what is going on in a company.

In summary, who uses financial accounting information? Everyone does, or at least everyone should. External financial reports come within the area of accounting referred to as financial accounting. Most of the data needed to prepare both internal and external reports is provided by the same accounting system. A major difference between management and financial accounting is the types of financial reports prepared. Internal reports are tailored to meet the needs of management and may vary considerably among businesses. General-purpose financial statements and other external reports, however, follow certain standards or guidelines and are thus more uniform among companies. The first eight chapters of *Survey of Accounting* focus on financial accounting, specifically on the primary financial statements (discussed and illustrated in Chapter 2). The remaining chapters, 9 through 15, focus on management accounting.

TO SUMMARIZE

Two major categories of reports are generated by the accounting cycle: internal and external. Management accounting focuses on providing reports for internal use by management to assist in making operating decisions and in planning and controlling a company's activities. Financial accounting provides information to meet the needs of external users. General-purpose financial statements are used by investors, creditors, and other external parties who are interested in a company's activities and results.

3 *Describe the environment of accounting, including the effects of generally accepted accounting principles, international business, ethical considerations, and technology.*

WITHIN WHAT KIND OF ENVIRONMENT DOES ACCOUNTING OPERATE?

Accounting functions in a dynamic environment. Changes in technology as well as economic and political factors can significantly influence accounting practice. Four particularly important factors are the development of "generally accepted accounting principles" (GAAP), international business, ethical considerations, and technology.

BUSINESS ENVIRONMENT ESSAY

The Evolution of Accounting It can be argued that accounting as a profession is very young; however, as a service activity it dates back several thousand years. Long before man invented numerical figures, designations for possessions and debts were established through natural means. Collections of pebbles, shells, or bones were used as representations of exchanges between people. Some maintained records of debt by carving notches in rods or canes. The ancient Peruvians used knotted strings before numerical symbols were invented. Regardless of the rudiments put into practice through the generations, it is obvious that accounting for ownership between parties drove man to invent new methods of record keeping and communication. In fact, Eric Hoffer discusses in his book *The Temper of Our Times* that accounting became the driving force of our written language.

> We are often told that the invention of writing in the Middle East about 3000 B.C. marked an epoch in man's career because it revolutionized the transmission of knowledge and ideas. Actually, for many centuries after its invention, writing was used solely to keep track of the intake and outgo of treasuries and warehouses. Writing was invented not to write books but to keep books. (Hoffer, p. 196)

Among the earliest known records are those of the Egyptians and Babylonians (from approximately 3000 B.C.), who recorded on clay tablets such transactions as the payment of wages and taxes. Multiple clay tablets giving listings of valuable items in treasuries and temples have been found at excavation sites in Sumeria and Babylon. It makes sense that accountants of old would only take the time to carve in these clay tablets instead of writing on papyrus if they regarded their contents to be of great importance. As a result, we have accurate knowledge of the wealth maintained in the treasuries, but little information relating to the persons who actually owned them.

Tied to the development of a written language came the ability to represent measures of tallied items with a single symbol. Differing numerical systems existed throughout the world. As empires gained and lost power, advances in culture and science spread among the different nations. In order for a ruler to maintain lands, he would dictate the use of more unified communication methods. Under Roman rule, nations of Europe, Africa, the Middle East, and some of Asia were forced to write and maintain business communications in Latin. During the Roman period (which lasted from approximately 500 B.C. to 500 A.D.), detailed tax records were maintained.

After the fall of Rome, trade continued to increase around the Mediterranean seaports. Italy found itself positioned between European consumers and Asian and Arabian producers. As trade increased in these port cities, the need to borrow and purchase on credit increased. In fact, the first bank of importance, Casa di San Georgio, was founded in Genoa, Italy, during the 12th century. During and after the crusades of 1096 to about 1270, a money stream had developed into and out of Italy by its European neighbors. Credit transactions rose in volume as traders in Florence, Pisa, and Venice became merchant-bankers. While accounting did not originate in Italy, its geographical location facilitated the formalization of a system of recording business transactions. In 1494, an Italian Franciscan monk, Luca Pacioli, published a treatise containing a small section titled "Particularis de Computis et Scripturis [Details of Accounting and Recording]," which contained the essential elements of the double-entry accounting system that is still in use today.

But accounting has not remained static. The Industrial Revolution brought about changes in business, and therefore in accounting. Beginning in England in the mid-1800s, manufacturing processes started to evolve from individualized, handicraft systems to mass-production, factory systems. Technological advances not only provided new machinery but required new types of expenditures as well. Cost accounting systems had to be developed to analyze and control the financial operations of these increasingly complex manufacturing processes.

Governmental laws and requirements also have caused changes in the business environment and have stimulated the growth of accounting services. For example, the Companies Act in England in the 1850s established compulsory independent audits by chartered accountants. In the United States, the 1913 Revenue Act instituted the personal federal income tax, which created a need for income tax accounting. The 1934 Securities Exchange Act established the Securities and Exchange Commission (SEC), which monitors the reporting procedures of companies that sell stock publicly.

These and other factors have produced changes in the types of accounting services needed, and in many instances they have affected the accounting procedures themselves. Thus, the profession of accounting has evolved to meet the needs of the people it serves in an ever-changing and increasingly complex business environment.

As this brief history makes clear, accounting is not an exact science. It is constantly evolving, changing to meet the needs of users and adapting itself to the economic environment in which it operates.

Source: Eric Hoffer, *The Temper of Our Times,* Harper & Row, 1966.

The Significance and Development of Accounting Standards

Imagine a company that compensates a key employee in the following ways:

- Paying a cash salary of $80,000.
- Giving a new car with a value of $30,000.
- Offering the option to become, a year from now, a 10% owner of the company in exchange for an investment of $200,000.

If the company does well in the coming year, the company will increase in value, the $200,000 price tag for 10% ownership will look like a great deal, and the employee will exercise the option. If the company does poorly, it will decline in value, the $200,000 price will be too high, and the employee will throw the option away and forget the whole thing. Assume the company then sells the ownership option to interested outside investors for $25,000.

The accounting question is how to summarize in one number the company's compensation cost associated with this employee. We would probably all agree to include the $110,000 ($80,000 + $30,000) compensation cost from the cash salary and the new car. What about the option? The following two arguments could be put forward:

1. If the employee were to buy the option from the company, just like any other outside investor, the employee would have to pay $25,000. Therefore, giving the option to the employee is just like paying him or her $25,000 cash. The $25,000 value of the option should be added to compensation cost.
2. The option doesn't cost the company a thing. In fact, the option merely increases the probability that the employee will invest $200,000 in the company in the future. The option doesn't add a penny to compensation cost.

So, which argument is right? Should each company decide for itself whether to include the $25,000 option value as part of compensation cost, or should there be an overall accounting standard followed by all companies? And if there is a standard, who sets it?[3]

There are many situations in business, such as the option compensation case just described, in which reasonable people can disagree about how certain items should be handled for accounting purposes. And, since financial accounting information is designed to be used by people outside a company, it is important that outsiders understand the rules and assumptions used by the company in constructing its financial statements. This would be extremely difficult and costly for outsiders to find out if every company formulated its own set of accounting rules. Accordingly, in most countries in the world there exists a committee or board that establishes the accounting rules for that country.

The Financial Accounting Standards Board

Financial Accounting Standards Board (FASB) The private organization responsible for establishing the standards for financial accounting and reporting in the United States.

In the United States, accounting standards are set by the **Financial Accounting Standards Board (FASB)**. The FASB is based in Norwalk, Connecticut, and its seven full-time members are selected from a variety of backgrounds—professional accounting, business, government, and academia. The FASB receives about one-third of its $20 million annual operating budget through donations from the accounting profession and from businesses. The remaining two-thirds is generated through sales of publications and other services (e.g., a CD-ROM version of all the existing accounting standards). An important thing to note about the FASB is that it is *not* a government agency; the FASB is a private body established and supported by the joint efforts of the U.S. business community, financial analysts, and practicing accountants. Because the FASB is not a government agency, it has no legal power to enforce the accounting standards it sets. The FASB gets its authority to establish rules from the Securities and Exchange Commission (discussed later).

The FASB maintains its influence as the accounting standard setter for the United States (and the most influential accounting body in the world) by carefully protecting its prestige and reputation for setting good standards. In doing so, the FASB must walk a fine line between constant improvement of accounting practices to provide more full and fair information for external users, and practical constraints on financial disclosure to appease businesses who are reluctant to disclose too much information to outsiders. To balance these opposing forces, the FASB seeks consensus by requesting written comments and sponsoring public hearings on all its proposed standards. The end result of this public process is a set of accounting rules that are described as being **generally accepted accounting principles (GAAP)**. Without general acceptance by the business community, FASB standards would merely be theoretical essays by a powerless body, and the FASB would be disbanded. This may sound overly dramatic, but the FASB was created in 1973 to replace the previously existing accounting standards body (the Accounting Principles Board or APB) which had lost its credibility with the business community because it was seen as being completely controlled by accountants.

generally accepted accounting principles (GAAP) Authoritative guidelines that define accounting practice at a particular time.

As you study this text, you will be intrigued by the interesting conceptual issues the FASB must wrestle with in setting accounting standards. The FASB has deliberated over the correct way to compute motion picture profits, the appropriate treatment of the cost of dismantling a nuclear power plant, the best approach for reflecting the impact of changes in foreign currency exchange rates, and the proper accounting for complex financial instruments such as commodity futures and interest rate swaps. And since U.S. companies are always suspicious that any change in the accounting rules will make them look worse on paper, almost all FASB decisions are made in the midst of controversy.

(STOP & THINK)

Why is it important for the FASB to remain completely independent?

3. Just to show how influential accounting can be, this exact issue was debated on the floor of the U.S. Senate.

Other Organizations

In addition to the FASB, several other organizations impact accounting standards and are important in other ways to the practice of accounting. Some of these organizations are discussed below.

Securities and Exchange Commission (SEC) The government body responsible for regulating the financial reporting practices of most publicly owned corporations in connection with the buying and selling of stocks and bonds.

certified public accountant (CPA) A special designation given to an accountant who has passed a national uniform examination and has met other certifying requirements.

American Institute of Certified Public Accountants (AICPA) The national organization of CPAs in the United States.

Securities and Exchange Commission

In response to the Stock Market Crash of 1929, Congress created the **Securities and Exchange Commission (SEC)** to regulate U.S. stock exchanges. Part of the job of the SEC is to make sure that investors are provided with full and fair information about publicly traded companies. The SEC is not charged with protecting investors from losing money; instead, the SEC seeks to create a fair information environment in which investors can buy and sell stocks without fear that companies are hiding or manipulating financial data.

As part of its regulatory role, the SEC has received from Congress specific legal authority to establish accounting standards for companies soliciting investment funds from the American public. For now, the SEC refrains from exercising this authority and allows the FASB to set U.S. accounting standards. The SEC has generally been content to be publicly supportive of the FASB and to privately work out any disagreements. Remember, however, that the SEC is always looming in the background, legally authorized to take over the setting of U.S. accounting standards should the FASB lose its credibility with the public.

American Institute of Certified Public Accountants

There are two different uses of the label "CPA"—there are individuals who are CPAs and there are CPA firms. A **certified public accountant (CPA)** is someone who has taken a minimum number of college-level accounting classes, has passed the CPA exam administered by the **American Institute of Certified Public Accountants (AICPA)**, and has met other requirements set by his or her state. In essence, the CPA label guarantees that the person has received substantial accounting training. However, not all CPAs work as accountants. CPAs work in law firms; as business consultants; as corporate managers; for the government; and even some as accounting professors.

FYI

Other tasks accountants perform are planning for acquisitions and mergers, measuring efficiency improvements from new technology, managing quality, and developing accounting software.

The second use of the label "CPA" is in association with a CPA firm. A CPA firm is a company that performs accounting services, just as a law firm performs legal services. Obviously, a CPA firm employs a large number of accountants, not all of whom have received the training necessary to be certified public accountants. CPA firms also employ attorneys, information technology specialists, experts in finance, and other business specialists. CPA firms help companies establish accounting systems, formulate business plans, redesign their operating procedures, and just about anything else you can think of. A good way to think of a CPA firm is as a freelance business-advising firm with a particular strength in accounting issues. CPA firms are also hired to perform independent audits of the financial statements of a company.

Institute of Management Accountants (IMA) The organization in the United States most concerned with the management accounting function; publishes *Management Accounting* and administers the CMA exam.

certified management accountant (CMA) A person who has been certified by the Institute of Management Accountants after having passed a qualifying examination similar in rigor to the CPA exam.

Institute of Management Accountants

Most accountants do not work for public accounting firms. Many work in industry, and for those individuals, the CPA designation is less relevant. There is still, however, a need to certify the competency of those accountants who work in industry. The **Institute of Management Accountants (IMA)** is the organization most actively and directly concerned with the management accounting function. The IMA publishes a monthly journal, *Management Accounting,* which addresses current issues and developments relating to internal reporting. The IMA also sponsors the **Certified Management Accounting (CMA)** designation, a certification that requires individuals to pass a qualifying exam similar in rigor to the CPA exam.

FYI

Other accounting-related certifications also exist. Examples include the Certified Internal Auditor (CIA) and the Certified Fraud Examiner (CFE).

BUSINESS ENVIRONMENT ESSAY

Do You Have What It Takes? There are many opportunities in the field of accounting, but in order to be an accountant, specific requirements must be met. First, the accounting field requires a formal education. For example, while individual state laws vary, by the year 2000, most accounting students in the United States will be required to have completed 150 hours of college education to become Certified Public Accountants (CPAs). During this educational period, accounting students often participate in some type of internship or on-the-job training for a future accounting career. This experience helps to prepare students for the actual accounting work environment. Next, aspiring accountants must pass an examination based on the skills obtained from their education. This ensures that accountants are competent enough to perform independent services for the community. In addition to the examination, field experience requirements must be met to satisfy state licensing laws for CPAs.

Due to challenging work environments, which sometimes place demands on an accountant's integrity, society is in need of accountants who exhibit high ethical standards and responsible behavior. Other skills an accountant should possess include strong people and communication skills, initiative, selling abilities, analytical skills, and computer proficiency. As computer technology rapidly develops, the need for computer skills increases. Because computerized accounting systems are continually improving, there is a high demand for information systems expertise in the accounting field.

Source: William H. Sagar, "Characteristics of a Profession," National Public Accountant, March 1995, p. 6, and "Career Paths in Accounting," Convergence Multimedia/CD-ROM.

Internal Revenue Service

Imagine that you have a contract to design a computerized accounting system for a local business. Your fee is $100,000, which will be paid in full when the job is finished. By the end of the year, you have collected nothing but you estimate that you have completed 80% of the work on the contract.

If you are asked by a potential business partner how much money you have earned during the past year, what will you say? To say that you made $0, the amount you've collected on the contract, significantly understates the value of the work you have completed. If the 80% estimate is a fair reflection of the work you've done, it would seem reasonable for you to report to the potential partner that you've earned $80,000 ($100,000 × 0.80) during the year. And, as you'll see later in the text, this is exactly what you would report according to financial accounting rules.

Internal Revenue Service (IRS) A government agency that prescribes the rules and regulates the collection of tax revenues in the United States.

Now, if you are asked by the **Internal Revenue Service (IRS)** to state your income for the year, how much should you report? You don't have much leeway in the matter, since the IRS has very specific rules about what is considered taxable income. Assume that IRS rules state that you must pay income tax on the $80,000 income from the estimated amount of the contract that you have completed. Two practical problems would arise:

1. You don't have the money to pay the tax. You won't be able to pay the tax until the job is completed and you have collected your entire fee.
2. You could have endless arguments with the IRS about the completion percentage. The IRS could send an agent to dispute your estimate. The whole thing might end up in Tax Court.

This example illustrates that what works for financial accounting purposes does not necessarily work for income tax purposes. Financial accounting reports are designed to provide information about the economic performance and health of a company. Tax rules are designed to tax income when the tax can be paid and to provide concrete rules to minimize inefficient arguing between taxpayers and the IRS.

The implication of this separation between financial accounting and tax accounting is that companies must maintain two sets of books—one set from which the financial statements can be prepared and the other set to comply with income tax regulations. There is nothing shady or underhanded about this. Financial accounting and tax accounting involve different sets of rules because they are designed for different purposes.

International Business

One of the significant environmental changes in recent years has been the expansion of business activity on a worldwide basis. As consumers, we are familiar with the wide array of products from other countries, such as electronics from Japan and clothing made in China. On the other hand, many U.S. companies have operating divisions in foreign countries. Other American companies are located totally within the United States but have extensive transactions with foreign companies. The economic environment of today's business is truly based on a global economy. As an example, in 1996 over 60% of **Microsoft**'s sales were to individuals and companies located outside the United States.

International Accounting Standards Committee (IASC) The committee formed in 1973 to develop worldwide accounting standards.

FYI

Since international accounting standards often differ from GAAP, foreign companies may be required to adjust their books to be listed on the New York Stock Exchange. For example, when Germany's **Daimler-Benz** (makers of Mercedes Benz) became a NYSE-listed company in 1994, its GAAP-adjusted books showed a loss of $748 million, whereas its German standard books reported earnings of $636 million.

Accounting practices among countries vary widely. Attempts are being made to make those practices more consistent among countries. In an attempt to harmonize conflicting national standards, the **International Accounting Standards Committee (IASC)** was formed in 1973 to develop worldwide accounting standards. This body now represents more than 100 accountancy bodies from 82 countries (including the United States).

IASC standards are gaining increasing acceptance throughout the world. For example, in an ongoing revamping of its national accounting system, China is rewriting its accounting rules to be in very close agreement with IASC standards. IASC standards are increasingly accepted worldwide, but not in the United States. FASB rules are universally considered to be the most extensive and stringent in the world. Thus, doing away with the FASB and adopting IASC standards in the United States would result in a decline in the quality of financial reporting. However, the FASB and the IASC are starting to work in cooperation on new accounting standards, as evidenced by their joint work on a standard (dealing with "earnings per share") released in 1997.

At numerous points throughout this text, we will point out certain international applications of accounting as well as some differences that might exist in accounting rules between the United States and other countries. In addition, each chapter includes a case in the end-of-chapter material dealing with an international accounting issue.

(STOP & THINK)

Why is it so difficult to make international accounting standards consistent?

Ethics in Accounting

Another environmental factor affecting accounting, and business in general, is the growing concern over ethics. This concern is highlighted as major incidents of improper acts are reported by the news media. Examples of impropriety are found in all areas of activity; for example, the **Bre-X Minerals** scandal (called "the greatest gold scam ever") and the collapse of **Phar-Mor** in retailing.

FYI

The AICPA's *Code of Professional Conduct* can be found on its Web site at www.aicpa.org.

Recognizing the importance of ethical behavior, numerous organizations within the accounting profession and among individual companies have adopted codes or standards of conduct that provide guidance for members of those organizations. For example, the AICPA has a *Code of Professional Conduct* that holds as key principles integrity, objectivity, and independence. Members of the AICPA are expected to abide by these principles and are subject to disciplinary action should they knowingly violate the *Code of Professional Conduct*. Likewise, the IMA has developed *Standards for Ethical Conduct for Management Accountants* that provide CMAs with guidance in confronting ethical issues involving such things as competence, confidentiality, objectivity, and integrity. The accounting profession recognizes its responsibility to protect the public's interest and has developed guidelines to assist its members in confronting and resolving ethical issues.

Don't let yourself naively think that ethical dilemmas in business are rare. Such issues arise quite frequently. To help prepare you to enter the business world and to recognize and deal with ethical issues, we have included at the end of each chapter at least one ethics case. Ethics is an important topic that should be considered carefully, with the ultimate goal of improving individual and collective behavior in society.

Technology

Few things have changed the way business is conducted as have computers. Technology allows businesses to do things that twenty years ago were unimaginable. Consider being able to use your desktop computer to track the status of a package shipped from Los Angeles to New York. Companies like **UPS** and **Federal Express** incorporate this type of technology as an integral part of their business. Financial institutions use technology to wire billions of dollars each day to locations around the world.

So how has technology changed the way accounting is done? That question can be addressed on several levels. First, technology allows companies to easily gather vast amounts of information about individual transactions. For example, information relating to the customer, the salesperson, the product being sold, and the method of payment can be easily gathered for each transaction using computer technology. Prior to today's technology, the cost of gathering this information was prohibitive.

Second, computer technology allows large amounts of data to be compiled quickly and accurately, thereby significantly reducing the likelihood of errors. As you will soon discover, a large part of the mechanics of accounting involves moving numbers from various accounting records as well as adding and subtracting a lot of figures. Technology has made this process virtually invisible. What once occupied a large part of an accountant's time can now be done in an instant.

Third, in the precomputer world of limited analytical capacity, it was essential for lenders and investors to receive condensed summaries of a company's financial activities. Now, lenders and investors have the ability to receive and process gigabytes of information, so why should the report of **Microsoft**'s financial performance be restricted to three short financial statements? Why can't Microsoft provide access to much more detailed information on-line? In fact, why can't Microsoft allow investors to directly tap into Microsoft's own internal accounting database? Information technology has made this type of information acquisition and analysis possible; the question accountants face right now is how much information companies should be required to make available to outsiders. Ten years ago, the only way you could get a copy of Microsoft's financial statements was to call or write to receive paper copies in the mail. Now you can download those summary financial statements from Microsoft's Web site. How will you get financial information ten years from now? No one knows, but the rapid advance in information technology guarantees that it will be different from anything we are familiar with now.

get connected
http://www.swcollege.com
net work

Access Microsoft's Web site at microsoft.com. Identify the different kinds of information found on Microsoft's home page, e.g., marketing, product information, etc.

Can you find any financial information?

www.microsoft.com

Finally, and most importantly, while technology has changed the way in which certain aspects of accounting are carried out, on a fundamental level the mechanics of accounting are still the same as they were 500 years ago. People are still required to analyze complex business transactions and input the results of that analysis into the computer. Technology has not replaced judgment.

So if you are asking the question—"Why do I need to understand accounting—can't computers just do it?"—the answer is a resounding, "No!" You need to know what the computer is doing if you are to be able to understand and interpret the information resulting from the accounting process. You need to understand that since judgment was required when the various pieces of information were put into the accounting systems, judgment will be required to appropriately use that information. We have included numerous end-of-chapter opportunities for you to experience how technology helps in the accounting process. These opportunities will illustrate the important role that technology can play in the accounting process as well as emphasize the critical role that the accountant plays as well.

TO SUMMARIZE

Accounting functions in a dynamic environment. Generally accepted accounting principles (GAAP) have developed over time. The primary standard-setting body for the private sector is the Financial Accounting Standards Board (FASB). The accounting environment includes business activity that is conducted on an international basis. Consequently, accounting practices often must be modified to reflect the accounting standards of different countries. Attempts are being made to establish comparable international accounting practices. There is increasing concern in society over ethics. High standards of ethical conduct are important, especially for accountants who assume a special responsibility to the public. CPAs and CMAs have adopted standards of conduct that contain principles and rules as guidelines for the performance of accounting services. Technology has changed the way in which accounting information is collected, analyzed, and used. The use of computers in the accounting process has increased significantly, and while this increase now allows more information to be gathered and used, computers have not replaced the accountant nor eliminated the need for qualified decision makers.

4 *Analyze the reasons for studying accounting.*

SO, WHY SHOULD I STUDY ACCOUNTING?

You may still be asking yourself the question, "But why do I need to study accounting?" Even if you have no desire to be an accountant, at some point in your life you will need financial information to make certain decisions. Those decisions may relate to buying versus leasing an automobile, budgeting your monthly income, deciding where you might invest your savings, or financing your (or your child's) college education. You can make each of these decisions without using financial information and then hope everything turns out okay, but that would be bad decision making. As noted in the discussion of Exhibit 1-3, a good decision does not guarantee a good outcome, but a bad decision guarantees one of two things—a bad outcome or a lucky outcome. And you cannot count on lucky outcomes time after time. On a personal level, each of us needs to understand how to collect and use accounting information.

Odds are that each of you will have the responsibility of providing some form of income for you and your family. Would you prefer working for a company that is doing well and has a promising future or one that is on the brink of bankruptcy? Of course we all want to work for companies that are doing well. But how would you know? Accounting information will allow you to evaluate your employer's short- and long-term potential.

FYI

The Bureau of Labor Statistics projects a 34% increase in accounting job openings from 1996 to the year 2005. The projected growth occurs in areas such as tax, health care, and government.

When you graduate and secure employment, it is almost certain that accounting information will play some role in your job. Whether your responsibilities include sales (where you will need information about product availability and costs), production (where you will need information regarding the costs of materials, labor, and overhead), quality control (where you will need information relating to variances between expected and actual production), or human resources (where you will need information relating to the costs of employees), you will use accounting information. The more you know about where accounting information comes from, how it is accumulated, and how it is best used, the better you will be able to perform your job.

Everyone is affected by accounting information. Saying you don't need to know accounting doesn't change the fact that you are affected by accounting information. Ignoring the value of that information simply puts you at a disadvantage. Those who recognize the value of accounting information and learn how to use it to make better decisions will have a competitive advantage over those who don't. It's as simple as that.

REVIEW OF LEARNING OBJECTIVES

1 Describe the purpose of accounting and explain its role in business and society. Accounting is a service activity designed to assist individuals and organizations in deciding how to allocate scarce resources and reach their financial objectives. It is used to accumulate, measure, and communicate economic data about organizations and to assist in the decision-making process.

2 Identify the primary users of accounting information. The primary users of accounting information are lenders, investors, management, and other interested individuals and organizations. Management accounting deals primarily with the internal accounting functions of planning, implementing, and control. Financial accounting is concerned with reporting business activities and results to external parties. The objectives of both areas of accounting are measurement and communication of information for decision-making purposes.

3 Describe the environment of accounting, including the effects of generally accepted accounting principles, international business, ethical considerations, and technology. Accounting functions in a dynamic environment. The principles of accounting have evolved over time to meet the changing demands of the business environment. They are therefore not absolute. Only if they prove useful do they become generally accepted. Accounting principles provide comparable data for external users and need to be applied with judgment.

Since the 1930s, several organizations have been involved in the development of accounting principles in the United States. The American Institute of Certified Public Accountants (AICPA), the Securities and Exchange Commission (SEC), and the Financial Accounting Standards Board (FASB) are among the most prominent. The FASB is currently the primary standard-setting body for accounting principles in the private sector.

Accounting is practiced in an international environment. Accounting procedures in the United States sometimes must be modified to accommodate foreign operations. Attempts are being made to establish consistent and comparable accounting practices throughout the world, primarily through the efforts of the International Accounting Standards Committee (IASC).

Ethical considerations affect society and are particularly important for accountants, who have a special responsibility to the public. CPAs and CMAs have adopted standards of conduct to guide them in the performance of their duties.

Technology has changed the way accounting information is accumulated and analyzed. What once occupied a large part of an accountant's time is now done quickly by computers, thereby freeing the accountant to be involved in more productive tasks. But technology has not removed the accountant from the decision-making process. Accounting judgment is still essential.

4 Analyze the reasons for studying accounting. Knowing how to use accounting information will help individuals make better decisions in their personal life as well as in their employment. Whatever the job, it is likely that accounting information plays a part. Knowing where information comes from, how it is accumulated, and how it is best used, will result in better decision making.

KEY TERMS AND CONCEPTS

accounting 5
accounting cycle 8
accounting system 4
American Institute of Certified Public Accountants (AICPA) 15
annual report 9
bookkeeping 4
business 6
certified management accountant (CMA) 15
certified public accountant (CPA) 15
financial accounting 9
Financial Accounting Standards Board (FASB) 14
financial statements 9
generally accepted accounting principles (GAAP) 14
Institute of Management Accountants (IMA) 15
Internal Revenue Service (IRS) 16
International Accounting Standards Committee (IASC) 17
management accounting 8
nonprofit organization 6
Securities and Exchange Commission (SEC) 15

DISCUSSION QUESTIONS

1. What are the three functions of an accounting system?
2. What are the essential elements in decision making, and how does accounting fit into the process?
3. What types of personal decisions have required you to use accounting information?
4. What does the term *business* mean to you?
5. Why is accounting often referred to as the "language of business"?
6. In what ways are the needs of internal and external users of accounting information the same? In what ways are they different?
7. What are generally accepted accounting principles (GAAP)? Who currently develops and issues GAAP? What is the purpose of GAAP?
8. Why is it important for financial statements and other external reports to be based on generally accepted accounting principles (GAAP)?
9. What are the respective roles of the Securities and Exchange Commission (SEC), the American Institute of CPAs (AICPA), and the Internal Revenue Service (IRS) in the setting of accounting standards?
10. For you as a potential investor, what is the problem with different countries having different accounting standards? For you as the president of a multinational company, what is the problem with different countries having different accounting standards?
11. Ethical considerations affect all society. Why are ethical considerations especially important for accountants?
12. Given significant technological advances, can we expect to see less demand for accountants and accounting-type services?
13. Other than it is a requirement for your major or your mom or dad is making you, why should you study accounting?

DISCUSSION CASES

CASE 1-1 TO LEND OR NOT TO LEND—THAT IS THE QUESTION

Sam Love is vice president and chief lending officer of the Meeker First National Bank. Recently, Bill McCarthy, a new farmer, moved to town. Sam has not dealt with Bill previously, and knows little about the Mountain Meadow Ranch that Bill operates. Bill would like to borrow $100,000 to purchase some equipment and yearling steers for his ranch. What information does Sam need to help make the lending decision? What type of information should Bill collect and analyze before even requesting the loan?

CASE 1-2

INFORMATION NEEDS TO REMAIN COMPETITIVE

In a recent article in *U.S. News & World Report,* Dan McGraw describes how two computer giants, **Dell** and **Compaq**, are poised to do battle in the personal computer market. Compaq has 13.2% of the U.S. market share for personal computers to Dell's 8.8%. However, Dell's market share has more than doubled in the last four years while Compaq has increased less than one percent. What type of information, accounting or otherwise, do you think the management of Compaq may want and need as they compete with Dell and the other PC companies?

Source: Dan McGraw, "Shootout at PC Corral," *U.S. News & World Report* (June 23, 1997), pp. 37–38.

CASE 1-3

INTERNATIONAL HAPPENINGS

July 1, 1997, marked a historic date as Hong Kong reverted to political and economic control by mainland China. Despite uncertainties caused by this change, traditional Hong Kong stocks have performed well. At the same time, "red-chip offerings" (stocks of companies controlled by mainland China interests that are listed on the Hong Kong stock exchange) have sizzled. As an international investor, what accounting information might be helpful as you consider investing in the Hong Kong stock market? What variables are present in this situation for which accounting information is not likely to be very helpful?

EXERCISES

EXERCISE 1-1
The Role and Importance of Accounting

Assume that you are applying for a part-time job as an accounting clerk in a retail clothing establishment. During the interview, the store manager asks how you expect to contribute to the business. How would you respond?

EXERCISE 1-2
Accounting Information and Decision Making

You are the owner of Automated Systems, Inc., which sells **Apple** computers and related data processing equipment. You are currently trying to decide whether to continue selling the Apple computer line or distribute the **IBM** personal computer instead. What information do you need to consider in order to determine how successful your business is or will be? What information would help you decide whether to sell the Apple or the IBM personal computer line? Use your imagination and general knowledge of business activity.

EXERCISE 1-3
Users of Financial Information

Why might each of the following individuals or groups be interested in a firm's financial statements? (A) The current stockholders of the firm, (B) The creditors of the firm, (C) The management of the firm, (D) The prospective stockholders of the firm, (E) The Internal Revenue Service (IRS), (F) The SEC, (G) The firm's major labor union.

EXERCISE 1-4
Investing in the Stock Market

Assume your grandparents have just gifted you $20,000 on the condition that you will invest the money in the stock market. As you contemplate making your investment choice, what accounting information do you want to help identify the companies that will have high future rates of return?

EXERCISE 1-5
Allocation of Limited Resources

Assume you are a small business owner trying to increase your company's profits. How can accounting information help you to efficiently allocate limited resources to maximize your business profit?

EXERCISE 1-6
Management vs. Financial Accounting

This chapter discusses two areas of accounting: management and financial accounting. Contrast management and financial accounting with respect to the following:

- overall purpose
- type of financial reports used (i.e., external, internal, or both)
- users of the information

Also, in what ways are these two fields of accounting similar?

EXERCISE 1-7
The Role of the SEC

It is not often that the federal government has allowed the private sector to govern itself, but that is exactly what has happened with the field of accounting. The SEC has delegated the responsibility of rule making to the FASB, a group of seven accountants who are hired full-time to discuss issues, research areas of interest, and determine what GAAP is and will be. What are the advantages of allowing the private sector to determine accounting standards? Identify any advantages that might be available to the SEC if it established the rules that govern the practice of accounting.

EXERCISE 1-8
Why Two Sets of Books?

This past year you were married. This coming April you will be faced with preparing your first tax return since Mom and Dad said "you are now on your own." As you review the IRS regulations, you notice several differences from what you learned in your accounting class. It appears that businesses must keep two sets of books: one for the IRS and one in accordance with GAAP. Why aren't GAAP and IRS rules the same?

EXERCISE 1-9
Differences in Accounting Across Borders

In the United States, accounting for inventory is a difficult issue. Inventory is comprised of those items either purchased or manufactured to be resold at a profit. Numerous methods are available to account for inventory for financial reporting purposes. A very commonly used method—called LIFO (last-in, first-out)—is the one that minimizes a company's tax obligation. In the United Kingdom, however, LIFO is not permitted for tax purposes and thus is not used very often for financial reporting. In Turkey, severe restrictions are placed on the use of LIFO, and in Russia, LIFO is a foreign term. Only in Germany, where the tax laws have been modified to allow the use of LIFO, can one see LIFO being adopted. Different accounting methods are available in accounting for numerous other issues. Identify some major problems associated with comparing the financial statements of companies from different countries.

EXERCISE 1-10
Ethics in Accounting

The text has pointed out that ethics is an important topic, especially for CPAs and CMAs. Derek Bok, former law professor and president of Harvard University, has suggested that colleges and universities have a special opportunity and obligation to train students to be more thoughtful and perceptive about moral and ethical issues. Other individuals have concluded that it is not possible to "teach" ethics. What do you think? Can ethics be taught? If you agree that colleges and universities can teach ethics, how might the ethical dimensions of accounting be presented to students?

EXERCISE 1-11
Career Opportunities in Accounting

You are scheduled to graduate from college with a degree in accounting and your mother would like to know what you plan to do with the rest of your life. She assumes that your only option is to be a bookkeeper like Bob Cratchit in the story *A Christmas Carol.* What can you tell Mom regarding the options available to you with your degree in accounting?

EXERCISE 1-12
Why Do I Need to Know Accounting?

One of your college friends recently graduated from school with a major in Music (specifically piano). He has told you that he is going to start his own piano instructional business. He plans to operate the business from home. You ask him how he is going to account for his business and his reply is, "I graduated in music, not accounting. I am going to teach music, not number crunching. I didn't need accounting in college and I don't need it now!" Is your friend right? What financial information might he find useful in operating his business?

EXERCISE 1-13

Challenges to the Accounting Profession

As the business world continues to change the way in which business is conducted, accountants are faced with the challenge of accounting for these changes. Who, for example, could have anticipated the risks associated with asbestos? Or the decline of communism? Or the increased litigious environment in the United States? Each of these events, and many more, has influenced business—which has, in turn, influenced accounting. From your general understanding of accounting and the current business environment, what are some of the challenges you see facing the accounting profession?

Analyzing Real Company Information

International Case

Ethics Case

Writing Assignment

The Debate

Internet Search

Accounting is more than just doing textbook problems. These Competency Enhancement Opportunities provide practice in critical thinking, oral and written communication, research, teamwork, and consideration of ethical issues.

ANALYZING REAL COMPANY INFORMATION

• Analyzing 1-1 (Microsoft)

In the Appendix at the back of this text is Microsoft's complete annual report for the year ended June 30, 1997. Review the annual report and identify the major areas contained in this report. Of the report, how many pages are devoted to a narrative of the prior three years' performance? How many pages focus on explaining technical accounting and business-related issues and procedures? In your opinion, given your limited knowledge of accounting, what is the most interesting part of the annual report? What is the least interesting?

• Analyzing 1-2 (General Motors)

Below is a condensed listing of the assets and liabilities of General Motors as of December 31, 1996. All amounts are in millions of U.S. dollars.

Assets		*Liabilities*	
Cash	$ 22,262	Loans Payable	$ 85,300
Loans Receivable	57,550	Pensions	7,599
Inventories	11,898	Other Retiree Benefits	43,190
Property & Equipment	67,616	Other Liabilities	62,635
Other Assets	62,816		
Total Assets	$222,142	Total Liabilities	$198,724

1. Among its assets, General Motors lists more than $57 billion in loans receivable. This represents loans that General Motors has made and expects to collect in the future. This is exactly the kind of asset reported among the assets of banks. Given what you know about General Motors' business, how do you think General Motors acquired these loans receivable?

2. The difference between the reported amount of General Motors' assets and liabilities is $23.418 billion ($222,142 − $198,724). What does this difference represent?

INTERNATIONAL CASE

• Should the SEC choose the FASB or the IASC?

The SEC has received from Congress the legal authority to set accounting standards in the United States. Historically, the SEC has allowed the FASB to set those standards. In addition, the SEC has refused to allow foreign companies to seek investment funds in the United States unless they agree to provide U.S. investors with financial statements prepared using FASB rules.

The number of foreign companies seeking to list their shares on U.S. stock exchanges is increasing. Even more would likely sell stock to the American public if the SEC were to agree to accept financial statements prepared according to usually less stringent IASC standards.

Why do you think the SEC has so far insisted on financial statements prepared using FASB rules? Do you agree with its policy? Explain.

ETHICS CASE

• Disagreement with the boss

You recently graduated with your degree in accounting and have accepted an entry-level accounting position with BigTec, Inc. One of your first responsibilities is to review expense reports submitted by various executives. The expense reports include such items as receipts for taking clients to dinner as well as hotel receipts for business travel. In conducting this review, you note that your boss has submitted for reimbursement several items that are clearly outside the established guidelines of the corporation. In questioning your boss about the items, he told you to process the items and not worry about it. What would you do?

WRITING ASSIGNMENTS

• The language of business

Accounting is known as "the language of business." Prepare a one- to two-page paper explaining why all business students should have some accounting education. Also include how accounting applies to at least five different types of businesses, such as a grocery store, a university, or a movie theater.

• Visiting an accounting professional

Select a field of accounting you are interested in. Visit a professional who works in that area and discuss the career opportunities available in that specific accounting field. After the visit, prepare a one-to two-page paper summarizing what you learned from your discussion with the accounting professional.

THE DEBATE

• Insulate the FASB

As mentioned in the text, the FASB conducts public hearings concerning any new accounting standards that it is considering. In addition, the FASB invites interested parties (businesses, trade groups, user groups, accounting professors) to send in written comments on proposed standards. This "due process" system occasionally exposes the FASB to intense lobbying pressure for and against proposed standards. For example, when the FASB was deliberating over the proper accounting for option compensation (see the example in the chapter), some companies, upset at the FASB's proposed approach, appealed to Congress to pass a bill outlawing the FASB's standard. Can the FASB establish good accounting standards in such a heated, public environment?

Divide your group into two teams.

- One team represents the "Open Door Policy." Prepare a two-minute oral argument supporting the continuation of the FASB's policy of adopting accounting standards only after public debate.
- The other team represents the "Insulate the FASB Movement." Prepare a two-minute oral argument outlining why it is impossible for the FASB to design conceptually correct accounting standards while being bombarded with the complaints and threats of self-interested companies and lobbyists.

INTERNET SEARCH

• The Financial Accounting Standards Board

The FASB's Web address is www.rutgers.edu/Accounting/raw/fasb/welcome.htm. Sometimes Web addresses change; so if this address does not work, access the Web site for this textbook (stice.swcollege.com) for an updated link.

Once you have gained access to the site, answer the following questions.

1. What is the mission of the FASB?
2. How many FASB statements are there? When was the most recent statement issued?
3. When was the first statement issued and what is it about? What other statements are related to Statement No. 1?
4. In what ways are the following three types of FASB pronouncements different: (1) Statements of Financial Accounting Standards (SFAS), (2) Interpretations of SFAS, and (3) Statements of Financial Accounting Concepts?

CHAPTER

2 FINANCIAL STATEMENTS: AN OVERVIEW

LEARNING OBJECTIVES

After studying this chapter, you should be able to:

1. *Understand the basic elements and formats of the three primary financial statements—balance sheet, income statement, and statement of cash flows.*
2. *Recognize the need for financial statement notes and identify the types of information included in the notes.*
3. *Describe the purpose of an audit report and the incentives the auditor has to perform a good audit.*
4. *Use financial ratios to identify a company's strengths and weaknesses and to forecast its future performance.*
5. *Explain the fundamental concepts and assumptions that underlie financial accounting.*

SETTING THE STAGE

In addition to founding the brokerage firm of **Merrill Lynch**, in 1926 Charles Merrill was instrumental in the consolidation of several grocery store chains in the western United States, forming one big holding company called **Safeway**. In 1955, control of Safeway passed to Robert Magowan, Merrill's son-in-law. Under Magowan's leadership, Safeway expanded to become the second largest supermarket chain in the United States. Shortly after Magowan retired in 1971, Safeway passed **The Great Atlantic and Pacific Tea Company (A&P)** to become the largest chain.

During the 1970s, Safeway became too cautious and conservative (in the view of many). It was whispered that Safeway would become the A&P of the West: a fallen giant no longer willing to make the bold moves that had created its success in the first place. In 1980, Robert Magowan's 37-year-old son, Peter (who had started out in Safeway as a teenager bagging groceries), became chairman of the board of directors. As he assumed leadership of Safeway, Magowan faced a host of problems: an overall decrease in the size of the grocery market due to an increased tendency by Americans to eat at fast-food restaurants; union contracts that resulted in higher labor costs for Safeway than many of its competitors; high corporate overhead; and stores that were too small and too close together. As a result of these problems, between 1976 and 1980 Safeway lost market share in 9 of the 14 major markets in which it operated. As one executive put it, "[Losing market share] in the food business [is] a hell of an indicator you're not giving the customer what he wants." By 1981, Safeway's financial performance had hit disappointing lows.

Under Peter Magowan's leadership, Safeway eliminated 2,000 office and warehouse jobs and embarked upon an impressive program of new construction and remodeling. During much of the early 1980s, Safeway spent more on capital expenditures than any other U.S. company, averaging nearly $600 million per year. In November 1986, Safeway was acquired by **Kohlberg, Kravis, Roberts & Co. (KKR)** for $5.3 billion in what was then the second-largest leveraged buyout (LBO) of all time. An LBO involves a group of private investors, sometimes joined by company managers, supplying only a small amount of money to buy an entire corporation. The bulk of the purchase price is provided by banks and other lenders, with the assets of the acquired company serving as collateral for the loans. As an indication of how leveraged the Safeway buyout was, the KKR investors put only $130 million of their own money into the $5.3 billion deal.

So, how is Safeway doing today? With 1996 sales of $17.3 billion, the 1996 Fortune 500 survey places Safeway as only the third-largest food and drug chain in the United States, behind **Kroger** ($25.2 billion in sales) and **American Stores** ($18.7 billion).[1] In fact, Safeway's 1996 sales are significantly below its peak sales of $20.3 billion in 1986. However, sales volume isn't the only financial measure that can be used to evaluate a company. For example, Safeway's net income in 1996 was $461 million, higher than the net income for both Kroger and American Stores. Also, Safeway's cash income ("cash from operations") was $825 million. Further, Safeway earned 38.8 cents of profit for every dollar invested by its stockholders—a decent one-year return on investment (a dollar invested in a certificate of deposit during the same period would have earned only about 4 cents).

1. Coincidentally, American Stores traces its roots back to the Skaggs family, whose stores also formed the backbone of the original Safeway chain organized by Charles Merrill in 1926.

To adequately answer the question of how Safeway is doing today, one must have a working knowledge of financial statements. In this chapter, you will learn that the financial statements are summary reports that show how a business is doing and where its successes and failures lie. The financial statements covered in this chapter are the same as those used every day by millions of business owners, investors, and creditors to evaluate how well or poorly organizations are doing.

You will also be introduced to the use of financial ratios, which are the tools of financial statement analysis. You will learn how to compute and interpret ratios such as return on equity, asset turnover, and price-earnings (PE) ratio. Hopefully, you will come away from this chapter convinced that the purpose of accounting is not to fill out dull reports that are then filed away in dusty cabinets, but rather to prepare summary financial performance measures to be used as the basis for thousands of economic decisions every day.

1 *Understand the basic elements and formats of the three primary financial statements—balance sheet, income statement, and statement of cash flows.*

primary financial statements The balance sheet, income statement, and statement of cash flows, used by external groups to assess a company's economic standing.

balance sheet (statement of financial position) The financial statement that reports a company's assets, liabilities, and owners' equity at a particular date.

income statement (statement of earnings) The financial statement that reports the amount of net income earned by a company during a period.

statement of cash flows The financial statement that reports the amount of cash collected and paid out by a company during a period of time.

THE FINANCIAL STATEMENTS

Because financial statements are used by so many different groups (investors, creditors, managers, etc.), they are sometimes called *general-purpose financial statements.* The three **primary financial statements** are the balance sheet, the income statement, and the statement of cash flows. These statements provide answers to the following questions:

1. What is the company's current financial status?
2. What were the company's operating results for the period?
3. How did the company obtain and use cash during the period?

The **balance sheet** (or **statement of financial position**) reports the resources of a company (assets), the company's obligations (liabilities), and the difference between what is owned (assets) and what is owed (liabilities), called owners' equity. The **income statement** (or **statement of earnings**) reports the amount of net income earned by a company during a period, with annual and quarterly income statements being the most common. (Net income is discussed later in the chapter.) The income statement represents the accountant's best effort at measuring the economic performance of a company. The **statement of cash flows** reports the amount of cash collected and paid out by a company in the following three types of activities: operating, investing, and financing. As an illustration, the 1997 financial statements from **Microsoft** are reproduced in Appendix A at the end of the book. The Microsoft statements are referred to throughout this chapter and the rest of the book.

The Balance Sheet

In the movie "The Princess Bride," the hero, Wesley, was "mostly dead all day" until being revived by a miracle pill. Wesley was immediately challenged to come up with a plan to stop the imminent marriage of his true love, Buttercup, to the evil Prince Humperdinck. In formulating his plan, Wesley's first question to his conspirators was "What are our liabilities?" followed by "What are our assets?" In essence, the recently revived hero was saying, "Let me see a balance sheet." Similarly, the first questions about any business by potential investors and creditors are "What are the resources of the business?" and "What are its existing obligations?" The balance sheet answers these questions.

The three categories of the balance sheet—assets, liabilities, and owners' equity—are each explained below.

Assets

assets Economic resources that are owned or controlled by a company.

Assets are economic resources that are owned or controlled[2] by a company. Assets for a typical company include cash, accounts receivable (amounts owed to the company by customers), inventory (goods held for sale), land, buildings, equipment, and even intangible items, such as copyrights and patents. To be summarized and aggregated on a balance sheet, each asset must be assigned a dollar amount. A balance sheet wouldn't be very useful with the following asset listing: one bank account, two warehouses full of goods, three trucks, and four customers who owe us money. As emphasized throughout this text, the monetary measurement and valuation of assets is an area in which accountants must exercise considerable professional judgment.

FYI

The insurmountable difficulties in valuing some assets can cause important economic assets to be excluded from a company's balance sheet. For example, how does one put a monetary value on the worldwide reputation of Coca-Cola or on the genius and leadership of Bill Gates? These assets, though incredibly valuable, are not listed in the balance sheets of The Coca-Cola Company or of Microsoft.

Liabilities

liabilities Obligations to pay cash, transfer other assets, or provide services to someone else.

Liabilities are obligations to pay cash, transfer other assets, or provide services to someone else. Your personal liabilities might include unpaid phone bills, the remaining balance on an automobile loan, or an obligation to complete work for which you have already been paid. Some common liabilities of a company are accounts payable (amounts owed by the company to suppliers), notes payable (amounts owed to banks or others), and mortgages payable (amounts owed for purchased property, such as land or buildings). Like assets, liabilities must be measured in monetary amounts. And, as with assets, quantifying the amount of a liability can require extensive judgment. As one example, consider the difficulties faced by a company to quantify its obligation to clean up a particular toxic waste site when the cleanup will take years to complete; the exact extent of the environmental damage at the site is still in dispute; and legal responsibility for the toxic mess is still debated in the courts. Properly valuing a company's liabilities is one of the biggest (if not *the* biggest) challenges that an accountant faces.

Owners' Equity

owners' equity The ownership interest in the net assets of an entity; equals total assets minus total liabilities.

net assets The owner's equity of a business; equal to total assets minus total liabilities.

The remaining claim against the assets of a business, after the liabilities have been deducted, is **owners' equity**. Thus, owners' equity is a residual amount; it represents the **net assets** (total assets minus total liabilities) available after all obligations have been satisfied. Obviously, if there are no liabilities (an unlikely situation, except at the start of a business), then the total assets are exactly equal to the owners' claims against those assets—the owners' equity.

In order to get a business started, investors transfer resources, usually cash, to the business in return for part ownership. Ownership of a company can be restricted to one person (a sole proprietorship), to a small group (a partnership), or to a diffuse group of owners who often don't even know one another (a corporation). When owners initially invest money in a corporation, they receive evidence of their own-

2. An example of an asset that a company does not technically own, but does economically control, is a building that the company uses under a long-term, noncancelable lease agreement.

stockholders (shareholders) The owners of a corporation.

stockholders' equity The owners' equity section of a corporate balance sheet.

dividends Distributions to the owners (stockholders) of a corporation.

retained earnings The amount of accumulated earnings of the business that have not been distributed to owners.

ership in the form of shares of stock, represented by stock certificates. These shares of stock may then be privately traded among existing owners of the corporation, privately sold to new owners, or traded publicly on an organized stock exchange such as the New York Stock Exchange (NYSE) (where Safeway's shares are traded) or the NASDAQ exchange (where Microsoft's shares are traded). The owners of a corporation are called **stockholders** or **shareholders**, and the owners' equity section of a corporate balance sheet is sometimes referred to as **stockholders' equity**.

Owners' equity is increased when owners make additional investments in a business or when the business generates profits that are retained in the business. Since business profits belong to the owners, retaining the profits in the business is equivalent to giving the profits to the owners and then having them immediately reinvest that amount back into the business.

Owners' equity is decreased when the owners take back part of their investment. If the business is a corporation, distributions to the owners (stockholders) are called **dividends**. Owners' equity can also be decreased if operations generate a loss instead of a profit. In the extreme, very poor performance can result in the loss of all the assets originally invested by the owners. For a corporation, the amount of accumulated earnings of the business that have not been distributed to owners is called **retained earnings**. The portion of owners' equity contributed by owners in exchange for shares of stock is called **capital stock**. The amount of retained earnings plus the amount of capital stock equals the corporation's total owners' equity.

FYI

Although the emphasis in this book is on corporations, most of the same principles also apply to proprietorships and partnerships.

BUSINESS ENVIRONMENT ESSAY

Should I Incorporate? Pick up just about any business newspaper or magazine, look in the classified section, and you are sure to see advertisements offering to help you set up a corporation. "Incorporate in USA by Fax or Phone!!!" "Incorporate: All 50 States and Offshore." "Typical Incorporating Fees: Delaware, $199; Wyoming, $285; the Bahamas, $500; Isle of Man, £250." With all this eagerness to incorporate, there must be some advantages. To understand these advantages, as well as the disadvantages, it is necessary to review the three major types of business entities: proprietorships, partnerships, and corporations.

1. *Proprietorship.* A proprietorship is a business owned by one person. Almost always, the owner of the business also manages the operation. For example, many owners of small businesses (especially those that provide personal services) manage the day-to-day activities of, and receive the profits directly from, those businesses. Legally, a proprietorship is merely an extension of the owner. The owner is personally responsible for all the activities and obligations of the business.
2. *Partnership.* A partnership is a business association of two or more individuals. As in a proprietorship, the partners generally own and manage the business and are personally responsible for all the obligations of the business. A partnership organization makes sense when the work load and financial requirements associated with starting and operating a business are too much for one person.
3. *Corporation.* A corporation is a business that is chartered (incorporated) as a separate legal entity under the laws of a particular state or country. With a proprietorship or a partnership, the owners *are* the business. With a corporation, the operations and obligations of the business are legally separated from the personal affairs of the owners. Typically, stockholders in a corporation can freely buy and sell their interests, thus allowing the corporate ownership to change without dissolving the business. The stockholders elect a board of directors, which then hires executives to manage the corporation. The managers, as employees of the corporation, may or may not be stockholders. Thus, in a corporation there is a separation of ownership from management.

The primary advantages of incorporation are:

- Investment funds can be accumulated from many different individuals, allowing for the development of larger, more efficient companies.
- Individual owners can buy and sell their ownership shares without getting the permission of the other owners.
- The liability of the owners is limited. If the business does not flourish, the worst that can happen to the owners is that they lose their investment; their other personal assets are not at risk.

The primary disadvantages of incorporation are:

- Corporate income is taxed twice: once when it is earned by the corporation and again when it is paid out to shareholders in the form of dividends.
- Management of the business is separated from ownership. The owners must be cautious in monitoring the activities of their hired managers.

As shown below, the majority of business activity in the United States is conducted by corporations, although the actual number of proprietorships is greater.

Type of Business	Number of Businesses	Sales
Sole Proprietorships	15.848 million	$ 757 billion
Partnerships	1.467 million	627 billion
Corporations	3.965 million	11,814 billion

Source: U.S. Bureau of the Census, *Statistical Abstract of the United States: 1996* (116th edition), Washington, DC, 1996. Data are based on IRS information for 1993.

capital stock The portion of a corporation's owners' equity contributed by owners in exchange for shares of stock.

accounting equation An algebraic equation that expresses the relationship between assets (resources), liabilities (obligations), and owners' equity (net assets, or the residual interest in a business after all liabilities have been met): Assets = Liabilities + Owners' Equity.

double-entry accounting A system of recording transactions in a way that maintains the equality of the accounting equation.

Accounting Equation

The balance sheet presents information based on the basic **accounting equation**:

Assets = Liabilities + Owners' Equity

In fact, the name "balance sheet" comes from the fact that a proper balance sheet must always balance—total assets must equal the total of liabilities and owners' equity. The accounting equation is not some miraculous coincidence; it is true by definition. Liabilities and owners' equity are just the sources of funding used to buy the assets; that is, they are the claims (creditors' claims and owners' claims) against the assets. So, another way to view the accounting equation is that the total amount of the assets is equal to the total amount of funding needed to buy the assets. The total resources, therefore, equal the claims against those resources. This is illustrated in Exhibit 2-1.

The accounting equation is presented here merely to give you a glimpse of **double-entry accounting**. Chapter 3 gives an in-depth discussion of the equation elements and the mechanics of double-entry accounting.

The Format of a Balance Sheet

A simple balance sheet, adapted from **Microsoft**'s 1997 balance sheet reproduced in Appendix A at the end of the book, is shown in Exhibit 2-2.

Note that a balance sheet is presented for a particular date because it reports a company's financial position at a point in time. The balance sheet in Exhibit 2-2 presents Microsoft's financial position as of June 30, 1997.

As illustrated, the balance sheet is divided into the three major sections we have described: assets, liabilities, and owners' equity. The asset section identifies the types of assets owned by Microsoft (cash, for example) and the monetary amounts asso-

EXHIBIT 2-1

Elements of the Accounting Equation

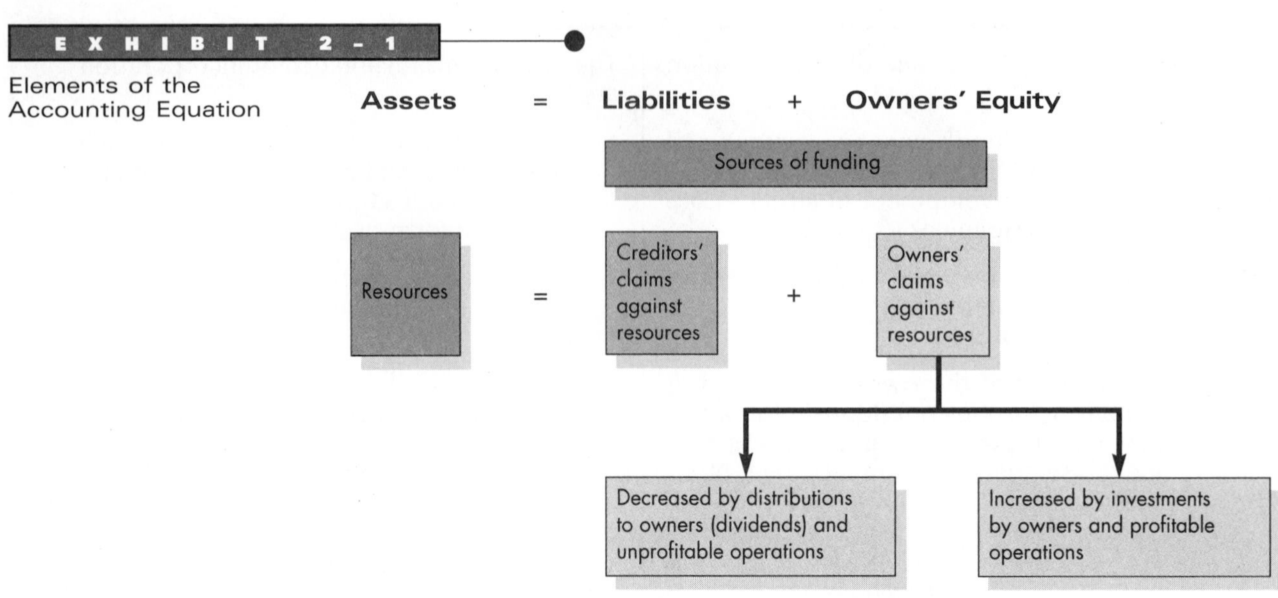

EXHIBIT 2-2

Simplified Balance Sheet for Microsoft

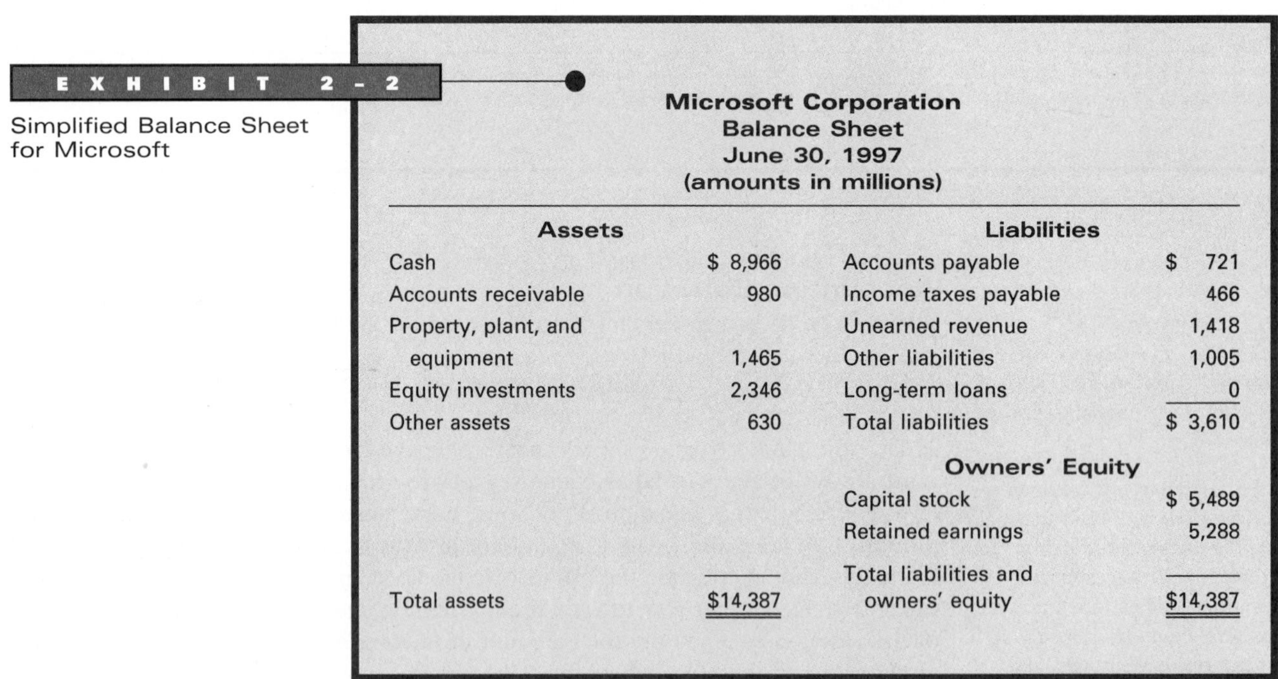

Microsoft Corporation
Balance Sheet
June 30, 1997
(amounts in millions)

Assets		**Liabilities**	
Cash	$ 8,966	Accounts payable	$ 721
Accounts receivable	980	Income taxes payable	466
Property, plant, and equipment	1,465	Unearned revenue	1,418
		Other liabilities	1,005
Equity investments	2,346	Long-term loans	0
Other assets	630	Total liabilities	$ 3,610
		Owners' Equity	
		Capital stock	$ 5,489
		Retained earnings	5,288
Total assets	$14,387	Total liabilities and owners' equity	$14,387

ciated with those assets. The liability section defines the extent and nature of Microsoft's debts (income taxes not yet paid, for example).

(STOP & THINK)

Actually, the Microsoft balance sheet is quite unusual. Very few companies have the large amount of cash ($9 billion) and low amount of long-term debt ($0) that Microsoft has. Is it good for a company to have so much cash?

Remember that the balance sheet is not merely a report to be prepared and forgotten; it is a summary of important information that is useful to investors and creditors. For example, if you were a banker, would you give a loan to Microsoft based on the information from the June 30, 1997, balance sheet? Of course you would, because you see that Microsoft already has enough cash on hand ($9 billion) to be able to pay off all existing liabilities ($3.6 billion) more than two times over. Based on the balance sheet information, you can see that any loan to Microsoft could be easily repaid.

Owners' equity completes the balance sheet. This section identifies the portion of Microsoft's resources that were contributed by owners, either in exchange for shares of stock or as undistributed earnings since Microsoft's inception. Together with liabilities, owners' equity indicates how a company is financed (whether by borrowing or by owner contributions and operating profits). You can see that Microsoft has been financed primarily through owner investment. Almost half of this owner investment ($5.3 billion) has been in the form of retained earnings.

Classified and Comparative Balance Sheets

Imagine that two people each owe you $10,000. You ask to see the balance sheets of each. Borrower A has assets of $10,000 in the form of cash. Borrower B has assets of $10,000 in the form of undeveloped land. If you need to collect the loan in the next two weeks, which of the two borrowers is more likely to be able to pay you back? Borrower A is more likely to be able to repay you quickly because the assets of A are more *liquid,* meaning that they are in the form of cash or can be easily converted into cash. Assets such as undeveloped land are said to be *illiquid* in that it takes time and effort to convert them into cash. This illustration shows that not all assets are the same. For some purposes, it is very important to distinguish between current assets, which are generally more liquid, and long-term assets. A balance sheet that distinguishes between current and long-term assets is called a **classified balance sheet**.

classified balance sheet A balance sheet in which assets and liabilities are subdivided into current and long-term categories.

CAUTION

Don't worry about fully understanding all the items in Safeway's classified balance sheet, such as the "Property under capital leases" and the "Cumulative translation adjustments." If there was nothing else to learn, this book would be much shorter and this accounting class would last for only two weeks.

To illustrate a classified balance sheet, we consider the balance sheet for **Safeway**, the supermarket chain described in the opening scenario of this chapter. In Exhibit 2-3, Safeway's assets are classified as current, or short-term, and long-term.

Current assets include cash and other assets that are expected to be converted to cash within a year. Current assets generally are listed in decreasing order of **liquidity**; cash is listed first, followed by the other current assets, such as accounts receivable. **Long-term assets**, such as land, buildings, and equipment, are those that a company needs in order to operate its business over an extended period of time.

Like assets, liabilities usually are classified as either current (obligations expected to be paid within a year) or long-term. Accounts payable, for example, usually would be paid within 30 to 60 days, whereas a mortgage may remain on the books for 20 to 30 years before it is fully paid.

current assets Cash and other assets that can be easily converted to cash within a year.

liquidity The ability of a company to pay its debts in the short run.

long-term assets Assets that a company needs in order to operate its business over an extended period of time.

comparative financial statements Financial statements in which data for two or more years are shown together.

Safeway's balance sheet in Exhibit 2-3 includes financial information for both the current year and the preceding year. Most companies prepare such **comparative financial statements** so that readers can identify any significant changes in particular items. For example, notice that Safeway's total assets increased by $350.9 million ($5,545.2 million − $5,194.3 million) from 1995 to 1996. Where did the money come from to finance this increase in assets? Most of it came from an increased amount of profits retained in the business (retained earnings increased by $460.6 million). In fact, this retained earnings increase was also enough to allow Safeway to repay some long-term debt (long-term notes and debentures decreased by $215.5 million).

Limitations of a Balance Sheet

Although the balance sheet is useful in showing the financial status of a company, it does have some limitations. The primary limitation of the balance sheet is that it does not reflect the current value or worth of a company. Refer back to the balance sheet numbers for **Microsoft** in Exhibit 2-2. If the balance sheet were perfect, meaning that it included all economic assets reported at their current market values, then

EXHIBIT 2-3

Classified Balance Sheets for Safeway

Safeway Inc.
Balance Sheet
December 28, 1996 and December 30, 1995
(amounts in millions)

	1996	1995
Assets		
Current assets:		
Cash	$ 79.7	$ 74.8
Accounts receivable	160.9	152.7
Merchandise inventories	1,283.3	1,191.8
Prepaid expenses and other current assets	130.5	95.5
Total current assets	$1,654.4	$1,514.8
Property:		
Land	$ 438.3	$ 419.4
Buildings	1,286.9	1,213.2
Leasehold improvements	957.2	858.5
Fixtures and equipment	2,108.5	1,912.7
Property under capital leases	278.7	283.4
Total property	$5,069.6	$4,687.2
Less accumulated depreciation and amortization	2,313.2	2,094.3
Total property, net	$2,756.4	$2,592.9
Other assets:		
Goodwill	$ 312.5	$ 323.8
Prepaid pension costs	328.7	322.4
Investments in unconsolidated affiliates	362.4	336.0
Other assets	130.8	104.4
Total assets	$5,545.2	$5,194.3
Liabilities and Stockholders' Equity		
Current liabilities:		
Accounts payable	$1,153.1	$1,040.0
Accrued salaries and wages	231.2	234.6
Other current liabilities	645.7	664.4
Total current liabilities	$2,030.0	$1,939.0
Long-term debt:		
Notes and debentures	$1,568.1	$1,783.6
Obligations under capital leases	160.4	166.2
Total long-term debt	$1,728.5	$1,949.8
Deferred income taxes	223.8	108.5
Accrued claims and other liabilities	376.1	401.5
Total liabilities	$4,358.4	$4,398.8
Stockholders' equity:		
Common stock: par value $0.01 per share	$ 2.2	$ 2.1
Additional paid-in capital	750.3	684.9
Unexercised warrants purchased	(322.7)	(196.2)
Cumulative translation adjustments	12.0	20.3
Retained earnings	745.0	284.4
Total stockholders' equity	$1,186.8	$ 795.5
Total liabilities and stockholders' equity	$5,545.2	$5,194.3

the amount of owners' equity would be equal to the market value of the company. In the case of Microsoft, the value of the company would be $10.777 billion, which is the amount of assets that would remain after all the liabilities were repaid. However, the actual market value of Microsoft on June 30, 1997, was $152 billion. How could the balance sheet be so wrong?

The discrepancy between recorded balance sheet value and actual market value is the result of the following two factors:

market value The value of a company as measured by the number of shares of stock outstanding multiplied by the current market price of the stock; the current value of a business.

1. Accountants record many assets at their purchase cost, not at their current market value. **Market value** is the price that would have to be paid to buy the same asset today. For example, if land was obtained ten years ago, it would still be reported on the balance sheet at its original cost, even though its market value may have increased dramatically.
2. Not all economic assets are included in the balance sheet. For example, important economic assets of Microsoft are its proven track record of successful products, the genius of Bill Gates, and a strong, established position in the marketplace (ask **Novell**, **WordPerfect**, **Lotus**, and **Netscape** what it is like to compete against Microsoft). These intangible factors are all very valuable economic assets. In fact, they are by far the most valuable assets Microsoft has. However, these important economic assets are outside the normal accounting process.

book value The value of a company as measured by the amount of owners' equity; that is, assets less liabilities.

Because the balance sheet can underreport the value of some long-term assets, and not report other important economic assets, the accounting **book value** of a company (measured by the amount of owners' equity) is usually less than the company's market value, measured by the market price per share times the number of shares of stock. This is illustrated in Exhibit 2-4 using data for the ten largest companies (in terms of market value) in the United States.

Despite its deficiencies, the balance sheet is a useful source of information regarding the financial position of a business. A lender would never loan a company money without knowing what assets the company has and what other loans the

EXHIBIT 2-4 Book Value and Market Value for the Ten Largest U.S. Firms

Company Name	Accounting Book Value (Owners' Equity)	Market Value (Shares × Price per Share)*
General Electric	$31,125	$169,388
Coca-Cola	6,156	147,619
Exxon	43,542	125,597
Microsoft	6,908	119,112
Intel	16,872	113,195
Merck	11,970	106,633
Philip Morris	14,218	104,591
Procter & Gamble	11,722	85,443
Johnson & Johnson	10,836	77,073
IBM	21,628	74,333

*Accounting book value and market value are in millions of dollars.

Source: Fortune 500 listing, 1996. Market values are as of March 14, 1997. Accounting book values are for the end of the immediately preceding fiscal year. Accessible at fortune.com.

company is already obligated to repay. An investor shouldn't pay money in exchange for ownership in a company without knowing something about the company's existing resources and obligations. When a balance sheet is classified, and when comparative data are provided, the balance sheet provides an informative picture of a company's financial position.

TO SUMMARIZE

The balance sheet provides a summary of the financial position of a company at a particular date. It helps external users assess the financial relationship between assets (resources) and liabilities and owners' equity (claims against those resources). Assets and liabilities are usually classified as either current or long-term and are presented in descending order of liquidity. For a corporation, owners' equity consists of directly invested funds as well as retained earnings. Classified and comparative balance sheets provide useful information for readers of financial statements. Because not all economic assets are included on the balance sheet, the book value as shown in the balance sheet is usually less than the market value of the company.

The Income Statement

Almost every day, *The Wall Street Journal* includes a section called "Digest of Earnings Reports" that contains the net income, or earnings, figures announced by companies the day before. The stock prices of companies go up or down depending on whether their announced earnings meet the expectations of investors. For example, on April 19, 1997, **Microsoft** stock shot up from $98.125 to $107.625 per share in response to news of an 85% increase in Microsoft's net income as compared to the previous year. This high level of interest centered on net income makes it apparent that investors find this accounting number useful in evaluating the health and performance of a business.

Net income is reported in the income statement. The income statement shows the results of a company's operations for a period of time (a month, a quarter, or a year). The income statement summarizes the revenues generated and the costs incurred (expenses) to generate those revenues. The "bottom line" of an income statement is net income (or net loss), the difference between revenues and expenses. To help you understand an income statement, we must first define its elements—revenues, expenses, and net income (or net loss).

Revenues

revenue Increase in a company's resources from the sale of goods or services.

Revenue is the amount of assets created through business operations. Think of revenue as another way for a company to acquire assets. In the same way that assets can be acquired by borrowing or by owners' investment, assets can also be acquired by providing a product or service for which customers are willing to pay. Manufacturing and merchandising companies receive revenues from the sale of merchandise. For example, **Safeway**'s revenue is the cash that customers pay in exchange for groceries. A service enterprise generates revenues from the fees it charges for the services it performs. For example, a portion of the sales price of **Microsoft** software is not payment for the software itself, but instead is an advance payment for the customer support service that Microsoft promises. Companies might also earn revenues from other activities, such as charging interest or collecting rent. When goods are sold or services performed, the resulting revenue is in the form of cash or accounts receivable (a promise from the buyer to pay for the goods or services by a specified date in the future). Revenues thus generally represent an increase in total assets. These new assets are not tied to any liability obligation; therefore, the assets belong to the owners and thus represent an increase in owners' equity.

expenses Costs incurred in the normal course of business to generate revenues.

net income (net loss) An overall measure of the performance of a company; equal to revenues minus expenses for the period.

Expenses

Expenses are the amount of assets consumed through business operations. Expenses are the costs incurred in normal business operations to generate revenues. Employee salaries and utilities used during a period are two common examples of expenses. For Safeway, the primary expense is the wholesale cost of the groceries that it sells to its customers at retail. Just as revenues represent an increase in assets and equity, expenses generally represent a decrease in assets and in equity.

In considering revenues and expenses, remember that not all inflows of assets are revenues; nor are all outflows of assets considered to be expenses. For example, cash may be received by borrowing from a bank, which is an increase in a liability, not a revenue. Similarly, cash may be paid for supplies, which is an exchange of one asset for another asset, not an expense. The details of properly identifying revenues and expenses will be discussed further in Chapter 3.

et connected
p://www.swcollege.com
net work

In its Web site, *Fortune* magazine (fortune.com) provides selected stories from current issues as well as summaries of its famous lists: the Fortune 500 (largest companies in the United States) and the Global 500 (largest companies in the world).

1. Search the Fortune 500 Top Performers to find out which U.S. company has the most assets.
2. Search the Global 500 Top Performers and identify which company employs more people than any other company in the world.

fortune.com

Net Income (or Net Loss)

Net income, sometimes called earnings or profit, is an overall measure of the performance of a company. Net income reflects the company's accomplishments (revenues) in relation to its efforts (expenses) during a particular period of time. If revenues exceed expenses, the result is called net income (Revenues − Expenses = Net Income). If expenses exceed revenues, the difference is called net loss. Because net income results in an increase in resources from operations, owners' equity is also increased; a net loss decreases owners' equity. Exhibit 2-5 lists the ten U.S. companies with the highest net incomes in 1996.

It is important to note the difference between revenues and net income. Both concepts represent an increase in the net assets (assets − liabilities) of a firm. However, revenues represent total resource increases; expenses are subtracted from revenues to derive income or loss. Thus, whereas revenue is a "gross" concept, income (or loss) is a "net" concept.

EXHIBIT 2-5

Top Ten U.S. Companies, Ranked by Net Income

Company Name	Net Income*
Exxon	$7,510
General Electric	7,280
Philip Morris	6,303
AT&T	5,908
IBM	5,429
Intel	5,157
General Motors	4,963
Ford	4,446
Merck	3,881
Citicorp	3,788

*Net income is in millions of dollars.

Source: Fortune 500 listing, 1996. Accessible at fortune.com.

The Format of an Income Statement

Comparative income statements, which have been modified to a "multi-step format," for Safeway are presented in Exhibit 2-6. In contrast to the balance sheet, which is "as of" a particular date, the income statement refers to the "year ended." Remember, the income statement covers a period of time; the balance sheet is a report at a point in time. The multi-step format illustrated here highlights several profit measurements including gross profit, operating income, and net income.

The income statement usually shows two main categories, revenues and expenses, although several subcategories may also be presented (as illustrated). Revenues are listed first. Typical operating expenses for most businesses are employee salaries, utilities, and advertising. For Safeway, as with any retail firm, the largest expense is for cost of goods sold. The difference between sales and cost of goods sold represents the difference between the retail price Safeway receives from a grocery sale and the wholesale cost of the groceries that are sold. This difference (sales − cost of goods sold) is called **gross profit** or **gross margin**.

gross profit (gross margin) The excess of net sales revenue over the cost of goods sold.

Expenses are sometimes divided into operating and nonoperating categories. The primary nonoperating expenses are interest and income taxes. These expenses are called nonoperating because they have no connection with the specific nature of the operation of the business. For example, Safeway deals with interest and income taxes in a way similar to that of Microsoft, even though the two companies operate in completely different industries.

Two other items that frequently appear in the income statement are **gains** and **losses**. Gains and losses refer to money made or lost on activities outside the normal business of a company. For example, when Safeway receives cash for selling groceries, it is called revenue. But when Safeway makes money by selling an old delivery truck, the amount is called a gain, not revenue, because Safeway is not in the business of selling trucks.

gains (losses) Money made or lost on activities outside the normal operation of a company.

EXHIBIT 2-6

Adapted Comparative Income Statements for Safeway

Safeway Inc.
Income Statement
For the Years Ended December 28, 1996
and December 30, 1995
(in millions)

	1996	1995
Revenues:		
Sales	$17,269.0	$16,397.5
Other revenue	54.4	28.9
Total revenue	$17,323.4	$16,426.4
Less: Cost of goods sold	12,494.8	11,905.1
Gross profit	$ 4,828.6	$ 4,521.3
Less: Operating and administrative expense	3,882.5	3,765.0
Operating income	$ 946.1	$ 756.3
Less: Interest expense	178.5	199.8
Income tax expense	307.0	228.2
Extraordinary loss	0.0	2.0
Net income	$ 460.6	$ 326.3
Earnings per share	$ 1.93	$ 1.34

earnings (loss) per share (EPS) The amount of net income (earnings) related to each share of stock; computed by dividing net income by the number of shares of stock outstanding during the period.

One final bit of information required on the income statements of corporations is **earnings (loss) per share (EPS)**. This EPS amount is computed by dividing the net income (earnings or loss) for the current period by the number of shares of stock outstanding during the period. Earnings per share information tells the owner of a single share of stock how much of the net income for the year belongs to him or her.

Like the balance sheet, the income statement usually shows the comparative results for two or more periods; allowing investors and creditors to evaluate how profitable an enterprise has been during the current period as compared with earlier periods. For example, examination of Safeway's comparative income statements in Exhibit 2-6 shows that net income in 1996 was 41% higher [($460.6 − $326.3) ÷ $326.3] than in 1995. Further analysis of the income statement is introduced later in this chapter and reinforced throughout the text. (For another illustration of a comparative income statement, see the income statement for **Microsoft** in Appendix A at the back of the book.)

Some other factors impacting a company's performance are excluded from the income statement and listed in a separate measure of "comprehensive income." An example is the impact of foreign currency exchange rate fluctuations on a multinational company with subsidiaries operating all over the world. Comprehensive income will be covered in detail in Chapter 6.

The Statement of Retained Earnings

statement of retained earnings A report that shows the changes in retained earnings during a period of time.

In addition to an income statement, corporations sometimes prepare a **statement of retained earnings**. This statement identifies changes in retained earnings from one accounting period to the next. As illustrated in Exhibit 2-7, the statement shows a beginning retained earnings balance, the net income for the period, a deduction for any dividends paid, and an ending retained earnings balance. For **Safeway Corporation**, which paid no dividends during 1996, its statement of retained earnings would be as follows:

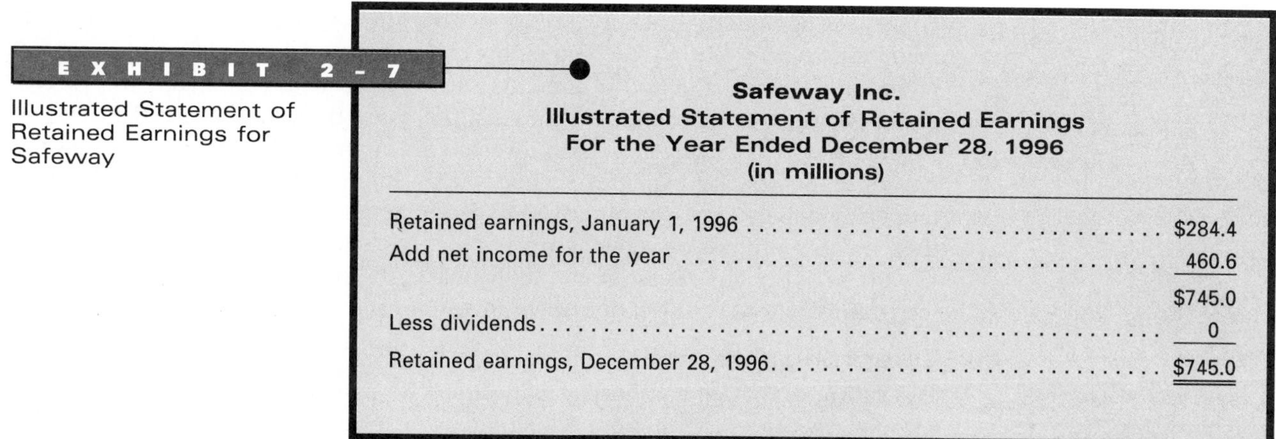

EXHIBIT 2-7

Illustrated Statement of Retained Earnings for Safeway

Safeway Inc.
Illustrated Statement of Retained Earnings
For the Year Ended December 28, 1996
(in millions)

Retained earnings, January 1, 1996	$284.4
Add net income for the year	460.6
	$745.0
Less dividends	0
Retained earnings, December 28, 1996	$745.0

Note how the accounting equation is impacted by the elements reported in the Statement of Retained Earnings. Net income results in an increase in net assets and a corresponding increase in Retained Earnings, which increases Owners' Equity.

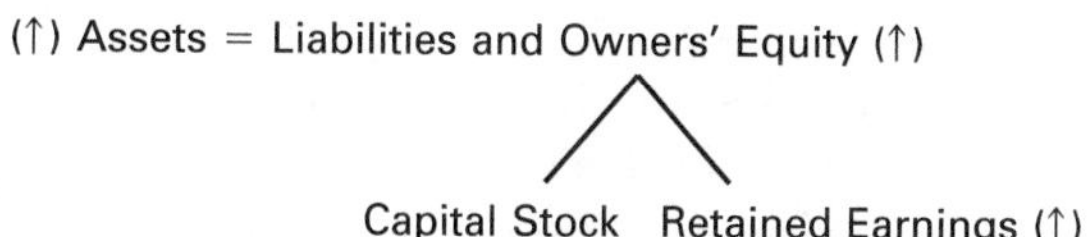

Dividends reduce assets (e.g., cash) and similarly reduce Retained Earnings, which reduces Owners' Equity.

(↓) Assets = Liabilities and Owners' Equity (↓)

Capital Stock   Retained Earnings (↓)

Corporations sometimes present a ***statement of stockholders' equity*** instead of a statement of retained earnings. The statement of stockholders' equity, illustrated for **Microsoft** in Appendix A at the back of the book, is more detailed and includes changes in capital stock as well as changes in retained earnings.

TO SUMMARIZE

The income statement provides a measure of the success of an enterprise over a specified period of time. The income statement shows the major sources of revenues generated and the expenses associated with those revenues. The difference between those revenues and expenses is net income or net loss. Gains and losses refer to money made or lost on activities outside the normal activities of a business. The income statements of corporations must also include earnings per share. Like balance sheets, income statements are usually prepared on a comparative basis. A statement of retained earnings or statement of stockholders' equity is often provided by corporations in their annual reports to shareholders.

The Statement of Cash Flows

Net income is the single best measure of a company's economic performance. However, anyone who has paid for rent or for college tuition knows that bills must be paid with cash, not with "economic performance." Accordingly, in addition to net income, investors and creditors also desire to know how much actual cash a company's operations generate during a period and how that cash is used. The statement of cash flows shows the cash inflows (receipts) and cash outflows (payments) of an entity during a period of time. As shown in Exhibit 2-8, companies receive cash primarily by selling goods or providing services, by selling other assets, by borrowing, and by receiving cash from investments by owners. Companies use cash to pay current operating expenses such as wages, utilities, and taxes; to purchase additional buildings, land, and otherwise expand operations; to repay loans; and to pay their owners a return on the investments that have been made.

In the statement of cash flows, individual cash flow items are classified according to three main activities: operating, investing, and financing.

Operating Activities

operating activities Activities that are part of the day-to-day business of a company.

Operating activities are those activities that are part of the day-to-day business of a company. Cash receipts from selling goods or from providing services is the major operating cash inflow. Major operating cash outflows include payments to purchase inventory and to pay wages, taxes, interest, utilities, rent, and similar expenses.

Investing Activities

investing activities Activities associated with buying and selling long-term assets.

The primary **investing activities** are the purchase and sale of land, buildings, and equipment. You can think of investing activities as those activities associated with buying and selling long-term assets.

Financing Activities

financing activities Activities whereby cash is obtained from or repaid to owners and creditors.

Financing activities are those activities whereby cash is obtained from or repaid to owners and creditors. For example, cash received from owners' investments, cash proceeds from a loan, or cash payments to repay loans would all be classified under financing activities.

EXHIBIT 2-8

Cash Flows

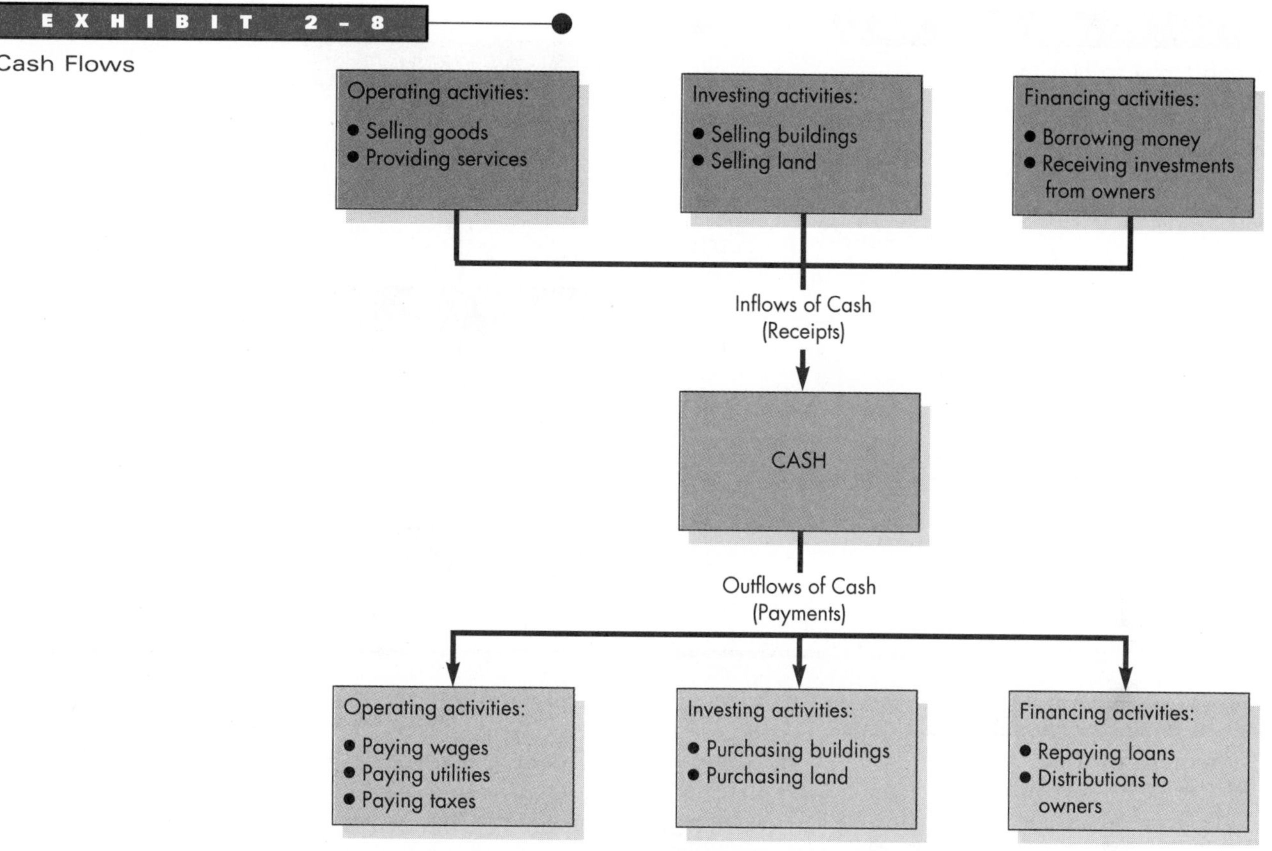

Conceptually, the statement of cash flows is the easiest to prepare of the three primary financial statements. Imagine examining every check and deposit slip you have written in the past year and sorting them into three piles—operating, investing, and financing. You would have to exercise some judgment in deciding which pile some items go into (for example, is the payment of interest an operating or a financing activity?). But overall, the three-way categorization of cash flows is not that difficult. In essence, this is all that is involved in the preparation of a statement of cash flows. However, as you will see in Chapter 8, actual preparation of a statement of cash flows can sometimes be challenging. The reason for this is that traditional accounting systems are designed to streamline the computation of net income. So, instead of preparing the statement of cash flows directly from the raw cash flow data, the process is as shown in Exhibit 2-9. The raw cash flow data are transformed into revenue and expense data using the accounting adjustments, assumptions, and estimates that you will learn about in this text. Then, to prepare the statement of cash flows, all of those adjustments must be undone to get back to the raw cash flow data. Challenging, but by the time we get to Chapter 8, you will be ready for it.

Exhibit 2-10 contains the statement of cash flows for the **Boston Celtics** for the year ended June 30, 1996. As sports fans know, the Boston Celtics is the NBA team with the most championships in history. What is not widely known is that ownership shares in the Boston Celtics can be purchased by the general public and are traded on the New York Stock Exchange. Because the Celtics is a publicly traded company, it must make its financial statements publicly available, thus providing the information for Exhibit 2-10. As with balance sheets and income statements, companies usually provide comparative statements of cash flows. However, we have elected not to show comparative statements of cash flows, in order to keep the Celtics illustration simple. (The **Microsoft** financial statements in Appendix A provide comparative statements of cash flows.)

EXHIBIT 2-9

Cash Flow to Net Income to Cash Flow

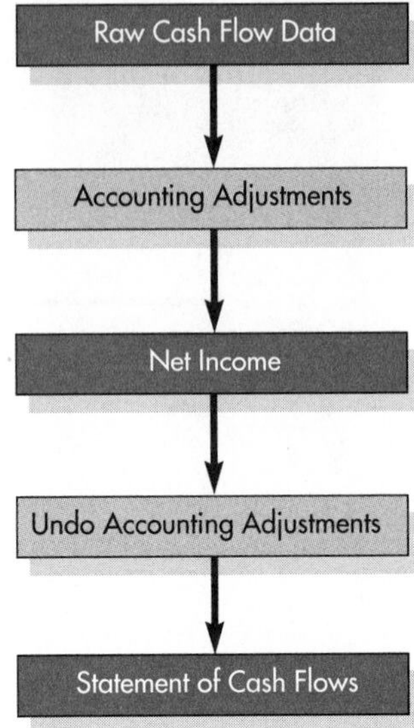

EXHIBIT 2-10

Statement of Cash Flows for the Boston Celtics

BOSTON CELTICS LIMITED PARTNERSHIP
Statement of Cash Flows
For the Year Ended June 30, 1996

CASH FLOWS FROM OPERATING ACTIVITIES		
Receipts:		
Basketball regular season receipts:		
Ticket sales	$31,323,249	
Television and radio broadcast rights fees	19,908,800	
Other (principally promotional advertising)	8,424,038	
Basketball playoff receipts	360,895	
		60,016,982
Outflows:		
Basketball regular season expenditures:		
Team expenses	26,066,875	
Game expenses	2,481,007	
Basketball playoff expenses	0	
General and administrative expenses	13,996,805	
Selling and promotional expenses	1,333,238	
		43,877,925
		16,139,057
Interest income		9,553,938
Interest expense		(4,624,043)
Ticket refunds paid		(504)
Proceeds from league expansion		4,490,673
Payment of income taxes		(4,973,883)
Payment of deferred compensation		(5,226,095)
Other operating cash outflows		(2,931,742)
NET CASH FLOWS FROM OPERATING ACTIVITIES		12,427,401

(continued)

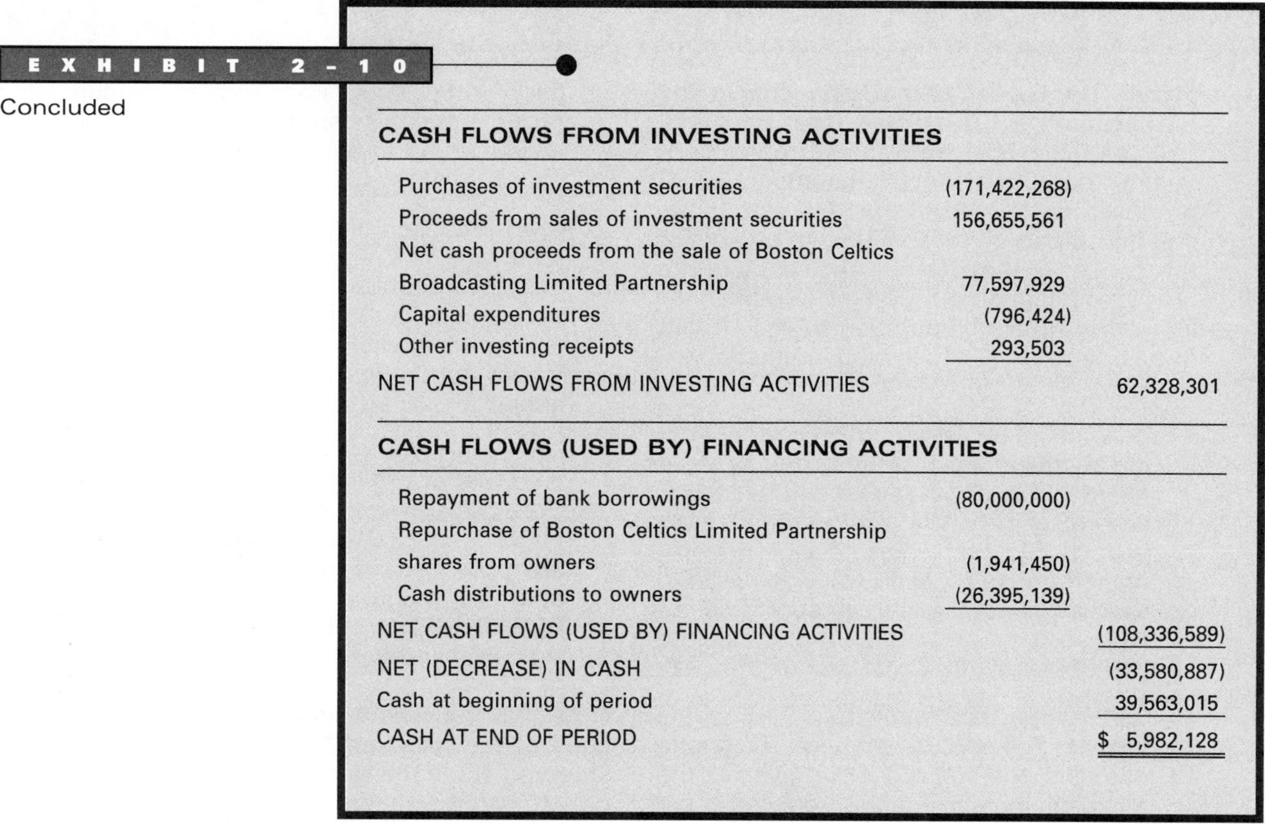

EXHIBIT 2-10

Concluded

CASH FLOWS FROM INVESTING ACTIVITIES		
Purchases of investment securities	(171,422,268)	
Proceeds from sales of investment securities	156,655,561	
Net cash proceeds from the sale of Boston Celtics Broadcasting Limited Partnership	77,597,929	
Capital expenditures	(796,424)	
Other investing receipts	293,503	
NET CASH FLOWS FROM INVESTING ACTIVITIES		62,328,301
CASH FLOWS (USED BY) FINANCING ACTIVITIES		
Repayment of bank borrowings	(80,000,000)	
Repurchase of Boston Celtics Limited Partnership shares from owners	(1,941,450)	
Cash distributions to owners	(26,395,139)	
NET CASH FLOWS (USED BY) FINANCING ACTIVITIES		(108,336,589)
NET (DECREASE) IN CASH		(33,580,887)
Cash at beginning of period		39,563,015
CASH AT END OF PERIOD		$ 5,982,128

FYI

Notice that the **Boston Celtics** has chosen June 30 as the end of its fiscal year. About two-thirds of large U.S. companies choose December 31. The Boston Celtics uses June 30 because that coincides with a natural lull in its business (the playoffs are over and the next regular season is months away). **Safeway** chooses the last Saturday of the year to make sure that each fiscal year contains a whole number of weeks.

One interesting item to note in the Celtics' cash flow statement is the $5.2 million payment for deferred compensation. This represents players' salaries that were earned (and reported as expenses) in prior years but not paid until 1996. Also notice the large amount of activity in buying and selling investment securities—$171 million in securities purchased and $157 million sold. And you thought that the Celtics only played basketball.

TO SUMMARIZE

The statement of cash flows is one of the three primary financial statements. It shows the significant cash inflows (receipts) and cash outflows (payments) of a company for a period of time. These cash flows are classified according to operating, investing, and financing activities. The statement of cash flows is discussed and illustrated in Chapter 8.

How the Financial Statements Tie Together

articulation The interrelationships among the financial statements.

Although we have introduced the primary financial statements as if they were independent of one another, they are interrelated and tie together. In accounting language, they "articulate." **Articulation** refers to the relationship between an operat-

BUSINESS ENVIRONMENT ESSAY

How To Get Your Own Copy of Microsoft's Financial Statements
The complete Microsoft annual report containing the 1997 financial statements is reproduced at the end of this text. Is this secret information, available only to owners of this book? No. Anyone can get a copy of the most recent annual report of Microsoft or any other public corporation in the United States. Any of the following methods will work:

- Become an investor in Microsoft by buying shares of stock in the company. As a Microsoft investor, you are entitled to receive a copy of the annual report each year. In fact, according to U.S. government regulations, Microsoft is required to send a copy of the annual report to all of its investors within three months of the end of Microsoft's fiscal year on June 30.
- Call, write, fax, or e-mail Microsoft's Investor Relations department. The phone numbers and addresses are given in the Microsoft annual report reproduced at the back of this book. For promotional purposes, companies are happy to mail their annual report to anyone who asks.
- Download a copy of the annual report from Microsoft's Web site at microsoft.com. On the Web sites of most companies (Microsoft included), the annual report is not easy to find. You have to skirt past games, promotional material, and lots of nonfinancial information, but the annual report is usually there somewhere.
- Download a copy of the annual report (and lots of other information) from the U.S. government archives at sec.gov/edgarhp.htm. These government filings are pure text documents (no pictures) and are made available through the EDGAR (Electronic Data Gathering, Analysis, and Retrieval) system.

Now that you know how to get your own copy of the Microsoft annual report, make sure you study the rest of this book to learn how to use the report.

ing statement (the income statement or the statement of cash flows) and comparative balance sheets, whereby an item on the operating statement helps explain the change in an item on the balance sheet from one period to the next.

Exhibit 2-11 shows how the financial statements tie together. Note that the beginning amount of cash from the 1998 balance sheet is added to the net increase or decrease in cash (from the statement of cash flows) to derive the cash balance as reported on the 1999 balance sheet. Similarly, the retained earnings balance as reported on the 1999 balance sheet comes from the beginning retained earnings balance (1998 balance sheet) plus net income for the period (from the income statement) less dividends paid. As you study financial statements, these relationships will become clearer and you will understand the concept of articulation better.

2 *Recognize the need for financial statement notes and identify the types of information included in the notes.*

notes to the financial statements
Explanatory information considered an integral part of the financial statements.

NOTES TO THE FINANCIAL STATEMENTS

The three primary financial statements contain a lot of information. Still, three summary reports cannot possibly tell financial statement users everything they want to know about a company. Additional information is given in the **notes to the financial statements**. In fact, in a typical annual report, whereas the primary financial statements fill only three pages, the notes go on for 15 pages or more. The notes tell about the assumptions and methods used in preparing the financial statements and also give more detail about specific items.

The financial statement notes are of the following four general types:

1. Summary of significant accounting policies.
2. Additional information about the summary totals found in the financial statements.

EXHIBIT 2-11

How the Financial Statements Tie Together

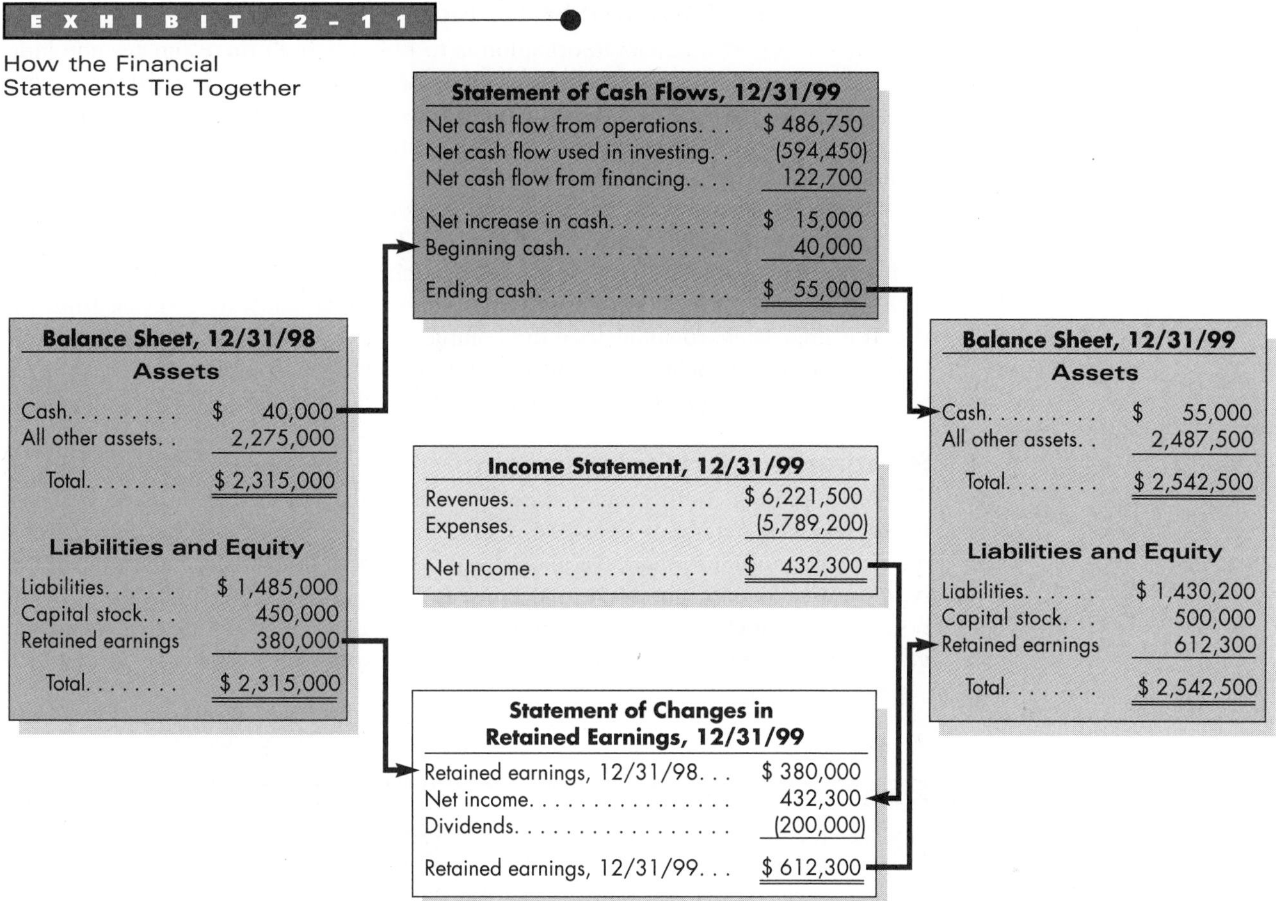

Statement of Cash Flows, 12/31/99
Net cash flow from operations. . . $ 486,750
Net cash flow used in investing. . (594,450)
Net cash flow from financing. . . . 122,700
Net increase in cash. . . . . $ 15,000
Beginning cash. 40,000
Ending cash. . . . . $ 55,000
Balance Sheet, 12/31/98
Assets
Cash. . . . . $ 40,000
All other assets. . 2,275,000
Total. . . . . . . $ 2,315,000
Liabilities and Equity
Liabilities. . . . . $ 1,485,000
Capital stock. . . 450,000
Retained earnings 380,000
Total. . . . . . . $ 2,315,000
Income Statement, 12/31/99
Revenues. . . . . $ 6,221,500
Expenses. . . . . (5,789,200)
Net Income. . . . . $ 432,300
Balance Sheet, 12/31/99
Assets
Cash. . . . . $ 55,000
All other assets. . 2,487,500
Total. . . . . . . $ 2,542,500
Liabilities and Equity
Liabilities. . . . . $ 1,430,200
Capital stock. . . 500,000
Retained earnings 612,300
Total. . . . . . . $ 2,542,500
Statement of Changes in Retained Earnings, 12/31/99
Retained earnings, 12/31/98. . . $ 380,000
Net income. 432,300
Dividends. . . . . (200,000)
Retained earnings, 12/31/99. . . $ 612,300

FYI

In its 1920 annual report, IBM included zero pages of notes (and the dollar amounts were carried out to the penny). In 1966, there were four pages of notes (and dollar amounts were rounded to the nearest dollar). In 1996, IBM's annual report included 26 pages of notes (and dollar amounts were rounded to the nearest million).

3. Disclosure of important information that is not recognized in the financial statements.
4. Supplementary information required by the FASB or the SEC.

Summary of Significant Accounting Policies

As mentioned earlier, accounting involves making assumptions, estimates, and judgments. In addition, in some settings, there is more than one acceptable method of accounting for certain items. For example, there are a variety of acceptable ways of estimating how much a building depreciates (wears out) in a year. In order for financial statement users to be able to properly interpret the three primary financial statements, they must know what procedures were used in preparing those statements. This information about accounting policies and practices is given in the financial statement notes.

Additional Information About Summary Totals

For a large company, such as Microsoft or Safeway, one summary number in the financial statements represents literally thousands of individual items. For example, the $1.568 billion in long-term loans included in Safeway's 1996 balance sheet (see Exhibit 2-3) represents loans of U.S. dollars, loans of Canadian dollars, mortgages, senior secured debentures, senior subordinated debentures, an unsecured bank credit agreement, and more. The balance sheet includes only one number, with the details in the notes.

Disclosure of Information Not Recognized

One way to report financial information is to boil down all the estimates and judgments into one number and then report that one number in the financial statements. This is called *recognition.* The key assumptions and estimates are then described in a note to the financial statements. Another approach is to skip the financial statements and just rely on the note to convey the information to users. This is called *disclosure.* Disclosure is the accepted way to convey information to users when the information is too uncertain to be recognized. For example, in July 1988, **Safeway** suffered a fire in one of its warehouses in Richmond, California. As of January 9, 1997, there were still 3,000 unsettled lawsuits against Safeway resulting from the fire. It is impossible to summarize the complexity of the potential outcome of these lawsuits in one financial statement number; so, Safeway describes the situation, in some detail, in the notes to the financial statements.

Supplementary Information

The FASB and SEC both require supplementary information that must be reported in the financial statement notes. For example, the FASB requires the disclosure of quarterly financial information and of business segment information. A sample of this type of disclosure can be seen in **Microsoft**'s annual report in Appendix A. In the notes to its financial statements, Microsoft reports that 56% of its 1997 revenue was generated through international sales; either U.S. export sales or sales by foreign subsidiaries of Microsoft.

TO SUMMARIZE

The notes to the financial statements contain additional information not included in the financial statements themselves. The notes explain the company's accounting assumptions and practices, provide details of financial statement summary numbers and additional disclosure about complex events, and report supplementary information required by the SEC or the FASB.

3 *Describe the purpose of an audit report and the incentives the auditor has to perform a good audit.*

THE EXTERNAL AUDIT

Refer back to the opening scenario for this chapter. Following the November 1986 leveraged buyout by **Kohlberg, Kravis, Roberts & Co. (KKR)**, **Safeway** decided to again issue shares to the public. In April 1990, Safeway issued shares at a price of $11.25 per share. The $11.25 price implied that the market value of KKR's initial investment had risen from $130 million to $731 million. The $11.25 price was determined by investment bankers and potential investors after examining the financial statements of Safeway. Now, consider the following questions:

- Who controlled the preparation of the Safeway financial statements used by investors in arriving at the $11.25 price? The owners and managers of Safeway, led by KKR.

- Did KKR have any incentive to bias the reported financial statement numbers? Absolutely. The better the numbers, the higher the stock offering price and the greater the profit made by KKR.

- Since KKR had control of the preparation of the financial statements and stood to benefit substantially if those statements looked overly favorable, how could the financial statements be trusted? Good question.

This situation illustrates a general truth: the owners and managers of a company have an incentive to report the most favorable results possible. Poor reported financial performance can make it harder to get loans, can lower the amount that managers receive as salary bonuses, and can lower the stock price when shares are issued to the public. With these incentives to stretch the truth, the financial statements would not be reliable unless they were reviewed by an external party.

To provide this external review, a company's financial statements are often audited by an independent certified public accountant (CPA). A CPA firm issues an **audit report** that expresses an opinion about whether the statements fairly present a company's financial position, operating results, and cash flows in accordance with generally accepted accounting principles. Note that the financial statements are the responsibility of a company's management and not of the CPA. Although not all company records have to be audited, audits are needed for many purposes. For example, a banker may not make a loan without first receiving audited financial statements from a prospective borrower. As another example, most securities cannot be sold to the general public until they are registered with the Securities and Exchange Commission. This registration process requires inclusion of audited financial statements.

audit report A report issued by an independent CPA that expresses an opinion about whether the financial statements present fairly a company's financial position, operating results, and cash flows in accordance with generally accepted accounting principles.

FYI

Notice that **Microsoft**'s audit report is dated July 17, 1997. This means that it took less than three weeks (from the end of the fiscal year on June 30) for the completion of the audit. Obviously, much audit work was conducted during the year to make this happen.

Though an audit report does not guarantee accuracy, it does provide added assurance that the financial statements are not misleading since they have been examined by an independent professional. However, the CPA cannot examine every transaction upon which the summary figures in the financial statements are based. The accuracy of the statements must remain the responsibility of the company's management. An example of a typical audit report is found in Appendix A in **Microsoft**'s 1997 annual report. Microsoft's financial statements were audited by **Deloitte & Touche**, one of the large international audit firms.

One final question: Who hires and pays Deloitte & Touche to do the audit of Microsoft's financial statements? Microsoft does. At first glance, this situation appears to be similar to allowing students in an accounting class to choose and pay the graders of the examinations. However, two economic factors combine to allow us to trust the quality of the audit, even though the company being audited is the one who hires the auditor:

- *Reputation.* Deloitte & Touche, as one of the large accounting firms (and almost all independent auditors in the United States), has a reputation for doing high-quality audits. It would be very reluctant to risk this reputation by signing off on a questionable set of financial statements.
- *Lawsuits.* Auditors are sued all the time, even when they conduct a perfect audit. Investors who lose money claim that they lost the money by relying on bogus financial statements that were certified by an external auditor. If even honest auditors get sued, then an auditor who intentionally approves a false set of financial statements is at great risk of losing a big lawsuit.

TO SUMMARIZE

An audit report is issued by an independent CPA firm attesting to the conformity of a set of financial statements with generally accepted accounting principles. CPA firms have an economic incentive to perform credible audits in order to preserve their reputations and to avoid lawsuits.

4 *Use financial ratios to identify a company's strengths and weaknesses and to forecast its future performance.*

FINANCIAL STATEMENT ANALYSIS

financial statement analysis Examining both the relationships among financial statement amounts and the trends in those numbers over time.

financial ratios Ratios that show relationships between financial statement amounts.

Financial statements are prepared so that they can be used. One important use is in analyzing a company's economic health. **Financial statement analysis** involves the examination of both the relationships among financial statement numbers and the trends in those numbers over time. One purpose of financial statement analysis is to use the past performance of a company to predict how it will do in the future. Another purpose of financial statement analysis is to evaluate the performance of a company with an eye toward identifying problem areas. Financial statement analysis is both diagnosis, identifying where a firm has problems, and prognosis, predicting how a firm will perform in the future.

Relationships between financial statement amounts are called **financial ratios**. For example, net income divided by sales is a financial ratio called "return on sales." Return on sales tells you how many pennies of profit a company makes on each dollar of sales. The return on sales for Microsoft is 30.4%, meaning that Microsoft makes $0.30 worth of profit for every dollar of software sold. There are hundreds of different financial ratios, each shedding light on a different aspect of the health of a company. Some of the more common ratios are introduced in the following section. The numbers from the Safeway balance sheet (Exhibit 2-3) and income statement (Exhibit 2-6) will be used to illustrate the ratio calculations.

Debt Ratio

debt ratio A measure of leverage, computed by dividing total liabilities by total assets.

Comparing the amount of liabilities to the amount of assets shows the extent to which a company has borrowed money to leverage the owners' investments and increase the size of the company. One frequently used measure of leverage is the **debt ratio**, computed as total liabilities divided by total assets. The debt ratio represents the proportion of borrowed funds used to acquire the company's assets. For Safeway, the 1996 debt ratio is computed as follows:

$$\text{Debt ratio: } \frac{\text{Total liabilities}}{\text{Total assets}} = \frac{\$4{,}358.4}{\$5{,}545.2} = 78.6\%$$

In other words, Safeway borrowed 78.6% of the money it needed to buy its assets.

Is 78.6% a good debt ratio, a bad debt ratio, or is it impossible to tell? If you are a banker thinking of lending money to Safeway, you want Safeway to have a low debt ratio; a smaller amount of other liabilities increases your chances of being repaid. If you are a Safeway stockholder, you want a higher debt ratio; you want the company to add borrowed funds to your investment dollars in order to expand the business. There is some middle ground where the debt ratio is not too high for creditors, nor too low for investors. The general rule of thumb is that debt ratios should be around 50%. However, this general benchmark varies widely from one industry to the next. The 78.6% debt ratio for Safeway is not unusual for a supermarket chain.

Current Ratio

current (or working capital) ratio A measure of the liquidity of a business; equal to current assets divided by current liabilities.

An important concern about any company is its *liquidity*. If a firm cannot meet its short-term obligations, it may not live to enjoy the long run. The most commonly used measure of liquidity is the **current** (or **working capital**) **ratio**, a comparison of the current assets (cash, receivables, and inventory) to the current liabilities. The current ratio is computed by dividing total current assets by total current liabilities. For Safeway, the 1996 current ratio is computed as follows:

$$\text{Current ratio: } \frac{\text{Current assets}}{\text{Current liabilities}} = \frac{\$1{,}654.4}{\$2{,}030.0} = 0.815$$

Historically, a current ratio below 2.0 suggests the possibility of liquidity problems. However, advances in information technology have enabled companies to be much more effective in minimizing the need to hold cash, inventories, and other current assets. As a result, current ratios for successful companies are frequently less than 1.0. The 0.815 current ratio for Safeway is similar to that for other supermarket chains.

Minimum current ratio requirements are frequently included in loan agreements. A typical agreement might state that if the current ratio falls below a certain level, the lender can declare the loan in default and require immediate repayment. This type of minimum current ratio restriction forces the borrower to maintain its liquidity and gives the lender increased assurance that the loan will be repaid.

Asset Turnover

asset turnover A measure of company efficiency, computed by dividing sales by total assets.

The balance sheet of Safeway reveals total assets of $5.545 billion at December 28, 1996. Are those assets being used efficiently? The **asset turnover** ratio gives an overall measure of company efficiency and is computed as follows:

$$\text{Asset turnover: } \frac{\text{Sales}}{\text{Total assets}} = \frac{\$17{,}269.0}{\$5{,}545.2} = 3.11$$

Safeway's 1996 asset turnover ratio of 3.11 means that for each dollar of assets, Safeway is able to generate $3.11 in sales. The higher the asset turnover ratio, the more efficient the company is at using its assets to generate sales.

Return on Sales

return on sales A measure of the amount of profit earned per dollar of sales, computed by dividing net income by sales.

As mentioned at the beginning of this section, Microsoft makes 30.4 cents of profit on each dollar of sales. This ratio is called **return on sales** and (using Safeway's 1996 numbers) is computed as follows:

$$\text{Return on sales: } \frac{\text{Net income}}{\text{Sales}} = \frac{\$460.6}{\$17{,}269.0} = 2.67\%$$

Clearly, the return on sales for Safeway of 2.67 cents per dollar is dramatically below that for Microsoft. However, as with all ratios, the return on sales value for Safeway must be evaluated within the appropriate industry. Return on sales in the supermarket industry is frequently between 1% and 2%; so, the Safeway value is very good indeed. In addition, Safeway's 1996 return on sales of 2.67% represents an improvement over its 1995 return on sales of 2.0%.

Return on Equity

return on equity A measure of the amount of profit earned per dollar of investment, computed by dividing net income by owners' equity.

What investors really want to know is how much profit they earn for each dollar they invest. This amount, called the **return on equity**, is the overall measure of the performance of a company. Return on equity for Safeway for 1996 is computed as follows:

$$\text{Return on equity: } \frac{\text{Net income}}{\text{Owners' equity}} = \frac{\$460.6}{\$1{,}186.8} = 38.8\%$$

Safeway's return on equity of 38.8% means that 38.8 cents of profit was earned for each dollar of stockholder investment in 1996. If your intuition tells you that this seems high, you are right. Good companies typically have return on equity values between 15% and 25%. Safeway had a great year in 1996.

Price-Earnings Ratio

price-earnings (PE) ratio A measure of growth potential, earnings stability, and management capabilities; computed by dividing market price per share by earnings per share.

If a company earned $100 this year, how much should you pay to buy that company? If you expect the company to make more in the future, you would be willing to pay a higher price than if you expected the company to make less. Also, you would probably be willing to pay a bit more for a stable company than for one experiencing wild swings in earnings. The **price-earnings (PE) ratio** measures the relationship between the market value of a company and that company's current earnings. This ratio is computed by dividing the market price per share of stock by the earnings per share. Safeway's PE ratio at the end of 1996 was:

$$\text{PE ratio: } \frac{\text{Market price per share}}{\text{Earnings per share}} = \frac{\$42.75}{\$1.93} = 22.2$$

In the United States, PE ratios typically range between 5 and 30. High PE ratios are associated with firms for which strong growth is predicted in the future. Refer back to Exhibits 2-4 and 2-5 and notice that Coca-Cola and Microsoft are included in the list of companies with the highest market values but are not among those with high net incomes. The reason Coca-Cola and Microsoft are valued so highly is that they are expected to continue to grow rapidly; their current incomes are small compared to what investors are expecting in the future. This expected future growth is reflected in the PE ratios for these companies, which are 42.3 for Coca-Cola and 54.3 for Microsoft.

A summary of the financial ratios discussed in this section is presented in Exhibit 2-12.

EXHIBIT 2-12

Summary of Selected Financial Ratios

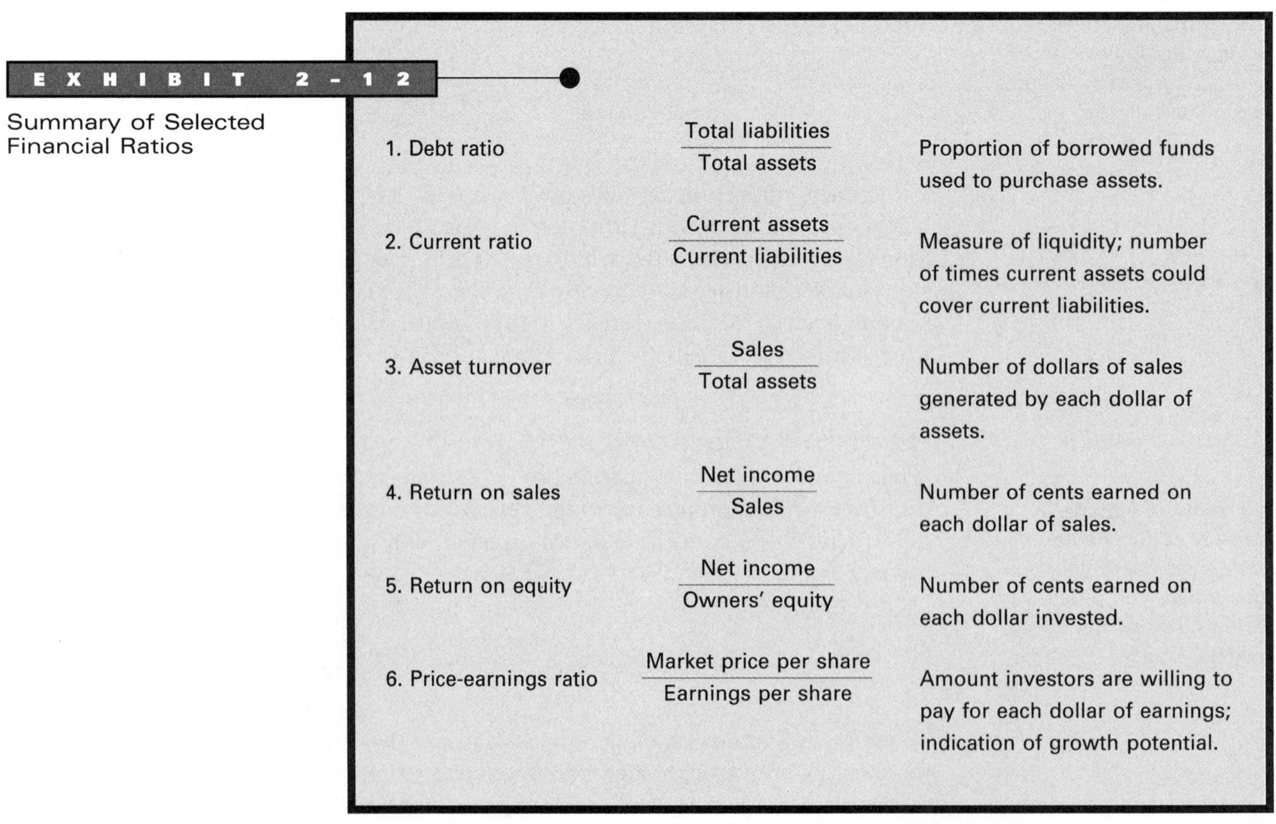

Ratio	Formula	Description
1. Debt ratio	$\frac{\text{Total liabilities}}{\text{Total assets}}$	Proportion of borrowed funds used to purchase assets.
2. Current ratio	$\frac{\text{Current assets}}{\text{Current liabilities}}$	Measure of liquidity; number of times current assets could cover current liabilities.
3. Asset turnover	$\frac{\text{Sales}}{\text{Total assets}}$	Number of dollars of sales generated by each dollar of assets.
4. Return on sales	$\frac{\text{Net income}}{\text{Sales}}$	Number of cents earned on each dollar of sales.
5. Return on equity	$\frac{\text{Net income}}{\text{Owners' equity}}$	Number of cents earned on each dollar invested.
6. Price-earnings ratio	$\frac{\text{Market price per share}}{\text{Earnings per share}}$	Amount investors are willing to pay for each dollar of earnings; indication of growth potential.

TO SUMMARIZE

This overview of financial ratios is intended to emphasize that the preparation of the financial statements by the accountant is not the end of the process, but just the beginning. Those financial statements are then analyzed by investors, creditors, and management to detect signs of existing deficiencies in performance and to predict how the firm will perform in the future. Proper interpretation of a ratio depends on comparing a firm's ratio value to the value for the same firm in the previous year, as well as to values for other firms in the same industry.

5 *Explain the fundamental concepts and assumptions that underlie financial accounting.*

FUNDAMENTAL CONCEPTS AND ASSUMPTIONS

Certain fundamental concepts and assumptions underlie financial accounting practice and the resulting financial statements. These ideas are so fundamental to any economic activity that they usually are taken for granted in conducting business. However, it is important to be aware of them because these assumptions, together with certain basic concepts and procedures, determine the rules and set the boundaries of accounting practice. They indicate which events will be accounted for and in what manner. In total, they provide the essential characteristics of the traditional **accounting model**.

accounting model The basic accounting assumptions, concepts, principles, and procedures that determine the manner of recording, measuring, and reporting a company's transactions.

This section will describe the separate entity concept, the assumption of arm's-length transactions, the cost principle, the monetary measurement concept, and the going concern assumption. The concept of double-entry accounting was already introduced on page 31 as the basis for the accounting equation. As noted, this concept will be explained in much more detail in Chapter 3. Additional concepts and assumptions will be covered in later chapters. Remember that accounting is the language of business, and it takes time to learn a new language. The terms and concepts we introduce here will become much more familiar as your study continues.

The Separate Entity Concept

Because business involves the exchange of goods or services between entities, it follows that accounting records should be kept for those entities. For accounting purposes, an **entity** is defined as the organizational unit for which accounting records are maintained—for example, IBM Corporation. It is a focal point for identifying, measuring, and communicating accounting data. Furthermore, the entity is considered to be *separate* from its individual owners.

entity An organizational unit (a person, partnership, or corporation) for which accounting records are kept and about which accounting reports are prepared.

We are all engaged in a variety of economic activities. For example, John Scott works for a large corporation, owns some real estate, is president of the local Little League baseball organization, and manages the family estate on behalf of his brothers and sister. The **separate entity concept** is the idea that, when John Scott is called upon to report the financial activities of the local Little League, he must make sure not to include any of his personal or family financial activities in the results. Similarly, the accounting records of a small business must be kept separate from the personal finances of the owner.

separate entity concept The idea that the activities of an entity are to be separated from those of the individual owners.

Applying the separate entity concept to large corporations can also be difficult. Large corporations, such as General Electric and IBM, own networks of subsidiaries (and those subsidiaries own subsidiaries) with complex business ties among the members of the group. A key part of the accounting process for such an organization is carefully defining what is part of General Electric and what is not. For example, one difficult accounting issue (covered in advanced accounting courses) is deciding how much of another company General Electric must own (20%? 45%? 51%? 100%?) before that other company is considered part of the General Electric reporting entity.

The Assumption of Arm's-Length Transactions

transactions Exchange of goods or services between entities (whether individuals, businesses, or other organizations), as well as other events having an economic impact on a business.

Accounting is based on the recording of economic transactions. Viewed broadly, **transactions** include not only exchanges of economic resources between separate entities, but also events that have an economic impact on a business independently. The borrowing and lending of money and the sale and purchase of goods or services are examples of the former. The loss in value of equipment due to obsolescence or fire is an example of the latter. Collectively, transactions provide the data that are included in accounting records and reports.

arm's-length transactions Business dealings between independent and rational parties who are looking out for their own interests.

Accounting for economic transactions enables us to measure the success of an entity. However, the data for a transaction will not accurately represent that transaction if any bias is involved. Therefore, unless there is evidence to the contrary, accountants assume **arm's-length transactions**. That is, they make the assumption that both parties—for example, a buyer and a seller—are rational and free to act independently; each trying to make the best deal possible in establishing the terms of the transaction.

To illustrate, assume you are preparing a personal balance sheet and want to list the value of your minivan. You bought the three-year-old minivan for $5,000. Of course, you should list the minivan on your balance sheet at the $5,000 price you paid for it. That should be a good reflection of the value of the vehicle. However, what if you bought the minivan from your brother (who gave you a good deal) and the real market value of the minivan is $11,000? The problem here is that the $5,000 price negotiated between you and your brother is not a market price. Market prices can be thought of as prices negotiated between two strangers who are both competing to get the best deal possible. Thus, a necessary assumption for financial statements to be informative is that the reported financial results come from arm's-length transactions. Without this assumption, the numbers in the financial statements (like the $5,000 for the minivan you bought from your brother) do not reflect true values.

historical cost The dollar amount originally exchanged in an arm's-length transaction; an amount assumed to reflect the fair market value of an item at the transaction date.

An illustration of the accounting problems that can arise from the lack of arm's-length transactions is provided by the labor problems of major league baseball. The team owners and the players are always arguing about the profitability of the teams. The players do not believe the numbers in the owners' financial statements; reported important transactions are between the baseball teams and other businesses controlled by the owners, such as television stations. Since the revenues received in these deals (between the baseball teams and related businesses) are not from arm's-length transactions, the players question whether the full value of the deals is reflected in the owners' financial reports.

cost principle The idea that transactions are recorded at their historical costs or exchange prices at the transaction date.

The Cost Principle

CAUTION

When reading accounting reports, remember that the reported values are historical costs, reflecting exchange prices at various transaction dates.

To further ensure objective measurements, accountants record transactions at **historical cost**, the amount originally paid or received for goods and services in arm's-length transactions. The historical cost is assumed to represent the fair market value of the item at the date of the transaction because it reflects the actual use of resources by independent parties. In accounting, this convention of recording transactions at cost is often referred to as the **cost principle**.

The Monetary Measurement Concept

monetary measurement The idea that money, as the common medium of exchange, is the accounting unit of measurement, and that only economic activities measurable in monetary terms are included in the accounting model.

Accountants do not record all the activities of economic entities. They record only those that can be measured in monetary terms. Thus, the concept of **monetary measurement** becomes another important characteristic of the accounting model. For example, employee morale cannot be measured directly in monetary terms and is not reported in the accounting records. Wages paid or owed, however, are quantifiable in terms of money and are reported. In accounting, all transactions are recorded in monetary amounts, whether or not cash is involved. In the United States, the dollar is the unit of exchange and is thus the measuring unit for accounting purposes.

As noted earlier in discussing the limitations of a balance sheet, the listed values may not be the same as actual market values for two reasons. The first is due to the cost principle. Because of such factors as inflation (an increase in the general price level of goods and services), the recorded amount of an item may be quite different from the amount required at a later time to buy or replace the item. The second reason results from the monetary measurement concept. Not all economic assets are recorded, because they are too difficult or impossible to measure in monetary amounts.

The Going Concern Assumption

going concern assumption The idea that an accounting entity will have a continuing existence for the foreseeable future.

The Safeway balance sheet in Exhibit 2-3 was prepared under the assumption that Safeway would continue in business for the foreseeable future. This is called the **going concern assumption**. Without this assumption, preparation of the balance sheet would be much more difficult. For example, the $1.3 billion inventory for Safeway in 1996 is reported at the cost originally paid to purchase the inventory. This is a reasonable figure because, in the normal course of business, Safeway can expect to sell the inventory for this amount, plus some profit. But if it were assumed that Safeway would go out of business tomorrow, the inventory would suddenly be worth a lot less. Imagine the low prices you could get on Safeway merchandise if it had to conduct a one-day, going-out-of-business sale! The going concern assumption allows the accountant to record assets at what they are worth to a company in normal use, rather than what they would sell for in a liquidation sale.

TO SUMMARIZE

In conducting economic activities, entities enter into transactions that form the basis of accounting records. An accounting model has been developed for recording, measuring, and reporting an entity's transactions. This model is founded on certain fundamental concepts and several important assumptions, principles, and procedures. First, the organizational unit being accounted for is a separate entity. The entity may be small or large, but it is the organizational unit for which accounting records are kept and financial reports prepared. Second, the transactions are assumed to be arm's-length. Third, transactions are recorded at historical cost. Fourth, transactions must be measurable in monetary amounts. Fifth, the accounting entity is assumed to be a going concern.

REVIEW OF LEARNING OBJECTIVES

1 Understand the basic elements and formats of the three primary financial statements—balance sheet, income statement, and statement of cash flows. The balance sheet provides a summary of the financial position of a company at a particular date. It lists a company's assets, liabilities, and owners' equity. Assets and liabilities are usually classified as either current or long-term. For a corporation, owners' equity consists of directly invested funds as well as retained earnings.

The income statement shows the major sources of revenues generated and the expenses associated with those revenues. The difference between revenues and expenses is net income or net loss. The income statements of corporations must also include earnings per share.

The statement of cash flows shows the significant cash inflows (receipts) and cash outflows (payments) of a company for a period of time. These cash flows are classified according to operating, investing, and financing activities.

2 Recognize the need for financial statement notes and identify the types of information included in the notes. The notes to the financial statements contain additional information not included in the financial statements themselves. The notes explain the company's accounting assumptions and practices, provide details of financial statement summary numbers and additional disclosure about complex events, and report supplementary information required by the SEC and the FASB.

3 Describe the purpose of an audit report and the incentives the auditor has to perform a good audit. An audit report is issued by an independent CPA firm attesting to the conformity of a set of financial statements with generally accepted accounting principles. CPA firms have an economic incentive to perform credible audits in order to preserve their reputations and to avoid lawsuits.

4 Use financial ratios to identify a company's strengths and weaknesses and to forecast its future performance. Financial statements are analyzed by investors, creditors, and management to detect signs of existing deficiencies in performance and to predict how the firm will perform in the future. Proper interpretation of a financial ratio depends on comparing a firm's ratio value to the value for the same firm in the previous year, as well as to values for other firms in the same industry.

5 Explain the fundamental concepts and assumptions that underlie financial accounting. Certain fundamental concepts underlie the practice of accounting. First, a business must be accounted for as an economic entity separate from the personal affairs of the owners and separate from other businesses. Second, the transactions are assumed to be arm's-length, so that the negotiated prices reflect true market values at the dates of the transactions. Third, transactions are recorded at historical cost. Fourth, only those transactions and events that can be measured in monetary terms are reported. Fifth, the accounting entity is assumed to be a going concern.

KEY TERMS AND CONCEPTS

accounting equation 31
accounting model 51
arm's-length transactions 52
articulation 43
asset turnover 49
assets 29
audit report 47
balance sheet (statement of financial position) 28
book value 35
capital stock 31
classified balance sheet 33
comparative financial statements 33
cost principle 52
current assets 33
current (or working capital) ratio 48
debt ratio 48
dividends 30
double-entry accounting 31
earnings (loss) per share (EPS) 39
entity 51
expenses 37
financial ratios 48
financial statement analysis 48
financing activities 40
gains (losses) 38
going concern assumption 53
gross profit (gross margin) 38
historical cost 52
income statement (statement of earnings) 28
investing activities 40
liabilities 29
liquidity 33
long-term assets 33
market value 35
monetary measurement 52
net assets 29
net income (net loss) 37
notes to the financial statements 44
operating activities 40
owners' equity 29
price-earnings (PE) ratio 50
primary financial statements 28
retained earnings 30
return on equity 49
return on sales 49
revenue 36
separate entity concept 51
statement of cash flows 28
statement of retained earnings 39
stockholders (shareholders) 30
stockholders' equity 30
transactions 52

REVIEW PROBLEM

The Income Statement and the Balance Sheet

Shirley Baum manages The Copy Shop. She has come to you for help in preparing an income statement and a balance sheet for the year ended December 31, 2000. Several amounts, determined as of December 31, 2000, are presented below. No dividends were paid this year.

Capital stock (10,000 shares outstanding)	$ 40,000	Mortgage payable	$72,000
Retained earnings (12/31/99)	12,400	Accounts payable	6,000
Advertising expense	2,000	Land	24,000
Cash	17,000	Supplies	2,000
Rent expense	2,400	Salary expense	20,000
Building (net)	100,000	Revenues	42,000
Interest expense	700	Other expenses	1,300
		Accounts receivable	3,000

Required:

1. Prepare an income statement for the year ended December 31, 2000, including EPS.
2. Determine the amount of retained earnings at December 31, 2000.
3. Prepare a classified balance sheet as of December 31, 2000.
4. Calculate the current ratio for The Copy Shop. What does the current ratio tell you about the company?

Solution

1. Income Statement

The first step in solving this problem is to separate the balance sheet items from the income statement items. Asset, liability, and owners' equity items reflect the company's financial position and appear on the balance sheet; revenues and expenses are reported on the income statement.

Balance Sheet Items	Income Statement Items
Capital stock	Advertising expense
Retained earnings	Rent expense
Cash	Interest expense
Building (net)	Salary expense
Mortgage payable	Revenues
Accounts payable	Other expenses
Land	
Supplies	
Accounts receivable	

After the items have been separated, the income statement and the balance sheet may be prepared using a proper format.

The Copy Shop
Income Statement
For the Year Ended December 31, 2000

Revenues		$42,000
Expenses:		
Advertising expense	$ 2,000	
Rent expense	2,400	
Interest expense	700	
Salary expense	20,000	
Other expenses	1,300	26,400
Net income		$15,600

EPS = $15,600 ÷ 10,000 shares = $1.56

2. Retained Earnings

The amount of retained earnings at December 31, 2000, may be calculated as follows:

Retained earnings (12/31/99)	$12,400
Add: Net income for year	15,600
Subtract: Dividends for year	(0)
Retained earnings (12/31/00)	$28,000

Since no dividends were paid during 2000, the ending balance in Retained Earnings is simply the beginning balance plus net income for the year.

3. Balance Sheet

The Copy Shop
Balance Sheet
December 31, 2000

Assets			Liabilities and Owners' Equity		
Current assets:			**Current liabilities:**		
Cash	$ 17,000		Accounts payable	$ 6,000	
Accounts receivable	3,000				
Supplies	2,000	$ 22,000	**Long-term liabilities:**		
			Mortgage payable	72,000	
Long-term assets:			Total liabilities		$ 78,000
Land	$ 24,000				
Building (net)	100,000	124,000	**Owners' equity:**		
			Capital stock	$40,000	
			Retained earnings	28,000*	68,000
			Total liabilities and		
Total assets		$146,000	owners' equity		$146,000

*See item 2 for calculation.

4. Current Ratio

CR = Current Assets/Current Liabilities
CR = $22,000/$6,000 = 3.67

The current ratio shows the relationship of total current assets to total current liabilities. It indicates whether a company can pay its current obligations with its current assets, and therefore helps short-term creditors assess a company's liquidity. The Copy Shop has almost four times the amount of current assets as its current liabilities (3.67:1). In other words, The Copy Shop has $3.67 of current assets for every $1 of current liabilities, which shows a favorable liquidity position.

DISCUSSION QUESTIONS

1. As an external user of financial statements, perhaps an investor or creditor, what type of accounting information do you need?
2. What is the major purpose of:
   a. A balance sheet?
   b. An income statement?
   c. A statement of cash flows?
3. Assume you want to invest in the stock market, and your friends tell you about a company's stock that is "guaranteed" to have an annual growth rate of 150 percent. Should you trust your friends and invest immediately or should you research the company's financial statements before investing? Explain.
4. Why are classified and comparative financial statements generally presented in annual reports to shareholders?
5. Why are owners' equity and liabilities considered the "sources" of assets?
6. Owners' equity is not cash; it is not a liability; and it generally is not equal to the current worth of a business. What is the nature of owners' equity?
7. What are the limitations of the balance sheet? Why is it important to be aware of these when evaluating a company's growth potential?
8. Some people feel that the income statement is more important than the balance sheet. Do you agree? Why or why not?
9. How might an investor be misled by only looking at the "bottom line" (the net income or EPS number) on an income statement?
10. Why is it important to classify cash flows according to operating, investing, and financing activities?
11. You are thinking of investing in one of two companies. In one annual report, the auditor's opinion states that the financial statements were prepared in accordance with generally accepted accounting

principles. The other makes no such claim. How important is that to you? Explain.

12. Some people think that auditors are responsible for ensuring the accuracy of financial statements. Are they correct? Why or why not?
13. What are the four general types of financial statement notes typically included in annual reports to stockholders?
14. What are the primary purposes of financial statement analysis?
15. Indicate how each of the following financial ratios is computed and describe what the ratio is attempting to explain:
    a. Debt ratio
    b. Current ratio
    c. Asset turnover
    d. Return on sales
    e. Return on equity
    f. Price-earnings ratio
16. Explain why each of the following is important in accounting:
    a. The separate entity concept
    b. The assumption of arm's-length transactions
    c. The cost principle
    d. The monetary measurement concept
    e. The going concern assumption

DISCUSSION CASES

CASE 2-1

CREDITOR AND INVESTOR INFORMATION NEEDS

Ink Spot is a small company that has been in business for two years. Wilford Smith, the president of the company, has decided that it is time to expand. He needs $10,000 to purchase additional equipment and to pay for increased operating expenses. Wilford can either apply for a loan at First City Bank, or he can issue more stock (1,000 shares are outstanding) to new investors. Assuming that you are the loan officer at First City Bank, what information would you request from Ink Spot before deciding whether to make the loan? As a potential investor in Ink Spot, what information would you need to make a good investment decision? What financial ratios might you consider as a potential lender or investor before making a decision?

CASE 2-2

ANALYZING TRENDS AND KEY FINANCIAL RELATIONSHIPS

An investor may choose from several investment opportunities: the stocks of different companies; rental property or other real estate; or savings accounts, money market certificates, and similar financial instruments. When considering an investment in the stock of a particular company, comparative financial data presented in the annual report to stockholders helps an investor identify key relationships and trends. As an illustration, comparative operating results for Prime Properties, Inc., from its 2000 annual report are provided. (Dollars are presented in thousands except for earnings per share.)

	Year Ended December 31		
	2000	1999	1998
Revenues:			
Property management fees	$ 58,742	$ 63,902	$ 66,204
Appraisal fees	55,641	60,945	62,320
Total revenues	$114,383	$124,847	$128,524

(continued)

	Year Ended December 31		
	2000	1999	1998
Expenses:			
Selling and advertising	$ 64,371	$ 75,403	$ 80,478
Administrative expenses	30,671	31,115	31,618
Other expenses	9,265	9,540	9,446
Interest expense	2,047	1,468	26
Total expenses	$106,354	$117,526	$121,568
Income before taxes	$ 8,029	$ 7,321	$ 6,956
Income taxes	2,409	2,196	2,087
Net income	$ 5,620	$ 5,125	$ 4,869
*Earnings per share	$2.25	$2.05	$1.95

*2.5 million shares outstanding

What trends are indicated by the comparative income statement data for Prime Properties, Inc.? Which of these trends would be of concern to a potential investor? What additional information would an investor need in order to make a decision about whether to invest in this company?

CASE 2-3

ACCOUNTING FOR THE PROPER ENTITY

You have been hired to prepare the financial reports for White River Building Supply, a proprietorship owned by Bill Masters. Upon encountering several payments made from the company bank account to a nearby university, you contact Bill Masters to find out how to classify these payments. Masters explains that those checks were written to pay his daughter's tuition and to purchase her textbooks and miscellaneous supplies. He then tells you to include the payments with other expenses of the business. "This way," he explains, "I can deduct the payments on my tax return. Why not, since it all comes out of the same pocket?" How would you respond to Masters?

EXERCISES

EXERCISE 2-1
Classification of Financial Statement Elements

Indicate for each of the following items whether it would appear on a balance sheet (BS) or an income statement (IS). If a balance sheet item, is it an asset (A), a liability (L), or an owners' equity item (OE)?

1. Accounts Payable
2. Sales Revenue
3. Accounts Receivable
4. Advertising Expense
5. Cash
6. Supplies
7. Consulting Revenue
8. Land
9. Capital Stock
10. Rent Expense
11. Equipment
12. Interest Receivable
13. Mortgage Payable
14. Notes Payable
15. Buildings
16. Salaries & Wages Expense
17. Retained Earnings
18. Utilities Expense

EXERCISE 2-2
Accounting Equation

Compute the missing amounts for companies A, B, and C.

	A	B	C
Cash	$25,000	$ 9,000	$12,000
Accounts receivable	20,000	15,000	7,000
Land and buildings	50,000	?	40,000
Accounts payable	?	6,000	14,000
Mortgage payable	30,000	10,000	15,000
Owners' equity	55,000	30,000	?

EXERCISE 2-3
Comprehensive Accounting Equation

Assuming no additional investments by or distributions to owners, compute the missing amounts for companies X, Y, and Z.

	X	Y	Z
Assets: January 1, 2000	$360	$?	$230
Liabilities: January 1, 2000	280	460	?
Owners' equity: January 1, 2000	?	620	150
Assets: December 31, 2000	380	?	310
Liabilities: December 31, 2000	?	520	90
Owners' equity: December 31, 2000	?	720	?
Revenues in 2000	80	?	400
Expenses in 2000	100	116	?

EXERCISE 2-4
Computing Elements of Owners' Equity

From the information provided determine:

1. The amount of retained earnings at December 31.
2. The amount of revenues for the period.

Totals	January 1	December 31
Current assets	$ 5,000	$ 10,000
All other assets	150,000	160,000
Liabilities	25,000	30,000
Capital stock	50,000	?
Retained earnings	80,000	?

Additional data:
Expenses for the period were $35,000.
Dividends paid were $7,500.
Capital stock increased by $5,000 during the period.

EXERCISE 2-5
Balance Sheet Relationships

Correct the following balance sheet.

Canfield Corporation
Balance Sheet
December 31, 2000

Assets		Liabilities and Owners' Equity	
Cash	$ 55,000	Buildings	$325,000
Accounts payable	65,000	Accounts receivable	75,000
Interest receivable	20,000	Mortgage payable	150,000
Capital stock	200,000	Sales revenue	350,000
Rent expense	60,000	Equipment	85,000
Retained earnings	145,000	Utilities expense	5,000
Total assets	$545,000	Total liabilities and owners' equity	$990,000

EXERCISE 2-6
Balance Sheet Preparation

From the following data, prepare a classified balance sheet for Low Price Company at December 31, 2000.

Accounts payable	$ 46,500
Accounts receivable	99,000
Buildings	325,500
Owners' equity, 1/1/00	150,000
Cash	116,250
Distributions to owners during 2000	18,750
Supplies	2,250
Land	165,000
Mortgage payable	412,500
Net income for 2000	117,750
Owners' equity, 12/31/00	?

EXERCISE 2-7
Income Statement Computations

Following are the operating data for an advertising firm for the year ended December 31, 2000.

Revenues	$175,000
Supplies expense	45,000
Salaries expense	70,000
Rent expense	1,500
Administrative expense	6,000
Income taxes (30% of income before taxes)	?

For 2000, determine:

1. Income before taxes.
2. Income taxes.
3. Net income.
4. Earnings per share (EPS), assuming there are 15,000 shares of stock outstanding.

EXERCISE 2-8
Income Statement Preparation

The following selected information is taken from the records of Sel Tec Corporation.

Accounts payable	$ 25,000
Accounts receivable	49,000
Advertising expense	7,500
Cash	15,500
Supplies expense	23,000
Rent expense	5,000
Utilities expense	1,500
Income taxes (30% of income before taxes)	?
Miscellaneous expense	2,200
Owners' equity	125,000
Salaries expense	88,000
Fees (revenues)	242,000

1. Prepare an income statement for the year ended December 31, 2000. (Assume that 5,000 shares of stock are outstanding.)
2. Explain what the EPS ratio tells the reader about Sel Tec Corporation.

EXERCISE 2-9
Cash Flow Computations

From the following selected data, compute:

1. Net cash flow provided (used) by operating activities.
2. Net cash flow provided (used) by investing activities.
3. Net cash flow provided (used) by financing activities.
4. Net increase (decrease) in cash during the year.
5. The cash balance at the end of the year.

Cash receipts from:	
Customers	$270,000
Investments by owners	54,000
Sale of building	90,000
Proceeds from bank loan	60,000
Cash payments for:	
Wages	$ 82,000
Utilities	3,000
Advertising	4,000
Rent	36,000
Taxes	67,000
Dividends	20,000
Repayment of principal on loan	40,000
Purchase of land	106,000
Cash balance at beginning of year	$386,000

EXERCISE 2-10
Income and Retained Earnings Relationships

Assume that retained earnings increased by $240,000 from December 31, 1999, to December 31, 2000, for Miller Corporation. During the year, a cash dividend of $140,000 was paid.

1. Compute the net income for the year.
2. Assume that the revenues for the year were $920,000. Compute the expenses incurred for the year.

EXERCISE 2-11
Retained Earnings Computations

During 2000, Safe Lite Corporation had revenues of $180,000 and expenses, including income taxes, of $100,000. On December 31, 1999, Safe Lite had assets of $400,000, liabilities of $100,000, and capital stock of $250,000. Safe Lite paid a cash dividend of $40,000 in 2000. No additional stock was issued. Compute the retained earnings on December 31, 1999, and 2000.

EXERCISE 2-12
Preparation of Income Statement and Retained Earnings

Prepare an income statement and a statement of retained earnings for Big Sky Corporation for the year ended June 30, 2000, based on the following information:

Capital stock (1,500 shares @ $100)		$150,000
Retained earnings, July 1, 1999		76,800
Dividends		6,500
Ski rental revenue		77,900
Expenses:		
Rent expense	$ 6,000	
Salaries expense	38,600	
Utilities expense	2,400	
Advertising expense	7,500	
Miscellaneous expense	7,700	
Income taxes	2,100	64,300

EXERCISE 2-13
Articulation: Relationships Between a Balance Sheet and an Income Statement

The total assets and liabilities of Roloflex Company at January 1 and December 31, 2000, are presented below.

	January 1	December 31
Assets	$76,000	$112,000
Liabilities	26,000	28,800

Determine the amount of net income or loss for 2000, applying each of the following assumptions concerning the additional issuance of stock and dividends paid by the firm. Each case is independent of the others.

1. Dividends of $10,800 were paid and no additional stock was issued during the year.
2. Additional stock of $4,800 was issued and no dividends were paid during the year.
3. Additional stock of $62,000 was issued and dividends of $15,600 were paid during the year.

EXERCISE 2-14
Cash Flow Classifications

For each of the following items, indicate whether it would be classified and reported under the Operating Activities (OA), Investing Activities (IA), or Financing Activities (FA) section of a statement of cash flows:

a. Cash receipts from selling merchandise
b. Cash payments for wages and salaries
c. Cash proceeds from sale of stock
d. Cash purchase of equipment
e. Cash dividends paid
f. Cash received from bank loan
g. Cash payments for inventory
h. Cash receipts from services rendered
i. Cash payments for taxes
j. Cash proceeds from sale of property no longer needed as expansion site

EXERCISE 2-15
Current Ratio

Using the data in Exercise 2-6, compute the current ratio for Low Price Company. What does the current ratio show?

EXERCISE 2-16
Debt Ratio

Using the data in Exercise 2-6, compute the debt ratio for Low Price Company. What does the debt ratio explain?

EXERCISE 2-17
Return on Equity and Price-Earnings Ratio

Using the data in Exercise 2-6, and assuming 20,000 shares of stock outstanding and a market price per share of $36.00, compute the return on equity and PE ratios for Low Price Company. Does the PE ratio seem reasonable relative to other U.S. stocks?

EXERCISE 2-18
Notes to Financial Statements

Refer to **Microsoft**'s annual report in Appendix A at the end of the book. How important are the notes to financial statements? What are the major types of notes that Microsoft includes in its annual report?

EXERCISE 2-19
The Cost Principle

On January 1, 2000, Save-More Construction Company paid $150,000 in cash for a parcel of land to be used as the site of a new office building. During March, the company petitioned the City Council to rezone the area for professional office buildings. The City Council refused, preferring to maintain the area as a residential zone. After nine months of negotiation, Save-More Construction convinced the Council to rezone the property for commercial use, thus raising its value to $200,000.

For accounting purposes, what value should be used to record the transaction on January 1, 2000? At what value would the property be reported at year-end, after the City Council rezoning? Explain why accountants use historical costs to record transactions.

EXERCISE 2-20
The Monetary Measurement Concept

Many successful companies, such as **Ford Motor Company**, **Exxon**, and **Marriott Corporation**, readily acknowledge the importance and value of their employees. In fact, the employees of a company are often viewed as the most valued asset of the company. Yet in the asset section of the balance sheets of these companies there is no mention of the asset employees. What is the reason for this oversight and apparent inconsistency?

EXERCISE 2-21
The Going Concern Assumption

Assume that you open an auto repair business. You purchase a building and buy new equipment. What difference does the going concern assumption make with regard to how you would account for these assets?

PROBLEMS

PROBLEM 2-1
Balance Sheet Classifications and Relationships

Tu'aa Corporation has the following balance sheet elements as of December 31, 2000.

Land	$ 69,000	Mortgage payable	$300,000
Cash	?	Capital stock	135,000
Building	178,000	Retained earnings	88,000
Accounts payable	100,000	Supplies	17,000
Notes payable (short-term)	105,000	Accounts receivable	88,000
Equipment	350,000		

Required:

Compute the total amount of:

1. Current assets.
2. Long-term assets.
3. Current liabilities.
4. Long-term liabilities.
5. Stockholders' equity

PROBLEM 2-2
Preparation of a Classified Balance Sheet

Following are the December 31, 2000, account balances for Siraco Company.

Cash	$ 1,950
Accounts receivable	2,500
Supplies	1,800
Equipment	11,275
Accounts payable	3,450
Wages payable	250
Dividends paid	1,500
Capital stock	775
Retained earnings, January 1, 2000	12,000
Revenues	10,000
Miscellaneous expense	1,550
Supplies expense	3,700
Wages expense	2,200

Required:

1. Prepare a classified balance sheet as of December 31, 2000.
2. **Interpretive Question:** On the basis of its 2000 earnings, was this company's decision to pay dividends of $1,500 a sound one?

PROBLEM 2-3
Balance Sheet Preparation with a Missing Element

The following data are available for Sunshine Products Inc. as of December 31, 2000.

Cash	$10,000
Accounts payable	14,000
Capital stock	35,200
Accounts receivable	20,000
Building	28,000
Supplies	1,200
Retained earnings	?
Land	10,000

Required:

1. Prepare a balance sheet for Sunshine Products, Inc.
2. Determine the amount of retained earnings at December 31, 2000.
3. **Interpretive Question:** In what way is a balance sheet a depiction of the basic accounting equation?

PROBLEM 2-4
Income Statement Preparation

Listed below are the results of Rulon Candies' operations for 1999 and 2000. (Assume 4,000 shares of outstanding stock for both years.)

	2000	1999
Sales	$300,000	$350,000
Utilities expenses	15,000	8,500
Employee salaries	115,000	110,000
Advertising expenses	10,000	20,000
Income tax expense	9,000	36,500
Interest expense	25,000	15,000
Cost of goods sold	115,000	85,000
Interest revenue	10,000	10,000

Required:

1. Prepare a comparative income statement for Rulon Candies, Inc., for the years ended December 31, 2000 and 1999. Be sure to include figures for gross margin, operating income, income before taxes, net income, and earnings per share.
2. **Interpretive Question:** What advice would you give Rulon Candies, Inc., to improve its profitability for the year 2001?

PROBLEM 2-5
Income Statement Preparation

The following information is taken from the records of Hill, Dunn, & Associates for the year ended December 31, 2000.

Income taxes	$ 10,800
Service revenues	150,000
Rent expense	5,500
Salaries expense	35,000
Miscellaneous expense	380
Utilities expense	1,230
Administrative expense	12,300

Required: Prepare an income statement for Hill, Dunn, & Associates for the year ended December 31, 2000. (Assume that 4,000 shares of stock are outstanding.)

PROBLEM 2-6
Expanded Accounting Equation

At the end of 2000, Morgan Systems Inc. had a fire that destroyed a majority of its accounting records. Morgan Systems Inc. was able to gather the following financial information for 2000.

a. Retained earnings was only changed as a result of net income and a $50,000 dividend payment to Morgan's investors.
b. All other account changes for the year are listed below. The amount of change for each account is shown as a net increase or decrease.

	Increase or (Decrease)
Cash	$ 25,000
Interest receivable	(15,000)
Inventory	100,000
Accounts receivable	(22,500)
Building	315,000
Accounts payable	45,000
Mortgage payable	275,000
Wages payable	(27,250)
Capital stock	52,500

Required: Using the accounting equation, compute Morgan's net income for 2000.

PROBLEM 2-7
Income Statement Preparation

Precision Corporation has been a leading supplier of magnetic storage disks for three years. Following are the results of Precision's operations for 2000.

Sales revenue	$68,000
Advertising expense	1,530
Income taxes	4,360
Delivery expense	480
Packaging expense	355
Salaries expense	18,350
Supplies expense	8,410
EPS = $3.45	

Required:

1. Prepare an income statement for the year ended December 31, 2000.
2. How many shares of stock were outstanding?

PROBLEM 2-8
Statement of Cash Flows

Southwestern Rentals Inc. rents equipment to customers ranging from homeowners to large construction companies. The financial information shown below was gathered from its accounting records for 2000. Assume any increase or decrease in the balances from 1/1/00 to 12/31/00 resulted from either receiving or paying cash in the transaction. For example, during 2000 the balance on loans for land holdings increased $150,000 because the company received $150,000 in cash by taking out an additional loan on the land.

Items	Balance as of 1/1/00	Balance as of 12/31/00
Cash	$ 20,000	$ 50,000
Cash receipts from customers	—	600,000
Loans on land holdings	100,000	250,000
Cash distributions to owners	—	150,000
Loan on building	100,000	70,000
Investments in securities	850,000	1,050,000
Cash payments for other expenses	—	50,000
Cash payments for taxes	—	55,000
Cash payments for operating expenses	—	135,000
Cash payments for wages and salaries	—	100,000

Required:

1. Prepare a statement of cash flows for Southwestern Rentals Inc. for the year ended December 31, 2000.
2. **Interpretive Question:** Does Southwestern Rentals Inc. appear to be in good shape from a cash flow standpoint? What other information would help you analyze the situation?

PROBLEM 2-9
Statement of Cash Flows

The cash account for Kwon Enterprises shows the following for the year ended December 31, 2000.

Beginning cash balance	$?
Cash receipts during year from:	
Services	1,351,000
Investments by owners	82,000
Sale of land	135,000
Cash payments during year for:	
Operating expenses	963,000
Taxes	114,000
Purchase of building	326,000
Distributions to owners	55,000
Ending cash balance	850,000

Required:

Prepare a statement of cash flows for Kwon Enterprises for the year ended December 31, 2000.

PROBLEM 2-10
Unifying Concepts: Net Income and Financial Ratio Analysis

A summary of the operations of Streuling Company for the year ended May 31, 2000, is shown below.

Advertising expense	$ 2,760
Supplies expense	37,820
Rent expense	1,500
Salaries expense	18,150
Miscellaneous expense	4,170
Dividends	12,400
Retained earnings (6/1/99)	156,540
Income taxes	21,180
Consulting fees (revenues)	115,100
Administrative expense	7,250

Required:

1. Determine the net income for the year by preparing an income statement. (Assume that 3,000 shares of stock are outstanding.)
2. Compute the return on equity (ROE) for Streuling Company, assuming total owners' equity is $255,000.
3. **Interpretive Question:** What does the ROE ratio explain about Streuling's profitability?
4. **Interpretive Question:** Assuming an operating loss for the year, is it a good idea for Streuling to still pay its shareholders dividends?

PROBLEM 2-11
Unifying Concepts: Net Income and Statement of Retained Earnings

A summary of the operations of Stellenbach Company for the year ended May 31, 2000, is shown below.

Advertising expense	$ 2,760
Supplies expense	37,820
Rent expense	1,500
Salaries expense	18,150
Miscellaneous expense	4,170
Dividends	12,400
Retained earnings (6/1/99)	156,540
Income taxes	21,180
Consulting fees (revenues)	115,100
Administrative expense	7,250

Required:

1. Determine the net income for the year by preparing an income statement. (There are 2,000 shares of stock outstanding.)
2. Prepare a statement of retained earnings for the year ended May 31, 2000.
3. Prepare a statement of retained earnings assuming that Stellenbach had a net loss for the year of $25,000.
4. **Interpretive Question:** Assuming a loss as in (3), is it a good idea for Stellenbach to still pay its shareholders dividends?

PROBLEM 2-12
Financial Ratios

The following information for High Flying Company is provided.

High Flying Company	
Current assets	$ 145,000
Long-term assets	750,000
Current liabilities	75,000
Long-term liabilities	300,000
Owners' equity	520,000
Sales for year	1,425,000
Net income for year	105,000
Average market price per share	145.00
Average number of shares outstanding	10,000

Required:

1. Compute the current ratio, debt ratio, return on sales, return on equity, asset turnover, and price-earnings ratio.
2. **Interpretive Question:** What do these ratios show for High Flying Company?

PROBLEM 2-13
Comprehensive Financial Statement Preparation

The following information was obtained from the records of Uptown, Inc., as of December 31, 2000.

Land	$ 37,500
Buildings	145,050
Salaries expense	40,050
Utilities expense	9,750
Accounts payable	25,650
Revenues	397,800
Supplies	69,450
Retained earnings (1/1/00)	272,550
Capital stock (1,000 shares outstanding)	45,000
Accounts receivable	46,500
Supplies expense	207,900
Cash	?
Notes payable (long-term)	25,800
Rent expense	25,650
Dividends in 2000	60,750
Other expenses	13,050
Income taxes	52,800

Required:

1. Prepare an income statement for the year ended December 31, 2000.
2. Prepare a classified balance sheet as of December 31, 2000.
3. Compute the current ratio as of December 31, 2000.
4. Compute the debt ratio as of December 31, 2000.
5. **Interpretive Question:** What does the current ratio tell about Uptown's liquidity?
6. **Interpretive Question:** What does the debt ratio tell about Uptown's leverage?
7. **Interpretive Question:** Why is the balance in Retained Earnings so large as compared with the balance in Capital Stock?

PROBLEM 2-14
Elements of Comparative Financial Statements

The following report is supplied by Smith Brothers Company.

Smith Brothers Company
Comparative Balance Sheets
As of December 31, 2000 and 1999

Assets	2000	1999	Liabilities and Owners' Equity	2000	1999
Cash	$13,000	$15,000	Accounts payable	$ 5,000	$ 4,000
Accounts receivable	18,000	11,000	Salaries and commissions payable	8,000	8,000
Notes receivable	11,000	10,000	Notes payable	25,000	27,000
Land	38,000	38,000	Capital stock	20,000	20,000
			Retained earnings	22,000	15,000
Total assets	$80,000	$74,000	Total liabilities and owners' equity	$80,000	$74,000

Operating expenses for the year included utilities of $4,500, salaries and commissions of $44,800, and miscellaneous expenses of $1,500. Income taxes for the year were $3,000, and the company paid dividends of $5,000.

Required:

1. Compute the total expenses, including taxes, incurred in 2000.
2. Compute the net income or net loss for 2000.
3. Compute the total revenue for 2000.
4. **Interpretive Question:** Why are comparative financial statements generally of more value to users than statements for a single period?

Analyzing Real Company Information

International Case

Ethics Case

Writing Assignment

The Debate

Internet Search

Accounting is more than just doing textbook problems. These Competency Enhancement Opportunities provide practice in critical thinking, oral and written communication, research, teamwork, and consideration of ethical issues.

ANALYZING REAL COMPANY INFORMATION

• Analyzing 2–1 (Microsoft)

The 1997 annual report for **Microsoft** is included in Appendix A. Locate that annual report and answer the following questions:

1. Locate Microsoft's 1997 balance sheet. What percentage of its total assets consists of cash and short-term investments? Compute Microsoft's current ratio. How does its current ratio compare to yours? How much long-term debt does Microsoft have?
2. Find Microsoft's 1997 income statement. Have revenues increased or decreased over the last three years? Is the rate of increase rising? Compute Microsoft's return on sales. Is it increasing?
3. Compute Microsoft's return on equity. How does that return compare to the rate of return you might earn if you were to invest your money in a savings account at a local bank?

COMPETENCY ENHANCEMENT OPPORTUNITIES

4. Review Microsoft's statement of cash flows. What activity generates most of Microsoft's cash? What is Microsoft doing with all its money—buying back its own stock, investing in other companies, or something else?

• Analyzing 2-2 (Safeway)

At the start of this chapter you learned a little about **Safeway** and its history. Now let's take a look at the company's financial performance in recent years. Safeway's income statement and balance sheet are shown below and on pages 69–70.

SAFEWAY INC. AND SUBSIDIARIES
Consolidated Income Statements
For the Years Ended December 28, 1996, December 30, 1995, and December 31, 1994
(in millions, except per-share amounts)

	1996	1995	1994
Sales	$17,269.0	$16,397.5	$15,626.6
Cost of goods sold	(12,494.8)	(11,905.1)	(11,339.3)
Gross profit	4,774.2	4,492.4	4,287.3
Operating and administrative expense	(3,882.5)	(3,765.0)	(3,675.2)
Operating income	891.7	727.4	612.1
Interest expense	(178.5)	(199.8)	(221.7)
Equity in earnings of unconsolidated affiliates	50.0	26.9	27.3
Other income—net	4.4	2.0	6.4
Income before taxes and extraordinary loss	767.6	556.5	424.1
Income taxes	(307.0)	(228.2)	(173.9)
Income before extraordinary loss	460.6	328.3	250.2
Extraordinary loss related to early retirement of debt, net of income tax benefit of $1.3 and $6.7	—	(2.0)	(10.5)
Net income	$ 460.6	$ 326.3	$ 239.7
Earnings per common share and common share equivalent:			
Primary income before extraordinary loss	$ 1.94	$ 1.36	$ 1.02
Extraordinary loss	—	(0.01)	(0.04)
Net income	$ 1.94	$ 1.35	$ 0.98
Fully diluted income before extraordinary loss	$ 1.93	$ 1.35	$ 1.01
Extraordinary loss	—	(0.01)	(0.04)
Net income	$ 1.93	$ 1.34	$ 0.97
Weighted average common shares and common share equivalents:			
Primary	237.8	240.6	244.1
Fully diluted	238.4	243.5	247.1

SAFEWAY INC. AND SUBSIDIARIES
Consolidated Balance Sheets
As of December 28, 1996, and December 30, 1995
(in millions, except per-share amounts)

	1996	1995
Assets		
Current assets:		
Cash and equivalents	$ 79.7	$ 74.8
Receivables	160.9	152.7
Merchandise inventories, net of LIFO reserve of $79.2 and $74.3	1,283.3	1,191.8
Prepaid expenses and other current assets	130.5	95.5
Total current assets	1,654.4	1,514.8
Long-term assets:		
Land	438.3	419.4
Buildings	1,286.9	1,213.2
Leasehold improvements	957.2	858.5
Fixtures and equipment	2,108.5	1,912.7
Property under capital leases	278.7	283.4
	5,069.6	4,687.2
Less accumulated depreciation and amortization	2,313.2	2,094.3
Total long-term assets, net	2,756.4	2,592.9
Goodwill, net of accumulated amortization of $116.4 and $106.3	312.5	323.8
Prepaid pension costs	328.7	322.4
Investments in unconsolidated affiliates	362.4	336.0
Other assets	130.8	104.4
Total assets	$5,545.2	$5,194.3

	1996	1995
Liabilities and Stockholders' Equity		
Current liabilities:		
Current maturities of notes and debentures	$ 237.3	$ 221.4
Current obligations under capital leases	18.4	19.0
Accounts payable	1,153.1	1,040.0
Accrued salaries and wages	231.2	234.6
Other accrued liabilities	390.0	424.0
Total current liabilities	2,030.0	1,939.0
Long-term liabilities:		
Notes and debentures	1,568.1	1,783.6
Obligations under capital leases	160.4	166.2
Total long-term liabilities	1,728.5	1,949.8
Deferred income taxes	223.8	108.5
Accrued claims and other liabilities	376.1	401.5
Total liabilities	4,358.4	4,398.8

(continued)

	1996	1995
Commitments and contingencies		
Stockholders' equity:		
Common stock: par value $0.01 per share; 750 shares authorized; 221.4 and 213.7 shares outstanding	$ 2.2	$ 2.1
Additional paid-in capital	750.3	684.9
Unexercised warrants purchased	(322.7)	(196.2)
Cumulative translation adjustments	12.0	20.3
Retained earnings	745.0	284.4
Total stockholders' equity	1,186.8	795.5
Total liabilities and stockholders' equity	$5,545.2	$5,194.3

Based on information contained in these financial statements, answer the following questions:

1. Compute Safeway's debt ratio for the past two years. Has this ratio increased or decreased? Why?
2. Compute the company's current ratio. Do you notice anything unusual about Safeway's current ratio? How can a company stay in business with a current ratio this low?
3. Compute Safeway's return on sales for 1996. Does the size of this number surprise you? Now compute the company's asset turnover. Considering return on sales and asset turnover together, what does the result indicate?

INTERNATIONAL CASE

• Thorn EMI

While the balance sheet, income statement, and statement of cash flows are common titles seen around the world, sometimes that is where the commonalities end. For example, take a look at the balance sheet for Thorn EMI, a music company based in England. Based on your knowledge of American accounting disclosure, answer the following questions about Thorn's balance sheet shown on pages 71 and 72.

1. Can you identify any major differences between Microsoft's and Thorn's balance sheets in terms of the order in which major categories are displayed?
2. What is Thorn EMI's total assets? Is it as easy to determine as Microsoft's total assets?
3. Take a look at the following list of accounts and identify, given your knowledge of assets, liabilities, and owners' equity, what

Thorn EMI
Balance Sheets
at 31 March 1996

		Group		Company	
		1996	**1995**	**1996**	**1995**
	Notes	**£m**	**£m**	**£m**	**£m**
Fixed assets					
Music publishing copyrights	11	**409.3**	379.5	—	—
Tangible fixed assets	12	**1,478.3**	1,401.2	**14.6**	43.5
Investments	13	**33.8**	52.3	**4,761.9**	3,506.9
Investments: own shares	14	**24.1**	38.8	**24.1**	38.8
		1,945.5	1,871.8	**4,800.6**	3,589.2
Current assets					
Stocks	15	**217.4**	216.0	—	—
Debtors: amounts falling due within one year	16	**934.6**	746.0	**160.1**	489.0
Debtors: amounts falling due after more than one year	16	**104.9**	124.5	**34.3**	51.4
Investments	17	**112.6**	74.5	—	—
Cash at bank and in hand	17	**247.8**	217.0	**42.4**	11.0
		1,617.3	1,378.0	**236.8**	551.4
Creditors: amounts falling due within one year					
Borrowings	17	**(411.2)**	(247.9)	**(27.2)**	(13.9)
Other creditors	20	**(1,778.6)**	(1,616.5)	**(1,297.7)**	(1,246.5)
		(2,189.8)	(1,864.4)	**(1,324.9)**	(1,260.4)
Net current assets (liabilities)		**(572.5)**	(486.4)	**(1,088.1)**	(709.0)
Total assets less current liabilities		**1,373.0**	1,385.4	**3,712.5**	2,880.2
Creditors: amounts falling due after more than one year					
Borrowings	17	**(340.6)**	(406.9)	**(57.6)**	(76.4)
Other creditors	21	**(35.7)**	(16.4)	**(1,424.8)**	(916.5)
		(376.3)	(423.3)	**(1,482.4)**	(992.9)
Provisions for liabilities and charges					
Deferred taxation	22	**(25.7)**	(17.2)	**(3.7)**	(3.7)
Other provisions	23	**(346.7)**	(287.0)	**(35.8)**	(14.3)
		(372.4)	(304.2)	**(39.5)**	(18.0)
		624.3	657.9	**2,190.6**	1,869.3

(continued)

	Notes	Group 1996 £m	Group 1995 £m	Company 1996 £m	Company 1995 £m
Capital and reserves					
Called-up share capital	24	**107.7**	106.9	**107.7**	106.9
Share premium account	24	**913.3**	899.8	**913.3**	899.8
Other reserves	25	**615.6**	625.0	**640.6**	640.6
Profit and loss reserve	25	**534.0**	469.6	**529.0**	222.0
Goodwill	25	**(1,612.4)**	(1,517.5)	**—**	—
Equity shareholders' funds		**558.2**	583.8	**2,190.6**	1,869.3
Minority interests (equity)	**26**	**66.1**	74.1	**—**	—
		624.3	657.9	**2,190.6**	1,869.3

the American equivalent of those accounts might be (you might want to reference Microsoft's balance sheet for comparison):

- Stocks
- Debtors
- Called-up share capital
- Profit and loss reserve

ETHICS CASE

• Violating a covenant

Often banks will require companies that borrow money to agree to certain restrictions on the companies' activities in order to protect the lending institution. These restrictions are called "debt covenants." An example of a common debt covenant is requiring a company to maintain its current ratio at a certain level, say 2.0.

Your boss has just come to you and asked, "How can you make our current ratio higher?" You know that the company has a line of credit with a local bank that requires the company to maintain its current ratio at 1.5. You also know that the company was dangerously close to violating this covenant during the previous quarter. The end of the fiscal period is next week, and some action must be taken to increase the current ratio. If the covenant is violated, the lending agreement gives the bank the right to significantly modify the terms of the debt (in the bank's favor) as well as giving the bank a seat on the company's board of directors. Management would prefer not to have the bank involved in the day-to-day affairs of the business, nor do they want to alter the terms of the lending agreement.

Identify ways in which the current ratio can be increased. Would any of the alternatives you identify be good for the business? For example, selling equipment might raise the current ratio, but would that be good for the business? Should a company engage in these types of transactions?

WRITING ASSIGNMENT

• The most important financial statement

As you have discovered, there are three primary financial statements—balance sheet, income statement, and statement of cash flows. In no more than two pages, answer the following question: If you could have access to only one of the primary financial statements, which would it be and why? As you provide support for the financial statement of your choice, also provide reasons as to why you would not pick the other two statements.

THE DEBATE

• Save the notes

As pointed out in the chapter, IBM's annual report in 1920 included zero pages of notes to the financial statements. In 1996, the notes had grown to 26 pages. While the number of financial statements has remained constant, the number of notes to the financial statements continues to grow.

Divide your group into two teams and prepare two-minute presentations representing the following points of view.

- The first team represents "Kill the Notes." You are to take the position that financial statements providing information relating to a firm's current asset and liability position, a summary of its operations, and its cash inflows and outflows, are all that is needed to make good resource allocation decisions. The three primary financial statements are all that need to be provided to current and potential investors and creditors. In other words, the notes do not add value to the financial reports.
- The other team represents "Save the Notes." You are to argue that the notes represent essential information that must be used when interpreting the data contained in the financial statements themselves.

INTERNET SEARCH

• Microsoft

While you have a copy of Microsoft's annual report in Appendix A, let's go see what its most current financial statements look like. Access Microsoft's Web site at microsoft.com. Sometimes addresses change, so if this Microsoft address doesn't work, access the Web site for this textbook (stice.swcollege.com) for an updated link to Microsoft.

Once you have accessed Microsoft's Web site, answer the following questions (you may have to search a bit to answer some of these questions):

1. When was Micro-Soft founded? (That's right, the company's name originally had a hyphen.)

2. Make your way to the shareholder information and locate the company's most recent income statement. Detail the steps you had to take to find this financial statement.
3. How has the company done since its 1997 financial statements were issued? Are sales still increasing? Are profits still on the rise?
4. Microsoft was one of the first companies to provide an income statement in multiple languages. Take a look at Microsoft's income statement based on accounting principles accepted in the United Kingdom. Do you recognize any of the terms? Now look at the German version of the income statement. Even though you probably don't speak German, can you guess what the German word is for "Revenues"?

ACCOUNTING FOR EXTERNAL USERS: BUSINESS ACTIVITIES

PART 2

CHAPTERS

CHAPTER 3 THE MECHANICS OF ACCOUNTING

SETTING THE STAGE

Ray Kroc, a 51-year-old milkshake machine distributor, first visited the McDonald brothers' drive-in (in San Bernardino, California) in July of 1954 because he wanted to know just why a single "hamburger stand" would need ten milkshake machines. That first day, Kroc spent the lunch rush hour watching the incredible volume of business the small drive-in was able to handle. Before leaving town, Kroc had received a personal briefing on the "McDonald's Speedee System" by Dick and Mac McDonald and had secured the rights to duplicate the system throughout the United States.

In his first outlet in Chicago, Ray Kroc soon discovered that duplicating the McDonald's system involved more than just signing a licensing agreement. Kroc's french fries, for example, were mushy, even though he closely copied the McDonald brothers' process. Feverish detective work finally revealed that Dick and Mac McDonald had been storing their potatoes in an outside bin before turning them into french fries. This aging process allowed some of the natural sugars in the potatoes to turn into starch, resulting in fries that would cook all the way through without burning. Further research revealed the optimal temperature for the cooking oil, the best type of potato to use, and how to make frozen french fries that taste as good as fresh. The end product, the McDonald's french fry, was instrumental in establishing the McDonald's reputation for consistent quality.

As the number of McDonald's locations expanded (to 21,022 at the end of 1996), so did the menu. Originally, the McDonald's menu contained just 15-cent hamburgers, 12-cent french fries, 20-cent milkshakes, cheeseburgers, three flavors of soft drinks, milk, coffee, potato chips, and pie. The first addition to this menu was the Filet-O-Fish sandwich in the early 1960s. The Big Mac started in Pittsburgh in 1967, and the Egg McMuffin debuted in Santa Barbara in 1971. Not all of the McDonald's menu innovations caught on—the McLean Deluxe (a low-fat hamburger held together with a seaweed-based filler) and the Hulaburger, one of Ray Kroc's personal favorites (a cheeseburger with a big slice of pineapple), are among the items that are no longer offered.

The essence of McDonald's business seems fairly simple: revenues come from selling Big Macs, Happy Meals, Chicken McNuggets, etc.; operating costs include the costs of the raw materials to produce the

LEARNING OBJECTIVES

After studying this chapter, you should be able to:

1. *Understand the process of transforming transaction data into useful accounting information.*
2. *Analyze transactions and determine how those transactions affect the accounting equation (step one of the accounting cycle).*
3. *Record the effects of transactions using journal entries (step two of the accounting cycle).*
4. *Summarize the resulting journal entries through posting and prepare a trial balance (step three of the accounting cycle).*
5. *Understand the need for adjusting entries, how financial statements are prepared, and how the books are closed (step four of the accounting cycle).*

food items, labor costs, building rentals, income taxes, and so forth. But the magnitude of McDonald's operations in terms of volume (sales average nearly $100 million per day) as well as geography (McDonald's has locations in over 100 countries throughout the world) makes compiling this information a challenge. In order to prepare its year-end financial reports, McDonald's must accumulate financial information from its various locations throughout the world, summarize that information according to U.S. accounting standards, and make the report available to the public in less than four weeks. In fact, McDonald's annual report for the period ended December 31, 1996, was finished on January 23, 1997.

With the number of transactions that occur on a daily basis, the accounting for McDonald's would be impossible were it not for a systematic method for analyzing these transactions and collecting and recording transaction-related information. What is the process by which McDonald's and other entities transform raw transaction data into useful information? Certainly, shareholders and others would not understand how McDonald's has performed if the company merely published volumes of raw transaction data. How are millions of transactions summarized and eventually reported in the primary financial statements? This transformation process is referred to as the **accounting cycle**.

accounting cycle The procedures for analyzing, recording, summarizing, and reporting the transactions of a business.

In the first two chapters, we provided an overview of accounting. We discussed the environment of accounting and its objectives, some basic concepts and assumptions of accounting, and the primary financial statements. Now we begin our study of the "accounting cycle." This simply means that we will examine the procedures for analyzing, recording, summarizing, and reporting the transactions of a business.

1 *Understand the process of transforming transaction data into useful accounting information.*

HOW CAN WE COLLECT ALL THIS INFORMATION?

Suppose you were asked this question, "What was the total cost, to the nearest dollar, of your college education last year?" To answer this question would require that you (1) gather information (in the form of receipts, credit card statements, and canceled checks) relating to all your expenditures, (2) analyze that information to determine which outflows relate to your college education, and (3) summarize those outflows into one number—the cost of your college education. Once you have answered that question, answer this one, "How much did you spend on food last year?" Again you would have to go through the same process of collecting data, analyzing it to identify those expenditures relating to food, and then summarizing those expenditures into one number. From these two examples you can see that, without a method for gathering day-to-day financial data, answers to seemingly routine questions can get quite complex.

Now you may be thinking, "Doesn't my checkbook allow me to easily answer these questions?" Your check register would certainly help, but its limitation is that it tracks only the transactions that go through your checking account. It does not track the cash in your pocket, in your savings accounts, or in other investment accounts. So if any of your expenditures for food were made with cash, your check register may not include those expenses. In addition, you would still be required to review each check and determine to what it related. Your check register provides good information for calculating exactly how much money you have in your checking account at any point in time. It is less effective for determining exactly how your money was spent.

Now consider the dilemma for businesses. They typically have far more transactions than you, and the kinds of transactions are more varied. Businesses buy and sell goods or services; borrow and invest money; pay wages to employees; purchase land, buildings, and equipment; distribute earnings to their owners; and pay taxes to the government. These activities are referred to as "exchange transactions" be-

business documents Records of transactions used as the basis for recording accounting entries; includes invoices, check stubs, receipts, and similar business papers.

cause the entity is actually trading (exchanging) one thing for another. A college bookstore, for example, exchanges textbooks for cash. **Business documents**, such as a sales invoice, a purchase order, or a check stub, are often used (1) to confirm that an arm's-length transaction has occurred, (2) to establish the amounts to be recorded, and (3) to facilitate the analysis of business events.

To determine how well an entity is managing its resources, the results of transactions must be analyzed. The accounting cycle makes the analysis possible by recording and summarizing an entity's transactions and preparing reports that present the summary results. Exhibit 3-1 shows the sequence of the accounting cycle. Later, we will discuss these general categories and the specific steps of the cycle.

Keeping track of a company's transactions requires a system of accounting that is tailor-made to the needs of that particular enterprise. Obviously, the accounting system of a large multinational corporation with millions of business transactions each day will be much more complex than the system needed by a small drugstore. The more complex and detailed the accounting system, the more likely it is to be automated. Historically, of course, all accounting systems had to be maintained by hand. The image of the accountant with green eyeshade and quill pen, sitting on a high stool, meticulously maintaining the accounting records, reflects those early manual systems. Today, few accounting systems are completely manual. Even small companies generally use some type of automated equipment, such as cash registers and computers. Such equipment helps reduce the number of routine clerical functions and improves the accuracy and timeliness of the accounting records.

EXHIBIT 3-1

Sequence of the Accounting Cycle

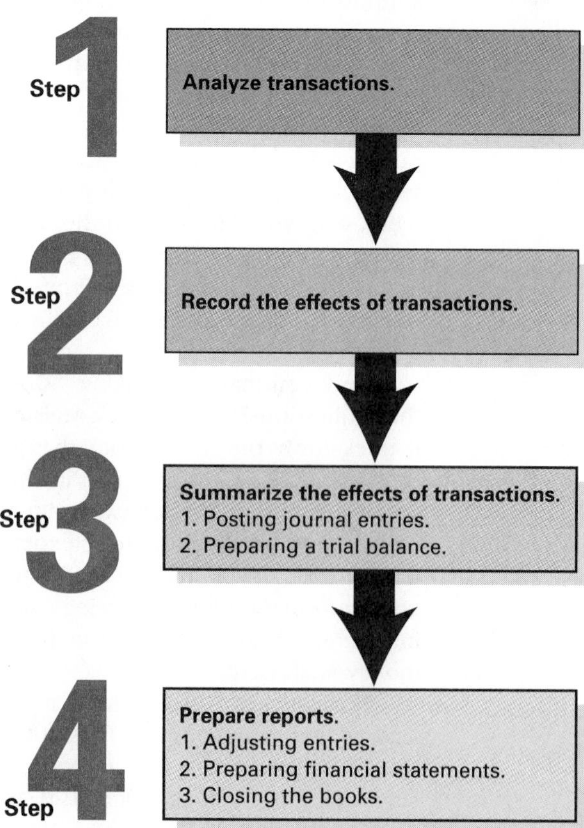

Exchange Transactions
(Businesses enter into exchange transactions signaling the beginning of the accounting cycle)
Step 1
Analyze transactions.
Step 2
Record the effects of transactions.
Step 3
Summarize the effects of transactions.
1. Posting journal entries.
2. Preparing a trial balance.
Step 4
Prepare reports.
1. Adjusting entries.
2. Preparing financial statements.
3. Closing the books.

Although a computer-based system is faster and requires less labor than a manual system, the steps in the process are basically the same for both: transactions are recorded on source documents; they are then analyzed, journalized, and posted to the accounts; and the resulting information is summarized, reported, and used for evaluation purposes. The difference lies in who (or what) does the work. With a computer-based system, the computer transforms the recorded data, summarizes the data into categories, and prepares the financial statements and other reports. However, human judgment is still essential in analyzing and recording transactions, especially those of a nonroutine nature.

Because a manual accounting system is easier to understand, we will use a manual system for the examples in this text. As you begin studying the steps in the accounting cycle, it is important that you understand the accounting equation and double-entry accounting more fully. This concept was briefly introduced in Chapter 2. You will recall that the accounting model is built on this basic equation. You now need to learn how to use the equation in accounting for the transactions of a business.

TO SUMMARIZE

Businesses enter into exchange transactions. Evidence of these transactions is provided by business documents. Accounting is designed to accumulate and report in summary form the results of a company's transactions, therefore transforming the financial data into useful information for decision making.

2 *Analyze transactions and determine how those transactions affect the accounting equation (step one of the accounting cycle).*

HOW DO TRANSACTIONS AFFECT THE ACCOUNTING EQUATION?

Suppose you are the keeper of the archives at **McDonald's** assigned to protect the secret ingredient mix for the Big Mac special sauce. You came to work this morning only to hear that **Burger King** has cracked the secret ingredient recipe and plans to come out with a Big Mac clone at half the price. How would this event be reflected in the financial statements?

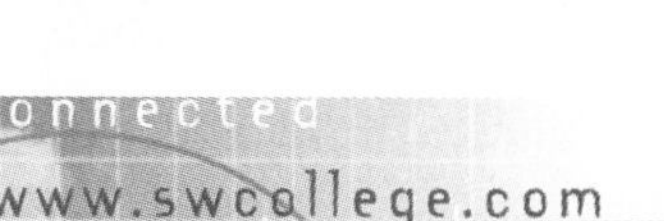

Access **McDonald's** Web site and compare it to **Burger King**'s.

In your opinion, which Web site is the easiest to navigate? How easy is it to find information on, for example, nutrition? Which site provides the easiest access to the company's financial information?

mcdonalds.com
burgerking.com

Often, the most difficult aspect of accounting is determining which events are to be reflected in the accounting records and which are not. In this example, the proliferation of Big Mac clones could have a serious impact on the future of the firm. However, as discussed in Chapter 2, events that cannot be measured in monetary terms will not be reflected in the financial statements. It would be virtually impossible to reliably quantify the impact that Big Mac clones could have on the future profitability of McDonald's, and thus, that information would not be reflected in the financial statements.

Now you may be saying to yourself, "We have an obligation to inform financial statement users about this attack on the Big Mac." We would all agree that this information should be shared, but the financial statements are not the place to do it. As you review **Microsoft**'s annual report (in Appendix A), you'll notice that the financial statements are one part of the information provided to users. Information relating to the competitive environment, product development, and marketing and sales efforts is included in the annual report, but not as part of the accounting information.

After quantifying an event's monetary impact, the event must be analyzed to determine if an arm's-length transaction has occurred. Accounting is concerned primarily with reflecting the effects of transactions between two independent entities. So a mining company's oil strike on the North Slope of Alaska would not be reflected in the financial statements until that oil is sold. Likewise, signing a promising young financial analyst directly out of college for a salary of $80,000 per year involves an exchange of promises. No accounting entry would be made until the analyst actually worked and received a paycheck.

Transactions between independent parties must be analyzed to determine their effect on the accounting equation. This analysis is often what separates an accountant from a bookkeeper. While many transactions are routine, some business events are quite complex and require a comprehensive analysis to determine how the event should be reflected in the financial statements. Consider the following examples:

- An employee works for one year, earning a base salary of $60,000. In addition, if the employee stays with the company for at least five years, the company promises to make a contribution to the employee's pension fund equal to 15% of salary. Approximately 60% of employees who start with the company stay for five years. Also, by working for one year, the employee earns 15 extra vacation days. Those vacation days can be saved and used any time in the future. How do we record compensation cost associated with this employee for the year?
- A company buys a building. In addition to paying $20,000 cash, the company agrees to pay $10,000 per year for the next ten years. The company will also pay a $2,000 property tax bill associated with the building from last year. As part of the purchase, the company gave the former owners of the building 500 shares of stock. Finally, the building will require $23,000 worth of repairs and renovations before it can be used. How much should be recorded as the cost of the building?

As these examples illustrate, transactions can become quite complex and the accounting for these types of transactions reflects that complexity. The good news is that the transaction analysis framework introduced in this chapter allows you to break complex transactions into manageable pieces and also provides a self-checking mechanism to ensure that you haven't forgotten anything. Once a transaction is properly

BUSINESS ENVIRONMENT ESSAY

The Importance of Accurate and Reliable Accounting Data Is accounting an art or a science? Actually, it's both. An accountant needs to know the clearcut standards of accounting procedure; considerable experience and good business judgment are also needed in order to succeed.

The discovery of errors in a company's accounting data has left many corporate managers and Wall Street analysts shell-shocked, as the following examples indicate:

- In the first six months of 1997, **Bre-X**, a Canadian mining company, reported an inventory of gold deposits from its Indonesian site of 71 million ounces, with a value of about $25 billion. One Bre-X official estimated the total deposits, both mined and unmined, to exceed 400 million ounces. Trouble was, there was no gold—the whole thing was a scam.
- On August 12, 1993, the stock of **T2 Medical Inc.** plunged to slightly less than half its August 11 closing value. The cause of this catastrophe was the announcement of a problem in the company's handling of its accounts receivable. T2 was consistently receiving less from its customers than it was billing them. The result was a downward course of total earnings for the first three quarters of 1993 from $52.7 million to about $36 million.

In both of these examples, investors lost millions and many members of each company's management team were replaced. In the case of Bre-X, the company's chief geologist leaped to his death from a helicopter to avoid the controversy that would follow the discovery of the fraud. This is a further reminder that the importance of accurate and reliable accounting data cannot be overestimated.

Sources: Richard Behar, "Jungle Fever," *Fortune*, June 9, 1997. "T2 Medical Skids on Accounting Errors," Reuters, Limited, BC Cycle, August 12, 1993.

analyzed and the affected accounts identified (along with the direction of those effects), the remainder of the accounting cycle can proceed without much difficulty.

The Accounting Equation

So let's begin our analysis of transactions by first reviewing some of the basics. Recall that the fundamental accounting equation is:

Assets	=	**Liabilities**	+	**Owners' Equity**
[Resources]		[Creditors' claims against resources]		[Owners' claims against resources]

Since the accounting equation is an equality, it must always remain in balance. To see how this balance is maintained when accounting for business transactions, consider the following activities:

Business Activity (Transaction)	**Effect in Terms of the Accounting Equation**
1. Investment of $50,000 by owners	Increase asset (Cash), increase owners' equity (Capital Stock): A ↑ $50,000 = OE ↑ $50,000
2. Borrowed $25,000 from bank	Increase asset (Cash), increase liability (Notes Payable): A ↑ $25,000 = L ↑ $25,000
3. Purchased $14,000 worth of inventory on credit. The inventory is to be resold at a later date.	Increase asset (Inventory), increase liability (Accounts Payable): A ↑ $14,000 = L ↑ $14,000
4. Purchased equipment costing $15,000 for cash	Decrease asset (Cash), increase asset (Equipment): A ↓ $15,000 = A ↑ $15,000

For each of the transactions, the terms in parentheses are the specific accounts affected by the transactions, as will be explained in the next section.

In each case, the equation remains in balance because an identical amount is added to both sides, subtracted from both sides, or added to and subtracted from the same side of the equation. Following each transaction, we can ensure that the accounting equation balances. Note how the following spreadsheet keeps track of the equality of the accounting equation:

Transaction #	**ASSETS**		**LIABILITIES**		**OWNERS' EQUITY**
Beginning Balance	$ 0	=	$ 0	+	$ 0
1	+50,000				+50,000
Subtotal	$50,000	=	$ 0	+	$50,000
2	+25,000		+25,000		
Subtotal	$75,000	=	$25,000	+	$50,000
3	+14,000		+14,000		
Subtotal	$89,000	=	$39,000	+	$50,000
4	+15,000 −15,000				
Total	$89,000	=	$39,000	+	$50,000

Using Accounts to Categorize Transactions

In Chapter 2, the balance sheet and the income statement were introduced as two of the primary financial statements. We learned that the elements of the balance sheet are assets, liabilities, and owners' equity; the elements of the income statement are revenues and expenses. Now we must learn how each of these elements is composed of many different accounts.

account An accounting record in which the results of transactions are accumulated; shows increases, decreases, and a balance.

An **account** is a specific accounting record that provides an efficient way to categorize transactions. Thus, we may designate asset accounts, liability accounts, and owners' equity accounts. Examples of asset accounts are Cash, Inventory, and Equipment. Liability accounts include Accounts Payable and Notes Payable. The equity accounts for a corporation are Capital Stock and Retained Earnings. You can think of an individual account as a summary of every transaction affecting a certain item (such as cash); the summary may be recorded on one page of a book, or in one computer file, or in one column of a spreadsheet (as seen below).

	ASSETS				LIABILITIES			OWNERS' EQUITY
Transaction #	Cash	Inventory	Equipment		Accounts Payable	Notes Payable		Capital Stock
Beginning Balance	$ 0	$ 0	$ 0	=	$ 0	$ 0	+	$ 0
1	+50,000							+50,000
Subtotal	$50,000	$ 0	$ 0	=	$ 0	$ 0	+	$50,000
2	+25,000					+25,000		
Subtotal	$75,000	$ 0	$ 0	=	$ 0	$25,000	+	$50,000
3		+14,000			+14,000			
Subtotal	$75,000	$14,000	$ 0	=	$14,000	$25,000	+	$50,000
4	−15,000		+15,000					
Total	$60,000	$14,000	$15,000	=	$14,000	$25,000	+	$50,000

Using the previous transactions, we can easily see how the accounting equation can be expanded to include specific accounts under the headings of assets, liabilities, and owners' equity. We can also see that after each transaction, the equality of the accounting equation can be determined simply by adding up the balances of all the asset accounts and comparing the total to the sum of all the liability and owners' equity accounts.

Now suppose that a company has 200 accounts and 10,000 transactions each month—this spreadsheet would quickly get very big. Today, computers help in compiling this massive amount of data. Five hundred years ago, when double-entry accounting was formalized, all the adding and subtracting was done by hand. You can imagine the difficulties of tracking multiple accounts, involving hundreds of transactions, using the spreadsheet method described above while doing all the computations by hand. The mixing of "+" or "−" in one column would provide ample opportunity to make mistakes.

T-account A simplified depiction of an account in the form of a letter T.

This problem was solved by separating the "+" and the "−" for each account into separate columns, totaling each column, and then computing the difference between the columns to arrive at an ending balance. The simplest, most fundamental format is the configuration of the letter T. This is called a **T-account**. Note that a T-account is an abbreviated representation of an actual account (illustrated later) and is used as a teaching and learning tool. The following are examples of T-accounts, representing the transactions described previously.

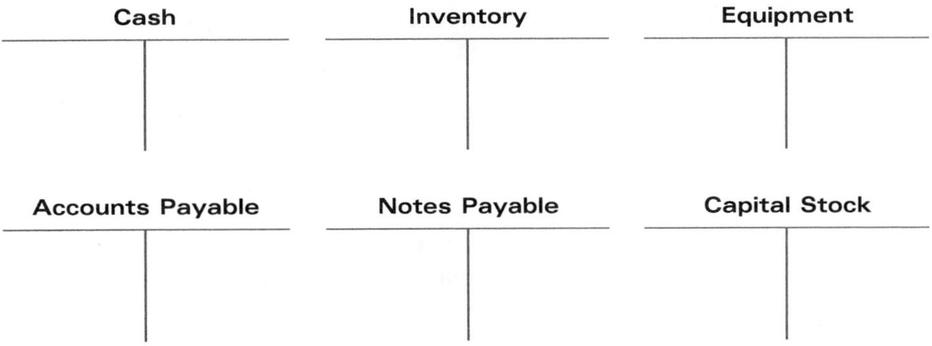

debit An entry on the left side of a T-account.

credit An entry on the right side of a T-account.

The account title (Cash, for example) appears at the top of the T-account. Transaction amounts may be recorded on both the left side and the right side of the T-account. Instead of using the terms left and right to indicate which side of a T-account is affected, terms unique to accounting were developed. **Debit** is used to indicate the left side of a T-account, and **credit** is used to indicate the right side of a T-account. Debit means left, credit means right; nothing more, nothing less. The appropriate debit (abbreviated DR) and credit (abbreviated CR) entries for the above T-accounts are:

Cash		Inventory		Equipment	
DR	CR	DR	CR	DR	CR

Accounts Payable		Notes Payable		Capital Stock	
DR	CR	DR	CR	DR	CR

F Y I

Where does the "DR" come from when the term debit doesn't have an "r" in it? Recall that accounting, as we know it today, was formalized in the 1500s in Italy. The Italian and Latin (a common language back then) verb forms of debit are *addebitare* and *debere*, respectively. Thus, the "DR" represents an Italian or Latin abbreviation of debit.

Besides representing the left and right sides of an account, the terms debit and credit take on additional meaning when coupled with a specific account. By convention, for asset accounts, debits refer to increases and credits to decreases. For example, to increase the Cash account, we debit it; to decrease the Cash account, we credit it. Since we expect the total increases in the cash account to be greater than the decreases, the cash account will usually have a debit balance after accounting for all transactions. Thus, we can make this generalization—asset accounts will have debit balances. The opposite relationship is true of liability and owners' equity accounts; they are decreased by *debits* and increased by *credits*. As a result, liability and owners' equity accounts will typically have credit balances. The effect of this system is shown here, with an increase indicated by (+) and a decrease by (−).

Assets		=	Liabilities		+	Owners' Equity	
DR (+)	CR (−)		DR (−)	CR (+)		DR (−)	CR (+)

CAUTION

Just a reminder that asset accounts will typically have debit balances, whereas liabilities and owners' equity accounts will typically have credit balances.

In addition to assets equaling liabilities and owners' equity, debits also equal credits. If you fully grasp the meaning of these two equalities, you are well on your way to mastering the mechanics of accounting. Debits and credits allow us to take a shortcut to ensure that the accounting equation balances. If, for every transaction, debits equal credits, then the accounting equation will balance.

To understand why this happens, keep in mind three basic facts regarding double-entry accounting:

1. Debits are always entered on the left side of an account and credits on the right side.
2. For every transaction, there must be at least one debit and one credit.
3. Debits must always equal credits for each transaction.

Now notice what this means for one of the business transactions shown earlier (page 81): investment by owners. An asset account (Cash) is debited; it is increased. An owners' equity account (Capital Stock) is credited; it is also increased. There is both a debit and a credit for the transaction, and we have increased accounts on both sides of the equation by an equal amount, thus keeping the equation in balance.

Be careful not to let the general, nonaccounting meanings of the words credit and debit confuse you. In general conversation, credit has an association with plus and debit with minus. But on the asset side of the accounting equation, where debit means increase and credit means decrease, this association can lead you astray. In accounting, debit simply means left and credit simply means right. To make sure you understand the relationship between debits and credits, the various accounts, and the accounting equation, let us examine further the transactions listed on page 81.

Business Activity (Transaction)	**Effect in Terms of the Accounting Equation**							
	Assets		=	**Liabilities**		+	**Owners' Equity**	
1. Investment by owners	Cash DR (+)							Capital Stock CR (+)
2. Borrowed money from bank	Cash DR (+)				Notes Payable CR (+)			
3. Purchased inventory on credit	Inventory DR (+)				Accounts Payable CR (+)			
4. Purchased equipment for cash	Equipment DR (+)	Cash CR (−)						

Note that every time an account is debited, other accounts have to be credited for the same amount. This is the major characteristic of the double-entry accounting system: *the debits must always equal the credits.* This important characteristic creates a practical advantage: the opportunity for "self-checking." If debits do not equal credits, an error has been made in analyzing and recording the entity's activities.

Before proceeding any further, let's stop for a moment and review the relationship between the various types of accounts and debits and credits. It is in your best interest not to go on until you understand these relationships.

Account Type			Debit or Credit?	Ending Balance
Asset	Increase (+)	results in	Debit	Debit
	Decrease (−)	results in	Credit	
Liability	Increase (+)	results in	Credit	Credit
	Decrease (−)	results in	Debit	
Owners' Equity	Increase (+)	results in	Credit	Credit
	Decrease (−)	results in	Debit	

Expanding the Accounting Equation to Include Revenues, Expenses, and Dividends

At this point, we must bring revenues and expenses into the picture. Obviously, they are part of every ongoing business. Revenues provide resource inflows; they are increases in resources from the sale of goods or services. Expenses represent resource outflows; they are costs incurred in generating revenues. Note that revenues are not synonymous with cash or other assets, but are a way of describing where the assets came from. For example, cash received from the sale of a product would be considered revenue. Cash received by borrowing from the bank would not be revenue, but an increase in a liability. By the same token, expenses are a way of describing how an asset has been used. Thus, cash paid for interest on a loan is an expense, but cash paid to buy a building represents the exchange of one asset for another.

How do revenues and expenses fit into the accounting equation? Remember that revenues minus expenses equals net income; and net income is a major source of change in owners' equity from one accounting period to the next. Revenues and expenses, then, may be thought of as *temporary* subdivisions of owners' equity. Revenues increase owners' equity and so, like all owners' equity accounts, are increased by credits. Expenses reduce owners' equity and are therefore increased by debits. As will be explained later in this chapter, all revenue and expense accounts are "closed" into the retained earnings account at the end of the accounting cycle.

dividends Distributions to the owners (stockholders) of a corporation.

One other temporary account affects owners' equity. It is the account that shows distributions of earnings to owners. For a corporation, this account is called **Dividends**. Since dividends reflect payments to the owners, therefore reducing owners' equity, the dividends account is increased by a debit and decreased by a credit. The dividends account, like revenues and expenses, is also "closed" into the retained earnings account.

Using the corporate form of business as an example, the accounting equation may be expanded to include revenues, expenses, and dividends, as shown in Exhibit 3-2.

CAUTION

We stated previously that owners' equity accounts will have credit balances. However, expenses, a component of retained earnings, will almost always have debit balances. Since revenues will usually exceed expenses, the net effect on retained earnings will result in a credit balance.

Keep in mind that in actual business practice, when a manual accounting system is used, the T-account is an integral feature of a more formal and complete account. Exhibit 3-3 is an example of such an account. Note that in addition to the debits and credits in the T-account portion (drawn in heavy lines in this example), the account has a title, Cash; an account number, 101; and columns for a transaction date, an explanation of the transaction, a posting reference (a cross-reference to other accounting records), and a balance.

EXHIBIT 3-2

Expanded Accounting Equation

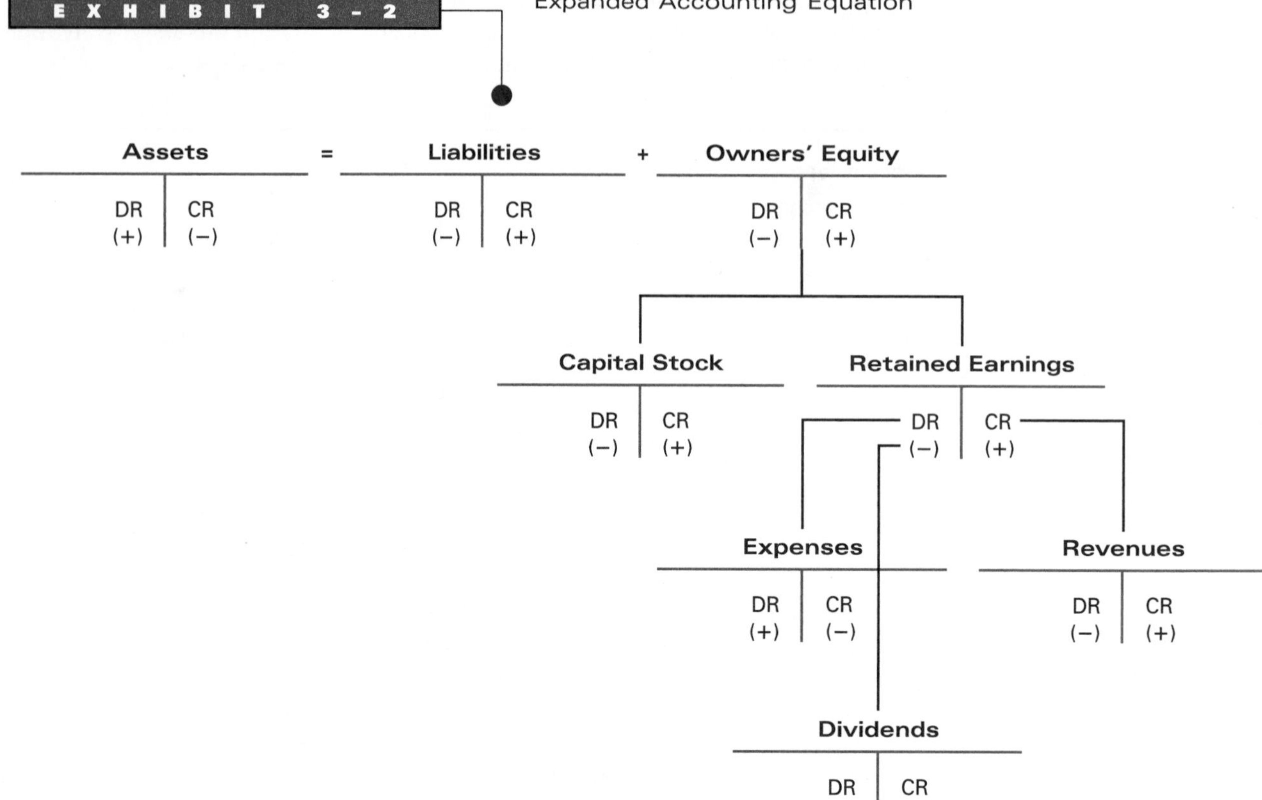

EXHIBIT 3-3

Typical Account

ACCOUNT: Cash ACCOUNT NO. 101

Date	Explanation	Post. Ref.	Debits	Credits	Balance

TO SUMMARIZE

Regardless of the size or complexity of a business, or the manner in which the records are maintained (manual or automated system), the steps of the accounting cycle are the same. The entire process is based on double-entry accounting and the basic accounting equation. Accounts accumulate the results of transactions. Debits are always entered on the left side of an account, and credits are always entered on the right side. Debits increase asset, expense, and dividend accounts and decrease liability, owners' equity, and revenue accounts. Credits decrease asset, expense, and dividend accounts and increase liability, owners' equity, and revenue accounts. Revenues increase owners' equity, whereas expenses and dividends decrease owners' equity. Therefore, under a double-entry system of accounting, it is always possible to check the accounting records to see that Assets = Liabilities + Owners' Equity and debits equal credits.

3 *Record the effects of transactions using journal entries (step two of the accounting cycle).*

HOW DO WE RECORD THE EFFECTS OF TRANSACTIONS?

With our knowledge of the different types of accounts (assets, liabilities, and owners' equity) and the use of the terms debit and credit (debit means left and credit means right), we are now ready to actually record the effects of transactions.

The second step in the accounting cycle is to record the results of transactions in a **journal**. Known as "books of original entry," journals provide a chronological record of all entity transactions. They show the dates of the transactions, the amounts involved, and the particular accounts affected by the transactions. Sometimes a detailed description of the transaction is also included.

journal An accounting record in which transactions are first entered; provides a chronological record of all business activities.

This chronological recording of transactions provides a company with a complete record of its activities. If amounts were recorded directly in the accounts, it would be difficult, if not impossible, for a company to trace a transaction that occurred, say, six months previously.

Smaller companies, such as a locally owned pizza restaurant, may use only one book of original entry, called a "General Journal," to record all transactions. Larger companies having thousands of transactions each year may use special journals (for example, a cash receipts journal) as well as a general journal.

A specific format is used in **journalizing** (recording) transactions in a general journal. The debit entry is listed first; the credit entry is listed second and is indented to the right. Normally, the date and a brief explanation of the transaction are considered essential parts of the **journal entry**. (In the text, we often ignore dates and explanations to simplify the examples, but they are used in practice.) Dollar signs usually are omitted. Unless otherwise noted, this format will be used whenever a journal entry is presented.

journalizing Recording transactions in a journal.

journal entry A recording of a transaction where debits equal credits; usually includes a date and an explanation of the transaction.

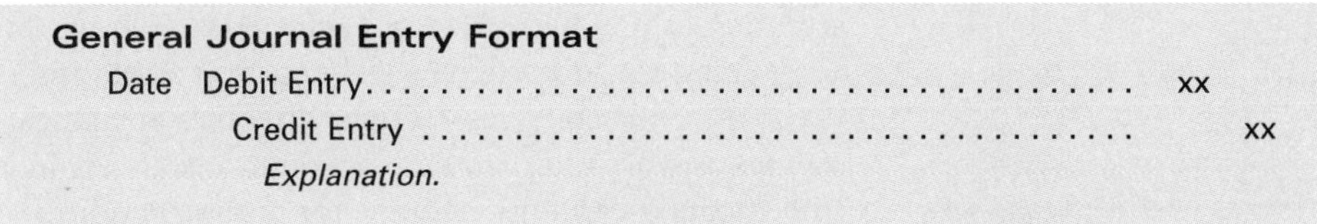

General Journal Entry Format

Date	Debit Entry	xx	
	Credit Entry		xx
	Explanation.		

Exhibit 3-4 is a partial page from a general journal, showing typical journal entries. Study this exhibit carefully because the entire accounting cycle is based on journal entries. If journal entries are incorrect, the resulting financial information will be inaccurate.

To give you additional exposure to analyzing transactions and recording journal entries, we are going to start our own business. Rather than spend the summer flipping burgers at the local hamburger house, you decide that you want to have an outdoor job—one that allows you to enjoy the summer sun, to be involved in rigorous physical activity, and sharpen your skills as an entrepreneur. You are going to start

EXHIBIT 3-4 General Journal

JOURNAL Page 1

Date	Description	Post. Ref.	Debits	Credits
2000 July 1	Cash		2,000	
	Capital Stock			2,000
	Issued 200 shares of capital stock at $10 per share.			
5	Truck		800	
	Cash			800
	Purchased a used truck.			
5	Equipment		250	
	Accounts Payable			250
	Purchased a lawnmower on account.			
5	Supplies		180	
	Cash			180
	Purchased supplies for cash.			

your own landscaping business. This business will involve mowing lawns, pulling weeds, trimming and planting shrubs, etc. We will use your new business to illustrate the journal entries used to record some common transactions of a business enterprise.[1] These transactions fit into the following four general categories: acquiring cash, acquiring other assets, selling goods or providing services, and collecting cash and paying obligations. Obviously, we cannot present all possible transactions in this chapter. In studying the illustrations, strive to understand the conceptual basis of transaction analysis rather than memorizing specific journal entries. Pay particular attention to the dual effect of each transaction on the company in terms of the basic accounting equation (that is, its impact on assets and on liabilities and owners' equity). Remember that business activity involves revenues, expenses, and distributions to owners as well, and that these accounts eventually increase or decrease owners' equity (the retained earnings account for a corporation).

Acquiring Cash, Either from Owners or by Borrowing

Your first task in starting this business is to acquire cash, either through owners' investments or by borrowing. Your parents indicate that they will match any funds that you are going to put into your business. You have $1,000 in savings, and coupled with your parents' matching funds, you decide to issue 200 shares of stock.

1. Normally, a small business like this one would be started as a sole proprietorship or as a partnership. We assume a corporation here to show a complete set of transactions.

Example 1

The following transaction illustrates investments by owners:

assets (+)	Cash.	2,000	
owners' equity (+)	Capital Stock.		2,000
	Issued 200 shares of capital stock at $10 per share.		

This transaction increases cash as a result of capital stock being issued to investors, or stockholders. The cash account is debited, and the capital stock account is credited. The economic impact of this situation may be summarized as follows:

Assets	=	Liabilities	+	Owners' Equity
(increase $2,000)		(no change)		(increase $2,000)

Example 2

Suppose that instead of coming up with the money yourself or from your parents, you went to a bank and convinced the loan officer to loan you the money. The journal entry for such a transaction would be:

assets (+)	Cash.	2,000	
liabilities (+)	Notes Payable.		2,000
	Borrowed $2,000 from First National Bank, signing a 12-month note at 12% interest.		

Here, the cash account is debited, and the notes payable account is credited. The accounting model captures the economic impact of borrowing the money as follows:

Assets	=	Liabilities	+	Owners' Equity
(increase $2,000)		(increase $2,000)		(no change)

Acquiring Other Assets

Now that you have obtained the funds necessary to start your business, either from owner investment or by borrowing, you can use that money to acquire other assets needed to operate the business. Such assets include supplies (such as fertilizer), inventory (perhaps shrubs that you will plant), and equipment (for example, a lawnmower and a truck for hauling). These assets may be purchased with cash or on credit. Credit purchases require payment after a period of time, for example, 30 days. Normally, interest expense is incurred when assets are bought on a time-payment plan that extends beyond two or three months. (To keep our examples simple here, we will not include interest expense. We will show how to account for interest on page 94, where we discuss the payment of obligations.) Examples of transactions involving the acquisition of noncash assets follow.

Example 1

The first thing you need is a lawnmower and some form of transportation. You find an old 1978 pickup truck for sale for $800 and you buy it paying cash.

assets (+)	Truck.	800	
assets (−)	Cash.		800
	Purchased a used truck.		

The accounting equation shows:

Assets	=	Liabilities	+	Owners' Equity
(increase $800; decrease $800)		(no change)		(no change)

Next, you drive to the local Sears store and purchase a Craftsman lawnmower and gas can for $250. Instead of paying for the mower with cash, you open a charge account, which will allow you to pay for the mower in 30 days with no interest charge. (If you wait and pay beyond this 30-day grace period, an interest charge will apply.) The journal entry to record this purchase is:

assets (+)	Equipment	250	
liabilities (+)	Accounts Payable		250
	Purchased a lawnmower and gas can on account.		

The accounting equation shows:

Assets	=	Liabilities	+	Owners' Equity
(increase $250)		(increase $250)		(no change)

When you pay for the mower, cash will be reduced, and the liability, Accounts Payable, will also be reduced, thus keeping the equation in balance.

Example 2

Off you go to the neighborhood Eagle Hardware & Garden Shop to purchase fertilizer, gloves, a rake, a shovel, and other assorted supplies. The total cost is $180, which you pay in cash; an increase in one asset (supplies) results in a decrease in another asset (cash).

assets (+)	Supplies	180	
assets (−)	Cash		180
	Purchased supplies for cash.		

The accounting equation shows:

Assets	=	Liabilities	+	Owners' Equity
(increase $180; decrease $180)		(no change)		(no change)

Example 3

On your way home from the hardware store, you drive past a greenhouse and notice a big sign indicating a "50% off" sale on shrubs. Since you anticipate that planting shrubs will be part of your business, you stop and purchase for cash $150 worth of shrubs as inventory. Your plan with the shrubs is to make money in two ways: (1) revenue from the labor associated with planting them and (2) a profit on selling the shrubs for more than you paid. (This is fair; after all, you are saving your client the time and trouble of having to go to the greenhouse.)

assets (+)	Inventory	150	
assets (−)	Cash		150
	Purchased inventory for cash.		

The accounting equation shows:

Assets	=	Liabilities	+	Owners' Equity
(increase $150; decrease $150)		(no change)		(no change)

Selling Goods or Providing Services

Now that you have your lawnmower, your transportation, your supplies, and your inventory, it is time to go to work. The next category of common transactions involves the sale of services or merchandise. Revenues are generated and expenses incurred during this process. Sometimes services or merchandise are sold for cash; at other times, they are sold on credit (on account) and a receivable is established for collection at a later date. Therefore, revenues indicate the source not only of cash but of other assets as well, all of which are received in exchange for the merchandise or services provided. Similarly, expenses may be incurred and paid for immediately by cash, or they may be incurred on credit—that is, they may be "charged," with a cash payment to be made at a later date. Illustrative transactions follow. Note that the effect of revenues and expenses on owners' equity is indicated in brackets for each transaction.

Example 1

As soon as people find out that you are in the lawn care and landscaping business, your phone begins ringing off the hook. While most of your clients pay you immediately when you perform the service, some prefer to pay you once a month. As a result, a portion of your revenues is received immediately in cash, while the balance becomes receivables. The journal entry to record your first week's revenue for lawn care services is:

		Debit	Credit
assets (+)	Cash	270	
assets (+)	Accounts Receivable	80	
revenues (+) [equity (+)]	Lawn Care Revenue		350
	To record revenue for lawn care services.		

compound journal entry A journal entry that involves more than one debit or more than one credit or both.

As the journal entry illustrates, more than two accounts can be involved in recording a transaction. This type of entry is called a **compound journal entry**.

Because revenues increase owners' equity, the accounting equation shows:

Assets	=	Liabilities	+	Owners' Equity (Revenues)
(increase $350)		(no change)		(increase $350)

Example 2

One of your customers asks if you will plant some shrubs in her backyard. You mention that you have some shrubs, describe them to her, and she is thrilled that you have just the shrubs she wants, thereby saving her a trip to the greenhouse. You use one-half of your inventory of shrubs in this customer's yard, and it takes you three hours to complete the job. She pays you in cash. In this instance, we are dealing with two different types of revenue—profit from the sale of the shrubs and revenue from your labor. Let's deal with each type of revenue separately.

Sale of Shrubs Sales, whether made on account or for cash, require entries that reflect not only the sale, but also the cost of the inventory sold. The "cost of goods sold" is an expense and, as such, is offset with the sales revenue to determine the profitability of sales transactions. The special procedures for handling inventory are described in Chapter 5. It is sufficient here to show an example of the impact of the transaction on the accounting equation.

In this example, you charged your customer $90 for one-half of the shrubs you purchased earlier.

assets (+)	Cash	90	
revenues (+) [equity (+)]	Sales Revenue		90
	Sold inventory for cash.		
expenses (+) [equity (−)]	Cost of Goods Sold	75	
assets (−)	Inventory		75
	To record the cost of inventory sold and to reduce inventory for its cost.		

In this example, inventory costing you $75 is being sold for $90. The effect on the accounting equation for each transaction is:

Sales on Account

Assets	=	Liabilities	+	Owners' Equity (Revenues)
(increase $90)		(no change)		(increase $90)

Cost of Goods Sold

Assets	=	Liabilities	+	Owners' Equity (Expenses)
(decrease $75)		(no change)		(decrease $75)

(STOP & THINK)

Could the two journal entries relating to the sale of inventory be combined into one journal entry?

Labor for Planting In addition to making a profit on the sale of the shrubs, you also generated revenue planting them. The journal entry to record this revenue is:

assets (+)	Cash	45	
revenues (+) [equity (+)]	Landscaping Revenue		45
	To record revenue for landscaping services.		

The effect on the accounting equation of the transaction is:

Assets	=	Liabilities	+	Owners' Equity (Revenues)
(increase $45)		(no change)		(increase $45)

Example 3

In addition to expenses relating to the sale of inventory, other expenses are also incurred in operating a business. Examples include gas for your lawnmower and your truck and the wages you agreed to pay your little brother for working for you (Mom said you had to let him help). The following journal entries illustrate how these expenses would be accounted for:

expenses (+) [equity (−)]	Gasoline Expense	50	
assets (−)	Cash		50
	Paid cash for gas for the truck and the mower.		
expenses (+) [equity (−)]	Wages Expense	60	
assets (−)	Cash		60
	Paid wages expense.		

The effect on the accounting equation of the gasoline expense is:

Assets	=	Liabilities	+	Owners' Equity (Expense)
(decrease $50)		(no change)		(decrease $50)

The entry for Wages Expense affects the equation in the same manner, the only difference being the amount, $60.

Collecting Cash and Paying Obligations

Obviously, once merchandise or services are sold on account, the receivables must be collected. The cash received is generally used to meet daily operating expenses and to pay other obligations. Excess cash can be reinvested in the business or distributed to the owners as a return on their investment.

Example 1

The collection of accounts receivable is an important aspect of most businesses. Receivables are created when you allow certain customers to pay for your services at a later date. When receivables are collected, that asset is reduced and cash is increased, as shown here.

		Debit	Credit
assets (+)	Cash	80	
assets (−)	Accounts Receivable		80
	Collected $80 of receivables.		

The effect of collecting the receivables on the accounting equation is:

Assets	=	Liabilities	+	Owners' Equity
(increase $80; decrease $80)		(no change)		(no change)

Note that no revenue is involved here. Revenue is recorded when the original sales transaction creates the accounts receivable. The cash collection on account merely involves exchanging one asset for another.

Example 2

Remember that lawnmower and gas can you purchased on account? Well, now you have to pay for them. The entry to record the payment of obligations with cash is:

		Debit	Credit
liabilities (−)	Accounts Payable	250	
assets (−)	Cash		250
	Paid $250 for the lawnmower and gas can previously purchased.		

After payment of accounts payable, the accounting equation shows:

Assets	=	Liabilities	+	Owners' Equity
(decrease $250)		(decrease $250)		(no change)

Remember that two parties are always involved in exchange transactions. What one buys, the other sells. When sales are on credit, the seller will record a receivable and the buyer will record a payable. The two accounts are inversely related. The seller of merchandise records a receivable and a sale, and simultaneously records an expense for the cost of goods sold and a reduction of inventory (as in Example 2 on page 92). The buyer records the receipt of the merchandise and, at the same time, records an obligation to pay the seller at some future time. When payment is made, the buyer reduces Accounts Payable and Cash (as in this example), whereas the seller increases Cash and reduces Accounts Receivable (as in Example 1).

Example 3

On page 89, we showed the entry required when cash was borrowed from the bank. In that entry, you borrowed $2,000 to be paid over twelve months. Suppose you are required to make monthly loan payments of $178 with a portion of each payment being attributed to interest and a portion to reducing the liability—just like a mortgage on a house. As the following compound journal entry shows, a note payable or similar obligation requires an entry for payment, as well as for the interest due. Note that "interest" is the amount charged for using money, as will be more fully explained in later chapters.

liabilities (−)	Notes Payable	158	
expenses (+) [equity (−)]	Interest Expense	20	
assets (−)	Cash.		178
	Paid first monthly payment on note with interest ($2,000 × 0.12 × 1/12).		

Analysis of this transaction reveals that assets have decreased for two reasons. First, a portion of a liability has been paid with cash. Second, interest expense at 12% for one month on the note payable has been paid. This relationship will generally be present in most long-term and some short-term liability transactions. Since the interest charge is an expense and decreases owners' equity, the impact of the entry on the accounting equation is:

Assets	=	Liabilities	+	Owners' Equity (Expense)
(decrease $178)		(decrease $158)		(decrease $20)

Example 4

Recall that you had two ways for obtaining the cash needed to start your business—investors (you, Mom, and Dad) or the bank. In the previous journal entry, we illustrated how the bank receives a return on its investment. Well, Mom and Dad would like a return as well. Corporations that are profitable generally pay dividends to their stockholders. "Dividends" represent a distribution to the stockholders of part of the earnings of a company. The following entry illustrates the payment of a cash dividend:

dividends (+) [equity (−)]	Dividends	50	
assets (−)	Cash		50
	Paid a $50 cash dividend.		

As noted earlier, dividends, like revenues and expenses, affect owners' equity. Unlike revenues and expenses, dividends are a distribution of profits and, therefore, are not considered in determining net income. Because dividends reduce the retained earnings accumulated by a corporation, they decrease owners' equity. The payment of a $50 dividend affects the accounting equation as follows:

Assets	=	Liabilities	+	Owners' Equity (Dividends)
(decrease $50)		(no change)		(decrease $50)

(STOP & THINK)

Why are dividends NOT considered to be an expense?

A Note on Journal Entries

When preparing a journal entry, a systematic method may be used in analyzing every transaction. A journal entry involves a three-step process:

1. Identify which accounts are involved.
2. For each account, determine if it is increased or decreased.
3. For each account, determine by how much it has changed.

FYI

Many students have a little trouble getting used to debits, credits, and journal entries. So you are not alone if you are feeling a little overwhelmed. But remember, riding a bike wasn't easy the first time either. Like riding a bike, you will soon find that debits, credits, and journal entries aren't that difficult.

The answer to step one tells you if the accounts involved are asset, liability, or owners' equity accounts. The answer to step two, when considered in light of your answer to step one, tells you if the accounts involved are to be debited or credited. Consider the instance where $25,000 is borrowed from a bank. The two accounts involved are Cash and Notes Payable. Cash increased, and since Cash is an asset and assets increase with debits, then Cash must be debited. Notes Payable increased (we owe more money), and since Notes Payable is a liability and liabilities increase with credits, then Notes Payable must be credited. The answer to step three completes the journal entry. Cash is debited for $25,000, and Notes Payable is credited for $25,000.

This three-step process will always work, even for complex transactions. Consider the case where inventory costing $60,000 is sold on account for $75,000. Using the three-step process results in the following:

1. *Step One:* What accounts are involved?
   - Accounts Receivable (an asset), Inventory (an asset), Cost of Goods Sold (an expense—part of owners' equity), and Sales Revenue (a revenue account—part of owners' equity).
2. *Step Two:* Did the accounts increase or decrease?
   - Accounts Receivable increased (customers owe us more money). Since Accounts Receivable is an asset, it is increased with a debit.
   - Inventory decreased (we don't have it anymore). Since Inventory is an asset, it is decreased with a credit.
   - Cost of Goods Sold increased (an expense causing owners' equity to decrease). Since owners' equity decreases with a debit, Cost of Goods Sold must be debited.
   - Sales Revenue increased (a revenue causing owners' equity to increase). Since owners' equity increases with a credit, Sales Revenue must be credited.
3. *Step Three:* By how much did each account change?
   - The answer to step three results in the following journal entries:

Account	Debit	Credit
Accounts Receivable.	75,000	
Sales Revenue.		75,000
Cost of Goods Sold	60,000	
Inventory.		60,000

TO SUMMARIZE

Journal entries are used to summarize the effects of business transactions. Journal entries are prepared or analyzed by answering three questions: (1) what accounts are involved, (2) did those accounts increase or decrease, and (3) by how much did each account change. By correctly answering these three questions, transactions will be properly accounted for and the accounting equation will always balance.

4 *Summarize the resulting journal entries through posting and prepare a trial balance (step three of the accounting cycle).*

posting The process of transferring amounts from the journal to the ledger.

ledger A book of accounts in which data from transactions recorded in journals are posted and thereby summarized.

CAUTION

Common mistakes when posting include posting a debit to the credit side of an account, transposing numbers (e.g., a 45 magically becomes a 54), and posting to the wrong account (e.g., Supplies instead of Inventory). The lesson—be very careful or mistakes will creep into your work.

POSTING JOURNAL ENTRIES AND PREPARING A TRIAL BALANCE

Once transactions have been analyzed and recorded in a journal, it is necessary to classify and group all similar items. This is accomplished by the bookkeeping procedure of **posting** all the journal entries to appropriate accounts. As indicated earlier, accounts are records of like items. They show transaction dates, increases and decreases, and balances. For example, all increases and decreases in cash arising from transactions recorded in the journal are accumulated in one account called Cash. Similarly, all sales transactions are grouped together in the sales revenue account. Exhibit 3-5 shows how the transactions from the general journal (Exhibit 3-4, page 88) would be posted to the cash account.

Posting is no more than sorting all journal entry amounts by account and copying those amounts to the appropriate account. No analysis is needed; all the necessary analysis is performed when the transaction is first recorded in the journal.

All accounts are maintained in an accounting record called the "general ledger." A **ledger** is a "book of accounts." Exhibit 3-6 shows how the three cash transactions in the general journal would be posted to the cash account in the general ledger, with arrows depicting the posting procedures. Observe that a number has been inserted in the "posting reference" column in both books. This number serves as a cross-reference between the general journal and the accounts in the general ledger. In the journal, it identifies the account to which the journal entry has been posted. In the ledger, it identifies the page on which the entry appears in the general journal. For example, the GJ1 notation in the cash account for the July 1 entry means that the $2,000 has been posted from page 1 of the general journal. As you will discover, these

EXHIBIT 3-5 Cash Account in General Ledger

ACCOUNT: Cash | ACCOUNT NO. 101

Date	Explanation	Post. Ref.	Debits	Credits	Balance
2000 July 1	Balance				0
1	Issued 200 shares of capital stock at $10 per share	GJ1	2,000		2,000
5	Purchased a used truck	GJ1		800	1,200
5	Purchased supplies	GJ1		180	1,020

EXHIBIT 3-6 Posting to the General Ledger

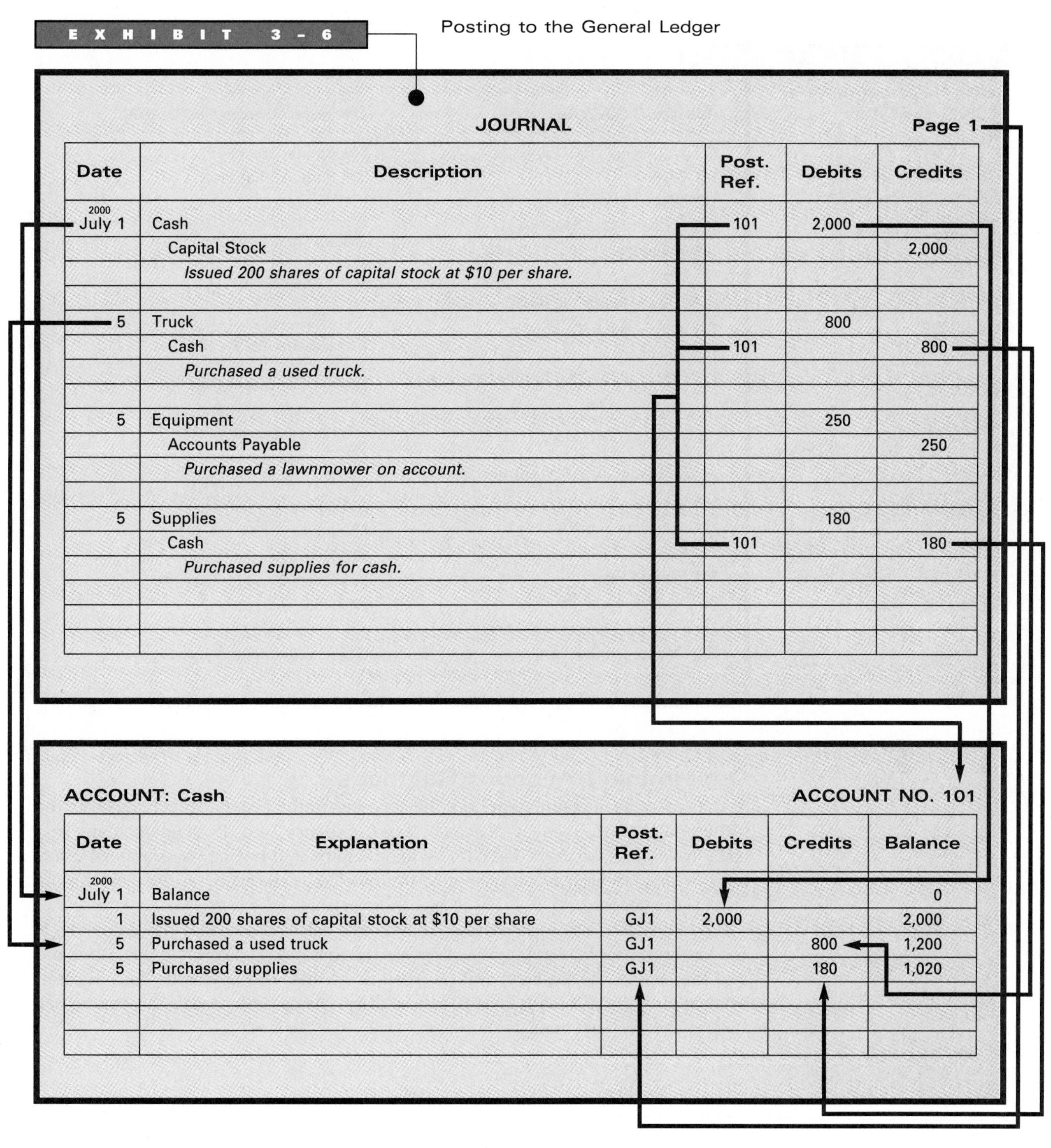

JOURNAL — Page 1

Date	Description	Post. Ref.	Debits	Credits
2000 July 1	Cash	101	2,000	
	Capital Stock			2,000
	Issued 200 shares of capital stock at $10 per share.			
5	Truck		800	
	Cash	101		800
	Purchased a used truck.			
5	Equipment		250	
	Accounts Payable			250
	Purchased a lawnmower on account.			
5	Supplies		180	
	Cash	101		180
	Purchased supplies for cash.			

ACCOUNT: Cash — **ACCOUNT NO. 101**

Date	Explanation	Post. Ref.	Debits	Credits	Balance
2000 July 1	Balance				0
1	Issued 200 shares of capital stock at $10 per share	GJ1	2,000		2,000
5	Purchased a used truck	GJ1		800	1,200
5	Purchased supplies	GJ1		180	1,020

posting references are useful in tracking down mistakes. With a computer system, the software automatically generates these posting references.

chart of accounts A systematic listing of all accounts used by a company.

A particular company will have as many (or as few) accounts as it needs to provide a reasonable classification of its transactions. The list of accounts used by a company is known as its **chart of accounts**. The normal order of a chart of accounts is assets (current and long-term), then liabilities (current and long-term), followed by owners' equity, sales, and expenses. Exhibit 3-7 shows some accounts that might appear in a typical company's chart of accounts.

EXHIBIT 3-7

Chart of Accounts for a Typical Company

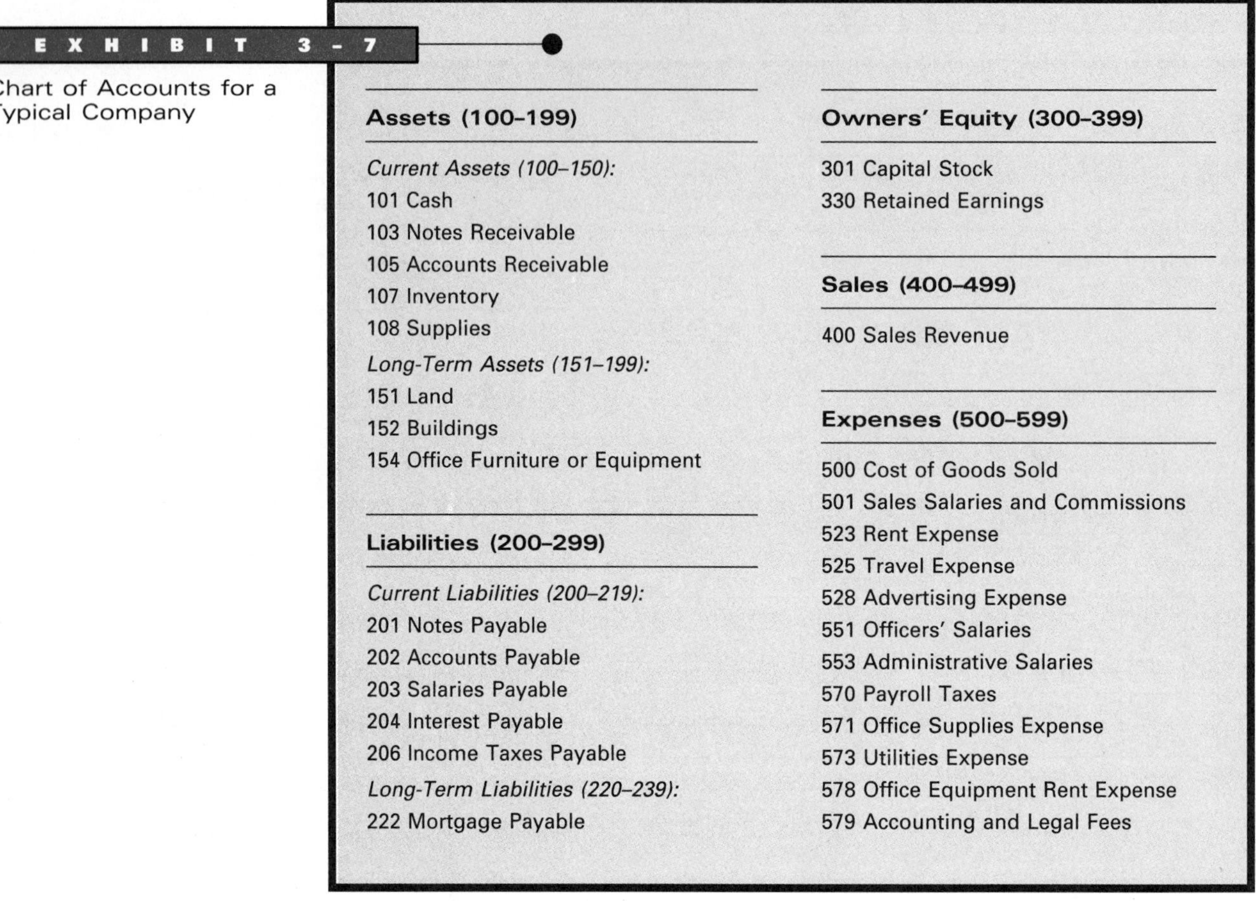

Assets (100–199)

Current Assets (100–150):
101 Cash
103 Notes Receivable
105 Accounts Receivable
107 Inventory
108 Supplies
Long-Term Assets (151–199):
151 Land
152 Buildings
154 Office Furniture or Equipment

Liabilities (200–299)

Current Liabilities (200–219):
201 Notes Payable
202 Accounts Payable
203 Salaries Payable
204 Interest Payable
206 Income Taxes Payable
Long-Term Liabilities (220–239):
222 Mortgage Payable

Owners' Equity (300–399)

301 Capital Stock
330 Retained Earnings

Sales (400–499)

400 Sales Revenue

Expenses (500–599)

500 Cost of Goods Sold
501 Sales Salaries and Commissions
523 Rent Expense
525 Travel Expense
528 Advertising Expense
551 Officers' Salaries
553 Administrative Salaries
570 Payroll Taxes
571 Office Supplies Expense
573 Utilities Expense
578 Office Equipment Rent Expense
579 Accounting and Legal Fees

Determining Account Balances

At the end of an accounting period, the accounts in the general ledger are reviewed to determine each account's balance. Asset, expense, and dividend accounts normally have debit balances; liability, owners' equity, and revenue accounts normally have credit balances. In other words, the balance is normally on the side that increases the account.

To illustrate how to determine an account balance, consider the following T-account from our landscaping business for the first month, assuming that Mom and Dad invested in the business and received dividends. The beginning cash account balance plus all Cash debit entries, less total credits to Cash, equals the ending balance in the Cash account.

Cash

Beg. Bal.	0	
(From Mom & Dad)	2,000	800 (Truck)
(From customers)	270	180 (Supplies)
(From customers)	90	150 (Inventory)
(From customers)	45	50 (Gasoline)
(From customers)	80	60 (Wages)
		250 (Accounts payable)
		50 (Dividends)
	2,485	1,540
	(1,540) ←	
End. Bal.	945	

Illustration of the First Three Steps in the Accounting Cycle

We have introduced the first three steps in the accounting cycle. A simple illustration will help reinforce what you have learned about the relationship of assets, liabilities, and owners' equity; including revenues, expenses, and dividends, and the mechanics of double-entry accounting. Katherine Kohler established the Double K Corporation in 2000. The following transactions occurred.

a. Initial capital contribution of $20,000, for which she received 1,000 shares of capital stock.
b. Double K Corporation paid $10,000 cash for inventory.
c. Borrowed $20,000 from a bank to buy some land, signing a long-term note with the bank.
d. Land was purchased for $25,000 cash.
e. During the year 2000, Double K Corporation sold 20 percent, or $2,000, of the inventory purchased. The company sold that inventory for $3,200, and the sale was originally made on credit.
f. The company paid $200 in selling expenses and $100 in miscellaneous expenses.
g. The company collected the full amount of the receivable in cash.

The inventory purchases are verified by invoices showing the actual items purchased, dates, amounts, and so forth. There is a $20,000 note payable to the bank. Other business documents indicate the sale of inventory and the expenses incurred. Through analysis of these transactions and supporting documents (step 1), the pertinent facts are obtained and the transactions are recorded in a journal (step 2). The journal entries to record the transactions of Double K Corporation are as follows. (Note that letters are used in place of dates.)

Business Transaction	Account Category and Direction	Journal Entries	Debits	Credits
Issued stock	assets (+)	(a) Cash	20,000	
	owners' equity (+)	Capital Stock		20,000
		Issued 1,000 shares of capital stock for $20,000.		
Purchased inventory	assets (+)	(b) Inventory	10,000	
	assets (−)	Cash		10,000
		Purchased $10,000 of inventory for cash.		
Borrowed money	assets (+)	(c) Cash	20,000	
	liabilities (+)	Notes Payable		20,000
		Borrowed $20,000 from a bank.		
Purchased land	assets (+)	(d) Land	25,000	
	assets (−)	Cash		25,000
		Purchased land for cash.		
Sold inventory	assets (+)	(e) Accounts Receivable	3,200	
	revenues (+)	Sales Revenue		3,200
		Sold $3,200 of inventory on account.		
	expenses (+)	Cost of Goods Sold	2,000	
	assets (−)	Inventory		2,000
		To record the cost of goods or inventory sold.		
Paid expenses	expenses (+)	(f) Selling Expenses	200	
	expenses (+)	Miscellaneous Expenses	100	
	assets (−)	Cash		300
		Paid selling and miscellaneous expenses.		
Collected cash	assets (+)	(g) Cash	3,200	
	assets (−)	Accounts Receivable		3,200
		Collected accounts receivable.		

Next, the transactions are posted to the ledger accounts (step 3, part 1). T-accounts are used to illustrate this process, with the letters (a) through (g) showing the cross-references to the journal entries. A balance is shown for the end of the period. (Where only one transaction is involved, the amount of the transaction is also the account balance.)

Cash

	Debit		Credit
(a)	20,000	(b)	10,000
(c)	20,000	(d)	25,000
(g)	3,200	(f)	300
Bal.	7,900		

Accounts Receivable

	Debit		Credit
(e)	3,200	(g)	3,200
	0		

Inventory

	Debit		Credit
(b)	10,000	(e)	2,000
Bal.	8,000		

Land

	Debit		Credit
(d)	25,000		

Notes Payable

	Debit		Credit
		(c)	20,000

Capital Stock

	Debit		Credit
		(a)	20,000

Sales Revenue

	Debit		Credit
		(e)	3,200

Cost of Goods Sold

	Debit		Credit
(e)	2,000		

Selling Expenses

	Debit		Credit
(f)	200		

Miscellaneous Expenses

	Debit		Credit
(f)	100		

trial balance A listing of all account balances; provides a means of testing whether total debits equal total credits for all accounts.

After the account balances have been determined, a trial balance is usually prepared (step 3, part 2). A **trial balance** lists each account with its debit or credit balance, as shown in Exhibit 3-8. By adding all the debit balances and all the credit balances, the accountant can see whether total debits equal total credits. Even if the trial balance does show total debits equal to total credits, there may be errors. A transaction may be omitted completely, or it may have been recorded incorrectly or posted to the wrong account. These types of errors will not be discovered by preparing a trial balance; additional analysis would be required. In this case, total debits equal total credits. Thus, the accounting equation is in balance. The balances are taken from each ledger account.

EXHIBIT 3-8

Trial Balance

Double K Corporation
Trial Balance
December 31, 2000

	Debits	Credits
Cash	$ 7,900	
Accounts Receivable	0	
Inventory	8,000	
Land	25,000	
Notes Payable		$20,000
Capital Stock		20,000
Sales Revenue		3,200
Cost of Goods Sold	2,000	
Selling Expenses	200	
Miscellaneous Expenses	100	
Totals	$43,200	$43,200

From the data in the trial balance, an income statement and a balance sheet can be prepared. Exhibit 3-9 shows these two financial statements for Double K Corporation.

EXHIBIT 3-9

Income Statement and Balance Sheet

Double K Corporation
Income Statement
For the Year Ended December 31, 2000

Sales revenue		$3,200
Expenses:		
Cost of goods sold	$2,000	
Selling expenses	200	
Miscellaneous expenses	100	2,300
Net income		$ 900*
EPS ($900 ÷ 1,000 shares)		$ 0.90

*Beginning retained earnings + net income − dividends.

Double K Corporation
Balance Sheet
December 31, 2000

Assets		Liabilities and Owners' Equity	
Cash	$ 7,900	Notes payable	$20,000
Inventory	8,000	Capital stock (1,000 shares)	20,000
Land	25,000	Retained earnings	900
Total assets	$40,900	Total liabilites and owners' equity	$40,900

TO SUMMARIZE

Once journal entries have been made and posted to the related accounts, account balances are computed by summing the debit and credit entries in each account. A trial balance is prepared by listing each account along with its balance. An income statement and a balance sheet can be prepared from this trial balance. A statement of cash flows is prepared by analyzing the inflows and outflows of cash as detailed in the cash account.

5 *Understand the need for adjusting entries, how financial statements are prepared, and how the books are closed (step four of the accounting cycle).*

time-period (or periodicity) concept The idea that the life of a business is divided into distinct and relatively short time periods so that accounting information can be timely.

COMPLETING THE ACCOUNTING CYCLE

Accrual accounting is the process of adjusting raw transaction data into refined measures of a firm's past economic performance and current economic condition. This accrual process is necessary because business requires periodic, timely financial reports and accrual information better measures a firm's performance than does cash flow data.

The financial picture of a company—its success or failure in meeting its economic objectives—cannot really be complete until the "life" of a business is over. However, managers, owners, and creditors cannot wait 10, 20, or 100 years to receive an exact accounting of a business. In order to provide timely accounting information, the **time-period concept** divides the life of an enterprise into distinct

fiscal year An entity's reporting year, covering a 12-month accounting period.

and relatively short (generally 12 months or less) accounting periods. The 12-month accounting period is referred to as the **fiscal year**.

Although periodic reporting is vital to a firm's success, the frequency of reporting forces accountants to use some data that are based on judgments and estimates. As you will see, the shorter the reporting period (for example, a month instead of a year), the less exact are the measurements of assets and liabilities and the recognition of revenues and expenses. Ideally, accounting judgments are made carefully and estimates are based on reliable evidence, but the limitations of accounting reports should be understood and kept in mind.

(STOP & THINK)

Since almost all companies have their financial records on computer, what stops them from preparing financial statements every day?

accrual-basis accounting A system of accounting in which revenues and expenses are recorded as they are earned and incurred, not necessarily when cash is received or paid.

Closely related to the time-period concept is the concept of **accrual-basis accounting**. This important characteristic of the traditional accounting model simply means that revenues are recognized (recorded) when earned without regard for when cash is received; expenses are recorded as incurred without regard for when they are paid. Accrual accounting requires that revenues and expenses be assigned to their proper accounting periods, which do not necessarily coincide with the periods in which cash is received or paid.

revenue recognition principle The idea that revenues should be recorded when (1) the earnings process has been substantially completed and (2) cash has either been collected or collectibility is reasonably assured.

How do we assign revenues to particular periods? The **revenue recognition principle** states that revenues are recorded when two main criteria have been met.

1. The earnings process is substantially complete; generally, a sale has been made or services have been performed.
2. Cash has been collected or collectibility is reasonably assured.

These two criteria ensure that both parties to the transaction have fulfilled their commitment or are formally obligated to do so. In simple terms, satisfying the first criterion demonstrates that the seller has done something; satisfying the second criterion demonstrates that the buyer has done something. The seller generally records sales revenue when goods are shipped or when services are performed. When this occurs, the seller has completed his or her part of the transaction. The seller assumes, when shipment is made or services performed, that the buyer has given a valid promise to pay (if this promise is not implied, then the seller probably will not ship). The promise to pay, or the actual payment, would complete the buyer's part of the transaction.

matching principle The concept that all costs and expenses incurred in generating revenues must be recognized in the same reporting period as the related revenues.

Once a company determines which revenues should be recognized during a period, how does it identify the expenses incurred? The **matching principle** requires that all costs and expenses incurred to generate revenues must be recognized in the same accounting period as the related revenues. The cost of the merchandise sold, for example, should be matched to the revenue derived from the sale of that merchandise during the period. Expenses that cannot be matched with revenues are assigned to the accounting period in which they are incurred. For example, the exact amount of electricity used to make an automobile generally cannot be determined, but since the amount used for a month or a year is known, that amount can be matched to the revenues earned during the same period.

As discussed previously, transactions generally are recorded in a journal in chronological order and then posted to the ledger accounts. The entries are based on the best information available at the time. Although the majority of accounts are up to date at the end of an accounting period and their balances can be included in the financial statements, some accounts require adjustment to reflect current circumstances. In general, these accounts are not updated throughout the period because it is impractical or inconvenient to make such entries on a daily or weekly basis. At the end of each accounting period, in order to report all asset, liability, and owners' equity amounts properly and to recognize all revenues and expenses for the period on an accrual basis, accountants are required to make any necessary adjust-

adjusting entries
Entries required at the end of each accounting period to recognize, on an accrual basis, revenues and expenses for the period and to report proper amounts for asset, liability, and owners' equity accounts.

ments prior to preparing the financial statements. The entries that reflect these adjustments are called **adjusting entries**.

One difficulty with adjusting entries is that the need for an adjustment is not signaled by a specific event such as the receipt of a bill or the receipt of cash from a customer. Rather, adjusting entries are recorded on the basis of an analysis of the circumstances at the close of each accounting period. This analysis involves just two steps:

1. Determine whether the amounts recorded for all assets and liabilities are correct. If not, debit or credit the appropriate asset or liability account. In short, fix the balance sheet.
2. Determine what revenue or expense adjustments are required as a result of the changes in recorded amounts of assets and liabilities indicated in step one. Debit or credit the appropriate revenue or expense account. In short, fix the income statement.

It should be noted that these two steps are interrelated and may be reversed. That is, revenue and expense adjustments may be considered first to fix the income statement, indicating which asset and liability accounts need adjustment to fix the balance sheet. As you will see, each adjusting entry involves at least one income statement account and one balance sheet account.

To illustrate why adjustment entries are needed and how they are made, we will assume that on December 31, 2000, our landscaping company has determined the following:

1. Your brother has worked for the company since its inception. He is paid every two weeks. The next payday is on Friday, January 5, 2001. On that day, your brother will be paid $700, the amount he earns every two weeks. Since December 31 falls halfway through the pay period, one-half of his wages should be allocated to 2000.
2. Recall that one of our options for financing our company was to borrow money from a bank. We borrowed $2,000 with the promise that on the first of every month we would make a $178 payment—a portion of that payment being attributed to interest[1] and a portion to principal. Our next payment is due on January 1, 2001, but the interest expense associated with that payment should be attributed to the period in which the money was actually used—December 2000. Assume that interest of $20 must be recognized on December 31, 2000.

To represent its current financial position and earnings, our landscaping company must record the impact of these events in the accounts, even though cash transactions have not yet occurred. The wages will not be paid until 2001. However, under accrual-basis accounting, these costs are expenses of 2000 and should be recognized on this year's income statement, with the corresponding liability shown on the balance sheet as of the end of the year. To fix the balance sheet, Wages Payable must be credited (increased) for $350. The debit of this adjusting entry is to Wages Expense, resulting in the proper inclusion of this expense in the 2000 income statement. The adjusting journal entry is as follows:

Dec. 31	Wages Expense.	350	
	Wages Payable		350
	To record obligation for wages.		

1. As noted previously, interest is the cost of using money. The amount borrowed or lent is the *principal.* The *interest rate* is an annual rate stated as a percentage. The *period of time* involved may be stated in terms of a year. For example, if interest is to be paid for 3 months, time is 3/12, or 1/4 of a year. If interest is to be paid for 90 days, time is 90/365 of a year. Thus, the formula for computing interest is Interest = Principal × Interest Rate × Time (fraction of a year).

The liability for the interest for the month of December is recorded by a credit (increase) to Interest Payable; this fixes the balance sheet. The debit of the adjusting entry is to Interest Expense, which properly includes this expense on the 2000 income statement. The adjusting entry is:

Dec. 31	Interest Expense	20	
	Interest Payable		20
	To record interest incurred.		

CAUTION

A liability is not recorded for the total amount of interest that will have to be paid over the entire life of the loan. If we repay the loan on December 31, the future interest will not have to be paid, but the interest for the month of December that has passed will still be due.

The wages expense and interest expense would be shown on the income statement for the year ended December 31, and the liabilities (wages payable and interest payable) would be shown on the balance sheet as of December 31. Because of the adjusting entries, both the income statement and balance sheet will more accurately reflect the financial situation of our landscaping company.

Financial Statement Preparation

Once all transactions have been analyzed, journalized, and posted and all adjusting entries have been made, the accounts can be summarized and presented in the form of financial statements. Financial statements can be prepared directly from the data in the adjusted ledger accounts. The data must only be organized into appropriate sections and categories so as to present them as simply and clearly as possible. Once the financial statements are prepared, explanatory notes are written. These notes clarify the methods and assumptions used in preparing the statements. In addition, the auditor must review the financial statements to make sure they are accurate, reasonable, and in accordance with generally accepted accounting principles. Finally, the financial statements are distributed to external users who analyze them in order to learn more about the financial condition of the company.

To illustrate the preparation of financial statements from adjusted ledger accounts, a simplified adjusted trial balance for **NIKE, Inc.**, as of May 31, 1997, is provided in Exhibit 3-10. From these data, an income statement and a balance sheet may be prepared for NIKE, as shown in Exhibits 3-11 and 3-12.

The ending retained earnings balance for NIKE for 1997 ($2,973,663), as reported on the balance sheet, is computed as follows:

Beginning retained earnings balance (from the adjusted trial balance)	$2,286,120
Add: Net income for the period (from the income statement)	795,822
Subtract: Dividends for the period (from the adjusted trial balance)	(108,279)
Ending retained earnings balance	$2,973,663

This follows the computation of retained earnings discussed in Chapter 2.

A statement of cash flows is not shown here. In order to prepare a statement of cash flows, we need more detailed information about the nature of the cash receipts and cash disbursements during the year. The preparation of a statement of cash flows will be illustrated in Chapter 8.

The Notes

As discussed in Chapter 2, the notes to the financial statements tell about the assumptions and methods used in preparing the financial statements and also give more

EXHIBIT 3-10

Simplified Adjusted Trial Balance

NIKE, Inc.
Simplified Adjusted Trial Balance
May 31, 1997
(in thousands)

	Debits	Credits
Cash and Equivalents	$ 445,421	
Accounts Receivable (net)	1,754,137	
Inventories	1,338,640	
Property, Plant, and Equipment (net)	922,369	
Intangible Assets and Goodwill	464,191	
Other Assets	436,449	
Notes Payable		$ 555,369
Accounts Payable		687,121
Accrued Liabilities		570,504
Income Taxes Payable		53,923
Long-Term Debt		296,020
Other Liabilities		42,432
Common Stock		182,175
Retained Earnings		2,286,120
Dividends	108,279	
Revenues		9,186,539
Cost of Sales	5,502,993	
Selling and Administrative Expenses	2,303,704	
Interest Expense	52,343	
Other Income/Expense	32,277	
Income Tax Expense	499,400	
Totals	$13,860,203	$13,860,203

EXHIBIT 3-11

Income Statement

NIKE, Inc.
Statement of Income
For the Year Ended May 31, 1997
(in thousands, except per share data)

Revenues		$9,186,539
Costs and expenses:		
Cost of sales	$5,502,993	
Selling and administrative expenses	2,303,704	
Interest expense	52,343	
Other income/expense	32,277	7,891,317
Income before taxes		$1,295,222
Income tax expense		499,400
Net income		$ 795,822
Net income per common share		$2.68
Average number of common equivalent shares		297,000

Note: This statement of income is not an exact replica of NIKE's actual income statement due to simplifying modifications for this exhibit.

EXHIBIT 3-12

Balance Sheet

NIKE, Inc.
Balance Sheet
May 31, 1997
(in thousands)

Assets		
Current assets:		
Cash and equivalents	$ 445,421	
Accounts receivable (net)	1,754,137	
Inventories	1,338,640	
Total current assets		$3,538,198
Long-term assets:		
Property, plant, and equipment (net)	$ 922,369	
Intangible assets and goodwill	464,191	
Other assets	436,449	
Total long-term assets		1,823,009
Total assets		$5,361,207
Liabilities and Owners' Equity		
Current liabilities:		
Notes payable	$ 555,369	
Accounts payable	687,121	
Accrued liabilities	570,504	
Income taxes payable	53,923	
Total current liabilities		$1,866,917
Long-term debt		296,020
Other liabilities		42,432
Total liabilities		$2,205,369
Owners' equity:		
Common stock	$ 182,175	
Retained earnings	2,973,663	
Total owners' equity		3,155,838
Total liabilities and owners' equity		$5,361,207

Note: This balance sheet is not an exact replica of NIKE's actual balance sheet due to simplifying modifications for this exhibit.

detail about specific items. A sample of the kind of information that appears in the notes for NIKE's financial statements is illustrated in Exhibit 3-13.

The financial statement notes serve to augment the summarized, numerical information contained in the financial statements. To highlight the importance of the notes, many financial statements have the following message printed at the bottom: "The notes are an integral part of these financial statements."

The Audit

As mentioned in Chapter 2, an independent audit, by CPAs from outside the company, is often conducted to ensure that the financial statements have been prepared in conformity with generally accepted accounting principles. With respect to the financial statements of NIKE, the audit procedures conducted by the external auditor would probably include the following checks.

EXHIBIT 3-13

Notes to the Financial Statements

NIKE, Inc.
Notes to the Financial Statements (partial list)
For the Year Ended May 31, 1997

Recognition of Revenues:

Revenues recognized include sales plus fees earned on sales by licensees.

Cash and Equivalents:

Cash and equivalents represent cash and short-term, highly liquid investments with original maturities three months or less.

Endorsement Contracts:

Accounting for endorsement contracts is based upon specific contract provisions. Generally, endorsement payments are expensed uniformly over the term of the contract after giving recognition to periodic performance compliance provisions of the contracts. Contracts requiring prepayments are included in prepaid expenses or other assets depending on the length of the contract.

Management Estimates:

The preparation of financial statements in conformity with generally accepted accounting principles requires management to make estimates, including estimates relating to assumptions that affect the reported amounts of assets and liabilities and disclosure of contingent assets and liabilities at the date of the financial statements and the reported amounts of revenues and expenses during the reporting period. Actual results could differ from these estimates.

Review of Adjustments As you learned in the first part of this chapter, adjusting entries usually require more analysis, and more judgment, than do the regular journal entries recorded throughout the year. As part of the audit, the auditor will review these adjusting entries. Auditors pay particular attention to the adjustments involving unrecorded expenses. As mentioned in the text, companies don't like making these adjusting entries, because they increase reported liabilities and reduce reported net income. Accordingly, the auditor should review the business events of the year to make sure that no expenses have been left unrecorded.

Sample of Selected Accounts For a number of accounts, the auditor undertakes a sampling process to see whether the items reported in the balance sheet actually exist. For example, NIKE reports an ending cash and equivalents balance of $445,421. The auditor will ask to see bank statements and will probably call the bank(s) to verify the existence of the cash. For inventory, the auditor will ask to physically see the inventory and will conduct a spot check to see whether the company inventory records match what is actually in the warehouse.

Review of Accounting Systems The auditor will also evaluate NIKE's accounting systems. If a company has a good accounting system, with all transactions being recorded in an efficient, orderly way, then the auditor has greater reason to be confident that the financial statements are reliable. On the other hand, if the company's accounting system is haphazard, with many missing documents and unexplained discrepancies, then the auditor must do more detailed work to verify the financial statements.

If the auditor finds that the financial statements have been prepared in conformance with generally accepted accounting principles, then the auditor provides a report to that effect. This report is attached and distributed as part of the financial statements.

BUSINESS ENVIRONMENT ESSAY

Annual Report to Stockholders—Read Carefully Financial statements are the end product of the accounting cycle and report a company's financial position, results of operations, and cash flows. The financial statements of corporations are presented in the annual report to stockholders. Major U.S. corporations spend millions of dollars to publish annual reports that will impress their stockholders and potential investors. To some extent, the annual report is a public relations document. In addition to the financial statements, annual reports typically include several pages of discussion and analysis prepared by management to describe the company's operations, its past performance, and expectations for the future. In addition, the annual report typically contains a letter to the shareholders from the chief executive officer (CEO) of the company. As might be expected, this letter tends to reflect an optimistic outlook. All the information in the annual report should be read and evaluated carefully, as the following examples illustrate:

- In fiscal year 1995, Kmart lost $571 million. In the letter to the shareholders, Kmart's CEO said: "I am encouraged by Kmart's progress and excited about the future . . . Excellence will make Kmart the retailer of choice for our customers, the buyer of choice for our suppliers, the employer of choice for our associates—and the investment of choice for you, our shareholders."
- Apple Computer posted an $816 million loss in fiscal 1996. In the letter to the shareholders, Apple's CEO chose to accentuate the positive: "Apple's late-year course corrections have been moving the Company in a positive direction toward renewed health."
- On October 2, 1996, Millennium Chemicals Inc. was created by being spun off from Hanson PLC. In its first set of financial statements, Millennium reported a loss of $2.7 billion. However, the CEO sounded very upbeat in the first letter to the shareholders: "I'd like to take the opportunity in this, our first Annual Report, to share not only a summary of results, but also, importantly, our strategy for creating value at the new Millennium. Value creation is our guiding principle, one that we will not compromise and one that is sweeping through the organization in these formative days."

Sources: Kmart 1995 Annual Report, Apple Computer 1996 Annual Report, Millennium Chemicals Inc. 1996 Annual Report.

Closing the Books

We have almost reached the end of the accounting cycle. Thus far, the accounting cycle has included analyzing documents, journalizing transactions, posting to the ledger accounts, determining account balances, preparing a trial balance, making adjusting entries, and preparing the financial statements. Just two additional steps are needed: (1) journalizing and posting closing entries and (2) preparing a post-closing trial balance.

real accounts
Accounts that are not closed to a zero balance at the end of each accounting period; permanent accounts appearing on the balance sheet.

nominal accounts
Accounts that are closed to a zero balance at the end of each accounting period; temporary accounts generally appearing on the income statement.

Real and Nominal Accounts

To explain the closing process, we must first define two new terms. Certain accounts are referred to as **real accounts**. These accounts report the cumulative increases and decreases in certain account balances from the date the company was organized. Real accounts (assets, liabilities, and owners' equity) appear on the balance sheet and are permanent; they are not closed to a zero balance at the end of each accounting period. Balances existing in real accounts at the end of a period are carried forward to the next period.

Other accounts are known as **nominal accounts**. These accounts (revenues, expenses, and dividends) are temporary; they are really just subcategories of Retained Earnings and are reduced to a zero balance through the closing process at the end of each accounting period. Thus, nominal accounts begin with a zero balance at the start of each accounting cycle. Transactions throughout the period (generally a year) are journalized and posted to the nominal accounts. These are used to accumulate and classify all revenue and expense items, and also dividends, for that period. At the end of the accounting period, adjustments are made, the income statement is prepared, and the balances in the temporary accounts are then closed to Retained Earnings, a permanent account. These closing entries bring the income statement accounts back to a zero balance, which makes the accounts ready for a new accounting period. In addition, the closing entries transfer the net income or loss for the accounting period to Retained Earnings and reduce Retained Earnings for any dividends. Without closing entries, revenue and expense balances would extend from period to period, making it difficult to isolate the operating results of each accounting period.

FYI

In a proprietorship or a partnership, the nominal accounts are closed to the owners' permanent capital accounts instead of to Retained Earnings.

Closing Entries

The actual mechanics of the closing process are not complicated. Revenue accounts normally have credit balances and are closed by being debited; expense accounts generally have debit balances and are closed by being credited. The difference between total revenues and total expenses represents the net income (or net loss) of the entity. For a corporation, net income is credited to Retained Earnings, since income increases owners' equity. A net loss would be debited to Retained Earnings since a loss decreases owners' equity.

To illustrate the closing process, we will again refer to NIKE's financial information as discussed earlier on pages 105–106. The closing journal entry is:

May 31	Revenues	9,186,539	
	Cost of Sales		5,502,993
	Selling and Administrative Expenses		2,303,704
	Interest Expense		52,343
	Other Expenses		32,277
	Income Tax Expense		499,400
	Retained Earnings		795,822
	To close revenues and expenses to Retained Earnings.		

closing entries Entries that reduce all nominal, or temporary, accounts to a zero balance at the end of each accounting period, transferring their preclosing balances to a permanent balance sheet account.

Closing entries must be posted to the appropriate ledger accounts. Once posted, all nominal accounts will have a zero balance, that is, they will be "closed."

The dividends account is also a nominal (temporary) account that must be closed at the end of the accounting period. However, dividends are not expenses and will not be reported on an income statement; they are distributions to stockholders of part of a corporation's earnings. Thus, dividends reduce retained earnings. When dividends are declared by the board of directors of a corporation, the amount that will be paid is debited to Dividends and credited to a liability account, Dividends Payable, or to Cash if paid immediately. Since Dividends is a temporary account, it must be closed to Retained Earnings at the end of the accounting period. The dividends account is closed by crediting it and by debiting Retained Earnings, thereby reducing owners' equity, as illustrated below for NIKE.

CAUTION

Don't close real accounts! Consider the negative implications of eliminating all your asset accounts at the end of the year. Nominal accounts are closed because they are just temporary subaccounts of Retained Earnings.

May 31	Retained Earnings	108,279	
	Dividends		108,279
	To close Dividends to Retained Earnings.		

The books are now ready for a new accounting cycle. The closing process for the revenues, expenses, and dividends of a corporation is shown schematically in Exhibit 3-14.

EXHIBIT 3-14

The Closing Process

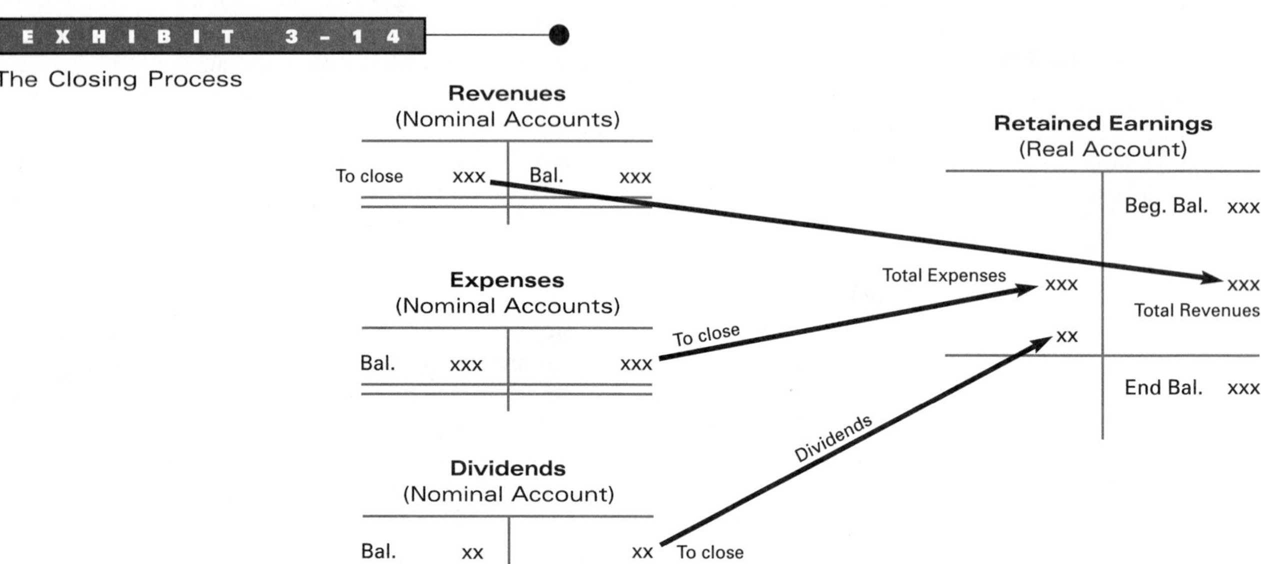

Preparing a Post-Closing Trial Balance

post-closing trial balance A listing of all real account balances after the closing process has been completed; provides a means of testing whether total debits equal total credits for all real accounts prior to beginning a new accounting cycle.

An optional last step in the accounting cycle is to balance the accounts and to prepare a **post-closing trial balance**. The accounts are to be balanced—debits and credits added and a balance determined—only after the closing entries have been recorded and posted in the General Ledger. The information for the post-closing trial balance is then taken from the ledger. The nominal accounts will not be shown since they have been closed and thus have zero balances. Only the real accounts will have current balances. This step is designed to provide some assurance that the previous steps in the cycle have been performed properly, prior to the start of a new accounting period. Exhibit 3-15 illustrates a post-closing trial balance for **NIKE, Inc.**

TO SUMMARIZE

To present financial statements that accurately report the financial position and the results of operations on an accrual basis for specific periods of time, adjusting entries must be made. Once adjusting entries are made, an adjusted trial balance is prepared. This adjusted trial balance provides the raw material for the preparation of the balance sheet and the income statement. The notes to the financial statements provide further information about the methods and assumptions used in preparing the financial statements as well as further detail about certain financial statement items. Once financial statements are prepared, all nominal (temporary) accounts are closed to a zero balance. All real (permanent) accounts (balance sheet accounts for assets, liabilities, and owners' equity) are carried forward to the next reporting period.

EXHIBIT 3-15

Post-Closing Trial Balance

NIKE, Inc.
Post-Closing Trial Balance
May 31, 1997
(in thousands)

	Debits	Credits
Cash and Equivalents	$ 445,421	
Accounts Receivable (net)	1,754,137	
Inventories	1,338,640	
Property, Plant, and Equipment (net)	922,369	
Intangible Assets and Goodwill	464,191	
Other Assets	436,449	
Notes Payable		$ 555,369
Accounts Payable		687,121
Accrued Liabilities		570,504
Income Taxes Payable		53,923
Long-Term Debt		296,020
Other Liabilities		42,432
Common Stock		182,175
Retained Earnings		2,973,663
Totals	$5,361,207	$5,361,207

REVIEW OF LEARNING OBJECTIVES

1 **Understand the process of transforming transaction data into useful accounting information.** The objective of the accounting process is to gather and transform transaction data into useful information that measures and communicates the results of business activity. The accounting system used to keep track of the many financial activities of a business should be tailor-made for that business, and may be a manual or an automated system, depending on the organization's needs.

2 **Analyze transactions and determine how those transactions affect the accounting equation.** The procedures for processing accounting data are based on double-entry accounting and the fundamental accounting equation: Assets = Liabilities + Owners' Equity. Revenues increase retained earnings, whereas expenses and dividends decrease retained earnings. Thus, these accounts have a direct impact on the amount of owners' equity. In terms of the increase/decrease relationship of accounts, assets, expenses, and dividends are increased by debits; liabilities, owners' equity, and revenues are increased by credits. The double-entry system of accounting ensures that the accounting equation will always balance because debit entries require equal credit entries; that is, total debits must always equal total credits when transactions are properly recorded.

3 **Record the effects of transactions using journal entries.** The effects of business events are recorded in the accounting system using journal entries. Journal entries detail the accounts involved in a transaction, whether the accounts increased or decreased, and the amount by which each account is affected. Each journal entry requires an equal amount of debits and credits. This equality ensures that the accounting equation will always be in balance.

4 **Summarize the resulting journal entries through posting and prepare a trial balance.** Once journal entries are made, they are posted to individual accounts. The posting process involves simply copying each debit and credit from a journal entry into the associated account. A trial balance can be prepared to ensure that debits equal credits and that the accounting equation is in balance. From the trial balance, the primary financial statements can be prepared.

5 **Understand the need for adjusting entries, how financial statements are prepared, and how the books are closed (step four of the accounting cycle).** At the end of an accounting period,

there are potentially many important events that have as yet not been recorded. Some important events occur outside the normal accounting process, while other events occur slowly over time. An important part of the accounting process is to review the financial condition and operating activities of the company for the period to make sure that all assets, liabilities, revenues, and expenses have been recorded. These year-end adjustments are called adjusting entries.

After the adjusting entries have been posted to the accounts, an adjusted trial balance is prepared. This adjusted trial balance provides the raw data for the preparation of the balance sheet and the income statement; preparation of the statement of cash flows requires more detailed information about cash receipts and cash disbursements. The notes to the financial statements provide further information about the methods and assumptions used in preparing the financial statements as well as further detail about certain financial statement items.

Once adjusting entries have been journalized and posted to the accounts and the financial statements have been prepared, the accounting records should be made ready for the next accounting cycle. This is accomplished by journalizing and posting closing entries for all nominal (temporary) accounts. Revenue accounts are closed by being debited; expense accounts and the dividends account are closed by being credited. Revenues, expenses, and dividends are closed to Retained Earnings.

KEY TERMS AND CONCEPTS

account 82
accounting cycle 77
accrual-basis accounting 102
adjusting entries 103
business documents 78
chart of accounts 97
closing entries 109
compound journal entry 91
credit 83
debit 83
dividends 85
fiscal year 102
journal 87
journal entry 87
journalizing 87
ledger 96
matching principle 102
nominal accounts 108
post-closing trial balance 110
posting 96
real accounts 108
revenue recognition principle 102
T-account 82
time-period concept 101
trial balance 100

REVIEW PROBLEM

The Accounting Cycle

Journal entries are given below for January 2000, the first month of operation for the Svendsen Service Company.

Date	Account	Debit	Credit
Jan. 2	Cash	40,000	
	Capital Stock		40,000
	Issued capital stock for cash.		
2	Insurance Expense	500	
	Cash		500
	Purchased a one-month insurance policy.		
2	Rent Expense	750	
	Cash		750
	Paid rent for the month of January.		
3	Shop Equipment	8,000	
	Cash		8,000
	Purchased shop equipment for cash.		
4	Supplies	3,000	
	Accounts Payable		3,000
	Purchased shop supplies on account.		
5	Automotive Equipment	11,500	
	Cash		3,500
	Notes Payable		8,000
	Purchased a truck. Paid $3,500 cash and issued a 30-day note for the balance.		

(continued)

Jan. 8	Cash	1,750	
	Service and Repair Revenue		1,750
	Received cash for repairs.		
9	Advertising Expense	300	
	Cash		300
	Paid cash for radio spot announcements.		
12	Automotive Expense	200	
	Cash		200
	Paid gas, oil, and service costs on the truck.		
14	Accounts Payable	3,000	
	Cash		3,000
	Paid $3,000 on account.		
16	Accounts Receivable	1,200	
	Service and Repair Revenue		1,200
	Repaired truck for Acme Drilling Company on account.		
18	Telephone Expense	75	
	Cash		75
	Paid for installation and telephone service for one month.		
19	Automotive Expense	180	
	Cash		180
	Paid for minor repairs on the truck.		
20	Cash	1,000	
	Notes Receivable	1,450	
	Service and Repair Revenue		2,450
	Collected $1,000 cash from Jones for truck repairs; accepted a 60-day note for the balance.		
24	Repairs and Maintenance Expense	150	
	Cash		150
	Paid cleaning and painting expenses on the building.		
25	Cash	1,500	
	Service and Repair Revenue		1,500
	Received cash for repairs and services from Hamilton, Inc.		
27	Supplies	2,500	
	Cash		2,500
	Purchased shop supplies.		
29	Office Equipment	1,250	
	Cash		1,250
	Purchased a computer.		
30	Cash	1,200	
	Accounts Receivable		1,200
	Collected receivables from Acme Drilling Company.		
31	Utilities Expense	900	
	Cash		900
	Paid the monthly utility bill.		
31	Automotive Expense	350	
	Cash		350
	Paid for gas, oil, and servicing of the truck.		

Required: Set up T-accounts, post all journal entries to the accounts, balance the accounts, and prepare a trial balance. From the trial balance, prepare an income statement and a balance sheet.

Solution The first step in solving this problem is to set up T-accounts for each item; then post all journal entries to the appropriate ledger accounts, as shown. Once the amounts are properly posted, account balances can be determined.

Cash

1/2	40,000	1/2	500
1/8	1,750	1/2	750
1/20	1,000	1/3	8,000
1/25	1,500	1/5	3,500
1/30	1,200	1/9	300
		1/12	200
		1/14	3,000
		1/18	75
		1/19	180
		1/24	150
		1/27	2,500
		1/29	1,250
		1/31	900
		1/31	350
Bal.	23,795		

Notes Receivable

1/20	1,450		

Accounts Receivable

1/16	1,200	1/30	1,200
Bal.	0		

Supplies

1/4	3,000		
1/27	2,500		
Bal.	5,500		

Shop Equipment

1/3	8,000		

Automotive Equipment

1/5	11,500		

Office Equipment

1/29	1,250		

Notes Payable

		1/5	8,000

Accounts Payable

1/14	3,000	1/4	3,000
		Bal.	0

Capital Stock

		1/2	40,000

Service and Repair Revenue

		1/8	1,750
		1/16	1,200
		1/20	2,450
		1/25	1,500
		Bal.	6,900

Insurance Expense

1/2	500		

Rent Expense

1/2	750		

Advertising Expense

1/9	300		

Automotive Expense

1/12	200		
1/19	180		
1/31	350		
Bal.	730		

Telephone Expense

1/18	75		

Repairs and Maintenance Expense

1/24	150		

Utilities Expense

1/31	900		

The final step is to prepare a trial balance to see whether total debits equal total credits for all accounts. List all the accounts with balances; then enter the balance in each account.

Svendsen Service Company
Trial Balance
January 31, 2000

	Debits	Credits
Cash	$23,795	
Accounts Receivable	0	
Notes Receivable	1,450	
Supplies	5,500	
Shop Equipment	8,000	
Automotive Equipment	11,500	
Office Equipment	1,250	
Accounts Payable		$ 0
Notes Payable		8,000
Capital Stock		40,000
Service and Repair Revenue		6,900
Insurance Expense	500	
Rent Expense	750	
Advertising Expense	300	
Automotive Expense	730	
Telephone Expense	75	
Repairs and Maintenance Expense	150	
Utilities Expense	900	
Totals	$54,900	$54,900

Svendsen Service Company
Income Statement
For the Month Ended January 31, 2000

Service and repair revenue		$6,900
Expenses:		
Insurance expense	$500	
Rent expense	750	
Advertising expense	300	
Automotive expense	730	
Telephone expense	75	
Repairs and maintenance expense	150	
Utilities expense	900	3,405
Net income		$3,495

Svendsen Service Company
Balance Sheet
January 31, 2000

Assets		
Cash	$23,795	
Accounts receivable	0	
Notes receivable	1,450	
Supplies	5,500	
Shop equipment	8,000	
Automotive equipment	11,500	
Office equipment	1,250	
Total assets		$51,495
Liabilities and Owners' Equity		
Accounts payable	$ 0	
Notes payable	8,000	
Total liabilities		$ 8,000
Capital stock	$40,000	
Retained earnings*	3,495	
Total owners' equity		43,495
Total liabilities and owners' equity		$51,495

*Retained earnings = Beginning balance + Net income − Dividends
= $0 + $3,495 − $0
= $3,495

DISCUSSION QUESTIONS

1. What is the basic objective of the accounting cycle?
2. Explain the first three steps in the accounting cycle.
3. What are the advantages of a computer-based accounting system? Does such a system eliminate the need for human judgment? Explain.
4. In a double-entry system of accounting, why must total debits always equal total credits?
5. Explain the increase/decrease, debit/credit relationship of asset, liability, and owners' equity accounts.
6. How are revenues, expenses, and dividends related to the basic accounting equation?
7. In what ways are dividend and expense accounts similar, and in what ways are they different?
8. Distinguish between a journal and a ledger.
9. Assume that Company A buys $1,500 of merchandise from Company B. The merchandise originally cost Company B $1,000. What entries should the buyer and seller make, and what is the relationship of the accounts for this transaction?
10. Indicate how each of the following transactions affects the accounting equation.
    a. Purchase of supplies on account.
    b. Payment of wages.
    c. Cash sales.
    d. Payment of monthly utility bills.
    e. Purchase of a building with a down payment of cash plus a mortgage.
    f. Cash investment by a stockholder.
    g. Payment of a cash dividend.
    h. Sale of goods on account for more than their cost.
    i. Sale of land at less than its cost.
11. What is a chart of accounts? What is its purpose?
12. If a trial balance appears to be correct (debits equal credits), does that guarantee complete accuracy in the accounting records? Explain.
13. Why are adjusting entries necessary?
14. Since there are usually no source documents for adjusting entries, how does the accountant know when to make adjusting entries and for what amounts?
15. Which are prepared first: the year-end financial statements or the general journal adjusting entries? Explain.
16. Of what value are the notes to the financial statements and the audit report, both of which are usually included in the annual report to shareholders?
17. Distinguish between real and nominal accounts.
18. What is the purpose of closing entries?
19. What is the purpose of the post-closing trial balance? Explain where the information for the post-closing trial balance comes from.

DISCUSSION CASES

CASE 3-1 HOW DOES MICROSOFT (AND OTHER COMPANIES) DO IT?

Microsoft's revenues exceeded $11 billion in 1997. These revenues were generated by millions of transactions all over the world—in the United States, Canada, Europe, South America, and Asia. What is the process used by Microsoft to transform this tremendous amount of transaction data into summarized information reported to the general public in the form of financial statements?

CASE 3-2 ADVANTAGES AND DISADVANTAGES OF A COMPUTERIZED ACCOUNTING SYSTEM

Your soon-to-be father-in law owns a small retail store. He has manually kept his business accounting records for over 20 years, but he is currently thinking about switching to a computerized accounting system. What advice would you give him about the advantages and the disadvantages of using a computerized accounting system?

CASE 3-3 WHEN IS A DEBIT A DEBIT?

Your new roommate, Susan, is confused. She has just received a notice from her bank indicating her account has been debited for the cost of new checks. This has reduced her cash account. Susan just learned in her introductory accounting class that debiting Cash increases the account. She wonders why the bank has reduced her account by debiting it. How can you help Susan understand this situation?

CASE 3-4

UNDERSTANDING THE MECHANICS OF ACCOUNTING

As the CFO (Chief Financial Officer) of Rollins Engineering Company, you are looking for someone to fill the position of office manager. Part of the job description is to maintain the company's accounting records. This means that the office manager must be able to journalize transactions, post them to the ledger accounts, and prepare monthly trial balances. You have just interviewed the first applicant, Jay McMahon, who claims that he has studied accounting. As an initial check on his understanding of the basic mechanics of accounting, you give Jay a list of accounts randomly ordered and with assumed balances and ask him to prepare a trial balance. Jay prepares the following.

Trial Balance

	Debits	Credits
Accounts Payable		$ 4,500
Salaries Expense		175,000
Consulting Revenues	$269,000	
Cash	82,100	
Utilities Expense	12,000	
Accounts Receivable		44,000
Supplies	11,000	
Rent Expense	30,000	
Capital Stock		77,000
Supplies Expense	33,000	
Office Equipment	15,000	
Retained Earnings		24,000
Other Expenses	6,400	
Salaries Payable	34,000	
Totals	$492,500	$324,500

Based solely on your assessment of Jay McMahon's understanding of accounting, would you hire him as office manager? Explain. Prepare a corrected trial balance that you can use as a basis for your discussion with Jay and future applicants. Explain how the basic accounting equation and the system of double-entry accounting provide a check on the accounting records.

CASE 3-5

WRESTLING WITH YOUR CONSCIENCE AND GAAP

You are the controller for South Valley Industries. Your assistant has just completed the financial statements for the current year and has given them to you for review. A copy of the statements also has been given to the president of the company. The income statement reports a net income for the year of $50,000 and earnings per share of $2.50.

In reviewing the statements, you realize that the assistant neglected to record adjusting entries. After making the necessary adjustments, the company shows a net loss of $10,000. The difference is due to an unusually large amount of unrecorded expenses at year-end. You realize that these expenses are not likely to be found by the independent auditors.

You wonder if it would be better to delay the recording of the expenses until the first part of the subsequent year in order to avoid reporting a net loss on the income statement for the current year. A significant increase in revenues is expected in the coming year and the expenses in question could be "absorbed" by the higher revenues.

What issues are involved in this case? What course of action would you take?

EXERCISES

EXERCISE 3-1
Basic Accounting Equation

The fundamental accounting equation can be applied to your personal finances. For each of the following transactions, show how the accounting equation would be kept in balance. Example: Paid for semester's tuition (decrease assets: cash account; decrease owners' equity: expense account increases).

1. Took out a school loan for college.
2. Paid this month's rent.
3. Sold your old computer for cash at no gain or loss.
4. Received week's paycheck from part-time job.
5. Received interest payment on savings account.
6. Paid monthly payment on car loan (part of the payment is principal; the remainder is interest).

EXERCISE 3-2
Accounting Elements: Increase/Decrease, Debit/Credit Relationships

The text describes the following accounting elements: assets, liabilities, owners' equity, capital stock, retained earnings, revenues, expenses, and dividends. Which of these elements are increased by a debit entry, and which are increased by a credit entry? Give a transaction for each item that would result in a net increase in its balance.

EXERCISE 3-3
Expanded Accounting Equation

Payless Department Store had the following transactions during the year:

1. Purchased inventory on account.
2. Sold merchandise for cash, assuming a profit on the sale.
3. Borrowed money from a bank.
4. Purchased land, making cash down payment and issuing a note for the balance.
5. Issued stock for cash.
6. Paid salaries for the year.
7. Paid a vendor for inventory purchased on account.
8. Sold a building for cash and notes receivable at no gain or loss.
9. Paid cash dividends to stockholders.
10. Paid utilities.

Using the following column headings, identify the accounts involved and indicate the net effect of each transaction on the accounting equation (+ increase; − decrease; 0 no effect). Transaction 1 has been completed as an example.

Transaction	Assets	=	Liabilities	+	Owners' Equity
1	+ (Inventory)		+ (Accounts Payable)		0

EXERCISE 3-4
Classification of Accounts

For each of the accounts listed, indicate whether it is an asset (A), a liability (L), or an owners' equity (OE) account. If it is an account that affects owners' equity, indicate whether it is a revenue (R), or expense (E) account.

1. Cash
2. Sales
3. Accounts Receivable
4. Cost of Goods Sold
5. Insurance Expense
6. Capital Stock
7. Mortgage Payable
8. Salaries and Wages Expense
9. Retained Earnings
10. Salaries Payable
11. Accounts Payable
12. Interest Revenue
13. Inventory
14. Interest Receivable
15. Notes Payable
16. Equipment
17. Office Supplies
18. Utilities Expense
19. Interest Payable
20. Rent Expense

EXERCISE 3-5
Normal Account Balances

For each account listed in Exercise 3-4, indicate whether it would normally have a debit (DR) balance or a credit (CR) balance.

EXERCISE 3-6
Journalizing Transactions

Record each of the following transactions in Guerrero's General Journal. (Omit explanations.)

1. Issued capital stock for $50,000 cash.
2. Borrowed $10,000 from a bank. Signed a note to secure the debt.
3. Purchased inventory from a supplier on credit for $8,000.
4. Paid the supplier for the inventory purchased in (3) above.
5. Sold inventory that cost $1,200 for $1,500 on credit.
6. Collected $1,500 from customers.
7. Paid salaries and rent of $25,000 and $1,200, respectively.

EXERCISE 3-7
Journal Entries

During June 2000, Husky Inc. completed the following transactions. Prepare the journal entry for each transaction.

June 1 Received $200,000 for 2,000 shares of capital stock.
2 Purchased $50,000 of equipment, paying 25 percent for cash and 75 percent on a note payable.
5 Paid utilities of $1,500 in cash.
9 Sold equipment for $25,000 cash (no gain or loss).
13 Purchased $100,000 of inventory, paying 50 percent for cash and 50 percent for credit.
14 Paid $5,000 cash insurance premium for June.
15 Sold inventory costing $30,000 for $45,000 to customers on account to be paid at a later date.
20 Collected $3,000 from accounts receivable.
24 Sold inventory costing $50,000 for $69,500 to customers for cash.
25 Paid yearly property taxes of $2,000.
30 Paid $50,000 of accounts payable for inventory purchased on June 13.

EXERCISE 3-8
Posting Journal Entries

Post the journal entires prepared in Exercise 3-7 to T-accounts, and determine the final balance for each account. (Assume all beginning account balances are zero.)

EXERCISE 3-9
Journalizing and Posting Transactions

Given the following T-accounts, describe the transaction that took place on each specified date during July:

Cash

7/5	9,500	7/1	3,420
7/28	8,000	7/23	2,000
		7/25	5,000
		7/30	5,500
Bal.	1,580		

Accounts Receivable

7/14	18,000	7/5	9,500
		7/28	8,000
Bal.	500		

Inventory

7/10	20,000	7/14	15,000
Bal.	5,000		

Equipment

7/30	1,500		

Land

7/30	4,000		

Accounts Payable

7/25	5,000	7/10	20,000
		Bal.	15,000

Sales Revenue

		7/14	18,000

Cost of Goods Sold

7/14	15,000		

Rent Expense

7/23	2,000		

Advertising Expense

7/1	3,420		

EXERCISE 3-10
Trial Balance

The account balances from the ledger of Yakamoto Inc. as of July 31, 2000, are listed here in alphabetical order. The balance for Retained Earnings has been omitted. Prepare a trial balance, and insert the missing amount for Retained Earnings.

Accounts Payable	$ 8,600	Fees Earned	$26,000
Accounts Receivable	2,000	Insurance Expense	3,600
Buildings	20,000	Land	19,000
Capital Stock	10,000	Miscellaneous Expenses	1,400
Retained Earnings	?	Mortgage Payable (due 2003)	24,000
Cash	19,600	Salary Expense	10,000
Rent Expense	3,000	Supplies	600
Equipment	16,000	Utilities Expense	400

EXERCISE 3-11
Relationships of the Expanded Accounting Equation

Domino, Inc., had the following information reported. From these data, determine the amount of:

1. Capital stock at December 31, 1999.
2. Retained earnings at December 31, 2000.
3. Revenues for the year 2000.

	December 31, 1999	December 31, 2000
Total assets	$250,000	$300,000
Total liabilities	60,000	70,000
Capital stock	?	50,000
Retained earnings	150,000	?
Revenues for 2000		?
Expenses for 2000		205,000
Dividends paid during 2000		5,000

EXERCISE 3-12
Adjusting Entries

Boswell Group is a professional corporation providing management consulting services. Give the entry that Boswell would use to record each of the following transactions on the date it occurred. Prepare the adjusting entries needed on December 31, 2000.

1. On July 1, 2000, the company paid a 3-year premium of $7,200 on an insurance policy that is effective July 1, 2000, and expires June 30, 2003.
2. On February 1, 2000, Boswell paid its property taxes for the year February 1, 2000 to January 31, 2001. The tax bill was $1,800.
3. On May 1, 2000, the company paid $180 for a 3-year subscription to an advertising journal. The subscription starts May 1, 2000, and expires April 30, 2003.
4. Boswell received $1,800 on September 15, 2000, in return for which the company agreed to provide consulting services for 18 months beginning immediately.
5. Boswell rented part of its office space to Bristle Brush Company. Bristle paid $1,200 on November 1, 2000, for the next six months' rent.
6. Boswell loaned $100,000 to a client. On November 1 the client paid $24,000, which represents two years' interest in advance (November 1, 2000 through October 31, 2002).

EXERCISE 3-13
Adjusting Entries

Shop Rite Services is ready to prepare its financial statements for the year ended December 31, 2000. The following information can be determined by analyzing the accounts:

1. On August 1, 2000, Shop Rite received a $4,800 payment in advance for rental of office space. The rental period is for one year beginning on the date payment was received. Shop Rite recorded the receipt as unearned rent.
2. On March 1, 2000, Shop Rite paid its insurance agent $3,000 for the premium due on a 24-month corporate policy. Shop Rite recorded the payment as prepaid insurance.
3. Shop Rite pays its employee wages the middle of each month. The monthly payroll (ignoring payroll taxes) is $22,000.

4. Shop Rite received a note from a customer on June 1, 2000, as payment for services. The amount of the note is $1,000 with interest at 12%. The note and interest will be paid on June 1, 2002.
5. On December 20, 2000, Shop Rite received a $2,500 check for services. The transaction was recorded as unearned revenue. By year-end, Shop Rite had completed three-fourths of the contracted services. The rest of the services won't be completed until at least the middle of January 2001.
6. On September 1, Shop Rite purchased $500 worth of supplies. At December 31, 2000, one-fourth of the supplies had been used. Shop Rite initially recorded the purchase of supplies as an asset.

Where appropriate, prepare adjusting journal entries at December 31, 2000, for each of these items.

EXERCISE 3-14
Real and Nominal Accounts

Classify each of the following accounts as either a real account (R) or a nominal account (N):

1. Cash
2. Sales Revenue
3. Accounts Receivable
4. Cost of Goods Sold
5. Prepaid Insurance
6. Capital Stock
7. Retained Earnings
8. Insurance Expense
9. Salaries Payable
10. Interest Expense
11. Insurance Premiums Payable
12. Salaries Expense
13. Accounts Payable
14. Prepaid Salaries
15. Utilities Expense
16. Notes Payable
17. Inventory
18. Property Tax Expense
19. Rent Expense
20. Interest Payable
21. Income Taxes Payable
22. Dividends
23. Buildings
24. Office Supplies
25. Income Tax Expense

EXERCISE 3-15
Closing Entry

Revenue and expense accounts of Rushford Publishing Co. for November 30, 2000, are given below. Prepare a compound journal entry that will close the revenue and expense accounts to the retained earnings account.

	Debits	Credits
Sales Revenue		$250,500
Cost of Goods Sold	$124,500	
Salaries Expense	35,000	
Interest Expense	1,000	
Rent Expense	9,300	
Insurance Expense	1,700	
Property Tax Expense	800	
Supplies Expense	1,000	
Advertising Expense	10,000	

EXERCISE 3-16
Closing Dividends and Preparing a Post-Closing Trial Balance

Below is a listing of account balances taken from the adjusted ledger account balances of Goldsmith Corporation.

Cash	$25,500
Accounts Receivable	24,000
Inventory	60,000
Prepaid Advertising	5,500
Building	95,000
Land	35,000
Accounts Payable	20,000
Wages Payable	5,000
Income Taxes Payable	4,000
Mortgage Payable	55,000
Notes Payable	27,500
Unearned Rent	2,500
Capital Stock	95,500
Dividends	15,500
Retained Earnings	51,000

All revenues and expense accounts have been closed to Retained Earnings. Dividends has not yet been closed.

Prepare (1) the closing entry for Dividends and (2) a post-closing trial balance for December 31, 2000.

PROBLEMS

PROBLEM 3-1
Journal Entries and Trial Balance

As of January 1, 2000, Kendrick Corp. had the following balances in its general ledger:

	Debits	Credits
Cash	$ 31,500	
Accounts Receivable	23,500	
Inventory	92,000	
Office Building	208,000	
Accounts Payable		$ 16,500
Mortgage Payable		180,000
Notes Payable		68,500
Capital Stock		57,500
Retained Earnings		32,500
Totals	$355,000	$355,000

Kendrick had the following transactions during 2000. All expenses were paid in cash, unless otherwise stated.

a. Accounts payable as of January 1, 2000, were paid off.
b. Purchased inventory for $35,000 cash.
c. Collected $21,000 of receivables.
d. Sold $185,000 of merchandise, 85 percent for cash and 15 percent for credit. The cost of goods sold was $98,500.
e. Paid $25,000 mortgage payment, of which $15,000 represents interest expense.
f. Paid salaries expense of $60,000.
g. Paid utilities of $6,300.
h. Paid installment of $5,000 on note.

Required:

1. Prepare journal entries to record each listed transaction. (Omit explanations.)
2. Set up T-accounts with the proper account balances at January 1, 2000, and post the journal entries to the T-accounts and prepare a trial balance for Kendrick Corp. at December 31, 2000.
3. **Interpretive Question:** If the debit and credit columns of the trial balance are in balance, does this mean that no errors have been made in journalizing the transactions? Explain.

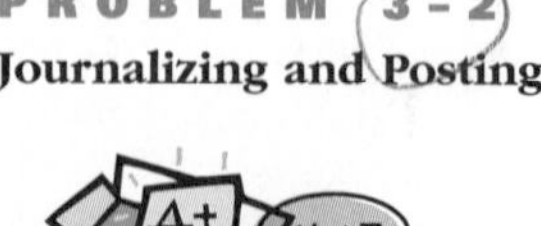

PROBLEM 3-2
Journalizing and Posting

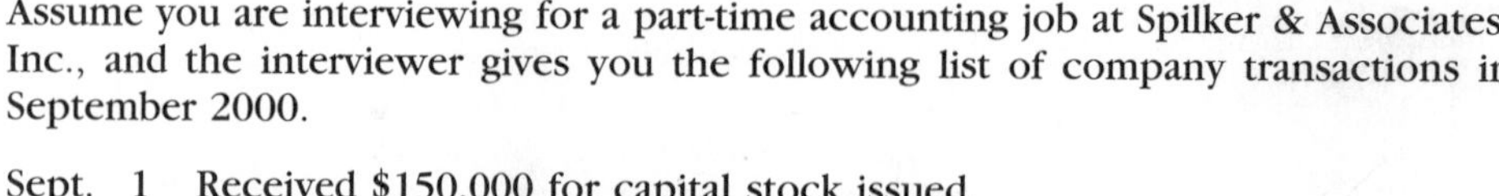

Assume you are interviewing for a part-time accounting job at Spilker & Associates, Inc., and the interviewer gives you the following list of company transactions in September 2000.

Sept. 1 Received $150,000 for capital stock issued.
2 Paid $20,000 cash to employees for wages earned in September 2000.
4 Purchased $75,000 of running shoes and clothing on account for resale.
5 Paid utilities of $1,800 for September 2000.
9 Paid $1,500 cash for September's insurance premium.
11 Sold inventory of running shoes and clothing costing $35,000 for $70,000, with $20,000 received in cash and the remaining balance on credit.
15 Purchased $2,500 of supplies on account.
21 Received $25,000 from customers as payments on their accounts.
25 Paid $75,000 of accounts payable.

Required:

1. Journalize each of the transactions for September. (Omit explanations.)
2. Set up T-accounts, and post each of the journal entries made in (1).
3. **Interpretive Question:** If the business owners wanted to know at any given time how much cash the company had, where would you tell the owners to look? Why?

PROBLEM 3-3
Journal Entries from Ledger Analysis

T-accounts for RAM Technology, Inc., are shown below.

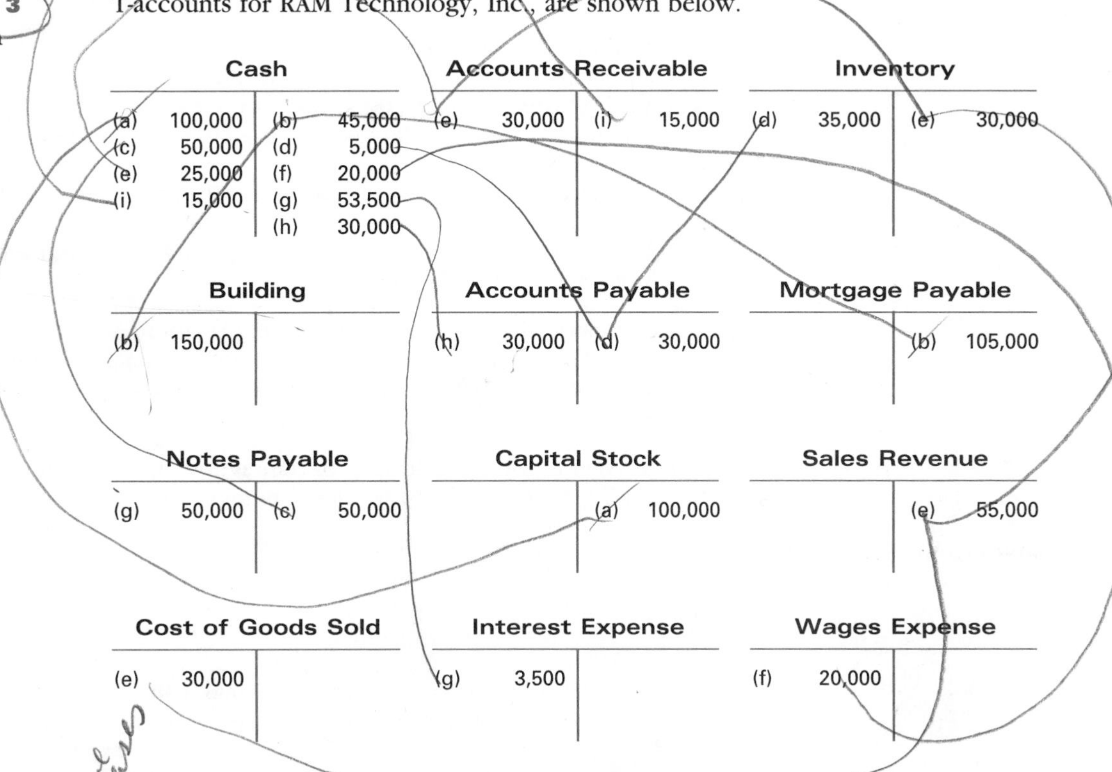

Cash

(a)	100,000	(b)	45,000
(c)	50,000	(d)	5,000
(e)	25,000	(f)	20,000
(i)	15,000	(g)	53,500
		(h)	30,000

Accounts Receivable

(e)	30,000	(i)	15,000

Inventory

(d)	35,000	(e)	30,000

Building

(b)	150,000		

Accounts Payable

(h)	30,000	(d)	30,000

Mortgage Payable

		(b)	105,000

Notes Payable

(g)	50,000	(c)	50,000

Capital Stock

		(a)	100,000

Sales Revenue

		(e)	55,000

Cost of Goods Sold

(e)	30,000		

Interest Expense

(g)	3,500		

Wages Expense

(f)	20,000		

Required:

1. Analyze these accounts and detail the appropriate journal entries that must have been made by RAM Technology, Inc. (Omit explanations.)
2. Determine the amount of net income/loss from the account information.

PROBLEM 3-4
Journalizing and Posting Transactions

Pat Bjornson, owner of Pat's Beauty Supply, completed the following business transactions during March 2000.

Mar.	1	Purchased $53,000 of inventory on credit.
	4	Collected $5,000 from customers as payments on their accounts.
	5	Purchased equipment for $3,000 cash.
	6	Sold inventory that cost $30,000 to customers on account for $40,000.
	10	Paid rent for March, $1,050.
	15	Paid utilities for March, $100.
	17	Paid a $300 monthly salary to the part-time helper.
	20	Collected $33,000 from customers as payments on their accounts.
	22	Paid $53,000 cash on account payable. (See March 1 entry.)
	25	Paid property taxes of $1,200.
	28	Sold inventory that cost $20,000 to customers for $30,000 cash.

Required:

1. For each transaction, give the entry to record it in the company's general journal. (Omit explanations.)
2. Set up T-accounts, and post the journal entries to their appropriate accounts.

PROBLEM 3-5
Unifying Concepts: Compound Journal Entries, Posting, Trial Balance

J&W Merchandise Company had the following transactions during 2000.

a. Sam Jeakins began business by investing the following assets, receiving capital stock in exchange:

Cash	$ 20,000
Inventory	37,000
Land	25,500
Building	160,000
Equipment	12,500*
Totals	$255,000

*A note of $5,000 on the equipment was assumed by the company.

b. Sold merchandise that cost $30,000 for $45,000; $15,000 cash was received immediately and the other $30,000 will be collected in 30 days.
c. Paid off the note of $5,000 plus $300 interest.
d. Purchased merchandise costing $12,000, paying $2,000 cash and issuing a note for $10,000.
e. Exchanged $2,000 cash and $8,000 in capital stock for office equipment costing $10,000.
f. Purchased a truck for $15,000 with $3,000 down and a one-year note for the balance.

Required:

1. Journalize the transactions. (Omit explanations.)
2. Post the journal entries using T-accounts for each account.
3. Prepare a trial balance at December 31, 2000.

PROBLEM 3-6
Unifying Concepts: T-Accounts, Trial Balance, and Income Statement

The following list is a selection of transactions from Trafalga Inc.'s business activities during 2000, the first year of operations.

a. Received $50,000 cash for capital stock.
b. Paid $5,000 cash for equipment.
c. Purchased inventory costing $18,000 on account.
d. Sold $25,000 of merchandise to customers on account. Cost of goods sold was $15,000.
e. Signed a note with a bank for a $10,000 loan.
f. Collected $9,500 cash from customers who had purchased merchandise on account.
g. Purchased land, $10,000, and a building, $60,000, for $15,000 cash and a 30-year mortgage of $55,000.
h. Made a first payment of $2,750 on the mortgage principal plus $2,750 in interest.
i. Paid $12,000 of accounts payable.
j. Purchased $1,500 of supplies on account
k. Paid $2,500 of accounts payable.
l. Paid $7,500 in wages earned during the year.
m. Received $10,000 cash and $3,000 of notes in settlement of customers' accounts.
n. Received $3,000 in payment of a note receivable plus interest of $250.
o. Paid $600 cash for a utility bill.
p. Sold excess land for its cost of $3,000.
q. Received $1,500 in rent for an unused part of a building.
r. Paid off $10,000 note, plus interest of $1,200.

Required:

1. Set up T-accounts, and appropriately record the debits and credits for each transaction. Leave room for a number of entries in the cash account.
2. Prepare a trial balance.
3. Prepare an income statement for the period. (Ignore income taxes and the EPS computation.)

PROBLEM 3-7
Correcting a Trial Balance

The trial balance at the top of the following page was prepared by a new employee.

Required:

Prepare the corrected company trial balance. (Assume all accounts have "normal" balances and the recorded amounts are correct.)

Trial Balance
Alden Company, Inc.
For Year Ended November 30, 2000

	Credits	Debits
Cash	$ 18,250	
Mortgage Payable		$ 78,900
Advertising Expense	9,600	
Capital Stock		102,000
Equipment	36,900	
Notes Payable		187,350
Inventory	148,000	
Wages Expense	87,150	
Notes Receivable	5,000	
Accounts Payable		19,750
Accounts Receivable		5,300
Rent Expense		8,750
Wages Payable	9,000	
Furniture		15,000
Other Expenses	2,950	
Sales Revenue		235,600
Buildings	104,700	
Cost of Goods Sold	113,050	
Property Tax Expense		1,300
Land		87,850
Retained Earnings		14,400
Utilties Expense	3,200	
Totals	$537,800	$756,200

PROBLEM 3-8
Unifying Concepts: First Steps in the Accounting Cycle

The following balances were taken from the general ledger of Benson Company on January 1, 2000:

	Debits	Credits
Cash	$13,500	
Short-Term Investments	10,000	
Accounts Receivable	12,500	
Inventory	15,000	
Land	25,000	
Buildings	75,000	
Equipment	20,000	
Notes Payable		$17,500
Accounts Payable		12,500
Salaries and Wages Payable		2,500
Mortgage Payable		37,500
Capital Stock (7,000 shares outstanding)		70,000
Retained Earnings		31,000

During 2000, the company completed the following transactions:

a. Purchased inventory for $110,000 on credit.
b. Issued an additional $25,000 of capital stock (2,500 shares) for cash.
c. Paid property taxes of $4,500 for the year 2000.
d. Paid advertising and other selling expenses of $8,000.
e. Paid utilities expenses of $6,500 for 2000.
f. Paid the salaries and wages owed for 1999. Paid additional salaries and wages of $18,000 during 2000.
g. Sold merchandise costing $105,000 for $175,000. Of total sales, $45,000 were cash sales and $130,000 were credit sales.
h. Paid off notes of $17,500 plus interest of $1,600.
i. On November 1, 2000, received a loan of $10,000 from the bank.

j. On December 30, 2000, made annual mortgage payment of $2,500 and paid interest of $3,700.
k. Collected receivables for the year of $140,000.
l. Paid off accounts payable of $112,500.
m. Received dividends and interest of $1,400 on short-term investments during 2000. (Record as Miscellaneous Revenue.)
n. Purchased additional short-term investments of $15,000 during 2000. (Note: Short-term investments are current assets.)
o. Paid 2000 corporate income taxes of $11,600.
p. Paid cash dividends of $7,600.

Required:

1. Journalize the 2000 transactions. (Omit explanations.)
2. Set up T-accounts with the proper account balances at January 1, 2000, and post the journal entries to the T-accounts.
3. Determine the account balances, and prepare a trial balance at December 31, 2000.
4. Prepare an income statement and a balance sheet. (Remember that the dividends account and all revenue and expense accounts are temporary retained earnings accounts.)
5. **Interpretive Question:** Why are revenue and expense accounts used at all?

PROBLEM 3-9
Adjusting Entries

The information presented below is for Sun Marketing, Inc.

a. Salaries for the period December 26, 2000, through December 31, 2000, amounted to $14,240 and have not been recorded or paid. (Ignore payroll taxes.)
b. Interest of $6,000 is payable for three months on a 15 percent, $160,000 loan and has not been recorded.
c. Rent of $24,000 was paid for six months in advance on December 1 and debited to Prepaid Rent.
d. Rent of $82,000 was credited to an unearned revenue account when received. Of this amount, $33,400 is still unearned at year-end.
e. The expired portion of an insurance policy is $1,000. Prepaid Insurance was originally debited.
f. Interest revenue of $300 from a $2,000 note has been earned but not collected or recorded.

Required:

Prepare the adjusting entries that should be made on December 31, 2000. (Omit explanations.)

PROBLEM 3-10
Account Classifications and Debit-Credit Relationships

Using the format provided, for each account identify (1) whether the account is a balance sheet (B/S) or an income statement (I/S) account; (2) whether it is an asset (A), a liability (L), an owners' equity (OE), a revenue (R), or an expense (E) account; (3) whether the account is a real or a nominal account; (4) whether the account will be "closed" or left "open" at year-end; and (5) whether the account normally has a debit or a credit balance. The following example is provided:

Account Title	(1) B/S or I/S	(2) A, L, OE, R, E	(3) Real or Nominal	(4) Closed or Open	(5) Debit/ Credit
Cash	B/S	A	Real	Open	Debit

1. Accounts Receivable
2. Accounts Payable
3. Prepaid Insurance
4. Mortgage Payable
5. Rent Expense
6. Sales Revenue
7. Cost of Goods Sold
8. Dividends
9. Capital Stock
10. Inventory
11. Retained Earnings
12. Prepaid Rent
13. Supplies on Hand
14. Utilities Expense
15. Income Taxes Payable
16. Interest Revenue
17. Notes Payable
18. Income Tax Expense
19. Wages Payable
20. Unearned Rent Revenue
21. Land
22. Unearned Consulting Fees
23. Interest Receivable
24. Consulting Fees

PROBLEM 3-11
Unifying Concepts: Analysis of Accounts

The bookkeeper for Careless Company accidentally pressed the wrong computer key and erased the amount of Retained Earnings. You have been asked to analyze the following data and provide some key numbers for the board of directors meeting, which is to take place in 30 minutes. With the exception of Retained Earnings, the following account balances are available at December 31, 2000.

Cash	$122,000	Accounts Receivable	$ 98,000
Furniture (net)	80,000	Inventory	320,000
Accounts Payable	240,000	Notes Payable	500,000
Land	520,000	Supplies on Hand	20,000
Buildings (net)	480,000	Capital Stock	600,000
Sales Revenue	830,000	Dividends	40,000
Salaries Expense	100,000	Retained Earnings	?
Cost of Goods Sold	440,000		

Required:

1. Compute the amount of total assets at December 31, 2000.
2. Compute the amount of net income for the year ended December 31, 2000.
3. After all closing entries are made, what is the amount of Retained Earnings at December 31, 2000.
4. What was the beginning Retained Earnings balance at January 1, 2000?

Analyzing Real Company Information

International Case

Ethics Case

Writing Assignment

The Debate

Internet Search

Accounting is more than just doing textbook problems. These Competency Enhancement Opportunities provide practice in critical thinking, oral and written communication, research, teamwork, and consideration of ethical issues.

ANALYZING REAL COMPANY INFORMATION

• Analyzing 3-1 (Microsoft)

The 1997 annual report for Microsoft is included in Appendix A. Locate that annual report and consider the following questions:

1. Find Microsoft's 1997 income statement. Assume that research and development expenditures were paid for in cash. What journal entry did Microsoft make in 1997 to record research and development?
2. Find Microsoft's 1997 cash flow statement. What journal entry did Microsoft make in 1997 to record the issuance of common stock?
3. Again, looking at the cash flow statement—what journal entry did Microsoft make in 1997 to record the purchase of property, plant, and equipment?
4. Using information from the cash flow statement, re-create the journal entry Microsoft made in 1997 to record the purchase of short-term investments. Comment on the change in the balance of the short-term investments account between the beginning of 1997 and the end of 1997.

• Analyzing 3-2 (McDonald's)

A brief history of the origin of the **McDonald's Corporation** is given at the start of this chapter. The following questions are adapted from information appearing in McDonald's 1996 annual report.

1. In 1996, total sales at all McDonald's stores worldwide were $31.8 billion. There were 21,000 McDonald's stores operating in 1996. *Estimate* how many customers per day visit an average McDonald's store.
2. For the stores owned by the McDonald's Corporation (as opposed to those owned by franchisees), total sales in 1996 were $7.571 billion, and total cost of food and packaging was $2.547 billion. What journal entries would McDonald's make to record a $10 sale and to record the cost of food and packaging associated with the $10 sale?
3. McDonald's reported payment of cash dividends of $232 million in 1996. What journal entry was required?
4. McDonald's reported that the total income tax it owed for 1996 was $645.5 million. However, only $558.1 million in cash was paid for taxes during the year. What compound journal entry did McDonald's make to record its income tax expense for the year?

INTERNATIONAL CASE

• Shanghai Petrochemical Company Limited

In July 1993, **Shanghai Petrochemical Company Limited** became the first company organized under the laws of the Peoples' Republic of China to publicly issue its shares on the worldwide market. Shanghai Petrochemical's shares now trade on the stock exchanges in Shanghai, Hong Kong, and New York. The following questions are adapted from information appearing in Shanghai Petrochemical's 1995 annual report.

1. In 1995, Shanghai Petrochemical reported sales of 11.835 billion renminbi (US$ 1 = 8.33 RMB) and cost of sales of RMB 9.016 billion. Make the necessary journal entries, using renminbi as the currency.
2. In 1995, Shanghai Petrochemical declared cash dividends of RMB 851.5 million. However, cash paid for dividends during the year was only RMB 818.8 million. Make the necessary compound journal entry to record the declaration and payment of cash dividends for the year.
3. In China, a 17% value added tax (VAT) is added to the invoiced value of all sales. This VAT is collected by the seller from the buyer and then held to be forwarded to the government. What journal entry would Shanghai Petrochemical make to record the sale, on account, of crude oil with an invoice sales value of $100 and a cost of $70?

ETHICS CASE

• Should you go the extra mile?

You work in a small convenience store. The store is very low-tech; you ring up the sales on an old-style cash register that merely records the amount of the sale. The store owner uses this cash register tape at the end of each day to verify that the correct amount of cash is in the cash register drawer. On a day-to-day basis, no other financial information is collected about store operations.

Since you started studying accounting, you have become a bit uneasy about your job because you see many ways that store operations could be improved through the gathering and use of financial information. Even though you are not an expert, you are quite certain that you could help the store owner set up an improved information system. However, you also know that this will take extra effort on your part, with no real possibility of receiving an increase in pay.

Should you say anything to the store owner, or should you just keep quiet and save yourself the trouble?

WRITING ASSIGNMENT

• Accounting is everywhere!

Financial accounting information is frequently used in newspaper and magazine articles to provide background data on companies. Prepare a one-page report on the use of financial accounting data by the press. Proceed as follows:

1. Scan the articles in a recent copy of one of the popular business periodicals (such as *The Wall Street Journal, Forbes, Fortune,* or *Business Week*) for examples of the use of financial accounting data.
2. Identify and describe three interesting examples:
   - Detail the nature of the accounting data used.
   - Outline the point that the writer is trying to make by using the particular accounting data.

THE DEBATE

• Are computers the hero or the villain?

Computers have changed the way we think about information. When accounting was done by hand, it was not possible to match individual sales with specific products, specific customers, the exact time of day of the sale, the income level of the customer, the customer's favorite TV shows and magazines, etc. In short, computers have made it possible to use the raw financial data to track much more than just revenues and expenses. How far should the use of computers go?

Divide your group into two teams.

- One team represents the computer technology group, "To Infinity, and Beyond!" Prepare a two-minute oral presentation supporting the notion that firms have a right to use their computer database systems to gather as much information about customers as possible, and even to sell that information to other firms. Now is the Information Age, and computers have made it possible to easily buy and sell information just like any other commodity.
- The other team represents "Right to Privacy." Prepare a two-minute oral presentation arguing that firms have no right to maintain databases containing individual customer information. A company's information system should relate to that company's products and processes, and customers have the right to interact with the firm anonymously.

INTERNET SEARCH

• McDonald's

Access **McDonald's** Web site at mcdonalds.com. Sometimes Web addresses change, so if this McDonald's address doesn't work, access the Web site for this textbook (stice.swcollege.com) for an updated link to McDonald's.

Once you've gained access to McDonald's Web site, answer the following questions:

1. Which has more calories—two hamburgers or one Big Mac?
2. How much money do you need to purchase a McDonald's franchise in the United States? What else is required to purchase a franchise?
3. Sometimes it isn't easy to find a company's financial statements in its Web site. Describe what you had to do to find a copy of McDonald's most recent annual report.
4. What information is contained in McDonald's most recent financial press release?

CHAPTER

OPERATING ACTIVITIES—INFLOWS 4

LEARNING OBJECTIVES

After studying this chapter, you should be able to:

1. *Understand the three basic types of business activities: operating, investing, and financing.*
2. *Use the two revenue recognition criteria to decide when the revenue from a sale or service should be recorded in the accounting records.*
3. *Properly account for the collection of cash and describe the business controls necessary to safeguard cash.*
4. *Record the losses resulting from credit customers who do not pay their bills.*
5. *Evaluate a company's management of its receivables by computing and analyzing appropriate financial ratios.*
6. *Match revenues and expenses by estimating and recording future warranty and service costs associated with a sale.*

SETTING THE STAGE

ZZZZ Best was a Los Angeles-based company specializing in carpet cleaning and insurance restoration.[1] Prior to allegations of fraud, and its declaration of bankruptcy in 1988, ZZZZ Best was touted as one of the hottest stocks on Wall Street. In 1987, after only six years in business, the company had a market valuation exceeding $211 million, giving its "genius" president a paper fortune of $109 million. Lawsuits, however, alleged that the company was nothing more than a massive fraud scheme that fooled major banks, two CPA firms, an investment banker, and a prestigious law firm.

ZZZZ Best was started as a carpet-cleaning business by Barry Minkow, a 15-year-old high-school student, in 1981. Although ZZZZ Best had impressive growth as a carpet-cleaning business, the growth was not nearly fast enough for the impatient Minkow. In 1985, ZZZZ Best reported that it was expanding into the insurance restoration business, restoring buildings that had been damaged by fire, floods, and other disasters. During 1985 and 1986, ZZZZ Best reported undertaking several large insurance restoration projects. The company reported high profits from these restoration jobs. A public stock offering in 1986 stated that 86 percent of ZZZZ Best Corporation's business was in the insurance restoration area.

Based on the company's high growth and reported income in 1987, a spokesperson for a large brokerage house was quoted in *Business Week* as saying that "Barry Minkow is a great manager and ZZZZ Best is a great company." He recommended that his clients buy ZZZZ Best stock. That same year, the Association of Collegiate Entrepreneurs and the Young Entrepreneurs' Organization placed Minkow on their list of the top 100 young entrepreneurs in America; and the mayor of Los Angeles honored Minkow with a commendation that said that Minkow had "set a fine entrepreneurial example of obtaining the status of a millionaire at the age of 18."

1. This description is based on articles in *The Wall Street Journal, Forbes,* and investigative proceedings of the U.S. House of Representatives, Subcommittee on Energy and Commerce hearings: *The Wall Street Journal,* July 7, 1987, p. 1; July 9, 1987, p. 1; August 23, 1988, p. 1; U.S. House of Representatives, Subcommittee on Oversight and Investigation of the Committee on Energy and Commerce, January 27, 1988; U.S. House of Representatives, Subcommittee on Oversight and Investigation of the Committee on Energy and Commerce, February 1, 1988; Daniel Akst, "How Barry Minkow Fooled the Auditors," *Forbes,* October 2, 1989, p. 126.

Unfortunately, ZZZZ Best's insurance business, its impressive growth, and its high reported income were totally fictitious. In fact, the company never once made a legitimate profit. Barry Minkow himself later said that he was a "fraudster" who convincingly deceived almost everyone involved with the company. Through the use of widespread collusion among company officials, Minkow was even able to hide the fraud from ZZZZ Best's external auditor. For example, when ZZZZ Best reported an $8.2 million contract to restore a building in San Diego, the external auditor demanded to see the building; this was difficult since neither the building nor the job existed. However, officials of ZZZZ Best gained access to a construction site and led the auditor through a tour of an unfinished building in San Diego to show that the "restoration" work was ongoing. The situation became very complicated for ZZZZ Best when the auditor later requested to see the finished job. ZZZZ Best had to spend $1 million to lease the building and hire contractors to finish six of the eight floors in ten days. The auditor was led on another tour and wrote a memo saying, "Job looks very good." The auditor was subsequently faulted for looking only at what ZZZZ Best officials chose to show, without making independent inquiries.

Minkow's house of cards finally came crashing down as it became apparent to banks, suppliers, investors, and the auditors that the increasing difficulty ZZZZ Best was having with paying its bills was entirely inconsistent with a company reporting so much revenue and profit. In January 1988, a federal grand jury in Los Angeles returned a 57-count indictment, charging 11 individuals—including ZZZZ Best founder and president, Barry Minkow—with engaging in a massive fraud scheme. Barry Minkow was later convicted and sentenced to 25 years in a federal penitentiary in Colorado.

ZZZZ Best was able to report high revenue and high income because Barry Minkow knew the power of a very simple journal entry: debit Accounts Receivable and credit Sales Revenue. In this chapter, you will study the accounting rules governing the proper recognition of revenue. You will also learn how to account for cash collections and how to handle customer accounts that are uncollectible. Selling goods and services, collecting the cash, and handling customer accounts are fundamental to the operation of any business. Accordingly, properly recording these activities is fundamental to the practice of accounting.

1 *Understand the three basic types of business activities: operating, investing, and financing.*

MAJOR ACTIVITIES OF A BUSINESS

In the first three chapters, you were introduced to the accounting environment, the basic financial statements, and the accounting cycle (the way business transactions are entered into the accounting records). That material was necessary for you to understand some basic terminology and procedures used in accounting. Accounting has often been called the language of business. By studying the first three chapters, you should now be somewhat familiar with this new business language.

With the basics behind us, it is now time to use accounting to understand how businesses work, how the various activities of business are accounted for, and how businesses report their operating results to investors. The activities of most businesses can be divided into three groups:

- operating activities
- investing activities
- financing activities

operating activities Transactions and events that involve selling products or services and incurring the necessary expenses associated with the primary activities of the business.

Operating activities involve selling products or services, buying inventory for resale, and incurring and paying for necessary expenses associated with the primary activities of the business. The operating activities of a motel, for example, would include renting rooms (the selling activity); buying soap, shampoo, and other supplies to operate the motel; and incurring and paying for electricity, heat, water, cleaning, television and telephone service, and salaries and taxes of workers. The operating activities of a grocery store would include buying produce, meats, canned goods, and other items for resale; selling products to customers; and incurring and paying for expenses associated with the store's operations such as utilities, salaries, and taxes. It is easy to identify operating activities because they are always associated with the primary purpose of a business.

In this chapter we cover the operating activities for selling products and services, the recognition of revenues from those sales, accounting for cash, and problems associated with collecting receivables arising from sales. In Chapter 5 we examine the purchase of inventory for resale to customers and the necessary accounting procedures and conclude our discussion of operating activities by considering other operating expenses, and how revenues and expenses are combined to compute the net income of a business. These other operating expenses include employee compensation, insurance, advertising, research and development, and income taxes.

investing activities Transactions and events that involve the purchase and sale of property, plant, equipment, and other assets not generally held for resale.

Investing activities involve the purchase of assets for use in the business. The assets purchased as part of investing activities include property, plant, and equipment, as well as financial assets such as investments in stocks and bonds of other companies. Investing activities are distinguishable from operating activities because they occurr less frequently and the amounts involved in each transaction are usually quite large. For example, while most businesses buy and sell inventory or services to customers on a daily basis (operating activities), only rarely do they buy and sell buildings, equipment, and stocks and bonds of other companies. It is important to note that buying inventory for resale is an operating activity, *not* an investing activity. Investing activities are covered in Chapter 7.

financing activities Transactions and events whereby resources are obtained from, or repaid to, owners (equity financing) and creditors (debt financing).

Financing activities involve raising money to finance a business by means other than operations. In addition to earning money through profitable operations, there are two other ways to fund a business: (1) money can be borrowed from creditors (debt financing) or (2) money can be raised by selling stock or ownership interests in the business to investors (equity financing). Debt and equity financing will be discussed in Chapter 6.

Once you have studied Chapters 4 through 7, you will have a good understanding of how businesses operate, invest, and are financed. That knowledge should be helpful in the future if you own your own business, invest in companies as a stockholder, work for a financial institution (or other lender of funds), or work in any position where a knowledge of business is essential.

After studying the operating, investing, and financing activities of a business, you will be ready to combine your knowledge of how businesses operate with the basic accounting knowledge you gained from Chapters 1 through 3. To do this, we will study in detail the statement of cash flows, which is structured around the three activities of a business (Chapter 8). You will discover that preparation of a statement of cash flows requires a sound understanding of the balance sheet and the income statement, as well as a good grasp of how the activities of a business tie together. Exhibit 4–1 provides a graphical road map of the business and reporting activities that will be discussed in the subsequent five chapters.

Although Chapters 4 through 7 are organized around business activities, it is important to understand how these activities relate to the basic financial statements. To help you understand these relationships, at the beginning of each of the next five chapters, we present basic financial statements that highlight the accounts that will be covered in that chapter. As you can see in Exhibit 4–2, Cash, Accounts Receivable, and Warranty Liability on the balance sheet; Sales, Bad Debt Expense, and Warranty Expense on the income statement; and Receipts from Customers on the statement of cash flows are covered in Chapter 4.

EXHIBIT 4-1

Major Activities of a Business

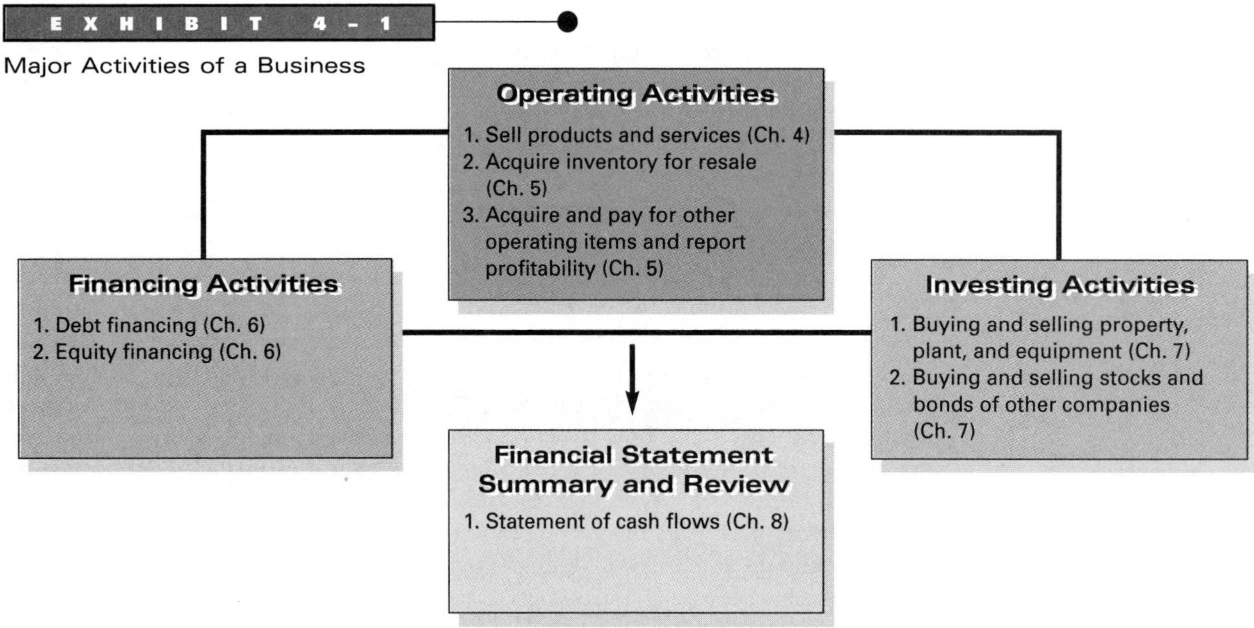

EXHIBIT 4-2

Basic Financial Statements

Balance Sheet

Current assets:		*Current liabilities:*	
Cash	Ch. 4	Accounts payable	Ch. 5
Investments	Ch. 7	Taxes payable	Ch. 5
Accounts receivable	Ch. 4	Wages payable	Ch. 5
Inventory	Ch. 5	Warranty liability	Ch. 4
Property, plant, and equipment	Ch. 7	Unearned revenues	Ch. 5
Intangible assets	Ch. 7	*Long-term liabilities:*	
Long-term investments	Ch. 7	Long-term debt	Ch. 6
Total assets		Pension costs	Ch. 5
		Stockholders' equity:	
		Common stock	Ch. 6
		Retained earnings	Ch. 6
		Unrealized increase/decrease in value of securities	Ch. 7
		Total liabilities and stockholders' equity	

Income Statement

Sales of goods and services	Ch. 4
Cost of goods sold	Ch. 5
Gross margin	
Expenses:	
Salaries expense	Ch. 5
Taxes expense	Ch. 5
Depreciation expense	Ch. 7
Bad debt expense	Ch. 4
Warranty expense	Ch. 4
Other revenues and expenses:	
Gains and losses on sales of securities	Ch. 7
Unrealized gains and losses on securities	Ch. 7
Interest expense	Ch. 6
Interest revenue	Ch. 7
Net income	

EXHIBIT 4-2 Concluded

Statement of Cash Flows

Operating activities:	
Receipts from customers	**Ch. 4**
Payments for inventory	Ch. 5
Payments for salaries	Ch. 5
Payments for interest	Ch. 5
Payments for taxes	Ch. 5
Purchase of trading securities	Ch. 7
Sale of trading securities	Ch. 7
Investing activities:	
Purchase of property, plant, and equipment	Ch. 7
Proceeds from sale of property, plant, and equipment	Ch. 7
Purchase of debt and equity securities other than trading securities	Ch. 7
Sale of debt and equity securities other than trading securities	Ch. 7
Financing activities:	
Sale of stock	Ch. 6
Purchase of treasury stock	Ch. 6
Proceeds from borrowing	Ch. 6
Repayments of borrowing	Ch. 6
Payments of dividends	Ch. 6
Net cash flows for the period	

TO SUMMARIZE

Activities of a business can be divided into (1) operating activities, (2) investing activities, and (3) financing activities. Operating activities involve selling products or services, buying inventory for resale, and incurring and paying for necessary expenses associated with the primary activities of a business. Investing activities include purchasing assets for use in the business and making investments in such items as stocks and bonds. Financing activities include raising money to finance a business by means other than operations.

2 *Use the two revenue recognition criteria to decide when the revenue from a sale or service should be recorded in the accounting records.*

RECOGNIZING REVENUE

The operations of a business revolve around the sale of a product or a service. **McDonald's** sells fast food; **Microsoft** sells software and continuing customer support; **Chase Manhattan** loans money and sells financial services. Just as the sale of a product or service is at the heart of any business, proper recording of the revenue from sales and services is fundamental to the practice of accounting. A simple time line illustrating the business issues involved with a sale is given in Exhibit 4-3.

Consideration of this time line raises a number of very interesting accounting questions:

- When should revenue be recognized—when the good or service is provided, when the cash is collected, or later, when there is no longer any chance that the customer will return the product or demand a refund because of faulty service?
- What accounting procedures are used to manage and safeguard cash as it is collected?

EXHIBIT 4-3 Time Line of Business Issues Involved with a Sale

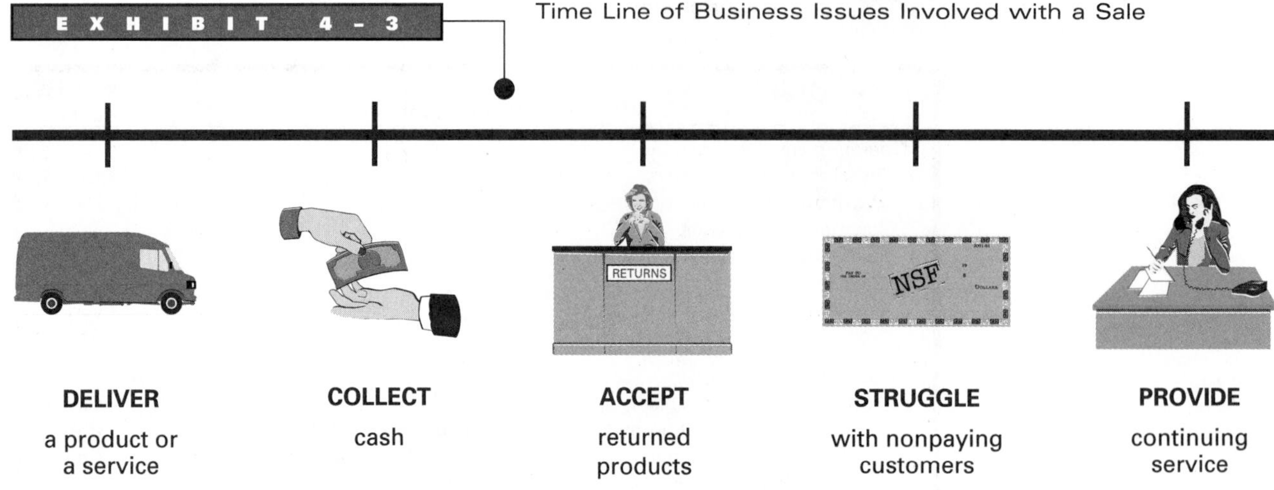

- How do you account for bad debts, that is, customers who don't pay their bills?
- How do you account for the possibility that sales this year may obligate you to make warranty repairs and provide continuing customer service for many years to come?

The following sections will address these accounting issues, beginning with the important question of when to recognize revenue.

When Should Revenue Be Recognized?

revenue recognition The process of recording revenue in the accounting records; occurs after (1) the work has been substantially completed and (2) cash collection is reasonably assured.

Revenue recognition is the phrase that accountants use to refer to the recording of a sale through a journal entry in the formal accounting records. Revenue is usually recognized when two important criteria have been met:

1. The work has been substantially completed (the company has done something), and
2. Cash, or a valid promise of future payment, has been received (the company has received something in return).

As a practical matter, most companies record sales when goods are shipped to customers. Credit sales are recognized as revenues before cash is collected, and revenue from services is usually recognized when the service is performed, not necessarily when cash is received.

To illustrate, we will assume that on a typical business day Farm Land Products sells 30 sacks of fertilizer for cash and 20 sacks on credit, all at $10 per sack. Given these data, the $500 of revenue is recorded as follows:

FYI

In the majority of companies, the most frequent types of journal entries are those to record sales, cash collections, purchases, and payments to suppliers. Because such transactions are so frequent, most firms maintain four separate special journals: (1) the sales journal, (2) the purchases journal, (3) the cash receipts journal, and (4) the cash disbursements journal.

Cash	300	
Accounts Receivable	200	
Sales Revenue		500
Sold 30 sacks of fertilizer for cash and 20 sacks on credit.		

Although the debit entries are made to different accounts, the credit entry for the full amount is to a revenue account. Thus, accrual-basis accounting requires the recognition of $500 in revenue instead of the $300 that would be recognized if the focus were merely on cash collection.

This example is a simple illustration of how sales are recorded and revenue is recognized. In reality, sales transactions are usually more complex, involving such things as uncertainty about exactly when the transaction is actually completed, and whether a valid promise of payment has actually been received from the customer. These difficulties are compounded by the fact that companies often have an understandable desire to report revenue as soon as possible in order to enhance their reported performance and make it easier to get loans or attract investors. As described in the opening scenario of this chapter, Barry Minkow, founder of **ZZZZ Best**, found that he could generate a lot of interest from lenders and investors just by recording the following journal entry:

Accounts Receivable	8,200,000	
Sales Revenue		8,200,000
ZZZZ Best entry to record fictitious San Diego restoration job.		

Note that this bogus entry improves both the balance sheet (increase in assets) and the income statement (increase in revenue), even though no customer had agreed to pay the $8.2 million and the revenue was completely fictitious. The discussion below will further examine the two revenue recognition criteria (work done and cash collectible) to see how accountants apply these rules to ensure that reported revenue fairly reflects the economic performance of a business.

Application of the Revenue Recognition Criteria

The Farm Land example was used to illustrate a straightforward case of revenue recognition at the time a sale is made. The Farm Land customers bought $500 worth of fertilizer, paying $300 cash and promising to pay $200 later; the $500 of revenue was recognized immediately. But what if the terms of the sale had also required Farm Land to deliver the fertilizer to the customers at no extra charge? In this case, proper application of the "work done" revenue recognition criterion would require that the revenue not be recorded until actual delivery had taken place. Alternatively, assume that the fertilizer sale was accompanied by a guarantee that, within 30 days, customers could return the unused portion of fertilizer for a full refund. If very few customers ever seek a refund, revenue should still be recognized at the time of sale. But, for example, if over 70% of fertilizer customers later seek refunds, the "cash collectible" revenue recognition criterion suggests that no revenue should be recognized until the completion of the 30-day return period; Farm Land then becomes reasonably assured of the amount of cash it will collect from the $500 in sales. This situation illustrates the need for accountants to exercise professional judgment and account for the economic reality of a transaction instead of blindly relying on technical legal rules about whether a sale has taken place. We will examine other common situations concerning the application of the revenue recognition criteria in the following three sections.

Airplane Tickets

Almost all of us pay for airplane tickets before we actually take the flight. Should **United Airlines** recognize the flight revenue when it collects the money from us or later when the actual flight takes place? The "work done" revenue recognition criterion indicates that airlines should delay recognizing flight revenue until they provide the promised flight service. This is exactly what airlines do. In fact, in its 1996 balance sheet, United Airlines reported an "Advance ticket sales" liability of $1.189 billion, reflecting the amount of revenue it could not currently recognize because it had collected the cash but had not yet provided the service.

Season Tickets

Many entertainment organizations sell season tickets to their productions. You can buy season tickets to a series of plays, concerts, art shows, or sporting contests. Should the sponsoring organization recognize these season ticket sales as revenue when the sale is made or wait until the end of the season to recognize the revenue? At first glance, the "work done" criterion seems to suggest that one must delay revenue recognition until the end of the season, when the season ticketholders have been given all the shows for which they paid. However, another way to view this transaction is that the work is done in pieces throughout the season. For example, the **Boston Celtics** of the NBA recognize revenue from season ticket sales in proportion to the number of games that they have played. This type of "proportional performance" technique is commonly used to recognize revenue for long-term projects. Revenue for a five-year construction project would be similarly recognized, in proportion to the percentage of the project that had been completed. For its software sales, **Microsoft** recognizes some revenue immediately, with the remainder recognized later in proportion to the amount of promised software upgrades and customer support service that has been provided.

Electricity

When you get your electric bill, the electric utility is asking you to pay for electricity you have already used. Since the utility has already done the work of providing the electricity, it should recognize the revenue before it collects the cash from you, *if* it is reasonably assured of the collectibility of the cash. For utilities, the fraction of customers who fail to pay for their service is quite small and predictable. Accordingly, the utility would recognize the revenue when the service was provided, and then do some additional accounting (explained later in this chapter) for those customer accounts that are uncollectible. In other cases, if cash collection is sufficiently uncertain, the company providing the product or service should wait until collecting the cash before recognizing any revenue. For example, immediate revenue recognition from furniture "sales" by some rent-to-own companies has been criticized because of the high probability that customers will stop making their payments before the entire rent-to-own contract is completed.

As mentioned initially, the accounting for most sales transactions is straightforward—the revenue is recognized when the sale is made. However, as illustrated by the discussion in this section, when the "work" associated with a sale extends over a significant period of time, or when cash collectibility is in doubt, the accountant must use professional judgment in applying the revenue recognition criteria to determine the proper time to record the sale.

(STOP & THINK)

Many colleges and universities prepare financial statements that are released to the public. When do you think a college or university should recognize revenue from student tuition?

TO SUMMARIZE

Revenue is recognized when the work is done and when cash collectibility is reasonably assured. The entries to record revenue from the sale of merchandise or from the performance of a service involve debits to Cash or Accounts Receivable and credits to Sales Revenue or Service Revenue.

BUSINESS ENVIRONMENT ESSAY

Worried About Revenues! Today the tobacco industry faces an unprecedented antismoking onslaught. An increasing number of lawsuits are alleging that smoking, and even second-hand smoke, causes cancer and other diseases, and that the tobacco companies are at fault because their sales practices get people hooked on addictive drugs. (By the way, if you wish to read a careful assessment of the health risks associated with cigarettes, read the financial reports of the tobacco companies. By federal law, these reports must be provided to all interested investors, and, in order to ensure that investors are not misled, the Securities and Exchange Commission monitors these disclosures to make sure that they are not overly optimistic. Accordingly, these financial statement disclosures contain a much more even-handed view than do most public statements on this controversial issue.) While being very large and extremely profitable, the tobacco companies are worried about future revenues. They are concerned that antismoking activity will result in fewer smokers and fewer sales. As a result, the big tobacco companies have been quietly diversifying into other businesses, so that now a significant amount of their revenues come from nontobacco sales. For example, three large tobacco companies now own the following:

	Philip Morris	RJR Nabisco	Loews
Major Cigarette Brands	Marlboro Benson & Hedges Merit Virginia Slims Basic	Winston Salem Camel Vantage	Newport Kent True
Other Major Businesses and Products	Post Cereals Jell-O Kool-Aid Oscar Mayer Miller Beer Kraft	Oreo Ritz Chips Ahoy Wheat Thins Fleischmann's Life Savers	14 Hotels Diamond Offshore Drilling CNA Financial Bulova
1996 Revenues (billions)	$69.2	$17.1	$20.4
% of Revenue from Cigarette Sales	53%	48%	11%

Sources: 1996 Form 10-K filings by Philip Morris, RJR Nabisco, and Loews.

3 *Properly account for the collection of cash and describe the business controls necessary to safeguard cash.*

CASH COLLECTION

Recall the Farm Land Products example in which fertilizer was sold, partially for cash and partially on credit. The sales were recorded by Farm Land as follows:

Cash	300	
Accounts Receivable	200	
Sales Revenue		500
Sold 30 sacks of fertilizer for cash and 20 sacks on credit.		

Subsequent collection of the $200 accounts receivable is recorded as follows:

Cash	200	
Accounts Receivable		200
Collected cash for $200 credit sale.		

Note that Sales Revenue is not credited again when the cash is collected; the revenue was already recognized when the sale was made.

The following T-accounts show that the net result of these two transactions is an increase in Cash and Sales Revenue of $500.

	Cash (Dr.)	Cash (Cr.)	Accounts Receivable (Dr.)	Accounts Receivable (Cr.)	Sales Revenue (Dr.)	Sales Revenue (Cr.)
Original sale	300		200			500
Collection of account	200			200		
Final balances	500					500
	To balance sheet					To income statement

These two entries illustrate simple sales and collection transactions. Many companies, however, offer sales discounts and must deal with merchandise returns. The accounting for discounts and returns is explained below.

Sales Discounts

sales discount A reduction in the selling price that is allowed if payment is received within a specified period.

In many sales transactions, the buyer is given a discount if the bill is paid promptly. Such incentives to pay quickly are called **sales discounts**, or cash discounts, and the discount terms are typically expressed in abbreviated form. For example, 2/10, n/30 means that a buyer will receive a 2 percent discount from the selling price if payment is made within 10 days of the date of purchase, but that the full amount must be paid within 30 days or it will be considered past due. (Other common terms are 1/10, n/30 and 2/10, EOM. The latter means that a 2 percent discount is granted if payment is made within 10 days after the date of sale, otherwise the balance is due at the end of the month.) A 2 percent discount is a strong incentive to pay within 10 days because it is equivalent to charging the customer an annual interest rate of about 36 percent to wait and pay after the discount period.[2] In fact, if the amount owed is substantial, most firms will borrow money, if necessary, to take advantage of a sales discount. This is because the interest rate they will have to pay a lending institution to borrow the money is considerably less than the effective interest rate of missing the sales discount.

If an account receivable is paid within a specified discount period, the entry to record the receipt of cash is different from the cash receipt entry shown earlier. Thus, if the $200 in Farm Land credit sales were made with discount terms of 2/10, EOM, and if the customers paid within the discount period, the entry to record the receipt of cash is:

Cash	196	
Sales Discounts ($200 × 0.02)	4	
Accounts Receivable		200
Collected cash within the discount period for $200 credit sale.		

contra account An account that is offset or deducted from another account.

Sales Discounts is a **contra account** (specifically, a contra-revenue account), which means that it is deducted from sales revenue on the income statement. This account is included with other revenue accounts in the general ledger, but unlike other revenue accounts, it has a debit balance rather than a credit balance.

2. This is calculated by computing an annual interest rate for the period that the money is "sacrificed." With terms 2/10, n/30, a buyer who pays on the 10th day instead of the 30th "sacrifices" the money for 20 days. Since 2 percent is earned in 20 days, and there are just over 18 periods of 20 days in a year, earnings would be 18 × 2 percent, or approximately 36 percent annual interest.

Sales Returns and Allowances

Customers often return merchandise, either because the item is defective or for a variety of other reasons. Most companies generally accept merchandise returns in order to maintain good customer relations. When merchandise is returned, the company must make an entry to reduce revenues and to reduce either Cash (a cash refund) or Accounts Receivable (an adjustment to the customer's account). A similar entry is required when the sales price is reduced because the merchandise was defective or damaged during shipment to the customer.

To illustrate the type of entry needed, we will assume that before any payments on account are made, Farm Land customers return goods costing $150; $100 in returns were made by cash customers, and $50 in returns were made by credit customers. The entry to record the return of merchandise is:

Sales Returns and Allowances	150	
Cash		100
Accounts Receivable		50
Received $150 of returned merchandise; $100 from cash customers and $50 from credit customers.		

sales returns and allowances A contra-revenue account in which the return of, or allowance for reduction in the price of, merchandise previously sold is recorded.

The credit customers will be sent a credit memorandum for the return, stating that credit has been granted and that the balance of their accounts (in total) is now $150 ($200 original credit purchase − $50 returns). Like Sales Discounts, **Sales Returns and Allowances** is a contra account that is deducted from sales revenue on the income statement. The income statement presentation for the revenue accounts, assuming payment within the discount period on the $150 balance in accounts receivable, is as follows:

Income Statement

Sales revenue	$500	
Less: Sales discounts*	(3)	
Sales returns and allowances	(150)	
Net sales revenue		$347

*($200 − $50) × 0.02 = $3

Note that when merchandise is returned, sales discounts for the subsequent payment are granted only on the selling price of the merchandise not returned.

It might seem that the use of contra accounts (Sales Discounts and Sales Returns and Allowances) involves extra steps that would not be necessary if discounts and returns of merchandise were deducted directly from Sales Revenue. Although such direct deductions would have the same final effect on net income, the contra accounts separate initial sales from all returns, allowances, and discounts. This permits a company's management to analyze the extent to which customers are returning merchandise, receiving allowances, and taking advantage of discounts. If management finds that excessive amounts of merchandise are being returned, they may decide that the company's sales returns policy is too liberal or that the quality of its merchandise needs improvement.

gross sales Total recorded sales before deducting any sales discounts or sales returns and allowances.

net sales Gross sales less sales discounts and sales returns and allowances.

A company's total recorded sales, before any discounts or returns and allowances, is referred to as **gross sales**. When sales discounts or sales returns and allowances are deducted from gross sales, the resulting amount is referred to as **net sales**.

Control of Cash

cash Coins, currency, money orders, checks, and funds on deposit with financial institutions; the most liquid of assets.

Cash includes coins, currency, money orders and checks (made payable or endorsed to the company), and money on deposit with banks or savings institutions that are available for use to satisfy the company's obligations. All the various transactions involving these forms of cash are usually summarized and reported under a single balance sheet account, Cash.

FYI

In its balance sheet (see Appendix A), Microsoft follows the common practice of combining cash and short-term investments (bonds and U.S. Treasury securities) for the total cash amount.

Because it is the easiest asset to spend if it is stolen, cash is a tempting target and must be carefully safeguarded. Several control procedures have been developed to help management monitor and protect cash. Of course, controls exist to safeguard all of a company's assets. However, because cash is particularly vulnerable to loss or misuse, we will discuss three important controls that are an integral part of accounting for cash.

One of the most important controls for cash is that the handling of cash be separated from the recording of cash. The purpose of this separation of duties is to make it difficult for theft or errors to occur with two or more people involved. If the cash records are maintained by an employee who also has access to the cash itself, cash can be stolen or "borrowed," and the employee can cover up the shortage by falsifying the accounting records.

FYI

Consider the case of an employee who both receives payments and keeps the books. He or she could pocket a cash payment from one customer and not record the receipt until payment is received from a second customer. The recording of the second customer's payment could be made when a third customer pays, and so on. This type of delayed recording of payments is called *lapping;* it allows an employee to use company money for extended periods of time.

A second cash control practice is to require that all cash receipts be deposited daily in bank accounts. This disciplined, rigid process ensures that personal responsibility for the handling of cash is focused on the individual assigned to make the regular deposit. In addition, this process prevents the accumulation of a large amount of cash—even the most trusted employee can be tempted when enticed by a large cash hoard.

A third cash control practice is to require that all cash expenditures (except those paid out of a miscellaneous petty cash fund) be made with prenumbered checks. As we all know from managing our personal finances, payments made with pocket cash are quickly forgotten and easily concealed. In contrast, payments made by check are well documented, both in our personal check registers and by our bank.

In addition to safeguarding cash, a business must ensure that cash is wisely managed. In fact, many businesses establish elaborate control and budgeting procedures for monitoring cash balances and estimating future cash needs. Companies also try to keep only minimum balances in no-interest or low-interest checking accounts; other cash is kept in more high-yielding investments such as certificates of deposit.

BUSINESS ENVIRONMENT ESSAY

E. F. Hutton's Overaggressive Cash Management Practices In the early 1980s, E. F. Hutton & Company challenged its branch managers to invigorate their cash management practices. The managers responded by developing a way to use cash at no interest. In anticipation of the collection of receivables (or sometimes even without the receivables), branch managers would write checks on accounts they knew were insufficiently funded. Later, before the checks cleared through the banking system, deposits would be made so that the bad checks would be covered. Using this method (known as "kiting" or "using the float"), the managers were able to use and earn interest on money that didn't even belong to the firm. E. F. Hutton commended managers who effectively used this technique, and before long, Hutton was kiting checks on four hundred of its banks.

Hutton intentionally opened accounts in small, rural banks because the collection process for such banks is slower. Hutton particularly liked doing business with banks in Watertown, New York, on the eastern shore of Lake Ontario; heavy winter snowstorms could be expected to delay mail deliveries and thus slow down the check-clearing process even further. Hutton also created chains of bank accounts, transferring funds by writing a check on one bank and depositing it in another. During the check-clearing interval, the funds would be earning interest in both banks.

At the time, Hutton apparently felt it was shrewdly taking full advantage of the banking system's check-clearing procedures and tolerant bankers. However, in 1986, when their overaggressive cash management techniques netted them 2,000 counts of mail and wire fraud, E. F. Hutton agreed to pay millions of dollars in fines, as well as all costs relating to the government investigation into the firm's banking practices. In the end, several of Hutton's officers found themselves without jobs, as the company was subsequently purchased by **Shearson Lehman Brothers Inc.**, another investment firm.

Sources: Saul W. Gellerman, "Why Good Managers Make Bad Ethical Choices," *Harvard Business Review,* July–August 1986, p. 85. Anthony Bianco and G. David Wallace, "What Did Hutton's Managers Know—And When Did They Know It?" *Business Week,* May 20, 1985, p. 110.

TO SUMMARIZE

The amount of cash collected from customers can be reduced because of sales discounts and sales returns and allowances. On the income statement, sales discounts and sales returns and allowances are subtracted from gross sales to arrive at net sales. Cash is a tempting target for fraud or theft, so companies must carefully monitor and control the way cash is handled and accounted for. Common controls include (1) separation of duties in handling and accounting for cash, (2) daily deposits of all cash receipts, and (3) payment of all expenditures by prenumbered checks.

4 *Record the losses resulting from credit customers who do not pay their bills.*

ACCOUNTING FOR CREDIT CUSTOMERS WHO DON'T PAY

receivables Claims for money, goods, or services.

The term **receivables** refers to a company's claims for money, goods, or services. Receivables are created through various types of transactions; the two most common being the sale of merchandise or services on credit and the lending of money. On a personal level, we are all familiar with credit. Because credit is so readily available, we can buy such items as cars, refrigerators, and big-screen TVs, that perhaps we could not afford to pay cash for. Major retail companies such as **Sears**, oil companies such as **Shell**, and credit card companies such as **Visa**, **Mastercard**, and **American Express** have made credit available to almost every responsible person in the United States. We live in a credit world; not only on the individual level, but also at the wholesale and manufacturing business levels.

accounts receivable A current asset representing money due for services performed or merchandise sold on credit.

In business, credit sales give rise to the most common type of receivables: accounts receivable. **Accounts receivable** are the amounts owed to a business by its credit customers and are usually collected in cash within 10 to 60 days. Accounts receivable result from informal agreements between a company and its credit customers; a more formal contract, including interest on the unpaid balance, is called a note receivable. Other receivables may result from loans to officers or employees of a company, for example. To identify and maintain the distinction between these receivables, businesses establish a separate general ledger account for each classification. If the amount of a receivable is material, it is separately identified on the balance sheet. Those that are to be converted to cash within a year (or the normal op-

bad debt An uncollectible account receivable.

FYI

Credit card sales can be viewed as a way for a business to reap the benefit of increased credit sales without being required to set up a bookkeeping and collection service for accounts receivable. The credit card company screens customers based on their credit-worthiness, sends out the bills, collects the cash, and bears the cost of any uncollectible accounts. The business that accepts credit card sales pays a fee ranging from 1 to 5 percent of credit card sales.

erating cycle) are classified as current assets and listed on the balance sheet below Cash. In this section of the chapter, we discuss the accounting issues associated with credit customers who don't pay.

When companies sell goods and services on credit (as most do), there are usually some customers who do not pay for the merchandise they purchase; these are referred to as **bad debts**. In fact, most businesses expect a small percentage of their receivables to be uncollectible. If a firm tries too hard to eliminate the possibility of losses from nonpaying customers, it usually makes its credit policy so restrictive that valuable sales are lost. On the other hand, if a firm extends credit too easily, the total cost of maintaining the accounts receivable system (due to the number of accounts to track and uncollectible receivables to try to collect) may exceed the benefit gained from attracting customers by allowing them to buy on credit. Because of this dilemma, most firms carefully monitor their credit sales and accounts receivable to ensure that their policies are neither too restrictive nor too liberal.

BUSINESS ENVIRONMENT ESSAY

Overstating Receivables One of the easiest ways to overstate income is to overstate receivables. As Barry Minkow of **ZZZZ Best** said, "Receivables are a wonderful thing. You make up a fictitious receivable and BOOM, the credit goes to revenues which increases income." Another company that overstated receivables and income was **Coated Sales, Inc.** Michael Weinstein, former chairman and chief executive officer of Coated Sales, Inc., orchestrated a financial fraud scheme that ultimately cost investors close to $100 million. Coated Sales, Inc. was a New Jersey company that manufactured textiles coated with special chemicals, used for making such products as yacht sails, bullet-proof vests, conveyor belts, and parachutes. The company was best known for supplying the fabric used in the sails of the America's Cup winning yacht—Stars and Stripes.

Coated Sales was started as the second career of millionaire entrepreneur Michael Weinstein, who had "retired" in his 30s and sold the discount drug store chain he built. Looking for a new business, he became interested in textiles through a friend. The proposition was simple: take unfinished textiles, known as gray goods, and finish them with specialized coatings or treatments. The company's earnings, though minuscule at first, began to double and even triple every year; sometimes every six months.

The fraud was instigated by inflating Coated's sales and earnings through the creation of phony invoices purporting to show sales of goods. Coated officials "prebilled" invoices to customers so they could obtain payment for goods before they were shipped. Coated then began sending out false invoices to customers, recording receivables, and obtaining funds for sales that never occurred. To prevent the customers from denying the sales, the company involved the customers in the racket. For example, Robert Solomon of **Globe Sports Products** paid the fictitious bills and would then receive the money back from Weinstein. Due to the inflated sales and receivables, the value of Coated's stock rose from $1.50 per share in its initial public offering to over $12 per share in 1987. From 1984 to 1987, sales allegedly rose from $9.9 million to over $90 million.

In addition, Weinstein inflated accounts receivable by billing fictitious customers. He used the inflated accounts receivable account to secure large bank loans. For example, **BancBoston Financial Co.** loaned Coated $45 million, based on the supposed existence of $51 million in accounts receivable that served as collateral for the loan.

Coated Sales' auditor, **KPMG Peat Marwick**, withdrew because of its suspicions. Within days, Coated Sales' stock value tumbled from $8 to $2 a share. Shortly thereafter, the corporation's credit dried up, forcing it to declare bankruptcy.

Source: Graham Button, "Homeless Jailbird," *Forbes*, Aug. 17, 1992, p. 13.

When an account receivable becomes uncollectible, a firm incurs a bad-debt loss. This loss is recognized as a cost of doing business, so it is classified as a selling expense. There are two ways to account for losses from uncollectible accounts: the direct write-off method and the allowance method.

Direct Write-Off Method

direct write-off method The recording of actual losses from uncollectible accounts as expenses during the period in which accounts receivable are determined to be uncollectible.

With the **direct write-off method**, an uncollectible account is recognized as an expense at the time it is determined to be uncollectible. For example, assume that during the year 2000, Farm Land Products had total credit sales of $300,000. Of this amount, $250,000 was subsequently collected in cash during the year, leaving a year-end balance in accounts receivable of $50,000 ($300,000 − $250,000). The summary journal entries to record this information are:

Accounts Receivable	300,000	
Sales Revenue		300,000
To record total credit sales for the year.		
Cash	250,000	
Accounts Receivable		250,000
To record total cash collections for the year.		

Assume that one credit customer, Jake Palmer, has an account balance of $1,500 which remains unpaid for several months in 2001. If, after receiving several past-due notices, Palmer still does not pay, Farm Land will probably turn the account over to an attorney or a collection agency. Then, if collection attempts fail, the company may decide that the Palmer account will not be collected and write it off as a loss. The entry to record the expense under the direct write-off method is:

Bad Debt Expense.	1,500	
Accounts Receivable		1,500
To write off the uncollectible account of Jake Palmer.		

bad debt expense An account that represents the portion of the current period's credit sales that are estimated to be uncollectible.

Bad Debt Expense is usually considered a selling expense on the income statement. Although the direct write-off method is objective (the account is written off at the time it proves to be uncollectible), it most likely would violate the matching principle, which requires that all costs and expenses incurred in generating revenues be identified with those revenues period by period. With the direct write-off method, sales made near the end of one accounting period may not be recognized as uncollectible until the next period. In this example, the revenue from the sale to Jake Palmer is recognized in 2000, but the expense from the bad debt is not recognized until 2001. As a result, expenses are understated in 2000, and overstated in 2001. This makes the direct write-off method unacceptable from a theoretical point of view. The direct write-off method is only allowable if bad debts involve small, insignificant amounts.

The Allowance Method

allowance method The recording of estimated losses due to uncollectible accounts as expenses during the period in which the sales occurred.

The **allowance method** satisfies the matching principle since it accounts for uncollectibles during the same period in which the sales occurred. With this method, a firm uses its experience (or industry averages) to estimate the amount of receivables arising from this year's credit sales that will ultimately become uncollectible. That estimate is recorded as bad debt expense in the period of sale. Although the use of estimates may result in a somewhat imprecise expense figure, this is generally thought to be a less serious problem than the direct write-off method's failure to match bad debt expenses with the sales that caused them. In addition, with experience, these estimates tend to be quite accurate.

To illustrate the allowance method, assume that Farm Land Products estimates that the bad debts created by its $300,000 in credit sales in 2000 will ultimately total $4,500. Note that this is a statistical estimate—on average, bad debts will be $4,500, but Farm Land does not yet know exactly which customers will be the ones who will fail to pay. The entry to record this estimated bad debt expense for 2000 is:

Bad Debt Expense	4,500	
Allowance for Bad Debts.		4,500
To record the estimated bad debt expense for the current year.		

allowance for bad debts A contra account, deducted from Accounts Receivable, that shows the estimated losses from uncollectible accounts.

Bad Debt Expense is a selling expense on the income statement, and **Allowance for Bad Debts** is a contra account to Accounts Receivable on the balance sheet. An allowance account is used because the company does not yet know which receivables will not be collected. Later on, for example in 2001, as actual losses are recognized, the balance in Allowance for Bad Debts is reduced. For example, if in 2001 the receivable of Jake Palmer for $1,500 is not collected, the entry is:

Allowance for Bad Debts	1,500	
Accounts Receivable		1,500
To write off the uncollectible account of Jake Palmer.		

Note that the write-off entry in 2001 does not impact net income in 2001. Instead, the net income in 2000, when the credit sale to Jake Palmer was originally made, already reflects the estimated bad debt expense. Think of this entry as follows: The $1,500 Jake Palmer account has been shown to be bad, so it is "thrown away" via a credit to Accounts Receivable. In addition, the Allowance for Bad Debts, which is a general estimate of the amount of bad accounts, is reduced by $1,500 because the bad Palmer account has been specifically identified and eliminated. In one entry, the amounts in Accounts Receivable and Allowance for Bad Debts have been reduced. Assume that the balance in Accounts Receivable was $50,000 and the balance in the Allowance for Bad Debts was $4,500 before the Palmer account was written off. The net amount in Accounts Receivable after the $1,500 write-off is exactly the same as it was before the entry, as shown here.

Before write-off entry		After write-off entry	
Accounts receivable	$50,000	Accounts receivable ($50,000 − $1,500)	$48,500
Less allowance for bad debts	4,500	Less allowance for bad debts ($4,500 − $1,500).	3,000
Net balance.	$45,500	Net balance	$45,500

net realizable value of accounts receivable The net amount that would be received if all receivables considered collectible were collected; equal to total accounts receivable less the allowance for bad debts.

The net balance of $45,500 reflects the estimated **net realizable value of accounts receivable**, that is, the amount of receivables the company actually expects to collect.

The following T-account shows the kinds of entries that are made to Allowance for Bad Debts:

Allowance for Bad Debts	
Actual writeoffs of uncollectible accounts	Estimates of uncollectible accounts

Occasionally, a customer whose account has been written off as uncollectible later pays the outstanding balance. When this happens, the company reverses the entry that was used to write off the account, and then recognizes the payment. For example, if the $1,500 is collected from Jake Palmer after his account has already been written off, the entries to correct the accounting records are:

Accounts Receivable.	1,500	
Allowance for Bad Debts.		1,500
To reinstate the balance previously written off as uncollectible.		
Cash.	1,500	
Accounts Receivable		1,500
Received payment in full of previously written-off accounts receivable.		

Sears allows customers to purchase products and services using a Sears credit card. Access Sears' annual report.

How long does Sears wait until writing off a customer's account as uncollectible? Hint: Look in the notes to the financial statements.

www.sears.com

Because customers sometimes pay their balances after their accounts are written off, it is important for a company to have good control over both the cash collection procedures and the accounting for accounts receivable. Otherwise, such payments as the previously written-off $1,500 could be pocketed by the employee who receives the cash, and it would never be missed. This is one reason that most companies separate the handling of cash from the recording of cash transactions in the accounts.

Because the amount recorded in Bad Debt Expense affects both the reported net realizable value of the receivables and net income, companies must be careful to use good estimation procedures. These estimates can focus on either the total number of credit sales during the period or on an examination of the outstanding receivables at year-end to determine their collectibility.

Estimating Uncollectible Accounts Receivable as a Percentage of Credit Sales

One method of estimating bad debt expense is to estimate uncollectible receivables as a percentage of credit sales for the period. If a company were to use this method, the amount of uncollectibles would be a straight percentage of the current year's credit sales. That percentage would be a projection based on experience in prior years, modified for any changes expected for the current period. For example, in the Farm Land example, credit sales for the year of $300,000 were expected to generate bad debts of $4,500, indicating that 1.5 percent of all credit sales are expected to be uncollectible ($4,500 ÷ $300,000 = 1.5%). Farm Land would evaluate the percentage each year, in light of its continued experience, to see whether the same percentage still seemed reasonable. In addition, if economic conditions have changed for Farm Land's customers (such as the onset of a recession making it more likely that debts might remain uncollected), the percentage would be adjusted.

When this percentage of sales method is used, the existing balance (if there is one) in Allowance for Bad Debts is not included in the adjusting entry to record bad debt expense. The 1.5 percent of the current year's sales that is estimated to be uncollectible is calculated and entered separately, and then added to the existing balance. For example, if the existing credit balance is $2,000, the $4,500 would be added, making the new credit balance $6,500. The rationale for not considering the existing $2,000 balance in Allowance for Bad Debts is that it relates to previous periods' sales and reflects the company's estimate (as of the beginning of the year) of prior years' accounts receivable that are expected to be uncollectible.

In determining the percentage of credit sales that will be uncollectible, a company must estimate the total amount of loss on the basis of experience or industry averages. Obviously, a company that has been in business for several years should be able to make more accurate estimates than a new company. Many established companies will use a 3- or 5-year average as the basis for estimating losses from uncollectible accounts.

(STOP & THINK)

Should a company work to reduce its bad debt expense to zero? Explain.

Estimating Uncollectible Accounts Receivable as a Percentage of Total Receivables

Another way to estimate uncollectible receivables is to use a percentage of total receivables. Using this method, the amount of uncollectibles is a percentage of the total receivables balance at the end of the period. Assume that Farm Land decides to use this method and determines that 12 percent of the $50,000 in the year-end accounts receivable will ultimately be uncollectible. Accordingly, the credit balance in Allowance for Bad Debts should be $6,000 ($50,000 × 0.12). If there is no existing balance in Allowance for Bad Debts representing the estimate of bad accounts left over from prior years, then an entry for $6,000 is made. However, if the account has an existing balance, only the net amount needed to bring the credit balance to $6,000 is added. For example, an existing credit balance of $2,000 in Allowance for Bad Debts results in the following adjusting entry:

Bad Debt Expense	4,000	
Allowance for Bad Debts.		4,000
To adjust the Allowance account to the desired balance ($6,000 − $2,000 = $4,000).		

In all cases, the ending balance in Allowance for Bad Debts should be the amount of total receivables estimated to be uncollectible.

In estimating bad debt expense, the percentage of sales method focuses on an estimation based directly on the level of current year's credit sales. With the percentage of total receivables method, the focus is on estimating total bad debts existing at the end of the period; this number is compared to the leftover bad debts from prior years and the difference is bad debt expense, the new bad debts created in the current period. These two techniques are merely alternative estimation approaches. In practice, a company would probably use both to ensure that the alternative estimation procedures yield roughly consistent results.

Aging Accounts Receivable. In the example just given, the correct amount of the ending Allowance for Bad Debts balance was computed by applying the estimated uncollectible percentage (12%) to the entire accounts receivable balance ($50,000). A more refined method of estimating the appropriate ending balance in Allowance for Bad Debts requires that a company base its calculations on how long its receivables have been outstanding. With this procedure, called **aging accounts receivable**, each receivable is categorized according to age, such as current, 1–30 days past due, 31–60 days past due, 61–90 days past due, 91–120 days past due, and over 120 days past due. Once the receivables in each age classification are totaled, each total is multiplied by an appropriate uncollectible percentage (as determined by experience), recognizing that the older the receivable, the less likely the company is to collect. Exhibit 4-4 shows how Farm Land could use an aging accounts receivable analysis to estimate the amount of its $50,000 ending balance in accounts receivable that will ultimately be uncollectible.

aging accounts receivable The process of categorizing each account receivable by the number of days it has been outstanding.

EXHIBIT 4-4 Aging Accounts Receivable

Customer	Balance	Current	Days Past Due 1–30	31–60	61–90	91–120	Over 120
A. Adams	$10,000	$10,000					
R. Bartholomew	6,500			$ 5,000			$1,500
F. Christiansen	6,250	5,000	$1,250				
G. Dover	7,260			7,260			
M. Ellis	4,000	4,000					
G. Erkland	2,250				$2,250		
R. Fisher	1,500		500			$1,000	
J. Palmer	1,500		1,500				
E. Zeigler	10,740	4,000	6,740				
Totals	$50,000	$23,000	$9,990	$12,260	$2,250	$1,000	$1,500

Estimate of Losses from Uncollectible Accounts

Age	Balance	Percentage Estimated to Be Uncollectible	Amount
Current	$23,000	1.5	$ 345
1–30 days past due	9,990	4.0	400
31–60 days past due	12,260	20.0	2,452
61–90 days past due	2,250	40.0	900
91–120 days past due	1,000	60.0	600
Over 120 days past due	1,500	80.0	1,200
Totals	$50,000		$5,897*

*Receivables that are likely to be uncollectible.

The allowance for bad debts estimate obtained using the aging method is $5,897. If the existing credit balance in Allowance for Bad Debts is $2,000, the required adjusting entry is:

Bad Debt Expense	3,897	
Allowance for Bad Debts..................................		3,897
To adjust the Allowance account to the desired ending balance ($5,897 − $2,000 = $3,897).		

CAUTION

The aging method is merely a more refined technique for estimating the desired balance in Allowance for Bad Debts.

The aging of accounts receivable is probably the most accurate method of estimating uncollectible accounts. It also enables a company to identify its problem customers. Companies that base their estimates of uncollectible accounts on credit sales or total outstanding receivables also often age their receivables as a way of monitoring the individual accounts receivable balances.

TO SUMMARIZE

Accounts receivable arise from credit sales to customers. Even though companies monitor their customers carefully, there are usually some who do not pay for the merchandise they purchase. There are two ways of accounting for losses from uncollectible receivables: the direct write-off method and the allowance method. The allowance method is generally accepted in practice because it is consistent with the matching principle. Two ways of estimating losses from uncollectible receivables are (1) as a percentage of credit sales, and (2) as some fraction of total outstanding receivables. A common method for applying the latter technique uses an aging of accounts receivable.

5 *Evaluate a company's management of its receivables by computing and analyzing appropriate financial ratios.*

ASSESSING HOW WELL COMPANIES MANAGE THEIR RECEIVABLES

An important element of overall company performance is the efficient use of assets. With regard to accounts receivable, inefficient use means that too much cash is tied up in the form of receivables. A company that collects its receivables on a timely basis has cash to pay its bills. Companies that do not do a good job of collecting receivables are often cash poor; paying interest on short-term loans to cover their cash shortage or losing interest that could be earned by investing cash.

There are several methods of evaluating how well an organization is managing its accounts receivable. The most common method includes computing two ratios, accounts receivable turnover and average collection period. The **accounts receivable turnover** ratio is an attempt to determine how many times during the year a company is "turning over" or collecting its receivables. It is a measure of how many times old receivables are collected and replaced by new receivables. Accounts receivable turnover is calculated as follows:

accounts receivable turnover A measure used to indicate how fast a company collects its receivables; computed by dividing sales by average accounts receivable.

$$\text{Accounts Receivable Turnover} = \frac{\text{Sales}}{\text{Average Accounts Receivable}}$$

Notice that the numerator of this ratio is sales, not credit sales. Conceptually, one might consider comparing the level of accounts receivable to the amount of credit sales instead of total sales. However, companies rarely, if ever, disclose how much of their sales are credit sales. For this ratio, you can think of cash sales as credit sales with a very short collection time (0 days). Also note that the denominator uses average accounts receivable instead of the ending balance. This recognizes that sales are generated throughout the year; the average accounts receivable balance is an approximation of the amount that prevailed during the year. If the accounts receivable balance is relatively unchanged during the year, then using the ending accounts receivable is acceptable and common. The accounts receivable turnover ratios for two well-known companies for 1996 are presented below.

$$\text{Wal-Mart} \quad \frac{\$104.859 \text{ billion}}{\$0.845 \text{ billion}} = 124.09 \text{ times}$$

$$\text{Boeing} \quad \frac{\$22.681 \text{ billion}}{\$1.988 \text{ billion}} = 11.41 \text{ times}$$

From this analysis, you can see that **Wal-Mart** turns its receivables over much more often than does **Boeing**. This is not surprising given the different nature of the two businesses. Wal-Mart sells primarily to retail customers for cash. Remember, from Wal-Mart's standpoint, a credit card sale is the same as a cash sale since Wal-Mart receives its money instantly; it is the credit card company that must worry about collecting the receivable. Boeing, on the other hand, sells to airlines and governments that have established business credit relationships with Boeing. Thus, the nature of its business dictates that Boeing has a much larger fraction of its sales tied up in the form of accounts receivable than does Wal-Mart.

average collection period A measure of the average number of days it takes to collect a credit sale; computed by dividing 365 days by the accounts receivable turnover.

Accounts receivable turnover can then be converted into the number of days it takes to collect receivables by computing a ratio called **average collection period**. This ratio is computed by dividing 365 (or the number of days in a year) by the accounts receivable turnover as follows:

$$\text{Average Collection Period} = \frac{365}{\text{Accounts Receivable Turnover}}$$

Computing this ratio for both Wal-Mart and Boeing shows that it takes Wal-Mart only 2.94 days (365 ÷ 124.09) on average to collect its receivables, while Boeing takes an average of 31.99 days (365 ÷ 11.41).

Consider what might happen to Boeing's average collection period during an economic recession. During a recession, purchasers are often strapped for cash and try to delay paying on their accounts for as long as possible. Boeing might be faced with airlines who still want to buy airplanes but wish to stretch out the payment period. The result would be a rise in Boeing's average collection period; more of Boeing's resources would be tied up in the form of accounts receivable. In turn, Boeing would have to increase its borrowing in order to pay its own bills since it would be collecting less cash from its slow-paying customers. Proper receivables management involves balancing the desire to extend credit in order to increase sales with the need to collect the cash quickly in order to pay off your own bills.

TO SUMMARIZE

Careful management of accounts receivable is a balance between extending credit to increase your sales and collecting cash quickly to reduce your need to borrow. Two ratios commonly used in monitoring the level of receivables are accounts receivable turnover and average collection period. The level of these ratios is determined by how well a company manages its receivables, as well as by what kind of business the company is in.

6 *Match revenues and expenses by estimating and recording future warranty and service costs associated with a sale.*

RECORDING WARRANTY AND SERVICE COSTS ASSOCIATED WITH A SALE

Let's return to the Farm Land example in which 50 sacks of fertilizer were sold for \$500. Assume that as part of each sale, Farm Land offers to send a customer service representative to the home or place of business of any purchaser who wants more detailed instruction on how to apply the fertilizer. Historical experience suggests that the buyer of one fertilizer sack in ten will request a visit from a Farm Land representative, and the material and labor cost of each visit averages \$35. So, with 50 sacks of fertilizer sold, Farm Land has obligated itself to provide, on average, \$175 in future customer service [(50 ÷ 10) × \$35]. Proper matching requires that this \$175 expense be estimated and recognized in the same period in which the associated sale is recognized. Otherwise, if you wait to record customer service expense until the actual visits are requested, this period's sales revenue would be reported in the same income statement with customer service expense arising from last period's sales. The accountant is giving up some precision because the service expense must be estimated in advance. This sacrifice in precision is worth the benefit of being able to better match revenues and expenses.

The entry to recognize Farm Land's estimated service expense from the sale of 50 sacks of fertilizer is as follows:

Customer Service Expense	175	
Estimated Liability for Service		175
Estimated customer service costs on sales [(50 ÷ 10) × $35].		

The credit entry, Estimated Liability for Service, is a liability. When actual expenses are incurred in providing the customer service, the liability is eliminated with the type of entry shown as follows:

Estimated Liability for Service	145	
Wages Payable (to service employees)		100
Supplies		45
Actual customer service costs incurred.		

This entry shows that supplies and labor were required to honor the service agreements. This procedure results in the service expense being recognized at the time of sale, not necessarily when the actual service occurs.

After these two journal entries are made, the remaining balance in Estimated Liability for Service will be $30, shown as follows:

Estimated Liability for Service

	Debit	Credit
Estimate at time of sale		175
Actual service costs incurred	145	
Remaining balance		30

The $30 balance represents the estimated amount of service that still must be provided in the future resulting from the sale of the 50 sacks of fertilizer. If actual experience suggests that the estimated service cost is too high, a lower estimate would be made in connection with subsequent fertilizer sales. If estimated liability for service is too low, a higher estimate is made for subsequent sales. The important point is that the accountant would not try to go back and "fix" an estimate that later proves to be inexact; the accountant merely monitors the relationship between the estimated and actual service costs in order to adjust future estimates accordingly.

The accounting just shown for estimated service costs is the same procedure used for estimated warranty costs. For example, General Motors promises automobile buyers that it will fix, at no charge to the buyer, certain mechanical problems for a certain period of time. GM estimates and records this warranty expense at the time the automobile sales are made. At the end of 1996, GM reported an existing liability for warranty costs of $13.7 billion. This amount is what GM estimates it will have to spend on warranty repairs in 1997 (and later years) on cars sold in 1996 (and earlier).

TO SUMMARIZE

In addition to bad debt expense, there are other costs that must be estimated and recognized at the time a sale is made in order to ensure the proper matching of revenues and expenses. If a company makes promises about future warranty repairs or continued customer service as part of the sale, the value of these promises should be estimated and recorded as an expense at the time of the sale.

REVIEW OF LEARNING OBJECTIVES

1 Understand the three basic types of business activities: operating, investing, and financing. The three major types of business activities are: (1) operating activities, (2) investing activities, and (3) financing activities. Operating activities include selling products or services, buying inventory for resale, and incurring and paying for necessary expenses associated with the primary activities of a business. Investing activities include purchasing property, plant, and equipment for use in the business; or purchasing investments, such as stocks and bonds of other companies. Financing activities include raising money by means other than operations to finance a business. The two common financing activities are borrowing (debt financing) and selling ownership or equity interests (equity financing) in the company.

2 Use the two revenue recognition criteria to decide when the revenue from a sale or service should be recorded in the accounting records. Revenue is recognized when the work is done and when cash collectibility is reasonably assured. The entries to record revenue from the sale of merchandise or from the performance of a service involve debits to Cash or Accounts Receivable and credits to Sales Revenue or Service Revenue. In general, revenues are recognized at the time of a sale. However, if cash is collected before a service is provided or a product is delivered, then revenue should not be recognized until the promised action has been completed. Revenue for long-term contracts is recognized in proportion to the amount of the contract completed.

3 Properly account for the collection of cash and describe the business controls necessary to safeguard cash. The amount of cash collected from customers can be reduced because of sales discounts and sales returns and allowances. Sales discounts are reductions in the payments required of customers who pay their accounts quickly. Sales returns and allowances are payment reductions granted to dissatisfied customers. On an income statement, sales discounts and sales returns and allowances are subtracted from gross sales to arrive at net sales. Cash is a tempting target for fraud or theft, so companies must carefully monitor and control the way cash is handled and accounted for. Common controls include (1) separation of duties in the handling of and accounting for cash, (2) daily deposits of all cash receipts, and (3) payment of all expenditures by prenumbered checks.

4 Record the losses resulting from credit customers who do not pay their bills. Accounts receivable balances are generally collected from 10 to 60 days after the date of sale. There are two ways to account for losses from uncollectible receivables: the direct write-off method and the allowance method. Only the allowance method is generally acceptable because it matches expenses with revenues. Losses from uncollectible receivables can be estimated (1) as a percentage of total credit sales for the period, or (2) as a percentage of total outstanding receivables. One technique for estimating uncollectible receivables as a percentage of total receivables is to perform an aging of accounts receivable.

5 Evaluate a company's management of its receivables by computing and analyzing appropriate financial ratios. Careful management of accounts receivable is a balance between extending credit to increase sales and collecting cash quickly to reduce the need to borrow. Two ratios commonly used in monitoring the level of receivables are accounts receivable turnover and average collection period. The level of these ratios is determined by how well a company manages its receivables, as well as by what kind of business the company is in.

6 Match revenues and expenses by estimating and recording future warranty and service costs associated with a sale. If a company makes promises about future warranty repairs or continued customer service as part of a sale, the value of these promises is estimated and recorded as an expense at the time of the sale. If experience suggests that the original estimate was in error, adjustments are made to the estimates made in relation to subsequent sales; however, no attempt is made to go back and "fix" the original estimates.

KEY TERMS AND CONCEPTS

gross sales 141
investing activities 133
net realizable value of accounts receivable 146
net sales 141
operating activities 132
receivables 143
revenue recognition 136
sales discounts 140
sales returns and allowances 141

REVIEW PROBLEM

Accounting for Receivables and Warranty Obligations

Douglas Company sells furniture. Approximately 10 percent of its sales are cash; the remainder are on credit. During the year ended December 31, 2000, the company had net credit sales of $2,200,000. As of December 31, 2000, total accounts receivable were $800,000 and Allowance for Bad Debts had a debit balance of $1,100 prior to adjustment. In the past, approximately 1 percent of credit sales have proven to be uncollectible. An aging analysis of the individual accounts receivable revealed that $32,000 of the accounts receivable balance appeared to be uncollectible.

The largest credit sale during the year occurred on December 4, 2000, for $72,000 to Aaron Company. Terms of the sale were 2/10, n/30. On December 13, Aaron Company paid $60,000 of the receivable balance and took advantage of the 2 percent discount. The remaining $12,000 was still outstanding on March 31, 2001, when Douglas Company learned that Aaron Company had declared bankruptcy. Douglas wrote the receivable off as uncollectible.

On December 31, 2000, Douglas Company estimated that it would cost $11,000 in labor and various expenditures to service the furniture it sold (under 90-day warranty agreements) during the last three months of 2000. During January 2001, the company spent $430 in labor and $600 for supplies to perform service on defective furniture that was sold during the year 2000.

Required: Prepare the following journal entries:

1. The sale of $72,000 of furniture on December 4, 2000, to Aaron Company on credit.
2. The collection of $58,800 from Aaron Company on December 13, 2000, assuming the company allows the discount on partial payment.
3. Record Bad Debt Expense on December 31, 2000, using the percentage of credit sales method.
4. Record Bad Debt Expense on December 31, 2000, using the aging of receivables method.
5. Record estimated warranty expense on December 31, 2000.
6. Record actual expenditures to service defective furniture under the warranty agreement on January 31, 2001.
7. Write off the balance of the Aaron Company receivable as uncollectible, March 31, 2001.

Solution The journal entries would be recorded as follows:

1. Dec. 4, 2000	Accounts Receivable.	72,000	
	Sales Revenue		72,000
	Sold $72,000 of furniture to Aaron Company on credit.		
2. Dec. 13, 2000	Cash.	58,800	
	Sales Discounts	1,200	
	Accounts Receivable		60,000
	Collected $58,800 from Aaron Company on December 4 sale and recognized the 2 percent discount taken (0.02 × $60,000 = $1,200).		

		Debit	Credit
3. Dec. 31, 2000	Bad Debt Expense	22,000	
	Allowance for Bad Debts		22,000
	Recorded bad debt expense as 1 percent of credit sales of $2,200,000 ($2,200,000 × 0.01 = $22,000).		

Note: When using the percentage of credit sales method to estimate bad debt expense, the existing balance in the account is ignored.

		Debit	Credit
4. Dec. 31, 2000	Bad Debt Expense	33,100	
	Allowance for Bad Debts		33,100
	Recorded bad debt expense using the aging of accounts receivable method ($32,000 + $1,100 debit balance).		

Note: When using the percentage of total receivables method (e.g., by aging receivables) to estimate bad debt expense, the existing balance in Allowance for Bad Debts must be taken into consideration so that the new balance is the amount of receivables not expected to be collected.

		Debit	Credit
5. Dec. 31, 2000	Customer Service Expense	11,000	
	Estimated Liability for Service		11,000
	Estimated customer service (warranty) costs on furniture sold during the last three months of 2000. (The warranty period is 90 days.)		
6. Jan. 31, 2001	Estimated Liability for Service	1,030	
	Wages Payable (to service employees)		430
	Supplies		600
	Actual customer service costs incurred.		
7. March 31, 2001	Allowance for Bad Debts	12,000	
	Accounts Receivable		12,000
	Wrote off the balance in the Aaron Company account as uncollectible.		

DISCUSSION QUESTIONS

1. What are the three types of basic business activities?
2. Why is the purchase of inventory for resale to customers classified as an operating activity rather than an investing activity?
3. When should revenues be recognized and reported?
4. Why do you think misstatements of revenues (e.g., recognizing revenues before they are earned) is one of the most common ways to manipulate financial statements?
5. Why is it important to have accounts for Sales Returns and Allowances and Sales Discounts? Wouldn't it be much easier to directly reduce the sales revenue account for these adjustments?
6. Why do companies usually have more controls for cash than for other assets?
7. What are three generally practiced controls for cash, and what is the purpose of each control?
8. Why do most companies tolerate having a small percentage of uncollectible accounts receivable?
9. Why does the accounting profession require use of the allowance method of accounting for losses due to bad debts rather than the direct write-off method?
10. Why is the net balance, or net realizable value, of accounts receivable the same after the write-off of a receivable as it was prior to the write-off of the uncollectible account?
11. Why is the "aging" of accounts receivable usually more accurate than basing the estimate on total receivables?
12. Why is it important to monitor operating ratios such as accounts receivable turnover?
13. Why must the customer service expense (warranty) sometimes be recorded in the period prior to when the actual customer services will be performed?

DISCUSSION CASES

CASE 4-1

RECOGNIZING REVENUES

HealthCare Incorporated* operates a number of medical testing facilities around the United States. Drug manufacturers, such as **Merck** and **Bristol-Myers Squibb**, contract with HealthCare for testing of their newly-developed drugs and other medical treatments. HealthCare Incorporated advertises, gets patients, and then administers the drug or other experimental treatments, under a doctor's care, to determine their effectiveness. The Food & Drug Administration requires such human testing before allowing the drugs to be prescribed by doctors and sold by pharmacists. A typical contract might read as follows:

> HealthCare Incorporated will administer the new drug, "Lexitol," to 50 patients, once a week for 10 weeks, to determine its effectiveness in treating male baldness. Merck will pay HealthCare Incorporated $100 per patient visit, to be billed at the conclusion of the test period. The total amount of the contract is $50,000 (50 patients × 10 visits × $100 per visit).

Given these kinds of contracts, when should HealthCare recognize revenue—when contracts are signed, when patient visits take place, when drug manufacturers are billed, or when cash is collected?

*The name of the actual company has been changed.

CASE 4-2

CREDIT POLICY REVIEW

The president, vice president, and sales manager of Moorer Corporation were discussing the company's present credit policy. The sales manager suggested that potential sales were being lost to competitors because of Moorer Corporation's tight restrictions on granting credit to consumers. He stated that if credit policies were loosened, the current year's estimated credit sales of $3,000,000 could be increased by at least 20 percent next year with an increase in uncollectible accounts receivable of only $10,000 over this year's amount of $37,500. He argued that because the company's cost of sales is only 25 percent of revenues, the company would certainly come out ahead.

The vice president, however, believed that a better alternative to easier credit terms would be to accept consumer credit cards such as **VISA** or **MasterCard**. He believed this alternative could increase sales by 40 percent. The credit card finance charges to Moorer Corporation would be 4 percent of the additional sales.

At this point, the president interrupted by saying that he wasn't at all sure that increasing credit sales of any kind was a good thing. In fact, he suggested that the $37,500 of uncollectible accounts receivable was altogether too high. He wondered whether or not the company should discontinue offering sales on account.

With the information given, determine whether Moorer Corporation would be better off under the sales manager's proposal or the vice president's proposal. Also, address the president's suggestion that credit sales of all types be abolished.

EXERCISES

EXERCISE 4-1
Recognizing Revenue

Supposedly, there is over a 200-year wait to buy **Green Bay Packers** season football tickets. The fiscal year end (when they close their books) for the Green Bay

Packers is March 30 of each year. When the Packers sell their season football tickets in February for the coming football season, when should the revenue from those ticket sales be recognized?

EXERCISE 4-2
Recognizing Revenue—Long-Term Construction Projects

In the year 2002, Salt Lake City, Utah, will host the Winter Olympics. To get ready for the Olympics, most of the major roads and highways in and around Salt Lake City are being renovated. It will take over three years to complete the highway projects and **Wasatch Constructors**, the construction company performing the work, probably doesn't want to wait until the work is completed to recognize revenue. How would you suggest that the revenue on these highway construction projects be recognized?

EXERCISE 4-3
Revenue Recognition

Yummy, Inc., is a franchiser that offers for sale an exclusive franchise agreement for $30,000. Under the terms of the agreement, the purchaser of a franchise receives a variety of services associated with the construction of a Yummy Submarine and Yogurt Shop, access to various product supply services, and continuing management advice and assistance once the retail unit is up and running. The contract calls for the franchise purchaser to make cash payments of $10,000 per year for three years to Yummy, Inc.

How should Yummy, Inc., account for the sale of a franchise contract? Specifically, when should the revenue and receivable be recognized?

EXERCISE 4-4
Control of Cash

Molly Maloney is an employee of Marshall Company, a small manufacturing concern. Her responsibilities include opening the daily mail, depositing the cash and checks received into the bank, and making the accounting entries to record the receipt of cash and the reduction of receivables. Explain how Maloney might be able to misuse some of Marshall's cash receipts. As a consultant, what control procedures would you recommend?

EXERCISE 4-5
Recording Sales Transactions

On June 24, 2000, Hansen Company sold merchandise to Jill Selby for $80,000 with terms 2/10, n/30. On June 30, Selby paid $39,200 on her account and was allowed a discount for the timely payment. On July 20, Selby paid $24,000 on her account and returned $16,000 of merchandise, claiming that it did not meet contract terms.

Record the necessary journal entries on June 24, June 30, and July 20.

EXERCISE 4-6
Recording Sales Transactions

Lopez Company sold merchandise on account to Atlantic Company for $4,000 on June 3, 2000, with terms 2/10, n/30. On June 7, 2000, Lopez Company received $200 of returned merchandise from Atlantic Company and issued a credit memorandum for the appropriate amount. Lopez Company received payment for the balance of the bill on June 21, 2000.

Record the necessary journal entries on June 3, June 7, and June 21.

EXERCISE 4-7
Estimating Bad Debts

The trial balance of Stardust Company at the end of its 2000 fiscal year included the following account balances:

Account	
Accounts Receivable	$48,900
Allowance for Bad Debts	2,500 (debit balance)

The company has *not yet* recorded any bad debt expense for 2000.

Determine the amount of bad debt expense to be recognized by Stardust Company for 2000 assuming the following independent situations:

1. An analysis of the aging of accounts receivables indicates that probable uncollectable accounts receivable at year end amounts to $4,500.

2. Company policy is to maintain a provision for uncollectible accounts receivable equal to 3 percent of outstanding accounts receivables.
3. Company policy is to estimate uncollectible accounts receivable equal to 0.5 percent of the previous year's annual sales, which were $200,000.

EXERCISE 4-8
Accounting for Bad Debts

The following data were associated with the accounts receivable and uncollectible accounts of Hilton, Inc., during 2000:

a. The opening credit balance in Allowance for Bad Debts was $900,000 at January 1, 2000.
b. During 2000, the company realized that specific accounts receivable totaling $920,000 had gone bad and had been written off.
c. An account receivable of $50,000 was collected during 2000. This account had previously been written off as a bad debt in 1999.
d. The company decided that Allowance for Bad Debts would be $920,000 at the end of 2000.

1. Prepare journal entries to show how these events would be recognized in the accounting system using:
   a. The direct write-off method.
   b. The allowance method.
2. Discuss the advantages and disadvantages of each method with respect to the matching principle.

EXERCISE 4-9
Accounting for Uncollectible Accounts Receivable

Dodge Company had the following information relating to its accounts receivable at December 31, 1999, and for the year ended December 31, 2000:

Accounts receivable balance at 12/31/99	$ 900,000
Allowance for bad debts at 12/31/99 (credit balance)	50,000
Gross sales during 2000 (all credit)	5,000,000
Collections from customers during 2000	4,500,000
Accounts written off as uncollectible during 2000	60,000
Estimated uncollectible receivables at 12/31/00	110,000

1. At December 31, 2000, what is the balance of Dodge Company's Allowance for Bad Debts? What is the bad debt expense for 2000?
2. At December 31, 2000, what is the balance of Dodge Company's gross accounts receivable?

EXERCISE 4-10
Aging of Accounts Receivable

Cicero Company's accounts receivable reveals the following balances:

Age of Accounts	Receivable Balance
Current	$600,000
1–30 days past due	320,000
31–60 days past due	80,000
61–90 days past due	50,000
91–120 days past due	9,000

The credit balance in Allowance for Bad Debts is now $26,000. After a thorough analysis of the collection history, the company estimated that the following percentages of receivables would eventually prove uncollectible:

Current	0.4%
1–30 days past due	3.0
31–60 days past due	12.0
61–90 days past due	60.0
91–120 days past due	90.0

Prepare an aging schedule for the accounts receivable, and give the journal entry for recording the necessary change in the allowance for bad debts account.

EXERCISE 4-11
Direct Write-Off vs. Allowance Method

The vice president for Tres Corporation provides you with the following list of accounts receivable written off in the current year. (These accounts were recognized as bad debt expense at the time they were written off; i.e., they were using the direct write-off method.)

Date	Customer	Amount
March 30	Rasmussen Company	$12,000
July 31	Dodge Company	7,500
September 30	Larsen Company	10,000
December 31	Peterson Company	12,000

Tres Corporation's sales are all on a n/30 credit basis. Sales for the current year total $3,600,000, and analysis has indicated that uncollectible receivable losses historically approximate 1.5 percent of sales.

1. Do you agree or disagree with Tres Corporation's policy concerning recognition of bad debt expense? Why or why not?
2. If Tres were to use the percent of sales method for recording bad debt expense, by how much would net income change for the current year?

EXERCISE 4-12
Accounting for Uncollectible Receivables—Percentage of Sales Method

The trial balance of Sporting House, Inc., shows a $100,000 outstanding balance in Accounts Receivable at the end of 1999. During 2000, 75 percent of the total credit sales of $4,000,000 was collected, and no receivables had been written off as uncollectible. The company estimated that 1.5 percent of the credit sales would be uncollectible. During 2001, the account of Larry Johnson, who owed $1,200, was judged to be uncollectible and was written off. At the end of 2001, the amount previously written off was collected in full from Mr. Johnson.

Prepare the necessary journal entries for recording all the preceding transactions relating to the books of Sporting House, Inc., on uncollectibles.

EXERCISE 4-13
Ratio Analysis

The following are summary financial data for Parker Enterprises, Inc., and Boulder, Inc., for three recent years:

	Year 3	Year 2	Year 1
Net sales (in millions):			
Parker Enterprises, Inc.	$ 3,700	$ 3,875	$ 3,882
Boulder, Inc.	17,825	16,549	15,242
Net accounts receivable (in millions):			
Parker Enterprises, Inc.	1,400	1,800	1,725
Boulder, Inc.	5,525	5,800	6,205

1. Using the above data, compute the accounts receivable turnover and average collection period for each company for years 2 and 3.
2. Which company appears to have the better credit management policy?

EXERCISE 4-14
Assessing How Well Companies Manage Their Receivables

Assume the Hickory Company has the following data related to its accounts receivable:

	1999	2000
Net sales	$1,425,000	$1,650,000
Net receivables:		
Beginning of year	375,000	333,500
End of year	420,000	375,000

Use these data to compute accounts receivable turnover ratios and average collection periods for 1999 and 2000. Based on your analysis, is Hickory Company managing its receivables better or worse in 2000 than it did in 1999?

EXERCISE 4-15
Accounting for Warranties

Rick Procter, president of Sharp Television Stores, has been concerned recently with declining sales due to increased competition in the area. Rick has noticed that many of the national stores selling television sets and appliances have been placing heavy emphasis on warranties in their marketing programs. In an effort to revitalize sales, Rick has decided to offer free service and repairs for one year as a warranty on his television sets. Based on experience, Rick believes that first-year service and repair costs on the television sets will be approximately 5 percent of sales. The first month of operations following the initiation of Rick's new marketing plan showed significant increases in sales of TV sets. Total sales of TV sets for the first 3 months under the warranty plan were $10,000, $8,000, and $12,000, respectively.

1. Assuming that Rick prepares adjusting entries and financial statements for his own use at the end of each month, prepare the appropriate entry to recognize customer service (warranty) expense for each of these first 3 months.
2. Prepare the appropriate entry to record services provided to repair sets under warranty in the second month, assuming that the following costs were incurred: labor (paid in cash), $550; supplies, $330.

EXERCISE 4-16
Accounting for Warranties

Johnson Auto sells used cars and trucks. During 2000, it sold 51 cars and trucks for a total of $1,350,000. Johnson provides a 12-month, 12,000 mile warranty on the used cars and trucks sold. Johnson estimates that it will cost $25,000 in labor and $13,000 in parts to service (during the following year) the cars and trucks sold in 2000.

In January 2001, Steve Martin brought his truck in for warranty repairs. Johnson Auto fixed the truck under its warranty agreement. It cost Johnson $400 in labor and $275 in parts to fix Steve Martin's truck. Prepare the journal entries to record (1) Johnson Auto's estimated customer service liability as of December 31, 2000 and (2) the costs incurred in repairing the truck in January 2001.

PROBLEMS

PROBLEM 4-1
Sales Transactions

Company R and Company S entered into the following transactions.

a. Company R sold merchandise to Company S for $40,000, terms 2/10, n/30.
b. Prior to payment, Company S returned $3,000 of the merchandise for credit.
c. Company S paid Company R in full within the discount period.
d. Company S paid Company R in full after the discount period. (Assume that transaction (c) did not occur.)

Required: Prepare journal entries to record the transactions for Company R (the seller).

PROBLEM 4-2
Analysis of Allowance for Bad Debts

Boulder View Corporation accounts for uncollectible accounts receivable using the allowance method.

As of December 31, 1999, the credit balance in Allowance for Bad Debts was $130,000. During 2000, credit sales totaled $10,000,000, $90,000 of accounts receivable were written off as uncollectible, and recoveries of accounts previously written off amounted to $15,000. An aging of accounts receivable at December 31, 2000, showed the following:

Classification of Receivable	Accounts Receivable Balance as of December 31, 2000	Percentage Estimated Uncollectible
Current	$1,140,000	2%
1–30 days past due	600,000	10
31–60 days past due	400,000	23
Over 60 days past due	120,000	75
	$2,260,000	

Required:

1. Prepare the journal entry to record bad debt expense for 2000, assuming bad debts are estimated using the aging of receivables method.
2. Record journal entries to account for the actual write-off of $90,000 uncollectible accounts receivable, and the collection of $15,000 in receivables that had previously been written off.

PROBLEM 4-3
Accounting for Accounts Receivable

Assume that Dome Company had the following balances in its receivable accounts on December 31, 1999:

Accounts receivable	$400,000
Allowance for bad debts	10,200 (credit balance)

Transactions during 2000 were as follows:

Gross credit sales	$1,600,000
Collections of accounts receivable ($1,560,000 less cash discounts of $20,000)	1,540,000
Sales returns and allowances (from credit sales)	10,000
Accounts receivable written off as uncollectible	6,000
Balance in Allowance for Bad Debts on December 31, 2000 (based on percent of total accounts receivable)	12,000

Required:

1. Prepare entries for the 2000 transactions.
2. What amount will Dome Company report for:
   a. Net sales in its 2000 income statement?
   b. Total accounts receivable on its balance sheet of December 31, 2000?

PROBLEM 4-4
Analysis of Receivables

Juniper Company was formed in 1990. Sales have increased on the average of 5 percent per year during its first 10 years of existence, with total sales for 1999 amounting to $400,000. Since incorporation, Juniper Company has used the allowance method to account for uncollectible accounts receivable.

On January 1, 2000, the company's Allowance for Bad Debts had a credit balance of $5,000. During 2000, accounts totaling $3,500 were written off as uncollectible.

Required:

1. What does the January 1, 2000, credit balance of $5,000 in Allowance for Bad Debts represent?
2. Since Juniper Company wrote off $3,500 in uncollectible accounts receivable during 2000, was the prior year's estimate of uncollectible accounts receivable overstated?
3. Prepare journal entries to record:
   a. The $3,500 write-off of receivables during 2000.
   b. Juniper Company's 2000 bad debt expense, assuming an aging of the December 31, 2000, accounts receivable indicates that potential uncollectible accounts at year-end total $9,000.

PROBLEM 4-5
Computing and Recording Bad Debt Expense

During 2000, Wishbone Corporation has a total of $5,000,000 in sales, of which 80 percent are on credit. At year-end, the accounts receivable balance shows a total of $2,300,000, which has been aged as follows:

Age	Amount
Current	$1,900,000
1–30 days past due	200,000
31–60 days past due	100,000
61–90 days past due	70,000
Over 90 days past due	30,000
	$2,300,000

Prepare the journal entry required at year-end to record the bad debt expense under each of the following independent conditions. Assume, where applicable, that Allowance for Bad Debts has a credit balance of $5,500 immediately before these adjustments.

Required:

1. Use the direct write-off method. (Assume that $60,000 of accounts are determined to be uncollectible and are written off in a single year-end entry.)
2. Based on experience, uncollectible accounts existing at year-end are estimated to be 3 percent of total accounts receivable.
3. Based on experience, uncollectible accounts are estimated to be the sum of:

   1 percent of current accounts receivable
   6 percent of accounts 1–30 days past due
   10 percent of accounts 31–60 days past due
   20 percent of accounts 61–90 days past due
   30 percent of accounts over 90 days past due

PROBLEM 4-6
Unifying Concepts: Aging of Accounts Receivable and Uncollectible Accounts

Delta Company has found that, historically, 1/2 percent of its current accounts receivable, 1 percent of accounts 1 to 30 days past due, 1 1/2 percent of accounts 31 to 60 days past due, 3 percent of accounts 61 to 90 days past due, and 10 percent of accounts over 90 days past due are uncollectible. The following schedule shows an aging of the accounts receivable as of December 31, 2000:

		Days Past Due			
	Current	1–30	31–60	61–90	Over 90
Balance	$45,600	$9,850	$4,100	$850	$195

The balances at December 31, 2000, in selected accounts are as follows. (Assume that the allowance method is used.)

Sales revenue	$120,096
Sales returns	1,209
Allowance for bad debts	113 (credit balance)

Required:

1. Given these data, make the necessary adjusting entry (or entries) for uncollectible accounts receivable on December 31, 2000.
2. On February 14, 2001, Lori Jacobs, a customer, informed Delta Company that she was going bankrupt and would not be able to pay her account of $46. Make the appropriate entry (or entries).
3. On June 29, 2001, Lori Jacobs was able to pay the amount she owed in full. Make the appropriate entry (or entries).
4. Assume that Allowance for Bad Debts at December 31, 2000, had a debit balance of $113 instead of a credit balance of $113. Make the necessary adjusting journal entry that would be needed on December 31, 2000.

PROBLEM 4-7
Estimating Uncollectible Accounts

Ulysis Corporation makes and sells clothing to fashion stores throughout the country. On December 31, 2000, before adjusting entries were made, it had the following account balances on its books:

Accounts receivable	$ 2,320,000
Sales revenue, 2000 (60% were credit sales)	16,000,000
Allowance for bad debts (credit balance)	4,000

Required:

1. Make the appropriate adjusting entry on December 31, 2000, to record the allowance for bad debts if uncollectible accounts receivable are estimated to be 3 percent of accounts receivable.
2. Make the appropriate adjusting entry on December 31, 2000, to record the allowance for bad debts if uncollectible accounts receivable are estimated on the basis of an aging of accounts receivable; the aging schedule reveals the following:

	Balance of Accounts Receivable	Percent Estimated to Become Uncollectible
Current	$1,200,000	1/2 of 1 percent
1–30 days past due	800,000	1 percent
31–60 days past due	200,000	4 percent
61–90 days past due	80,000	20 percent
Over 90 days past due	40,000	30 percent

3. Now assume that on March 3, 2001, it was determined that a $64,000 account receivable from Petite Corners is uncollectible. Record the bad debt, assuming:
   a. The direct write-off method is used.
   b. The allowance method is used.
4. Further assume that on June 4, 2001, Petite Corners paid this previously written off debt of $64,000. Record the payment, assuming:
   a. The direct write-off method had been used on March 3 to record the bad debt.
   b. The allowance method had been used on March 3 to record the bad debt.
5. **Interpretive Question:** Which method of accounting for bad debts, direct write-off or allowance, is generally used? Why?

Analyzing Real Company Information

International Case

Ethics Case

Writing Assignment

The Debate

Internet Search

Accounting is more than just doing textbook problems. These Competency Enhancement Opportunities provide practice in critical thinking, oral and written communication, research, teamwork, and consideration of ethical issues.

ANALYZING REAL COMPANY INFORMATION

• Analyzing 4–1 (Microsoft)

The 1997 annual report for **Microsoft** is included in Appendix A. Locate that annual report and consider the following questions:

1. Provide the summary journal entry that would be made by Microsoft to record its revenue for the fiscal year ended June 30, 1997 (assume all sales were on account).

COMPETENCY ENHANCEMENT OPPORTUNITIES

2. Given Microsoft's beginning and ending balances in accounts receivable, along with your journal entry from Part 1, estimate the amount of cash collected from customers during the year.
3. Notice that Microsoft has an unearned revenue account. The balance in that account increased from 1996 to 1997. Provide the journal entry that was made to record that increase.
4. Locate Microsoft's note on revenue recognition. What is Microsoft's revenue recognition policy?

• Analyzing 4–2 (Bank of America)

Bank of America is one of the oldest banks in America, as well as being the second largest. Founded in the late 1800s, Bank of America has grown from being strictly a California-based bank to one with operations in over 20 states. Information from Bank of America's annual report is given below. (Amounts are in millions.)

	1996	1995
Bad debt expense	$ 885	N/A
Allowance for bad debts	3,523	$3,554

Using this information, answer the following questions:

1. Provide the journal entry made by Bank of America to record bad debt expense for 1996.
2. Provide the journal entry made by Bank of America to record actual bad debts for 1996.

• Analyzing 4–3 (Microsoft and IBM)

Information from comparative income statements and balance sheets for **Microsoft** and **IBM** is given below. (Amounts are in millions.)

	Microsoft		IBM	
	1997	1996	1996	1995
Sales	$11,358	N/A	$75,944	N/A
Accounts receivable	980	$639	23,167	$23,402

Use this information to answer the following questions:

1. Compute Microsoft's average collection period receivable for 1997.
2. Compute IBM's average collection period for 1996.
3. Why do you think these two very profitable companies can have such large differences in their average collection period?

INTERNATIONAL CASE

• Revenue from foreign transactions

The global economy is requiring many businesses to conduct transactions with numerous foreign companies. While these transactions do not present any accounting problems when the transactions are denominated in

American dollars, problems arise if the transactions are denominated in a foreign currency. For example, consider what happens when a sale is made with a Japanese company and the invoice is to be paid in Japanese yen.

1. American Inc. sells one widget to Japanese Co. at an agreed upon price of 1,000,000 yen. On the day of the sale, one yen is equal to $0.01. American Inc. maintains its accounting records in American dollars. Therefore, the amount in yen must be converted to dollars. Provide the journal entry that would be made by American Inc. on the day of the sale, assuming Japanese Co. pays for the widget on the day of the sale.
2. Most sales are on account, meaning that payment will not be received for 30 days or even longer. What issues will arise for American Inc. if the sale is made with payment due in 30 days? (Hint: What might happen to the value of the yen in relation to the dollar during the 30-day period?)
3. Suppose that 30 days from the date of the sale the value of one yen is equal to $0.008. What journal entry would be made when the 1,000,000 yen are received by American Inc? (Hint: A loss will be recognized. Use an account entitled "Exchange Loss.")

ETHICS CASE

• Changing our estimates

John Verner is the controller for BioMedic Inc., a biotechnology company. John is finishing his preparation of the preliminary financial statements for a meeting of the board of directors scheduled for later in the day. At the board's prior meeting, members discussed the need to achieve a certain income level and profit margin for two reasons: (1) to comply with loan agreements, and (2) to prepare for a stock offering in the near future.

Unfortunately for John and the company, the preliminary net income figure is coming up short. John knows that the board will take a serious look at the estimates and assumptions made in preparing the income statement. In anticipation of the board's review, John has identified the following two issues:

1. In the past, bad debt expense has been computed using the percentage of sales method. The percentage used has varied between 3 and 3.5 percent. This year, John assumed a rate of 3 percent. If he were to modify his estimate of bad debt expense to be 2.5 percent of sales, income would increase by $700,000.
2. BioMedic Inc. offers a warranty on many of the products it sells. Like bad debt expense, warranty expense is computed as a percentage of sales. John is considering modifying his estimates of warranty expense from 1.4 percent of sales down to 1.1 percent. This modification would result in a $420,000 increase in net income.

These two changes, considered together, would result in the firm being able to report that it achieved its targeted net income figure, thereby satisfying lenders and potential investors.

What issues should John consider before he makes the changes to the income statement? Would John be doing something wrong by making these changes? Would John be breaking the law?

WRITING ASSIGNMENT

• Revenue recognition for health clubs

Health fitness has become increasingly popular in the 90s. Health clubs have popped up all over, and with these clubs come some interesting accounting issues. Members typically sign up for one year and pay an upfront fee, followed by a monthly payment. The upfront fee covers, among other things, a health assessment by a club expert as well as a customized training program. For the monthly fee, members get the use of the facilities. The big accounting question is: how should the upfront fee be accounted for? Can the entire amount of the upfront fee be recognized at the beginning of the contract or should it be recognized over the course of the year? Prepare a one- to two-page paper explaining your point of view.

THE DEBATE

• The direct write-off method vs. the allowance method

When it comes to recognizing bad debt expense, the allowance method is used because it complies with the matching principle (i.e., expenses are matched with revenues in the period in which those revenues are earned). However, the allowance method requires estimation and the estimates may not be reliable. An alternative is to use the direct write-off method. When a receivable is deemed worthless, it is written off and the bad debt is recognized. This method requires no estimates and is thus more reliable.

Divide your group into two teams.

- One team represents "The Direct Write-Off Method." Prepare a two-minute oral argument supporting the use of this method.
- The other team represents "The Allowance Method." Prepare a two-minute presentation supporting your position.

INTERNET SEARCH

• Boeing Company

Boeing Company is the largest manufacturer of airplanes in the world. Access Boeing's Web site at www.boeing.com. Sometimes Web addresses change, so if this address doesn't work, access the Web site for this textbook (stice.swcollege.com) for an updated link.

Once you've gained access to Boeing's Web site, answer the following questions:

1. In addition to manufacturing commercial airplanes, for what other industry segments does Boeing manufacture products?
2. Recently, Boeing merged with another large aerospace company. Can you identify that company?
3. Compute the company's average collection period for the most recent year.
4. Review Boeing's note disclosure relating to revenue recognition. How does the company recognize revenue in its various industry segments?

CHAPTER 5

OPERATING ACTIVITIES—EXPENDITURES

LEARNING OBJECTIVES

After studying this chapter, you should be able to:

1. *Identify what items and costs should be included in inventory and cost of goods sold.*
2. *Account for inventory purchases and sales using both a perpetual and a periodic inventory system, calculate cost of goods sold using the results of an inventory count, and understand the impact of errors in ending inventory on reported cost of goods sold.*
3. *Apply the four inventory cost flow alternatives: specific identification, FIFO, LIFO, and average cost.*
4. *Discuss and account for additional day-to-day activities related to the operating cycle.*
5. *Prepare an income statement summarizing operating activities as well as other revenues and expenses, extraordinary items, and earnings per share.*
6. *Analyze a company's inventory level and liquidity position using various analysis techniques.*

SETTING THE STAGE

Sears, Roebuck and Co. began as the result of an inventory mistake. In 1886, a shipment of gold watches was mistakenly sent to a jeweler in Redwood Falls, Minnesota. When the jeweler refused to accept delivery of the unwanted watches, they were purchased by an enterprising railroad agent who saw an opportunity to make some money. Richard Sears sold all of those watches, ordered more, and started the **R.W. Sears Watch Company**. The next year, Sears moved his operation to Chicago, found a partner in watchmaker Alvah Roebuck, and in 1893 they incorporated under the name "Sears, Roebuck and Co."

The initial growth of Sears was fueled by mail-order sales to farmers. Sears bought goods in volume from manufacturers. Then, taking advantage of cheap parcel post and rural free delivery (RFD) rates, Sears shipped the goods directly to the customers, thus bypassing the profit markups of the chain of middlemen usually standing between manufacturers and farmers. Sales growth was partially driven by Richard Sears' persuasive advertising copy in the famous Sears catalog. In fact, Sears' early product descriptions have been politely called "fanciful." But the company compensated by backing its products with an unconditional money-back guarantee for dissatisfied customers.

The next wave of growth at Sears began in 1925 when the first Sears retail store was opened in Chicago. The shift from mail-order catalog sales to retail outlet sales paralleled the rise in popularity of the automobile in the United States. The automobile made it practical for rural customers to shop in the city. Reflecting the importance of the automobile, Sears pioneered the placement of free parking lots next to its stores. In the post-World War II boom, Sears' sales skyrocketed, leaving chief rival **Montgomery Ward** far behind.

The 1980s was a decade of diversification at Sears. However, the diversification actually began in 1931 when Sears started selling **Allstate** auto insurance, first by mail and then from its retail locations. In the 1980s, Sears acquired **Dean Witter**, a financial services firm, and **Coldwell Banker**, a real estate firm. In addition, Sears launched the Discover® credit card and backed Prodigy®, the first widespread online service (a joint project with **IBM** and **CBS**).

In the early 1990s, the diversified Sears empire began to show increasing weakness, culminating in a reported loss of almost $2.3 billion in 1992. The response of Sears' management was to go back to the basics of retail marketing. The financial services operations (including the Discover card) and the real estate operations (along with the famous Sears Tower in Chicago) were sold. Sears focused on clothing sales in its mall-based stores and appliance and automotive product sales in its off-the-mall stores. In addition, Sears returned to emphasizing its in-house Sears credit card, with over 55 million cardholders. This focused strategy appears to be working. In 1996, Sears' chief executive officer (CEO), Arthur Martinez, was selected as *Financial World's* CEO of the Year. More importantly for shareholders, Sears' stock price increased from $15 per share in 1992 to as high as $64 per share in 1997.

Sources: Sears Company History at sears.com/company/pubaff; "Sears, Roebuck and Co.," *International Directory of Company Histories,* Vol. 18 (Detroit: St. James Press, 1997), pp. 475–479.

Most companies are in the business of selling goods or services for a profit. In Chapter 4, we discussed the sales transaction and noted that a company recognizes revenue when it has provided goods or services to a customer and *when the customer has paid or provided a promise of payment. Whether a company provides a product (either as a manufacturer, a wholesaler, or a retailer) or a service (such as legal or accounting), the issues associated with recording a sale are the same. An asset account (either Cash or Accounts Receivable) is increased at the same time a revenue account is increased. We also noted that the sales event does not end with the initial exchange. Companies must also account for the potential of sales discounts, bad debts, and warranties.*

For firms that sell a product, the cost of the inventory sold typically represents the largest expense for that business. For example, cost of goods sold for **H. J. Heinz** *(the ketchup maker) in 1997 represented over 68 percent of revenues. In this chapter, we discuss issues relating to cost of goods sold and inventory. Inventory is purchased (often on account) and then resold at a profit. Two methods for recording day-to-day inventory transactions are introduced—perpetual and periodic. We also discuss the various methods for valuing inventory at the end of a period—FIFO, specific identification, LIFO, and average cost.*

While cost of goods sold represents a significant expense for those companies who manufacture and/or sell a product, it is certainly not the only expense. And for those companies who sell a service, other expenses can be just as significant as cost of goods sold. For example, **KPMG Peat Marwick** *(one of the large international accounting firms) disclosed in its 1996 annual report that personnel costs amounted to 41 percent of revenues.*

In this chapter, we also discuss a number of these other significant operating issues. We will begin with two significant operating expenses that are incurred by almost every firm: employee compensation and taxes. Exhibit 5-1 highlights the accounts that will be discussed in this chapter.

Also in this chapter we discuss issues relating to the format of the income statement and information relating to earnings per share. This chapter concludes with a discussion of how information relating to the operations of a firm can be used by investors and creditors in making resource allocation decisions. We review the uses of a common-size income statement, and we also analyze the cash flow cycle of a business and how certain ratios are useful in assessing a firm's operations.

EXHIBIT 5-1 Basic Financial Statements

Balance Sheet

Current assets:		*Current liabilities:*	
Cash	Ch. 4	**Accounts payable**	Ch. 5
Investments	Ch. 7	**Taxes payable**	Ch. 5
Accounts receivable	Ch. 4	**Wages payable**	Ch. 5
Inventory	Ch. 5	Warranty liability	Ch. 4
Property, plant, and equipment	Ch. 7	**Unearned revenues**	Ch. 5
Intangible assets	Ch. 9	*Long-term liabilities:*	
Long-term investments	Ch. 7	Long-term debt	Ch. 6
Total assets		**Pension costs**	Ch. 5
		Stockholders' equity:	
		Common stock	Ch. 6
		Retained earnings	Ch. 6
		Unrealized increase/decrease in value of securities	Ch. 7
		Total liabilities and stockholders' equity	

Income Statement

Sales of goods and services	Ch. 4
Cost of goods sold	Ch. 5
Gross margin	
Expenses:	
Salaries expense	Ch. 5
Taxes expense	Ch. 5
Depreciation expense	Ch. 7
Bad debt expense	Ch. 4
Warranty expense	Ch. 4
Other revenues and expenses:	
Gains and losses on sales of securities	Ch. 7
Unrealized gains and losses on securities	Ch. 7
Interest expense	Ch. 6
Interest revenue	Ch. 7
Net income	

Statement of Cash Flows

Operating activities:	
Receipts from customers	Ch. 4
Payments for inventory	Ch. 5
Payments for salaries	Ch. 5
Payments for interest	Ch. 5
Payments for taxes	Ch. 5
Purchase of trading securities	Ch. 7
Sale of trading securities	Ch. 7
Investing activities:	
Purchase of property, plant, and equipment	Ch. 7
Proceeds from sale of property, plant, and equipment	Ch. 7
Purchase of debt and equity securities other than trading securities	Ch. 7
Sale of debt and equity securities other than trading securities	Ch. 7
Financing activities:	
Sale of stock	Ch. 6
Purchase of treasury stock	Ch. 6
Proceeds from borrowing	Ch. 6
Repayments of borrowing	Ch. 6
Payments of dividends	Ch. 6
Net cash flows for the period	

1 *Identify what items and costs should be included in inventory and cost of goods sold.*

inventory Goods held for resale.

cost of goods sold The expenses incurred to purchase or manufacture the merchandise sold during a period.

INVENTORY AND COST OF GOODS SOLD

Inventory is the name given to goods that are either manufactured or purchased for resale in the normal course of business. A car dealer's inventory is comprised of automobiles; a grocery store's inventory consists of vegetables, meats, dairy products, canned goods, and bakery items; Sears' inventory is composed of shirts, appliances, DieHard® batteries, and more. Like other items of value, such as cash or equipment, inventory is classified as an asset and reported on the balance sheet. When products are sold, they are no longer assets. The costs to purchase or manufacture the products must be removed from the asset classification (inventory) on the balance sheet and reported on the income statement as an expense—**cost of goods sold**.

The time line in Exhibit 5-2 illustrates the business issues involved with inventory.

EXHIBIT 5-2 Time Line of Business Issues Involved with Inventory

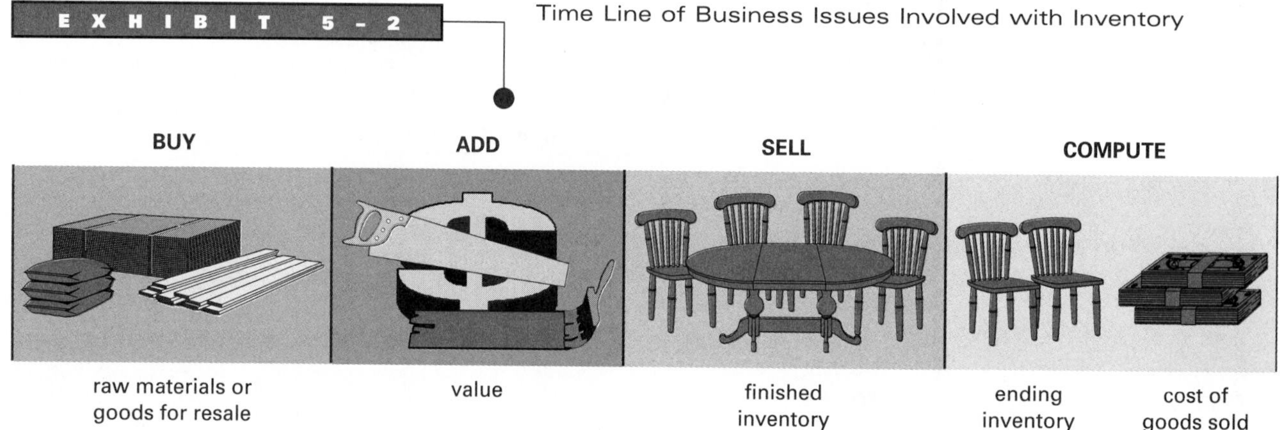

The accounting questions associated with the items in the time line are as follows:

- When is inventory considered to have been purchased—when it is ordered, shipped, received, or paid for?
- Similarly, when is the inventory considered to have been sold?
- Which of the costs associated with the "value-added" process are considered to be part of the cost of inventory and which are simply business expenses for that period?
- How should total inventory cost be divided between the inventory that was sold (cost of goods sold) and the inventory that remains (ending inventory)?

These questions are addressed in the following sections of the chapter.

What Is Inventory?

In a merchandising firm, either wholesale or retail, inventory is composed of the items that have been purchased in order to be resold. In a supermarket, milk is inventory, a shopping cart is not. In a manufacturing company, there are three different types of inventory: raw materials, work in process, and finished goods.

Raw Materials

raw materials Materials purchased for use in manufacturing products.

Raw materials are goods acquired in a relatively undeveloped state that will eventually compose a major part of the finished product. If you are making bicycles, one of the raw materials is tubular steel. For a computer assembler, raw materials inventory is composed of plastic, wires, and Intel® chips.

Work in Process

work in process Partially completed units in production.

Work in process consists of partially finished products. When you take a tour of a manufacturing plant, you are seeing work-in-process inventory.

Finished Goods

finished goods Manufactured products ready for sale.

Finished goods are the completed products waiting for sale. A completed car rolling off the automobile assembly line is part of finished goods inventory.

What Costs Are Included in Inventory Cost?

Inventory cost consists of all costs involved in buying the inventory and preparing it for sale. In the case of raw materials or goods acquired for resale by a merchandising firm, cost includes the purchase price, freight, and receiving and storage costs.

The cost of work-in-process inventory is the sum of the costs of the raw materials, the production labor, and some share of the manufacturing overhead required to keep the factory running. The cost of an item in finished goods inventory is the total of the materials, labor, and overhead costs used in the production process for that item. As you can imagine, accumulating these costs and calculating a cost per unit is quite a demanding task. The cost of a finished automobile includes the cost of the steel and rubber; the salaries and wages of assembly workers, inspectors, and testers; the factory insurance; the workers' pension benefits; and much more. This costing process is a key part of management accounting and is covered in Chapter 10.

The costs just described are all costs expended in order to get inventory produced and ready to sell. These costs are appropriately included in inventory costs. Those costs incurred in the sales effort itself are *not* inventory costs, but instead should be reported as operating expenses in the period in which they are incurred. For example, the costs of maintaining the finished goods warehouse or the retail showroom are period expenses. Salespersons' salaries are period expenses, as is the cost of advertising. In addition, general nonfactory administrative costs are also period expenses. Examples are the costs of the corporate headquarters and the company president's salary.

Ending Inventory and Cost of Goods Sold

cost of goods available for sale The cost of all merchandise available for sale during the period; equal to the sum of beginning inventory and net purchases.

Inventory purchased or manufactured during the period is added to beginning inventory and the total cost of this inventory is called the **cost of goods available for sale**. At the end of an accounting period, total cost of goods available for sale must be allocated between inventory still remaining (to be reported in the balance sheet as an asset) and inventory sold during the period (to be reported in the income statement as an expense, Cost of Goods Sold).

This cost allocation process is extremely important. This importance is apparent from the fact that the more cost that is said to remain in ending inventory, the less cost is reported as cost of goods sold in the income statement. For this reason, accountants must be careful of inventory errors since they directly impact reported net income. The impact of inventory errors is illustrated later in the chapter.

The cost allocation process also involves a significant amount of accounting judgment. Because identical inventory items are usually purchased at varying prices throughout the year, the accountant must determine which items (the low cost or high cost) remain and which were sold in order to calculate the amount of ending inventory and cost of goods sold. Again, this decision can directly impact the amount of reported cost of goods sold and net income. The use of inventory cost flow assumptions is discussed later in the chapter.

TO SUMMARIZE

Inventory is composed of goods held for sale in the normal course of business. Cost of goods sold is the cost of inventory sold during the period. For a manufacturing firm, the three types of inventory are raw materials, work in process, and finished goods. All costs incurred in producing and getting inventory ready to sell should be added to inventory cost. The costs associated with the selling effort itself are operating expenses of the period. At the end of an accounting period, the total cost of goods available for sale during the period must be allocated between ending inventory and cost of goods sold.

2 *Account for inventory purchases and sales using both a perpetual and a periodic inventory system, calculate cost of goods sold using the results of an inventory count, and understand the impact of errors in ending inventory on reported cost of goods sold.*

ACCOUNTING FOR INVENTORY PURCHASES AND SALES

To begin a more detailed study of inventory accounting, we must first establish a solid understanding of the journal entries used to record inventory transactions. The accounting procedures for recording purchases and sales using both a periodic and a perpetual inventory system are detailed in this section.

Overview of Perpetual and Periodic Systems

Some businesses track changes in inventory levels on a continuous basis, recording each individual purchase and sale to maintain a running total of the inventory balance. This is called a perpetual inventory system. Other businesses rely on quarterly or yearly inventory counts to reveal which inventory items have been sold. This is called a periodic inventory system.

Perpetual

You own a discount appliance superstore. Your biggest-selling items are washers, dryers, refrigerators, microwaves, and dishwashers. You advertise your weekly sale items on local TV stations and your sales volume is quite heavy. You have 50 salespeople who work independently of one another. You have found that customers get very upset if they come to buy an advertised item and you have run out. In this business environment, would it make sense to keep a running total of the quantity remaining of each inventory item, updated each time a sale is made? Yes, the benefit of having current information on each inventory item would make it worthwhile to spend a little extra time when a sale is made to update the inventory records.

perpetual inventory system A system of accounting for inventory in which detailed records of the number of units and the cost of each purchase and sales transaction are prepared throughout the accounting period.

This appliance store would probably use a **perpetual inventory system**. With a perpetual system, inventory records are updated whenever a purchase or a sale is made. In this way, the inventory records at any given time reflect how many of each inventory item should be in the warehouse or out on the store shelves. A perpetual system is most often used when each individual inventory item has a relatively high value or when there are large costs to running out of or overstocking specific items.

Periodic

You operate a newsstand in a busy metropolitan subway station. Almost all of your sales occur during the morning and the evening rush hours. You sell a diverse array of items—newspapers, magazines, pens, snacks, and other odds and ends. During rush hour, your business is a fast-paced pressure cooker; the longer you take treating one customer, the more chance there is that the busy commuters waiting in line for service will tire of waiting and you will lose sales. In this business environment, would it make sense to make each customer wait while you meticulously check off on an inventory sheet exactly which items were sold? No, the delay caused by this detailed bookkeeping would cause you to lose customers. It makes more sense to wait until the end of the day, count up what inventory you still have left, compare that to what you started with, and use those numbers to deduce how many of each inventory item you sold during the day.

periodic inventory system A system of accounting for inventory in which cost of goods sold is determined and inventory is adjusted at the end of the accounting period, not when merchandise is purchased or sold.

This subway newsstand scenario is an example of a situation where a **periodic inventory system** is appropriate. With a periodic system, inventory records are not updated when a sale is made; only the dollar amount of the sale is recorded. Periodic systems are most often used when inventory is composed of a large number of diverse items, each with a relatively low value.

Impact of Information Technology

Over the past 25 years, advances in information technology have lowered the cost of maintaining a perpetual inventory system, causing more businesses to adopt perpetual systems in order to more closely track inventory levels. The most visible manifestation of this trend is in supermarkets. In your parents' day, the check-out clerk rang up the price of each item on a cash register. After you walked out of the store with your groceries, the store knew the total amount of your purchase but did not know what individual items you had purchased. This was a periodic inventory system. Now, with laser scanning equipment tied into the supermarket's computer system, most supermarkets operate under a perpetual system. The store manager knows exactly what you bought and exactly how many of each item should still be left on the store shelves.

(S T O P & T H I N K)

If you buy your groceries with a credit card or a bank debit card, what kind of information can the supermarket accumulate about you?

Perpetual and Periodic Journal Entries

The following transactions for Grantsville Clothing Store will be used to illustrate the differences in bookkeeping procedures between a business using a perpetual system and one using a periodic system:

a. Purchased on account: 1,000 shirts at a cost of $10 each for a total of $10,000.
b. Purchased on account: 300 pairs of pants at a cost of $18 each for a total of $5,400.
c. Paid cash for separate shipping costs on the shirts purchased in (a), $970. The supplier of the pants purchased in (b) included the shipping costs in the $18 purchase price.
d. Returned 30 of the shirts (costing $300) to the supplier because they were stained.
e. Paid for the shirt purchase. A 2% discount was given on the $9,700 bill ([1,000 purchased − 30 returned] × $10) because of payment within the 10-day discount period (payment terms were 2/10, n/30).
f. Paid $5,400 for the pants purchase. No discount was allowed because payment was made after the discount period.
g. Sold on account: 600 shirts at a price of $25 each for a total of $15,000.
h. Sold on account: 200 pairs of pants at a price of $40 each for a total of $8,000.
i. Accepted return of 50 shirts by dissatisfied customers.

The journal entries for the perpetual system should seem familiar to you—a perpetual system has been assumed in all earlier chapters of the text. A perpetual system was assumed because it is logical and is the system all companies would choose if there were no cost to updating the inventory records each time a sale or purchase is made. As mentioned, a periodic system is sometimes a practical necessity.

Purchases

With a perpetual system, all purchases are added (debited) directly to Inventory. With a periodic system, the inventory balance is only updated using an inventory count at the end of the period; inventory purchases during the period are recorded in a temporary holding account called Purchases. As will be illustrated later, at the end of the period, the balance in Purchases is closed to Inventory in connection with the computation of cost of goods sold.

Entries (a) and (b) to record the shirt and pants purchases are given below:

	Perpetual			Periodic		
a.	Inventory	10,000		Purchases	10,000	
	Accounts Payable		10,000	Accounts Payable		10,000
b.	Inventory	5,400		Purchases	5,400	
	Accounts Payable		5,400	Accounts Payable		5,400

Transportation Costs

The cost of transporting the inventory is an additional inventory cost. Sometimes, as with the pants in the Grantsville Clothing example, the shipping cost is already included in the purchase price and a separate entry to record the transportation costs is not needed. When a separate payment is made for transportation costs, it is recorded as follows:

	Perpetual			Periodic		
c.	Inventory	970		Freight In	970	
	Cash		970	Cash		970

With a perpetual system, transportation costs are added directly to the inventory balance. With a periodic system, another temporary holding account is created, Freight In, and transportation costs are accumulated in this account during the period. As with the Purchases account, Freight In is closed to Inventory at the end of the period in connection with the computation of cost of goods sold.

Purchase Returns

With a perpetual system, the return of unsatisfactory merchandise to the supplier results in a decrease in Inventory. In addition, since no payment will have to be made for the returned merchandise, Accounts Payable is reduced by the same amount. With a periodic system, the amount of the returned merchandise is recorded in yet another temporary holding account called Purchase Returns. Purchase Returns is a contra-account to Purchases and is also closed to Inventory as part of the computation of cost of goods sold.

	Perpetual			Periodic		
d.	Accounts Payable	300		Accounts Payable	300	
	Inventory		300	Purchase Returns		300

If the returned merchandise had already been paid for, the supplier would most likely return the purchase price. In this case, the debit would be to Cash instead of to Accounts Payable.

Purchase Discounts

As discussed in Chapter 4, sellers sometimes offer inducements for credit customers to pay quickly. In this example, Grantsville Clothing takes advantage of purchase discounts to save money on the payment for the shirts. The amount of the purchase discount is $194 ($9,700 × 0.02) and the total payment amount for the shirts is $9,506 ($9,700 − $194). The amount recorded for inventory should reflect the actual amount paid to purchase the inventory. With a perpetual system, this is shown by subtracting the purchase discount amount from the inventory account. With a periodic system, another holding account is created to accumulate purchase discounts taken during the period.

	Perpetual			Periodic		
e.	Accounts Payable	9,700		Accounts Payable	9,700	
	Inventory		194	Purchase Discounts		194
	Cash		9,506	Cash		9,506
f.	Accounts Payable	5,400		Accounts Payable	5,400	
	Cash		5,400	Cash		5,400

FYI

In practice, this same inventory adjustment information (e.g., Freight In, Purchase Returns, etc.) would probably be maintained in supplemental records under a perpetual system. Such information would be useful to management in evaluating company purchasing practices, for example.

Note that the payment for the pants is made after the discount period so the full amount must be paid. Since this transaction had no impact on Inventory, the entry is the same for both the perpetual and the periodic systems.

In terms of journal entries, you should recognize that the difference between a perpetual and a periodic system is that all adjustments to inventory under a perpetual system are entered directly in the inventory account; all inventory adjustments with a periodic system are accumulated in an array of temporary holding accounts: Purchases, Freight In, Purchase Returns, and Purchase Discounts.

Sales

The sale of shirts and pants would be recorded as follows:

	Perpetual			Periodic		
g.	Accounts Receivable	15,000		Accounts Receivable	15,000	
	Sales (600 × $25)		15,000	Sales		15,000
	Cost of Goods Sold	6,000		no entry		
	Inventory (600 × $10)		6,000			
h.	Accounts Receivable	8,000		Accounts Receivable	8,000	
	Sales (200 × $40)		8,000	Sales		8,000
	Cost of Goods Sold	3,600		no entry		
	Inventory (200 × $18)		3,600			

These entries reflect the primary difference between a perpetual and a periodic system—with a periodic system, no attempt is made to recognize cost of goods sold on a transaction-by-transaction basis. In fact, with a periodic system, Grantsville Clothing would not even know how many shirts and how many pairs of pants had been sold. Instead, only total sales of $23,000 ($15,000 + $8,000) would be known.

For simplicity, we have recorded the cost of goods sold for the shirts as $10 each. The actual cost per shirt, after adjusting for freight in and purchase discounts, is $10.80, computed as follows:

Total purchase price (1,000 shirts)	$10,000
Plus: Freight in	970
Less: Purchase returns (30 shirts)	(300)
Less: Purchase discounts	(194)
Total cost of shirts (970 shirts)	$10,476

Total cost $10,476 ÷ 970 shirts = $10.80 per shirt

In practice, it is unlikely that a firm using a perpetual system would bother to adjust unit costs for the effects of freight cost and purchase discounts on an ongoing basis. The cost of doing these calculations could easily outweigh any resulting improvement in the quality of cost information.

Sales Returns

As discussed in Chapter 4, dissatisfied customers sometimes return their purchases. The journal entries to record the return of 50 shirts are as follows:

	Perpetual			Periodic		
i.	Sales Returns (50 × $25)	1,250		Sales Returns	1,250	
	Accounts Receivable		1,250	Accounts Receivable		1,250
	Inventory (50 × $10)	500		no entry		
	Cost of Goods Sold		500			

(STOP & THINK)

Should the returned inventory be recorded at its original cost of $10 per shirt?

Under the perpetual system, not only are the sales for the returned items canceled, but the cost of the returned inventory is also removed from cost of goods sold and restored to the inventory account.

Closing Entries

After all the journal entries are posted to the ledger, the T-accounts for Inventory and Cost of Goods Sold, under a perpetual system, would appear as follows:

Inventory

	Debit		Credit
(a)	10,000	(d)	300
(b)	5,400	(e)	194
(c)	970	(g)	6,000
(i)	500	(h)	3,600
Bal.	6,776		

Cost of Goods Sold

	Debit		Credit
(g)	6,000	(i)	500
(h)	3,600		
Bal.	9,100		

These numbers, after being verified by a physical count of the inventory (as described in the next section), would be reported in the financial statements—the $6,776 of inventory in the balance sheet and the $9,100 of cost of goods sold in the income statement.

Review the journal entries (a) through (i) under the periodic system and notice that none of the amounts have been entered in either Inventory or Cost of Goods Sold. As a result, both of these accounts will have zero balances at year end. Actually, the inventory account would have the same balance it had at the beginning of the period which, in this example, we will assume to be zero.

With a periodic inventory system, the correct balances are recorded in Inventory and Cost of Goods Sold through a series of closing entries. Two entries are made:

1. Accumulate and add all the temporary holding accounts to the inventory account balance. At this point, the inventory account balance is equal to the cost of goods available for sale (beginning inventory plus the net cost of purchases for the period).
2. Reduce Inventory by the amount of Cost of Goods Sold. At this point, the inventory account balance is equal to the ending inventory amount and the appropriate cost of goods sold amount is also recognized.

To illustrate, the information for Grantsville Clothing will be used. The entry to accumulate all the temporary holding accounts is as follows:

Inventory	15,876	
Purchase Returns	300	
Purchase Discounts	194	
Freight In		970
Purchases		15,400
Closing of temporary inventory accounts for periodic system.		

net purchases The net cost of inventory purchased during a period, after adding the cost of freight in and subtracting returns and discounts.

The inventory debit of $15,876 is the amount of **net purchases** for the period. Notice that, after this entry has been posted, the balances in all the temporary holding accounts will have been reduced to zero. As mentioned, after the addition of net purchases, the inventory account balance represents cost of goods available for sale (the sum of beginning inventory and net purchases). Remember that, in this example, beginning inventory is assumed to be zero.

The second closing entry involves the adjustment of Inventory to its appropriate ending balance. If the year-end physical count indicates that the ending inventory balance should be $6,776, the appropriate entry is as follows:

Cost of Goods Sold	9,100	
Inventory ($15,876 − $6,776)		9,100
Adjustment of inventory account to appropriate ending balance.		

In this example, the values for both ending inventory ($6,776) and cost of goods sold ($9,100) are the same using either a perpetual or a periodic system. So, what is the practical difference between the two systems? One difference is that a perpetual system can tell you the inventory balance and the cumulative cost of goods sold at any time during the period. With a periodic system, on the other hand, you must wait until counting the inventory at the end of the period to compute inventory or cost of goods sold. Another difference is that, with a perpetual system, you can compare the inventory records to the amount of inventory actually on hand and thus determine whether any inventory has been lost or stolen. As described in the next section, this comparison is not possible with a periodic system.

Counting Inventory and Calculating Cost of Goods Sold

Regular physical counts of the existing inventory are essential to maintaining reliable inventory accounting records. With a perpetual system, the physical count can be compared to the recorded inventory balance to see whether any inventory has been lost or stolen. With a periodic system, a physical count is the only way to get the information necessary to compute cost of goods sold.

Taking a Physical Count of Inventory

No matter which inventory system a company is using, periodic physical counts are a necessary and important part of accounting for inventory. With a perpetual inventory system, the physical count either confirms that the amount entered in the accounting records is accurate or it highlights shortages and clerical errors. If, for example, employees have been stealing inventory, the theft will show up as a difference between the balance in the inventory account and the amount physically counted.

A physical count of inventory involves two steps:

1. *Quantity count.* In most companies, physically counting all inventory is a time-consuming activity. Because sales transactions and merchandise deliveries can complicate matters, inventory is usually counted on holidays or after the close of business on the inventory day. Special care must be taken to ensure that all inventory owned, wherever its location, is counted.
2. *Inventory costing.* When the physical count has been completed, each type of merchandise is assigned a unit cost. The quantity of each type of merchandise is multiplied by its unit cost to determine the dollar value of the inventory. These amounts are then added to obtain the total ending inventory for the business. This is the amount reported as Inventory on the balance sheet. The ending balance in the inventory account may have to be adjusted for any shortages discovered.

To illustrate the impact of a physical inventory count on the accounting records for both a periodic and a perpetual system, we will refer back to the Grantsville Clothing Store example used earlier. Assume that a physical count, combined with inventory costing analysis, suggests that the correct amount for ending inventory is $5,950. This information can be combined with previous information from the accounting system as follows:

	Periodic System	Perpetual System	
Beginning inventory	$ 0	$ 0	
Plus: Net purchases	15,876	15,876	
Cost of goods available for sale	$15,876	$15,876	
Less: Ending inventory	5,950	6,776	(from inventory system)
Cost of goods sold	$ 9,926	$ 9,100	(from inventory system)
Goods lost or stolen	unknown	826	($6,776 − $5,950)
Total cost of goods sold, lost, or stolen	$ 9,926	$ 9,926	

Recall that, in this example, the beginning inventory is assumed to be zero. The amount of net purchases is a combination of the items affecting the amount paid for inventory purchases during the period: purchase price, freight in, purchase returns, and purchase discounts. The $15,876 amount for net purchases was computed earlier in connection with the closing entry for the periodic system.

This cost of goods sold computation highlights the key difference between a periodic and a perpetual system. With a periodic system, the company does not know what ending inventory *should be* when the inventory count is performed. The best the company can do is count the inventory and assume that the difference between the cost of goods available for sale and the cost of goods still remaining (ending inventory) must represent the cost of goods that were sold. Actually, a business using a periodic system has no way of knowing whether these goods were sold, lost, stolen, or spoiled—all they know for sure is that the goods are gone.

With a perpetual system, the accounting records themselves yield the cost of goods sold during the period, as well as the amount of inventory that *should be* found when the physical count is made. In the Grantsville Clothing example, the predicted ending inventory is $6,776 (from the T-account shown earlier); the actual ending inventory, according to the physical count, is only $5,950. The difference of $826 ($6,776 – $5,950) represents inventory lost, stolen, or spoiled during the period. This amount is called **inventory shrinkage**. The adjusting entry needed to record this inventory shrinkage is as follows:

inventory shrinkage The amount of inventory that is lost, stolen, or spoiled during a period; determined by comparing perpetual inventory records to the physical count of inventory.

Inventory Shrinkage	826	
Inventory ($6,776 – $5,950)		826
Adjustment of perpetual inventory balance to reflect inventory shrinkage.		

FYI

In the notes to its 1994 financial statements, **Kmart** disclosed that, as a result of the year-end inventory count, inventory shrinkage of $17 million was discovered.

For internal management purposes, the amount of inventory shrinkage would be tracked from one period to the next in order to detect whether the amount of "shrinkage" for any given period is unusually high. For external reporting purposes, the shrinkage amount would probably be combined with normal cost of goods sold and the title "Cost of Goods Sold" given to the total. Notice that if this practice is followed, reported cost of goods sold would be the same under both a perpetual and a periodic system. The difference is that, with a perpetual system, company management knows how much of the goods were actually sold and how much represents inventory shrinkage.

With a periodic inventory system, no journal entry for inventory shrinkage is made because the amount of shrinkage is unknown. Instead, the ending inventory amount derived from the physical count would be used to make the second periodic inventory closing entry (refer back to the previous section). Using the $5,950 ending inventory amount, the appropriate periodic inventory closing entry is:

Cost of Goods Sold	9,926	
Inventory ($15,876 – $5,950)		9,926
Adjustment of inventory account to appropriate ending balance.		

The Income Effect of an Error in Ending Inventory

As shown in the previous section, the results of the physical inventory count directly impact the computation of cost of goods sold with a periodic system and inventory shrinkage with a perpetual system. Errors in the inventory count will cause the amount of cost of goods sold or inventory shrinkage to be misstated. To illustrate, assume that the correct inventory count for Grantsville Clothing is $5,950 but that the ending inventory value is mistakenly computed to be $6,450. The impact of this $500 ($6,450 – $5,950) inventory overstatement is as follows:

	Periodic System	Perpetual System
Beginning inventory	$ 0	$ 0
Plus: Net purchases	15,876	15,876
Cost of goods available for sale	$15,876	$15,876
Less: Ending inventory	6,450	6,776 (from inventory system)
Cost of goods sold	$ 9,426	$ 9,100 (from inventory system)
Goods lost or stolen	unknown	326 ($6,776 – $6,450)
Total cost of goods sold, lost, or stolen	$ 9,426	$ 9,426

The $500 inventory overstatement reduces the reported cost of goods sold, lost, or stolen by $500, from $9,926 (computed earlier) to $9,426. This is because if we mistakenly think that we have more inventory remaining, then we will also mistakenly think that we must have sold less. Conversely, if the physical count understates ending inventory, total cost of goods sold will be overstated.

Since an inventory overstatement decreases reported cost of goods sold, it will also increase reported gross margin and net income. For this reason, the managers of a firm that is having difficulty meeting profit targets are sometimes tempted to "mistakenly" overstate ending inventory. Because of this temptation, auditors must take care to review a company's inventory counting process and also to physically observe a sample of the actual inventory.

TO SUMMARIZE

With a perpetual inventory system, the amount of inventory and cost of goods sold for the period are tracked on an ongoing basis. With a periodic inventory system, inventory and cost of goods sold are computed using an end-of-period inventory count. With a periodic system, inventory-related items are recorded in temporary holding accounts that are closed to the inventory account at the end of the period. A physical inventory count is necessary to ensure that inventory records match with the actual existing inventory. If a perpetual system is used, an inventory count can be used to compute the amount of inventory shrinkage during the period. An error in the reported ending inventory amount can have a significant effect on reported cost of goods sold, gross margin, and net income. For example, overstatement of ending inventory results in understatement of cost of goods sold and overstatement of net income.

BUSINESS ENVIRONMENT ESSAY

Inventory Fraud One of the most common ways of committing major financial statement fraud and reporting income that is higher than it should be is to overstate a company's inventory. If ending inventory is overstated, cost of goods sold is understated and net income is overstated. The overstatement of inventories and income can attract investors and boost stock prices. In addition, since inventory can often be pledged as collateral to borrow money from banks, its overstatement increases a company's borrowing power. Each of these scenarios is illustrated by the following actual cases.

Crazy Eddie Inc. [1]At one point, Crazy Eddie Inc. was one of the hottest names in consumer electronics. What began in 1970 as a single store selling TVs, stereos, and other electronic products mushroomed into an empire with so many stores that *The New Yorker* magazine once ran a cartoon in which all roads led to Crazy Eddie. The piercing slogan "C-r-r-r-azy Eddie! His prices are ins-a-a-a-ne!" blurted incessantly on radio and TV stations and brought customers in droves. At one point, Crazy Eddie stock traded for as much as $43.25 per share.

In 1987, however, the company ended up under court-protected bankruptcy because of much-publicized inventory problems. As much as $65 million in inventory was suddenly inexplicably missing or phantom. When new management took over the company in a desperate rescue attempt in 1987, the $65 million inventory write-off more than erased all the earnings the company had ever reported. It seems that during the inventory counts, company officers had drafted phony inventory count sheets and improperly included merchandise so that the reported ending inventory and net income would be higher. The resulting artificially high profits and stock price allowed its founder, Eddie Antar, to rake in $68.4 million from stock sales through 1986.

The Great Salad Oil Case [2]The **Allied Crude Vegetable Oil** (Great Salad Oil) Case is one of the most well-known inventory frauds of all time. Founded in 1957 by Tino De Angelis, the company was set up on an old petroleum tank farm in Bayonne, New Jersey. De Angelis used the soybean oil that was supposedly in the tanks as collateral to borrow money from financial institutions. He then hired **American Express Warehousing, Ltd.** (a subsidiary of **American Express**) to take charge of storing, inspecting, and documenting the oil. The warehousing receipts issued by the warehouse workers were used as evidence of the oil.

De Angelis handpicked 22 men to work at the tank farm, and they fooled the American Express inspectors with considerable ease. For example, one of them would climb to the top of a tank, drop in a weighted tape measure, and then shout down to the inspector that the tank was full. In most cases the tanks were empty, although some were filled with seawater and topped with a thin slick of oil. Moreover, the tanks were connected by a jungle of pipes which allowed the men to pump whatever oil there was from one tank to another.

The maneuvers gave De Angelis an "endless" supply of oil and borrowing power. If anyone had checked a statistical report issued by the U.S. Census Bureau, he or she would have found that the oil supposedly stored at the tank farm totaled twice as much as all the oil in the country. By the close of 1963, the warehouse receipts represented 937 million pounds of oil when actually only 100 million pounds existed.

The salad oil scandal was revealed when De Angelis was unable to make payments on an investment. The ensuing investigation revealed a fraud that was conservatively estimated at $200 million. Most of the losses were borne by 51 major banking and brokerage houses in the United States and Europe, 20 of which collapsed.

De Angelis pleaded guilty to four federal counts of fraud and conspiracy and was given a 20-year sentence. The millions of dollars loaned to De Angelis were never found, and it is generally believed that the missing oil never existed. In fact, when one oil tank that supposedly had $3,575,000 worth of oil was opened, seawater ran out for 12 consecutive days.

Sources: [1]Jeff Tannenbaum, "Short Circuit," *The Wall Street Journal,* Monday, July 10, 1989, p. A1, Col. 6. [2]Marshall B. Romney and W. Steve Albrecht, "The Use of Investigative Agencies by Auditors," *The Journal of Accountancy,* October 1979, p. 61.

3 *Apply the four inventory cost flow alternatives: specific identification, FIFO, LIFO, and average cost.*

INVENTORY COST FLOW ASSUMPTIONS

Consider the following transactions for the Ramona Rice Company for the year 2000.

Mar. 23 Purchased 10 kilos of rice, $4 per kilo.
Nov. 17 Purchased 10 kilos of rice, $9 per kilo.
Dec. 31 Sold 10 kilos of rice, $10 per kilo.

The surprisingly difficult question to answer with this simple example is "How much money did Ramona make in 2000?" As you can see, it depends on which rice she sold on December 31. There are three possibilities:

	Case #1 Sold Old Rice	Case #2 Sold New Rice	Case #3 Sold Mixed Rice
Sales ($10 × 10 kilos)	$100	$100	$100
Cost of goods sold (10 kilos)	40	90	65
Gross margin	$ 60	$ 10	$ 35

FIFO (first in, first out) An inventory cost flow whereby the first goods purchased are assumed to be the first goods sold so that the ending inventory consists of the most recently purchased goods.

In Case #1, it is assumed that the 10 kilos of rice sold on December 31 were the old ones, purchased on March 23 for $4 per kilo. Accountants call this a **FIFO (first in, first out)** assumption. In Case #2, it is assumed that the new rice was sold, that pur-

LIFO (last in, first out) An inventory cost flow whereby the last goods purchased are assumed to be the first goods sold so that the ending inventory consists of the first goods purchased.

average cost An inventory cost flow assumption whereby cost of goods sold and the cost of ending inventory are determined by using an average cost of all merchandise available for sale during the period.

chased on November 17 for $9 per kilo. Accountants call this a **LIFO (last in, first out)** assumption. In Case #3, it is assumed that all the rice is mixed together and the $6.50 cost per kilo is the average cost of all the rice available for sale [($40 + $90) ÷ 20 kilos]. Accountants call this an **average cost** assumption.

The point of the Ramona Rice example is this: in most cases, there is no feasible way to track exactly which units were sold. Accordingly, in order to compute cost of goods sold, the accountant must make an assumption. Note that this is not a case of tricky accountants trying to manipulate the reported numbers; instead, this is a case in which income simply cannot be computed unless the accountant uses his or her judgment and makes an assumption.

All three of the assumptions described in the example—FIFO, LIFO, and average cost—are acceptable under U.S. accounting rules. An interesting question is whether a company would randomly choose one of the three acceptable methods, or whether the choice would be made more strategically. For example, if Ramona were preparing financial statements to be used to support a bank loan application, which assumption would you suggest that she make? On the other hand, if Ramona were completing her income tax return, which assumption would be the best? This topic of strategic accounting choice will be discussed later in this chapter.

In the following sections, we will examine in more detail the different cost flow assumptions used by companies to determine inventories and cost of goods sold.

Specific Identification Inventory Cost Flow

specific identification A method of valuing inventory and determining cost of goods sold whereby the actual costs of specific inventory items are assigned to them.

One alternative is to specifically identify the cost of each particular unit that is sold. This approach, called **specific identification**, is often used by automobile dealers and other businesses that sell a limited number of units at a high price. To illustrate the specific identification inventory costing method, we will consider the September 2000 records of Nephi Company, which sells one type of bicycle.

Sept. 1 Beginning inventory consisted of 10 bicycles costing $200 each.
3 Purchased 8 bicycles costing $250 each.
18 Purchased 16 bicycles costing $300 each.
20 Purchased 10 bicycles costing $320 each.
25 Sold 28 bicycles, $400 each.

These inventory records show that during September the company had 44 bicycles (10 from beginning inventory and 34 that were purchased during the month) that it could have sold. However, only 28 bicycles were sold, leaving 16 on hand at the end of September. Using the specific identification method of inventory costing requires that the individual costs of the actual units sold be charged against revenue as cost of goods sold. To compute cost of goods sold and ending inventory amounts with this alternative, a company must know which units were actually sold and what the unit cost of each was.

Suppose that of the 28 bicycles sold by Nephi on September 25, eight came from the beginning inventory, four came from the September 3 purchase, and 16 came from the September 18 purchase. With this information, cost of goods sold and ending inventory are computed as follows:

	Bicycles	Costs
Beginning inventory	10	$ 2,000
Net purchases	34	10,000
Goods available for sale	44	$12,000
Ending inventory	16	4,600
Cost of goods sold	28	$ 7,400

The cost of ending inventory is the total of the individual costs of the bicycles still on hand at the end of the month, or:

2 bicycles from beginning inventory, $200 each	$ 400
4 bicycles purchased on September 3, $250 each	1,000
0 bicycles purchased on September 18, $300 each	0
10 bicycles purchased on September 20, $320 each	3,200
Total ending inventory (16 units)	$4,600

Similarly, the cost of goods sold is the total of the costs of the specific bicycles sold, or:

8 bicycles from beginning inventory, $200 each	$1,600
4 bicycles purchased on September 3, $250 each	1,000
16 bicycles purchased on September 18, $300 each	4,800
0 bicycles purchased on September 20, $320 each	0
Total cost of goods sold (28 units)	$7,400

For many companies, it is impractical, if not impossible, to keep track of specific units. When that is the case, an assumption must be made as to which units were sold during the period and which are still in inventory, as illustrated in the Ramona Rice example given earlier.

It is very important to remember that the accounting rules do not require that the assumed flow of goods for costing purposes match the actual physical movement of goods purchased and sold. In some cases, the assumed cost flow may be similar to the physical flow, but firms are not required to match the assumed accounting cost flow to physical flow. A grocery store, for example, usually tries to sell the oldest units first to minimize spoilage. Thus, the physical flow of goods would reflect a FIFO pattern, but the grocery store could use a FIFO, LIFO, or average cost assumption in determining the ending inventory and cost of goods sold numbers to be reported in the financial statements. On the other hand, a company that stockpiles coal must first sell the coal purchased last since it is on top of the pile. That company might use the LIFO cost assumption, which reflects physical flow, or it might use one of the other alternatives.

In the next few sections, we will illustrate the FIFO, LIFO, and average inventory costing methods. The bicycle inventory data for Nephi Company will again be used in illustrating the different inventory cost flows.

FIFO Cost Flow Assumption

With FIFO, it is assumed that the oldest units are sold and the newest units remain in inventory. The ending inventory and cost of goods sold for Nephi Company if using the FIFO inventory cost flow assumption are:

	Bicycles	Costs
Beginning inventory	10	$ 2,000
Net purchases	34	10,000
Goods available for sale	44	$12,000
Ending inventory	16	5,000
Cost of goods sold	28	$ 7,000

The $7,000 cost of goods sold and $5,000 cost of ending inventory are determined as follows:

FIFO cost of goods sold (oldest 28 units):	
10 bicycles from beginning inventory, $200 each	$2,000
8 bicycles purchased on September 3, $250 each	2,000
10 bicycles purchased on September 18, $300 each	3,000
Total FIFO cost of goods sold	$7,000

FIFO ending inventory (newest 16 units):	
10 bicycles purchased on September 20, $320 each	$3,200
6 bicycles purchased on September 18, $300 each	1,800
Total FIFO ending inventory	$5,000

LIFO Cost Flow Assumption

LIFO is the opposite of FIFO. With LIFO, the cost of the most recent units purchased is transferred to cost of goods sold. When prices are rising, as they are in the Nephi Company example, LIFO provides higher cost of goods sold, and hence lower net income, than FIFO. This is because the newest (high-priced) goods are assumed to have been sold. The ending inventory and cost of goods sold for Nephi Company with the LIFO inventory cost flow assumption are:

	Bicycles	Costs
Beginning inventory	10	$ 2,000
Net purchases	34	10,000
Goods available for sale	44	$12,000
Ending inventory	16	3,500
Cost of goods sold	28	$ 8,500

The $8,500 cost of goods sold and $3,500 cost of ending inventory are determined as follows:

LIFO cost of goods sold (newest 28 units):	
10 bicycles purchased on September 20, $320 each	$3,200
16 bicycles purchased on September 18, $300 each	4,800
2 bicycles purchased on September 3, $250 each	500
Total LIFO cost of goods sold	$8,500

LIFO ending inventory (oldest 16 units):	
10 bicycles from beginning inventory, $200 each	$2,000
6 bicycles purchased on September 3, $250 each	1,500
Total LIFO ending inventory	$3,500

Average Cost Flow Assumption

With average costing, an average cost must be computed for all the inventory available for sale during the period. The average unit cost for Nephi Company during September is computed as follows:

	Bicycles	Costs
Beginning inventory	10	$ 2,000
Net purchases	34	10,000
Goods available for sale	44	$12,000
$12,000 ÷ 44 units = $272.73 per unit		

With the average cost assumption, cost of goods sold is computed by multiplying the number of units sold by the average cost per unit. Similarly, the cost of ending inventory is computed by multiplying the number of units in ending inventory by the average cost per unit. These calculations are as follows:

Average cost of goods sold: 28 units	×	$272.73 per unit	=	$7,636 (rounded)
Average ending inventory: 16 units	×	$272.73 per unit	=	$4,364 (rounded)

This information can be shown as follows:

	Bicycles	Costs
Beginning inventory	10	$ 2,000
Net purchases	34	10,000
Goods available for sale	44	$12,000
Ending inventory	16	4,364
Cost of goods sold	28	$ 7,636

A Comparison of All Inventory Costing Methods

The cost of goods sold and ending inventory amounts we have calculated using the three cost flow assumptions are summarized along with the resultant gross margins as follows:

	FIFO	LIFO	Average
Sales revenue (28 × $400)	$11,200	$11,200	$11,200
Cost of goods sold	7,000	8,500	7,636
Gross margin	$ 4,200	$ 2,700	$ 3,564
Ending inventory	$ 5,000	$ 3,500	$ 4,364

Note that the net result of each of the inventory cost flow assumptions is to allocate the total cost of goods available for sale of $12,000 between cost of goods sold and ending inventory.

Conceptual Comparison

From a conceptual standpoint, LIFO gives a better reflection of cost of goods sold in the income statement than does FIFO because the most recent goods ("last in"), with the most recent costs, are assumed to have been sold. Thus, LIFO cost of goods sold matches current revenues with current costs. Average cost is somewhere between LIFO and FIFO. However, on the balance sheet, FIFO gives a better measure of inventory value because, with the FIFO assumption, the "first in" units are sold and the remaining units are the newest ones with the most recent costs. In summary, LIFO gives a conceptually better measure of income, but FIFO gives a conceptually better measure of inventory value on the balance sheet.

Financial Statement Impact Comparison

As illustrated in the Nephi Company example, in times of rising inventory prices (which is the most common situation in the majority of industries today), cost of goods sold is highest with LIFO and lowest with FIFO. As a result, gross margin, net income, and ending inventory are lowest with LIFO and highest with FIFO. This might make you wonder why any company would ever voluntarily choose to use

LIFO (during times of inflation) because the impact on the reported financial statement numbers is uniformly bad. It might further surprise you to learn that, since 1974, hundreds of U.S. companies have switched from FIFO to LIFO voluntarily and that over half of the large companies in the United States currently use LIFO in accounting for at least some of their inventories.

The attractiveness of LIFO can be explained with one word—TAXES. If a company uses LIFO in a time of rising prices, reported cost of goods sold is higher, reported taxable income is lower, and cash paid for income taxes is lower. In fact, LIFO was invented in the 1930s in the United States for the sole purpose of allowing companies to lower their income tax payments. In most instances where accounting alternatives exist, firms are allowed to use one accounting method for tax purposes and another for financial reporting. However, in 1939 when the Internal Revenue Service (IRS) approved the use of LIFO, it ruled that firms may use LIFO for tax purposes only if they also use LIFO for financial reporting purposes. Therefore, companies must choose between reporting high profits and paying high taxes with FIFO or reporting low profits and paying low taxes with LIFO.

(STOP & THINK)

Over the entire life of a company—from its beginning with zero inventory until its final closeout when the last inventory item is sold—is aggregate cost of goods sold more, less, or the same as aggregate purchases? How is this impacted by the inventory cost flow assumption used?

TO SUMMARIZE

Specific identification can be used by some companies as a method of valuing inventory and determining cost of goods sold. However, in most cases, an accountant must make an inventory cost flow assumption in order to compute cost of goods sold and ending inventory. With FIFO (first in, first out) it is assumed that the oldest inventory units are sold first. With LIFO (last in, first out) it is assumed that the newest units are sold first. With the average cost assumption, the total goods available for sale are used to compute an average cost per unit for the period; this average cost is then used in calculating cost of goods sold and ending inventory. LIFO produces a better matching of current revenues and current expenses in the income statement; FIFO yields a balance sheet inventory value that is closer to the current value of the inventory. The primary practical attraction of LIFO is that it lowers the payment of income taxes.

4 *Discuss and account for additional day-to-day activities related to the operating cycle.*

ADDITIONAL BUSINESS EVENTS RELATED TO THE OPERATING CYCLE

Employee compensation issues are critical for every business. Not only must companies worry about current payroll, but thought must be given to employee compensation to be paid in the future. In addition, taxes affect every company. We begin our discussion of additional business events by examining these two issues.

Employee Compensation

Often, one of the largest operating expenses of a business is the salaries and wages of its employees. But the cost of employees is not simply the expense associated with the current period's wages. As the following time line illustrates, issues associated with employee compensation can extend long after the employee has retired.

Employee Compensation Event Line

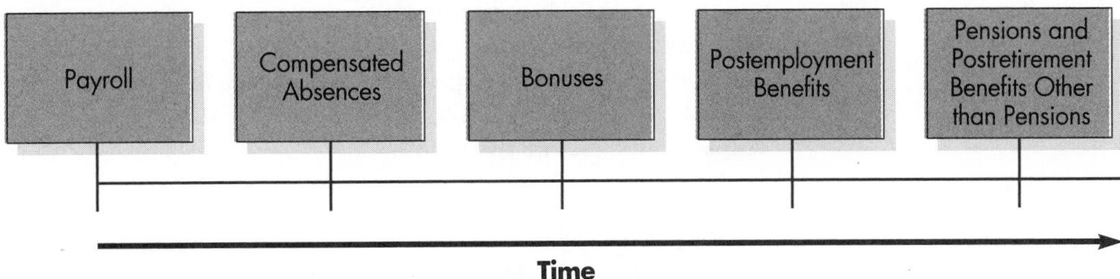

Payroll relates to the salaries and wages earned by employees for work done in the current period. Wages are paid anywhere from weekly to monthly, depending on the company. Compensated absences exist when an employer agrees to pay workers for sick days or vacation days. These obligations must be estimated and accrued in the period that the employee earns those days off. Many employees are paid bonuses based on some measure of performance (such as income or sales volume). Those bonuses are often paid quarterly or annually. In some cases, employees may earn what are termed "postemployment benefits," which kick in if an employee is laid off or terminated. Finally, firms offer benefits to their employees upon retirement. We will discuss each of these items in further detail in the sections that follow.

Payroll

In its simplest form, accounting for payroll involves debiting Salaries Expense and crediting Salaries Payable when employees work and then debiting Salaries Payable and crediting Cash when wages are paid. However, accounting for salaries and related payroll taxes is never quite that simple and can, in fact, be quite complex. This is primarily because every business is legally required to withhold certain taxes from employees' salaries and wages.

Very few people receive their full salary as take-home pay. For example, an employee who earns $30,000 a year probably takes home between $20,000 and $25,000. The remainder is withheld by the employer to pay the employee's federal and state income taxes, **social security (FICA) taxes**,[2] and any voluntary or contractual withholdings that the employee has authorized (such as union dues, medical insurance premiums, and charitable contributions). Thus, the accounting entry to record the expense for an employee's monthly salary (computed as 1/12 of $30,000) might be:

social security (FICA) taxes Federal Insurance Contributions Act taxes imposed on employee and employer; used mainly to provide retirement benefits.

Salaries Expense	2,500	
FICA Taxes Payable, Employee		191
Federal Withholding Taxes Payable		400
State Withholding Taxes Payable		200
Salaries Payable		1,709
To record Mary Perrico's salary for July.		

All the credit amounts (which are arbitrary in this example) are liabilities that must be paid by the employer to the federal and state governments and to the employee. It should be noted that these withholdings do not represent an additional expense to the employer, since the employee actually pays them. The employer merely serves as an agent for the governments for collecting and paying these withheld amounts.

2. Congress has split FICA taxes into two parts—Social Security and Medicare. For the purposes of this chapter, we will combine the two.

In addition to remitting employees' income and FICA taxes, companies must also pay certain payroll-related taxes, such as the employer's portion of the FICA tax (an amount equal to the employee's portion) and state and federal unemployment taxes. The payroll-related taxes paid by employers are expenses to the company and are included in operating expenses on the income statement. An entry to record the company's share of payroll taxes relating to Mary Perrico's employment (again using arbitrary amounts) would be:

Payroll Tax Expense	279	
FICA Taxes Payable, Employer		191
Federal Unemployment Taxes Payable		18
State Unemployment Taxes Payable		70
To record employer payroll tax liabilities associated with Mary Perrico's salary for July.		

The different liabilities recorded in the preceding two entries for payroll would be eliminated as payments are made. The entries to account for the payments are:

FICA Taxes Payable	382	
Federal Withholding Taxes Payable	400	
Federal Unemployment Taxes Payable	18	
Cash		800
Paid July withholdings and payroll taxes to federal government.		
State Withholding Taxes Payable	200	
State Unemployment Taxes Payable	70	
Cash		270
Paid July withholdings and payroll taxes to state government.		
Salaries Payable	1,709	
Cash		1,709
Paid July salary to Mary Perrico.		

As these entries show, three checks are written for payroll-related expenses: one to the federal government, one to the state, and one to the employee.

One further point about salaries and wages needs to be made. The period of time covered by the payroll may not coincide with the last day of the year for financial reporting. Thus, if the reporting year ends on Wednesday, December 31, and the salaries and wages for that week will be paid Monday, January 5 of the following year, then the company must show the salaries and wages earned from Monday through Wednesday (December 29, 30, and 31) as a liability on the December 31 balance sheet. To accomplish this, the company would record an end-of-year adjusting entry to record the salaries and wages earned for those three days.

Compensated Absences

Suppose that you work for a business that provides each employee one day of sick leave for each full month of employment. When should that sick day (or compensated absence) be accounted for? when it is taken by the employee? when it is earned by the employee? And how much of an accrual should be associated with the compensated absences?

The matching principle requires that the expense associated with the compensated absence be accounted for in the period in which it is earned by the employee. Some of the conceptual issues associated with accounting for compensated absences are similar to those addressed in accounting for bad debts. In the case of bad debts, if we waited until we were sure a customer wasn't going to pay, then we could be certain regarding our bad debt expense. But we may not find out that we are not going to be paid until several periods later, and as a result, the bad debt expense would be reflected in the wrong accounting period. So instead of waiting until accounts are dishonored, we estimate the expense for each period. The same is true with compensated absences. While we could wait until those sick days are taken and then know exactly what they will cost, it may be years before we know. Rather than wait, we estimate instead. For example, if you earn both $100 a day and one sick day per month, then it makes sense for your employer to recognize an expense (and accrue a liability) of $100 per month related to your sick pay. This would be done with the following journal entry:

Salaries Expense	100	
Sick Days Payable		100
To recognize accrued sick pay.		

When you take that sick day (and let's not forget that the government will take its share of your sick pay also), the journal entry would be:

Sick Days Payable	100	
Various Taxes Payables		20
Cash.		80
To record payment of sick day net of FICA, federal, and state taxes.		

The same procedures would apply when accounting for accrued vacation pay or other types of compensated absences.

Bonuses

Many companies offer employees bonus plans that provide them additional compensation should certain objectives be achieved. These objectives, or targets, are mostly financial in nature. An example would be the company president receiving a bonus of 10 percent of her salary if the company's gross margin exceeds a predetermined amount, such as last year's gross margin figure. Suppose that the president's salary is $100,000 per year and that the company did in fact achieve the target figure. The journal entry would be:

Salaries Expense	10,000	
Various Taxes Payable		2,000
Bonus Payable		8,000
To record bonus earned by company president.		

Bonuses can be calculated based on a number of possibilities—income before taxes and bonus, income from operations, income from a particular segment, number of units sold, etc. Regardless of the calculations involved in computing the bonus, the journal entry given above would be used to account for it.

stock options Rights given to employees to purchase shares of stock of a company at a predetermined price.

In some instances, other types of compensation might be substituted for a cash bonus. For example, **stock options** have become increasingly popular. Employees, generally top management, may be given the option to purchase stock in the future at a price specified today. A typical example would be to give management stock options that allow them to purchase, say, 1,000 shares of the company's stock at $20 per share at some future date. And generally the stock would be selling today at an amount below the option price of $20. The objective of this type of compensation is to incent management to run the business effectively so that the stock price of the company increases. If the stock price rises above $20, then shareholders win and management wins. If the price of the stock remains below $20, then managers have received nothing and the company has provided nothing. The accounting for stock option compensation can get very complicated and is beyond the scope of this textbook.

FYI

The issue of accounting for stock options is so controversial and its potential impact so significant that it was debated on the floor of the United States Senate.

Postemployment Benefits

postemployment benefits Benefits paid to employees who have been laid off or terminated.

Postemployment benefits are perhaps the least common of the topics covered in this section on employee compensation. **Postemployment benefits** are those benefits that are incurred after an employee has ceased to work for an employer but before that employee retires. A common example is a company-provided severance package for employees who have been laid off. This severance package might include salary for a certain time period, retraining costs, education costs, etc. While the company may not know the exact postemployment cost, accounting standards require that the amount be estimated and accrued in the period in which the decision is made to cut back the labor force. For example, suppose a company decides to close a segment of its operations, thereby laying off a certain percentage of its labor force. The company must estimate the costs associated with the benefits offered to those laid-off employees and would record the following journal entry:

Salaries Expense	xxx	
Benefits Payable.		xxx
To record postemployment benefits for laid-off employees.		

When the benefits are paid, a journal entry would be made to reduce the payable and to record the cash outflow.

Pensions

pension An agreement between an employer and employees that provides for benefits upon retirement.

Next to the current period's payroll, pensions are perhaps the next most significant employee cost. A **pension**, as you probably know, is compensation received by an employee after that employee has retired. Various types of pension plans exist. Some involve the employer setting aside money that will be paid to the employee following retirement. This type of plan is called a *defined contribution plan*—the employee gets whatever was contributed plus the earnings on those contributions. Others involve providing pension benefits based on factors such as number of years worked by the employee. This type of plan is called a *defined benefit plan*—the employee gets whatever benefit is defined in the plan.

The accounting for pension plans can get particularly complex, especially in the case of defined benefit plans. General Motors, for example, details in its annual report notes the computations and related assumptions of its $80 billion projected benefit obligation. While the computations may be involved, the objective of this accounting is the same as in the case of compensated absences and postemployment benefits. A company attempts to do its best to determine the costs to be paid out in the future and records an estimate of those costs in the current period—the period in which those costs are actually earned by the employee.

Northern Life Insurance Company's Web site features a fun "Dream Retirement Game." Play the game and see how you fare.

How much money do you need to save per month to reach your dream retirement income?

www.northernlifetsa.com

(STOP & THINK)

Who bears the risks associated with a defined contribution plan—the employer or the employee? Which party bears the risks associated with a defined benefit plan?

Taxes

In addition to the payroll taxes described in the previous section, companies are responsible for paying several other taxes to federal, state, and/or local governments, including sales taxes, property taxes, and income taxes. The accounting for these taxes is described next.

Sales Taxes

Most states and some cities charge a sales tax on retail transactions. These taxes are paid by customers to the seller, who in turn forwards them to the state or city. Sales taxes collected from customers represent a current liability until remitted to the appropriate governmental agency. For example, assume that a sporting goods store in Denver prices a pair of skis at $200 and that the state of Colorado charges a 5 percent sales tax. When the stores sells the skis, it collects $210 and records the transaction as follows:

Cash	210	
Sales Revenue		200
Sales Tax Payable		10
Sold a pair of skis for $200. Collected $210, including 5 percent sales tax.		

sales tax payable Money collected from customers for sales taxes that must be remitted to local governments and other taxing authorities.

The sales revenue is properly recorded at $200, and the $10 is recorded as **Sales Tax Payable**, a liability. Then, on a regular basis, a sales tax return is completed and filed with the state or city tax commission, and sales taxes collected are paid to those agencies. Note that the collection of the sales tax from customers creates a liability to the state but does not result in the recognition of revenue when collected or an expense when paid to the state. The company acts as an agent of the state in collecting the sales tax and recognizes a liability only until the collected amount is remitted to the state.

Property Taxes

Property taxes are usually assessed by county or city governments on land, buildings, and other company assets. The period covered by the assessment of property taxes is often from July 1 of one year to June 30 of the next year. If a property taxpayer is on a calendar-year financial reporting basis (or on a fiscal-year basis ending on a day other than June 30), the property tax assessment year and the company's financial reporting year will not coincide. Therefore, when the company prepares its financial statements at calendar-year end, it must report a prepaid tax asset (if taxes are paid at the beginning of the tax year) or a property tax liability (if taxes are paid at the end of the tax year) for the taxes associated with the first portion of the assessment year. To illustrate, assume that Yokum Company pays its property taxes of $3,600 on June 30, 1999, for the period July 1, 1999, to June 30, 2000. If the company is on a calendar-year basis and records the prepayment as an asset, then the adjusting entry at December 31, 1999, would be:

Property Tax Expense	1,800	
Prepaid Property Taxes		1,800
To record property tax expense for 6 months.		

The prepaid property taxes account balance of $1,800 would be shown on Yokum's balance sheet at December 31, 1999, as a current asset. On June 30, 2000, property tax expense would be recognized for the period January 1, 2000, through June 30, 2000, with the following entry:

Property Tax Expense	1,800	
Prepaid Property Taxes.		1,800
To record property tax expense for the property assessment period January 1–June 30, 2000.		

Income Taxes

Another operating expense of most companies is income taxes. This expense reflects the amount expected to be paid to the federal and state governments based on the income before taxes reported on the current year's income statement. To illustrate, assume that Salem Company's 2000 income before income taxes was computed at $186,000 and that the company's 2000 income tax rate for the reporting year (for both federal and state income taxes) will be 30 percent. Based on these facts, an adjusting entry would be prepared at year-end showing a tax expense and liability of $55,800:

Income Tax Expense.	55,800	
Income Taxes Payable.		55,800
To record the income tax expense and tax liability on $186,000 of income before income taxes for the year 2000 using a 30 percent effective tax rate ($186,000 × 0.30).		

income taxes payable The amount expected to be paid to the federal and state governments based on the income before taxes reported on the income statement.

The **income taxes payable** account would be shown on the year-end balance sheet as a current liability. As shown on the partial income statement that follows, the income tax expense is subtracted from income before income taxes to arrive at net income of $130,200:

Income before income taxes	$186,000
Income taxes	55,800
Net income	$130,200

TO SUMMARIZE

In addition to cost of goods sold, there are several other types of operating expenses. The most significant of these expenses is usually payroll expenses, such as salaries and wages or unemployment and FICA taxes. Employee compensation is not limited to just the current period's payroll. The cost of employees also includes compensated absences, bonuses, postemployment benefits, and pensions. Tax liabilities, such as sales taxes, property taxes, and income taxes, which must be paid to governmental agencies, comprise another category of operating expenses.

5 *Prepare an income statement summarizing operating activities as well as other revenues and expenses, extraordinary items, and earnings per share.*

SUMMARIZING OPERATIONS ON AN INCOME STATEMENT

Having now completed our discussion of operating revenues and expenses, you are ready to examine an income statement, such as the one in Exhibit 5-3, and see how operating results are communicated to investors and creditors. The numbers in the income statement do not relate to any previous examples; they are shown here for illustrative purposes only.

This income statement shows that with net sales revenue of $2,475,000, P&L Company had net income of $385,000. The income statement classifies and accounts for the other $2,090,000 ($2,475,000 − $385,000). Sales revenue, cost of goods sold,

EXHIBIT 5-3

Sample Income Statement

P & L Company
Income Statement
For the Year Ended December 31, 2000

Revenues:			
Gross sales revenue		$2,500,000	
Less: Sales returns		(12,000)	
Sales discounts		(13,000)	
Net sales revenue			$2,475,000
Cost of goods sold			1,086,000
Gross margin			$1,389,000
Operating expenses:			
Selling expenses:			
Sales salaries expense	$200,000		
Sales commissions expense	60,000		
Advertising expense	45,000		
Delivery expense	14,000		
Total selling expenses		$ 319,000	
General and administrative expenses:			
Administrative salaries expense	$278,000		
Rent expense, office equipment	36,000		
Property tax expense	22,000		
Miscellaneous expenses	8,000		
Total general & administrative expenses		344,000	
Total operating expenses			663,000
Operating income			$ 726,000
Other revenues and expenses:			
Dividend revenue		$ 5,000	
Gain on sale of land		4,000	
Interest expense		(85,000)	
Net other revenues and expenses			(76,000)
Income from operations before income taxes			$ 650,000
Income taxes on operations (30%)			195,000
Income before extraordinary item			$ 455,000
Extraordinary item:			
Flood loss		$ (100,000)	
Income tax effect (30%)		30,000	(70,000)
Net income			$ 385,000
Earnings per share (100,000 shares outstanding):			
Income before extraordinary item			$4.55
Extraordinary loss			(0.70)
Net income			$3.85

and operating expenses (which are separated into selling expenses and general and administrative expenses on the income statement) have already been explained. It is important to note that operating income of $726,000 shows how much was earned by P&L Company from carrying on its major operations. These items constitute the major ongoing components of the income statement. Items shown at the bottom of the income statement are not part of the main operations of the business or are unusual and nonrecurring in nature.

Other Revenues and Expenses

other revenues and expenses Items incurred or earned from activities that are outside of, or peripheral to, the normal operations of a firm.

Other revenues and expenses are those items incurred or earned from activities outside of, or peripheral to, the normal operations of a firm. For example, a manufacturing company that receives dividends from its investments in the stock of another firm would show those dividend revenues as "Other Revenues and Expenses." This way, investors can see how much of a firm's income is from its major operating activity and how much is from peripheral activities, such as investing in other companies. The most common items reported in this section are interest and investment revenues and expenses. The other revenues and expenses category also includes gains and losses from the sale of assets other than inventory, such as land and buildings.

Extraordinary Items

extraordinary items Nonoperating gains and losses that are unusual in nature, infrequent in occurrence, and material in amount.

The **extraordinary items** section of an income statement is reserved for reporting special nonoperating gains and losses. This category is restrictive and includes only those items that are (1) unusual in nature, (2) infrequent in occurrence, and (3) material in amount. They are separated from other revenues and expenses so that readers can identify them as one-time, or nonrecurring, events. Extraordinary items are rare but can include losses or gains from floods, fires, earthquakes, and so on. For example, in 1980 when Mount St. Helens erupted in Washington, much of the **Weyerhaeuser Company**'s timberlands were adversely affected by the mudslides and flooding. Weyerhaeuser reported an extraordinary loss of $66,700,000 in 1980 to cover standing timber, buildings, equipment, and other damaged items. Certain other types of gains and losses are required by generally accepted accounting principles to be reported as extraordinary items. These involve technical accounting issues that are discussed in more advanced texts.

FYI

Another item that is disclosed in the extraordinary items section of the income statement relates to discontinued operations. When a company decides to cease the operations of a segment or a division, it must provide careful disclosure as to the past profitability of the segment and the expected costs associated with closing the segment.

If a firm has an extraordinary loss, its taxes are lower than they would be on the basis of ordinary operations. P&L Company, for example, actually paid only $165,000 ($195,000 based on operations less a $30,000 tax benefit from the extraordinary loss) in taxes. On the other hand, if a firm has an extraordinary gain, its taxes are increased. So that the full effect of the gain or loss can be presented, extraordinary items are always shown together with their tax effects so that a net-of-tax amount can be seen. Thus, income tax expense may appear in two places on the income statement: below operating income before income taxes and in the extraordinary items section.

Earnings per Share

earnings per share (EPS) The amount of net income (earnings) related to each share of stock; computed by dividing net income by the number of shares of stock outstanding during the period.

As noted in Chapter 2, a company is required to show **earnings per share (EPS)** on the income statement. If extraordinary items are included on the income statement, a firm will report EPS figures on income before extraordinary items, on extraordinary items, and on net income. Earnings per share is calculated by dividing a firm's net income by the number of shares of stock outstanding during the period. Exhibit 5-3 assumes that 100,000 shares of stock are outstanding. Earnings per share amounts are important because they allow potential investors to compare the profitability of all firms, whether large or small. Thus, the performance of a company earning $200 million and having 200,000 shares of stock outstanding can be compared with a company earning $60,000 and with 30,000 shares outstanding.

CAUTION

Actual earnings per share computations are much more complicated than shown here. Changes in the shares outstanding during the period must be considered when calculating EPS. In addition, there is another EPS figure, called diluted earnings per share, that considers the potential effect on EPS of things like the exercising of stock options by shareholders.

Examples of Differing Formats

The income statement featured in Exhibit 5-4 demonstrates detailed disclosure of a company's operations. Most companies do not provide that level of detail. The information contained in income statements varies from company to company. For example, **Microsoft** (see Appendix A) summarizes the results of its operations in 12 lines. **IBM**, on the other hand, provides detailed revenue and cost figures on the face of its income statements for each operating segment (see Exhibit 5-4). **Ford Motor Company** provides detail in its income statements (see Exhibit 5-5 on page 196) as to the operations of its two very different lines of business—automotive and financial services. (Note that Ford has made more money from financing cars than from selling cars in 1995 and 1996.) Keep in mind that the format of the income statement will vary across companies, but the information contained in the income statement is the same—revenues and expenses.

EXHIBIT 5-4 IBM's Income Statements for 1994, 1995, and 1996

(Dollars in millions except per share amounts) For the Year Ended December 31:	1996	1995*	1994
Revenue:			
Hardware sales	$36,316	$35,600	$32,344
Services	15,873	12,714	9,715
Software	13,052	12,657	11,346
Maintenance	6,981	7,409	7,222
Rentals and financing	3,725	3,560	3,425
Total revenue	75,947	71,940	64,052
Cost:			
Hardware sales	23,396	21,862	21,300
Services	12,647	10,042	7,769
Software	4,082	4,428	4,680
Maintenance	3,659	3,651	3,635
Rentals and financing	1,624	1,590	1,384
Total cost	45,408	41,573	38,768
Gross profit	30,539	30,367	25,284
Operating expenses:			
Selling, general and administrative	16,854	16,766	15,916
Research, development and engineering	4,654	4,170	4,363
Purchased-in-process research and development	435	1,840	—
Total operating expenses	21,943	22,776	20,279
Operating income	8,596	7,591	5,005
Other income, principally interest	707	947	1,377
Interest expense	716	725	1,227
Earnings before income taxes	8,587	7,813	5,155
Provision for income taxes	3,158	3,635	2,134
Net earnings	5,429	4,178	3,021
Preferred stock dividends and transaction costs	20	62	84
Net earnings applicable to common shareholders	$ 5,409	$ 4,116	$ 2,937
Net earnings per share of common stock	$ 10.24	$ 7.23	$ 5.02

Average number of common shares outstanding:
1996—528,352,094; 1995—569,384,029; 1994—584,958,699

*Reclassified to conform to 1996 presentation.

EXHIBIT 5-5 Ford's Income Statements for 1994, 1995, and 1996

For the Years Ended December 31, 1996, 1995 and 1994
(in millions, except amounts per share)

	1996	1995	1994
AUTOMOTIVE			
Sales (Note 1)	**$118,023**	$110,496	$107,137
Costs and expenses (Notes 1 and 15):			
Costs of sales	**108,882**	101,171	95,887
Selling, administrative and other expenses	**6,625**	6,044	5,424
Total costs and expenses	**115,507**	107,215	101,311
Operating income	**2,516**	3,281	5,826
Interest income	**841**	800	665
Interest expense	**695**	622	721
Net interest income/(expense)	**146**	178	(56)
Equity in net (loss)/income of affiliated companies (Note 1)	**(6)**	(154)	271
Net expense from transactions with Financial Services (Note 1)	**(85)**	(139)	(44)
Income before income taxes—Automotive	**2,571**	3,166	5,997
FINANCIAL SERVICES			
Revenues (Note 1)	**28,968**	26,641	21,302
Costs and expenses (Note 1):			
Interest expense	**9,704**	9,424	7,023
Depreciation	**6,875**	6,500	4,910
Operating and other expenses	**6,217**	5,499	4,607
Provision for credit and insurance losses	**2,564**	1,818	1,539
Asset write-downs and dispositions (Note 15)	**121**	—	475
Total costs and expenses	**25,481**	23,241	18,554
Net revenue from transactions with Automotive (Note 1)	**85**	139	44
Gain on sale of The Associates' common stock (Note 15)	**650**	—	—
Income before income taxes—Financial Services	**4,222**	3,539	2,792
TOTAL COMPANY			
Income before income taxes	**6,793**	6,705	8,789
Provision for income taxes (Note 6)	**2,166**	2,379	3,329
Income before minority interests	**4,627**	4,326	5,460
Minority interests in net income of subsidiaries	**181**	187	152
Net income	**$ 4,446**	$ 4,139	$ 5,308
Income attributable to Common and Class B Stock after preferred stock dividends (Note 1)	**$ 4,381**	$ 3,839	$ 5,021
Average number of shares of Common and Class B Stock outstanding	**1,179**	1,071	1,010
AMOUNTS PER SHARE OF COMMON AND CLASS B STOCK (Note 1)			
Income	**$ 3.72**	$ 3.58	$ 4.97
Income assuming full dilution	**$ 3.64**	$ 3.33	$ 4.44
Cash dividends	**$ 1.47**	$ 1.23	$ 0.91

TO SUMMARIZE

The results of operating activities are summarized and reported on an income statement. On an income statement, cost of goods sold is subtracted from net sales to arrive at gross margin, or the amount a company marks up its inventory. Operating expenses are then subtracted from gross margin to arrive at operating income. Nonoperating items, such as other revenues and expenses, extraordinary items, and earnings per share, are reported on the income statement below operating income.

6 *Analyze a company's inventory level and liquidity position using various analysis techniques.*

OPERATING CYCLE RATIOS AND ANALYSIS

We have discussed the operating cycle of a business and the accounts involved. Analyzing a company's operating position involves assessing changes in expenditure patterns from year to year as well as assessing how well a company is managing its short-term assets and liabilities that are affected by current operations. In this section, we first examine how a common-size income statement may be used to provide insight into a firm's operations. Next, we analyze a firm's liquidity position. **Liquidity** is basically a measure of how well a company can meet its current obligations. If a firm cannot meet its obligations in the short run, it may not have a chance to be profitable or to experience growth in the long run. The two most commonly used measures of liquidity are the current ratio and the acid-test ratio. We also introduce other ratios that assist users in assessing a company's liquidity position.

liquidity A company's ability to meet current obligations with cash or other assets that can be quickly converted to cash.

Common-Size Income Statement

Try comparing IBM's income statement from Exhibit 5-4 with Microsoft's from Appendix A. IBM had sales in 1996 of $76 billion, compared to Microsoft's $11 billion. It is difficult to make meaningful comparisons when there is such a great difference in the numbers. Common-size financials statements allow us to get around this problem.

Common-sizing an income statement involves dividing each income statement component by revenues. Doing this over several years allows a financial statement user to detect trends. Comparing common-size income statements across companies enables users to detect differences between firms. As an example, common-size income statements for Campbell Soup Company for the three years ended August 3, 1997, are given in Exhibit 5-6.

When Campbell Soup Company's income is analyzed using a common-size format, trends become apparent. For example, cost of products sold has decreased markedly for each of the past three years. However, marketing and selling expenses and other expenses have been increasing. Research and development expenses, as a percentage of revenues, is declining slowly. Also of interest is the fact that interest expense is slowly increasing. This simple analysis technique can reveal potential problem areas for a firm as well as aid in comparing the results of companies of different sizes.

Current Ratio

The comparison of current assets with current liabilities is regarded as a fundamental measure of a company's liquidity. Known as the **current (working capital) ratio**, this measurement is computed by dividing total current assets by total current liabilities.

current (working capital) ratio A measure of the liquidity of a business; equal to current assets divided by current liabilities.

The current ratio is a measure of the ability of a business to meet current obligations. Since it measures liquidity, care must be taken to determine that proper items have been included in the current asset and current liability categories. A ratio of current assets to current liabilities of less than 2 to 1 for a trading or man-

EXHIBIT 5-6

Common-Size Income Statements for Campbell Soup Company

	1997	1996	1995
Net Sales	100.0	100.0	100.0
Cost and Expenses:			
Cost of Products Sold	54.1	56.8	58.7
Marketing and Selling Expenses	20.5	19.5	18.9
Administrative Expenses	4.1	4.5	4.5
Research and Development Expenses	1.0	1.1	1.2
Other Expenses	1.7	1.0	0.8
Restructuring Charge	2.7	—	—
Total Costs and Expenses	84.1	82.9	84.1
Earnings Before Interest and Taxes	15.9	17.1	15.9
Interest Expense	(2.0)	(1.6)	(1.5)
Interest Income	0.1	0	0.1
Earnings Before Taxes	14.0	15.5	14.5
Taxes on Earnings	5.0	5.1	4.7
Net Earnings	9.0	10.4	9.8

ufacturing unit has historically been considered unsatisfactory. In any case, because liquidity needs are different for various industries and companies, any such arbitrary measure should not be viewed as meaningful or appropriate in all cases. A comfortable margin of current assets over current liabilities suggests that a company will be able to meet maturing obligations even in the event of unfavorable business conditions or losses on such assets as short-term investments, receivables, and inventories.

To illustrate current ratio calculations, we will use information from the 1997 **The Gap, Inc.**, annual report:

(in thousands)	1997	1996
Current assets	$1,329,255	$1,280,045
Current liabilities	$774,896	$551,744
Current ratio	1.72	2.32

A current ratio of 1.72 means that The Gap could liquidate its total current liabilities 1.72 times using only its current assets, and it has $1.72 of current assets for every $1 of current liabilities. It is possible to overemphasize the importance of a high current ratio. Assume that a company is normally able to carry on its operations with current assets of $200,000 and current liabilities of $100,000. If the company has current assets of $500,000 and current liabilities remain at $100,000, its current ratio has increased from 2 to 5. The company now has considerably more working capital than it requires. It should also be observed that certain unfavorable conditions may be accompanied by a higher ratio. For example, a company's cash balance may rise due to a slowdown in business and the postponement of advertising and research programs or building and equipment repairs and replacements. At the same time, slower customer collections may result in rising trade receivables, and reduced sales volume may result in rising inventories. These items would have a positive effect on the current ratio but are signs of deteriorating health of the business or economy.

Acid-Test Ratio

acid-test (quick) ratio A measure of a firm's ability to meet current liabilities; more restrictive than the current ratio, it is computed by dividing net quick assets (all current assets, except inventories and prepaid expenses) by current liabilities.

A test of a company's immediate liquidity is made by comparing the sum of cash, securities held for sale, notes receivable, and accounts receivable (known as "quick assets") with current liabilities. The total quick assets divided by current liabilities gives the **acid-test (quick) ratio**. Considerable time may be required to convert raw materials, goods in process, and finished goods into receivables and then into cash. A company with a satisfactory current ratio may be in a relatively poor liquidity position when inventories comprise most of the total current assets. This is revealed by the acid-test ratio. In developing the ratio, the receivables and securities included in the total quick assets should be examined closely. In some cases these items may actually be less liquid than inventories.

Usually, a ratio of quick assets to current liabilities of at least 1 to 1 is considered desirable. Again, special conditions of the particular business must be evaluated. Questions such as the following should be considered: What is the composition of the quick assets? What special requirements are made by current activities upon these assets? How soon are current payables due?

To illustrate acid-test ratio calculations, we will again use information from The Gap:

	1997	1996
Total quick assets	$621,276	$669,072
Total current liabilities	$774,896	$551,744
Acid-test ratio	0.80	1.21

The acid-test ratio indicates that The Gap's liquidity position has decreased from 1996 to 1997. At the end of its 1997 fiscal year, the company has $0.80 in quick assets for every dollar of liabilities.

Evaluating the Level of Inventory

Money tied up in the form of inventories cannot be used for other purposes. Therefore, companies try hard to minimize the necessary investment in inventories while at the same time trying to have enough inventory on hand to meet customer demand.

inventory turnover A measure of the efficiency with which inventory is managed; computed by dividing cost of goods sold by average inventory for a period.

Two widely used measurements of how effectively a company is managing its inventory are the inventory turnover ratio and number of days' sales in inventory. **Inventory turnover** provides a measure of how many times a company turns over, or replenishes, its inventory during a year. The calculation is similar to the accounts receivable turnover discussed in Chapter 4. It is calculated by dividing cost of goods sold by average inventory as follows:

$$\text{Inventory turnover} = \frac{\text{Cost of goods sold}}{\text{Average inventory}}$$

The average inventory amount is the average of the beginning and ending inventory balances. The inventory turnover ratios for Sears, Safeway, and Caterpillar for 1996 are as follows (dollar amounts are in billions):

	Sears	Safeway	Caterpillar
Cost of goods sold	$24.925	$12.495	$11.832
Beginning inventory	4.033	1.192	1.921
Ending inventory	4.646	1.283	2.222
Average inventory	4.340	1.238	2.072
Inventory turnover	5.740	10.090	5.710

From this analysis, you can see that Safeway, the supermarket, turns its inventory over more frequently than does Sears, the department store, and Caterpillar, the equipment dealer. This matches what we would have predicted given the differences among these three companies in the nature of the business and the nature of the inventory.

number of days' sales in inventory An alternative measure of how well inventory is being managed; computed by dividing 365 days by the inventory turnover ratio.

Inventory turnover can also be converted into the **number of days' sales in inventory**. This ratio is computed by dividing 365, or the number of days in a year, by the inventory turnover, as follows:

$$\text{Number of days' sales in inventory} = \frac{365}{\text{Inventory turnover}}$$

CAUTION

Sometimes these two inventory ratios are computed using ending inventory rather than average inventory. This is appropriate if the inventory balance does not change much from the beginning to the end of the year.

Computing this ratio for Sears, Safeway, and Caterpillar yields the following:

	Number of Days' Sales in Inventory
Sears	63.6 days
Safeway	36.2 days
Caterpillar	63.9 days

Individuals analyzing how effective a company's inventory management is would compare these ratios with other firms in the same industry and with comparable ratios for the same firm in previous years.

CAUTION

Number of days' sales in accounts payables, as we have defined it, assumes that inventory is the only item purchased on account. It is likely that Accounts Payable includes such items as supplies purchased on account. However, the purchase of inventory is typically the most significant element of Accounts Payable.

Number of Days' Sales in Accounts Payable

In Chapter 4, we introduced the ratio of number of days' sales in accounts receivable. Above, we discussed number of days' sales in inventory. Taken together, these two ratios indicate the length of a firm's operating cycle. These two ratios measure the amount of time it takes, on average, from the point when inventory is purchased to the point when cash is collected from the customer who purchased the inventory. For example, the length of NIKE's operating cycle for 1997 is depicted below.

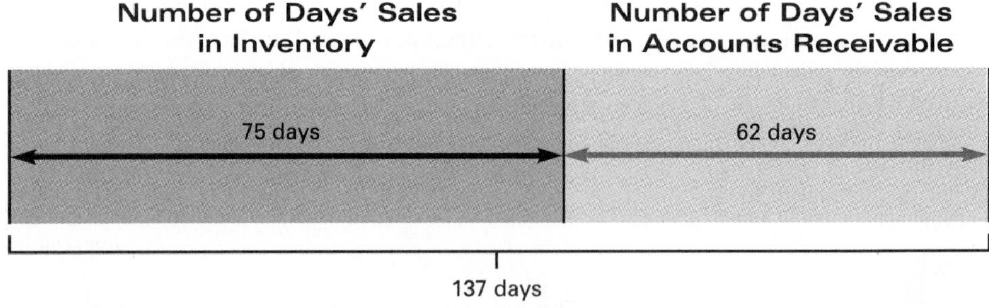

Is NIKE's operating cycle too long, too short, or just right? That is difficult to tell without information from prior years and information from competitors. But by including one additional ratio in the analysis, we can determine if NIKE is facing a cash flow problem.

number of days' sales in accounts payable The average number of days from the purchase of inventory from suppliers until payment is made.

By computing **number of days' sales in accounts payable** we can determine how long the company must finance its operating cycle with either internally generated or borrowed funds. The number of days' sales in accounts payables is computed by dividing cost of goods sold by average accounts payable and then dividing the result into 365 days:

$$\text{Number of days' sales in accounts payable} = \frac{\text{365 days}}{\text{Cost of goods sold/Average accounts payable}}$$

The number of days' sales in accounts payable indicates how long it takes for a company to pay its suppliers. For example, NIKE's number of days' sales in accounts payable is computed as follows:

$$\text{Number of days' sales in accounts payable} = \frac{\text{365 days}}{\$5{,}502{,}993{,}000/\$571{,}077{,}500}$$

$$= \text{38 days}$$

NIKE pays its suppliers in 38 days, while it waits for 137 days before receiving the cash from its customers. How does NIKE finance the remaining 99 days (137 days − 38 days) of its operating cycle? It must either borrow from the bank, sell stock or other assets, or use its cash on hand. Perhaps this explains, in part, why NIKE's total debt from notes payable and long-term debt increased from $462 million in 1996 to $851 million in 1997.

TO SUMMARIZE

Proper inventory management seeks a balance between keeping a lower inventory level to avoid tying up excess resources and maintaining a sufficient inventory balance to ensure smooth business operation. Companies assess how well their inventory is being managed by using two ratios: (1) inventory turnover and (2) number of days' sales in inventory. A company's choice of inventory cost flow assumption can significantly impact the values of these inventory ratios; intelligent ratio analysis requires considering possible accounting differences among companies.

Common-size income statements can be used to compare a firm's performance across time or across competitors at the same point in time. Common-size financial statements eliminate the size differences across companies and focus on financial statement relationships. Several ratios are used to evaluate a firm's liquidity position. The current (working capital) ratio is computed by dividing current assets by current liabilities. The acid-test (quick) ratio is computed by dividing cash, marketable securities, notes receivables, and accounts receivables by total current liabilities. The number of days' sales in accounts payable ratio indicates how many days a company's suppliers typically wait before getting paid. Considered along with the number of days' sales in inventory and the number of days' sales in accounts receivable ratios discussed in prior chapters, these three ratios can give an indication of the liquidity position of a firm.

REVIEW OF LEARNING OBJECTIVES

1 Identify what items and costs should be included in inventory and cost of goods sold. Inventory is composed of goods held for sale in the normal course of business. Cost of goods sold is the cost of inventory sold during the period. For a manufacturing firm, the three types of inventory are raw materials, work in process, and finished goods. All costs incurred in producing and getting inventory ready to sell should be added to inventory cost. The costs associated with the selling effort itself are operating expenses of the period. Inventory should be recorded on the books of the company holding legal title. Goods in transit belong to the company paying for the shipping. Goods on consignment belong to the supplier/owner, not to the business holding the inventory for possible sale. At the end of an accounting period, the total cost of goods available for sale during the period must be allocated between ending inventory and cost of goods sold.

2 **Account for inventory purchases and sales using both a perpetual and a periodic inventory system, calculate cost of goods sold using the results of an inventory count, and understand the impact of errors in ending inventory on reported cost of goods sold.** With a perpetual inventory system, the inventory account is adjusted for every sale or purchase transaction. Discounts on purchases, returns of merchandise, and the cost of transporting goods intended for resale into the firm are also adjustments made directly to the inventory account. With a periodic inventory system, inventory-related items are recorded in temporary holding accounts that are closed to Inventory at the end of the period. The closing entries for a periodic system involve closing Purchases, Freight In, Purchase Returns, and Purchase Discounts to Inventory, and then adjusting the Inventory balance to reflect the appropriate amount given the results of the ending inventory physical count. Obtaining an accurate inventory amount involves counting the physical units and then properly computing the cost of those units. When a perpetual inventory system is used, the ending inventory count provides an opportunity to compute inventory shrinkage. When ending inventory is not correctly counted, both cost of goods sold and net income will be reported incorrectly. For example, an overstatement in ending inventory leads to an overstatement in reported net income.

3 **Apply the four inventory cost flow alternatives: specific identification, FIFO, LIFO, and average cost.** The four major costing methods used in accounting for inventories are specific identification, FIFO, LIFO, and average cost. Each of these may result in different dollar amounts of ending inventory, cost of goods sold, gross margin, and net income. A firm may choose any costing alternative without regard to the way goods physically flow through that firm. With FIFO, the oldest units are assumed to be sold first; with LIFO, the newest units are assumed to be sold first. LIFO matches current revenues and current expenses in the income statement; FIFO results in current values being reported in the balance sheet. During an inflationary period, LIFO provides the lowest reported income and, therefore, lower taxes.

4 **Discuss and account for additional day-to-day activities related to the operating cycle.** In addition to cost of goods sold, organizations incur a variety of other expenses in operating their businesses. The largest of these is usually employee compensation items such as salaries and wages and payroll taxes. Accounting for payroll is complicated by the fact that organizations must withhold several different types of taxes, including federal and state income taxes and FICA taxes, as well as other items from employees' salaries. Employee compensation includes more than just the current period's payroll. Compensated absences, stock options, and bonuses also generally affect employee compensation in the current period. Long-term employee compensation issues include postemployment benefits and postretirement benefits.

Other operating expenses that are incurred are sales, income, and property taxes of the organization. Interest expense often plays a role in reporting the results of operations of a company. Additional operating activities include prepaid expenses, such as insurance and supplies; accrued expenses, such as rent and utilities; and obligations to perform services. The accounting for these items depends on the timing of the payment relative to the incurrence of the expense.

5 **Prepare an income statement summarizing operating activities as well as other revenues and expenses, extraordinary items, and earnings per share.** The income statement is the means of reporting net income. Its major sections are revenues, cost of goods sold, operating expenses, operating income, other revenues and expenses, extraordinary items, net income, and earnings per share.

In addition to cost of goods sold expense, businesses incur many other operating expenses. With accrual accounting these are reported on the income statement as they are incurred, not when they are paid. Interest and other nonoperating revenues and expenses are classified separately below operating income. The income statement is not complete until all extraordinary items and earnings-per-share amounts have been included.

6 **Analyze a company's inventory level and liquidity position using various analysis techniques.** One of the major concerns in the current operating activities of most businesses is liquidity—that is, whether or not they can pay their current obligations as they become due. Various analysis techniques are available to assist financial statement users in assessing a firm's liquidity. For example, common-size financial statements allow users to compare a company's performance with other firms and with the same firm across time. Ratio analysis also provides insight into a company's liquidity position. Common measures of liquidity are the current ratio (current assets divided by current liabilities) and the acid-test ratio (current assets minus inventory and prepaid expenses divided by current liabilities). Companies assess how well their inventory is being managed by using two ratios: (1) inventory turnover and (2) number of days' sales in inventory. Inventory turnover is computed as cost of goods sold divided by average inventory; it tells how many times during the period the company turned over, or replenished, its inventory. The number of days' sales in inventory is computed by dividing 365 by the inventory turnover value. A company's choice of inventory cost flow assumption can significantly impact the values of these inventory ratios. The ratio of number of days' sales in accounts payable, combined with number of days' sales in inventory and number of days' sales in accounts receivable, allows the user to assess the firm's needs with regard to financing the operating cycle.

KEY TERMS AND CONCEPTS

acid-test (quick) ratio 199
average cost 182
cost of goods available for sale 171
cost of goods sold 170
current (working capital) ratio 197
earnings per share (EPS) 194
extraordinary items 194
FIFO (first in, first out) 181
finished goods 171
income taxes payable 192
inventory 170
inventory shrinkage 179
inventory turnover 199
LIFO (last in, first out) 182
liquidity 197
net purchases 177
number of days' sales in accounts payable 200
number of days' sales in inventory 200
other revenues and expenses 194
pension 190
periodic inventory system 173
perpetual inventory system 172
postemployment benefits 190
raw materials 170
sales tax payable 191
social security (FICA) taxes 187
specific identification 182
stock options 189
work in process 171

REVIEW PROBLEMS

The Income Statement

From the following information prepare, in good form, an income statement for Southern Corporation for the year ended December 31, 2000. Assume that there are 200,000 shares of stock outstanding.

Sales Returns	$ 50,000
Sales Discounts	70,000
Gross Sales Revenue	9,000,000
Flood Loss	80,000
Income Taxes on Operations	500,000
Administrative Salaries Expense	360,000
Sales Salaries Expense	800,000
Rent Expense (General and Administrative)	32,000
Utilities Expense (General and Administrative)	4,000
Supplies Expense (General and Administrative)	16,000
Delivery Expense (Selling)	6,300
Payroll Tax Expense (Selling)	6,000
Automobile Expense (General and Administrative)	3,800
Insurance Expense (General and Administrative)	34,000
Advertising Expense (Selling)	398,000
Interest Revenue	6,000
Interest Expense	92,000
Insurance Expense (Selling)	7,000
Entertainment Expense (Selling)	7,200
Miscellaneous Selling Expenses	15,000
Miscellaneous General and Administrative Expenses	10,800
Tax rate applicable to flood loss	30%
Cost of Goods Sold	5,950,000

Solution The first step in preparing an income statement is classifying items, as follows:

Revenue Accounts	
Sales Returns	$ 50,000
Sales Discounts	70,000
Gross Sales Revenue	9,000,000

Cost of Goods Sold Accounts	
Cost of Goods Sold	$5,950,000

Selling Expense Accounts	
Sales Salaries Expense	$800,000
Delivery Expense	6,300
Payroll Tax Expense	6,000
Advertising Expense	398,000
Insurance Expense	7,000
Entertainment Expense	7,200
Miscellaneous Selling Expenses	15,000

General and Administrative Expense Accounts	
Administrative Salaries Expense	$360,000
Rent Expense	32,000
Utilities Expense	4,000
Supplies Expense	16,000
Automobile Expense	3,800
Insurance Expense	34,000
Miscellaneous General and Administrative Expenses	10,800

Other Revenue and Expense Accounts	
Interest Revenue	$ 6,000
Interest Expense	92,000

Miscellaneous Accounts	
Income Taxes on Operations	$500,000

Extraordinary Item Accounts	
Flood Loss	$80,000
Tax Rate	30%

Once the accounts are classified, the income statement is prepared by including the accounts in the following format:

Net Sales Revenue (Gross Sales Revenue − Sales Returns − Sales Discounts)
− Cost of Goods Sold
= Gross Margin
− Selling Expenses
− General and Administrative Expenses
= Operating Income
+/− Other Revenues and Expenses (add Net Revenues, subtract Net Expenses)
= Income Before Income Taxes
− Income Taxes on Operations
= Income Before Extraordinary Items
+/− Extraordinary Items (add Extraordinary Gains, subtract Extraordinary Losses, net of applicable taxes)
= Net Income

After net income has been computed, earnings per share is calculated and added to the bottom of the statement. It is important that the proper heading be included.

Southern Corporation
Income Statement
For the Year Ended December 31, 2000

Revenues:			
Gross sales revenue		$9,000,000	
Less: Sales returns		(50,000)	
Sales discounts		(70,000)	
Net sales revenue			$8,880,000
Cost of goods sold			5,950,000
Gross margin			$2,930,000
Operating expenses:			
Selling expenses:			
Sales salaries expense	$800,000		
Delivery expense	6,300		
Payroll tax expense	6,000		
Advertising expense	398,000		
Insurance expense	7,000		
Entertainment expense	7,200		
Miscellaneous expenses	15,000		
Total selling expenses		$1,239,500	
General and administrative expenses:			
Administrative salaries expense	$360,000		
Rent expense	32,000		
Utilities expense	4,000		
Supplies expense	16,000		
Automobile expense	3,800		
Insurance expense	34,000		
Miscellaneous expenses	10,800		
Total general and administrative expenses		460,600	
Total operating expenses			1,700,100
Operating income			$1,229,900

(continued)

Operating income		$1,229,900
Other revenues and expenses:		
Interest revenue	$ 6,000	
Interest expense	(92,000)	
Total other expenses and revenues		(86,000)
Income from operations before income taxes		$1,143,900
Income taxes on operations		500,000
Income before extraordinary item		$ 643,900
Extraordinary item:		
Flood loss	$ (80,000)	
Income tax effect (30%)	24,000	(56,000)
Net income		$ 587,900
Earnings per share:		
Before extraordinary items	$3.22 ($643,900 ÷ 200,000 shares)	
Extraordinary loss	(0.28) ($ 56,000 ÷ 200,000 shares)	
Net income	$2.94 ($587,900 ÷ 200,000 shares)	

Inventory Cost Flow Alternatives

Lehi Wholesale Distributors buys printers from manufacturers and sells them to office supply stores. During January 2000, its inventory records showed the following:

Jan. 1	Beginning inventory consisted of 26 printers at $200 each.
10	Purchased 10 printers at $220 each.
15	Purchased 20 printers at $250 each.
28	Purchased 9 printers at $270 each.
31	Sold 37 printers.

Required: Calculate ending inventory and cost of goods sold, using:

1. FIFO inventory.
2. LIFO inventory.
3. Average cost.

Solution When computing ending inventory and cost of goods sold, it is usually easiest to get an overview first. The following calculations are helpful:

Beginning inventory, 26 units at $200 each	$ 5,200
Purchases: 10 units at $220	$ 2,200
20 units at $250	5,000
9 units at $270	2,430
Total purchases (39 units)	$ 9,630
Cost of goods available for sale (65 units)	$14,830
Less ending inventory (28 units)	?
Cost of goods sold (37 units)	?

Given a beginning inventory, only ending inventory and cost of goods sold will vary with the different inventory costing alternatives. Because ending inventory and cost of goods sold are complementary numbers whose sum must equal total goods available for sale, you can calculate only one of the two missing numbers in each case, and then compute the other by subtracting the first number from goods available for sale. Thus, in the calculations that follow, we will always calculate ending inventory first.

1. FIFO Inventory
Since we know that 28 units are left in ending inventory, we look for the last 28 units purchased because the first units purchased would all be sold. The last 28 units purchased were:

9 units at $270 each on January 28 =	$2,430
19 units at $250 each on January 15 =	4,750
Ending inventory	$7,180

Ending inventory is $7,180, and cost of goods sold is $7,650 ($14,830 − $7,180).

2. LIFO Inventory
The first 28 units available would be considered the ending inventory (since the last ones purchased are the first ones sold). The first 28 units available were:

Beginning inventory: 26 units at $200 =	$5,200
January 10 purchase: 2 units at $220 =	440
Ending inventory	$5,640

Thus,

Cost of goods available for sale.	$14,830
Ending inventory.	5,640
Cost of goods sold	$ 9,190

3. Average Cost
Total units available for sale is divided into total cost of goods available for sale to get a weighted average cost.

$$\frac{\text{Cost of goods available for sale}}{\text{Units available for sale}} = \frac{\$14,830}{65} = \$228.15 \text{ per unit}$$

Cost of goods available for sale.	$14,830
Less ending inventory (28 units at $228.15)	6,388
Cost of goods sold (37 units at $228.15)	$ 8,442

Note: With the average cost alternative, the computed amounts may vary slightly due to rounding.

DISCUSSION QUESTIONS

1. In wholesale and retail companies, inventory is comprised of the items that have been purchased for resale. What types of inventory does a manufacturing firm have?
2. What comprises the cost of inventory?
3. Why is it more difficult to account for the inventory of a manufacturing firm than for that of a merchandising firm?
4. When is the cost of inventory transferred from an asset to an expense?
5. Which inventory method (perpetual or periodic) provides better control over a firm's inventory?
6. Is the accounting for purchase discounts and purchase returns the same with the perpetual and the periodic inventory methods? If not, what are the differences?
7. Are the costs of transporting inventory into and out of a firm treated the same way? If not, what are the differences?
8. Why is it usually important to take advantage of purchase discounts?
9. Why are the closing entries for inventory under a periodic system more complicated than those for a perpetual system?

10. Why is it necessary to physically count inventory when the perpetual inventory method is being used?
11. What adjusting entries to Inventory are required when the perpetual inventory method is used?
12. Explain the difference between cost flow and the movement of goods.
13. Which inventory cost flow alternative results in paying the least amount of taxes when prices are rising?
14. Would a firm ever be prohibited from using one inventory costing alternative for tax purposes and another for financial reporting purposes?
15. Why is it necessary to know which inventory cost flow alternative is being used before the financial performances of different firms can be compared?
16. Why is the accounting for payroll-related liabilities more complicated than the accounting for other current liabilities?
17. If the period of time covered by a company's payroll does not coincide with the last day of the year for financial reporting, how is accounting for the payroll affected by this situation?
18. Why is an end-of-year adjusting entry for property taxes often necessary?
19. When and how does a company record the amount owed to the government for income taxes for a given year?
20. What types of items would be included on an income statement as "other revenues and expenses"?
21. More than ever before, there seems to be tremendous attention paid to a company's earnings-per-share number. Why do you think investors and creditors pay so much attention to earnings per share?
22. What can the inventory turnover ratio tell us?
23. What is the difference between the current ratio and the acid-test ratio?
24. Some people might argue that a current ratio that is too high could mean a company is operating inefficiently. On what do you think they base this argument?

DISCUSSION CASES

CASE 5-1

WHY USE A PERPETUAL SYSTEM?

You are a consultant for the ABC Consulting Company. You have been hired by Eddie's Electronics, a company that owns 25 electronics stores selling radios, televisions, compact disk players, stereos, and other electronic equipment. Since the company began business 10 years ago, it has been using a periodic inventory system. However, Mark Eddie just returned from a seminar where some of his competitors told him he should be using the perpetual inventory method. Mr. Eddie is not sure whether he should believe his competitors. He wants you to advise him about his inventory choices and make a recommendation about the inventory method he should use.

CASE 5-2

SHOULD WE REDUCE INVENTORY?

It has now been two years since you advised Mr. Eddie to switch to the perpetual inventory method. He is very happy with the additional information he has about inventory levels and theft. He has hired you for advice once again. This time, Mr. Eddie has been to an inventory management seminar where he heard that most companies have too much money tied up in inventory and that his company could be much more profitable if it reduced its inventory levels. What would you tell him?

CASE 5-3

COMPARISON OF CURRENT RATIOS

You are comparing the current ratios of two companies in the same industry. Company A has a current ratio of 2.2, while Company B has a current ratio of 1.4. You ask two analysts which company is in better financial shape. The first analyst says that Company A is in better shape because its current ratio is higher. The second analyst says that Company A has too much money tied up in inventory and receivables, and therefore, Company B is in the better shape. Which analyst should you believe?

EXERCISES

EXERCISE 5-1
Recording Sales Transactions—Perpetual Inventory Method

On June 24, 2000, Hansen Company sold merchandise to Jill Selby for $80,000 with terms 2/10, n/30. On June 30, Selby paid $39,200, receiving the cash discount on her payment, and returned $16,000 of merchandise, claiming that it did not meet contract terms.

Assuming that Hansen uses the perpetual inventory method, record the necessary journal entries on June 24 and June 30. The cost of merchandise to Hansen Company is 70 percent of its selling price.

EXERCISE 5-2
Perpetual Inventory Method

Oakwood Furniture purchases and sells dining room furniture. Its management uses the perpetual method of inventory accounting. Journalize the following transactions that occurred during April 2000:

Apr.	2	Purchased on account $15,000 of inventory with payment terms 2/10, n/30, and paid $250 in cash to have it shipped from the vendor's warehouse to the Oakwood showroom.
	5	Sold inventory costing $3,000 for $5,400 on account.
	10	Paid $6,860 on account (from April 2 purchase).
	14	Returned two damaged tables purchased on April 2 (costing $800 each) to the vendor.
	19	Received payment of $1,000 from customers.
	20	Paid the balance of the account from April 2 purchase.
	22	Sold inventory costing $6,000 for $7,000 on account.
	26	A customer returned a dining room set that she decided didn't match her home. She paid $2,500 for it, and its cost to Oakwood was $1,500.

Assuming the balance in the inventory account is $8,000 on April 1, and no other transactions relating to inventory occurred during the month, what is the inventory balance at the end of April?

EXERCISE 5-3
Adjusting Inventory (Perpetual Method)

Deer Company's perpetual inventory records show an inventory balance of $120,000. Deer Company's records also show cost of goods sold totaling $240,000. A physical count of inventory on December 31, 2000, showed $92,000 of ending inventory.

Adjust the inventory records assuming that the perpetual inventory method is used.

EXERCISE 5-4
Recording Sales Transactions—Periodic Inventory Method

On June 24, 2000, Mowen Company sold merchandise to Jack Simpson for $80,000 with terms 2/10, n/30. On June 30, Simpson paid $39,200, receiving the cash discount on his payment, and returned $16,000 of merchandise, claiming that it did not meet contract terms.

Assuming that Mowen Company uses the periodic inventory method, record the necessary journal entries on June 24 and June 30.

EXERCISE 5-5
Adjusting Inventory and Closing Entries (Periodic Method)

As of December 31, 2000, Deer Company had the following account balances:

Inventory (beginning)	$120,000
Purchases	220,000
Purchase returns	4,000

A physical count of inventory on December 31, 2000, showed $92,000 of ending inventory. Prepare the closing entries that are needed to adjust the inventory records and close the related purchases accounts, assuming that the periodic inventory method is used.

EXERCISE 5-6
Cost of Goods Sold Calculation

The accounts of Meeks Company have the following balances for 2000:

Purchases	$260,000
Inventory, January 1, 2000	40,000
Purchase returns	7,640
Purchase discounts	880
Freight in	12,400
Freight out (selling expense)	2,400
Cash	4,000

The inventory count on December 31, 2000, is $48,000. Using the information given, compute the cost of goods sold for Meeks Company for 2000.

EXERCISE 5-7
Cost of Goods Sold Calculations

Complete the Cost of Goods Sold section for the income statements of the following five companies:

	Able Company	Baker Company	Carter Company	Delmont Company	Eureka Company
Beginning inventory	$16,000	$24,800	______	______	$19,200
Purchases	26,500	______	$43,000	$89,500	______
Purchase returns	______	1,000	1,800	200	2,200
Cost of goods available for sale	42,100	______	58,300	______	81,500
Ending inventory	______	22,200	15,200	28,800	______
Cost of goods sold	33,400	67,200	______	93,400	68,400

EXERCISE 5-8
Journalizing Inventory Transactions

Fleming Machinery uses the periodic method of inventory accounting.

1. Journalize the following transactions relating to the company's purchases in 2000:

Jan. 21	Purchased $8,000 of inventory on credit, terms 2/10, n/30.
30	Paid $7,840 to pay off the debt from the January 21 purchase.
Mar. 14	Purchased $125,000 of inventory on credit, terms 2/10, n/30. Paid $500 in cash for transportation.
Apr. 1	Returned defective machinery worth $20,000 to manufacturer.
13	Paid $105,000 to pay off the debt from the March 14 purchase.

2. Assuming these were the only purchases in 2000, compute the cost of goods sold. Beginning inventory was $13,000 and ending inventory was $22,000.

EXERCISE 5-9
Adjusting Inventory Records for Physical Counts

Spartacas Inc., which uses the perpetual inventory method, recently had an agency count its inventory of frozen chickens. The agency left the following inventory sheet:

Type of Merchandise	Date Purchased	Quantity on Hand	Unit Cost	Inventory Amount
Chicken grade A	2/12/00	30	$5.00	(a)
Chicken grade B	2/18/00	16	(b)	$54.40
Chicken grade C	2/08/00	(c)	$2.50	$60.00
Chicken grade D	2/15/00	46	(d)	$52.90

Complete the inventory calculations for Spartacas (items a-d) and provide the journal entry necessary to adjust ending inventory, if necessary. The balance in Inventory before the physical count was $305.05.

EXERCISE 5-10
Specific Identification Method

E's Diamond Shop is computing its inventory and cost of goods sold for November 2000. At the beginning of the month, these items were in stock:

	Quantity	Cost	Total
Ring A	8	$600	$ 4,800
Ring A	10	650	6,500
Ring B	5	300	1,500
Ring B	6	350	2,100
Ring B	3	450	1,350
Ring C	7	200	1,400
Ring C	8	250	2,000
			$19,650

During the month, purchases of four type A rings at $600, two type B rings at $450, and five type C rings at $300 and the following sales were made:

Ring Type	Quantity Sold	Price	Cost
A	2	$1,000	$600
A	3	1,050	600
A	1	1,200	650
B	2	850	450
B	2	800	350
C	4	450	200
C	3	500	250
C	1	550	250

Because of the high cost per item, E's uses specific identification inventory costing.

1. Calculate cost of goods sold and ending inventory balances for November.
2. Calculate the gross margin for the month.

EXERCISE 5-11
Inventory Costing Methods

For each of the descriptions listed below, identify the inventory costing method to which it applies. The costing methods are: average cost, LIFO, and FIFO.

1. The value of ending inventory does not include the cost of the most recently acquired goods.
2. In a period of rising prices, cost of goods sold is highest.
3. In a period of rising prices, ending inventory is highest.
4. Ending inventory is between the levels of the other two methods.
5. The balance of the inventory account may be unrealistic because inventory on hand is valued at old prices.

EXERCISE 5-12
FIFO, LIFO Inventory Costing

Jefferson's Jewelry Store is computing its inventory and cost of goods sold for November 2000. At the beginning of the month, the following jewelry items were in stock (rings were purchased in the order listed below):

	Quantity	Cost	Total
Ring A	8	$600	$ 4,800
Ring A	10	650	6,500
Ring B	5	300	1,500
Ring B	6	350	2,100
Ring B	3	450	1,350
Ring C	7	200	1,400
Ring C	8	250	2,000
			$19,650

During the month, the following rings were purchased: four type A rings at $600, two type B rings at $450, and five type C rings at $300. Also during the month, the following sales were made:

Ring Type	Quantity Sold	Price
A	2	$1,000
A	3	1,050
A	1	1,200
B	2	850
B	2	800
C	4	450
C	3	500
C	1	550

Jefferson's uses the periodic inventory method. Calculate cost of goods sold and ending inventory balances for November using FIFO and LIFO.

EXERCISE 5-13

FIFO, LIFO, and Average Cost Calculations (Periodic Inventory Method)

The following transactions took place with respect to Model M computers in Alpha's Computer Store during April 2000:

April 1	Beginning inventory	40 computers at $1,200
5	Purchase of Model M computers	15 computers at $1,300
11	Purchase of Model M computers	16 computers at $1,350
24	Purchase of Model M computers	10 computers at $1,400
30	Sale of Model M computers	32 computers at $3,000

Assuming the periodic inventory method, compute the cost of goods sold and ending inventory balances using the following inventory costing alternatives: (a) FIFO, (b) LIFO, and (c) average cost.

EXERCISE 5-14

Payroll Accounting

Stockbridge Stores Inc. has three employees, Frank Wall, Mary Jones, and Susan Wright. Summaries of their 2000 salaries and withholdings are as follows:

Employee	Gross Salaries	Federal Income Taxes Withheld	State Income Taxes Withheld	FICA Taxes Withheld
Frank Wall	$54,000	$6,500	$2,500	$3,825
Mary Jones	39,000	4,800	1,900	2,984
Susan Wright	34,000	4,250	1,500	2,601

1. Prepare the summary entry for salaries paid to the employees for the year 2000.
2. Assume that, in addition to FICA taxes, the employer has incurred $192 for federal unemployment taxes and $720 for state unemployment taxes. Prepare the summary journal entry to record the payroll tax liability for 2000, assuming no taxes have yet been paid.
3. **Interpretive Question:** What other types of items are frequently withheld from employees' paychecks in addition to income taxes and FICA taxes?

EXERCISE 5-15

Bonus Computation and Journal Entry

Pete Mehling is the president of Mehling Company, and his cousin, John Mehling, is the vice president. Their compensation package includes bonuses of 3 percent for Pete Mehling and 2 percent for John Mehling of net income that exceeds $200,000. Net income for the year 2000 has just been computed to be $990,000.

1. Compute the amount of bonuses to be paid to Pete and John Mehling.
2. Prepare the journal entries to record the accrual and payment of the bonuses. Include all withholding taxes in an account called Various Taxes Payable, similar to the one in the chapter. Taxes payable on the bonuses total $9,200 for Pete and $6,300 for John.

EXERCISE 5-16
Accounting for Property Taxes

In July 2000, Reynolds Company received a bill from the county government for property taxes on its land and buildings for the period July 1, 1999, through June 30, 2000. The amount of the tax bill is $7,600, and payment is due August 1, 2000. The tax rate for the period July 1, 2000, to June 30, 2001, will not change, and the company does not plan to acquire any additional taxable assets during that period. Reynolds Company uses the calendar year for financial reporting purposes.

1. Prepare the journal entries to record payment of the property taxes on August 1, 2000, assuming no entry has been made to record a liability for the property taxes.
2. Prepare the adjusting entry for property taxes on December 31, 2000.

EXERCISE 5-17
Preparing an Income Statement

Willow Company is preparing financial statements for the calendar year 2000. The following totals for each account have been verified as correct:

Office Supplies on Hand	$ 300
Insurance Expense	120
Gross Sales Revenue	6,000
Cost of Goods Sold	3,220
Sales Returns	200
Interest Expense	100
Accounts Payable	120
Accounts Receivable	260
Extraordinary Loss	1,080
Selling Expenses	360
Office Supplies Used	80
Cash	300
Revenue from Investments	280
Number of Shares of Capital Stock	90

Prepare an income statement. Assume a 20 percent income tax rate on both income from operations and extraordinary items. Include EPS numbers.

EXERCISE 5-18
Unifying Concepts: The Income Statement

Use the following information to prepare an income statement for Fairchild Corporation for the year ending December 31, 2000. You should show separate classifications for revenues, cost of goods sold, gross margin, selling expenses, general and administrative expenses, operating income, other revenues and expenses, income before income taxes, income taxes, and net income. (*Hint:* Net income is $27,276.)

Sales Returns	$ 4,280
Income Taxes	26,000
Interest Revenue	2,400
Office Supplies Expense (General and Administrative)	400
Utilities Expense (General and Administrative)	3,980
Office Salaries Expense (General and Administrative)	12,064
Miscellaneous Selling Expenses	460
Insurance Expense (Selling)	1,160
Advertising Expense	6,922
Sales Salaries Expense	40,088
Sales Discounts	3,644
Interest Expense	1,170
Miscellaneous General and Administrative Expenses	620
Insurance Expense (General and Administrative)	600
Payroll Tax Expense (General and Administrative)	3,600
Store Supplies Expense (Selling)	800
Delivery Expense (Selling)	2,198
Inventory, January 1, 2000	79,400
Sales Revenue	395,472
Average number of shares of stock outstanding	10,000
Cost of Goods Sold	262,610
Purchases	230,560
Purchases Discounts	3,050
Inventory, December 31, 2000	44,300

EXERCISE 5-19
Inventory Ratios

The following data for 2000, regarding the inventory of two companies, is available:

	Atkins Computers	Burbank Electronics
Beginning inventory	$ 40,000	$ 80,000
Ending inventory	48,000	95,000
Cost of goods sold	690,000	910,000

Compute inventory turnover and number of days' sales in inventory for both companies. Which company is handling its inventory more efficiently?

EXERCISE 5-20
Common-Size Income Statements

Rex Company has the following income statements for the years 2000 and 1999.

	12/31/2000	12/31/1999
Sales revenue	$480,000	$400,000
Cost of goods sold	380,000	270,000
Gross margin	$100,000	$130,000
Selling expenses	40,000	42,000
General & administrative expenses	50,000	48,000
Income before income taxes	$ 10,000	$ 40,000
Income taxes	3,000	12,000
Net income	$ 7,000	$ 28,000

1. Prepare common-size income statements for Rex Company.
2. **Interpretive Question:** Explain why net income decreased in the year 2000.

EXERCISE 5-21
Ratio Analysis

The following information was taken from the Embassy Company's balance sheets:

	in 000's	
	December 31, 2000	December 31, 1999
Cash	$ 150	$ 100
Accounts receivable	700	800
Inventory	1,400	2,000
Total current assets	$2,250	$2,900
Total current liabilities	$1,600	$1,800

1. Calculate the acid-test ratios for Embassy Company for 2000 and 1999.
2. Calculate the current ratios for Embassy Company for 2000 and 1999.

EXERCISE 5-22
Ratio Analysis

The following information was extracted from Morgan Company's balance sheets.

	in 000's	
	December 31, 2000	December 31, 1999
Cash	$ 200	$ 300
Securities held for resale	500	500
Accounts receivable	1,400	1,700
Inventory	4,200	1,900
Total current assets	$6,300	$4,400
Total current liabilities	$6,100	$4,400

1. Compute Morgan Company's acid-test ratios for 2000 and 1999.
2. Compute Morgan Company's current ratios for 2000 and 1999.
3. **Interpretive Question:** How do you explain the change in opposite directions of the acid-test and current ratios from 1999 to 2000?

PROBLEMS

PROBLEM 5-1
Perpetual and Periodic Journal Entries

The following transactions for Goodmonth Tire Company occurred during the month of March 2000.

a. Purchased 500 automobile tires on account at a cost of $40 each for a total of $20,000.
b. Purchased 300 truck tires on account at a cost of $80 each for a total of $24,000.
c. Paid cash of $1,300 for separate shipping costs on the automobile tires purchased in (a). The supplier of the truck tires included the shipping costs in the $80 price.
d. Returned 12 automobile tires to the supplier because they were defective.
e. Paid for the automobile tires. A 1 percent discount was given on the amount owed. (*Hint:* Remember that some of the automobile tires were returned.) Payment terms were 1/20, n/30.
f. Paid for half the truck tires, receiving a discount of 2 percent. Terms were 2/10, n/30.
g. Paid the remaining balance owed on the truck tires. No discount was received because payment was made after the discount period.
h. Sold on account 400 automobile tires at a price of $90 each for a total of $36,000.
i. Sold on account 200 truck tires at a price of $150 each for a total of $30,000.
j. Accepted return of 7 automobile tires from dissatisfied customers.

Required:

1. Prepare journal entries to account for the above transactions assuming a periodic inventory system.
2. Prepare journal entries to account for the above transactions assuming a perpetual inventory system.
3. Assume that inventory levels at the beginning of March (before these transactions) were 100 automobile tires at a cost of $40 each, and 70 truck tires at a cost of $80 each. Also, assume that a physical count of inventory at the end of March revealed that 184 automobile tires and 164 truck tires were on hand. Given these inventory amounts, prepare the closing entries to account for inventory and related accounts as of the end of March.

PROBLEM 5-2
Income Statement Calculations

Waukesha Company has gross sales of 160 percent of cost of goods sold. It has also provided the following information for the calendar year 2000:

Inventory balance, January 1, 2000	$100,000
Total cost of goods available for sale	300,000
Sales returns	13,000
Purchase returns	5,000
Freight in	2,000
Sales (net of returns)	407,000
Operating expenses	27,000

Required:

Using the available information, compute the following. (Ignore income taxes.)

1. Gross sales for 2000.
2. Net purchases and gross purchases for 2000.
3. Cost of goods sold for 2000.
4. Inventory balance at December 31, 2000.
5. Gross margin for 2000.
6. Net income for 2000.

PROBLEM 5-3
Income Statement Calculations

	Company A	Company B	Company C	Company D
Sales revenue	$2,000	(4)	$480	$1,310
Beginning inventory	200	76	0	600
Purchases	(1)	423	480	249
Purchase returns. . .	(20)	(19)	(0)	(8)
Ending inventory. . .	300	110	(6)	195
Cost of goods sold .	1,200	370	(7)	(9)
Gross margin	(2)	(5)	155	(10)
Operating expenses	108	22	34	129
Net income	(3)	107	121	546

Required: Complete the income statement calculations by filling in all missing numbers.

PROBLEM 5-4
Inventory Cost Flow Alternatives

Stocks, Inc. sells weight-lifting equipment. The sales and inventory records of the company for January through March 2000 were as follows:

	Weight Sets	Unit Cost	Total Cost
Beginning inventory, Jan. 1	460	$30	$13,800
Purchase, Jan. 16.	110	32	3,520
Sale, Jan. 25 ($45 per set)	216		
Purchase, Feb. 16.	105	36	3,780
Sale, Feb. 27 ($40 per set)	307		
Purchase, March 10	150	28	4,200
Sale, March 30 ($50 per set).	190		

Required:

1. Determine the amounts for ending inventory, cost of goods sold, and gross margin under the following costing alternatives. Use the periodic inventory method, which means that all sales are assumed to occur at the end of the period no matter when they actually occurred. Round amounts to the nearest dollar.
   a. FIFO
   b. LIFO
   c. Average cost
2. **Interpretive Question:** Which alternative results in the highest gross margin? Why?

PROBLEM 5-5
Periodic Inventory Cost Flow Method

Dudley Wholesale buys peaches from farmers and sells them to canneries. During August 2000, Dudley's inventory records showed the following:

		Cases	Price
August 1	Beginning inventory	4,100	$10.50
4	Purchase	1,500	11.00
9	Sale	950	19.95
13	Purchase	1,000	11.00
19	Sale	1,450	19.95
26	Purchase	1,700	11.50
30	Sale	1,900	19.95

Dudley Wholesale uses the periodic inventory method to account for its inventory, which means that all sales are assumed to occur at the end of the period no matter when they actually occurred.

Required:

Calculate the cost of goods sold and ending inventory using the following cost flow alternatives. (Calculate unit costs to the nearest tenth of a cent.)

1. FIFO
2. LIFO
3. Average cost

PROBLEM 5-6
Payroll Accounting

Orange County Bank has three employees, Albert Myers, Juan Moreno, and Michi Endo. During January 2000, these three employees earned $6,000, $4,200, and $4,000, respectively. The following table summarizes the required withholding rates on each individual's income for the month of January:

Employee	Federal Income Tax Withholdings	State Income Tax Withholdings	FICA Tax
Albert Myers	33%	3%	7.65%
Juan Moreno	28	4	7.65
Michi Endo...........	28	5	7.65

You are also informed that the bank is subject to the following unemployment tax rates on the salaries earned by the employees during January 2000:

Federal Unemployment Tax	0.8%
State Unemployment Tax	3.0%

Required:

1. Prepare the journal entry to record salaries payable for the month of January.
2. Prepare the journal entry to record payment of the January salaries to employees.
3. Prepare the journal entry to record the bank's payroll taxes for the month of January.

PROBLEM 5-7
Unifying Concepts: The Income Statement

From the following information, prepare an income statement for Notem Incorporated for the year ended December 31, 2000. (*Hint:* Net income is $119,100.) Assume that there are 10,000 shares of capital stock outstanding.

Gross Sales Revenue	$3,625,000
Income Taxes	140,000
Cost of Goods Sold..........	2,415,000
Sales Salaries Expense	410,000
Rent Expense (Selling)	16,000
Payroll Tax Expense (Selling)	3,100
Entertainment Expense (Selling)	2,000
Miscellaneous Selling Expenses	7,800
Miscellaneous General and Administrative Expenses	5,400
Automobile Expense (Selling)	3,500
Insurance Expense (General and Administrative)..........	1,900
Interest Expense	46,000
Interest Revenue	3,000
Sales Returns	10,000
Advertising and Promotion Expense	199,000
Insurance Expense (Selling)	17,000
Delivery Expense (Selling)..........	3,100
Office Supplies Expense (General and Administrative)	8,000
Utilities Expense (General and Administrative)	1,100
Administrative Salaries Expense	180,000
Fire Loss (net of tax)..........	40,000

PROBLEM 5-8
Income Statement Analysis

The following table represents portions of the income statements of Brinkerhoff Company for the years 1998–2000:

	2000	1999	1998
Gross sales revenue	$42,000	$ (9)	$25,800
Sales discounts	0	100	100
Sales returns	0	200	700
Net sales revenue	42,000	(10)	(1)
Beginning inventory	(15)	8,000	(2)
Purchases	24,800	(11)	15,000
Purchases discounts	700	300	500
Freight-in	(16)	0	500
Cost of goods available for sale	29,000	25,000	(3)
Ending inventory	3,800	(12)	(4)
Cost of goods sold	(17)	(13)	(5)
Gross margin	(18)	14,000	(6)
Selling expenses	4,000	(14)	(7)
General and administrative expenses	(19)	3,200	3,000
Income before income taxes	9,000	8,000	4,000
Income taxes	4,500	4,000	(8)
Net income	(20)	4,000	2,000

Required:

Fill in the missing numbers. Assume that gross margin is 40 percent of net sales revenue.

PROBLEM 5-9
Calculating and Interpreting Inventory Ratios

Captain Geech Boating Company sells fishing boats to fisherman. Its beginning and ending inventories for 2000 are $462 million and $653 million, respectively. It had cost of goods sold of $1.578 billion for the year ended December 31, 2000. Merchant Marine Company also sells fishing boats. Its beginning and ending inventories for the year 2000 are $120 million and $90 million, respectively. It had cost of goods sold of $1.1 billion for the year ended December 31, 2000.

Required:

1. Calculate the inventory turnover and number of days' sales in inventory for the two companies.
2. **Interpretive Question:** Are the results of these ratios what you expected? Which company is managing its inventory more efficiently?

PROBLEM 5-10
Common-Size Income Statements

Mako Company has the following income statements for the three years ended December 31, 1998, 1999, and 2000.

	Dec. 31, 2000	Dec. 31, 1999	Dec. 31, 1998
Sales revenue	$150,000	$120,000	$95,000
Cost of goods sold	95,000	70,000	50,000
Gross margin	$ 55,000	$ 50,000	$45,000
Selling expenses	18,333	16,667	15,000
Administrative expenses	11,000	10,000	9,000
Income before income taxes	$ 25,667	$ 23,333	$21,000
Income taxes	5,133	4,667	4,200
Net income	$ 20,534	$ 18,666	$16,800

pg 198

Required:

1. Prepare common-size income statements.
2. The manager of the company believes that she should get a raise because net income increased each year. Do you agree that she should get a raise?

PROBLEM 5-11
Ratio Analysis

Margo Company and Shiprock Company have the following financial information:

	in 000's	
	Margo Company	Shiprock Company
Cash	$ 1,500	$ 4,500
Investments held for sale	2,000	5,000
Accounts receivable	4,500	9,000
Inventory	22,000	10,000
Total current assets	$30,000	$28,500
Total current liabilities	$20,000	$20,000

Required:

1. Compute the acid-test ratios for the two companies.
2. Compute the current ratios for the two companies.
3. **Interpretive Question:** Assume you are a banker and that the two companies have come to you for a $10,000,000 loan. Both companies belong to an industry where products change very rapidly. Which company would you have the greatest concern about and why?

PROBLEM 5-12
Liquidity Ratios

Towers Company is interested in monitoring its liquidity as closely as possible. This means that it wants to have the supplier finance its inventory as long as possible and collect cash owed to it as quickly as possible. The company had the following financial statement accounts as of December 31, 1998, December 31, 1999, and December 31, 2000.

	in 000's		
	Dec. 31, 2000	Dec. 31, 1999	Dec. 31, 1998
Relevant balance sheet accounts:			
Cash	$ 2,200	$ 2,500	$ 2,000
Accounts receivable	16,000	17,000	15,000
Inventory	33,000	35,000	31,000
Accounts payable	19,000	20,000	18,000
Relevant income statement accounts:			
Sales	$280,000	$310,000	$252,000
Costs of goods sold	155,000	160,000	150,000

Required:

1. Calculate the accounts payable turnover for 1999 and 2000.
2. Calculate the number of days' sales in payables for 1999 and 2000.
3. Calculate the accounts receivable turnover and number of days' sales in accounts receivable for 1999 and 2000.
4. Calculate the inventory turnover and number of days' sales in inventory for 1999 and 2000.
5. Answer the following questions:
   a. On average, how long does it take from the time Towers buys inventory until it collects cash?
   b. What percentage of the time in answer (a) is financed by Towers suppliers?
   c. What percentage of the time in answer (a) is financed by Towers Company?
   d. Can Towers Company speed up its cash collections most by focusing on inventory or accounts receivable management?

Analyzing Real Company Information

International Case

Ethics Case

Writing Assignment

The Debate

Internet Search

Accounting is more than just doing textbook problems. These Competency Enhancement Opportunities provide practice in critical thinking, oral and written communication, research, teamwork, and consideration of ethical issues.

ANALYZING REAL COMPANY INFORMATION

• Analyzing 5-1 (Microsoft)

Using Microsoft's 1997 annual report in Appendix A, answer the following questions:

1. What type of items compose Microsoft's inventory?
2. Review Microsoft's balance sheet to determine the amount of inventory on hand on June 30, 1997. Does this mean Microsoft has absolutely no inventory? Where would Microsoft's inventory probably be disclosed?
3. Review the management's discussion note disclosure on operating expenses, specifically the discussion relating to cost of revenue. Does this discussion help explain what might make up some of Microsoft's inventory?

• Analyzing 5-2 (Archer Daniels Midland)

Selected financial statement information relating to inventories for Archer Daniels Midland (ADM) is given below:

	1997	1996
Cost of goods sold	$12,552,718	$11,853,070
Inventory—FIFO valuation	2,138,903	1,981,277
Inventory—LIFO valuation	2,094,092	1,790,636

ADM accounts for approximately 75 percent of its inventories using the FIFO method. However, some of its inventories are accounted for using the LIFO method. Thus, the differences reflected in the above table represent those inventories accounted for using the two methods.

1. Compute ADM's number of days' sales in inventory for 1997 using (a) the FIFO valuation for inventory and (b) the LIFO valuation for inventory. Are the differences significant enough to concern you?
2. Suppose that ADM purchases its inventory with the terms "net 30 days." That is, ADM's creditors expect payment in 30 days. Is ADM going to have a cash flow problem?

• Analyzing 5-3 (La-Z-Boy and McDonald's)

The following information is taken from the 1997 financial statements of La-Z-Boy Inc., makers of recliners and other home furnishings, and the 1996 financial statements of McDonald's, makers of the Big Mac® and other fast foods.

	La-Z-Boy	McDonald's
Cost of goods sold	$744.7*	$2,546.6
Beginning inventory	79.2	58.0
Ending inventory	78.8	69.6

*Amounts in millions.

1. Before you do any computations, forecast which of the two companies will have a lower number of days' sales in inventory.
2. Compute each company's number of days' sales in inventory ratio. Was your forecast in (1) correct?
3. How can these two very successful companies have number of days' sales in inventory ratios that are so different?

INTERNATIONAL CASE

• Why no LIFO?

The LIFO method of accounting for inventory is primarily a U.S. invention. Many countries around the world will not allow LIFO to be used and other countries discourage its use. For example, the International Accounting Standards Committee calls LIFO an undesirable but "allowable" method. In the United Kingdom, LIFO is allowable under corporate law but is unacceptable by professional accounting standards.

Why do you think other countries have such an unfavorable opinion of LIFO? Think about these issues: In periods of rising prices, does the amount shown on the balance sheet relating to inventory reflect current cost? If a company's inventory on the balance sheet reflected costs from years past, what would happen to the income statement if suddenly those inventory costs were moved to Cost of Goods Sold? Would the result reflect a firm's actual performance?

ETHICS CASE

• Shipping bricks

In 1989 the United States Department of Justice Criminal Division discovered a massive inventory fraud that was being conducted by officials at **MiniScribe Corporation**. MiniScribe manufactured and sold computer disk drives. The fraud included placing bricks in disk drive boxes, shipping those boxes to customers, and recording a sale when the box was shipped. MiniScribe officials also knowingly shipped defective drives and recorded sales even though they knew those drives would be returned.

What would be the effect on the income statement and the balance sheet of shipping bricks and recording those shipments as sales? (*Hint:* Think about the journal entry that would have been made by MiniScribe accountants when a box of bricks was shipped to customers who were expecting disk drives.) Would company officials be able to fool financial statement users for a long time using this type of deception? What could financial statement users have looked for to detect this type of fraud?

WRITING ASSIGNMENT

• Computing the total compensation for a professor

Eunice Burns is a new assistant professor of phrenology at the University of Winnemucca. Her academic year salary is $30,000. In addition, she receives a summer salary equal to two-ninths (approximately 22 percent) of her academic year salary. The university agrees to contribute an amount equal to 7 percent of Eunice's academic year salary into a pension fund. Eunice acquires legal title to these pension contributions only if she stays at the university for five years or more. Historically, approximately 60 percent of new assistant professors have remained with the university at least five years. The university withholds $840 per year from Eunice's salary as her contribution to medical coverage. It costs the university $3,000 per year per employee for medical coverage. Eunice has a term-life insurance policy through the university because of the favorable group rate she can get. The $300 annual cost is withheld from her salary. If she were to get the same insurance on her own, it would cost $450. The FICA tax rate is 7.65 percent. This amount is withheld from Eunice's pay, and in addition, the university must match this amount and pay it to the federal government. Federal income taxes totaling 15 percent of income are withheld from Eunice's pay. Both the FICA tax and the federal income tax withholding are applied only to Eunice's academic year salary; no amounts are withheld from her summer salary.

You have just been hired as an assistant to the chief financial officer of the university. You have been asked to compute what the total cost to the university is of having Eunice Burns on the faculty. Write a one-page memo to the chief financial officer of the university outlining your calculations. Be sure to explain any assumptions that you make.

THE DEBATE

• One method for all

As you know, we have periodic and perpetual inventory methods, along with LIFO, FIFO, and average cost variations of each. How can we compare the financial statements of different companies if different inventory methods are being used? This debate focuses on the idea that perhaps financial statement users would be better able to compare information if all companies used the same inventory method.

Divide your group into two teams and prepare a 5-minute presentation defending the following positions:

- One team represents "What's Good for One Is Good for All." To make financial statements comparable, all companies should be required to use the same inventory method. Which one? Rather than fight over the pros and cons of LIFO and FIFO, a compromise position would be to require all firms to use perpetual average cost. With the availability of computers, the computational problems associated with this method no longer exist. The resulting information would then allow more comparability across firms.

- The other team represents "It's OK to Be Different." Firms are different. One size does not fit all, and one inventory method is not appropriate for all firms. Firms should be allowed to use the inventory method(s) best suited for their unique operations.

INTERNET SEARCH

• Sears

We began this chapter with a discussion of **Sears Roebuck & Co.** Access its Web site at www.sears.com. Sometimes Web addresses change, so if this address doesn't work, access the Web site for this textbook (stice.swcollege.com) for an updated link.

Once you have located the company's Web site, answer the following questions:

1. Locate the portion of the Web site dedicated to Sears' history. Can you find information about Sears' beginnings (similar to the narrative at the beginning of this chapter)? In what year did Sears issue the first large general catalog?
2. Locate Sears' balance sheet. Have inventories, as a percentage of total assets, increased or decreased over the time period presented?
3. Compute Sears' number of days' sales in inventory. Is it increasing or decreasing over the time period presented?
4. Locate Sears' note information relating to inventory. Which inventory methods does Sears employ? Does Sears disclose the effects that different inventory methods might have on the income statement? If so, what would have been the effects in the most recent year?

CHAPTER

6 FINANCING ACTIVITIES

SETTING THE STAGE

Charles Dow and Edward Jones were young newspaper reporters who in 1882 teamed up to provide the Wall Street financial community with handwritten news bulletins. By 1889, the staff of **Dow Jones & Company** had grown to 50, and it was decided to convert the bulletin service into a daily newspaper. The first issue of *The Wall Street Journal* appeared on July 8, 1889. Clarence Barron, who operated a financial news service in Boston, was *The Wall Street Journal*'s first out-of-town reporter. Barron purchased Dow Jones & Company in 1902 for $130,000, and his heirs still hold majority control of the company today.

In the 1940s, *The Wall Street Journal* began publishing more than just business news, expanding coverage to economics, politics, and general news. Today, *The Wall Street Journal* has a daily paid circulation of 1.8 million and is read by an estimated 4.9 million people per day. Dow Jones also publishes *The Wall Street Journal Europe, The Asian Wall Street Journal,* and each day contributes special business pages to Spanish and Portuguese language newspapers in 21 Latin American countries. *The Wall Street Journal* is also a leader in Web-based news, with 150,000 paid subscribers. This is particularly impressive since the Web is an environment where all of us are accustomed to getting our information for free.

The Wall Street Journal is the flagship of the company, but the name "Dow Jones" is best known because of the Dow-Jones industrial average that is cited in the news every day. "The Dow" is widely used to reflect the general health of the U.S. economy. So, what is it? Simply put, the Dow-Jones industrial average measures the average movement of the stock prices of selected U.S. companies. The very first value of the average was 40.94 on May 26, 1896. This value was computed by Charles Dow by adding the share prices of 12 important companies chosen by him (**General Electric** was one of them) and then dividing by 12. Thus, the average price per share for these 12 companies was $40.94. Since 1928, the average has included 30 companies that are chosen by the editors of *The Wall Street Journal.* The computation of the average is no longer a simple averaging of share prices, but the underlying concept remains the same. Changes in the compa-

LEARNING OBJECTIVES

After studying this chapter, you should be able to:

1. *Use present value concepts to measure long-term liabilities.*
2. *Account for long-term liabilities, including notes payable, mortgages payable, and lease obligations.*
3. *Account for bonds, including the original issuance, the payment of interest, and the retirement of bonds.*
4. *Distinguish between debt and equity financing and describe the advantages and disadvantages of organizing a business as a proprietorship or a partnership.*
5. *Describe the basic characteristics of a corporation and the nature of common and preferred stock.*
6. *Account for the issuance and repurchase of common and preferred stock.*
7. *Understand the factors that impact retained earnings, describe the factors determining whether a company can and should pay cash dividends, and account for cash dividends.*
8. *Compute the common ratios that are used to evaluate the capital structure of a company.*

nies included in the average are rare; since 1990, seven companies have been replaced to reflect the decreasing importance of manufacturing in the U.S. economy. For example, Bethlehem Steel, which had been included in "The Dow" since 1928, was replaced in March 1997 by Wal-Mart. The 30 companies included in the average are listed every day in *The Wall Street Journal,* usually on page C3.

Sources: Dow Jones & Company History at dowjones.com; Dow Jones & Company, *International Directory of Company Histories,* Vol. 19 (St. James Press, Detroit, MI, 1998), pp. 128–131.

Dow Jones & Company is an appropriate symbol of capitalism—a corporation that has done business in and around the spiritual heart of capitalistic finance, the New York Stock Exchange, for over one hundred years. With the disintegration of the former Soviet Union and the rapid conversion of China into a "socialist market" economy, it seems that capitalism has defeated communism in the economic battle of the twentieth century. But, as illustrated by the history of many of the companies profiled in earlier chapters (Microsoft, Sears, Intel, General Electric), the true story of capitalism is not of rich "capitalists" exploiting the masses. Instead, capitalism is the story of unknown individuals using a free market to find outside investor financing in order to turn their ideas into reality. Accounting for investor financing is the topic of this chapter. In this chapter, we will first discuss financing through borrowing (debt financing), and then we will discuss financing by selling stock (equity financing).

In discussing debt financing, we will introduce various types of long-term liabilities. We will explain a concept used in measuring the present value of an obligation due in the future. This concept—the time value of money—is useful for computing the value of bonds and notes, as well as for computing mortgage payments and pension obligations. We also discuss the measurement of long-term liabilities and introduce numerous types of long-term liabilities—notes, mortgages, leases, and bonds. The basic accounting procedures associated with several of these liabilities are also discussed.

Another way organizations raise money to finance operations is from investments by owners. In corporations, those investments take the form of stock purchases. In proprietorships and partnerships, they take the form of capital investments in the business. Exhibit 6-1 shows the financial statement items that will be covered in this chapter.

Certain basic characteristics are common to all investor financing, no matter what the form of business. The first is that owner investments affect the equity accounts of the business. Second, together with the liabilities, these owners' equity accounts show the sources of the cash that was used to buy the assets. There are three primary ways to bring money into a business: borrowing (debt financing), selling owners' interests (equity financing), and earning profits (also reflected in the equity accounts through the retained earnings account).

et connected
p://www.swcollege.com
net work

Speaking of debt, let's take a look at our government's debt situation. To see what the national debt is to the penny, go to www.publicdebt.treas.gov/opd/opd.htm.

What was the national debt 100 years ago? 200 years ago?

www.publicdebt.treas.gov/opd/opd.htm

1 *Use present value concepts to measure long-term liabilities.*

MEASURING LONG-TERM LIABILITIES

Conceptually, the value of a liability is the cash that would be required to pay the liability in full today. Since money has a time value, most people are willing to accept less money today than they would if a liability were paid in the future. Therefore, with the exception of Accounts Payable, liabilities to be paid in the future usually involve interest.

EXHIBIT 6-1

Basic Financial Statements

Balance Sheet

Current assets:		*Current liabilities:*	
Cash	Ch. 4	Accounts payable	Ch. 5
Investments	Ch. 7	Taxes payable	Ch. 5
Accounts receivable	Ch. 4	Wages payable	Ch. 5
Inventory	Ch. 5	Warranty liability	Ch. 4
Property, plant, and equipment	Ch. 7	Unearned revenues	Ch. 5
Intangible assets	Ch. 7	*Long-term liabilities:*	
Long-term investments	Ch. 7	**Long-term debt**	**Ch. 6**
Total assets		Pension costs	Ch. 5
		Stockholders' equity:	**Ch. 6**
		Common stock	**Ch. 6**
		Retained earnings	**Ch. 6**
		Unrealized increase/decrease in value of securities	Ch. 7
		Total liabilities and stockholders' equity	

Income Statement

Sales of goods and services	Ch. 4
Cost of goods sold	Ch. 5
Gross margin	
Expenses:	
Salaries expense	Ch. 5
Taxes expense	Ch. 5
Depreciation expense	Ch. 7
Bad debt expense	Ch. 4
Warranty expense	Ch. 4
Other revenues and expenses:	
Gains and losses on sales of securities	Ch. 7
Unrealized gains and losses on securities	Ch. 7
Interest expense	**Ch. 6**
Interest revenue	Ch. 7
Net income	

Statement of Cash Flows

Operating activities:	
Receipts from customers	Ch. 4
Payments for inventory	Ch. 5
Payments for salaries	Ch. 5
Payments for interest	**Ch. 6**
Payments for taxes	Ch. 5
Purchase of trading securities	Ch. 7
Sale of trading securities	Ch. 7
Investing activities:	
Purchase of property, plant, and equipment	Ch. 7
Proceeds from sale of property, plant, and equipment	Ch. 7
Purchase of debt and equity securities other than trading securities	Ch. 7
Sale of debt and equity securities other than trading securities	Ch. 7
Financing activities:	
Sale of stock	**Ch. 6**
Purchase of treasury stock	**Ch. 6**
Proceeds from borrowing	**Ch. 6**
Repayments of borrowing	**Ch. 6**
Payments of dividends	**Ch. 6**
Net cash flows for the period	

long-term liabilities Debts or other obligations that will not be paid within one year.

Accounting for **long-term liabilities** is complex because usually payments of interest, or in some cases principal and interest, are made periodically over the period in which the liability is outstanding. Further, in some cases the amount of the liability in a noncash transaction may not be readily apparent. Measurement and recording of these liabilities are based on the time value of money concept.

Present Value and Future Value Concepts

present value of $1 The value today of $1 to be received or paid at some future date, given a specified interest rate.

The concepts of present value and future value are used to measure the effect of time on the value of money. To illustrate, if you are to receive $100 one year from today, is it worth $100 today? Obviously not, because if you had the $100 today you could either use it now or invest it and earn interest. If the $100 isn't to be received for one year, those options are not available. The **present value of $1** is the value today of $1 to be received or paid in the future, given a specified interest rate. To determine the value today of money to be received or paid in the future, we must "discount" the future amount (reduce the amount to its present value) by an appropriate interest rate. For example, if money can earn 10 percent per year, $100 to be received one year from now is approximately equal to $90.91 received today.

Putting it another way, if $90.91 is invested today in an account that earns 10 percent interest for one year, the interest earned will be $9.09 ($90.91 × 10% × 1 year = $9.09). The sum of the $90.91 principal plus $9.09 interest would equal $100 at the end of one year. Thus, the present value of $100 to be received (or paid) in one year with 10 percent interest is $90.91. This present value relationship can be diagrammed as follows:

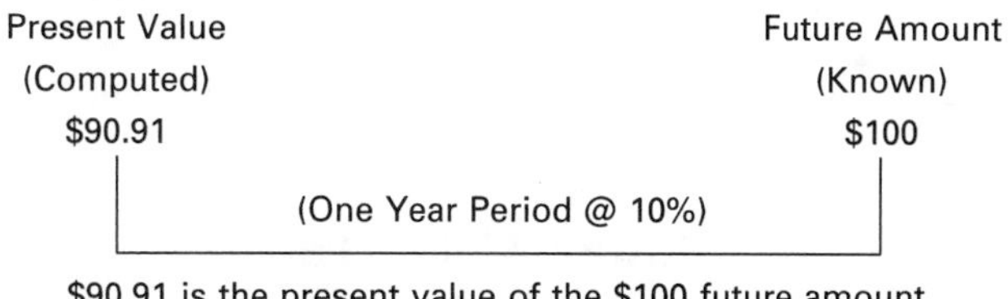

$90.91 is the present value of the $100 future amount.

The relationships in this diagram can be described in two ways. We have just looked at the relationship by recognizing that the $90.91 is the present value of $100 to be received one year from now when interest is 10 percent. In this example, the $100 to be received one year from now is known, and the present value of $90.91 must be computed. We are computing a present value amount from a known future value amount.

Another way to look at the relationship is on a future value basis. Future values apply when the amount today ($90.91) is known, and the future amount must be calculated. Future values are exactly the opposite of present values. Thinking in terms of future values, $100 is the future amount we can expect to receive in one year, given a present known amount of $90.91 when the interest rate is 10 percent. We can diagram this relationship as follows:

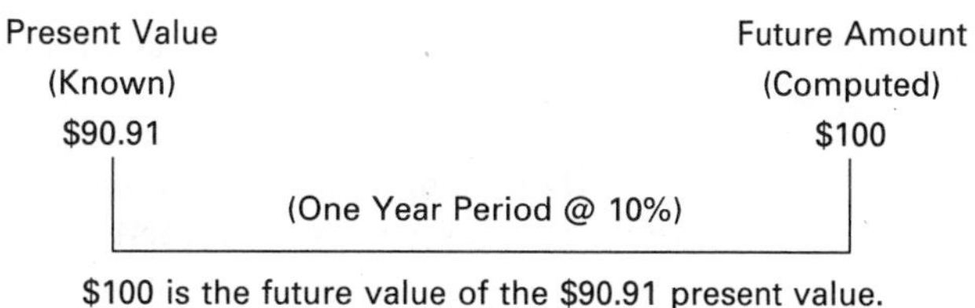

$100 is the future value of the $90.91 present value.

Present and future values can be calculated using formulas. However, if more than one period is involved, the calculations become rather complicated. Therefore, it is more convenient to use either a present value table or a calculator that gives the present value of $1 for various numbers of periods and interest rates (see Table I, page 260) or a future value table that gives the future value of $1 for various numbers of periods and interest rates (see Table III, page 262). We will illustrate the use of both a present value table and a future value table.

Present Value Table

To use a present value table, you simply locate the appropriate number of periods in the leftmost column and the interest rate in the row at the top of the table. The intersection of the row and column is the factor representing the present value of $1 for the number of periods and the relevant interest rate. To find the present value of an amount other than $1, multiply the factor in the table by that amount.

To illustrate the use of a present value table (Table I) to find the present value of a known future amount, assume that $10,000 is to be paid four years from today when the interest rate is 10 percent. What is the present value of the $10,000 payment?

Amount of payment	$10,000
Present value factor of $1 to be paid in 4 periods at 10% interest (from Table I)	× 0.6830
Present value of payment	$ 6,830

This present value amount, $6,830, is the amount that could be paid today to satisfy the obligation that is due four years from now. As indicated, this procedure is sometimes referred to as "discounting." Thus, we say that $10,000 discounted for four years at 10 percent is $6,830. Stated another way, if $6,830 is invested today in an account that pays 10 percent interest, in four years the balance in that account would be $10,000.

Future Value Table

To find the future value of an amount that is known today, use a future value table. When using a future value table, simply locate the appropriate number of periods in the leftmost column and the interest rate in the row at the top of the table. The intersection of the row and column is the factor representing the future value of $1 for the number of periods and the relevant interest rate. To find the future value of an amount other than $1, multiply the factor in the table by that amount.

To illustrate the use of a future value table (Table III), we will use the same information that was presented before, except that we will now assume that the present value of $6,830 is known, not the future amount of $10,000. Assume that we have a savings account with a current balance of $6,830 that earns interest of 10%. What will be the balance in that account in four years?

Present value in savings account	$ 6,830
Future value factor of $1 in 4 periods at 10% interest (from Table III)	× 1.4641
Future value	$10,000*

*Rounded; other calculations in chapter will also be rounded.

When computing future values, we often use the term *compounding* to mean the frequency with which interest is added to the principal. Thus, we say that interest of 10 percent has been compounded once a year (annually) to arrive at a future value at the end of four years of $10,000. If the interest is added more or less frequently than once a year, the future amount will be different.

compounding period The period of time for which interest is computed.

The preceding example assumed an annual **compounding period** for interest. If the 10 percent interest had been compounded semiannually (twice a year) for four years, the calculation would have involved using a 5% (one-half of the 10%) rate for 8 periods (4 years × 2 periods per year) instead of 10% for 4 periods. To illustrate, what is the present value of $10,000 to be paid in four years if interest of 10% is compounded semiannually?

Amount of payment	$10,000
Present value factor of $1 to be paid in 8 periods at 5% interest (from Table I)	× 0.6768
Present value of payment	$ 6,768

Thus, the present value of $10,000 to be paid in four years is $6,768 if interest is compounded semiannually. Likewise, if semiannual compounding is used to determine the future value of $6,768 in four years at 10 percent compounded semiannually, the result is as follows:

Present value in savings account	$ 6,768
Future value factor of $1 in 8 periods at 5% interest (from Table III)	× 1.4775
Future value	$10,000

Note that the present value ($6,768) is lower with semiannual compounding than with annual compounding ($6,830). The more frequently that interest is compounded, the greater the total amount of interest deducted (in computing present values) or added (in computing future values).

(STOP & THINK)

Without referencing the present value tables, answer these questions: "As interest rates increase, what would you expect to happen to the present value factors? Would you expect them to increase or decrease? Why?"

Since interest may also be compounded quarterly, monthly, or for some other period, you should learn the relationship of interest to the compounding period. Semiannual interest means that you double the interest periods and halve the annual interest rate; with quarterly interest you quadruple the periods and take one-fourth of the annual interest rate. The formula for interest rate is:

$$\frac{\text{Yearly interest rate}}{\text{Compounding periods per year}} = \text{Interest rate per compounding period}$$

The number of interest periods is simply the number of periods per year times the number of years. That formula is:

$$\text{Compounding periods per year} \times \text{Number of years} = \text{Number of interest periods}$$

The Present Value of an Annuity

In discussing present values and future values, we have assumed only a single present value or future value with one of the amounts known and the other to be computed. With liabilities, we generally know the future amount that must be paid and would like to compute the present value of that future payment. Since this chapter focuses on liabilities, we will concentrate on present value calculations.

annuity A series of equal amounts to be received or paid at the end of equal time intervals.

present value of an annuity The value today of a series of equally spaced, equal-amount payments to be made or received in the future given a specified interest rate.

Many long-term liabilities involve a series of payments rather than one lump-sum payment. For example, a company might purchase equipment under an installment agreement requiring payments of $5,000 each year for five years. Determining the value today (present value) of a series of equally spaced, equal amount payments (called an **annuity**) is more complicated than determining the present value of a single future payment. If you were to try to calculate the **present value of an annuity** by hand, you would have to discount the first payment for one period, the second payment for two periods, and so on, and then add all the present values together. Because such calculations are time-consuming, a table is generally used (see Table II, page 261). The factors in the table are the sums of the individual present values of all future payments. Based on the present value of an annuity of $1, the table provides factors for various interest rates and number of payments.

CAUTION

Use care when referencing the present value and future value tables. You can do all your computations correctly, but if you pull the factor from the wrong table, your answer will be wrong.

To illustrate the use of a present value of an annuity table (Table II), we will assume that $10,000 is to be paid at the end of each of the next 10 years. If the interest rate is 12% compounded annually, Table II shows a present value factor of 5.6502. This factor means that the present value of $1 paid each year for 10 years discounted at 12 percent is approximately $5.65. Applying this factor to payments of $10,000 results in the following:

Amount of the annual payment....................	$10,000
Present value factor of an annuity of $1	
discounted for 10 payments at 12%	× 5.6502
Present value	$56,502

This amount, $56,502, is the amount (present value) that could be paid today to satisfy the obligation if interest is 12%.

TO SUMMARIZE

Long-term liabilities are debts or other obligations that will not be paid or satisfied within one year. Present value concepts, which equate the value of money received or paid in different periods, are used to measure long-term liabilities. Although present values can be computed using formulas, it is usually more convenient to use a table, such as Table I or II on pages 260–261. If a future lump-sum payment is involved, Table I can be used to determine the present value. Table II is used to compute the present value of an annuity, which is a series of equally spaced, equal amount payments. To determine the value of an amount at some point in the future, future value tables can be used. Tables III and IV allow one to compute the future value of a lump sum or an annuity, respectively. In calculating present and future values, you must consider the compounding period and the interest rate. For other than annual payments, the number of periods used is the number of periods per year times the number of years; the interest rate used is the annual rate divided by the number of periods per year.

2 *Account for long-term liabilities, including notes payable, mortgages payable, and lease obligations.*

ACCOUNTING FOR LONG-TERM LIABILITIES

Now that we have explained how present value concepts are applied in measuring long-term liabilities, we are ready to discuss the accounting for those liabilities. The time line in Exhibit 6–2 illustrates the business events associated with long-term liabilities.

EXHIBIT 6-2 Time Line of Business Issues Involved with Long-Term Liabilities

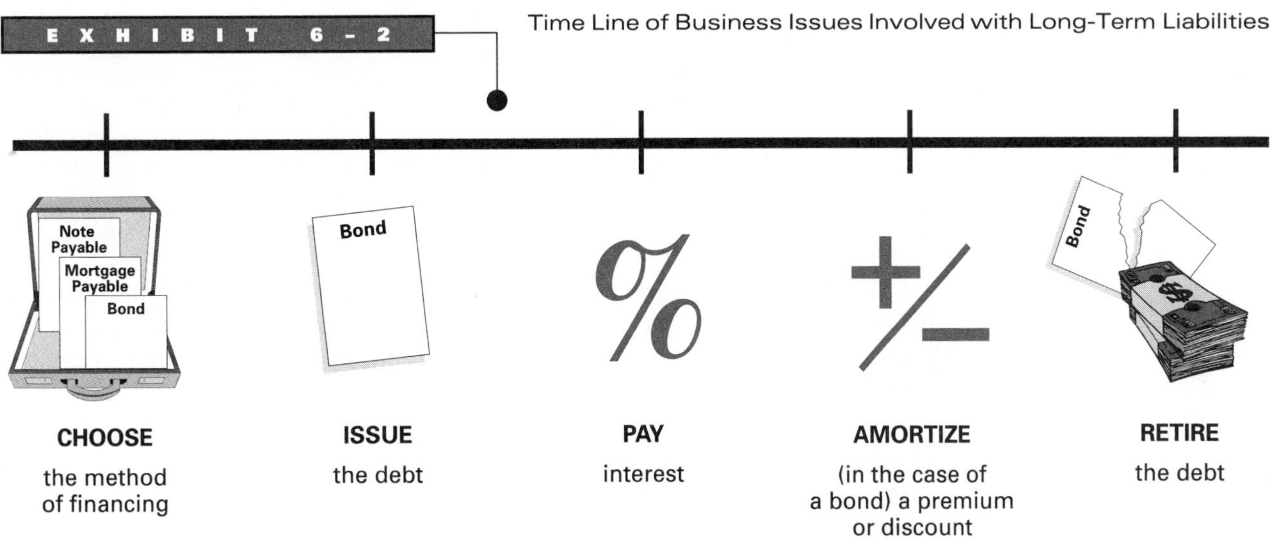

A company's first decision is to determine the type of long-term financing to use. In this chapter we will discuss four different types of debt financing: notes payable, mortgages payable, obligations under capital leases, and bonds. There are advantages and disadvantages to each type of financing. For example, bonds (which are sold in $1,000 increments) allow a company to borrow a little bit of money from a lot of different people, whereas notes involve borrowing a lot of money from one lender (or perhaps a consortium of lenders). The benefit of a mortgage is typically a lower interest rate because the property being purchased is used as collateral on the loan, thereby providing the lender with less risk. Leases have the advantage of typically requiring a lower down payment as there are no risks associated with product obsolescence. (At the end of the lease, the asset being leased is returned to the owner.) Once the pros and cons of the various types of financing are analyzed, and the company selects an option, the accounting differs, depending upon the type of financing chosen. In this section, we will discuss the recording of long-term debt, including notes payable, mortgages payable, and obligations under capital leases.

Interest-Bearing Notes

To illustrate the accounting for a long-term interest-bearing note payable, assume that on January 1, 2000, Giraffe Company borrowed $10,000 from City Bank for three years at 10 percent interest. Assume also that interest is payable annually on December 31. The entries to account for the note are:

2000			
Jan. 1	Cash.	10,000	
	Note Payable.		10,000
	Borrowed $10,000 from City Bank for three years.		
Dec. 31	Interest Expense.	1,000	
	Cash		1,000
	Made first annual interest payment on City Bank note ($10,000 × 0.10).		
2001			
Dec. 31	Interest Expense.	1,000	
	Cash		1,000
	Made second annual interest payment on City Bank note ($10,000 × 0.10).		*(continued)*

2002			
Dec. 31	Interest Expense	1,000	
	Note Payable	10,000	
	Cash		11,000
	Made final interest payment ($10,000 × 0.10) and repaid principal on City Bank note.		

When an interest-bearing note is issued for cash, present value computations are not necessary because the amount of cash received or paid is always equal to the present value. However, to show that the present value of the note in the example is $10,000, we can compute the present value as shown here:

Present value of interest payments:		
Amount of each interest payment	$ 1,000	
Table II factor for 3 payments at 10%	× 2.4869	
Present value of annuity		$ 2,487
Present value of principal payment:		
Amount of principal payment	$ 10,000	
Table I factor for 3 periods at 10%	× 0.7513	
Present value of lump-sum payment		7,513
Present value of interest and principal		$10,000

The total present value is the sum of the present values of the interest payments (an annuity) and the lump-sum principal payment due in three years.

Mortgages Payable

mortgage payable A written promise to pay a stated amount of money at one or more specified future dates; a mortgage is secured by the pledging of certain assets, usually real estate, as collateral.

A **mortgage payable** is similar to a note payable in that it is a written promise to pay a stated sum of money at one or more specified future dates. It is different from a note in the way it is applied. Whereas money borrowed with a note can often be used for any business purpose, mortgage money is usually related to a specific asset, typically real estate. Assets purchased with a mortgage are usually pledged as security or collateral on the loan. For individuals, home mortgages are common, and for companies, plant mortgages are frequent. In either case, mortgages generally require periodic (usually monthly) payments of principal plus interest.

To illustrate the accounting for a mortgage, we will assume that McGiven Automobile Company borrows $100,000 on January 1 to purchase a new showroom and signs a mortgage agreement pledging the showroom as collateral on the loan. If the mortgage is at 8 percent for 30 years, and the monthly payment is $733.76, payable on January 31 with subsequent payments due at the end of each month thereafter, the entries to record the acquisition of the mortgage and the first monthly payment are:

Cash	100,000	
Mortgage Payable		100,000
Borrowed $100,000 to purchase the automobile showroom.		
Mortgage Payable	67.09	
Interest Expense	666.67	
Cash		733.76
Made first month's mortgage payment.		

As this entry shows, only $67.09 of the $733.76 payment is applied to reduce the mortgage; the remainder is interest ($100,000 × 0.08 × 1/12). In each successive month, the amount applied to reduce the mortgage will increase slightly until, toward the end of the 30-year mortgage, almost all the payment will be for principal. A **mortgage amortization schedule** identifies how much of each mortgage payment is interest and how much is principal reduction, as shown in Exhibit 6-3. Note that during the first 20 years of McGiven's $100,000, 8 percent, 30-year mortgage, more of each mortgage payment is for interest than for principal.

mortgage amortization schedule A schedule that shows the breakdown between interest and principal for each payment over the life of a mortgage.

At the end of each year, a mortgage is reported on the balance sheet in two places: (1) The principal to be paid during the next year is shown as a current liability, and (2) the balance of the mortgage payable is shown as a long-term liability. Further, any accrued interest on the mortgage is reported as a current liability, and the interest expense for the year is included with other expenses on the income statement.

EXHIBIT 6-3

Mortgage Amortization Schedule ($100,000, 30-Year Mortgage at 8%)

End-of-Year Totals

Year	Monthly Payment	Principal Paid During Year	Interest Paid During Year	Outstanding Mortgage Balance
1	$733.76	$ 835	$7,970	$99,165
2	733.76	905	7,900	98,260
3	733.76	980	7,825	97,280
4	733.76	1,061	7,744	96,219
5	733.76	1,149	7,656	95,070
10	733.76	1,712	7,093	87,725
15	733.76	2,551	6,254	76,783
20	733.76	3,800	5,005	60,080
25	733.76	5,661	3,144	36,793
30	733.76	8,434	371	0

Total payments over life of mortgage: $264,154*

*733.76 × 360 payments = $264,154.

TO SUMMARIZE

Long-term interest-bearing notes are obligations that will be repaid over several years. Interest on the note is computed by multiplying the outstanding balance of the note times the rate of interest. Mortgages payable are long-term liabilities that arise when companies borrow money to buy land, construct buildings, or purchase additional operating assets. Mortgages are tied to specific assets. They are amortized over a period of time and involve periodic, usually monthly, payments that include both principal and interest.

Lease Obligations

A company may choose to lease rather than purchase an asset. If a lease is a simple, short-term rental agreement, called an operating lease, lease payments are recorded as Rent Expense by the lessee and as Rent Revenue by the lessor. However, with some leases, the transaction is classified as a capital lease and is accounted for as if

BUSINESS ENVIRONMENT ESSAY

How Interest Rates Affect Mortgage Payments The interest rate on a mortgage is as important as the amount of the loan in determining whether a person can afford a mortgage. This is because the amount of interest paid over an extended period of time will be at least equal to, or even two or three times, the amount of the loan. The following table shows the monthly payments on a $100,000, 25-year mortgage at interest rates from 7 to 14 percent, as well as the qualifying annual income.

The qualifying annual income is the minimum amount a person can earn in order to afford payments at each interest rate. The **Federal Home Loan Mortgage Corporation,** and most lending institutions, recommend that the monthly payments not exceed 28 percent of a person's monthly gross income. If, for example, you earn $30,000 a year, you should pay no more than $700 a month on a mortgage, which would be a $100,000 mortgage at 7 percent, or a $58,000 mortgage at 14 percent. For this reason, most people "shop around" for the lowest mortgage rates—and even then, many will not qualify for a loan.

To calculate monthly payments on smaller or larger mortgages, divide the amount by $100,000, then multiply that percentage by the figure in the table. For example, the monthly payment on a $60,000 mortgage at 9 percent is $503.40 [($60,000/$100,000) × $839].

$100,000, 25-Year Mortgage

Interest Rate	Monthly Payment	Total Amount Paid	Qualifying Annual Income
7%	$ 707	$212,100	$30,300
8%	772	231,600	33,084
9%	839	251,700	35,957
10%	909	272,700	38,957
11%	980	294,000	42,000
12%	1,053	315,900	45,129
13%	1,128	338,400	48,348
14%	1,204	361,200	51,600

the asset had been purchased with long-term debt. The lessee records the leased property as an asset and recognizes a liability to the lessor.

To illustrate the measurement and recording of a capital lease, we will assume that Malone Corporation leases a mainframe computer from Macro Data, Inc., on December 31, 1999. The lease requires annual payments of $10,000 for 10 years, with the first payment due on December 31, 2000.[1] The rate of interest applicable to the lease is 14 percent compounded annually.

FYI

Many companies structure their lease agreements so as not to meet the lease capitalization criteria. In these cases, the companies must still disclose their expected future lease payments in the notes to the financial statements.

Assuming the lease meets criteria for a capital lease, the computer and the related liability will be recorded by Malone Corporation at the present value of the future lease payments. From Table II, on page 261, the factor for the present value of an annuity for 10 payments at 14 per-

1. Readers should be aware that the illustration of a capital lease presented here assumes that lease payments are made at the end of each year, with the present values based on an ordinary annuity. Usually lease payments are made at the beginning of each lease period, which requires present value calculations using the concept of an annuity in advance or "annuity due." These calculations are explained in intermediate accounting texts.

cent is 5.2161. This factor is multiplied by the annual lease payment to determine the present value. The entry to record the lease on Malone's books is:

1999			
Dec. 31	Leased Computer.	52,161	
	Lease Liability.		52,161
	Leased a computer from Macro Data, Inc., for $10,000 a year for 10 years discounted at 14% ($10,000 × 5.2161 = $52,161).		

If Malone Corporation uses a calendar year for financial reporting, the December 31, 2000, balance sheet will report the leased asset in the property, plant, and equipment section and the lease liability in the liabilities section.

A schedule of the computer lease payments is presented in Exhibit 6-4. Each year the lease liability account balance is multiplied by 14 percent to determine the amount of interest included in each of the annual $10,000 lease payments.

EXHIBIT 6-4

Schedule of Computer Lease Payments

Year	Annual Payment	Interest Expense (0.14 × Lease Liability)	Principal	Lease Liability
				$52,161
1	$10,000	(0.14 × $52,161) = $7,303	$2,697	49,464
2	10,000	(0.14 × 49,464) = 6,925	3,075	46,389
3	10,000	(0.14 × 46,389) = 6,494	3,506	42,883
4	10,000	(0.14 × 42,883) = 6,004	3,996	38,887
5	10,000	(0.14 × 38,887) = 5,444	4,556	34,331
6	10,000	(0.14 × 34,331) = 4,806	5,194	29,137
7	10,000	(0.14 × 29,137) = 4,079	5,921	23,216
8	10,000	(0.14 × 23,216) = 3,250	6,750	16,466
9	10,000	(0.14 × 16,466) = 2,305	7,695	8,771
10	10,000	(0.14 × 8,771) = 1,229	8,771	0

Note that this is the same procedure as is used with a mortgage when determining the amount of each payment that is applied to reduce the principal and the amount that is considered interest expense.

The remainder of the payment is a reduction in the liability. For example, the first lease payment is recorded as follows:

2001			
Dec. 31	Interest Expense	7,303	
	Lease Liability	2,697	
	Cash.		10,000
	Paid annual lease payment for computer ($52,161 × 0.14 = $7,303; $10,000 − $7,303 = $2,697).		

Similar entries would be made in each of the remaining nine years of the lease, except that the principal payment (reduction in Lease Liability) would increase while the interest expense would decrease. Interest expense decreases over the lease term because a constant rate (14 percent) is applied to a decreasing principal balance.

Although the asset and liability accounts have the same balance at the beginning of the lease term, they seldom remain the same during the lease period. The asset and the liability are accounted for separately, with the asset being depreciated using one of the methods that will be discussed in Chapter 7.

TO SUMMARIZE

A lease is a contract whereby the lessee makes periodic payments to the lessor for the use of an asset. A simple short-term rental agreement, or operating lease, involves only the recording of rent expense by the lessee and rent revenue by the lessor. A capital lease is accounted for as a debt-financed purchase of the leased asset. Both the asset and liability are initially recorded by the lessee at the present value of the future lease payments discounted at the applicable interest rate. Subsequently, the asset is depreciated and the lease liability is written off as periodic payments are made. Part of each lease payment is interest expense, computed at a constant interest rate, and the remainder is a reduction of the principal amount of the liability.

3 *Account for bonds, including the original issuance, the payment of interest, and the retirement of bonds.*

THE NATURE OF BONDS

A **bond** is a contract between the borrowing company (issuer) and the lender (investor) in which the borrower promises to pay a specified amount of interest at the end of each period the bond is outstanding and to repay the principal at the maturity date of the bond contract. Bonds generally have maturity dates exceeding ten years and, as a result, are another example of a long-term liability.

bond A contract between a borrower and a lender in which the borrower promises to pay a specified rate of interest for each period the bond is outstanding and repay the principal at the maturity date.

debentures (unsecured bonds) Bonds for which no collateral has been pledged.

secured bonds Bonds for which assets have been pledged in order to guarantee repayment.

registered bonds Bonds for which the names and addresses of the bondholders are kept on file by the issuing company.

coupon bonds Unregistered bonds for which owners receive periodic interest payments by clipping a coupon from the bond and sending it to the issuer as evidence of ownership.

Types of Bonds

Bonds can be categorized on the basis of certain characteristics. A three-way classification system is:

1. The extent to which bondholders are protected.
   a. **Debentures** (or **unsecured bonds**). Bonds that have no underlying assets pledged as security, or collateral, to guarantee their repayment.
   b. **Secured bonds**. Secured bonds are bonds that have a pledge of company assets, such as land or buildings, as a protection for lenders. If the company fails to meet its bond obligations, the pledged assets can be sold and used to pay the bondholders. Bonds that are secured with the issuer's assets are often referred to as "mortgage bonds."
2. How the bond interest is paid.
   a. **Registered bonds**. Bonds for which the issuing company keeps a record of the names and addresses of all bondholders and pays interest only to those individuals whose names are on file.
   b. **Coupon bonds**. Unregistered bonds for which the issuer has no record of current bondholders but instead pays interest to anyone who can show evidence of ownership. Usually these bonds contain a printed coupon for each interest payment. When a payment is due, the bondholder clips the coupon from the certificate and sends it to the issuer as evidence of bond ownership. The issuer then sends an interest payment to the bondholder.

3. How the bonds mature.
   a. **Term bonds**. Bonds that mature in one lump sum on a specified future date.
   b. **Serial bonds**. Bonds that mature in a series of installments.
   c. **Callable bonds**. Term or serial bonds that the issuer can redeem at any time at a specified price.
   d. **Convertible bonds**. Term or serial bonds that can be converted to other securities, such as stocks, after a specified period, at the option of the bondholder. (The accounting for this type of bond is discussed in advanced accounting texts.)

term bonds Bonds that mature in one lump sum at a specified future date.

serial bonds Bonds that mature in a series of installments at specified future dates.

callable bonds Bonds for which the issuer reserves the right to pay the obligation before its maturity date.

convertible bonds Bonds that can be traded for, or converted to, other securities after a specified period of time.

In addition to these more traditional bond features, other, more unique types of bonds have been developed in the last decade and have become increasingly popular. Two such examples include zero-interest bonds and junk bonds. **Zero-interest bonds** are bonds that are issued with no promise of interest payments. The company issuing the bonds promises only to repay a fixed amount at the maturity date. While the idea of having to make no interest payments might be initially appealing to the issuer, remember that the present value of the bond is affected by both the lump sum payment at the end of the life of the bond as well as the annuity payment. If this annuity (interest) payment will not be part of the bond, potential buyers of the bond will pay much less for the bond. For this reason, these bonds are often referred to as *deep-discount bonds.*

zero-interest bonds Bonds issued with no promise of interest payments; only a lump sum payment will be made.

Junk bonds are high-risk bonds issued by companies in weak financial condition or with large amounts of debt already outstanding. These bonds typically yield returns of at least 12 percent, but some may return in excess of 20 percent. Of course, with these high returns comes greater risk. For example, in April of 1991 one of the largest insurance companies in California was closed by the state. The reason cited for the closure was that the company had invested over 50 percent of its available funds in junk bonds whose value had declined considerably. This significant decline jeopardized the long-term solvency of the insurance company and caused the state to step in to prevent a collapse of the firm.

junk bonds Bonds issued by companies in weak financial condition with large amounts of debt already outstanding; these bonds yield high rates of return because of high risk.

Characteristics of Bonds

When an organization issues bonds, it usually sells them to underwriters (brokers and investment bankers), who in turn sell them to various institutions and to the public. At the time of the original sale, the company issuing the bonds chooses a trustee to represent the bondholders. In most cases, the trustee is a large bank or trust company to which the company issuing bonds delivers a contract called a bond indenture, deed of trust, or trust indenture. The **bond indenture** specifies that in return for an investment of cash by investors, the company promises to pay a specific amount of interest (based on a specified, or stated, rate of interest) each period the bonds are outstanding and to repay the **principal** (also called **face value**, or **maturity value**) of the bonds at a specified future date (the **bond maturity date**). It is the duty of the trustee to protect investors and to make sure that the bond issuer fulfills its responsibilities.

FYI

Bonds are bought and sold on trading markets just like stocks. The New York Bond Exchange is the largest exchange of this type.

bond indenture A contract between a bond issuer and a bond purchaser that specifies the terms of a bond.

principal (face value or maturity value) The amount that will be paid on a bond at the maturity date.

bond maturity date The date at which a bond principal or face amount becomes payable.

The total value of a single "bond issue" often exceeds several million dollars. A bond issue is generally divided into a number of individual bonds, which may be of varying denominations. The principal or face value of each bond is usually $1,000, or a multiple thereof. Note that the price of bonds is quoted as a percentage of $1,000 face value. Thus, a bond quoted at 98 is selling for $980 (98% × $1,000), and a bond quoted at 103 is selling for $1,030 (103% × $1,000). By issuing bonds in small denominations, a company increases the chances that a broad range of investors will be able to compete for the purchase of the bonds. This increased demand usually results in the bonds selling for a higher price.

In most cases, the market price of bonds is influenced by (1) the riskiness of the bonds and (2) the interest rate at which the bonds are issued. The first factor, riskiness of the bonds, is determined by general economic conditions and the financial status of the company selling the bonds, as measured by organizations (**Moody**'s or **Standard and Poor**'s, for instance) that regularly assign a rating, or a grade, to all corporate bonds.

Companies strive to earn as high a bond rating as possible because the higher the rating, the lower the interest rate they will have to pay to attract buyers. A high-risk bond, on the other hand, will have a low rating, which means that the company will have to offer a higher rate of interest to attract buyers.

TO SUMMARIZE

Bonds are certificates of debt issued by companies or government agencies, guaranteeing a stated interest rate and repayment of the principal at a specified maturity date. Corporations issue bonds as a form of long-term borrowing to finance the acquisition of operating assets, such as land, buildings, and equipment. Bonds can be classified by their level of security (debentures versus secured bonds), by the way interest is paid (registered versus coupon bonds), and by the way they mature (term bonds, serial bonds, callable bonds, and convertible bonds).

Determining a Bond's Issuance Price

When a company issues bonds, it is generally promising to make two types of payments: (1) a payment of interest of a fixed amount at equal intervals (usually semiannually but sometimes quarterly or annually) over the life of the bond and (2) a lump-sum payment—the principal, or face value, of the bond—at the maturity date. For example, assume that Denver Company issues 10 percent, 5-year bonds with a total face value of \$800,000. Interest is to be paid semiannually. This information tells us that Denver Company agrees to pay \$40,000 (\$800,000 × 0.10 × 1/2 year) in interest every six months and also agrees to pay to the investors the principal amount of \$800,000 at the end of five years. The following diagram reflects this agreement between Denver Company and the bond investors:

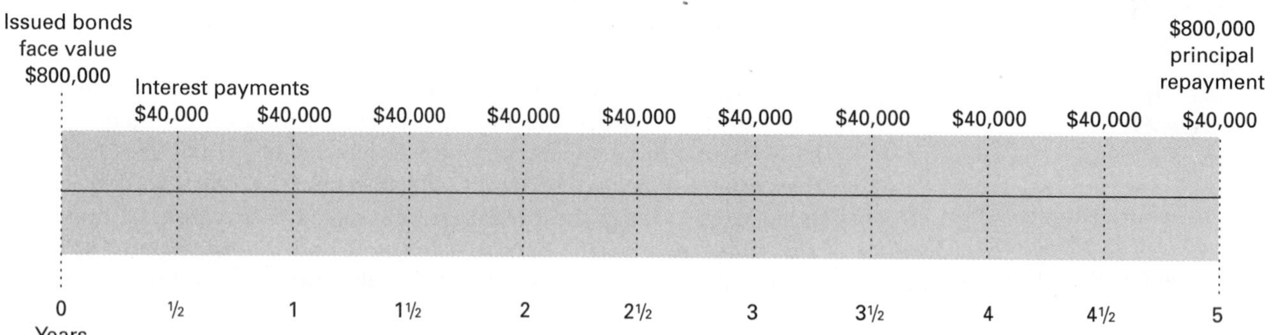

(STOP & THINK)

If the market rate of interest is higher than the rate of interest stated on the bonds, will the bonds sell at a price higher or lower than the face value? Think about it this way. Is the higher rate more attractive to investors, and if it is, what would investors do as a result?

In this example, it was assumed that the bonds were issued at their face value of \$800,000. However, bonds are frequently issued at a price that is more or less than their face value. The actual price at which bonds are issued is affected by what interest rate investors are seeking at the time the bonds are sold in relation to the interest rate specified by the borrower in the bond indenture. How, then, is the issuance price of bonds determined?

Essentially, present value concepts are used to measure the effect of time on the value of money. The price should equal the present value of the interest payments (an annuity) plus the present value of the bond's lump-sum face value at maturity. These present values are computed using the **market rate of interest** (also called the **effective rate** or **yield rate**), which is the rate investors expect to earn on their investment. It is contrasted with the **stated rate of interest**, which is the rate printed on the bond (10 percent in the Denver Company example).

market rate (effective rate or yield rate) of interest The actual interest rate earned or paid on a bond investment.

stated rate of interest The rate of interest printed on the bond.

bond discount The difference between the face value and the sales price when bonds are sold below their face value.

bond premium The difference between the face value and the sales price when bonds are sold above their face value.

If the effective rate is equal to the stated rate, the bonds will sell at face value (that is, at $800,000). If the effective rate is higher than the stated rate, the bonds will sell at a **bond discount** (at less than the face value) because the investors desire a higher rate than the company is promising to pay. Likewise, if the effective rate is lower than the stated rate, the bonds will sell at a **bond premium** (at more than face value) because the company is promising to pay a higher rate than the market is paying at that time.

Consider the following scenario: If Company A is issuing bonds with a stated rate of 12 percent while the market rate for similar bonds is 10 percent, what will happen to the price of the bonds? Investors, eager to receive a 12 percent return, will bid the price of the bonds up until the price at which the bonds sell will yield a 10 percent return. The amount paid for the bonds over and above the maturity value is the bond premium. If Company A were issuing bonds with a stated rate of 8 percent, no one would buy the bonds until the price was lowered sufficiently to allow investors to earn a return of 10 percent. The difference between the selling price and the maturity value would be the amount of the bond discount.

We will use the Denver Company bonds example (from page 238) to explain how the price is computed in each situation.

Bonds Issued at Face Value

Denver Company has agreed to issue $800,000 bonds and pay 10 percent interest, compounded semiannually. Assume that the effective interest rate demanded by investors for bonds of this level of risk is also 10 percent. Using the effective interest rate, which happens to be the same as the stated rate, the calculation to determine the price at which the bonds will be issued is shown below. (Note that since the interest is compounded semiannually, the interest rate is halved and the 5-year bond life is treated as ten 6-month periods.)

The calculation shows why the bonds sell at face value. At the effective rate, the sum of the present value of the interest payments and the payment at maturity is $800,000, which is the issuance price at the stated rate. This equality of present values will occur only when the effective rate and the stated rate are the same.

1.	Semiannual interest payments	$ 40,000	
	Present value of an annuity of 10 payments of $1 at 5% (Table II)	× 7.7217	
	Present value of interest payments		$308,868
2.	Maturity value of bonds	$800,000	
	Present value of $1 received 10 periods in the future discounted at 5% (Table I)	× 0.6139	
	Present value of principal amount		491,132*
3.	Issuance price of bonds (total present value)		$800,000

*Difference is due to the rounding of the present value factor.

Bonds Issued at a Discount

The Denver Company will sell its bonds at less than the face value of $800,000 (at a discount) if the stated rate of interest is less than the effective rate that investors are seeking. To illustrate the issuance of bonds at a discount, assume that the effective rate is 12 percent compounded semiannually; the stated rate remains 10 percent compounded semiannually. In this case, the bonds will be issued at a price of $741,124, as shown here.

1.	Semiannual interest payments	$ 40,000	
	Present value of an annuity of 10 payments of $1 at 6% (Table II)	× 7.3601	
	Present value of interest payments		$294,404
2.	Maturity value of bonds	$800,000	
	Present value of $1 received 10 periods in the future discounted at 6% (Table I)	× 0.5584	
	Present value of principal amount		446,720
3.	Issuance price of bonds (total present value)		$741,124

Denver Company will receive less than the $800,000 face value because the stated rate of interest is lower than the effective rate. In this case, there is a discount of $58,876 ($800,000 − $741,124).

Bonds Issued at a Premium

The Denver Company bonds will be issued for more than $800,000 (at a premium) when the stated interest rate is higher than the effective rate. Let us now assume that the effective rate is 8 percent compounded semiannually and that the stated rate is still 10 percent compounded semiannually. In this case, the bonds will be issued at $864,916, as shown here.

1.	Interest payments	$ 40,000	
	Present value of an annuity of 10 payments of $1 at 4% (Table II)	× 8.1109	
	Present value of interest payments		$324,436
2.	Maturity value of bonds	$800,000	
	Present value of $1 received 10 periods in the future discounted at 4% (Table I)	× 0.6756	
	Present value of principal amount		540,480
3.	Issuance price of bonds (total present value)		$864,916

Denver Company will receive more than the $800,000 face value when the bonds are issued because the company has agreed to pay the investors a higher rate of interest than the market rate.

In all three situations, the 10 percent stated rate determined the amount of each interest payment. The price of the bonds was determined by discounting the $40,000 of interest payments and the $800,000 lump sum at maturity by the effective rate of interest, which may vary from day to day, depending on market conditions. In essence, the issuance price depends on four factors: (1) face value of the bonds, (2) periodic interest payments (face value × stated interest rate), (3) time period, and (4) effective interest rate. Although the bond price is the exact amount that allows investors to earn the interest rate they are seeking, it also reflects the real cost of money to the borrowing company.

TO SUMMARIZE

The price at which bonds are issued is a function of the interest rate investors are seeking when the bonds are issued in relation to the interest rate the borrowing company is promising to pay. The bond's face value, or principal, and future interest payments (face value × stated interest rate) are discounted by the interest rate desired by investors (the effective, yield, or market rate) to arrive at the issuance price of the bonds. Bonds will sell at their face value if the stated interest rate is equal to the effective rate. If the effective rate is higher than the stated rate, the bonds will sell at a discount. If the effective rate is lower than the stated rate, the bonds will sell at a premium. The effective rate used to discount the payments promised by the borrower reflects the real cost of the money borrowed.

Accounting for Bonds Payable Issued at Face Value

When a company issues bonds, it must account for the issuance (sale) of the bonds, for the interest payments, and for the amortization of any bond premium or discount. Then, at or before maturity, the company must account for the bond's retirement.

The accounting for these four elements depends on the issuance price of the bonds and on the date of issuance in relation to the date on which interest is paid. In the following sections, we explain the accounting for bonds when the issue price is equal to face value. The accounting for bonds issued at a premium or at a discount involves a periodic adjustment to interest expense and is not illustrated in this text. For most of this discussion, we will use the following data:

Issuing company	Central Trucking Company
Accounting year	Calendar year ending December 31
Face value of bonds issued	$100,000
Stated interest rate	12 percent
Effective interest rate when issued	12 percent
Initial date of issuance	January 1, 2000
Date of maturity	January 1, 2010
Interest payment dates	January 1 and July 1

Central Trucking Company issued $100,000 bonds with a stated interest rate of 12 percent on January 1, 2000. The bonds were issued at face value because 12 percent is the effective, or market, rate of interest for similar bonds. The journal entry to record their issuance on January 1, 2000, is as follows:

Cash	100,000	
Bonds Payable		100,000
Issued $100,000, 12%, 10-year bonds at face value.		

The entry to record the first payment of interest on July 1, 2000, is:

Bond Interest Expense	6,000	
Cash		6,000
Paid semiannual interest on the $100,000, 12%, 10-year bonds ($100,000 × 0.12 × 1/2 year).		

Since Central Trucking operates on a calendar-year basis, it will need to make the following adjusting entry on December 31, 2000, to account for the interest expense between July 1 and December 31, 2000:

Bond Interest Expense	6,000	
Bond Interest Payable		6,000
To recognize expense for the six months July 1 to December 31, 2000 ($100,000 × 0.12 × 1/2 year).		

At the end of the accounting period (December 31, 2000), the financial statements will report the following:

Income Statement	
Bond interest expense ($6,000 × 2)	$12,000
Balance Sheet	
Current liabilities:	
Bond interest payable	$ 6,000
Long-term liabilities:	
Bonds payable (12%, due January 1, 2010)	$100,000

On January 1, 2001, when the semiannual interest is paid, the bond interest payable account is eliminated. The January 1 entry is:

Bond Interest Payable	6,000	
Cash		6,000
Paid semiannual bond interest.		

The entries to record the interest expense payments during the remaining nine years will be the same as those made during 2000 and on January 1, 2001. The only other entry required in accounting for these bonds is the recording of their retirement on January 1, 2010. That entry, assuming that all interest has been accounted for, will be:

Bonds Payable	100,000	
Cash		100,000
Retired the $100,000, 10-year, 12% bonds.		

As the preceding entries illustrate, accounting for the issuance of bonds, the payment of the interest, and the retirement of the bonds is relatively simple when the bonds are issued at face value.

Bond Retirements Before Maturity

Bond issues are, by definition, an inflexible form of long-term debt. The issuing company has a set schedule of interest payments and a specified maturity date, usually at least five or ten years from the issuance date. In many cases, however, a company may want to pay off (redeem) and retire its bonds before maturity. This situation might occur when interest rates fall—a company uses the money obtained by issuing new bonds at a lower interest rate to retire the older, higher-interest bonds. As a result, the company retains the money it needs for expansion or other long-range projects but pays less interest for using that money.

As noted earlier, callable bonds are issued with an early redemption provision. Although the company usually has to pay a premium (penalty) for the privilege of redeeming (calling) the bonds, the amount of the penalty will probably be less than the amount gained in paying a lower interest rate. With bonds that are not callable, the company simply purchases the bonds in the open market, as available, at the going price.

To illustrate the retirement of bonds before maturity, assume that the Central Trucking Company bonds were now selling in the bond market at 109 and are callable at 110. The company decides to take advantage of lower interest rates (8 percent) by issuing new bonds and using the proceeds to pay off the outstanding bonds. Given that the bonds were issued at their face value, the penalty (the call premium) is $10,000. The entry to record the retirement of the bonds at 110 is:

Bonds Payable	100,000	
Loss on Bond Retirement	10,000	
Cash ($100,000 × 1.10).		110,000
To retire $100,000 of bonds at a call price of 110.		

In this case, the bonds were retired at a loss of $10,000. The loss is probably tolerable because the company expects to pay significantly less interest over the life of the new bond issue than it would have had to continue to pay on the old bonds. Gains and losses on the early retirement of bonds are reported on the income statement as extraordinary gains and losses.

TO SUMMARIZE

Accounting for bonds involves three steps: (1) accounting for their issuance, (2) accounting for the periodic interest payments, and (3) accounting for their retirement. When bonds are retired at maturity, there is no gain or loss since the amount paid is equal to the face value of the bonds. When bonds are retired before maturity, a gain or loss often results since the price paid to retire the bonds can be different from the carrying value of the bonds. The gain or loss on retirement of bonds is reported on the income statement as an extraordinary item.

4 *Distinguish between debt and equity financing and describe the advantages and disadvantages of organizing a business as a proprietorship or a partnership.*

RAISING EQUITY FINANCING

Thus far we have discussed various types of loans—or debt financing. We now turn our attention to equity financing. Equity financing is different from debt financing in that with equity financing an organization is selling ownership in its business, whereas with debt financing the company is borrowing money that must be repaid. The business issues associated with investor financing are summarized in the time line in Exhibit 6-5.

The factors impacting the choice between borrowing and seeking additional investment funds are described in this section of the chapter. This section also outlines the advantages and disadvantages of organizing a business as a proprietorship or partnership. The decision to incorporate and the process that a corporation follows in soliciting investor funds are described in the next section. The remainder of the chapter is devoted to the accounting procedures used to give a proper reporting of stockholders' equity to the investors. Of course, proper financial reporting to current and potential investors is one of the primary reasons for the existence of financial accounting.

EXHIBIT 6-5 Time Line of Business Issues Involved with Investor Financing

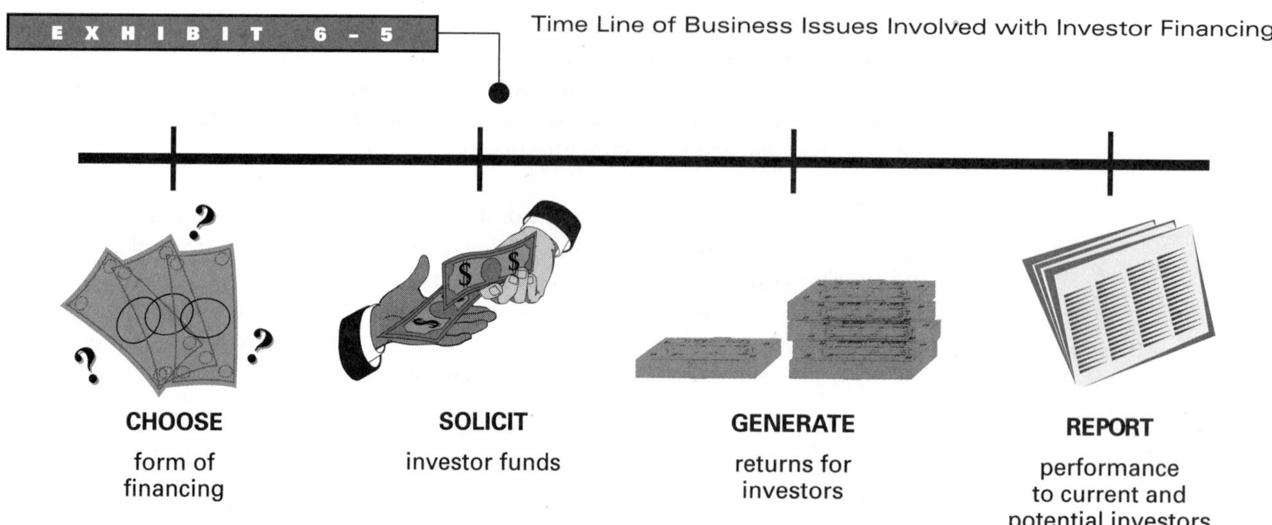

Difference Between a Loan and an Investment

Imagine that you own a small business and need $40,000 for expansion. What is the difference between borrowing the $40,000 and finding a partner who will invest the $40,000? If you borrow the money, you must guarantee to repay the $40,000 with interest. If you fail to make these payments, the lender can haul you into court and use the power of the law to force repayment. On the other hand, if your company does very well and you generate more than enough cash to repay the $40,000 plus interest, the lender does not get to share in your success. You owe the lender $40,000 plus interest and not a penny more. So, a loan is characterized by a fixed, legal obligation to repay a specified amount, whether the borrowing company performs poorly or performs well.

If you receive $40,000 in investment funds from a new partner, the partner now shares in your company's failures and successes. If business is bad and the investor is never able to recover his or her $40,000 investment—well, that's the way it goes. The law will not help the investor recover the investment because the very nature of an investment is that the investor accepts the risk of losing everything. However, in exchange for accepting this risk, the investor also gets to share in the success if the company does well. For example, if you had loaned $40,000 to Bill Gates for **Microsoft** expansion back in 1986, you would have been repaid the $40,000 plus a little interest. However, if you had invested that same $40,000 in Microsoft, your investment would now be worth about $6 million. Thus, an investment is characterized by a higher risk of losing your money, balanced by the chance of sharing in the wealth if the company does well.

FYI

The law does not help an investor recover lost investment funds unless it is shown that the investor was tricked (by false financial reports, for example) into making the investment.

Proprietorships and Partnerships

As explained in Chapter 2, a business can be organized as a proprietorship, a partnership, or a corporation. These three types of organization are merely different types of legal contracts that define the rights and responsibilities of the owner or owners of the business. The advantages and disadvantages of proprietorships and partnerships are discussed below. Corporations are discussed in the next section.

A **proprietorship** is a business owned by one person. A **partnership** is a business owned by two or more persons or entities. In most respects, proprietorships and partnerships are similar to each other but very different from corporations. Both a proprietorship and a partnership are characterized by ease of formation, limited life, and unlimited liability.

proprietorship A business owned by one person.

partnership An association of two or more individuals or organizations to carry on economic activity.

Ease of Formation

Proprietorships and partnerships can be formed with few legal formalities. When a person decides to establish a proprietorship, he or she merely acquires the necessary cash, inventory, equipment, and other assets; obtains a business license; and begins providing goods or services to customers. The same is true for a partnership, except that since two or more persons are involved, they must decide together which assets will be acquired and how business will be conducted.

Limited Life

Because proprietorships and partnerships are not legal entities that are separate and distinct from their owners, they are easily terminated. In the case of a proprietorship, the owner can decide to dissolve the business at any time. For a partnership, anything that terminates or changes the contract between the partners legally dissolves the partnership. Among the events that dissolve a partnership are:

1. the death or withdrawal of a partner,
2. the bankruptcy of a partner,
3. the admission of a new partner,
4. the retirement of a partner, or
5. the completion of the project for which the partnership was formed.

The occurrence of any of these events does not necessarily mean that a partnership must cease business; rather, the existing partnership is legally terminated, and another partnership must be formed.

Unlimited Liability

Proprietorships and partnerships have unlimited liability, which means that the proprietor or partners are personally responsible for all debts of the business. If a partnership is in poor financial condition, creditors first attempt to satisfy their claims from the assets of the partnership. After those assets are exhausted, creditors may seek payment from the personal assets of the partners. In addition, since partners are responsible for one another's actions (within the scope of the partnership), creditors may seek payment for liabilities created by a departed or bankrupt partner from the personal assets of the remaining partners. This unlimited liability feature is probably the single most significant disadvantage of a proprietorship or partnership. It can deter a wealthy person from joining a partnership for fear of losing personal assets.

TO SUMMARIZE

A loan is a fixed, legal obligation to repay a specified amount, whether the borrowing company performs poorly or performs well. With an investment, the investor risks losing the investment funds if the company performs poorly but shares in the wealth if the company does well. A proprietorship is a business owned by one person. A partnership is a business owned by two or more persons. Both types of businesses are easy to start and easy to terminate. A major disadvantage of proprietorships and partnerships is the unlimited liability of the owner or partners.

5 *Describe the basic characteristics of a corporation and the nature of common and preferred stock.*

CORPORATIONS AND CORPORATE STOCK

Corporations are the dominant form of business enterprise in the United States. Established as separate legal entities, **corporations** are legally distinct from the persons responsible for their creation. In many respects, they are accorded the same rights as individuals; they can conduct business, be sued, enter into contracts, and own property. Firms are incorporated by the state in which they are organized and are subject to that state's laws and requirements.

corporation A legal entity chartered by a state; ownership is represented by transferable shares of stock.

Characteristics of a Corporation

Corporations have several characteristics that distinguish them from proprietorships and partnerships. These characteristics are discussed below.

Limited Liability

limited liability The legal protection given stockholders whereby they are responsible for the debts and obligations of a corporation only to the extent of their capital contributions.

Limited liability means that in the event of corporate bankruptcy, the maximum financial loss any stockholder can sustain is his or her investment in the corporation (unless fraud can be proved). Since a corporation is a separate legal entity and is responsible for its own acts and obligations, creditors cannot usually look beyond the corporation's assets for satisfaction of their claims. This is not true of other forms of business organizations. In a partnership, for example, the partners can usually be held liable for the debts of the partnership, even to the extent of their personal assets. This limited liability feature has probably been most responsible for the phenomenal growth of the corporate form of business because it protects investors from sustaining losses beyond their investments. In most cases of bankruptcy, however, stockholders will lose most of their investment, since the claims of creditors must be satisfied before stockholders receive anything.

Easy Transferability of Ownership

Shares of stock in a corporation can be bought, sold, passed from one generation to another, or otherwise transferred without affecting the legal or economic status of the corporation. In other words, most corporations have perpetual existence—the life of the corporation continues by the transfer of shares of stock to new owners.

Ability to Raise Large Amounts of Capital

The sale of shares of stock permits many investors, both large and small, to participate in ownership of the business. Some corporations actually have thousands of individual stockholders. In its 1997 annual report, **Microsoft** reports that it has 53,390 stockholders of record. Because of this widespread ownership, large corporations are said to be publicly owned.

Double Taxation

Because corporations are separate legal entities, they are taxed independently of their owners. This often results in a disadvantage, however, because the portion of corporate profits that is paid out in dividends is taxed twice. First, the profits are taxed to the corporation; second, the owners, or stockholders, are taxed on their dividend income.

FYI

There are some hybrid organizations that have characteristics of both partnerships and corporations. For example, several of the large international accounting firms are organized as limited liability partnerships (LLPs). An LLP offers the advantages of a partnership structure but also provides each partner with limited liability for lawsuit costs caused by the actions of his or her partners.

Close Government Regulation

Because large corporations may have thousands of stockholders, each with only small ownership interests, the government has assumed the task of monitoring certain corporate activities. Examples of government regulation are the requirements that all major corporations be audited and that they issue periodic financial statements. As a result, in certain respects, major corporations often enjoy less freedom than do partnerships and proprietorships.

Starting a Corporation

Suppose that you wanted to start a corporation. First, you would study your state's corporate laws (usually with the aid of an attorney). Then you would apply for a charter with the appropriate state official. In the application you would give the intended name of your corporation, its purpose (that is, the type of activity it will engage in), the type and amount of stock you plan to have authorized for your corporation, and in some cases, the names and addresses of the potential stockholders. Finally, if the state approves your application, you will be issued a "charter" (also called "articles of incorporation"), giving legal status to your corporation.

Of course, the primary purpose of forming a corporation is to then sell stock in the corporation in order to obtain business financing. If the business you intend to establish will operate across state lines and if you intend to seek investment funds from the general public, then you must register your intended stock issue with the Securities and Exchange Commission in Washington, D.C. You are required to provide a **prospectus** to each potential investor; the prospectus outlines your business plan, sources of financing, significant risks, etc. Finally, you can sell your shares to the public in what is called an "initial public offering" (IPO). You will receive the proceeds from the IPO, minus the commission charged by the investment banker sponsoring the issue.

prospectus Report provided to potential investors that presents a company's financial statements and explains its business plan, sources of financing, and significant risks.

When an investor buys stock in a corporation, he or she receives a stock certificate as evidence of ownership. For convenience, these stock certificates are frequently held by the stockbroker through whom the investor purchased the shares. The investors in a corporation are called **stockholders**, and they govern the corporation through an elected **board of directors**. In most corporations, the board of directors then chooses a management team to direct the daily affairs of the corporation. In smaller companies, the board of directors is usually made up of members of that management team.

stockholders Individuals or organizations that own a portion (shares of stock) of a corporation.

board of directors Individuals elected by the stockholders to govern a corporation.

Several types of stock can be authorized by the charter and issued by the corporation. The most familiar types are common stock and preferred stock, and the major difference between them concerns the degree to which their holders are allowed to participate in the rights of ownership of the corporation.

Common Stock

Certain basic rights are inherent in the ownership of **common stock**. These rights are as follows:

common stock The most frequently issued class of stock; usually it provides a voting right but is secondary to preferred stock in dividend and liquidation rights.

1. The right to vote in corporate matters such as the election of the board of directors or the undertaking of major actions such as the purchase of another company.
2. The preemptive right, which permits existing stockholders to purchase additional shares whenever stock is issued by the corporation. This allows common stockholders to maintain the same percentage of ownership in the company if they choose to do so.
3. The right to receive cash dividends *if* they are paid. As explained later, corporations do not have to pay cash dividends, and the amount received by common stockholders is sometimes limited.
4. The rights to ownership of all corporate assets once obligations to everyone else have been satisfied. This means that once all loans have been repaid and the claims of the preferred stockholders have been met (as discussed below), all the excess assets belong to the common stockholders.

FYI

Occasionally a corporation will have more than one class of common stock. For example, Dow Jones & Company has Common Stock and Class B Common Stock. Each Class B share gets ten votes in corporate matters, and most of the Class B shares are owned by the descendants of Clarence Barron.

In essence, the common stockholders of a corporation are the true owners of the business. They delegate their decision-making authority to the board of directors, who in turn delegate authority for day-to-day operations to managers hired for that purpose. Thus, a distinguishing characteristic of business ownership as a common stockholder of a corporation is a clear separation between owning the business and operating the business.

Preferred Stock

The term "preferred stock" is somewhat misleading because it gives the impression that **preferred stock** is better than common stock. Preferred stock isn't better; it's different. A good way to think of preferred stock is that preferred stockholders give up some of the ownership rights of the common stockholders in exchange for some of the protection enjoyed by lenders.

preferred stock A class of stock that usually provides dividend and liquidation preferences over common stock.

BUSINESS ENVIRONMENT ESSAY

Investing in the Stock Market "October," said Mark Twain, "is one of the peculiarly dangerous months to speculate in stocks. Others are July, January, September, April, November, May, March, June, December, August, and February." Despite Mark Twain's warning, stocks have always been one of the most prestigious and desired investments. These days, stock trading is easier than ever. There are scores of Internet stock trading firms that will allow you to buy and sell as many shares as you wish for less than $10 per trade. For some people, Internet stock trading has become the ultimate video game, with shooting lasers and fighting ninjas being replaced by stock price charts and the Federal Reserve Board.

This textbook won't make you an expert in picking promising stocks. In fact, you should be suspicious of any book or investment advisor claiming to have the secrets to deciphering the stock market. Here are some practical guidelines to help you avoid some of the pitfalls when deciding to buy stock:

1. Do not make hasty, emotional decisions about buying and selling stocks.
2. Do not "fall in love" with stocks so that you are no longer objective in your appraisal of them.
3. Remember, you will seldom, if ever, buy stocks at their lowest price and sell them at their highest price.
4. There are stock market "fads," so when you buy at the height of a stock's popularity, you almost always pay too much.
5. Don't invest in stocks unless you can afford to lose the money you invest or at least have no access to it for a long time.
6. Plan to hold your stock investments for a long time. Most stock-market millionaires were not speculators, and commissions on frequent sales and purchases will eat up your short-term gains.

Source: W. S. Albrecht, *Money Wise* (Salt Lake City, Utah: Deseret Book Company, 1983), pp. 134–139.

In most cases, preferred stockholders are not allowed to vote for the corporate board of directors. In addition, preferred stockholders are usually only allowed to receive a fixed cash dividend, meaning that if the company does well, preferred stockholders do not get to share in the success. In exchange for these limitations, preferred stockholders are entitled to receive their cash dividends and have their claims fully paid in case the corporation is liquidated, before any cash is paid to common stockholders.

convertible preferred stock Preferred stock that can be converted to common stock at a specified conversion rate.

Preferred stock may also include other types of privileges, the most common of which is convertibility. **Convertible preferred stock** is preferred stock that can be converted to common stock at a specified conversion rate. For example, the notes to **Microsoft**'s 1997 financial statements (see Appendix A) reveal that the investors who purchased 12.5 million shares of Microsoft convertible preferred stock in December 1996 will be able to exchange those preferred shares (if they wish) for Microsoft common stock beginning in December 1999. Convertible preferred stock can be very appealing to investors. They can enjoy the dividend privileges of the preferred stock while having the option to convert to common stock if the market value of the common stock increases significantly. By issuing shares of stock with varying rights and privileges, companies can appeal to a wider range of investors.

TO SUMMARIZE

A corporation is a business entity that has a legal existence separate from that of its owners; it can conduct business, own property, and enter into contracts. The five major features of a corporation are (1) limited liability for stockholders, (2) easy transferability of ownership, (3) the ability to raise large amounts of capital, (4) separate taxation, and (5) for large corporations, closer regulation by government. Common stock confers four basic rights upon its owners: (1) the right to vote in corporate matters, (2) the right to maintain proportionate ownership, (3) the right to receive cash dividends, and (4) the ownership of all excess corporate assets upon liquidation of a corporation. Preferred stock typically carries preferential claims to dividend and liquidation privileges but has no voting rights.

6 *Account for the issuance and repurchase of common and preferred stock.*

ACCOUNTING FOR STOCK

In this section we focus on the accounting for the issuance of stock as well as the accounting for stock repurchases.

Issuance of Stock

par value Nominal value assigned to and printed on the face of each share of a corporation's stock.

Each share of common stock usually has a **par value** printed on the face of the stock certificate. For example, the common stock of Dow Jones & Company has a $1 par value. This par value has little to do with the market value of the shares. In February 1998, each Dow Jones common share with a $1 par value was selling for about $50 per share. When par-value stock sells for a price above par, it is said to sell at a premium. In most states it is illegal to issue stock for a price below par value. If stock were to be issued at a discount (below par), stockholders could be held liable to later make up the difference between their investment and the par value of the shares they purchased. The par value multiplied by the total number of shares outstanding is usually equal to a company's "legal capital," and it represents the amount of the invested funds that cannot be returned to the investors as long as the corporation is in existence. This legal capital requirement was intended to provide a means of protecting a company's creditors; without it, excessive dividends could be paid, leaving nothing for creditors. The par value really was of more importance 100 years ago and is something of a historical oddity today. These days, most states allow the sale of no-par stock.

FYI

Most companies establish a very low par value, such as $0.10 or $1 per share. This strategy usually eliminates the possibility of stock ever selling below par value.

When par-value stock is issued by a corporation, usually Cash is debited, and the appropriate stockholders' equity accounts are credited. For par-value common stock, the equity accounts credited are Common Stock, for an amount equal to the par value, and Paid-In Capital in Excess of Par, Common Stock, for the premium on the common stock.

To illustrate, we will assume that the Boston Lakers Basketball Team (a corporation) issued 1,000 shares of $1 par-value common stock for $50 per share. The entry to record the stock issuance is:

Cash (1,000 shares × $50)	50,000	
Common Stock (1,000 shares × $1 par value)		1,000
Paid-In Capital in Excess of Par,		
Common Stock (1,000 shares × $49)		49,000
Issued 1,000 shares of $1 par-value common stock at $50 per share.		

contributed capital The portion of owners' equity contributed by investors (the owners) in exchange for shares of stock.

A similar entry would be made if the stock being issued were preferred stock. The total par value of the common and preferred stock, along with the associated amounts of paid-in capital in excess of par, constitute a corporation's **contributed capital**.

get connected
http://www.swcollege.com
net work

Do you want to try your hand at buying some shares of stock? Go to ameritrade.com, the Web site for one of the leading Internet stock trading companies.

How much does it cost in commissions to execute one stock trade?

ameritrade.com

This illustration points out two important elements in accounting for the issuance of stock: (1) The equity accounts identify the type of stock being issued (common or preferred), and (2) the proceeds from the sale of the stock are divided into the portion attributable to its par value and the portion paid in excess of par value. These distinctions are important because the owners' equity section of the balance sheet should correctly identify the specific sources of capital so that the respective rights of the various stockholders can be known.

If the stock being issued has no par value, only one credit is included in the entry. To illustrate, assume that the Lakers' stock does not have a par value and that the corporation issued 1,000 shares for $50 per share. The entry to record this stock issuance would be:

Cash	50,000	
Common Stock		50,000
Issued 1,000 shares of no-par stock at $50 per share.		

Although stock is usually issued for cash, other considerations may be involved. To illustrate the kinds of entries made when stock is issued for noncash considerations, we will assume that a prospective stockholder exchanged a piece of land for 5,000 shares of the Boston Lakers' $1 par-value common stock. Assuming the market value of the stock at the date of the exchange was $40 per share, the entry is:

Land (5,000 shares × $40)	200,000	
Common Stock (5,000 shares × $1)		5,000
Paid-In Capital in Excess of Par, Common Stock (5,000 shares × $39)		195,000
Issued 5,000 shares of $1 par-value common stock for land (5,000 shares × $40 per share = $200,000).		

When noncash considerations are received in payment for stock, the assets or services received should be recorded at the current market value of the stock issued. If the market value of the stock cannot be determined, the market value of the assets or services received should be used as the basis for recording the transaction.

Accounting for Stock Repurchases

treasury stock Issued stock that has subsequently been reacquired by the corporation.

Sometimes, when a company has excess cash or needs some of its shares of stock back from investors, it may purchase some of its own outstanding stock. This repurchased stock is called **treasury stock** by accountants. There are many reasons for a firm to buy its own stock. Five of the most common are that management:

1. may want the stock for a profit-sharing, bonus, or stock-option plan for employees,
2. may feel that the stock is selling for an unusually low price and is a good buy,
3. may want to stimulate trading in the company's stock,
4. may want to remove some shares from the market in order to avoid a hostile takeover, and
5. may want to increase reported earnings per share by reducing the number of shares of stock outstanding.

Many successful U.S. companies have ongoing stock repurchase plans. For example, **Microsoft** disclosed in its 1997 annual report (Appendix A) that it spent $3.1 billion in 1997 to repurchase 37 million of its own shares. **Coca-Cola** spent $4.5 billion in the years 1993–1996 repurchasing its own shares. The most aggressive stock buyback program is **General Electric**'s—GE has announced its intention to spend a total of $13 billion buying back its own shares and, as of the end of 1996, had already spent $11.3 billion.

When a firm purchases stock of another company, the investment is included as an asset on the balance sheet. However, a corporation cannot own part of itself, so treasury stock is not considered an asset. Instead, it is a contra-equity account and is included on the balance sheet as a deduction from stockholders' equity. Think of it this way: When a corporation issues shares, its equity is increased; when the corporation buys those shares back, its equity is reduced. The reporting of treasury stock is illustrated in the stockholders' equity section of the balance sheet for General Electric in Exhibit 6-6.

EXHIBIT 6-6

Share Owners' Equity for General Electric

General Electric Company
December 31, 1996 and 1995
Share Owners' Equity
(in millions of U.S. dollars)

	1996	1995
Common stock	$ 594	$ 594
Unrealized gains on investment securities—net	671	1,000
Other capital	2,498	1,663
Retained earnings	38,670	34,528
Less common stock held in treasury	(11,308)	(8,176)
Total share owners' equity	$31,125	$29,609

Notice that the $11.308 billion spent by General Electric to buy back its own shares as of December 31, 1996, is shown as a subtraction from total share owners' equity. By the way, the "other capital" included in GE's equity section is primarily composed of paid-in capital in excess of par.

(STOP & THINK)

For **General Electric**, the total amount invested by stockholders is $3,092 million, which is the sum of common stock at par ($594 million) and paid-in capital in excess of par (other capital of $2,498 million). And yet GE has spent $11,308 million buying back shares from stockholders. How is this possible?

Treasury stock is usually accounted for on a cost basis; that is, the stock is debited at its cost (market value) on the date of repurchase. To illustrate, we assume that 100 shares of the $1 par-value common stock were reacquired by the Boston Lakers for $60 per share. The entry to record the repurchase is:

Treasury Stock, Common	6,000	
Cash (100 shares × $60)		6,000
Purchased 100 shares of treasury stock at $60 per share.		

CAUTION

Do not credit a gain when treasury stock is reissued at a price greater than its cost. Gains are associated with a company's operations, not with a company buying and selling its own shares.

The effect of this entry is to reduce both total assets (cash) and total stockholders' equity by $6,000.

When treasury stock is reissued, the treasury stock account must be credited for the original amount paid to reacquire the stock. If the treasury stock's reissuance price is greater than its cost, an additional credit must be made to an account called Paid-In Capital, Treasury Stock. Together, these credits show the net increase in total stockholders' equity.

At the same time, the cash account is increased by the total amount received upon reissuance of the treasury stock.

To illustrate, we assume that 40 of the 100 shares of the treasury stock that were originally purchased for $60 per share are reissued at $80 per share. The entry to record that reissuance is:

Cash (40 shares × $80)	3,200	
Treasury Stock, Common (40 shares × $60 cost)		2,400
Paid-In Capital, Treasury Stock [40 × ($80 − $60)]		800
Reissued 40 shares of treasury stock at $80 per share.		

The company now has a balance of $3,600 in the treasury stock account (60 shares at $60 per share).

Sometimes the reissuance price of treasury stock is less than its cost. As before, the entry involves a debit to Cash for the amount received and a credit to Treasury Stock for the cost of the stock. However, since an amount less than the repurchase cost has been received, an additional debit is required. The debit is to Paid-In Capital, Treasury Stock if there is a balance in that account from previous transactions, or to Retained Earnings if there is no balance in the paid-in capital, treasury stock account.

To illustrate, we will consider two more treasury stock transactions. First, we assume that another 30 shares of treasury stock are reissued for $40 per share, $20 less than their cost. Since Paid-In Capital, Treasury Stock has a balance of $800, the entry to record this transaction is:

Cash (30 shares × $40)	1,200	
Paid-In Capital, Treasury Stock	600	
Treasury Stock, Common (30 shares × $60 cost)		1,800
Reissued 30 shares of treasury stock at $40 per share; original cost was $60 per share.		

Note that after this transaction is recorded, the balance in Paid-In Capital, Treasury Stock is $200 ($800 − $600).

Next, we assume that the company reissues 20 additional shares at $45 per share. The entry to record this transaction is:

Cash (20 shares × $45)	900	
Paid-In Capital, Treasury Stock	200	
Retained Earnings	100	
Treasury Stock (20 shares × $60 cost)		1,200
Reissued 20 shares of treasury stock at $45 per share; original cost was $60 per share.		

In this transaction, the selling price was $300 less than the cost of the treasury stock. Since the paid-in capital, treasury stock account had a balance of only $200, Retained Earnings was debited for the remaining $100.

Balance Sheet Presentation

We have discussed the ways in which stock transactions affect owners' equity accounts. We will now show how these accounts are summarized and presented on the balance sheet. The following data, with the addition of the preferred stock information in (1), summarize the stock transactions of the Boston Lakers shown earlier.

1. $40 par value preferred stock: issued 1,000 shares at $45 per share.
2. $1 par value common stock: issued 1,000 shares at $50 per share.
3. $1 par value common stock: issued 5,000 shares for land with a fair market value of $200,000.
4. Treasury stock, common: purchased 100 shares at $60; reissued 40 shares at $80; reissued 30 shares at $40; reissued 20 shares at $45.

With these data, and assuming a Retained Earnings balance of $100,000, the stockholders' equity section would be as shown in Exhibit 6-7.

EXHIBIT 6-7

Stockholders' Equity for Boston Lakers

Boston Lakers Basketball Team
Stockholders' Equity

Preferred stock ($40 par value, 1,000 shares issued and outstanding)	$ 40,000
Common stock ($1 par value, 6,000 shares issued, 5,990 shares outstanding)*	6,000
Paid-in capital in excess of par, preferred stock	5,000
Paid-in capital in excess of par, common stock	244,000
Total contributed capital	$295,000
Retained earnings (to be discussed)	100,000
Total contributed capital and retained earnings	$395,000
Less treasury stock (10 shares of $1 par common at cost of $60 per share)	(600)
Total stockholders' equity	$394,400

**Note:* Treasury shares are described as being issued but not outstanding. Thus, 6,000 common shares have been issued, but only 5,990 are outstanding since 10 are held by the Boston Lakers as treasury shares.

TO SUMMARIZE

When a company issues stock, it debits Cash or a noncash account (property, for example) and credits various stockholders' equity accounts. Shares typically are assigned a par value which is usually small in relation to the market value of the shares. Amounts received upon issuance of shares are divided into par value and paid-in capital in excess of par. A company's own stock that is repurchased is known as treasury stock and is included in the financial statements as a contra-stockholders' equity account. Treasury stock is usually accounted for on a cost basis. The stockholders' equity section of a balance sheet contains separate accounts for each type of stock issued, amounts paid in excess of par values, treasury stock, and retained earnings.

7 *Understand the factors that impact retained earnings, describe the factors determining whether a company can and should pay cash dividends, and account for cash dividends.*

RETAINED EARNINGS

There are two ways for common stockholders to invest money in a corporation. First, as described in the previous section, common stockholders can buy shares of stock. Second, when the corporation makes money, the common stockholders can allow the corporation to keep those earnings to be reinvested in the business.

retained earnings The portion of a corporation's owners' equity that has been earned from profitable operations and not distributed to stockholders.

Retained earnings is the name given to the aggregate amount of corporate earnings that have been reinvested in the business. The retained earnings balance is increased each year by net income and decreased by losses, dividends, and some treasury stock transactions (as illustrated earlier).

Remember, retained earnings is not the same as cash. In fact, a company can have a large retained earnings balance and be without cash, or it can have a lot of cash and a very small retained earnings balance. For example, on December 31, 1996, Dow Jones & Company had a cash balance of $6.8 million but a retained earnings balance of $1.6 *billion*. Although both cash and retained earnings are usually increased when a company has earnings, the amounts by which they are increased are usually different. This occurs for two reasons: (1) The company's net income, which increases retained earnings, is accrual-based, not cash-based; and (2) cash from earnings may be invested in productive assets, such as inventories, used to pay off loans, or spent in any number of ways, many of which do not affect net income or retained earnings. In summary, Cash is an asset; Retained Earnings is one source of financing (along with borrowing and direct stockholder investment) that a corporation can use to get funds to acquire assets.

Cash Dividends

dividends Distributions to the owners (stockholders) of a corporation.

cash dividend A cash distribution of earnings to stockholders.

If you had your own business and wanted to withdraw money for personal use, you would simply withdraw it from the company's checking account or cash register. In a corporation, a formal action by the board of directors is required before money can be distributed to the owners. In addition, such payments must be made on a pro rata basis. That is, each owner must receive a proportionate amount on the basis of ownership percentage. These pro rata distributions to owners are called **dividends**. When these dividends are paid in the form of cash, they are called **cash dividends**. The amount of dividends an individual stockholder receives depends on the number of shares owned and on the per-share amount of the dividend.

Should a Company Pay Cash Dividends?

Note that a company does not have to pay cash dividends. Theoretically, a company that does not pay dividends should be able to reinvest its earnings in assets that will enable it to grow more rapidly than its dividend-paying competitors. This added growth will presumably be reflected in increases in the per-share price of the stock. In practice, most public companies pay regular cash dividends, but some well-known companies do not. For example, Microsoft has never paid cash dividends to its common stockholders.

So, should a corporation pay cash dividends or not? Well, the surprising answer is that no one knows the answer to that question. Ask your finance professor what he or she thinks. While no one knows the theoretically best dividend policy, three general observations can be made:

- Stable companies pay out a large portion of their income as cash dividends.
- Growing companies (such as Microsoft) pay out a small portion of their income as cash dividends. They keep the funds inside the company for expansion.
- Companies are very cautious about raising dividends to a new level, because once investors begin to expect a certain level of dividends, they see it as very bad news if the company reduces the dividends back to the old level.

(STOP & THINK)

If you were a Microsoft shareholder, would you want to receive a high level of cash dividends or would you prefer that Bill Gates use your share of the profits for business expansion?

Although cash dividends are the most common type of dividend, corporations can distribute other types of dividends as well. A stock dividend is a distribution of additional shares of stock to stockholders. A property dividend is a distribution of corporate assets (for example, the stock of another firm) to stockholders. Property dividends are quite rare. In this chapter, only the accounting for cash dividends will be discussed.

Accounting for Cash Dividends

declaration date The date on which a corporation's board of directors formally decides to pay a dividend to stockholders.

Three important dates are associated with dividends: (1) declaration date, (2) date of record, and (3) payment date. The first is when the board of directors formally declares its intent to pay a dividend. On this **declaration date**, the company becomes legally obligated to pay the dividends. Assuming that the board of directors votes on December 15, 2000, to declare an $8,000 dividend, this liability may be recorded as follows:

Dividends	8,000	
Dividends Payable		8,000
Declared dividend on December 15, 2000.		

At the end of the year, the account Dividends is closed to Retained Earnings by the following entry:

Retained Earnings	8,000	
Dividends		8,000
To close Dividends to Retained Earnings.		

From this entry, you can see that a declaration of dividends reduces Retained Earnings and, eventually, the amount of cash on hand. Thus, though not considered to be an expense, dividends do reduce the amount a company could otherwise invest in productive assets.

An alternative way of recording the declaration of dividends involves debiting Retained Earnings directly. However, using the dividends account instead of Retained Earnings allows a company to keep separate records of dividends paid to preferred and common stockholders. Whichever method is used, the end result is the same: a decrease in Retained Earnings.

date of record The date selected by a corporation's board of directors on which the stockholders of record are identified as those who will receive dividends.

dividend payment date The date on which a corporation pays dividends to its stockholders.

The second important dividend date is the **date of record**. Falling somewhere between the declaration date and the payment date, this is the date selected by the board of directors on which the stockholders of record are identified as those who will receive dividends. Since many corporate stocks are in flux—being bought and sold daily—it is important that the stockholders who will receive the dividends be identified. No journal entry is required on the date of record; the date of record is simply noted in the minutes of the directors' meeting and in a letter to stockholders.

As you might expect, the third important date is the **dividend payment date**. This is the date on which, by order of the board of directors, dividends will be paid. The entry to record a dividend payment would typically be:

Dividends Payable	8,000	
Cash		8,000
Paid dividends declared on December 15, 2000.		

As mentioned earlier, once a dividend-paying pattern has been established, the expectation of dividends is built into the per-share price of the stock. A reduction in the dividend pattern usually produces a sharp drop in the price. Similarly, an increased dividend usually triggers a stock price increase. Dividend increases are usually considered to set a precedent, indicating that future dividends will be at this per-share amount or more. With this in mind, boards of directors are careful about increasing or decreasing dividends.

Dividend Preferences

When cash dividends are declared by a corporation that has both common and preferred stock outstanding, allocation of the dividends to the two classes of investors depends on the rights of the preferred stockholders. These rights are identified when the stock is approved by the state. Two "dividend preferences," as they are called, are (1) current-dividend preference and (2) cumulative-dividend preference.

Current-Dividend Preference. Preferred stock has a dividend percentage associated with it and is typically described as follows: "5% preferred, $40 par value stock, 1,000 shares outstanding." The first figure—"5%" in this example—is a percentage of the par value and can be any amount, depending on the particular stock. So, $2.00 per share (0.05 × $40 par) is the amount that will be paid in dividends to preferred stockholders each year that dividends are declared. The fact that preferred stock dividends are fixed at a specific percentage of their par value makes them somewhat similar to the interest paid to bondholders. The **current-dividend preference** requires that when dividends are paid, this percentage of the preferred stock's par value be paid to preferred stockholders before common stockholders receive any dividends.

current-dividend preference The right of preferred stockholders to receive current dividends before common stockholders receive dividends.

To illustrate the payment of different types of dividends, the following data from the Boston Lakers Basketball Team will be used throughout this section. (The various combinations of dividend preferences illustrated over the next few pages are summarized in Cases 1 to 4 in Exhibit 6-8.) As a reminder, the outstanding stock includes:

- Preferred stock: 5%, $40 par value, 1,000 shares issued and outstanding
- Common stock: $1 par value, 6,000 shares issued, 5,990 shares outstanding

To begin, note that, as with all preferred stock, the Lakers' 5% preferred stock has a current-dividend preference: Before any dividends can be paid to common stockholders, preferred stockholders must be paid a total of $2,000 ($40 × 0.05 × 1,000 shares). Thus, if only $1,500 of dividends were declared (Case 1), preferred stockholders would receive the entire dividend payment. If $3,000 were declared (Case 2), preferred stockholders would receive $2,000 and common stockholders, $1,000.

Cumulative-Dividend Preference. The **cumulative-dividend preference** can be quite costly for common stockholders because it requires that preferred stockholders be paid current dividends plus all unpaid dividends from past years before common stockholders receive anything. If dividends have been paid in all previous years, then only the current 5% must be paid to preferred stockholders. But if dividends on preferred stock were not paid in full in prior years, the cumulative deficiency must be paid before common stockholders receive anything.

cumulative-dividend preference The right of preferred stockholders to receive current dividends plus all dividends in arrears before common stockholders receive any dividends.

EXHIBIT 6-8

Dividend Preferences: Summary of Cases 1 to 4

Case	Preferred-Dividend Feature	Years in Arrears	Total Dividend	Preferred Dividend	Common Dividend
1	5%, Noncumulative	Not applicable	$ 1,500	$1,500	$ 0
2	5%, Noncumulative	Not applicable	3,000	2,000	1,000
3	5%, Cumulative	2	5,000	5,000	0
4	5%, Cumulative	2	11,000	6,000	5,000

dividends in arrears
Missed dividends for past years that preferred stockholders have a right to receive under the cumulative-dividend preference if and when dividends are declared.

With respect to the cumulative feature, it is important to repeat that companies are not required to pay dividends. Such past unpaid dividends are called **dividends in arrears**. Since they do not have to be paid unless dividends are declared in the future, dividends in arrears do not represent actual liabilities and thus are not recorded in the accounts. Instead, they are reported in the notes to the financial statements.

To illustrate the distribution of dividends for cumulative preferred stock, we will assume that the Boston Lakers Basketball Team has not paid any dividends for the last two years but has declared a dividend in the current year. The Lakers must pay $6,000 in dividends to preferred stockholders before they can give anything to the common stockholders. The calculation is as follows:

Dividends in arrears, 2 years	$4,000
Current dividend preference	
($40 × 0.05 × 1,000 shares)	2,000
Total	$6,000

Therefore, if the Lakers paid only $5,000 in dividends (Case 3), preferred stockholders would receive all the dividends, common stockholders would receive nothing, and there would still be dividends in arrears of $1,000 the next year. If $11,000 in dividends were paid (Case 4), preferred stockholders would receive $6,000, and common stockholders would receive $5,000.

The entries to record the declaration and payment of dividends in Case 4 are:

Date of Declaration

Dividends, Preferred Stock	6,000	
Dividends, Common Stock	5,000	
Dividends Payable.		11,000
Declared dividends on preferred and common stock.		

Date of Payment

Dividends Payable	11,000	
Cash		11,000
Paid dividends on preferred and common stock.		

Constraints on Payment of Cash Dividends

Earlier in this section, the question was asked whether a company should pay cash dividends. A related question is: Can the company legally pay cash dividends? To illustrate, consider the following exaggerated scenario. Tricky Company obtains a corporate charter, borrows $1,000,000 from Naïve Bank, pays out a $1,000,000 cash dividend to the stockholders, and all the stockholders disappear to the Bahamas. Is this a legal possibility? No, it isn't, because the corporate right to declare cash dividends is regulated by state law in order to protect creditors. The right to declare cash dividends is often linked to a company's retained earnings balance.

In many states, a company is not allowed to pay cash dividends in an amount that would cause the retained earnings balance to be negative. Thus, if the retained earnings balance of the Boston Lakers was $8,500, the $11,000 dividend in Case 4 discussed above could not be paid, even if the Lakers had the available cash to make the payment. The incorporation laws in many states are less restrictive and allow the payment of cash dividends in excess of the retained earnings balance if, for example, current earnings are strong or the market value of the assets is high.

FYI

Delaware has a reputation for having the least restrictive dividend laws. This is one reason many of the major U.S. companies are incorporated in the state of Delaware.

Frequently, lenders do not rely on state incorporation laws to protect them from excess cash dividend payments by corporations to which they lend money. Instead, the loan contract itself includes restrictions on the payment of cash dividends during the period that the loan is outstanding. In this way, lenders are able to prevent cash that should be used to repay loans from being paid to stockholders as dividends.

TO SUMMARIZE

The retained earnings account reflects the total undistributed earnings of a business since incorporation. It is increased by net income and decreased by dividends, net losses, and some treasury stock transactions. The important dates associated with a cash dividend are the date of declaration, the date of record, and the payment date. Preferred stockholders can be granted a current and a cumulative preference for dividends over the rights of common stockholders. In some states, the payment of cash dividends is limited to an amount not to exceed the existing retained earnings balance.

8 *Compute the common ratios that are used to evaluate the capital structure of a company.*

USING FINANCING RATIOS TO EVALUATE CAPITAL STRUCTURE

capital structure The relationship between the quantities of debt and equity a company has used for financing.

debt ratio A measure of leverage, computed by dividing total liabilities by total assets.

debt-equity ratio The number of dollars of borrowed funds for every dollar invested by owners; computed as total liabilities divided by total equity.

Analysts and others who study financial statements often use ratios to determine how well a company is doing. They use ratios such as inventory turnover and accounts receivable turnover to measure efficiency. They use ratios such as return on sales to assess profitability. And, they use debt and equity ratios to assess the capital structure of a firm. **Capital structure** is the name given to the relationship between the quantities of debt and equity a company has used for financing.

As mentioned in Chapter 2, the **debt ratio** is a commonly used measure of a company's capital structure. The debt ratio is interpreted as the percentage of total financing that has been acquired through borrowing and is computed as follows:

$$\text{Debt ratio} = \frac{\text{Total liabilities}}{\text{Total assets}}$$

A similar ratio is called the **debt-equity ratio** and is computed as follows:

$$\text{Debt-equity ratio} = \frac{\text{Total liabilities}}{\text{Total equity}}$$

The debt-equity ratio is interpreted as the number of dollars of borrowed funds a company has received for each dollar of invested funds. As you can see, these two ratios are very similar. In fact, they measure the same thing—the relative quantities of debt and equity in a firm's capital structure. However, be careful when using these ratios. Although they measure the same general relationship, the values are not directly comparable. For example, if a company has total liabilities of $40, total equity of $60, and total assets of $100, the debt ratio is 0.40 ($40/$100), but the debt-equity ratio is 0.67 ($40/$60). Make sure when interpreting either one of these capital structure ratios that you are comparing it to a value computed by using the same formula.

Debt ratio and debt-equity ratio values for **Dow Jones** (1996), **Microsoft** (1997), and **General Electric** (1996) are computed on the following page. All amounts are in millions of dollars.

	Dow Jones	Microsoft	General Electric
Total liabilities	$1,116	$ 3,610	$241,277
Total equity	1,644	10,777	31,125
Total assets	2,760	14,387	272,402
Debt ratio	40.4%	25.1%	88.6%
Debt-equity ratio	0.679	0.335	7.752

First, notice that both the debt ratio and the debt-equity ratio tell the same story—Microsoft has borrowed very little, General Electric has borrowed a lot, and Dow Jones is in between. The high level of borrowing by General Electric stems from GE's large financing subsidiary (**GE Capital Services**). Banks and other financial institutions routinely have capital structures composed of more than 90% debt. This is because the financial assets of banks serve as good collateral for this high level of borrowing. As a general rule of thumb, large U.S. corporations normally have debt ratios somewhere between 40 and 60 percent.

dividend payout ratio A measure of the percentage of earnings paid out in dividends; computed by dividing cash dividends by net income.

Another ratio of interest to stockholders is the **dividend payout ratio**. This ratio is interpreted as the percentage of net income paid out during the year in the form of cash dividends and is computed as follows:

$$\text{Dividend payout ratio} = \frac{\text{Cash dividends}}{\text{Net income}}$$

Dividend payout ratio values for Dow Jones, Microsoft, and General Electric are computed below.

	Dow Jones	Microsoft	General Electric
Cash dividends	$ 93	$ 15	$3,138
Net income	190	3,454	7,280
Dividend payout ratio	48.9%	0.4%	43.1%

Both Dow Jones and GE pay out approximately half of their annual income as dividends, a normal level for large U.S. corporations. The low dividend payout ratio of Microsoft is indicative of a rapidly expanding company. In fact, before the $15 million in preferred stock dividends paid in 1997, Microsoft had never paid any cash dividends in its history.

TO SUMMARIZE

The relationship between the amount of a firm's borrowing and the amount of its equity is called the firm's capital structure. Two ratios used to measure the capital structure are the debt ratio (total liabilities divided by total assets) and the debt-equity ratio (total liabilities divided by total equity). The dividend payout ratio (cash dividends divided by net income) reveals the percentage of net income that is paid out as cash dividends.

TABLE I The Present Value of $1 Due in *n* Periods*

Period	1%	2%	3%	4%	5%	6%	7%	8%	9%	10%	12%	14%	15%	16%	18%	20%
1	.9901	.9804	.9709	.9615	.9524	.9434	.9346	.9259	.9174	.9091	.8929	.8772	.8696	.8621	.8475	.8333
2	.9803	.9612	.9426	.9246	.9070	.8900	.8734	.8573	.8417	.8264	.7972	.7695	.7561	.7432	.7182	.6944
3	.9706	.9423	.9151	.8890	.8638	.8396	.8163	.7938	.7722	.7513	.7118	.6750	.6575	.6407	.6086	.5787
4	.9610	.9238	.8885	.8548	.8227	.7921	.7629	.7350	.7084	.6830	.6355	.5921	.5718	.5523	.5158	.4823
5	.9515	.9057	.8626	.8219	.7835	.7473	.7130	.6806	.6499	.6209	.5674	.5194	.4972	.4761	.4371	.4019
6	.9420	.8880	.8375	.7903	.7462	.7050	.6663	.6302	.5963	.5645	.5066	.4556	.4323	.4104	.3704	.3349
7	.9327	.8706	.8131	.7599	.7107	.6651	.6227	.5835	.5470	.5132	.4523	.3996	.3759	.3538	.3139	.2791
8	.9235	.8535	.7894	.7307	.6768	.6274	.5820	.5403	.5019	.4665	.4039	.3506	.3269	.3050	.2660	.2326
9	.9143	.8368	.7664	.7026	.6446	.5919	.5439	.5002	.4604	.4241	.3606	.3075	.2843	.2630	.2255	.1938
10	.9053	.8203	.7441	.6756	.6139	.5584	.5083	.4632	.4224	.3855	.3220	.2697	.2472	.2267	.1911	.1615
11	.8963	.8043	.7224	.6496	.5847	.5268	.4751	.4289	.3875	.3503	.2875	.2366	.2149	.1954	.1619	.1346
12	.8874	.7885	.7014	.6246	.5568	.4970	.4440	.3971	.3555	.3186	.2567	.2076	.1869	.1685	.1372	.1122
13	.8787	.7730	.6810	.6006	.5303	.4688	.4150	.3677	.3262	.2897	.2292	.1821	.1625	.1452	.1163	.0935
14	.8700	.7579	.6611	.5775	.5051	.4423	.3878	.3405	.2992	.2633	.2046	.1597	.1413	.1252	.0985	.0779
15	.8613	.7430	.6419	.5553	.4810	.4173	.3624	.3152	.2745	.2394	.1827	.1401	.1229	.1079	.0835	.0649
16	.8528	.7284	.6232	.5339	.4581	.3936	.3387	.2919	.2519	.2176	.1631	.1229	.1069	.0930	.0708	.0541
17	.8444	.7142	.6050	.5134	.4363	.3714	.3166	.2703	.2311	.1978	.1456	.1078	.0929	.0802	.0600	.0451
18	.8360	.7002	.5874	.4936	.4155	.3503	.2959	.2502	.2120	.1799	.1300	.0946	.0808	.0691	.0508	.0376
19	.8277	.6864	.5703	.4746	.3957	.3305	.2765	.2317	.1945	.1635	.1161	.0829	.0703	.0596	.0431	.0313
20	.8195	.6730	.5537	.4564	.3769	.3118	.2584	.2145	.1784	.1486	.1037	.0728	.0611	.0514	.0365	.0261
25	.7798	.6095	.4476	.3751	.2953	.2330	.1842	.1460	.1160	.0923	.0588	.0378	.0304	.0245	.0160	.0105
30	.7419	.5521	.4120	.3083	.2314	.1741	.1314	.0994	.0754	.0573	.0334	.0196	.0151	.0116	.0070	.0042
40	.6717	.4529	.3066	.2083	.1420	.0972	.0668	.0460	.0318	.0221	.0107	.0053	.0037	.0026	.0013	.0007
50	.6080	.3715	.2281	.1407	.0872	.0543	.0339	.0213	.0134	.0085	.0035	.0014	.0009	.0006	.0003	.0001
60	.5504	.3048	.1697	.0951	.0535	.0303	.0173	.0099	.0057	.0033	.0011	.0004	.0002	.0001	†	†

*The formula used to derive the values in this table was $PV = F \frac{1}{(1+i)^n}$ where PV = present value, F = future amount to be discounted, i = interest rate, and n = number of periods.

†The value of 0 to four decimal places.

TABLE II

The Present Value of an Annuity of $1 per Number of Payments*

Number of Payments	1%	2%	3%	4%	5%	6%	7%	8%	9%	10%	12%	14%	15%	16%	18%	20%
1	0.9901	0.9804	0.9709	0.9615	0.9524	0.9434	0.9346	0.9259	0.9174	0.9091	0.8929	0.8772	0.8596	0.8621	0.8475	0.8333
2	1.9704	1.9416	1.9135	1.8861	1.8594	1.8334	1.8080	1.7833	1.7591	1.7355	1.6901	1.6467	1.6257	1.6052	1.5656	1.5278
3	2.9410	2.8839	2.8286	2.7751	2.7232	2.6730	2.6243	2.5771	2.5313	2.4869	2.4018	2.3216	2.2832	2.2459	2.1743	2.1065
4	3.9820	3.8077	3.7171	3.6299	3.5460	3.4651	3.3872	3.3121	3.2397	3.1699	3.0373	2.9137	2.8550	2.7982	2.6901	2.5887
5	4.8884	4.7135	4.5797	4.4518	4.3295	4.2124	4.1002	3.9927	3.8897	3.7908	3.6048	3.4331	3.3522	3.2743	3.1272	2.9906
6	5.7985	5.6014	5.4172	5.2421	5.0757	4.9173	4.7665	4.6229	4.4859	4.3553	4.1114	3.8887	3.7845	3.6847	3.4976	3.3255
7	6.7282	6.4720	6.2303	6.0021	5.7864	5.5824	5.3893	5.2064	5.0330	4.8684	4.5638	4.2883	4.1604	4.0386	3.8115	3.6046
8	7.6517	7.3255	7.0197	6.7327	6.4632	6.2098	5.9713	5.7466	5.5348	5.3349	4.9676	4.6389	4.4873	4.3436	4.0776	3.8372
9	8.5660	8.1622	7.7861	7.4353	7.1078	6.8017	6.5152	6.2469	5.9952	5.7590	5.3282	4.9464	4.7716	4.6065	4.3030	4.0310
10	9.4713	8.9826	8.5302	8.1109	7.7217	7.3601	7.0236	6.7101	6.4177	6.1446	5.6502	5.2161	5.0188	4.8332	4.4941	4.1925
11	10.3676	9.7868	9.2526	8.7605	8.3064	7.8869	7.4987	7.1390	6.8052	6.4951	5.9377	5.4527	5.2337	5.0286	4.6560	4.3271
12	11.2551	10.5733	9.9540	9.3851	8.8633	8.3838	7.9427	7.5361	7.1607	6.8137	6.1944	5.6603	5.4206	5.1971	4.7932	4.4392
13	12.1337	11.3484	10.6350	9.9856	9.3936	8.8527	8.3577	7.9038	7.4869	7.1034	6.4235	5.8424	5.5831	5.3423	4.9095	4.5327
14	13.0037	12.1062	11.2961	10.5631	9.8986	9.2950	8.7455	8.2442	7.7862	7.3667	6.6282	6.0021	5.7245	5.4675	5.0081	4.6106
15	13.8651	12.8493	11.9379	11.1184	10.3797	9.7122	9.1079	8.5595	8.0607	7.6061	6.8109	6.1422	5.8474	5.5755	5.0916	4.6755
16	14.7179	13.5777	12.5611	11.6523	10.8378	10.1059	9.4466	8.8514	8.3126	7.8237	6.9740	6.2651	5.9542	5.6685	5.1624	4.7296
17	15.5623	14.2919	13.1661	12.1657	11.2741	10.4773	9.7632	9.1216	8.5436	8.0216	7.1196	6.3729	6.0472	5.7487	5.2223	4.7746
18	16.3983	14.9920	13.7535	12.6593	11.6896	10.8276	10.0591	9.3719	8.7556	8.2014	7.2497	6.4674	6.1280	5.8178	5.2732	4.8122
19	17.2260	15.6785	14.3238	13.1339	12.0853	11.1581	10.3356	9.6036	8.9501	8.3649	7.3658	6.5504	6.1982	5.8775	5.3162	4.8435
20	18.0456	16.3514	14.8775	13.5903	12.4622	11.4699	10.5940	9.8181	9.1285	8.5136	7.4694	6.6231	6.2593	5.9288	5.3527	4.8696
25	22.0232	19.5235	17.4131	15.6221	14.0939	12.7834	11.6536	10.6748	9.8226	9.0770	7.8431	6.8729	6.4641	6.0971	5.4669	4.9476
30	25.8077	22.3965	19.6004	17.2920	15.3725	13.7648	12.4090	11.2578	10.2737	9.4269	8.0552	7.0027	6.5660	6.1772	5.5168	4.9789
40	32.8347	27.3555	23.1148	19.7928	17.1591	15.0463	13.3317	11.9246	10.7574	9.7791	8.2438	7.1050	6.6418	6.2335	5.5482	4.9966
50	39.1961	31.4236	25.7298	21.4822	18.2559	15.7619	13.8007	12.2335	10.9617	9.9148	8.3045	7.1327	6.6605	6.2463	5.5641	4.9995
60	44.9550	34.7609	27.6756	22.6235	18.9293	16.1614	14.0392	12.3766	11.0480	9.9672	8.3240	7.1401	6.6651	6.2482	5.5553	4.9999

*The formula used to derive the values in this table was $PV = F\left(\frac{1 - \frac{1}{(1+i)^n}}{i}\right)$ where PV = present value, F = periodic payment to be discounted, i = interest rate, and n = number of payments.

TABLE III

Amount of $1 Due in *n* Periods

Period	1%	2%	3%	4%	5%	6%	7%	8%	9%	10%	12%	14%	15%	16%	18%	20%
1	1.0100	1.0200	1.0300	1.0400	1.0500	1.0600	1.0700	1.0800	1.0900	1.1000	1.1200	1.1400	1.1500	1.1600	1.1800	1.2000
2	1.0201	1.0404	1.0609	1.0816	1.1025	1.1236	1.1449	1.1664	1.1881	1.2100	1.2544	1.2996	1.3225	1.3456	1.3924	1.4400
3	1.0303	1.0612	1.0927	1.1249	1.1576	1.1910	1.2250	1.2597	1.2950	1.3310	1.4049	1.4815	1.5209	1.5609	1.6430	1.7280
4	1.0406	1.0824	1.1255	1.1699	1.2155	1.2625	1.3108	1.3605	1.4116	1.4641	1.5735	1.6890	1.7490	1.8106	1.9388	2.0736
5	1.0510	1.1041	1.1593	1.2167	1.2763	1.3382	1.4026	1.4693	1.5386	1.6105	1.7623	1.9254	2.0114	2.1003	2.2878	2.4883
6	1.0615	1.1262	1.1941	1.2653	1.3401	1.4185	1.5007	1.5869	1.6771	1.7716	1.9738	2.1950	2.3131	2.4364	2.6996	2.9860
7	1.0721	1.1487	1.2299	1.3159	1.4071	1.5036	1.6058	1.7138	1.8280	1.9487	2.2107	2.5023	2.6600	2.8262	3.1855	3.5832
8	1.0829	1.1717	1.2668	1.3686	1.4775	1.5938	1.7182	1.8509	1.9926	2.1436	2.4760	2.8526	3.0590	3.2784	3.7589	4.2998
9	1.0937	1.1951	1.3048	1.4233	1.5513	1.6895	1.8385	1.9990	2.1719	2.3579	2.7731	3.2519	3.5179	3.8030	4.4355	5.1598
10	1.1046	1.2190	1.3439	1.4802	1.6289	1.7908	1.9672	2.1589	2.3674	2.5937	3.1058	3.7072	4.0456	4.4114	5.2338	6.1917
11	1.1157	1.2434	1.3842	1.5395	1.7103	1.8983	2.1049	2.3316	2.5804	2.8531	3.4785	4.2262	4.6524	5.1173	6.1759	7.4031
12	1.1268	1.2682	1.4258	1.6010	1.7959	2.0122	2.2522	2.5182	2.8127	3.1384	3.8960	4.8179	5.3502	5.9360	7.2876	8.9161
13	1.1381	1.2936	1.4685	1.6651	1.8856	2.1329	2.4098	2.7196	3.0658	3.4523	4.3635	5.4924	6.1528	6.8858	8.5994	10.699
14	1.1495	1.3195	1.5126	1.7317	1.9799	2.2609	2.5785	2.9372	3.3417	3.7975	4.8871	6.2613	7.0757	7.9875	10.147	12.839
15	1.1610	1.3459	1.5580	1.8009	2.0789	2.3966	2.7590	3.1722	3.6425	4.1772	5.4736	7.1379	8.1371	9.2655	11.973	15.407
16	1.1726	1.3728	1.6047	1.8730	2.1829	2.5404	2.9522	3.4259	3.9703	4.5950	6.1304	8.1372	9.3576	10.748	14.129	18.488
17	1.1843	1.4002	1.6528	1.9479	2.2920	2.6928	3.1588	3.7000	4.3276	5.0545	6.8660	9.2765	10.761	12.467	16.672	22.186
18	1.1961	1.4282	1.7024	2.0258	2.4066	2.8543	3.3799	3.9960	4.7171	5.5599	7.6900	10.575	12.375	14.462	19.673	26.623
19	1.2081	1.4568	1.7535	2.1068	2.5270	3.0256	3.6165	4.3157	5.1417	6.1159	8.6128	12.055	14.231	16.776	23.214	31.948
20	1.2202	1.4859	1.8061	2.1911	2.6533	3.2071	3.8697	4.6610	5.6044	6.7275	9.6463	13.743	16.366	19.460	27.393	38.337
30	1.3478	1.8114	2.4273	3.2434	4.3219	5.7435	7.6123	10.062	13.267	17.449	29.959	50.950	66.211	85.849	143.37	237.37
40	1.4889	2.2080	3.2620	4.8010	7.0400	10.285	14.974	21.724	31.409	45.259	93.050	188.88	267.86	378.72	750.37	1469.7
50	1.6446	2.6916	4.3839	7.1067	11.467	18.420	29.457	46.901	74.357	117.39	289.00	700.23	1083.6	1670.7	3927.3	9100.4
60	1.8167	3.2810	5.8916	10.519	18.679	32.987	57.946	101.25	176.03	304.48	897.59	2595.9	4383.9	7370.1	20555.	56347.

TABLE IV Amount of an Annuity of $1 per Number of Payments

Number of Payments	1%	2%	3%	4%	5%	6%	7%	8%	9%	10%	12%	14%	15%	16%	18%	20%
1	1.0000	1.0000	1.0000	1.0000	1.0000	1.0000	1.0000	1.0000	1.0000	1.0000	1.0000	1.0000	1.0000	1.0000	1.0000	1.0000
2	2.0100	2.0200	2.0300	2.0400	2.0500	2.0600	2.0700	2.0800	2.0900	2.1000	2.1200	2.1400	2.1500	2.1600	2.1800	2.2000
3	3.0301	3.0604	3.0909	3.1216	3.1525	3.1836	3.2149	3.2464	3.2781	3.3100	3.3744	3.4396	3.4725	3.5056	3.5724	3.6400
4	4.0604	4.1216	4.1836	4.2465	4.3101	4.3746	4.4399	4.5061	4.5731	4.6410	4.7793	4.9211	4.9934	5.0665	5.2154	5.3680
5	5.1010	5.2040	5.3091	5.4163	5.5256	5.6371	5.7507	5.8666	5.9847	6.1051	6.3528	6.6101	6.7424	6.8771	7.1542	7.4416
6	6.1520	6.3081	6.4684	6.6330	6.8019	6.9753	7.1533	7.3359	7.5233	7.7156	8.1152	8.5355	8.7537	8.9775	9.4420	9.9299
7	7.2135	7.4343	7.6625	7.8983	8.1420	8.3938	8.6540	8.9228	9.2004	9.4872	10.8090	10.7305	11.0668	11.4139	12.1415	12.9159
8	8.2857	8.5830	8.8923	9.2142	9.5491	9.8975	10.2598	10.6366	11.0285	11.4359	12.2997	13.2328	13.7268	14.2401	15.3270	16.4991
9	9.3685	9.7546	10.1591	10.5828	11.0266	11.4913	11.9780	12.4876	13.0210	13.5795	14.7757	16.0853	16.7858	17.5185	19.0859	20.7989
10	10.4622	10.9497	11.4639	12.0061	12.5779	13.1808	13.8164	14.4866	15.1929	15.9374	17.5487	19.3373	20.3037	21.3215	23.5213	25.9587
11	11.5668	12.1687	12.8078	13.4864	14.2068	14.9716	15.7836	16.6455	17.5603	18.5312	20.6546	23.0445	24.3493	25.7329	28.7551	32.1504
12	12.6825	13.4121	14.1920	15.0258	15.9171	16.8699	17.8885	18.9771	20.1407	21.2843	24.1331	27.2707	29.0017	30.8502	34.9311	39.5805
13	13.8093	14.6803	15.6178	16.6268	17.7130	18.8821	20.1406	21.4953	22.9534	24.5227	28.0291	32.0887	34.3519	36.7862	42.2187	48.4966
14	14.9474	15.9739	17.0863	18.2919	19.5986	21.0151	22.5505	24.2149	26.0192	27.9750	32.3926	37.5811	40.5047	43.6720	50.8180	59.1959
15	16.0969	17.2934	18.5989	20.0236	21.5786	23.2760	25.1290	27.1521	29.3609	31.7725	37.2797	43.8424	47.5804	51.6595	60.9653	72.0351
16	17.2579	18.6393	20.1569	21.8248	23.6575	25.6725	27.8881	30.3243	33.0034	35.9497	42.7535	50.9804	55.7178	60.9250	72.9390	87.4421
17	18.4304	20.0121	21.7616	23.6975	25.8404	28.2129	30.8402	33.7502	36.9737	40.5447	48.8837	59.1176	65.0751	71.6730	87.0680	105.9306
18	19.6147	21.4123	23.4144	25.6454	28.1324	30.9057	33.9990	37.4502	41.3013	45.5992	55.7497	68.3941	75.8364	84.1407	103.7403	128.1167
19	20.8190	22.8406	25.1169	27.6712	30.5390	33.7600	37.3790	41.4463	46.0185	51.1591	63.4397	78.9692	88.2118	98.6032	123.4135	154.7400
20	22.0190	24.2974	26.8704	29.7781	33.0660	36.7856	40.9955	45.7620	51.1601	57.2750	72.0524	91.0249	102.4436	115.3797	146.6280	186.6880
30	34.7849	40.5681	47.5754	56.0849	66.4388	79.0582	94.4608	113.2832	136.3075	164.4940	241.3327	356.7868	434.7451	530.3117	790.9480	1181.8816
40	48.8864	60.4020	75.4013	95.0255	120.7998	154.7620	199.6351	259.0565	337.8824	442.5926	767.0914	1342.0251	1779.0903	2360.7572	4163.2130	7343.8578
50	64.4632	84.5794	112.7969	152.6671	209.3480	290.3359	406.5289	573.7702	815.0836	1163.9085	2400.0182	4994.5213	7217.7163	10435.6488	21813.0937	45497.1908
60	81.6697	114.0515	163.0534	237.9907	353.5837	533.1282	813.5204	1253.2133	1944.7921	3034.8164	7471.6411	18535.1333	29219.9916	46057.5085	114189.6665	281732.5718

REVIEW OF LEARNING OBJECTIVES

1 **Use present value concepts to measure long-term liabilities.** Obligations that will not be paid or otherwise satisfied within one year are classified on the balance sheet as long-term liabilities. Some common types of long-term liabilities are notes payable, mortgages payable, lease obligations, and pension obligations. The present value of a long-term liability is the current value, which is computed by discounting the known future amount using the current interest rate. If the present value amounts of assets or liabilities are known and a future amount is desired, then the present value must be compounded to arrive at a future amount that includes both principal and interest.

2 **Account for long-term liabilities, including notes payable, mortgages payable, and lease obligations.** Interest-bearing notes are recorded on the books of the issuer at face value. Interest expense is incurred based on the rate of interest, the carrying value of the note, and the passage of time. Interest Expense is debited for the amount of interest incurred and Cash or Interest Payable is credited.

Mortgage liabilities are paid by a series of regular payments that include interest expense and a reduction of the principal of the mortgage note. The balance sheet liability at any given time is the present value of the remaining mortgage payments.

A firm can acquire new assets by either purchasing or leasing them. Leasing involves periodic payments over the life of the lease. The lease is classified as an operating lease if it is short term and does not meet any of the criteria of a capital lease. If the lease meets one of the specified criteria, it is treated as a purchase and referred to as a capital lease. As such, it is recorded as both an asset and a long-term liability. The asset is depreciated and the liability is reduced as lease payments are made.

3 **Account for bonds, including the original issuance, the payment of interest, and the retirement of bonds.** Accounting for bonds by the borrowing company (the issuer) includes three elements: accounting for their issuance, for interest payments, and for their retirement. If bonds are sold at face value, Cash is debited and Bonds Payable is credited. However, bonds are more often sold at a premium or a discount. The bond liability is recorded at face value in the bonds payable account, whereas the premium or discount is recorded in a separate account and added to (in the case of a premium) or subtracted from (in the case of a discount) Bonds Payable on the balance sheet. When interest is paid, Bond Interest Expense is debited and Cash is credited. An adjustment is made to bond interest expense if the bond is sold at a premium or discount. At the date a bond matures, the borrowing company pays the face value to the investors and the bonds are canceled. If the bonds are retired before maturity, a gain or loss will be recognized when the carrying value of the bonds differs from the amount paid to retire the bonds.

4 **Distinguish between debt and equity financing and describe the advantages and disadvantages of organizing a business as a proprietorship or a partnership.** Borrow-ing money imposes a legal obligation to repay the amount borrowed, plus interest. Receiving investment funds does not obligate the company to repay investors. Investors stand to lose their investments if the company does poorly, but they also stand to share in the wealth if the company does well. Proprietorships are owned by one person; partnerships are owned by two or more persons or entities. Partnerships and proprietorships share three characteristics: (1) ease of formation, (2) limited life, and (3) unlimited liability.

5 **Describe the basic characteristics of a corporation and the nature of common and preferred stock.** A corporation is a business entity that is legally separate from its owners and is chartered by a state. It is independently taxed, and it can incur debts, conduct business, own property, and enter into contracts. Among the benefits of the corporate form of business are that ownership interests are easily transferred and that the liability of the owners is limited to the amount of their investment. Common stockholders are the true owners of a corporation. They have the right to vote in corporate matters and own all corporate assets that are left after the claims of others have been satisfied. Preferred stockholders are entitled to receive their full cash dividend payments before any dividends can be paid to common stockholders. Preferred stockholders are entitled to a fixed amount of the corporate assets, and that amount does not increase when the company is successful.

6 **Account for the issuance and repurchase of common and preferred stock.** Stock that is issued often has a par value associated with each share. This par value is a legal technicality and represents the minimum amount that must be invested. When stock is issued in exchange for a noncash item, the transaction is recorded at the market value of the noncash item. Repurchased stock is called treasury stock. When treasury stock is purchased by a corporation, it is accounted for at cost and deducted from total stockholders' equity as a contra-equity account.

7 **Understand the factors that impact retained earnings, describe the factors determining whether a company can and should pay cash dividends, and account for cash dividends.** Retained earnings is increased by net income and is decreased by a net loss, by dividends, and by some treasury stock transactions. Corporations usually distribute cash dividends to their owners. The three important dates in accounting for cash dividends are the declaration date, the date of record, and the payment date. Dividends are not a liability until they are declared. If a company has common and preferred stock, the allocation of dividends between the two types of stock depends on the dividend preferences of the preferred stock. According to the incorporation laws in some states, the ability of a company to pay cash dividends can be restricted by the balance in retained earnings. In addition, private lending agreements sometimes constrain a company's ability to pay cash dividends.

8 **Compute the common ratios that are used to evaluate the capital structure of a company.** The debt ratio and the debt-equity ratio are used to measure how much debt a company has relative to its equity. This relationship is called a company's capital structure. The debt ratio is computed as total liabilities divided by total assets. The debt-equity ratio is computed as total liabilities divided by total equity. The dividend payout ratio, which is cash dividends divided by net income, reveals what percentage of a company's income it is paying out in dividends.

KEY TERMS AND CONCEPTS

annuity 230
board of directors 247
bond 236
bond discount 239
bond indenture 237
bond maturity date 237
bond premium 239
callable bonds 237
capital structure 258
cash dividend 254
common stock 247
compounding period 229
contributed capital 249
convertible bonds 237
convertible preferred stock 248
corporation 245
coupon bonds 236
cumulative-dividend preference 256
current-dividend preference 256
date of record 255
debentures (unsecured bonds) 236
debt ratio 258
debt-equity ratio 258
declaration date 255
dividend payment date 255
dividend payout ratio 259
dividends 254
dividends in arrears 257
junk bonds 237
limited liability 246
long-term liabilities 227
market rate (effective rate or yield rate) of interest 239
mortgage amortization schedule 233
mortgage payable 232
par value 249
partnership 244
preferred stock 247
present value of $1 227
present value of an annuity 230
principal (face value or maturity value) 237
proprietorship 244
prospectus 247
registered bonds 236
retained earnings 254
secured bonds 236
serial bonds 237
stated rate of interest 239
stockholders 247
term bonds 237
treasury stock 250
zero-interest bonds 237

REVIEW PROBLEMS

Accounting for Long-Term Liabilities

Energy Corporation had the following transactions relating to its long-term liabilities for the year:

a. Issued a $30,000, 3-year, 8% note payable to White Corporation for a truck purchased on January 2. Interest is payable annually on December 31 of each year.
b. Issued $300,000 of 12%, 10-year bonds on July 1. The market rate on the date of issuance was 12%. Interest payments are made on June 30 and December 31 of each year.
c. Purchased a warehouse on December 1 by borrowing $250,000. The terms of the mortgage call for monthly payments of $2,194 for 30 years to be made at the end of each month. The interest rate on the mortgage is 10%.

Required: Make all journal entries required during the year to account for the above liabilities. Energy Corporation reports on a calendar-year basis.

Solution

Date	Account	Debit	Credit
Jan. 2	Truck	30,000	
	Note Payable		30,000
	Purchased a truck by issuing a note.		
July 1	Cash	300,000	
	Bonds Payable		300,000
	Issued 12%, 10-year bonds with a face value of $300,000.		
Dec. 1	Warehouse	250,000	
	Mortgage Payable		250,000
	Purchased a warehouse by issuing a 10%, 30-year mortgage.		
31	Interest Expense	2,400	
	Cash		2,400
	Paid yearly interest on the 3-year, 8% note ($30,000 × 8% = $2,400).		
	Bond Interest Expense	18,000	
	Cash		18,000
	Paid semiannual interest payment on 12%, 10-year bonds ($300,000 × 0.12 × 6/12 = $18,000).		
	Interest Expense	2,083	
	Mortgage Payable	111	
	Cash		2,194
	Paid first monthly payment on 30-year mortgage (Interest: $250,000 × 0.10 × 1/12 = $2,083; Reduction in principal: $2,194 − $2,083 = $111).		

Stockholders' Equity

Clarke Corporation was organized during 1973. At the end of 2000, the equity section of the balance sheet was:

Contributed capital:	
Preferred stock (8%, $30 par, 6,000 shares authorized, 5,000 shares issued and outstanding)	$150,000
Common stock ($5 par, 50,000 shares authorized, 20,000 shares issued, 17,000 shares outstanding)	100,000
Paid-in capital in excess of par, common stock	80,000
Total contributed capital	$330,000
Retained earnings	140,000
Total contributed capital plus retained earnings	$470,000
Less treasury stock (3,000 shares of common stock at cost, $10 per share)	(30,000)
Total stockholders' equity	$440,000

During 2000, the following stockholders' equity transactions occurred in chronological sequence:

a. Issued 800 shares of common stock at $11 per share.
b. Reissued 1,200 shares of treasury stock at $12 per share.
c. Issued 300 shares of preferred stock at $33 per share.
d. Reissued 400 shares of treasury stock at $9 per share.
e. Declared and paid a dividend large enough to meet the current-dividend preference on the preferred stock and to pay the common stockholders $1.50 per share.
f. Net income for 2000 was $70,000, which included $400,000 of revenues and $330,000 of expenses.
g. Closed the dividends accounts for 2000.

Required:

1. Journalize the transactions.
2. Set up T-accounts with beginning balances and post the journal entries to the T-accounts, adding any necessary new accounts. (Assume a beginning balance of $20,000 for the cash account.)
3. Prepare the stockholders' equity section of the balance sheet as of December 31, 2000.

Solution

1. Journalize the Transactions

a.	Cash	8,800	
	Common Stock		4,000
	Paid-in Capital in Excess of Par, Common Stock		4,800
	Issued 800 shares of common stock at $11 per share.		

Cash received is $11 × 800 shares; common stock is par value times the number of shares ($5 × 800); paid-in capital is the excess.

b.	Cash	14,400	
	Treasury Stock		12,000
	Paid-in Capital, Treasury Stock		2,400
	Reissued 1,200 shares of treasury stock at $12 per share.		

Cash is $12 × 1,200 shares; treasury stock is the cost times the number of shares sold ($10 × 1,200 shares); paid-in capital is the excess.

c.	Cash	9,900	
	Preferred Stock		9,000
	Paid-in Capital in Excess of Par, Preferred Stock		900
	Issued 300 shares of preferred stock at $33 per share.		

Cash is $33 × 300 shares; preferred stock is par value times the number of shares issued ($30 × 300); paid-in capital is the excess.

d.	Cash	3,600	
	Paid-in Capital, Treasury Stock	400	
	Treasury Stock		4,000
	Reissued 400 shares of treasury stock at $9 per share.		

Cash is $9 × 400 shares; treasury stock is the cost times the number of shares sold ($10 × 400); paid-in capital is decreased for the difference. If no paid-in capital, treasury stock balance had existed, Retained Earnings would have been debited.

e.	Dividends, Preferred Stock	12,720	
	Dividends, Common Stock	29,100	
	Cash		41,820
	Declared and paid cash dividend.		

Calculations:

Preferred Stock	Number of Shares	Par-Value Amount
Original balance	5,000	$150,000
Entry (c)	300	9,000
Total	5,300	$159,000
		× 0.08
		$ 12,720

Common Stock	Number of Shares
Original balance (excludes treasury stock)	17,000
Entry (a)	800
Entry (b)	1,200
Entry (d)	400
Total	19,400 shares
	× $1.50
	$29,100
Total preferred stock dividend	$12,720
Total common stock dividend	29,100
Total dividend	$41,820

		Debit	Credit
f.	Revenues (individual revenue accounts)	400,000	
	Expenses (individual expense accounts)		330,000
	Retained Earnings		70,000
	To close net income to Retained Earnings.		
g.	Retained Earnings	41,820	
	Dividends, Preferred Stock		12,720
	Dividends, Common Stock		29,100
	To close the dividends accounts for 2000.		

2. Set Up T-Accounts and Post to the Accounts

Cash

Debit		Credit	
Beg. Bal.	20,000	(e)	41,820
(a)	8,800		
(b)	14,400		
(c)	9,900		
(d)	3,600		
Bal.	14,880		

Preferred Stock

Debit		Credit	
		Beg. Bal.	150,000
		(c)	9,000
		Bal.	159,000

Paid-In Capital in Excess of Par, Preferred Stock

Debit		Credit	
		(c)	900
		Bal.	900

Common Stock

Debit		Credit	
		Beg. Bal.	100,000
		(a)	4,000
		Bal.	104,000

Paid-In Capital in Excess of Par, Common Stock

Debit		Credit	
		Beg. Bal.	80,000
		(a)	4,800
		Bal.	84,800

Treasury Stock

Debit		Credit	
Beg. Bal.	30,000	(b)	12,000
		(d)	4,000
Bal.	14,000		

Paid-In Capital, Treasury Stock

Debit		Credit	
(d)	400	(b)	2,400
		Bal.	2,000

Retained Earnings

Debit		Credit	
(g)	41,820	Beg. Bal.	140,000
		(f)	70,000
		Bal.	168,180

Dividends, Preferred Stock

(e)	12,720	(g)	12,720
Bal.	0		

Dividends, Common Stock

(e)	29,100	(g)	29,100
Bal.	0		

Revenues

(f)	400,000	Beg. Bal.	400,000
		Bal.	0

Expenses

Beg. Bal.	330,000	(f)	330,000
Bal.	0		

3. Prepare Stockholders' Equity Section of the Balance Sheet

Clarke Corporation
Partial Balance Sheet
December 31, 2000

Stockholders' Equity

Contributed Capital:	
Preferred stock (8%, $30 par, 6,000 shares authorized, 5,300 shares issued and outstanding)	$159,000
Common stock ($5.00 par, 50,000 shares authorized, 20,800 shares issued, 19,400 outstanding)	104,000
Paid-in capital in excess of par, preferred stock	900
Paid-in capital in excess of par, common stock	84,800
Paid-in capital, treasury stock	2,000
Total contributed capital	$350,700
Retained earnings	168,180
Total contributed capital plus retained earnings	$518,880
Less treasury stock (1,400 shares of common stock at cost, $10 per share)	(14,000)
Total stockholders' equity	$504,880

Transaction	Common Stock Issued	Common Stock Authorized	Treasury Stock
Number of shares originally issued	20,000	50,000	3,000
Entry (a)	800		
Entry (b)			(1,200)
Entry (d)			(400)
Total	20,800	50,000	1,400

DISCUSSION QUESTIONS

1. The higher the interest rate, the lower the present value of a future amount. Why?
2. What is an annuity?
3. When does the stated amount of a liability equal its present value?

4. What is the difference between a note payable and a mortgage payable?
5. When a mortgage payment is made, a portion of it is applied to interest and the balance is applied to reduce the principal. How is the amount applied to reduce the principal computed?
6. If a lease is recorded as a capital lease, what is the relationship of the lease payments and the lease liability?
7. To whom do companies usually sell bonds?
8. What are two important characteristics that determine the issuance price of a bond?
9. Identify four different ways in which bonds can mature or be eliminated as liabilities.
10. If a bond's stated interest rate is below the market interest rate, will the bond sell at a premium or at a discount? Why?
11. If you think the market interest rate is going to drop in the near future, should you invest in bonds?
12. When do you think bonds will sell at or near face value?
13. Explain why bonds retired before maturity may result in a gain or loss to the issuing company.
14. What are the primary differences between debt financing and equity financing?
15. What are the major differences between a partnership and a corporation?
16. In which type of business entity do all owners have limited liability?
17. In what way is there a double taxation of corporate profits?
18. How are common and preferred stock different from each other?
19. What is the purpose of having a par value for stock?
20. Why would a company repurchase its own shares of stock that it previously issued?
21. Is treasury stock an asset? If not, why not?
22. How is treasury stock usually accounted for?
23. In what way does the stockholders' equity section of a balance sheet identify the sources of the assets?
24. What factors impact the retained earnings balance of a corporation?
25. Is it possible for a firm to have a large Retained Earnings balance and no cash? Explain.
26. When is a company legally barred from paying cash dividends?
27. Why should a potential common stockholder carefully examine the dividend preferences of a company's preferred stock?

DISCUSSION CASES

CASE 6-1 PRESENT VALUE CONCEPTS

Hamburg Company recently began business and purchased a large facility to make beach clothing. Hamburg Company managed to make a small profit in its initial year of operations, although it has used all its cash to purchase inventory and equipment. After preparing its tax return for the year, Hamburg's managers realized that they could pay less taxes than they thought. Because IRS accelerated depreciation methods allow for higher depreciation expense than the straight-line method the company is using for financial reporting purposes, Hamburg can claim more depreciation expense than they thought they could and can reduce taxable income by $30,000. However, Hamburg's managers know that the two depreciation methods will eventually even out and that the difference is only temporary and will create a deferred income tax liability, which must be recorded on the books. Hamburg's management is very conservative, though, and would rather pay the additional taxes now than record a liability that must be paid in the future, even if it means borrowing the money from a bank to pay the extra taxes. They have come to you for advice. What would you tell them?

CASE 6-2 DEBT AND EQUITY FINANCING

Berlin Company is in a world of hurt. For the past 15 years, the company has been the exclusive toy supplier to Infants-R-Us toy stores. Unfortunately for Berlin Company, Infants-R-Us just declared bankruptcy and went out of business. Berlin is the supplier for a few local toy stores, but Infants-R-Us was by far its largest customer. Berlin's management believes that it can save the company if it can raise enough money to develop a new product line of the popular toy, "Nano Babies." Developing the new product line will require a considerable investment, however.

Berlin is trying to decide the best way to finance the investment. It has found a bank that will loan it the money at 18 percent, a very high rate but the only one it can get because of its precarious financial position. Berlin can also issue bonds to raise the money, but because of investors' concerns about the future viability of the company, the only kind of bonds investors will buy are high-interest junk bonds at an interest rate of 17 percent. Even then, there is concern that the bonds will be discounted when they are marketed. Which financing alternative would you recommend to the company? If you were an investor, would you buy Berlin Company's bonds?

CASE 6-3

TO PAY OR NOT TO PAY DIVIDENDS

Assume Lenny Company manufactures specialized computer peripheral parts such as speakers, modems, etc. It is a new company that has been in operation for just two years. During those two years, Lenny Company's stock price has increased over 400 percent. Lenny Company does not pay dividends nor does the company plan to do so in the future. However, the company's stock seems to be heavily traded. Why do you think there is so much interest in buying Lenny Company's stock if stockholders do not receive dividends?

EXERCISES

EXERCISE 6-1

Computing the Present Value of a Lump Sum

Find the present value (rounded to the nearest dollar) of:

1. $15,000 due in 5 years at 8 percent compounded annually.
2. $25,000 due in 8½ years at 10 percent compounded semiannually.
3. $9,500 due in 4 years at 12 percent compounded quarterly.
4. $20,000 due in 20 years at 8 percent compounded semiannually.

EXERCISE 6-2

Computing the Future Value of a Lump Sum

Compute the future value (rounded to the nearest dollar) of the following investments.

1. $10,209 invested to earn interest at 8 percent compounded annually for 5 years.
2. $10,908 invested to earn interest at 10 percent compounded semiannually for 8½ years.
3. $5,920 invested to earn interest at 12 percent compounded quarterly for 4 years.
4. $4,166 invested to earn interest at 8 percent compounded semiannually for 20 years.

EXERCISE 6-3

Computing the Present Value of an Annuity

What is the present value (rounded to the nearest dollar) of an annuity of $8,000 per year for 5 years if the interest rate is:

1. 8 percent compounded annually.
2. 10 percent compounded annually.

EXERCISE 6-4

Accounting for Long-Term Note Payable

Silmaril Inc. borrowed $25,000 from First National Bank by issuing a 3-year, 10 percent note dated July 1, 1999. Interest is payable semiannually on December 31 and June 30. The principal amount is to be repaid in full on June 30, 2002. Silmaril Inc. reports on a calendar-year basis. Prepare all journal entries relating to the note during 1999, 2000, 2001, and 2002.

EXERCISE 6-5

Accounting for a Mortgage

On January 1, 2000, Gandalf Inc. borrowed $50,000 to finance the purchase of machinery. The terms of the mortgage require payments to be made at the end of every month with the first payment being due on January 31, 2000. The length of the mortgage is 5 years and the mortgage carries an interest rate of 12 percent.

1. Compute the amount of the monthly payment.
2. Prepare a mortgage amortization schedule for 2000.
3. Prepare the journal entry to be made on January 31, 2000, when the first payment is made.
4. For the remainder of the year, how will the journal entries relating to the mortgage differ from the one made on January 31?

EXERCISE 6-6
Lease Accounting

Temple Corporation signed a lease to use a machine for four years. The annual lease payment is $10,500 payable at the end of each year.

1. Record the lease, assuming that the lease should be accounted for as a capital lease and the applicable interest rate is 10 percent. (Round to the nearest dollar.)
2. For the initial year, record the annual lease payment.

EXERCISE 6-7
Issuance Price of Bonds

Hanover Company issued 5-year bonds on January 1. The face value of the bonds is $56,000. The stated interest rate on the bonds is 10 percent. The market rate of interest at the time of issuance was 8 percent. The bonds pay interest semiannually. Calculate the issuance price of the bonds.

EXERCISE 6-8
Issuance Price of Bonds

Bremen Company issued 5-year bonds on January 1. The face value of the bonds is $56,000. The stated interest rate on the bonds is 8 percent. The market rate of interest at the time of issuance was 10 percent. The bonds pay interest semiannually. Calculate the issuance price of the bonds.

EXERCISE 6-9
Accounting for Bonds Issued at Face Value

Rikker Co. issued $600,000 of 12%, 10-year bonds at face value on October 1, 2000. The bonds pay interest on April 1 and October 1. Rikker uses the calendar year for financial reporting purposes.

1. Provide the journal entry to record the bond issuance on October 1, 2000.
2. Provide the journal entry to record interest expense on December 31, 2000.
3. Provide the journal entries made during 2001 relating to the bond.
4. On February 14, 2001, Rikker elected to retire the bond issue early. The market price on the day of retirement was $605,000. Provide the journal entries to record the bond retirement.
5. Why do you think Rikker elected to retire the bonds early?

EXERCISE 6-10
Issuance of Stock

Brockbank Corporation was organized on July 15, 2000. Record the journal entries for Brockbank to account for the following:

a. The state authorized 30,000 shares of 7 percent preferred stock ($20 par) and 100,000 shares of no-par common stock.
b. Peter Brockbank gave 6,000 shares of common stock to his attorney in return for her help in incorporating the business. Fees for this work are normally about $18,000. (Note: The debit is to Organization Costs, an intangible asset.)
c. Brockbank Corporation gave 15,000 shares of common stock to a friend who contributed a building worth $50,000.
d. Brockbank Corporation issued 5,000 shares of preferred stock at $25 per share.
e. Peter Brockbank paid $70,000 cash for 30,000 shares of common stock.
f. Another friend donated a $15,000 machine and received 4,000 shares of common stock.
g. The attorney sold all her shares to her brother-in-law for $18,000.

EXERCISE 6-11
No Par Stock Transactions

Parker Maintenance Corporation was organized in early 2000 with 40,000 shares of no-par common stock authorized. During 2000, the following transactions occurred:

a. Issued 17,000 shares of stock at $36 per share.
b. Issued another 2,400 shares of stock at $38 per share.
c. Issued 2,000 shares for a building appraised at $40,000.
d. Declared dividends of $1 per share.
e. Earned net income of $99,000 for the year, including $200,000 of revenues and $101,000 of expenses.
f. Closed the dividends accounts.

Given this information:

1. Journalize the transactions.
2. Present the stockholders' equity section of the balance sheet as it would appear on December 31, 2000.

EXERCISE 6-12
Treasury Stock Transactions

Provide the necessary journal entries to record the following:

a. Fayette Corporation was granted a charter authorizing the issuance of 100,000 shares of $16 par-value common stock.
b. The company issued 40,000 shares of common stock at $20 per share.
c. The company reacquired 2,000 shares of its own stock at $22 per share, to be held in treasury.
d. Another 2,000 shares of stock were reacquired at $24 per share.
e. Of the shares reacquired in (c), 800 were reissued for $26 per share.
f. Of the shares reacquired in (d), 1,400 were reissued for $18 per share.
g. Given the preceding transactions, what is the balance in the treasury stock account?

EXERCISE 6-13
Stock Issuance and Cash Dividends

Stillwater Corporation was organized in January 2000. The state authorized 100,000 shares of no-par common stock and 50,000 shares of 10 percent, $20 par, preferred stock. Record the following transactions that occurred in 2000.

a. Issued 10,000 shares of common stock at $30 per share.
b. Issued 2,000 shares of preferred stock for a building appraised at $60,000.
c. Declared a cash dividend sufficient to meet the current-dividend preference on preferred stock and pay common shareholders $2 per share.

EXERCISE 6-14
Stock Issuance, Treasury Stock, and Dividends

On January 1, 2000, Snow Company was authorized to issue 100,000 shares of common stock, par value $10 per share and 10,000 shares of 8 percent preferred stock, par value $20 per share. Record the following transactions for 2000:

a. Issued 70,000 shares of common stock at $25 per share.
b. Issued 8,000 shares of preferred stock at $30 per share.
c. Reacquired 5,000 shares of common stock at $20 per share.
d. Reissued 2,000 shares of treasury stock for $46,000.
e. Declared a cash dividend sufficient to meet the current-dividend preference on preferred stock and pay common shareholders $1 per share.

EXERCISE 6-15
Stock Transactions and Dividends

Marion Corporation was organized in January 2000. The state authorized 200,000 shares of no-par common stock and 100,000 shares of 10 percent, $10 par, preferred stock. Record the following transactions that occurred in 2000.

a. Issued 20,000 shares of common stock at $20 per share.
b. Issued 8,000 shares of preferred stock for a piece of land appraised at $90,000.
c. Declared a cash dividend sufficient to meet the current-dividend preference on preferred stock and paid common shareholders $1 per share.
d. How would your answer to (c) change if the dividend declared were not sufficient to meet the current-dividend preference on preferred stock?

EXERCISE 6-16
Dividend Calculations

On January 1, 2000, Oldroyd Corporation had 130,000 shares of common stock issued and outstanding. During 2000, the following transactions occurred (in chronological order).

a. 10,000 new shares of common stock were issued.
b. 2,000 shares of stock were reacquired for use in the company's employee stock option plan.
c. At the end of the option period, 1,200 shares had been purchased by corporate officials.

Given this information, compute the following:

1. After the foregoing three transactions have occurred, what amount of dividends must Oldroyd Corporation declare in order to pay 50 cents per share? to pay $1 per share?
2. What is the dividend per share if $236,640 is paid?
3. If all 2,000 treasury shares had been purchased by corporate officials through the stock option plan, what would the dividends per share have been, again assuming $236,640 in dividends were paid? (Round to the nearest cent.)

EXERCISE 6-17
Dividend Calculations

Stewart Corporation has the following stock outstanding:

Preferred stock (5%, $20 par value, 20,000 shares)	$400,000
Common stock ($5 par value, 80,000 shares)	400,000

For the two independent cases that follow, compute the amount of dividends that would be paid to preferred and common shareholders. Assume that total dividends paid are $86,000. No dividends have been paid for the past two years.

Case A, Preferred is noncumulative.
Case B, Preferred is cumulative.

EXERCISE 6-18
Stock Issuance, Treasury Stock, and Dividends

During 2000, Doxey Corporation had the following transactions and related events:

Jan. 15	Issued 6,500 shares of common stock at par ($16 per share), bringing the total number of shares outstanding to 121,300.
Feb. 6	Declared a 50-cent-per-share dividend on common stock for stockholders of record on March 6.
Mar. 6	Date of record.
8	Pedro Garcia, a prominent banker, purchased 20,000 shares of Doxey Corporation common stock from the company for $346,000.
Apr. 6	Paid dividends declared on February 6.
June 19	Reacquired 800 shares of common stock as treasury stock at a total cost of $9,350.
Sep. 6	Declared dividends of 55 cents per share to be paid to common stockholders of record on October 15, 2000.
Oct. 6	The Dow-Jones industrial average plummeted 300 points, and Doxey's stock price fell $3 per share.
15	Date of record.
Nov. 6	Paid dividends declared on September 6.
Dec. 15	Declared and paid a 6 percent cash dividend on 18,000 outstanding shares of preferred stock (par value $32).

Given this information:

1. Prepare the journal entries for these transactions.
2. What is the total amount of dividends paid to common and preferred stockholders during 2000?

EXERCISE 6-19
Analysis of Stockholders' Equity

The stockholders' equity section of Kay Corporation at the end of the current year showed:

Preferred stock (6%, $40 par, 10,000 shares authorized, 6,000 shares issued and outstanding)	$?
Common stock ($6 par, 80,000 shares authorized, 53,000 issued, 52,650 shares outstanding)	318,000
Paid-in capital in excess of par, preferred stock	?
Paid-in capital in excess of par, common stock	129,000
Retained earnings	86,000
Less treasury stock (350 shares at cost)	(2,000)
Total stockholders' equity	$?

1. What is the dollar amount to be reported for preferred stock?
2. What is the average price for which common stock was issued? (Round to the nearest cent.)
3. If preferred stock was issued at an average price of $43 per share, what amount should appear in the Paid-In Capital in Excess of Par, Preferred Stock account?
4. What is the average cost per share of treasury stock? (Round to the nearest cent.)
5. Assuming that the preferred stock was issued for an average price of $43 per share, what is total stockholders' equity?
6. If net income for the year were $67,000 and if only dividends on preferred stock were paid, by how much would retained earnings increase?

EXERCISE 6-20
Preparing the Stockholders' Equity Section

The following account balances, before any closing entries, appear on the books of Spring Company as of December 31, 2000:

Retained Earnings (balance at Jan. 1, 2000)	$240,000
Dividends, Preferred Stock	15,000
Dividends, Common Stock	35,000
Common Stock ($5 par, 100,000 shares authorized, 70,000 issued and outstanding)	350,000
Paid-In Capital in Excess of Par, Common Stock	350,000
Preferred Stock (6%, $50 par, 50,000 shares authorized, 5,000 issued and outstanding)	250,000
Paid-In Capital in Excess of Par, Preferred Stock	25,000

Based on these account balances, and assuming net income for 2000 of $80,000, prepare the stockholders' equity section of the December 31, 2000, balance sheet for Spring Company.

EXERCISE 6-21
Ratios

Carver Company had the following financial statement balances (in millions of dollars) at the end of December 31, 2000.

	2000
Long-term debt	$12.58
Total liabilities	62.10
Total stockholders' equity	36.89
Total assets	98.99

Based on these data, compute the following ratios:

1. Debt ratio
2. Debt-equity ratio.

PROBLEMS

PROBLEM 6-1
Present and Future Value Computations

Required:

1. Determine the present value in each of the following situations.
   a. A $5,000 loan to be repaid in full at the end of three years. Interest on the loan is payable quarterly. The interest rate is 12 percent compounded quarterly.
   b. A 2-year note for $8,000 bearing interest at an annual rate of 10 percent, compounded semiannually. Interest is payable semiannually.
   c. A 5-year mortgage to be paid in monthly installments of $1,000. The interest rate is 12 percent compounded monthly.
2. Determine the future value in each of the following situations:
   a. An investment of $10,000 today to earn interest at 6% compounded semiannually to provide for a down payment on a house five years from now.
   b. An investment of $25,000 today to earn interest at 8% compounded quarterly that is designated for a charitable contribution 10 years from now when the donor retires.

PROBLEM 6-2
Present and Future Value Computations

Required:

1. Compute the present value for each of the following situations, assuming a rate of interest of 10 percent compounded annually. (Round amounts to the nearest dollar.)
   a. A lump-sum payment of $30,000 due on a mortgage five years from now.

b. A series of payments of $5,000 each, due at the end of each year for five years.
c. A 5-year, 10% loan of $25,000, with interest payable annually, and the principal due in five years.

2. Compute the future value amounts (rounded to the nearest dollar) in each of the following situations:
   a. A $20,000 lump-sum investment today that will earn interest at 10% compounded annually over five years.
   b. A $5,000 lump-sum investment today that will earn interest at 8%, compounded quarterly to provide money for a child's college education 15 years from now.

PROBLEM 6-3
Accounting for Notes Payable

During 1999, Kenan Corporation had the following transactions relating to long-term liabilities:

Apr. 1 Purchased a machine costing $200,000 from Perry Corporation. Issued a 2-year, interest-bearing note with interest payable on April 1 of each year. The note matures on April 1, 2001, and carries an interest rate of 9 percent.

July 1 Borrowed $30,000 from Northern National Bank. The terms of the note require semiannual payments of interest on December 31 and June 30. The note matures in two years and carries an interest rate of 8 percent.

Required:

1. Prepare the journal entries made on April 1 and July 1 to record the issuance of these two notes.
2. Prepare the adjusting entries made on December 31, 1999.
3. Prepare all journal entries made during 2000.

PROBLEM 6-4
Accounting for a Mortgage

On November 1, 2000, Hill Company arranges with an insurance company to borrow $200,000 on a 20-year mortgage to purchase land and a building to be used in its operations. The land and the building are pledged as collateral for the loan, which has an annual interest rate of 12 percent, compounded monthly. The monthly payments of $2,200 are made at the end of each month, beginning on November 30, 2000.

Required:

1. Prepare the journal entry to record the purchase of the land and building, assuming that $40,000 of the purchase price is assignable to the land.
2. Prepare the journal entries on November 30 and December 31 for the monthly payments on the mortgage.
3. **Interpretive Question:** Explain generally how the remaining liability at December 31, 2000, will be reported on the company's balance sheet dated December 31, 2000.

PROBLEM 6-5
Lease Accounting

On January 1, 1999, Linda Lou Foods, Inc., leased a tractor. The lease agreement qualifies as a capital lease and calls for payments of $7,000 per year (payable each year on January 1, starting in 2000) for eight years. The annual interest rate on the lease is 8 percent. Linda Lou Foods uses a calendar-year reporting period.

Required:

1. Prepare the journal entries for the following dates:
   a. January 1, 1999, to record the leasing of the tractor.
   b. December 31, 1999, to recognize the interest expense for the year 1999.
   c. January 1, 2000, to record the first lease payment.
2. Prepare the appropriate journal entries at December 31, 2000, and January 1, 2001.
3. **Interpretive Question:** Explain briefly how the leased asset is accounted for annually.

PROBLEM 6-6
Insurance Price of Bonds

Patterson Company issued 30-year bonds on June 30. The face value of the bonds is $750,000. The stated interest rate on the bonds is 6 percent. The market rate of interest at the time of issuance was 4 percent. Patterson also issued another set of bonds on August 31. These bonds were 20-year bonds and had a face value of $556,000. The stated rate of interest on these bonds was 5 percent. The market rate of interest at the time these bonds were issued was 8 percent. Both sets of bonds pay interest semiannually.

Required:

Calculate the issuance price of these bonds.

PROBLEM 6-7
Accounting for Bonds

On July 1, 2000, Paramount Inc. issued $500,000, 8 percent, 30-year bonds with interest paid semiannually on January 1 and July 1. The bonds were sold when the market rate of interest was 8 percent. On October 1, 2003, the bonds were retired when their fair market value was $495,000.

Required:

1. Demonstrate, using the present value tables, that the bonds were sold for $500,000.
2. Provide the journal entry made on July 1 to record the issuance of the bonds.
3. Provide the journal entry made on December 31, 2000, relating to interest.
4. Provide the journal entries to record the retirement of the bonds.

PROBLEM 6-8
Reporting Liabilities on the Balance Sheet

The following amounts are shown on the Plymouth Company's adjusted trial balance for the year 2000:

Accounts Payable	$ 36,000
Property Taxes Payable	6,300
Short-Term Notes Payable	44,000
Mortgage Payable (Due within one year)	28,000
Mortgage Payable (Due after one year)	300,000
Accrued Interest on Mortgage Payable	3,000
Lease Liability (Current Portion)	58,000
Lease Liability (Long Term)	414,000
Rent Payable	70,000
Income Taxes Payable	50,000
Federal & State Unemployment Taxes Payable	16,000

Required:

Prepare the liabilities section of Plymouth Company's balance sheet at December 31, 2000.

PROBLEM 6-9
Stock Transactions and Analysis

The following selected items and amounts were taken from the balance sheet of Quale Company as of December 31, 2000:

Cash	$ 93,000
Property, plant, and equipment	850,000
Accumulated depreciation	150,000
Liabilities	50,000
Preferred stock (7%, $100 par, noncumulative, 10,000 shares authorized, 5,000 shares issued and outstanding)	500,000
Common stock ($10 par, 100,000 shares authorized, 80,000 shares issued and outstanding)	800,000
Paid-in capital in excess of par, preferred stock	1,000
Paid-in capital in excess of par, common stock	125,000
Paid-in capital, treasury stock	1,000
Retained earnings	310,000

Required:

For each of parts (1) to (5), (a) prepare the necessary journal entry (or entries) to record each transaction, and (b) calculate the amount that would appear on the December 31, 2000, balance sheet as a consequence of this transaction only for the account given. (*Note:* In your answer to each part of this problem, consider this to be the only transaction that took place during 2000.)

1. Two hundred shares of common stock are issued in exchange for cash of $4,000.
   a. Entry
   b. Paid-in capital in excess of par, common stock
2. Two hundred shares of preferred stock are issued at a price of $102 per share.
   a. Entry
   b. Paid-in capital in excess of par, preferred stock
3. Five hundred shares of common stock are issued in exchange for a building. The common stock is not actively traded, but the building was recently appraised at $11,000.
   a. Entry
   b. Property, plant, and equipment

4. One thousand shares of common stock were reacquired from a stockholder for $23,000 and subsequently reissued for $21,500 to a different investor. (*Note:* Make two entries.)
   a. Entries
   b. Paid-in capital, treasury stock
5. The board of directors declared dividends of $75,000. This amount includes the current-year dividend preference on preferred stock, with the remainder to be paid to common stockholders.
   a. Entry
   b. Retained earnings

PROBLEM 6-10
Stock Transactions and the Stockholders' Equity Section

The following is West Valley Company's stockholders' equity section of the balance sheet on December 31, 1999.

Preferred stock (8%, $60 par, noncumulative, 16,000 shares authorized, 8,000 shares issued and outstanding)	$480,000
Common stock ($10 par, 120,000 shares authorized, 80,000 shares issued and outstanding)	800,000
Paid-in capital in excess of par, preferred stock	130,000
Paid-in capital in excess of par, common stock	252,000
Retained earnings	330,000

1. Journalize the following 2000 transactions:
   a. Issued 2,000 preferred shares at $70 per share.
   b. Reacquired 1,000 common shares for the treasury at $13 per share.
   c. Declared and paid a $2-per-share dividend on common stock in addition to paying the required preferred dividends. (*Note:* Debit Retained Earnings directly.)
   d. Reissued 600 treasury shares at $14 per share.
   e. Reissued the remaining treasury shares at $12 per share.
   f. Earnings for the year were $92,000, including $200,000 of revenues and $108,000 of expenses.
2. Prepare the stockholders' equity section of the balance sheet for the company at December 31, 2000.

PROBLEM 6-11
Recording Stockholders' Equity Transactions

Zina Corporation was organized during 1999. At the end of 1999, the stockholders' equity section of the balance sheet appeared as follows:

Contributed capital:	
Preferred stock (8%, $40 par, 10,000 shares authorized, 5,000 shares issued and outstanding)	$200,000
Common stock ($20 par, 30,000 shares authorized, 12,000 issued, 10,000 outstanding)	240,000
Paid-in capital in excess of par, preferred stock	50,000
Total contributed capital	$490,000
Retained earnings	110,000
Total contributed capital plus retained earnings	$600,000
Less treasury stock (2,000 shares at cost of $25 per share)	(50,000)
Total stockholders' equity	$550,000

During 1999, the following transactions occurred in the order given:

a. Issued 1,000 shares of common stock at $24 per share.
b. Reissued 1,000 shares of treasury stock at $27 per share.
c. Reissued 500 shares of treasury stock at $20 per share.

Required: Record the transactions.

PROBLEM 6-12

Stock Transactions and Stockholders' Equity Section

The balance sheet for Lakeland Corporation as of December 31, 1999, is as follows:

Assets		$750,000
Liabilities		$410,000
Stockholders' equity:		
Preferred stock, convertible (5%, $20 par)	$ 50,000	
Common stock ($10 par)	150,000	
Paid-in capital in excess of par, common stock	30,000	
Retained earnings	116,000	
	$346,000	
Less treasury stock, common (500 shares at cost)	(6,000)	340,000
Total liabilities and stockholders' equity		$750,000

During 2000, the following transactions were completed in the order given:

a. 750 shares of outstanding common stock were reacquired by the company at $7 per share.
b. 150 shares of common stock were reacquired in settlement of an account receivable of $1,500.
c. Semiannual cash dividends of 75 cents per share on common stock and 50 cents per share on preferred stock were declared and paid.
d. Each share of preferred stock is convertible into three shares of common stock. Five hundred shares of preferred stock were converted into common stock. (*Hint:* Shares are converted at par values, and any excess reduces Retained Earnings.)
e. The 900 shares of common treasury stock acquired during 2000 were sold at $13. The remaining treasury shares were exchanged for a machine with a fair market value of $6,300.
f. 3,000 shares of common stock were issued in exchange for land appraised at $39,000.
g. Semiannual cash dividends of 75 cents per share on common stock and 50 cents per share on preferred stock were declared and paid.
h. Closed net income of $35,000 to Retained Earnings, which included $135,000 of revenues and $100,000 of expenses.
i. Closed dividends accounts to Retained Earnings.

Required:

1. Give the necessary journal entries to record the transactions listed.
2. Prepare the stockholders' equity section of the balance sheet as of December 31, 2000.

PROBLEM 6-13

Dividend Calculations

Salty Corporation was organized in January 1997 and issued shares of preferred and common stock as shown. As of December 31, 2000, there have been no changes in outstanding stock.

Preferred stock (8%, $10 par, 20,000 shares issued and outstanding)	$200,000
Common stock ($40 par, 10,000 shares issued and outstanding)	400,000

Required:

For each of the following independent situations, compute the amount of dividends that would be paid for each class of stock in 1999 and 2000. Assume that total dividends of $10,000 and $80,000 are paid in 1999 and 2000, respectively.

1. Preferred stock is noncumulative.
2. Preferred stock is cumulative, and no dividends are in arrears in 1999.
3. Preferred stock is cumulative, and no dividends have been paid during 1997 and 1998.

PROBLEM 6-14
Stockholders' Equity Calculations

A computer virus destroyed important financial information pertaining to Denton Company's stockholders' equity section. Your expertise is needed to compute the missing account balances. The only information you can recover from the computer's back-up system is as follows:

a. During 2000, 8,000 shares of common stock with a par value of $10 were issued when the market price per share was $22.
b. Cash dividends of $30,000 were paid to preferred shareholders.
c. Denton Company acquired 4,000 shares of common stock at $15 to hold as treasury stock.
d. Denton Company reissued 3,000 shares of treasury stock for $18.

	December 31, 1999	December 31, 2000
Preferred stock.	$ 2,000	$ 2,000
Common stock.	6,000	?
Paid-in capital in excess of par, preferred stock	750	750
Paid-in capital in excess of par, common stock	1,750	?
Paid-in capital, treasury stock.	0	?
Retained earnings	4,500	5,250
Treasury stock	0	(15,000)
Total stockholders' equity	15,000	?

1. Calculate the account balances for the following accounts:
   a. Common stock
   b. Paid-in capital in excess of par, common stock
   c. Paid-in capital, treasury stock
   d. Stockholders' equity
2. How much net income did Denton Company report for 2000?

PROBLEM 6-15
Unifying Concepts: Stock Transactions and the Stockholders' Equity Section

Richard Corporation was founded on January 1, 2000, and entered into the following stock transactions during 2000.

a. Received authorization for 100,000 shares of $20 par-value common stock, 50,000 shares of 6 percent preferred stock with a par value of $5, and 50,000 shares of no-par common stock.
b. Issued 25,000 shares of the $20 par-value common stock at $24 per share.
c. Issued 10,000 shares of the preferred stock at $8 per share.
d. Issued 5,000 shares of the no-par common stock at $22 per share.
e. Reacquired 1,000 shares of the $20 par-value common stock at $25 per share.
f. Reacquired 500 shares of the no-par common stock at $20 per share.
g. Reissued 250 of the 1,000 reacquired shares of $20 par-value common stock at $23 per share.
h. Reissued all the 500 reacquired shares of no-par common stock at $23 per share.
i. Closed the $14,000 net income to Retained Earnings. Revenues and expenses for the year were $90,000 and $76,000 respectively.

Required:

1. Prepare journal entries to record the 2000 transactions in Richard Corporation's books.
2. Prepare the stockholders' equity section of Richard Corporation's balance sheet at December 31, 2000. Assume that the transactions represent all the events involving equity accounts during 2000.

PROBLEM 6-16
Unifying Concepts: Stockholders' Equity

Icon Corporation was organized during 1998. At the end of 1999, the equity section of its balance sheet appeared as follows:

Contributed capital:		
Preferred stock (6%, $20 par, 10,000 shares authorized, 5,000 shares issued and outstanding)	$100,000	
Common stock ($10 par, 50,000 shares authorized, 11,000 shares issued, 10,000 outstanding).	110,000	
Paid-in capital in excess of par, preferred stock	20,000	
Total contributed capital		$230,000
Retained earnings		100,000
Total contributed capital plus retained earnings		$330,000
Less treasury stock (1,000 shares of common at cost)		(12,000)
Total stockholders' equity		$318,000

During 2000, the following stockholders' equity transactions occurred (in chronological sequence):

a. Issued 500 shares of common stock at $13 per share.
b. Reissued 500 shares of treasury stock at $13 per share.
c. Issued 1,000 shares of preferred stock at $25 per share.
d. Reissued 500 shares of treasury stock at $10 per share.
e. Declared a dividend large enough to meet the current-dividend preference of the preferred stock and to pay the common stockholders $2 per share. Dividends are recorded directly in the retained earnings account.
f. Closed net income of $65,000 to Retained Earnings. Revenues were $400,000; expenses were $335,000.

Required:

1. Journalize the transactions.
2. Prepare the stockholders' equity section of the balance sheet at December 31, 2000.

PROBLEM 6-17
Ratios

Jenson Company and Marshall Company operate in the same industry. At the end of 2000, selected information from their financial statements (in millions of dollars) was as follows:

	Jenson Company	Marshall Company
Long-term debt	$22.1	$34.1
Total liabilities.	35.4	57.2
Total stockholders' equity	22.4	33.3

Required:

Based on the above information for Jenson Company and Marshall Company, make the following computations and answer the interpretive question:

1. Compute the debt ratios for the two companies.
2. Compute the debt-equity ratios for the two companies.
3. **Interpretive Question:** Which company do you think is the stronger (i.e., which would you rather invest in)?

Analyzing Real Company Information

International Case

Ethics Case

Writing Assignment

The Debate

Internet Search

Accounting is more than just doing textbook problems. These Competency Enhancement Opportunities provide practice in critical thinking, oral and written communication, research, teamwork, and consideration of ethical issues.

ANALYZING REAL COMPANY INFORMATION

• Analyzing 6–1 (Microsoft)

The 1997 annual report for **Microsoft** is included in Appendix A. Locate that annual report and consider the following questions:

1. Examine Microsoft's balance sheet as of June 30, 1997. Do you notice anything unusual in connection with Microsoft's reported long-term debt?
2. During fiscal 1997, Microsoft issued $980 million in convertible preferred stock. The terms of this preferred stock are that the investors agreed to give Microsoft $980 million, and Microsoft agreed to pay them a fixed amount of $27 million per year in dividends. Starting in 1999, these preferred stockholders can exchange their shares for Microsoft common stock, which will entitle them to all the rights of Microsoft owners. In what ways is this $980 million investment in Microsoft similar to a loan? In what ways is it different from a loan?

• Analyzing 6–2 (Microsoft)

The 1997 annual report for **Microsoft** is included in Appendix A. Microsoft's statement of stockholders' equity provides details of equity transactions of the company during the 1997 fiscal year. Locate that statement and consider the following questions:

1. What was the major reason that stockholders' equity increased for the year?
2. How much did common stockholders receive in dividends during the year? How much did preferred shareholders receive?
3. Did Microsoft issue more shares than it repurchased during the year or vice versa? How can you tell? (*Hint:* You should look in the notes to the statements to answer this question.)

• Analyzing 6–3 (Citicorp)

The **City Bank of New York** was chartered on June 16, 1812, just two days before the start of the War of 1812 between the United States and Great Britain. In order to get around twentieth-century bank holding laws, a holding company was organized to own the bank. This holding company took the name of **Citicorp** in 1974, and the bank itself is now called **Citibank**. Citibank is one of the largest banks in the United States.

Following are a simplified balance sheet for Citicorp as of December 31, 1996, and a schedule outlining the interest rate on Citicorp's outstanding long-term debt.

Citicorp
Balance Sheet
December 31, 1996

	(Millions of Dollars)
Cash	$ 6,905
Investment securities	81,752
Loans receivable	169,109
Other assets	23,252
Total	$281,018
Deposit liabilities	$184,955
Other liabilities	56,491
Long-term debt	18,850
Stockholders' equity	20,722
Total	$281,018

Interest Rates Prevailing on Parent and Subsidiary Loans for Loans Outstanding on December 31, 1996

Type of Loan	Interest Rate Range	Average Interest Rate
PARENT COMPANY		
Fixed interest rate loans	2.42% to 10.50%	7.32%
Floating interest rate loans	3.50% to 8.23%	5.99%
SUBSIDIARIES		
Fixed interest rate loans	3.50% to 18.69%	9.07%
Floating interest rate loans	3.00% to 32.84%	11.51%

1. Citicorp's simplified balance sheet is representative of most banks' balance sheets. Using the information about relative sizes of assets and liabilities given in that balance sheet, write a brief description of the primary operating activity of a bank.
2. Compute Citicorp's debt ratio (total liabilities divided by total assets). Comment on whether the value seems high or low to you.
3. In its long-term debt of $18.850 billion, Citicorp has both fixed rate loans and floating rate (or variable rate) loans. What is the advantage of borrowing with a fixed-rate loan? What is the advantage of borrowing with a variable-rate loan?
4. Citicorp includes the following information in its 1996 financial statement note on long-term debt: "Approximately 5% . . . of subsidiary long-term debt was guaranteed by Citicorp, and of the debt not guar-

anteed by Citicorp, approximately 35% . . . was secured by the assets of the subsidiary." When Citicorp guarantees the long-term debt of one of its subsidiaries, does that raise or lower the interest rate that the subsidiary must pay on the debt? Explain. Is the interest rate on a loan higher when it is secured by assets or when it is unsecured? Explain.

INTERNATIONAL CASE

• British Petroleum

In May 1901, William Knox D'Arcy convinced the Shah of Persia (present-day Iran) to allow him to hunt for oil. The oil discovered in Persia in 1908 was the first commercially significant amount of oil found in the Middle East. The company making the discovery called itself the **Anglo-Persian Oil Company**, later named **British Petroleum**, or BP. Today, BP is one of the largest oil and gas exploration and refining companies in the world.

The information below comes from Note 20 (Finance debt) of British Petroleum's 1996 financial statements. All amounts are in millions of British pounds.

	Loans	Finance Leases
Payments due within:		
1 year	£1,020	£ 58
2 to 5 years	1,294	426
after 5 years	1,196	2,578
	£3,510	£3,062
Less finance charge	0	2,040
Net obligation	£3,510	£1,022

1. In Great Britain, a finance lease is what we in the United States would call a capital lease. According to Note 20, British Petroleum expects to make total lease payments under finance leases of £3.062 billion. However, only a liability of £1.022 billion is reported on the balance sheet. Why is there a difference between the two amounts?
2. The £3.062 billion payment amount for the finance leases reflects the total of all lease payments that will be made under the agreements. Does the £3.510 billion amount reported for loans reflect the amount of all payments that will be made under the loan agreements? Explain.
3. The future loan and finance lease payments are separated into amounts to be repaid within one year, within two to five years, and after five years. How would a financial statement user find this payment timing information to be useful?

ETHICS CASE

• Buying your own shares back

You are the chief financial officer for Esoteric Inc., a company whose stock is publicly traded. The stock market has recently experienced an overall downturn and the price of your company's stock has decreased by about 15 percent. This significantly affects the compensation of the executives of your company as their bonuses are based on the company's stock price. The bonus plan promotes company executives who take actions to increase the value of the company to stockholders. The reasoning is that if management increases the value of the company to stockholders, management should be rewarded.

As you consider ways to increase the value of the company, when the market itself is slumping, the following idea pops into your head: We will buy back our own stock. It will cause the value of the remaining outstanding stock to increase in value, which is good for those individuals holding that stock. And it will also result in you and the other corporate executives receiving sizeable bonuses.

Do you think this plan of action to increase stock price was what the designers of the compensation plan had in mind when they linked executive bonuses to company stock price? Does buying back the company's own stock add value to the company as a whole? Should the compensation plan prohibit activities like buying stock back? Consider these issues and be prepared to discuss them.

WRITING ASSIGNMENT

• My contract's bigger than your contract!

You are an agent for professional athletes. One of your clients is a superstar in the NBA. Last month you negotiated a new deal for your client that pays him $22 million per year for each of the next six years. Your client was very pleased with this $132 million contract, especially since it was a bigger contract than any of the other players on his team.

This morning, while you were relaxing in your Jacuzzi, you got an angry cellular call from your client. It seems that one of his teammates just signed a $150 million deal, paying him $15 million per year for each of the next ten years. Your client is outraged, since you guaranteed him that no one on his team would be receiving a bigger contract this season. Your client has threatened to terminate his agreement with you and also to spread the word among all his friends that you are not trustworthy.

Write a one-page memo to your client explaining that the actual value of his $132 million contract is greater than the $150 million contract signed by his teammate. Your client has had some exposure to the concept of the time value of money, since he has a marketing degree from an ACC school.

THE DEBATE

• Microsoft should share the wealth!

Turn to **Microsoft**'s annual report in Appendix A and notice its cash balance. As of June 30, 1997, the company had almost $9 billion in cash. It is likely that the company has a lot more cash on hand now. Should Microsoft use some of that cash to pay a dividend to its common shareholders?

Divide your group into two teams.

- The first team represents the position that "Bill Knows Best—Don't Pay a Dividend." Prepare a two-minute presentation outlining the reasons why Microsoft's no-dividend policy is appropriate.
- The second team represents the position that "A Dividend Should Be Paid." Prepare a two-minute presentation outlining reasons why Microsoft should use some of its stockpile of cash to reward common shareholders who have never received a dividend.

INTERNET SEARCH

• Dow Jones & Company

We began this chapter with a look at the history of **Dow Jones & Company**. Let's continue our examination of this company using its Internet site. Access Dow Jones' site at www.dowjones.com. Sometimes Web addresses change, so if this address doesn't work, access the Web site for this book at stice.swcollege.com for an updated link to Dow Jones & Company.

Once you have gained access to the company's Web site, answer the following questions:

1. What business publications is the company responsible for? What other services does the company provide?
2. Locate the company's most recent annual report. Which of the company's business segments is the most profitable as measured by operating income as a percentage of revenues?
3. Did the company pay a dividend in the most recent year? If so, how much per share? Compute the company's dividend payout ratio.
4. Review the note disclosure relating to the company's executive incentive plan. What is the objective of this plan?

CHAPTER

INVESTING ACTIVITIES 7

LEARNING OBJECTIVES

After studying this chapter, you should be able to:

1. *Identify the two major categories of long-term operating assets: property, plant, and equipment and intangible assets.*
2. *Understand the factors important in deciding whether to acquire a long-term operating asset.*
3. *Record the acquisition of property, plant, and equipment through a simple purchase and as part of the purchase of several assets at once.*
4. *Compute straight-line and units-of-production depreciation expense for plant and equipment.*
5. *Record the discarding and selling of property, plant, and equipment.*
6. *Account for the acquisition and amortization of intangible assets and understand the special difficulties associated with accounting for intangibles.*
7. *Understand why companies invest in other companies.*
8. *Understand the different classifications for securities.*
9. *Account for the purchase, recognition of revenue, and sale of trading and available-for-sale securities.*
10. *Account for changes in the value of securities.*

SETTING THE STAGE

Thomas Edison received $300,000 in investment funds in 1878 in order to start his Edison Electric Light Company. Today, **General Electric** is the direct descendant of Edison's company and, with a market value of $255 billion (as of February 1998), is the most valuable company in the world. General Electric has been a fixture in corporate America since the late 1800s and is the only one of the 12 companies included in the original Dow Jones Industrial Average that is still included among the 30 companies making up the Dow today.

The stated purpose of the creation of the **Edison Electric Light Company** was the development of an economically practical electric light bulb. After a year of experimentation, Thomas Edison discovered that carbonized bamboo served as a long-lasting light filament that was also easy to produce. Edison quickly found that delivering electric light to people's homes required more than a light bulb. So, Edison developed an entire electricity generation and distribution system, inventing new pieces of equipment when he couldn't find what he needed. The first public electric light system was built in London, followed soon after by the Pearl Street Station system in New York City in 1882. In 1892, Edison's company was merged with the **Thomson-Houston Electric Company** (developer of alternating-current [AC] equipment that could transmit over longer distances than Edison's direct-current [DC] system), and the General Electric Company was born.

From the beginning, the strength of General Electric has been research. In addition to improvements in the design of the light bulb (including the development in the early 1900s of gas-filled, tungsten-filament bulbs that are the model for bulbs still used today), GE was also instrumental in the development of almost every familiar household appliance—the iron, washing machine, refrigerator, range, air conditioner, dishwasher, and more. In addition, GE research scientists helped create FM radio, aircraft jet engines, and nuclear-power reactors.

Today, General Electric operates in a diverse array of businesses, ranging from train locomotives to medical CT scanners to consumer financing to the NBC television network. When Jack Welch became CEO of GE in 1981, his goal was to make GE number one or number two in each market segment in which it operates, or else get out of that particular line of business. This strategy has continued the success of GE and has seen GE's market value grow by an average of 22 percent per year over the past 17 years.

In order to support its broad array of businesses, GE maintains a vast quantity of long-term assets that cost over $71 billion to acquire. In 1996 alone, GE spent an additional $13.3 billion in acquiring long-term operating assets and received $1.4 billion for disposing of old assets. This collection of long-term assets includes $2.1 billion in rail cars, $6.3 billion in buildings, $17.8 billion in machinery, and $20.6 billion in "intangible" assets.

Sources: General Electric Company History at ge.com/ibhis0.htm; General Electric Company, *International Directory of Company Histories,* Vol. 12 (St. James Press, Detroit, MI, 1996), pp. 193–197; 1996 Annual Report of the General Electric Company.

In Chapter 5, the operating activities of a business and the assets and liabilities arising from those operations were discussed. In Chapter 6, we discussed debt and equity financing. In this chapter, investments in long-term operating assets as well as investments in stocks and bonds (securities) of other companies are discussed. Exhibit 7-1 shows the balance sheet and income statement accounts as well as the cash flow items that will be covered in this chapter.

Profitable companies like General Electric must decide what to do with the cash generated from operations. Should those funds be returned to stockholders,

EXHIBIT 7-1 Basic Financial Statements

Balance Sheet

Current assets:		*Current liabilities:*	
Cash	Ch. 4	Accounts payable	Ch. 5
Investments	**Ch. 7**	Taxes payable	Ch. 5
Accounts receivable	Ch. 4	Wages payable	Ch. 5
Inventory	Ch. 5	Warranty liability	Ch. 4
Property, plant, and equipment	**Ch. 7**	Unearned revenues	Ch. 5
Intangible assets	**Ch. 7**	*Long-term liabilities:*	
Long-term investments	**Ch. 7**	Long-term debt	Ch. 6
Total assets		Pension costs	Ch. 5
		Stockholders' equity:	Ch. 6
		Common stock	Ch. 6
		Retained earnings	Ch. 6
		Unrealized increase/decrease in value of securities	**Ch. 7**
		Total liabilities and stockholders' equity	

Income Statement

Sales of goods and services	Ch. 4
Cost of goods sold	Ch. 5
Gross margin	
Expenses:	
Salaries expense	Ch. 5
Taxes expense	Ch. 5
Depreciation expense	**Ch. 7**
Bad debt expense	Ch. 4
Warranty expense	Ch. 4
Other revenues and expenses:	
Gains and losses on sales of securities	**Ch. 7**
Unrealized gains and losses on securities	**Ch. 7**
Interest expense	Ch. 6
Interest revenue	**Ch. 7**
Net income	

EXHIBIT 7-1

Concluded

Statement of Cash Flows	
Operating activities:	
Receipts from customers	Ch. 4
Payments for inventory	Ch. 5
Payments for salaries	Ch. 5
Payments for interest	Ch. 6
Payments for taxes	Ch. 5
Purchase of trading securities	Ch. 7
Sale of trading securities	Ch. 7
Investing activities:	
Purchase of property, plant, and equipment	Ch. 7
Proceeds from sale of property, plant, and equipment	Ch. 7
Purchase of debt and equity securities other than trading securities	Ch. 7
Sale of debt and equity securities other than trading securities	Ch. 7
Financing activities:	
Sale of stock	Ch. 6
Purchase of treasury stock	Ch. 6
Proceeds from borrowing	Ch. 6
Repayments of borrowing	Ch. 6
Payments of dividends	Ch. 6
Net cash flows for the period	

reinvested in operating assets, or invested in other companies? This chapter addresses the latter two options—reinvesting the money in operating assets and investing in other companies. The first part of this chapter deals with long-term operating assets. This type of asset can be subdivided into two categories: (1) property, plant, and equipment and (2) intangible assets. The second part of this chapter discusses the issues associated with investing in the debt or equity securities of another company.

1 *Identify the two major categories of long-term operating assets: property, plant, and equipment and intangible assets.*

NATURE OF LONG-TERM OPERATING ASSETS

Businesses make money by selling products and services. A company needs an infrastructure of long-term operating assets in order to profitably produce and distribute these products and services. For example, General Electric needs factories in which to manufacture the locomotives and light bulbs that it sells. GE also needs patents on its unique technology to protect its competitive edge in the market place. A factory is one example of a long-term operating asset that is classified as property, plant, and equipment. A patent is an example of an intangible asset. **Property, plant, and equipment** refers to tangible, long-lived assets acquired for use in business operations. This category includes land, buildings, machinery, equipment, and furniture. **Intangible assets** are long-lived assets that are used in the operation of a business but do not have physical substance. In most cases, they provide their owners with competitive advantages over other firms. Typical intangible assets are patents, licenses, franchises, and goodwill.

property, plant, and equipment Tangible, long-lived assets acquired for use in business operations; includes land, buildings, machinery, equipment, and furniture.

intangible assets Long-lived assets without physical substance that are used in business, such as licenses, patents, franchises, and goodwill.

The time line in Exhibit 7-2 illustrates the important business issues associated with long-term operating assets.

The following section outlines the process used in deciding whether to acquire a long-term operating asset. The subsequent sections discuss the accounting issues that arise when a long-term operating asset is acquired: accounting for the acquisition of the asset, recording periodic depreciation, accounting for new costs and changes in asset value, and properly removing the asset from the books upon disposition.

EXHIBIT 7-2 Time Line of Business Issues Involved with Long-Term Operating Assets

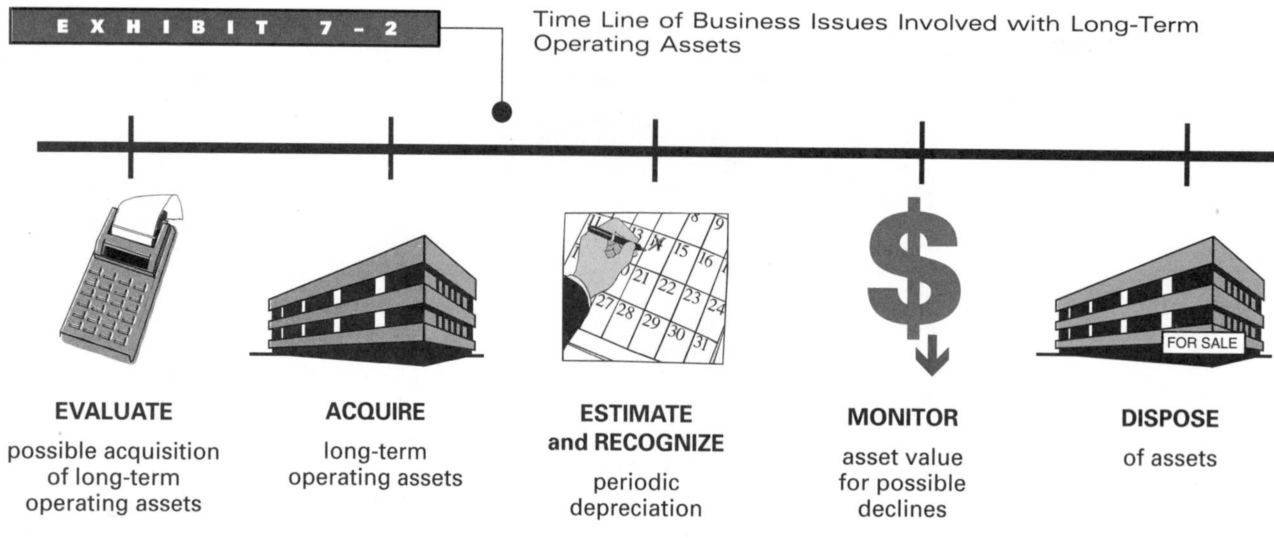

TO SUMMARIZE

Long-term operating assets provide an infrastructure in which to conduct operating activities. The category of property, plant, and equipment refers to tangible, long-lived assets such as land and equipment. Examples of intangible assets are patents and licenses.

2 *Understand the factors important in deciding whether to acquire a long-term operating asset.*

DECIDING WHETHER TO ACQUIRE A LONG-TERM OPERATING ASSET

As mentioned in the previous section, long-term operating assets are acquired to be used over the course of several years. The decision to acquire a long-term asset depends on whether the future cash flows generated by the asset are expected to be large enough to justify the asset cost. The process of evaluating a long-term project is called **capital budgeting**. This process is briefly introduced here and is covered in more detail in Chapter 15.

capital budgeting Systematic planning for long-term investments in operating assets.

Assume that Yosef Manufacturing makes joysticks and other computer game accessories. Yosef is considering expanding its operations by buying an additional production facility. The cost of the new factory is $100 million. Yosef expects to be able to sell the joysticks and other items made in the factory for $80 million per year. At that level of production, the annual cost of operating the factory (wages, insurance, materials, maintenance, etc.) is expected to total $65 million. The factory is expected to remain in operation for 20 years. Should Yosef buy the new factory for $100 million?

To summarize the information in the preceding paragraph, Yosef must decide whether to pay $100 million for a factory that will generate a net profit of $15 million ($80 million − $65 million) per year for 20 years. At first glance, you might think that the decision is obvious since the factory costs only $100 million but will generate $300 million in profit ($15 million × 20 years) during its 20-year life. But this analysis ignores the important fact that dollars received far in the future are not worth as much as dollars received right now. For example, if you can invest your money and earn 10 percent, receiving $1 today is the same as receiving $6.73 20 years from now because the $1 received today could be invested and would grow to $6.73 in 20 years. This important concept is called the **time value of money** and is essential to properly evaluating whether to acquire any long-term asset.

time value of money The concept that a dollar received now is worth more than a dollar received far in the future.

Using the time value of money calculations that were explained in Chapter 6, it can be shown that receiving the future cash flows from the factory of $15 million per year for 20 years is the same as receiving $128 million in one lump sum right now, if the prevailing interest rate is 10%. Thus, the decision to acquire the factory boils down to the following comparison: Should we pay $100 million to buy a factory now if the factory will generate future cash flows that are worth the equivalent of $128 million now? The decision is yes, since the $128 million value of the expected cash inflows is greater than the $100 million cost of the factory. On the other hand, if the factory were expected to generate only $10 million per year, then, using the computations that will be explained in Chapter 10, it can be calculated that the value of the cash flows would be only $85 million, and the factory should not be purchased for $100 million.

The important concept to remember here is that long-term operating assets have value because they are expected to help a company generate cash flows in the future. If events occur to change the expectation concerning those future cash flows, then the value of the asset changes. For example, if consumer demand for computer joysticks dries up, the value of a factory built to produce joysticks can plunge overnight even though the factory itself is still as productive as it ever was. Accounting for this type of decline in the value of a long-term operating asset is discussed later in the chapter.

TO SUMMARIZE

Long-term operating assets have value because they help companies generate future cash flows. The decision to acquire a long-term operating asset involves comparing the cost of the asset to the value of the expected cash inflows, after adjusting for the time value of money. An asset's value can decrease or disappear if events cause a decrease in expectations about the future cash flows generated by the asset.

3 *Record the acquisition of property, plant, and equipment through a simple purchase as well as through a lease, self-construction, and as part of the purchase of several assets at once.*

ACCOUNTING FOR ACQUISITION OF PROPERTY, PLANT, AND EQUIPMENT

Like all other assets, property, plant, and equipment are initially recorded at cost. The cost of an asset includes not only the purchase price but also any other costs incurred in acquiring the asset and getting it ready for its intended use. Examples of these other costs include shipping, installation, and sales taxes.

Property, plant, and equipment are usually acquired by purchase. Also, a company can in one transaction purchase several different assets or even another entire company. The accounting for each of these types of acquisition is explained below.

Assets Acquired by Purchase

A company can purchase an asset by paying cash, incurring a liability, exchanging another asset, or by a combination of these methods. If a single asset is purchased for cash, the accounting is relatively simple. To illustrate, we assume that Wheeler Resorts, Inc., purchases a new delivery truck for $15,096 (purchase price, $15,000, less 2% discount for paying cash, plus sales tax of $396). The entry to record this purchase is:

Delivery Truck	15,096	
Cash		15,096
Purchased a delivery truck for $15,096 ($15,000 − $300 cash discount + $396 sales tax).		

In this instance, cash was paid for a single asset, the truck. An alternative would be to borrow part of the purchase price. If the company had borrowed $12,000 of the $15,096 from a bank, the entry would have been:

Delivery Truck	15,096	
Cash		3,096
Notes Payable		12,000
Purchased a delivery truck for $15,096; paid $3,096 cash and issued a note for $12,000 to Chemical Bank.		

The $12,000 represents the principal of the note; it does not include any interest charged by the lending institution. (The interest is recognized later as interest expense.)

When one long-term operating asset is acquired in exchange for another, the cost of the new asset is usually set equal to the market value of the asset given up in exchange. However, there are some exceptions to this rule. Asset exchanges can be complicated and are not discussed in this text.

Acquisition of Several Assets at Once

basket purchase The purchase of two or more assets acquired together at a single price.

A **basket purchase** involves two or more assets acquired together at a single price. A typical basket purchase is the purchase of a building along with the land on which the building sits. Because there are differences in the accounting for land and buildings, the purchase price must be allocated between the two assets on some reasonable basis. The relative fair market values of the assets are usually used to determine the respective costs to be assigned to the land and the building.

To illustrate, we will assume that Wheeler Resorts purchases a 40,000-square-foot building on 2.6 acres of land for $3,600,000. How much of the total cost should be assigned to the land and how much to the building? If an appraisal indicates that the fair market values of the land and the building are $1,000,000 and $3,000,000, respectively, the resulting allocated costs would be $900,000 and $2,700,000, calculated as follows:

Asset	Fair Market Value	Percentage of Total Value	Apportionment of Lump-Sum Cost
Land	$1,000,000	25%	0.25 × $3,600,000 = $ 900,000
Building	3,000,000	75	0.75 × $3,600,000 = 2,700,000
Total	$4,000,000	100%	$3,600,000

In this case, the fair market value of the land is $1,000,000, or 25 percent of the total market value of the land and building. Therefore, 25 percent of the actual cost, or $900,000, is allocated to the land and 75 percent of the actual cost, or $2,700,000, is allocated to the building. The journal entry to record this basket purchase is:

Land	900,000	
Building	2,700,000	
Cash		3,600,000
Purchased 2.6 acres of land and a 40,000-square-foot building.		

If part of the purchase price is financed by a bank, an additional credit to Notes Payable or Mortgage Payable would be included in the entry.

Sometimes one company will buy all the assets of another company. For example, in its 1997 annual report (included in Appendix A), **Microsoft** discloses that, on August 1, 1997, it purchased **WebTV Networks** for $425 million. The purchase of an entire company raises a number of accounting issues. The first, already discussed above, is how to allocate the purchase price to the various assets acquired. In general, all acquired assets are recorded on the books of the acquiring company at their fair values as of the acquisition date.

goodwill An intangible asset that exists when a business is valued at more than the fair market value of its net assets, usually due to strategic location, reputation, good customer relations, or similar factors; equal to the excess of the purchase price over the fair market value of the net assets purchased.

The second major accounting issue associated with the purchase of an entire company is the recording of goodwill. **Goodwill** represents all the special competitive advantages enjoyed by a company, such as a trained staff, good credit rating, reputation for superior products and services, and an established network of suppliers and customers. These factors allow an established business to earn more profits than would a new business, even though the new business might have the same type of building, the same equipment, and the same type of production processes.

When one company purchases another established business, the excess of the purchase price over the value of the identifiable net assets is assumed to represent the purchase of goodwill. The accounting for goodwill is illustrated later in the chapter.

TO SUMMARIZE

When property, plant, and equipment assets are purchased, they are recorded at cost, which includes all expenditures associated with acquiring and getting them ready for their intended use, such as sales tax, shipping, and installation. When two or more assets are acquired for a single price in a basket purchase, the relative fair market values are used to determine the respective costs.

4 *Compute straight-line and units-of-production depreciation expense for plant and equipment.*

CALCULATING AND RECORDING DEPRECIATION EXPENSE

depreciation The process of cost allocation that assigns the original cost of plant and equipment to the periods benefited.

The second element in accounting for plant and equipment is the allocation of an asset's cost over its useful life. The matching principle requires that this cost be assigned to expense in the periods benefited from the use of the asset. The allocation procedure is called **depreciation**, and the allocated amount, recorded in a period-ending adjusting entry, is an expense that is deducted from revenues in order to determine income. It should be noted that the asset "plant" normally refers to buildings only; land is recorded as a separate asset and is not depreciated because it is usually assumed to have an unlimited useful life.

book value For a long-term operating asset, book value is equal to the asset's original cost less any accumulated depreciation.

salvage value The amount expected to be received when an asset is sold at the end of its useful life.

Accounting for depreciation is often confusing because students tend to think that depreciation expense reflects the decline in an asset's value. The concept of depreciation is nothing more than a systematic write-off of the original cost of an asset. The undepreciated cost is referred to as **book value**, which represents that portion of the original cost not yet assigned to the income statement as an expense. A company never claims that an asset's recorded book value is equal to its market value. In fact, market values of assets could increase at the same time that depreciation expense is being recorded.

To calculate depreciation expense for an asset, you need to know (1) its original cost, (2) its estimated useful life, and (3) its estimated salvage, or residual, value. **Salvage value** is the amount expected to be received when the asset is sold at the end of its useful life. When an asset is purchased, its actual life and salvage value are obviously unknown. They must be estimated as realistically as is feasible, usually on the basis of experience with similar assets. In some cases, an asset will have little or no salvage value. If the salvage value is not significant, it is usually ignored in computing depreciation.

There are several methods that can be used for depreciating the costs of assets for financial reporting. In the main part of this chapter we describe two: straight-line and units-of-production. In the expanded material section of this chapter we describe two more depreciation methods: sums-of-the-years'-digits and declining-balance.

straight-line depreciation method The depreciation method in which the cost of an asset is allocated equally over the periods of an asset's estimated useful life.

units-of-production method The depreciation method in which the cost of an asset is allocated to each period on the basis of the productive output or use of the asset during the period.

The **straight-line depreciation method** assumes that an asset will benefit all periods equally and that the cost of the asset should be assigned on a uniform basis for all accounting periods. If an asset's benefits are thought to be related to its productive output (miles driven in an automobile, for example), the **units-of-production method** is usually appropriate.

To illustrate straight-line and units-of-production depreciation methods, we assume that Wheeler Resorts purchased a van on January 1 for transporting hotel guests to and from the airport. The following facts apply:

Acquisition cost	$24,000
Estimated salvage value	$2,000
Estimated life:	
In years	4 years
In miles driven	60,000 miles

Straight-Line Method of Depreciation

The straight-line depreciation method is the simplest depreciation method. It assumes that an asset's cost should be assigned equally to all periods benefited. The formula for calculating annual straight-line depreciation is:

$$\frac{\text{Cost} - \text{Salvage value}}{\text{Estimated useful life (years)}} = \text{Annual depreciation expense}$$

With this formula, the annual depreciation expense for the van is calculated as:

$$\frac{\$24{,}000 - \$2{,}000}{4 \text{ years}} = \$5{,}500 \text{ depreciation expense per year}$$

When the depreciation expense for an asset has been calculated, a schedule showing the annual depreciation expense, the total accumulated depreciation, and the asset's book value (undepreciated cost) for each year can be prepared. The depreciation schedule for the van (using straight-line depreciation) is shown in Exhibit 7-3.

EXHIBIT 7-3

Depreciation Schedule with Straight-Line Depreciation

	Annual Depreciation Expense	Accumulated Depreciation	Book Value
Acquisition date	—	—	$24,000
End of year 1	$ 5,500	$ 5,500	18,500
End of year 2	5,500	11,000	13,000
End of year 3	5,500	16,500	7,500
End of year 4	5,500	22,000	2,000
	$22,000		

The entry to record straight-line depreciation each year is:

Depreciation Expense	5,500	
Accumulated Depreciation, Hotel Van		5,500
To record annual depreciation for the hotel van.		

Depreciation Expense is reported on the income statement. Accumulated Depreciation is a contra-asset account that is offset against the cost of the asset on the balance sheet. Book value is equal to the asset account balance, which retains the original cost of the asset as a debit balance, minus the credit balance in the accumulated depreciation account.

FYI

A comparison of the amounts of cost and accumulated depreciation reveals how old the plant and equipment is relative to its total expected life.

At the end of the first year, the acquisition cost, accumulated depreciation, and book value of the van are presented on the balance sheet as follows:

Property, Plant, and Equipment:	
Hotel van	$24,000
Less: Accumulated depreciation	5,500
Book value	$18,500

Units-of-Production Method of Depreciation

The units-of-production depreciation method allocates an asset's cost on the basis of use rather than time. This method is used primarily when a company expects that asset usage will vary significantly from year to year. If the asset's usage pattern is uniform from year to year, the units-of-production method will produce the same depreciation pattern as the straight-line method. Assets with varying usage patterns for which this method of depreciation may be appropriate are automobiles and other vehicles whose life is estimated in terms of numbers of miles driven. It is also used for certain machines whose life is estimated in terms of number of units produced or number of hours of operating life. The formula for calculating the units-of-production depreciation for the year is:

$$\frac{\text{Cost} - \text{Salvage value}}{\text{Total estimated life in units, hours, or miles}} \times \text{Number of units, hours, or miles produced or used during the year} = \text{Current year's depreciation expense}$$

To illustrate, we again consider Wheeler Resorts' van, which has an expected life of 60,000 miles. With the units-of-production method, if the van is driven 12,000 miles during the first year, the depreciation expense for that year is calculated as follows:

$$\frac{(\$24{,}000 - \$2{,}000)}{60{,}000 \text{ miles}} \times 12{,}000 \text{ miles} = \$4{,}400 \text{ depreciation expense}$$

The entry to record units-of-production depreciation at the end of the first year of the van's life is:

Depreciation Expense	4,400	
Accumulated Depreciation, Hotel Van		4,400
To record depreciation for the first year of the hotel van's life.		

The depreciation schedule for the four years is shown in Exhibit 7-4. This exhibit assumes that 18,000 miles were driven the second year, 21,000 the third year, and 9,000 the fourth year.

EXHIBIT 7-4

Depreciation Schedule with Units-of-Production Depreciation

	Miles Driven	Depreciation Expense	Accumulated Depreciation	Book Value
Acquisition date	—	—	—	$24,000
End of year 1	12,000	$ 4,400	$ 4,400	19,600
End of year 2	18,000	6,600	11,000	13,000
End of year 3	21,000	7,700	18,700	5,300
End of year 4	9,000	3,300	22,000	2,000
		$22,000		

Note that part of the formulas for straight-line and units-of-production depreciation are the same. In both cases, cost − salvage value is divided by the asset's useful life. With straight-line, life is measured in years; with units-of-production, life is in miles or hours. With units-of-production, the depreciation per mile or hour must then be multiplied by the usage for the year to determine depreciation expense.

What if the van lasts for longer than four years or is driven for more than 60,000 miles? Once the $22,000 difference between cost and salvage value has been recorded as depreciation expense, there is no further expense to record. Thus, any additional years or miles are "free" in the sense that no depreciation expense will be recognized in connection with them. However, as other vans are purchased in the future, the initial useful life estimates for those vans will be adjusted to reflect the experience with previous vans.

What if the van lasts for less than four years or is driven for less than 60,000 miles? This topic is covered later in the chapter in connection with the accounting for the disposal of property, plant, and equipment.

A Comparison of Depreciation Methods

The amount of depreciation expense will vary according to the depreciation method used by a company. Exhibit 7-5 compares the annual depreciation expense for Wheeler Resorts' van under the straight-line and units-of-production depreciation methods. This schedule makes it clear that the total amount of depreciation is the same regardless of which method is used.

EXHIBIT 7-5

Comparison of Depreciation Expense Using Different Depreciation Methods

	Straight-Line Depreciation	Units-of-Production Depreciation
End of year 1	$ 5,500	$ 4,400
End of year 2	5,500	6,600
End of year 3	5,500	7,700
End of year 4	5,500	3,300
Totals	$22,000	$22,000

Straight-line is by far the most commonly used depreciation method because it is the simplest method to apply and because it makes intuitive sense. For example, in the notes to its 1997 financial statements (see Appendix A), **Microsoft** discloses that it depreciates its property, plant, and equipment using the straight-line method.

Partial-Year Depreciation Calculations

Thus far, depreciation expense has been calculated on the basis of a full year. However, because businesses purchase assets at all times during the year, partial-year depreciation calculations are often required. To compute depreciation expense for less than a full year, first calculate the depreciation expense for the year and then distribute it evenly over the number of months the asset is held during the year.

To illustrate, assume that Wheeler Resorts purchased its $24,000 van on July 1 instead of January 1. The depreciation calculations for the first one and one-half years, using straight-line depreciation, are shown in Exhibit 7-6. The units-of-production method has been omitted from the exhibit; midyear purchases do not complicate the calculations with this method since it involves numbers of miles driven, hours flown, and so on, rather than time periods.

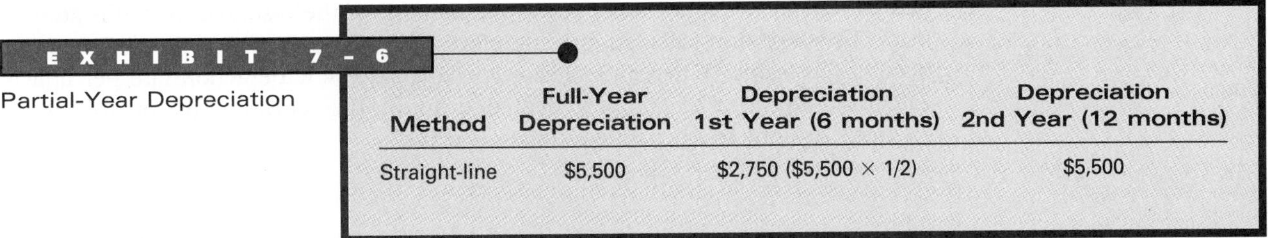

EXHIBIT 7-6

Partial-Year Depreciation

Method	Full-Year Depreciation	Depreciation 1st Year (6 months)	Depreciation 2nd Year (12 months)
Straight-line	$5,500	$2,750 ($5,500 × 1/2)	$5,500

In practice, many companies simplify their depreciation computations by taking a full year of depreciation in the year an asset is purchased and none in the year the asset is sold, or vice versa. This is allowed because depreciation is based on estimates, and in the long run, the difference in the amounts is usually immaterial.

Units-of-Production Method with Natural Resources

natural resources Assets that are physically consumed or waste away, such as oil, minerals, gravel, and timber.

depletion The process of cost allocation that assigns the original cost of a natural resource to the periods benefited.

Another common use for the units-of-production method is with natural resources. **Natural resources** include such assets as oil wells, timber tracts, coal mines, and gravel deposits. Like all other assets, newly purchased or developed natural resources are recorded at cost. This cost must be written off as the assets are extracted or otherwise depleted. This process of writing off the cost of natural resources is called **depletion** and involves the calculation of a depletion rate for each unit of the natural resource. Conceptually, depletion is exactly the same as depreciation; with plant and equipment, the accounting process is called depreciation, whereas with natural resources it is called depletion.

To illustrate, assume that Power-T Company purchases a coal mine for $1,200,000 cash. The entry to record the purchase is:

Coal Mine	1,200,000	
Cash..		1,200,000
Purchased a coal mine for $1,200,000.		

If the mine contains an estimated 200,000 tons of coal deposits (based on a geologist's estimate), the depletion expense for each ton of coal extracted and sold will be $6 ($1,200,000/200,000 tons). Here, the unit of production is the extraction of one ton of coal. If 12,000 tons of coal are mined and sold in the current year, the depletion entry is:

Depletion Expense	72,000	
Accumulated Depletion, Coal Mine		72,000
To record depletion for the year: 12,000 tons at $6 per ton.		

After the first year's depletion expense has been recorded, the coal mine is shown on the balance sheet as follows:

Coal mine	$1,200,000
Less: Accumulated depletion	72,000
Book value	$1,128,000

But how do you determine the number of tons of coal in a mine? Since most natural resources cannot be counted, the amount of the resource owned is an estimate. The depletion calculation is therefore likely to be revised as new information becomes available. When an estimate is changed, a new depletion rate per unit is calculated and used to compute depletion during the remaining life of the natural resource or until another new estimate is made.

TO SUMMARIZE

Depreciation is the process whereby the cost of an asset is allocated over its useful life. Two common and simple methods of depreciation are straight-line and units-of-production. The straight-line and units-of-production methods allocate cost proportionately over an asset's life on the bases of time and use, respectively. Regardless of which method is used, depreciation is only an allocation of an asset's cost over the periods benefited and is not a method of valuation. Natural resources are assets, such as gravel deposits or coal mines, that are consumed or that waste away. The accounting process of depreciation for natural resources is called depletion.

5 *Record the discarding and selling of property, plant, and equipment.*

DISPOSAL OF PROPERTY, PLANT, AND EQUIPMENT

Plant and equipment eventually become worthless or are sold. When a company removes one of these assets from service, it has to eliminate the asset's cost and accumulated depreciation from the accounting records. There are basically three ways to dispose of an asset: (1) discard or scrap it, (2) sell it, or (3) exchange it for another asset.

Discarding Property, Plant, and Equipment

When an asset becomes worthless and must be scrapped, its cost and its accumulated depreciation balance should be removed from the accounting records. If the asset's total cost has been depreciated, there is no loss on the disposal. If, on the other hand, the cost is not completely depreciated, the undepreciated cost represents a loss on disposal.

To illustrate, we assume that Wheeler Resorts, Inc., purchases a computer for $15,000. The computer has a 5-year life and no estimated salvage value and is depreciated on a straight-line basis. If the computer is scrapped after five full years, the entry to record the disposal is as follows:

Accumulated Depreciation, Computer	15,000	
Computer		15,000
Scrapped $15,000 computer.		

If it costs Wheeler $300 to have the computer dismantled and removed, the entry to record the disposal is:

Accumulated Depreciation, Computer	15,000	
Loss on Disposal of Computer	300	
Computer		15,000
Cash		300
Scrapped $15,000 computer and paid disposal costs of $300.		

If the computer is scrapped after only four years of service (and after $12,000 of the original cost has been depreciated), there would be a loss on disposal of $3,300 (including the disposal cost), and the entry would be:

Accumulated Depreciation, Computer	12,000	
Loss on Disposal of Computer	3,300	
Computer		15,000
Cash		300
Scrapped $15,000 computer and recognized loss of $3,300 (including $300 disposal costs).		

Don't think of the losses recognized above as "bad" or the gains as "good." A loss on disposal simply means that, given the information we now have, it looks as if we didn't record enough depreciation expense in previous years. As a result, the book value of the asset is higher than what we can get on disposal. Similarly, a gain means that too much depreciation expense was recognized in prior years, making the book value of the asset low compared to its actual disposal value.

Selling Property, Plant, and Equipment

A second way of disposing of property, plant, and equipment is to sell it. If the sales price of the asset exceeds its book value (the original cost less accumulated depreciation), there is a gain on the sale. Conversely, if the sales price is less than the book value, there is a loss.

To illustrate, we refer again to Wheeler's $15,000 computer. If the computer is sold for $600 after five full years of service, assuming no disposal costs, the entry to record the sale is:

Cash	600	
Accumulated Depreciation, Computer	15,000	
Computer		15,000
Gain on Sale of Computer		600
Sold $15,000 computer at a gain of $600.		

Since the asset was fully depreciated, its book value was zero and the $600 cash received represents a gain. If the computer had been sold for $600 after only four years of service, there would have been a loss of $2,400 on the sale, and the entry to record the sale would have been:

Cash	600	
Accumulated Depreciation, Computer	12,000	
Loss on Sale of Computer	2,400	
Computer		15,000
Sold $15,000 computer at a loss of $2,400.		

The $2,400 loss is the difference between the sales price of $600 and the book value of $3,000 ($15,000 − $12,000). The amount of a gain or loss is thus a function of two factors: (1) the amount of cash received from the sale, and (2) the book value of the asset at the date of sale. The book value can vary from the market price of the asset for two reasons: (1) The accounting for the asset is not intended to show market value in the financial statements, and (2) it is difficult to estimate salvage value and useful life at the outset of an asset's life.

Exchanging Property, Plant, and Equipment

A third way of disposing of property, plant, and equipment is to exchange it for another asset. Such exchanges occur regularly with cars, trucks, machines, and other types of large equipment. Accounting for exchanges can be more complicated than accounting for disposals and sales and is not covered in this text.

TO SUMMARIZE

There are three ways of disposing of assets: (1) discarding (scrapping), (2) selling, and (3) exchanging. If a scrapped asset has not been fully depreciated, a loss equal to the undepreciated cost or book value is recognized. When an asset is sold, there is a gain if the sales price exceeds the book value and a loss if the sales price is less than the book value.

6 *Account for the acquisition and amortization of intangible assets and understand the special difficulties associated with accounting for intangibles.*

ACCOUNTING FOR INTANGIBLE ASSETS

Intangible assets are rights and privileges that are long-lived, are not held for resale, have no physical substance, and usually provide their owner with competitive advantages over other firms. Familiar examples are patents, franchises, licenses, and goodwill. Although intangible assets have no physical substance, they are accounted for in the same way as other long-term operating assets. That is, they are originally recorded at cost and the cost is allocated over the useful or legal life, whichever is shorter. The periodic allocation to expense of an intangible asset's cost is called **amortization**. Conceptually, depreciation (with plant and equipment), depletion (with natural resources), and amortization (with intangible assets) are exactly the same thing. Straight-line amortization is generally used for intangible assets.

amortization The process of cost allocation that assigns the original cost of an intangible asset to the periods benefited.

The traditional accounting model is designed for manufacturing and merchandising companies. Accordingly, accountants have developed intricate and sophisticated accounting methods for use with buildings, equipment, inventory, and receivables. The accounting procedures for gathering and reporting useful information about intangible assets is not as well developed. A big challenge facing the accounting profession is the task of improving the accounting for intangible assets in a business environment dominated increasingly by information, service, and reputation.

The importance of intangible assets can be illustrated by considering **Microsoft**. As mentioned in Chapter 2, if the balance sheet were perfect, the amount of owners' equity would be equal to the market value of the company. On June 30, 1997, Microsoft's reported equity was equal to $10.777 billion. The actual market value of Microsoft on June 30, 1997, was $152 billion. The reason for the large difference between the recorded value of the company and the actual value of the company is that a traditional balance sheet excludes many important intangible economic assets. Examples of Microsoft's important intangible economic assets are its track record of successful products and its entrenched market position. These intangible factors are by far the most valuable assets owned by Microsoft, but they fall outside the traditional accounting process.

As with many accounting issues, accounting for intangibles involves a trade-off between relevance and reliability. Information concerning intangible assets is relevant, but to meet the standard for recognition in the financial statements, the recorded amount for the intangible must also be reliable. As a result, accounting for intangibles focuses on identifying the costs associated with securing or developing the intangible assets. This is illustrated below with a discussion of the accounting for patents, franchises, and licenses.

et connected
p://www.swcollege.com
net work

Fortune magazine posts its *Fortune 500* list on its Web site. The information posted includes the reported equity and market values for the 500 largest companies in the United States.

What are the differences between reported equity and the market value of equity for The Coca-Cola Company and for General Motors Corporation?

fortune.com

Patents

patent An exclusive right granted for 17 years by the federal government to manufacture and sell an invention.

A **patent** is an exclusive right to produce and sell a commodity that has one or more unique features. In the United States, patents are issued to inventors by the federal government and have a legal life of 17 years. Patents may be obtained on new products developed in a company's own research laboratories, or they may be purchased from others. If a patent is purchased from others, its cost is simply the purchase price, and it is recorded as an asset (patent). The cost of the patent is amortized over the useful life of the patent, which may or may not coincide with the patent's legal life.

The cost of a patent for a product developed within a firm is difficult to determine. Should it include research and development costs as well as legal fees to obtain the patent? Should other company expenses such as administrative costs be included? Because of the high degree of uncertainty about their future benefits, U.S. accounting rules dictate that research and development costs must be expensed in the period in which they are incurred. Therefore, all research and development costs of internally developed patents are expensed as they are incurred.

FYI

The U.S. rule for accounting for research and development differs from the international rule. According to international accounting rules, research and development costs that are incurred after the technological feasibility of a project has been demonstrated should be capitalized as an asset.

To illustrate the accounting for patents, assume that Wheeler Resorts, Inc., acquires, for $200,000, a patent granted seven years earlier to another firm. The entry to record the purchase of the patent is:

Patent	200,000	
Cash		200,000
Purchased patent for $200,000.		

Because seven years of its 17-year legal life have already elapsed, the patent now has a legal life of only 10 years, although it may have a shorter useful life. If its useful life is assumed to be eight years, one-eighth of the $200,000 cost should be amortized each year for the next eight years. The entry each year to record the patent amortization expense is:

Amortization Expense, Patent	25,000	
Patent		25,000
To amortize one-eighth of the cost of the patent.		

Notice that in the above entry, the patent account was credited. Alternatively, a contra-asset account, such as Accumulated Amortization, could have been credited. In practice, however, crediting the intangible asset account directly is more common. This is different from the normal practice of crediting accumulated depreciation for buildings or equipment.

Franchises and Licenses

franchise An entity that has been licensed to sell the product of a manufacturer or to offer a particular service in a given area.

license The right to perform certain activities, generally granted by a governmental agency.

Issued either by companies or by government agencies, **franchises** and **licenses** are exclusive rights to perform services in certain geographical areas. For example, **McDonald's Corporation** sells franchises to individuals to operate its hamburger outlets in specific locations. Similarly, local airports issue licenses to airlines allowing them to use a specified number of boarding gates for a specified length of time. Like patents, the cost of a franchise or license is amortized over its useful or legal life, whichever is shorter.

Goodwill

When businesses are purchased, the negotiated price often exceeds the total fair market value of the individual assets purchased minus the outstanding liabilities assumed by the buyer. As mentioned earlier, this excess in purchase price that cannot be allocated to specific assets is called goodwill and is an intangible asset. The emergence of goodwill in such a transaction is considered an indication that the purchased business is worth more than its net assets, due to such favorable characteristics as a good reputation, a strategic location, product superiority, or management skill.

Goodwill is recorded only if its value can be objectively determined by a transaction. Therefore, even though two businesses may enjoy the same favorable characteristics, goodwill will be recognized only when it is purchased; that is, when one company buys another company. This disparity in accounting exists because the action of a buyer in paying a premium for a firm is objective evidence that goodwill exists and has a specific value.

CAUTION

Goodwill is recorded only when it is purchased. A company's reported goodwill balance does not reflect the company's own homegrown goodwill. So, **Microsoft**'s goodwill is not recognized in Microsoft's balance sheet, but it would be recognized in your balance sheet if you were to purchase Microsoft.

As you can imagine, estimating the useful life of goodwill is extremely difficult. In order to give companies some direction in estimating the useful life of goodwill, accounting standard setters have established some guidelines. In the United States, for example, the accounting rule is that the estimated life of goodwill must be 40 years or less. According to international accounting standards, goodwill usually is assumed to have a life of five years or less, although a life of up to 20 years is sometimes justifiable. Most U.S. companies simply assume that any goodwill they purchase has a life of 40 years.

To illustrate the accounting for goodwill, assume that, in order to cater to the medicinal needs of its guests, Wheeler Resorts purchases Valley Drug Store for $400,000. At the time of purchase, the recorded assets and liabilities of Valley Drug have the following fair market values:

Inventory	$220,000
Long-term operating assets	110,000
Other assets (prepaid expenses, etc.)	10,000
Liabilities	(20,000)
Total net assets	$320,000

Note that Wheeler Resorts records these items at their fair market values on the date purchased, just as it does when purchasing individual assets.

Because Wheeler was willing to pay $400,000 for Valley Drug, there must have been other favorable, intangible factors worth approximately $80,000. These factors are called goodwill, and the entry to record the purchase of the drug store is:

Inventory	220,000	
Long-Term Operating Assets	110,000	
Other Assets	10,000	
Goodwill	80,000	
Liabilities		20,000
Cash		400,000
Purchased Valley Drug Store for $400,000.		

If Wheeler decides to use 40 years as the useful life of the goodwill, the yearly amortization entry is:

Amortization Expense, Goodwill	2,000	
Goodwill		2,000
To record annual straight-line amortization of goodwill ($80,000/40 years).		

Difficulties of Accounting for Intangible Assets: The Case of Brand Names

Brand names offer a good illustration of the difficulty associated with accounting for intangible assets. As shown in Exhibit 7-7, a brand name can be an extremely valuable asset. According to *Financial World* magazine, if you were to try to buy the worldwide rights to the exclusive use of the name "*Marlboro*," you would have to pay in excess of $44 billion. A valuable brand name such as "*Marlboro*" or "*Coca-Cola*" arises as an integral part of improving products, advertising, strategic expansion, and so forth. Accordingly, it is very difficult to identify which costs associated with brand name sales are normal business expenses and which actually contribute to brand name value. Therefore, even though a brand name might have significant economic value, it is unlikely that the value, or the costs associated with developing the brand name, could be separately and reliably identified.

As mentioned earlier in the chapter, a useful technique for valuing tangible long-term assets is to estimate the present value of the future cash flows expected to be

EXHIBIT 7-7

Ten Most Valuable Brands in the World—1996

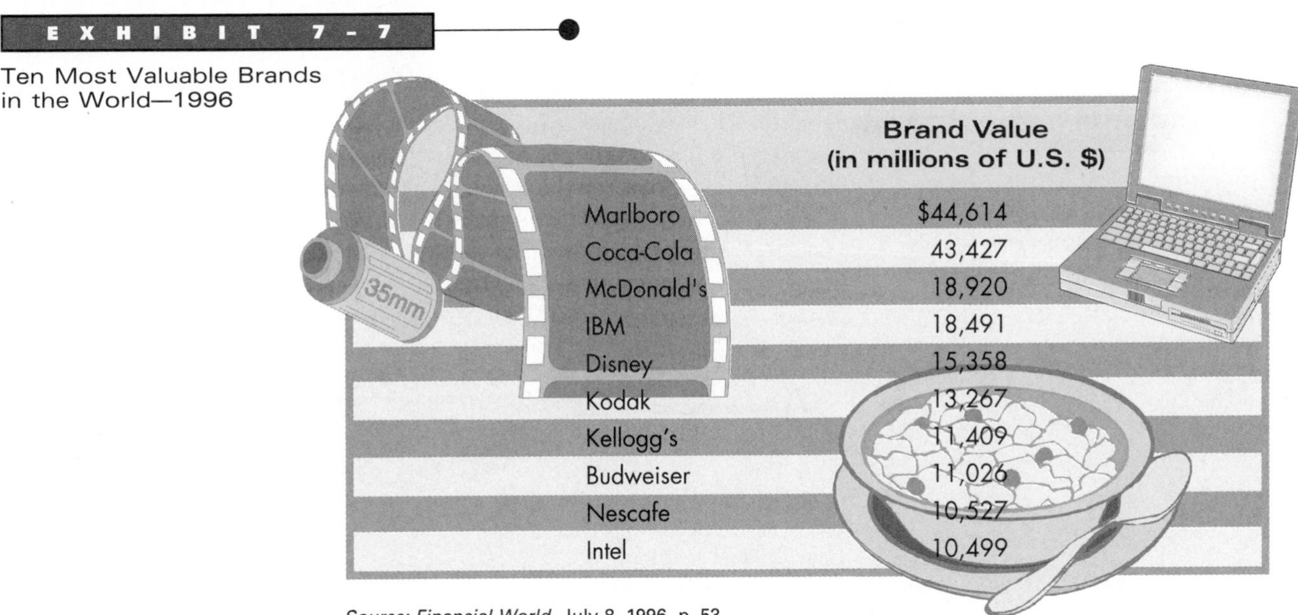

	Brand Value (in millions of U.S. $)
Marlboro	$44,614
Coca-Cola	43,427
McDonald's	18,920
IBM	18,491
Disney	15,358
Kodak	13,267
Kellogg's	11,409
Budweiser	11,026
Nescafe	10,527
Intel	10,499

Source: *Financial World,* July 8, 1996, p. 53.

associated with the asset. This technique is impractical for most intangible assets because the value of the intangible is inextricably connected with its use in conjunction with other assets. Thus, identifying the future cash flows associated with the intangible asset itself is nearly impossible.

In summary, the accounting for intangibles is still in its infancy. As accountants strive to meet the information demands of business decision makers, we will see a rapid development in the standards of accounting for intangibles.

TO SUMMARIZE

Intangible assets are long-term rights and privileges that have no physical substance but provide competitive advantages to owners. Common intangible assets are patents, franchises, licenses, and goodwill. The cost of an intangible asset is amortized over the economic life of the asset. Because it is often difficult to trace the development of specific intangible assets to specific costs, it is difficult to reliably recognize the assets in the financial statements.

7 *Understand why companies invest in other companies.*

WHY COMPANIES INVEST IN OTHER COMPANIES

Thus far in this chapter we have discussed investments in long-term operating assets—those assets used in a business to produce and distribute products and services. Sometimes organizations buy another type of long-term asset—the debt and equity securities of other companies. Companies invest in the debt and equity securities of other companies for a variety of reasons. A major reason is to earn a return on their excess cash. Most businesses are cyclical or seasonal; that is, their cash inflows and outflows vary significantly throughout the year. At certain times (particularly when inventories are being purchased), a company's cash supply is low. At other times (usually during or shortly after heavy selling seasons), there is excess cash on hand. A typical cash flow pattern for a retail firm is illustrated in Exhibit 7-8. The time line shows that the company has insufficient cash for inventory buildup for the Christmas rush, followed by large amounts of accounts receivable (from credit sales), and then an excess of cash immediately after Christmas.

When a company needs cash to meet current obligations, funds can be obtained through such means as borrowing from financial institutions or selling (factoring)

EXHIBIT 7-8 A Cash Flow Pattern

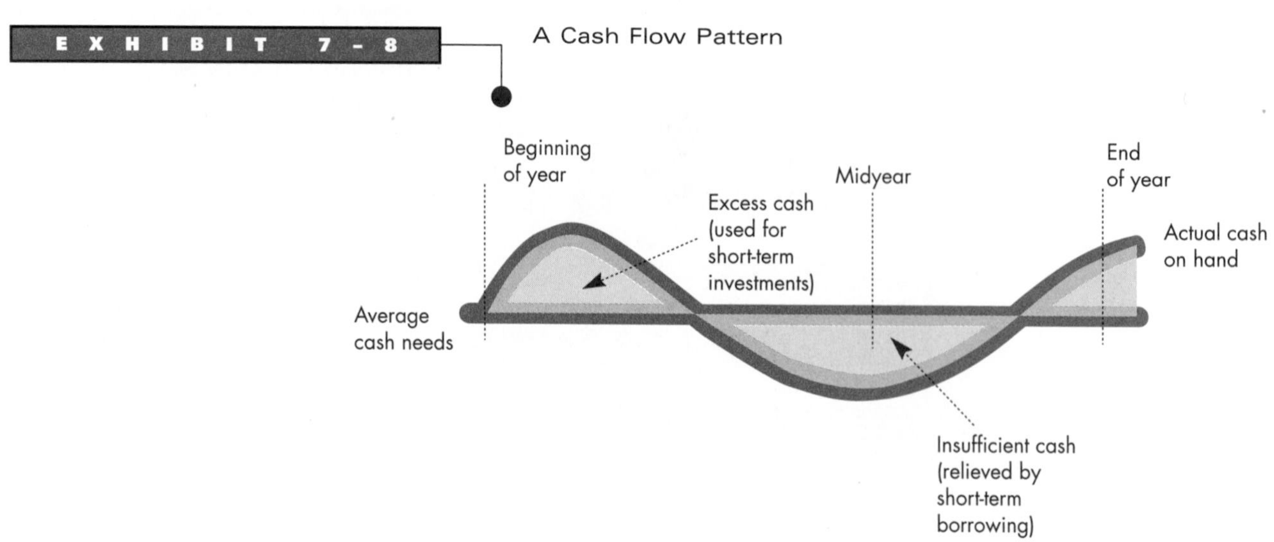

accounts receivable or other assets. During those periods of time when excess cash exists, firms usually prefer to invest that money and earn a return. A firm can place its money in a bank and earn a fixed return. However, most firms are not satisfied with the low interest rates offered by financial institutions and have turned to other investment alternatives. Investing in the stocks (equity) and bonds (debt) of other companies allows a firm to earn a higher rate of return by accepting a higher degree of risk. Consider an extreme example of a company whose sole purpose is to invest in the debt and equity securities of other companies. College Retirement Equities Fund (CREF), registered with the Securities and Exchange Commission as a management investment company, was formed to assist nonprofit educational and research organizations in providing retirement benefits to their employees. Eligible individuals contribute funds to CREF and CREF invests those funds. As of December 31, 1996, CREF had a portfolio of investments with a fair market value of over $83 billion. Its 1996 audited financial statements include over 80 pages detailing its debt and equity investments.

Firms invest in other companies for reasons other than to earn a return. The ability to ensure a supply of raw materials, to influence the board of directors, or to diversify their product offerings are additional reasons for companies to invest in other companies. For example, Coca-Cola Company owns 44 percent of Coca-Cola Enterprises and 51 percent of Coca-Cola Amatil Ltd. Co. These two companies bottle many of Coke's products, and Coca-Cola Company maintains a significant ownership to ensure that the bottling facilities remain available.

Rather than investing in the research and development required to develop a product or an area of expertise, many companies find it cheaper to purchase all or part of another company that has already expended the effort and the time to develop the desired product or know-how. As an example, to complement its existing software, Novell (a computer company specializing in networking) purchased WordPerfect and Quattro Pro, word-processing and spreadsheet software packages, respectively. This purchase then allowed Novell to assemble a menu of software packages to compete with Microsoft's Word, Excel, PowerPoint, and Access software packages. Novell's attempt to compete with Microsoft failed, and the company eventually sold WordPerfect to Corel.

(S T O P & T H I N K)

Can you think of additional reasons why companies would purchase interests in other companies?

TO SUMMARIZE

Companies invest in other companies for a variety of reasons. In most cases, the objective is to earn a return on the investment, either through the receipt of interest or dividends, or through an increase in the value of the investment. Firms also invest in other companies for the purpose of being able to influence the operating decisions of that company. In some cases, companies find it cheaper to buy another company to gain access to its assets rather than to expend the resources necessary to develop the assets on their own.

8 *Understand the different classifications for securities.*

CLASSIFYING A SECURITY

debt securities Financial instruments issued by a company that carry with them a promise of interest payments and the repayment of principal.

Two general types of securities are purchased by companies—debt securities and equity securities. **Debt securities** are financial instruments that carry with them the promise of interest payments and the repayment of the principal amount. Bonds are the most common type of debt security. Debt securities are issued by companies when the need for cash arises. These securities are often traded on public exchanges such as the New York Bond Exchange. Investors often prefer debt securities rather than equity securities because of the certainty of the income stream (interest) and of the relative safety (low risk) of debt as an investment. Investors in corporate debt securities have priority over investors in equity securities, both for the yearly interest payments and for the return of principal if the issuing corporation gets into financial difficulty. The most common type of debt securities are bonds issued by corporations (recall from Chapter 6 that a bond is typically issued in multiples of $1,000). Once the bonds are issued, ownership of the entire bond issuance, or just a portion, can change hands frequently.

equity securities (stock) Shares of ownership in a corporation that can change significantly in value and that provide for a return to investors in the form of dividends.

On the other hand, **equity securities** (or **stock**), also traded on public exchanges, represent actual ownership interest in a corporation. The owner of equity securities is allowed to vote on such corporate matters as executive compensation policies, who will serve on the board of directors of the corporation, and who will be the outside auditor. In addition to voting, the owner of stock often receives a return on that investment in the form of a dividend. A second type of return often accumulates to the stockholder as well—appreciation in stock price. Many investors invest in a company not for the dividend but for the potential increase in stock price. High-tech companies typically do not pay dividends, instead electing to funnel their profits back into the company. Investors know that their return in high-tech companies will come in the form of an increased stock price, not a dividend. With the potential increased stock price also comes a risk—the stock price could fall. Holders of debt securities, barring extreme financial difficulties by the issuer, will always receive the face amount of the bond upon maturity. Equity holders do not have that same promise. The value of stock can greatly increase or become worthless.

get connected
http://www.swcollege.com
net work

Do you follow the stock price of individual companies? How can you get a company's stock price history? You can find the current stock price for any company that is publicly traded on the major stock exchanges at www.quote.yahoo.com.

At what price is Microsoft (trading symbol MSFT) currently trading?

www.quote.yahoo.com

As mentioned earlier, investors can purchase both debt and equity securities with different goals in mind. Some may purchase to receive interest or dividend payments or to realize quick gains on price changes, while others may invest for more long-term reasons. Accounting standard setters have developed different methods of accounting for investments depending on the intentions of the holder of the security. Exhibit 7-9 outlines the major classifications of debt and equity securities.

Held-to-Maturity Securities

held-to-maturity security Debt security purchased by an investor with the intent of holding the security until it matures.

If a debt security is purchased with the intent of holding the security until it matures, it is classified as a **held-to-maturity security** and is accounted for using techniques similar to those discussed in Chapter 6 for the bond issuer. The investor and the issuer record the same amounts but in a different way. With bond liabilities, the face

EXHIBIT 7-9 Classifications of Debt and Equity Securities

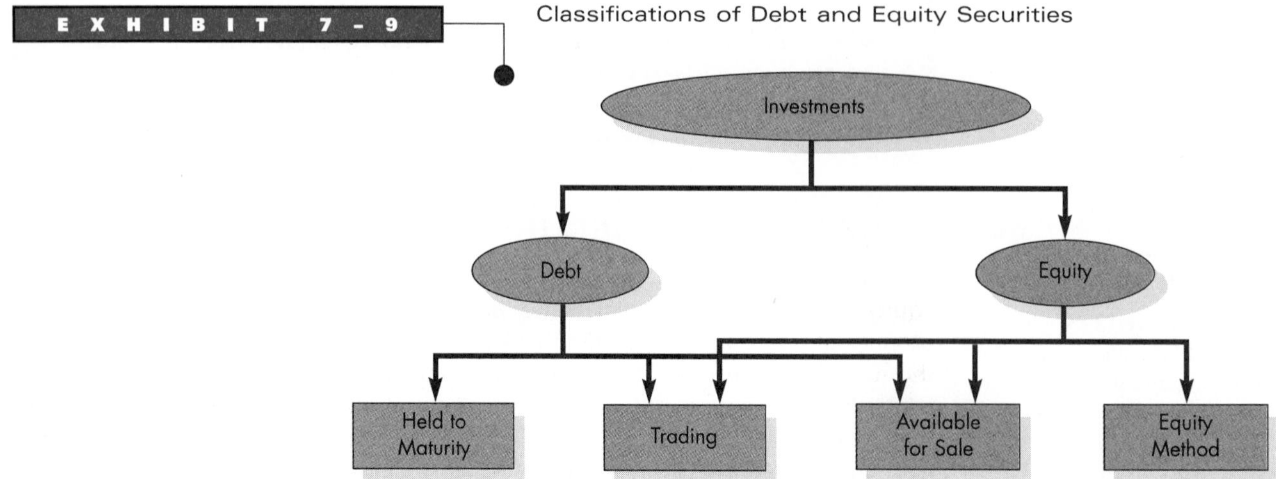

FYI

Equity securities cannot be classified as held-to-maturity securities.

value of the bonds is recorded in Bonds Payable, and a separate contra account is maintained for any discount or premium. Amortization of the discount or premium is then recorded in these contra accounts. With bond investments, the actual amount paid for the bonds (the cost of the asset), not the face value, is originally debited to the investment account. The amortization of any bond premium or discount is then recorded directly in the investment account. Thus, if you recall the accounting for Bonds Payable as presented in Chapter 6, you already know most of what there is to accounting for a bond investment that is expected to be held to maturity and those procedures are not repeated here. Note that equity securities cannot be classified as held-to-maturity; equity securities typically do not mature.

FYI

Debt securities cannot be classified as equity method securities.

Equity Method Securities

In the case of equity securities, accounting standard setters have determined that if securities are held with the objective being to significantly influence the operations of the investee, then the security should be accounted for using the **equity method**. The equity method records changes in the value of the investment as the net assets of the investee change. The assumption underlying the equity method is that if the investor can influence the operating decisions of the investee, then any change in the net assets of the investee should be reflected on the books of the investor. In determining what constitutes significant influence, the Accounting Principles Board suggests that, unless evidence exists to the contrary, ownership of at least 20 percent of the outstanding common stock of a company, but less than 50 percent, indicates the existence of significant influence. If ownership exceeds 50 percent, then a controlling interest is assumed and the accounting becomes far more complex. Generally, the parent company (the acquiring company) and the subsidiary company (the acquired company) are required to combine their financial statements into one set of statements as if they were one economic entity. Such combined statements are called **consolidated financial statements**. The preparation of consolidated financial statements is covered in advanced accounting courses.

equity method Method used to account for an investment in the stock of another company when significant influence can be imposed (presumed to exist when 20 to 50 percent of the outstanding voting stock is owned).

consolidated financial statements Statements that report the combined operating results, financial position, and cash flows of two or more legally separate but affiliated companies as if they were one economic entity.

Trading and Available-for-Sale Securities

In those instances where securities are not being held to maturity (in the case of debt) or to control or significantly influence an investee (in the case of equity), the Financial Accounting Standards Board has developed two other classes of securities—trading and available-for-sale. **Trading securities** are those debt and equity securities held with the intent of selling the securities should the need for cash arise or to realize gains arising from short-term changes in price. These types of securities are purchased simply to earn a return on excess cash. **Available-for-sale securities** are publicly traded securities that are classified as neither held-to-maturity nor trading (in the case of debt securities). In the case of equity securities, they represent securities that are not trading securities nor are they accounted for using the equity method.

trading securities Debt and equity securities purchased with the intent of selling them should the need for cash arise or to realize short-term gains.

available-for-sale securities Debt and equity securities not classified as trading, held-to-maturity, or equity method securities.

Why the Different Classifications?

Why are there different classifications for debt and equity securities? Why not simply classify all securities as "investments"? The reason for the distinction lies in the different treatments of accounting for changes in market value. In the case of securities classified as held-to-maturity, changes in the security's value between the date of purchase and the maturity date do not affect the amount to be received at maturity. That amount is fixed on the day the bonds are issued. Thus, temporary changes in the value of securities classified as held-to-maturity are not recognized on the investor's books. Similar reasoning applies to securities accounted for under the

BUSINESS ENVIRONMENT ESSAY

Following the Stock Market Stocks are sold in a variety of markets in the same way that bonds are sold. Original issues of stocks are usually sold by an investment banking group, referred to as the underwriters. After stocks are originally sold, they are traded in the market place, either on the New York Stock Exchange, the American Stock Exchange, regional market exchanges, or in the over-the-counter market. A selected portion of stocks traded on the New York Stock Exchange on Friday, February 20, 1998, is listed here as they were reported in *The Wall Street Journal* on Monday, February 23, 1998. The quotations show the following information for each stock: (1) 52-week high and low, (2) name of the company, (3) the trading symbol for that company, (4) the current dividend, (5) the yield percentage in relation to the purchase price, (6) the price-earnings ratio, (7) the volume of sales for that day, (8) the high, low, and closing prices for that day, and (9) the net change from the closing price of the previous day's trading. To illustrate how to read the quotation, the information for AT&T common stock is as follows: The 52-week high was 66⅜ ($66.375), and the low was 30¾ ($30.75). The annual dividend rate is $1.32, with a current yield of 2.1 percent. The current price is 22 times the annual earnings. A total of 43,270,000 shares were traded on Friday, February 20, 1998, with the high price for the day being 63 13/16 ($63.8125) and the low price being 61¾ ($61.75). The stock closed for the day at 62 ($62.00), which was 1⅝ ($1.625) lower than the close on Thursday, February 19, 1998.

NEW YORK STOCK EXCHANGE COMPOSITE TRANSACTIONS

Quotations as of 5 p.m. Eastern Time
Friday, February 20, 1998

	52 Weeks Hi	Lo		Stock	Sym	Div	Yld %	PE	Vol 100s	Hi	Lo	Close		Net Chg
				-A-A-A-										
	24¾	21½	♣	AMLI Resdntl	AML	1.76	7.8	16	664	22½	22⅜	22½		...
	56 11/16	33⅛	♣	AMP	AMP	1.08f	2.5	21	3076	43⅝	42⅞	43 7/16	+	3/16
	136½	78½		AMR	AMR		...	11	22769	128 11/16	122	123⅞	−	5 13/16
	51¼	40⅞	♣	ARCO Chm	RCM	2.80	6.0	40	229	46 9/16	46⅛	46 9/16		...
	37⅝	19		ASA	ASA	80m	3.8	...	904	21 13/16	21	21 3/16	−	¾
	66⅜	30¾		AT&T	T	1.32	2.1	22	43270	63 13/16	61¾	62	−	1⅝
▲	46⅝	29¼		AXA UAP	AXA	.65p	...	...	1555	48 1/16	47⅛	47½	+	2⅛
s	32⅜	9⅝		AamesFnl	AAM	.13	1.0	13	1295	12 9/16	12 3/16	12 7/16	+	5/16
	26 15/16	24½		AbbeyNtl		2.19	8.2	...	28	26⅝	26 9/16	26⅝	−	⅛
	75¾	52⅛		AbbotLab	ABT	1.20f	1.6	28	14846	74⅜	73¼	74¼	+	½
	39	12¾		Abercrombie A	ANF		...	...	4277	35¾	34⅛	35 5/16	−	⅜
	21	11½		Abitibi g	ABY	.40	...	...	838	14 1/16	13⅝	13⅞	+	¼
	28⅝	17¾	♣	AcceptIns	AIF		...	11	412	24 7/16	24⅛	24⅜	−	⅛
	32	15¾		AccuStaff	ASI		...	30	6471	29 5/16	28½	28 15/16	+	1/16

Source: *The Wall Street Journal*, February 23, 1998.

equity method. These securities are purchased, not with the intent of selling them in the future, but instead to be able to exercise influence over a corporation. Again, temporary changes in these securities are not recognized on the investor's books.

Trading securities are purchased with the intent of earning a return—through interest or dividends and through short-term resale of the security. Firms are required to recognize these two types of returns on the income statement. For example, assume that XYZ Co. purchases 100 shares of ABC Inc. stock for $5 per share. During the year, ABC pays a $1 dividend per share and the value of the stock increases to $7 per share. XYZ will recognize, as income, $100 in dividend income as well as $200 in unrealized market gains. While the $100 in dividends was actually received, the $200 gain was not. The securities would have to have been sold in order to actually receive the $200 increase in value. Recognizing this gain, even though it was not realized through an arm's-length transaction, represents a major departure from the historical cost principle that has guided accounting for centuries. In 1994, the FASB determined that because the fair market value of many debt and equity securities can be objectively determined (via market quotes) and easily sold (one phone call to a broker), it would be appropriate to include any unrealized gains or losses on changes in value of trading securities on the income statement.

FYI

Many companies avoid the issue of what to include on the income statement by classifying all their investment securities as being available-for-sale. IBM and Microsoft are examples of companies who use this classification scheme.

Changes in the value of securities classified as available-for-sale are recorded on the balance sheet. However, no gain or loss is realized on the income statement. Instead, an adjustment is made directly to a stockholders' equity account—Unrealized Increase/Decrease in Value of Available-for-Sale Securities Equity. The obvious question is "Why aren't changes in the value of these securities reflected on the income statement?" The answer lies in the intent behind holding the securities. With trading securities, it is probable that the securities will be sold sooner rather than later. We cannot make that same assumption with available-for-sale securities. We are less certain as to the likelihood of their being sold. Because of this uncertainty surrounding when the change in value will actually be realized, the FASB elected to go around the income statement in reporting changes in value relating to available-for-sale securities. Exhibit 7-10 summarizes the classification and disclosure issues relating to investments in debt and equity securities.

EXHIBIT 7-10

Classification and Disclosure of Securities

Classification of Securities	Types of Securities	Disclosed at	Reporting of Temporary Changes in Fair Value
Trading	Debt and equity	Fair value	Income statement
Available-for-sale	Debt and equity	Fair value	Stockholders' equity
Held-to-maturity	Debt	Amortized cost	Not recognized
Equity method	Equity	Cost adjusted for changes in net assets of investee	Not recognized

TO SUMMARIZE

Securities are classified depending upon the intent of management. If management's intent is to hold the investment until maturity (debt) or to influence the decisions of an investee (equity), then the held-to-maturity (debt) and equity method (equity) classifications are appropriate. If the securities are being held for other reasons, then management may classify them as either trading or available-for-sale. The importance of classification becomes apparent when accounting for changes in value.

9 *Account for the purchase, recognition of revenue, and sale of trading and available-for-sale securities.*

ACCOUNTING FOR TRADING AND AVAILABLE-FOR-SALE SECURITIES

There are four issues associated with accounting for securities: (1) accounting for the purchase, (2) accounting for the revenue earned, (3) accounting for the sale, and (4) accounting for the changes in value. The first three of these issues are fairly straightforward and are presented in this section. Accounting for changes in the value of securities is discussed in the following section. The time line in Exhibit 7-11 illustrates the important business issues associated with buying and selling investment securities.

EXHIBIT 7-11 Time Line of Business Issues Involved with Buying and Selling Investment Securities

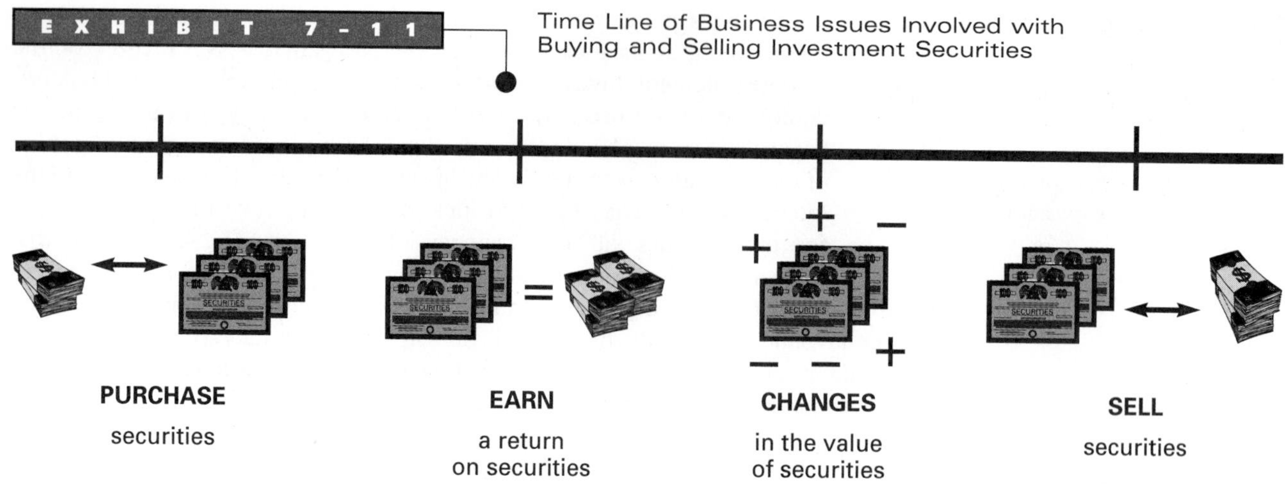

Accounting for the Purchase of Securities

Investments in securities, like all other assets, are recorded at cost when purchased. This is the case whether the security being purchased is debt or equity or whether it is being held with the intent to sell it quickly or hold it for the long term. Cost includes the market price of the security plus any extra expenditures required in making the purchase (such as a stockbroker's fee).

To illustrate the accounting for securities, we will use the following information throughout the chapter. On July 1, 1999, Far Side Incorporated purchased the following securities:

Security	Type	Classification	Cost (including broker's fees)
1	Debt	Trading	$ 5,000
2	Equity	Trading	27,500
3	Debt	Available-for-sale	17,000
4	Equity	Available-for-sale	9,200

The initial entry to record the investments is as follows:

Investment in Trading Securities	32,500	
Investment in Available-for-Sale Securities.	26,200	
Cash		58,700

Though investments in securities are all recorded at cost, each of the four classifications of securities is accounted for differently subsequent to purchase. As a result, separate accounts are used to record the initial purchase. Securities 1 and 2 were purchased by management with the intent of earning a return on their investment and selling the securities should the need for cash arise. Therefore, those securities are classified as "trading." Securities 3 and 4 were also purchased to earn a return on excess cash but have been classified by management as "available-for-sale." While the journal entry illustrated above combines all securities of the same classification into one account, subsidiary records will be kept for each individual security purchased.

Accounting for the Return Earned on an Investment

While a firm invests in the debt or equity of another firm with the intent of earning a return on its investment, how that return is accounted for varies depending on the classification of the investment. Recall from Chapter 6 that when debt securities are sold, a premium or discount can arise as a result of differences between the stated rate of interest and the market rate of interest. The resulting premium or discount must then be amortized over the life of the investment, thereby affecting the amount of interest expense recorded by the issuer. Theoretically, the purchaser of that debt security must also account for the difference between the purchase price and the eventual maturity value. However, we are assuming in the discussion that follows that for debt securities classified as "trading" or as "available-for-sale," the time for which the investor anticipates holding the securities is not long enough for any amortization of premium or discount to materially affect interest expense.

With this caveat in mind, the accounting for dividends and interest received on trading and available-for-sale securities becomes relatively straightforward. Cash received relating to interest and dividends is credited to Interest Revenue and Dividend Revenue, respectively. Interest earned but not yet received or dividends that have been declared but not paid are also recorded as revenue with a corresponding receivable. Continuing our example, interest and dividends received during 1999 relating to our securities investments were as follows:

Security	Interest	Dividends
1	$225	
2		$825
3	850	
4		644

The appropriate journal entry to record the receipt of interest and dividends is:

Cash	2,544	
Interest Revenue..............................		1,075
Dividend Revenue..............................		1,469

Accounting for the Sale of Securities

Suppose that Far Side sells all of its investment in Security 2 for $28,450 on October 31, 1999. As Security 2 was purchased for $27,500, the security has increased in value and that increase must be recorded. The journal entry to record the sale is:

Cash..	28,450	
Investment in Trading Securities.......................		27,500
Realized Gain on Sale of Trading Securities		950

If Security 2 had been sold for less then $27,500, a loss would have been recorded. If a broker's fee had been charged on the transaction, the fee would reduce the amount of cash received and decrease the gain recognized. If the broker's fee were to exceed $950, a loss would be recorded on the books of the seller.

At the end of the accounting period, any gain or loss on the sale of securities must be included on the income statement. In the above example, the "Realized Gain on Sale of Securities" would be included with Other Revenues and Expenses

BUSINESS ENVIRONMENT ESSAY

Following the Bond Market Bonds are sold in a variety of markets. Original issues of bonds, both industrial and governmental, are usually sold by an investment banking group referred to as the underwriters. Bonds are then traded in the marketplace, either on the New York Bond Exchange or over-the-counter through brokers who make a market for a particular company's bonds. Following is an excerpt from *The Wall Street Journal* showing some composite information regarding bond transactions, as well as price quotations involving specific bond issues. The composite information gives investors a sense of the overall activity level of the bond market in relation to previous years. In this case, it shows that sales through February 20, 1998, were lower than in either 1997 or 1996 for comparable time periods. Using a representative sample of bonds trading in the marketplace, it also gives the high and low prices for 1998 and 1997.

The listings for specific bonds give the stated interest rate; the year of maturity; the current yield (effective rate); the sales volume for that trading date (with 000s omitted); the closing price for the day; and the net change from the closing price on the previous day that the bond market was open. Looking at the IBM bond issue listed, we can deduce the following: the bonds have a stated interest rate of 6 3/8 percent and mature in 2000. The current yield (effective interest) on the bonds is 6.3 percent. Trading volume for the day was $106,000 face value, and the market price of the bonds at the end of the day was 101 1/2 (101.5) percent of face value, an increase of 1/8 point from the previous day's closing price. Thus, each $1,000 bond was selling for $1,015.00.

Source: *The Wall Street Journal,* February 23, 1998.

NEW YORK EXCHANGE BONDS

Quotations as of 4 p.m. Eastern Time
Friday, February 20, 1998

Volume $13,677,000

SALES SINCE JANUARY 1
(000 omitted)

1998	1997	1996
$597,262	$932,448	$1,019,447

	Domestic Fri.	Domestic Thu.	All Issues Fri.	All Issues Thu.
Issues traded	252	251	261	260
Advances	91	94	97	95
Declines	108	98	111	103
Unchanged	53	59	53	62
New highs	12	6	14	6
New lows	1	1	1	1

Dow Jones Bond Averages

-1997- High	-1997- Low	-1998- High	-1998- Low		---1998--- Close	---1998--- Chg.	---1998--- % Yld	--1997-- Close	--1997-- Chg.
105.13	101.09	105.48	104.92	20 Bonds	105.21	+0.04	6.81	103.48	−0.07
102.89	97.64	103.02	102.19	10 Utilities	102.58	+0.07	6.91	100.24	−0.10
105.13	101.09	105.48	104.92	10 Industrials	105.21	+0.04	6.81	103.48	−0.07

Bonds	Cur Yld	Vol	Close		Net Chg.
GMA dc6s11	6.3	65	95	−	⅛
GMA zr12	...	17	380½	+	2⅜
GMA zr15	...	12	320⅛	−	1¼
Genesc 10⅜03	10.0	5	103⅝	−	1
GenesisH 9⅝05	9.2	1	106½		...
GrandCas 10⅛03	9.3	150	109	−	¼
Hallwd 7s00	7.3	27	96		...
Hills 12½03	14.6	232	85⅝	+	⅛
Hilton 5s06	cv	26	105½	−	1½
HomeDpt 3¼01	cv	34	149½		...
ITT Cp 7⅜15	7.7	10	95⅝	+	⅛
ITT Cp 7¾25	8.1	280	96¼		...
ITT 8⅝03	8.5	5	105	−	1½
IllBel 7⅝06	7.5	2	101⅝	−	⅜
IntgHlt 6s03	cv	3	112	+	4¾
IBM 6⅜00	6.3	106	101½	+	⅛
NatData 5s03	cv	1	102½		...
NStl 8⅜06	8.3	25	101¼	+	¾
Natnsbk 8½99	8.3	10	103	+	1
NETelTel 4⅝99	4.7	5	98½	+	⅜
NETelTel 5⅝00	5.7	100	100¼	+	¼
NETelTel 6⅛06	6.2	2	98½	−	⅜
NETelTel 7⅜07	7.3	5	101⅜		...
NETelTel 6⅝08	6.4	15	100	+	⅝
NETelTel 7⅞22	7.5	5	105⅝	+	1⅜
NETelTel 6⅞23	6.9	10	100⅜	−	⅝
NJBTl 7¼11	7.2	20	101¼	−	⅛
NYTel 7½09	7.4	2	101⅜	−	⅜
NYTel 7⅜11	7.3	100	101	−	⅛
NYTel 7⅞17	7.6	50	103	−	⅛
NYTel 7s25	7.0	240	100		...
NYTel 7s33	7.1	45	99¼	+	½
Noram 6s12	cv	10	95	+	1
Novacr 5½2000	cv	3	95½	−	⅛
OcciP 10⅜01	9.1	5	111½	+	⅛
OcciP 11⅝19	10.0	8	111⅝	−	⅛
OffDep zr07	...	16	74	+	1
OffDep zr08	...	37	66		...
OhBIT 7½11	7.4	49	101¼	−	⅜
OreStl 11s03	10.0	12	110⅛	+	⅛
Oryx 7½14	cv	35	100½	+	¼
PacBell 6¼05	6.2	253	101⅝	−	⅛
PacBell 6⅞23	6.8	5	101¼	−	¾
PacBell 7⅛33	7.3	40	103⅜	+	⅜
ParkElc 5½06	cv	15	99		...
ParkerD 5½04	cv	6	104½	−	1

realized gains and losses Gains and losses resulting from the sale of securities in an arm's-length transaction.

on the income statement. Note the term "realized." **Realized gains and losses** indicate that an arm's-length transaction has occurred and the securities have actually been sold. This distinction is important because in the next section we focus on accounting for unrealized gains and losses—those gains and losses that occur while a security is still being held and no arm's-length transaction has taken place.

TO SUMMARIZE

Investments in debt and equity securities are recorded at cost, which includes the fair value of the security plus any other expenditures required to purchase the security. When purchased, the security is classified into one of four categories: held-to-maturity, equity method, trading, or available-for-sale securities. Revenues from securities take the form of interest, dividends, or gains or losses when selling the securities and are included under Other Revenues and Expenses on the income statement.

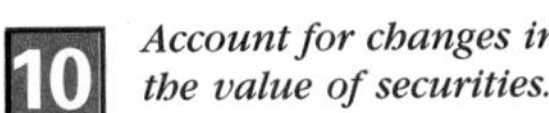

10 *Account for changes in the value of securities.*

ACCOUNTING FOR CHANGES IN THE VALUE OF SECURITIES

Investments in debt and equity securities are initially recorded at cost. If the value of a security changes after it is purchased, should that change in value be recorded on the investor's books? As stated previously in the chapter, the answer is "it depends." It depends on management's intent regarding that security. In the case of trading and available-for-sale securities, changes in market value are recorded on the books of the investor. For held-to-maturity securities and equity method securities, changes in value are not recorded unless they are considered permanent. To illustrate the accounting for changes in value of securities, we will continue the Far Side example. On December 31, 1999, the following market values were available:[1]

Security	Classification	Historical Cost	Market Value (December 31, 1999)
1	Trading	$ 5,000	$ 5,200
3	Available-for-sale	17,000	16,700
4	Available-for-sale	9,200	9,250

Changes in the Value of Trading Securities

At the end of 1999, Far Side computes the market value of its trading securities portfolio and compares it to the historical cost of the portfolio. In this instance, market value is $200 greater than historical cost. The journal entry to record this increase in value is:

Market Adjustment—Trading Securities	200	
Unrealized Gain on Trading Securities—Income		200

unrealized gains and losses Gains and losses resulting from changes in the value of securities that are still being held.

This journal entry recognizes the $200 increase in the value of the trading securities and records the unrealized gain on the income statement. **Unrealized gains and losses** indicate that the securities have changed in value and are still being

1. Remember that Security 2 was sold on October 31, 1999.

Market Adjustment—Trading Securities An account used to track the difference between the historical cost and the market value of a company's portfolio of trading securities.

held. This journal entry also introduces a new account—**Market Adjustment—Trading Securities**. This account is combined with the trading securities account and reported on the balance sheet. Thus, the balance sheet will reflect the trading securities at their fair market value. Why not adjust the trading securities account directly instead of creating this market adjustment account? The reason is that the use of a valuation account, Market Adjustment—Trading Securities, allows a record of historical cost to be maintained. With this approach, a company can easily determine realized and unrealized gains. Perhaps the most important reason for keeping a record of historical cost is that, for tax purposes, only realized gains and losses are relevant. Other decisions made within a firm also rely on this historical cost information.

Changes in the Value of Available-for-Sale Securities

A market adjustment account is also employed when adjusting available-for-sale securities to their fair market value. However, the change in value is not recorded on the income statement but is instead recorded in the account "Unrealized Increase/Decrease in Value of Available-for-Sale Securities—Equity." This account is disclosed in the stockholders' equity section of the balance sheet and its balance is carried forward from year to year. To illustrate, the available-for-sale portfolio of Far Side has a fair market value of $25,950 at year-end and a historical cost of $26,200. The appropriate adjustment is:

Unrealized Increase/Decrease in Value of Available-for-Sale Securities—Equity	250	
Market Adjustment—Available-for-Sale Securities		250

This journal entry adjusts the portfolio of available-for-sale securities to its fair market value at year-end and records the difference in the equity account.

Subsequent Changes in Value

Assume that no securities were bought or sold by Far Side Inc. during 2000. At the end of 2000, its portfolio of securities had the following fair market values:

Security	Classification	Historical Cost	Market Value (December 31, 2000)
1	Trading	$ 5,000	$ 4,850
3	Available-for-sale	17,000	16,900
4	Available-for-sale	9,200	9,150

The value of the trading securities has declined to $4,850. Since the market adjustment account relating to trading securities should reflect the difference between historical cost and market, an entry is made to adjust the balance in Market Adjustment—Trading Securities from its previous $200 debit balance to the required $150 credit balance ($5,000 − $4,850). Where did this $200 debit balance come from? It came from the adjusting entry made on December 31, 1999. Remember that the market adjustment account is a real (balance sheet) account and is not closed at the end of an accounting period. Its balance carries forward from year to year. The required adjusting entry is:

Unrealized Loss on Trading Securities—Income.	350	
Market Adjustment—Trading Securities		350

When this entry is posted, the Market Adjustment—Trading Securities T-account will appear as follows:

Market Adjustment—
Trading Securities

12/31/99	200		
		Adjustment	350
		12/31/00	150

CAUTION

The amount of the adjustment for the current period depends on the balance in the market adjustment account. Don't forget to factor that balance into your calculations.

The $150 credit balance will be netted against the $5,000 balance in the trading securities account and disclosed on the balance sheet as "Investment in Trading Securities (net)" for $4,850. The $350 unrealized loss would be included in the current period's net income and reported on the income statement. This adjustment procedure ensures that changes in the value of the trading securities portfolio are reflected in the period in which those changes in value occurred.

A similar procedure would be employed in valuing the available-for-sale securities portfolio, with the exception being that the stockholders' equity account is used instead of the income statement account. For Far Side, the market value of the available-for-sale securities portfolio is $26,050. In comparing this to the historical cost of $26,200, a $150 credit balance in the market adjustment account is required. Take a moment and read the information again. An adjustment to get to a $150 credit balance is required—not an adjustment *of* $150. Given the previous credit balance in Market Adjustment—Available-for-Sale Securities of $250, the following adjusting entry is required:

Market Adjustment—Available-for-Sale Securities	100	
Unrealized Increase/Decrease in Value of Available-for-Sale Securities—Equity		100

Once this entry is posted, Market Adjustment—Available-for-Sale Securities will have the required $150 credit balance as follows:

Market Adjustment—
Available-for-Sale Securities

		12/31/99	250
Adjustment	100		
		12/31/00	150

When individual securities from a portfolio are sold, a realized gain or loss is recognized for the difference between the original cost of the securities and the selling price, without regard to previous adjustments made to a market adjustment account. At the end of the period, the cost of the remaining securities is compared to the fair market value of the remaining securities, and the market adjustment account is updated to account for the difference.

TO SUMMARIZE

When the value of a trading or available-for-sale security changes, that change is reflected on the balance sheet using a market adjustment account. For trading securities, the unrealized gain or loss is reflected on the income statement for the period. For available-for-sale securities, the unrealized increase or decrease is recorded in a stockholders' equity account.

REVIEW OF LEARNING OBJECTIVES

1 Identify the two major categories of long-term operating assets: property, plant, and equipment and intangible assets. There are two major types of operating assets. Property, plant, and equipment are long-lived, tangible assets acquired for use in a business. This category includes land, buildings, machinery, equipment, and furniture. Intangible assets are long-lived assets used in a business, but they have no physical substance. Common intangible assets are patents, licenses, franchises, and goodwill.

2 Understand the factors important in deciding whether to acquire a long-term operating asset. The value of long-term operating assets stems from the fact that they help companies generate future cash flows. Capital budgeting is the name given to the process whereby decisions are made about acquiring long-term operating assets. Capital budgeting involves comparing the cost of the asset to the value of the expected cash inflows, after adjusting for the time value of money. The value of a long-term operating asset can disappear instantly if events lower the expectations about the future cash flows generated by the asset.

3 Record the acquisition of property, plant, and equipment through a simple purchase and as part of the purchase of several assets at once. When purchased, property, plant, and equipment is recorded at cost, which includes all expenditures associated with acquiring them and getting them ready for their intended use.

If two or more assets are acquired in a "basket" purchase, the relative fair market value method is used to assign costs to individual assets. If one company buys all the assets of another company, the excess of the purchase price over the aggregate fair value of the acquired net assets is recorded as goodwill, an intangible asset.

4 Compute straight-line and units-of-production depreciation expense for plant and equipment. Depreciation is the process of allocating the cost of plant and equipment to expense in the periods that are benefited from the use of the asset. The two most common and simple methods of depreciation are straight-line and units-of-production.

The straight-line method is the only method that results in the same amount of depreciation for each full year. The units-of-production method allocates cost over the useful life measured in units of output or usage. Both methods require salvage value to be subtracted from the original cost in computing depreciation expense.

The units-of-production method is also used with natural resources such as coal, gravel, and timber. Depletion expense for a year is computed by first computing a depletion rate by dividing the cost assigned to the natural resource by the estimated number of remaining units to be extracted. This depletion rate is multiplied by the number of units extracted for the year to arrive at the dollar amount of depletion for the year.

5 Record the discarding and selling of property, plant, and equipment. Property, plant, and equipment may be disposed of by discarding, selling, or exchanging. When an asset is sold, a gain is reported if the sales price exceeds the book value, or a loss is reported if the book value exceeds the sales price.

6 Account for the acquisition and amortization of intangible assets and understand the special difficulties associated with accounting for intangibles. Intangible assets are rights and privileges that are long-lived, are not held for resale, have no physical substance, and usually provide competitive advantages for the owner. Common examples are patents, franchises, licenses, and goodwill. Patents acquired by purchase are recorded at cost and amortized over the shorter of their economic life or their 17-year legal life. Research and development costs incurred internally in a firm are expensed as incurred even if they may result in the development of a legal patent. Franchises and licenses are exclusive rights to perform services or sell a product in certain geographical areas. The cost of acquiring a franchise or license is recorded as an asset, which is then amortized over its useful or legal life, whichever is shorter. Goodwill occurs when a business is purchased and the purchase price exceeds the total value of the identifiable assets less outstanding liabilities assumed. The excess purchase price that cannot be allocated to specific assets is called goodwill and is recorded as an intangible asset. Goodwill is amortized as an expense over its expected life, not to exceed 40 years. Because it is often difficult to trace the development of specific intangible assets to specific costs, it is difficult to reliably recognize the assets in the financial statements.

7 **Understand why companies invest in other companies.** Companies invest in the debt and equity securities of other companies for a variety of reasons. The primary reason these investments occur is to earn a return on invested funds. Bonds and stocks offer a higher potential return for investors than the interest rates offered by government-backed securities or savings rates offered by banks and other financial institutions. Along with the potential for higher returns comes the prospect of higher risks; these investments provide the possibility of earning little return or even losing money. Besides earning a return, companies invest in the securities of other companies for additional reasons. These reasons include establishing a long-term business relationship, ensuring an adequate supply of raw materials, ensuring a sales network for inventory, or gaining access to developed assets, such as software programs or oil reserves.

8 **Understand the different classifications for securities.** Debt and equity securities are classified according to management's intent in holding the securities. If the securities are being held for the short-term with the intent to sell the securities if cash is needed, the securities are accounted for as "trading" securities. If debt securities are expected to be held until they mature, the securities are classified as "held-to-maturity." If equity securities are purchased with the intent of being able to significantly influence the operating decisions of the investee (ownership of between 20 and 50 percent of outstanding common stock typically reflects the ability to significantly influence), the securities are accounted for using the equity method. Debt and equity securities not classified as trading, held-to-maturity, or equity method are classified as "available-for-sale." The importance of these distinctions comes into play when changes in the value of the securities are accounted for by the investee.

9 **Account for the purchase, recognition of revenue, and sale of trading and available-for-sale securities.** Investments in securities are initially recorded at cost. Cost includes the fair market value of the securities as well as broker's fees. For trading and available-for-sale securities, dividends or interest earned are recorded as revenue. For held-to-maturity securities and equity method securities, the recognition of revenue is more complex. When a security is sold, regardless of its classification, its carrying (book) value is compared to the selling price to determine any realized gain or loss on the sale. These realized gains and losses are disclosed on the income statement with Other Revenues and Expenses.

10 **Account for changes in the value of securities.** When the market value of a security changes, the classification of the security determines if the change in value is recorded on the financial statements. With held-to-maturity securities and equity method securities, since the intent of management is to hold these types of securities for long periods of time, changes in market value are not recognized. For securities classified as trading, any unrealized gains and losses are recognized on the income statement. A market adjustment account is offset against Investment in Trading Securities to value the securities at their fair market value on the balance sheet. Available-for-sale securities are also adjusted to fair market value using a market adjustment account. However, the offset is recorded in a stockholders' equity account.

KEY TERMS AND CONCEPTS

amortization 300
available-for-sale securities 307
basket purchase 292
book value 293
capital budgeting 290
consolidated financial statements 307
debt securities 305
depletion 297
depreciation 293
equity method 307
equity securities (stock) 306
franchise 302
goodwill 293
held-to-maturity securities 306
intangible assets 289
license 302
Market Adjustment—Trading Securities 314
natural resources 297
patent 301
property, plant, and equipment 289
realized gains and losses 313
salvage value 293
straight-line depreciation method 294
time value of money 290
trading securities 307
units-of-production method 294
unrealized gains and losses 313

REVIEW PROBLEMS

Property, Plant, and Equipment

Swift Motor Lines is a trucking company that hauls crude oil in the Rocky Mountain states. It presently has 20 trucks. The following information relates to a single truck:

a. Date truck was purchased, July 1, 1997.
b. Cost of truck:

Truck	$125,000
Paint job	3,000
Sales tax	7,000

c. Estimated useful life of truck, 120,000 miles.
d. Estimated salvage value of truck, $27,000.
e. 1999 expenditures on truck:
   (1) $6,000 on new tires and regular maintenance.
   (2) On Jan. 1, spent $44,000 to completely rework the truck's engine; increased the total life to 200,000 miles but left expected salvage value unchanged.
f. Miles driven:

1997	11,000
1998	24,000
1999 (after reworking of engine)	20,000
2000	14,000

Required:

Record journal entries to account for the following. (Use the units-of-production depreciation method.)

1. The purchase of the truck.
2. The expenditures on the truck during 1999.
3. Depreciation expense for:
   a. 1997
   b. 1998
   c. 1999
   d. 2000

Solution

1. Truck Purchase

The cost of the truck includes both the amount paid for it and all costs incurred to get it in working condition. In this case, the cost includes both the paint job and the sales tax. Thus, the entry to record the purchase is:

Truck	135,000	
Cash		135,000
Purchased truck for cash.		

2. Expenditures

The expenditure of $6,000 is an ordinary expenditure and is expensed in the current year. The engine overhaul is capitalized. The entries are:

Repairs and Maintenance Expense	6,000	
Cash		6,000
Recorded purchase of new tires and regular maintenance on truck.		
Truck	44,000	
Cash		44,000
Recorded major overhaul to truck's engine.		

3. Depreciation Expense

The formula for units-of-production depreciation on the truck is:

$$\frac{\text{Cost} - \text{Salvage value}}{\text{Total miles expected to be driven}} \times \frac{\text{Number of miles}}{\text{driven in any year}} = \text{Depreciation expense}$$

Journal entries and calculations are as follows:

a. 1997:

Depreciation Expense	9,900	
Accumulated Depreciation, Truck		9,900
Recorded depreciation expense for 1997.		

$$\frac{\$135{,}000 - \$27{,}000}{120{,}000 \text{ miles}} \times 11{,}000 \text{ miles} = \$9{,}900 \text{ or } \$0.90 \text{ per mile} \times 11{,}000 \text{ miles}$$

b. 1998:

Depreciation Expense	21,600	
Accumulated Depreciation, Truck		21,600
Recorded depreciation expense for 1998.		

$$\frac{\$135{,}000 - \$27{,}000}{120{,}000 \text{ miles}} \times 24{,}000 \text{ miles} = \$21{,}600 \text{ or } \$0.90 \text{ per mile} \times 24{,}000 \text{ miles}$$

c. 1999:

Depreciation Expense	14,600	
Accumulated Depreciation, Truck		14,600
Recorded depreciation expense for 1999.		

$$\frac{\$135{,}000 - \$9{,}900 - \$21{,}600 + \$44{,}000 - \$27{,}000}{\substack{165{,}000 \text{ miles} \\ (200{,}000 - 11{,}000 - 24{,}000)}} \times 20{,}000 \text{ miles} = \$14{,}600 \text{ or } \$0.73^{*} \text{ per mile} \times 20{,}000 \text{ miles}$$

*Rounded to the nearest cent.

d. 2000:

Depreciation Expense	10,220	
Accumulated Depreciation, Truck		10,220
Recorded depreciation expense for 2000.		

$0.73 × 14,000 miles = $10,220

Investments in Debt and Equity Securities

On January 1, 2000, Schultz Inc. purchased the following securities:

Security	Type	Classification	Cost
1	Debt	Trading	$2,500
2	Debt	Trading	1,500
3	Equity	Trading	1,750
4	Debt	Available-for-sale	4,300
5	Equity	Available-for-sale	2,750

On March 31, one-half of Security 2 was sold for $900. During the year, interest and dividends were received as follows:

Security	Interest	Dividends
1	$200	
2	85	
3		none
4	435	
5		$200

The following fair market values are available on December 31, 2000. Schultz had no balance in its market adjustment accounts on January 1, 2000.

Security	Market Value
1	$2,400
2	950
3	1,600
4	4,250
5	2,900

Required: Record all necessary journal entries to account for these investments during 2000.

Solution: To account for these investments, four events must be accounted for:

1. The initial purchase on January 1.
2. The sale of one-half of Security 2 on March 31.
3. The receipt of interest and dividends during the year.
4. The changes in value as of December 31.

1. The initial purchase

Jan. 1	Investment in Trading Securities	5,750	
	Investment in Available-for-Sale Securities	7,050	
	Cash		12,800
	To record the purchase of trading and available-for-sale securities.		

2. The sale of one-half of Security 2 on March 31

Mar. 31	Cash	900	
	Realized Gain on Sale of Securities		150
	Investment in Trading Securities		750
	Sold one-half of Security 2 ($750 book value) for $900. Recorded the $150 realized gain ($900 – $750).		

3. The receipt of interest and dividends during the year

Cash	920	
Interest Revenue		720
Dividend Revenue		200
Received $720 in interest during the year and $200 in dividends.		

Note: Even if cash were not received by year-end, the interest and dividends earned would need to be recorded, with the offsetting debit to a receivable account(s).

4. The changes in value as of December 31, 2000

Dec. 31	Unrealized Loss on Trading Securities	50	
	Market Adjustment—Trading Securities		50
	To account for the difference between book value ($5,000) and fair market value ($4,950) of trading securities.		

(*Note:* Remember that one-half of Security 2 was sold during the year.)

Dec. 31	Market Adjustment—Available-for-Sale Securities	100	
	Unrealized Increase/Equity in Value of Available-for-Sale Securities		100
	To account for the difference between book value ($7,050) and fair market value ($7,150) of available-for-sale securities.		

DISCUSSION QUESTIONS

1. What are the major characteristics of property, plant, and equipment?
2. When buying a long-term asset such as a building or piece of equipment, the time value of money must be considered. With respect to time value, it is often said that the last payment (say, 20 years in the future) doesn't cost as much as the next payment. Explain.
3. Why are expenditures other than the net purchase price included in the cost of an asset?
4. Why are fair market values used to determine the cost of operating assets acquired in a basket purchase?
5. Companies usually depreciate assets such as buildings even though those assets may be increasing in value. Why?
6. Why is it common to have a gain or loss on the disposal of a long-term operating asset? Is it true that if the useful life and salvage value of an asset are known with certainty and are realized, there would never be such a gain or loss?
7. When recording the disposal of a long-term operating asset, why is it necessary to debit the accumulated depreciation of the old asset?
8. Why are intangible assets considered assets if they have no physical substance?
9. Goodwill can only be recorded when a business is purchased. Does this result in similar businesses having incomparable financial statements?
10. Why do firms invest in assets that are not directly related to their primary business operations?
11. Describe the risk and return tradeoff of investments.
12. What are the four different classifications of debt and equity securities?
13. When would a security be classified as "trading"?
14. What types of securities can be classified as "held-to-maturity"?
15. To be classified as an equity method security, the investor must typically own at least a certain percentage of the outstanding common stock of the investee. What is that minimum percentage? That percentage of ownership represents the investor's ability to do what?
16. Identify the different types of returns an investor can realize when investing in debt and equity securities.
17. When a security is sold, what information must be known to account for that transaction?
18. What is the difference between a realized gain or loss and an unrealized gain or loss?
19. What does the account "Market Adjustment" represent?
20. How are changes in the value of trading securities accounted for on the books of the investor?
21. How are changes in the value of available-for-sale securities accounted for on the books of the investor?
22. For trading and available-for-sale securities, what is the process for adjusting the value of a security after a valuation account has been established?
23. Why aren't premiums and discounts on available-for-sale securities amortized?
24. Why aren't changes in the value of held-to-maturity and equity method securities accounted for on the books of the investor?
25. How are the changes in the values of trading and available-for-sale securities accounted for differently?

DISCUSSION CASES

CASE 7-1

INTANGIBLE ASSETS

Renford Company owns two restaurants. One, located in Tacoma, was purchased from a previous owner and the other, located in Seattle, was built by Renford Company after purchasing the franchise. The restaurant in Seattle has a $20,000 unamortized franchise on the books. (The franchise originally cost $200,000 and is being amortized over 10 years.) The restaurant was built nine years ago. The Tacoma restaurant was purchased last year and has goodwill of $550,000 on the books. As it turns out, the Seattle restaurant does twice as much business as the Tacoma restaurant and is much more profitable. The Seattle restaurant is in a prime location, and business keeps increasing each year. The Tacoma restaurant does about the same amount of business each year, and it doesn't look as if it will ever do any better. Does it make sense to you to have goodwill on the books of the least profitable restaurant? Should Renford record goodwill on the books of the Seattle restaurant or should it write off the goodwill on the Tacoma restaurant's books (which is being amortized over a 40-year period)?

CASE 7-2

WHICH INVESTMENT SHOULD WE MAKE?

Pentron Data Corporation has a significant amount of excess cash on hand and has decided to make a long-term investment in either debt or equity securities. After a careful analysis, the investment committee has recommended either one of the following two investments to the company treasurer. The first investment involves purchasing sixty $1,000, 8 percent bonds issued by the Andrea Company. The bonds mature in 4 years, pay interest semiannually, and are currently selling at 92. The second investment alternative involves purchasing 3,000 shares of Franklin Corporation common stock at $30 per share (including brokerage fees). The investment committee believes that the Franklin stock will pay an annual dividend of $3.50 per share and is likely to be saleable at the end of four years for $36 per share.

Discuss the following questions:

1. If Pentron wants to earn 12 percent per year, should it make either investment?
2. Which of the two investments would you advise the treasurer to invest in assuming the inherent risk is approximately equal? Your decision should be based on which investment provides the more attractive return, ignoring income tax effects.

CASE 7-3

CLASSIFICATION OF SECURITIES

Memphis Company has just purchased five securities; it intends to hold the stock until the price increases to a sufficiently high level, at which time it plans to sell the stock. In fact, it is unlikely that the company will hold the securities for more than a few months. However, management of the company has decided to classify the securities as available-for-sale rather than as trading securities. Why are they choosing this type of classification, and would you allow it if you were the auditor?

EXERCISES

EXERCISE 7-1
Acquisition Decision

Johnson Company is considering acquiring a new airplane. It has looked at two financing options. The first is to lease the airplane for 10 years with lease payments of $70,000 each year. The second is to purchase the airplane, making a down payment of $250,000 and annual payments of $40,000 for 10 years. If the present value of the two financing options is the same, what other factors must be considered in deciding whether to purchase or to lease?

EXERCISE 7-2
Computing Asset Cost and Depreciation Expense

Antique Furniture Company decided to purchase a new furniture-polishing machine for its store in New York City. After a long search, it found the appropriate polisher in Chicago. The machine costs $75,000, and has an estimated 10-year life and no salvage value. Antique Furniture Company made the following additional expenditures with respect to this purchase:

Sales tax	$4,000
Delivery costs (FOB shipping point)	1,500
Installation costs	2,200
Painting of machine to match the decor.	300

1. What is the cost of the machine to Antique Furniture Company?
2. What is the amount of the first full year's depreciation if Antique uses the straight-line method?

EXERCISE 7-3
Acquisition and Depreciation of Assets

Western Oil Company, which prepares financial statements on a calendar-year basis, purchased new drilling equipment on July 1, 2000, using check numbers 1015 and 1016. The check totals are shown here, along with a breakdown of the charges.

1015 (Payee—Oil Equipment, Inc.):	
Cost of drilling equipment	$ 75,000
Cost of cement platform.	25,000
Installation charges	13,000
Total.	$113,000
1016 (Payee—Red Ball Freight):	
Freight costs for drilling equipment	$2,000

Assume that the estimated life of the drilling equipment is 10 years and its salvage value is $5,000.

1. Record the disbursements on July 1, 2000, assuming that no entry had been recorded for the drilling equipment.
2. Disregarding the information given about the two checks, assume that the drilling equipment was recorded at a total cost of $95,000. Calculate the depreciation expense for 2000 using the straight-line method.

EXERCISE 7-4
Accounting for the Acquisition of Assets—Basket Purchase

Sealise Corporation purchased land, a building, and equipment for a total cost of $450,000. After the purchase, the property was appraised. Fair market values were determined to be $120,000 for the land, $280,000 for the building, and $80,000 for the equipment. Given these appraisals, record the purchase of the property by Sealise Corporation.

EXERCISE 7-5
Depreciation Calculations

Luric Company purchased a new car on July 1, 1999, for $15,000. The estimated life of the car was four years or 104,000 miles, and its salvage value was estimated to be $2,000. The car was driven 9,000 miles in 1999 and 27,000 miles in 2000.

1. Compute the amount of depreciation expense for 1999 and 2000 using the following methods:
   a. Straight-line.
   b. Units-of-production.
2. Which depreciation method reflects more closely the used-up service potential of the car? Explain.

EXERCISE 7-6
Depreciation Calculations

Denver Hardware Company has a giant paint mixer that cost $31,500 plus $400 to install. The estimated salvage value of the paint mixer at the end of its useful life in 15 years is estimated to be $1,900. Denver estimates that the machine can mix 850,000 cans of paint during its lifetime. Compute the second full year's depreciation expense, using the following methods:

1. Straight-line.
2. Units-of-production, assuming that the machine mixes 51,000 cans of paint during the second year.

EXERCISE 7-7
Accounting for the Disposal of Assets

Zimer Concrete Company has a truck that it wants to sell. The truck had an original cost of $60,000, was purchased three years ago, and was expected to have a useful life of five years with no salvage value.

Using straight-line depreciation, and assuming that depreciation expense for three full years has been recorded, prepare journal entries to record the disposal of the truck under each of the following independent conditions:

1. Zimer Concrete Company sells the truck for $25,000 cash.
2. Zimer Concrete Company sells the truck for $20,000 cash.
3. The old truck is wrecked and Zimer Concrete Company hauls it to the junkyard.

EXERCISE 7-8
Disposal of an Asset

Honey Bee Company purchased a machine for $91,000. The machine has an estimated useful life of 7 years and a salvage value of $7,000. Journalize the disposal of the machine under each of the following conditions. (Assume straight-line depreciation.)

1. Sold the machine for $72,000 cash after two years.
2. Sold the machine for $28,000 cash after five years.

EXERCISE 7-9
Accounting for Intangible Assets

Gaylord Research, Inc., has the following intangible assets:

Asset	Cost	Date Purchased	Expected Useful or Legal Life
Goodwill.	$ 16,000	January 1, 1991	40 years
Patent.	136,000	January 1, 1993	17 years
Franchise	180,000	January 1, 1994	10 years

1. Record the amortization expense for each of these intangible assets for 2000.
2. Prepare the intangible assets section of the balance sheet for Gaylord Research, Inc., as of December 31, 2000.

EXERCISE 7-10
Intangible Assets

On January 1, 1999, Landon Company purchased a franchise to operate a regionally owned fast-food restaurant for a cost of $250,000. On July 1, 1999, Landon Company purchased another existing business in a nearby city for a total cost of $750,000. The market value of the land, building, and equipment, and other tangible assets was $550,000. The excess $200,000 was recorded as goodwill, to be amortized over a 40-year period.

Assuming Landon Company amortizes franchises over a 10-year period, record the following:

1. The purchase of the franchise on January 1, 1999.
2. The amortization of the franchise and goodwill at December 31, 1999.
3. The amortization of the franchise and goodwill at December 31, 2000.

EXERCISE 7-11
Accounting for the Purchase of Securities

The Fishing Store is a chain of sporting goods stores. The Fishing Store is interested in using some of its excess cash to invest in securities. It decides to buy the following securities:

Security	Type	Price
Fea Company	Available-for-sale	$ 4,000
Herdsman Inc.	Trading	7,500
Lenny Company	Available-for-sale	3,200
White Company	Held-to-maturity	10,000

Prepare the journal entry to record the purchase of these securities.

EXERCISE 7-12
Investment in Trading Securities—Journal Entries

Prepare the journal entries to account for the following investment transactions of Clyde Company.

1999
July 1 Purchased 200 shares of Nickle Company stock at $36 per share plus a brokerage fee of $450. The Nickle stock is classified as trading.
Oct. 31 Received a cash dividend of $1.50 per share on the Nickle Company stock.
Dec. 31 At year-end, Nickle Company stock had a market price of $33 per share.

2000
Feb. 20 Sold 100 shares of the Nickle Company stock for $37 per share.
Oct. 31 Received a cash dividend of $1.70 per share on the Nickle Company stock.
Dec. 31 At year-end, Nickle Company stock had a market price of $39 per share.

EXERCISE 7-13
Investment in Available-for-Sale Securities—Journal Entries

Wishbone Corporation made the following available-for-sale securities transactions:

Jan. 14 Purchased 2,000 shares of Clarke Corporation common stock at $31.60 per share.
Mar. 31 Received a cash dividend of $0.30 per share on the Clarke Corporation stock.
Aug. 28 Sold 800 shares of Clarke Corporation stock at $37.50 per share.
Dec. 31 The market value of the Clarke Corporation stock was $36.00 per share.

Prepare journal entries to record the transactions.

EXERCISE 7-14
Investment in Debt and Equity Securities

In February 2000, Packard Corporation purchased the following securities. Prior to these purchases, Packard had no portfolio of investment securities.

Security	Type	Classification	Cost
1	Debt	Trading	$11,500
2	Equity	Trading	9,000
3	Equity	Available-for-sale	7,250
4	Debt	Available-for-sale	12,300

During 2000, Packard received $2,400 in interest and $1,800 in dividends. On December 31, 2000, Packard's portfolio of securities had the following market values:

Security	Fair Market Value
1	$12,000
2	8,750
3	7,500
4	12,500

Prepare the journal entries required to record each of these transactions.

EXERCISE 7-15
Investment in Securities—Changes in Value

Sharp Incorporated had the following portfolio of investment securities on January 1, 2000:

Security	Type	Classification	Historical Cost	Fair Market Value (12/31/99)
1	Debt	Trading	$1,000	$ 800
2	Equity	Trading	1,250	1,100
3	Debt	Trading	1,700	1,650
4	Debt	Available-for-sale	2,200	2,150
5	Debt	Held-to-maturity	1,800	1,750

Appropriate adjustments were made on 12/31/99. No securities were bought or sold during 2000. On December 31, 2000, Sharp's portfolio of securities had the following fair market values:

Security	Fair Market Value (12/31/00)
1	$ 650
2	1,200
3	1,700
4	2,250
5	1,850

Prepare the necessary adjusting entry(ies) on December 31, 2000.

EXERCISE 7-16
Accounting for the Sale of Securities

Jerrod Company owns the following securities, which it is interested in selling:

Security	Type	Cost	Market Adjustments	Market Price
Monsen Company	Available-for-sale	$ 4,000	$ 300 increase	$ 5,000
Jensen Company	Trading	7,500	1,000 decrease	5,500
Stic Company	Available-for-sale	3,200	500 increase	4,000
Larouse Company	Held-to-maturity	10,000	No change	11,000

Prepare the journal entry to record the sale of these securities.

PROBLEMS

PROBLEM 7-1
Acquisition, Depreciation, and Disposal of Assets

On January 2, 2000, Scott Company purchased a building and land for $440,000. The most recent appraisal values for the building and the land were $360,000 and $120,000, respectively. The building has an estimated useful life of 20 years and a salvage value of $10,000.

Required:

1. Assuming cash transactions and straight-line depreciation, prepare journal entries to record:
   a. Purchase of the building and land on January 2, 2000.
   b. Depreciation expense on December 31, 2000.
2. Assume that after three years the property (land and building) was sold for $350,000. Prepare the journal entry to record the sale.

PROBLEM 7-2
Purchasing Property, Plant, and Equipment

Jordon Company is considering replacing its automated stamping machine. The machine is specialized and very expensive. Jordon is considering three acquisition alternatives. The first is to lease a machine for 10 years at $1 million per year, after which time Jordon can buy the machine for $1 million. The second alternative is to pay cash for the machine at a cost of $7 million. The third alternative is to make a down payment of $3 million, followed by 10 annual payments of $550,000. The company is trying to decide which alternative to select.

Required:

1. Assuming the present value of the lease payments is $7.2 million and the present value of the 10 loan payments of $550,000 is $4.1 million, determine which alternative Jordon should choose.
2. **Interpretive Question:** Your decision in part (1) was based only on financial factors. What other qualitative issues may influence your decision?

PROBLEM 7-3
Acquisition of an Asset

Pacific Printing Company purchased a new printing press. The invoice price was $158,500. The company paid for the press within 30 days, so they were allowed a 3 percent discount. The freight to have the press delivered cost $2,500. A premium of $900 was paid for a special insurance policy to cover the transportation of the press. The company spent $2,800 to install the press and an additional $400 in start-up costs to get the press ready for regular production.

Required:

1. At what amount should the press be recorded as an asset?
2. What additional information must be known before the depreciation expense for the first year of operation of the new press can be computed?
3. **Interpretive Question:** What criterion is used to determine whether the start-up costs of $400 are included in the cost of the asset? Explain.

PROBLEM 7-4
Depreciation Calculations

On January 1, VICOM Company purchased a $68,000 machine. The estimated life of the machine was five years, and the estimated salvage value was $5,000. The machine had an estimated useful life in productive output of 75,000 units. Actual output for the first two years was: year 1, 20,000 units; year 2, 15,000 units.

Required:

1. Compute the amount of depreciation expense for the first year, using each of the following methods:
   a. Straight-line.
   b. Units-of-production.
2. What was the book value of the machine at the end of the first year, assuming that straight-line depreciation was used?
3. If the machine is sold at the end of the fourth year for $15,000, how much should the company report as a gain or loss (assuming straight-line depreciation)?

PROBLEM 7-5
Purchase of Multiple Assets for a Lump Sum

On April 1, 2000, Mission Company paid $360,000 in cash to purchase land, a building, and equipment. The appraised fair market values of the assets were as follows: land, $90,000; building, $260,000; and equipment, $50,000. The company incurred legal fees of $3,000 to determine that it would have a clear title to the land. Before the facilities could be used, Mission had to spend $2,500 to grade and landscape the land, $4,000 to put the equipment in working order, and $15,000 to renovate the building. The equipment was then estimated to have a useful life of six years with no salvage value, and the building would have a useful life of 20 years with a net salvage value of $15,000. Both the equipment and the building are to be depreciated on a straight-line basis. The company is on a calendar-year reporting basis.

Required:

1. Allocate the lump-sum purchase price to the individual assets acquired.
2. Prepare the journal entry to acquire the land, building, and equipment.
3. Prepare the journal entry to record the title search, put the equipment in working order, and renovate the building.
4. Prepare the journal entries on December 31, 2000, to record the depreciation on the building and the equipment.

PROBLEM 7-6
Basket Purchase and Partial-Year Depreciation

On April 1, 2000, Rosenberg Company purchased for $200,000 a tract of land on which was located a fully equipped factory. The following information was compiled regarding this purchase:

	Market Value	Seller's Book Value
Land	$ 75,000	$ 30,000
Building	100,000	75,000
Equipment	50,000	60,000
Totals	$225,000	$165,000

Required:

1. Prepare the journal entry to record the purchase of these assets.
2. Assume that the building is depreciated on a straight-line basis over a remaining life of 20 years and the equipment is depreciated on a straight-line basis over five years. Neither the building nor the equipment is expected to have any salvage value. Compute the depreciation expense for 2000 assuming the assets were placed in service immediately upon acquisition.

PROBLEM 7-7
Acquisition, Depreciation, and Sale of an Asset

On January 2, 1998, Union Oil Company purchased a new airplane. The following costs are related to the purchase:

Airplane, base price	$112,000
Cash discount	3,000
Sales tax	4,000
Delivery charges	1,000

Required:

1. Prepare the journal entry to record the payment of these items on January 2, 1998.
2. Ignore your answer to part 1 and assume that the airplane cost $90,000 and has an expected useful life of five years or 1,500 hours. The estimated salvage value is $3,000. Using units-of-production depreciation and assuming that 300 hours are flown in 1999, calculate the amount of depreciation expense to be recorded for the second year.
3. Ignore the information in parts 1 and 2 and assume that the airplane costs $90,000, that its expected useful life is five years, and that its estimated salvage value is $5,000. The company now uses the straight-line depreciation method. On January 1, 2001, the following balances are in the related accounts:

Airplane	$90,000
Accumulated Depreciation, Airplane	51,000

Prepare the necessary journal entries to record the sale of this airplane on July 1, 2001, for $40,000.

PROBLEM 7-8
Acquisition, Depreciation, and Sale of an Asset

On July 1, 2000, Philip Ward bought a used pickup truck at a cost of $5,300 for use in his business. On the same day, Ward had the truck painted blue and white (his company's colors) at a cost of $800. Mr. Ward estimates the life of the truck to be three years or 40,000 miles. He further estimates that the truck will have a $450 scrap value at the end of its life, but that it will also cost him $50 to transfer the truck to the junkyard.

Required:

1. Record the following journal entries:
   a. July 1, 2000: Paid all bills pertaining to the truck. (No previous entries have been recorded concerning these bills.)
   b. Dec. 31, 2000: The depreciation expense for the year, using the straight-line method.
   c. Dec. 31, 2001: The depreciation expense for 2001, again using the straight-line method.
   d. Jan. 2, 2002: Sold the truck for $2,600 cash.
2. What would the depreciation expense for 2000 have been if the truck had been driven 8,000 miles and the units-of-production method of depreciation had been used?
3. **Interpretive Question:** In part 1d, there is a loss of $650. Why did this loss occur?

PROBLEM 7-9
Accounting for Natural Resources

On April 30, 1998, Lindon Oil Company purchased an oil well, with reserves of an estimated 100,000 barrels of oil, for $1,000,000 cash.

Required: Prepare journal entries for the following:

1. Record the purchase of the oil well.
2. During 1998, 10,000 barrels of oil were extracted from the well. Record the depletion expense for 1998.
3. During 1999, 18,000 barrels of oil were extracted from the well. Record the depletion expense for 1999.

PROBLEM 7-10
Accounting for Intangible Assets (Goodwill)

On January 1, 2000, Universal Company purchased the following assets and liabilities from Grand Company for $250,000:

	Book Value	Fair Market Value
Inventory	$40,000	$ 50,000
Building	80,000	100,000
Land	50,000	60,000
Accounts receivable	20,000	20,000
Accounts payable	(10,000)	(10,000)

Required:

1. Prepare a journal entry to record the purchase of Grand by Universal.
2. Record amortization of goodwill as of December 31, 2000. (Assume a 40-year amortization period for the goodwill.)

PROBLEM 7-11
Investment in Securities—Recording and Analysis

The following data pertain to the securities of Linford Company during 2000, the company's first year of operations:

a. Purchased 400 shares of Corporation A stock at $40 per share plus a commission of $200. This security is classified as trading.
b. Purchased $6,000 of Corporation B bonds. These bonds are classified as trading.
c. Received a cash dividend of 50 cents per share on the Corporation A stock.
d. Sold 100 shares of Corporation A stock for $46 per share.
e. Received interest of $240 on the Corporation B bonds.
f. Purchased 50 shares of Corporation C stock for $3,500. Classified the stock as available-for-sale.
g. Received interest of $240 on the Corporation B bonds.
h. Sold 150 shares of Corporation A stock for $28 per share.
i. Received a cash dividend of $1.40 per share on the Corporation C stock.
j. Interest receivable at year-end on the Corporation B bonds amounts to $60.

Required: Prepare journal entries to record the preceding transactions. Post the entries in T-accounts, and determine the amount of each of the following for the year:

1. Dividend revenue.
2. Bond interest revenue.
3. Net gain or loss from selling securities.

PROBLEM 7-12
Investments in Trading Securities

In December 2000, the treasurer of Marble Company concluded that the company had excess cash on hand and decided to invest in Sandy Corporation stock. The company intends to hold the stock for a period of 6 to 12 months and classifies the security as trading. The following transactions took place:

Jan. 1 Purchased 5,500 shares of Sandy Corporation stock for $82,500.
Apr. 15 Received a cash dividend of $0.65 per share on the Sandy Corporation stock.
May 22 Sold 1,500 shares of the Sandy Corporation stock at $20 per share for cash.
July 15 Received a cash dividend of 45 cents per share on the Sandy Corporation stock.
Aug. 31 Sold the balance of the Sandy Corporation stock at $8 per share for cash.

Required: Prepare the appropriate journal entries to record each of these transactions.

PROBLEM 7-13
Recording Investment Transactions

The following data pertain to the investments of Sumner Company during 2000, the company's first year of operations.

a. Purchased 200 shares of Corporation A stock at $40 per share, plus brokerage fees of $100. Classified as trading.
b. Purchased $10,000 of Corporation B bonds at face value. Classified as trading.
c. Received a cash dividend of 50 cents per share on the Corporation A stock.
d. Received interest of $600 on the Corporation B bonds.
e. Purchased 50 shares of Corporation C stock for $3,500. Classified as available-for-sale.
f. Received interest of $600 on the Corporation B bonds.
g. Sold 80 shares of Corporation A stock for $32 per share due to a significant decline in the market.
h. Received a cash dividend of $1.40 per share on the Corporation C stock.
i. Interest receivable at year-end on the Corporation B bonds amounts to $200.
j. Market value of securities at year end: Corporation A stock, $42 per share; Corporation B bonds, $10,200; Corporation C stock, $3,450.

Required:

Enter these transactions in T-accounts, and determine each of the following for the year:

1. Dividend revenue.
2. Bond interest revenue.
3. Net gain or loss from selling securities.
4. Unrealized gain or loss from holding securities.

PROBLEM 7-14
Investments in Available-for-Sale Securities

Durham Company often purchases common stocks of other companies as long-term investments. At the end of 1999, Durham held the common stocks listed. (Assume that Durham Company exercises no significant influence over these companies; i.e., they are classified as available-for-sale securities.)

Corporation	Number of Shares	Total Cost per Share
A	2,000	$ 70
B	3,000	50
C	1,500	148
D	1,000	82

Additional information for 1999:

Sep. 30 Durham received a cash dividend of $2.50 per share on Corporation A stock.
Dec. 31 The market prices were quoted as follows:
Corporation A stock, $64; Corporation B stock, $48;
Corporation C stock, $150; Corporation D stock, $78.

Required:

1. Illustrate how these investments would be reported on the balance sheet at December 31, 1999, and prepare the adjusting entry at that date.
2. What items and amounts would be reported on the income statement for 1999?
3. Prepare the journal entry for the sale of Corporation D stock for $74 per share in 2000.
4. **Interpretive Question:** Why are losses from the write-down of available-for-sale securities not included in the current year's income, whereas similar losses for trading securities are included?

PROBLEM 7-15
Investment Portfolio

General Corporation has the following investments in equity securities at December 31, 1999 (there are no existing balances in the market adjustment account):

Company	Classification	Shares	Percentage of Shares Owned	Cost	Market Price at 12/31/99
Clarke Corporation	Trading	1,000	2%	$75	$78
Marlin Company	Available-for-sale	4,000	15	34	32
Air Products, Inc.	Available-for-sale	3,000	10	46	43

Required:

1. Prepare any adjusting entries required at December 31, 1999.
2. Illustrate how these investments would be presented on General Corporation's balance sheet at December 31, 1999. The available-for-sale securities are expected to be held for two to five years.
3. Prepare the journal entry on April 10, 2000, when General Corporation sold the Clarke Corporation investment for $72 per share.
4. Assume that General Corporation still owns its investment in Marlin Company and Air Products at December 31, 2000; the market prices are $37 for Marlin and $44 for Air Products on that date. Prepare all adjusting journal entries needed at December 31, 2000.

Accounting is more than just doing textbook problems. These Competency Enhancement Opportunities provide practice in critical thinking, oral and written communication, research, teamwork, and consideration of ethical issues.

ANALYZING REAL COMPANY INFORMATION

• Analyzing 7–1 (Microsoft)

Using Microsoft's 1997 annual report contained in Appendix A, answer the following questions:

1. As a percentage of total assets, is Microsoft's investment in Property, Plant, and Equipment increasing or decreasing over time? Which of Microsoft's assets is increasing the fastest as a percentage of total assets? What does that indicate Microsoft is doing?
2. Reference the notes to the financial statements. What depreciation method does Microsoft use? Compute the average useful life of Microsoft's depreciable assets (i.e., not including land) by dividing the depreciation expense for the year by the ending balance in the depreciable asset accounts and then dividing the result into 1. Does the resulting estimated useful life seem reasonable?
3. Microsoft notes in its statement of cash flows that $499 million of property, plant, and equipment was purchased in 1997. Using that information along with the detailed information from the notes, compute (a) the original cost of the equipment disposed of during 1997 and (b) the accumulated depreciation associated with that equipment. *Hint:*

For property, plant, and equipment, beginning balance + purchases − disposals = ending balance; a similar calculation is used for accumulated depreciation.

• Analyzing 7-2 (Microsoft)

The 1997 annual report for **Microsoft** is included in Appendix A. Locate that annual report and consider the following questions:

1. Find Microsoft's note on significant accounting policies. Using the information in that note (under the heading "Financial instruments"), determine what fraction of Microsoft's investment securities are classified as "available-for-sale."
2. In its note on "Cash and short-term investments," Microsoft lists the general types of investments that make up its $8.966 billion portfolio. Certificates of deposit are listed both as "cash and cash equivalents" and as "short-term investments." What is the difference between these two categories? *Hint:* Go back to the note you looked at to answer (1).
3. Look at Microsoft's stockholders' equity statement. Where in the equity section does Microsoft report the unrealized gains and losses from available-for-sale securities?

• Analyzing 7-3 (Berkshire Hathaway)

Berkshire Hathaway is a diversified holding company primarily owned by Warren Buffett. It is one of the most profitable and successful companies in history. As you can see from this case, Berkshire Hathaway has ownership interests in a wide variety of companies. The following note comes from its 1996 annual report.

(5) Investments in equity securities

Aggregate data with respect to the consolidated investment in equity securities are shown below (in millions):

December 31, 1996

	Cost	Unrealized Gains	Carrying Value
Common stock of:			
American Express Company	$1,392.7	$ 1,401.6	$ 2,794.3
The Coca-Cola Company	1,298.9	9,226.1	10,525.0
The Walt Disney Company	1,533.2	183.6	1,716.8
Federal Home Loan Mortgage Corp.	449.7	1,323.1	1,772.8
The Gillette Company	600.0	3,132.0	3,732.0
McDonald's Corporation	1,265.3	103.1	1,368.4
Wells Fargo & Company	553.9	1,413.0	1,966.9
All other equity securities	2,058.3	1,816.1	3,874.4
	$9,152.0	$18,598.6	$27,750.6

(continued)

December 31, 1995

	Cost	Unrealized Gains	Carrying Value
Common stock of:			
American Express Company	$1,392.7	$ 653.6	$ 2,046.3
Capital Cities/ABC, Inc.	345.0	2,122.5	2,467.5
The Coca-Cola Company	1,298.9	6,126.1	7,425.0
Federal Home Loan Mortgage Corp.	260.1	783.9	1,044.0
GEICO Corporation	1,175.8	—	1,175.8
The Gillette Company	600.0	1,902.0	2,502.0
Wells Fargo & Company	423.7	1,043.2	1,466.9
All other equity securities	1,680.0	1,210.1	2,890.1
	$7,176.2	$13,841.4	$21,017.6

Berkshire Hathaway also discloses that it classifies each of these investments as an available-for-sale security.

1. All securities included in the tables in Berkshire Hathaway's Note 5 are classified as available-for-sale. Make all journal entries that were required in 1996 to account for Berkshire Hathaway's investments in:
   a. **The Cola-Cola Company**
   b. **Federal Home Loan Mortgage Corp.**
2. The notes to Berkshire Hathaway's financial statements also contain the following information:

> On January 4, 1996, shareholders of Capital Cities/ABC, Inc. ("Capital Cities") and The Walt Disney Company ("Disney") approved an agreement and plan of merger by and between Disney and Capital Cities. In March 1996, Berkshire received approximately 21 million shares of Disney common stock and $1.2 billion in cash in exchange for the common shares of Capital Cities.

Use this information, plus the information from Note 5, to answer the following questions:

a. This "merger" would be more accurately described as **Disney**'s acquisition of **Capital Cities/ABC**. When one company acquires another, the stockholders of the acquired company often receive a payment greater than the value of their investment in order to induce them to approve the acquisition. This is called a premium. Did the stockholders of Capital Cities/ABC receive a premium?
b. What was the price per share of the Disney shares when Berkshire Hathaway received them in March 1996?
c. By what percentage did the value of the Disney shares increase between March and December 1996?

INTERNATIONAL CASE

• Sony

Sony Corporation was organized in 1946 under the name **Tokyo Tsushin Kogyo**. The name "Sony" is a combination of the Latin word "sonus" (sound) and the English word "sonny"; it was given to a small transistor radio sold by the company in the United States, starting in 1954. The radio was so popular that the entire company changed its name to Sony in 1958.

In its 1997 annual report, Sony included the note to its financial statements shown below.

(9) Marketable securities and securities investments

March 31, 1997

(in millions of ¥)	Cost	Unrealized Gains	Unrealized Losses	Fair Market Value
Available for sale:				
Debt securities	¥531,968	¥ 22,001	¥1,338	¥552,631
Equity securities	49,512	124,682	2,364	171,830
Total	¥581,480	¥146,683	¥3,702	¥724,461

March 31, 1996

(in millions of ¥)	Cost	Unrealized Gains	Unrealized Losses	Fair Market Value
Available for sale:				
Debt securities	¥341,554	¥ 11,592	¥2,149	¥350,997
Equity securities	49,842	158,279	1,006	207,115
Total	¥391,396	¥169,871	¥3,155	¥558,112

1. In the notes to its English-language financial statements, Sony states that those statements "conform with accounting principles generally accepted in the United States." However, the official accounting records of Sony are maintained using Japanese accounting principles. Why would Sony go to the trouble of preparing a separate set of English-language financial statements using U.S. accounting principles?
2. Assuming that approximately the same equity securities were on hand in both 1996 and 1997, how well did Sony's equity investments perform in 1997?
3. What journal entries did Sony make during the year to record the purchase and revaluation of available-for-sale securities? Use only the total amounts (that is, don't use the separate amounts for debt and equity securities), and ignore the possibility that securities were sold during the year.

ETHICS CASE

• Is it OK to strategically classify securities?

You have recently been hired as a staff assistant in the office of the chairman of the board of directors of Clefton Inc. Since you have some background in accounting, the chairman has asked you to review the preliminary financial statements that were prepared by the company's accounting staff. After the financial statements are approved by the chairman of the board, they will be audited by external auditors. This is the first year that Clefton has had its financial statements audited by external auditors.

In examining the financial statement note on investment securities, you notice that all of the securities that had unrealized gains for the year have been classified as trading, whereas all of the securities that had unrealized losses have been classified as available-for-sale. You realize that this has the impact of placing all the gains on the income statement and hiding all the losses in the equity section of the balance sheet. You call the chief accountant who confirms that the securities are not classified until the end of the year, and that the classification depends on whether a particular security has experienced a gain or a loss during the year. The chief accountant states that this policy was adopted, with the approval of the chairman of the board, in order to maximize the reported net income of the company. The chief accountant tells you that investment security classification is based on how management intends to use those securities; therefore, management may classify the securities in any way it wishes.

You are uncomfortable with this investment security classification strategy. You are also dismayed that the chief accountant and the chairman of the board seem to have agreed on this scheme to maximize reported income. You are also worried about what the external auditors will do when they find out about this classification scheme. You have been asked to report to the chairman of the board this afternoon to give your summary of the status of the preliminary financial statements. What should you do?

WRITING ASSIGNMENT

• Why doesn't the gain go on the income statement?

You are the controller for Chong Lai Company. You just received a very strongly worded e-mail message from the president of the company. The president has learned that a $627,000 gain on a stock investment made by the company last year will not be reported in the income statement because you have classified the security as available for sale. With the gain, the company would report a record profit for the year. Without the gain, profits are actually down slightly from the year before. The president wants an explanation—*now.*

It has been your policy for the past several years to routinely classify all investments as available for sale. Your company is not in the business of actively buying and selling stocks and bonds. Instead, all investments are made to strengthen relationships with either suppliers or major customers. As such, your practice is to buy securities and hold them for several years.

Write a one-page memo to the president explaining the rationale behind your policy of security classification.

WRITING ASSIGNMENT

• Gains are good, losses are bad—right?

When a long-term asset is sold for more than its book value, we record a gain. When a long-term asset is sold for less than its book value, we record a loss.

Your assignment is to write a two-page memo addressing the following questions:

1. What factors affect a long-term asset's book value?
2. What factors affect a long-term asset's fair value?
3. Should financial statement users expect an asset's book value to equal its fair value?
4. In the case of an asset sold for a loss, if we knew when we purchased the asset what we know at the point of sale, how would depreciation expense have differed if our objective was to ensure that book value equaled fair value when the asset was sold?
5. Is recognizing a loss on the sale of a long-term asset a bad thing? Is a gain good?

THE DEBATE

• Market values do not belong in the financial statements!

Accounting traditionalists opposed the move to report investment securities in the balance sheet at their current market value. These traditionalists complain that inclusion of market values reduces the reliability of the financial statements and introduces an unnecessary amount of variability in the reported numbers. On the other hand, supporters of reporting market values claim that market values are extremely relevant and, for investment securities traded on active markets, are reliable as well.

Divide your group into two teams.

- One team represents "Market Value." Prepare a two-minute oral presentation arguing that the market value of investment securities should be reported on the balance sheet. To do otherwise is to make the statements an out-of-date curiosity rather than a useful tool.
- The other team represents "Historical Cost." Prepare a two-minute oral presentation arguing for a return to strict historical cost on the balance sheet.

INTERNET SEARCH

• General Electric

We began this chapter with a review of the history of **General Electric**. Let's go to GE's Web site and learn a little more about the company and its financial position. GE's Web address is ge.com. Sometimes Web addresses change, so if this General Electric address doesn't work, access the Web site for this textbook (stice.swcollege.com) for an updated link to General Electric.

Once you have gained access to General Electric's Web site, answer the following questions:

1. General Electric was formed in 1892. Can you identify at what worldwide event the company debuted? *Hint:* Access the Web page relating to company history.
2. Locate the company's most recent balance sheet. What percentage of total assets does property, plant, and equipment represent for General Electric? Is that percentage increasing, decreasing, or remaining constant?
3. Access the notes to the financial statements. What depreciation method does General Electric use for most of its manufacturing plant and equipment?
4. Find the note relating specifically to property, plant, and equipment. What types of property, plant, and equipment does General Electric own? Is GE strictly a company involved in producing light bulbs?

CHAPTER 8 STATEMENT OF CASH FLOWS

SETTING THE STAGE

In 1906, William T. Grant opened his first twenty-five-cent store in Lynn, Massachusetts. Twenty-two years later, stock of the W. T. Grant Company was offered for sale to the public. By 1953, the company had expanded to include over 500 stores and the company's expansion continued into the 1960s. In 1969 alone, 410 new stores were opened. In 1973, the company's stock was selling at nearly 20 times earnings and peaked at $70 5/8 per share. As late as September 1974, a group of banks loaned the company $600 million.

However, a careful analysis of W. T. Grant's financial statements would have indicated that while the company was reporting profits through 1974, cash flows from operations were almost always negative from 1966 to 1975. Once the market realized the magnitude of W. T. Grant's cash flow problems, it reacted quickly. In December 1974, the company's stock was trading at $2 per share. The company closed 107 stores and laid off 7,000 employees in September 1975. On

LEARNING OBJECTIVES

After studying this chapter, you should be able to:

1. *Understand the purpose of a statement of cash flows.*
2. *Recognize the different types of information reported in the statement of cash flows.*
3. *Prepare a simple statement of cash flows.*
4. *Analyze financial statements to prepare a statement of cash flows.*
5. *Use information from the statement of cash flows to make decisions.*

EXHIBIT 8-1

Financial History of W. T. Grant Company 1966–1975

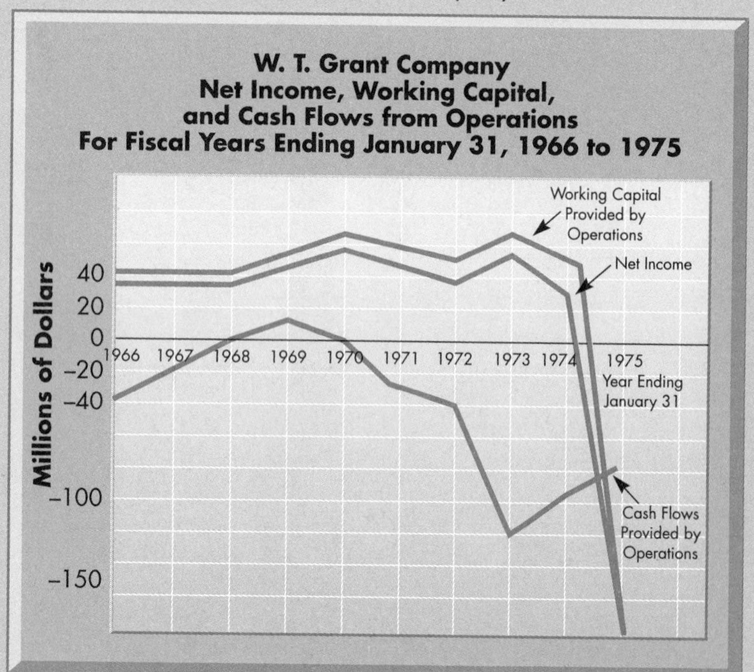

October 2, 1975, the nation's largest retailer filed for protection under Chapter XI of the National Bankruptcy Act. Only four months later, the creditors' committee voted for liquidation, and W. T. Grant ceased to exist.

Why couldn't creditors and stockholders see W. T. Grant's impending problems any sooner? As the chart in Exhibit 8–1 shows, net income and working capital provided by operations were of little help in predicting W. T. Grant's problems, but a careful analysis of the company's cash flows would have revealed the problems as much as a decade before the collapse.

How could this happen? Oddly enough, information regarding a firm's cash flows was not required to be provided to investors and creditors until 1987. Prior to that time, companies prepared a statement of changes in financial position, which measured changes in current assets and current liabilities. This statement of changes in financial position provided information that, if not carefully interpreted, could lead one to believe that a buildup of inventory and receivables was as good as money in the bank (as was the case with W. T. Grant).

In this chapter, we will study the statement of cash flows. You will learn that this statement provides one of the earliest warning signs of cash concerns and receivables collection problems of the type experienced by W. T. Grant. The statement of cash flows alerts financial statement readers to increases and decreases in cash as well as to the reasons and trends for the changes.

It is not enough in today's business environment to just monitor earnings and earnings per share measurements. The financial position of an entity and especially the inflows and outflows of cash are also critical elements that determine the financial success of an organization.

Each of the three primary financial statements was introduced and illustrated in Chapter 2. In subsequent chapters, we examined in detail the components of the balance sheet and income statement. For our discussion of the statement of cash flows, we will first describe the purpose and general format of a statement of cash flows. We will then show how easy it is to prepare a statement of cash flows if detailed cash flow information is available. A statement of cash flows can also be prepared based on an analysis of balance sheet and income statement accounts. We will also distinguish between the direct and indirect methods of reporting operating cash flows and discuss the usefulness of the statement of cash flows. Finally, we will explain how the statement of cash flows can be used to make investment and lending decisions.

Understand the purpose of a statement of cash flows.

WHAT'S THE PURPOSE OF A STATEMENT OF CASH FLOWS?

statement of cash flows The financial statement that shows an entity's cash inflows (receipts) and outflows (payments) during a period of time.

The **statement of cash flows**, as its name implies, summarizes a company's cash flows for a period of time. It provides answers to such questions as, "Where did our money come from?" and "Where did our money go?" The statement of cash flows explains how a company's cash was generated during the period and how that cash was used.

You might think that the statement of cash flows is a replacement for the income statement. However, the two statements have two different objectives. The income statement, as you know, measures the results of operations for a period of time. Net income is the accountant's best estimate at reflecting a company's economic performance for a period. The income statement provides details as to how the retained earnings account changes during a period and ties together, in part, the owners' equity sections of comparative balance sheets.

The statement of cash flows, on the other hand, provides details as to how the cash account changed during a period. The statement of cash flows reports the period's transactions and events in terms of their impact on cash. In Chapter 4, we compared the cash-basis and accrual-basis methods of measuring income and explained why accrual-basis income is considered a better measure of periodic income. The statement of cash flows provides important information from a cash-basis perspective that complements the income statement and balance sheet, thus providing a more complete picture of a company's operations and financial position. It is important to note that the statement of cash flows does not include any transactions or accounts that are not already reflected in the balance sheet or the income statement. Rather, the statement of cash flows simply provides information relating to the cash flow effects of those transactions.

Users of financial statements, particularly investors and creditors, need information about a company's cash flows in order to evaluate the company's ability to generate positive net cash flows in the future to meet its obligations and to pay dividends. In some cases, careful analysis of cash flows can provide early warning of impending financial problems, as would have been the case with the **W. T. Grant Company**.

Before moving on, it is important to reiterate that the statement of cash flows does not replace the income statement. The income statement summarizes the results of a company's operations whereas the statement of cash flows summarizes a company's inflows and outflows of cash. Information contained in the income statement can be used to facilitate the preparation of a statement of cash flows; information in the statement of cash flows sheds some light on the company's ability to generate income in the future. The statement of cash flows and the income statement provide complementary information about different aspects of a business.

TO SUMMARIZE

The statement of cash flows, one of the three primary financial statements, provides information about the cash receipts and payments of an entity during a period. It provides important information that complements the income statement and balance sheet.

2 *Recognize the different types of information reported in the statement of cash flows.*

cash equivalents Short-term, highly liquid investments that can be converted easily into cash.

WHAT INFORMATION IS REPORTED IN THE STATEMENT OF CASH FLOWS?

Accounting standards include specific requirements for the reporting of cash flows. The general format for a statement of cash flows, with details and dollar amounts omitted, is presented in Exhibit 8-2. As illustrated, the inflows and outflows of cash must be divided into three main categories: operating activities, investing activities, and financing activities. Further, the statement of cash flows is to be presented in a manner that reconciles the beginning and ending balances of cash and cash equivalents. **Cash equivalents** are short-term, highly liquid investments that can be converted easily into cash. Generally, only investments with maturities of three months or less qualify as cash equivalents. Examples are U.S. Treasury bills, money market funds, and commercial paper (short-term debt issued by corporations). In this chapter, as is common in practice, the term *cash* will be used to include cash and cash equivalents.

get connected
ttp://www.swcollege.com
net work

Speaking of cash, what is the largest denomination ever printed by the United States Treasury Department? Go to www.ustreas.gov/currency to find out.

www.ustreas.gov/currency

EXHIBIT 8-2

General Format for a Statement of Cash Flows

Cash provided by (used in):	
Operating activities	$XXX
Investing activities	XXX
Financing activities	XXX
Net increase (decrease) in cash and cash equivalents	$XXX
Cash and cash equivalents at beginning of year	XXX
Cash and cash equivalents at end of year	$XXX

Major Classifications of Cash Flows

Exhibit 8-3 shows the three main categories of cash inflows and outflows—operating, investing, and financing. Exhibit 8-4 summarizes the specific activities included in each category. Beginning with operating activities, each of the cash flow categories will be explained. We will also discuss the reporting of significant noncash transactions and events.

Operating Activities

operating activities Transactions and events that enter into the determination of net income.

Operating activities include those transactions and events that enter into the determination of net income. Cash receipts from the sale of goods or services are the major cash inflows for most businesses. Other inflows are cash receipts for interest revenue, dividend revenue, and similar items. Major outflows of cash are for the purchase of inventory and for the payment of wages, taxes, interest, utilities, rent, and similar expenses. As we will explain later, the amount of cash provided by (or used in) operating activities is a key figure and should be highlighted on the statement of cash flows.

EXHIBIT 8-3

The Flow of Cash

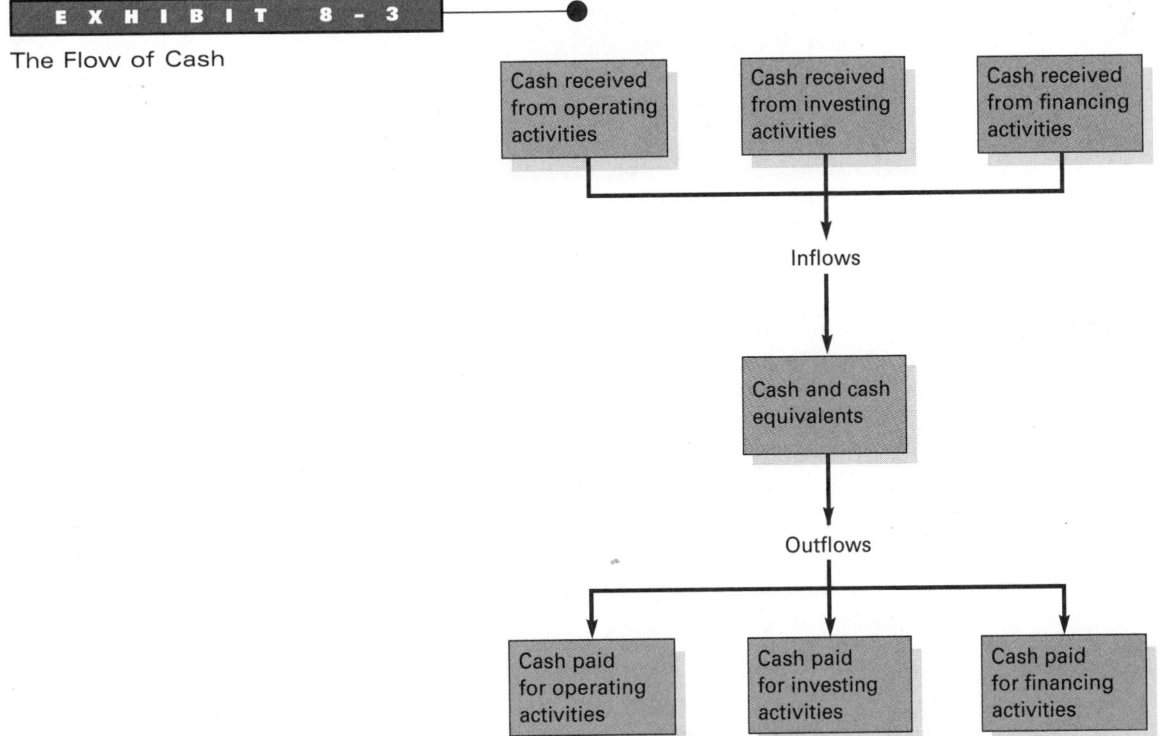

EXHIBIT 8-4

Major Classification of Cash Flows

Operating Activities

Cash receipts from:

- Sale of goods or services
- Interest revenue
- Dividend revenue
- Sale of investments in trading securities

Cash payments to:

- Suppliers for inventory purchases
- Employees for services
- Governments for taxes
- Lenders for interest expense
- Brokers for purchase of trading securities
- Others for other expenses (e.g., utilities, rent)

Investing Activities

Cash receipts from:

- Sale of property, plant, and equipment
- Sale of a business segment
- Sale of investments in securities other than trading securities
- Collection of principal on loans made to other entities

Cash payments to:

- Purchase property, plant, and equipment
- Purchase debt or equity securities of other entities (other than trading securities)
- Make loans to other entities

Financing Activities

Cash receipts from:

- Issuance of own stock
- Borrowing (e.g., bonds, notes, mortgages)

Cash payments to:

- Stockholders as dividends
- Repay principal amounts borrowed
- Repurchase an entity's own stock (treasury stock)

FYI

Although cash inflows from interest and dividends logically might be classified as financing activities, the FASB has decided to classify them as operating activities, which conforms to their presentation on the income statement.

Note that our focus in analyzing operating activities is to determine cash flows from operations. An analysis is required to convert income from an accrual-basis to a cash-basis number. How will this be done? We will begin with the net income figure, remove all items relating to investing activities (such as depreciation and gains/losses on the sale of equipment) and financing activities (such as gains/losses on retirement of debt), and then adjust for changes in those current assets and current liabilities that involve cash and relate to operations (which are most of the current assets and current liabilities).

FYI

The purchase and sale of trading securities is classified as an operating activity.

Investing Activities

Transactions and events that involve the purchase and sale of securities (other than trading securities), property, buildings, equipment, and other assets not generally held for resale, and the making and collecting of loans

investing activities Transactions and events that involve the purchase and sale of securities (excluding cash equivalents), property, plant, equipment, and other assets not generally held for resale, and the making and collecting of loans.

are classified as **investing activities**. These activities occur regularly and result in cash inflows and outflows. They are not classified under operating activities since they relate only indirectly to the central, ongoing operations of the entity, which is usually the sale of goods or services.

The analysis of investing activities involves identifying those accounts on the balance sheet relating to investments (typically long-term asset accounts), and then explaining how those accounts changed and the cash flow effects of those changes for the period.

Financing Activities

financing activities Transactions and events whereby resources are obtained from, or repaid to, owners (equity financing) and creditors (debt financing).

Financing activities include transactions and events whereby resources are obtained from or paid to owners (equity financing) and creditors (debt financing). Dividend payments, for example, fit this definition. As noted earlier, the receipt of dividends and interest and the payment of interest are classified under operating activities simply because they are reported as a part of income on the income statement. The receipt or payment of the principal amount borrowed or repaid (but not the interest) is considered a financing activity.

Analyzing the cash flow effects of financing activities involves identifying those accounts relating to financing (typically long-tem debt and common stock) and explaining how changes in those accounts affected the company's cash flows. Exhibit 8-5 summarizes the activities reflected on the statement of cash flows and how the balance sheet and income statement accounts relate to the various activities.

FYI

The activities are typically listed in this order: operating, investing, and financing. However, there is no requirement that they be listed in this order. **Microsoft**, for example, uses the order operating, financing, and investing.

Noncash Investing and Financing Activities

Some investing and financing activities do not affect cash. For example, equipment may be purchased with a note payable, or land may be acquired by issuing stock. These noncash transactions are not reported in the statement of cash flows. However, if a company has significant noncash financing and investing activities, they should be disclosed in a separate schedule or in a narrative explanation. The disclosures may be presented below the statement of cash flows or in the notes to the financial statements.

EXHIBIT 8-5 How Balance Sheet and Income Statement Accounts Relate to the Statement of Cash Flows

Cash Flow Activity	Related Balance Sheet and Income Statement Accounts	Examples	Chapters in Which Accounts Were Covered
Operating	All income statement accounts **except** those income statement items relating to:	Sales, Cost of Goods Sold, Salaries Expense, etc.	Chs. 4–5
	• Investing	Depreciation, Gains/Losses on Sale of Equipment	Ch. 7
	• Financing	Gains/Losses on Retirement of Debt	Ch. 6
	Current assets	Accounts Receivable	Ch. 4
		Inventory	Ch. 5
	Current liabilities	Accounts Payable	Ch. 5
Investing	Long-term assets	Property, Plant, and Equipment	Ch. 7
	Long-term investments	Available-for-Sale and Held-to-Maturity Securities	Ch. 7
Financing	Long-term debt	Bonds and Mortgages	Ch. 6
	Stockholders' equity (except for net income in Retained Earnings)	Common Stock	Ch. 6
		Dividends	Ch. 6

TO SUMMARIZE

The statement of cash flows is presented in a manner that highlights three major categories of cash flows: operating activities, investing activities, and financing activities. In addition, the format of the statement should provide a reconciliation of the beginning and ending balances of cash and cash equivalents (short-term, highly liquid investments). Any significant noncash investing and financing activities should be disclosed separately, either below the statement of cash flows or in the notes to the financial statements.

BUSINESS ENVIRONMENT ESSAY

The Statement of Cash Flows—A Historical Perspective The statement of cash flows is a relatively new financial statement. In 1987, the Financial Accounting Standards Board (FASB) issued an accounting standard, FASB Statement No. 95, requiring that the statement of cash flows be presented as one of the three primary financial statements. Previously, companies had been required to present a statement of changes in financial position, often called the funds statement. In 1971, APB Opinion No. 19 made the funds statement a required financial statement although many companies had begun reporting funds flow information several years earlier. The funds statement provided useful information, but it had several limitations. First, APB Opinion No. 19 allowed considerable flexibility in how funds could be defined and how they were reported on the statement. As a result, many companies reported on a working-capital basis (current assets minus current liabilities), whereas others reported on a cash basis or some other basis. Further, in each case, the individual company selected its own format. This inconsistency across companies made comparisons difficult.

Second, the funds statement, even when prepared on a cash basis, did not provide a complete and clear picture of a company's ability to generate positive cash flows. One reason is that APB Opinion No. 19 required that all investing and financing activities be reported in the statement, even those that did not affect cash or working capital. Another problem was that the funds statement usually included two sections—sources (inflows) and uses (outflows) of funds. Thus, the amount of working capital or cash provided or used by each major type of activity (operating, financing, and investing) was not identified.

The limitations of the funds statement often made it difficult to assess a company's ability to generate sufficient cash. Some companies were able to report favorable earnings in the income statement, even while experiencing serious cash flow problems that were not readily apparent from the information reported in the funds statement. For example, **Endo-Lase**, a distributor of medical lasers, reported a 200 percent increase in sales in one year. Unfortunately, due to poor collection performance, receivables increased at an even faster rate than sales and much of the reported increase in revenues took the form of IOUs. When many of these receivables were determined to be uncollectible, Endo-Lase had to restate its previously reported earnings. So, although reported earnings appeared strong, Endo-Lase's cash flows were actually negative, and eventually the company had to file for bankruptcy protection.

3 *Prepare a simple statement of cash flows.*

PREPARING A STATEMENT OF CASH FLOWS—A SIMPLE EXAMPLE

Now that we have reviewed the three types of cash flow activities disclosed on the statement of cash flows, let's start with a simple example to see how easy (conceptually) a statement of cash flows is to prepare. For this example, we will begin with the following trial balance information for Silmaril Inc.

Silmaril Inc.
Trial Balance
January 1, 1999

	Debit	Credit
Cash	$ 300	
Accounts Receivable	2,500	
Inventory	1,900	
Property, Plant, and Equipment	4,000	
Accumulated Depreciation		$1,200
Accounts Payable		1,700
Taxes Payable		40
Long-Term Debt		2,200
Common Stock		1,000
Retained Earnings		2,560
Totals	$8,700	$8,700

The following transactions were conducted by Silmaril Inc. during 1999:

1. Sales on account, $13,500.
2. Collections on account, $14,000.
3. Purchased inventory on account, $7,900.
4. Cost of goods sold, $8,000.
5. Paid accounts payable, $8,100.
6. Purchased property, plant, and equipment for cash, $1,700.
7. Sold property, plant, and equipment for cash, $500 (original cost, $1,200, accumulated depreciation, $800).
8. Paid long-term debt, $200.
9. Issued stock at par value, $450.
10. Recorded depreciation expense, $500.
11. Paid interest on debt, $180.
12. Recorded interest owed (accrued) but not paid, $20.
13. Paid miscellaneous expenses (e.g., wages, supplies, etc.) for the period, $3,200.
14. Recorded tax expense for the period, $450.
15. Paid taxes during the period, $440.

With this information, we can reconstruct the journal entries made by Silmaril Inc. during the year:

		Debit	Credit
1.	Accounts Receivable	13,500	
	Sales		13,500
2.	Cash	14,000	
	Accounts Receivable		14,000
3.	Inventory	7,900	
	Accounts Payable		7,900
4.	Cost of Goods Sold	8,000	
	Inventory		8,000
5.	Accounts Payable	8,100	
	Cash		8,100
6.	Property, Plant, and Equipment	1,700	
	Cash		1,700

7.	Cash	500	
	Accumulated Depreciation	800	
	Property, Plant, and Equipment		1,200
	Gain on Sale of Equipment		100
8.	Long-Term Debt	200	
	Cash		200
9.	Cash	450	
	Common Stock		450
10.	Depreciation Expense	500	
	Accumulated Depreciation		500
11.	Interest Expense	180	
	Cash		180
12.	Interest Expense	20	
	Interest Payable		20
13.	Miscellaneous Expenses	3,200	
	Cash		3,200
14.	Tax Expense	450	
	Taxes Payable		450
15.	Taxes Payable	440	
	Cash		440

When these journal entries are posted, the following trial balance results:

Silmaril Inc.
Trial Balance
December 31, 1999

	Debit	Credit
Cash	$ 1,430	
Accounts Receivable	2,000	
Inventory	1,800	
Property, Plant, and Equipment	4,500	
Accumulated Depreciation		$ 900
Accounts Payable		1,500
Interest Payable		20
Taxes Payable		50
Long-Term Debt		2,000
Common Stock		1,450
Retained Earnings		2,560
Sales		13,500
Gain on Sale of Equipment		100
Cost of Goods Sold	8,000	
Depreciation Expense	500	
Interest Expense	200	
Tax Expense	450	
Miscellaneous Expenses	3,200	
Totals	$22,080	$22,080

To this point, this is all a review—journalizing transactions, posting journal entries, and preparing a trial balance. From this trial balance, we can easily prepare an income statement and a balance sheet; but our objective here is to prepare a statement of cash flows. With information from the cash T-account, we can prepare a statement of cash flows. The cash T-account would contain the following information (journal entry reference numbers are in parentheses):

Cash

Beg. Bal.	300		
(2)	14,000	(5)	8,100
(7)	500	(6)	1,700
(9)	450	(8)	200
		(11)	180
		(13)	3,200
		(15)	440
End. Bal.	1,430		

Our task at this point is to simply categorize each cash inflow and outflow as an operating, investing, or financing activity. The inflows and outflows break down as follows:

Operating Activities:		
Collections on account (2)		$14,000
Payments for inventory (5)	$ 8,100	
Payments for miscellaneous expenses (13)	3,200	
Payment for interest (11)	180	
Payment for taxes (15)	440	(11,920)
Cash flows from operating activities		$ 2,080
Investing Activities:		
Sold equipment (7)	$ 500	
Purchased equipment (6)	(1,700)	
Cash flows from investing activities		(1,200)
Financing Activities:		
Issued stock (9)	$ 450	
Paid debt (8)	(200)	
Cash flows from financing activities		250
Net increase in cash		$ 1,130
Beginning cash balance		300
Ending cash balance		$ 1,430

As you can see, if we have access to the detailed transaction data from the Cash t-account, preparing a statement of cash flows involves determining the proper cash flow category (operating, investing, or financing) for each inflow or outflow and then properly formatting the statement. More advanced accounting software programs allow financial statement preparers to categorize each cash inflow and outflow as an operating, investing, or financing activity and to prepare a statement of cash flows with the press of a key. What was once considered one of the most difficult parts of accounting, preparing a statement of cash flows, has been greatly simplified as a result of computer technology.

If information is properly coded when input into a computerized accounting system, the preparation of a statement of cash flows is easy. As mentioned, the more advanced accounting software facilitates this process. But what happens if an accounting system does not classify cash transactions according to their activities? In the next section, we discuss how a statement of cash flows is prepared if one does not have ready access to detailed cash inflow and outflow information.

TO SUMMARIZE

If transactions are properly classified when input into the accounting system, the preparation of a statement of cash flows is straightforward. Cash inflows and outflows are segregated according to type of activity (operating, investing, or financing) and a statement of cash flows is prepared based on that information. As technology continues to advance, the preparation of a statement of cash flows gets easier.

4 *Analyze financial statements to prepare a statement of cash flows.*

ANALYZING THE OTHER PRIMARY FINANCIAL STATEMENTS TO PREPARE A STATEMENT OF CASH FLOWS

If detailed cash flow information is not accessible, the preparation of a statement of cash flows is more difficult. The income statement and comparative balance sheets must be analyzed to determine how cash was generated and how cash was used by a business. How can we determine a company's cash inflows and outflows by looking at balance sheets and an income statement? The secret lies in remembering the basics of double-entry accounting: each journal entry has two parts—a debit and a credit. In the case of the cash account, every time cash is debited, some other account is credited; every time cash is credited, some other account is debited. If we don't have access to the details of the cash account, we can infer those details based on our knowledge of accounting and by analyzing changes in accounts other than cash.

For example, consider the accounts receivable account. A debit to that account means what? Ninety-nine percent of the time, a debit to accounts receivable is associated with a sale on account. A credit to accounts receivable means what? Most likely, cash was collected. If you have the beginning and ending balances for the accounts receivable account (from comparative balance sheets) and sales for the period (from the income statement), you can infer the cash collected for the period. Consider the information taken from Silmaril's beginning trial balance and the year-end trial balance relating to accounts receivable (remember, we are assuming that the detailed journal entries are not available to us, only the resulting financial statements):

Accounts Receivable

Beg. Bal.	2,500		
Sales	13,500	Collections	?
End. Bal.	2,000		

To reconcile the accounts receivable account, we can only assume that cash collections of $14,000 occurred. With any other amount the account will not reconcile.[1] In other words, we can infer that the following journal entry must have been made:

Cash.	14,000	
Accounts Receivable		14,000

1. Some of you might be thinking that accounts receivable can be credited when accounts are written off. This is true, and write-offs would affect our analysis. However, our purpose here is to understand the concepts. A more complicated analysis including write-offs will be covered in an intermediate accounting class.

As you can see from this analysis, we don't necessarily need the detailed cash account information to prepare a statement of cash flows. We can use our knowledge of double-entry accounting to infer those details.

CAUTION

Every balance sheet account (except cash) must be analyzed to determine any cash flow effects. Then those effects must be classified by activity.

A similar analysis is conducted for every balance sheet account (except cash). The analyses combine our knowledge of the relationship between the income statement and balance sheet accounts and of what accounts are associated with operating, investing, and financing activities. Consider another example—common stock. First of all, we know that changes in the common stock account would be considered financing activities. Second, what do we know about credits to the common stock account? They would typically be associated with the issuance (sale) of stock. Debits to the common stock account? They would be associated with the retirement of common stock. Assume we are given comparative balance sheet information (transactions in a company's own stock are not reflected on the income statement) relating to the common stock account of Silmaril Inc. as follows:

	Beginning Balance	Ending Balance
Common stock	$1,000	$1,450

What would you infer about the cash flow activities of the company relating to its common stock account? Without any additional information, it would be safe to assume that the company sold stock for $450. If something out of the ordinary happened in the common stock account (like the retirement of stock), that information would generally be available in the notes to the financial statements and would be used to modify the analysis.

As an illustration of this type of complexity, consider Silmaril's property, plant, and equipment (PP&E) account. First of all, the PP&E account is associated with what type of cash flow activity? Investing. Increases in property, plant, and equipment would correspond to purchases of PP&E and decreases would relate to the sale of PP&E. Since the sale of PP&E is typically an out-of-the-ordinary type of transaction, we could look at the notes to the financial statements for information relating to any sales. In the case of Silmaril Inc. we find that equipment costing $1,200, with accumulated depreciation of $800, was sold for $500. Based on this information, and using information from the comparative balance sheets, we can infer the purchases made during the period as follows:

FYI

Buying and using PP&E would be considered common activities. Selling PP&E would be considered less common.

Property, Plant, and Equipment

Beg. Bal.	4,000		
Purchases	?	Sold	1,200
End. Bal.	4,500		

How much PP&E was purchased during the period? The only amount that will reconcile the PP&E account is $1,700. The journal entry would have been a debit to PP&E and a credit to Cash. Again, we see that we don't need the details of the cash account to be able to infer the cash inflows and outflows for the company. Our knowledge of double-entry accounting allows us to do a little detective work and infer what went on in the cash account.

A Six-Step Process for Preparing a Statement of Cash Flows

Is there a systematic method for analyzing the income statement and comparative balance sheets to prepare a statement of cash flows? Yes, the following six-step process can be used in preparing a statement of cash flows.

noncash items Items included in the determination of net income on an accrual basis that do not affect cash; examples are depreciation and amortization.

1. Compute the change in the cash and cash-equivalent accounts for the period of the statement. Seldom is one handed a check figure in real life, but such is the case when preparing a statement of cash flows. The statement of cash flows is not complete until you have explained the change from the beginning balance in the cash account to the balance at year end.
2. Convert the income statement from an accrual-basis to a cash-basis summary of operations. This is done in three steps: (1) eliminate from the income statement those expenses that do not involve cash (such **noncash items** would include depreciation expense that does not involve an outflow of cash in the current period even though income was reduced); (2) eliminate from the income statement the effects of nonoperating activity items (such items include gains and losses on the sale of long-term assets and gains and losses associated with the retirement of debt); (3) identify those current asset and current liability accounts associated with the income statement accounts, and adjust those income statement accounts for the changes in the associated current assets and current liabilities. For example, Sales will be adjusted for the change between the beginning and ending balance in Accounts Receivable to derive the cash collections for the period. The final result will be cash flows from operating activities.
3. Analyze the long-term assets to identify the cash flow effects of investing activities. Changes in property, plant, and equipment and in long-term investments may indicate that cash has either been spent or has been received.
4. Analyze the long-term debt and stockholders' equity accounts to determine the cash flow effects of any financing transactions. These transactions could be borrowing or repaying debt, issuing or buying back stock, or paying dividends.
5. Prepare a formal statement of cash flows by classifying all cash inflows and outflows according to operating, investing, and financing activities. The net cash flows provided by (used in) each of the three main activities of an entity should be highlighted. The net cash flows amount for the period is then added (subtracted) from the beginning cash balance to report the ending cash balance.
6. Report any significant investing or financing transactions that did not involve cash in a narrative explanation or in a separate schedule to the statement of cash flows. This would include such transactions as the purchase of land by issuing stock or the retirement of bonds by issuing stock.

(STOP & THINK)

Why must gains (losses) on the sale of equipment be subtracted (added) when computing cash flows from operations?

CAUTION

Make sure that the total net cash flows from the statement (the sum of net cash flows from operating, investing, and financing activities) is equal to the net increase (decrease) in cash as computed in Step 1.

An Illustration of the Six-Step Process

We will illustrate this six-step process using the information from the Silmaril Inc. example presented earlier. Remember that our assumption when preparing the statement of cash flows in this case is that we do not have access to the detailed cash flow information. Thus, we are going to have to make inferences about cash flows by examining all other balance sheet and income statement accounts other than the cash account.

Step 1. Compute the Change in the Cash and Cash-Equivalent Accounts for the Period of the Statement.

Recall that Silmaril began the year with a cash balance of $300 and ended with a cash balance of $1,430. Thus, our target in preparing the statement of cash flows is to explain why the cash account changed by $1,130 during the year.

Step 2. Convert the Income Statement from an Accrual Basis to a Cash Basis.

From the trial balance prepared at the end of the year, we can prepare the following income statement for Silmaril Inc.:

Sales	$13,500
Cost of goods sold	8,000
Gross margin	$ 5,500
Miscellaneous expenses	3,200
Depreciation expense	500
Income from operations	$ 1,800
Interest expense	(200)
Gain on sale of equipment	100
Income before taxes	$ 1,700
Tax expense	450
Net income	$ 1,250

Our objective at this point is to convert the income statement to cash flows from operations. Recall that this involves three steps: (1) eliminating expenses not involving cash, (2) eliminating the effects of nonoperating activities, and (3) adjusting the remaining figures from an accrual basis to a cash basis. We will use a work sheet to track the adjustments that will be made. The first two adjustments involve removing depreciation expense (since it does not involve an outflow of cash) and eliminating the gain on the sale of the equipment (since the sale of equipment is an investing activity, the effect of which will be disclosed in the investing activities section of the statement). The following worksheet reflects these adjustments:

	Income Statement	Adjustments	Cash Flows from Operations
Sales	$13,500		
Cost of goods sold	(8,000)		
Miscellaneous expenses	(3,200)		
Depreciation expense	(500)	**+500 (not a cash flow item)**	0
Interest expense	(200)		
Gain on sale of equipment	100	**−100 (not an operating activity)**	0
Tax expense	(450)		
	$ 1,250		

Note that since depreciation expense was initially subtracted to arrive at net income, our adjustment involves adding $500 back since no cash actually flowed out of the company relating to depreciation. The gain on the sale of the equipment should be reflected in the investing activities section of the statement of cash flows. Therefore, its effect must be removed from operations to avoid reporting the gain twice. Since the gain was initially added, we would subtract $100 as an adjustment to remove the effects of this investing activity from the operating activities section.

The adjustments now involve converting the remaining revenue and expense items from an accrual basis to a cash basis. Recall from our analysis earlier in this section that the amount of cash collected from customers differed from sales for the period. In fact, collections exceeded sales by $500 (explaining how the accounts receivable account declined by $500). An adjustment must be made to increase the accrual-basis sales figure to its cash-basis counterpart. We add $500 as illustrated below.

	Income Statement	Adjustments	Cash Flows from Operations
Sales	$13,500	**+500 (decrease in accounts receivable)**	$14,000
Cost of goods sold	(8,000)		
Miscellaneous expenses	(3,200)		
Depreciation expense	(500)	+500 (not a cash flow item)	0
Interest expense	(200)		
Gain on sale of equipment	100	−100 (not an operating activity)	0
Tax expense	(450)		
	$ 1,250		

Next, we turn our attention to cost of goods sold. The statement of cash flows should reflect the amount of cash paid for inventory during the period. We can compute that amount by adjusting cost of goods sold to reflect the inventory used this period but purchased last period, as well as inventory that was purchased last period and paid for this period.

Since inventory declined for the period from a beginning balance of $1,900 to an ending balance of $1,800, we must adjust the cost of goods sold to reflect that it includes inventory that was purchased last period and used this period (explaining how the inventory balance declined). To reduce cost of goods sold, our adjustment would involve adding $100. A similar adjustment would be made for the change in the balance in Accounts Payable. What event would cause Accounts Payable to decline? Obviously, Accounts Payable would most likely decline because more was paid for this period than was purchased this period. If more was paid for this period, we would be required to subtract an additional $200 to reflect the additional cash outflow. The net effect of these two adjustments is to convert the accrual-basis cost of goods sold figure to the amount of inventory paid for during the year. The following T-account analysis shows the net effect of these two adjustments:

Cash (Dr.)	Cash (Cr.)	Inventory (Dr.)	Inventory (Cr.)	Accounts Payable (Dr.)	Accounts Payable (Cr.)	Cost of Goods Sold (Dr.)	Cost of Goods Sold (Cr.)
	8,100[C]	1,900	8,000[A]		1,700	8,000[A]	
		7,900[B]		8,100[C]	7,900[B]		
		1,800			1,500		

[A]Cost of inventory sold during the period (from the income statement).
[B]Inventory purchased during the period [solved for based on the beginning and ending inventory balances and cost of goods sold (A)].
[C]Inventory paid for during the period [solved for based on the beginning and ending accounts payable balances and the inventory purchased during the period (B)].

Updating our work sheet results in the following:

	Income Statement	Adjustments	Cash Flows from Operations
Sales	$13,500	+500 (decrease in accounts receivable)	$14,000
Cost of goods sold	(8,000)	**+100 (decrease in inventory)** **−200 (decrease in accounts payable)**	(8,100)
Miscellaneous expenses	(3,200)		
Depreciation expense	(500)	+500 (not a cash flow item)	0
Interest expense	(200)		
Gain on sale of equipment	100	−100 (not an operating activity)	0
Tax expense	(450)		
	$ 1,250		

CAUTION

Remember that Cost of Goods Sold is subtracted from Sales. Adding $100 would serve to reduce the negative number, and subtracting $200 would make the cost of goods sold figure a larger negative number.

Since a miscellaneous expenses payable account does not exist, we can safely assume that all the miscellaneous expenses were paid for in cash. Therefore, there would be no adjustment.

Both Interest Expense and Tax Expense require adjustments similar to that done for Accounts Payable and/or Inventory. Let's first deal with adjusting Interest Expense from an accrual basis to a cash basis. Note that Interest Payable increased from $0 at the beginning of the period to $20 at the end of the period. How would that happen? Obviously, if a payable account increases, then we owe for products and services we have purchased or used. In this case what we have used is money. Interest expense for the period was $200, of which we have yet to pay $20 of that interest. Thus, the cash flow related to interest must be $180—requiring an adjustment of $20.

Tax Expense is adjusted in a similar fashion. Since the amount of taxes owed increased from the beginning to the end of the period, we must have paid a lesser amount relating to taxes than is reflected on the income statement. Reviewing the T-account for Taxes Payable helps us see how that can be:

Taxes Payable

		Beg. Bal.	40
Taxes paid during the period	?	Amount related to tax expense	450
		End. Bal.	50

As you can determine, the only amount that would balance the above t-account would be $440—the amount paid for taxes during the period. Since the income statement reflects expense of $450 related to taxes, yet the cash outflow was only $440, we must make an adjustment of $10. The work sheet, with these final adjustments, appears as follows:

	Income Statement	Adjustments	Cash Flows from Operations
Sales	$13,500	+500 (decrease in accounts receivable)	$14,000
Cost of goods sold	(8,000)	+100 (decrease in inventory) −200 (decrease in accounts payable)	(8,100)
Miscellaneous expenses	(3,200)	+0	(3,200)
Depreciation expense	(500)	+500 (not a cash flow item)	0
Interest expense	(200)	**+20 (increase in interest payable)**	(180)
Gain on sale of equipment	100	−100 (not an operating activity)	0
Tax expense	(450)	**+10 (increase in taxes payable)**	(440)
	$ 1,250	+830 net adjustment	$ 2,080

Note that the cash flows from operations figure obtained through an analysis of the income statement accounts and current asset and current liability accounts is the same figure obtained previously when we assumed access to the detailed cash account information. We should always get the same answer when the question is the same—"What were cash flows from operations?"

The Direct and Indirect Methods Our final task relating to cash flows from operations relates to preparing the Operating Activities section of the statement of cash flows. At this point, we have two alternatives to select from—the indirect method or the direct method.

indirect method A method of reporting net cash flows from operations that involves converting accrual-basis net income to a cash basis.

The **indirect method** begins with net income as reported on the income statement and then details the adjustments made to arrive at cash flows from operations. For Silmaril Inc., it would involve beginning with the net income figure and then listing the adjustments from the work sheet. In other words, the following highlighted portions of the work sheet would be used.

	Income Statement	Adjustments	Cash Flows from Operations
Sales	$13,500	+500 (decrease in accounts receivable)	$14,000
Cost of goods sold	(8,000)	+100 (decrease in inventory) −200 (decrease in accounts payable)	(8,100)
Miscellaneous expenses	(3,200)	+0	(3,200)
Depreciation expense	(500)	+500 (not a cash flow item)	0
Interest expense	(200)	+20 (increase in interest payable)	(180)
Gain on sale of equipment	100	−100 (not an operating activity)	0
Tax expense	(450)	+10 (increase in taxes payable)	(440)
	$ 1,250	+830 net adjustment	$ 2,080

The operating activities section would be formatted as follows:

Operating Activities:		
Net income		$1,250
Add: Depreciation expense	$500	
Decrease in accounts receivable	500	
Decrease in inventory	100	
Increase in interest payable	20	
Increase in taxes payable	10	
Less: Gain on sale of equipment	(100)	
Decrease in accounts payable	(200)	830
Cash flows from operations		$2,080

direct method A method of reporting net cash flows from operations that shows the major classes of cash receipts and payments for a period of time.

Using the **direct method**, the operating activities section of a statement of cash flows is, in effect, a cash-basis income statement. Unlike the indirect method, the direct method does not start with net income. Instead, this method directly reports the major classes of operating cash receipts and payments of an entity during a period. This information is obtained from the last column of the work sheet as follows:

	Income Statement	Adjustments	Cash Flows from Operations
Sales	$13,500	+500 (decrease in accounts receivable)	$14,000
Cost of goods sold	(8,000)	+100 (decrease in inventory) −200 (decrease in accounts payable)	(8,100)
Miscellaneous expenses	(3,200)	+0	(3,200)
Depreciation expense	(500)	+500 (not a cash flow item)	0
Interest expense	(200)	+20 (increase in interest payable)	(180)
Gain on sale of equipment	100	−100 (not an operating activity)	0
Tax expense	(450)	+10 (increase in taxes payable)	(440)
	$ 1,250	+830 net adjustment	$ 2,080

The resulting operating activities section, given below, looks a lot like the operating activities section we prepared when we had access to the detailed cash flow information.

Operating Activities:		
Collections from customers		$14,000
Payments for inventory	$8,100	
Payments for miscellaneous expenses	3,200	
Payments for interest	180	
Payments for taxes	440	(11,920)
Cash flows from operating activities		$ 2,080

Note that the same amount of cash flows from operating activities is derived using either the indirect method or the direct method.

(STOP & THINK)

Now that you have seen both methods for preparing the operating activities section of the statement of cash flows, which method do you prefer? Which method do you think is used most often by companies?

Why Two Methods? You may be asking yourself, "Why are there two methods for preparing a statement of cash flows when both methods always result in the same answer?" Good question. There are advantages and disadvantages to each method. The indirect method is favored and used by most companies because it is relatively easy to apply and reconciles the difference between net income and the net cash flows provided by operations. The direct method is favored by many users of financial statements because it reports directly the sources of cash inflows and outflows without the potentially confusing adjustments to net income. The accounting standard setters considered the arguments for both methods, and although they preferred the clarity of the direct method, they permitted either method to be used. Because they can choose either method and already have to compute net income, approximately 95 percent of large U.S. corporations use the indirect method when preparing a statement of cash flows.

Some Rules of Thumb While all this analysis may seem complex, the guidelines shown below will help you as you analyze accounts and prepare a statement of cash flows.

Accounts	Direction of Change During the Period	Adjustment to be Made
Current assets	Increase	Subtracted
Current assets	Decrease	Added
Current liabilities	Increase	Added
Current liabilities	Decrease	Subtracted

CAUTION

These guidelines will help you to understand how certain adjustments are made, but they will not help you understand *why* the adjustments are being made. To understand why, you must use your knowledge of accounting.

When current assets increase (decrease) during the period, the difference between the beginning and ending balances is subtracted (added) from the appropriate income statement account to arrive at cash flows for the period. As an example, if accounts receivable increase during the period, that means sales exceed collections and Sales on the income statement must be reduced to reflect the cash collected for the period. The reverse would be true when accounts receivable decrease.

In the case of current liabilities, an increase (decrease) requires that an adjustment be made to add (subtract) the difference between the beginning and ending balances. For example, when interest payable increases from the beginning to the end of the period, interest expense exceeds the cash paid during the period. Interest Expense must be reduced (by adding back) to reflect the cash paid during the period. Again, the reverse would be true if interest payable were to decrease during the period. Exhibit 8-6 summarizes the procedures for converting selected accounts from an accrual to a cash basis.

Step 3. Analyze the Long-Term Assets to Identify the Cash Flows Effect of Investing Activities.

The only long-term asset account for Silmaril Inc. is the property, plant, and equipment (PP&E) account with its associated accumulated depreciation. The balance in the PP&E account increased by $500 during the period. What would an increase in the PP&E account indicate? Obviously, something was purchased. If we had no additional information, we would assume that PP&E was purchased by paying $500. But we do have additional information. We know that PP&E was purchased during the period by paying $1,700. With that information, we can prepare the following PP&E T-account:

PP&E

Beg. Bal.	4,000		
Purchased	1,700	Sold	?
End. Bal.	4,500		

EXHIBIT 8-6

Guidelines for Converting from Accrual to Cash Basis

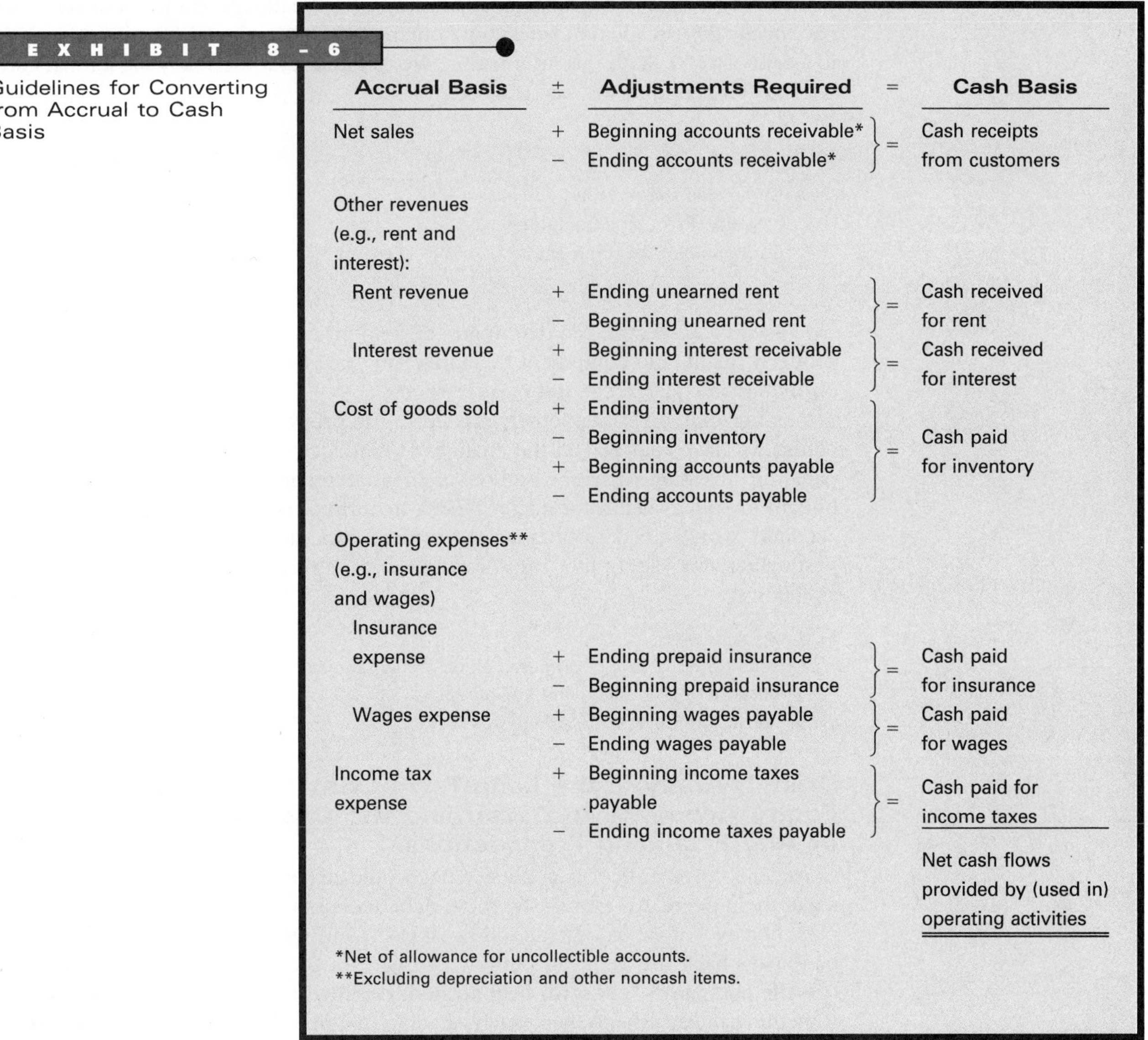

Accrual Basis	±	Adjustments Required	=	Cash Basis
Net sales	+	Beginning accounts receivable*	=	Cash receipts
	−	Ending accounts receivable*		from customers
Other revenues (e.g., rent and interest):				
Rent revenue	+	Ending unearned rent	=	Cash received
	−	Beginning unearned rent		for rent
Interest revenue	+	Beginning interest receivable	=	Cash received
	−	Ending interest receivable		for interest
Cost of goods sold	+	Ending inventory	=	Cash paid
	−	Beginning inventory		for inventory
	+	Beginning accounts payable		
	−	Ending accounts payable		
Operating expenses** (e.g., insurance and wages)				
Insurance expense	+	Ending prepaid insurance	=	Cash paid
	−	Beginning prepaid insurance		for insurance
Wages expense	+	Beginning wages payable	=	Cash paid
	−	Ending wages payable		for wages
Income tax expense	+	Beginning income taxes payable	=	Cash paid for income taxes
	−	Ending income taxes payable		
				Net cash flows provided by (used in) operating activities

*Net of allowance for uncollectible accounts.
**Excluding depreciation and other noncash items.

To make the T-account balance, equipment must have been sold. What was the original cost of the equipment that was sold? It must have been $1,200 (that is the only number that will make the T-account balance). What was the accumulated depreciation associated with the sold equipment? Let's take a look at the Accumulated Depreciation T-account. Entries on the debit side of that account track the accumulated depreciation associated with equipment that has been sold. Entries to the credit side are associated with depreciation expense for the period. Since we know depreciation expense for the period (from the income statement), and we know the beginning and ending balances in the account (from the balance sheet), we can infer the accumulated depreciation associated with the equipment that was sold.

Accumulated Depreciation

		Beg. Bal.	1,200
Sold	?	Depreciation Expense	500
		End. Bal.	900

The accumulated depreciation associated with the equipment that was sold must have been $800. In addition, we know from the income statement that the sale resulted in a gain of $100. With this information, we can infer that the following journal entry was made relating to the sale of PP&E:

Cash	500	
Accumulated Depreciation	800	
Property, Plant, and Equipment		1,200
Gain on Sale of Equipment		100

As you can see, we can determine the amount of cash received from the sale of property, plant, and equipment by monitoring the change in other related accounts on the income statement and balance sheet.

As our only investing activity related to the property, plant, and equipment account, we have analyzed all the changes in that account and are now ready to prepare the investing activities section of the statement of cash flows. Had Silmaril bought or sold available-for-sale or held-to-maturity securities during the year, these accounts would need to be analyzed to determine any cash flow effects. The investing activities section of the statement of cash flows for Silmaril Inc. would be as follows:

Investing Activities:		
Proceeds from the sale of property, plant, and equipment	$ 500	
Purchased property, plant, and equipment	(1,700)	
Cash flows from investing activities		$(1,200)

Step 4. Analyze the Long-Term Debt and Stockholders' Equity Accounts to Determine the Cash Flow Effects of Any Financing Transactions.

Consider long-term debt accounts. What would make them increase? What would make them decrease? Obviously, these debt accounts would increase when a company borrows more money (an inflow of cash) and would decrease when the company pays back the debt (an outflow of cash). In the case of Silmaril, we observe that the company's long-term debt account declined from $2,200 to $2,000. Unless something unusual happened (such as additional debt being issued and then some debt being repaid), we assume that the reason for the decrease was that cash was used to reduce the liability.

In the case of stockholders' equity accounts, we examine both the common stock and retained earnings accounts for increases and decreases resulting from cash flows. The common stock account will increase as a result of the sale of stock and decrease if any stock is repurchased and retired. Since the common stock account increased by $450 during the period, we assume that the increase resulted from the sale of stock. Again, if an unusual transaction had occurred, information relating to the transaction would be available in the notes. Retained Earnings increases from the recognition of net income (an operating activity) and decreases as a result of net losses (also an operating activity) or through the payment of dividends (a financing activity). In the case of Silmaril Inc., since no dividends are disclosed on the trial balance, the entire change in Retained Earnings results from net income; the cash flow effect has already been included in operating activities.

Silmaril Inc. would prepare the following information relating to its financing activities:

Financing Activities:		
Proceeds from the sale of stock	$ 450	
Repayment of long-term debt	(200)	
Cash flows from financing activities		$250

Step 5. Prepare a Formal Statement of Cash Flows.

Based on our analysis of all income statement and balance sheet accounts, we have identified all inflows and outflows of cash for Silmaril Inc. and categorized those cash flows based on the type of activity. The resulting statement of cash flows (prepared using the direct method)[2] would be as follows:

Operating Activities:		
Collections from customers		$14,000
Payments for inventory	$ 8,100	
Payments for miscellaneous expenses	3,200	
Payments for interest	180	
Payments for taxes	440	(11,920)
Cash flows from operating activities		$ 2,080
Investing Activities:		
Proceeds from the sale of property, plant, and equipment	$ 500	
Purchased property, plant, and equipment	(1,700)	
Cash flows from investing activities		(1,200)
Financing Activities:		
Proceeds from the sale of stock	$ 450	
Repayment of long-term debt	(200)	
Cash flows from financing activities		250
Net increase in cash		$ 1,130
Beginning cash balance		300
Ending cash balance		$ 1,430

Additional disclosure is required in the notes to the financial statements depending on the methods used. Other disclosures required by FASB Statement No. 95 include the amounts paid for interest and income taxes. When the indirect method is used to report cash flows from operating activities, cash paid for interest and income taxes is disclosed as supplemental. When the direct method is used to report cash flows from operating activities, these amounts are included in the statement of cash flows.

An additional disclosure required when the direct method is used is a schedule reconciling net income with net cash flows provided by (used in) operating activities. This schedule is, in effect, the same as the operating activities section of a statement of cash flows prepared using the indirect method.

noncash transactions Investing and financing activities that do not affect cash; if significant, they are disclosed below the statement of cash flows or in the notes to the financial statements.

Step 6. Report Any Significant Investing or Financing Transactions that Did Not Involve Cash.

If Silmaril had any significant **noncash transactions**, like purchasing PP&E by issuing debt or trading Silmaril stock for that of another company, these transactions would be disclosed in the notes to the financial statements or in a separate schedule below the statement of cash flows. In this example, no such transactions occurred.

TO SUMMARIZE

The cash inflows and outflows of an organization must be analyzed and classified into one of three categories: operating, investing, and financing. Operating activities include those transactions that enter into the determination of net income. The direct or the indirect method may be used to show the net cash flows provided by (used in) operating activities. The indirect method starts with net income, as reported on the income statement, and adds or subtracts adjustments to convert accrual net income to net

2. A statement of cash flows prepared using the indirect method is shown in the Review Problem on pages 363–366. The statement of cash flows for Microsoft, shown in Appendix A, was also prepared using the indirect method.

cash flows from operations. Adjustments to net income are made for increases and decreases in operating account balances, noncash items such as depreciation, and gains and losses from the sale of assets. The direct method shows the major classes of operating cash receipts and payments. The direct method requires analysis of cash transactions or an analysis of accrual revenues and expenses in order to convert them to cash receipts and payments. Both methods produce the same results, and either method is allowed under generally accepted accounting principles. Investing activities involve the purchase or sale of long-term assets like property, plant, and equipment or investment securities. Financing activities include transactions in which cash is obtained from or paid to owners and creditors.

5 *Use information from the statement of cash flows to make decisions.*

USING INFORMATION FROM THE STATEMENT OF CASH FLOWS TO MAKE DECISIONS

To this point in the text, we have reviewed numerous financial statement analysis techniques involving the income statement and the balance sheet. We have introduced and discussed numerous ratios that were computed using numbers from the income statement and the balance sheet. We can also use information from the statement of cash flows for analysis purposes.

Analysis using cash flow information is often restricted to an analysis of the relationships among the categories in the statement of cash flows. We do not perform vertical or horizontal analysis because, unlike the balance sheet and income statement, there is no guarantee that a specific number from the statement of cash flows will consistently serve as the denominator for scaling purposes. For example, all balance sheet accounts are compared to total assets when preparing a vertical analysis of the balance sheet. Why? Because total assets is always going to be the biggest number on the balance sheet. The same is true for the income statement. Revenue is used because it is, in almost every case, the biggest number on the income statement. In the case of the statement of cash flows, some years the cash flow from operations may be the largest number on the statement. In subsequent years, that number may be negative. Thus, horizontal and vertical analyses are rarely performed using the statement of cash flows because of scaling problems.

Although the statement of cash flows, like the other financial statements, reports information about the past, careful analysis of this information can help investors, creditors, and others assess the amounts, timing, and uncertainty of future cash flows. Specifically, the statement helps users answer questions such as how a company is able to pay dividends when it had a net loss, or why a company is short of cash despite increased earnings. A statement of cash flows may show, for example, that external borrowing or the issuance of capital stock provided the cash from which dividends were paid even though a net loss was reported for that year. Similarly, a company may be short on cash, even with increased earnings, because of increased inventory purchases, plant expansion, or debt retirement.

Trends are often more important than absolute numbers for any one period. Accordingly, cash flow statements usually are presented on a comparative basis. This enables users to analyze a company's cash flows over time.

Because companies are required to highlight cash flows from operating, investing, and financing activities, a company's operating cash flows and investing and financing policies can be compared with those of other companies. We can learn much about a company by examining patterns that appear among the three cash flow categories in the statement of cash flows. Exhibit 8–7 shows eight possible cash flow patterns and provides some insight into what each cash flow pattern indicates about the company.

EXHIBIT 8-7

Analysis of Cash Flows Statement: Patterns

	CF from Operating	CF from Investing	CF from Financing	General Explanation
#1	+	+	+	Company is using cash generated from operations, from sale of assets, and from financing to build up pile of cash—very liquid company—possibly looking for acquisition.
#2	+	−	−	Company is using cash flows generated from operations to buy fixed assets and to pay down debt or pay owners.
#3	+	+	−	Company is using cash from operations and from sale of fixed assets to pay down debt or pay owners.
#4	+	−	+	Company is using cash from operations and from borrowing (or from owner investment) to expand.
#5	−	+	+	Company's operating cash flow problems are covered by sale of fixed assets, by borrowing, or by stockholder contributions.
#6	−	−	+	Company is growing rapidly, but has short-falls in cash flows from operations and from purchase of fixed assets financed by long-term debt or new investment.
#7	−	+	−	Company is financing operating cash flow shortages and payments to creditors and/or stockholders via sale of fixed assets.
#8	−	−	−	Company is using cash reserves to finance operation shortfall and pay long-term creditors and/or investors.

Source: Michael T. Dugan, Benton E. Gup, and William D. Samson, "Teaching the Statement of Cash Flows," *Journal of Accounting Education,* Vol. 9, 1991, p. 36.

Positive cash flows from operations are necessary if a company is to succeed over the long term (patterns 1 through 4). The most common cash flow pattern is 2. Companies use cash flows from operations to purchase fixed assets or to pay down debt. Growing companies follow cash flow pattern 6. Cash is being borrowed to cover a shortage of cash from operations as well as to purchase fixed assets. Most (about 80 percent) of the publicly traded companies in the United States follow patterns 2, 4, and 6.

TO SUMMARIZE

Conducting financial statement analysis using information from the statement of cash flows is more difficult than analyses using information from the income statement and the balance sheet. The primary reason is that it is common for cash flows for certain categories to be negative, thereby making interpretation difficult. However, an analysis of the relationship among the categories on the statement of cash flows can provide insight into a company's performance.

REVIEW OF LEARNING OBJECTIVES

1 Understand the purpose of a statement of cash flows. The statement of cash flows is one of the three primary financial statements presented by companies in their annual reports. Its primary purpose is to provide information about the cash receipts and payments of an entity during a period. The statement of cash flows also explains the changes in the balance sheet accounts and the cash effects of the accrual-basis amounts reported in the income statement.

2 Recognize the different types of information reported in the statement of cash flows. The statement of cash flows reports an entity's inflows and outflows of cash for a period of time and reconciles the beginning and ending balances of cash and cash equivalents.

The inflows and outflows of cash should be classified and reported for three main categories: operating activities, investing activities, and financing activities. Cash receipts and payments classified under operating activities generally include all items that enter into the determination of net income. Examples include receipts from the sale of goods or services and from interest, and the payments for inventory, wages, utilities, taxes, and interest.

Investing activities include the purchase and sale of certain securities (other than cash equivalents, which are included with cash), buildings and equipment, and other assets that are not generally purchased for resale by the entity. Also included are the making and collecting of loans.

Financing activities include obtaining and repaying cash from owners (equity financing) and from creditors (debt financing). Selling stock, paying cash dividends, and borrowing money, for example, are included under this category.

Significant noncash transactions involving investing and financing activities should be reported in a note or in a separate schedule to the financial statements. Since they do not involve cash flows, they should not be reported in the statement of cash flows. An example would be the purchase of land by the issuance of stock.

3 Prepare a simple statement of cash flows. If cash inflows and outflows can be categorized according to the activity (operating, investing, or financing) when entered into the accounting system, the preparation of a statement of cash flows is straightforward. At the end of the period, inflows and outflows would be divided by category and type of cash flow, e.g., collections from customers, payments for inventory, etc. A statement of cash flows would then simply list those inflows and outflows by activity.

4 Analyze financial statements to prepare a statement of cash flows. Often, detailed cash flow information is not available. When that happens, the statement of cash flows is prepared by analyzing comparative balance sheets and the income statement. A six-step process can be employed to assist in the analysis. First, the change in the cash balance for the period is computed. Second, the income statement is converted from an accrual basis to a cash basis. The result is cash flows from operating activities. Third, long-term assets are analyzed to determine the cash flow effects of investing activities. Fourth, long-term liabilities and stockholders' equity accounts are analyzed to determine the cash flow effects of financing activities. Fifth, a formal statement of cash flows is prepared. And sixth, significant noncash transactions are disclosed in the notes to the financial statements or in a separate schedule at the bottom of the statement of cash flows.

5 Use information from the statement of cash flows to make decisions. A careful analysis of the statement of cash flows will indicate shifts in a company's operating, investing, and financing policies. The statement explains the change in the cash balance during the period by identifying the inflows and outflows of cash. This helps investors and creditors observe trends related to a company's use of operating income and to its use of external sources of capital such as the issuance of stock or bonds. Used with the income statement and the balance sheet, the statement of cash flows is a valuable source of information.

KEY TERMS AND CONCEPTS

REVIEW PROBLEMS

Classifying Cash Flows

Anna Dimetros is the bookkeeper for Russia Imports, Inc. (RII), a New York City-based company. Anna has collected the following cash flow information about RII for the most current year of operations. The cash balance at the beginning of the year was $105,000.

Cash receipts:	
Cash received from issuance of stock	$ 50,000
Cash received from customers	252,300
Cash received from interest at bank	4,600
Cash received from borrowing at bank	25,000
Total cash receipts	$331,900
Cash payments:	
Cash paid for wages of employees	$134,600
Cash paid to stockholders as dividends	5,500
Cash paid to bank for interest	7,200
Cash paid to bank to repay earlier loan	10,000
Cash paid for taxes	23,500
Cash paid for operating expenses	128,100
Cash paid for equipment	15,000
Total cash payments	$323,900

Required:

1. From the information provided, classify the cash flows for Russia Imports, Inc., according to operating, investing, and financing activities.
2. Determine the ending cash balance.

Solution

Russia Imports, Inc.
Cash Flows
20XX

1. *Cash flows from operating activities:*		
Cash receipts from:		
Customers	$252,300	
Bank (interest)	4,600	$256,900
Cash payments to:		
Employees (wages)	$134,600	
Bank (interest)	7,200	
Government (taxes)	23,500	
Various entities (operating expenses)	128,100	293,400
Net cash flows used in operating activities		$ (36,500)
Cash flows from investing activities:		
Cash payments to:		
Purchase equipment	$ (15,000)	
Net cash flows used in investing activities		$ (15,000)

(continued)

Cash flows from financing activities:		
Cash receipts from:		
Issuance of stock	$ 50,000	
Borrowing at bank	25,000	$ 75,000
Cash payments to:		
Stockholders (dividends)	$ (5,500)	
Repay earlier loan	(10,000)	(15,500)
Net cash flows provided by financing activities		$ 59,500
Total net cash flows for period		$ 8,000
2. Beginning cash balance		$105,000
Total net cash flows for period		8,000
Ending cash balance		$113,000*

*Alternatively, beginning balance ($105,000) + receipts ($331,900) − payments ($323,900) = ending balance ($113,000).

Preparing a Statement of Cash Flows

Snow Corporation produces clock radios. Comparative income statements and balance sheets for the years ended December 31, 2000 and 1999, are presented.

Snow Corporation
Comparative Income Statements
For the Years Ended December 31, 2000 and 1999

	2000	1999
Net sales revenue	$600,000	$575,000
Cost of goods sold	500,000	460,000
Gross margin	$100,000	$115,000
Operating expenses	66,000	60,000
Operating income	$ 34,000	$ 55,000
Interest expense	4,000	3,000
Income before taxes	$ 30,000	$ 52,000
Income taxes	12,000	21,000
Net income	$ 18,000	$ 31,000

Snow Corporation
Comparative Balance Sheets
December 31, 2000 and 1999

	2000	1999
Assets		
Current assets:		
Cash and cash equivalents	$ 11,000	$ 13,000
Accounts receivable (net)	92,000	77,000
Inventory	103,000	92,000
Prepaid expenses	6,000	5,000
Total current assets	$212,000	$187,000
Property, plant, and equipment:		
Land	$ 69,000	$ 66,000
Machinery and equipment	172,000	156,000
Accumulated depreciation, machinery and equipment	(113,000)	(102,000)
Total property, plant, and equipment	$128,000	$120,000
Total assets	$340,000	$307,000

(continued)

	2000	1999
Liabilities and Stockholders' Equity		
Current liabilities:		
Accounts payable	$ 66,000	$ 78,000
Dividends payable	2,000	0
Income taxes payable	3,000	5,000
Total current liabilities	$ 71,000	$ 83,000
Long-term debt	75,000	42,000
Total liabilities	$146,000	$125,000
Stockholders' equity:		
Common stock, no par	$ 26,000	$ 26,000
Retained earnings	168,000	156,000
Total stockholders' equity	$194,000	$182,000
Total liabilities and stockholders' equity	$340,000	$307,000

The following additional information is available.

a. Dividends declared during 2000 were $6,000.
b. Market price per share of stock on December 31, 2000, was $14.50.
c. Equipment worth $16,000 was acquired by the issuance of a long-term note ($10,000) and by paying cash ($6,000).
d. Land was acquired for $3,000 cash.
e. Depreciation of $11,000 was included in operating expenses for 2000.
f. There were no accruals or prepaid amounts for interest.

Required: Analyze the data provided to prepare a statement of cash flows. Use (1) the indirect method and (2) the direct method to report cash flows from operating activities.

Solution **1. Indirect Method**

Snow Corporation
Statement of Cash Flows (Indirect Method)
For the Year Ended December 31, 2000

Cash flows from operating activities:		
Net income	$18,000	
Add (deduct) adjustments to cash basis:		
Depreciation expense	11,000	
Increase in accounts receivable	(15,000)	
Increase in inventory	(11,000)	
Increase in prepaid expenses	(1,000)	
Decrease in accounts payable	(12,000)	
Decrease in income taxes payable	(2,000)	
Net cash flows used in operating activities		$(12,000)
Cash flows from investing activities:		
Cash payments for:		
Land	$ (3,000)	
Machinery and equipment	(6,000)	
Net cash flows used in investing activities		(9,000)
Cash flows from financing activities:		
Cash receipts from long-term borrowing	$23,000	
Cash payments for dividends	(4,000)*	
Net cash flows provided by financing activities		19,000
Net decrease in cash		$ (2,000)
Cash and cash equivalents at beginning of year		13,000
Cash and cash equivalents at end of year		$ 11,000

*Cash dividends declared ($6,000) less increase in dividends payable ($2,000).

(continued)

Supplemental disclosure:	
Cash payments for:	
Interest	$ 4,000
Income taxes	14,000
Noncash transaction	
Equipment was purchased by issuing a long-term note for $10,000.	

The statement of cash flows for Snow Corporation shows that although reported net income was positive for 2000, the net cash flows generated from operating activities were negative. Only by borrowing cash was Snow Corporation able to pay dividends and purchase land and equipment. Even then the cash account decreased by $2,000 during the period.

2. Direct Method

Snow Corporation
Statement of Cash Flows (Direct Method)
For the Year Ended December 31, 2000

Cash flows from operating activities:		
Cash receipts from customers		$585,000
Cash payments for:		
Inventory	$523,000	
Operating expenses	56,000	
Interest expense	4,000	
Income tax expense	14,000	597,000
Net cash flows used in operating activities		$ (12,000)
Cash flows from investing activities:		
Cash payments for:		
Land	$ (3,000)	
Machinery and equipment	(6,000)	
Net cash flows used in investing activities		(9,000)
Cash flows from financing activities:		
Cash receipts from long-term borrowing	$ 23,000	
Cash payments for dividends	(4,000)	
Net cash flows provided by financing activities		19,000
Net decrease in cash		$ (2,000)
Cash and cash equivalents at beginning of year		13,000
Cash and cash equivalents at end of year		$ 11,000

*Supplemental Disclosure**
Equipment was purchased by issuing a long-term note for $10,000.

*A schedule reconciling net income with net cash flow used by operating activities would also be presented, either with the statement of cash flows or in the notes to the financial statements. The information provided in the schedule is the same as the operating activities section of the statement of cash flows prepared using the indirect method (see part 1).

DISCUSSION QUESTIONS

1. What is the main purpose of a statement of cash flows?
2. What are cash equivalents, and how are they treated on a statement of cash flows?
3. Distinguish among cash flows from operating, investing, and financing activities, providing examples for each type of activity.

4. How are significant noncash investing and financing transactions to be reported?
5. Describe the process of converting from accrual revenues to cash receipts.
6. Describe the six-step process that can be used to prepare a statement of cash flows by analyzing the income statement and comparative balance sheets.
7. Distinguish between the indirect and direct methods of reporting net cash flows provided by (used in) operating activities.
8. How are depreciation and similar noncash items treated on a statement of cash flows?
9. What supplemental disclosures are likely to be required in connection with a statement of cash flows?
10. How might investors and creditors use a statement of cash flows?

DISCUSSION CASES

CASE 8-1

SHOULD WE MAKE THE LOAN?

Save More, Inc., a discount department store, has applied to its bankers for a loan. Although the company has been profitable, it is short of cash. The loan application includes the following information about current assets, current liabilities, net income, depreciation expense, and dividends for the past five years. (All numbers are rounded to the nearest thousand, with the 000's omitted.)

	Dec. 31, 1995	Dec. 31, 1996	Dec. 31, 1997	Dec. 31, 1998	Dec. 31, 1999
Cash and cash equivalents.	$ 5	$ 73	$ 10	$158	$ (189)
Accounts receivable (net). .	403	555	516	576	654
Inventory.	253	142	383	385	1,022
Accounts payable	19	17	281	253	52
Net income	454	492	467	440	481
Depreciation expense	50	50	55	60	60
Dividends paid	177	197	208	211	211

As a bank loan officer, you have been asked to review these figures in order to determine whether the bank should loan money to Save More, Inc.

1. Compute the net cash flows from operations for the last four years.
2. What caused the sudden decrease in cash flows from operations?
3. What factors would you focus on and what additional information would you need before deciding whether to make the loan?

CASE 8-2

ANALYZING THE CASH POSITION OF GOOD TIME, INC.

The following data show the account balances of Good Time, Inc., at the beginning and end of the company's fiscal year.

Debits	Aug. 31, 2000	Sept. 1, 1999
Cash and cash equivalents	$ 88,200	$ 29,000
Accounts receivable (net)	15,000	13,300
Inventory	10,500	12,700
Prepaid insurance	2,800	2,000
Long-term investments (cost equals market)	3,000	8,400
Equipment	40,000	33,000
Treasury stock (at cost)	5,000	10,000
Cost of goods sold	184,000	
Operating expenses	93,500	
Income taxes	18,800	
Loss on sale of equipment	500	
Total debits	$461,300	$108,400

Credits	Aug. 31, 2000	Sept. 1, 1999
Accumulated depreciation—equipment	$ 9,500	$ 9,000
Accounts payable	3,500	5,600
Interest payable	500	1,000
Income taxes payable	6,000	4,000
Notes payable—long-term	8,000	12,000
Common stock	55,000	50,000
Paid in capital in excess of par	16,000	15,000
Retained earnings	9,800*	11,800
Sales	352,000	
Gain on sale of long-term investments	1,000	
Total credits	$461,300	$108,400

*Preclosing balance

The following information concerning this year was also available:

a. All purchases and sales were on account.
b. Equipment with an original cost of $5,000 was sold for $1,500; a lost of $500 was recognized on the sale.
c. Among other items, the operating expenses included Depreciation Expense of $3,500; Interest Expense of $1,400; and Insurance Expense of $1,200.
d. Equipment was purchased by issuing common stock and paying the balance ($6,000) in cash.
e. Treasury stock was sold for $2,000 less than it cost; the decrease in stockholders' equity was recorded by reducing Retained Earnings.
f. No dividends were paid this year.

You are to examine Good Time's cash position by:

1. Preparing schedules showing the amount of cash collected from accounts receivable, cash paid for accounts payable, cash paid for interest, and cash paid for insurance.
2. Preparing a statement of cash flows for Good Time for the fiscal year 2000 using the direct method.
3. Identifying the major reasons why Good Time's cash and cash equivalents increased so dramatically during the year.
4. Commenting on whether the dividend policy seems appropriate under the current circumstances.

CASE 8-3

ANALYZING CASH FLOW PATTERNS

Paula Dalton is a security analyst for DJM, Inc. She claims that she can tell a great deal about companies by analyzing their cash flow patterns. Specifically, she looks at the negative or positive cash flow trends in the three categories on cash flow statements. Paula thinks that this information is even more valuable than net income trend data from income statements. She illustrates her theory with the following patterns of cash flows for Abbott Company over the past three years.

	2000	1999	1998
Net income	–	+	+
Cash flows from:			
Operating activities	–	–	+
Investing activities	+	+	+
Financing activities	+	+	+

How do you think Paula would analyze these results? Do you agree that analyzing cash flow patterns provides superior analytical information?

EXERCISES

EXERCISE 8-1
Classification of Cash Flows

Indicate whether each of the following items would be classified as a cash inflow (I), cash outflow (O), or noncash item (N), and under which category each would be reported on a statement of cash flows: Operating Activities (OA); Investing Activities (IA); Financing Activities (FA); or not on the statement (NOS). An example is provided.

Item	Classified As	Reported Under
Example: Sales Revenue	I	OA

1. Fees collected for services
2. Interest paid
3. Proceeds from sale of equipment
4. Cash (principal) received from bank on long-term note
5. Purchase of treasury stock for cash
6. Collection of loan made to company officer
7. Cash dividends paid
8. Taxes paid
9. Depreciation expense
10. Wages paid to employees
11. Cash paid for inventory purchases
12. Proceeds from sale of common stock
13. Interest received on loan to company officer
14. Purchase of land by issuing stock
15. Utility bill paid

EXERCISE 8-2
Classification of Cash Flows

The following items summarize certain transactions that occurred during the past year for Alta Inc. Show in which section of the statement of cash flows that the information would be reported by placing an X in the appropriate column. (Assume the direct method is used to report operating cash flows.)

Transaction	Reported In Statement of Cash Flows: Operating	Investing	Financing	Not Reported in Statement of Cash Flows
a. Collections from customers				
b. Depreciation expense				
c. Wages and salaries paid				
d. Cash dividends paid				
e. Taxes paid				
f. Utilities paid				
g. Building purchased in exchange for stock				
h. Stock of Western Co. purchased				
i. Inventory purchased for cash				
j. Interest on Alta's note to local bank paid				
k. Interest received from a note with a customer				
l. Delivery truck sold at no gain or loss				

EXERCISE 8-3
Transaction Analysis

Following are the transactions of Equine Company:

a. Sold equipment for $1,000. The original cost was $15,700; the book value is $1,700.
b. Purchased equipment costing $110,000 by paying cash of $20,000 and signing a $90,000 long-term note at 12 percent interest.
c. Received $5,000 of the principal and $450 in interest on a long-term note receivable.
d. Received $2,500 in cash dividends on stock held as a trading security. (Assume that the cost method is used.)
e. Purchased treasury stock for $3,000.

Complete the following:

1. Prepare journal entries for each of the transactions. (Omit explanations.)
2. For each transaction, indicate the amount of cash inflow or outflow. Then, note how each transaction would be classified on a statement of cash flows.

EXERCISE 8-4
Transaction Analysis

The Vikon Company had the following selected transactions during the past year:

a. Sold (issued) 1,000 shares of common stock, $10 par, for $25 per share.
b. Collected $100,000 of accounts receivable.
c. Paid dividends to current stockholders in the amount of $50,000 (assume dividends declared earlier, establishing a dividends payable account).
d. Received $1,500 interest on a note receivable from a company officer.
e. Paid the annual insurance premium of $1,200.
f. Recorded depreciation expense of $5,000.

1. Prepare appropriate journal entries for each of the above transactions. (Omit explanations.)
2. For each transaction, indicate the amount of cash inflow or outflow and also how each cash flow would be classified on a statement of cash flows.

EXERCISE 8-5
Preparing a Simple Cash Flow Statement

Assume you have access to the ledger (specifically the detail of the cash account) for New Company, represented by the following T-account.

Cash

Beg. Bal.	11,500	(2)	75,000
(1)	150,000	(3)	60,000
(4)	6,000	(5)	5,500
(6)	30,000	(7)	25,000
(8)	12,000	(9)	15,000
End. Bal.	29,000		

The transactions that are represented by posting entries (1) through (9) in the cash account are as follows:

1. Collections on account O
2. Payments for wages and salaries O
3. Payments for inventory O
4. Proceeds from sale of equipment I
5. Payments of dividends F
6. Proceeds from new bank loan F
7. Payments for other cash operating expenses O
8. Proceeds from sale of nontrading securities I
9. Payments for taxes F

From these data, prepare a statement of cash flows for New Company for the year ended December 31, 1999.

EXERCISE 8-6
Determining Cash Receipts and Payments

Assuming the following data, compute:

1. Cash collected from customers.
2. Cash paid for wages and salaries.
3. Cash paid for inventory purchases.
4. Cash paid for taxes.

	Income Statement Amount for Year	Balance Sheet	
		Beg. of Year	End of Year
Sales revenue	$225,000		
Accounts receivable (net)		$20,000	$22,000
Wages and salaries expense	55,000		
Wages payable		14,000	11,000
Cost of goods sold	105,000		
Accounts payable		24,500	26,000
Inventory		34,000	28,000
Income tax expense	35,000		
Income taxes payable		15,500	18,000

EXERCISE 8-7
Adjustments to Cash Flows from Operations (Indirect Method)

Assume that you are using the indirect method of preparing a statement of cash flows. For the changes listed, indicate which ones would be added to and which ones would be subtracted from net income in computing net cash flows provided by (used in) operating activities. If the change does not affect net cash flows provided by (used in) operating activities, so indicate.

1. Increase in Accounts Receivable (net)
2. Decrease in Accounts Payable
3. Increase in securities classified as cash equivalents
4. Gain on sale of equipment
5. Decrease in Inventory
6. Increase in Prepaid Insurance
7. Depreciation
8. Increase in Wages Payable
9. Decrease in Dividends Payable
10. Decrease in Interest Receivable

EXERCISE 8-8
Cash Flows from Operations (Direct Method)

Jane Ortiz is the proprietor of a small company. The results of operations for last year are shown, along with selected balance sheet data. From the information provided, determine the amount of net cash flows provided from operations, using the direct method.

Sales revenue	$200,000	
Cost of goods sold	140,000	
Gross margin		$60,000
Operating expenses:		
Wages expense	$ 25,000	
Utilities expense	1,800	
Rent expense	12,000	
Insurance expense	3,000	41,800
Net income		$18,200

	Beginning of Year	End of Year
Accounts receivable (net)	$ 22,000	$25,000
Inventory	35,000	30,000
Prepaid insurance	3,000	2,500
Accounts payable	14,000	17,000
Wages payable	4,000	2,000

EXERCISE 8-9
Cash Flows from Operations (Indirect Method)

Given the data in Exercise 8-8, show how the amount of net cash flows from operating activities would be calculated using the indirect method.

EXERCISE 8-10
Cash Flows Provided by Operations (Direct Method)

The following information was taken from the comparative financial statements of Imperial Corporation for the years ended December 31, 1999 and 2000.

Net income for 2000	$ 90,000
Sales revenue	500,000
Cost of goods sold	300,000
Depreciation expense for 2000	60,000
Amortization of goodwill for 2000	10,000
Interest expense on short-term debt for 2000	3,500
Dividends declared and paid in 2000	65,000

	Dec. 31, 2000	Dec. 31, 1999
Accounts receivable (net)	$30,000	$43,000
Inventory	50,000	42,000
Accounts payable	56,000	59,400

Use the direct method to compute cash flows provided by operating activities in 2000. (Hint: You need to calculate cash paid for operating expenses.)

EXERCISE 8-11
Cash Flows Provided by Operations (Indirect Method)

Given the data in Exercise 8-10, show how the amount of cash provided by operations for 2000 is computed using the indirect method.

EXERCISE 8-12
Cash Flows Provided by Operations (Direct Method)

The following information was taken from the comparative financial statements of Altec Industries Inc. for the years ended December 31, 1999 and 2000.

Net income for 2000	$175,000
Sales revenue	750,000
Cost of goods sold	425,000

(continued)

Depreciation expense for 2000	$ 45,000
Amortization of goodwill for 2000	5,000
Interest expense on short-term debt for 2000	8,000
Dividends declared and paid in 2000	30,000
Utilities expense	3,000

	Dec. 31, 2000	Dec. 31, 1999
Accounts receivable (net)	$45,000	$57,000
Inventory	62,500	50,000
Accounts payable	70,000	51,500

Use the direct method to compute cash flows provided by operating activities in 2000. (Hint: You need to calculate cash paid for operating expenses.)

EXERCISE 8-13
Cash Flows Provided by Operations (Indirect Method)

Given the data in Exercise 8-12, show how the amount of cash flows provided by operations for 2000 is computed using the indirect method.

EXERCISE 8-14
Net Cash Flows (Indirect Method)

Given the following selected data for Milton Corporation, using the indirect method to report cash flows from operating activities, determine the net increase (decrease) in cash for the year ended December 31, 2000.

Net income	$ 95,000
Depreciation	25,000
Other operating expenses	140,000
Cost of goods sold	240,000
Sales revenue	500,000
Increase in accounts receivable (net)	10,000
Decrease in accounts payable	5,000
Decrease in inventory	3,000
Increase in prepaid assets	7,000
Increase in wages payable	15,000
Equipment purchased for cash	40,000
Increase in bonds payable	100,000
Dividends declared and paid	40,000
Decrease in dividends payable	2,000

EXERCISE 8-15
Net Cash Flows (Direct Method)

Based on the following information, determine the net increase (decrease) in cash for Porter Corporation for the year ended December 31, 2000. Use the direct method to report cash flows from operating activities.

Cash received from interest revenue	$ 14,000
Cash paid for dividends	45,000
Cash collected from customers	349,000
Cash paid for wages	254,000
Depreciation expense for the period	25,000
Cash received from issuance of common stock	200,000
Cash paid for retirement of bonds at par	100,000
Cash received on sale of equipment at book value	5,000
Cash paid for land	85,000

EXERCISE 8-16
Statement of Cash Flows (Indirect Method)

North Western Company provides the following financial information. Prepare a statement of cash flows for 2000, using the indirect method to report cash flows from operating activities.

North Western Company
Comparative Balance Sheets
For the Years Ended December 31, 2000 and 1999

	2000	1999
Assets		
Cash and cash equivalents	$ 4,500	$ 9,000
Accounts receivable (net)	33,000	36,000
Inventory	75,000	60,000
Plant and equipment (net)	262,500	225,000
Total assets	$375,000	$330,000
Liabilities and Stockholders' Equity		
Accounts payable	$ 60,000	$ 54,000
Capital stock	225,000	217,500
Retained earnings	90,000	58,500
Total liabilities and stockholders' equity	$375,000	$330,000

North Western Company
Income Statement
For the Year Ended December 31, 2000

Sales	$412,500
Cost of goods sold	225,000
Gross margin	$187,500
Operating expenses	135,000
Net income	$ 52,500

Note: Dividends of $21,000 were declared and paid during 2000. Depreciation expense for the year was $22,500.

EXERCISE 8-17
Statement of Cash Flows (Direct Method)

By analyzing the information in Exercise 8-16, prepare a statement of cash flows. Use the direct method to report cash flows from operating activities.

EXERCISE 8-18
Analyzing Cash Flows

Study the comparative cash flow statements for **Microsoft** in Appendix A. What observations do you have about Microsoft's cash flow position? From a liquidity standpoint, is the trend over the last few years positive or negative? Explain.

PROBLEMS

PROBLEM 8-1
Transaction Analysis

Development Corporation reports the following summary data for the most current year.

a. Sales revenue totaled $251,500.
b. Interest revenue for the period was $2,200.
c. Interest expense for the period was $800.
d. Cost of goods sold for the period was $156,000.
e. Operating expenses, all paid in cash (except for depreciation of $15,000), were $48,000.
f. Income tax expense for the period was $8,000.
g. Accounts receivable (net) increased by $10,000 during the period.

h. Accounts payable decreased by $5,000 during the period.
i. Inventory at the beginning and end of the period was $25,000 and $35,000, respectively.
j. Cash increased during the period by $5,000.

Required:

Assume all other current asset and current liability accounts remained constant during the period.

1. Compute the amount of cash collected from customers.
2. Compute the amount of cash paid for inventory.
3. Compute the amount of cash paid for operating expenses.
4. Compute the amount of cash flows provided by (used in) operations.
5. **Interpretive Question:** What must have been the combined amount of cash flows provided by (used in) investing and financing activities?

PROBLEM 8-2

Analysis of the Cash Account

The following information, in T-account format, is provided for the M & M Company for the year 2000.

Cash Account

Beg. Bal.	15,400	(b)	56,500
(a)	147,000	(c)	23,000
(d)	3,500	(f)	59,700
(e)	15,000	(g)	1,600
		(h)	2,400
End. Bal.	37,700		

Additional information:

a. Sales revenue for the period was $145,000. Accounts receivable (net) decreased $2,000 during the period.
b. Net purchases of $58,000 were made during 2000, all on account. Accounts payable increased $1,500 during the period.
c. The equipment account increased by $18,000 during the year.
d. One piece of equipment that cost $5,000, with a net book value of $3,000, was sold for a $500 gain.
e. The company borrowed $15,000 from its bank during the year.
f. Various operating expenses were all paid in cash, except for depreciation of $1,800. Total operating expenses were $61,500.
g. Interest expense for the year was $1,200. The interest payable account decreased by $400 during the year.
h. Income tax expense for the year was $3,600. The income taxes payable account increased by $1,200 during the year.

Required:

1. From the information given, reconstruct the journal entries that must have been made during the year (omit explanations).
2. Prepare a statement of cash flows for M & M Company for the year ended December 31, 2000.

PROBLEM 8-3

Analyzing Cash Flows

The following information was provided by the treasurer of Surety, Inc., for the year 2000.

a. Cash sales for the year were $50,000; sales on account totaled $60,000.
b. Cost of goods sold was 50 percent of total sales.
c. All inventory is purchased on account.
d. Depreciation on equipment was $31,000 for the year.
e. Amortization of goodwill was $2,000.
f. Collections of accounts receivable were $38,000.

g. Payments on accounts payable for inventory equaled $39,000.
h. Rent expense paid in cash was $11,000.
i. 20,000 shares of $10 par stock were issued for $240,000.
j. Land valued at $106,000 was acquired by issuance of a bond with a par value of $100,000.
k. Equipment was purchased for cash at a cost of $84,000.
l. Dividends of $46,000 were declared but not yet paid.
m. $15,000 of dividends that had been declared the previous year were paid.
n. A machine used on the assembly line was sold for $12,000. The machine had a book value of $7,000.
o. Another machine with a book value of $500 was scrapped and was reported as an ordinary loss. No cash was received on this transaction.
p. The cash account increased $191,000 during the year to a total of $274,000.

Required:

1. Compute the beginning balance in the cash account.
2. How much cash was provided by (or used in) operating activities?
3. How much cash was provided by (or used in) investing activities?
4. How much cash was provided by (or used in) financing activities?
5. Would all the above items, (a) through (p), be reported on a cash flow statement? Explain.

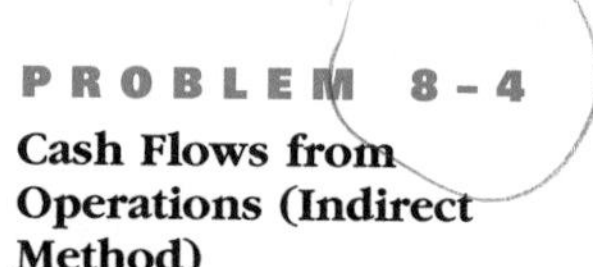

PROBLEM 8-4
Cash Flows from Operations (Indirect Method)

Gardner Enterprises reported a net loss of $40,000 for the year just ended. Relevant data for the company follow.

	Beginning of Year	End of Year
Cash and cash equivalents	$ 50,000	$ 20,000
Accounts receivable (net)	80,000	65,000
Inventory	123,000	130,000
Prepaid expenses	7,500	4,500
Accounts payable	55,000	60,000
Accrued liabilities	10,000	4,000
Dividends payable	25,000	35,000

Depreciation for the year, $43,000
Dividends declared, $35,000

Required:

1. Using the indirect method, determine the net cash flows provided by (used in) operating activities for Gardner Enterprises.
2. **Interpretive Question:** Explain how Gardner Enterprises can pay cash dividends during a year when it reports a net loss.

PROBLEM 8-5
Cash Flows from Operations (Direct Method)

Super Sales Inc. shows the following information in its accounting records at year-end:

Sales revenue	$890,000
Interest revenue	12,000
Cost of goods sold	425,000
Wages expense	225,000
Depreciation expense	50,000
Other (cash) operating expenses	84,000
Dividends declared	40,000

Selected balance sheet data are as follows:

	Beginning of Year	End of Year
Accounts receivable (net)	$ 55,000	$ 78,000
Interest receivable	10,000	12,000
Inventory	225,000	220,000
Accounts payable	42,000	35,000
Wages payable	20,000	25,000
Dividends payable	35,000	40,000

Required:

1. Using the direct method, compute the net cash flows provided by (used in) operating activities for Super Sales Inc.
2. **Interpretive Question:** Explain the main differences between the net amount of cash flows from operations and net income (loss).

PROBLEM 8-6
Cash Flows from Operations (Indirect and Direct Methods)

The following combined income and retained earnings statement, along with selected balance sheet data, are provided for Roper Company:

Roper Company
Combined Income and Retained Earnings Statement
For the Year Ended December 31, 2000

Net sales revenue		$85,000
Other revenues		4,500[1]
Total revenues		$89,500
Expenses:		
Cost of goods sold	$51,000	
Selling and administrative expenses	14,700	
Depreciation expense	3,200	
Interest expense	1,400	
Total expenses		70,300
Income before taxes		$19,200
Income taxes		5,760
Net income		$13,440
Retained earnings, January 1, 2000		33,500
		$46,940
Dividends declared and paid		2,500
Retained earnings, December 31, 2000		$44,440

[1]Gain on sale of equipment (Cost $9,500; book value, $6,000; sales price $10,500).

	Beginning of Year	End of Year
Accounts receivable (net)	$10,500	$11,000
Inventory	19,300	18,000
Prepaid expenses	950	700
Accounts payable	7,200	8,000
Interest payable	1,500	1,000
Income taxes payable	500	2,500

Required:

1. Using the indirect method, compute the net cash flows from operations for Roper Company for 2000.
2. Using the direct method, compute the net cash flows from operations for Roper Company for 2000.
3. What is the impact of dividends paid on net cash flows from operations? Explain.

PROBLEM 8-7
Computation of Net Income from Cash Flows from Operations (Direct Method)

The following partially completed work sheet is provided for ATM Corporation, which uses the direct method in computing net cash flows from operations:

ATM Corporation
Partial Work Sheet—Cash Flows from Operations
(Direct Method)
For the Year Ended December 31, 2000

	Accrual Basis	Adjustments Debits	Adjustments Credits	Cash Basis
Net sales revenue				150,000
Expenses:				
Cost of goods sold				75,000
Depreciation				0
Loss on sale of equipment				0
Other (cash) expenses				26,000
Total expenses				101,000
Net income (net cash flows from operations)				49,000

Key:
1. Decrease in Accounts Receivable (net), $4,500.
2. Loss on sale of equipment, $1,500.
3. Increase in Inventory, $10,000.
4. Increase in Accounts Payable, $3,000.
5. Depreciation for the year, $8,000.
6. Decrease in Prepaid Expenses, $1,000.
7. Increase in Accrued Liabilities, $2,500.

Required: Complete the worksheet with the key items above and compute the net income (loss) to be reported by ATM Corporation on its income statement for 2000.

PROBLEM 8-8
Income Statement from Cash Flow Data

Jackson Corporation computed the amount of cash flows from operations using both the direct and indirect methods, as follows:

Direct method:	
Collections from customers	$445,000
Payments to suppliers	(130,000)
Payments for operating expenses	(210,000)
Cash flows provided by operating activities	$105,000
Indirect method:	
Net income	$ 95,000
Depreciation	20,000
Gain on sale of equipment	(7,500)
Decrease in inventory	1,000
Decrease in accounts receivable (net)	1,500
Decrease in accounts payable	(7,500)
Increase in miscellaneous accrued payable	2,500
Cash flows provided by operating activities	$105,000

Required: Using the data provided, prepare an income statement for Jackson Corporation for the year 2000.

PROBLEM 8-9
Statement of Cash Flows (Indirect Method)

JEM Company's comparative balance sheets for 1999 and 2000 are provided.

JEM Company
Comparative Balance Sheets
December 31, 2000 and 1999

	2000	1999
Assets		
Cash and cash equivalents	$ 30,500	$ 10,000
Accounts receivable (net)	64,500	51,000
Inventory	100,000	115,000
Equipment	55,000	30,000
Accumulated depreciation—equipment	(21,500)	(14,000)
Total assets	$228,500	$192,000
Liabilities and Stockholders' Equity		
Accounts payable	$ 52,500	$ 46,000
Long-term notes payable	70,000	50,000
Capital stock	60,000	60,000
Retained earnings	46,000	36,000
Total liabilities and stockholders' equity	$228,500	$192,000

The following additional information is available:

a. Net income for the year 2000 (as reported on the income statement) was $50,000.
b. Dividends of $40,000 were declared and paid.
c. Equipment that cost $8,000 and had a book value of $1,000 was sold during the year for $2,500.

Required: Based on the information provided, prepare a statement of cash flows for JEM Company for the year ended December 31, 2000. Use the indirect method to report cash flows from operating activities.

PROBLEM 8-10
Statement of Cash Flows (Direct Method)

Financial statement data for Continental Stores Inc. are provided. (All numbers are shown rounded to the nearest thousand, with 000's omitted.)

Continental Stores Inc.
Income and Retained Earnings Statements
For the Year Ended December 31, 2000

Sales revenue	$1,290
Cost of goods sold	978
Gross margin	$ 312
Operating expenses:	
Sales and administrative expenses	$ 105
Depreciation expense	14
Other expenses	87
Total operating expenses	$ 206
Income before taxes	$ 106
Income taxes	51
Net income	$ 55
Dividends paid	10
Increase in retained earnings	$ 45

Continental Stores Inc.
Comparative Balance Sheets
December 31, 2000 and 1999

	2000	1999
Assets		
Cash and cash equivalents	$ 752	$ 725
Accounts receivable (net)	461	448
Inventory	226	953
Land	1,340	1,240
Store fixtures	369	369
Accumulated depreciation, store fixtures	(51)	(37)
Total assets	$3,097	$3,698
Liabilities and Stockholders' Equity		
Liabilities:		
Accounts payable	$ 175	$ 378
Short-term notes payable	525	768
Long-term debt	804	1,004
Total liabilities	$1,504	$2,150
Stockholders' equity:		
Common stock	$ 448	$ 448
Paid-in capital in excess of par	500	500
Retained earnings	645	600
Total stockholders' equity	$1,593	$1,548
Total liabilities and stockholders' equity	$3,097	$3,698

Required:

1. Compute the net cash flows from operations using the direct method.
2. **Interpretive Question:** Comment on the difference between net income and net cash flows from operations.
3. Prepare a statement of cash flows for Continental Stores Inc. for the period ended December 31, 2000.

PROBLEM 8-11
Statement of Cash Flows (Indirect Method)

Required:

1. Using the data from Problem 8-10, prepare a statement of cash flows. Use the indirect method to report cash flows from operating activities.
2. **Interpretive Question:** What are the main differences between a statement of cash flows prepared using the indirect method and one prepared using the direct method?

PROBLEM 8-12
Unifying Concepts: Analysis of Operating, Investing, and Financing Activities

Grant Kesler is the manager and one of three brothers who own the Rocky Mountain Auto Parts Company in Denver, Colorado. Grant is pleased that sales were up last year and that his new, small company has been able to expand and open a second store in Denver. After reviewing the balance sheet, however, Grant is concerned that cash shows a negative balance. He can't understand how his company can show net income, based on increased sales, yet have a negative cash position. He is concerned about what his banker is going to say when they meet next month to discuss a loan for the company to expand to a third store. Grant provides the following financial information and asks for your help.

Rocky Mountain Auto Parts Company
Income Statement
For the Year Ended December 31, 2000

Sales		$150,000
Less cost of goods sold		63,000
Gross margin		$ 87,000
Operating expenses:		
Salary and wages	$32,000	
Depreciation	4,500	
Other operating expenses	12,400	48,900
Net operating income		$ 38,100
Income taxes		8,200
Net income		$ 29,900

Rocky Mountain Auto Parts Company
Comparative Balance Sheets
As of December 31, 2000 and 1999

	2000	1999
Assets		
Current assets:		
Cash	$ (3,200)	$ 6,400
Accounts receivable (net)	3,100	2,700
Inventory	63,000	42,000
Total current assets	$ 62,900	$51,100
Other assets:		
Property, plant, and equipment	$ 82,300	$39,000
Less accumulated depreciation	(20,100)	(15,600)
Total other assets	$ 62,200	$23,400
Total assets	$125,100	$74,500
Liabilities and Stockholders' Equity		
Current liabilities:		
Accounts payable	$ 6,400	$ 5,700
Wages payable	1,500	1,300
Taxes payable	1,900	2,100
Total current liabilities	$ 9,800	$ 9,100
Other liabilities:		
Note payable	30,000	10,000
Total liabilities	$ 39,800	$19,100
Stockholders' equity:		
Capital stock	$ 40,000	$40,000
Retained earnings	45,300	15,400
Total stockholders' equity	$ 85,300	$55,400
Total liabilities and stockholders' equity	$125,100	$74,500

Required:

1. Using the direct method, compute the net cash flows from operations. Also determine net cash flows for investing and financing activities.
2. **Interpretive Question:** Is Rocky Mountain Auto Parts Company in a good liquidity position? As Mr. Kesler's banker, would you loan him more money to fund the company's expansion?

Analyzing Real Company Information

International Case

Ethics Case

Writing Assignment

The Debate

Internet Search

Accounting is more than just doing textbook problems. These Competency Enhancement Opportunities provide practice in critical thinking, oral and written communication, research, teamwork, and consideration of ethical issues.

ANALYZING REAL COMPANY INFORMATION

• Analyzing 8-1 (Microsoft)

The 1997 annual report for **Microsoft** is included in Appendix A. Locate that annual report and consider the following questions.

1. Does Microsoft present the three cash flow statement categories—operating, investing, and financing—in the same order as that illustrated in the chapter?
2. In 1997, Microsoft spent $3.089 billion on various investing activities. Were the cash flows from operations sufficient to pay for these investments?
3. In its 1997 operating activities section, Microsoft reports both $1.601 billion and a $0.743 billion in relation to unearned revenue. Exactly what does each of these numbers represent? Compare these numbers to the corresponding numbers in 1995 and comment on the reason for such a big difference.
4. Did Microsoft pay any cash dividends to common stockholders during 1997? Did Microsoft make any payments to common stockholders during the year?

• Analyzing 8-2 (The Coca-Cola Company)

The 1997 statement of cash flows for **The Coca-Cola Company** is given on page 383. Use the statement to answer the following questions.

1. Coca-Cola includes a line in its cash flow statement titled "Net cash provided by operations after reinvestment." How is this amount calculated? Interpret the results of the calculation for Coca-Cola for the period 1995–1997.
2. In its operating activities section, Coca-Cola subtracts gains on sales of assets in the computation of net cash provided by operating activities. Why are these gains subtracted?
3. Think of the dealings that The Coca-Cola Company has with its shareholders. The shareholders give money to the company by purchasing new shares of stock. In turn, the company returns cash to shareholders by paying cash dividends and by repurchasing shares of stock. For the three-year period 1995–1997, did The Coca-Cola Company receive more cash from its shareholders than it paid back to them, or did it pay more cash to its shareholders than it received? Show your calculations.
4. Look carefully at the statement of cash flows. Did the U.S. dollar get stronger or weaker during the three-year period 1995–1997?

The Coca-Cola Company and Subsidiaries
Consolidated Statements of Cash Flows
For the Years Ended December 31, 1995, 1996, 1997
(In millions)

	1997	1996	1995
Operating activities:			
Net income	$ 4,129	$ 3,492	$ 2,986
Depreciation and amortization	626	633	562
Deferred income taxes	380	(145)	157
Equity income, net of dividends	(108)	(89)	(25)
Foreign currency adjustments	37	(60)	(23)
Gains on issuances of stock by equity investees	(363)	(431)	(74)
Gains on sales of assets, including bottling interests	(639)	(135)	(16)
Other items	18	316	60
Net change in operating assets and liabilities	(47)	(118)	(299)
Net cash provided by operating activities	$ 4,033	$ 3,463	$ 3,328
Investing activities:			
Acquisitions and investments, principally bottling companies	$(1,100)	$ (645)	$ (338)
Purchases of investments and other assets	(459)	(623)	(403)
Proceeds from disposals of investments and other assets	1,999	1,302	580
Purchases of property, plant, and equipment	(1,093)	(990)	(937)
Proceeds from disposals of property, plant, and equipment	71	81	44
Other investing activities	82	(175)	(172)
Net cash used in investing activities	$ (500)	$(1,050)	$(1,226)
Net cash provided by operations after reinvestment	$ 3,533	$ 2,413	$ 2,102
Financing activities:			
Issuances of debt	$ 155	$ 1,122	$ 754
Payments of debt	(751)	(580)	(212)
Issuances of stock	150	124	86
Purchase of stock for treasury	(1,262)	(1,521)	(1,796)
Dividends	(1,387)	(1,247)	(1,110)
Net cash used in financing activities	$(3,095)	$(2,102)	$(2,278)
Net increase (decrease) in cash	438	311	(176)
Effect of exchange rate changes on cash and cash equivalents	(134)	(45)	(43)
Cash and cash equivalents:			
Net increase (decrease) during the year	304	266	(219)
Balance at beginning of year	1,433	1,167	1,386
Balance at end of year	$ 1,737	$ 1,433	$ 1,167

INTERNATIONAL CASE

• Glaxo Wellcome

Glaxo Wellcome, a British company, is one of the largest pharmaceutical firms in the world. The name "Glaxo" comes from the company's first major product line, baby food products that were sold with the slogan, "Builds Bonnie Babies." Growth of the company in recent years has been driven by sales of Zantac, an anti-ulcer drug.

Glaxo Wellcome's 1997 statement of cash flows is shown below. Look at the statement and answer the following questions. [Note: Translations of British accounting terms into American English are shown in square brackets.]

1. In a U.S. statement of cash flows, cash flows are sorted into three categories. How many categories does Glaxo Wellcome use?
2. List some of the items that Glaxo Wellcome has excluded from the computation of cash from operating activities that would be included in that computation if the statement of cash flows were prepared according to U.S. standards.
3. Given your answer in (2), which is a better indication of cash from operating activities: the number reported by Glaxo Wellcome using a British classification of cash flows, or the number that would be reported using a U.S. classification? Explain your answer.
4. If you were to redo Glaxo Wellcome's statement of cash flows for 1997 and use the U.S. classification scheme with just three categories, the total of these three categories would result in the same net change in cash, (101), as reported by Glaxo Wellcome using the British classification. Why is this?

Glaxo Wellcome plc
Consolidated Statement of Cash Flows
31st December 1997
(in millions of £)

	1997	**1996**
Trading profit	2,822	3,132
Depreciation	373	410
Profit on sale of tangible fixed assets	(4)	(5)
Increase in stocks [inventory]	(184)	(96)
Decrease/(increase) in debtors [accounts receivable]	49	(261)
(Decrease)/increase in creditors [accounts payable]	(59)	56
Decrease in pension and other provisions	(236)	(193)
Net cash inflow from operating activities	**2,761**	**3,043**
Returns on investment and servicing of finance		
Interest received	104	87
Interest paid	(231)	(278)
Cost of financing	(2)	(4)
Other	8	69
	(121)	**(126)**

(continued)

	1997	1996
Taxation paid		
Corporate taxation	(566)	(785)
Advance Corporation Tax	(252)	(263)
	(818)	**(1,048)**
Capital expenditure		
Purchase of tangible fixed assets	(415)	(401)
Sale of tangible fixed assets	222	33
	(193)	**(368)**
Acquisitions and disposals		
Purchase of fixed asset investments	(19)	(25)
Sale of fixed asset investments	0	3
Investment in associates	(32)	(46)
Purchase of businesses	(6)	(287)
Disposal of businesses	0	674
	(57)	**319**
Dividends paid	**(1,207)**	**(1,020)**
Net cash inflows before financing	**365**	**800**
Financing		
Management of liquid resources	(407)	(55)
Issue of ordinary share capital	184	215
Issue of shares to minority shareholders	4	0
Increase in long-term loans	244	382
Repayment of long-term loans	(14)	(26)
Net repayment of short-term loans	(490)	(1,229)
New obligations under finance [capital] leases	13	0
Net cash inflow from financing activities	**(466)**	**(713)**
(Decrease)/increase in cash in the year	**(101)**	**87**

ETHICS CASE

• Manipulating the federal budget deficit

Assume that you are the paymaster in charge of all U.S. Department of Defense (DOD) payroll matters. The total amount that you disburse in payroll checks in any given week is in excess of $1 billion.

Currently, Congress is struggling to reduce the reported federal budget deficit. It is an election year, and the Congresspersons are worried that they will be stuck with a "tax and spend" label if the reported deficit this year is too high. Of course, the Department of Defense budget has been scrutinized very carefully to reduce reported expenditures as much as possible.

Yesterday, a Congressional leader came to your office with a disturbing proposal. Since the federal budget numbers are reported on a cash basis, rather than on an accrual basis, expenses are reported when they are paid instead of when they are incurred. This year, the final DOD payday of the year happens to fall on the last day of the federal government's fiscal year (September 30). The Congressional leader suggested that you delay the issuance of the payroll checks by one day. This would push the actual payment of the cash into the next fiscal year. Thus, even though the payment would be for services performed in the current fiscal year, the expense wouldn't be reported until next year. With this simple trick, the reported deficit for this year (an election year) can be reduced by $1 billion.

What should you do?

WRITING ASSIGNMENT

• Convincing the old-timers of the need for cash flow data

You are the chief accountant for Harry Monst Company. The president of the company is a former accountant who worked her way up through the management ranks over the course of 30 years. She is a great manager, but her knowledge of accounting is outdated.

Harry Monst Company has a revolving line of credit with Texas Commercial Bank. A new loan officer has just been put in charge of the Harry Monst account. The new loan officer is surprised to see that Harry Monst has not been submitting a statement of cash flows along with the rest of the financial statements that comprise the annual loan review packet. The new loan officer called you and asked for a statement of cash flows.

You were surprised when you took the completed statement of cash flows to the president for her signature. She refused to sign, stating that she had never looked at or prepared a statement of cash flows in her career and she wouldn't start now.

Write a one-page memo to the president with the objective of convincing her of the usefulness of the statement of cash flows.

THE DEBATE

• No one can understand the indirect method!

Companies have the option of reporting cash flows from operating activities using either the direct or the indirect method. Many financial statement users think that the information provided with the direct method is easier to understand. In spite of this, over 95 percent of large U.S. companies use the indirect method.

Divide your group into two teams.

- One team represents the "Direct Method." Prepare a two-minute oral presentation arguing that the direct method is just what its name implies—direct and easy to understand. The indirect method is merely an attempt by accountants to confuse financial statement users.
- The other team represents the "Indirect Method." Prepare a two-minute oral presentation arguing that the direct method may seem easy to understand, but only to unsophisticated financial statement readers. The indirect method reveals much more useful information.

INTERNET SEARCH

• Compaq

Access **Compaq**'s Web site at compaq.com. Sometimes Web addresses change, so if this address does not work, access the Web site for this textbook [stice.swcollege.com] for an updated link.

Once you've gained access to the site, answer the following questions.

1. Use Compaq's Site Map to locate information on what Compaq is doing to make it easier for schools and universities to finance the purchase of Compaq computers.
2. Through its Web site, Compaq makes information available to people thinking about employment with the company. What does Compaq have to say about living in Houston (the location of Compaq's corporate headquarters)?
3. Use Compaq's Web site search facility to find out what connection there is between Compaq's company history and the Fortune 500 list of the largest companies in the United States.
4. Find Compaq's most recent set of financial statements. In its statement of cash flows, does Compaq use the direct method or the indirect method in reporting cash from operating activities?
5. In the most recent year, which is greater—Compaq's net income or Compaq's cash flows from operating activities?
6. Did Compaq pay any cash dividends in the most recent year?

ACCOUNTING FOR INTERNAL USERS: BUSINESS DECISIONS

PART 3

CHAPTERS

CHAPTER

9 INTRODUCTION TO MANAGEMENT ACCOUNTING

SETTING THE STAGE

You've probably never heard of E. I. du Pont de Nemours and Company, but you may be familiar with its more common name, DuPont. Some of this company's best known brands are Teflon® resins, SilverStone® non-stick finish, Lycra® spandex fiber, Stainmaster® stain-resistant carpet, Kevlar® fiber, and Mylar® polyester films. In 1996, DuPont had revenues of $43.8 billion, net income of $3.6 billion, and ranked number 14 in the Fortune 500 list. DuPont operates in approximately 70 countries worldwide with roughly 175 manufacturing and processing facilities. These facilities include 140 chemical and specialties plants, 27 natural gas processing plants, and 8 petroleum refineries. This is a *big* company! So what does this company have to do with you (outside of the fact that you probably use many of its products)? In 1903, the owners of DuPont created for themselves a challenge that no one had ever before attempted. The way they handled this challenge profoundly affected the way America manages its companies today and permanently changed our approach to management accounting. If you want to understand financial accounting in America, you need to study the underlying theories of generally accepted accounting principles (GAAP) and the process used by the Financial Accounting Standards Board (FASB) to create GAAP. But if you want to understand management accounting in America (as well as in many other countries around the world), you really need to put yourself in the shoes of three cousins, Alfred, Coleman, and Pierre du Pont.

One of the oldest continuously operating industrial enterprises in the world, the DuPont Company was established in 1802 near Wilmington, Delaware, by a French immigrant, Eleuthére Irénée du Pont de Nemours, to produce black powder. Essentially, E. I. du Pont built a product that ignited when it was supposed to. Public enthusiasm for du Pont's product continued, and the company grew into a major family corporation. However, the start of the twentieth century brought increased competition from other companies, and DuPont fell on hard times. Seizing the opportunity created by the crisis, three of E. I. du Pont's great-grandsons, Alfred I. du Pont, Thomas Coleman du Pont, and Pierre Samuel du Pont, offered to purchase the firm's assets from the family in exchange for bonds and stock in a new corporation (a transaction known today as a leveraged buy-out). The offer

LEARNING OBJECTIVES

After studying this chapter, you should be able to:

1. *Describe some of the history that defines modern management accounting.*
2. *Discuss the major differences in managing manufacturing, merchandising, and service organizations.*
3. *Define the common terms and measures found in modern management accounting.*
4. *Understand that successfully planning, controlling, and evaluating a business requires effective management of cost, quality, and time.*
5. *Describe the professional environment of management accountants today.*

was accepted. In 1902 the company was restructured to look for new business and create new products through research and development.

Alfred, Coleman, and Pierre had some pretty innovative ideas about running a business. In 1903, the gunpowder industry looked much like any other industry in America. Each of DuPont's competitors in the industry focused primarily on manufacturing. They purchased raw materials (such as charcoal, sodium nitrate, and crude glycerin) from suppliers and distributed their gunpowder products to customers using independent wholesalers and general merchants. For the du Pont cousins, the business they purchased looked a lot like the left side of Exhibit 9–1. After the purchase, they decided to expand the business beyond the manufacturing of high explosives, smokeless gunpowder, and black blasting powder. The DuPonts started "forward integrating" into the distribution business by creating their own network of branch sales offices scattered across the United States. They also "backward integrated" by buying out many (but not all) of their suppliers. When the dust finally settled, DuPont was America's first large-scale "vertically integrated" company (right side of Exhibit 9–1). Most of the profits usually earned by outside companies (either selling DuPont products to customers or selling raw materials to DuPont) were now consolidated within DuPont. While this type of organization is quite common today, it was a strange-looking company at the turn of the century. Although Alfred, Coleman, and Pierre were confident that their new way of doing business was going to make them a lot of money (and they were right!), they had created a serious challenge for themselves. They knew how to run a manufacturing business, but now they were in the purchasing and sales business as well. These were three very different businesses, each with its own way of communicating results and measuring success. The three cousins had a limited amount of time and resources to invest in developing their company. How were they going to be able to effectively plan schedules, control operations, and evaluate each division to determine additional investment needs? Essentially, Alfred, Coleman, and Pierre had an accounting problem. What would you have done if you were in their shoes in 1903? What the cousins did to handle the challenge was, to say the least, impressive.[1]

1. Historical sources: A.D. Chandler, *The Invisible Hand,* 1977 (HBS Press: Boston, MA); H.T. Johnson and R.S. Kaplan, *Relevance Lost,* 1987 (HBS Press: Boston, MA); The DuPont homepage at www.dupont.com/corp/gbl-company/history.html; Microsoft Encarta 1994.

A Comparative Look at the DuPont Company Before and After 1903

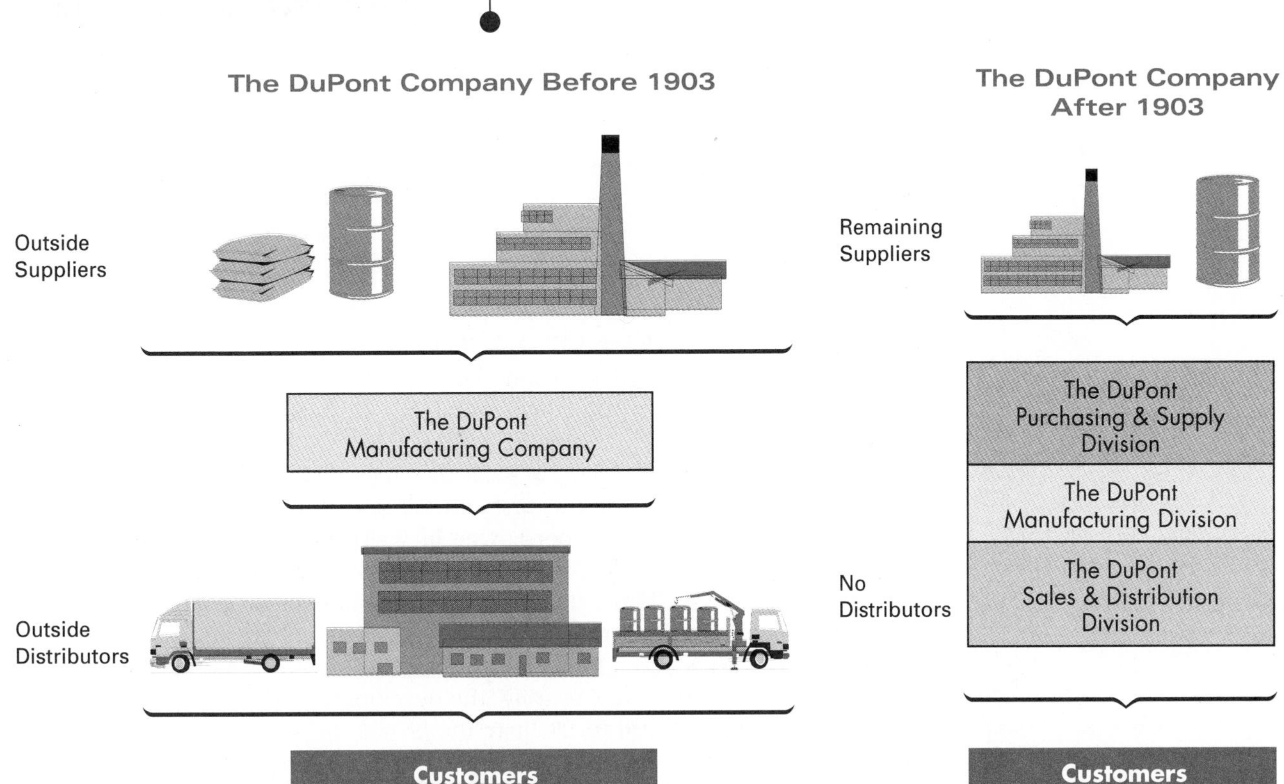

This chapter introduces management accounting and distinguishes it from financial accounting. We will consider some of the basic concepts and terms that have developed to support this discipline. It is important to understand that management accounting is essentially the result of the efforts of many individuals and organizations to create information that has a competitive value in the marketplace. To really comprehend management accounting, you need to grasp how manufacturing, merchandising, and service companies do business. It also needs to be clear that effective management in modern organizations requires management accountants to provide not only cost data, but also quality- and time-based information as well. This information is used to support the management process of planning, controlling, and evaluating. Hence, this chapter introduces three critical issues.

1. *The nature of manufacturing, merchandising, and service organizations.*
2. *The strategic issues of cost, quality, and time.*
3. *The management process of planning, controlling, and evaluating.*

All topics discussed in subsequent chapters will address these critical issues.

1 *Describe some of the history that defines modern management accounting.*

A LITTLE HISTORY

Prior to 1810, American business was basically made up of independent contractors, each of whom focused on doing one thing well. If you wanted to purchase groceries, you went down to a local market that was owned and operated by an independent proprietor. Go to the next town to buy groceries and you would deal with a different storeowner (i.e., there were no chain stores as we know them today!). If you needed a plow, you went to a blacksmith. If you needed a barrel, you went to a cooper. If you needed a wagon, you went to a wainwright. In turn, each of these small manufacturers generally had to deal with several independent suppliers of raw materials, such as lumber, coal, and iron. As you can imagine, the wheels of commerce turned rather slowly. On the other hand, businesses were fairly easy to manage. Business owners at the turn of the nineteenth century generally did not employ large numbers of people. They also did not have many complex processes within their company to manage. Cost accounting, if we can say it existed at all, was not a difficult procedure. If the wainwright wanted to know how much it cost to build a wagon for a customer, he simply added up the costs of buying lumber products from the sawmill, leather products from the tanner, and iron products from the blacksmith. He then set the price for a wagon high enough to be compensated for his assembly labor. Essentially, for most of these small businesses, market prices supplied every conceivable bit of information for decision making and control.

Nothing Feels Quite Like Cotton

Remember learning in high school about the Industrial Revolution? It began in Britain and spilled over to America sometime after 1812. Big businesses started appearing on the East Coast of America, beginning with the mechanized, integrated cotton textile factories of New England. In 1814, all the steps of an industrial process were combined under one roof for the first time at a cotton mill established by the American industrialist Francis Cabot Lowell in Waltham, Massachusetts. Instead of contracting with several small family-owned businesses to card, spin, and sew raw material into cloth, Lowell brought raw cotton fiber into a heavily equipped factory (staffed with workers who were organized by specialty) and created a finished product ready for sale! This was a new concept of doing business, and it really complicated the accounting process. (Actually, the development of management accounting probably did a great deal to facilitate the growth of these large-scale firms.) In order to run this textile mill, Lowell and his managers required some kind of a reporting system that would provide the information needed to plan, control, and evaluate work that they were not actually doing themselves. History shows that these early textile mills developed a remarkably good accounting system that tracked inventory, payroll, and production work. Most importantly, the "Waltham system" of accounting separately tracked direct and indirect costs of manufacturing and carefully noted the efficiency with which the company used cotton, labor time, and general overhead resources. Don't worry if you don't understand some of this terminology. You'll learn about direct and indirect costs, as well as overhead, later in this chapter, and we'll talk about efficiency variances in a subsequent chapter. The important thing to understand here is that the birth of management accounting was the result of an opportunity to obtain a competitive edge in the textile business. Just remember that the purpose of *financial accounting,* as defined by GAAP, is to comply with requests of outside investors, creditors, and regulators for fair and consistent reports of operations. But the *only* reason we do *management accounting* is to satisfy a competitive need!

BUSINESS ENVIRONMENT ESSAY

History of Financial Accounting
The Stock Market Crash of 1929 can be (and has been) blamed on the cavalier mentality of the "Roaring Twenties," Herbert Hoover, and Prohibition. Another suspect is financial accounting. The rapidly rising stock market in the 1920s enticed many companies to publicly issue shares for the first time. These share issues were often accompanied by little or no financial disclosure. Thus, stock traders were buying and selling shares based mainly on rumor, speculation, and deceit.

In the aftermath of the Crash, Congress established the Securities and Exchange Commission (SEC) to regulate the issuance and trading of securities in the United States. In addition to monitoring insider trading and stock broker behavior, the SEC also ensures that companies issuing securities for purchase by U.S. investors must provide full and fair disclosure of their financial status through the public release of financial statements prepared using a generally accepted set of accounting practices. The SEC has the legal authority to prescribe accepted accounting standards, but has generally allowed the accounting profession in the United States to establish those rules. Currently, the Financial Accounting Standards Board (FASB), a nongovernmental body supported by the business community and the accounting profession, is the acknowledged source of authoritative accounting standards in the United States.

A financial accounting issue currently facing the SEC is whether to allow foreign companies to issue shares in the United States while releasing financial statements prepared using their home-country accounting methods. So far, the SEC has said "no," arguing that companies listed on U.S. exchanges should comply with U.S. GAAP. As the global economy becomes increasingly integrated, it is certain that an international standard of financial accounting practice will emerge. The only question is, "Who will set these international standards?"

Bringing It Home on the Railroads

Shortly after the launch of the textile industry, the advent of the railroad business probably presented some of the most complex administrative problems of the nineteenth century. The practicability of the locomotive was demonstrated in 1829, and the locomotive quickly began replacing the horse and mule as the primary means of mass commercial travel in the United States. By 1869, the **Union Pacific Railroad** from the East and the **Central Pacific Railroad** from the West were joined at Promontory Point, Utah. Railroad companies soon grew to sizes that dwarfed the scale of the largest textile factories, and names like J. P. Morgan and Edward Henry Harriman became famous (or infamous, depending on your perspective). Managing these huge administrative entities required special record-keeping systems that recorded numerous daily transactions and summarized essential information for frequent internal reports to management. The real issue, though, was that railroads required a hierarchy of management, i.e., managers managing other managers. At a textile mill, the manager was right there in the factory working with a group of employees. On the other hand, given the vast and complex scale of the business, railroad managers were literally spread out all over the map! Owners and senior managers needed the same means of assessing performance of submanagers at terminals and yards across the country. The answer came in the 1860s from business professionals like Albert Fink, senior vice president of the **Louisville & Nashville Railroad**. Fink kept track of operating expenses in his railroad using a calculation called "costs per ton-mile" (the average cost to move a ton of material one mile). Using this measure, Fink could monitor costs throughout his company and pinpoint reasons for cost differences to specific stations and station managers. In addition, the "operating ratio" (a ratio of operating expenses to revenues) also provided competitive information that indicated how the performance of various submanagers would affect the company's total financial performance. The message to railroad submanagers was made obvious—keep the costs down! What was the message to executive managers and management accountants? Performance measures can be used to delegate responsibilities and to control and evaluate the business from a distance. This message contributed to the growing realization that good management accounting adds competitive value and allows companies to spread out geographically.

The Steely-Eyed Business Tycoon

At this point in time, management accounting, known as cost accounting, was strictly focused on cost measurement and cost management. Business owners were making a great deal of money using this information to build and expand large companies. However, no one understood cost information quite like Andrew Carnegie, who controlled about 25 percent of the American iron and steel production in 1899. One of the shrewdest entrepreneurs of his time, Carnegie was well educated in the textile mills and railroad companies of America. Although few persons have ever gained access to the accounting records of **Carnegie Steel Company**, those who have agree that Carnegie was obsessed with costs. One of his favorite sayings was "Watch the costs and the profits will take care of themselves."[2] Every department at Carnegie Steel reported the amount and cost of materials and labor on each order of steel as it passed through its production zone. Carnegie was always asking department heads the reasons for any change in costs. Carnegie went far beyond the railroads' efforts of using costs to evaluate the performance of department managers. He and his executive managers relied on their cost charts to check the quality and mix of raw materials, to evaluate improvements in processes and products, and to price contracts. Carnegie Steel would never accept a customer contract until its costs were carefully estimated. Was Andrew Carnegie's management accounting technique successful? In 1901 he sold his company to the **United States Steel Corp.** for $250 million and retired. During his lifetime he gave more than $350 million to various educational, cultural, and peace institutions, many of which bear his name. Not bad for a lad with no formal education.

Selling It!

While textile, railroad, and steel industries were making tremendous advances in the science of production and management, other businesses were paying attention. The last quarter of the nineteenth century brought with it an incredible outpouring of inexpensive, mass-produced goods and services for consumers. Large companies were able to develop and produce extremely high volumes of goods for consumption by the American public mainly due to the emergence of a new breed of busi-

2. Chandler, *The Invisible Hand,* p. 268.

wholesalers Top-tier merchants who typically deal directly with the original manufacturers to distribute products to retailers.

retailers Second-tier merchants who typically purchase products from wholesalers to distribute to end customers. Many large retailers, however, will often bypass wholesalers to purchase products directly from original manufacturers.

inventory turnover (stockturns) The number of times the inventory in the organization "turns over" during a period of time. It is often easier to think of inventory turnover as the number of times a dollar invested in inventory is sold during a period of time. Inventory turnover is computed as Cost of Goods Sold ÷ Average inventory value.

ness—**wholesalers** and **retailers**. Besides making many diverse items available for purchase from one source, these wholesalers and retailers provided other critical services, including distribution, delivery, and credit service on account. The emergence in the United States of the large-scale retailer began with companies such as **R. H. Macy & Company, Inc.**, in New York City and **Marshall Field** in Chicago. **Sears, Roebuck & Company** was also founded in Chicago in the latter part of the nineteenth century and became *the* mail-order catalog store for urban and rural communities throughout the country. By bridging the price gap between small local producers and huge mass producers, these retailers and distributors achieved tremendous financial success. Managers and accountants in this industry learned to focus on a very important idea: move the inventory! The success of the mass merchant hinged on **inventory turnover** (called "stockturns"). By selling goods faster than smaller local merchants, large-scale wholesalers and retailers could charge lower prices and still realize tremendous profit. Up to this point, big business in America had focused almost exclusively on costs. Now wholesalers and retailers introduced a new concept to management accounting. Companies could make a lot of money by controlling and evaluating the way managers use *assets* (in this case, inventory). As early as 1870, Marshall Field and other large-scale retailers began monitoring stockturns throughout their organizations with great interest. This was an important step toward modern-day techniques of asset (or capital) management.

DuPont Makes Accounting History

Now we're back to the DuPont story. By the time Alfred, Coleman, and Pierre du Pont had finished buying out suppliers and establishing sales offices throughout the country, they had created a giant organization. The fact that their company was big, however, is not what makes their situation interesting. Lowell, Morgan, Carnegie, and Macy each had already created and successfully managed huge companies. However, these companies were all focused on doing *one thing well*—making cloth, moving railway cars, producing steel, or selling goods. The du Ponts, on the other hand, were trying to combine within one company many different types of businesses: wholesale purchasing, raw materials and finished goods manufacturing, and retail distribution. They had a huge management hierarchy, complicated production processes, geographically dispersed business locations, and inventory that needed to turn over rapidly. Each of these divisions constantly required attention and additional capital investments in order to grow and flourish. The du Ponts knew they could make or lose money in any part of this new monstrous company. Obviously, neither they nor their capital could be everywhere at once. They needed to make trade-off decisions. The problem was, with very diverse divisions, how could they decide which divisions should receive additional investments of time and money? They couldn't really compare the cost reports of retail stores in Denver with a black powder manufacturing factory in Delaware or with a sodium nitrate processing plant in Chile. Having all these unique business activities also made it quite difficult to relate various measures of efficiency (such as operating ratios or stockturns) directly to overall company profit. The first thing the new DuPont management team did was develop extensive budgets to coordinate the flow of resources from raw materials to the final customer. But they still needed a measurement for comparing performance in the firm's separate divisions with performance of the whole company. Enter the accountant (actually, he was an electrical engineer turned accountant). Nevertheless, if a management accountant hall of fame existed, the bust of F. Donaldson Brown would grace its entrance!

Donaldson Brown, along with other executives at DuPont, realized that every division required an investment in capital (assets) in order to be in business. The overall goal of every business should be to effectively use its assets to make a profit. For example, an explosives plant earning $50,000 in profit with required capital investments of $1,000,000 would not be making the same contribution to overall

DuPont profits as a major distributing division earning an equal $50,000 in profit with only $500,000 in required capital assets. If you had a million dollars to invest, which division would receive your money? The distributing division is earning a 10% return ($50,000 ÷ $500,000) on the DuPont investment in inventory, equipment, and buildings. The explosives plant is earning only a 5% return on investment. Although this simple formula was not really new to American business in the first part of the twentieth century, Brown took the idea of **return on investment (ROI)** and turned it into a management technique that could be used to manage any kind of business operation at DuPont. Exhibit 9-2 illustrates how the DuPont ROI formula could be expanded into a comprehensive measurement system for performance. Study this exhibit for a moment. If any company division (or the company as a whole) is generating low ROI, the DuPont management team can immediately begin analyzing the problem. Is asset turnover too low? Perhaps the division needs to reduce its investment in assets or work to improve sales. Is the profit margin less than adequate? Maybe the division needs to concentrate on reducing selling expenses or manufacturing costs. The ROI tool allowed the du Pont cousins to greatly succeed in managing the country's first integrated company by combining cost management with asset management and raising it to an art form! It's likely that no management accounting technique has had as great an impact on business management

return on investment (ROI) A measure of operating performance and efficiency in utilizing assets; computed in its simplest form by dividing net income by average total assets.

EXHIBIT 9-2

An Illustration of the DuPont ROI Formula (simple and complex)

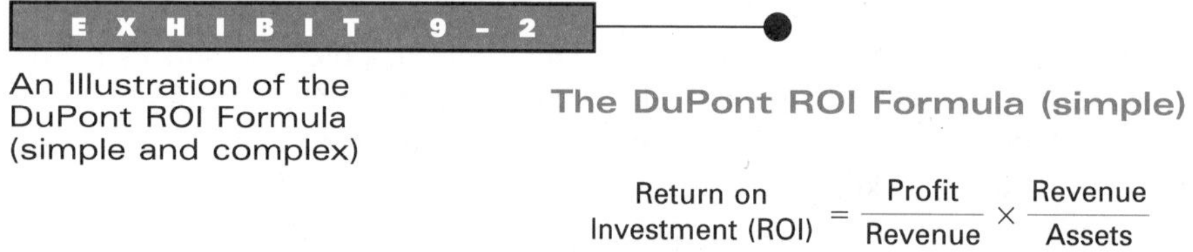

The DuPont ROI Formula (simple)
Return on Investment (ROI) = Profit / Revenue × Revenue / Assets

Later development of the DuPont formula expanded the model to include a measure of leverage (Assets/Equity). The effect of this modification is to create a return on equity (ROE) instead of ROI.

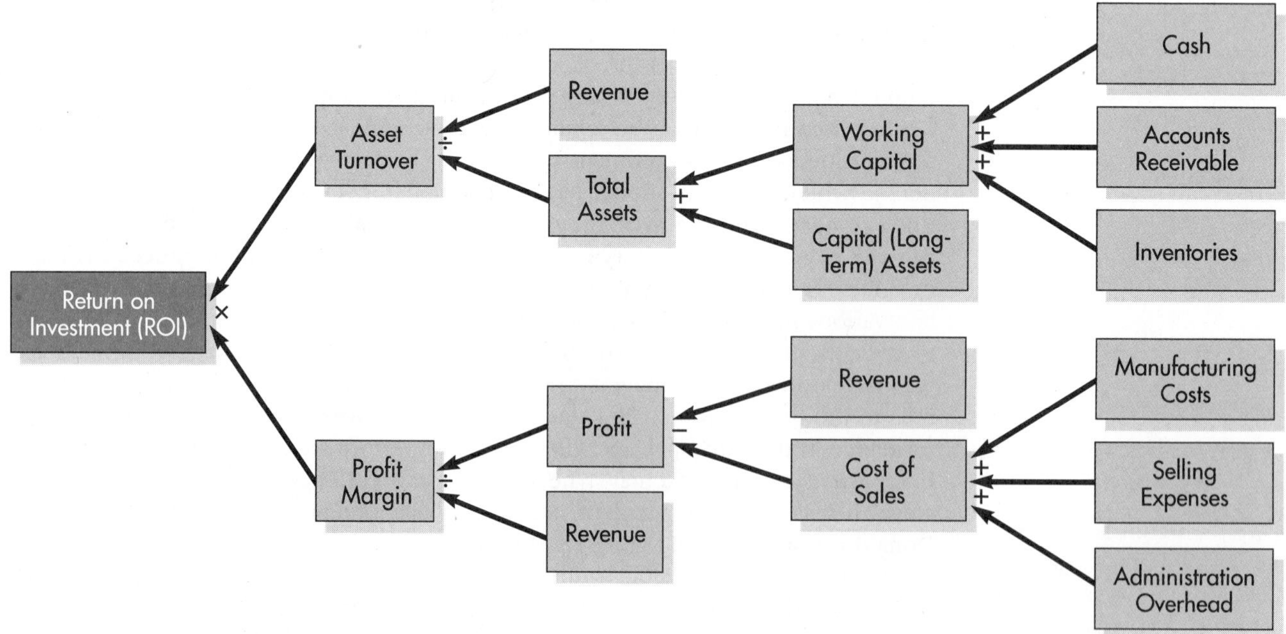

***Source:** T. C. Davis, "How the DuPont Organization Appraises Its Performance," in AMA *Financial Management Series No. 94* (American Management Association, New York, 1950), p. 7. Reprinted in Johnson and Kaplan, *Relevance Lost,* 1987 (HBS Press: Boston, MA), p. 85.

as the DuPont ROI formula. In fact, Donaldson Brown took the ROI approach with him when he followed Pierre du Pont to help rescue a little company in the midst of an inventory crisis in 1920. The name of the company was **General Motors**. The success of the DuPont technique at General Motors can be witnessed today in any parking lot in America.

Differences between Financial and Management Accounting

Why is it so important to understand the history of management accounting? First, many professionals have a difficult time separating the purposes of management accounting from financial accounting. Financial accounting, as established by GAAP, is intended to provide external users (such as investors, creditors, and suppliers) with useful information for making economic decisions. These decisions can include whether to invest in a company, to loan the company money, or to establish a long-term buyer-supplier relationship. The primary financial statements (the balance sheet, the income statement, and the statement of cash flows) provide information to external users in a standardized format using a common set of accounting practices. External users can then easily compare the financial statements for a vast array of companies.

planning Outlining the activities that need to be performed for an organization to achieve its objectives.

controlling Implementing management plans and identifying how plans compare with actual performance.

evaluating Analyzing results, rewarding performance, and identifying problems.

Second, it should be *very* clear to you now that management accounting is less precisely defined than financial accounting. A regulatory agency or an oversight board does not create it. Rather, management accounting is the result of individuals and companies striving to create an information system that has competitive value. Every company is different; each has a different strategy for success and its own definition of success. As a result, management accounting is really a unique process for every organization. Each company creates its own customized view of how it does business. That view is (or should be) reflected in the kinds of performance measures and planning documents it creates from its management accounting system. On the other hand, there are some rather consistent management accounting practices for organizations both in America and throughout the world. Every organization must be involved in a process of **planning** for the future, **controlling** present operations, and **evaluating** past events. Hence, regardless of the type of business you may be in someday, you will deal with the realities of planning, controlling, and evaluating. Watching how other successful businesses approach the process of planning, controlling, and evaluating is how management accounting continues to develop today. Someone has a novel information-tracking idea that provides a competitive edge; the rest of us watch and then try to duplicate and improve on the effort.

CAUTION

Don't think management accounting is not important just because it is not as precisely defined as financial accounting. As evidenced by our brief review of business history, management accounting is critical to the success of businesses throughout the world.

(STOP & THINK)

We have described some differences in financial and management accounting. Why is it important for an accounting system to provide both types of accounting information?

TO SUMMARIZE

Management accounting is the product of many years of business owners and managers experimenting with methods for capturing and using information about their organizations that would give them a competitive edge (in contrast to financial accounting rules established by an authoritative body). The development of management accounting is a story of evolution that begins with the Industrial Revolution in America nearly 200 years ago. Resulting from the need to manage a large production process in textile mills, managers needed some kind of reporting system that provided the information needed to plan, control, and evaluate work they were not actually doing themselves. As railroad companies later spread geographically across the nation, executive-level managers created long-distance cost performance measures to evaluate the efforts of subordinates. Toward the end of the nineteenth century, Andrew Carnegie lifted cost management to new heights with his use of cost sheets to specifically track the exact costs to produce his steel products. The advent of large-scale wholesalers and retailers shifted attention to the need to effectively manage inventory assets using inventory turnover (stockturn) measures. Donaldson Brown and the du Pont cousins finally consolidated all these important developments into the famous DuPont ROI management accounting model at the beginning of the twentieth century. Management accounting thus established itself as a mature business discipline.

BUSINESS ENVIRONMENT ESSAY

The Cost of Bad Information The focus of management accounting is to provide useful information to management for decision making. However, once in a while bad information is provided, usually with devastating results. Take the case of Starship, for example. Starship was to be a radically new, high-technology, corporate jet produced by **Beech Aircraft**. Instead of being made with aluminum, as most planes are, it was to be made entirely of plastics and carbon fiber. Being 15 to 20 percent lighter than competitors, Starship was to deliver jet performance at propeller plane price.

Unfortunately, the plane was not successful. To quote a 1994 *Fortune* article, "It's a Dud. A Fiasco. A Little Bighorn with Wings." Over a period of five and one-half years, Beech sold only 15; **Cessna** sold over 390 comparable jets during the same period.

Why was the plane so unsuccessful? The problem lies in bad information, which created delays. The delays first came in months. Then years. As the years passed, costs climbed. By 1994, Beech spent $350 million on the aircraft. The plane was such a flop that if the company had instead used $1,000 bills laminated three-ply to build the planes, it still would have saved over $50 million!

Beech didn't act on the information it had available. Ignoring FAA standards, cost overruns, and customer concerns, it forged ahead. The result of this myopic vision was a product more repudiated by the market than almost any other product made. Indeed, the Starship will find its resting place next to Edsel and New Coke.

Source: Adapted from Alan Farnham, "It's a Bird, It's a Plane, It's a Flop!" *Fortune,* May 2, 1994, pp. 108–110.

2 *Discuss the major differences in managing manufacturing, merchandising, and service organizations.*

manufacturing organizations Organizations that focus on using labor and/or machinery to convert raw materials into marketable products.

merchandising organizations Organizations that focus on procuring tangible products and distributing them to customers.

BUSINESS ORGANIZATIONS

It should be obvious that there are many different kinds of business organizations. Donaldson Brown identified a performance measure (ROI) that could be used to manage all kinds of businesses. Still, different types of organizations also have their own specific methods of planning budgets, controlling costs, and evaluating performance. Generally, businesses can be divided into **manufacturing**, **merchandising**, and **service organizations**. Think for a moment about our accounting history lesson. Each of the companies we talked about falls into one of these three categories. For example, the **Carnegie Steel Company** is clearly a manufacturing organization; **Sears, Roebuck & Company** is in the merchandising business; the **Union Pacific Railroad Corporation** provides a service (transportation) to its customers. Many governmental, nonprofit, and for-profit organizations (such as law and accounting firms) fall into this last group. America's "big business" originally began in the manufacturing industries. Today, industry in the United States is shifting more

service organizations Organizations that focus on delivery of marketable services, such as legal advice or education, to individuals or other organizations.

toward merchandising and service companies. Service organizations are America's fastest growing business segment.

It is important that you clearly understand both the differences and the similarities of running a manufacturing organization versus merchandising or service organizations. Think about the types of products that each of these organizations provides to its customers. Manufacturers invest a lot of resources into building large factories, hiring managers, and employing production personnel who take materials (such as raw cotton) and convert them into a finished product (such as a bolt of cloth). It is important that manufacturers are able to effectively track and manage the costs of these raw materials and laborers, as well as the administrative costs of managing long-term assets (such as a large factory).

Like manufacturers, merchandisers also sell inventory to customers. The important difference is that merchandisers generally purchase their inventory from manufacturers and resell it to their customers. Merchandisers do not have to invest in and manage the purchase of raw materials, the payment of production labor, and the costs of running a large factory. Sounds simple, right? However, merchandisers *are* faced with the challenge of *logistics.* Getting the right inventory to the right place at the right time for the right price is a very involved business process, particularly for large-scale merchants who are spread across broad geographic areas.

Finally, service firms really do not have to deal with inventory at all. The product they provide to customers is service. Nevertheless, service firms have to carefully manage the costs and delivery of their product, just like manufacturers and merchants. For some service firms, like railroads and airlines, a large part of service costs is related to large assets like trains, planes, and terminals. Other service firms, like accounting firms and law firms, find that the bulk of their service costs is related to paying for the expertise of highly trained professionals. As you can see, for all three types of organizations, cost and performance management is a critical process in a successful business.

The DuPont ROI formula is a pretty terrific tool for *evaluating* the financial performance of all three kinds of organizations. On the other hand, *planning* and *controlling* business processes in order to produce strong financial results often require management accounting tools that are fairly unique to each organization type. Therefore, you should try to become aware of management needs and the management accounting methods that are more applicable, for example, to merchants than to manufacturers or service providers.

FYI

In 1996, U.S corporations reported earnings of nearly $1.9 trillion. When we break this number down by industries, manufacturers earned $822 billion, merchandisers earned $350 billion, and service and transportation companies earned $728 billion. You should note, however, that governmental and nonprofit organizations do not report earnings. Therefore, service industries are even bigger than these numbers would indicate!

Source: U.S. Department of Commerce, Bureau of Economic Analysis, 1996

net connected ://www.swcollege.com **net work**

The Bureau of Economic Analysis is known as the economic accountant for the U.S. Department of Commerce. Go to its Web site and investigate the "Industry & wealth data." Within these data you can find overviews of key economic information such as Gross Domestic Product (GDP) by industry. (GDP is the dollar value of final goods and services produced in the economy during any particular year.) Look at the "Overview of 1987-96" table.

What were the 1987 GDP and 1996 GDP in current dollars for all manufacturing industries? What were the 1987 GDP and 1996 GDP in current dollars for all service industries (not including transportation)?

www.bea.doc.gov/

TO SUMMARIZE

Industry basically can be grouped into manufacturers, merchandisers, and service firms. In order to provide products to their customers, manufacturers have to manage the costs of raw materials, laborers, and administration of large factory assets. Merchants, on the other hand, purchase finished inventory and must manage the logistics of distributing inventory to store locations and customers. Service firms do not sell inventory. Rather, these firms must manage the costs of capital assets, such as railroads, or expert professionals, like lawyers and doctors. All three of these business types must effectively plan, control, and evaluate costs and performance in the process of successfully delivering their products to customers.

3 *Define the common terms and measures found in modern management accounting.*

TRADITIONAL MANAGEMENT ACCOUNTING TERMINOLOGY

As indicated before, business professionals and management accountants work hard to create information systems and performance measures that add value to their organizations. A good information and performance measurement system helps define the vocabulary used in communication between company employees and managers. Since we also pay attention to other companies' successful use of management accounting techniques, a set of common management accounting terms has evolved. So, before we discuss traditional and cutting-edge management accounting practices, it is probably a good idea to define a few basic terms. Remember, an official regulatory body of professionals has not defined these terms. As you work in various organizations later in your career, you will likely find that these definitions can become ambiguous. Depending on the decision context, a particular cost can have several titles. It is very important that you understand this fact! If you like playing card games such as bridge or canasta, you understand that it is often very important in the game to distinguish between cards of different suits—hearts, spades, clubs, or diamonds. On the other hand, for some decisions in the card game it may be more useful to concentrate on the value of the card—ace, 10, deuce, etc. So, sometimes you care about the ace of hearts because of its "heartness," and at other times you are really more interested in its "aceness." Similarly, a *product cost* may also be a *variable cost.* Depending on the management setting, you may choose to categorize costs as *fixed* or *variable* versus *product* or *period* or *direct* or *indirect* (we'll discuss all these terms next).

CAUTION

In business conversations (discussions concerning costs, for example), never assume you are talking about the same concept as another individual. You always need to be sure that everyone has the same definition of a management accounting term or concept before you let the conversation get too far.

Differences among Costs, Assets, Expenses, and Losses

Management accountants often use the term *cost.* You should pay attention to this term because it has many meanings. There are many specific types of costs, but used by itself the term **cost** generally means the cash or cash-equivalent value sacrificed for goods and services that are expected to provide current or future benefits (usually revenues) to an organization. Did you catch the use of the term "future benefits"? Cost is usually used in the context of an *asset purchase*. For example, if $600 cash and a piece of machinery having a cash-equivalent value of $800 are exchanged for supplies, the cost of those supplies is $1,400. For financial statement purposes, the $1,400 expended for the supplies is reported as an asset if the supplies have future benefits or value. As assets are used up, thus having no future value, the costs of these assets turn into **expenses**. Both expenses (expired costs) and assets (unexpired costs) provide benefits to an organization and help generate revenues. Costs that provide no current or future benefit to an organization are called **losses**.

cost Cash or cash-equivalent value sacrificed for goods and services that are expected to provide benefits to an organization.

expenses Costs incurred in the normal course of business to generate revenues.

losses Costs that provide no benefit to an organization.

Product and Period Costs

In all three types of organizations, costs associated with the products or services offered are called **product costs**. In a manufacturing company, for example, prod-

product costs Costs associated with products or services offered.

uct costs (often referred to as manufacturing costs) are all costs necessary to create finished goods ready for sale. They include all costs related to production: the factory manager's salary, depreciation and taxes on the factory building, wages of the factory workers, and the materials that go into the product. In a merchandising company, product costs are the costs incurred to purchase goods and get them ready for resale to customers. In a service company, product costs (sometimes called cost of services) involve labor, supplies, and other costs directly related to providing services to customers. At Kelly Services, Inc., for example, labor costs for all personnel who provide part-time or temporary services for clients are classified as contract service costs and are subtracted from revenues to arrive at gross margin. A major difference between Kelly Services, Inc., and manufacturers or merchandisers is inventory. Kelly sells services. Can we put service labor into inventory? Think about this idea, as we'll discuss it shortly. In manufacturing and merchandising organizations, the product costs of units still on hand at the end of the period clearly form the basis for the dollar amount of inventory carried on the balance sheet. The product costs of units sold during the accounting period are used to determine cost of goods sold, which is shown on the income statement as part of the calculation of gross margin for the period.

period costs Costs not directly related to a product, service, or asset that are charged as expenses to the income statement in the period in which they are incurred.

Period costs are all costs incurred that cannot be associated with or assigned to a product or service. These costs are usually not associated with inventory or any other kind of asset. For example, the most common period costs are selling and administrative costs. Examples of selling costs are sales salaries, advertising, and delivery costs. Examples of administrative costs are salaries of the president and controller, depreciation or rent on office buildings, taxes on assets used in administration, and other office expenditures such as postage, supplies, and utilities. The management accountant typically treats period costs very differently from product costs. Instead of using these costs to establish a value for inventory, period costs are usually recognized as an expense on the income statement in the period in which they are incurred. For example, if Sears, Roebuck & Company sells two-thirds of the inventory it purchased during November, only the cost of the inventory sold becomes an expense (Cost of Goods Sold) on that month's income statement. The other third of the inventory cost remains an asset (Inventory) on the balance sheet. Regardless of how many products are sold during the month, the president's entire salary for November is recognized as an expense on the monthly income statement. Now do you see why we call these "period" costs? Because period costs are always expensed in the period (e.g., month) in which they are incurred.

As you might imagine, it is sometimes difficult to determine whether a cost is a product or a period cost. For example, many companies have their entire operation—factory, sales, and corporate offices—in one building. Is building depreciation a product or a period cost? If it is a period cost, is it a selling or an administrative expense? Generally, such costs are divided on some equitable basis, such as square feet of space occupied. If, for example, the building has 100,000 square feet, with the factory occupying 75,000 square feet, then 75 percent (75,000 ÷ 100,000) of the building depreciation might logically be assigned to product cost (manufacturing) and 25 percent to period cost (nonmanufacturing).

Types of Product Costs

Now let's examine how we measure product and period costs in each of the three types of organizations. How would one measure product costs for a merchandiser? Actually, that is a fairly easy question. The resources Macy's spends to acquire store inventory for resale to customers clearly are product costs. As products are sold, these inventory costs become an expense on the income statement. What about the wages and salaries of Macy's store clerks and managers? Macy's will likely categorize these costs as part of its selling and administrative expenses and treat them as a period cost on the income statement. That's not too difficult. Now consider the same question for **Arthur Andersen LLP**, one of the largest certified public accounting (CPA) firms in the world. What are the products sold by this service firm? Arthur Andersen sells the time of its tax accountants, auditors, and consultants. The salaries of these professionals represent the costs of its "product." Arthur Andersen also employs many other people (such as clerks, secretaries, and office managers) to support the professionals and administer office needs. The wages and salaries of these clerks and office managers, along with costs of office rent, desk supplies, and computers, are likely treated as period costs and recognized as selling and administrative expenses on the income statement.

When identifying product costs, the most challenging organization to analyze is manufacturing. Does **DuPont** purchase inventory for resale? Actually, it does purchase some inventory, such as basic chemicals. But it doesn't simply turn around and sell these basic chemicals to customers. Manufacturing has to take place before these raw materials become a finished product ready for sale. DuPont must employ laborers to work on these chemicals. In addition, DuPont builds factory buildings and purchases manufacturing equipment. DuPont must also employ managers and other support personnel (such as engineers and custodians) to support the line workers' efforts to convert basic chemicals into saleable product. These are all product costs. Basically, any cost required to get the product manufactured and ready for sale is a product cost. To help management analyze the manufacturing cost of its products, product costs are divided into three components: (1) direct materials, (2) direct labor, and (3) manufacturing overhead. **Direct materials** are materials that become part of the product and are traceable to it. **Direct labor** consists of the wages that are paid to those who physically work on the direct materials to transform them into a finished product. **Manufacturing overhead** includes all other costs incurred in the manufacturing process not specifically identified as direct materials or direct labor.

direct materials Materials that become part of the product and are traceable to it.

direct labor Wages that are paid to those who physically work on the direct materials to transform them into a finished product and are traceable to specific products.

manufacturing overhead All costs incurred in the manufacturing process other than direct materials and direct labor.

It is important to emphasize that costs are typically classified as direct materials or direct labor only if they are clearly identifiable with manufactured products and traceable to them. Some labor and many minor materials may be incurred in manufacturing a product, but they are not traced to specific products because it is either too difficult or too expensive to do so. Glue and nails, for example, are usually part of a finished piece of furniture, but their costs are so minor and their specific uses so difficult to trace that they are not assigned to individual products; rather they are considered indirect materials and are included in manufacturing overhead. Similarly, the wages paid to factory supervisors and management, maintenance workers, and factory security guards are treated as indirect labor and assigned to manufacturing overhead. Besides indirect materials and indirect labor, the costs assigned to manufacturing overhead include: depreciation, insurance, and taxes on the factory building and machinery; repairs to manufacturing equipment; and the cost of utilities to operate the factory.

Andrew Carnegie and his executive team learned a long time ago that it is fairly easy to assign direct materials and direct labor to products. However, assigning the depreciation of the factory building (a manufacturing overhead cost) to cost sheets of specific products likely proved to be a decision nightmare for Carnegie. Better than most business owners in his time, Andrew Carnegie realized that if manufacturing overhead costs are not assigned to products accurately, products may not be properly priced and operating decisions and competitive strategies might be less than optimal. The cost assignment decision is even tougher today. The more automated and less labor-intensive manufacturing facilities become, the greater the portion of the total product cost that is categorized as manufacturing overhead.

Exhibit 9-3 summarizes the relationship between product costs and period costs in various types of organizations.

EXHIBIT 9-3

Product Costs and Period Costs in Business Organizations

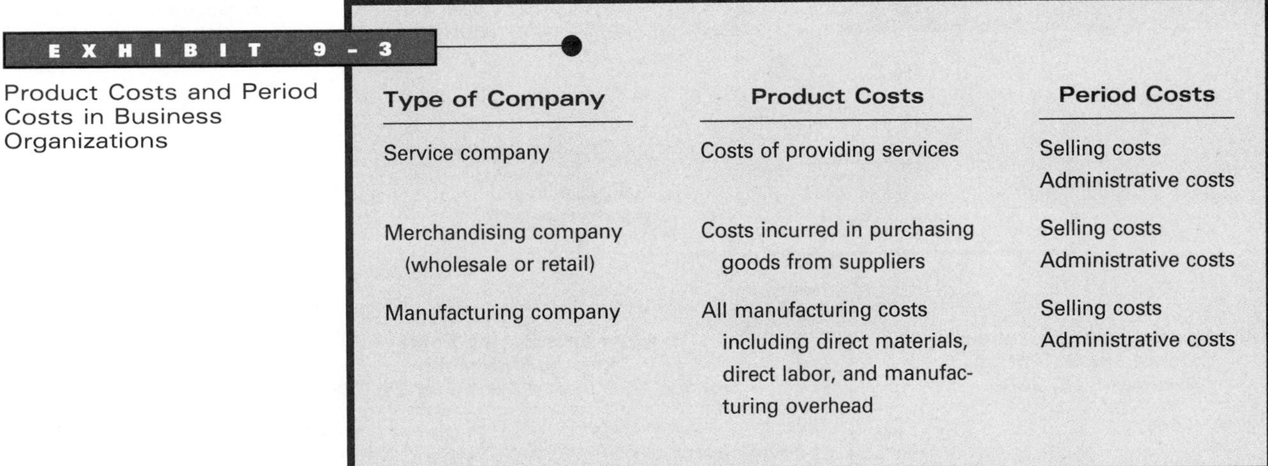

Type of Company	Product Costs	Period Costs
Service company	Costs of providing services	Selling costs Administrative costs
Merchandising company (wholesale or retail)	Costs incurred in purchasing goods from suppliers	Selling costs Administrative costs
Manufacturing company	All manufacturing costs including direct materials, direct labor, and manufacturing overhead	Selling costs Administrative costs

Product Cost Flows and Inventories

A service firm like Arthur Andersen LLP has lots of supplies and equipment, but the main product it sells to its customers is time and knowledge. Interestingly, many service companies do create an account resembling inventory for holding client-related costs. In contrast, a merchandising firm has lots of inventory to sell. All product costs for this inventory are recorded in one inventory account, Merchandise Inventory. A manufacturing firm has three inventory accounts through which product costs must flow: (1) Raw Materials, (2) Work in Process, and (3) Finished Goods.

Exhibit 9-4 shows the flow of product costs and period costs in each of three (service, merchandising, and manufacturing) imaginary firms. Look at the income statement and balance sheet for the Bigelow Engineering Company. As this service firm pays for labor, supplies, and other costs directly associated with providing engineering services to its clients, these product costs are accumulated in Cost of Services or a similarly titled account. At the end of an accounting period, service costs that have been incurred but not billed are classified as a current asset similar to inventory. When service is complete and customers have been billed, service costs are transferred from the balance sheet to the income statement as Cost of Services. On the income statement, cost of services is subtracted from service revenues to arrive at gross margin.

Sharpe Office Supply, Inc., is a merchandising firm. Its inventory account is debited for the cost of merchandise purchased. Of that amount, the cost of merchandise sold during a period is transferred to Cost of Goods Sold and is reported on the income statement. The unsold merchandise remains in the inventory account and is reported as a current asset on the balance sheet at the end of the accounting period. Selling and administrative expenses for both Bigelow and Sharpe are period expenses that flow directly to the income statement for the period in which they are incurred.

raw materials inventory The inventory of raw (or direct) materials that have not yet begun the production process.

work-in-process inventory Inventory that is partly completed in the production process, but not yet ready for sale to customers.

finished goods inventory Inventory that has completed the production process and is ready for sale to customers.

In the Lever Soap Company, materials purchased for use in manufacturing its products are initially recorded in the **raw materials inventory** account. As these materials are used in production, their cost is transferred to **work-in-process inventory**. As direct labor costs are incurred, they too are recorded in Work-in-Process Inventory. Manufacturing overhead costs, including indirect materials and indirect labor, are also accumulated and transferred to Work-in-Process Inventory.

When products are completed, the total cost is transferred from Work-in-Process Inventory to **Finished Goods Inventory**. The subsequent accounting for these costs is similar to the accounting for inventory in a merchandising firm. When the finished goods are sold, the cost of the units sold is transferred to Cost of Goods Sold on the income statement, and the cost of the unsold units remains in Finished Goods Inventory reported on the balance sheet.

EXHIBIT 9-4 The Flow of Product and Period Costs in Service, Merchandising, and Manufacturing Organizations

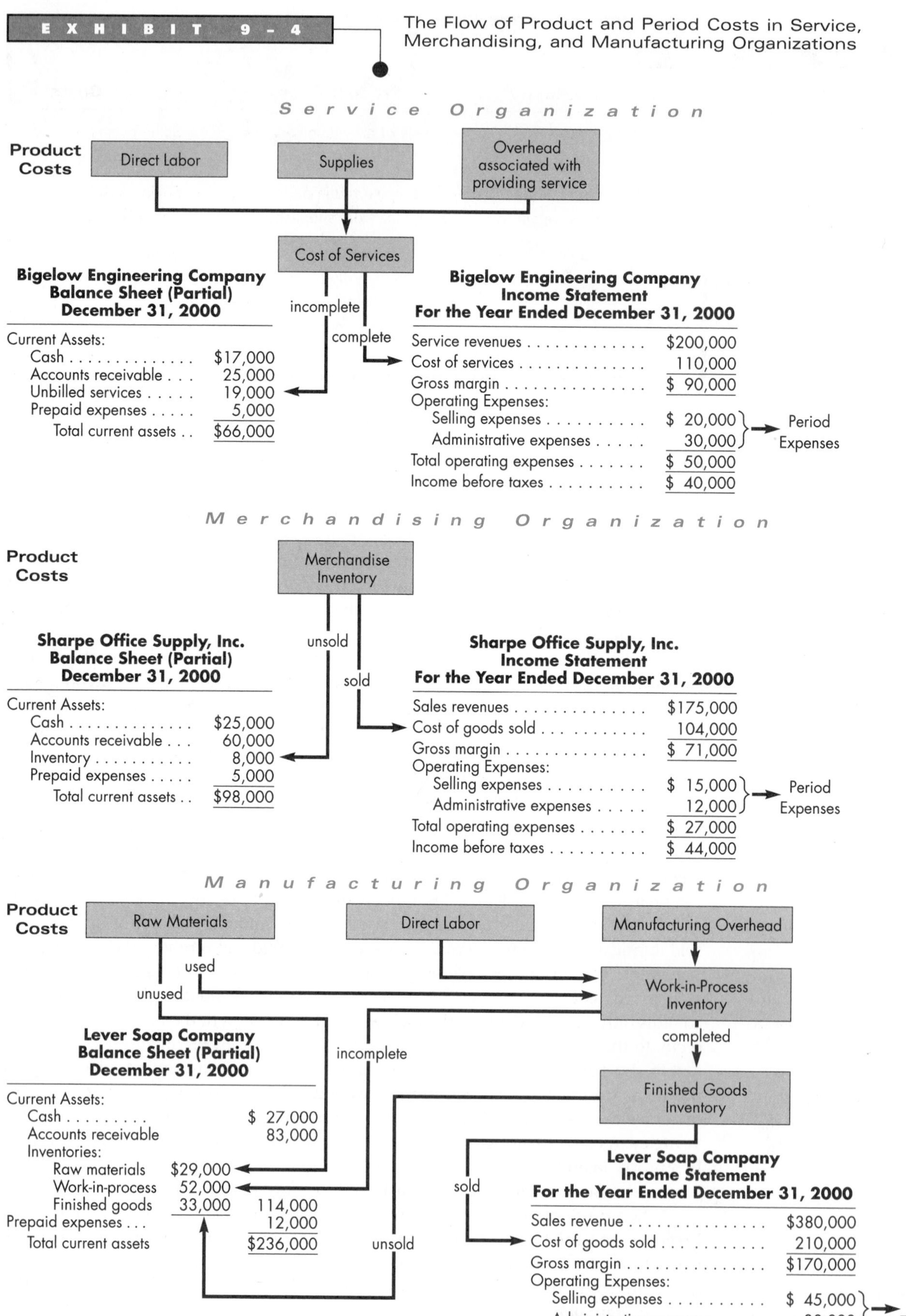

Essentially, the whole point of Exhibit 9-4 is to illustrate that product costs initially are assets on the balance sheet. When the product is sold, these costs are transferred to the income statement as expired costs or expenses. Costs incurred during an accounting period that are not product costs are recorded as expenses and reported on the income statement. We will spend a lot more time on the product cost calculations for manufacturing, merchandising, and service firms in Chapter 10.

Now that you better understand the difference between product and period costs for all three types of business organizations, we will discuss other terms commonly used by management accountants. Organizations need cost information for many different types of decisions: to evaluate performance, to assess alternative action plans, and to make other planning and strategic decisions. Different types of decisions require different cost information.

CAUTION

In theory, distinguishing between variable and fixed costs sounds simple. If the activity, such as production volume or sales volume, increases and the cost in question increases, then it must be a variable cost. Otherwise, it is a fixed cost. However, there are many complexities involved in actually identifying and managing variable and fixed costs. Subsequent chapters, particularly Chapter 11, will focus on variable and fixed costs.

Variable and Fixed Costs

Total **variable costs** change in direct proportion to changes in activity level. Product costs and period costs can be either variable or fixed. One example of a variable product cost is the costs of direct materials (such as bolts of cloth in a clothing factory), which vary proportionately with the number of units produced. Sales commissions, which vary proportionately with sales volume, are an example of a variable period cost. **Fixed costs** remain constant in total, regardless of activity level, at least over a certain range of activity. Examples of fixed period costs are institutional advertising, insurance, and executives' salaries. Examples of fixed product costs are plant depreciation and supervisors' salaries. Regardless of changes in sales or production output, these costs typically remain constant.

variable costs Costs that change in total in direct proportion to changes in activity level.

fixed costs Costs that remain constant in total, regardless of activity level, at least over a certain range of activity.

direct costs Costs that are specifically traceable to a unit of business or segment being analyzed.

indirect costs Costs normally incurred for the benefit of several segments within the organization. Indirect costs are sometimes called common costs.

Direct and Indirect Costs

A cost classification useful for evaluating performance is direct costs and indirect costs. **Direct costs** are costs that can be obviously and physically traced to a unit of business or segment being analyzed. The unit may be a sales territory, product line, division, plant, or any other subdivision for which information is accumulated for analysis. Direct costs are often described as those costs that would be saved if the segment were to be discontinued. Typically, many types of direct costs are variable, yet some are fixed. For example, if the segment being considered were a branch sales office, the cost of inventory and labor to run the store would be direct costs that are variable. On the other hand, the costs to rent the building would be a direct cost that is fixed. **Indirect costs**—sometimes referred to as common, or joint, costs—are costs that are normally incurred for the benefit of several segments. Indirect costs can also be either fixed or variable, although these costs are often fixed. Sometimes these costs are allocated in order to be assigned to a segment. For example, consider a sales manager's salary. If a segment is defined as a branch sales office and a sales manager supervises only one segment, the manager's salary is likely a direct cost of that sales office. However, if the manager is responsible for several segments, the company may choose to allocate it to each sales office. In this case, the manager's salary would be an indirect cost to the sales offices. Indirect costs, such as the manager's salary, normally do not change if one or more of the segments were to be discontinued. Another example of an indirect cost may be manufacturing overhead. Manufacturing overhead is usually not directly identifiable with any product line and is, therefore, an indirect cost. These types of costs are incurred as a consequence of general or overall operating activities.

Costs are designated as either direct or indirect so that a segment can be evaluated on the basis of only those costs directly traceable or chargeable to it. Although companies sometimes allocate indirect costs among

FYI

Activity-based costing (ABC) is a relatively new method of cost assignment, which we will discuss in Chapter 10. A major emphasis of ABC is to directly connect costs with certain activities. One result of ABC is the increase in number of costs that can be classified as direct costs.

segments, such allocations often confuse the analysis of the segment's operations. By focusing only on direct costs, management can both identify segments where performance needs to be improved and recognize segments where performance is outstanding and should be rewarded.

Differential Costs and Sunk Costs

differential costs Future costs that change as a result of a decision; also called incremental or relevant costs.

sunk costs Costs, such as depreciation, that are past costs and do not change as the result of a future decision.

When evaluating alternative actions, managers must distinguish differential costs from sunk costs. The **differential costs**, sometimes called incremental or relevant costs, of a decision are the future costs that change as a result of that decision. (The term *differential* is also commonly applied to future revenues that will be affected by the decision.) **Sunk costs**, on the other hand, are past costs that do not change as the result of a decision.

To illustrate, assume that you own Middle East Fire Fighters, Inc., a company that specializes in extinguishing oil well fires. A customer wants you to put out 500 oil well fires immediately. To bid on the job, you need to know what it will cost. You need to know what additional equipment will be necessary, how many additional people you'll need to hire, and what other costs, such as travel, will be incurred. Costs resulting from accepting the job are the differential costs. For example, the cost of the additional workers needed to extinguish the fires, the expenditures for additional equipment to fight the fires, and the expenses for travel to the fires are differential because they will be incurred as a result of the decision to accept the job. If the job is not accepted, the additional workers will not be hired, the extra equipment would not be needed, and other costs, such as travel, would not be incurred.

Sunk costs are costs that already are committed, but that won't change because of this new job. A cost such as depreciation on existing equipment to be used on this job is a sunk cost. Such a cost is not a future cost (depreciation is an allocation of a past cost), nor does it change as a result of the decision to accept this job. Thus, sunk costs are never relevant to a decision. If, for example, Middle East Fire Fighters decides not to accept the job because depreciation on its existing equipment is too high, it is using the wrong decision criterion. If the new job is profitable and can pay for new equipment that must be purchased, the job should be accepted (other factors being held constant).

Many individuals and companies make poor decisions because of a failure to correctly distinguish between differential costs and sunk costs. As an example, assume you have season tickets to a school's basketball games. On the night of a game, a friend asks you to go to a movie with her. It is a movie you have wanted to see for a long time. If you decline because you have already purchased the basketball tickets and believe you must therefore go to the basketball game, you may have made the wrong decision. The cost of the basketball ticket is a sunk cost. The only costs that are relevant to the decision are costs associated with going to the movie, such as the ticket price and popcorn and other goodies you might buy.

Out-of-Pocket Costs and Opportunity Costs

out-of-pocket costs Costs that require an outlay of cash or other resources.

At the most general level, costs can be separated into out-of-pocket costs and opportunity costs. **Out-of-pocket costs** require an outlay of cash or other resources. All the costs, expenses, assets, and losses discussed thus far in this chapter (other than sunk costs) could be called out-of-pocket costs. If a company is deciding whether or not to accept a special order, the costs of materials needed to produce that order are out-of-pocket costs. If a fast-food restaurant is considering installing a drive-up window, the cost of construction is an out-of-pocket cost. Naïve individuals and organizations usually consider only out-of-pocket costs when making decisions. For example, an individual deciding whether or not to attend a movie might consider only the $7 cost of the ticket required to gain admittance.

opportunity costs
The benefits lost or forfeited as a result of selecting one alternative course of action over another.

Though opportunity costs do not require an outlay of resources, they are as important as out-of-pocket costs to good management decision making. **Opportunity costs** are the benefits lost or forfeited as a result of selecting one alternative course of action over another. For example, choosing to go to a movie instead of working two hours at $6 per hour has an opportunity cost of $12, as well as an out-of-pocket cost of $7 for the ticket. If Middle East Fire Fighters chooses to accept a contract to put out a series of fires in one part of the world, it could preclude the organization from accepting another larger contract that may arrive next week. Installing a drive-up window at a fast-food outlet may have several opportunity costs, such as lost seating or lost parking available to customers.

Opportunity costs are important in all organizations but are especially critical in situations where there are defined limits on available resources. Professional basketball teams, for example, have league-imposed salary caps that dictate the maximum total amount of salaries they can pay to team members. (In 1996–1997, the salary cap was approximately $24.3 million per team.) When an exceptional player, such as Shaquille O'Neal (Shaq) of the **Los Angeles Lakers**, comes up for salary negotiations, the team's management must consider both out-of-pocket and opportunity costs when deciding whether or not to pay the salary requested. For example, Shaq signed a seven-year contract in 1996 with the Los Angeles Lakers for $123 million; that works out to a little more than $17.5 million per year! Before agreeing to the contract, the Lakers management had to decide whether yearly ticket sales and TV revenues would be sufficient to meet the out-of-pocket cost of $17.5 million. Management also had to consider what other player(s) they could sign for $17.5 million per year and whether or not, with a salary cap of $24.3 million, they would be able to pay other current and prospective players enough. Paying $17.5 million per year to Shaq means other players cannot be paid that money and thus is a high opportunity cost for a professional basketball team.[3]

(STOP & THINK)

Which of the following costs are typically recorded within the traditional accounting system: product costs, fixed costs, indirect costs, out-of-pocket costs, sunk costs, opportunity costs?

TO SUMMARIZE

Management accountants have created their own specialized vocabulary. Management must consider many different ways to define costs depending on the types of decisions to be made. Those organizations that best understand and manage their costs are usually the most successful. Costs are quite different from expenses and losses. Service, merchandising, and manufacturing firms all have product and period costs. In a service company, product costs are costs of providing a service to customers. In a merchandising company, product costs are costs incurred to purchase goods and get them ready for resale. In a manufacturing company, product costs are often referred to as manufacturing costs and include the costs of direct materials, direct labor, and manufacturing overhead incurred to produce goods. The product costs for these three organizations are also used on the balance sheet to measure the unbilled services asset account for service firms; the merchandise inventory account for merchandise firms; and the raw materials, work-in-process, and finished goods inventory accounts for manufacturing firms. In contrast to product costs, period costs generally include all costs not directly related to the materials, labor, and overhead involved in providing products to customers. Period costs are used strictly to compute the selling and general administrative expenses on the income statement.

There are also terms used to describe other costs. Variable costs are costs that change in total in direct proportion to changes in activity level. Fixed costs remain constant in total, regardless of activity level, at least over a certain range of activity.

3. *Time*, July 29, 1996.

Direct costs are costs that are specifically traceable to a segment. Indirect costs, or common costs, are costs that are normally incurred for the benefit of several segments. Differential costs are future costs that change as the result of a decision. Sunk costs are past costs that do not change because of a specific decision. Out-of-pocket costs require an outlay of resources. Opportunity costs are measured as the benefits lost by choosing one alternative over another.

4 *Understand that successfully planning, controlling, and evaluating a business requires effective management of cost, quality, and time.*

MANAGEMENT ACCOUNTING TODAY AND IN THE FUTURE

The foundation of management accounting has, historically, been built around concepts and measurements related to costs. However, the effect of increasing competition in today's international marketplace requires that modern management accounting be broadened to include noncost information. In addition, modern management accounting must continue to carefully focus on supporting all aspects of the process of managing today's organizations.

Just-in-Time (JIT) Inventory Systems

Now that you are familiar with the idea of product costs and inventories, it is time to introduce you to a relatively new product cost management concept that Andrew Carnegie and Donaldson Brown would have loved. In describing product costs in a manufacturing environment in the preceding section, three types of inventories were introduced: (1) raw materials, (2) work-in-process, and (3) finished goods. What is the purpose of inventory in a manufacturing plant? This seems pretty obvious. In the past, manufacturers stockpiled inventories in order to avoid shutdowns or slowdowns and to meet customer needs if suppliers were late or if production or delivery was slow. Occasionally (sometimes more than occasionally!), suppliers deliver raw materials that contain some defects, or the production process ruins some work-in-process, or a customer returns an unacceptable product. How do we deal with these unexpected surprises? Again the answer has been to "have a little extra on hand" in order to replace bad parts or products without having to interrupt the manufacturing process. Not surprisingly, production managers can get a little nervous when the inventory levels get too low.

Because of concerns with risks due to scheduling and quality problems, companies used to establish policies to keep inventory levels at or above some minimal level (usually called a "safety stock"). However, a few years ago some cagey accountants and business owners in Japan created a new competitive view of inventory management. They (like everyone else) realized that maintaining these inventories can be very expensive because of warehousing costs, interest costs incurred to finance inventory, and the opportunity cost of money tied up in stockpiled inventory. The real insight these Japanese business professionals had was that inventories are really only "buffers" that mask inefficient operations or product quality problems. Eliminate these timing and quality problems, and you no longer need the inventory buffers. By concentrating on improving product quality and timely deliveries, many Japanese companies became much more efficient and profitable as inventories were kept to a minimum or even eliminated. The emerging inventory system that allows for the elimination of inventory stockpiles, inefficiency, and waste is referred to as "just-in-time" (JIT) inventory. The competitive value of this management system soon caught on and came to America. For now, you should know

BUSINESS ENVIRONMENT ESSAY

The Japanese Focus on Inventory

Henry Ford, the famous automotive production industrialist, lifted the Ford Motor Company to great success during the early and mid-1900s by achieving tremendous cost efficiencies in producing cars. He believed in long production runs where low-skilled workers could build the same car part over and over again. As a result, high manufacturing costs per automobile plummeted and he was able to bring cars to the public at extremely competitive prices. However, this production approach required high levels of inventories in raw materials, work in process, and finished goods.

Meanwhile, across the ocean in Japan, Taiichi Ohno, an industrial scientist, and Eliji Toyoda, an executive vice president at Toyota Motor Corporation, were experimenting with a different approach to large-scale production. While other Toyota executives thought that Toyoda's ideas were impractical, in 1949, in a machine shop in Koromo, Eliji Toyoda began experimenting with a new production control approach using the concepts of a just-in-time (JIT) inventory system. By 1953, the Koromo machine shop had a fully implemented *Kanban* system, which was based on the concept that supplies should be "pulled" through the production process as they were needed. Interestingly, Eliji Toyoda copied this idea from the sales methods of U.S. supermarkets. Mr. Toyoda was able to demonstrate that *Kanban* eliminated waste due to the over-production of parts, reduced or eliminated the need of buffer inventories in the plant, and dramatically reduced production defects. In 1963, top management decided on the full application of *Kanban* as a means of transforming the production control system. Cost accountants were charged with developing and maintaining performance measures that tracked defects, excess inventory, and throughput time. The rest, as they say, is history.

Source: M. Udagawa, "The development of production management at the Toyota Motor Corporation" *Business History,* 1995, pp. 107–120.

that JIT inventory systems have dramatically changed the cost structures of many manufacturing companies. Inventory balances have been reduced significantly and product costs have decreased, primarily because of increased efficiency and reduced costs of handling inventory.

A New Marriage in Strategic Performance Measures: Cost, Quality, and Time

Nobody could have fully anticipated the effect that the JIT concept has had on the process of managing companies today. Essentially, the benefits of JIT didn't stop with simply decreasing the *costs* of inventory management. The additional emphases of improving the *quality* of products and the *timelines* of production and distribution systems have become a whole new way of competing in manufacturing, merchandising, and service companies. Businesses today create a competitive advantage by delivering more value to customers in less cycle time than competitors. As a firm creates and exploits a competitive advantage in cost, quality, and time, it creates increased shareholder value. In other words, if you make your customers happy, you create greater financial outcomes and, therefore, you make the owners (shareholders) of the business happy! As a result, new performance measures related to cost, quality, and time are being accumulated, tracked, and monitored by firms in many industries and have become a hot topic for research among management accountants. Some examples of the new performance measures being tracked by management accountants in the strategic areas of cost, quality, and time are displayed in Exhibit 9-5. We'll discuss many of these performance measures in later chapters.

EXHIBIT 9-5 New Measures of Cost, Quality, and Time

Cost Measures	Quality Measures	Time Measures
Engineering cost performance	Manufacturing first-pass yield	On-time delivery
Rework and scrap costs	Warranty returns	Master schedule stability
Cost versus features/benefits delivered	Vendor supply quality	New product development cycle time
Costs of quality	Service and support events	Manufacturing cycle time
Life cycle costs	Successful availability events	Recovery-response time
Target costs	Alignment with customer expectations	Time to market
Learning costs	Six sigma error rate	Order fulfillment cycle time
Activity costs	Waste, scrap, and rework rates	Rework & other non-value-added time

The idea of extending beyond cost to also compete on quality and time is having a major impact in industries across the world. These competitive developments present a real opportunity for today's management accountants to jump in and be a part of the process! Frankly, some accountants are not paying attention to this recent shift in management information needs. These accountants continue to focus on providing cost data only. Apparently, they haven't learned their history lesson. Success and profits flow to the business that creates new views of information it can use to gain a competitive edge in the market place. On the other hand, some farsighted accountants see the trend and are currently bringing together "balanced scorecards" that combine cost, quality, and time data to support decision making that can literally redefine customer and client service.

BUSINESS ENVIRONMENT ESSAY

One Company's Experience with Cost, Quality, and Time Developing measures of cost, quality, and time is a highly proprietary strategic activity. Many organizations are very reluctant to disclose the specifics of their efforts to develop competitive information in these three areas. One company (a medium-sized aerospace corporation in the Pacific Northwest who chooses to remain anonymous) provides a good illustration of the process of creating cost, quality, and time strategic measures. In 1989, the executive team started work to develop new competitive information for this company. They first conducted a survey of key customers, asking about product design, quality, and reliability; the company's ability to meet delivery schedules and other commitments; pricing and perceived value; service and the capability to recover from mistakes; and the overall ease of doing business with the company.

The results were surprising. Contrary to expectations, customers weren't concerned with the company's technological innovations that management had been proud of for years. Instead, customers were concerned with cost, quality, and delivery performance. To their dismay, the executives discovered that customers were dissatisfied with the company's performance in these three areas. Some said they continued to buy from the company only because it was easy to do business with and it resolved problems quickly. Clearly, the company was at risk of losing their customers to a competitor unless some changes were made!

In order to refocus the company on the needs of its customers, an executive staff team was formed to meet weekly to develop a new performance measurement system. The meetings turned into prolonged debates over the number and kind of measures to use. Hours of brainstorming eventually led to the following list:

Cost Measures

- Engineering cost performance
- Production efficiency
- Rework and scrap costs

Quality Measures

- Quality of supplier's products
- Manufacturing first-pass yield
- Warranty returns

Time Measures

- New-product development cycle time
- Master schedule stability
- Manufacturing cycle time
- On-time delivery

The executive team assigned the company's controller to collect performance data for each of these ten measures and issue a monthly report. Graphs of the results were posted for employees and customers to see and became a critical part of any meeting in which management reviewed performance. Some adjustments to these measures were made based on feedback from employees and customers. Eventually, this new approach to performance measures played a crucial role in the company's overall efforts to increase its competitive position. By 1993, it achieved the following performance improvements:

- Customer-quoted delivery times were cut by 50%.
- On-time shipments rose 89%.
- Product-development cycle time fell 35%.
- Manufacturing costs as a percentage of manufacturing sales fell 10%.

Source: K. V. Ramanathan and D. S. Schaffer, "How Am I Doing?" *Journal of Accountancy,* May 1995, pp. 79–82.

The Management Process

We began this chapter with a brief history of management accounting in order to emphasize that the purpose of management accounting is to provide managers with information that has competitive value. To accomplish this, management accountants must understand the types of decisions being made and how these decisions affect the processes of managing a successful organization. Exhibit 9-6 illustrates the general management process.

The center circle in Exhibit 9-6 is labeled decision making. Critical to the success experienced by great companies in the past like **DuPont**, **Union Pacific Railroad**, and **Marshall Field** was intelligent decision making by individuals supported by competitive management accounting information. As we prepare to move into the twenty-first century, strategic performance measures of cost, quality, and time will continue to support and improve decisions that build organizations both in the profit and not-for-profit sectors of our society. Managers will always need to make choices. What should be produced? What should be sold? What does this client need? Which supplier should be used? Who should be promoted? How should financing be obtained? How should products be shipped?

The decision-making circle intersects three other circles, each representing a major management function. This intersection is meant to show that each of these functions requires decision making. The three management functions of planning, controlling, and evaluating generally follow a natural order—at least in theory. In practice, managers and management accountants are often required to work with processes, customers, and employers requiring all three functions at once. Life can move pretty fast in business!

EXHIBIT 9-6

The Management Process

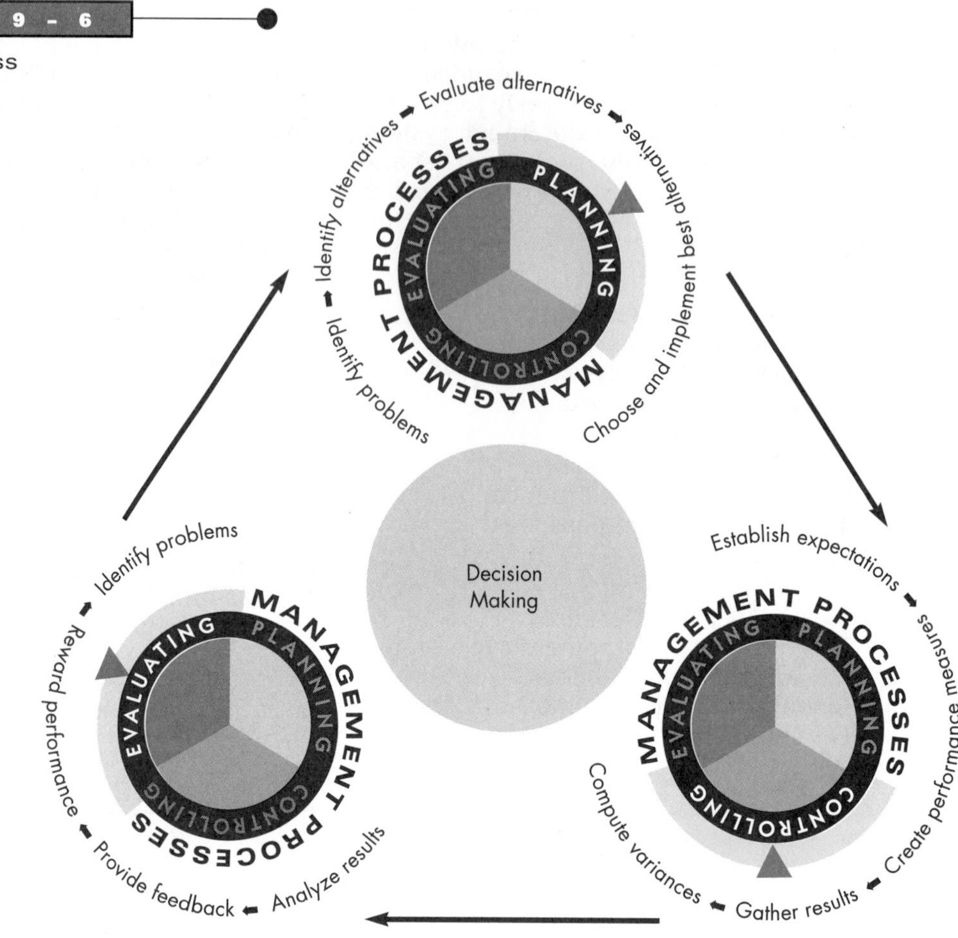

Planning

Management planning involves a process of identifying problems or opportunities, identifying alternatives, evaluating alternatives, then choosing and implementing the best alternative(s). There are two basic types of planning:

1. Long-run or strategic planning
2. Short-run planning, which includes:
   a. Short-run operating decisions
   b. Short-run nonroutine decisions

strategic planning Broad, long-range planning, usually conducted by top management.

Long-run planning involves making decisions whose effects extend several years into the future—usually three to five years, but sometimes longer. This includes broad-based decisions about products, markets, productive facilities, and financial resources. Long-run planning is often called strategic planning. **Strategic planning**, likely the most critical decision-making process that takes place at the executive level in any organization today, usually involves identifying an organization's mission, the goals flowing from that mission, and strategies and action steps to accomplish those goals. Successful executives, such as Pierre du Pont or Andrew Carnegie, have always displayed great skill in studying the market, identifying customer needs, evaluating competitors' strengths and weaknesses, and defining the right investments and processes their organizations need for success. Good management accounting supports good strategic planning by providing the internal information needed by executives to evaluate and adjust their strategic plans. One

capital budgeting Systematic planning for long-term investments in operating assets.

short-run operating decisions Managerial decisions about current operations and those of the immediate future characterized by their regularity and frequency.

short-run nonroutine decisions Managerial decisions that require more extensive analysis than short-run operating decisions but less than long-run asset purchase decisions.

significant aspect of strategic planning is planning for the purchase and use of major assets to help the company meet its long-range goals. This type of long-run planning is called **capital budgeting**.

Short-run planning is divided into two categories on the basis of frequency and type of decision. Some decisions have to do with operations in the current period and may be made as often as daily or weekly. Such decisions are characterized by their regularity and frequency and are referred to as **short-run operating decisions**. The second category of short-run planning has to do with **short-run nonroutine decisions**. These decisions require more analysis than short-run operating decisions but less than long-run asset purchase decisions. The key question in long-run asset purchases (capital budgeting) usually is: What additional major assets, such as plant and equipment, are needed to meet the company's long-run goals? Short-run nonroutine decisions, on the other hand, involve the question: What is the best use of existing resources? Typical nonroutine decisions include whether to enter or exit a market for a particular service or product, whether to make or buy a component, whether to sell a product before or after additional processing, and what prices to charge for services and products.

Controlling

Controlling involves a process of establishing expectations, creating performance measures, gathering results, and computing variances. Beginning with Francis Lowell's textile mill in Massachusetts, good managers have always established expectations using budgets. As you would expect from our history lesson, the first budgets focused on costs. Today, sophisticated budgets establish expectations regarding prices to be paid for material, labor, overhead, and administrative costs. Operating budgets also determine the desired amounts of labor, materials, and administrative support that will be used to efficiently achieve the right outputs of products and services. Today's operating budgets go beyond cost and quantity inputs. Management accounting is expanding its influence to establish expectations and create performance measures for the other two strategic imperatives—quality and time.

Gathering results requires that expected inputs of costs, expected outputs of quality, and expected timelines be compared with actual performance. This comparison typically results in information called *variances*, which tells management how well the organization is achieving its plans. Such information has two important functions. First, it provides a signal to managers about operations. If performance is in accordance with the plan, the variances signal that operations are in control and no unusual management action is necessary. If performance is substantially different from the plan, management needs to decide how to alter operations in order to improve future performance. As you would expect, past work in management accounting has traditionally focused on cost variances. Today, management accountants also gather information to compute variances on quality and time issues.

Evaluating

Evaluating involves analyzing results, providing feedback to managers and other employees, rewarding performance, and identifying problems. Upper-level management must evaluate how well lower-level managers performed the activities assigned to them in the original planning stage. Feedback enables management to evaluate performance and provide direction for future improvements, an important aspect of growth in the organization. If performance is good, management needs to consider rewards; if performance is poor, corrective action must be taken. Too many companies fail to clearly link incentive compensation with management goals in order to ensure that everyone is focused on low cost, high quality, and timely delivery of goods and services expected by customers and clients.

This third function in the management process, evaluating, brings us back to the point at which we started, planning. The information gained through the evaluation function is used in planning for the following period. Remember that as a manager *evaluates* performance in the last period, he or she may also be making *planning* decisions to improve operations for the next period while gathering and receiving results to *control* the current period.

TO SUMMARIZE

Just-in-time (JIT) inventory management is a rather recent competitive strategy imported to America from Japan. This business process is perhaps the first new management innovation to recognize that management requires information regarding cost, quality, and time if it is to effectively compete in today's fast-paced, international environment. Low cost, high quality, and timely delivery are expected of companies who plan to be in business in the twenty-first century. Management accountants, if they expect to have jobs as key decision-support professionals in the twenty-first century, must provide data that encompasses all three of these strategic imperatives.

The essential purpose of management accounting is to support decision making that adds value to the organization. Effective decision making is the key to the management process, and it is central to the management functions of planning, controlling, and evaluating. Planning is the process of making decisions about future operations and investments. Controlling involves establishing expectations, creating performance measures, gathering results, and comparing the plan to actual performance. Evaluating is a process of analyzing results and providing feedback. The natural end result of evaluating is identification of problems and opportunities, and from there, the next stage of planning begins.

5 *Describe the professional environment of management accountants today.*

THE MANAGEMENT ACCOUNTING PROFESSION

Management accountants have come a long way since the beginning of their profession in the 1800s. Today, management accountants play a key role within many organizations. The nature of their work continues to expand as computer technology grows in importance in the gathering and use of information by decision makers. Given their critical role as information stewards in the organization, management accountants must always be conscious of ethical issues they regularly face in their profession.

The Management Accountant's Role in the Organization

FYI

Management accountants can obtain a professional certificate that is much like the CPA certification. The Certificate in Management Accounting (CMA) is sponsored by the Institute of Management Accountants (IMA), a national organization of professional management accountants. Five areas of study are emphasized on the CMA exam: (1) economics and finance, (2) organizational behavior, (3) public reporting, (4) periodic reporting for internal and external purposes, and (5) decision analysis, including modeling and information systems.

The management accountant's function in the organization is to support competitive decision making by collecting, processing, and communicating information that helps management plan, control, and evaluate business processes and company strategy. The top accountant in most organizations is called the controller. In many organizations, management accountants report to the controller. The controller usually reports to a financial vice president who, in turn, reports to the organization's president or chief executive officer (CEO). As the chief accounting officer, the controller supervises all accounting departments. He or she usually has overall responsibility for all financial and management accounting duties. The organization of the accounting function in a typical large corporation is shown in Exhibit 9-7.

As should be clear by now, management accounting has the responsibility to supply to management relevant information to make decisions. In contrast, the internal audit department has the responsibility to ensure that controls are followed and operations are efficient. Financial account-

EXHIBIT 9-7 Management Accountants in an Organization

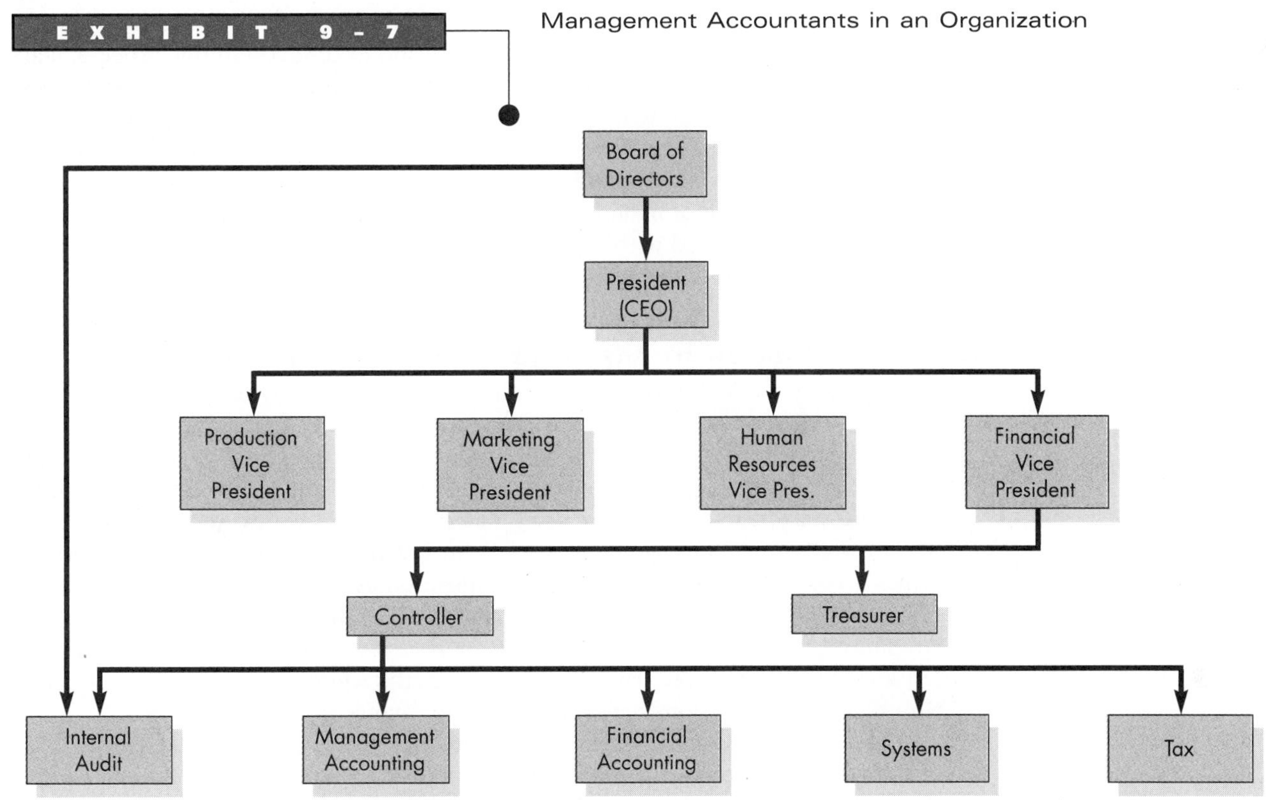

ing provides information to outsiders, such as creditors, investors, and government agencies. Systems has the responsibility to process information so that it is available to management in formats useful for decision making. Tax is made up of experts who make sure that tax laws are complied with and that the organization pays no more than its legally obligated tax liability. The controller is an integral part of the planning, controlling, evaluating, and decision-making activities of an organization.

Technology and the Management Accountant

Hopefully, as you have read this introductory chapter to management accounting, you have noticed that the goals of management accounting information provided to the management and executive teams inside the organization are quite different from the financial accounting information provided to groups outside of the organization, such as investors, creditors, and regulators. You may even ask how information and performance measures regarding quality and time can be provided by a typical general ledger system that is limited to debits and credits of dollar amounts. This is a good question! For most of the twentieth century, management accountants have been able to successfully produce management accounting information using the general ledger systems of financial accounting. This marriage of management accounting and financial accounting information systems worked as long as the goal of management accounting was strictly to track cost information. However, the emergence of JIT, coupled with increased competition in a worldwide market, has forced most organizations to compete on issues of quality and timeliness, as well as cost. The problem is that it is very difficult to use a debit/credit system to track organizational performance regarding quality and time. Thankfully, computerized information systems, specifically database systems, have progressed to a point where it is economically feasible for organizations to track just about any kind of information. Now the real challenge for current and future management accountants is to organize

FYI

To address the increased importance of technology in business society, many organizations have recently created a new position to manage the technology function, the Chief Information Officer (CIO). The CIO's job is to design, implement, and manage all information systems. However, there may be a bit of a conflict here. Do CIOs also handle the *accounting* information systems? Should accounting information systems now be strictly limited to financial data? Who should management accountants report to? The CIO or the Controller? Organizations are grappling with these issues as they work to include this new position in their management structure.

the immense amount of data that can be provided to support decision making without creating information overload in managers and executives. In this process, management accountants should understand how to use the most current technology. Typically, developing knowledge and skills in computer technologies will require additional courses of study for the future business professional. The goal of the remainder of this book is to provide you with a framework for developing cost, quality, and time-based information that supports the management process. This framework must then be used with top-notch technology in order to provide information that truly adds competitive value to organizations!

Ethical Issues in Management Accounting

Unfortunately, ethical dilemmas in both large and small organizations are not rare. As white-collar crime continues to rise, management accountants are often confronted with ethical issues on the job and need to be prepared to deal with them on a rational basis. A sampling of some of the ethical dilemmas that management accountants may be exposed to are listed in Exhibit 9–8. If your career path leads you to the position of a management accountant (or any position as a business professional!), you will find that dealing with these types of ethical indiscretions is not easy. The situation is often complicated by the fact that violators are often people you know and work with. Further, your role as a member of the management team requires that you work to handle questions of ethics internally as much as possible. However, some occasions may require you to involve outside authorities.

The Institute of Management Accountants (IMA) has provided standards of ethical conduct to help management accountants resolve ethical issues in their profession. Essentially, the IMA notes that management accountants are ethically required to (1) be competent in their profession, (2) not disclose confidential information, (3) act with both actual and apparent integrity in all situations, and (4) maintain objectivity in communicating information to decision makers. If confronted with situations that may involve ethical conflicts, the management accountant should consider the following courses of action: (1) Discuss the problem with the immediate supervisor (only when the supervisor is involved should higher management levels be involved). (2) Confidentially use an objective advisor to help clarify the issues. (3) Resign from the organization and submit an informative report to an appropriate representative of the organization (after exhausting all levels of internal communication).

FYI

The full text of the IMA's *Standards of Ethical Conduct for Management Accountants* can be viewed at the following URL: www.rutgers.edu/Accounting/raw/ima/imaethic.htm

Although the IMA has a formal code of ethics, there really isn't a perfect set of rules you can follow to help you resolve every conflict. Therefore,

EXHIBIT 9-8

Ethical Dilemmas Faced by Management Accountants

Ethical internal dilemmas

- Padding expense accounts
- Theft in the workplace
- Inflating profits on financial reports
- Violating a firm's purchasing policies
- Understating or postponing recognition of costs to achieve higher bonuses or make the financial statements look better
- Using company assets for personal use

Ethical issues involving third-party transactions

- Bid rigging to give business to favored suppliers
- Taking kickbacks on purchase contracts
- Adjusting inspection reports to reflect higher quality of product
- Withholding unfavorable information

you need to be developing values and skills right now in order to prepare for future challenges. The ethics cases at the end of each chapter have been included to aid in that preparation. Perhaps more than anything else you do, developing a commitment to and an understanding of good ethics will help you grow into a great business professional and will ultimately improve our society.

TO SUMMARIZE

The management accountant holds a key position in organizations today. The top accountant in most organizations is the controller. All accounting functions report to this individual, including the management accountants, the financial and tax accountants, the internal auditors, and systems support personnel. The role played by management accountants is being significantly affected by dramatic improvements in computer technology. Today's technology allows the management accountant to track performance information that goes beyond the cost-based information of historic general ledger systems. The important role of management accountants, coupled with the opportunity to manage a wide variety of critical information, often forces the management accounting professional to confront internal ethical issues. Management accountants need to anticipate and be prepared to deal with various ethical dilemmas.

REVIEW OF LEARNING OBJECTIVES

1 **Describe some of the history that defines modern management accounting.** The development of management accounting today is a product of the managers and owners reacting to competitive forces throughout the history of the Industrial Revolution. The textile mills of the early 1800s created the first need for formal management information systems. Beginning in the mid-1800s, the railroads developed measures that allowed executives to assess the cost performance of managers who were geographically distanced from the home office. Andrew Carnegie took what he learned in the textile mills and railroads and created rigorous cost evaluation systems to run his steel mills. Merchandisers in the late 1800s effectively focused on managing assets as well as costs using inventory turnover measures. At the turn of the century, the DuPont Corporation combined all these innovations into a new performance evaluation model based on the return on investment (ROI) measure. The development trend of management accounting is in contrast to legislative and regulatory forces that began defining financial accounting after the market crash of 1929.

2 **Discuss the major differences in managing manufacturing, merchandising, and service organizations.** The first large businesses in the United States were manufacturing organizations. Today's business economy now increasingly includes more merchandising and service firms. Merchandising firms, such as wholesalers and retailers, sell inventory manufactured by another organization. Service firms, including transportation organizations such as railroads and airlines, sell services rather than inventories. These differences are important when we attempt to define product costs for expense and inventory measurement purposes, as well as other performance measures.

3 **Define the common terms and measures found in modern management accounting.** For manufacturing firms, product costs include direct materials, direct labor, and manufacturing overhead. In a merchandising company, product costs are costs incurred to purchase goods and get them ready for resale. For service firms, product costs are costs of providing a service to customers. These costs are used to determine both asset values on the balance sheet and cost of goods sold on the income statement. In contrast to product costs, period costs are used strictly to compute the selling and general administrative expenses on the income statement. Management accountants also use a number of terms to categorize other costs. These include fixed and variable costs, direct and indirect (common) costs, differential costs, sunk costs, out-of-pocket costs, and opportunity costs.

4 **Understand that successfully planning, controlling, and evaluating a business requires effective management of cost, quality, and time.** The emergence of just-in-time (JIT) inventory management expanded management accountants' view of performance measures to include quality and time measures, as well as cost measures. As a result, management

accountants today must be well versed in using cost, quality, and time information to support the management functions of long- and short-run planning, controlling, and evaluating the business processes and resources.

Describe the professional environment of management accountants today. In large organizations today, management accountants, along with financial and tax accountants, internal auditors, and systems support personnel, typically report to the corporate controller. Computer technology continues to grow in importance to the management accountant's job of tracking performance information for the organization. The central prominance of management accounting to the management process requires that management accountants be prepared to deal with ethical dilemmas.

KEY TERMS AND CONCEPTS

DISCUSSION QUESTIONS

1. **DuPont** was America's first large-scale "vertically integrated" company. What does "vertically integrated" mean?
2. The chapter talks about the birth of management accounting being the result of an opportunity to obtain a competitive edge in business. Explain how management accounting provides a competitive edge.
3. How can management accounting information be useful in helping companies to be competitive and profitable?
4. How did the large railroad companies change management accounting?
5. What is the difference between a manufacturing company and a merchandising company? Between a merchandising company and a service company?
6. What exactly did Donaldson Brown, the accountant for **DuPont**, develop and why was it so revolutionary?
7. Management accounting and financial accounting provide different information for different purposes. Explain what this means and provide an example that contrasts management and financial accounting.
8. Managers need not be concerned about external financial statements. Do you agree or disagree with this statement? Explain.
9. Why is GAAP so important for external financial reporting but not for internal management reporting?
10. Explain the difference between a product cost and a period cost.
11. What are the three components of manufacturing costs? Briefly describe them.
12. What similarities and differences exist among the costs of merchandising, manufacturing, and service firms?
13. How do nonmanufacturing costs and indirect costs differ?
14. What classification determines whether materials used in the production of a product are direct materials or indirect materials? Is the classification always simple to determine? What are some examples of direct materials and indirect materials used in the production of a chair?
15. How do variable costs and fixed costs differ?
16. Analyze your personal expenses on a variable and fixed basis. What are some of your personal fixed costs and variable costs? What would cause them to change?
17. What is the difference between sunk costs and differential costs? Give an example of each.
18. How can out-of-pocket costs and opportunity costs be applied to your personal financial decisions?
19. While a minimum level of inventory was deemed desirable by most companies, how did the concept of JIT change that view? Use the measures of cost, quality, and time as you prepare your answer.
20. Identify the three management functions relating to the decision-making process. Briefly define each function.
21. Identify some ethical dilemmas that might be faced by management accountants.

DISCUSSION CASES

CASE 9-1

DEVELOPING MANAGEMENT ACCOUNTING INFORMATION (DUPONT)

The story of **E. I. du Pont de Nemours and Company** detailed at the beginning of this chapter provides key insights into the development of management accounting. Particularly, we see how the structure of a business affects the kinds of information required for planning, controlling, and evaluating purposes. Consider the decision to "vertically integrate" the company. What were the potential risks to **DuPont** of this decision? What accounting information would have been required to determine if the decision to vertically integrate was successful? Does the traditional accounting system designed to produce external financial reports provide the required information in an easily obtainable fashion?

CASE 9-2

SUPPORTING THE MANAGEMENT PROCESS (IBM)

International Business Machines Corporation (IBM) has faced challenges lately due to increased competition in the home-consumer segment of the personal computer (PC) market. When IBM introduced the PC in the early '80s, the PC was a huge success. The PC market grew immensely and competition was on the rise.

Although the PC was initially marketed towards businesses, a home-consumer market emerged as well. In 1995, IBM, under the direction of CEO Louis V. Gerstner, set up a home-consumer-PC division to augment its business-PC division. IBM hoped that with the two divisions each employing its own design, manufacturing, and marketing personnel, it could better focus on the needs of its various customers and increase total sales.

IBM's consumer division quickly developed PC's that had high customer appeal. In early 1996, the division released its "Aptiva" PC in a sleek, dark-gray color. The model was equipped with many high-tech features. Also, IBM's good reputation allowed the consumer division to charge a higher price for the PC's. (In December 1996, IBM PC's sold for an average of $1,880, whereas other companies charged as little as $1,300 – $1,400.)

Initially, the manufacturing department in IBM's consumer division could not keep up with consumer demand. However, IBM is now losing its share in the consumer market to companies such as **Dell**, **Compaq**, and **Packard Bell**. These companies are finding that consumers choose low price over the extra "frills" that IBM offers in its computers. Furthermore, IBM is discovering that many consumers are no longer willing to pay higher prices for IBM's good reputation. IBM, the company that once dominated the PC market, has plummeted to a market share of just 4.4% and is now considering shutting down its consumer division and returning to its previous one-division system for all PC's.

1. Did IBM make a good decision in setting up its consumer division? How so?
2. Analyze the series of IBM decisions and actions involving the consumer division. Try to categorize these decisions and actions following the three-fold management process of planning, controlling, and evaluating.
3. Based on the three-fold management process of planning, controlling, and evaluating, where do you think IBM was weakest in its decision-making practice with respect to the consumer division? Where do you think it was strongest?
4. If you were Louis V. Gerstner, what information would you want from your management accountants in order to effectively plan, control, and evaluate the decision to either shut down or to continue the consumer division?

Source: Raju Narisetti, "IBM to Revamp Struggling Home-PC Business," *Wall Street Journal,* October 14, 1997, p. B1.

EXERCISES

EXERCISE 9-1
Changes in Business Affecting Management Accounting

You are at the student union having lunch with a friend who is attending law school. In the course of your conversation, you tell your friend that, in contrast to financial accounting or tax accounting, management accounting has had a "natural evolution." Further, management accounting is more important in business today than ever before, and only those organizations that best control costs and improve quality are competitive. Your friend asks you two questions:

1. What do you mean by a "natural evolution"?
2. Why is it more important for management accountants to provide useful information to management today than it was before?

EXERCISE 9-2
Characteristics of Accounting Reports

For each of the following, note whether it is characteristic of financial accounting reports, management accounting reports, or both:

1. They are used primarily by creditors and investors.
2. They aid management in identifying problems.
3. They are based on generally accepted accounting principles.
4. They are standardized across companies.
5. They provide information for decision making by management.
6. They measure performance and isolate differences between planned and actual results.
7. They are created based on competitive needs that are unique to the organization.

EXERCISE 9-3
Financial and Management Accounting

A friend who is thinking about majoring in accounting has asked you to distinguish between the work of a financial accountant and a management accountant. What is your response?

EXERCISE 9-4
Period and Product Costs

Bright Inc., a producer of educational toys for children, incurs the following types of costs:

a. Depreciation on the production plant
b. Depreciation on the corporate offices
c. Paper, toner, and miscellaneous supplies for the office copy machines
d. Wages of production line employees
e. Raw materials used in the production of toys
f. Wages of the corporate headquarter's secretarial staff
g. Maintenance costs on the production equipment
h. Advertising costs
i. Shipping costs for products sold
j. Salaries of plant supervisors
k. Interest on bank loans
l. Property tax on the production plant
m. Property tax on the corporate offices
n. Commissions paid to sales personnel
o. Administrative salaries of corporate executives

Classify the costs as period costs or product costs. For each item classified as a product cost, indicate whether it would usually be included in direct materials, direct labor, or manufacturing overhead.

EXERCISE 9-5
Manufacturing Costs

Jordan Industries is a manufacturing company that produces solid oak office equipment. During the year, the following costs were incurred. The building depreciation and the utilities are allocated 3/4 to production and 1/4 to administration. The cost of furniture parts can be traced to specific production runs.

Oak wood	$ 50,000
Miscellaneous supplies (glue, saw blades, varnish, etc.)	10,000
Furniture parts (wheels, locks, etc.)	5,500
Payroll—plant manager's salary	25,000
Payroll—administrative salaries	100,000
Payroll—production line employees' wages	45,500
Building depreciation	28,000
Maintenance—plant and equipment	5,000
Utilities	16,000
Income taxes	8,500

1. Classify the costs into the following four categories: direct materials, direct labor, manufacturing overhead, and period costs.
2. Calculate the total amount of cost for each category.

EXERCISE 9-6
Manufacturing and Nonmanufacturing Costs

The Benson Manufacturing Company produces rides for amusement parks. Parts for the rides are purchased from other suppliers. Rides are then assembled in various company plants.

Recently, Benson Manufacturing hired two new employees. One will be working in an assembly plant, and the other will be working in the marketing division of the corporate offices as a sales representative.

The assembly plant employee will be paid an annual salary of $25,000, or $12.50 per hour. Her time will be charged to the individual rides that she assembles.

The marketing division employee will receive an annual salary of $20,000 plus commission. He will be responsible for both advertising and selling. His salary is for advertising responsibilities, and he will be paid a commission on sales of amusement rides.

Answer the following questions:

1. Should the salary of the assembly plant employee be classified as a manufacturing or a nonmanufacturing cost? Should the salary of the marketing division employee be classified as a manufacturing or a nonmanufacturing cost? How is this classification made?
2. After classifying their salaries as manufacturing or nonmanufacturing costs, determine how the salary costs will affect the cost of assembling the amusement rides. Classify the employee costs as direct, indirect, fixed, variable, product, or period. (Each cost can be classified in more than one way.)

EXERCISE 9-7
JIT Inventory

The president of Penman Corporation, John Burton, has asked you, the company's controller, to advise him on whether Penman should develop a just-in-time (JIT) inventory system.

Your research concludes that there is a high cost associated with inventory storage facilities; that inventories use a large portion of the company's cash flow; and because of the nature of the inventory, there is a significant amount of shrinkage. Research of the competition shows that neither of Penman's two competitors uses a JIT inventory system.

Most of Penman's employees are trained to do only one job and belong to a local union. The union is strong and, in the past, has been opposed to major production changes. The union believes major changes will cause job termination of union employees.

Your research indicates that Penman's major production item (a fairly new product in the market) should continue to have strong sales growth.

Using the information provided, advise John Burton to either continue the present system or work to develop a JIT inventory system.

EXERCISE 9-8
Performance Measurement

Refer to Exercise 9-7.

1. Is the decision facing John Burton an example of a long-run decision, a short-run operating decision, or a short-run nonroutine decision? Be sure to defend your answer.

2. Assume John decides to develop a JIT inventory system. He plans to evaluate the system after one year. List at least four possible performance measures John could use to evaluate the effectiveness of the JIT system. Describe what information these measures would provide John.

EXERCISE 9-9
Cost Classifications

The following are costs associated with manufacturing firms, merchandising firms, or service firms:

a. Miscellaneous materials used in production
b. Salesperson's commission in a real estate firm
c. Administrators' salaries for a furniture wholesaler
d. Administrators' salaries for a furniture manufacturer
e. Freight costs associated with inventories of a grocery store
f. Office manager's salary in a doctor's office
g. Utilities for the corporate offices of a toy manufacturer
h. Line supervisor's salary for a clothing-manufacturing firm
i. Training seminar for sales staff of a service firm
j. Fuel used in a trucking firm
k. Paper used at a printing business
l. Oil for machinery at a plastics manufacturing firm
m. Food used at a restaurant
n. Windshields used for a car manufacturer

Classify the costs as (1) product or period, (2) variable or fixed, and (3) direct materials, direct labor, or manufacturing overhead. Write "not applicable (NA)" if a category doesn't apply.

EXERCISE 9-10
Cost Classifications

The following are costs associated with manufacturing firms, merchandising firms, or service firms:

a. Legal services for an accounting firm
b. Car leases for company management
c. Oil used to service manufacturing equipment
d. Office supplies for a grocery store
e. Entertainment expense
f. Travel expenses for doctors in a medical firm
g. Plastic used in making computers
h. Collection costs of account receivables
i. Electricity to run saws at a lumber yard
j. Food for a company banquet
k. Advertising expense
l. Continuing education for a doctor
m. Commissions paid to salespersons
n. Depreciation on sports equipment by a professional football team
o. Calculators used by office employees
p. Earplugs used at an airport
q. Toll charges incurred because of business travel
r. Fuel used in manufacturing equipment

1. Classify the costs as period or product.
2. Classify the costs as fixed or variable.
3. For those costs that are product costs, classify them as direct materials, direct labor, or manufacturing overhead. Write "not applicable (N/A)" if a category doesn't apply.

Accounting is more than just doing textbook problems. These Competency Enhancement Opportunities provide practice in critical thinking, oral and written communication, research, teamwork, and consideration of ethical issues.

ANALYZING REAL COMPANY INFORMATION

• Analyzing 9–1 (Microsoft)

1. In his 1997 letter to **Microsoft** shareholders, Bill Gates emphasized that Microsoft is focusing on helping individual users and company system administrators lower the "Total Cost of Ownership" of their computer systems. List the costs that you think are part of the "Total Cost of Ownership" for an individual computer owner.
2. Microsoft is increasingly selling its software as part of "integrated suites," such as Microsoft Office, instead of as individual programs (e.g., Word, Excel, PowerPoint). What kinds of information (both sales data and cost data) would Microsoft need to assemble in order to intelligently make the decision to switch from selling individual programs to integrated suites?
3. In 1996, Microsoft increased its spending on research and development by 67%; R&D spending increased by another 34% in 1997. Microsoft reports that part of this increase stems from greater use of outside software developers who contract with Microsoft to work on specific projects. What factors does Microsoft need to consider in deciding to assign a research project to an outside contractor rather than to its internal software development staff?

• Analyzing 9–2 (DuPont)

As described in the chapter, the challenge facing **DuPont** in the early part of the twentieth century was how to manage the diverse set of businesses operating under the control of the DuPont management team. This diversity still exists today. In its 1996 annual report, DuPont described its business segments as follows:

> "The company has six principal segments that manufacture and sell a wide range of products to many different markets, including energy, transportation, textile, construction, automotive, electronics, printing, health care, packaging and agricultural products. The company sells its products worldwide; however, about 50 percent and 36 percent of sales are made in the United States and Europe, respectively."

Summary segment results for 1996 are as follows:

	Chemicals	Fibers	Polymers	Petroleum	Life Sciences	Diversified Businesses
Total Revenue	$4,331	$7,226	$6,912	$20,579	$2,472	$3,180
After-Tax Operating Income	563	802	909	860	679	205
Identifiable Assets at December 31, 1996	3,723	6,805	4,535	13,018	1,749	2,835

Instructions:

1. Which segment has the highest profit margin? The lowest?
2. Which segment has the highest asset turnover? The lowest?
3. Which segment has the highest return on investment? The lowest?
4. How could the segment with the lowest return on investment improve its financial performance?

INTERNATIONAL CASE

• Toyota

Toyota Motor Corporation was mentioned in the chapter as the place where just-in-time (JIT) inventory began. Toyota was started in 1918 by Sakichi Toyoda as the **Toyota Spinning and Weaving Co.**; in fact, a subsidiary of Toyota still makes spinning and weaving equipment today. In 1995, Toyota was the third-largest motor vehicle producer in the world, manufacturing 4,512,076 vehicles (behind **General Motors** at 7,997,794 and **Ford** at 6,401,495). In January 1997, Toyota made its 100 millionth vehicle.

In its 1997 annual report, Toyota said the following about its performance:

> "Consolidated net income rose 50.2%, to 385.9 billion yen ($3,112 million), in the fiscal year ended March 31, 1997. That rise in earnings is attributable principally to the weakening of the yen, continuing cost savings, and growth in sales volume. The yen/dollar exchange rate averaged 112 yen during the past fiscal year, compared with 96 yen in the previous year... The capacity for achieving cost savings on a continuing basis is integral to management at Toyota. New cost savings therefore will continue to contribute to earnings in the years ahead... Our cost savings resulted from value-engineering improvements in designs and also from improvements in manufacturing processes and in logistics. Unending, systematic improvements in product designs and production processes will yield continuing cost savings."

Instructions:

1. Toyota attributes its 50% increase in net income to three factors: the weakening of the yen, cost savings, and growth in sales volume. Consider conducting a performance evaluation on the following people, and decide which of the three factors should be considered in the evaluation of:
   a. an assembly line worker
   b. a factory manager
   c. a sales manager
   d. the company president
2. In relation to its cost savings, Toyota reports that the savings stem from improvements in engineering design, improvements in manufacturing processes, and improved logistics. Consider conducting a performance evaluation on the following people, and decide which (and why!) of the three cost savings factors should be considered in the evaluation of:
   a. an assembly line worker
   b. a factory manager
   c. a purchasing manager
   d. the company president

ETHICS CASE

• Whom to tell about MediCare overbilling?

Professor Mary Allen is sitting in her office one day when Mark Sullivan, an accounting graduate from five years ago, knocks on her door. Mark had been an exceptionally good student and had started with Peat and Price CPA firm upon graduation. After three years with that firm, he joined MiniCare Health Company as the chief accountant and is now serving as its controller. After being invited in, Mark asks if he can talk with Professor Allen in confidence. Once comfortably seated, Mark proceeds to tell Professor Allen the following:

"Two years ago, I started working for MiniCare. Not long after I was promoted to controller, I noticed that the officers of the company were doing things that I didn't think were right. They were overbilling Medicare on several occasions, and senior management executives were misusing their positions by taking company perks that were against the company code of ethics. I have talked to my superior, the financial vice president, and he has, in essence, told me to mind my own business—that accountants are to report results and assist management, not question them."

Mark informs Professor Allen that he is making $100,000 a year, far more than he could earn in another company at this stage in his career. He asks Professor Allen for advice. What should Professor Allen recommend that he do? Should he quit his job? Should he talk to someone else? If so, who? Should he go public with his information?

WRITING ASSIGNMENT

- **Sunk Costs: They may be sunk, but they aren't forgotten.**

You are the manager of the tire manufacturing subdivision of Uniyear Diversified Products. Last year, you were successful in convincing corporate executives that your division needed to purchase a new warehouse facility costing $40 million to house raw materials. You argued at the time that you could be much more productive if delays in getting materials from suppliers could be eliminated.

During the past 18 months, your company has worked hard to adopt JIT inventory and total quality control. You have successfully placed online terminals at key supplier locations, and the lag time in getting the raw materials you need has dropped from an average of four weeks to six hours.

Your problem now is that you no longer need the $40 million warehouse. It is a sunk cost. However, you are afraid if you reveal that fact to the corporate executives, they will penalize or even fire you for being so shortsighted.

Instructions:
Draft a one-page memo to the president of Uniyear Diversified Products that explains why the $40 million warehouse is no longer needed. Remember that the memo has two purposes: to inform the president that the warehouse is no longer needed and to do so in a way that doesn't cost you your job.

THE DEBATE

- **When should you surrender?**

You are a partner in a CPA firm. For over 15 years, you conducted the audit of XYZ Corporation. However, three years ago the company went bankrupt. To your surprise, a class-action lawsuit was filed against your firm for $5 million, alleging you failed to warn stockholders that the company was in financial difficulty. Your audit fee for XYZ Corporation was only $15,000 per year. Thus far you have spent $957,000 on legal fees and expert witness costs. Your attorney has worked out a settlement with the plaintiffs that would involve you paying the plaintiff $750,000. You believe your defense is excellent, that the quality of your audits of XYZ Corporation was high, and that you will win the lawsuit. However, you also believe it will cost another $800,000 in legal fees to successfully defend the case. Should you settle?

Divide your group into two teams.

- One team represents the "Fight to the Death" group. Prepare a two-minute oral presentation supporting the notion that you should not pay a penny to settle the lawsuit when you know that you did nothing wrong. You believe that the best long-run business strategy is to vigorously fight every lawsuit in order to discourage future suits.

- The other team represents the "Cut Our Losses" group. Prepare a two-minute oral presentation arguing that the past litigation costs are sunk and that the only reasonable comparison is between the cost of settling now and the cost of continuing the lawsuit.

INTERNET SEARCH

• DuPont

Access **DuPont**'s Web site at www.dupont.com. Sometimes Web addresses change, so if this DuPont address doesn't work, access the Web site for this textbook (stice.swcollege.com) for an updated link to DuPont.

Once you've gained access to DuPont's Web site, answer the following questions:

1. Who is the current chief executive officer (CEO) of DuPont? How long has he or she been with the company? What is his or her background (e.g., legal, accounting, engineering, etc.)?
2. As mentioned in the chapter, the DuPont organization includes many diverse types of businesses. How many employees does DuPont have? In how many countries does DuPont operate? How many manufacturing facilities does DuPont operate? What fraction of DuPont's business is conducted outside the United States?
3. The history of DuPont, and some of its well-known products, is summarized in the chapter. DuPont's Web site offers further information. When did DuPont's polymer chemists invent nylon? What is Kevlar® used for?
4. DuPont reports a corporate commitment to moving toward zero emissions, zero employee injuries, and zero material waste. What progress does DuPont report in its effort to reduce air carcinogenic emissions?

CHAPTER

10 COST SYSTEMS

SETTING THE STAGE

For several years, the two best selling cars in the United States have been the Honda Accord and the Ford Taurus. In fact, at times, **Ford** and **Honda** have been so preoccupied with being number one that they have accused each other of inflating sales figures and selling cars at prices below manufacturing cost. One year, for example, Ford supposedly offered tremendously low prices to rental car companies as an incentive for them to replace their Honda rental cars with the Ford Taurus; they then counted those fleet sales to edge out the Honda Accord as the number one selling car in the United States. To maximize sales, both Ford and Honda have done everything possible to keep the costs of the Accord and Taurus as low as possible, while continuously improving the quality.

Even with this intense competition between Ford and Honda, the manufacturer's suggested retail prices of both the Honda Accord and the Ford Taurus have nearly doubled in the past ten years. However, for 1998, Honda has not only maintained the costs of its new Accord, but has made the car bigger, more powerful, and better equipped than the 1997 model, *and* reduced the average suggested retail price by nearly $1,000 per car. It is the first time that either the Accord or Taurus (or almost any car) has had a significant price reduction. The 1998 Honda Accord LX V-6, for example, has a sticker price of $21,945 compared to $22,895 for the same car in 1997.

How can Honda reduce the price of its Accord when there is modest inflation? Remember, 1997 was a year when the economy was humming, unemployment was at an all-time low, and there was moderate inflation. With an inflation rate of 1.6 percent in 1997, you would have expected Honda prices to have increased by at least 1.6 percent, even without consideration of additional options and more power, right? According to Honda, the company can lower the price of its Accord because it has better tracked its manufacturing costs and re-engineered its manufacturing processes to eliminate high cost manufacturing activities and simplify the manufacturing process; the savings from these lower manufacturing costs are being passed on to Honda's customers.

It turns out that Honda is not the only company using more accurate product costing information to simplify manufacturing processes and reduce manufacturing costs. In fact, prices of many consumer goods

LEARNING OBJECTIVES

After studying this chapter, you should be able to:

1. *Explain the flow of goods in a manufacturing firm.*
2. *Understand the difficulty, yet importance, of having accurate product cost information.*
3. *Identify and compare conventional product costing systems.*
4. *Describe and apply job order costing procedures for a manufacturing firm.*
5. *Understand how merchants manage cost information in their organizations.*
6. *Understand how service organizations manage their cost information.*

actually fell in 1997. For example, the box of Kleenex tissues that cost $1.17 at Wal-Mart in 1996 was only $0.87 at the same store in 1997. The DeWalt 9.6 volt electric drill that cost $140 at Home Depot in 1996 was only $129 at the same store in 1997. These kinds of price drops used to be associated only with technology items, such as personal computers or compact disc players. Now, big price cuts can be found on just about anything. Consider the following price decreases on the same products from 1996 to 1997:

	1996 Price	1997 Price
Maytag refrigerator	$799.00	$699.00
Bic round-stick pens	0.86	0.81
GE light bulbs	2.60	2.08
Long-distance call (LA to NY)	3.10	2.90

Like the Accord, the new Maytag refrigerator has fewer parts than the older model. Bic pens are cheaper because the manufacturer incorporated better inventory management methods and speeded up the manufacturing process. Whereas it used to take several hours to make a Bic pen, the company can now turn a lump of plastic and a glob of ink into a pen in eight minutes. By better understanding and managing their manufacturing costs, these companies not only have reduced prices, but increased the quality of their products, accelerated production, and delivered their products to customers faster than ever before.

Source: *USA Today*, Monday, September 29, 1997, p. 3B.

As described in the opening scenario, Honda was able to reduce the price of its new Accord because the company has simplified the manufacturing process and lowered manufacturing costs. Unfortunately, accurately tracking manufacturing costs, especially in multiple-product firms, is very difficult. Indeed, many companies have sold their products at prices they thought covered all manufacturing costs, only to discover later (through bankruptcy proceedings) that they had been selling their products at prices much lower than their production and selling costs. While accurately determining the manufacturing costs of products is difficult, it is one of the most important tasks for the management accountant and one of the most useful pieces of information for business decision makers. Without accurate cost information, it is difficult to set appropriate prices, evaluate performance, reward employees, or make production decisions. It is even difficult to know whether or not a company should be competing in a specific market.

In this chapter, you will learn how goods are produced in manufacturing companies and how the costs incurred in manufacturing products are tracked and accumulated. You will also learn terminology used in product costing and how the costs of products are determined. You will also learn about product costing for service companies, such as legal, accounting, and consulting firms, and for merchandising companies.

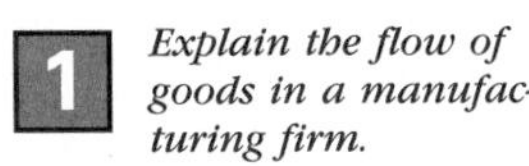

Explain the flow of goods in a manufacturing firm.

THE FLOW OF GOODS IN A MANUFACTURING FIRM

To understand why it is so difficult to accurately measure product costs in a manufacturing firm, it is helpful to see how products flow through a manufacturing organization. Consider the floor plan for a simple, hypothetical manufacturing company shown in Exhibit 10-1.

This floor plan is for a manufacturer of furniture, Broyman Furniture Company. The floor plan shows a building that is partitioned into two sections. The administrative offices include office space for various vice presidents, the sales staff, the president, and word-processing staff. The manufacturing facility encompasses the offices of the vice president of manufacturing, the plant manager, and the controller; the raw materials and finished goods warehouses; and the factory floor, where production takes place. When purchased, raw materials are delivered to the raw materials warehouse where they are stored until requisitioned for production. When req-

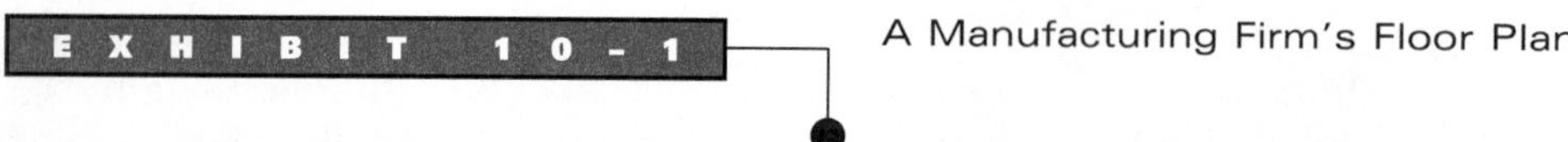

A Manufacturing Firm's Floor Plan

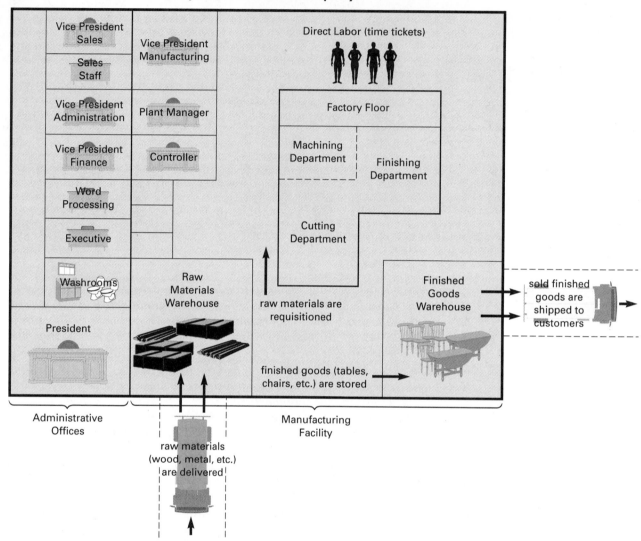

Broyman Furniture Company

Vice President Sales
Sales Staff
Vice President Manufacturing
Vice President Administration
Plant Manager
Vice President Finance
Controller
Word Processing
Executive
Washrooms
President
Direct Labor (time tickets)
Factory Floor
Machining Department
Finishing Department
Cutting Department
Raw Materials Warehouse
raw materials are requisitioned
finished goods (tables, chairs, etc.) are stored
Finished Goods Warehouse
sold finished goods are shipped to customers
Administrative Offices
Manufacturing Facility
raw materials (wood, metal, etc.) are delivered

uisitioned, they are moved out onto the factory floor. The factory floor includes three different manufacturing departments: cutting, machining, and finishing. Whereas some furniture products require work in all three areas, others may require work in only one or two. On the factory floor, factory employees combine materials with their labor to produce finished products. The finished products are then moved into the finished goods warehouse and stored until sold.

While the movement of goods through this simple factory is straightforward, tracking the costs of goods manufactured is not always so simple. (Later in the chapter, we will illustrate in detail how this company tracks the costs of making a custom-ordered table.) Certainly, the costs of the raw materials and the wages of factory employees who work in production are manufacturing costs that can be traced to specific products. But what about the salaries of the vice president of manufacturing, the plant manager, the controller, and the individuals working in the administrative offices? Should any part of their salaries be included in product costs? What about the utility bills to heat and light the building, the depreciation or rent on the building, the cost of the parking lot, paper towels for the washrooms, and other miscellaneous expenditures? Should any part of these expenses be included in manufacturing costs?

Since the individuals working in the administrative offices perform administrative and selling duties, rather than manufacturing functions, their salaries should probably not be classified as product costs. Likewise, the costs to pay for electricity, heat, and other expenses for the administrative offices are probably not manufacturing costs. However, the vice president of manufacturing, the plant manager, and the controller all perform functions related to manufacturing and, as a result, their salaries should probably be included as product costs. However, although these employees perform administrative functions within the manufacturing facility, the work they perform cannot easily be identified with or assigned to specific products, unlike the factory employees who work directly on the products. Similarly, the heat, power, and depreciation related to the manufacturing facility should be included as manufacturing costs but cannot be easily traced to specific products. What about the costs of delivering purchased raw materials to the plant or the delivery of finished goods to customers? Should these delivery costs be classified as manufacturing, administrative, or selling expenses?

As you can see, accurately determining the costs of manufactured products can be challenging, even in a simple firm with one product and one location. When we introduce the complexities of multiple products being produced in the same facility, changing prices and labor rates, multiple manufacturing locations (perhaps some international locations), and individuals performing multiple functions, it becomes very challenging to accurately determine product costs. In order to accurately measure product costs, management accountants must be able to:

1. Determine which costs relate to manufacturing and which relate to administrative and selling functions.
2. Accurately identify and measure all costs associated with manufacturing.
3. Determine appropriate ways to assign costs incurred to products manufactured.

These issues are discussed in the following sections.

BUSINESS ENVIRONMENT ESSAY

Costs and the Medical Profession

Have you ever gone to the doctor's office, spent 20 minutes in the waiting room, then another 20 minutes in the examination room before the doctor comes in? When she finally comes in, she examines you for ten minutes and then sends you on your way, charging you $50 for the visit. No wonder medical doctors make so much money—or do they? Does the doctor put your $50 right in her pocket?

What costs must your $50 cover? Unfortunately, you must help the doctor pay for office medical supplies, rent on the office, utilities, salaries of nurses and office personnel, fees charged by hospitals to use their facilities, and costs of training seminars to remain current in her field. While these costs are expensive, perhaps the most rapidly rising cost is for malpractice insurance. As an example, in many communities in the United States, the cost of obstetrical malpractice insurance is so high that some doctors will no longer deliver babies.

Where does the doctor get the money to cover these costs? By charging you $50 for your visit. Medicine is a business. The doctor is pricing patient visits to cover all costs incurred in providing that service. Costs must be covered and we, the consumers, must pay for them. The next time you visit the doctor, take a look around the waiting room, enjoy those pictures, and read those magazines. After all, you paid for them!

TO SUMMARIZE

In a manufacturing firm, raw materials are worked on by factory employees to produce finished goods. While it is easy to see how goods flow through a manufacturing firm, tracking the costs of manufactured products is very difficult. The cost of raw materials, as well as the wages and benefits of factory employees who work directly on products, can easily be applied to specific products. However, other manufacturing costs cannot easily be "connected" to specific products. They must be assigned to products on some arbitrary, but rational, basis.

2 *Understand the difficulty, yet importance, of having accurate product cost information.*

WHY HAVING ACCURATE PRODUCT COSTS IS SO DIFFICULT, YET IMPORTANT

As discussed in Chapter 9, management is constantly making decisions regarding planning, control, and evaluation. Managers need accurate product cost information to plan for the future, to control current operations, and to evaluate past performance. They also need accurate product cost information so they can deliver high-quality products to customers at the lowest price and at the fastest speed.

We have just described how difficult it is to accurately determine product costs, even in an unrealistically simple manufacturing firm. Regardless of the difficulty, however, having accurate product cost information is critical for a business. Without knowledge of accurate product costs, managers could easily over- or underprice products and make other poor decisions. What if, for example, **Honda** sells its 1998 Accord LX for $21,945 (its intended sales price), but the actual cost of producing the car is $24,000? How long could Honda stay in business losing $2,055 per car? In this case, buyers will probably rush to buy Accords; the Hondas will be priced much less than other comparable cars because competing dealers will have priced their cars to cover total manufacturing costs. Not only will Honda lose money on every car it sells, but the more cars Honda sells, the greater its losses will be. What if Honda attempts to sell its Accord LX for $21,945, but the true and accurate cost of making the car is only $16,000? If the true and accurate cost is only $16,000, other manufacturers, such as **Ford**, will sell their cars for much less than Honda; sales of Accords will dwindle. If Honda really believes its costs are higher than $16,000, say $20,500, it will not lower prices to the point where the company can compete with Ford and other manufacturers. The competitors that better understand their own costs will probably reduce prices, leaving Honda behind in the market. With lower (maybe even zero) sales, Honda will again lose money because it won't sell enough cars to cover its operating expenses. As you can see, having accurate product cost information helps managers in many ways, including making planning, controlling, and evaluating decisions such as the following:

get connected
http://www.swcollege.com
net work

Access Honda's Web site. The base price for a 1998 Accord LX V-6 is $21,945.

How much does the price increase by adding floor mats, a security system, and a CD player? How do these features affect Honda's manufacturing costs?

www.honda.com

1. As part of the planning process, a company can determine whether it can or should compete in certain markets. It is possible that prices of competitors in some markets are already lower than the manufacturing costs would be for a new company trying to compete.
2. When controlling operations, a company can analyze the relationship between production levels and costs and determine whether to increase or decrease production levels of certain products. These control data will help the company in planning future operations because it can determine if the increased cost of additional production would be less than the revenue that would be derived from sales of those products.

3. In the evaluation process, a company can decide whether to reward employees for holding manufacturing costs down or to penalize employees for allowing manufacturing costs to become too high.

CAUTION

Product costs are only one element management must consider when establishing prices for its products. Pricing is a complex issue and management usually looks to its own strategy and to the market to set prices (competitors' prices, market's ability to pay, and so forth). Assuming that management only looks at product costs to set prices is a wrong assumption.

Having accurate product cost information also allows a company to identify and eliminate costly, complicated manufacturing processes so higher-quality, lower-priced products can be delivered to customers in increasingly shorter manufacturing times. Accurate cost information allows management to determine the appropriate level at which to operate, to assess the long-term profitability of various products, and to manage the costs of production activities.

Manufacturing Overhead: The Problem in Determining Accurate Product Costs

In the previous chapter, you learned that the costs of manufacturing products can be broken down into three elements: (1) direct materials, (2) direct labor, and (3) manufacturing overhead. Direct materials include the cost of raw materials that are used directly in the manufacture of products. Direct materials are kept in the raw materials warehouse (see Exhibit 10–1) until used and include such things as rubber used in making tires, steel used to make cars, wood used to make tables, and plastic used to make glasses. Direct labor includes the wages and other payroll-related expenses of factory employees who work directly on products. Direct labor includes the cost of wages and benefits for assembly line workers, but it does not include the wages and benefits of the factory custodians or the factory controller because, even though they work in the factory, they don't work directly on making products. Manufacturing overhead includes all manufacturing costs that are not classified as direct materials or direct labor. This includes miscellaneous materials used in production, such as glue or nails; wages for the factory supervisor, controller, and custodians who work in the factory but not directly on products; and other manufacturing costs such as utilities, depreciation of manufacturing facilities, insurance, and property taxes.

While it is easy to assign direct materials and direct labor costs to specific products, it is extremely difficult to assign manufacturing costs, such as rent or the custodian's salary, to specific manufactured products. One of the major reasons for this difficulty is that many of these overhead costs are "lumpy" in nature and do not match the production of goods. To be more specific, production output in a manufacturing plant tends to occur in an even flow throughout the year. Similarly, the cost of raw materials and direct labor used also follows a generally even pattern throughout the year. On the other hand, most manufacturing overhead costs are not related to the flow of production. For example, think about the way car insurance generally works. Most insurance companies send a bill twice a year for the next six months' worth of car insurance. The car insurance is "used" every day, but paying for this cost on such an occasional basis makes it difficult to budget for and to apply it to daily use. Companies face the same problem. They have insurance and tax bills that are part of manufacturing overhead costs that must be paid only once or twice a year. Further, utility costs, like heating and air conditioning in the plant, vary from month to month, sometimes significantly! The occasional repairs and maintenance on equipment are similarly difficult to predict and to budget for accurately. Nevertheless, most management accountants are required by their organizations to relate these "lumpy" costs back to the volume of production output. In addition, accurate product pricing is even more difficult because the actual amount of all manufacturing overhead costs isn't known until the end of the period, long after some products have been completed and even sold. Exhibit 10–2 shows this product costing problem.

While direct materials and direct labor are directly related or associated to the manufacture of certain products, the various expense items that comprise manu-

EXHIBIT 10-2 Assignment of Product Costs

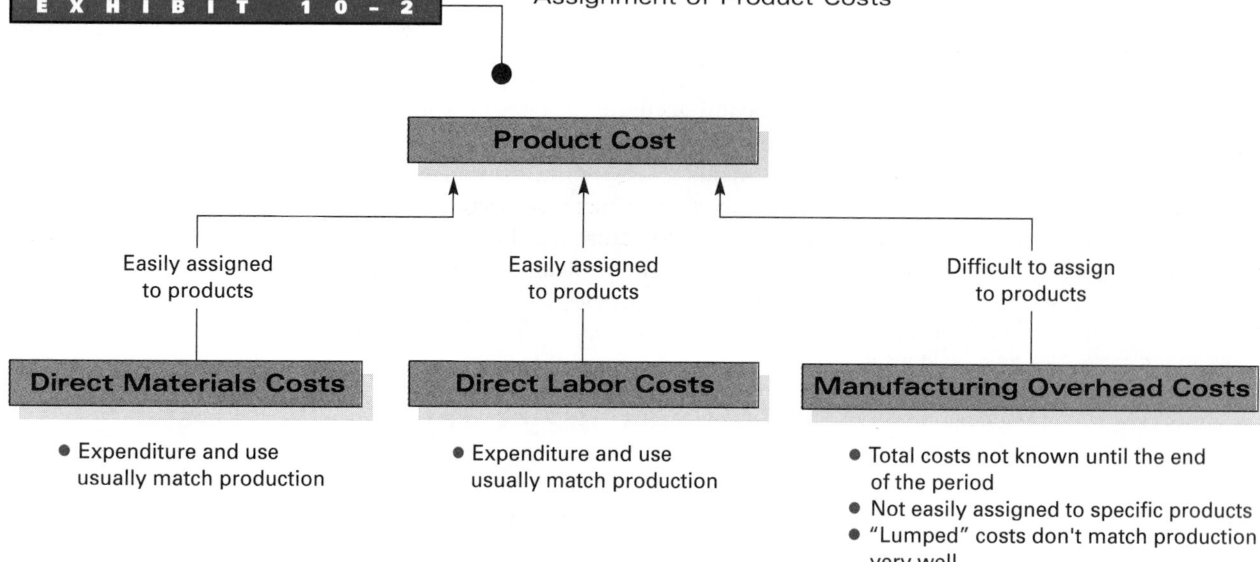

facturing overhead are not. Therefore, management accountants must find some artificial (but hopefully logical) and fair way to "allocate" or "assign" manufacturing overhead costs to products produced. This "artificial allocation" often results in inaccurate product costs and can lead to serious problems when making planning, controlling, and evaluating decisions.

Problems with Conventional Cost Systems

Most product costing systems were initially designed for the purpose of assigning direct materials, direct labor, and manufacturing overhead costs to individual products. This would then determine which costs should flow to Cost of Goods Sold (as each product is sold) to be matched with revenues and which costs should be used to value the remaining inventory on the balance sheet. Because the emphasis was on financial and tax accounting, there sometimes wasn't much emphasis on accurately allocating manufacturing overhead to specific products. Product cost information was used primarily for external financial reporting (to measure the assets and income for an accounting period) and for income tax reporting (to measure taxable income). Because product costing systems were driven primarily by external reporting rules and needs, they did not necessarily provide the best information for management decision making. It has only been in recent years that the emphasis has developed for good management accounting systems that provide cost information useful for decision making: planning (e.g., how much direct materials should we buy?); controlling (e.g., which products are costing more to produce than expected?); and evaluating (e.g., which plants are operating efficiently?).

New Methods of Cost Accumulation

As a wave of modernization sweeps across America, manufacturing companies are discovering that by both integrating the computer into production and assembly facilities and more accurately monitoring manufacturing activities, they can reduce costs, improve quality, and increase productivity. These changes in technology and manufacturing processes have made it virtually impossible to accurately measure manufacturing costs using traditional cost accounting systems. Whereas the bulk of a product's cost used to be comprised of direct materials and direct labor, many costs now fall into the manufacturing overhead category. Automation, robotics, and other innovations have replaced workers, thereby shifting many costs from direct

FYI

Hardly a day goes by without one company (or more) announcing changes that will save significant manufacturing costs while, at the same time, making their products better. For example, in a recent month, there were newspaper articles about savings in product costs at the following companies: **Ford Motor Co.**, **Breyers Ice Cream**, **Delta Air Lines, Inc.**, **Chock Full o' Nuts**, **RCA**, **Product Genesis**, and others.

labor to manufacturing overhead. To provide accurate product costs, new and better ways of assigning manufacturing overhead to products have had to be developed.

Management accountants are now working with manufacturing workers to develop radically different product costing systems. These new types of cost systems are providing information so different from that of conventional cost systems that many businesses have been able to refocus their manufacturing efforts and dramatically increase their profits (while reducing prices, as was shown in the opening scenario). With better product cost information, manufacturers have been able to eliminate high-cost, low-productivity processes and replace them with lower-cost, less-complex processes for manufacturing. Researchers and manufacturers have spent more time trying to determine ways to provide accurate product cost information than they have spent on any other management accounting topic. The result has been the introduction of several new product costing methods including *activity-based costing* (ABC).

Activity-based costing is an attempt to better track overhead costs and more accurately assign them to products. ABC systems relate overhead costs to specific cost drivers thought to create those costs. Advocates maintain that activity-based costing can provide management with a more accurate assignment of overhead to products and therefore a better understanding of profitability. ABC systems use direct material and direct labor cost information in the same way as conventional systems. Where ABC systems differ is in their accounting for overhead costs. ABC advocates claim that traditional cost accounting distorts product costs by allocating overhead costs in irrelevant ways, which may lead to inaccurate and potentially damaging decisions.

As you study the simple costing systems in this chapter, realize that they reflect only the outline of an actual costing system for a real business. Identification of underlying cost drivers and the proper assigning of overhead costs is a very important topic, but it is one that is beyond the scope of this book.

TO SUMMARIZE

While it is difficult to determine true product costs, having accurate product cost information is extremely important. Without accurate costs, management can easily over- or underprice products and make bad business decisions. While it is easy to allocate direct material and direct labor costs to specific products, manufacturing overhead costs make accurate product costing difficult. Traditionally, product cost information has been used primarily for financial reporting and tax purposes, without much emphasis on accurately assigning manufacturing overhead costs to manufacturing products. Recently, however, a number of innovative approaches to product costing have been developed. The new methods of cost accumulation offer significant potential benefits to manufacturing companies. Management needs accurate product cost information to plan for the future, control current operations, and evaluate past performance.

3 *Identify and compare conventional product costing systems.*

CONVENTIONAL PRODUCT COST ACCUMULATION SYSTEMS

In support of the management process (planning, controlling, and evaluating business activities), cost accumulation is critical to controlling costs in the organization. Unless the management accountant is able to provide useful cost data, it is almost impossible for managers to establish expectations and performance measures, then determine how actual results compare to the expectations. The two conventional methods for accumulating product costs and assigning them to individual products are job order and process costing. The specific method used by an organization depends on the nature of the manufacturing process. If manufacturing involves the production of custom-ordered goods or goods where the costs associated with each identifiable job is recorded separately, **job order costing** is used. Usually, when job order costing is used, each item tends to be unique; management is interested in how much it costs to produce that item (or batch of items) regardless of whether the job took a few hours, a few days, or a few months. Job order costing is usually applied to high-cost, low-volume goods. Examples of situations where job order costing would probably be used are the printing of wedding announcements (and other special printing orders), the construction of a building or aircraft, and the manufacture of custom equipment.

job order costing A method of product costing whereby each job, product, or batch of products is costed separately.

Alternatively, the manufacturing process may involve the production of large numbers of similar or standardized products. When all finished products are essentially identical, management is interested in the total manufacturing costs over a specific period of time, such as a week or a quarter. Since all units are similar and have the same applicable costs, total period costs are divided by the number of units made (during that period) to determine an average cost for each unit produced. The method used to collect these costs is called **process costing**. Process costing is generally applied to high-volume, low-cost goods, where individual units cannot be separately identified during the manufacturing process. Process costing is often used, for example, by producers of bricks, chemicals, textiles, plastics, paints, gasoline, flour, and various foods. We will discuss job order costing here. Process costing, which is more complicated, is covered in managerial accounting textbooks.

process costing A method of product costing whereby costs are accumulated by process or work centers and averaged over all products manufactured in those centers.

TO SUMMARIZE

Job order and process costing are the two conventional ways of accumulating and assigning manufacturing costs to products produced. With job order costing, each job (or batch of production) is costed separately because of its uniqueness. Process costing is used for products that are mass-produced. With process costing, the cost of individual products is determined by dividing total manufacturing costs by the number of units produced over a specified period of time.

4 *Describe and apply job order costing procedures for a manufacturing firm.*

THE JOB ORDER COSTING SYSTEM

In discussing the conventional product costing methods, we focus on job order costing for two reasons: (1) it is a logical system, clearly conveying an understanding of how costs are traditionally tracked and accumulated in a manufacturing firm, and (2) it is the basis for costing used in many service firms, which are becoming increasingly important in the U.S. economy. Indeed, the United States has now moved to an information society, with manufacturing comprising a smaller and smaller portion of the U.S. economy. The cost accounting for merchandising and service firms is discussed later in the chapter.

As we discuss the mechanics of job order costing, remember the big picture. Job order costing is only one of several potential methods used to track and compute the cost of manufactured products. Regardless of the costing method, product cost information is used to plan future operations (e.g., at what level of production should we operate?), to control current operations (e.g., are our costs too high?), and to evaluate performance (e.g., were our costs and performance last period good or bad?). Product costs are used to support continuous decisions about production costs, product quality, and manufacturing time and efficiency.

The Job Cost Sheet

job cost sheet A document prepared for each manufacturing job that is job order costed; it contains a summary of direct materials, direct labor, and overhead costs.

In a job order costing system, all manufacturing costs for each job are accumulated on a computerized job order form or on a document called a **job cost sheet**. The job cost sheet (or computerized job order form) serves as a basis for determining the cost of the completed job. This "cost" is transferred to the finished goods inventory and becomes the cost of goods sold amount when the product is sold to a customer. Although it is helpful to visualize the job cost sheet as a sheet of paper (as shown in Exhibit 10-3) on which costs are listed, in most companies this "document" is a computer file.

EXHIBIT 10-3 Job Cost Sheet

Broyman Furniture Company
Job Cost Sheet

52
Job order number

Product was made for stock ___ Yes *x* No
Product was specially ordered *x* Yes ___ No
Customer name *Marlin Dockweiler*
Mahogany Table 4′ × 8′
Date started *January 3, 2000* Date completed *January 6, 2000*

Machining department

Direct materials			Direct labor			Manufacturing overhead		
Date	Requisition number	Amount	Time ticket number	Hours	Amount	Machine hours	Rate	Amount
1/3/00	*872*	*$100.00*	*25*	*8*	*$80*	*8*	*$4 per*	*$32*
							machine	
							hour	

Finishing department

Direct materials			Direct labor			Manufacturing overhead		
Date	Requisition number	Amount	Time ticket number	Hours	Amount	Direct labor hours	Rate	Amount
1/6/00	*876*	*$30.00*	*61*	*3*	*$36*	*4.5*	*$3 per*	*$13.50*
1/6/00	*877*	*5.00*	*75*	*1.5*	*18*		*direct*	
							labor	
							hour	

Cost summary

	Machining	Finishing	Total
Direct materials	*$100.00*	*$ 35.00*	*$135.00*
Direct labor	*80.00*	*54.00*	*134.00*
Manufacturing overhead	*32.00*	*13.50*	*45.50*
Total cost	*$212.00*	*$102.50*	*$314.50*
Unit cost			*$314.50*

Exhibit 10–3 is the completed job cost sheet for a mahogany table manufactured by Broyman Furniture Company for a particular customer, Marlin Dockweiler. It shows that the production of the table is a custom job requiring two operations: machining (preparing the mahogany) and finishing (assembling and staining the table). (You will recall that there were three manufacturing areas in Exhibit 10–1. This table does not require work in the cutting department.)

Job cost sheets are prepared by a firm's accounting and/or production department upon notification that a sales order has been received and production has started. Production begins only after the sales department has confirmed in writing that the price, shipment date, quantity, and other terms have been agreed to by the customer.

manufacturing overhead rate The rate at which manufacturing overhead is assigned to products; estimated manufacturing overhead for the period divided by the number of units of the activity base being used.

Exhibit 10–3 shows that the mahogany table cost $314.50 to make. This amount includes $135 of direct materials, $134 of direct labor, and $45.50 of manufacturing overhead (which includes utilities, depreciation on plant and machinery, and so on). Looking at the job cost sheet, we can see that the hourly wage rate for direct labor is $10 per hour ($80 ÷ 8 hours) in machining and $12 per hour ($36 ÷ 3 hours) in finishing; the manufacturing overhead rate is $4 per machine hour in machining and $3 per direct labor hour in finishing. The **manufacturing overhead rate** is an estimate of the overhead that will be incurred for each unit (in this case, allocated on the basis of machine and direct labor hours). In this example, an average of $4 of overhead is incurred by the company for every hour the machine is run in the machining department. Thus, each job that requires the use of the machine is allocated a portion of the overhead costs. The use of different manufacturing overhead rates is common. Each department will allocate manufacturing overhead to products on the basis of the most meaningful activity in that department. (Remember the problem discussed earlier in accurately estimating and allocating manufacturing overhead to products.) The machining department is more automated, so activity is tied more closely to machine hours; the finishing department requires more handwork, so activity is tied more closely to direct labor hours. Later in the chapter, we will explain the calculation of manufacturing overhead rates, as well as the method of assigning overhead costs to products.

Direct Materials Costs

To illustrate the accounting for direct materials costs, we will assume that Broyman purchased a supply of mahogany and placed it in a materials storeroom. The entry to record this purchase is:

Raw Materials Inventory	50,000	
Accounts Payable (or Cash)		50,000
Purchased 25,000 board feet of mahogany at $2 per foot.		

When raw materials are needed (such as for the manufacture of the table), the machining department would send a request to the storeroom (usually via computer) identifying the quantity and type of materials needed. When the raw materials warehouse fills the request, it records the transfer of goods to the factory floor by making an entry (usually by computer) that serves as the basis for the accounting records. The storeroom manager sends the transfer information to the accounting department, where the unit cost is entered and the total cost calculated. The accounting entry made to record the transfer of mahogany from storage to machining is:

Work-in-Process Inventory	100	
Raw Materials Inventory		100
Issued 50 board feet of mahogany to production at $2 per foot.		

The 50 board feet of mahogany were used directly in the manufacture of the table; the cost is assigned as direct materials for the Dockweiler job. Because the amount of direct materials used varies proportionately with the level of production, direct materials are almost always variable costs.

Indirect materials and supplies used in production (classified as manufacturing overhead costs), such as glue, nails, and varnish, are ordered from the storeroom in the same manner. Although some inexpensive materials, such as glue, are used directly in the manufactured products and others are used to support production, it is generally not cost-beneficial to trace such miscellaneous items to a particular job. These miscellaneous items are treated as indirect materials costs and recorded in the manufacturing overhead account (explained later in the chapter). Manufacturing overhead consists of numerous expenditures such as indirect labor, indirect materials, utilities, rent, etc. The sum of these various expenditures provides the balance in the manufacturing overhead account. The following entry records the requisition for indirect materials by the machining department:

Manufacturing Overhead (indirect materials)	xxx	
Raw Materials Inventory.		xxx
Issued miscellaneous materials and supplies to the machining department.		

At the end of a period, the amount of materials and supplies that remain on hand in the raw materials warehouse is shown on the balance sheet as Raw Materials Inventory.

Direct Labor Costs

The method of charging direct labor costs to production jobs is similar to that for direct materials costs. Most factories have a time clock where employees punch in and record their hourly activities. These time clocks often allow workers to identify specific jobs worked on. When the time clocks do not capture specific job information, the information is noted by making entries in the computer or on manual time tickets. The job cost sheet, shown in Exhibit 10-3, reveals that employees worked on the mahogany table for 8 hours on January 3, 2000. Since the wage rate was $10 per hour in machining, the total direct labor cost in machining was $80 ($10 per hour × 8 hours). The entry to record the direct labor costs (ignoring payroll taxes) is:

Work-in-Process Inventory	80	
Wages Payable		80
To record the machining department's direct labor costs on job #52.		

Within certain limits, direct labor costs vary proportionately with the number of products made and, thus, can be considered variable costs.

Like materials, labor costs can be either direct or indirect. Indirect labor costs include the wages of employees who perform functions not related to a specific job, such as maintenance and custodial. Usually, these employees still punch time clocks, but their wages become part of the indirect labor costs that are included in manufacturing overhead, as discussed in the next section. The entry to record indirect labor costs is:

Manufacturing Overhead (indirect labor)	xxx	
Wages Payable		xxx
To record indirect labor costs.		

(S T O P & T H I N K)

In the example, we have illustrated making a mahogany table using two operations: machining and finishing. When making a real table, how many separate operations do you think would be necessary?

Manufacturing Overhead Costs

In contrast to direct materials and direct labor, manufacturing overhead (the third type of product cost) involves more complex accounting procedures and estimation problems. While direct materials and direct labor can be readily assigned to specific jobs or products, manufacturing overhead costs are difficult to trace directly to the production of a single item and must often be estimated in advance of their incurrence. By definition, most manufacturing overhead costs benefit all products made in a department or a company during a period. The depreciation on equipment and the wages paid for maintenance in the machining department, for example, ensure the smooth operation of the entire department for the period; these cannot be traced directly to individual items produced during the period.

Some manufacturing overhead costs, such as property taxes and repairs, are not known until the end of an accounting period. However, managers need current product cost information (for pricing similar jobs, estimating costs for next year, and so forth), so each job is assigned a share of *estimated* manufacturing overhead costs. In accounting terminology, manufacturing overhead costs are applied to (or absorbed by) jobs or products.

Measuring and Assigning Manufacturing Overhead Costs

The way management accountants assign manufacturing overhead costs to products is similar to the concept of depreciation. You will recall that we assign the "lump sum" costs to plant and equipment uniformly across periods of time, or to equipment use, by using a depreciation procedure such as the straight-line or units-of-production depreciation method. The classic straight-line depreciation method simply takes the initial costs of an asset and divides it by the number of years the company expects to use the asset to determine a depreciation rate per year. Similarly, a company takes the expected annual costs of overhead and divides this estimated amount by the direct labor hours (or another selected activity base, e.g., machine hours) expected to be used during the year. (These estimations are determined on the basis of experience and analysis.) The result is an allocation rate per direct labor hour that is used to uniformly assign a "lumpy" cost to production volume throughout the year. This rate is called the **predetermined overhead rate**.

predetermined overhead rate A rate at which estimated manufacturing overhead costs are assigned to products throughout the year; equals total estimated manufacturing overhead costs divided by a suitable allocation base, such as number of units produced, direct labor hours, direct materials used, or direct labor costs.

The process of assigning (applying) manufacturing overhead costs to individual jobs involves two steps. First, the predetermined overhead rate is computed (as described above). Second, the predetermined overhead rate is multiplied by the actual amount of the activity used to complete a job to arrive at the amount of manufacturing overhead to be applied to that job. Exhibit 10-4 illustrates the two-step process of applying manufacturing overhead to individual jobs.

Applying Manufacturing Overhead to Products

Step One

$$\frac{\text{Annual expected (budgeted) manufacturing overhead}}{\text{Annual expected (budgeted) activity level (e.g., direct labor hours)}} = \text{Predetermined overhead rate}$$

Step Two

Predetermined overhead rate × Actual activity level per job = Allocated manufacturing overhead assigned to job

cost driver Base used to allocate costs of activities consumed in manufacturing to the products using those activities.

In applying overhead costs to products, two problems can arise. First, total overhead costs must be estimated accurately. This is often difficult since some costs are not known until after a period is over. Second, a good measure of activity level by which costs can be assigned to products may not be found. The best way to assign manufacturing overhead costs to products is to use an activity base that "drives" or influences the overhead costs. A **cost driver** is a measure of activity, such as machine hours or direct labor hours, that is a causal factor in the incurrence of manufacturing overhead costs in a department or an organization. If a base is used to compute overhead rates that does not "drive" overhead costs, the result will be inaccurate rates and distorted product costs.

To illustrate these problems, we will continue the example of job order number 52 for Broyman Furniture Company (see Exhibit 10-3). First, we will explain the calculations for manufacturing overhead related to the machining department; then, we will calculate manufacturing overhead for the finishing department. At the beginning of the period, the accountants estimated the total manufacturing overhead costs to be incurred in the machining department during the year based on the expected level of activity. Assuming that machine hours are used as the measure of activity level and that the accountants and production personnel estimated 42,000 machine hours for the year 2000, the following manufacturing overhead costs may be calculated for the machining department. Note that these costs have been separated into fixed and variable components.

Variable manufacturing overhead:		
Indirect labor	$20,000	
Indirect materials	15,000	
Utilities	7,000	$ 42,000
Fixed manufacturing overhead:		
Rent	$72,000	
Depreciation	30,000	
Insurance	24,000	126,000
Total expected manufacturing overhead cost for the year 2000 (machining)		$168,000

CAUTION

After studying financial accounting, some students have a difficult time with the accounting for manufacturing overhead. For example, in financial accounting, we accounted for salaries by debiting Salaries Expense and crediting Salaries Payable, the correct entry when the salaries are for sales or other nonmanufacturing personnel. However, when the wages are related to manufacturing, the debit is to Work-in-Process Inventory for direct labor and Manufacturing Overhead for indirect labor. Thus, in management accounting, it is important to determine first whether salaries are for manufacturing or for nonmanufacturing personnel. Then, for manufacturing personnel, it must be determined whether the individuals worked directly on the product (Work-in-Process Inventory) or indirectly on the product (Manufacturing Overhead). The same is true for other costs such as depreciation and rent. If these costs relate to manufacturing, they are debited to Manufacturing Overhead; costs not related to manufacturing are debited to Depreciation Expense, Rent Expense, and so forth. The manufacturing costs will eventually become expenses when the products are sold (Cost of Goods Sold).

Using these data, the accountants then computed the predetermined overhead rate in the machining department to be $4 per machine hour, as follows:

$$\frac{\text{Total estimated manufacturing overhead cost for the year 2000}}{\text{Total estimated machine hours for 2000}} = \frac{\$168{,}000}{42{,}000} = \$4 \text{ per hour}$$

The job cost sheet indicates that it took 8 machine hours to produce the mahogany table components in the machining department. Therefore, based on the predetermined overhead rate of $4 per machine hour, a total of $32 of manufacturing overhead cost was included on the job cost sheet for the machining department (8 hours × $4).

The same procedure was followed in determining the manufacturing overhead cost to be applied in the finishing department. The job cost sheet indicates that direct labor hours was the measure of activity used. If the accountants estimated that the finishing department would incur total manufacturing overhead costs of $150,000 in the year 2000 and use 50,000 direct labor hours, then the predetermined overhead rate would be:

$$\frac{\text{Total estimated manufacturing overhead cost for the year 2000}}{\text{Total estimated direct labor hours for 2000}} = \frac{\$150{,}000}{50{,}000} = \$3 \text{ per hour}$$

BUSINESS ENVIRONMENT ESSAY

Medicare and Overhead Cost Allocation Finding an appropriate way to allocate overhead costs is probably the most difficult part of product costing. Medicare has faced this same problem in deciding how much hospitals and clinics can bill them for services performed. To ensure comparability across vendors, Medicare uses an allocation method based on the ratio-of-cost-to-charges (RCC). For example, patients with kidney failure can be treated using two different methods: (1) hemodialysis, which requires patients to visit a dialysis clinic three times each week to receive treatments using dialyzer equipment or (2) peritoneal dialysis, which allows patients to administer their own treatments daily at home. Because Medicare reimburses providers $129.70 for a hemodialysis treatment and only $55.59 per treatment for peritoneal dialysis, each hemodialysis treatment carries a larger burden of overhead than does peritoneal dialysis, regardless of the actual amount of overhead expended on each treatment. For example, if total overhead were estimated to be $100,000, with 70% hemodialysis treatment and 30% peritoneal dialysis treatment, and there were 1,000 treatments of each type, each hemodialysis treatment would bear $70 of overhead and each peritoneal dialysis would bear $30 of overhead.

This calculation is shown below.

	Medicare Reimbursement	Percentage	Total Overhead	Treatments	Overhead per Treatment
Hemodialysis	$129.70	70%	$ 70,000	1,000	$70
Peritoneal Dialysis	55.59	30%	30,000	1,000	$30
Total	$185.29	100%	$100,000		

Source: T.D. West and D.A. West, "Applying ABC to Healthcare," *Management Accounting,* February 1997, pp. 22–33.

The job cost sheet also indicates that it took 4.5 direct labor hours to complete the mahogany table in the finishing department. Based on a predetermined overhead rate of $3 per direct labor hour, a total of $13.50 of manufacturing overhead cost was included on the job cost sheet for the finishing department (4.5 hours × $3).

Adding the amount of manufacturing overhead applied in the machining department to the amount applied in finishing, we have a total of $45.50 of manufacturing overhead being applied to job #52. This information is recorded as follows:

Work-in-Process Inventory	45.50	
Manufacturing Overhead.		45.50
To apply manufacturing overhead to job #52.		

Notice that as *actual* overhead costs are incurred (as with indirect materials and indirect labor), the manufacturing overhead account is debited. As overhead costs are *applied* to products, the manufacturing overhead account is credited. This relationship is illustrated and discussed a bit later in the chapter.

Transferring the Costs of Completed Jobs and Computing Unit Costs

While a job is in process, the costs of direct materials, direct labor, and manufacturing overhead are accounted for separately. When the job is completed, however, these costs (in total) are transferred from Work-in-Process Inventory to Finished Goods Inventory. In the Broyman Furniture Company example, the total cost assigned to Job #52 was $314.50, as shown in Exhibit 10-3 and summarized here.

Type of Cost	Machining	Finishing	Total
Direct materials	$100.00	$ 35.00	$135.00
Direct labor (DL)	80.00 (8 DL hrs. × $10)	54.00 (4.5 DL hrs. × $12)	134.00
Manufacturing overhead	32.00 (8 mach. hrs. × $4)	13.50 (4.5 DL hrs. × $3)	45.50
Totals	$212.00	$102.50	$314.50

The entry to transfer the completed cost of job #52 to Finished Goods Inventory is:

Finished Goods Inventory	314.50	
Work-in-Process Inventory		314.50
To record the completion of job #52.		

At the completion of each job, the unit cost is computed by adding the direct materials, direct labor, and manufacturing overhead costs and dividing the total by the number of units produced. (Of course, if only one unit is produced, the unit cost is simply the total.) The job is transferred from the production floor (Finishing Department in Exhibit 10-1) to the Finished Goods Warehouse. The job cost sheet is then sent to the Finished Goods Inventory file, and the cost data are used in pricing similar jobs, estimating costs for the next year, and measuring income.

Transferring the Costs of Products That Are Sold

When a product is sold, the costs assigned to it are transferred to Cost of Goods Sold. For example, when the mahogany table, which cost $314.50 to make, is shipped to Marlin Dockweiler, the table is loaded from the warehouse onto the truck; the cost of the table is transferred from Finished Goods Inventory to Cost of Goods Sold, using the following entry:

Cost of Goods Sold	314.50	
Finished Goods Inventory		314.50
To record the cost of goods sold for job #52.		

With this entry, costs have been traced all the way through the production cycle and onto the income statement. Two major tasks have been accomplished: (1) the total cost of producing an item has been summarized on the job cost sheet or computer job order form and (2) the proper entries have been made in the accounting records to account for the production costs. These entries are necessary so that the correct amount of net income and the financial position of a company can be reported at any point in time. For the manufacturing of the table for Marlin Dockweiler, the flow of costs through the accounts is charted in Exhibit 10-5.

Note that direct labor, when incurred, and raw materials, when used, are debited directly to Work-in-Process Inventory. Manufacturing overhead costs, on the other hand, are entered first as debits to Manufacturing Overhead and

(S T O P & T H I N K)

Compare Exhibit 10-1 with Exhibit 10-5. Try to identify the physical location (from Exhibit 10-1) with each type of accounting cost in Exhibit 10-5.

EXHIBIT 10-5 Flow of Costs—Job Order Costing

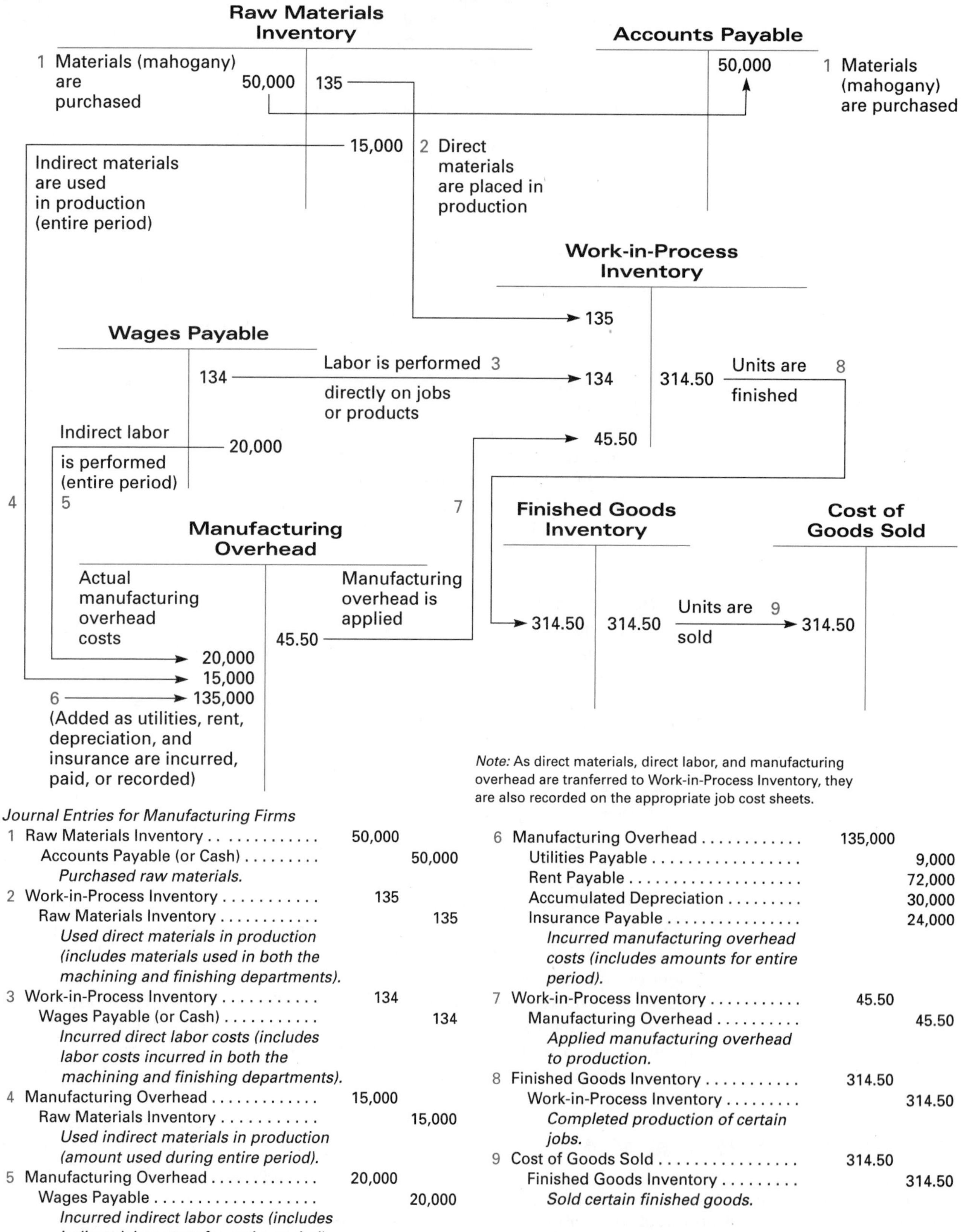

Note: As direct materials, direct labor, and manufacturing overhead are tranferred to Work-in-Process Inventory, they are also recorded on the appropriate job cost sheets.

Journal Entries for Manufacturing Firms

	Account	Debit	Credit
1	Raw Materials Inventory	50,000	
	Accounts Payable (or Cash)		50,000
	Purchased raw materials.		
2	Work-in-Process Inventory	135	
	Raw Materials Inventory		135
	Used direct materials in production (includes materials used in both the machining and finishing departments).		
3	Work-in-Process Inventory	134	
	Wages Payable (or Cash)		134
	Incurred direct labor costs (includes labor costs incurred in both the machining and finishing departments).		
4	Manufacturing Overhead	15,000	
	Raw Materials Inventory		15,000
	Used indirect materials in production (amount used during entire period).		
5	Manufacturing Overhead	20,000	
	Wages Payable		20,000
	Incurred indirect labor costs (includes indirect labor costs for entire period).		
6	Manufacturing Overhead	135,000	
	Utilities Payable		9,000
	Rent Payable		72,000
	Accumulated Depreciation		30,000
	Insurance Payable		24,000
	Incurred manufacturing overhead costs (includes amounts for entire period).		
7	Work-in-Process Inventory	45.50	
	Manufacturing Overhead		45.50
	Applied manufacturing overhead to production.		
8	Finished Goods Inventory	314.50	
	Work-in-Process Inventory		314.50
	Completed production of certain jobs.		
9	Cost of Goods Sold	314.50	
	Finished Goods Inventory		314.50
	Sold certain finished goods.		

then are transferred to Work-in-Process Inventory by crediting Manufacturing Overhead. Be careful to note that in Exhibit 10-5, entry 1 is for mahogany that will be used on several jobs; entries 4, 5, and 6 are actual manufacturing costs incurred for the entire accounting period in which the table was manufactured. Entries 2, 3, 7, 8, and 9 are entries associated with the mahogany table for Marlin Dockweiler. At the end of the period, the company will usually have three inventory balances: raw materials, work-in-process, and finished goods inventory.

TO SUMMARIZE

When a job order costing system is used, all direct labor, direct materials, and manufacturing overhead costs are accumulated on a job cost sheet or on a computer job order form. Because the exact amount of manufacturing overhead cannot be determined until the accounting period is completed, an estimated amount of manufacturing overhead is applied to jobs. To estimate the amount of manufacturing overhead to be applied to a job, a predetermined overhead rate is calculated for each department involved in production, using an appropriate measure of activity. This rate is multiplied by the actual quantity of the activity used to complete the job. Total costs for completed jobs are then transferred from Work-in-Process Inventory to Finished Goods Inventory. When manufactured goods are sold, costs are transferred from Finished Goods Inventory to Cost of Goods Sold.

Actual Versus Applied Manufacturing Overhead

In discussing the flow of costs in a job order costing system, we have used estimated manufacturing overhead. However, accountants must also keep track of actual manufacturing overhead costs. Estimated costs are useful for pricing and similar decisions, but actual costs are needed for accurate determination of income and for computing a company's income tax liability. Both actual and applied (estimated) manufacturing overhead costs are typically accounted for on a monthly basis. As previously discussed, actual costs are recorded on the debit side of the manufacturing overhead account, and applied manufacturing overhead costs are recorded on the credit side of the manufacturing overhead account, as illustrated in Exhibit 10-6.

EXHIBIT 10-6

Recording Costs in the Manufacturing Overhead Account

Manufacturing Overhead	
Actual manufacturing overhead costs are entered as debits on a regular basis as they are incurred.	Estimated overhead costs are entered as credits as production takes place; costs are applied to work-in-process on the basis of a predetermined overhead rate.

If the estimates are perfectly accurate, at the end of the period we should have applied as much overhead to work-in-process as was actually incurred, and the ending balance in the manufacturing overhead account would be $0 (this rarely happens). Typically, though, the ending balance in the manufacturing overhead account is not very large. The procedures for handling any balance left in manufacturing overhead are discussed in the next section.

To illustrate the accounting for the difference between actual and applied manufacturing overhead costs, we will assume that during March 2000, the machining department of Broyman Furniture Company incurred the following actual manufacturing overhead costs: $100, indirect labor; $175, indirect materials; $115, repairs; $600, rent; $300, insurance; and $200, depreciation. The total of these costs would be debited to Manufacturing Overhead, whereas the individual amounts would be credited to their respective accounts, as shown here.

Manufacturing Overhead	1,490	
Wages Payable		100
Raw Materials Inventory		175
Accounts Payable		115
Rent Payable		600
Prepaid Insurance		300
Accumulated Depreciation		200
To record actual manufacturing overhead costs.		

Applied costs, as shown earlier, would be credited to Manufacturing Overhead. If the machining department had used a total of 360 machine hours while working on jobs during March 2000, a total of $1,440 (360 machine hours × $4 per machine hour) would have been applied to jobs worked on that month. At the end of March, the manufacturing overhead account for machining would appear as follows:

Manufacturing Overhead, Machining

Actual costs	1,490	Costs applied to work-in-process inventory	1,440

A comparison of the debit and credit sides of the manufacturing overhead account shows that actual manufacturing overhead costs incurred by the machining department were $50 higher than applied costs. A difference this small could be ignored until year-end because management is concerned with immediate decisions, for which current estimates are adequate. However, at year-end this difference must be accounted for (as explained in the next section), not only to balance the books, but also to show actual costs in measuring income.

The procedure for collecting actual manufacturing overhead costs and for applying estimated manufacturing overhead costs to jobs for the finishing department of Broyman Furniture Company would follow the same pattern as for the machining department.

(STOP & THINK)

What would it mean if the debit (actual overhead) and credit (applied overhead) amounts in the manufacturing overhead account were vastly different?

Disposition of Over- and Underapplied Manufacturing Overhead

underapplied manufacturing overhead The excess of actual manufacturing overhead costs over the applied overhead costs for a period.

overapplied manufacturing overhead The excess of applied manufacturing overhead (based on a predetermined application rate) over the actual manufacturing overhead costs for a period.

At the end of the year, the balance in Manufacturing Overhead must be eliminated and the account must be brought to a zero balance. When total actual manufacturing overhead exceeds the amount applied, the account will have a debit balance referred to as **underapplied manufacturing overhead**. If applied manufacturing overhead exceeds actual costs, the account will have a credit balance representing **overapplied manufacturing overhead**.

Which is better to have—under- or overapplied overhead? If overhead is underapplied, then the total cost of jobs will be understated. If a company were to price its products in the future based on this understated cost, the company could lose money, since it may not cover its actual manufacturing overhead costs. On the other hand, overapplied manufacturing overhead indicates that jobs were overcharged for overhead and costs were overstated. If future pricing decisions were made based on these overstated costs, the company would soon find customers looking elsewhere for more reasonably priced products. Neither under- nor overapplied overhead is desirable. A company's objective is to attempt to anticipate overhead costs and accurately charge those costs to the various jobs.

There are two methods of treating over- and underapplied manufacturing overhead:

1. Close over- or underapplied manufacturing overhead directly to Cost of Goods Sold.
2. Allocate over- or underapplied manufacturing overhead to Work-in-Process Inventory, Finished Goods Inventory, and Costs of Goods Sold, on the basis of the ending balances in those accounts.

The first method is easier and more commonly used, especially if the over- or underapplied amount is small, because it requires only a single entry to correct the amount of manufacturing overhead applied. In the Broyman Furniture Company example, manufacturing overhead for the machining department was underapplied by $50 ($1,490 − $1,440) during March. Assume that at year-end, when total actual and applied manufacturing overhead have been recorded, manufacturing overhead for the machining department was still underapplied, but by $1,000. The entry to assign this underapplied manufacturing overhead to Cost of Goods Sold would be:

Cost of Goods Sold	1,000	
Manufacturing Overhead		1,000
To recognize the excess of actual manufacturing overhead costs for the machining department over the applied manufacturing overhead for 2000.		

This entry will increase the cost of goods sold for the year by $1,000. Companies that have very small or zero inventory balances would normally charge any over- or underapplied overhead to Cost of Goods Sold.

The second method is more accurate because, theoretically, any difference between applied and actual manufacturing overhead should be allocated proportionately to all items in production during the period. The items in production include those produced and sold (Cost of Goods Sold), those produced and not sold (Finished Goods Inventory), and those still being produced (Work-in-Process Inventory). If the estimate had been accurate, manufacturing overhead costs would have been allocated proportionately to all products. Therefore, those products actually sold should not be burdened with, or relieved of, the entire amount of the estimation error. However, because this alternative requires detailed calculations and several journal entries, it is more complicated and will not be illustrated here. When differences between actual and applied overhead are small, this more accurate method is usually not worth the extra effort.

BUSINESS ENVIRONMENT ESSAY

Simplifying Product Costing by Outsourcing One way to simplify operations and product costing is for a company to only perform the core, or strategic, functions inside the company and to outsource all support activities to a network of external companies that specialize in each function. These types of companies, sometimes referred to as virtual corporations, form functional alliances to manufacture products or provide services for customers. The goal of a virtual corporation is to position itself at the center of these relationships and serve as the catalyst that draws these cooperating companies together and organizes how the work will flow. Supposedly, this allows a company to maximize the return from these partnerships while making the minimum investment in permanent staff, fixed assets, and working capital. One such company is **Super Bakery, Inc.**, which was formed by former Pittsburgh Steelers' running back Franco Harris in 1983. Super Bakery, Inc., is a supplier of donuts and other baked goods to the institutional food market. Since its inception, it has been gaining market share and establishing a firm foothold in the highly competitive institutional baked goods market. Instead of creating a large multifunctional organization to administer the business, the management of Super Bakery outsources selling to a network of independent brokers and contracts out manufacturing, warehousing, and shipping. Super Bakery handles strategic planning, marketing, research and development, and finance/accounting in-house. The company also purchases ingredients and formulates and produces its own dough. Super Bakery's product costing problem is significantly reduced by outsourcing so many functions. In essence, Franco Harris is letting other companies worry about many different aspects of product costing.

Source: Tim R.V. Davis and B.L. Darling, "ABC in a Virtual Corporation," *Management Accounting,* October 1996, pp. 18–26.

Cost of Goods Manufactured Schedule

cost of goods manufactured schedule A schedule supporting the income statement; summarizes the total cost of goods manufactured during a period, including direct materials, direct labor, and manufacturing overhead.

Exhibit 10–5 showed how manufacturing costs are accumulated in Work-in-Process, then flow to Finished Goods Inventory, and finally to Cost of Goods Sold. These costs are also usually summarized on a **cost of goods manufactured schedule**, which supports the cost of goods sold calculation on the income statement.

The cost of goods manufactured schedule shows the specific costs that have been incurred to manufacture goods during a period. Exhibit 10–7 shows the cost of goods manufactured schedule for Broyman Furniture Company. Many of the numbers in this schedule are arbitrary because the cost of goods manufactured schedule is for an entire period, while the example in this chapter was for one table manufactured during the period. While we do use the overhead amounts provided earlier, for now just focus on the format.

The cost of goods manufactured schedule provides the calculations that support the flow of costs for a manufacturing firm. In our example, the schedule shows that raw materials costing $290,000 were combined with direct labor costs of $300,000 and manufacturing overhead costs of $174,000 to transfer $764,000 of manufacturing costs to work-in-process inventory. The $764,000 was then adjusted for the beginning and ending work-in-process inventories to determine the $774,000 cost of goods manufactured for the period. Knowing the total cost of goods manufactured makes it easy to determine the total cost of goods sold. The cost of goods manufactured amount is added to beginning finished goods inventory (assume $60,000) and adjusted for any over- or underapplied manufacturing overhead (assume $6,000 overapplied) to arrive at cost of goods available for sale of $828,000. The ending finished goods inventory (assume $40,000) is then subtracted to determine the cost of goods sold ($788,000). This calculation of cost of goods sold is shown below.

Cost of Goods Sold	
Beginning finished goods inventory	$ 60,000
Add: Cost of goods manufactured	774,000
Less: Overapplied manufacturing overhead	(6,000)
Total cost of goods available for sale	$828,000
Less: Ending finished goods inventory	(40,000)
Cost of goods sold	$788,000

EXHIBIT 10-7

Cost of Goods Manufactured Schedule

Broyman Furniture Company
Cost of Goods Manufactured Schedule
For the Year Ended December 31, 2000

Direct materials:		
Beginning raw materials inventory	$ 50,000	
Add: Raw materials purchased	270,000	
Total raw materials available	$320,000	
Less: Ending raw materials inventory	30,000	
Raw materials used in production		$290,000
Direct labor		300,000
Manufacturing overhead:		
Indirect labor	$ 20,000	
Utilities	7,000	
Rent	72,000	
Depreciation	30,000	
Indirect materials	15,000	
Insurance	24,000	
Total actual manufacturing overhead	$168,000	
Add: Overapplied manufacturing overhead	6,000	
Applied manufacturing overhead		174,000
Total manufacturing costs		$764,000
Add: Beginning work-in-process inventory		90,000
Less: Ending work-in-process inventory		(80,000)
Cost of goods manufactured		$774,000

CAUTION

Remember that over- or underapplied overhead is usually charged to cost of goods sold. Thus, in the cost of goods sold calculation, underapplied overhead is added to cost of goods manufactured and overapplied overhead is subtracted from cost of goods manufactured.

Total cost of goods manufactured should include only those costs that have gone through the work-in-process account during the period. Thus, applied (rather than actual) overhead costs are included in the cost of goods manufactured schedule. As a result, overhead costs listed on the schedule must be adjusted for the amount of over- or underapplied overhead. On the cost of goods manufactured schedule, underapplied manufacturing overhead is subtracted from actual overhead costs, or overapplied overhead is added to actual manufacturing overhead costs.

Analyzing Cost of Goods Sold

In the preceding example, cost of goods sold was determined to be $788,000. You should note that this is a summary number that is used in the financial statements and is the number to which auditors will attest. However, because it is a summary number, it is not useful for internal decision making. To be useful, management would want to determine the cost of goods sold on a product-by-product basis, a period-by-period basis, and a department-by-department basis. By breaking costs down by product, period, and department, management can determine which units and products are performing well and which are performing poorly. In evaluating products and departments, cost is only one criterion examined by management. In most cases, management is just as interested in indicators of product quality and production speed as they are in costs of production. Exhibit 10-8 shows cost, quality, and time data that would be examined by management for a hypothetical company with three divisions and six products.

EXHIBIT 10-8 Divisional Performance Report

	DIVISION A		DIVISION B		DIVISION C	
	Product 1	Product 2	Product 3	Product 4	Product 5	Product 6
Cost to produce	Higher than last period	Same as last period	Lower than last period	Lower than last period	Higher than last period	Higher than last period
Quality of product	Happier customers, fewer defects	No change in customer attitudes	Happier customers, fewer defects	Happier customers, fewer defects	Increase in complaints	Increase in complaints
Average time to produce	Same as last period	One day less	Two days less	One day less	Two days more	Six days more

Obviously, management could have many different measures for the cost, quality, and time attributes it monitors. In this hypothetical example, the summary information suggests that both products in Division B have improved performance over the last period, while both products in Division C show decreased performance over the prior period. Obviously, comparing performance with the last period is only one measure that could be used. Management may want to compare the performance of products versus each other or "benchmark" the performance of its products with those of other companies.

Management would also use the inventory numbers to calculate days in inventory and inventory turnover ratios for raw materials, work-in-process, and finished goods inventories. Using inventory management methods, which will be discussed in later courses, management will do everything possible to minimize the company's investment in inventory.

TO SUMMARIZE

Actual manufacturing overhead costs are accumulated and debited to Manufacturing Overhead throughout the year. Applied (or estimated) manufacturing overhead costs are assigned to jobs on the basis of a predetermined overhead rate. These costs are credited to Manufacturing Overhead and debited to Work-in-Process Inventory. Any difference between actual and applied manufacturing overhead must be accounted for in order to properly measure income. When total actual manufacturing overhead exceeds total applied overhead, the excess is referred to as underapplied manufacturing overhead. When total applied overhead exceeds total actual overhead, the excess is referred to as overapplied manufacturing overhead. The easiest and most commonly used method of eliminating over- or underapplied manufacturing overhead is to transfer it directly to Cost of Goods Sold. In some cases, the over- or underapplied manufacturing overhead is allocated among Work-in-Process Inventory, Finished Goods Inventory, and Cost of Goods Sold to arrive at a more accurate assignment of costs. Manufacturing costs are summarized on a cost of goods manufactured schedule. The cost of goods manufactured is added to the beginning finished goods inventory to determine cost of goods available for sale. Ending finished goods inventory is then subtracted from this number to compute cost of goods sold. Cost of goods sold is a summary number that is audited and used in the financial statements, but is not very useful for internal mangement decision making. For decision making, management would examine costs, as well as quality and time measures, on a product-by-product, period-by-period, and department-by-department basis.

5 *Understand how merchants manage cost information in their organizations.*

COST ACCUMULATION IN MERCHANDISING ORGANIZATIONS

In the preceding section, we focused on discussing the nature of manufacturing companies and how management accountants accumulate costs for these organizations. Traditionally, accounting textbooks have not gone much beyond manufacturing to discuss how management accounting works in merchandising and service organizations. This may have been appropriate given how manufacturing used to dominate the economy in the United States. However, manufacturing is no longer the dominate type of business today. Merchandising and service organizations continue to increase their prevalence in the world economy. While both merchandising and service organizations borrow much of their management accounting from the manufacturing industry, there are some important differences. Many of these differences are the result of needs to support management decision processes in merchandising and service organizations that are very different from the decision processes required in the manufacturing business.

Inventory Flow and the Income Statement

In comparison to accounting for manufacturing businesses, the flow of costs through the merchandising accounting system is relatively simple. Examine Exhibit 10-9 and compare it to Exhibit 10-3 (page 437). Notice how simple the flow of inventory costs are in Exhibit 10-9. Essentially, accounting for inventory in merchan-

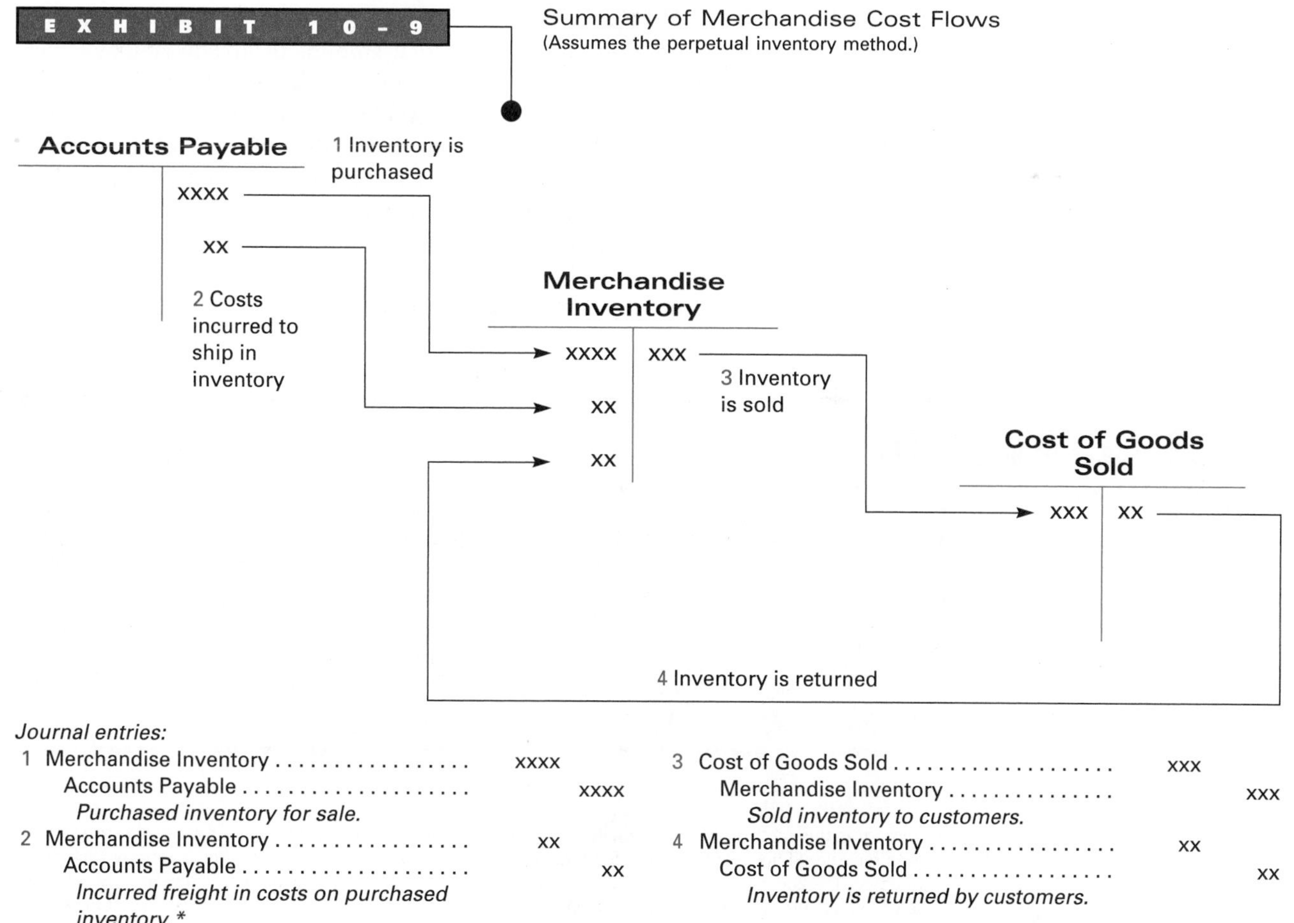

Journal entries:

1 Merchandise Inventory	XXXX		3 Cost of Goods Sold	XXX	
Accounts Payable		XXXX	Merchandise Inventory		XXX
Purchased inventory for sale.			*Sold inventory to customers.*		
2 Merchandise Inventory	XX		4 Merchandise Inventory	XX	
Accounts Payable		XX	Cost of Goods Sold		XX
*Incurred freight in costs on purchased inventory.**			*Inventory is returned by customers.*		

**Note:* Freight in is considered part of the purchase cost and should be added to inventory, eventually to be split between Cost of Goods Sold and the ending balance in Merchandise Inventory as goods are sold. In practice, the entire cost of freight in for a period is often simply debited directly to Cost of Goods Sold.

dising organizations is a fairly straightforward process. There are no raw materials, manufacturing overhead, or work-in-process accounts. Merchandise inventory, by definition, is essentially complete and ready for sale when purchased. Hence, inventory is debited to Merchandise Inventory throughout the year as it is acquired.[1] Conceptually, the inventory costs for a merchant should also include all costs required to purchase the inventory, transport it to the merchant's place of business, and ready it for sale (unpacking, displaying, etc.). Hence, the inventory cost *should* include the purchase price, shipping costs (freight in), insurance while in transit, administrative costs incurred by the merchant related to purchasing and handling activities, and storage costs prior to sale. In practice, though, most of these overhead-related costs, other than freight in costs, are difficult to allocate to specific inventory items. As a result, overhead costs related to merchandise inventory are often expensed as a period cost and included in Selling and General Administrative Expenses.

As inventory is sold, the cost of inventory is credited from Merchandise Inventory and debited to Cost of Goods Sold. When customers return merchandise that can be resold, Cost of Goods Sold is credited and the inventory account is debited. (If the returned merchandise cannot be resold, then nothing happens in either of these accounts.)

It looks as if tracking inventory costs in a merchant's accounting system is a fairly easy conceptual process. However, developing useful information on merchandise inventory for managers who need to plan, control, and evaluate inventory and inventory costs is a bit more involved.

Managing Inventory Costs

Merchants are always very conscious of the total amount of inventory that is currently in the retail store or in the distribution center. Managing this inventory takes careful and detailed planning. The detail in these plans results from merchants having *many* different types of inventory items, each with its own particular supplier source and targeted customer. Merchants must also be very careful in planning their inventory levels since there are critical issues involved in having either too little or too much inventory. These issues are listed in Exhibit 10-10. If management accountants are aware of these issues, they can help their organizations avoid a variety of unnecessary out-of-pocket costs or opportunity costs.

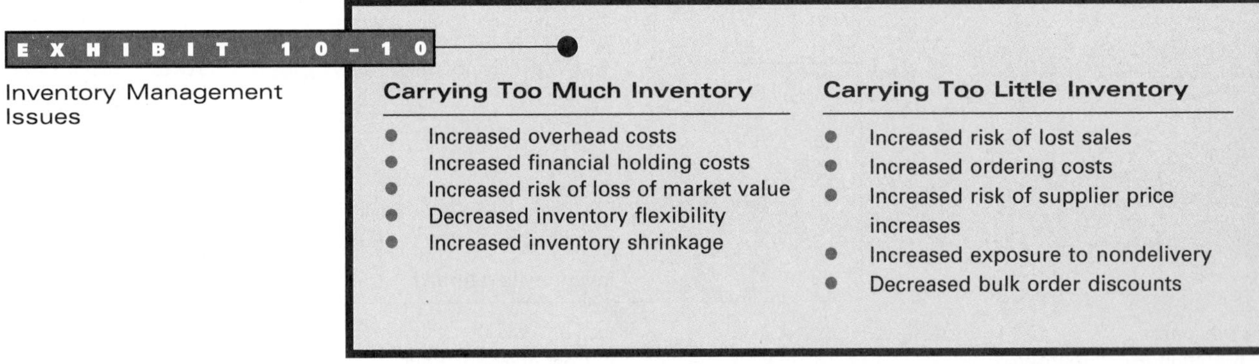

EXHIBIT 10-10

Inventory Management Issues

Carrying Too Much Inventory	Carrying Too Little Inventory
• Increased overhead costs	• Increased risk of lost sales
• Increased financial holding costs	• Increased ordering costs
• Increased risk of loss of market value	• Increased risk of supplier price increases
• Decreased inventory flexibility	• Increased exposure to nondelivery
• Increased inventory shrinkage	• Decreased bulk order discounts

1. Recall that this method of continuously debiting and crediting Merchandise Inventory as inventory is purchased (and crediting Cost of Goods Sold as inventory is sold) is called the *perpetual* inventory method of accounting. The alternative to the perpetual method is the *periodic* inventory method. There are several more accounts involved with the periodic inventory method, including Purchases, Purchase Discounts, and Purchase Returns. A significant difference between the perpetual and periodic inventory methods is that the periodic inventory method adjusts Merchandise Inventory *only at the end* of each period when cost of goods sold is calculated for the income statement.

Carrying Too Much Inventory

Financial accounting has always recorded inventory as an asset. However, financial accountants and financial analysts have long understood that having too much of this asset is actually a negative signal on the performance of a company. Having inventory is certainly necessary for most merchants if they expect to do business with their customers. However, accumulating as much inventory as possible is *not* the purpose of merchandising (or manufacturing) companies. Good business management entails having the right assets at the right place in the right time and in the right quantity (always a challenging endeavor!). The advent of the just-in-time (JIT) inventory management concept has clearly taught us that too much inventory creates a lot of management problems. First of all, it should be clear to you that there are many out-of-pocket costs involved in having inventory on site, including costs of storage, security, and record keeping. What may not be as clear is the financial opportunity cost (sometimes called the **holding cost**) of the inventory investment. Every dollar that is invested in inventory cannot be used in alternative business investments, such as expanding another part of the business or simply investing in the stock market or in a bank savings account. Whatever money we *could* make by investing the money elsewhere is the holding cost of the current inventory investment. Management accountants measure and report holding costs all the time.

holding costs The financial opportunity costs that result from investing money in an asset such as inventory. Whatever income the money could generate in an alternative investment is the holding cost of the current investment.

inventory shrinkage The disorder, spoilage, and theft that result when a company chooses to maintain inventory on site, resulting in additional out-of-pocket costs to replace inventory.

Increased overhead costs and holding costs are not the only issues involved in carrying too much inventory. The more inventory a merchant elects to carry, the more risk the merchant has that the inventory will decrease in market value before it can be sold (inventory may unexpectedly increase in market value as well). In addition, when a merchant invests in a lot of one type of inventory, it becomes difficult to shift to another inventory type that customers may suddenly want to buy. Finally, every merchant understands the tough reality that inventories "shrink" over time. **Inventory shrinkage** happens in a lot of ways. The type of shrinkage we hear about most often is theft (either by customers or employees). However, when inventory is being moved, stacked, stored, retrieved, and rotated, things get broken, parts get lost, and items become mislabeled. Liquid and gas stocks spill or evaporate. Cloth material becomes soiled. Grocery items spoil or become stale. As inventory is piled up around the store or distribution center, this disorder, spoilage, and theft is revealed every time the company makes an annual inventory count, resulting in additional out-of-pockets costs to replace inventory.

FYI

In the notes to its 1995 annual report, Kmart Corporation revealed that, in the fourth quarter of 1994, it had discovered inventory shrinkage totaling $17 million. Avoiding this shrinkage would have increased Kmart's profits for the year by 6.5 percent. Even more significant was the fact that Kmart's decision to mark down discontinued and seasonal merchandise reduced profits by $171 million!

Carrying Too Little Inventory

As implied earlier, it is not always clear that inventory is an asset. Clearly having too much inventory is a poor use of resources. However, poor planning that results in not having enough inventory on hand is also a source of trouble that the accountant needs to help management understand. It is obvious to most managers and owners that they lose potential sales when they have to turn away customers because of a lack of inventory. Management accountants can support good inventory management when they are able to quantify these opportunity costs for decision makers. However, as can be seen in Exhibit 10-10, there are also other costs of inadequate inventory levels in the organization. For example, initiating an order with a wholesaler or manufacturer for the delivery of goods often requires a number of business processes, including counting inventory, preparing purchase orders, receiving and inspecting shipments of goods, and initiating payments for purchases. Most merchants have to initiate and pay for each of these steps every time they purchase inventory. Merchants who maintain low inventory levels will generally have to make more purchases, and pay for additional employee time, to replenish their stock.

Prices for most types of inventory increase with time. Some items are particularly susceptible to sudden price increases. Have you ever had the experience of awakening one morning to hear the morning newscast report of a sudden surge in automobile gasoline prices? When you go out to your car to discover the gas tank nearly empty, don't you wish you had filled the tank yesterday? One reason some merchants will purchase large amounts of inventory is to temporarily protect themselves from sudden increases in prices. Companies without similar foresight will experience greater out-of-pocket expenses if prices do increase. Companies that keep very low levels of inventory are most likely to have to pay for every price increase. In addition, these same companies are much more dependent on their suppliers to *always* meet their delivery commitments. If a supplier is late in making promised shipments, or delivers inventory that is damaged or of the wrong type, the supplier may miss making sales to some customers. Finally, merchants who regularly purchase large levels of inventory often enjoy price discounts from their suppliers. Merchants making smaller purchases should be aware of the opportunity cost related to missing these potential bulk purchase discounts.

FYI

How important is the Christmas buying season for a toy merchant? The 1995 annual report for **Toys Я Us, Inc.**, reports that approximately 48 percent of its sales occur in the months of November, December, and January.

Example of Inventory Management Costs

We'll use the fictitious example of two large retailers of children's toys, Kids N Toys, Inc., and Child's Delight, Inc., to illustrate the issues and costs involved in inventory management. As you might expect, the Christmas buying season is a big deal for a toy retailer. Management and buyers for these companies study trend reports and catalogs all year in order to properly plan their investments for December. Both companies have limited resources that can be invested in inventory for the holiday season. Given the necessary **lead time**, as well as the size of the investment, these decisions are absolutely critical to both companies. Once December has arrived, it becomes very difficult to make many adjustments to preplanned inventory types and levels.

lead time Generally, the time interval between initiating a request and finally fulfilling the request.

A wholesaler of children's dolls has announced the availability of a new doll for Christmas this year, the Burzee Doll. Based on the manufacturer's reputation, as well as the fact that the manufacturer of the doll intends to do a lot of promotional advertising, the wholesaler is confident that the Burzee Doll will sell very well this year. To help make planning decisions, each retailer has its management accountants prepare some forecasts on potential revenues and costs related to the issues listed in Exhibit 10-10. Based on the projections of its management accountants, Kids N Toys, Inc., decides to invest very heavily in the Burzee Doll and orders 50,000 dolls for delivery on November 1. Because of the size of its order, the wholesaler offers Kids N Toys a discount of $2 per doll. On the other hand, the management accountants' projections of revenues and costs at Child's Delight, Inc., are not as optimistic. As a result, Child's Delight orders only 5,000 dolls and pays the full wholesale price of $12 per doll. Both retailers follow the manufacturer's recommendation to set customer price at $30 per doll.

(STOP & THINK)

These two companies now have two very different levels of inventory in Burzee Dolls. With its very large inventory investment, what additional inventory costs are now a factor for Kids N Toys? What additional inventory costs is Child's Delight susceptible to with its relatively small inventory investment?

Exhibit 10-11 outlines all the Burzee Doll events that take place during the holiday season, as well as the resulting revenues and costs for the two companies. As it turns out, the Burzee Dolls are a real hit during the holiday buying season. Child's Delight keeps running out of inventory and must reorder dolls three times during the season. As you can see in Exhibit 10-11, each time Child's Delight reorders dolls, it is not hard for the management accountants to note the amount of inventory shrinkage. Occasionally, dolls are stolen, misplaced, or destroyed in the process of

EXHIBIT 10-11 Management Events in the Burzee Doll Inventory

Date	Event	Kids N Toys, Inc.	Child's Delight, Inc.
Nov. 1	Retailers prepare the Burzee Doll inventory.	Company buys 50,000 dolls at $10 per doll. Customer price is set at $30.	Company buys 5,000 dolls at $12 per doll. Customer price is set at $30.
30	Sales on the doll start increasing.	Company has sold 7,500 dolls.	Company has sold 4,950 dolls and is out of stock. Reorders another 5,000 dolls at $12 per doll.
Dec. 10	Sales on the doll are really strong.	Company has sold another 12,000 dolls.	Company has sold another 4,970 dolls and is out of stock again. Reorders another 5,000 dolls at $15 per doll (supplier has increased price).
20	Sales on the doll continue to be very strong.	Company has sold another 15,000 dolls.	Company has sold another 4,990 dolls and is out of stock again. Reorders another 5,000 dolls at $15 per doll.
31	Sales have nearly halted in the last few days.	Company has sold another 7,000 dolls.	Company has sold another 4,940 dolls and is out of stock again. Chooses not to reorder.
Jan. 15	Sales are nearly nonexistent.	Company has sold another 500 dolls and now puts dolls on sale at cost ($10).	Out of Burzee Doll business.
30	Sales pick up a little.	Company has sold another 2,000 dolls and now sells the remaining 4,400 usable dolls to a small merchant for $3 per doll.	Out of Burzee Doll business.
31	Evaluate inventory shrinkage.	Sold a total of 48,400 units, indicating that 1,600 units were lost due to shrinkage.	Sold a total of 19,850 units, indicating that 150 units were lost due to shrinkage.

moving, sorting, and stacking. On the other hand, Kids N Toys has dolls all over the store, making it difficult to know much about shrinkage without taking a very expensive inventory count. The management accountants at Kids N Toys elect to wait until all the inventory is sold before measuring inventory shrinkage.

By the end of December, Child's Delight has sold all of its dolls and elects not to place a fifth order. On the other hand, Kids N Toys still has a large number of dolls remaining. Since the buying craze for Burzee Dolls appears to be finished, Kids N Toys puts the dolls on sale at cost ($10 per doll) in mid-January. At the end of January, the store liquidates the remaining 4,400 dolls to another retailer at $3 per doll.

The Financial Accounting Report

When all Burzee Doll sales are totaled, Kids N Toys sold 48,400 dolls (indicating inventory shrinkage over the last three months of 1,600 dolls); Child's Delight sold 19,850 dolls (indicating inventory shrinkage of 150 dolls). Which of the two retailers did better with the Burzee Dolls? Exhibit 10-12 provides a financial accounting report based on what each company spent on inventory purchases and received in inventory sales. When you look at a gross margin of $793,200 for Kids N Toys, it appears that this company did a much better job selling Burzee Dolls than its competitor, Child's Delight, based on its gross margin of only $325,500.

EXHIBIT 10-12

Financial Accounting Report on the Burzee Doll Inventory

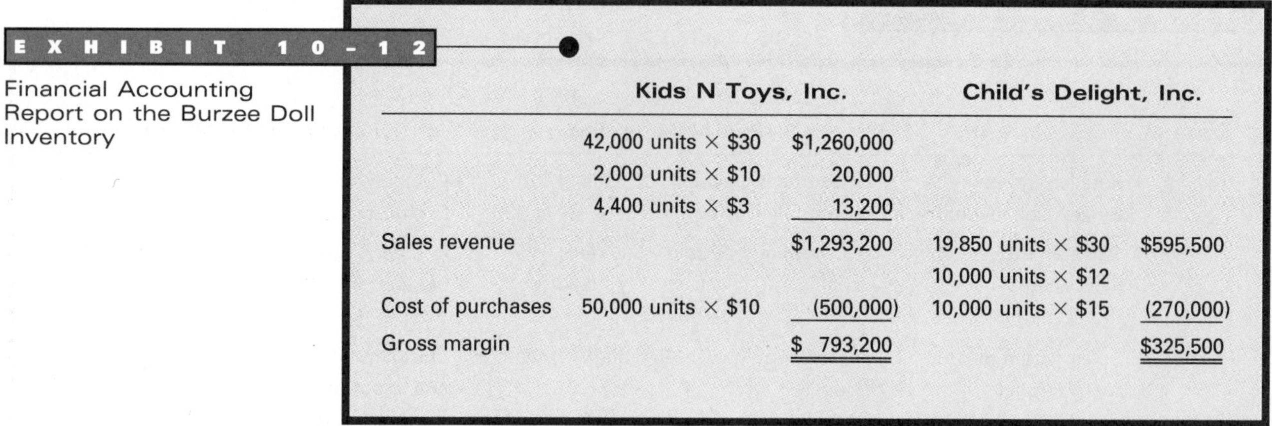

	Kids N Toys, Inc.		Child's Delight, Inc.	
	42,000 units × $30	$1,260,000		
	2,000 units × $10	20,000		
	4,400 units × $3	13,200		
Sales revenue		$1,293,200	19,850 units × $30	$595,500
			10,000 units × $12	
Cost of purchases	50,000 units × $10	(500,000)	10,000 units × $15	(270,000)
Gross margin		$ 793,200		$325,500

(STOP & THINK)

Is there anything wrong with using the financial accounting analysis presented in Exhibit 10-12 to evaluate management performance in these two companies? What costs may be missing?

Return on Investment (ROI)

The accounting numbers presented in Exhibit 10-12 are acceptable for financial reporting. The reporting of both revenues and costs of purchases follow all the requirements of GAAP. However, if you had money to invest in these companies, you might actually like Child's Delight's retail work on Burzee Dolls better than the work done by Kids N Toys. Think about the average size of the inventory investment each company maintained. Kids N Toys initially spent $500,000 to acquire 50,000 dolls. By the end of January, this inventory had been fully liquidated back into cash. Hence, Kids N Toys had quite a bit of cash tied up in Burzee Doll inventory! On average, how much cash did it have invested in this inventory during its selling period? On November 1, Kids N Toys had $500,000 in Burzee Doll inventory. On January 30, it had no Burzee Doll inventory. On average, Kids N Toys had about a $250,000 investment in inventory during its three-month selling period ($500,000 ÷ 2).[2]

How does Kids N Toys' average inventory investment compare to its competitor's investment? Rather than one large inventory purchase at the beginning of November, Child's Delight made four smaller investments as needed during November and December. The average initial investment amount was $67,500 [($60,000 + $60,000 + $75,000 + $75,000) ÷ 4]. On December 31, it had no Burzee Doll inventory. On average, then, Child's Delight had only about a $33,750 investment in inventory during its two-month selling period ($67,500 ÷ 2).

Obviously, the difference between the two companies' gross margins reported in Exhibit 10-12 is dramatic. However, the difference in Kids N Toys' average inventory investment of $250,000 versus the $33,750 average inventory investment at Child's Delight is also impressive. Remember from Chapter 9 that the DuPont approach to business recognizes that it is just as important to manage the money outflow for asset investment as it is to manage the money inflow from profits. This is the logic underlying Pierre du Pont and Donaldson Brown's ROI (return on investment) formula. Remember that the ROI formula has two parts (see Exhibit 9-2 on page 396 if you need a review):

$$\underset{\text{(Profit} \div \text{Revenue)}}{\text{Profit Margin}} \times \underset{\text{(Revenue} \div \text{Total assets)}}{\text{Asset Turnover}} = \text{ROI}$$

2. Be careful with this calculation! The fact that Kids N Toys held its doll inventory for three months (or two months, or four months) does not change the fact that average inventory for the company is $250,000. The formal calculation here is (Beginning balance + Ending balance) ÷ 2. Instead of having no inventory, what if Kids N Toys still had $50,000 worth of Burzee Dolls on January 30? The average inventory investment would then be $275,000 [($500,000 + $50,000) ÷ 2].

Based on an ROI-view of these two companies, which one has created the most revenue for each dollar invested in its Burzee Doll inventory asset? Answering this question is really a function of the "asset turnover" section of the ROI formula. Notice, however, that rather than *total* revenue and *total* assets, we are focusing only on Burzee Doll revenue and the value of the Burzee doll inventory asset. Actually this fact really doesn't present a problem. Rather than measuring how much total revenue is generated per dollar of total assets, we will simply measure how much *specific revenue is generated per dollar of a specific inventory item*. Hence, how many times does Kids N Toys turn over its Burzee Doll inventory compared to Child's Delight?

Kids N Toys: Revenue ÷ Average inventory
$1,293,200 ÷ $250,000 = 5.17

Child's Delight: Revenue ÷ Average inventory
$595,500 ÷ $33,750 = 17.64

Note that organizations have a limited amount of resources to invest. Using the ROI formula, the DuPont Company was able to wisely manage the task of maximizing the value of its investments by knowing where in the massive organization to invest its resources. Looking at the asset turnover numbers above, which company made the best use of limited purchasing dollars to manage the Burzee Doll inventory in order to create sales revenue?

These numbers provide a good lesson as you develop your analytical abilities. You need to be *very* careful in how you interpret these numbers. Asset turnover in the ROI formula is Revenue ÷ Total assets. When we measure the turnover of the Burzee Doll inventory, we are basically measuring stockturns. Typically, inventory turnover (i.e., stockturns) is measured using costs of goods sold rather than revenue. Either approach, however, may be appropriate as long as one approach is used consistently to evaluate different decision alternatives.[3] Further, we are considering only *part* of each company's income and assets. The information presented suggests that Child's Delight is the better company. This may not be true. Overall, Kids N Toys may be a much better managed company if it is able to keep total sales up and total costs down while employing an overall leaner investment in working capital (which includes cash, accounts receivable, and inventory), capital equipment, and buildings.

There are many important issues (as listed in Exhibit 10–10) involving the day-to-day effort to manage the Burzee Doll inventory. Even the ROI measures above do not provide Kids N Toys and Child's Delight management with the data necessary to address all issues as they *plan* for future inventory investments and *control* and *evaluate* the current inventory acquisition and selling process. This is where good management accounting can provide real value in management's effort to improve a merchandising operation. Exhibit 10–13 provides a management accounting view of the two companies' retail work with the Burzee Doll line of operations. Study both Exhibit 10–13 and Exhibit 10–10 for a moment. What information in Exhibit 10–13 could help a manager trying to work with some of the issues described in Exhibit 10–10?

3. Notice that using cost of goods sold to measure stockturns provides the same information as using revenue to measure asset turnover (Child's Delight is doing the best job of managing its inventory investments in Burzee Dolls).

Kids N Toys: Cost of goods sold ÷ Average inventory
$500,000 ÷ $250,000 = 2

Child's Delight: Cost of goods sold ÷ Average inventory
$270,000 ÷ $33,750 = 8

The Management Accounting Report on Kids N Toys' Net Operating Profit

net operating profit The difference between normal business sales and normal business expenses.

As you can see in Exhibit 10–13, we are identifying some additional out-of-pocket costs on the Burzee Doll operation for each company. Note that the gross margin for each company is the same as that calculated in the financial accounting report in Exhibit 10–12. However, we're approaching the calculation of gross margin differently, as well as identifying some other relevant costs to calculate **net operating profit** for each company. Net operating profit is useful in measuring the performance of these operations. Much more important, though, are the insights gained in the management accounting numbers used to calculate gross margin and net operating profit. These numbers, presented in Exhibit 10–13, are extremely useful for planning, controlling, and evaluating the Burzee Doll retail operations.

Let's work with Kids N Toys first. This company originally purchased 50,000 units with the intent of selling all of them for $30. Why didn't it then have $1,500,000 in revenue? This question cannot be answered using the financial accounting report in Exhibit 10–12, but the answer is obvious in the management accounting report in Exhibit 10–13. Somehow, 1,600 dolls that Kids N Toys planned to sell were broken, misplaced, or stolen. Based on an intended $30 selling price, this cost the company $48,000 in lost revenue. In addition, the market demand changed while Kids N Toys still had dolls to sell. As a result, the store had to sell some dolls for prices lower than the planned $30. Specifically, Kids N Toys reduced expected revenue by $40,000 when it sold 2,000 dolls for $10, and reduced expected revenue by another $118,800 when it sold 4,400 dolls for $3. This loss of market value is a risk that Kids N Toys management should consider when planning for next year's purchases. Further, management should also evaluate the information on inventory shrinkage to better control the inventory operation.

EXHIBIT 10-13

Management Accounting Report on the Burzee Doll Inventory

In addition to cost of purchases, note the following additional inventory costs:

- Average inventory overhead costs are $1.10 per unit per month.
- Average costs to initiate and receive a purchase order are $1,250 per event.

	Kids N Toys, Inc.		Child's Delight, Inc.	
Expected revenue	50,000 units × $30 standard price	$1,500,000	20,000 units × $30 standard price	$600,000
Shrinkage loss	1,600 units × $30	(48,000)	150 units × $30	(4,500)
Market loss	2,000 units × ($30 − $10) + 4,400 units × ($30 − $3)	(158,800)		(0)
Actual revenue		$1,293,200		$595,500
Purchase costs	50,000 units × $10 standard cost	(500,000)	20,000 units × $10 standard cost	(200,000)
Lost discount		(0)	20,000 units × $2 lost discount	(40,000)
Price increase		(0)	10,000 units × $3 price increase	(30,000)
Gross margin		$ 793,200		$325,500
Overhead costs	50,000 units ÷ 2 = 25,000 average inventory level × $1.10 × 3 months	(82,500)	5,000 units ÷ 2 = 2,500 average inventory level × $1.10 × 2 months	(5,500)
Order costs	1 order × $1,250	(1,250)	4 orders × $1,250	(5,000)
Net operating profit		$ 709,450		$315,000

Recall that the idea of activity-based costing (ABC) was introduced earlier in the chapter. Briefly, ABC is an approach to tracking the relationship between activities and costs and is generally used to better allocate manufacturing overhead costs to products. This concept can also be used to analyze overhead costs in merchandising organizations. Managing the Burzee Doll inventory requires some overhead costs. In this example, let's assume an ABC analysis reveals that the cost for storage, security, and other supervisory activities works out to be about $1.10 per doll per month. In addition, the effort to count inventory and prepare the purchase order, as well as to receive and pay for the inventory, requires about $1,250 in administrative costs each time inventory is purchased. As we've indicated previously, financial accounting generally uses only the direct cost of inventory purchases to measure gross margin. These overhead and purchasing costs related to managing the Burzee Doll inventory are typically combined with all other administrative costs to form Selling and General Administrative Expenses on the income statement. However, the management accounting report in Exhibit 10-13 has specifically identified and related these costs to the Burzee Doll inventory. This information allows management to see exactly how the Burzee Doll product line is contributing to Kids N Toys' overall net operating profit. Further, management can evaluate how having a lot of inventory leads to higher overhead costs. On the other hand, though, purchasing all these dolls at once saved Kids N Toys additional purchasing costs.

The Management Accounting Report on Child's Delight's Net Operating Profit

Now let's evaluate operations at Child's Delight using the management accounting report in Exhibit 10-13. During November and December, Child's Delight purchased a total of 20,000 units with the intent of selling all of them for $30. Similar to Kids N Toys, the difference between expected revenue and actual revenue is explained by the inventory shrinkage of 150 units. Compared to Kids N Toys, why does Child's Delight have a much lower percentage of dolls being broken, misplaced, or stolen? It seems reasonable to expect that Child's Delight found it much easier to maintain and keep track of its much smaller level of inventory. Can this shrinkage be further reduced? Child's Delight should carefully consider this question as it plans for the next buying season.

As noted in Exhibit 10-10, keeping the inventory levels low helps protect the organization against certain types of costs and risks. However, this can be a challenging balance since there are other costs that occur as a result of low inventory levels; Child's Delight incurred three of these costs. First, because Child's Delight made small inventory purchases, bulk discounts were unavailable to the company. The effect of losing these discounts, $40,000, was to pay $2 more per doll (20,000 dolls × $2). Second, each time Child's Delight ran out of inventory and had to reorder, it had to pay the current market rate. Given the high popularity of Burzee Dolls during the holiday buying spree, it is not surprising that the manufacturer raised the price. This cost was passed through the distributor to Child's Delight, who had to pay an additional $3 per doll for its last two shipments. Overall, this resulted in an additional $30,000 in cost (10,000 dolls × $3). Finally, each purchase event at Child's Delight adds to the management activities that must take place. If we assume that both companies have similar inventory acquisition activities (note, this is a *big* assumption), then Child's Delight must have $5,000 in purchase order costs (4 purchases × $1,250 activity costs). Again, though, low inventory levels have their advantage. Since Child's Delight orders only 5,000 dolls at a time, its inventory will range from 0 to 5,000 dolls. On average, it will generally have on hand 2,500 dolls. Based on an average monthly overhead rate of $1.10 per doll, selling Burzee Dolls led to relatively low overhead costs of $5,500 (again, assuming similar ABC costs for storage,

CAUTION

Remember that financial accounting reports are dictated by GAAP. However, management accounting reports differ across organizations. Hence, the format of the management accounting report in Exhibit 10-13 is not regulated by anyone! The management accountants for one particular retailer will customize the report to best support their own management processes of planning, controlling, and evaluating. The cost calculations displayed in Exhibit 10-13 are used by many, but not all, organizations in the merchandising industry.

security, and other supervisory activities for Child's Delight and Kids N Toys). Clearly, Child's Delight management should pay attention to all these numbers as it evaluates this year's operations and make plans for next year.

TO SUMMARIZE

Because wholesalers and retailers generally do not have to deal with raw materials or work in process, the process of accounting for inventory in a merchandising business is not nearly as complicated as it is in a manufacturing business. However, *managing* inventory costs is both complicated and critical for a merchant. Having too much inventory creates unnecessary overhead costs, financial holding costs, costs due to loss of market value, and costs due to inventory shrinkage. Not having enough inventory may result in unnecessary ordering costs and loss of bulk order discounts, as well as opportunity costs due to lost sales and increased supplier prices. While measuring some of these costs presents a challenge to management accountants, the information is very important to the processes of planning, controlling, and evaluating gross margins and net operating profits for individual product lines.

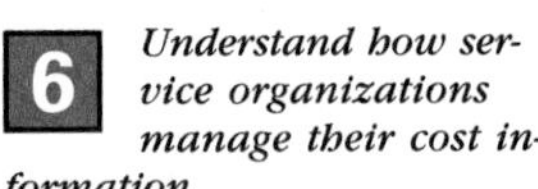

Understand how service organizations manage their cost information.

COST ACCUMULATION IN SERVICE ORGANIZATIONS

There are a number of accounting similarities between manufacturing and service organizations. The most important similarity is that both manufacturing and service organizations will have a significant amount of direct labor involved in producing their products. In addition, there are typically large amounts of overhead costs that are allocated to individual products. Similar to many manufacturers, service businesses will often allocate overhead on the basis of direct labor hours. One important difference is that manufacturers also have large amounts of raw materials costs to be managed while the materials included in the services sold by service companies are typically limited to insignificant amounts of supplies used in the service process.

FYI

Over the past 100 years, costs for raw materials in manufacturing firms have averaged nearly 50 percent of total product costs.

"Inventory" Flow and the Income Statement in Service Companies

Exhibit 10-14 summarizes the flow of costs for a service company. Comparing Exhibit 10-14 to Exhibit 10-9 illustrates the fact that accounting for service cost flows can be more complicated than accounting for merchandise inventory cost flows. In fact, the cost flow for service companies is quite similar to the manufacturing cost flow discussed earlier. Materials (e.g., supplies), labor, and overhead costs are all involved in, and should be assigned to, the process of creating and delivering a service product to the customer.

The overhead for service firms can involve nearly any kind of management costs—service firms generally do not distinguish between manufacturing and administrative overhead costs. Allocating overhead to service activities generally involves factoring an *overhead rate* into the billing rate used to charge customers. Think about all the services you buy and use. Often some type of a billing rate per hour or per event is used to determine the price you pay for the service. For example, accountants, lawyers, consultants, programmers, and repair shops often charge by the hour. When you get the bill, you understand that the *huge* rate per hour does not solely represent the wage or salary of the professional who provided a service to you. This rate has been enhanced (sometimes significantly!) in order to

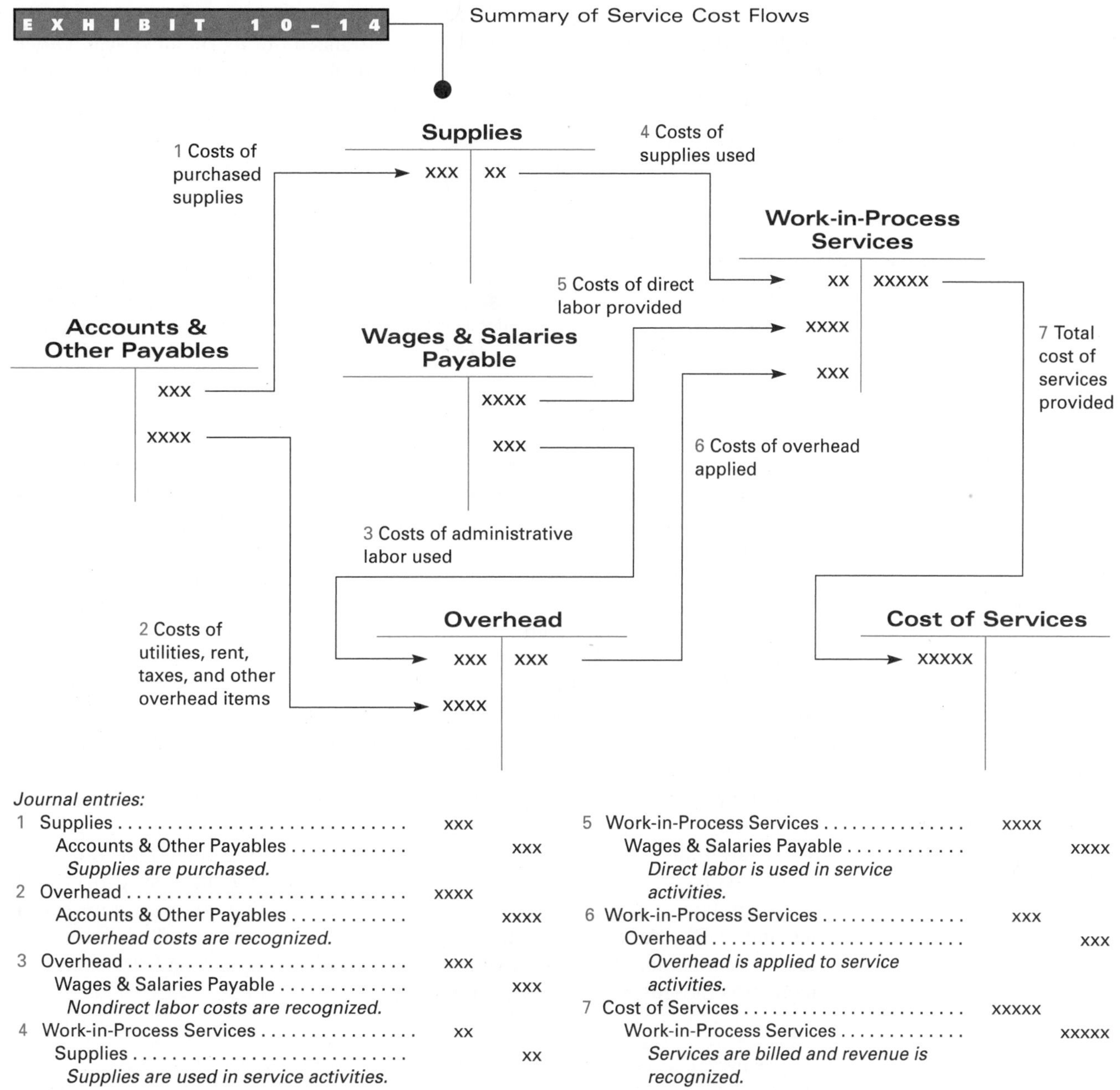

Journal entries:

		Debit	Credit
1	Supplies	xxx	
	Accounts & Other Payables		xxx
	Supplies are purchased.		
2	Overhead	xxxx	
	Accounts & Other Payables		xxxx
	Overhead costs are recognized.		
3	Overhead	xxx	
	Wages & Salaries Payable		xxx
	Nondirect labor costs are recognized.		
4	Work-in-Process Services	xx	
	Supplies		xx
	Supplies are used in service activities.		
5	Work-in-Process Services	xxxx	
	Wages & Salaries Payable		xxxx
	Direct labor is used in service activities.		
6	Work-in-Process Services	xxx	
	Overhead		xxx
	Overhead is applied to service activities.		
7	Cost of Services	xxxxx	
	Work-in-Process Services		xxxxx
	Services are billed and revenue is recognized.		

cover all the overhead and supplies costs necessary to support the work done by the service professional. Similarly, doctors, trainers, entertainers, and transportation companies usually charge by event. You understand that the doctor isn't paid the full $175 charge when he or she gives you a physical exam. Much of that amount goes to pay for the costs of staff, equipment, and building occupancy necessary to support the actual service provided by your doctor.

Assigning overhead costs to a service event follows a pattern very similar to that of manufacturing firms. Total overhead for the service organization is estimated for a period of time, generally a year. This estimated overhead is then divided by an appropriate activity measure. For an accountant, this activity measure may be billable hours. The measure for a bank could be the number of teller transactions or number of accounts. For a cable TV company, it could be the average number of accounts expected for the year. The activity measure for an electric company might be the expected number of kilowatts produced during the next year. Other examples of possible overhead rate calculations for several types of service companies are presented below.

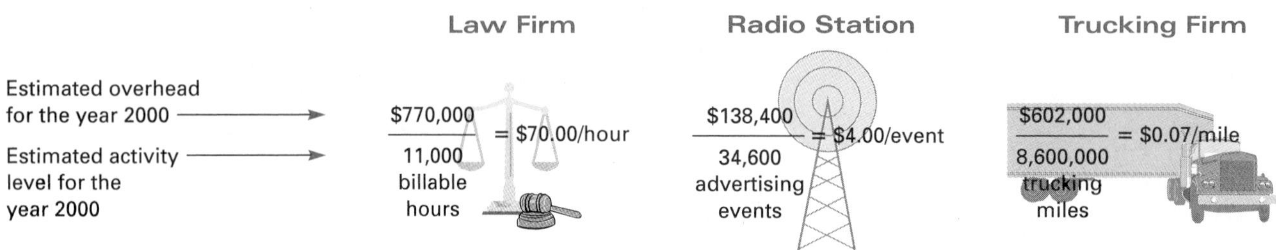

With a predetermined overhead rate, service companies are able to allocate overhead costs to service events as they occur. This method of allocating overhead helps managers control overhead costs, establish prices for services provided, and measure profit on each service event or contract. The overhead account for a service company is used in much the same manner as a manufacturing firm. As actual overhead costs are incurred, they are debited to the overhead account rather than being debited to an expense account. Then, as the appropriate overhead activities actually take place (e.g., consulting hours, teller transactions, and kilowatts), overhead costs are allocated to Work-in-Process Services (more about this account in the next section). As services are actually billed, these overhead costs are combined with the direct labor costs of the service professionals (if any) and any incidental costs of supplies and debited to Cost of Services (an account very similar to the cost of goods sold account used by manufacturers and merchants). At the end of the year (or any other time period relevant to the company), the total actual overhead costs are compared to the total allocated overhead costs to determine an over- or underapplied overhead amount. If overhead is overapplied, there will be a credit balance in the service company's overhead account. This balance means that too much overhead cost was allocated to the cost of service activities. The overapplied costs are removed (and the overhead account is closed) with the following entry:

Overhead	xxx	
Cost of Services		xxx

If overhead is underapplied, then there will be a debit balance in the overhead account and Cost of Services is adjusted (increased) by closing the overhead account with the following entry:

Cost of Services	xxx	
Overhead		xxx

Similar to manufacturing firms, the service company may choose to apportion the over- or underapplied overhead amount between Cost of Services and Work-in-Process Services. The question you might be asking at this point is, "Why would a service organization have a work-in-process inventory account?" Good question! We'll talk about this account in the next section.

Who Has Work-In-Process Inventory?

In manufacturing companies, accounting for work-in-process inventory is a significant part of the product cost accounting effort. Costs of resources used in the process of creating a product are attached to that product. At the end of an income period (e.g., a month, a quarter, or a year), there are typically a number of products still in process. There can be a significant amount of costs tied up in these in-process products. GAAP requires that these costs be capitalized (identified as assets) and assigned to the balance sheet until the products are actually sold. Only at the time that goods are sold and revenue is recognized can the related costs be charged to the income statement. The basic underlying accounting concept behind this approach is the all-important matching principle.

The logic for identifying work-in-process inventory as a balance sheet asset applies to both manufacturing and service businesses. Service companies typically earn revenue as the service is provided to the customer. However, at the end of an accounting period, there may be situations in which significant effort and resources have been invested in a service product that is not yet completed for the customer. As a result, revenue is not yet earned and the costs invested at this point should not be recognized as expenses. In other words, service companies have work in process.

Some examples of work in process that are likely to exist at the end of an accounting period for various types of service companies are:[4]

- Accounting/Legal—An audit that will take three months to complete is in its initial stage.
- Architectural/Engineering—The blueprints for a large construction project are only partially completed.
- Banking/Financial—The fieldwork has been completed and the lending documents are being finalized for a large loan that will be closed next month.
- Marketing/Advertising—Three weeks of effort have been expended on the development of a new advertising campaign that will not be ready for presentation to the client for another three weeks.
- Transportation—A large shipment of coal is being held in a Midwest freight yard en route to its shipping point on the East Coast.

In each of these examples, resources have been invested in creating a service that the customer has not yet received. As a result, work in process exists and should be recognized on the balance sheet. As you can see in Exhibit 10-14, as supplies and labor costs are directly invested in the process of creating a service for customers, these amounts are debited to Work-in-Process Services. As overhead costs such as utilities, rent, taxes, and support staff salaries are incurred, these costs are debited to the overhead account and are subsequently allocated to Work-in-Process Services using an overhead rate. When the service is completed and delivered to the customer, then the revenue earning process is complete and the service costs are transferred out of Work-in-Process Services and into Cost of Services.[5]

4. O.B. Martinson, *Cost Accounting in the Service Industry: A Critical Assessment* (Institute of Management Accountants: Montvale, NJ) 1989, pp. 47–48.

5. Some fairly large long-term service contracts are sometimes designed to allow the provider to bill and receive partial payments as the contract is completed. In these cases, as the revenue process is partially completed, some service costs can be transferred out of Work-in-Process Services and into Cost of Services. Learning about this type of accounting is reserved for more advanced accounting coursework.

TO SUMMARIZE

Costs flow through a service firm in a manner very similar to a manufacturing firm. Costs of supplies (usually insignificant in size) and direct labor (usually significant in size) accumulate in an account called Work-in-Process Services. This account performs much the same function as a work-in-process account in a manufacturing firm. In addition, overhead must often be applied to Work-in-Process Services as service activities take place. The process of applying overhead is typically done using a predetermined overhead application rate.

SUMMARY OF DIFFERENCES IN INCOME STATEMENT FORMATS

Now that we have worked through the flow of costs for manufacturing firms and for merchandising and service firms, let's review all three types of firms. Exhibit 10-15 compares the income statements for three fictitious firms. The exhibit also presents some balance sheet accounts for comparison. Let's carefully examine this exhibit to be sure you understand the differences and similarities in the accounting for manufacturing, service, and merchandising organizations.

As you can see, the income statement in Exhibit 10-15 follows a typical income statement format:

Sales revenue	$XXX,XXX
Costs of goods sold	(XX,XXX)
Gross margin	$ XX,XXX
Selling and general administrative expenses	(X,XXX)
Operating income	$ X,XXX

There are two important items you should note in Mason Tool's cost of goods sold calculation versus Brown Engineering's Cost of Services calculation. First of all, notice that Brown is using a rather insignificant amount of supplies to create their service product; especially when compared with Mason Tool, which is using a very significant amount of raw materials to create its tools. This difference underscores the fact that some supplies are often used in the process of creating and delivering a service product, but these costs are typically not a significant component of Cost of Services. Secondly, as with most service organizations, Brown Engineering does not hold finished service products for later sale to its customers. Only Mason Tool and Smith Office Supply, Inc., need to adjust cost of goods sold by the change in either finished goods inventory or merchandise inventory.

Smith Office Supply does not create the products it sells. As a result, the cost of goods sold calculation for a merchant requires only that Smith adjust the total amount of merchandise it purchased in 2000 by the change in its sold inventory account.

The income statement differences and similarities for the manufacturing, service, and merchandising firms are underscored in the balance sheet information presented at the bottom of Exhibit 10-15. As you can see, all three firms have accounts receivable, supplies inventory, and accounts payable accounts. Because Brown uses supplies directly in providing engineering services to its clients, this account is used in the cost of services calculation. On the other hand, cost of supplies for Mason Tool and Smith Office Supply are included in the overhead and administrative expenses accounts. In addition, you can see that Mason Tool has three inventory accounts; Smith Office Supply has one inventory account to record costs of goods until the goods are sold to customers. Brown does not have a raw materials inventory, finished goods inventory, or merchandise inventory account. However, its work-in-process services account acts much like Mason Tool's work-in-process inventory account and is similarly used to adjust the Cost of Services expense account in Brown's income statement.

EXHIBIT 10-15 Financial Statement Comparison: Manufacturing, Service, and Merchandising Firms

Income Statements for Different Types of Firms
For the Year Ended December 31, 2000

	Manufacturing Firm	Service Firm	Merchandising Firm
	Mason Tool Company	Brown Engineering, Inc.	Smith Office Supply, Inc.
Sales revenues	$4,000,000	$5,000,000	$2,500,000
Cost of goods sold/Cost of services:			
Cost of goods manufactured/Cost of services:			
Beginning raw materials/supplies inventory	$ 234,000	$ 2,300	
+ Purchases of raw materials/supplies	1,153,000	11,400	
Total raw materials/supplies available	$1,387,000	$ 13,700	
− Ending raw materials/supplies inventory	(205,000)	(1,800)	
Raw materials/supplies used	$1,182,000	$ 11,900	
+ Direct labor	445,000	1,890,000	
+ Manufacturing/service overhead	1,003,000	798,000	
Total manufacturing/service costs	$2,630,000	$2,699,900	
+ Beginning work in process	245,000	755,000	
− Ending work in process	(192,000)	(843,000)	
Cost of goods manufactured/Cost of services	$2,683,000	$2,611,900	
Underapplied overhead	307,000	22,100	
Adjusted cost of goods mfd./Cost of services	$2,990,000	$2,634,000	
Merchandise purchases			$1,713,000
+ Beginning finished goods/merchandise inventory	354,000		378,000
− Ending finished goods/merchandise inventory	(407,000)		356,000
Total cost of goods sold/Cost of services	$2,937,000		$1,735,000
Gross margin	$1,063,000	2,366,000	$ 765,000
Selling and general administrative expenses:			
Selling expenses	$ 256,000	$ 367,000	$ 406,000
Administrative expenses	474,000	1,003,000	188,000
Total selling and general administrative expenses	$ 730,000	$1,370,000	$ 594,000
Net operating income	$ 333,000	$ 996,000	$ 171,000

Selected Balance Sheet Information
For the Year Ended December 31, 2000

	Manufacturing Firm	Service Firm	Merchandising Firm
Accounts receivable	$744,000	$639,000	$ 39,000
Raw materials inventory	205,000		
Work-in-process inventory	192,000		
Work-in-process services		843,000	
Finished goods inventory	407,000		
Merchandise inventory			356,000
Supplies inventory	7,500	1,800	450
Accounts payable	298,000	106,000	489,000

REVIEW OF LEARNING OBJECTIVES

1 **Explain the flow of goods in a manufacturing firm.** In a manufacturing firm, employees work with raw materials to make finished goods to be sold to customers. When purchased, raw materials are stored in a raw materials warehouse; when completed, goods are stored in a finished goods warehouse. The costs of raw materials and direct labor (factory employees who work directly in production) are combined with manufacturing overhead costs as goods are being produced to make up the cost of finished goods.

2 **Understand the difficulty, yet importance, of having accurate product cost information.** It is relatively easy to associate direct materials and direct labor costs to specific products. However, it is very difficult, and often even arbitrary, to assign manufacturing costs to specific products. It is difficult to accurately determine the cost of products manufactured because manufacturing overhead costs have to be estimated before being incurred; they often cannot be easily assigned to units produced; and they are often "lumpy." Regardless of the difficulty, however, having accurate product cost information is critical for management to make good planning, control, and evaluation decisions.

3 **Identify and compare conventional product costing systems.** A major purpose of management accounting is to provide management with accurate cost information for pricing and other decision making. Job order costing and process costing are the two conventional ways of accumulating product costs. Job order costing is used for costing products that are custom-ordered or where the costs associated with each identifiable job (item or batch) can be recorded separately. Process costing is appropriate for firms in which identical products are mass-produced by passing them through a series of uniform production steps or processes. A problem with conventional product costing systems is that they are designed primarily to meet external financial reporting and tax requirements and are not adequate for management's cost information needs. This problem, combined with the modernizing of U.S. businesses, has led to new product costing methods, such as activity-based costing.

4 **Describe and apply job order costing procedures for a manufacturing firm.** The job cost sheet is the primary document used in a job order costing system. It is used to record direct materials, direct labor, and manufacturing overhead costs and to calculate unit costs. When materials are purchased by a manufacturing firm, their costs are recorded in a raw materials inventory account. As direct materials are used, costs are removed from this account and debited to Work-in-Process Inventory. Direct labor and manufacturing overhead costs are also debited to Work-in-Process Inventory. As units are completed, the costs in Work-in-Process Inventory are transferred to Finished Goods Inventory. When sold, the costs are transferred to Cost of Goods Sold. Whereas direct materials and direct labor costs assigned to products are actual costs, manufacturing overhead is assigned to products on the basis of some predetermined overhead rate. Expected manufacturing overhead costs for a period are estimated at the beginning of the period so that products can be costed as they are produced. As actual manufacturing overhead costs are incurred, they are debited to Manufacturing Overhead. This account is credited, and Work-in-Process Inventory is debited, as overhead costs are assigned to specific jobs on the basis of the predetermined rate. At the end of the period, any debit (underapplied) or credit (overapplied) balance in the manufacturing overhead account is either closed directly to Cost of Goods Sold or allocated among Cost of Goods Sold, Finished Goods Inventory, and Work-in-Process Inventory.

5 **Understand how merchants manage cost information in their organizations.** Because merchants basically purchase inventory in a finished state, the process of accounting for inventory in a merchandising business is not nearly as complicated as it is in a manufacturing business. There are a number of important issues associated with managing the inventory in order to maximize sales and minimize a variety of inventory costs. For example, having too much inventory creates unnecessary overhead costs, financial holding costs, costs due to loss of market value, and costs due to inventory shrinkage. Not having enough inventory may result in unnecessary ordering costs and loss of bulk order discounts, as well as opportunity costs due to lost sales and increased supplier prices. Measuring these costs allows management accountants to prepare detailed cost reports that support effective management of gross margins and net operating profits for individual product lines.

6 **Understand how service organizations manage their cost information.** There are a number of similarities between accounting for service organizations and manufacturing organizations. Materials, labor, and overhead costs accumulate in an account called Work-in-Process Services. This account performs much the same function as Work-in-Process Inventory in a manufacturing firm. In addition, overhead is applied to Work-in-Process Services as service

activities take place using a predetermined overhead application rate. When the firm has completed and delivered the contracted service, the relevant costs are transferred from Work-in-Process Services to Cost of Services (an account similar to the cost of goods sold account used by manufacturing and merchandising firms).

KEY TERMS AND CONCEPTS

cost driver 441
cost of goods manufactured schedule 448
holding costs 453
inventory shrinkage 453
job cost sheet 437
job order costing 436
lead time 454
manufacturing overhead rate 438
net operating profit 458
overapplied manufacturing overhead 446
predetermined overhead rate 440
process costing 436
underapplied manufacturing overhead 446

REVIEW PROBLEMS

Job Order Costing

Salem Manufacturing Company applies manufacturing overhead costs on the basis of direct materials costs. That is, for every dollar of direct materials costs, 60 cents of overhead is applied ($180,000 ÷ $300,000 = $0.60). The year 2000 estimates are:

Direct materials costs.	$300,000
Manufacturing overhead	180,000

Following are the Salem Manufacturing Company transactions for 2000: (Round entries to the nearest dollar.)

a. Purchased materials for cash, $500,000.
b. Issued $400,000 of materials to production (80 percent direct, 20 percent indirect).
c. Incurred direct labor costs of $250,000.
d. Incurred indirect labor costs of $70,000.
e. Incurred costs for administrative and sales salaries of $70,000 and $60,000, respectively.
f. Incurred manufacturing overhead costs: property taxes on manufacturing plant, $6,000; plant utilities, $14,000; insurance on plant and equipment, $3,000. (Assume these expenses have not yet been paid.)
g. Recorded depreciation on manufacturing plant and equipment of $18,000 and $6,000, respectively.
h. Applied manufacturing overhead.
i. Transferred 65 percent of Work-in-Process Inventory to Finished Goods Inventory. Beginning Work-in-Process Inventory was $13,000.
j. Sold 90 percent of finished goods on account at a markup of 60 percent of cost. There was no beginning inventory of finished goods.
k. Closed the balance in Manufacturing Overhead to Cost of Goods Sold.

Required: Prepare a journal entry for each transaction.

Solution

a.	Raw Materials Inventory	500,000	
	Cash.		500,000
	Purchased raw materials.		
b.	Manufacturing Overhead	80,000	
	Work-in-Process Inventory	320,000	
	Raw Materials Inventory		400,000
	Used raw materials in production.		
c.	Work-in-Process Inventory	250,000	
	Wages Payable (or Cash)		250,000
	Incurred direct labor costs.		

d.	Manufacturing Overhead	70,000	
	Wages Payable (or Cash)		70,000
	Incurred indirect labor costs.		
e.	Salaries Expense, Administrative	70,000	
	Salaries Expense, Sales	60,000	
	Salaries Payable (or Cash)		130,000
	Incurred sales and administrative salaries expense.		
f.	Manufacturing Overhead	23,000	
	Property Taxes Payable		6,000
	Utilities Payable		14,000
	Insurance Payable		3,000
	Incurred manufacturing overhead costs.		
g.	Manufacturing Overhead	24,000	
	Accumulated Depreciation—Plant		18,000
	Accumulated Depreciation—Equipment		6,000
	Recorded depreciation on plant and equipment.		
h.	Work-in-Process Inventory	192,000	
	Manufacturing Overhead		192,000
	Applied manufacturing overhead to Work-in-Process Inventory.		

The predetermined overhead rate is equal to estimated total manufacturing overhead divided by estimated direct materials costs ($180,000 ÷ $300,000), or 60 percent of direct materials costs. In this case, $192,000 ($320,000 × 0.60) is applied because direct materials costs were $320,000 ($400,000 × 0.80).

i.	Finished Goods Inventory	503,750	
	Work-in-Process Inventory		503,750*
	Transferred Work-in-Process Inventory to Finished Goods Inventory (0.65 × $775,000).		

*The amount transferred is determined as follows:

Work-in-Process Inventory

Beginning Balance	13,000		
(b)	320,000		
(c)	250,000		
(h)	192,000		
	775,000	(i)	503,750
Ending Balance	271,250		

j.	Accounts Receivable	725,400	
	Sales		725,400
	Cost of Goods Sold	453,375	
	Finished Goods Inventory		453,375
	Sold 90% of Finished Goods Inventory.		

Since Finished Goods Inventory is $503,750 (i), Cost of Goods Sold is $453,375 ($503,750 × 0.90). Since Finished Goods Inventory is marked up 60 percent, Sales is $725,400 ($453,375 × 1.6).

k.	Cost of Goods Sold	5,000	
	Manufacturing Overhead		5,000*
	Closed underapplied manufacturing overhead.		

*The amount of underapplied manufacturing overhead is determined as follows:

Manufacturing Overhead

Actual Overhead	(b)	80,000	(h)	192,000	Applied Overhead
	(d)	70,000			
	(f)	23,000			
	(g)	24,000			
	Balance	5,000			

Accounting for Overhead in a Service Business

Columbus & Hercules, a public accounting firm, is computing the overhead rates to use when billing customers and bidding on jobs. Columbus & Hercules provides the following estimates relating to overhead costs for the year 2000:

Utilities	$ 12,000
Rent	30,000
Equipment depreciation	22,000
Office supplies	20,000
Support staff salaries	120,000
Total estimated overhead costs	$204,000

In addition, Columbus & Hercules offers the following annual estimates (based on a 50-week work year) regarding the salaries and estimated hours associated with the professionals employed by the firm:

Position	Total Estimated Salaries	Total Estimated Billable Hours
Partners (2 × $100,000)	$200,000	4,400
Managers (3 × $70,000)	210,000	6,600
Seniors (6 × $50,000)	300,000	13,200
Staff auditors (10 × $25,000)	250,000	22,000

Columbus & Hercules computes a chargeable hourly rate for each position which is the sum of the following: (1) each position's hourly rate (based on salary), (2) an overhead rate, and (3) a markup of 20 percent of (1) and (2). The overhead rate allocates estimated overhead costs to each position, then relates the allocated costs to the hours expected to be worked by each position. Travel and materials costs are directly traceable and billed to each job.

Columbus & Hercules have no client projects in process on January 1, 2000. During January of 2000, Columbus & Hercules worked on several auditing and accounting jobs and incurred the following costs:

Jan. 1 Paid rent for January, $2,500.
4 Purchased office supplies on account, $1,200.
9 Paid $4,500 for payables from last year.
15 Paid office support salaries, $5,000.
15 Paid biweekly salaries of professionals: partners, $8,000; managers, $8,400; seniors, $12,000; staff, $10,000.
15 Applied overhead costs based on billable hours: partners, 170 hours; managers, 270 hours; seniors, 500 hours; staff, 900 hours.
18 Used office supplies totaling $800 to prepare client materials.
21 Purchased office supplies on account, $1,100.
25 Received and paid invoice from office supply store for purchase on January 4.
27 Billed clients for the following jobs using the computed hourly rate for each position:

	Job #1	Job #2
Partner	90 hours	80 hours
Manager	150 hours	140 hours
Senior	320 hours	200 hours
Staff	560 hours	400 hours

Jan. 27 Transferred costs from Work-in-Process Services to Cost of Services based on information from January 27.
31 Estimated utility costs for the month of January to be $1,000.
31 Paid office support salaries, $5,400.
31 Made an adjusting entry for the depreciation of office equipment, $1,900.
31 Paid biweekly salaries of professionals: partners, $8,000; managers, $8,400; seniors, $12,000; staff, $10,000.
31 Applied overhead costs based on billable hours: partners, 180 hours; managers, 280 hours; seniors, 525 hours; staff, 950 hours.

Required:

1. Compute the billing rate to be used for each position.
2. Provide the journal entries made by Columbus & Hercules for January.
3. Compute the ending balance in Work-in-Process Services.
4. Compute the ending balance in Overhead.

Solution

1. Billing rate

Overhead allocation rate: $204,000 ÷ $960,000 = $0.2125 per dollar of salary.

Position	Estimated Salaries	Preliminary Rate	Allocated Overhead	Hours	Overhead Rate per Hour
Partner	$200,000	$0.2125	$ 42,500	4,400	$9.66
Manager	210,000	0.2125	44,625	6,600	6.76
Senior	300,000	0.2125	63,750	13,200	4.83
Staff	250,000	0.2125	53,125	22,000	2.41
Total	$960,000		$204,000		

Billable Rate for Each Position

Position	Hourly Rate (1)	Overhead Rate (2)	Markup [(1) + (2)] × .20 = (3)	Billable Rate (1) + (2) + (3)
Partner	$45.45[1]	$9.66	$11.02	$66.13
Manager	31.82[2]	6.76	7.72	46.30
Senior	22.73[3]	4.83	5.51	33.07
Staff	11.36[4]	2.41	2.75	16.52

[1]$200,000 ÷ 4,400 hours = $45.45 per hour
[2]$210,000 ÷ 6,600 hours = $31.82 per hour
[3]$300,000 ÷ 13,200 hours = $22.73 per hour
[4]$250,000 ÷ 22,000 hours = $11.36 per hour

2. Journal entries

		Debit	Credit
Jan. 1	Overhead	2,500	
	Cash		2,500
	Paid rent for the month of January.		
4	Office Supplies	1,200	
	Accounts Payable		1,200
	Purchased office supplies on account.		

Date	Account	Debit	Credit
Jan. 9	Accounts Payable	4,500	
	Cash		4,500
	Paid accounts payable from prior period.		
15	Overhead	5,000	
	Cash		5,000
	Paid office support salaries.		
15	Work-in-Process Services	38,400	
	Cash		38,400
	Paid salaries of professionals.		

Partners	$ 8,000
Managers	8,400
Seniors	12,000
Staff	10,000
Total	$38,400

Date	Account	Debit	Credit
15	Work-in-Process Services	8,051	
	Overhead		8,051
	Allocated overhead based on billable hours.		

Partners—170 hours × $9.66	$1,642
Managers—270 hours × $6.76	1,825
Seniors—500 hours × $4.83	2,415
Staff—900 hours × $2.41	2,169
Total	$8,051

Date	Account	Debit	Credit
18	Work-in-Process Services	800	
	Office Supplies		800
	Used office supplies on behalf of clients.		
21	Office Supplies	1,100	
	Accounts Payable		1,100
	Purchased office supplies on account.		
25	Accounts Payable	1,200	
	Cash		1,200
	Paid for supplies purchased on Jan. 4.		
27	Accounts Receivable	57,724	
	Service Revenue		57,724
	Billed clients for Jobs #1 and #2.		

Partners—170 hours × $66.13	$11,242
Managers—290 hours × $46.30	13,427
Seniors—520 hours × $33.07	17,196
Staff—960 hours × $16.52	15,859
Total	$57,724

Date	Account	Debit	Credit
27	Cost of Services	48,107	
	Work-in-Process Services		48,107
	Transferred completed work in process to cost of services; comprised of each position's hourly rate and overhead rate.		

Partners—170 hours × ($45.45 + $9.66)	$ 9,369
Managers—290 hours × ($31.82 + $6.76)	11,188
Seniors—520 hours × ($22.73 + $4.83)	14,331
Staff—960 hours × ($11.36 + $2.41)	13,219
Total	$48,107

Date	Account	Debit	Credit
31	Overhead	1,000	
	Utilities Payable		1,000
	To record estimated utilities expense for the month.		

Jan. 31	Overhead	5,400	
	Cash		5,400
	Paid office support salaries.		
31	Overhead	1,900	
	Accumulated Depreciation—Office Equipment		1,900
	To record depreciation expense for the month.		
31	Work-in-Process Services	38,400	
	Cash		38,400
	Paid salaries of professionals.		

Partners	$ 8,000
Managers	8,400
Seniors	12,000
Staff	10,000
Total	$38,400

31	Work-in-Process Services	8,458	
	Overhead		8,458
	Allocated overhead based on billable hours.		

Partners—180 hours × $9.66	$1,739
Managers—280 hours × $6.76	1,893
Seniors—525 hours × $4.83	2,536
Staff—950 hours × $2.41	2,290
Total	$8,458

3. Ending balance in Work-in-Process Services

Work-in-Process Services

1/15	38,400	1/27	48,107
1/15	8,051		
1/18	800		
1/31	38,400		
1/31	8,458		
End. bal.	46,002		

4. Ending balance in Overhead

Overhead

1/1	2,500	1/15	8,051
1/15	5,000	1/31	8,458
1/31	1,000		
1/31	5,400		
1/31	1,900		
		End. bal.	709

DISCUSSION QUESTIONS

1. Why is it difficult to track the costs of manufactured products?
2. Why do managers need accurate product cost information?

3. For financial reporting, which costs are usually in-cluded as product costs in a manufacturing company?
4. Why should a firm know how much it costs to manufacture its products?
5. How can manufacturing companies improve quality while also reducing costs?
6. What is the major difference between job order costing and process costing?
7. What is the difference in accounting treatment for direct materials and indirect materials?
8. Why are actual manufacturing overhead costs not assigned directly to products as they are incurred?
9. What is the normal flow of costs in a job order costing system?
10. What are some common bases for applying manufacturing overhead costs to products?
11. Why might Manufacturing Overhead be referred to as a "clearing account"?
12. How does a firm dispose of over- or underapplied manufacturing overhead costs?
13. Should managers concentrate only on the costs of production (e.g., the cost of goods sold number), or are there other costs and factors they should also consider?
14. Name three problems associated with carrying too much inventory.
15. Name three problems associated with carrying too little inventory.
16. What is inventory shrinkage? Name three things that can cause inventory shrinkage.
17. How can the ROI formula be used to evaluate the management of inventory?
18. What is the principal "product cost" for a service company?
19. Which three costs go into the work-in-process services account for a service company? How does this account differ between service and manufacturing firms?

DISCUSSION CASES

CASE 10-1 PACKARD INC.

Packard Inc. produces and sells mousetraps. The cost of a mousetrap can be broken down as follows:

Direct materials	$0.23
Direct labor	0.09
Manufacturing overhead	0.12
Cost per trap	$0.44

The traps are then sold for 120% of cost, or $0.53 each. The manufacturing overhead is applied based on direct labor costs and was computed at the beginning of the year using the following estimates:

Estimated manufacturing overhead for the period	$540,000
Estimated direct labor costs	$405,000
Predetermined overhead rate (per direct labor dollar)	$1.33

During the year, several changes in the production process were made. The result is that expected overhead costs have been significantly reduced below the original estimate of $540,000. For the first six months of the year, overhead costs of $272,000 were actually incurred. For that same time period, actual direct labor costs were $204,000. For the last six months of the year, overhead costs are expected to be $225,000 and direct labor costs are expected to be $202,500.

1. What changes (if any) should be made in the predetermined manufacturing overhead rate for Packard Inc.?

2. Assuming that direct materials and direct labor costs will remain the same for the last six months of the year, determine the new cost of a single mousetrap.
3. Since the cost of producing mousetraps dropped during the second half of the year, Packard can reduce the price of its traps and still earn its 20 percent markup on cost. Should the company reduce the price of its mousetraps? What factors would affect your decision?

CASE 10-2

US MACDONALD CORPORATION

You work for US MacDonald Corporation (USMC), an airplane manufacturer. USMC makes airplanes for commercial airlines such as **United**, **American**, and **Delta**, and for the **U.S. Air Force**. Many parts are common to all planes made by USMC. The market for commercial planes is extremely competitive, with **General Dynamics**, **Lockheed**, and European manufacturer **AIRBUS** often bidding lower than your company. However, USMC's contract with the Air Force allows you to bill them at your cost plus a 9 percent profit.

Times have been tough lately for your company. In fact, if you can't find a way to increase profits, your company is considering laying off 5,000 employees.

A colleague has just presented you with an idea that he believes will increase profits. He suggests that instead of using direct labor hours to allocate overhead costs among airplanes, you should allocate costs on the basis of the number of each type of airplane made. Since you make far more, smaller, less expensive planes for the Air Force, more of the overhead costs will be allocated to those planes. This action will not only decrease your cost per unit on commercial planes (allowing you to be competitive in that market), but it will also increase your profits on Air Force planes, since the cost per plane will be higher.

You are not sure about your colleague's suggested action. You do know that your allocation base of direct labor hours is quite arbitrary and probably does not correspond well to the way overhead costs are consumed.

1. What is an appropriate allocation basis? Would adopting the suggestion be ethical?
2. Would you change your mind if you learned that competitors were allocating overhead on the basis of number of each type of plane made?
3. Is your action appropriate, from both a business and an ethical point of view, if direct labor hours is not an accurate allocation base?

CASE 10-3

SERVICE COST FLOWS

The CPA firm you work for has just been hired by Phillips Attorneys at Law to perform an audit. In the process of the audit, you notice that Phillips' accountant has been inconsistent in accounting for the company president's salary. You notice that sometimes he has accounted for the company president's salary as follows:

Overhead	20,000	
Salaries and Wages Payable		20,000
To record the company president's salary.		

Other times, the accountant has debited Salaries and Wages Expense instead of Overhead. When you confront the accountant about the inconsistency, he gets somewhat defensive and says that it doesn't matter which method is used because both methods result in an expense; net income will be the same either way.

1. Assuming that the company president's tasks are exclusively administrative, do you agree with the accountant? Why?
2. Which journal entry is correct? Why?

EXERCISES

EXERCISE 10-1
Manufacturing Costs

Springville Manufacturing Company uses a job order costing system. For Job #151, the production manager requisitioned $1,200 of materials and used 40 hours of direct labor at $18 per hour. Manufacturing overhead is applied on the basis of direct labor hours, using a predetermined overhead rate. At the beginning of the year, $800,000 of manufacturing overhead costs were estimated based on a forecast of 200,000 direct labor hours. Prepare the cost summary section of a job cost sheet for Job #151. (*Note:* You have to calculate the predetermined overhead rate.)

EXERCISE 10-2
Manufacturing Costs

The Make-It-Right Company manufactures special wheelchairs for handicapped athletes. The company uses a job order costing system. Partial data for a particular job include:

Direct materials	$450
Direct labor	375
Manufacturing overhead	?
Total cost	$?

The company allocates manufacturing overhead on the basis of direct labor hours. The estimated total manufacturing costs for the year are $750,000 and the total estimated direct labor hours are 150,000. Factory workers are paid $15 per hour.

1. Compute the predetermined manufacturing overhead rate.
2. What is the allocated manufacturing overhead cost and the total cost of the above referenced job?

EXERCISE 10-3
Predetermined Manufacturing Overhead Rates

Memphis Corporation uses a job order costing system. Thus, management must establish a predetermined overhead rate for applying manufacturing overhead. During the past three years, the following data have been accumulated:

	1998	1999	2000
Direct labor hours	40,000	52,000	65,000
Machine hours	80,000	65,000	45,000
Direct materials costs	$400,000	$250,000	$390,000
Total budgeted manufacturing overhead	$80,000	$65,000	$45,000

1. What would the predetermined overhead rate be for each of the three years, if based on: (a) direct labor hours, (b) machine hours, (c) direct materials costs?
2. **Interpretive Question:** Which allocation basis would you recommend be used in the future for applying manufacturing overhead? Why?

EXERCISE 10-4
Predetermined Manufacturing Overhead Rates

East Lake Corporation uses a job order costing system and applies manufacturing overhead using a predetermined overhead rate. The following data are available for the past two years.

	1999	2000
Direct labor hours	104,000	130,000
Direct materials costs	$500,000	$780,000
Machine hours	100,000	70,000
Total budgeted manufacturing overhead	$130,000	$90,000

1. Compute the predetermined overhead rate for each of the two years, based on: (a) direct labor hours, (b) direct materials costs, and (c) machine hours.
2. **Interpretive Question:** Which allocation basis would you recommend for applying manufacturing overhead? Why?

EXERCISE 10-5
Work-in-Process Analysis

Matt Jones, a recently hired internal auditor, is currently auditing the work-in-process inventory account. Matt has forgotten some basic cost accounting concepts and asks for your assistance. Identify the four types of transactions or events that affect the work-in-process inventory account in a job order costing system. Prepare and explain a sample journal entry for each type of transaction.

EXERCISE 10-6
Flow of Manufacturing Costs

Post the following cost data to the appropriate T-accounts to trace the flow of costs from the time they are incurred until the product is completed and sold. (Assume that purchases and expenses are credited to Cash or Accounts Payable.)

a.	Direct materials purchased	$ 60,000
b.	Direct materials used	50,000
c.	Indirect materials purchased	9,000
d.	Indirect materials used	7,000
e.	Wages payable, direct	60,000
f.	Wages payable, indirect	12,000
g.	Selling and administrative expenses	32,000
h.	Actual manufacturing overhead costs other than indirect materials and indirect labor	25,000
i.	Manufacturing overhead applied	40,000
j.	Work-in-process completed	120,000
k.	Finished goods sold	135,000

Raw Materials Inventory

Beg. Bal.	9,000	

Manufacturing Overhead

Work-in-Process Inventory

Beg. Bal.	30,000	

Finished Goods Inventory

Beg. Bal.	20,000	

Cash (Accounts Payable)

Wages Payable

Cost of Goods Sold

Selling and Administrative Expenses

EXERCISE 10-7
Applying Manufacturing Overhead

Newstar Company has four manufacturing subsidiaries: A, B, C, and D. Each subsidiary keeps a separate set of accounting records. Manufacturing cost forecasts for 2000 for each subsidiary are:

	Subsidiaries			
	A	B	C	D
Materials to be used (lbs.)	80,000	80,000	60,000	52,500
Direct labor hours	30,000	40,000	25,000	40,000
Direct labor costs	$12,000	$10,000	$3,750	$7,000
Machine hours	25,000	15,000	9,500	40,000
Manufacturing overhead	$30,000	$45,000	$20,000	$50,000

The predetermined overhead rates for each subsidiary are based on the following:

A: Machine hours
B: Direct labor costs
C: Materials to be used
D: Direct labor hours

1. Compute the predetermined overhead rate to be used in 2000 by each subsidiary.
2. If Subsidiary B actually had $8,000 of direct labor costs and $37,500 of manufacturing overhead, will overhead be over- or underapplied and by how much?
3. If Subsidiary C used 66,000 pounds of materials in 2000, what will be the applied manufacturing overhead?
4. **Interpretive Question:** Identify the two most commonly used methods to dispose of under- or overapplied manufacturing overhead. What is the major advantage of each method?

EXERCISE 10-8
Applying Manufacturing Overhead

Valtec Company has three manufacturing divisions: A, B, and C. Each division has its own job order costing system and forecasts the following manufacturing costs for the year 2000:

	Division		
	A	B	C
Materials to be used (lbs.)	120,000	100,000	80,000
Direct labor hours	45,000	60,000	25,000
Machine hours	40,000	25,000	15,000
Total budgeted manufacturing overhead	$50,000	$70,000	$45,000

The predetermined overhead rates for each division are based on the following:

A: Machine hours
B: Materials to be used
C: Direct labor hours

1. Compute the predetermined overhead rate to be used in 2000 by each division.
2. If Division A actually had 37,000 machine hours and $49,000 of manufacturing overhead, will overhead be over- or underapplied and by how much?
3. If Division B used 95,000 pounds of materials in 2000, what will be the applied manufacturing overhead?
4. **Interpretive Question:** Of the two commonly used methods to dispose of over- or underapplied manufacturing overhead, which method would you recommend and why?

EXERCISE 10-9
Assigning Manufacturing Costs to Jobs

Noah Manufacturing Company uses a job order costing system. All relevant information for Jobs #609 and #610, which were completed during June, is provided here. No other jobs were in process during the month of June.

	Job #609	Job #610
Direct materials cost	$5,000	$6,500
Direct labor cost	$3,900	$5,400
Direct labor hours on job	400	700
Units produced	500	875

A predetermined overhead rate of $6 per direct labor hour is used to apply manufacturing overhead costs to jobs. Actual manufacturing overhead for the month of June totaled $9,000. All completed products are delivered to customers immediately after completion, so costs are transferred directly to Cost of Goods Sold without going through Finished Goods Inventory.

1. How much manufacturing overhead will be assigned to each job completed during June?
2. Compute the total cost of each job.
3. Compute the unit cost for each job.
4. Compute the over- or underapplied manufacturing overhead for June.

5. Prepare the journal entries to transfer the cost of direct materials, direct labor, and manufacturing overhead to Work-in-Process Inventory, and to transfer the cost of completed jobs to Cost of Goods Sold. (Omit explanations.)
6. **Interpretive Question:** How would the company have computed its predetermined overhead rate of $6 per direct labor hour? Explain.

EXERCISE 10-10
Using Job Cost Sheets to Assign Manufacturing Costs to Jobs

Remington Company uses predetermined overhead rates in assigning manufacturing overhead costs to jobs. The rates are based on machine hours in the Machining Department and on direct labor hours in the Assembly Department. Estimated costs, machine hours, and direct labor hours for the year in each department are:

	Machining	Assembly
Direct labor cost	$64,000	$100,000
Manufacturing overhead	$90,000	$50,000
Direct labor hours	12,000	32,000
Machine hours	18,000	2,500

During the month of April, the job cost sheet for Job #402X included the following data for 50 completed units of product:

	Machining	Assembly
Direct materials cost	$400	$700
Direct labor cost	$650	$2,300
Direct labor hours	120	740
Machine hours	900	80

1. What predetermined overhead rates would be used by the company in assigning manufacturing overhead costs to Job #402X in machining and in assembly? (*Note:* You should round all rates you calculate to two decimal places.)
2. Using the overhead rates you calculated in (1), how much manufacturing overhead is applied to Job #402X?
3. What is the unit cost for Job #402X? (Round the unit cost to two decimal places.)
4. **Interpretive Question:** How is the total cost accumulated on the job cost sheet used?

EXERCISE 10-11
Analyzing Manufacturing Costs and a Cost of Goods Manufactured Schedule

The following T-accounts represent inventory costs as of December 31, 2000.

Raw Materials Inventory

Debit		Credit
Bal. 12/31/99	140,000	400,000
	350,000	
Bal. 12/31/00	90,000	

Finished Goods Inventory

Debit		Credit
Bal. 12/31/99	79,000	673,000
	700,000	
Bal. 12/31/00	106,000	

Work-in-Process Inventory

Debit		Credit
Bal. 12/31/99	25,000	700,000
	400,000	
	249,000	
	172,000	
Bal. 12/31/00	146,000	

Manufacturing Overhead

Debit	Credit
49,000	249,000
52,000	
60,000	
72,000	

1. Determine the direct labor costs for 2000.
2. Determine the cost of goods manufactured for 2000.
3. Determine the cost of goods sold for 2000.

4. Compute over- or underapplied manufacturing overhead for 2000.
5. Determine actual indirect manufacturing costs for 2000.

EXERCISE 10-12
Service Cost Flows

Xavier & Associates Law Firm estimated its total overhead costs for 2000 to be $1.8 million. It allocates overhead based on direct labor hours. Xavier employs a total of 11 attorneys, each working an average of 2,000 hours per year. The average annual salary for Xavier attorneys is $140,000, or approximately $70 per hour. Xavier attorneys worked a total of 23 hours and used $150 of supplies in doing work for Mr. Bailey, one of Xavier's clients.

1. What is Xavier's overhead rate?
2. Prepare the journal entry to record the overhead for the Bailey job.
3. Prepare the journal entry to record the cost of supplies for the Bailey job.
4. Prepare the journal entry to record the cost of labor for the Bailey job.

EXERCISE 10-13
Service Cost Flows

Pierce Engineers incurred the following costs in 2000:

Use of supplies for clients	$ 3,500
Utilities	8,000
Property taxes	12,000
Engineers' salaries	100,000
Support staff salaries	35,000
Applied overhead	50,000

Prepare the journal entries to account for the costs given. Close the overhead account to Work-in-Process Services.

EXERCISE 10-14
Predetermined Service Overhead Rates

The following data are available for Haul-It-Away Truckers:

	1999	2000
Budgeted direct labor hours	135,000	140,000
Planned number of moving jobs	300	310
Total miles to be driven	450,000	597,000
Total budgeted overhead	$900,000	$1,200,000

1. Compute the predetermined overhead rate for each of the two years, if based on: (a) direct labor hours, (b) number of moving jobs, and (c) total miles driven.
2. **Interpretive Question:** Which allocation basis would you recommend for applying overhead? Why?

EXERCISE 10-15
Applying Overhead

Lemon Schools teaches private drivers' education courses. It applies overhead based on instructor hours, i.e., direct labor hours. The following information was forecasted for 2000:

Direct labor	$360,000
Property tax on cars	$3,600
Supplies	$12,000
Rent	$24,000
Support staff salaries	$160,000
Instructor hours	24,000

1. Calculate the predetermined overhead rate for 2000.
2. If Lemon actually had 23,000 instructor hours and spent $170,000 on overhead, will overhead be under- or overapplied for 2000? By how much?

EXERCISE 10-16
Inventory Turnover

Both Dave and Kelly own auto parts stores. The following information is available for 1999 and 2000:

	Dave	Kelly
Gross margin		
1999	$150,000	$300,000
2000	130,000	350,000
Ending inventory		
1999	75,000	225,000
2000	55,000	255,000

1. Calculate each company's turnover for inventory for 2000.
2. Which owner manages its inventory better? Explain your answer.

EXERCISE 10-17
Service Costs

The following information is available for a particular job performed by Newland Business Consultants in 2000:

Direct labor	$4,000
Supplies	500
Overhead	???
Total cost	$???

Newland applies overhead on the basis of consulting hours, i.e., direct labor hours. The estimated total overhead costs for 2000 are $6.2 million, and the estimated total consulting hours are 150,000. Newland pays its consultants $40 per hour.

1. Compute the predetermined overhead rate.
2. What is the allocated overhead cost and the total cost of this particular job?

PROBLEMS

PROBLEM 10-1
Job Order Costing—Journal Entries

Following are transactions for Montigo Manufacturing Company. Assume that the company has no beginning Work-in-Process Inventory.

1. Montigo purchased $600,000 of raw materials, paying 10 percent down, with the remainder to be paid in 10 days.
2. $260,000 of materials was requisitioned by the production manager (90 percent for direct use and the remainder for indirect purposes).
3. The liability incurred in (1) was paid in full.
4. 24,000 hours of direct labor and 2,000 hours of indirect labor were incurred. (Assume an average hourly wage rate of $9.00 for both direct and indirect labor.)
5. The following salaries were paid:

Factory supervisor (a product cost)	$80,000
Administrative executives	70,000
Sales personnel	90,000

6. Rent and utilities for the building of $30,000 and $7,000, respectively, were paid. Three-fourths of these expenses are applicable to manufacturing and the remainder to administration.
7. Depreciation on factory equipment was $15,000.
8. Advertising costs for the year totaled $15,000.
9. Manufacturing overhead is applied at a rate of $6.90 per direct labor hour.
10. All but $35,000 of Work-in-Process Inventory was completed and transferred to Finished Goods Inventory.
11. The sales price of finished goods that were sold was 130 percent of manufacturing costs. Assume a perpetual inventory system and that all finished goods were sold.
12. Close over- or underapplied overhead directly to cost of goods sold.

Required: Prepare journal entries for the transactions.

PROBLEM 10-2
Accounting for Manufacturing Transactions—Journal Entries

Payson Company uses a job order costing system. The following is a partial list of the company's accounts. (*Note:* Additional accounts may be needed.)

Cash
Manufacturing Overhead
Sales
Cost of Goods Sold
Sales Commissions Expense
Administrative Expenses
Accounts Receivable
Commissions Payable

Required:

1. Prepare journal entries for each of the following transactions (omit explanations).
2. Prepare T-accounts and post the journal entries to the T-accounts. Transaction (a) has been completed as an example.
   a. Raw materials previously purchased on account were paid for in cash, $700.

Cash		Accounts Payable	
	(a) 700	(a) 700	

   b. Raw materials were purchased for $1,500 on account.
   c. Direct labor costs of $3,000 were recorded.
   d. Raw materials costing $1,100 were issued directly to production.
   e. Depreciation of $1,500 on manufacturing equipment was recorded. (Assume this is a product cost.)
   f. Property taxes payable of $2,600 were recorded, half to manufacturing and half to administration.
   g. Manufacturing overhead costs of $400 were applied to a job in process.
   h. Materials previously purchased on account were paid for in cash, $1,500.
   i. Sales commissions of $240 were recorded.
   j. Goods costing $2,700 were transferred from Work-in-Process Inventory to Finished Goods Inventory.
   k. Finished goods costing $2,300 were sold for $3,200 on credit, and the cost of goods sold was recorded.

PROBLEM 10-3
Manufacturing Cost Flows

Tremonton Corporation uses a job order costing system in its manufacturing operation. For the year 2000, Tremonton's predetermined overhead rate was 90 percent of direct labor costs. For September 2000, the company incurred the following costs:

Purchased raw materials on account	$140,000
Issued raw materials to manufacturing process	130,000
Incurred direct labor costs ($10 per hour × 15,000 hrs)	150,000
Actual manufacturing overhead costs	128,500
Cost of goods completed and sold	483,000

The company's inventories at the beginning of September 2000 were as follows:

Raw materials	$ 24,000
Work-in-process	115,000

The costs of all completed orders are transferred directly from Work-in-Process Inventory to Cost of Goods Sold.

Required:

1. Compute the following amounts.
   a. Work-in-Process Inventory balance at the end of September 2000.
   b. Over- or underapplied manufacturing overhead for the month of September.
2. Prepare journal entries to reflect the flow of costs into and out of Work-in-Process Inventory during September (omit explanations).

PROBLEM 10-4
Manufacturing Costs—Job Order Costing

The following data apply to the Newton and Alexander companies:

	Newton	Alexander
Raw materials inventory, January 1, 2000	(1) $____	$ 4,000
Raw materials purchased	21,000	(4) ____
Raw materials inventory, December 31, 2000	6,000	3,000
Manufacturing overhead (actual)	8,000	(5) ____
Manufacturing overhead (applied)	(2) ____	16,000
Selling and administrative expenses	14,000	25,000
Work-in-process inventory, January 1, 2000	(3) ____	20,000
Work-in-process inventory, December 31, 2000	16,000	22,000
Direct (raw) materials used in production	15,000	(6) ____
Direct labor costs	25,000	30,000
Cost of goods manufactured	49,000	55,000
Overapplied (or underapplied) manufacturing overhead	(2,000)	4,000

Required: Fill in the unknowns for the two cases. (*Hint:* Indirect materials are not used in either company.)

PROBLEM 10-5
Job Order Cost Flows Using T-Accounts

High Country Furniture Company manufactures custom furniture only and uses a job order costing system to accumulate costs. Actual direct materials and direct labor costs are accumulated for each job, but a predetermined overhead rate is used to apply manufacturing overhead costs to individual jobs. Manufacturing overhead is applied on the basis of direct labor hours. In computing a predetermined overhead rate, the controller estimated that manufacturing overhead costs for 2000 would be $80,000 and direct labor hours would be 20,000. The following information is available for the year 2000:

a. Direct materials purchased, $22,000.
b. Direct materials used in production, $19,500.
c. Wages and salaries paid for the year: direct labor (18,000 hours), $117,000; indirect labor, $12,000; sales and administrative salaries, $21,000.
d. Depreciation on machinery and equipment, $9,000.
e. Rent and utilities for building (75 percent factory), $16,000.
f. Miscellaneous manufacturing overhead, $51,500.
g. Advertising costs, $12,000.
h. Manufacturing overhead is applied to Work-in-Process Inventory.
i. Eighty percent of Work-in-Process Inventory was completed and transferred to Finished Goods Inventory.

Required:

1. Compute the predetermined overhead rate at which manufacturing overhead costs will be applied to jobs.
2. Set up T-accounts and post the transactions.
3. Compute the under- or overapplied manufacturing overhead. Prepare a journal entry to close Manufacturing Overhead and transfer the balance to Cost of Goods Sold.

PROBLEM 10-6
Applying Manufacturing Overhead

Pinegor Corporation has four independent manufacturing divisions. The following data apply to the divisions for the year ended December 31, 2000:

	A	B	C	D
Direct materials costs	$120,000	$140,000	$80,000	$65,000
Direct labor hours	40,000	30,000	24,000	14,000
Direct labor costs	$110,000	$65,000	$70,000	$42,000
Actual manufacturing overhead	$120,000	$60,000	$70,000	$16,500
Machine hours worked	20,000	6,000	14,000	8,000
Number of units produced	100,000	2,000	15,000	5,000
Predetermined overhead rate	90% of direct labor costs	57% of direct materials costs	$1.25 per direct labor hour	$2 per machine hour

Required:

1. For each of the four divisions, calculate:
   a. Applied manufacturing overhead.
   b. Over- or underapplied manufacturing overhead.
   c. Cost of goods manufactured, assuming no work-in-process inventories.
   d. Average cost per unit produced.
2. **Interpretive Question:** How would you recommend that the over- or underapplied manufacturing overhead be disposed of in each division? Why?

PROBLEM 10-7
Applying Manufacturing Overhead

Openshaw Manufacturing Company made the following estimates at the beginning of the year:

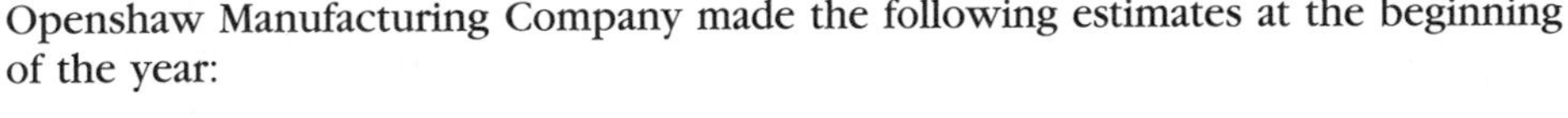

	Department G	Department H
Direct labor costs	$219,000	$166,980
Manufacturing overhead	$86,700	$153,340
Machine hours	17,000	12,500
Direct labor hours	30,000	22,000

Manufacturing overhead is applied on the basis of machine hours in Department G, and on the basis of direct labor hours in Department H. During the year, the following two jobs were completed:

	Job #29	
	Department G	Department H
Direct materials used	$16,000	$9,200
Direct labor costs	$18,250	$14,420
Direct labor hours	2,500	1,900
Machine hours	1,410	1,080

	Job #30	
	Department G	Department H
Direct materials used	$17,500	$8,100
Direct labor costs	$19,710	$13,920
Direct labor hours	2,700	1,800
Machine hours	1,530	1,020

Required:

1. Compute the predetermined overhead rate for each department.
2. Determine the amount of manufacturing overhead to be applied to each job.
3. Determine the total cost of each job.
4. Given that the actual manufacturing overhead costs for the year in Department G and H were $88,200 and $152,500, respectively; that the actual machine hours in Department G were 18,100; and that the direct labor hours in Department H were 21,600; compute the amount of over- or underapplied manufacturing overhead.
5. **Interpretive Question:** Why is the predetermined overhead rate based on estimated rather than actual information?

PROBLEM 10-8
Unifying Concepts: Job Order Costing and Cost of Goods Manufactured Schedule

Itsu Manufacturing Company applies manufacturing overhead on the basis of direct materials costs. The estimates for 2000 were:

Direct materials costs	$500,000
Manufacturing overhead	150,000

Following are the transactions of Itsu Manufacturing Company for 2000:

a. Raw materials purchased on account, $550,000.
b. Raw materials issued to production, 90 percent for direct use and 10 percent for indirect use, for a total of $350,000.
c. Direct labor costs, $500,000.
d. Indirect labor costs, $50,000.
e. Administrative and sales salaries, $140,000 and $90,000, respectively.
f. Utilities, $21,000; plant depreciation, $40,000; maintenance, $15,000; miscellaneous manufacturing overhead, $4,000. (These costs are allocated on the basis of plant floor space—administrative facilities, 500 square feet; manufacturing, 2,500 square feet; sales facilities, 1,000 square feet.)
g. Manufacturing equipment depreciation, $12,000.
h. Additional raw materials issued to production for direct use, $250,000.
i. Manufacturing overhead is applied.
j. Recorded factory foreman's salary, $54,000.
k. Ninety percent of existing Work-in-Process Inventory is transferred to Finished Goods Inventory. (Work-in-Process beginning inventory was $30,000.)
l. All finished goods are sold. (Assume no beginning or ending inventories. Sales are marked up 50 percent of cost.)
m. Over- or underapplied manufacturing overhead is closed to Cost of Goods Sold.

Required:

1. Prepare a journal entry for each of the transactions. (Assume that all manufacturing overhead is a product cost.)
2. Given the following beginning inventory amounts, prepare a cost of goods manufactured schedule for 2000 for Itsu Manufacturing Company. Assume all beginning and ending raw materials amounts include only direct materials.

Raw materials inventory......	$80,000
Work-in-process inventory	30,000
Finished goods inventory	-0-

3. **Interpretive Question:** Comparing actual manufacturing overhead with estimates for 2000, what would you recommend that Itsu Manufacturing Company estimate for manufacturing overhead costs in 2001?

PROBLEM 10-9

Unifying Concepts: Job Order Costing and Cost of Goods Manufactured Schedule

Delta Manufacturing Company applies manufacturing overhead to jobs on the basis of machine hours. The 2000 estimates of manufacturing overhead and machine hours were:

Manufacturing overhead	$1,825,000
Machine hours	365,000

Delta had the following transactions for October 2000:

a. Raw materials of $420,000 were purchased on account.
b. Raw materials of $400,000 were issued to production; 90 percent were direct materials and the balance were indirect materials.
c. Direct labor costs incurred, $300,000.
d. Indirect labor costs incurred, $55,000.
e. Selling, general, and administrative expenses incurred, $150,000.
f. Manufacturing overhead costs incurred:

Plant depreciation (factory)..	$25,000
Equipment depreciation (factory)	14,000
Utilities (factory)...	7,000
Factory maintenance	9,000
Factory taxes and insurance..	5,000
Miscellaneous manufacturing overhead	6,000

g. Machine hours for the month, 30,400.
h. Eighty-five percent of Work-in-Process Inventory was transferred to Finished Goods Inventory. Assume that beginning Work-in-Process Inventory amounted to $95,000.
i. *All* finished goods are sold. (There is no beginning or ending finished goods inventory.)
j. Over- or underapplied manufacturing overhead is charged to Cost of Goods Sold, and overhead accounts are closed.

Required:

1. Prepare journal entries to reflect the flow of costs incurred during October.
2. Assuming that beginning raw materials inventory was $16,000 and beginning work-in-process inventory was $95,000 (h), prepare a cost of goods manufactured schedule for October 2000.

PROBLEM 10-10
Analysis of Job Order Cost Flows

The following T-accounts represent manufacturing cost flows for Kanton Manufacturing Company for the year 2000.

Direct Materials Inventory

	Debit	Credit
1/1	70,000	250,000
	210,000	
12/31	30,000	

Work-in-Process Inventory

	Debit	Credit
1/1	80,000	700,000
	250,000	
	310,000	
	140,000	
12/31	80,000	

Finished Goods Inventory

	Debit	Credit
1/1	90,000	740,000
	700,000	
12/31	50,000	

Manufacturing Overhead

Debit	Credit
30,000	140,000
22,000	
16,000	
38,000	
40,000	

Required:

1. Compute the following amounts for 2000:
   a. Direct labor cost.
   b. Cost of goods manufactured.
   c. Cost of goods sold.
   d. Actual manufacturing overhead costs.
2. Prepare a cost of goods manufactured schedule for 2000.
3. Prepare a cost of goods sold schedule for 2000.
4. **Interpretive Question:** Explain how the over- or underapplied manufacturing overhead is usually accounted for.

PROBLEM 10-11
Unifying Concepts: Job Order Costing

Jones Custom Furniture Manufacturing, Inc., made the following estimates at the beginning of the year, 2000:

Budgeted direct labor costs	$300,000
Budgeted direct labor hours	20,000
Budgeted manufacturing overhead	$520,000

Jones applies manufacturing overhead to specific job orders on the basis of direct labor hours.

During the month of January, the following transactions occurred for Job #345, an order for 10 custom oak chairs, manufactured in the first week of January 2000:

Jan. 3 Requisitioned direct materials (lumber, fabric, paint), $876 (requisition #11042); put into production on Job #345.

3 Requisitioned indirect materials (glue, staples, sandpaper, and equipment grease), $154 (#11045), for use in manufacturing the 10 chairs for Job #345 and other subsequent jobs.

Jan. 7 Processed time card #6655 for Employee #214; 25 direct labor hours attributed to Job #345 at wage rate of $15 per hour.
7 Applied manufacturing overhead at the predetermined rate to Job #345, based on the actual direct labor hours.
7 Processed the manufacturing supervisor's weekly salary of $1,000. (This salary is considered indirect labor because the supervisor oversees all jobs in process and does not account for his time on a job-by-job basis.)
7 Job #345 was completed and transferred to the finished goods warehouse to await shipment to the customer.
9 The 10 oak chairs (Job #345) were shipped to the customer. The sales invoice reflects a sales price of $3,000 on account.

In addition to Job #345, Jones completed 47 other job orders in January, and had seven others in process at month-end. The following information summarizes additional manufacturing transactions for Jones for the month of January (not relating to Job #345).

a. Raw materials purchased on account, $102,675.
b. Requisitioned raw materials to specific job orders, $90,430; 80 percent direct materials, and the remainder indirect materials not directly attributable to any one specific job.
c. Incurred and paid direct labor wages totaled, $24,600; an average of $15 per hour for 1,640 total direct labor hours for January.
d. Applied manufacturing overhead at the predetermined rate to all jobs in progress on the basis of the actual direct labor hours incurred by job.
e. Incurred and paid supervisor salaries and other indirect manufacturing labor (e.g., maintenance labor) totaled, $7,000.
f. Incurred and paid the following costs associated with the manufacturing process and facility:

Factory rent	$ 7,600
Factory utilities	2,700
Insurance	1,200
Miscellaneous	1,900
	$13,400

g. Recorded depreciation of manufacturing equipment for the month, $5,500.
h. The cost of the 47 jobs completed during the month as summarized by their individual job cost sheets totaled $125,446.
i. Shipped all completed jobs to customers by month-end at a total sales price of $200,714 on account.
j. Incurred and paid selling and administrative costs (e.g., administrative salaries, sales commissions, office supplies, office rent, etc.), $46,514.

Required:

1. a. Calculate Jones' predetermined overhead rate for the year 2000.
   b. Prepare journal entries for the first seven transactions (relating to Job #345). Omit explanations.
   c. Create a job cost sheet, and record the accumulation of costs for Job #345. Determine the total cost of manufacturing the 10 oak chairs.
   d. Determine the gross margin earned on the 10 oak chairs.
2. Prepare the journal entries for transactions (a)–(j). Omit explanations.
3. Close Manufacturing Overhead to Cost of Goods Sold (include all transactions noted for Job #345).
4. Calculate Jones' total gross margin for January, including Job #345.
5. Calculate Jones' total operating income for January.
6. Determine the ending January balances in the raw materials, work-in-process inventory, and finished goods inventories (assume no beginning balances).

PROBLEM 10-12
Computing Overhead Rates and Client Billing in a Service Firm

Morgan Engineering Company employs three professional engineers, each having a different specialty. Don Corbin specializes in structural engineering; Bob Rouse, electrical engineering; and Bill Phillips, mechanical engineering. The firm expects to incur the following operating costs for 2000; travel and materials costs are billed separately to clients.

Office salaries and wages	$ 36,000
Office supplies	20,000
Utilities and telephone	15,400
Depreciation	16,200
Taxes and insurance	10,300
Miscellaneous expenses	2,100
Total estimated costs for 2000	$100,000

The salaries and billable hours of the three engineers are expected to be as follows:

	Expected Salary	Expected Hours
Corbin	$ 60,000	2,000
Rouse	48,000	1,760
Phillips	42,000	1,925
Total	$150,000	5,685

Required:

1. Compute the overhead cost rate that should be used for each of the engineers (based on the expected hours to be billed, with overhead cost rates varying in proportion to each engineer's compensation) to ensure that the total expected operating costs for 2000 will be recovered from clients. (*Hint:* Allocate total estimated overhead costs to each engineer based on relative salaries, then relate the allocated costs to the hours expected to be worked by each.)
2. Using the overhead cost rates determined in (1), determine the costs associated with the firm's work for Seaside Company with the following engineering services and related costs: Corbin, 100 hours; Rouse, 40 hours; Phillips, 10 hours; transportation and supplies costs, $1,600.

PROBLEM 10-13
Service Costing—Journal Entries

Following are transactions for Andersen Custodial Inc. Assume the company's beginning work-in-process services account balance is zero.

1. Purchased supplies costing $5,000 for cash.
2. Received and immediately paid a utility bill, $800.
3. Used supplies costing $3,000 in doing work for a customer.
4. 3,000 hours of direct labor and 1,500 hours of indirect labor were incurred and paid. The average hourly wage rate for both direct and indirect labor is $7.
5. Monthly rent payment was made, $2,000.
6. Applied overhead at $4.50 per direct labor hour.
7. Andersen bills its customers at a rate of $20 per direct labor hour. All work in process was moved to Cost of Services.
8. All under- or overapplied overhead is closed to Cost of Services.

Required: Prepare the journal entries for the above transactions.

PROBLEM 10-14
Service Costing—Journal Entries

Blake Accounting Services has the following transactions. Its beginning work-in-process services account balance is zero.

a. Purchased supplies costing $11,000 on account.
b. Paid property tax, $20,000.
c. Paid rent, $2,000; and utilities, $700.
d. Paid support staff salaries, $35,000.

e. Used supplies costing $9,000.
f. Paid direct labor salaries, $50,000. Average rate was $10 per hour.
g. Applied overhead at $11.50 per direct labor hour.
h. Transferred $100,000 from work in process to Cost of Services and billed customers for 4,500 hours of work. Blake bills its customers $40 per direct labor hour.
i. Closed under- or overapplied overhead to cost of services.

Required:

1. Prepare the journal entries for the above transactions.
2. Determine the ending balance in the work-in-process services account.

PROBLEM 10-15
Service Cost Flows

Tolman Company had the following balances at the beginning of 2000:

	Debit	Credit
Accounts receivable	$22,000	
Supplies	5,000	
Work-in-process services	15,000	
Accounts payable (related to supplies)		$ 3,500
Salaries and wages payable		35,000
Utilities payable		1,200
Rent payable		1,500

Tolman estimates that its total 2000 overhead will amount to $200,000. It allocates overhead based on direct labor hours. Tolman estimates that its total 2000 direct labor hours will be 50,000 hours. Because it produces monthly financial statements, Tolman makes adjusting entries at the end of each month. However, over- or underapplied overhead is not closed to Cost of Services until the end of the year.

During January 2000, Tolman had the following transactions:

Jan. 1 Paid rent. Tolman has a two-year, $72,000 lease. Rent is payable on the 1st of each month.
4 Paid all utilities payable from 1999.
5 Paid all salaries and wages payable from 1999. $23,000 was for direct labor; $12,000 was for indirect labor.
8 Paid for all supplies purchased in 1999.
10 Used supplies, $450.
19 Collected $15,000 from a customer for services performed and billed in December 1999.
23 Purchased supplies, $600.
25 Used supplies, $1,300.
31 Paid all employees for January labor. Total direct labor costs for the month of January were $25,000, direct labor hours, 4,000. Indirect labor costs were $15,000.
31 Tolman estimates its January utility expenses to be $1,000.
31 Tolman completed and billed jobs costing $40,000. The company billed customers $55,000.

Required:

1. Prepare all journal entries necessary for the month of January.
2. What is the balance in the work-in-process services account at the end of January?
3. Compute the balance in the overhead account on January 31.

Analyzing Real Company Information

International Case

Ethics Case

Writing Assignment

The Debate

Internet Search

Accounting is more than just doing textbook problems. These Competency Enhancement Opportunities provide practice in critical thinking, oral and written communication, research, teamwork, and consideration of ethical issues.

ANALYZING REAL COMPANY INFORMATION

• Analyzing 10-1 (Microsoft)

1. Is Microsoft a service business, a manufacturing business, or a merchandising business? Explain.
2. Microsoft's 1997 income statement (Appendix A) lists research and development expense of $1.925 billion for the year. The notes to the financial statements say that "research and development costs are expensed as incurred" in accordance with generally accepted accounting principles. Do you think that Microsoft treats R&D costs any differently in its internal accounting reports? Explain.
3. In its management's discussion and analysis (Appendix A), Microsoft describes its three primary sales channels. What are they?

• Analyzing 10-2 (Schrader Bellows)

Schrader Bellows is a division of Parker Hannifin Corporation. Schrader Bellows manufactures pneumatic control products. What's a pneumatic control device? You've got one sticking out from each of the tires on your car or bicycle. You probably call it an air valve stem. Pneumatic devices control air passing from one place to another and can be fairly complex in certain heavy industrial settings. Schrader Bellows was owned by Scoville, Inc. until the mid-1980s. However, serious cost problems at Schrader Bellows, coupled with a cash shortage within its parent company, led Scoville to sell Schrader Bellows to one of its primary competitors, Parker Hannifin Corporation. A few years after the acquisition, some interesting product cost data were made available on the manufacturing operations at Schrader Bellows.

Prior to being acquired by Parker Hannifin, Schrader Bellows had eight support departments providing service to four production departments that manufactured over 2,700 pneumatic control devices. Support departments in most large manufacturing organizations exist to provide all the necessary nonproduction activities in the plant, such as maintenance, supervision, security, etc. Costs of these support departments, prior to the Parker Hannifin acquisition, were essentially allocated to production departments using direct labor hours. In 1983, direct labor rates in the production departments ranged from $6.50 to $10.00 per hour. Additional 1983 cost data are provided at the top of the next page.

Example Cost Report on One Pneumatic Device (Valve #60073)

Product Cost Category	Unit Cost
Materials cost	$1.52
Labor cost	0.57
Overhead cost	3.08
Total cost	$5.17

Source: From Exhibit 9, p. 15, Standard Cost Report, Schrader Bellows (A).

Total Overhead Budget by Department

Production Departments	
Assembly	$ 337,000
Automatic Manufacturing	671,000
Plating	290,000
Packing	352,000
General Machining	955,000
Total	$2,605,000
Support Departments	
Work-in-Process Inventory Management	$ 104,000
Finished Goods Inventory Management	256,000
Production Control	564,000
Purchasing	357,000
Raw Materials Inventory Management	77,000
Setup Control	1,560,000
Quality Control	531,000
Manufacturing Engineering	1,243,000
Total	$4,692,000

Source: From Exhibit 10, p. 16, Schrader Bellows (A).

Source: Adapted from Robin Cooper, Schrader Bellows: A Strategic Cost Analysis, Software Module, 9-186-272. Boston: Harvard Business School, 1986. Copyright © 1986 by the President and Fellows of Harvard College. Reprinted by permission.

1. Look at the cost breakdown on Valve #60073. What do you notice about the ratio between the three categories of product costs? What does this suggest about the total product costs at Schrader Bellows?

Try to approximate the total costs of direct materials and direct labor at Schrader Bellows.

2. Look at the total overhead budget by departments. What is important about these numbers?

• Analyzing 10-3 (Pump, Inc.)

Acquiring management accounting data on real companies can be a challenge, since this information is generally highly proprietary and of significant competitive value. The cost data below are for a medium-sized family-owned pump manufacturing business located in the Midwest. (This business chooses to remain anonymous in order to keep its competitors from using these data to compete against them.) We'll simply refer to this company as Pump, Inc.

Pump, Inc., had reorganized much of its production into manufacturing "cells": self-supervising work centers that produce complete products. The cell program was initiated because of a strategic decision (with no management accounting data to support it) to improve customer service. The financial impact of the program was unclear; the operational causes and the financial effects were murky. As a result, the management team at Pump, Inc., was having a difficult time evaluating the effects of its strategic decision to change *most* of the company to manufacturing cells. (Some of the production process continued to be organized as a typical production line, similar to what is demonstrated in the chapter.) The current year's cost data are presented below in the standard format typically used by the management accountant for Pump, Inc.

Typical Cost Data Format

Cost Category	Cost	Percent of Cost
Direct materials	$433,966	54.55%
Direct labor	96,990	12.19%
Manufacturing overhead	264,583	33.26%
Total costs	$795,539	100.00%

The management team, however, had a difficult time using the cost data in the typical format to effectively control and evaluate their reorganizational decision. The management accountant was asked to try to reformat the data in order to make it more useful for the management team. After some analysis, the accountant decided to provide more detail by breaking down Manufacturing Overhead into subcategories organized by function: Indirect Materials, Indirect Labor, Factory Support, Occupancy Costs, and Non-Factory Support. The accountant also realized that she could divide all costs into two additional categories: People Costs (represent costs spent to pay for wages and salaries) and Purchased Costs (represent costs spent to pay for materials, supplies, and services acquired from outside agencies). The new report format is presented at the top of the next page.

New Cost Data Format

Cost Category	People Costs	Purchased Costs	Total Cost
Direct materials		$433,966	$433,966
Indirect materials		9,460	9,460
Direct labor	$ 96,990		96,990
Indirect labor (production line supervision)	29,100		29,100
Factory support (material handling, equipment depreciation, utilities, expediting, engineering, etc.)	80,953	71,310	152,263
Occupancy costs (rents, taxes, maintenance, etc.)	15,180	32,550	47,730
Non-factory support (cost accounting, personnel, etc.)	23,390	2,640	26,030
Total costs	$245,613	$549,926	$795,539

Source: Adapted from J.S. McGroarty and C.T. Horngren, "Functional Costing for Better Teamwork and Decision Support," *Journal of Cost Management,* Winter 1993, pp. 24–36. Reprinted with permission.

Consider the two reports on cost data for Pump, Inc.

1. Do you think the new report format provides any additional information value for controlling and evaluating the decision to change most of production process into manufacturing cells?
2. What costs do you think the management team at Pump, Inc., should pay careful attention to in its effort to better control costs in the production plant?
3. Most importantly, if you were on the management team at Pump, Inc., what *additional* data would you like to see the management accountant provide?

INTERNATIONAL CASE

• Andersen Worldwide

Andersen Worldwide is the parent company for two business units—**Arthur Andersen** and **Andersen Consulting**. Total revenues for the company were $11.3 billion for the year ended August 31, 1997. Andersen Worldwide has offices in 78 countries, and nearly half of its revenues are generated outside of North and South America.

Andersen Worldwide describes its two business units as follows:

- "Arthur Andersen is a global multidisciplinary professional services firm that helps its clients improve their business performance." (This is the unit that performs audits of external financial statements.)
- "Andersen Consulting is a global management and technology consulting organization whose mission is to help its clients change to be more successful."

1. What does Andersen Worldwide sell?
2. Arthur Andersen has an office in Quito, Ecuador. What type of company operating in Ecuador would hire Arthur Andersen or Andersen Consulting instead of a local Ecuadorian professional services firm?

3. Review the chapter discussion of cost information for service companies. What costs would be important to Arthur Andersen in deciding how much to bid on a consulting contract for a potential new client?

ETHICS CASE

• State Home Builders Inc.

You have recently been hired as an accountant for the largest residential construction company in the state. Your primary responsibility is to track costs for each home being constructed. Tracking the costs for direct materials and direct labor is relatively straightforward. Each home under construction has a job cost sheet. Materials requisitioned for each home site are carefully tracked, and the construction workers are very careful about assigning their time to the homes they work on.

Accounting for manufacturing overhead costs, on the other hand, presents quite a problem. In the past, overhead has been allocated on the basis of direct labor hours. As a result, since larger houses require more workers, those houses have been allocated a larger share of the overhead.

Your company was recently selected by the state to build a number of low-income housing complexes. The state has agreed to an arrangement whereby they will pay your costs plus a 10 percent profit. Construction of these low-income housing units will be relatively simple and will not require a great deal of materials or labor, compared to the average house the company builds.

At a meeting following the granting by the state of the construction contract, the production foreman proposes the following idea:

> Since the state has agreed to pay our costs plus ten percent, the higher the costs on the project, the more money we make. What we need to do is to funnel as much of our costs as possible to this low-income housing project. Now I don't want anyone to think I am proposing something unethical. I am not saying that we should charge the state for fictitious costs. What I am saying is that we should allocate as much overhead as possible to the low-income project. Therefore, I propose that we allocate overhead on a per-house basis with each house, regardless of size, being allocated the same amount of overhead.

You have analyzed the activities that drive overhead costs and have found that bigger houses, in addition to requiring more direct materials and direct labor, require more inspections, more supervision, etc. You can see that most in attendance at the meeting are being persuaded by the production foreman's idea. You slowly raise your hand. It takes about ten seconds before all the voices quiet. You look around the table and see ten of your colleagues staring at you. You open your mouth and . . .

1. What would you do in this situation? Is the overhead allocation method being proposed by the production foreman illegal? Is it unethical?
2. Suppose you argue that overhead should continue to be allocated on the basis of direct labor hours. After hearing your points, the group votes to go with the production foreman and allocate the overhead on a per-house basis. What would you do next?

WRITING ASSIGNMENT

• Consultant's report for a small-town supermarket

You have been hired as a financial consultant by a small-town supermarket. The supermarket is considering building a new, larger store and requests your expertise in evaluating the feasibility of the project. You know that the construction of the store will cost $3,000,000. You also know that the average gross margin percentage in supermarkets is 27 percent.

Draft a one-page memo to the owner of the supermarket requesting additional cost information to be used in your analysis. The store owner is a clever businessperson but has no experience in using quantitative data in making decisions. Therefore, your memo must be very specific in identifying the information that you will need to perform a useful analysis.

THE DEBATE

• When does a direct materials cost turn into an indirect cost (e.g., manufacturing overhead)?

Consider your automobile. What costs would be considered direct materials? What costs would be considered indirect materials? Are the fender panels direct or indirect materials? Are the rivets that connect the fender to the frame direct or indirect materials? Are the headlights direct or indirect materials? Are the screws that hold the headlights in place direct or indirect materials? In light of the intense price competition that takes place in the automobile industry, these are important cost questions: direct materials are assigned to a specific automobile (or automobile model), while indirect materials are gathered together in the pool of manufacturing overhead costs and generally allocated across all types of automobiles in the manufacturing plant.

Divide your group into two teams.

- One team represents: "Rivets and screws should be treated as direct costs." Prepare a two-minute oral argument supporting this view. Be careful that you don't make too many quick assumptions. Tracking direct materials costs to specific product units or product lines can be a very expensive process in a complex manufacturing organization.
- The other team represents: "Rivets and screws should be treated as indirect costs." Prepare a two-minute oral argument supporting this view. You must be careful that you don't make too many quick assumptions. Before you say that rivets and screws are indirect because their costs are small, consider that the Big Three automakers spend tens of millions of dollars each year on rivets and screws.

INTERNET SEARCH

• Wal-Mart

Access **Wal-Mart**'s Web site at wal-mart.com. Sometimes Web addresses change, so if this address doesn't work, access the Web site for this textbook (stice.swcollege.com) for an updated link.

Once you've gained access to the site, answer the following questions.

1. Use Wal-Mart's Store Locator to find the store nearest you.
2. What is Wal-Mart's Retail Link™?
3. Describe Wal-Mart's "Support American Made" program.
4. Wal-Mart's first non-U.S. store was opened in December 1991. Where? How many Wal-Mart stores are located in China?

CHAPTER

11 ANALYZING COST-VOLUME-PROFIT RELATIONSHIPS

SETTING THE STAGE

Recently, a profitable two-plant manufacturing company (that wishes to remain anonymous) built a new manufacturing facility less than one mile from its largest operating facility. This new facility provided no new features; it was built solely to provide additional manufacturing capacity. The company was expert in the design and manufacture of its products and, with the new facility coming on-line, would have the capacity to make and sell more of its products.

As the firm's management considered the new facility, all involved parties got caught up in the excitement of the new plant. Executive management wanted to be "a bigger player in the industry" and believed that the new plant was its key to being one; marketing said that the company easily could sell the "new capacity"; operations suggested that the new capacity would help the firm run more efficiently and facilitate manufacturing flow, thereby causing costs per unit to drop dramatically; and finance approved capital appropriations based on the most favorable scenarios provided by everyone else.

What actually happened to this company was that fixed costs tripled while sales increased marginally, by about 30 percent. Profits turned quickly into losses, inventory increased, and over time the stock price fell to less than one-fourth its pre-new facility level. In reality, the company had more than enough capacity in its pre-existing facility to manufacture 25–30 percent more product; and indeed could have done so without incurring any additional fixed costs. As in so many cases, the data were available to all concerned, but the ability to analyze, interpret, and then act upon that data was missing or, worse, squandered.

Source: John M. Brausch and Thomas C. Taylor, "Who Is Accounting For The Cost of Capacity?" *Management Accounting,* February 1997, p. 44.

LEARNING OBJECTIVES

After studying this chapter, you should be able to:

1. *Understand the key factors involved in cost-volume-profit (CVP) analysis and why CVP is such an important tool in management decision making.*
2. *Explain and analyze the basic cost behavior patterns—variable and fixed.*
3. *Describe the behavior patterns of mixed costs and stepped costs.*
4. *Analyze mixed costs using the scattergraph and high-low methods.*
5. *Analyze CVP relationships using the contribution margin, equation, and graphic approaches.*
6. *Describe potential changes in CVP variables and the effects these changes have on company profitability; identify the limiting assumptions of CVP analysis.*
7. *Explain the effects of sales mix on profitability.*
8. *Explain the issues of quality and time relative to CVP decisions.*

In Chapters 9 and 10, we discussed the costing of products and services in manufacturing, merchandising, and service companies. To review, some of those costs, such as direct materials and direct labor costs in a manufacturing firm, were costs that varied directly with the number of products or services produced. Other costs, such as some manufacturing overhead costs in a manufacturing firm, could not be as easily traced to products. Costs that vary proportionately with the level of products produced or services offered are variable costs, while costs that do not vary in total with changes in the level of production are fixed costs. In order to make decisions about the appropriate level of production and spending, you must learn more about the nature of various costs, including variable costs, fixed costs, and costs with both variable and fixed elements. You must learn how these costs change with changes in level of activity.

In this chapter, you will learn how to analyze relationships between variable costs, fixed costs, and revenues. You will learn that a key factor in making operating decisions is understanding ***cost behavior****—how costs change in relation to changes in activity level, such as number of patients in a hospital. An understanding of how costs behave in relation to levels of activity helps managers predict the effects of their decisions on future performance.*

cost behavior The way in which a cost is affected by changes in activity levels.

You will also use the knowledge of cost behavior patterns to analyze the kinds of decisions facing companies like the one in the opening scenario. You will learn, for example, to make calculations that will determine how profits will change in relation to changes in sales volume, fixed costs, and variable costs. The techniques for studying these relationships are referred to collectively as ***cost-volume-profit (CVP) analysis****. While cost-volume-profit analysis is often helpful in controlling operations and evaluating performance, it is critical in helping management plan future operations. Thus, we will be primarily focusing on planning. Since the techniques we discuss are equally applicable to all types of firms, we will use examples and have assignments affecting manufacturing, merchandising, and service entities. While the focus will be primarily on examining the financial implications of cost-volume-profit decisions, we will also pay attention to the effects these decisions have on quality and time issues as well.*

cost-volume-profit (CVP) analysis Techniques for determining how changes in revenues, costs, and level of activity affect the profitability of an organization.

1 *Understand the key factors involved in cost-volume-profit (CVP) analysis and why CVP is such an important tool in management decision making.*

UNDERSTANDING WHY COST-VOLUME-PROFIT (CVP) ANALYSIS IS IMPORTANT

Management must make many critical operating decisions that affect a firm's profitability. With respect to planning, management is often interested in what will be the impact on profitability if a particular action is taken. CVP analysis can help managers assess that impact. A sample of questions that can be answered with CVP analysis include:

1. What is the effect on profits if the selling price is increased 10 percent and the number of units sold declines 2 percent?
2. What is the effect on profits if the selling price is decreased 5 percent and the number of units sold increases 10 percent?
3. How many units must be sold to break even on a particular product if fixed costs are reduced by 10 percent?
4. How much sales revenue is needed to earn a pretax profit equal to $500,000?
5. What is the effect on profits if the advertising budget is increased $100,000 and the number of units sold increases by 3 percent?
6. What is the effect on profits if product line A is discontinued and product line B sales are increased 25 percent?

FYI

Obviously, management must consider quality and speed of production, as well as costs and selling prices when making decisions such as these. For example, in question 3, reducing fixed costs will require fewer goods to break even, but if it lowers quality or slows the speed of production, it may be a poor decision.

It should now be clear that CVP analysis involves studying the interrelationships between revenues, costs, level of activity, and profits. More specifically, the key factors involved in CVP analysis include:

1. The revenues derived from the prices charged for products and services.
2. The fixed and variable costs associated with products and services.
3. The level of activity as measured by sales volume.
4. The mix of products sold or services provided.
5. The effects making changes in costs and prices has on speed of production and on quality of goods and services.
6. The profits that result from the various combinations of the other factors.

In this chapter we will focus primarily on the first four factors, all of which relate to costs and revenues. However, quality of products and services and speed of production will also be considered. By understanding the relationships involved in CVP analysis, managers are better able to determine product prices, the mix of products, market strategy, appropriate sales commissions, advertising budgets, production schedules, and a host of other important planning decisions. While CVP analysis is most useful for planning, it can also be used to assist with controlling decisions (e.g., are the costs too high for the level of sales?), and evaluating decisions (e.g., should we reward employees for holding costs down or punish them for allowing costs to become too high?). Indeed, the concept of CVP analysis is pervasive in management accounting. It offers tremendous potential for helping management increase the profitability and effectiveness of an organization. This chapter will help you learn the mechanics of CVP analysis as well as how to use this important concept. Before studying CVP analysis, however, you need to have a better understanding of basic cost behavior patterns. Once you understand these cost behavior patterns and how to determine them, you can use them to make the planning, controlling, and evaluating decisions discussed above.

TO SUMMARIZE

CVP analysis is a very important concept in management accounting. Key factors involved in CVP analysis include (1) the revenues derived from the sales prices charged for goods and services, (2) the fixed and variable costs, (3) the sales volume, (4) the mix of products, (5) speed and quality of production, and (6) the resulting profits. Understanding the interrelationships of the key variables in CVP analysis can assist management in planning and in making critical controlling and evaluating decisions.

2 *Explain and analyze the basic cost behavior patterns—variable and fixed.*

BASIC COST BEHAVIOR PATTERNS

The two basic cost behavior patterns—variable and fixed—were introduced in Chapter 9. Other cost behavior patterns are variations of these two. Mixed costs, for example, exhibit characteristics of both variable and fixed costs; stepped costs may resemble either fixed or variable costs. In this section, we will explain variable and fixed costs; mixed and stepped costs will be discussed in the next section.

A cost is classified into one of the two basic categories by the way it reacts to changes in level of activity. The first task, then, is to define the activity involved and identify appropriate activity bases (referred to in Chapters 9 and 10 as cost drivers). Once the activity is defined, measurements of changes in activity level can be used to determine cost behavior patterns.

Measuring Level of Activity

Level of activity may be measured in terms of output, input, or a combination of the two. Some of the most common activity bases used are number of units sold and number of units produced in manufacturing firms; number of units sold in merchandising firms; and number of contract hours paid for or billed in service firms. Note that just because a cost doesn't vary with a particular activity base (e.g., total units sold or units produced) does not mean it isn't a variable cost. As we discussed with activity-based costing (Chapter 10), the cost may vary with another activity base that is more relevant. Managers must be careful to understand the various activity bases within their company so they can properly plan for and control costs.

Manufacturing and merchandising companies with a single product generally measure volume of activity in terms of output, for example, number of cars, television sets, or desks produced. However, many companies produce or sell several different products (refrigerators, toasters, and irons, for example) and a simple total of all the products manufactured or sold during a given period may not provide a good measure of activity. This is particularly true for manufacturing firms. It obviously takes more effort (and consequently costs more) to produce a refrigerator than an iron. In multiproduct situations, these manufacturing firms usually use input measures, such as direct labor hours worked, machine time used, or the time needed to set up a job, as the activity base. Such measures are often better cost drivers than the more general output measures.

Variable Costs

variable costs Costs that change in total in direct proportion to changes in activity level.

Total **variable costs** change in direct proportion to changes in activity level. Examples are costs of direct materials, which vary proportionately with the number of units produced, and sales commissions, which vary proportionately with the sales volume. As an example, an automobile manufacturer might define the activity as the production of cars and the cost driver as the number of cars produced. If engines, tires, axles, and steering wheels are purchased from suppliers, the related costs would be variable because the total cost of steering wheels, for example, would vary proportionately with the number of cars produced. If no cars are produced, there are no steering wheel costs; if 1,000 cars are manufactured during a period, the total cost for steering wheels and other purchased parts is 1,000 times the unit cost of each item. As more cars are produced, the total cost of each item increases. The unit cost, however, remains constant. For example, if an auto company pays $15 per steering wheel, the total cost of steering wheels for 200 cars is $3,000; for 500 cars, it is $7,500. At both levels of activity, however, the unit cost is still $15. This relationship between variable costs and level of activity is shown graphically in Exhibit 11-1, which relates the number of cars produced to the total cost of the steering wheels used in production.

CAUTION

The level of activity and the activity base are critical factors. Do not think that because a cost doesn't vary with production or sales, it cannot be a variable cost. A cost is variable if it is incurred as a direct result of the activity measure being considered. Thus, for example, in an engineering department, the activity base may be the number of engineering changes. Those costs that vary in total with the number of engineering changes made would be classified as variable costs for that activity.

In addition to sales commissions and materials, many other costs (such as labor) have a variable cost behavior pattern. For example, if it takes 4 hours of labor to assemble a frame and each hour costs $12, a unit labor cost of $48 per frame is a variable cost; the total labor cost would be $48 times the number of frames produced. As another example, if it generally requires $115 in materials and inspection time to do a quality check on a batch of chemicals being produced, then inspection costs of $115 per batch (regardless of the number of pounds of chemicals in the batch) is also a variable cost for batch-related activities. With respect to labor, however, a word of caution is in order. While the labor it takes to assemble a frame or perform quality checks varies proportionately with the number of frames assembled or quality checks performed, it isn't always easy to have exactly

EXHIBIT 11-1

An Example of Variable Costs

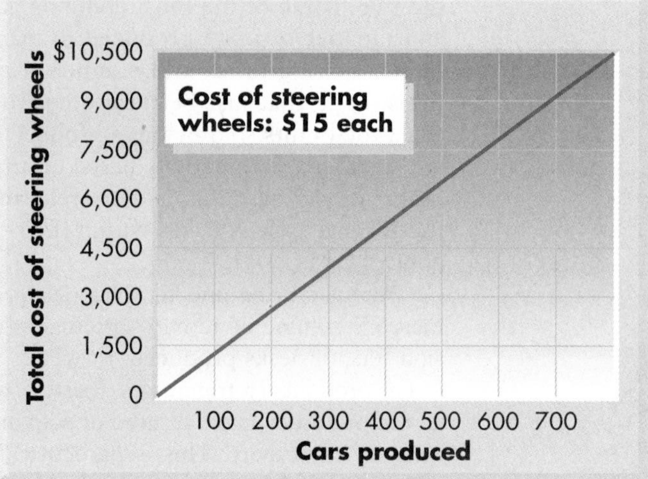

the right amount of labor on hand for various levels of production. When changes in production occur, it may take weeks or months to adjust labor costs to the amount that should be incurred.

The Relevant Range and Linearity

Our definition of the variable cost behavior pattern specifies that variable costs have a linear relationship to the level of activity; that is, when the level of activity increases, total variable costs rise at a directly proportional rate. In practice, a truly linear relationship usually does not exist; it is, however, approximated within a certain range of production, called the **relevant range**. For other ranges of activity, variable costs are actually **curvilinear costs**; that is, they vary at increasing or decreasing rates with changes in activity level. To illustrate, assume that an ice cream manufacturer uses milk, sugar, and other ingredients purchased from suppliers to make ice cream. Assuming that 1 gallon of milk is used to make 1 gallon of ice cream, if no ice cream is produced, there is no milk cost. If 500 gallons of ice cream are manufactured during a period, the total cost of milk is $1.60 per gallon or a total of $800. As more ice cream is produced, the total cost of milk increases, but the price per gallon decreases because of quantity discounts. At 1,000 gallons of milk purchased, the price is $1.50 per gallon, and at 2,000 gallons purchased, the price is $1.40 per gallon. The price decreases $0.10 per gallon for each additional 1,000 gallons purchased until a price of $1.00 per gallon is reached. The graph in Exhibit 11-2 shows how the curvilinear cost relationship is approximated by a linear segment within the relevant range of 2,000 to 4,000 gallons of milk purchased.

relevant range The range of operating level, or volume of activity, over which the relationship between total costs (variable plus fixed) and activity level is approximately linear.

curvilinear costs Variable costs that do not vary in direct proportion to changes in activity level but at decreasing or increasing rates due to economies of scale, productivity changes, and so on.

Relevant range is an important concept and should be kept in mind when considering cost behavior patterns. If activity increases or decreases significantly, cost relationships will probably change. If production volume soars, for example, such factors as overtime work and bulk-purchase discounts may subject direct labor and materials costs to fluctuations that destroy their proportional relationship to volume. That is why we say that the definition of variable costs—costs that in total have a linear relationship with volume of activity—is applicable only within relevant ranges. The important point to remember is that whenever we mention

EXHIBIT 11-2

Curvilinear Variable Costs

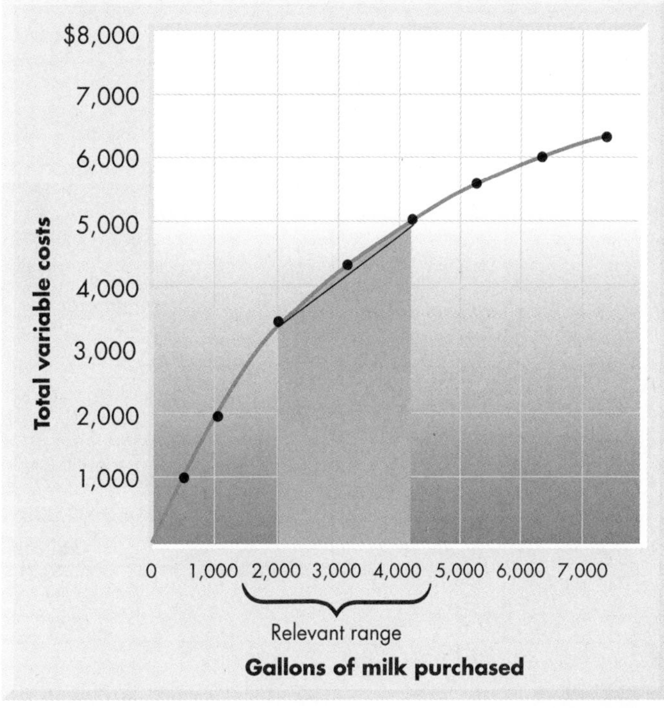

a particular variable cost, we are assuming that the cost is within the relevant range of activity.

fixed costs Costs which remain constant in total, regardless of activity level, at least over a certain range of activity.

Fixed Costs

Fixed costs remain constant in total, regardless of activity level, at least within the relevant range of activity. Examples include property taxes, insurance, executives' salaries, plant depreciation, and rent. Because total fixed costs remain constant as activity increases, the fixed cost per unit (total fixed cost ÷ level of activity) decreases, and vice versa. This is in contrast to variable costs, where the cost per unit remains constant through changes in the level of activity.

Exhibit 11-3 shows the relationship between the ice cream manufacturer's fixed manufacturing overhead cost and the total number of gallons of ice cream produced. As shown, within an activity range of 2,000 to 4,000 gallons of ice cream, the total fixed manufacturing overhead of $2,000 does not change. The per-unit fixed manufacturing overhead cost, on the other hand, will drop considerably as production increases. For example, when fixed manufacturing overhead is $2,000 and 2,000 gallons of ice cream are being produced, each gallon must bear an overhead burden of $1 ($2,000 ÷ 2,000 gallons). With production of 4,000 gallons, however, the burden is only $0.50 ($2,000 ÷ 4,000 gallons) per gallon.

Exhibit 11-3 also shows that if fewer than 2,000 gallons are produced, fixed manufacturing overhead can be reduced to $1,000 by laying off a production manager, for example. If

CAUTION

While total variable costs increase as production increases, the per-unit variable cost is constant across activity levels within the relevant range. In contrast, while total fixed costs are constant over the relevant range, the per-unit fixed cost changes with increases or decreases in production.

(STOP & THINK)

Assume you are buying a car by making monthly payments of $400 per month. Which would give you more money to spend each month—getting a raise at work of $400 per month or paying off the car? Remember, eliminating a fixed cost increases the amount of money you have to spend without incurring any additional income taxes.

EXHIBIT 11-3

An Example of Fixed Costs

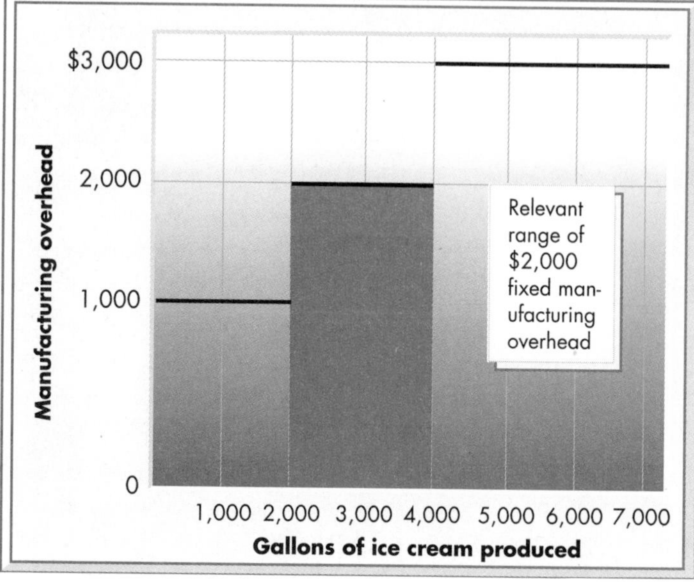

FYI

Have you ever wondered why you always wait so long and why there are so many patients at one time in a dentist's office? Think about the nature of the dentist's costs. Most costs are fixed—dentists' salaries, rent or depreciation, and so forth. When costs are mostly fixed, seeing a high volume of patients is important to cover the fixed costs. Then, once fixed costs are covered, almost all additional patient revenue becomes profit. Thus, by seeing only a few additional patients, dentists can increase their profits substantially.

more than 4,000 gallons are produced, fixed manufacturing overhead will increase to $3,000 (perhaps because a second production shift will require the addition of management personnel).

The Trend Toward Fixed Costs

As was stated earlier, over the past few decades, fixed costs have increased as a percentage of total costs for many manufacturing companies, primarily due to the increase in factory automation. As each manual job is replaced by a machine, costs change from variable labor costs to fixed depreciation or rental charges.

This greater proportion of fixed costs has a significant effect on the decision-making process. When costs are fixed, management is limited in its ability to influence costs with activity level decisions. With variable costs, management has more flexibility to change activity levels, and thereby increase or decrease total operating cost structures.

TO SUMMARIZE

Understanding cost behavior patterns is essential for making operating decisions. Cost behavior is the way a cost changes in response to changes in activity level. There are two basic cost behavior patterns, variable and fixed. Total variable costs change in direct proportion to changes in the level of activity over the relevant range; therefore, variable costs are constant per unit over this range. In analyzing variable costs, we generally assume a linear relationship between total costs and the level of activity within the relevant range; for other ranges, variable costs are usually curvilinear. Total fixed costs do not change over the relevant range; therefore, fixed costs decrease per unit as the level of activity increases within the relevant range. Because of such factors as automation, many costs that were once variable now exhibit fixed cost behaviors.

3 *Describe the behavior patterns of mixed costs and stepped costs.*

OTHER COST BEHAVIOR PATTERNS

Mixed and stepped costs, as we have noted, are variations of the basic fixed and variable cost behavior patterns. In the following sections, we will explain the behavior of these costs.

Mixed Costs

mixed costs Costs that contain both variable and fixed cost components.

Mixed costs are costs that contain both variable and fixed components. An example is rent that is based on a fixed rental fee plus a percentage of total sales. Thus, the rental terms for an automobile dealer's showroom might include a flat payment of $4,000 per month plus 1 percent of each month's sales. The 1 percent of sales is the variable portion, and the $4,000 is the fixed cost. The total rent, therefore, would be considered a mixed cost and could be diagrammed as shown in Exhibit 11-4. This exhibit shows that the cost of renting the showroom increases as sales increase. The total rent is $4,000 when there are no sales; $6,000 when sales are $200,000 [$4,000 + (0.01 × $200,000)]; and $8,000 when sales are $400,000 [$4,000 + (0.01 × $400,000)]. This increase is directly due to the variable cost element, which increases in total as activity level (car sales) increases.

Stepped Costs

stepped costs Costs that change in total in a stair-step fashion (in large amounts) with changes in volume of activity.

Stepped costs are costs that change in total in a stair-step fashion (that is, in large amounts) with changes in volume of activity. An example might be the labor charges for the maintenance of the tools and machinery in a small manufacturing plant. One maintenance worker can handle the upkeep of all the equipment during normal levels of activity. When there is a significant increase in activity, a second worker must be hired, and the maintenance cost approximately doubles.

How are stepped costs analyzed so that managers can make appropriate decisions? If the steps are wide compared to the relevant range, the costs are usually treated as fixed. If the steps are small compared to the relevant range, the costs are usually approximated with a variable cost line. Though this approximation is not perfect, it is better than making the more substantial error of ignoring the change in a stepped cost. Of course, the way management treats stepped (and mixed) costs may depend on the type of decision being made. For example, management may be more willing to treat stepped costs as fixed if they are evaluating performance rather than planning future production, because miscalculating how

EXHIBIT 11-4

An Example of Mixed Costs

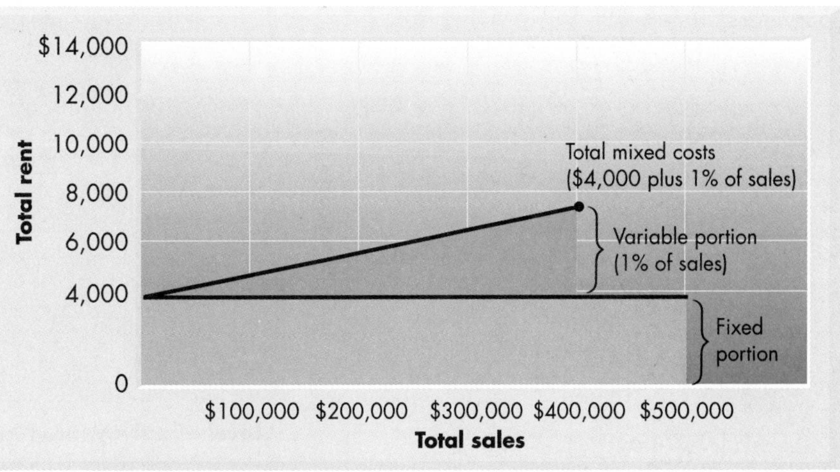

much an employee is paid is not as severe as miscalculating what future sales will be. It is always a good idea to determine how management will use information, for planning, controlling, or evaluating, before drawing conclusions about what type of analysis is best.

Exhibit 11-5 illustrates a stepped cost (warehouse salaries) that approximates a variable cost. The company has hired a number of full-time employees to prepare orders for shipment out of its warehouse. Each employee can prepare a maximum of 100 orders for shipment within one work week. Each employee receives a fixed amount, $200, for that period. Therefore, with eight employees, the company can prepare 800 orders at a cost of $1,600; a ninth employee will increase the warehouse salary cost to $1,800 and the shipping capacity to 900 orders. Each additional warehouse employee will cause costs to "step up" $200 and will allow the company to process an additional 100 orders.

Exhibit 11-6 illustrates a stepped cost (supervisors' salaries) that resembles the behavior of a fixed cost. It assumes that one supervisor is necessary to oversee each

EXHIBIT 11-5

Stepped Cost that Approximates a Variable Cost (Warehouse Salaries)

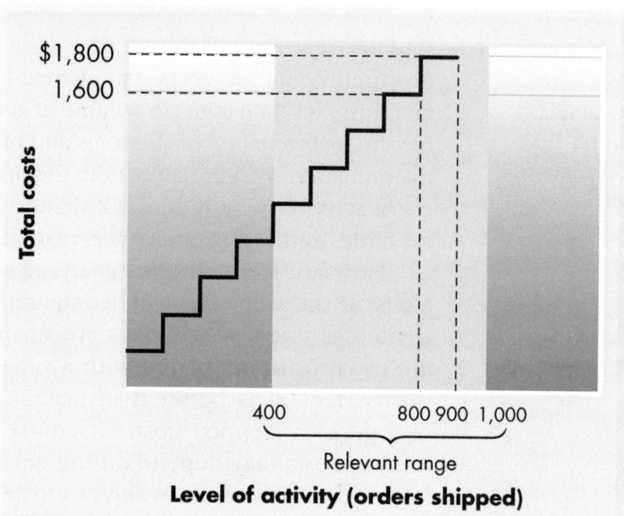

EXHIBIT 11-6

Stepped Cost that Approximates a Fixed Cost (Supervisors' Salaries)

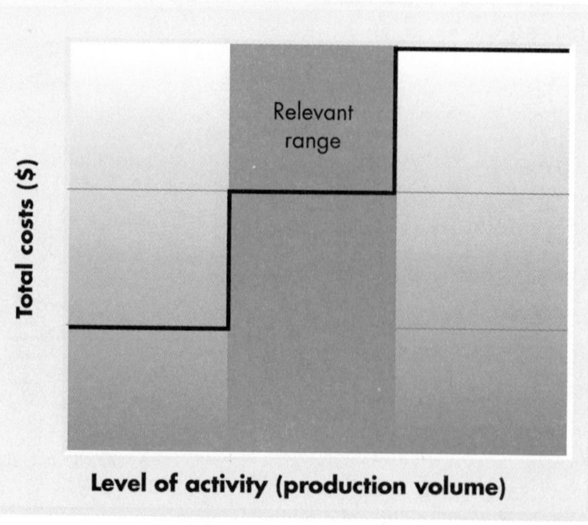

of the ten manufacturing departments in the factory; the company has two production shifts, requiring a total of 20 supervisors. If the factory is operating at capacity but is not filling all its orders, a third production shift may be needed. This added shift requires ten additional supervisors. Below a certain level of activity, on the other hand, the company would cut back to one shift and lay off ten supervisors. In both cases, the cost of supervisors' salaries changes dramatically. Because the production capacity of each shift is substantial, the level of activity would have to change significantly before management would decide to add or eliminate a shift.

The obvious difference between the capacity of a production shift and the capacity of a warehouse worker makes it clear that in the case of the supervisors' salaries, a much greater change in volume of activity is needed for costs to change. In this situation, then, the costs behave more like fixed costs within a relevant range.

TO SUMMARIZE

Mixed costs have both a variable and a fixed cost component. An increase in a mixed cost with a rising level of activity is due directly to the variable cost element. Stepped costs increase with the level of activity but not proportionately. If the steps are wide in relation to the relevant range, these costs can be treated as fixed; if the steps are narrow, they can be treated as variable.

4 *Analyze mixed costs using the scattergraph and high-low methods.*

ANALYSIS OF MIXED COSTS

We have shown how stepped costs can be classified as either fixed or variable. Mixed costs often are difficult to separate into variable and fixed components. Usually, the fixed portion represents the cost necessary to maintain a service (such as a telephone) or a facility (such as a building), and the variable portion covers actual use. Recall the example of the automobile showroom's rental cost, part of which was a flat monthly fee and part a percentage of sales. Other common mixed costs are certain types of leases and such overhead costs as electricity, repairs, telephone, and maintenance.

The most accurate way to separate the actual fixed and variable components of mixed costs is to analyze each invoice. On an electricity bill, for example, there may be a flat monthly service charge that would be classified as a fixed cost. Additional variable costs are those based on the amount of electricity actually used during the month. This approach would be time-consuming, however, and would probably not be cost-effective. (That is, it would cost more than the detailed information is worth.) A more useful approach would be to use, for each level of activity, the historical trend in past costs as the basis for classifying costs as fixed or variable. There are several methods of doing this. In this section we will concentrate on two: the scattergraph method and the high-low method.

scattergraph (visual-fit) method A method of segregating the fixed and variable components of a mixed cost by plotting on a graph total costs at several activity levels and drawing a regression line through the points.

regression line On a scattergraph, the straight line that most closely expresses the relationship between the variables.

variable cost rate The change in cost divided by the change in activity; the slope of the regression line.

The Scattergraph, or Visual-Fit, Method

Probably the simplest method of segregating mixed costs into their variable and fixed components is the **scattergraph (or visual-fit) method**. The total mixed cost for each level of activity is plotted on a graph, and a straight line (called the **regression line**) is visually fitted through the points. The fixed portion of the mixed cost is estimated to be the amount on the cost (vertical) axis at the point where it is intercepted by the regression line. The variable cost per unit (referred to as the **variable cost rate**) is equal to the slope of the regression line, which is simply the change in cost divided by the change in activity.

To illustrate the scattergraph method, we will assume the following electricity costs for an automobile manufacturer. In the analysis and calculations that follow, all costs are assumed to fall within the relevant range of activity. In this example, we use direct labor hours as a measure of the activity level.

Month	Direct Labor Hours Worked	Total Electricity Cost
January	7,000	$ 70,000
February	6,000	60,000
March	12,000	100,000
April	6,600	80,000
May	18,000	120,000
June	14,000	110,000

Exhibit 11-7 is the scattergraph on which these costs and hours have been plotted. It appears that the total fixed portion of electricity cost is about $40,000 per month, which is where the regression line intersects the cost axis. The variable cost rate is approximately $4.29 per direct labor hour, which is the slope of the regression line. To calculate the slope we use the following formula and the data points of zero and 14,000 direct labor hours, respectively.

$$\text{Variable cost rate} = \frac{\text{Change in (electricity) cost}}{\text{Change in activity (direct labor hours)}}$$

$$X = \frac{\$100{,}000 - \$40{,}000}{14{,}000 - 0}$$

$$X = \frac{\$60{,}000}{14{,}000}$$

$$X = \$4.29$$

EXHIBIT 11-7 Total Electricity Costs

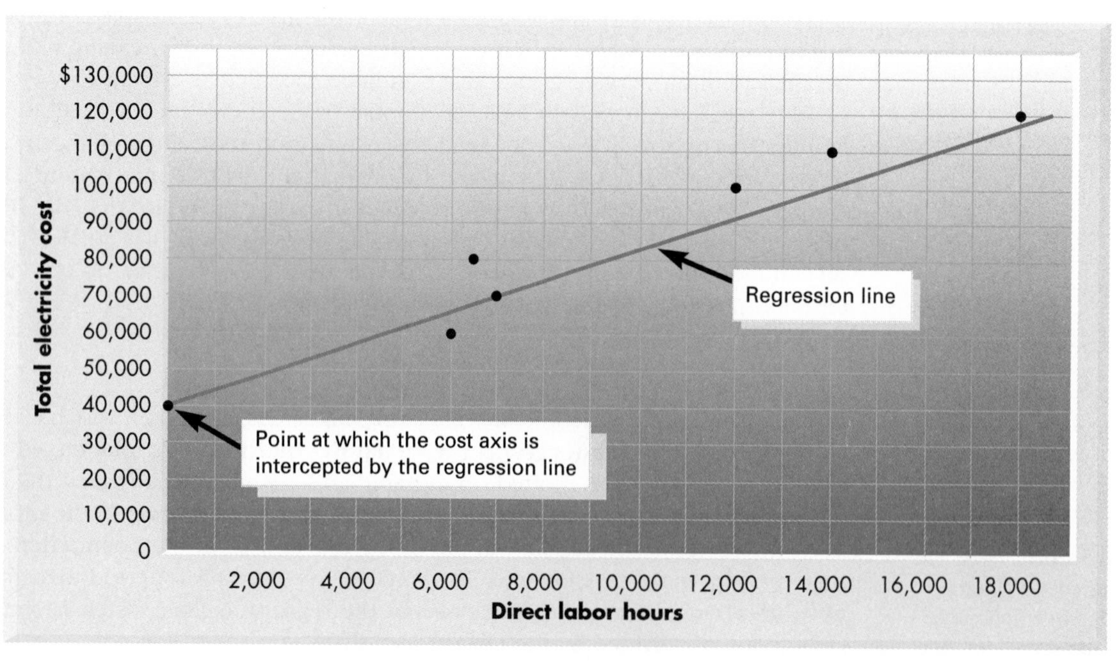

Notice that in this case we used activity levels of 0 and 14,000. Although the scattergraph provides only estimates of the fixed and variable portions of mixed costs, it can be an extremely useful tool for controlling operating costs. For instance, it shows at a glance any trends and abrupt changes in cost behavior patterns. It is also a means of checking whether costs are rising at a directly proportionate rate within the relevant range. As such, it can be used as a preliminary step to more sophisticated methods.

The High-Low Method

high-low method A method of segregating the fixed and variable components of a mixed cost by analyzing the costs at the high and the low activity levels within a relevant range.

A second approach is the **high-low method**, which analyzes mixed costs on the basis of total costs incurred at both the high and the low levels of activity. To illustrate this method, we refer again to the electricity costs of the automobile manufacturer.

Month	Direct Labor Hours Worked	Total Electricity Cost
January	7,000	$ 70,000
February	6,000	60,000
March	12,000	100,000
April	6,600	80,000
May	18,000	120,000
June	14,000	110,000

Although these two columns of figures do not show trends as clearly as the scattergraph does, they do suggest that as the activity level (direct labor hours) increases, total electricity costs increase. Given this relationship, the high-low method can be used to determine the fixed and variable portions of the electricity cost as follows:

1. Identify the highest and lowest activity levels (18,000 hours in May and 6,000 hours in February). These two months also represent the highest and lowest levels of electricity costs, or $120,000 and $60,000, respectively.
2. Determine the differences between the high and low points.

	Total Electricity Cost	Direct Labor Hours
High point (May)	$120,000	18,000
Low point (February)	60,000	6,000
Difference	$ 60,000	12,000

3. Calculate the variable cost rate (variable cost per unit). The formula is the same as the one used to compute the slope of the regression line in the scattergraph method. The results are different, of course, because the scattergraph method considers all the points, whereas the high-low method uses only the high and low points.

$$\text{Variable cost rate} = \frac{\text{Change in costs}}{\text{Change in activity}}$$

$$= \frac{\$60{,}000}{12{,}000}$$

$$= \$5 \text{ per direct labor hour}$$

4. Determine fixed costs based on the variable cost rate ($5 in this case). The formula for this computation is:

$$\text{Fixed costs} = \text{Total costs} - \text{Variable costs}$$

At the high level of activity, the calculation would be:

X = $120,000 − (18,000 × $5)
X = $120,000 − $90,000
X = $30,000

At the low level of activity, it would be:

X = $60,000 − (6,000 × $5)
X = $60,000 − $30,000
X = $30,000

In the case of either the high or low activity level, within the relevant range, the variable portion of the total electricity cost is $5 per direct labor hour, and the fixed portion is $30,000 per month. This means that $30,000 is the amount the company pays each month just to have electricity available, and $5 is the average additional electricity cost for each hour of direct labor worked.

A Comparison of the Scattergraph and High-Low Methods

As we have illustrated, the scattergraph and high-low methods may produce quite different results.

Method	Variable Cost Rate	Fixed Cost
Scattergraph	$4.29	$40,000
High-low	5.00	30,000

The scattergraph method takes all the data into account and therefore tends to be more accurate, although it is somewhat subjective (depending on how the line is drawn) and inconsistent because different people might draw the line through the points differently. The high-low method is useful for a quick approximation. To check whether the high and low points are representative of the costs incurred at all levels of activity, you could plot the data on a scattergraph. For example, if you examine the regression line in the scattergraph of Exhibit 11-7, you will notice that the low point lies below the line and the high point lies above the line, indicating that, in this case, a straight line drawn through the high and the low points would not be precisely representative of the six data points plotted. Nevertheless, both methods can be used to predict future costs. If, for example, management wants to know how much electricity will cost next month with 10,000 direct labor hours budgeted, you would make one of the following calculations:

Method	Formula	Estimated Cost
Scattergraph	$40,000 + 10,000 ($4.29)	$82,900
High-low	$30,000 + 10,000 ($5.00)	$80,000

TO SUMMARIZE

Two common techniques for analyzing mixed costs are the scattergraph and high-low methods. The scattergraph method consists of visually fitting a straight line (the regression line) through points plotted on a graph, then noting where the line intercepts the cost axis (the fixed cost) and calculating the slope of the line (the variable cost rate). With the high-low method, the high and the low levels of activity are used to first calculate the variable cost rate, and then the fixed cost component. These methods involve estimates and can lead to questionable decisions if they are not used with caution.

BUSINESS ENVIRONMENT ESSAY

Greatest Turnaround in Aviation History America West's emergence from Chapter 11 bankruptcy reorganization three years ago has been touted as the "greatest turnaround in aviation history." America West, like Continental and TWA before, spent several years in bankruptcy court seeking protection from creditors while it worked out its problems. Today, America West has one of the strongest balance sheets in the U.S. airline industry and has outstanding growth potential in its markets. (America West claims 41 percent of Phoenix fliers, making it that city's largest airline, and 22 percent of the Las Vegas market, two of the fastest growing cities in the United States.)

What has changed? How has America West taken what airline creditors wanted to liquidate and turned it into a viable competitor in its industry? For one thing, America West's management carefully analyzed its costs, divided those costs into fixed and variable components, and made several decisions to reduce fixed costs. For example, America West dropped several unprofitable routes, cut its work force by over 20 percent, and reduced its fleet of jets by one-third. In addition, America West shed over a billion dollars of debt, cutting its interest expense by over $20 million per year.

With fixed costs under control, America West became profitable. In fact, it is now one of the most profitable of all airlines. Because it cut costs, America West Airlines' passengers pay lower fares than on other airlines. These lower fares result in the airline filling more seats than most of its competitors. Since its costs are low, it is highly profitable. Fixed costs are now a smaller percentage of total costs at America West than at almost all other airlines.

Source: Adapted from Julie Schmit, "Airline Starts Over as Rising Star," *USA Today*, August 23, 1994, Section B1. Copyright 1994, *USA Today*. Reprinted with permission.

5 *Analyze CVP relationships using the contribution margin, equation, and graphic approaches.*

METHODS OF CVP ANALYSIS

Now that you have a better understanding of cost behaviors and can separate both mixed and stepped costs into their fixed and variable cost elements, you are ready to use your knowledge of cost behaviors to make planning, controlling, and evaluating decisions. As we noted at the beginning of the chapter, using fixed and variable cost relationships to make management decisions is referred to as cost-volume-profit (CVP) analysis.

There are three common and related ways to think about CVP analysis: (1) the contribution margin approach, (2) the equation approach, and (3) the graphic approach. We will introduce all three techniques, illustrating how each technique can help management understand how profits change in response to changes in variable costs, fixed costs, sales volume, and the mix of products sold.

contribution margin The difference between total sales and variable costs; it is the portion of sales revenue available to cover fixed costs and provide a profit.

The Contribution Margin Approach

Contribution margin is equal to sales revenue less variable costs; it is the amount of revenue that remains to cover fixed costs and provide a profit for an organization. Contribution margin is one of the most important management accounting concepts you will study because many operating decisions are made on the basis of how it will be affected. A company may decide, for example, to advertise one product more than others because it has a higher contribution margin.

The Contribution Margin Income Statement

To illustrate the concept of contribution margin, we will use the following format of a contribution margin income statement. The statement data for Jewels Corporation, a producer of high-quality baseball gloves, follow.[1]

Jewels Corporation
Contribution Margin Income Statement
For the Month Ended November 30, 2000

	Total	Per Unit
Sales revenue (1,000 gloves)	$200,000	$200
Less variable costs	110,000	110
Contribution margin	$ 90,000	$ 90
Less fixed costs	63,000	
Profit*	$ 27,000	

*In this chapter, the term "profit" means pretax income; the terms *income* and *profit* are interchangeable.

per-unit contribution margin The excess of the sales price of one unit over its variable costs.

As this income statement shows, for planning and internal decision-making purposes, Jewels Corporation computes its contribution margin on a per-unit (glove) and total-dollar basis. During November, Jewels' **per-unit contribution margin** is $90; the total contribution margin at a sales volume of 1,000 baseball gloves is $90,000.

The per-unit contribution margin tells us that $90 is available from each glove sold to cover fixed costs and provide a profit. By showing the $63,000 of fixed costs separately, this income statement also indicates that Jewels must generate sufficient contribution margin to cover these costs before a profit can be earned. With $200,000 of sales revenue, the contribution margin ($90,000) is sufficient to cover the fixed costs and provide a profit of $27,000.

This type of contribution margin income statement is particularly useful as a planning tool. It enables a company to project profits at any level of activity within the relevant range. For example, if Jewels Corporation forecasts sales at 1,200 baseball gloves next month, it could prepare a forecasted (or pro-forma) income statement (contribution margin format) as follows:

Jewels Corporation
Pro-Forma Contribution Margin Income Statement
For the Month Ended December 31, 2000

Sales revenue (1,200 gloves × $200)	$240,000
Less variable costs (1,200 gloves × $110)	132,000
Contribution margin	$108,000
Less fixed costs	63,000
Profit	$ 45,000

Notice that with an increase in sales of 200 baseball gloves, the contribution margin increases $18,000 ($108,000 − $90,000). This can be confirmed by multiplying the per-unit contribution margin by the increase in volume ($90 per unit × 200 gloves = $18,000). Since we assume that the increase in volume is still within the relevant range of activity, the fixed costs remain at $63,000, and profit increases by the $18,000 change in contribution margin.

1. In this example, it is assumed that there is only one model of baseball glove, which sells for $200.

CAUTION

Usually, fixed and variable costs are only appropriate over a relevant range. Be sure when making calculations that you do not assume that these same cost relationships exist across all possible production levels. For example, in the opening scenario, fixed costs tripled when a new plant was built, with a sales increase of only 30 percent.

The Contribution Margin Ratio

The contribution margin may be expressed as a percentage of sales revenue as well as on a per-unit or total-dollar basis. Knowing the **contribution margin ratio**, which is the percentage of sales revenue left after variable costs are deducted, management can compare the profitability of various products. For example, if product A has a 45 percent contribution margin ratio and the ratio of product B is only 30 percent, the company should emphasize product A, assuming that other factors are equal.

To illustrate the calculation of contribution margin ratios, we refer again to the initial Jewels Corporation example. The ratio would be computed as follows:

contribution margin ratio The percentage of net sales revenue left after variable costs are deducted; the contribution margin divided by net sales revenue.

	Total	Per Unit	Ratio (Percentage)
Sales revenue (1,000 gloves)	$200,000	$200	100%
Less variable costs	110,000	110	55%
Contribution margin	$ 90,000	$ 90	45%
Less fixed costs	63,000		
Profit	$ 27,000		

The contribution margin ratio is 45 percent of sales revenue ($90 ÷ $200), which means that for every $1.00 increase in sales revenue, the contribution margin increases by $0.45 (45 percent of $1.00). If fixed costs are already covered, profit will also increase by $0.45 for every $1.00 increase in sales. Notice also that the variable cost ratio ($110 ÷ $200 = 55%) plus the contribution margin ratio (45 percent) must equal 100 percent.

With contribution margin ratios, it is easy to analyze the impact of future changes in sales on the contribution margin. For example, if Jewels' management estimates that sales will increase by $20,000, it can apply the contribution margin ratio of 45 percent and estimate that the contribution margin will increase by $9,000 ($20,000 × 0.45). The higher the contribution margin ratio, the larger the share of each additional dollar of sales that goes toward covering fixed costs and increasing profit.

TO SUMMARIZE

The contribution margin is sales revenue less variable costs. It is the amount of revenue left to cover fixed costs and provide a profit. The contribution margin can be expressed in total dollars, on a per-unit basis, or on a percentage basis. Since fixed costs remain constant within a relevant range, once fixed costs have been covered, income increases by the amount of the per-unit contribution margin for every additional unit sold.

The Equation Approach

Cost-volume-profit analysis can also be expressed in an equation format. To highlight the important idea that CVP analysis depends on dividing costs into fixed and variable behavior patterns, we will develop the CVP equation in several steps.

1. Expressing a traditional income statement as an equation, we would have:

$$\text{Revenues} - \text{Costs} = \text{Profit}$$

F Y I

In deciding how to make tradeoffs between costs, quality, and other factors, it isn't always best to choose the lowest-cost alternative. Take major league baseball, for example. In 1997, the five teams with the highest player payrolls were: New York Yankees ($66 million), Baltimore Orioles ($63 million), Cleveland Indians ($60 million), Atlanta Braves ($58 million), and Florida Marlins ($55 million). Guess which five teams were the final teams remaining in the playoffs? You guessed it, these five. If winning the world series is the highest-quality outcome, then minimizing payroll costs is probably not a relevant goal.

Source: *USA Today,* October 7, 1997, C6.

2. Since all costs can be classified as either variable or fixed, we can modify the above to reflect the basic CVP equation as follows:

   Revenues − Variable costs − Fixed costs = Profit

3. Or, we can express the equation in units:

   (Sales price × Number of units) − (Variable cost × Number of units) − Fixed costs = Profit

4. Finally, we can express the equation using ratios:

   Revenues − (Variable cost ratio × Revenues) − Fixed costs = Profit

These equations are quick and useful methods for examining the financial aspects of CVP problems. To illustrate, we will use the data from the Jewels Corporation example and assume that sales of 1,200 baseball gloves are projected. What will Jewels' profit be?

(Sales price × Units) − (Variable cost × Units) − Fixed costs = Profit
($200 × 1,200) − ($110 × 1,200) − $63,000 = Profit
$240,000 − $132,000 − $63,000 = Profit
$45,000 = Profit

Note that a profit of $45,000 was also obtained using the contribution margin approach. This is no surprise since these are simply alternative routes to the same destination. Both methods are commonly used, depending on the individual preferences of management.

In summary, while there are many alternative ways to write the CVP formula, there is really only one formula, and it is not hard to remember: Revenues − Variable costs − Fixed costs = Profit. CVP analysis is basically a matter of simple algebra; you merely insert the known elements into the formula and solve for the one unknown element (X).

break-even point The amount of sales of the number of units sold at which total costs equal total revenues; the point at which there is no profit or loss.

Break-Even Point

Generally, management wants to know how many units need to be sold to break even, that is, to recover all costs. Thus, the **break-even point** is defined as the volume of activity at which total revenues equal total costs, or where profit or loss is zero. The break-even point may also be thought of as that volume of activity at which the contribution margin equals the fixed costs.

Although the goal of business planning is to make a profit, not just to break even, knowing the break-even point can be useful in assessing the risk of selling a new product, setting sales goals and commission rates, deciding on marketing and advertising strategies, and other similar operating decisions. Because the break-even point is, by definition, that activity level at which no profit or loss is earned, the basic CVP equation can be modified to reflect a break-even point as follows:

Revenues = Variable costs + Fixed costs + $0 Income

As you can see, to compute the break-even point, we first set income equal to zero, then solve for the unknown—typically either the number of units to be sold or the total revenues to be achieved.

Bank of America has a tool for analyzing a home loan refinancing decision. Use the following data: current loan balance, $140,000; current monthly payment, $1,445; market value, $206,000; interest rate, 7.5 percent; term, 15 years; estimated closing costs, $1,500; estimated mortgage points, 2 (i.e., 2 percent × new loan amount).

How many months would it take to "break even" on the new loan? Can you calculate the number of months on your own?

www.bofa.com/tools/refi_analysis.html

Again using the Jewels Corporation example, how many units must Jewels sell to break even? (Note that we use X to represent the unknown element, in this case, the number of baseball gloves.)

Sales price × Units (X) = [Variable cost × Units (X)] + Fixed costs
$200X = $110X + $63,000
$90X = $63,000
X = 700 units (baseball gloves)

In this case, if Jewels sells 700 baseball gloves, it will generate enough revenues to cover its variable and fixed costs, earning zero profits [($200 × 700) − ($110 × 700) − $63,000 = $0].

Determining Sales Volume to Achieve Target Income

Another way CVP analysis can be used in planning is to determine what level of activity is necessary to reach a target level of income. In this case, we obviously set income in the formula at the targeted level, and then use the formula to plan or predict what fixed costs, variable costs, sales prices, and sales volumes are needed to achieve the target level of income. **Target income** is usually defined as the amount of income that will enable management to reach its objectives—paying dividends, meeting analysts' predictions, purchasing a new plant and equipment, or paying off existing loans. It can be expressed either as a percentage of revenues or as a fixed amount.

target income A profit level desired by management.

BUSINESS ENVIRONMENT ESSAY

Does Professional Soccer Have Any Real Future in the United States? 1997 was the second season of Major League Soccer (MLS) in the United States. There have been many attempts to launch professional soccer as an American sport, but each attempt has failed. The last failure, that of the North American Soccer League (NASL)—which brought Pelé, Cruyff, Best, and Beckenbauer to the United States in the early 1970s—was especially hard because, with the big names, professional soccer looked so promising. One of the major reasons previous attempts have failed is because player salaries and other fixed costs have been too high for the small number of fans and meager TV revenues. Each attempt has ended up with negative contribution margins and the team owners losing money.

Aware of past losses, this time MLS has established itself in a different way. It has bet on an unusual single-entity structure, under which the league owns all the teams as well as all player contracts, and investors buy operating rights rather than setting up franchises. MLS says the structure allows it to "eliminate the financial disparities between large and small markets, control player salaries and other fixed costs, and offer commercial affiliates an integrated sponsorship and licensing program." It also gives MLS significant economies of scale and allows it to allocate fixed costs across several teams.

Even though the fan base shrunk and TV ratings dropped during the first two years, financially the league is ahead of forecasts. MLS lost $19 million in 1996, compared with anticipated losses of $22 million, and expects to lose $13 million more in 1997. The MLS is confident that the break-even point will come "by the end of the fourth year." The question is, does the MLS have the financial wherewithal, the management expertise, and the fan and TV support to make it long-term?

In the end, whether the MLS succeeds will depend on whether sufficient revenues can be generated to cover fixed and variable costs. While fixed costs, including player salaries, are low now, they may not always be. Already, 10 players, backed by the MLS Players Association, have filed a class action lawsuit arguing that the league's precious single-entity structure is designed expressly to hold down player salaries (fixed costs) and that, in doing so, it violates U.S. antitrust laws.

Source: John McLaughlin, *SKY,* October 1997, pp. 27–32.

To illustrate target income, suppose the management of Jewels Corporation would like to know how many baseball gloves must be sold to achieve a target income of $36,000, assuming no changes in per-unit variable costs or total fixed costs. The calculation is as follows:

$$[\text{Sales price} \times \text{Units (X)}] - [\text{Variable costs} \times \text{Units (X)}] - \text{Fixed costs} = \text{Target income}$$

$$\begin{aligned} \$200X - \$110X - \$63{,}000 &= \$36{,}000 \\ \$90X &= \$99{,}000 \\ X &= 1{,}100 \text{ units (gloves)} \end{aligned}$$

Thus, if Jewels could sell 1,100 baseball gloves at a contribution margin of $90 (assuming $63,000 of fixed costs), the company would earn a pretax profit of $36,000 [($90 × 1,100 units) − $63,000 = $36,000].

Notice that although the basic CVP equation has not changed, these last two illustrations are different in two important ways. First, the unknown factor in the preceding example is volume of activity (units), not income as in earlier examples (in one case, an assumed zero income and, in the other case, an assumed target income). Second, these last two illustrations identify the per-unit contribution margin ($90), which is the sales price per unit less the variable cost per unit. This leads us to a short-cut formula for computing break-even volume or a target income volume. The break-even formula is:

$$\text{Break-even sales (in units)} = \frac{\text{Fixed costs}}{\text{Contribution margin per unit}}$$

The target income formula is:

$$\text{Target sales (in units)} = \frac{\text{Fixed costs} + \text{Target income}}{\text{Contribution margin per unit}}$$

Plugging in the numbers for Jewels Corporation, the results are the same as shown earlier. For break-even:

$$\frac{\$63{,}000}{\$90} = 700 \text{ units}$$

For target sales:

$$\frac{\$63{,}000 + \$36{,}000}{\$90} = 1{,}100 \text{ units}$$

Short cuts are useful, but they should not be applied until you fully understand the basic relationships.

CAUTION

Remember, when making dollar value computations, the per-unit variable cost is not used. Rather, the per-unit variable cost ratio times sales and total fixed costs are subtracted from sales (in dollars) to arrive at income for a given level of sales. Many students make the mistake of multiplying the variable cost per unit times sales instead of the variable cost ratio times sales to get total variable costs.

Computation in Dollar Amounts Versus Units Before leaving the equation approach, we should note that a variable cost ratio is sometimes used instead of a per-unit variable cost. In such cases, the basic CVP equation is modified as follows:

$$\text{Sales} - (\text{Variable cost ratio} \times \text{Sales}) - \text{Fixed costs} = \text{Income}$$

Since the variable costs are stated as a percentage of sales dollars rather than on a per-unit basis, this approach expresses activity in terms of sales dollars, not units. For example, the break-even point for Jewels Corporation may be expressed as $140,000 in sales revenue ($200 per unit × 700 units) instead of 700 units as previously illustrated. This may be verified using the preceding equation and a 55 percent variable cost ratio as follows:

$$\text{Sales} - (0.55)\ \text{Sales} - \$63{,}000 = \$0$$
$$(0.45)\ \text{Sales} = \$63{,}000$$
$$\text{Sales} = \$140{,}000$$

The Graphic Approach

Cost-volume-profit relationships also can be expressed in graphic form. In fact, the graphic format may be the most effective method to communicate information to management. It allows managers to visualize and examine cost and revenue data over a range of activity rather than at a single volume. However, it is difficult to read precise information from a graph, so management may want to use the equation approach when a specific proposal is being considered.

On a CVP graph, volume or activity level usually is shown on the horizontal axis, and total dollars of sales and costs are shown on the vertical axis. Lines are then drawn to represent total fixed costs, total costs, and total revenues. Exhibit 11-8 shows a cost-volume-profit graph for Jewels Corporation.

Fixed and variable cost relationships are valid only for the relevant range of activity (the screened area on the graph in Exhibit 11-8). In this case, fixed costs are $63,000, and variable costs are $110 per glove over the range of activity be-

EXHIBIT 11-8 A Cost-Volume-Profit Graph

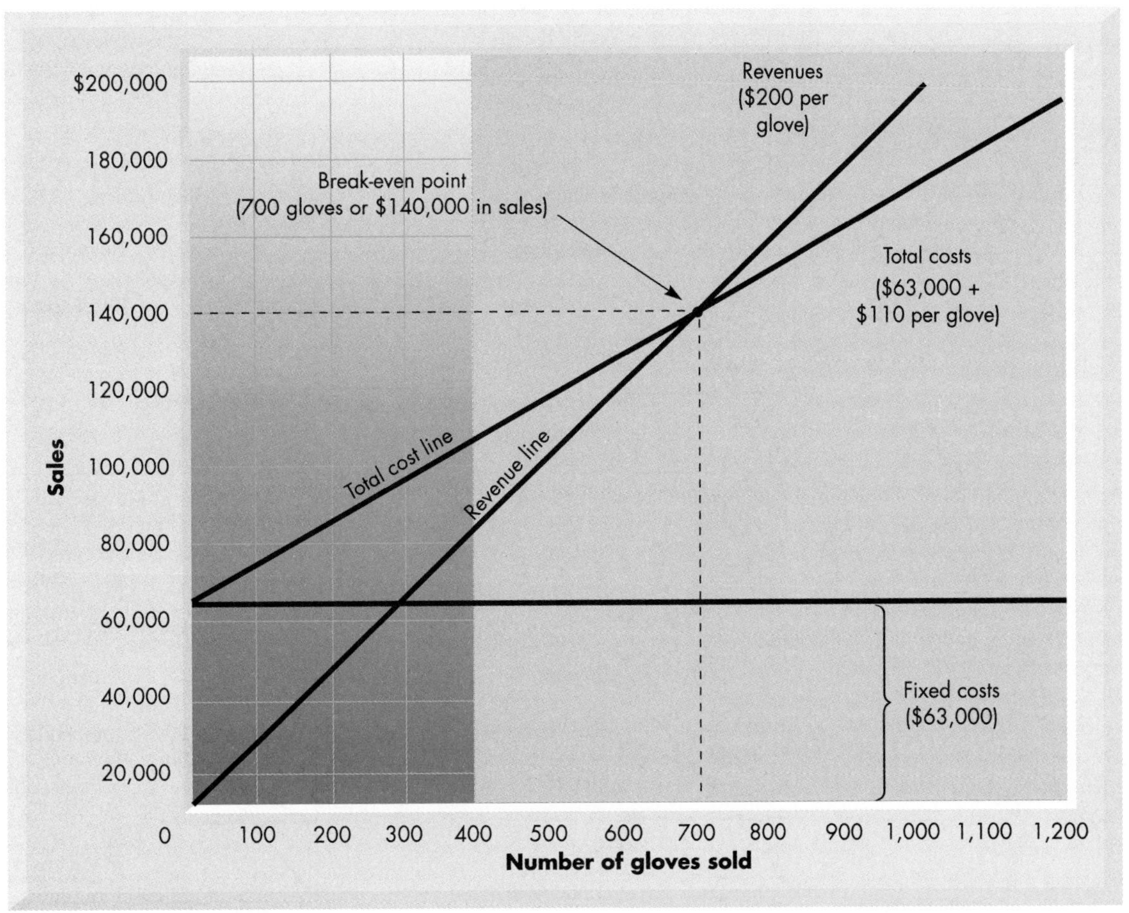

tween 400 and 1,200 gloves sold. Total costs are \$74,000 at 100 gloves [\$63,000 + (\$110 × 100 gloves)], \$85,000 at 200 gloves [\$63,000 + (\$110 × 200 gloves)], and so on. Similarly, total revenues are \$20,000 at 100 gloves (\$200 × 100 gloves), \$40,000 at 200 gloves, and \$60,000 at 300 gloves. The break-even point, the point at which total revenues equal total costs, is 700 gloves, or \$140,000 in sales.

As shown in Exhibit 11-9, the graphic format can be used to isolate such items of interest as total variable costs, total fixed costs, the area in which losses occur, the area in which profits will be realized, and the break-even point. Because cost-volume-profit graphs illustrate a wide range of activity, management can use them to quickly determine approximately how much profit or loss will be realized at various levels of sales.

The Profit Graph

profit graph A graph that shows how profits vary with changes in volume.

Some managers use another graphic approach, referred to as the **profit graph**, which plots only profits and losses and omits costs and revenues. Exhibit 11-10 shows a profit graph for Jewels Corporation.

Notice that though the horizontal axis of the profit graph is the same as those of the previous graphs, the vertical axis represents only profits and losses. As long as the contribution margin is positive, the maximum amount of losses that can occur is at a zero level of sales. With no sales, total losses will be the amount of the fixed costs. With the axes properly labeled, the profit line is drawn as follows:

1. Locate the loss for zero sales volume on the vertical axis. This is the total fixed cost, or negative \$63,000 in this case.
2. Locate the profit or loss at another sales volume. For example, at sales of 700 gloves, profits are zero [\$140,000 − (\$63,000 + \$77,000)], or at sales of 1,000 gloves, profits are \$27,000 [\$200,000 − (\$63,000 + \$110,000)].
3. After the two profit or loss points have been identified, draw a line through them back to the vertical axis.

EXHIBIT 11-9

Cost-Volume-Profit Graphs

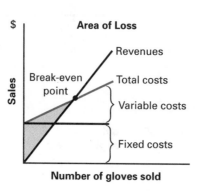

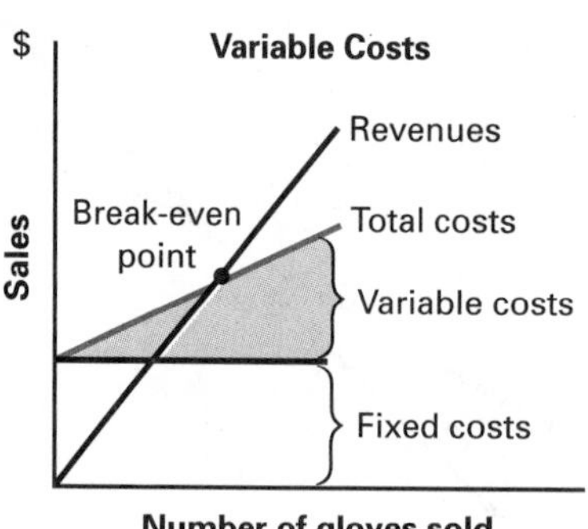

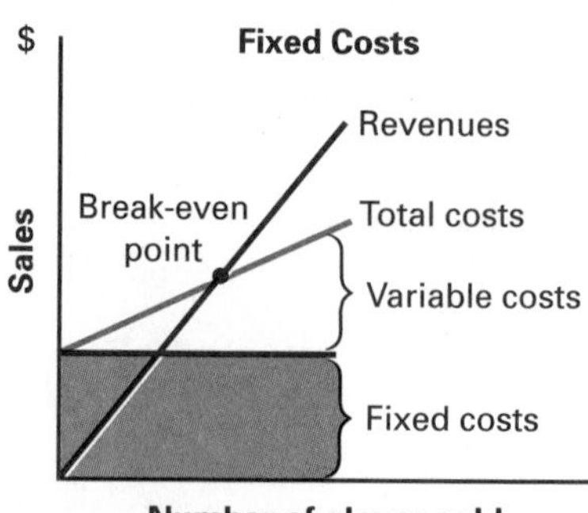

$
Area of Loss
Revenues
Break-even point
Total costs
Sales
Variable costs
Fixed costs
Number of gloves sold

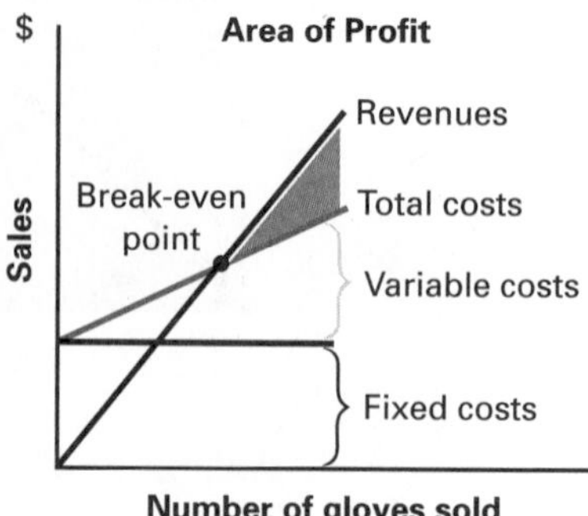

EXHIBIT 11-10

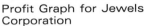

Profit Graph for Jewels Corporation

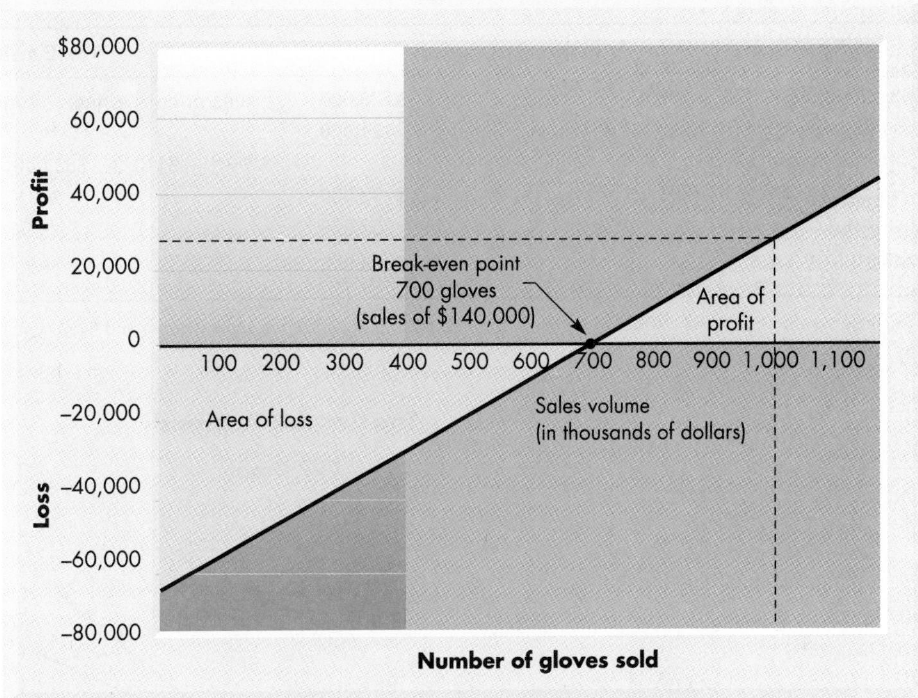

Because of its simplicity, the profit graph is widely used for making comparisons of competing projects. It has the disadvantage, however, of not showing how costs vary with changes in sales volume.

(STOP & THINK)

When analyzing costs, volume, and profit, why do you think most managers prefer the graphical approach over the contribution margin or equation approaches?

A Comparison of the Three CVP Approaches

The three CVP approaches (contribution margin, equation, and graphic) are merely alternative representations of the same calculation. To illustrate this point, we will use all three approaches to determine what volume of activity Jewels Corporation needs to reach a target income of $36,000. This was illustrated earlier with the equation approach, but it is repeated here to show that all approaches produce the same quantitative results. As shown in Exhibit 11-11, Jewels Corporation must sell 1,100 baseball gloves to reach a target income of $36,000.

A fixed dollar amount of income, such as the $36,000 that would be earned by selling 1,100 baseball gloves, is probably the most typical way of expressing a target income goal for many companies. However, because investors often evaluate companies partially on the basis of the **return on sales revenue** (or simply "return on sales"), management may want to state its goal as a percentage return as opposed to a fixed amount of income. For example, if a company set a target income of a 20 percent return on sales, the computation would be:

return on sales revenue A measure of operating performance; computed by dividing net income by total sales revenue.

$$\begin{aligned}
\text{Sales revenue} &= \text{Variable costs} + \text{Fixed costs} + 0.20\ \text{Sales revenue} \\
\$200X &= \$110X + \$63{,}000 + 0.2(\$200X) \\
\$200X &= \$110X + \$63{,}000 + \$40X \\
\$50X &= \$63{,}000 \\
X &= 1{,}260\ \text{gloves}
\end{aligned}$$

For Jewels Corporation, the 20 percent return on revenues would be earned by selling 1,260 baseball gloves.

EXHIBIT 11-11 Comparison of Three CVP Approaches

The Contribution Margin Approach*		The Equation Approach
Sales revenue (1,100 × $200)	$220,000	(Sales price × Units) − (Variable costs × Units) − Fixed costs = Profit
Less variable costs (1,100 × $110)	121,000	$200X − $110X − $63,000 = $36,000
Contribution margin ($99,000 ÷ $90 = 1,100)	$ 99,000	$90X = $99,000
Less fixed costs	63,000	X = 1,100 gloves
Profit	$ 36,000	

*This income statement was created by working from the bottom up, since we know income and fixed costs but not the number of gloves to be sold.

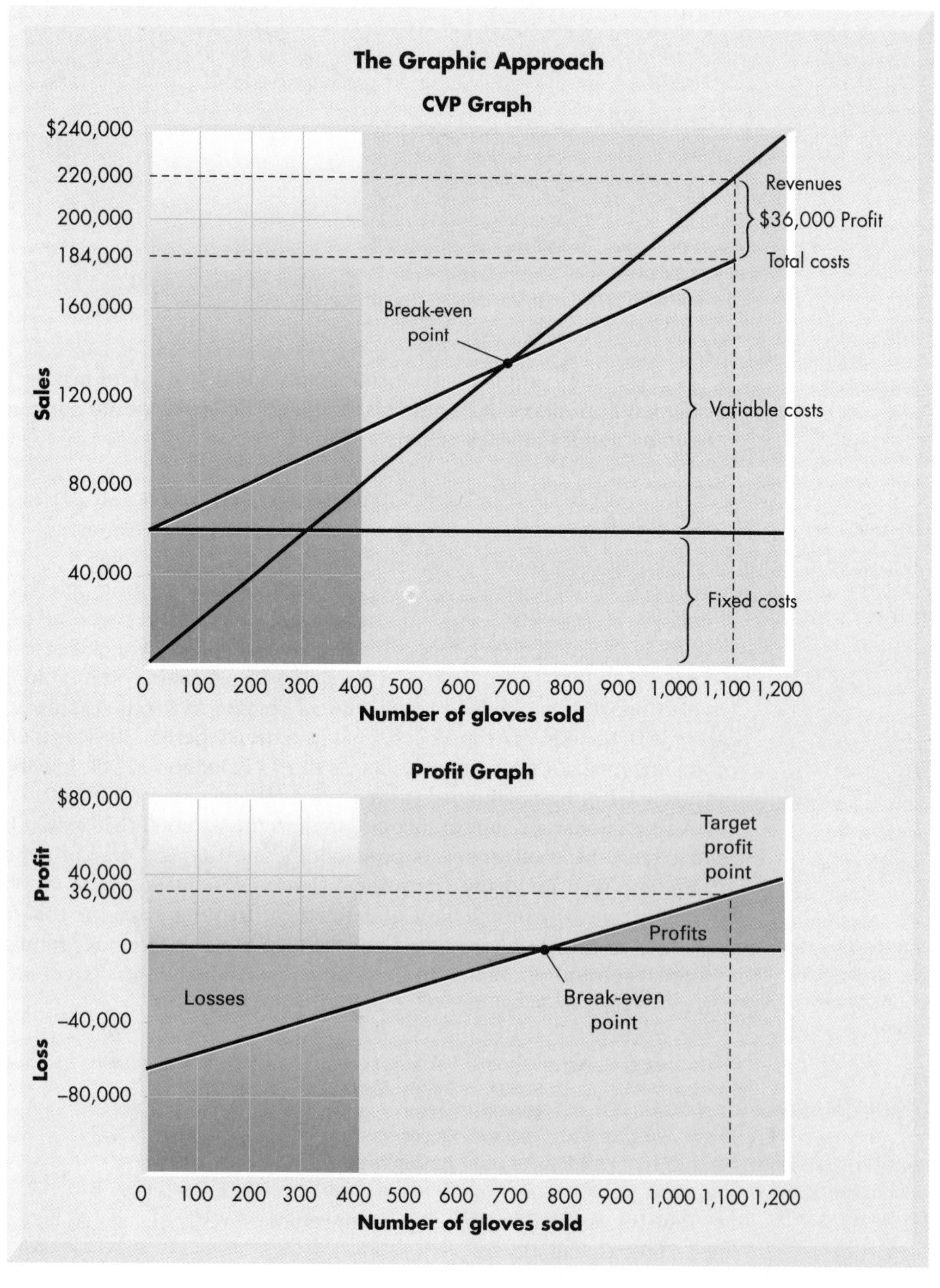

TO SUMMARIZE

In addition to the contribution margin approach, the financial effects on cost-volume-profit decisions can be examined by using either equations or graphs. These methods of analysis can be used to calculate the break-even point, which occurs at the point where total revenues equal total fixed costs plus total variable costs. These methods can also be used to project a target income level, with profit being equal to the excess of revenues over total costs. The graphic approaches can be useful because they highlight cost-volume-profit relationships over wide ranges of activity. The most common graphic approach involves plotting fixed costs as a horizontal line with variable costs above fixed costs. A profit graph, which shows only profit or loss and volume, is much simpler, but it does not show how costs vary with changes in sales volume. All three CVP approaches are based on the same calculations and on the underlying concept of fixed and variable cost behavior patterns.

6 *Describe potential changes in CVP variables and the effects these changes have on company profitability; identify the limiting assumptions of CVP analysis.*

THE EFFECT OF CHANGES IN COSTS, PRICES, AND VOLUME ON PROFITABILITY

The basic techniques of CVP analysis that we have covered in this chapter are used almost daily by management for making business decisions. (Of course, management is as interested in ways to improve product quality and speed of production as it is in reducing costs or increasing revenues.) Managers must be adept at evaluating the effects on profitability of the five most common changes in CVP variables: (1) the amount of fixed costs, (2) the variable cost rate, (3) the sales price, (4) the sales volume or the number of units sold, and (5) combinations of these variables. For these illustrations, we will use only the equation format since it is more concise and direct.

Changes in Fixed Costs

Many factors, an increase in property taxes or an increase in management's salaries, for example, will cause an increase in fixed costs. (Recall also from the opening scenario that building a new manufacturing facility can also increase fixed costs.) If all other factors remain constant, an increase in fixed costs always increases the number of units needed to break even. Obviously, the number of units needed to reach a target income will also increase. To illustrate, we will assume that Jewels Corporation's fixed costs increase from \$63,000 to \$81,000. Because of the added fixed costs, Jewels must now sell 1,300 baseball gloves, instead of 1,100, in order to earn a target income of \$36,000.

Target income of \$36,000:

$$\$200X - \$110X - \$81,000 = \$36,000$$
$$\$90X = \$117,000$$
$$X = 1,300 \text{ gloves}$$

Note that for decisions such as these, the basic CVP equation can be restated as follows:

Revenues = Variable costs + Fixed costs + Target income (R = VC + FC + TI)

By isolating sales revenue on the left, we highlight the goal of our calculation—to determine the number of baseball gloves that must be sold if fixed costs increase. We will use this form of the equation in the following sections.

The computations are quite simple. In fact, you may have found them unnecessary, realizing that if the fixed costs increase by \$18,000 (\$81,000 − \$63,000), and if the unit contribution margin remains \$90 per glove, 200 additional gloves

(\$18,000 ÷ \$90) will have to be sold in order to reach the \$36,000 target income (1,100 + 200 = 1,300).

Changes in the Variable Cost Rate

Like an increase in fixed costs, an increase in the variable cost rate also increases the number of units needed to break even or to reach target income levels, when all other factors remain constant. Suppose that the variable cost rate increased from \$110 per baseball glove to \$130 per glove because of increased wages for factory personnel, increased costs of direct materials, or other factors. With this increase, the number of units needed to reach the target income would be calculated as follows (assuming that fixed costs are again \$63,000 and rounding to the nearest unit):

Target income of \$36,000:

$$\begin{aligned} R &= VC + FC + TI \\ \$200X &= \$130X + \$63{,}000 + \$36{,}000 \\ \$70X &= \$99{,}000 \\ X &= 1{,}414 \text{ gloves} \end{aligned}$$

The increase in the variable cost rate reduces the unit contribution margin (from \$90 to \$70), which means that more gloves must be sold to maintain the same target income. With a unit contribution margin of \$90, the company would make a \$36,000 target income by selling 1,100 baseball gloves; with a unit contribution margin of only \$70, an additional 314 (1,414 − 1,100) gloves must be sold to earn a \$36,000 target income.

Changes in Sales Price

If all other variables remain constant, an increase in the sales price decreases the sales volume needed to reach a target income. This is because an increase in sales price increases the unit contribution margin per baseball glove, thereby decreasing the number of gloves that must be sold to earn the same amount of target income.

To illustrate, we will assume that the demand for baseball gloves is overwhelming and that Jewels cannot produce gloves fast enough. A decision is made to increase the price from \$200 to \$230 per glove. As a result of the price increase, the number of gloves that must be sold to reach the target income of \$36,000 decreases.

Target income of \$36,000:

$$\begin{aligned} R &= VC + FC + TI \\ \$230X &= \$110X + \$63{,}000 + \$36{,}000 \\ \$120X &= \$99{,}000 \\ X &= 825 \text{ gloves} \end{aligned}$$

With the sales price increase of \$30 per glove, the contribution margin also increased \$30 per glove to \$120; and with a \$120 contribution margin per glove, only 825 gloves need to be sold to reach the \$36,000 target income. Obviously, a decrease in the sales price would have the opposite effect; it would increase the number of units needed to reach the target income.

Changes in Sales Volume

As you probably have noticed, the sales volume (the number of gloves to be sold) for the target income has varied with each change in one of the other variables. When other variables remain constant, an increase in the sales volume will result in an increase in income. Very simply, the more gloves sold, the higher the income (as long as the contribution margin is positive). The degree of change in profits resulting from volume alterations depends on the size of the unit contribution margin. When the unit contribution margin is high, a slight change in volume results in a dramatic change in profit. With a lower unit contribution margin, the change in profit is less.

Simultaneous Changes in Several Variables

Thus far, we have examined changes in only one variable at a time. Individual changes are quite rare, however; more often, a decision will affect several variables, all at the same time. For example, should Jewels Corporation increase fixed advertising costs by $20,000 and reduce the sales price by 10 percent if the result would be to increase sales volume by 500 units? The impact on the target income from these proposed changes is as follows:

Initial Data		Proposed Changes
Sales price per glove	$200	$180 ($200 × 90%)
Variable costs per glove	$110	$110
Fixed costs	$63,000	$83,000 ($63,000 + $20,000)
Target income	$36,000	X
Sales volume	1,100 gloves	1,600 gloves (1,100 + 500)

Computations and result:

$$\begin{aligned} R &= VC + FC + TI \\ \$180 \times 1{,}600 &= (\$110 \times 1{,}600) + \$83{,}000 + X \\ \$288{,}000 &= \$176{,}000 + \$83{,}000 + X \\ \$29{,}000 &= X \text{ (target income)} \end{aligned}$$

The analysis shows that target income would drop by $7,000 ($36,000 − $29,000) as a result of these changes. So, the decision would be not to implement the proposed changes.

Consider another possible decision—should Jewels automate part of its production, thereby reducing (by $10) variable costs to $100 per unit and increasing (by $5,000) fixed costs to $68,000? The computation would be:

$$\begin{aligned} R &= VC + FC + TI \\ \$200 \times 1{,}100 &= (\$100 \times 1{,}100) + \$68{,}000 + X \\ \$220{,}000 &= \$110{,}000 + \$68{,}000 + X \\ \$42{,}000 &= X \text{ (target income)} \end{aligned}$$

CAUTION

Remember, any change that affects the level of sales (such as a price decrease) also affects the total amount of variable costs. Some students think only to change the number of units of sales, and not the number of units multiplied by the variable cost per unit.

This analysis shows that management should implement these proposed changes because they would increase target income by $6,000 ($42,000 − $36,000). Obviously, this is true only if the assumptions can be relied on—that is, if fixed costs will rise by no more than $5,000 and unit variable costs will decrease by a full $10.

Consider another example. Suppose Jewels Corporation could use part of the excess capacity of its operating facilities to make baseball bats. These bats would sell for $90 per unit, increase fixed costs by $40,000, and have a variable cost per unit of $45. Jewels wants to add this new product line only if it can increase income by $25,000. How many baseball bats must Jewels sell to reach this target income? The computation follows:

$$\begin{aligned} R &= VC + FC + TI \\ \$90X &= \$45X + \$40{,}000 + \$25{,}000 \\ \$45X &= \$65{,}000 \\ X &= 1{,}444 \text{ baseball bats} \end{aligned}$$

Management now must determine whether the company can produce and sell 1,444 baseball bats. If that sales goal seems attainable, the facilities should be used to make the bats.

BUSINESS ENVIRONMENT ESSAY

Gathering Information for CVP Accurately determining fixed and variable costs and performing CVP analysis is not an easy task, but the rewards of thorough work are well worth the effort. Through a detailed analysis of its costs, a manufacturing firm in the UK found that two of its three production processes were generating losses. Prices to its major customers had to be increased between 20 and 60 percent. However, only one customer stopped buying from the company as a result of the increase. Surprisingly, that same customer returned not long after and confessed to being unable to find a better deal elsewhere. With inaccurate cost information, the company had simply been pricing its products too low.

Source: "Which Products Make a Profit?" *Management Accounting,* June 1993, pp. 34–36.

Limiting Assumptions of CVP Analysis

CVP analysis is an extremely useful tool for assisting management in making short-term operating decisions. There are, however, some limiting assumptions of CVP analysis that must not be overlooked.

The key assumption is that the behavior of revenues and costs is linear throughout the relevant range. CVP analysis is valid only for a relevant range.

A second assumption is that all costs, including mixed costs, can be accurately divided into fixed and variable categories. As noted earlier in the chapter, some costs have characteristics of both fixed and variable costs. These costs sometimes are not easily classified into their fixed and variable components, which limits the accuracy of CVP analysis.

For companies with more than one product, a third major assumption in CVP analysis is required—that the mix of a company's products does not change over the relevant range. The sales mix is the proportion of the total units sold (or the total dollar sales) represented by each of a company's products. (Sales mix will be discussed in the next section.)

In addition to the three assumptions already identified, there are other limiting assumptions implicit in CVP analysis. For example, CVP analysis assumes that efficiency and productivity are held constant, that the prices of materials and other product components are constant, and that revenues and costs can be analyzed using a single activity base, such as volume. A related and very significant assumption, and one that clearly is not always valid, is that volume is the only or even the primary driver of costs.

Because of the above described limiting assumptions, the conclusions reached from CVP analysis must be considered with reasonable caution. Nevertheless, CVP analysis does provide a good model for predicting future operating results when specific relationships are defined and recognized.

TO SUMMARIZE

The effects of changes in costs, prices, and volume on profitability may be determined by CVP analysis. Changes in individual variables or simultaneous changes in several variables can be analyzed with this technique. CVP analysis is based on three critical and limiting assumptions: (1) that the behavior of revenues and costs is linear throughout the relevant range, (2) that all costs can be categorized as either fixed or variable, and (3) that the sales mix does not change.

7 *Explain the effects of sales mix on profitability.*

sales mix The relative proportion of total units sold (or total sales dollars) that is represented by each of a company's products.

SALES MIX

As we explained earlier in the chapter, **sales mix** is the proportion of the total units represented by each of a company's products. To keep our discussions simple, in a previous section of the chapter, we used examples of companies with only one product. However, because many companies have more than one product, we need to illustrate how sales mix issues are resolved. To illustrate how a change in sales mix can affect a company's CVP relationships, we assume that Multi-Product Inc. sells three different products. Following are the monthly revenues and costs for each type of product:

	Product A		Product B		Product C		Total	
	Amount	Percent	Amount	Percent	Amount	Percent	Amount	Percent
Sales revenue	$25,000	100%	$45,000	100.00%	$30,000	100%	$100,000	100%
Less variable costs	20,000	80	30,000	66.67	21,000	70	71,000	71
Contribution margin	$ 5,000	20%	$15,000	33.33%	$ 9,000	30%	$ 29,000	29%
Sales mix	25%		45%		30%		100%	

Total sales are $100,000, which in this example includes $25,000 in sales of Product A, $45,000 of Product B, and $30,000 of Product C. Therefore, the sales mix is 25 percent Product A ($25,000 ÷ $100,000), 45 percent Product B ($45,000 ÷ $100,000), and 30 percent Product C ($30,000 ÷ $100,000). With this sales mix, the average contribution margin ratio is 29 percent, which is determined by subtracting total variable costs of $71,000 from total sales of $100,000, and dividing the result ($29,000) by $100,000. If Multi-Product Inc. had fixed costs of $17,400 and desired a target income of $40,000, the necessary sales volume (in dollars) would be:

$$\begin{aligned} \text{Sales} - (0.71)\text{ Sales} - \$17{,}400 &= \$40{,}000 \\ (0.29)\text{ Sales} &= \$57{,}400 \\ \text{Sales} &= \$57{,}400 \div 0.29 \\ \text{Sales} &= \$197{,}931 \text{ (rounded)} \end{aligned}$$

FYI

Obviously, a computer can make sales mix and other CVP computations very easy. Using simulation or other programs, the financial effects of changes in the sales of one product or simultaneous changes in sales of several products can be quickly calculated.

Alternatively, the company could divide the average contribution margin ratio (29 percent) into fixed costs plus target income ($17,400 + $40,000). As you can see, this revised, more compact formula is simply a restatement of the preceding equation.

$$\frac{\text{Fixed costs + Target income}}{\text{Average contribution margin ratio}} = \frac{\$57{,}400}{0.29} = \$197{,}931 \text{ (rounded)}$$

Obviously, $197,931 in sales will make the target income only if the average contribution margin ratio, and therefore the sales mix, does not change. To illustrate the effect of a change in sales mix, assume that the total sales revenue and the sales prices of each product remain the same but that the sales mix changes as follows:

	Product A		Product B		Product C		Total	
	Amount	Percent	Amount	Percent	Amount	Percent	Amount	Percent
Sales revenue	$50,000	100%	$30,000	100.00%	$20,000	100%	$100,000	100%
Less variable costs	40,000	80	20,000	66.67	14,000	70	74,000	74
Contribution margin	$10,000	20%	$10,000	33.33%	$ 6,000	30%	$ 26,000	26%
Sales mix	50%		30%		20%		100%	

In this example, the contribution margin ratio for each product remains the same, but the sales mix changes. Product A now comprises 50 percent of total sales instead of 25 percent. Since Product A has a lower contribution margin ratio than Products B and C, the average contribution margin ratio decreases from 29 percent to 26 percent. Accordingly, the sales volume needed to generate $40,000 of target income increases to $220,769, computed as follows:

$$\frac{\text{Fixed costs} + \text{Target income}}{\text{Average contribution margin ratio}} = \frac{\$57,400}{0.26} = \$220,769 \text{ (rounded)}$$

As you can see, a sensible profit-maximizing strategy for management would be to maintain as large a contribution margin as possible on all products, and then to emphasize those products with the largest individual contribution margins. The remaining chapters of this text discuss procedures management can use to control costs and hence maintain high contribution margins. The second part of this strategy—emphasizing the products with the highest contribution margins—is a marketing function. Multi-Product Inc., for example, should promote Product B more aggressively than Product A. With other factors being equal, a company should spend more advertising dollars and pay higher sales commissions on its higher contribution margin products. In fact, instead of paying commissions based on total sales, a good strategy would be to base sales commissions on the total contribution margin generated. This way, the mix of products that maximizes the sales staff's commissions will be the mix that provides the company with the greatest overall profit.

(STOP & THINK)

Would maximizing the sales of the highest contribution margin products still be the best profit-maximizing strategy if there were production constraints where producing more of the highest contribution margin products severely limited the production of other products? What if producing the highest contribution margin product reduced the quality of, or speed at which, one or more of the products could be produced and/or delivered to customers?

TO SUMMARIZE

Sales mix is the proportion of the total units sold represented by each of a company's products. Changes in sales mix can change profits because not all products have the same contribution margin. Other things being equal, to maximize profits, management should put greater emphasis on the sale of products with higher contribution margin ratios.

8 *Explain the issues of quality and time relative to CVP decisions.*

ISSUES OF QUALITY AND TIME

The emphasis in this chapter has been primarily on costs and profits and how they change when changes in variable costs, fixed costs, sales prices, and sales volume are made. Remember, however, that financial results are just one element of performance management is interested in. Good managers are equally interested in how these changes will affect the quality of goods and services produced and sold, and the speed at which products and services can be delivered to customers. If, for example, reducing fixed costs means that goods will be produced slower or that the quality of manufactured products will be reduced, the decision to reduce fixed costs may be a poor one. On the other hand, if management can automate a function using robotics instead of high-cost laborers, for example, it may be possible to simultaneously reduce costs, increase quality and consistency, and improve speed of production.

To determine whether quality and speed of production are good or bad, management may need to compare its results with those of other firms, a process called *benchmarking*.

TO SUMMARIZE

When considering the effect on profits of changes in variable costs, fixed costs, sales prices, sales volume, and sales mix, it is important to also consider the effects these changes would have on quality of goods and services, and the speed at which products and services can be delivered to customers. Changes that increase quality, reduce costs, and speed up production are good changes and should be made; changes that result negatively in one or more of these variables must be carefully analyzed and tradeoffs considered.

REVIEW OF LEARNING OBJECTIVES

1 **Understand the key factors involved in cost-volume-profit (CVP) analysis and why CVP is such an important tool in management decision making.** CVP analysis is a very important management concept. It is a technique used by management to understand how profits may be expected to vary in relation to changes in key variables: sales price and volume, variable costs, fixed costs, and mix of products. CVP analysis is a particularly useful tool for planning and making operating decisions. It can provide data to stimulate increased sales efforts or cost reduction programs; assist in production scheduling or marketing strategy; and help establish company policies, for example, the appropriate product mix or the fixed cost structure of a company. Effective management requires a comprehensive understanding and use of CVP analysis.

2 **Explain and analyze the basic cost behavior patterns—variable and fixed.** Understanding cost behavior patterns can assist management in making key operating decisions. The two basic cost behavior patterns are variable and fixed. Costs that vary in total in direct proportion to changes in the level of activity are variable costs. Therefore, per-unit variable costs remain constant. Generally, we assume a linear relationship between variable costs and level of activity within the relevant range; for other ranges, variable costs are curvilinear. Costs that do not change in total with changes in activity level, within the relevant range, are fixed costs; thus, per-unit fixed costs decrease as level of activity increases. Because of factors such as automation, fixed costs are becoming a greater percentage of total costs in most manufacturing companies.

3 **Describe the behavior patterns of mixed costs and stepped costs.** Costs that contain both fixed and variable components are mixed costs. Stepped costs increase in total in a stair-step fashion with the level of activity. If the steps are wide, the cost is treated as a fixed cost for analysis purposes; if the steps are narrow, the cost is approximated as a variable cost.

4 **Analyze mixed costs using the scattergraph and high-low methods.** Before mixed costs can be analyzed and used in decision making, they must be divided into their fixed and variable components. The scattergraph and high-low methods are commonly used to analyze mixed costs. The scattergraph method involves visually plotting a straight line (the regression line) through points on a graph of cost data at various activity levels. With the high-low method, the highest and lowest levels of activity and the associated highest and lowest costs are used to calculate the variable cost rate and the total fixed costs.

5 **Analyze CVP relationships using the contribution margin, equation, and graphic approaches.** Three common methods of CVP analysis are (1) the contribution margin approach, (2) the equation approach, and (3) the graphic approach. Although all three approaches are variations of the same basic calculations, each has its advantages. For example, the graphic approach allows the simultaneous analysis of several different activity levels.

6 **Describe potential changes in CVP variables and the effects these changes have on company profitability; identify the limiting assumptions of CVP analysis.** CVP analysis is commonly used to assess break-even points and to compute target income levels. The equation approach is especially useful in assessing how profits can be expected to change when costs or revenues change. Increases in fixed or variable costs result in a larger number of sales being required to break even and reach target income levels. Increases in sales price or volume of units sold result in a decreased number of sales being required to break even and reach target income levels. There are several limiting assumptions of CVP analysis, including: (1) cost and revenue behavior patterns are linear and remain constant over the relevant range, (2) all costs can be categorized as either fixed or variable, and (3) the sales mix of products is constant over the relevant range.

7 **Explain the effects of sales mix on profitability.** Sales mix is the proportion of total units sold represented by each of a company's products. Because not all products have the same contribution margin ratios, changes in the sales mix of products sold can significantly affect total profits. The best profit-maximizing strategy is to maintain as large a contribution margin as possible on all products and then emphasize those products with the largest individual contribution margins.

8 **Explain the issues of quality and time relative to CVP decisions.** When making changes in costs, revenues, and volume, resulting changes in the quality of products or services and the speed at which those products and services can be delivered to customers must be considered. Changes that result in increased profits while decreasing product or service quality or slowing down delivery of products or services may not be good decisions.

KEY TERMS AND CONCEPTS

REVIEW PROBLEMS

1. Variable and Fixed Costs Analyses

Blade Corporation manufactures two types of inline skates—a basic model and a racing model. During the year 2000, Blade accumulated the following summary information about its two products:

	Racing Model	Basic Model
Selling price	$130	$65
Number of units manufactured and sold	14,000	9,000

	Racing Model		Basic Model	
	Units	Costs	Units	Costs
January	1,200	$ 112,000	800	$ 39,600
February	900	91,000	600	30,000
March	800	76,400	450	25,800
April	1,400	124,800	900	36,900
May	950	92,650	1,000	47,000
June	1,600	146,800	1,200	57,300
July	1,400	134,600	1,300	60,600
August	1,700	154,500	650	32,195
September	1,550	140,200	850	44,250
October	1,500	134,500	500	27,000
November	600	62,500	350	20,700
December	400	44,000	400	22,000
Totals	14,000	$1,313,950	9,000	$443,345

Required:

1. Use the high-low method to estimate the variable and fixed production costs of both the racing model and basic model skates.
2. All selling costs are fixed and they total $200,000 for the racing model and $80,000 for the basic model. Prepare a contribution margin income statement for each model at sales of 10,000 racing and 10,000 basic skates.

Solution

1. Variable and Fixed Costs

The high-low method involves finding the variable and fixed costs at the high and low levels of production. In this case:

	Racing Model	Basic Model
High production month	1,700 (Aug.)	1,300 (July)
Low production month	400 (Dec.)	350 (Nov.)
Difference	1,300	950
Total production costs of high month	$154,500	$60,600
Total production costs of low month	44,000	20,700
Difference	$110,500	$39,900

Once the differences are known, the change in units (production) is divided into the change in costs to determine the variable cost rate.

$$\frac{\text{Change in costs}}{\text{Change in units}} = \text{Variable cost rate}$$

$$\text{Racing Model: } \frac{\$110{,}500}{1{,}300} = \$85$$

$$\text{Basic Model: } \frac{\$39{,}900}{950} = \$42$$

Since total variable costs equal unit variable cost times number of units produced, and total costs equal total variable costs plus total fixed costs, fixed costs can now be calculated.

Total costs − (Variable cost per unit × Number of units) = Total fixed costs

	Racing Model	Basic Model
High production level (X) =	$154,500 − $85(1,700)	$60,600 − $42(1,300)
	X = $154,500 − $144,500	X = $60,600 − $54,600
	X = $10,000	X = $6,000
Low production level (X) =	$44,000 − $85(400)	$20,700 − $42(350)
	X = $44,000 − $34,000	X = $20,700 − $14,700
	X = $10,000	X = $6,000

Thus, we have the following:

	Racing Model	Basic Model
Variable cost rate	$ 85	$ 42
Total fixed costs	10,000	6,000

2. Contribution Margin Income Statements

Blade Corporation
Contribution Margin Income Statements
For the Year Ended December 31, 2000

	Racing Model	Basic Model
Sales revenue (at 10,000 units)	$1,300,000	$650,000
Less variable cost of goods sold*	(850,000)	(420,000)
Contribution margin	$ 450,000	$230,000
Less fixed cost of goods sold	(10,000)	(6,000)
Less fixed selling costs	(200,000)	(80,000)
Income	$ 240,000	$144,000

*$85 per unit for racing model; $42 per unit for basic model.

2. Assessing the Effects of Changes in Costs, Prices, and Volume on Profitability

K&D Company plans the following for the coming year:

Sales volume	100,000 units
Sales price	$2.50 per unit
Variable costs	$1.30 per unit
Fixed costs	$60,000

Required:

1. Determine K&D's target income.
2. Compute what the target income would be under each of the following independent assumptions:
   a. The sales volume increases 20 percent.
   b. The sales price decreases 20 percent.
   c. Variable costs increase 20 percent.
   d. Fixed costs decrease 20 percent.

Solution

1. Target Income

Basic CVP Equation: R = VC + FC + TI

Units sold × Sales price = (Units sold × Variable unit cost) + Fixed costs + Target income
100,000 × $2.50 = (100,000 × $1.30) + $60,000 + X
$250,000 = $130,000 + $60,000 + X
$250,000 = $190,000 + X
$60,000 = X

This answer can be validated by dividing fixed costs by the per-unit contribution margin to find the break-even point, and then multiplying the excess units to be sold above the break-even point by the per-unit contribution margin of $1.20 ($2.50 − $1.30).

$$\frac{\text{Fixed costs}}{\text{Per-unit contribution margin}} = \text{Break-even point}$$

$$\frac{\$60{,}000}{\$1.20} = 50{,}000 \text{ units}$$

Units sold	100,000
Less break-even point (units)	50,000
Excess	50,000
Per-unit contribution margin	× $1.20
Target income	$60,000

2a. The sales volume increases 20 percent

$$[100{,}000 + (0.20 \times 100{,}000)] \times \$2.50 = [100{,}000 + (0.20 \times 100{,}000)] \times \$1.30 + \$60{,}000 + X$$
$$120{,}000 \times \$2.50 = (120{,}000 \times \$1.30) + \$60{,}000 + X$$
$$\$300{,}000 = \$156{,}000 + \$60{,}000 + X$$
$$\$300{,}000 = \$216{,}000 + X$$
$$\$84{,}000 = X$$

In this case, the contribution margin does not change. Therefore, the answer can be validated by multiplying the units to be sold in excess of the break-even point by the per-unit contribution margin of $1.20 to find the target income.

Units sold	120,000
Less break-even point (units)	50,000
Excess	70,000
Per-unit contribution margin	× $1.20
Target income	$84,000

2b. The sales price decreases 20 percent

$$100{,}000 \times [\$2.50 - (0.20 \times \$2.50)] = (100{,}000 \times \$1.30) + \$60{,}000 + X$$
$$100{,}000 \times \$2.00 = \$130{,}000 + \$60{,}000 + X$$
$$\$200{,}000 = \$190{,}000 + X$$
$$\$10{,}000 = X$$

In this case, the contribution margin changes. Therefore, the answer can be validated by dividing fixed costs by the new per-unit contribution margin of $0.70 ($2.00 − $1.30) to find the new break-even point, and then multiplying the units to be sold in excess of the break-even point by the new per-unit contribution margin.

$$\frac{\$60{,}000 \text{ (fixed costs)}}{\$0.70 \text{ (new per-unit contribution margin)}} = 85{,}714 \text{ units (new break-even point)}$$

Units sold	100,000
Less break-even point (units)	85,714
Excess	14,286
Per-unit contribution margin	× $0.70
Target income	$10,000 (rounded)

2c. Variable costs increase 20 percent

$$100{,}000 \times \$2.50 = 100{,}000\ [\$1.30 + (0.20 \times \$1.30)] + \$60{,}000 + X$$
$$\$250{,}000 = (\$100{,}000 \times \$1.56) + \$60{,}000 + X$$
$$\$250{,}000 = \$156{,}000 + \$60{,}000 + X$$
$$\$250{,}000 = \$216{,}000 + X$$
$$\$34{,}000 = X$$

In this case, the contribution margin changes. Therefore, the answer can be validated by dividing fixed costs by the new per-unit contribution margin of $0.94 ($2.50 − $1.56) to find the new break-even point, and then multiplying the units to be sold in excess of the break-even point by the new per-unit contribution margin.

$$\frac{\$60{,}000 \text{ (fixed costs)}}{\$0.94 \text{ (new per-unit contribution margin)}} = 63{,}830 \text{ units (new break-even point)}$$

Units sold	100,000
Less break-even point (units)	63,830
Excess	36,170
Per-unit contribution margin	× $0.94
Target income	$34,000 (rounded)

2d. Fixed costs decrease 20 percent

$$100{,}000 \times \$2.50 = (100{,}000 \times \$1.30) + [\$60{,}000 - (0.20 \times \$60{,}000)] + X$$
$$\$250{,}000 = \$130{,}000 + (\$60{,}000 - \$12{,}000) + X$$
$$\$250{,}000 = \$130{,}000 + \$48{,}000 + X$$
$$\$250{,}000 = \$178{,}000 + X$$
$$\$72{,}000 = X$$

In this case, the contribution margin does not change, but fixed costs, and hence the break-even point, do. Therefore, the answer can be validated by dividing the per-unit contribution margin of $1.20 into the new fixed costs to find the break-even point, and then multiplying the units to be sold in excess of the break-even point by the per-unit contribution margin.

$$\frac{\$48{,}000 \text{ (new fixed costs)}}{\$1.20 \text{ (per-unit contribution margin)}} = 40{,}000 \text{ units (new break-even point)}$$

Units sold	100,000
Less break-even point (units)	40,000
Excess	60,000
Per-unit contribution margin	× $1.20
Target income	$72,000

DISCUSSION QUESTIONS

1. Explain how understanding cost behavior patterns can assist management.
2. Discuss how level of activity is measured in manufacturing, merchandising, and service firms.
3. What is meant by the linearity assumption, and why is it made? Relate this assumption to the relevant-range concept.
4. What factors seem to have caused the shift from variable to fixed cost patterns?
5. How should stepped costs be treated in the planning process?
6. Why must all mixed costs be segregated into their fixed and variable components?
7. What is the major weakness of the scattergraph, or visual-fit, method of analyzing mixed costs?
8. What is the major limitation of the high-low method of analyzing mixed costs?
9. What are three commonly used methods of CVP analysis?
10. What is the contribution margin and why is it important for managers to know the contribution margins of their products?
11. How much will profits increase for every unit sold over the break-even point?
12. What is the major advantage of the graphic approach of CVP analysis?
13. When other factors are constant, what is the effect on profits of an increase in fixed costs? of a decrease in variable costs?
14. What are the limiting assumptions of CVP analysis?
15. What effect is a change in the sales mix likely to have on a firm's overall contribution margin ratio?
16. How do the issues of quality and time relate to CVP decisions?

DISCUSSION CASES

CASE 11-1

COLORADO OUTDOORS FEDERATION

The Colorado Outdoors Federation sponsors an annual banquet. This year the guest speaker is a noted wildlife photographer and lecturer. In planning for the event, the group's treasurer has determined the following costs:

Rental of meeting facility	$250
Honorarium for speaker	800
Tickets and advertising	300
Cost of dinner (per person)	20
Door prizes	500

Last year, tickets were sold at $20 per person, and 350 people attended the banquet. This year the planning committee is hoping for an attendance of 450 at a price of $25 each.

Answer the following:

1. a. At $25 per person, how many people must attend the banquet for the Federation to break even?
   b. How much profit (loss) will occur if 450 people attend?
2. Should the Federation increase its advertising costs by $200 and its door prizes by $300 if it can expect another 100 people to attend the banquet?
3. If the Federation maintains its original expected costs but reduces the price per ticket from $25 to $22, it can expect 500 people to attend the banquet. Should the Federation reduce the price of its tickets to $22 per person?

CASE 11-2

ENTERTAINMENT ENTERPRISES

Entertainment Enterprises, a firm that sells magazine subscriptions, is experiencing increased competition from a number of companies. The president, Betty Kincher, has asked you, the controller, to prepare an income statement that will highlight the fixed and variable costs; this will provide more useful information for planning and control purposes. Sales revenues are $25 per subscription. An analysis of company costs for the past six months reveals the following:

Administrative salaries	$10,000 per month
Advertising expense	$2,000 per month
Cost of goods sold	$12.50 per subscription
Rent expense	$5,000 per month
Sales commissions	15% of sales

In addition, the company makes most sales contacts through an extensive telephone network. Consequently, the telephone expense is significant and has both fixed and variable components. Relevant data concerning the telephone expense for the past six months follow:

Month	Unit Sales	Telephone Expense
July	4,000	$10,200
August	5,000	12,300
September	3,500	9,150
October	4,500	11,250
November	5,200	12,720
December	5,500	13,350

Prepare a management report for the president that:

1. Computes the fixed and variable portions of the telephone expense using the high-low method. (*Note:* A scattergraph may be used to visually check your answer.)
2. Identifies the total variable and fixed costs for the past six months for Entertainment Enterprises.
3. Presents a budgeted (pro-forma) contribution margin income statement for Entertainment Enterprises for the next six months (January through June), assuming that it expects to sell 30,000 subscriptions at a price of $25 each.
4. Explains how the information provided in (3) might help the president make better management decisions.

EXERCISES

EXERCISE 11-1
Variable and Fixed Costs over the Relevant Range

Cook Corporation manufactures plastic garbage cans. In a typical year, the firm produces between 40,000 and 50,000 cans. At this level of production, fixed costs are $10,000 and variable costs are $2 per can.

1. Graph the cost of producing cans, with cost as the vertical axis and production output as the horizontal axis.
2. Indicate on the graph the relevant range of the $10,000 in fixed costs, and explain the significance of the relevant range.
3. What would total production costs be if 46,000 cans were produced?

EXERCISE 11-2
Fixed Costs—The Relevant Range

Flying A Company manufactures airplanes. The following schedule shows total fixed costs at various levels of airplane production:

Units Produced	Total Fixed Costs
0–200	$200,000
201–500	300,000
501–800	400,000

1. What is the fixed cost per unit when 50 airplanes are produced?
2. What is the fixed cost per unit when 250 airplanes are produced?
3. What is the fixed cost per unit when 800 airplanes are produced?
4. Plot total fixed costs on a graph similar to that shown in Exhibit 18-3.

EXERCISE 11-3
Scattergraph Method of Analyzing Mixed Costs

Wyoming Company makes windmills. The company has the following total costs at the given levels of windmill production:

Units Produced	Total Costs
20	$16,000
30	20,000
40	24,000
50	28,000

1. Use the scattergraph method to estimate the fixed and variable elements of Wyoming's total costs.
2. Compute the total cost of making 44 windmills, assuming that total fixed costs are $8,000 and that the variable cost rate computed in (1) does not change.

EXERCISE 11-4
Scattergraph Method of Analyzing Mixed Costs

Given the following mixed costs at various levels of production, complete the requirements.

Month	Units Produced	Mixed Costs
January	2	$13.75
February	3	16.50
March	1	11.00
April	5	22.00
May	2	13.75

1. Plot the data on a scattergraph, and visually fit a straight line through the points.
2. Based on your graph, estimate the monthly fixed cost and the variable cost per unit produced.
3. Compute the total cost of producing 8 units in a month, assuming that the same relevant range applies.
4. Why is it so important to be able to determine the components of a mixed cost?

EXERCISE 11-5
High-Low Method of Analyzing Mixed Costs

Sailmaster makes boats and has the following costs at the given levels of production:

Units Produced	Total Costs
200	$200,000
250	225,000
300	250,000
350	275,000
400	300,000
450	325,000

1. Use the high-low method to compute the variable and fixed elements of Sailmaster's total costs.
2. Compute the total cost of making 500 boats, assuming that total fixed costs and the variable cost rate do not change.

EXERCISE 11-6
High-Low Method of Analyzing Mixed Costs

The San Fernando Herald has determined that the annual printing of 600,000 newspapers costs 9 cents per copy. If production were to be increased to 900,000 copies per year, the per-unit cost would drop to 7 cents per copy.

1. Determine the total fixed and variable costs of printing 600,000 newspapers.
2. What would be the total cost of producing 800,000 copies?

EXERCISE 11-7
Contribution Margin Calculations

Jerry Stone owns and operates a small beach shop in a mall on Sanibel Island, Florida. For the last six months, Jerry has had a display of sunglasses in the front window. Largely because of the display, Jerry has sold 100 pairs of sunglasses per month at an average cost of $26 and selling price of $50. The sales volume has doubled since the display was put in the window. Twenty-five percent of Jerry's storage space is occupied by 190 ice coolers. The coolers have not been selling as well as Jerry hoped, but he is convinced that a front window display of coolers would increase sales by 50 percent. The coolers cost Jerry a total of $2,280 and have been selling at a rate of 100 per month at $28 each.

1. Assuming that cost of goods sold is the only variable cost, compute the contribution margin per unit for sunglasses and ice coolers.
2. Compute the total contribution margins for both sunglasses and ice coolers assuming window displays and no window displays for both items.
3. What are the economic costs associated with keeping the sunglasses display in the store window?
4. What are the economic costs associated with replacing the sunglasses display with an ice cooler display?

EXERCISE 11-8
Contribution Margin Income Statement

The following data apply to Gordon Company for 2000:

Sales revenue (10 units at $25 each) . .	$250
Variable selling expenses	45
Variable administrative expenses	25
Fixed selling expenses	30
Fixed administrative expenses	15
Direct labor	50
Direct materials	60
Fixed manufacturing overhead	5
Variable manufacturing overhead	3

1. Prepare a contribution margin income statement. Assume there were no beginning or ending inventories in 2000.
2. How much would Gordon Company have lost if only five units had been sold during 2000?

EXERCISE 11-9
Analysis of a Contribution Margin Income Statement

Fill in the missing amounts for the following three cases:

	Case I	Case II	Case III
Sales revenue	$100,000	$120,000	$ (7) ?
Variable cost of goods sold:			
Direct materials	$ 25,000	$ (4) ?	$10,000
Direct labor	(1) ?	30,000	10,000
Variable selling and administrative costs.	7,000	(5) ?	5,000
Contribution margin	$ (2) ?	$ 40,000	$ (8) ?
Gross margin	40,000	60,000	20,000
Fixed selling and administrative costs*	11,000	20,000	(9) ?
Rent expense on office building	(3) ?	10,000	1,000
Depreciation expense on delivery trucks	10,000	5,000	4,000
Income	$ 8,000	$ (6) ?	$ -0-

*Except rent and depreciation.

EXERCISE 11-10
Analysis of the Contribution Margin

Dr. Hughes and Dr. Hawkins, owners of the Spanish Fork Care Clinic, have $150,000 of fixed costs per year. They receive 20,000 patient visits in a year, charging each patient an average of $20 per visit; variable costs average $2 per visit (needles, medicines, and so on).

1. What is the contribution margin per patient visit?
2. What is the total contribution margin per year?
3. What is the total pretax profit for a year?
4. Drs. Hughes and Hawkins can bring in another doctor at a salary of $100,000 per year. If this new doctor can handle 5,000 patient visits per year, should the new doctor be hired? (Assume no additional fixed costs will be incurred.)

EXERCISE 11-11
Contribution Margin Analysis

Compute the missing amounts for the following independent cases. (Assume zero beginning and ending inventories.)

	Case I	Case II	Case III
Sales volume (units)	12,000	(5) ?	8,000
Sales price per unit	$5	$4	(9) ?
Variable costs (total)	(1) ?	$50,000	$25,000
Contribution margin (total)	(2) ?	(6) ?	$15,000
Contribution margin per unit (rounded)	$2	$1.50	(10) ?
Fixed costs (total)	(3) ?	(7) ?	(11) ?
Fixed costs per unit (rounded)	(4) ?	$1.00	(12) ?
Income	$10,000	(8) ?	$10,000

EXERCISE 11-12
Break-Even Point and Target Income

Detienne Company manufactures and sells one product for $20 per unit. The unit contribution margin is 40 percent of the sales price, and fixed costs total $80,000.

1. Using the equation approach, compute:
   a. The break-even point in sales dollars and units.
   b. The sales volume (in units) needed to generate a profit of $40,000.
   c. The break-even point (in units) if variable costs increase to 80 percent of the sales price and fixed costs increase to $100,000.
2. Using the contribution margin approach in units, recalculate 1(a), 1(b), and 1(c).

EXERCISE 11-13
Break-Even Point and Target Income

Household Products, Inc., estimates 2000 costs to be as follows:

Direct materials	$4 per unit
Direct labor	$6 per unit
Variable manufacturing overhead	$2 per unit
Variable selling and administrative expenses	$1 per unit
Fixed expenses	$50,000

1. Assuming that Household will sell 40,000 units, what sales price per unit will be needed to achieve a $60,000 profit?
2. Assuming that Household decides to sell its product for $16 per unit, determine the break-even sales volume in dollars and units.
3. Assuming that Household decides to sell its product for $16 per unit, determine the number of units it must sell to generate a $50,000 profit.

EXERCISE 11-14
Break-Even Point—Graphic Analysis

Using the following graph, complete the requirements.

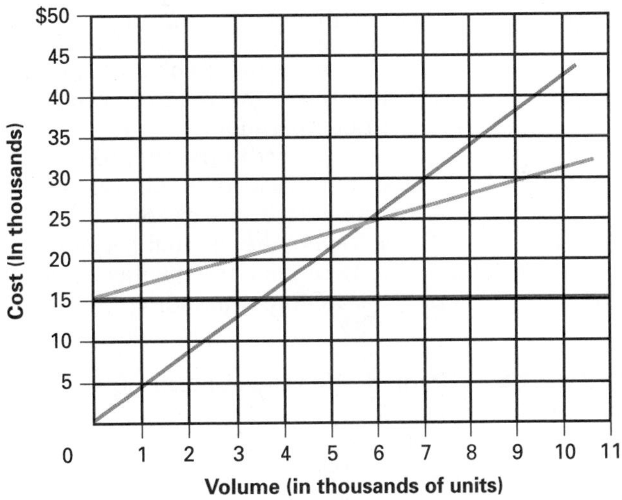

1. Copy the graph and identify (label) fixed costs, variable costs, total revenues, the total cost line, and the break-even point.
2. Determine the break-even point in both sales dollars and volume.
3. Suppose that as a manager you forecast sales volume at 7,000 units. At this level of sales, what would be your total fixed costs, approximate variable costs, and profit (or loss)?
4. At a sales volume of 3,000 units, what would be the level of fixed costs, variable costs, and approximate profit (or loss)?

EXERCISE 11-15
Profit Graph

Using the graph on page 536, answer the questions.

1. What is the break-even point in sales volume (in units)?
2. Approximately what volume of sales (in units) must this company have to generate an income of $300?
3. How much are the fixed costs?

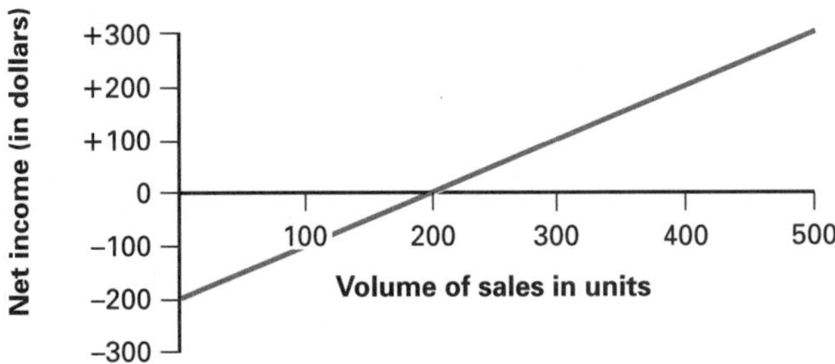

EXERCISE 11-16
Graphing Revenues and Costs

Montana Company manufactures chocolate candy. Its manufacturing costs are as follows:

Annual fixed costs	$15,000
Variable costs	$2 per box of candy

1. Plot variable costs, fixed costs, and total costs on a graph for activity levels of 0 to 30,000 boxes of candy.
2. Plot a revenue line on the graph, assuming that Montana sells the chocolates for $5 a box.

EXERCISE 11-17
CVP Analysis

The Last Outpost is a tourist stop in a western resort community. Kerry Yost, the owner of the shop, sells hand-woven blankets for an average price of $30 per blanket. Kerry buys the blankets from native Americans at an average cost of $21. In addition, he has selling expenses of $3 per blanket. Kerry rents the building for $300 per month and pays one employee a fixed salary of $500 per month.

1. Determine the number of blankets Kerry must sell to break even.
2. Determine the number of blankets Kerry must sell to generate an income of $1,000 per month.
3. Assume that Kerry can produce and sell his own blankets at a total variable cost of $16 per blanket, but that he would need to hire one additional employee at a monthly salary of $600.
   a. Determine the number of blankets Kerry must sell to break even.
   b. Determine the number of blankets Kerry must sell to generate an income of $1,000 per month.

EXERCISE 11-18
CVP Analysis—Changes in Variables

Stop & Shop Inc. estimates that next year's results will be:

Sales revenue (150,000 units)	$1,125,000
Less variable costs	(600,000)
Less fixed costs	(400,000)
Income	$ 125,000

Recompute income, assuming each of the following independent conditions:

1. 10 percent increase in the contribution margin.
2. 6 percent increase in the sales volume.
3. 6 percent decrease in the sales volume.
4. 6 percent increase in variable costs per unit.
5. 7 percent decrease in fixed costs.
6. 7 percent increase in fixed costs.
7. 7 percent increase in the sales volume and a 5 percent increase in fixed costs.

EXERCISE 11-19
CVP Analysis—Changes in Variables

Modern Fun Corporation sells electronic games. Its three salespersons are currently being paid fixed salaries of $30,000 each; however, the sales manager has suggested that it might be more profitable to pay the salespersons on a straight commission basis. He has suggested a commission of 15 percent of sales. Current data for Modern Fun Corporation are as follows:

Sales volume	15,000 units
Sales price	$40 per unit
Variable costs	$29 per unit
Fixed costs	$140,000

1. Assuming that Modern Fun Corporation has a target income of $50,000 for next year, which alternative is more attractive?
2. The sales manager believes that by switching to a commission basis, sales will increase 20 percent. If that is the case, which alternative is more attractive? (Assume that sales are expected to remain at 15,000 units under the fixed salary alternative.)

EXERCISE 11-20
Sales Mix

Klein Brothers sells products X and Y. Because of the nature of the products, Klein sells two units of product X for each unit of product Y. Relevant information about the products is as follows:

	X	Y
Sales price per unit	$20	$30
Variable cost per unit	16	24

1. Assuming that Klein's fixed costs total $140,000, compute Klein's break-even point in sales dollars and units of products X and Y.
2. Assuming that Klein sells two units of product Y for each unit of product X, and fixed costs remain at $140,000, compute Klein's break-even point in sales dollars and units of products X and Y.
3. Explain any differences in your answers to (1) and (2).

PROBLEMS

PROBLEM 11-1
Graphing Revenues and Costs

Cloward and Hawkins, CPAs, took in $350,000 of gross revenues this year. Besides themselves, they have two professional staff (one manager and one senior) and a full-time secretary. Fixed operating expenses for the office were $50,000 last year. This year the volume of activity is up 5 percent, and fixed costs are still $50,000. Total variable operating costs, except for bonuses, average $5 per billable hour. The billable time for all professionals is as follows:

Partners:	3,000 hours at $75/hour
Manager:	1,800 hours at $40/hour
Senior:	2,120 hours at $25/hour

Salaries for the professional staff are $40,000 and $28,000, respectively; the secretary is paid $18,000. The partners each draw salaries of $60,000; plus they share a 5 percent bonus based on gross revenues. The manager is given a 2 percent bonus, also based on gross revenues.

Required:

1. Plot the data on a graph clearly showing (a) fixed costs, (b) variable costs, (c) total costs, and (d) total revenues.
2. How much profit did the CPA firm make this year (after partners' salaries)?

PROBLEM 11-2
High-Low and Scattergraph Methods of Analysis

Woodfield Company makes bed linens. During the first six months of 2000, Woodfield had the following production costs:

Month	Units Produced	Total Costs
January	10,000	$ 68,000
February	20,000	100,000
March	15,000	90,000
April	8,000	52,000
May	17,000	94,000
June	12,000	74,000

Required:

1. Use the high-low method to compute the monthly fixed cost and the variable cost rate.
2. Plot the costs on a scattergraph.
3. **Interpretive Question:** Based on your scattergraph, do you think the fixed costs and the variable cost rate determined in (1) are accurate? Why?

PROBLEM 11-3
Contribution Margin Income Statement

Early in 2001, Delta Company (a retailing firm) sent the following income statement to its stockholders:

Delta Company
Income Statement
For the Year Ended December 31, 2000

Sales revenue (1,000 units)	$60,000	
Less cost of goods sold (variable)	40,000	
Gross margin		$20,000
Operating expenses:		
Selling	$ 6,000	
Administrative	4,000	
Depreciation (fixed)	1,000	
Insurance (fixed)	50	
Utilities ($20 fixed and $30 variable)	50	11,100
Income		$ 8,900

Required:

1. Prepare a contribution margin income statement. (Assume that the fixed components of the selling and administrative expenses are $3,000 and $2,000, respectively.)
2. **Interpretive Question:** Why is a contribution margin income statement helpful to management?
3. **Interpretive Question:** How would the analysis in (1) be different if the depreciation expense was considered a stepped cost with wide steps compared to the relevant range?

PROBLEM 11-4
Contribution Margin Income Statement

Susan Young is an attorney for a small law firm in Arizona. She is also a part-time inventor and an avid golfer. One day Susan's golf foursome included a man named Henry Jones, a manufacturer of Christmas ornaments. Henry explained to Susan that he manufactures an ornament everyone loves, but stores will not carry the ornaments because they are very fragile and often break during shipping. Susan told Henry about a plastic box she had developed recently that would protect such fragile items during shipping. After crash testing the plastic box, Henry offered Susan a contract to purchase 100,000 of the boxes for $2.20 each. Susan is convinced that the box has many applications and she can obtain future orders. Production of the plastic boxes will take one year. Estimated costs for the first year are as follows:

Lease payments on building	$800 per month
Lease payments on machine	$2,200 per month
Cost to retool machine	$10,000
Depreciation on machine	$9,600
Direct materials	$0.70 per box
Direct labor	$0.30 per box
Indirect materials and other manufacturing overhead	$10,000
Interest on loan	$2,500
Administrative salaries	$15,000

Required:

1. Using the information provided, determine Susan's contribution margin and projected net income at a sales level of 100,000 boxes.
2. If Susan's salary as an attorney is $44,500, determine how many boxes Susan must sell to earn profits equal to her salary.

PROBLEM 11-5
Functional and Contribution Margin Income Statements

Smooth Surface Inc. (SSI) is a retail outlet for customized speedboats. The average cost of a boat to the company is $12,500. SSI includes a markup of 30 percent of cost in the sales price. In 2000, SSI sold 33 boats and finished the year with the same amount of inventory it had at the beginning of the year. Additional operating costs for the year were as follows:

Selling expenses:	
Advertising (fixed)	$ 500 per month
Commissions (mixed)	4,500 per month plus 2% of sales
Depreciation (fixed)	300 per month
Utilities (fixed)	150 per month
Freight on delivery (variable)	100 per boat
Administrative expenses:	
Salaries (fixed)	$4,000 per month
Depreciation (fixed)	300 per month
Utilities (fixed)	150 per month
Clerical (variable)	25 per sale

Required:

1. Prepare a traditional income statement using the functional approach.
2. Prepare an income statement using the contribution margin format.
3. **Interpretive Question:** Which statement is more useful for decision making? Why?

PROBLEM 11-6
Contribution Margin and Functional Income Statements

The following information is available for Dabney Company for 2000:

Sales revenue (at $20 per unit)	$151,200
Fixed manufacturing costs	24,000
Variable manufacturing costs (at $8 per unit)	60,480
Fixed selling expenses	70,000
Variable selling expenses (at $2 per unit)	15,120

Required:

1. Prepare a contribution margin income statement.
2. Prepare a functional income statement.
3. Calculate the number of units sold.
4. Calculate the contribution margin per unit.
5. Calculate markup as a percentage of manufacturing costs.
6. **Interpretive Question:** Why is a knowledge of the contribution margin more useful than a knowledge of the markup per unit when management has to make a decision about profitability?

PROBLEM 11-7
Unifying Concepts: High-Low Method, Contribution Margins, and Analysis

Press Publishing Corporation has two major magazines: *Star Life* and *Weekly News.* During 2000, *Star Life* sold 3 million copies at $1.00 each, and *Weekly News* sold 2.1 million copies at $1.10 each. Press Publishing accumulated the following cost information:

	Star Life		*Weekly News*	
Month	Copies Produced	Manufacturing Cost	Copies Produced	Manufacturing Cost
January	400,000	$170,000	300,000	$170,000
February	300,000	150,000	150,000	105,000
March	400,000	180,000	130,000	100,000
April	200,000	120,000	120,000	90,000
May	250,000	140,000	200,000	130,000
June	200,000	125,000	250,000	150,000
July	240,000	130,000	150,000	110,000
August	200,000	130,000	200,000	135,000
September	180,000	110,000	150,000	105,000
October	230,000	130,000	150,000	108,000
November	200,000	125,000	150,000	115,000
December	200,000	126,000	150,000	112,500

Required

1. Use the high-low method to estimate the variable and fixed manufacturing costs of each magazine. (Round the variable cost rate to three decimal places.)
2. If all selling expenses are fixed and they total $500,000 for *Star Life* and $400,000 for *Weekly News,* prepare contribution margin income statements for the two magazines at sales of 3 million copies each.
3. Which magazine is more profitable at sales of 2 million copies?
4. **Interpretive Question:** If the same total dollar amount spent on either magazine will result in the same number of new subscriptions, which magazine should be advertised?

PROBLEM 11-8
Contribution Margin Analysis

Sunrise Company is a manufacturer of alarm clocks. The following information pertains to Sunrise's 2000 sales:

Sales price per unit	$ 15
Variable costs per unit	11
Total fixed costs	300,000

Required:

1. Determine Sunrise Company's unit contribution margin.
2. Using the contribution margin approach, compute:
   a. The break-even point in sales dollars and units.
   b. The sales volume (in dollars and units) needed to generate a target income of $50,000.
3. Using the equation approach of CVP analysis, compute:
   a. The break-even point in sales dollars and units.
   b. The sales volume (in dollars and units) needed to generate a 20 percent return on sales.

PROBLEM 11-9
Contribution Margin Analysis

Porter Company manufactures products X, Y, and Z. The following information relates to the three products:

	Product X	Product Y	Product Z
Sales volume (in units)	50,000	25,000	10,000
Sales revenue	$150,000	$125,000	$100,000
Variable costs	$100,000	$ 85,000	$ 70,000
Fixed costs	$ 30,000	$ 30,000	$ 30,000

Required:

1. At the current level of sales, which product provides the most profit?
2. With each additional unit of sales, which product provides the least contribution to profit?
3. If you could sell only 5,000 units, but all 5,000 must be either product X, Y, or Z, which would you sell?
4. If you could sell only 50,000 units, but all 50,000 must be either product X, Y, or Z, which would you sell?
5. **Interpretive Question:** If you had $5,000 for advertising and each dollar of advertising resulted in a one-unit increase in sales volume, which product would you advertise?

PROBLEM 11-10
Break-Even Analysis

Trudy Sorensen paid $150 to rent a carnival booth for four days. She has to decide whether to sell donuts or popcorn. Donuts cost $1.20 per dozen and can be sold for $2.40 per dozen. Popcorn will require a $75 rental fee for the popcorn maker and $0.05 per bag of popcorn for the popcorn, butter, salt, and bags; a bag of popcorn could sell for $0.30.

Required:

1. Compute the break-even point in dozens of donuts if Trudy decides to sell donuts exclusively and the break-even point in bags of popcorn if she decides to sell popcorn exclusively.
2. Trudy estimates that she can sell either 50 donuts or 30 bags of popcorn every hour the carnival is open (10 hours a day for four days). Which product should she sell?
3. Trudy can sell back to the baker at half cost any donuts she fails to sell at the carnival. Unused popcorn must be thrown away. If Trudy sells only 80 percent of her original estimate, which product should she sell? (Assume that she bought or produced just enough to satisfy the demands she originally estimated.)

PROBLEM 11-11
CVP Graphic Analysis

Using the following graph, complete the requirements.

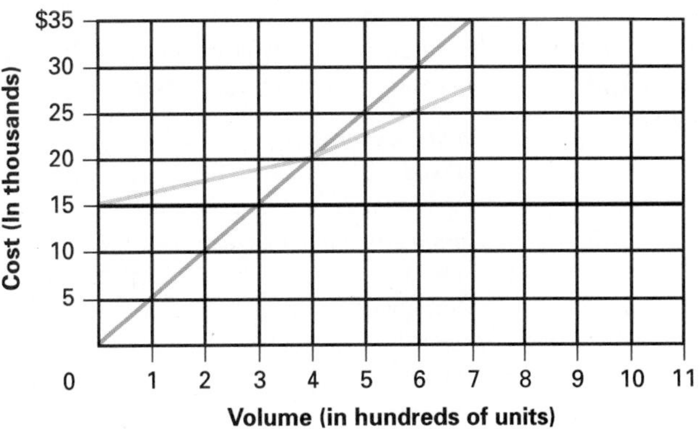

Required:

1. Determine the following:
   a. The break-even point in sales dollars and volume.
   b. The sales price per unit.
   c. Total fixed costs.
   d. Total variable costs at the break-even point.
   e. The variable cost per unit.
   f. The unit contribution margin.
2. What volume of sales must the company generate to reach a target income of $7,500?

PROBLEM 11-12
Contribution Margin Analysis—Changes in Variables

SMC Inc. is a producer of hand-held electronic games. Its 2000 income statement was as follows:

SMC Inc.
Contribution Margin Income Statement
For the Year Ended December 31, 2000

	Total	Per Unit
Sales revenue (150,000 games)	$5,250,000	$35
Less variable costs	3,750,000	25
Contribution margin	$1,500,000	$10
Less fixed costs	900,000	
Income	$ 600,000	

In preparing its budget for 2001, SMC is evaluating the effects of changes in costs, prices, and volume on income.

Required:

Evaluate the following independent cases, and determine SMC's 2001 budgeted income or loss in each case. (Assume that 2000 figures apply unless stated otherwise.)

1. Fixed costs increase $150,000.
2. Fixed costs decrease $100,000.
3. Variable costs increase $3 per unit.
4. Variable costs decrease $4 per unit.
5. Sales price increases $5 per unit.
6. Sales price decreases $5 per unit.
7. Sales volume increases 25,000 units.
8. Sales volume decreases 15,000 units.
9. Sales price decreases $4 per unit, sales volume increases 40,000 units, and variable costs decrease by $2.50 per unit.
10. Fixed costs decrease by $100,000, and variable costs increase $4 per unit.
11. Sales volume increases 30,000 units, with a decrease in sales price of $2 per unit. Variable costs drop $1.50 per unit, and fixed costs increase $50,000.

PROBLEM 11-13
Income Statement and Break-Even Analysis

Zimmerman Company records the following costs associated with the production and sale of a steel slingshot:

Selling expenses:	
Fixed	$6,500
Variable	$0.50 per unit sold
Administrative expenses:	
Fixed	$4,500
Variable	$0.25 per unit sold
Manufacturing costs:	
Fixed	$15,500
Variable	$7.50 per unit produced

Assume that in 2000 the beginning and ending inventories were the same. Also assume that 2000 sales were 11,000 units at $11.50 per slingshot.

Required:

1. Prepare a contribution margin income statement.
2. Determine the break-even point in sales dollars.
3. **Interpretive Question:** Zimmerman believes that sales volume could be improved 20 percent if an additional commission of $0.50 per unit were paid to the salespeople. Zimmerman also believes, however, that the same percentage increase could be achieved through an additional $3,000 investment in advertising. Which action, if either, should Zimmerman take? Why?

PROBLEM 11-14
CVP Analysis—Changes in Variables

Rougely Manufacturing Company produces electric carving knives. The firm has not been as profitable as expected in the past three years. As a result, there is excess capacity that could be used to produce an additional 10,000 knives per year. However, any production above that amount would require a capital investment of

$50,000. Operating results for the previous year are shown here. Assume that there is never any ending inventory.

Sales revenue (125,000 knives × $8)		$1,000,000
Variable costs (125,000 knives × $5)	$625,000	
Fixed costs	350,000	975,000
Income		$ 25,000

Required:

Respond to the following independent proposals, and support your recommendations:

1. The production manager believes that profits could be increased through the purchase of more automated production machinery, which would increase fixed costs by $100,000 and reduce the variable costs by $0.75 per knife. Is she correct if sales are to remain at 125,000 knives annually?
2. The sales manager believes that a 5 percent discount on the sales price would increase the sales volume to 135,000 units annually. If he is correct, would this action increase or decrease profits?
3. Would the implementation of both proposals be worthwhile?
4. The sales manager believes that an increase in sales commissions could improve the sales volume. In particular, he suggests that an increase of $0.50 per knife would increase the sales volume 30 percent. If he is correct, would this action increase profits?
5. The accountant suggests another alternative: Reduce administrative salaries by $10,000 so that prices can be reduced by $0.10 per unit. She believes that this action would increase the volume to 130,000 units annually. If she is correct, would this action increase profits?
6. The corporate executives finally decide to spend an additional $30,000 on advertising to bring the sales volume up to 135,000 units. If the increased advertising can bring in these extra sales, is this a good decision?

PROBLEM 11-15
CVP Analysis—Return on Sales

The federal government recently placed a ceiling on the selling price of sheet metal produced by MOB Company. In 2000, MOB was limited to charging a price that would earn a 20 percent return on gross sales. On the basis of this restriction, MOB had the following results for 2000:

Sales revenue (1,150,000 feet at $2.00 per foot)		$2,300,000
Variable costs (1,150,000 feet × $1.40)	$1,610,000	
Fixed costs	230,000	1,840,000
Income		$ 460,000

In 2001, MOB predicted that the sales volume would decrease to 900,000 feet of sheet metal. With this level of sales, however, the company anticipated no changes in the levels of fixed and variable costs.

Required:

1. Determine MOB's income for 2001 if all forecasts are realized. Compute both the dollar amount of profit and the percentage return on sales.
2. MOB plans to petition the government for a price increase so that the 2000 rate of return on sales (20 percent) can be maintained. What sales price should the company request, based on 2001 projections? (Round to the nearest cent.)
3. How much profit (in dollars) will MOB earn in 2001 if this sales price, as determined in (2), is approved?
4. **Interpretive Question:** What other factors must be considered by MOB and the government?

PROBLEM 11-16
Unifying Concepts: CVP Analysis and Changes in Variables

The 2000 pro-forma income statement for Cedar Co. is as follows (ignore taxes):

Cedar Co.
Pro-Forma Income Statement
For the Year Ended December 31, 2000

Sales (60,000 units)		$660,000
Cost of goods sold:		
Direct materials	$40,000	
Direct labor	75,000	
Variable manufacturing overhead	18,000	
Fixed manufacturing overhead	11,000	
Total cost of goods sold		144,000
Gross margin		$516,000
Selling expenses:		
Variable	$45,000	
Fixed	98,000	
Administrative expenses:		
Variable	17,000	
Fixed	77,000	
Total selling and administrative expenses		237,000
Income		$279,000

Required:

1. Compute how many units must be sold to break even.
2. Compute the increase (decrease) in income under the following independent situations:
   a. Sales increase 30 percent.
   b. Fixed selling and administrative expenses decrease 10 percent.
   c. Contribution margin decreases 20 percent.
3. Compute sales in units and dollars at the break-even point if fixed costs increase from $186,000 to $260,400.
4. Compute the number of units that must be sold if expected profit is $1 million.

PROBLEM 11-17
Sales Mix and Contribution Margin Not Realized

Mike's Ice Cream Company produces and sells ice cream in three sizes: quart, half-gallon, and gallon. Relevant information for each of the sizes is as follows:

	Quart	Half-Gallon	Gallon
Average sales price	$1.00	$1.85	$3.60
Less variable cost	0.80	1.40	2.40
Unit contribution margin	$0.20	$0.45	$1.20
Sales mix (% of sales)	15%	60%	25%

Mike anticipates sales of $500,000 and fixed costs of $120,000 in 2000.

Required:

1. Determine the break-even sales volume in dollars and units for 2000.
2. Determine Mike's 2000 projected income.
3. Assume that Mike's sales mix changes to 10 percent quarts, 40 percent half-gallons, and 50 percent gallons. Determine Mike's break-even sales volume in dollars and units.

Analyzing Real Company Information

International Case

Ethics Case

Writing Assignment

The Debate

Internet Search

Accounting is more than just doing textbook problems. These Competency Enhancement Opportunities provide practice in critical thinking, oral and written communication, research, teamwork, and consideration of ethical issues.

ANALYZING REAL COMPANY INFORMATION

• Analyzing 11-1 (Microsoft)

Annual revenues, as well as sales and marketing expenses, for the last ten years are provided below for **Microsoft Corporation.**

Microsoft Corporation (millions)

Year	Sales and Marketing Expenses	Annual Revenue
1988	$ 162	$ 591
1989	219	804
1990	317	1,183
1991	534	1,843
1992	854	2,759
1993	1,205	3,753
1994	1,384	4,649
1995	1,895	5,937
1996	2,657	8,671
1997	2,856	11,358

Operating output data, such as the number of computer products sold each year, are not provided in Microsoft's annual report. However, it seems sensible that changes in revenues should serve as an approximate measure of changes in the number of products sold by Microsoft. Use the high-low method to analyze the data above to determine if there is a relationship between revenues and sales and marketing expenses. What appears to be the amount of fixed costs in these expenses? Does this fixed cost amount make sense? (*Note:* Be sure to remember that the data above are in millions of dollars.)

• Analyzing 11-2 (Star Video)

It is likely that a number of grocery stores in your town have video rental departments. However, grocery stores generally do not focus much management attention on their small video rental businesses. The main purpose of having a video department is to encourage more customers to come into the store and purchase groceries! However, a grocery store cannot simply buy a large selection of video tapes, corner off a section of floor space, and start renting tapes. Successfully managing a rental business requires being aware of an unimaginably large number of video titles. Obviously, new movies are constantly being released, while old movies gradually lose their appeal and are eventually scrapped. Further, large-scale video rental chains such as **Blockbuster** constantly track shifting consumer tastes for certain titles and movie categories. These consumer preferences are quite different based on demographic data like geographic location, average age, ethnicity, average income, etc. A grocery store really can't manage all these data without losing focus on its main business. Hence, most grocery stores contract out their video rental business to a large-scale video management company. These management companies can purchase huge quantities of tapes, maintain large distribution warehouses, and track demographic data that allow them to manage and move specific inventories to the appropriate grocery store locations. In 1992, one such video management company, Star Video (not its real name), was managing 86 stores representing three supermarket chains in five states—Arizona, California, Montana, Washington, and Wyoming. Total revenue in 1992 for Star Video was $3.6 million. Star Video makes all the inventory investments and handles all management activities involved in providing video rentals at each of the 86 stores. Video rental revenue is then split between Star Video and each grocery store, with Star Video keeping the lion's share. Stores like this arrangement, since they make most of their money on grocery sales to customers who come to rent videotapes. Star Video needs to carefully manage revenue and costs at each store in order to stay profitable. Below are the data for six stores located in Washington.

Store Name	Monthly Revenue	Monthly Operating Expenses
Moses Lake	$ 6,408	$ 3,295
W. Kennewick	4,064	2,289
Pasco	4,038	2,270
S. Kennewick	3,692	2,142
E. Wenatchee	1,395	1,316
Richland	2,104	1,516
Total	$21,701	$12,828

Use the high-low method to analyze the operating expenses at these six stores. Determine if operating expenses are related to store revenue. What appear to be the fixed costs of operating each store? Create a graph and plot these costs using revenue on the horizontal axis and operating expenses on the vertical axis. Does the scattergraph agree or disagree with the results of your high-low analysis?

INTERNATIONAL CASE

• The Paper Company

The **Ghanata Group of Companies (GGC)** is a locally owned and controlled company in Ghana, West Africa. One of its principle operating divisions, **The Paper Company**, is one of Africa's most modern and largest manufacturers/distributors of paper products. For both operating and reporting purposes, The Paper Company is organized into product lines: scholastic, envelope, and stationery. During the 1980s, the economy in Ghana was stagnant. The country faced severe economic problems as a result of unfavorable trade terms with other countries. The official exchange rate of U.S. $1.00 to the local currency, the *cedi,* was about 39.00 as of the end of 1984. (The unofficial rate, e.g., the black market rate, was at least five times worse!) As a result of the economy, it became very difficult for GGC to secure direct materials for its divisions. If a division could secure direct materials, it could sell almost everything it produced. Hence, in terms of being able to predict sales volumes, there was a great deal of risk for GGC divisions. The 1985 budgeted operating data for the three departments in The Paper Company were as follows:

The Paper Company
1985 Budgeted Operations Data
(Cedi 000's)

	Scholastic	Envelope	Stationery
Budgeted sales..............	$1,785,000	$984,000	$3,334,050
Budgeted variable costs	(410,550)	(442,800)	(2,200,473)
Contribution margin..........	$1,374,450	$541,200	$1,133,577
Budgeted fixed costs	(1,267,350)	(482,160)	(933,534)
Income.....................	$ 107,100	$ 59,040	$ 200,043

The margin of safety (MOS) measures the excess of total sales over break-even volume in sales. In effect, the MOS defines that amount at which sales can decline before losses will occur for a company, and it is measured as follows:

Margin of safety (MOS) = Total sales − Break-even sales

MOS can also be calculated as a percentage by dividing the MOS in dollars by total sales dollars, as follows:

MOS percentage = MOS in dollars/Total sales

Compute the margin of safety (MOS) in both dollars and as a percentage for all three departments. Given the high-risk business environment in Ghana at this time, which department presents the highest risk to GGC? The lowest risk? Be sure to explain your answer in terms of operating leverage.

Source: A. Oppong, "The Paper Company," *The Journal of Accounting Case Research,* 1996, Vol. 3, No. 2, pp. 80–88. Permission to use has been granted by Captus Press Inc. and the Accounting Education Resource Centre of The University of Lethbridge. [Journal Subscription: Captus Press Inc., York University Campus, 4700 Keele Street, North York, Ontario, M3J 1P3, by calling (416) 736-5537, or by fax at (416) 736-5793, Email: info@captus.com, Internet: http://www.captus.com]

ETHICS CASE

• Pickmore International

Joan Hildabrand is analyzing some cost data for her boss, Ross Cumings. The data relate to a special sales order that Pickmore International is considering from a large customer in Singapore. The following data are applicable to the product being ordered:

Normal unit sales price	$49.95
Variable unit manufacturing costs	10.50
Variable unit selling and administrative expenses	18.25

The customer is requesting that the sales order be accepted on the following terms:

a. The unit sales price would equal the unit contribution margin plus 10 percent.
b. Freight would be paid by the customer.
c. Pickmore International would pay a $5,000 "facilitating payment" to a "friend of the customer" to get the product through customs more quickly.

In considering the order, Ross has indicated to Joan that this is a very important customer. Furthermore, Pickmore has no excess capacity right now, but this work would help some employees earn a little extra Christmas money with overtime.

1. What are the accounting and ethical issues involved in this case?
2. Should Joan recommend acceptance of the sales terms proposed for this special order?

WRITING ASSIGNMENT

• Issues of quality and time on CVP decisions

This chapter described how to analyze whether the difference between sales price and variable costs, as well as the volume of sales, are sufficient to pay for all fixed costs in an organization and provide a sufficient profit. A number of methods have been presented for analyzing these costs, volume, and price relationships. These methods all focus on *quantitative* issues that affect how a company manages its resources to maximize overall profits. However, there are a number of *qualitative* issues involving quality and time that should also affect decisions about what sales prices to set, how to manage fixed and variable costs, and which products should be emphasized within the organization. One way to trade off fixed costs for variable costs is to consider making large fixed costs investments into technology that result in automated production, merchandising, and service processes. These kinds of investments allow some variable costs, such as direct labor, to be reduced. Managing this cost tradeoff often has strong implications on the quality of the product or service, as well as the timeliness with which it can be delivered. Both of these qualitative issues eventually affect the quantitative issues of costs, volume, and price. Go to your library and find an article describing one organization's effort to invest in automation or other technologies in order to reduce costs. Determine what quality and time issues are affected by the investment. Write a one- to two-page memo describing what you found.

THE DEBATE

• Which cost analysis method is best?

Many costs within an organization are mixed costs, combining elements of both fixed and variable costs. Separating these types of costs into their fixed and variable cost components is necessary before CVP analysis work can be done. Two potential cost analysis methods are the scattergraph (visual-fit) approach and the high-low approach. Each of these methods has both disadvantages and advantages compared to the other.

Divide your group into two teams and prepare a two-minute oral argument supporting your assigned position.

- One team represents "The scattergraph (visual-fit) method is superior!" Explain why this method should be used for determining the variable and fixed cost components in a mixed cost.
- The other team represents "High-low; the way to go!" Explain why this method should be used for determining the variable and fixed cost components in a mixed cost.

INTERNET SEARCH

• Centre for Applied Ethics

We have discussed ethical issues for accountants in this text and have included an ethics case at the end of each chapter. Obviously, ethical issues are of concern to accountants and all other business professionals. There are a number of good resources on the Internet for those interested in better exploring ethical issues in business (hopefully, we're all interested in this topic!). One of the better sites is the Centre for Applied Ethics at the University of British Columbia (www.ethics.ubc.ca). Sometimes Web addresses change, so if this address doesn't work, access the Web site for this textbook (stice.swcollege.com) for an updated link to the Centre for Applied Ethics.

Go to this site and explore the materials regarding applied ethics resources on the World Wide Web. Find an article that discusses either business or professional ethics. Write a short paragraph that describes exactly where you found the article and give a brief summary.

CHAPTER

12 STANDARDS AND PERFORMANCE VARIANCES

SETTING THE STAGE

Just a few years ago, Caterpillar Inc. changed its overall corporate structure from a "functional bureaucratic" organization to a "profit center" organization and instituted performance measures appropriate to the new structure. The result has been increased performance in nearly every division in the company. Take the Wheel Loader and Excavators Division (WLED), based in Aurora, Illinois, for example. Since the restructuring, the division has achieved outstanding success and continuous improvement.

Until 1990, Caterpillar's organizational structure was divided into functional areas such as engineering, manufacturing, and accounting. The idea was that if each functional area achieved its goals and objectives, the customer would be happy and the corporation would prosper.

Then in mid-1990, Caterpillar restructured its functional organization into one comprised of 13 "profit center" divisions and four "service center" divisions. One goal of the reorganization and new performance measurement system was to increase responsiveness, flexibility, and customer focus, so Caterpillar created minibusinesses within the company that concentrate on each customer's product needs. This decentralized approach allows each division to focus on product design, manufacturing, pricing, and parts and service for each customer.

For example, under the previous structure, a customer who wanted to buy a hydraulic excavator would contact a dealer who would work with the massive Caterpillar organization. Today the same customer still contacts a Caterpillar dealer (whose role is unchanged), but the customer's needs are addressed by the Hydraulic Excavator Product Group within the WLED.

Another goal of the reorganization and new performance measurement system was to drive authority, responsibility, and decision making downward in the organization, thereby empowering employees and holding them accountable for results. By doing so, Caterpillar believed it would develop more broadly based businesspeople throughout the organization and allow them to make better use of their experience and innovativeness within their areas of expertise.

Caterpillar's changes were made after benchmarking (comparing) Caterpillar with such companies as AT&T, Texas Instruments, and IBM. Based on the

LEARNING OBJECTIVES

After studying this chapter, you should be able to:

1. *Explain why performance evaluation is such an important activity in organizations.*
2. *Describe the process of strategic planning in organizations.*
3. *Identify different kinds of organizational units in which performance evaluation occurs.*
4. *Explain how performance is evaluated in cost centers.*
5. *Explain how performance is evaluated in profit centers.*
6. *Explain how performance is evaluated in investment centers.*
7. *Explain why it is important for a company to have quality and time standards as well as financial standards.*

benchmarking, new performance measures were developed that related to the corporate mission, the new organizational structure, the desire to push authority and responsibility downward in the organization, and critical success factors. The new performance measures involved an integrated set of financial and nonfinancial measures that emphasized both long-term and short-term results. In the WLEDs, for example, the division and each of its four product groups are profit centers, i.e., where both revenues and expenses are accounted for. In addition, profit also is determined for major component groups such as machine structures, machine attachments, and parts, even though they aren't designated as formal profit centers. The benefit of determining profit by major component groups, as well as by product groups within divisions, is to push accountability to lower levels in the company and to create constructive competition among intraorganizational units. This approach aligns well with the strategy in place for "cost ownership" at the WLED. Cost ownership is a team concept where representatives from all functional areas (such as purchasing, engineering, accounting, manufacturing, and marketing) work together to minimize costs and maximize quality for each component and product. This level of profit analysis helps to identify areas of the business that are having difficulty and that require special efforts to improve profitability.

There are several reasons why companies reorganize their processes as **Caterpillar** *did in the opening scenario. A recent survey by the Institute of Management Accountants identified seven reasons, as shown in Exhibit 12-1. Note that for each reason we have identified whether it affects the cost, quality, or speed with which products and/or services are delivered to customers.*

In deciding to restructure, Caterpillar used benchmarking, *a process used by companies to target key areas for improvement within their operations so that they can increase their productivity, competitiveness, and quality. Benchmarking involves comparing a company's financial and operational performance against a competitor's performance or the performance of various internal departments against each other. Internal comparisons allow the best processes within a company to be identified so departments that aren't performing up to speed can find out why and adopt new performance standards. External comparisons let companies see how they stack up in the marketplace and discover areas in which they can improve.*

EXHIBIT 12-1 Reasons Why Companies Reorganize Their Processes

Improve key business processes (cost, quality, speed)	19% of respondents
Improve products (quality)	17%
Cost cutting (cost)	16%
Improve internal/external customer satisfaction (cost, quality, speed)	16%
Competitive issues (cost, quality, speed)	14%
Improve profits (cost)	9%
Reduce headcount (cost)	7%

Source: Dan Arisak, "The Controller As Business Strategist," *Management Accounting,* December 1996, pp. 48–49.

Benchmarking is only one way organizations evaluate their performance. There are other ways that will be discussed in this chapter. Before covering different types of performance evaluation systems, however, it is important that you understand why performance evaluation is such an important activity for a company.

1 *Explain why performance evaluation is such an important activity in organizations.*

WHY PERFORMANCE EVALUATION IS SO IMPORTANT

Today we live in an age where information is transmitted worldwide almost instantaneously. With accurate and timely information so readily available, it is absolutely critical that companies produce the highest quality products at the lowest possible price and faster than anyone else. If a U.S. automobile manufacturer produces a car that is more expensive or of a lower quality than cars made in Japan or Germany, for example, consumers will buy foreign automobiles because information about the Japanese and German cars is readily available to U.S. car buyers. Likewise, if a U.S. automobile company can buy higher quality tires at a lower price from a Korean tire manufacturer than it can from a U.S. tire manufacturer, it will buy Korean tires because information about the foreign tires is easily accessible by the U.S. automobile manufacturer. Similarly, if an investor has a limited amount of money to invest, he or she can just as easily buy stocks of European or Asian companies as stocks of U.S. companies because the information is available and the markets are easily accessible.

FYI

Much of the continuous improvement literature had its origin in Japan with Japanese companies. In fact, the term "kaizen" in Japanese means "continuous improvement." You will see the term "kaizen" used frequently, even in U.S. management accounting literature. Continuous improvement can take the form of continuous reduction in product defects, delivery time, material waste, inventory size, setup time, and so on. Under continuous improvement programs, one of the major responsibilities of managers and workers is to reduce total costs by continuous improvement in both monetary and nonmonetary standards.

This increased availability of up-to-date information and the ease with which products, services, and investments can be made or purchased internationally has made it critically important that companies operate as efficiently and effectively as possible. Because it is so important to be a high-performing or "world-class" company, organizations are placing more and more emphasis on evaluating their performance and continuously improving. Managers recognize that, in this information age, it is "survival of the fittest" and that only the highest performing companies will be able to compete in the long run.

Companies can be poor performers for several reasons. Some companies don't perform well because they don't develop appropriate corporate strategies or goals or they lack vision (planning). Some companies don't perform well because they have poor performance measurement methods or methods that don't fit their organizational structures and, therefore, really don't accurately assess how well they are doing. Perhaps most commonly, some companies don't perform well because they fail to execute their strategies and planned actions (controlling).

Performance evaluation is important for both planning and controlling decisions. With respect to planning, managers in manufacturing companies must determine how to acquire direct materials, employ direct labor, and provide sufficient manufacturing support to produce the products their companies sell. In merchandising companies, managers must know where to buy the highest quality goods at the lowest possible prices. In service companies, management must be able to plan manpower and other resource needs so that they can serve clients effectively. A sales forecast together with the results of past performance and future standards help management make these planning decisions. If, for example, a manufacturing company plans to sell 10,000 units of its product, management must know in advance how much material will be needed for production and how much each unit should cost. Management also needs to know what the percentage of defective units will be, how efficiently labor will perform, and what other costs will be incurred in making its products. Given a past cost of $5 per unit, management can plan not only to acquire $50,000 of direct materials but also to obtain appropriate financing to pay for the materials. Management can also determine if more or less materials and/or labor will be needed because of improved or worsening quality and performance. Information about past performance helps management avoid being caught short or having a costly oversupply of direct materials or labor.

Information about past performance also helps management decide whether the company can handle special orders or changes in customer demand. An analysis of past performance enables management to determine what is needed for each additional unit of product and whether a special order can be produced with existing facilities and resources.

Performance evaluation is also important for controlling decisions. Management must determine whether a product is being produced efficiently. An analysis of past performance or a benchmarking against other firms or standards may reveal, for example, that costs are too high as a result of factors beyond company control (the supplier raised prices, for example) or because a department is wasting materials or operating inefficiently. If production is inefficient, management must decide on a course of action to correct the problem. Benchmarking and standards are important because a comparison of the current period's performance with past periods' performances is not always a sufficient measure of efficiency. Even if performance has improved, a company may still be operating inefficiently. Accurately measuring efficiency requires that a company analyze its performance for continuous improvement against other companies and departments and against standards that have been carefully established. It is only possible to improve if you know how well you are doing. Performance evaluation allows organizations to plan better, to reward or penalize employees and segments for good or bad performance, and to more efficiently and effectively allocate resources.

In this chapter, we will discuss several ways companies organize and set goals and then measure their performance against those goals. As was the case with product cost determination discussed in Chapter 10, there have been significant performance evaluation research and changes in the past few years. Much of this research and many of the changes have emphasized developing performance systems that align performance measurement with an organization's strategic plan and objectives and that focus on customer and employee needs. Historically, many performance measures have been backward looking and have tended to report results too late to be useful and for corrective action to be taken. New performance measures link daily activities with ways that help organizations guide decisions and actions.

Obviously, to effectively evaluate performance, organizations must have goals, objectives, or benchmarks against which to assess their performance. Most organizations establish these goals and benchmarks through a process called strategic planning, which we will discuss next.

TO SUMMARIZE

Living in an age where information is inexpensive and readily available, it is important that companies offer the highest quality products at the lowest possible price and faster than their competitors. Because quality, speed, and price are so important, it is critical that organizations establish good performance evaluation methods and continuously improve. It isn't possible for a company to improve its performance until it knows how it is doing. Performance evaluation helps an organization plan better and control its operations more effectively.

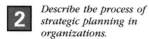

2 *Describe the process of strategic planning in organizations.*

strategic planning Broad, long-range planning, usually conducted by top management.

STRATEGIC PLANNING

To be effective, performance measures must relate to the goals of an organization. Most companies go through a process of **strategic planning** to determine how they will organize and operate their businesses. Essentially, strategic planning is the systematic and formalized effort of a company to establish basic company purposes, objectives, policies, and strategies and to develop detailed plans to implement policies and strategies to achieve objectives and company purposes. Usually, strategic planning begins by establishing a mission statement that guides the company. As an example, consider the mission statement shown in Exhibit 12-2, which guides the strategic planning at **Conair-Franklin**, a privately owned company that produces auxiliary equipment and production support systems for the plastics industry.

In strategic planning, mission statements are usually followed by goals or guidelines that identify what it is the organization will try to accomplish. The goals or guidelines are then broken down into specific actions that must be taken to accomplish the goals and mission. Performance measures, relating to quality, financial performance, and speed of delivery, are then developed to assess how well the actions are being accomplished. The assumption is that if a company performs its action steps well, it will be accomplishing its goals and fulfilling its mission.

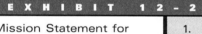

Mission Statement for Conair-Franklin

1. **Our Customer:**
   Conair-Franklin will be the **Best Company** in our industry segment as measured by our customer satisfaction index which is a function of:
   a. Improved Quality
   b. Better Service
   c. Shorter Delivery
   d. More Competitive Prices

   We will take care of our customers as **Priority One.**

2. **Our People:**
   As employees we will work together in teams to help each other grow in job skills and performance and help each other achieve excellence in all that we do.
   We will share and enjoy together all of the financial and psychological benefits which come to those who are clearly **Number One** in what they do.

3. **Our Results:**
   Conair-Franklin will achieve superior performance levels and profits by:
   Speeding everything up—finding faster ways.
   Simplifying everything we do.
   Flattening our organization to improve communications and accountability.
   Empowering every employee to improve things in his/her area.
   Eliminating waste everywhere.
   Reducing cost everywhere.

Source: Michael D. Akers and Grover L. Porter, "Strategic Planning at Five World-Class Companies," *Management Accounting,* July 1995, pp. 26–27.

While strategic planning varies from firm to firm and can be accomplished in different ways, it almost always involves these four steps:

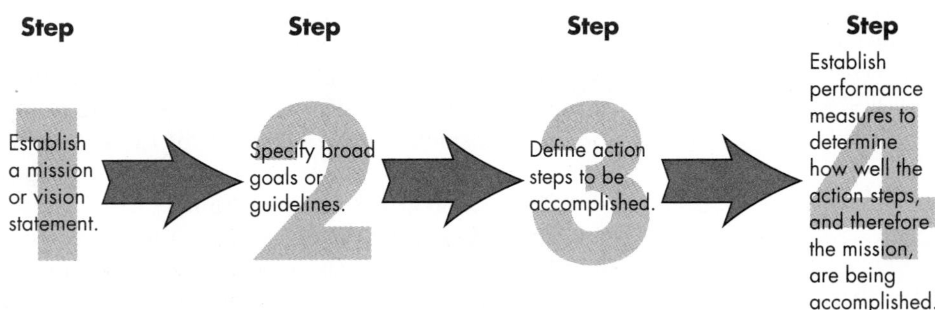
Step
1
Establish a mission or vision statement.
Step
2
Specify broad goals or guidelines.
Step
3
Define action steps to be accomplished.
Step
4
Establish performance measures to determine how well the action steps, and therefore the mission, are being accomplished.

et connected
p://www.swcollege.com
net work

Coca-Cola products are available in 195 countries around the world. In 1997, the people of the world consumed almost 1 billion servings of Coca-Cola products *each day.* Access the company's Web site.

What is The Coca-Cola Company's mission statement?

coca-cola.com

Whatever the specific model used, strategic planning usually involves several key aspects. First, strategic planning is future oriented, focusing on what a company will be in the future. Second, it includes a critical assessment of the strengths and weaknesses of the company. Third, it includes analyses of competitors, customers, and markets.

Obviously, strategic planning can take place at the division or group level as well as the corporate level. In fact, in most organizations, divisions develop strategic plans that are reviewed by the corporate office. The way a division strategically plans and evaluates its performance depends on the type of unit it is. In this chapter we will focus on the performance evaluation aspect of strategic planning. Although mission statements, goals, and activities are specifically tailored to individual companies, there are often similarities in the way organizations evaluate their performance. As was discussed in the opening scenario, Caterpillar was able to improve its performance by turning its various divisions into profit centers and evaluating them, in part, on the profits they made. In the next section, we will discuss different types of organizational units and examine key performance measures used for each.

(S T O P & T H I N K)

Why is it important that employees and other stakeholders (e.g., customers and investors) be involved in the strategic planning process of a company? In other words, is a strategic plan something that should be developed through broad-based participation or is it something that should be established only by top management?

TO SUMMARIZE

Strategic planning is a systematic effort to establish basic company purposes, objectives, policies, and strategies and to develop detailed plans to implement policies and strategies to achieve basic objectives and company purposes. Most strategic plans involve establishing a mission statement, specifying goals or objectives, defining action steps to be accomplished, and establishing performance measures to determine how well the action steps, and hence, the strategic plan have been accomplished. Strategic planning is future oriented; it involves a company assessing its strengths and weaknesses, as well as analyzing its competitors, customers, and markets.

3 *Identify different kinds of organizational units in which performance evaluation occurs.*

segments Parts of an organization requiring separate reports for evaluation by management.

PERFORMANCE EVALUATION IN DIFFERENT TYPES OF OPERATING UNITS

Most companies are made up of a number of relatively independent **segments** or sub-units, sometimes called groups, divisions, or subsidiaries.

As an example, Exhibit 12-3 shows an organizational chart for a hypothetical company that we will call International Manufacturing Corporation (IMC). IMC has three operating (subsidiary) companies: Acme Computer, Edison Automobile, and Jennifer Cosmetics. Although each of these companies has several divisions and other sub-segments, only a few of those for Edison Automobile are shown. Edison has three geographic bases: the United States, the Far East, and Europe. The making and selling of automobiles in the Far East division is further broken down into the Japanese and Korean units. The Japanese unit is separated into sales, manufacturing, and service. Edison Automobile's other geographic divisions have similar subsegments.

You will notice that IMC uses different criteria to define its segments at each level. At the highest level, product group (computers, autos, cosmetics) is used, prob-

EXHIBIT 12-3 An Organizational Chart

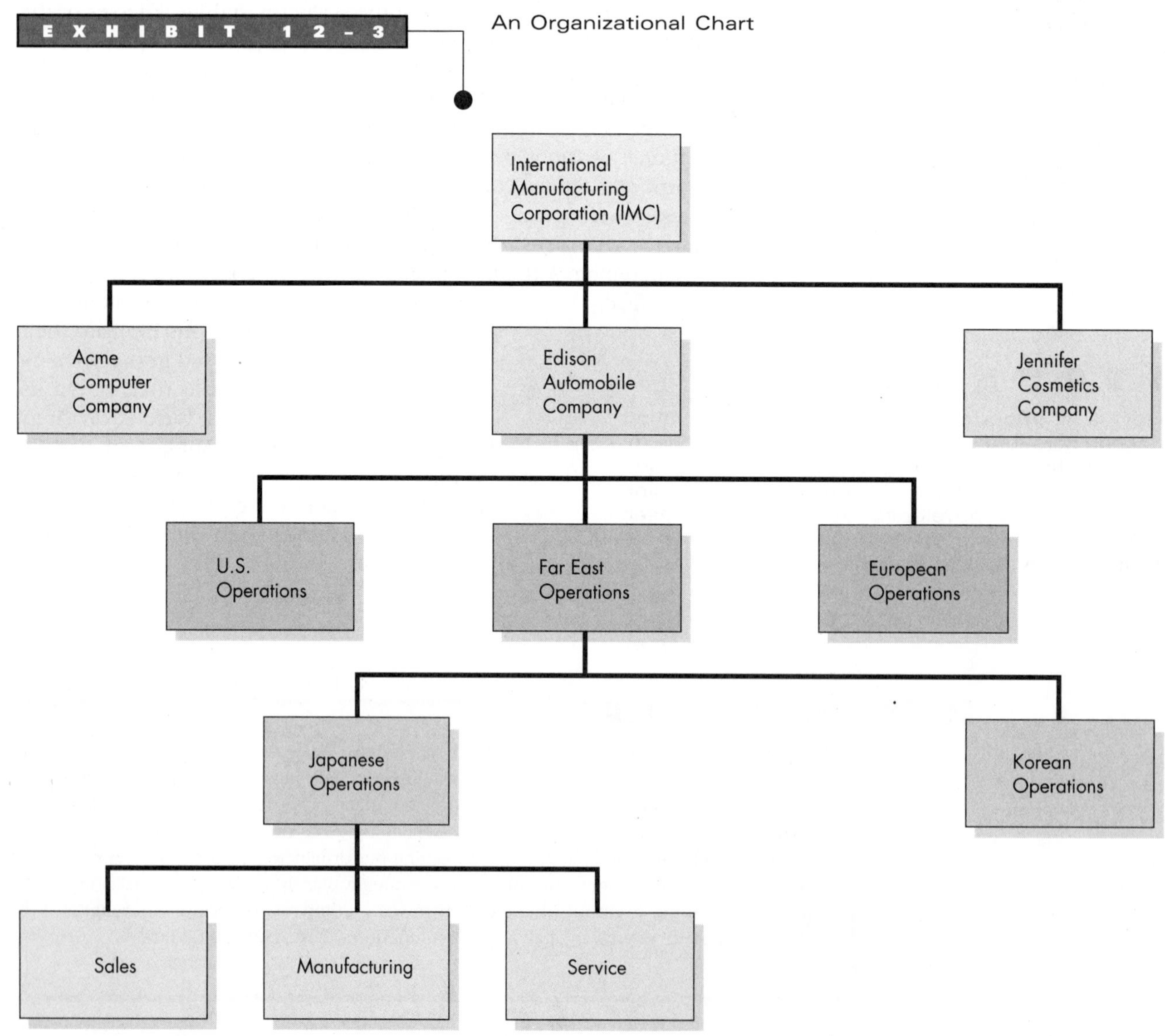

BUSINESS ENVIRONMENT ESSAY

Berkshire Hathaway As an example of how businesses are divided into segments, consider **Berkshire Hathaway, Inc.**, which is primarily owned by Warren E. Buffett, one of the richest individuals in the United States. In its 1996 annual report, Berkshire identified seven separate business segments: (1) candy, (2) encyclopedias and other reference materials, (3) home cleaning systems, (4) home furnishings, (5) newspapers, (6) shoes, and (7) insurance. These seven comprised 86 percent of Berkshire's revenues with another 26 smaller companies comprising the remaining 14 percent. The most profitable segment, based on operating profits before taxes, was the insurance division; the encyclopedias and other reference materials was the least profitable.

In addition to its own business segments, Berkshire Hathaway also owns 11 percent of **American Express**, 8 percent of **Coca-Cola**, 8 percent of **Federal Home Loan Mortgage Corporation**, 9 percent of **Gillette**, 4 percent of **McDonald's Corporation**, 4 percent of **Walt Disney Company**, 16 percent of the **Washington Post**, and 8 percent of **Wells Fargo & Company**. Warren Buffett is generally believed to be one of the most astute investors in the United States. As he states in his annual report, "We are interested in making investments that meet the following conditions:

1. It is a large purchase (at least $25 million of before tax earnings).
2. The company has demonstrated consistent earning power.
3. The business earns a good return on equity with little or no debt.
4. The management of the company is good and in place.
5. The company is involved in a 'simple business.'
6. There is an offering price which is realistic."

Source: 1996 Annual Report of Berkshire Hathaway, Inc., Copyright 1997 by Warren E. Buffett, Omaha, Nebraska.

ably because there is a significant difference in the business knowledge needed to produce and sell these products. At the middle level, segments are defined geographically because of the unique needs of each market and the distances involved. At the lowest level, each country unit is subdivided by function—sales, manufacturing, and service.

Given the organizational chart in Exhibit 12-3, how much autonomy should the executives of each division be granted by corporate management? If each company (Acme, Edison, and Jennifer) has its own president, vice presidents, and other officers, should these executives be allowed to operate independently of one another? If Acme, for example, is the most profitable company, should it be given more operating capital than Edison and Jennifer, or less? Should a decision for Acme to expand into laptop computers be made by Acme's executives or by IMC's corporate officers? Within Edison Automobile, how much autonomy should each of the geographic offices have? Should a decision to double the advertising budget or offer consumer rebates in the Far East operations be made by the manager of that division, by the top management of Edison Automobile, or by the president of IMC?

Questions such as these are difficult to answer. In fact, it would probably be difficult to find two companies that would answer them the same way. Assuming that IMC is basically a **decentralized company**, managers at all levels will have the authority to make decisions concerning the operations for which they are directly responsible. Regarding the question of rebates in the Far East, for example, the operating manager of that geographic division should probably decide whether to offer them. Likewise, the manager of the Japanese Manufacturing division should decide where to buy engine parts; the manager of the Service division should have

decentralized company An organization in which managers at all levels have the authority to make decisions concerning the operations for which they are responsible.

primary responsibility for the prices to charge for repairing a muffler in Japan. These managers would also be held accountable for the consequences of their decisions.

Benefits and Problems of Decentralization

To what degree should a company decentralize? In the opening scenario, you saw that the performance of Caterpillar improved when it decentralized and held managers of various subunits responsible for products, customers, and profits. Clearly, a large company employing thousands of people in different geographic areas could not remain completely centralized, with top management making all the decisions. The president of IMC would not know enough about the costs and varieties of paint in Japan, for example, or have enough time to make all the operating decisions for the manufacturing subsegment of the Japanese operations of Edison Automobile. Though such decisions would never be made by the president of a large international company, they would be made at a higher level in a **centralized company** than in a decentralized one.

centralized company An organization in which top management makes most of the major decisions for the entire company rather than delegating decisions to managers at lower levels.

Currently, the trend in most companies is to decentralize. The reasons often cited for making decisions at the lowest possible level in an organization are:

1. Segment managers usually have more information about matters within their area of responsibility than do managers at higher levels.
2. Segment managers are in a better position to see current problems and to react quickly to local situations.
2. Higher-level management can spend more time on broader policy and strategic issues because the burden of daily decision making is distributed.
4. Segment managers have a greater incentive to perform well, because they receive the credit (or blame) for performance resulting from their decisions.
5. Employees have greater incentives and motivation to perform well because there are more chances for advancement into leadership positions when a company is decentralized.
6. Managers and officers can be evaluated more easily because their responsibilities are more clearly defined.

Decentralization has its drawbacks as well. Decisions made by managers of decentralized units are sometimes not consistent with the overall objectives of the firm. For example, Edison Automobile might find it less expensive to buy computer parts for its automobiles from an outside source than from Acme Computer, or the Service division of Japanese operations may find it cheaper to buy repair parts from outsiders rather than from the Manufacturing division. Such decisions would allow the buying divisions to report lower costs, but the decisions might decrease the company's overall profitability.

There are two ways to prevent such problems. First, certain decisions should be centralized. For example, all decisions related to insurance coverage, which benefits the entire company, should probably be made at the corporate level. Second, a system of responsibility accounting should be established so that a manager's decisions will benefit not only the segment but also the firm as a whole. This **goal congruence**, whereby the goals of the company and all its segments are in harmony, can be achieved only if the responsibility accounting system is well designed. After discussing the concept of responsibility accounting and how performance is measured in cost, profit, and investment centers, we will describe and illustrate some specific problems of goal congruence in decentralized firms.

goal congruence The selection of goals for responsibility centers that are consistent, or congruent, with those of the company as a whole.

responsibility accounting A system of evaluating performance; managers are held accountable for the costs, revenues, assets, or other elements over which they have control.

Responsibility Accounting

Responsibility accounting is a system in which managers are assigned and held accountable for certain costs, assets, and/or revenues. There are two important behavioral considerations in assigning responsibilities to managers. First, the responsible manager should be involved in developing the plan for the unit over which the manager has control. Current research indicates that people are more motivated to achieve a goal (budget or standard) if they participate in setting it. Such participation assures that the goals will be reasonable and, more importantly, that they will be perceived to be reasonable by the managers.

Second, a manager should be held accountable only for those costs, assets, or revenues over which the manager has substantial control. Some costs may be generated within a segment, but control over them lies outside that unit. The manager of the Japanese Manufacturing division, for example, may be responsible for labor costs, but employee wages may be determined by a union scale controlled elsewhere. Admittedly, determining "substantial control" requires a judgment based on the circumstances, but if all relevant factors are considered, careful and fair judgments can be made.

Responsibility Accounting Reports

Regardless of the degree of autonomy given managers at various operating levels, responsibility accounting (performance) reports are needed at all levels of the organization. At the lowest levels, these reports tell managers where corrective action must be taken to control their segments' operations. At top levels, these reports keep management informed of the activities of all segments. They are then used to reward past performance and set incentives for future performance.

Exhibit 12-4 illustrates the kind of responsibility accounting reports a company might use. Note that reporting begins at the bottom and works upward, with each manager receiving information on the operations for which that manager is responsible, as well as summary information on the performance of lower-level managers. Note also that these reports are **exception reports**, meaning that variances from, or exceptions to, the budget are highlighted. In the report, unfavorable or negative variances are labeled "U" while favorable variances are labeled "F." Such reports direct management immediately to the areas requiring corrective action. To keep the example simple, Exhibit 19-4 focuses only on costs. In a real company, some units would report their profitability and even a return on investment.

exception reports Reports that highlight variances from, or exceptions to, the budget.

Responsibility accounting reports prepared for lower-level managers contain greater detail and are usually issued more frequently than those for upper-level managers. This is because lower-level managers are responsible for the detailed operations of the firm and need to take immediate action when some aspect of operations gets out of control; upper-level managers perform more of an overall review function. Furthermore, the responsibility accounting reports of lower-level managers in a decentralized operation would contain more items than they would in a centralized operation; with decentralization, managers are given broader areas of responsibility.

Responsibility Centers

In our example, the president of IMC is responsible for the entire organization and should be held accountable for the company's overall successes and failures. At lower levels, the president of Edison Automobile Company, the manager of Edison's operations in the Far East, the manager in charge of Japanese operations in Edison's Far East operations, and the manager of the Japanese Manufacturing division, for example, would be held responsible for operations within their respective units.

responsibility center An organizational unit in which a manager has control over and is held accountable for performance.

cost center An organizational unit in which a manager has control over and is held accountable for costs.

profit center An organizational unit in which a manager has responsibility for both costs and revenues.

Each unit is referred to as a **responsibility center** and, depending on the operation, it may be a cost, profit, or investment center. As the name implies, a **cost center** is any organizational unit in which the manager of that unit has control over the costs incurred. The manager of a cost center has no responsibility for revenues or assets, either because revenues are not generated or because they are under the control of someone else. The manufacturing unit of Japanese operations of IMC Corporation, for example, could be designated a cost center. A **profit center** manager, however, has responsibility for both costs and revenues. Profit centers are usually found at higher levels in an organization than are cost centers. The geographic

EXHIBIT 12-4 Responsibility Accounting Reports for Edison Automobile Company of IMC Corporation

President, Edison Automobile	**Responsibility Centers**	**Budgeted Costs**	**Actual Costs**	**Variance***
The president receives from each geographic area of operations a report summarizing its performance. The president can see where corrective action needs to be made by tracing the differences between budget and actual costs downward to their sources.	General Administration	x	x	x
	United States	x	x	x
	Far East	$58,000	$65,000	$7,000 U
	Europe	x	x	x

Far East Operations	**Responsibility Centers**	**Budgeted Costs**	**Actual Costs**	**Variance**
The manager of Far East operations receives a report from each country segment's head. These reports are then summarized and passed on to the president of Edison Automobile.	Japanese Operations	$21,000	$23,000	$2,000 U
	Korean Operations	x	x	x
	Total costs	$58,000	$65,000	$7,000 U

Japanese Operations	**Responsibility Centers**	**Budgeted Costs**	**Actual Costs**	**Variance**
The manager of Japanese operations receives from each unit a report summarizing its performance. These reports are combined and sent up to the next level, the manager of Far East operations.	Sales	x	x	x
	Manufacturing	$ 9,000	$10,200	$1,200 U
	Service	x	x	x
	Total costs	$21,000	$23,000	$2,000 U

Japanese Manufacturing Division	**Variable Costs of Manufacturing**	**Budgeted Costs**	**Actual Costs**	**Variance**
The Manufacturing division supervisor receives a performance report on the supervisor's center of responsibility. The totals from these reports are then communicated to the manager of Japanese operations, the next level of responsibility.	Direct materials	$ 2,000	$ 2,500	$ 500 U
	Direct labor	6,000	6,400	400 U
	Manufacturing overhead	1,000	1,300	300 U
	Total costs	$ 9,000	$10,200	$1,200 U

*U means unfavorable.

regions (United States, Far East, and Europe, as well as various country operations within the Far East region) of Edison Automobile would probably be profit centers.

investment center An organizational unit in which a manager has responsibility for costs, revenues, and assets.

In an **investment center**, the manager is responsible for costs, revenues, and assets. This means that the manager is responsible not only for operating costs, but also for determining the amount of funds to be invested in the center's plant and equipment and for the rate of return earned on those investments. Investment centers are usually found at relatively high levels in organizations. The different companies in IMC (Acme Computer, Edison Automobile, and Jennifer Cosmetics) would probably be investment centers.

TO SUMMARIZE

Most companies are divided into segments with specific responsibilities assigned to each segment manager. In a centralized organization, top management makes most of the operating decisions; in a decentralized organization, decision-making authority is delegated down the corporate ladder to the managers most immediately responsible. It is very important in a decentralized company that the goals of the company and all its segments are in harmony. This concept is referred to as goal congruence.

Regardless of the degree of decentralization, almost all companies use performance reports that show variances from budgeted amounts for each division, department, and unit. These reports pass upward through an organization so that supervisors and managers at all levels can assess the performance of the units serving under them. Decentralized companies are divided into fairly independent responsibility centers. There are three types of responsibility centers: cost, profit, and investment. Managers of responsibility centers usually have control over, and are held accountable for, the performance of the center.

4 *Explain how performance is evaluated in cost centers.*

EVALUATING PERFORMANCE IN COST CENTERS

As stated in the last section, managers of cost centers are responsible for costs incurred. Most cost centers usually have one type of cost that is more significant than any other. In service organizations, salaries are generally the major cost. In wholesale and retail businesses, the cost of merchandise purchased for resale is often the most significant cost. In manufacturing firms, costs incurred to make products (direct materials, direct labor, and manufacturing overhead) are usually most significant.

If managers are to be held responsible for the costs incurred in their centers, a control system must be developed that will provide objective information about these costs. The system should show whether costs are too high or too low, improving (decreasing) or getting worse (increasing), and whether or not they will allow the company to be competitive. The method most commonly used to provide such feedback in cost centers is called **standard costing**. With this method, standard costs are compared to actual costs and variances are computed. Standard cost systems can be used in service, merchandising, or manufacturing firms.

standard costing The method of comparing standard costs to actual costs and computing variances; commonly used in cost centers to provide objective information about costs.

standard cost system A cost-accumulation system in which standard costs are used as product costs instead of actual costs.

Standard Cost System

Companies that use standard costing design their accounting systems to incorporate standard costs and variances. This type of system, called a **standard cost system**, is a cost-accumulation process based on costs that should have been incurred rather than costs that were actually incurred. The steps in establishing and operating a standard cost system are:

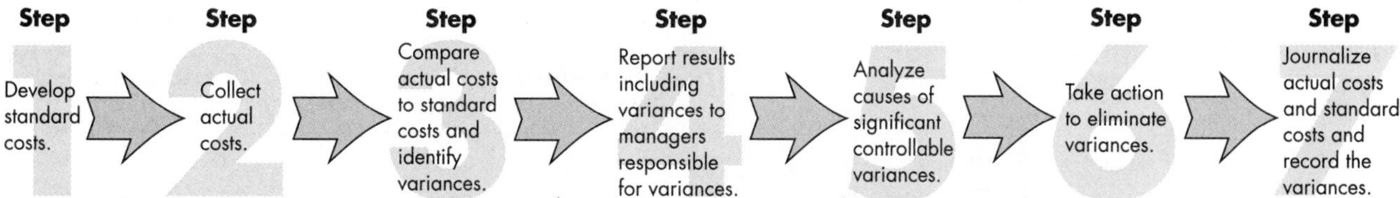
Step 1
Develop standard costs.
Step 2
Collect actual costs.
Step 3
Compare actual costs to standard costs and identify variances.
Step 4
Report results including variances to managers responsible for variances.
Step 5
Analyze causes of significant controllable variances.
Step 6
Take action to eliminate variances.
Step 7
Journalize actual costs and standard costs and record the variances.

These steps describe a typical standard cost system. You can find some or all of these elements in most organizations, but you will not likely find all seven elements in all firms. You are most likely to find an extensive standard cost system in manufacturing firms, which usually have standard costs for direct materials and direct labor and, to a lesser extent, for manufacturing overhead. These standard

standard cost cards An itemization of the components of the standard cost of a product.

costs usually are reported on **standard cost cards**, often stored in a computer. A standard cost card for Smell-Good Perfume made by Jennifer Cosmetics, a subsidiary of IMC Company, is shown in Exhibit 12-5. The data in Exhibit 12-5 will be used to illustrate how variances are calculated and analyzed.

Determining Standard Costs and Identifying Variances

In a manufacturing firm, standard costs are determined on the basis of careful analysis and the experience of many people, including accountants, industrial engineers, purchasing agents, and the managers of the departments to be judged. Accountants play an important role in developing standard costs because they have the data needed to determine how costs have changed in the past in relation to levels of activity. This is not an easy task. Changes in methods of production, technology, worker efficiency, and plant layout, for example, can affect the behavior of costs. Before they can serve as standard costs, past costs often have to be adjusted to take changes in operating conditions into account. These changes sometimes occur gradually and may not be easily noticeable, making it difficult for management accountants to identify cost characteristics that will be useful in setting standards for the future.

Engineers are often involved in setting standard costs because of their knowledge of the most efficient way of performing each task in relation to the existing technology of the operation. Managers who will be judged by the standard costs should be involved in the standard-setting process; they are more likely to be motivated to meet standards if they have participated in setting the standards and have accepted them. Of course, the participation of such managers also makes effective use of their experience and judgment.

variance Any deviation from standard.

management by exception The strategy of focusing attention on significant deviations from a standard.

Once management has established a standard quantity and a standard price for each resource (direct materials, direct labor, and manufacturing overhead), the standard quantity is multiplied by the standard price to arrive at a standard dollar cost for the manufactured product. Actual costs are then compared with these standards to calculate the **variance**, the amount by which the actual cost differs from the standard. This variance, if significant, is a signal to management that costs may be "out of control" and that corrective action should be taken to eliminate the variance. This process of using variances from a standard to isolate problem areas is called **management by exception**. It is the basis of the control function.

(STOP & THINK)

Is it possible for a company to have positive variances (actual costs are less than standard costs) and still have problems?

Since standard costs have a price (or rate) component and a quantity (or usage) component, a comparison of actual and standard costs can result in two variances: a price (rate) variance and a quantity (usage) variance. These vari-

EXHIBIT 12-5

Standard Cost Card

Jennifer Cosmetics
Standard Cost Card—Smell-Good Perfume

	(1) Standard Quantity	(2) Standard Price or Rate	(3) Standard Cost (1) × (2)
Inputs:			
Direct materials	2 ounces	$ 2.000	$ 4.00
Direct labor	2 hours	16.000	32.00
Manufacturing overhead:			
Variable	2 hours	1.500	3.00
Fixed	2 hours	2.375	4.75
Total standard cost per unit			$43.75

ances are usually computed for direct materials, direct labor, and variable manufacturing overhead.

Exhibit 12-6 is a general model for calculating variances. This model has two important characteristics. First, it is applicable to each of the manufacturing cost elements—direct materials, direct labor, and variable manufacturing overhead. Second, the analysis is essentially an input-output analysis. The price (rate) variance compares actual inputs used at the actual and standard prices. The actual quantities are used to isolate the effect of the price change on the cost of the resources actually acquired or used. The price variance, then, is the difference between the actual price and the standard price, times the actual quantity. The quantity (usage) variance compares the inputs actually used at the standard price with the inputs that should have been used at the standard price to produce the actual output. The standard price is used so that the quantity variances will not be influenced by price changes. The quantity variance is the difference between the actual quantity and the standard quantity, times the standard price.

EXHIBIT 12-6 General Model for Variance Analysis

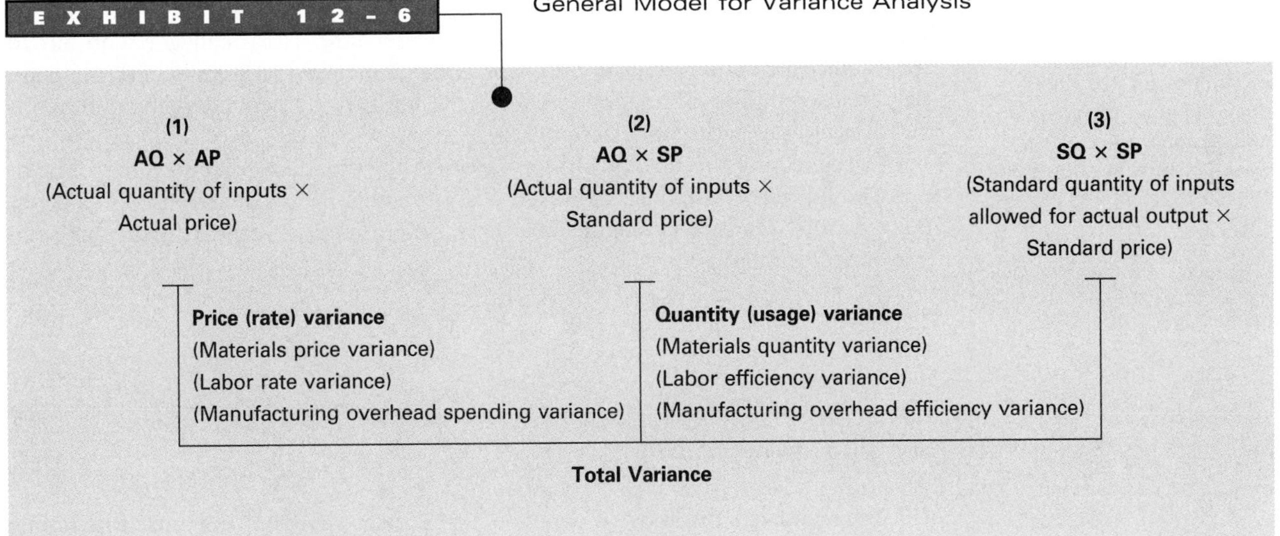

TO SUMMARIZE

Standard cost systems are used to accumulate costs based on standards rather than actual costs. Standard costs are predetermined costs that serve as benchmarks for judging what actual costs should be. Standard costs are usually expressed as the per-unit cost of materials, labor, and manufacturing overhead and are used by managers for planning, implementing, and controlling decisions. The total variance between actual and standard costs is made up of price and quantity variances. Standard costs are based on careful analysis by many people, including accountants, engineers, and managers. Standard costs are compared with actual costs incurred to determine variances, the amounts by which actual costs differ from standards. Significant variances alert management to specific problem areas that may require corrective action. The strategy of focusing on significant variances, called management by exception, is essential to the controlling function.

Direct Materials Variances

Variance analysis is an essential part of an effective standard cost system. We will first explain how direct materials variances are computed and analyzed. Then, we will explain the computation and analysis of direct labor variances.

To illustrate the computation of the price and quantity variances for direct materials, we will assume the following actual results of Smell-Good Perfume made by Jennifer Cosmetics:

Direct materials purchased	10,000 ounces at $1.85 per ounce
Direct materials used	8,300 ounces
Bottles of perfume produced	4,000

Keep in mind throughout the following discussion that the standard cost card (Exhibit 12-5) specifies that materials should cost $2 for each ounce and that each bottle produced should require 2 ounces of material. (Obviously, many ingredients would be mixed together to make perfume. We are assuming only one ingredient is used to keep the example simple.)

materials price variance The extent to which the actual price varies from the standard price for the quantity of materials purchased or used; computed by multiplying the difference between the actual and standard prices by the quantity purchased or used.

Materials Price Variance The **materials price variance** reflects the extent to which the actual price varies from the standard price for the actual quantity of materials purchased or used. Although the price variance can be calculated either when materials are purchased or when they are used, it is generally best to isolate the variance at purchase and report the variance to the purchasing manager who has responsibility for controlling the purchase price. If management waits until the materials are used before calculating variances, the information needed by the purchasing managers to take corrective action is delayed.

In calculating the materials price variance, the standard price per unit of materials should reflect the final, delivered cost of materials, net of any discounts taken. For example, Jennifer Cosmetics may have determined its standard materials price per ounce as follows:

Purchase price	$1.84
Freight	0.17
Handling costs	0.04
Less purchase discounts	(0.05)
Standard materials cost per unit	$2.00

The standard cost above assumes that the materials were purchased in certain lot sizes (for example, 50 gallon quantities) and delivered a certain way (by rail, for example). Handling costs and purchase discounts have also been included.

Assuming that variances are determined when materials are purchased and that 10,000 ounces of materials are purchased, the price variance is computed as follows:

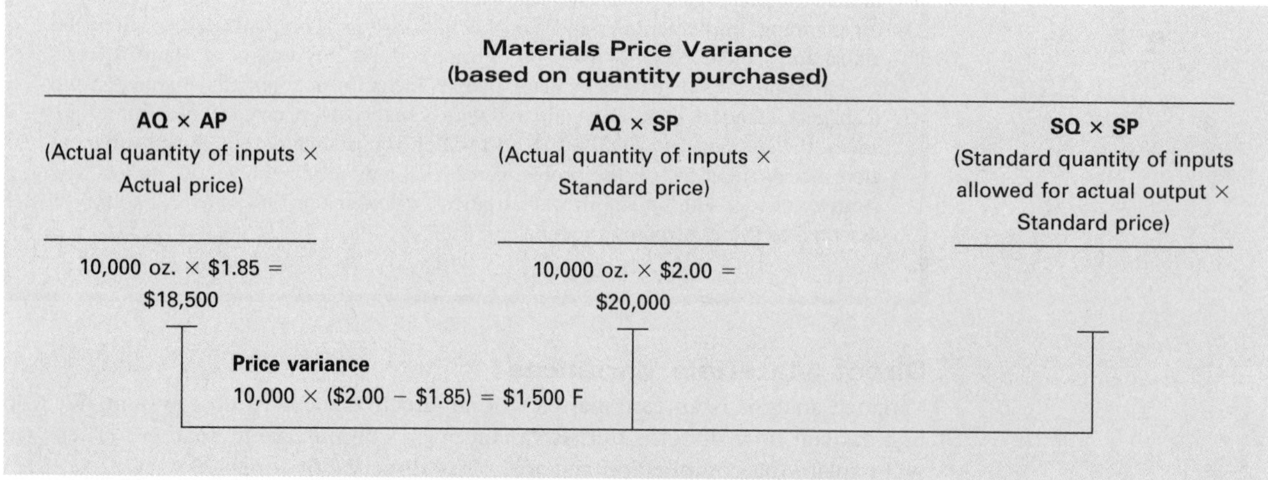

This variance indicates that the company spent $1,500 less than the standard cost for the direct materials purchased. Because less money was spent than the standard cost, the variance is labeled "F" meaning "favorable." If the amount expended had exceeded the standard cost, the variance would have been "unfavorable," designated with a "U."

Isolating materials price variances at the time of purchase has the advantage of providing immediate information on purchasing decisions. This also allows companies to carry inventory in the accounting records at the standard cost. Some companies, however, prefer to compute materials price variances at the time the materials are transferred to Work-in-Process Inventory. If 8,300 ounces were used in production, the variance would be based on that amount rather than on the 10,000 ounces purchased. In this case, a favorable price variance of $1,245 would result, as shown below.

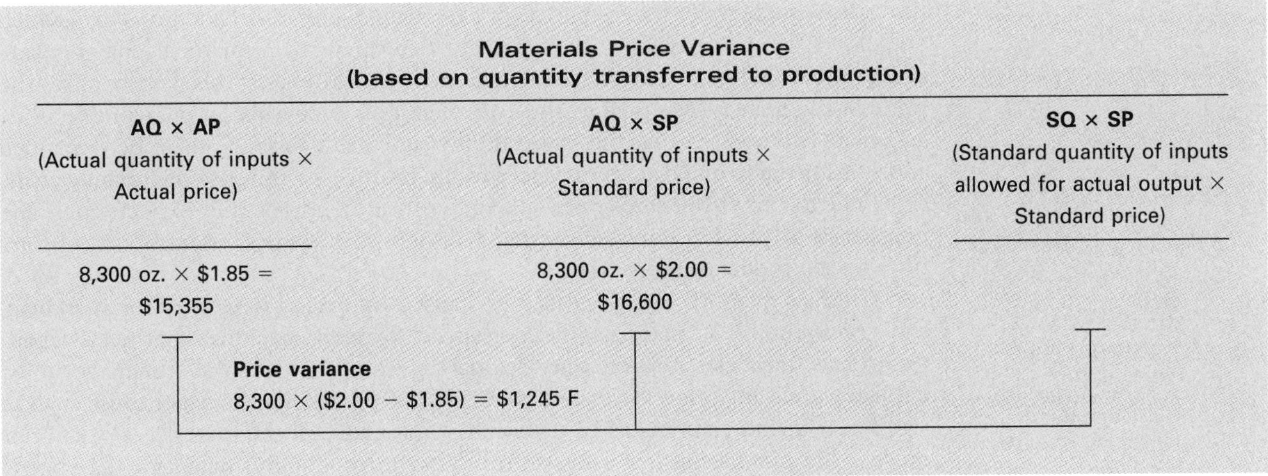

materials quantity variance The extent to which the actual quantity of materials varies from the standard quantity; computed by multiplying the difference between the actual quantity and the standard quantity of materials used by the standard price.

Materials Quantity Variance The standard quantity of materials should reflect the amount needed for each completed unit of product but should allow for normal waste, spoilage, and other unavoidable inefficiencies. The standard cost card indicates that 2 ounces of direct materials are allowed for each bottle of perfume produced. Because Jennifer Cosmetics produced 4,000 bottles of Smell-Good perfume last period, the standard quantity allowed is 8,000 ounces (2 ounces × 4,000 bottles). Actual use of materials amounted to 8,300 ounces. The computation of the **materials quantity variance** is:

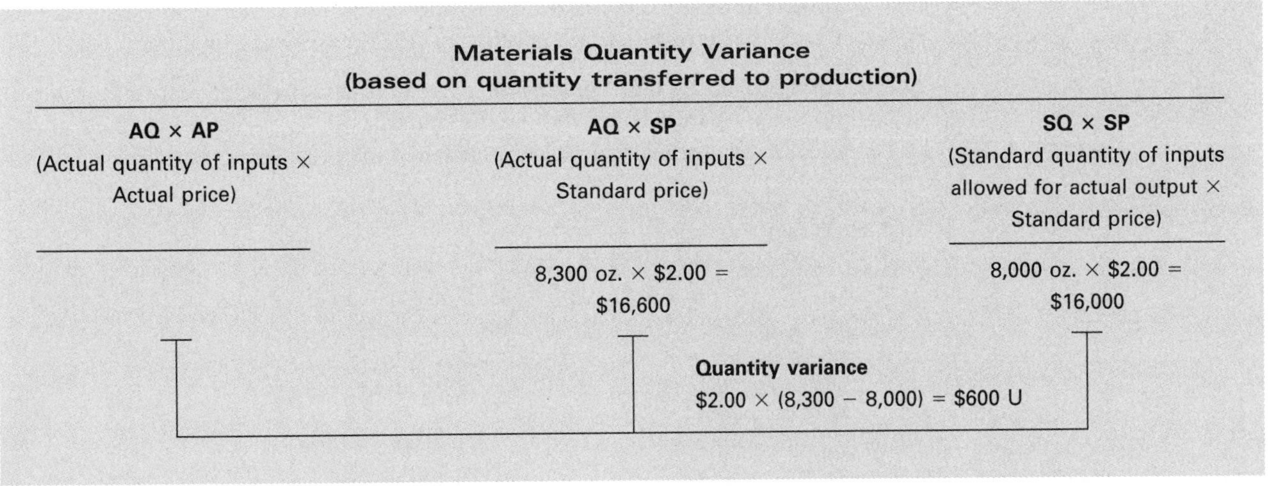

The company used 300 more ounces of material than expected, resulting in an unfavorable quantity variance of $600 (300 ounces × $2 per ounce).

Controlling Materials Variances Materials price variances are usually under the control of the purchasing department. The purchasing function involves getting a variety of price quotations; buying in economic lot sizes to take advantage of quantity discounts; buying and paying on a timely basis to obtain cash discounts; and paying attention to alternative forms of delivery to minimize shipping costs. Some of these factors will be less important when there are few suppliers or when purchase contracts with suppliers are for long periods. In any case, the existence of unfavorable price variances may suggest a problem that needs correcting.

The buyer responsible for these purchases should be able to explain the variance even though the buyer may not be able to control its occurrence. This may be the case, for example, when market prices change after the standard is set, which could be the explanation for the favorable price variance. Or materials may be damaged, requiring the reorder of a small quantity on a rush basis; this usually raises the price of the materials as well as the cost of shipping, causing an unfavorable price variance. The point is that the cause of any significant variance must be explained and steps taken to avoid such variances in the future. The purpose of variance analysis is not to browbeat employees for failing to meet impossible expectations; the purpose is to provide information that will help management identify ways of improving the production process.

Materials quantity variances may be caused by quality defects, poor workmanship, poor choice of materials, inexperienced workers, machines that need repair, or an inaccurate materials quantity standard. Just as the purchasing manager must explain significant price variances, generally the production manager must analyze significant quantity variances to determine their cause. If the material is of inferior quality, the purchasing manager, rather than the production manager, may be responsible for the variance. Again, the point is that the cause of the variance must be determined; only then can it be decided what action, if any, to take to prevent its recurrence. Production managers can be made aware of materials quantity variances on a timely basis if the company uses materials requisition forms. These forms should indicate when materials withdrawals from the storeroom exceed the standard quantity of materials specified for that production run. If the standard amount of materials for the production run is known at the start of the run, additional requisitions of materials can be "red-flagged" as being excessive. By using an excess materials requisition procedure as a nonmonetary standard, production managers will be alerted to a materials quantity variance before the monetary measure of the materials quantity variance is available. Thus, production managers can take quicker action to correct a problem than would be the case if they had to wait until the end of the reporting period to learn of materials quantity variances. Corrective action may involve returning excess materials to the storeroom rather than being careless about control in the production area that could lead to waste or theft.

Accounting for Materials Variances The journal entries for recording the purchase and use of materials, as well as the materials price variance (isolated at purchase) and the quantity variance (isolated when materials are used), are:

Materials Price Variance:

Direct Materials Inventory ($2.00 × 10,000 ounces)	20,000	
Materials Price Variance [($2.00 − $1.85) × 10,000 ounces]		1,500
Cash (or Accounts Payable) ($1.85 × 10,000 ounces)		18,500
Purchased 10,000 ounces of direct materials at $1.85 per ounce and entered the materials in inventory at the standard price of $2.00 per ounce.		

Materials Quantity Variance:		
Work-in-Process Inventory (8,000 ounces × $2.00)	16,000	
Materials Quantity Variance [(8,300 ounces − 8,000 ounces) × $2.00]. .	600	
Direct Materials Inventory (8,300 ounces × $2.00).		16,600
Transferred 8,300 ounces of materials out of inventory and recorded standard usage of 8,000 ounces of materials to produce 4,000 bottles of perfume.		

As shown, Materials Price Variance and Materials Quantity Variance are debited when the variances are unfavorable; they are credited when the variances are favorable. An unfavorable variance can be thought of as an expense; a favorable variance can be considered an expense reduction or savings. Note that the $16,000 debit to Work-in-Process Inventory is the standard cost for the 4,000 bottles (standard 8,000 ounces of materials × $2.00 standard price per ounce). The actual cost deviations from the standard costs are now in variance accounts. The variance accounts are usually transferred to Cost of Goods Sold at the end of the period. Thus, the income statement reports actual costs, where Work-in-Process Inventory and Finished Goods Inventory include only the standard costs of materials. Alternatively, as explained in Chapter 10, when variances are significant in amount, variance account balances at the end of a period should be allocated among Cost of Goods Sold, Work-in-Process Inventory, and Finished Goods Inventory instead of just transferred to Cost of Goods Sold.

TO SUMMARIZE

The difference between actual and standard costs of materials for a given production level can be separated into a materials price variance and a materials quantity variance. The materials price variance can be computed when the materials are purchased or when they are used in production. The managers responsible for the variances must determine their causes and, if the variances are outside an acceptable range, take action to eliminate them. The materials variances (price and quantity) are recorded in individual accounts when materials are acquired and used. The accounts for materials variances are generally closed into Cost of Goods Sold; work-in-process inventory and finished goods inventory accounts include only standard materials costs.

Direct Labor Variances

A direct labor rate variance and a direct labor efficiency variance are usually determined for manufacturing labor when a standard cost system is being used. These variances are computed in a manner similar to the materials price and quantity variances.

labor rate variance The extent to which the actual labor rate varies from the standard rate for the quantity of labor used; computed by multiplying the difference between the actual rate and the standard rate by the quantity of labor used.

Labor Rate Variance A **labor rate variance** is a price variance; it shows the difference between actual and standard wage rates. Unfavorable labor rate variances may occur when skilled workers with high hourly pay rates are placed in jobs intended for less skilled or lower-wage-rate employees. Unfavorable labor rate variances may also occur when employees work overtime at premium pay (time and a half or double time). Conversely, favorable labor rate variances occur when less skilled or lower-wage-rate employees perform duties intended for higher-paid workers.

For Jennifer Cosmetics, the standard cost card (Exhibit 12-5) indicates that the standard direct labor rate per bottle of perfume was 2 hours at $16 per hour. Actual labor used during the month to make 4,000 bottles was 8,352 hours at $16.20 per hour. The labor rate variance was thus $1,670 unfavorable, computed as follows:

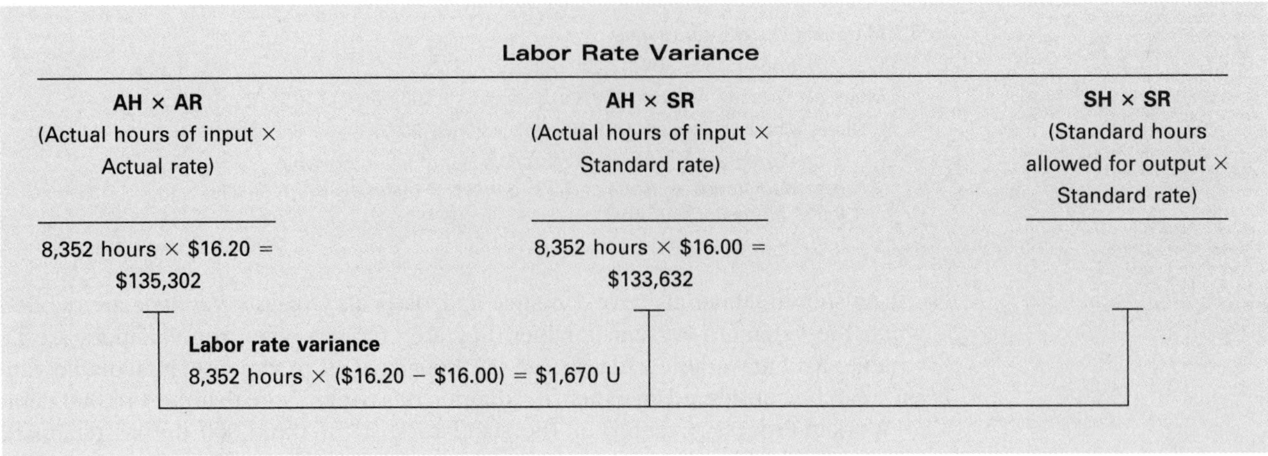

Labor Rate Variance
AH × AR
(Actual hours of input × Actual rate)
AH × SR
(Actual hours of input × Standard rate)
SH × SR
(Standard hours allowed for output × Standard rate)
8,352 hours × $16.20 = $135,302
8,352 hours × $16.00 = $133,632
Labor rate variance
8,352 hours × ($16.20 − $16.00) = $1,670 U

As this variance indicates, $1,670 more than the standard amount for the actual number of hours used was spent for direct labor because actual labor rates were higher than standard rates by $0.20 per hour. The company's guidelines would determine whether the variance should be investigated. Depending on the firm's hiring policies, and the degree of authority given to operating managers in setting wage rates and assigning workers to particular jobs, the operating managers may or may not be responsible for this labor rate variance. In general, labor rates are the responsibility of the manager who makes staffing decisions.

labor efficiency variance The extent to which the actual labor used varies from the standard quantity; computed by multiplying the difference between the actual quantity and the standard quantity of labor by the standard rate.

Labor Efficiency Variance The **labor efficiency variance** is a quantity variance. It measures the cost (or benefit) of using labor for more (or fewer) hours than prescribed by the standard. Computed in the same manner as the materials quantity variance, the labor efficiency variance computation is illustrated in the following schedule for Jennifer Cosmetics. Note that total standard hours are computed by multiplying the standard hours per unit by the actual number of bottles produced (2 hours × 4,000 bottles = 8,000 standard hours allowed).

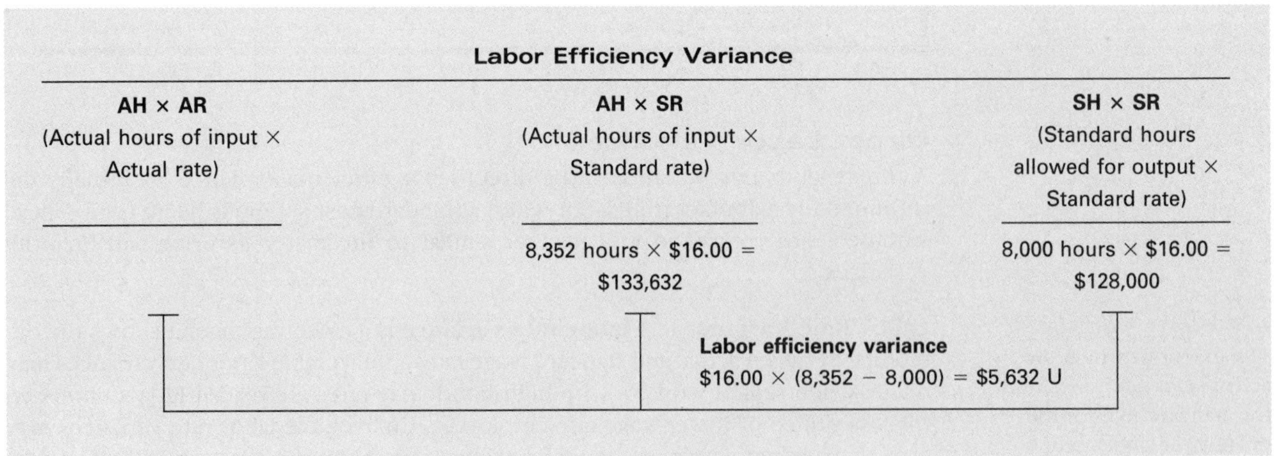

Labor Efficiency Variance
AH × AR
(Actual hours of input × Actual rate)
AH × SR
(Actual hours of input × Standard rate)
SH × SR
(Standard hours allowed for output × Standard rate)
8,352 hours × $16.00 = $133,632
8,000 hours × $16.00 = $128,000
Labor efficiency variance
$16.00 × (8,352 − 8,000) = $5,632 U

The manufacturing division used 352 more direct labor hours than the standard, which caused an unfavorable efficiency variance of $5,632 (352 hours × $16).

The labor efficiency variance shows how efficiently the workers performed and, hence, how productive a department was. The variances might be unfavorable for a variety of reasons, including poorly trained employees, poor-quality materials that

FYI

Organizations often try to encourage employees to work harder and faster by offering them rewards for productivity increases. However, employees are skeptical about whether rewards will actually be received. For example, a survey reported in 1997 found the following results:

- 81% of workers surveyed say they will not receive any reward for productivity increases.
- 60% of managers surveyed feel their compensation will not increase if their performance improves.
- Only 3% of base salary separates average from outstanding employees at companies surveyed.

Source: Craig Eric Schneider, "Capitalizing on Performance Management, Recognition, and Rewards Systems," *Compensation and Benefits Review,* March–April 1997, p. 23.

CAUTION

When computing variances, be careful not to confuse actual and standard hours and actual and standard rates. The rate variance is always the difference between the standard and actual rate times the actual hours. (To multiply it times standard hours would not tell you how much the rate increase actually cost or saved the company in total.) On the other hand, the efficiency variance is a time-based variance and, therefore, it is the difference between the standard and actual hours times the standard rate.

require extra processing time, old or faulty equipment, and improper supervision of employees. Note that the labor efficiency variance is probably the most important and closely watched manufacturing variance. It has become even more important in recent years as U.S. industries have tried to increase their productivity to match that of Japan, Korea, and other countries.

Controlling Labor Variances Whereas a materials price variance is usually the responsibility of the purchasing department, labor "price" or rate variances are normally the responsibility of the production manager who is responsible for employees' work assignments or personnel responsible for hiring employees. As indicated, rate variances are likely to be due to (1) certain tasks being performed by workers with different pay rates or (2) assigning a worker to a job calling for either more skill or less skill than the worker's pay scale would suggest. These variances may be manageable if there is care in assigning workers to jobs that are consistent with their skills and pay scales. Deviations may be necessary in certain situations because of vacations, sickness, or other employee absences. If the variances are caused by factors beyond the manager's control, he or she should not be held responsible for the unfavorable variance.

In a labor-intensive company, the labor efficiency variance is much more important than in a company that has low labor costs. The labor efficiency variance can be expressed in standard hours for a given activity or in monetary terms (standard hours × standard labor rate). If time standards are set for each activity and workers are required to report their actual hours of work on time tickets, managers have a basis for checking labor efficiency by comparing standard hours with the actual hours shown on time tickets. The variances can be separated into categories of causes so that judgments can be made about what corrective action should be taken. Some typical causes of labor inefficiency variances are absenteeism, machinery breakdowns, poor-quality materials, poor work environment, inadequate machinery, lack of employee skills on a given job, poor employee attitudes, lazy employees, and inaccurate standards. If these causes can be identified by analyzing time tickets, corrective action can be taken promptly. If the labor efficiency variance is expressed in monetary terms, the variances may not be available until end-of-period accounting reports are issued.

Accounting for Labor Variances Since the labor rate and labor efficiency variances are both computed for a given period of time or for a given amount of production, the labor costs and variances for Jennifer Cosmetics can be accounted for in a single journal entry.

Work-in-Process Inventory (8,000 hours × $16.00)	128,000	
Labor Rate Variance [($16.20 − $16.00) × 8,352 hours]	1,670	
Labor Efficiency Variance [(8,352 hours − 8,000 hours) × $16.00] . .	5,632	
Wages Payable (8,352 hours × $16.20)		135,302
To charge Work-in-Process Inventory for standard labor hours at the standard wage rate to produce 4,000 bottles of perfume; to set up unfavorable labor rate and efficiency variances to reflect the use of 352 hours above standard at an average wage rate of $0.20 above standard.		

As with all production variances, labor variances are closed to Cost of Goods Sold at the end of the period or allocated among Cost of Goods Sold, Work-in-Process Inventory, and Finished Goods Inventory. By closing variances from standard into Cost of Goods Sold, actual cost of goods sold will be reported on the income statement. Work-in-Process Inventory and Finished Goods Inventory include only the standard costs of labor.

BUSINESS ENVIRONMENT ESSAY

Gainsharing at a Box Company

There are many ways to motivate employees to work harder and be more productive. A new approach, called gainsharing, is becoming more and more popular. A Missouri company, employing about 180 factory workers and manufacturing corrugated boxes, shipping containers, inner packing, and displays, illustrates how gainsharing works in practice. Under pressure from an original equipment manufacturer (OEM) customer for lower prices, the box producer was forced to boost the workforce to higher productivity in order to slice unit costs, thereby permitting lower prices.

The gainsharing project began with an examination of the company's production records for the past two years. This research found that labor costs (including supervision, plant engineering, scheduling, and all indirect labor) hovered around 37 percent of total cost. That is, for every $1 million spent in producing corrugated products, $370,000 went to associated labor expense. The objective was to trim those costs.

With some expert guidance, the company proceeded to design a formula for rewarding the workforce for achieving lower labor costs. The formula showed that if the workers performed harder, smarter, neater, and more carefully, reducing labor costs to, say, $300,000, savings would be $70,000 on the next $1 million production run. The savings (gain) in that period would be shared equally: $35,000 for the workers, as a bonus of $194.44 for each employee, and a $35,000 savings for the company. The employee bonuses were over and above the normal wage rate.

The gainsharing at the company made a tremendous difference. Labor costs dropped to less than 30 percent of the total cost of making boxes.

Source: Woodruff Imberman, "Is Gainsharing the Wave of the Future?" *Management Accounting,* November 1995, p. 35.

TO SUMMARIZE

The labor rate variance is the difference between the actual and the standard labor rates multiplied by the actual hours worked. The labor efficiency variance is the difference between actual and standard hours multiplied by the standard wage rate. Labor variances are usually controllable by manufacturing division managers. The labor variances (rate and efficiency) are recorded in individual accounts when labor costs are incurred. Like materials variances, labor variances are closed to Cost of Goods Sold so that work-in-process inventory and finished goods inventory accounts include only standard labor costs.

Standard Costs in Nonmanufacturing Firms

In nonmanufacturing environments, standards are sometimes expressed only in quantitative terms; in other situations, the quantitative standards are converted to monetary standards as a basis for identifying monetary variances. For example, automobile service centers have standard times and standard labor costs for automobile repairs, tune-ups, oil changes, muffler replacements, and so forth. Organizations might have standard times for such activities as cleaning hotel rooms, taking blood samples, completing income tax returns, and meeting delivery schedules. These types of standards can be applied in not-for-profit and service organizations as well as in restaurants and merchandising firms. In the fast food area, for example, franchises, such as **McDonald's** and **Baskin-Robbins**, have standard quantities for meat in hamburgers and ice cream in cones.

BUSINESS ENVIRONMENT ESSAY

Standard Costing in the Legal Profession Variations on standard cost systems have been implemented in law firms to help analyze profitability for individual transactions or cases. Cost measurements have become even more important for firm profitability in recent years, since the use of fixed fees as opposed to per-hour billing has increased in the profession.

Here's how one system works. Revenues and costs are accumulated on a case-by-case basis. Revenues are based either on a prearranged fixed fee or on billing rates established for hours invested by firm members. Costs are collected as follows: (1) For all personnel whose time is billed to clients, total compensation (including annual salary and fringe benefits) is divided by a standard number of billable hours per year, which yields a standard cost-per-billable-hour for each paralegal, associate, and partner of the firm; (2) The number of hours charged to the case by each member is multiplied by that member's standard cost-per-billable-hour; (3) An overhead cost is charged to the case based on the number of partner hours invested times the overhead rate per partner billable hour. Overhead costs include administrative and other support salaries, rent and utilities, and equipment; this overhead rate is usually based on the last year's operating results.

Assuming billable hours is the production output, labor variance analysis at a law firm might be calculated as shown below. In calculating the efficiency variance, standard output ratio would be calculated as total hours worked divided by total billed hours.

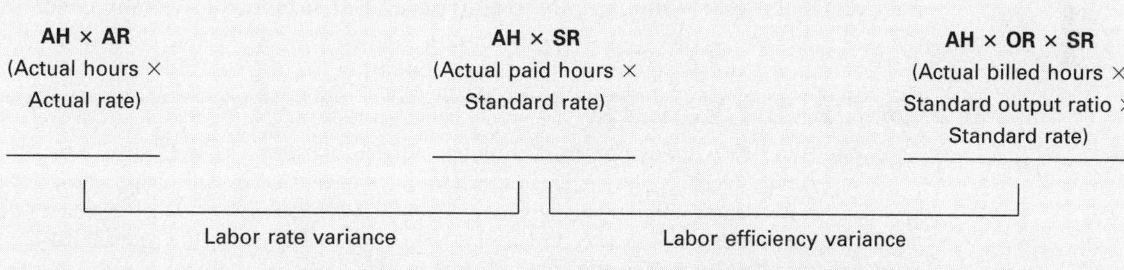

Source: Adapted from David Maister, "Analyzing Firm Performance Matter by Matter," *The Connecticut Law Tribune,* August 1, 1994, p. 30ff.

Evaluation of Standard Costing

Standard cost systems, such as those discussed here, have many advantages and disadvantages. The advantages include the following:

1. The setting of standard costs requires a careful analysis of operations. Such an analysis can lead to efficiencies and economies even before the standard cost system is fully operative.
2. Standard costs are useful for planning overall materials and labor.
3. A standard cost system is simpler to operate than a system using actual costs because the cost flows are recorded at standard.
4. A standard cost system helps identify and control problem areas; this leads to increased production efficiency.
5. Standard costs provide a basis for measuring performance by assigning variances to the responsible manager.
6. A standard cost system is compatible with the principle of management by exception, which contributes to the effective utilization of management's time and effort.

The disadvantages of standard costing include the following.

1. A standard cost system is expensive and time consuming to develop.
2. It is easy to misinterpret the causes of a variance because so many factors are involved.
3. Standard costs must be changed as conditions change (e.g., as the product, the materials, or the production methods change). Sometimes these changes occur so quickly that standards become out of date before management realizes it.
4. Workers tend to view measures of efficiency with mistrust. Responsibility for significant variances may be erroneously assigned, leading to morale problems.
5. The setting of standards is not an exact science. Standards are reported as specific figures but are treated by managers as ranges of acceptable performance. Random fluctuations are to be expected but often are hard to distinguish from situations requiring action.
6. Standards do not support continuous improvement.

Although the disadvantages noted here are real and should not be minimized, standard cost systems have generally been cost-beneficial and are widely used, even for nonmanufacturing activities. You should recognize that standards are also used for planning and controlling in nonmanufacturing activities and organizations. Manufacturing firms use standards and budgets for their nonmanufacturing activities, as do merchandising and service businesses. In essence, the concepts of standards and cost systems apply to all types of organizations in varying degrees.

TO SUMMARIZE

Standard costs can be used in nonmanufacturing firms, as well as manufacturing firms. Standard cost systems have both advantages and disadvantages. Most advantages center on achieving greater accuracy and efficiency. Most disadvantages center on the costs involved in setting standards and the inability to establish exact standards in a changing environment.

5 *Explain how performance is evaluated in profit centers.*

EVALUATING PERFORMANCE IN PROFIT CENTERS

As defined earlier, a profit center is an organizational unit (segment) in which a manager has responsibility for both costs and revenues. Profit centers both produce and market goods or services. For example, the U.S., Far East, and European operations of the Edison Automobile Company of IMC Corporation, illustrated in Exhibit 12-3, might be profit centers.

The Segment-Margin Income Statement

segment-margin income statement An income statement that identifies costs directly chargeable to a segment and further divides them into variable and fixed cost behavior patterns.

To evaluate the performance of profit centers and to decide how limited resources will be divided among profit centers, management needs a report that compares the revenues and costs of the profit centers being evaluated. One such report that is often used is the **segment-margin income statement**, such as the one presented in Exhibit 12-7 (pages 574-575) for IMC.

To keep Exhibit 12-7 simple, we are assuming that IMC has only two divisions: Acme Computer and Edison Automobile. Further, we have included only the regions of Edison Automobile. You will note that it includes three geographical regions; the Far East Region has operations in two countries—Japan and Korea. As you read across, note that the segment focus becomes narrower: from divisions to geographic regions to countries within geographic regions.

Before reviewing specific aspects of this segment-margin income statement, we want to remind you of a very important management accounting principle—segment managers should receive information about, and be evaluated on, only the items they can control or influence.

direct costs Costs that are specifically traceable to a unit of business or segment being analyzed.

indirect costs Costs normally incurred for the benefit of several segments or activities.

As was the case with cost centers, in evaluating profit centers it is important that managers be held responsible only for the controllable costs; the costs and revenues over which they have control are usually called **direct costs**. In Exhibit 12-7, we apply responsibility accounting to IMC by including in each segment report only the revenues and costs controlled by that segment manager. This implies that some costs, **indirect costs**, will not be assigned to a particular segment because the manager cannot control them. Company-wide, indirect costs total $1,500,000, which might include the president's salary and interest on company debt, for example.

CAUTION

Many students confuse the terms variable and fixed costs, controllable and noncontrollable costs, and direct and indirect costs. Costs are variable if they fluctuate with activity. If they don't fluctuate with activity, costs are fixed. Costs are controllable if they can be adjusted by the activity manager. If they can't be adjusted by the activity manager, costs are noncontrollable. Costs are direct if removing the activity results in the costs being eliminated. Costs that remain after an activity is eliminated are indirect.

Similarly, when Edison Automobile is broken down into smaller segments for analysis, we see an additional $200,000 of indirect costs that are not assigned to the Edison Automobile's three regions. Costs such as the division manager's salary and advertising for all regions are not controlled by the division manager and so are not allocated to the regions. You will note that as we move down the organizational hierarchy, from divisions to geographical regions to countries, indirect costs increase in total; managers at the lower levels have the narrowest range of responsibility and the fewest costs to control. The manager of manufacturing in Japan, for example, will be responsible for the items ordered for that unit but not for setting the salary of the manager of Far East operations; this is the responsibility of the manager of Edison Automobile. The salary of the manager of Far East operations is thus a direct and controllable cost of Edison Automobile and is a direct and noncontrollable cost to Japanese operations.

Interpreting Profit Center Performance Results

Given that the segment-margin income statement in Exhibit 12-7 was prepared in light of the principles of controllable and direct costs, how does management use the information it contains? First, the net income figure provides management with concrete information for evaluating the performance of the company as a whole. Second, the **segment margins** enable management to analyze company results by evaluating the performance of each segment.

segment margins The difference between segment revenue and direct segment costs; a measure of the segment's contribution to cover indirect fixed costs and provide profits.

segment-margin ratios The segment margin divided by the segment's net sales revenue; a measure of the efficiency of the segment's operating performance, and therefore of its profitability.

contribution-margin ratio The percentage of net sales revenue left after variable costs are deducted; the contribution margin divided by net sales revenue.

We are now ready to examine the operations of IMC segments in detail. In absolute terms, Edison Automotive has a smaller segment margin than Acme Computer ($3,000,000 versus $2,000,000). U.S. operations has earned more than the Far East and European Operations; the Japanese operations has a larger segment margin than Korean operations. Absolute profits, however, often favor those segments with a larger asset base—with larger manufacturing facilities, for example. A larger facility with more manufacturing capacity should naturally have higher production and higher sales and, hence, a higher segment margin and higher income. A more equitable way to assess performance is to compare **segment-margin ratios** (segment margin divided by net sales), because ratios focus on relationships rather than absolute dollar amounts. For example, though the segment margin of European operations is larger than that of Far East operations, the latter has a higher segment-margin ratio (25 percent versus 18 percent). Far East operations also has a higher **contribution-margin ratio** [30 percent versus 23 percent ($600 ÷ $2,000 = 30 percent for Far East; $700 ÷ $3,000 = 23 percent for Europe)].

In using segment-margin income statements to evaluate profit centers, it is important to review performance over several periods or months. A single period or month may not be typical of overall performance. In our example, September might have been an unusually bad profitability month for the Korean unit of Far East

EXHIBIT 12-7 A Segment-Margin Income Statement

International Manufacturing Corporation (IMC)
Segment-Margin Income Statement
September 2000
(in thousands of dollars)

		Corporation Breakdown Into Two Companies	
	Corporation as a Whole	Acme Computer	Edison Automobile
Net sales revenue	$25,000	$15,000	$10,000
Variable costs:			
Cost of goods sold	$15,000	$ 9,000	$ 6,000
Selling and administrative costs	3,000	1,700	1,300
Total variable costs	$18,000	$10,700	$ 7,300
Contribution margin	$ 7,000	$ 4,300	$ 2,700
Less fixed costs controllable by segment managers	2,000	1,300	700
Segment margin	$ 5,000	$ 3,000	$ 2,000
Less company indirect costs	1,500		
Net income	$ 3,500		
Segment-margin ratio		20%	20%

operations because of a slump in the Korean economy or a labor strike. In fact, the performance can only be evaluated by looking at cost and profit trends over several periods and by comparing the results of these units with those of other similar units. (This comparison is consistent with the process of benchmarking introduced earlier.)

TO SUMMARIZE

Profit center managers are usually evaluated on both costs and revenues. The most common profit center measurement tool is the segment-margin income statement. This statement identifies both direct and indirect costs and charges only the direct costs to segments. Segment-margin income statements subdivide direct costs into their variable and fixed cost components. Nonmonetary as well as monetary measures should be used to evaluate profit centers.

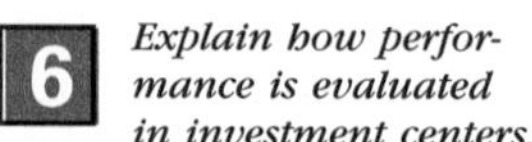
6 *Explain how performance is evaluated in investment centers.*

EVALUATING PERFORMANCE IN INVESTMENT CENTERS

An investment center was defined earlier as an organizational unit in which a manager has responsibility for costs, revenues, and assets. Overall, companies would be considered investment centers, as would the independent segments of decentralized companies. For example, the Acme Computer, Edison Automobile, and Jennifer Cosmetics subsidiaries of IMC (see Exhibit 12-3) would probably all be investment

International Manufacturing Corporation (IMC)
Segment-Margin Income Statement (continued)
September 2000
(in thousands of dollars)

Possible Breakdown of Edison Automobile (Only)				Possible Breakdown of Edison Automobile (Far East Operations)		
Not Allocated	U.S. Operations	Far East Operations	European Operations	Not Allocated	Japanese Operations	Korean Operations
—	$5,000	$2,000	$3,000	—	$1,200	$800
—	$2,900	$1,100	$2,000	—	$ 700	$400
—	700	300	300	—	170	130
—	$3,600	$1,400	$2,300	—	$ 870	$530
—	$1,400	$ 600	$ 700	—	$ 330	$270
$ 200	250	100	150	$ 30	60	10
$(200)	$1,150	$ 500	$ 550	$(30)	$ 270	$260
	23%	25%	18%		23%	33%

centers. Officers of such segments are responsible for acquiring and managing the assets required to manufacture and market their products, as well as for managing the revenues and costs related to those products. The assets include inventory, accounts receivable, and long-term operating assets such as equipment and delivery trucks.

In business, the distinction between profit and investment centers often becomes blurred or even nonexistent. Many companies refer to segments as profit centers when they are really investment centers. However, because the distinction between profit and investment centers is useful for defining responsibilities and determining how performance will be evaluated, we discuss them separately.

There are several methods of evaluating the performance of an investment center. When a segment operates almost as a separate company, the rate of return on invested assets and the residual income are usually measured.

Return on Investment (ROI)

return on investment (ROI) A measure of operating performance and efficiency in utilizing assets; computed in its simplest form by dividing net income by total assets.

As you will recall, we discussed **return on investment (ROI)** (sometimes called return on total assets[1]) to evaluate a company's overall performance. ROI is a measure of how much has been earned on the assets of a company; it is equal to net income divided by total assets. For example, if a company earned $1,000 on $10,000 of assets for one year, its ROI would be $1,000 ÷ $10,000, or 10 percent.

1. In this chapter, we will use the term *ROI* instead of the term "return on total assets" because it is more commonly used in management decision making. We also use total assets instead of average total assets to keep the calculations simple.

Because an investment center operates as if it were an independent company, its performance can also be evaluated using ROI. In calculating the ROI for an investment center, however, management must be sure to consider only the assets, revenues, and costs controlled by that center. In other words, assets used and costs incurred for the benefit of several investment centers should not be included in the calculation. To stress this concept, we will restate the basic ROI formula as:

$$\text{Investment center ROI} = \frac{\text{Investment center income}}{\text{Investment center assets}}$$

Generally, when an investment center's ROI is analyzed, this formula is divided into its components—the profit margin (sometimes called operating performance) and asset turnover ratios—as follows:

$$\text{Profit margin} \times \text{Asset turnover} = \text{ROI}$$

$$\frac{\text{Net income}}{\text{Revenue}} \times \frac{\text{Revenue}}{\text{Total assets}} = \frac{\text{Net income}}{\text{Total assets}}$$

Clearly, we could have eliminated the two revenue figures because they cancel each other out, making ROI equal to net income divided by total assets. However, the inclusion of revenue draws attention to the important concept that ROI is a function of both operating performance and asset turnover.

The expanded formula shown above helps us identify the three ways an investment center can improve its ROI: (1) It can decrease costs to increase its **profit margin (operating performance) ratio** (net income divided by revenue), (2) it can decrease assets to increase its **asset turnover ratio** (revenue divided by total assets), or (3) it can increase revenue with a corresponding increase in net income. An investment center requiring a major investment in assets (such as a steel mill) will necessarily have a low asset turnover and will therefore have to rely primarily on a higher operating performance to increase its return. An investment center with few operating assets (such as a grocery store) has a more rapid asset turnover, and can sustain a lower profit margin ratio while still earning an attractive ROI. For example, a grocery store might make only 2 cents profit per dollar of product sold, but its asset turnover of 12 times a year makes its ROI 24 percent. A steel mill with an asset turnover of 2 times a year would have to earn 12 cents per dollar of sales to produce an ROI of 24 percent.

profit margin (operating performance) ratio An overall measure of the profitability of operations during a period; computed by dividing net income by revenue.

asset turnover ratio An overall measure of how effectively assets are used during a period; computed by dividing revenue by total assets.

To illustrate the three ways of increasing ROI, we will assume that Acme Computer has revenue of \$10,000,000, net income of \$1,000,000, and total assets of \$5,000,000. The ROI is:

$$\text{Profit margin} \times \text{Asset turnover} = \text{ROI}$$

$$\frac{\$1{,}000{,}000}{\$10{,}000{,}000} \times \frac{\$10{,}000{,}000}{\$5{,}000{,}000} = \text{ROI}$$

$$10\% \times 2 = 20\%$$

The following examples show how each of the three alternatives increases ROI:

1. Increase ROI by reducing expenses by \$400,000, providing a net income of \$1,400,000:

$$\frac{\$1{,}400{,}000}{\$10{,}000{,}000} \times \frac{\$10{,}000{,}000}{\$5{,}000{,}000} = \text{ROI}$$

$$14\% \times 2 = 28\%$$

2. Increase ROI by reducing total assets to $4,000,000:

$$\frac{\$1{,}000{,}000}{\$10{,}000{,}000} \times \frac{\$10{,}000{,}000}{\$4{,}000{,}000} = \text{ROI}$$

$$10\% \times 2.5 = 25\%$$

3. Increase ROI by increasing revenue to $12,000,000 (assume that profits increase proportionately):[2]

$$\frac{\$1{,}200{,}000}{\$12{,}000{,}000} \times \frac{\$12{,}000{,}000}{\$5{,}000{,}000} = \text{ROI}$$

$$10\% \times 2.4 = 24\%$$

Although ROI is an effective way of evaluating managers of investment centers, it has certain drawbacks. For example, assume that an investment center currently has an ROI of 22 percent, but the company has an overall ROI of only 16 percent. If a new project or investment that promises a return of 19 percent becomes available to the investment center manager, it might be rejected because the center's ROI would be reduced, even though the company's overall ROI would be increased.

Residual Income

residual income The amount of net income earned above a specified minimum rate of return on assets; used to evaluate investment centers.

Although ROI is widely used to evaluate investment centers, because of its drawbacks, some companies use a closely related measure called **residual income**, which is the amount of net income an investment center is able to earn above a certain minimum rate of return on assets. Exhibit 12-8 compares the residual income and ROI approaches. Assuming that the specified minimum rate of return on assets is 15 percent and that an investment center earns a $25,000 net income on total assets of $100,000, we see that residual income is $10,000 ($25,000 net income − $15,000 minimum return on assets).

To further illustrate why many companies prefer to use residual income over ROI for evaluating investment center performance, assume that the division for which data were given in Exhibit 12-8 has an opportunity to invest $40,000 in a new project that will generate a return of 20 percent ($8,000 per year). A manager being evaluated on ROI would probably reject this investment opportunity

EXHIBIT 12-8

A Comparison of ROI and Residual Income

	ROI	Residual Income
Total assets	$100,000	$100,000
Net income	$ 25,000	$ 25,000
ROI ($25,000 ÷ $100,000)	25%	
Minimum rate of return on assets (15% × $100,000)		15,000
Residual income		$ 10,000

2. When revenue increases, fixed costs may remain the same. The result is that both the operating performance and asset turnover ratios are likely to increase when revenue goes up. We are ignoring these CVP considerations in order to keep the example simple.

because, as the following analysis shows, it would reduce the division's overall ROI from 25 to 23.6 percent.

	Without the New Investment	With the New Investment	Total
Total assets	$100,000	$40,000	$140,000
Net income	$ 25,000	$ 8,000	$ 33,000
ROI	25%	20%	23.6%

On the other hand, a manager being evaluated on residual income (with a minimum rate of return of 15 percent) would probably be quite enthusiastic about the project because it increases residual income from $10,000 to $12,000.

	Without the New Investment	With the New Investment	Total
Total assets	$100,000	$40,000	$140,000
Net income	$ 25,000	$ 8,000	$ 33,000
Minimum rate of return	15,000*	6,000**	21,000
Residual income	$ 10,000	$ 2,000	$ 12,000

*$100,000 × 15% = $15,000
**$40,000 × 15% = $6,000

Whether or not the investment should actually be made also depends on several other factors, including what other alternatives are or will be available. The advantage of residual income is that it encourages managers to make as much profit as possible rather than merely achieving a certain ROI; this means making investments that benefit not only their centers but also the company as a whole.

TO SUMMARIZE

Managers of investment centers are usually held responsible for costs, revenues, and assets. The most common performance measures used in investment centers are ROI and residual income. ROI is a function of both operating performance and asset turnover. Residual income is the amount of net income left over after a certain minimum rate of return has been earned on assets. Both ROI and residual income must be used with care because they can encourage managers to maximize short-run profits at the expense of long-term profitability.

7 *Explain why it is important for a company to have quality and time standards as well as financial standards.*

QUALITY AND TIME STANDARDS

In discussing responsibility accounting and performance evaluation, we have focused primarily on monetary considerations. Nonmonetary measures of effective performance are just as important. For example, one well-known fast-food chain's managers are evaluated not only on the profitability of their unit, but also on such quality standards as cleanliness and the kind of service provided to customers. In another company, some managers receive more points for developing new technologies and making innovations than for keeping costs in line. At another company, production employees are rewarded on how much they can reduce the delivery time of products to customers. Other nonmonetary measures of performance include creating good employee morale, maintaining equipment in good running order, and so forth.

For a performance evaluation system to be successful, the criteria by which managers and supervisors are evaluated should be well defined, objective, and measurable. Usually, qualitative criteria are much harder to evaluate than objective cost measures and resulting variances, but that does not diminish their importance. In fact, quality and time standards are often as important to a firm's success as are financial results. Those companies that can deliver the highest-quality products quickest and at the most competitive price will usually be most successful. Some companies have even developed "best supplier" awards to recognize those suppliers who deliver products at the lowest price, with the highest quality and with the minimum number of late orders. Criteria used in making these awards usually include such elements as cost reductions, delivery improvement (frequency as well as timeliness), percentage of defects, and so forth.

In evaluating quality and time considerations, quality is usually defined as the total features and characteristics of a product or service that bear on its ability to satisfy stated or implied needs. Generally, the final measure of quality must be viewed from a customer perspective as determined by acceptance in the market place. One writer has suggested that quality includes the following eight dimensions:[3]

1. *Performance*—a product's primary operating characteristic. Examples are automobile acceleration and a television set's picture clarity.
2. *Features*—supplements to a product's basic functioning characteristics, such as power windows on a car.
3. *Reliability*—a probability of not malfunctioning during a specified period.
4. *Conformance*—the degree to which a product's design and operating characteristics meet established standards.
5. *Durability*—a measure of product life.
6. *Serviceability*—the speed and ease of repair.
7. *Aesthetics*—how a product looks, feels, tastes, and smells.
8. *Perceived quality*—as seen by a customer.

As an example of how management might apply these quality components to a specific product, consider an automobile tire. Its quality may be measured by treadwear rate, handling, traction, impact on gas mileage, noise levels, resistance to punctures, and appearance. As another example, the tax service of a CPA may be measured by timely completion of tax returns, tax savings, number of audits or letters from the IRS, suggestions made for future investment opportunities, fees charged, and personal attention given.

This discussion of quality suggests that performance evaluation must be viewed more broadly and from a different perspective than it has been in the past. Controlling costs is still essential, but the emphasis should also be on quality and improvement in processes, products, and services. Some people argue that the competitive advantage of some Japanese companies is the direct result of acceptance of this quality philosophy, attributed to W. Edwards Deming. The Deming chain reaction is depicted in Exhibit 12-9.

With a broader perspective, managers can seek ways to measure all aspects of company performance. The emphasis should be on the critical activities of the company. The goal is to identify and concentrate on those activities that add the most value to products or services.

In addition to quality, performance evaluation now often considers the time it takes to get a product to the market place. In fact, it has been this emphasis on

3. David A. Garvin, "Competing on the Eight Dimensions of Quality," *Harvard Business Review*, 65, November–December 1987, pp. 101–109.

EXHIBIT 12-9

Deming Chain Reaction

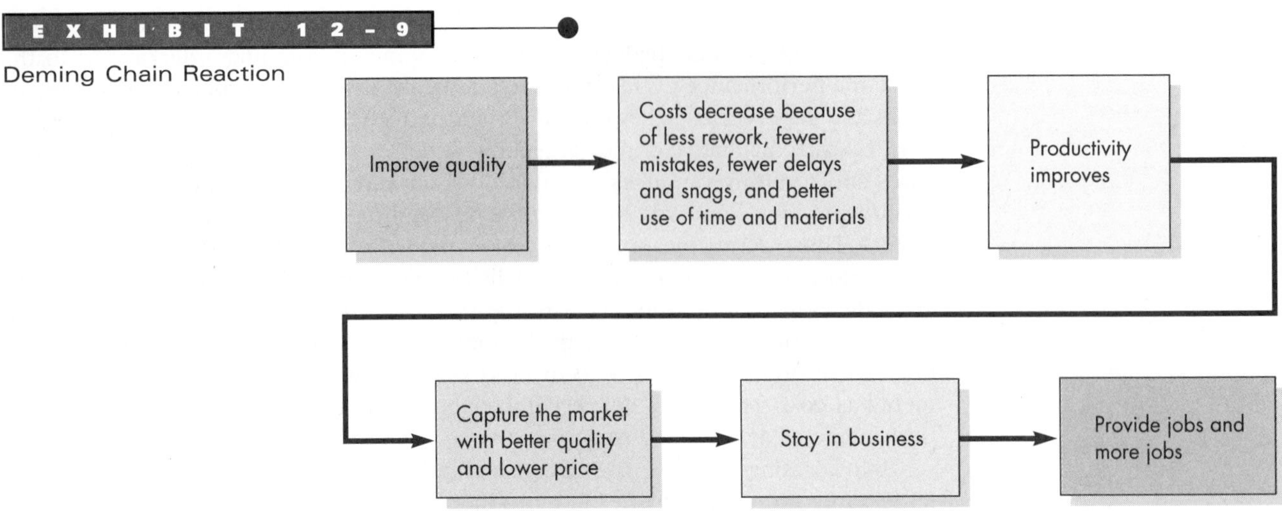

speeding up production that has primarily been responsible for just-in-time (JIT) inventory systems.

The challenge is to integrate cost, quality, and speed considerations into evaluation systems effectively. The objectives of zero defects, continuous improvement, decreasing manufacturing and delivery time, and meeting customer expectations of quality are admirable. Developing and effectively implementing performance measures that help achieve these objectives is not an easy task, but it is certainly worthy of management's effort. In the end, those organizations that

BUSINESS ENVIRONMENT ESSAY

Nonmonetary Standards at Xerox

Customer surveys at Xerox's Omaha district indicated that 18 percent of customers were dissatisfied with billing accuracy. This figure prompted an evaluation of billing accuracy, revealing the district's billing error rate to be 3.54 percent. Further, estimates were made of the costs required to correct billing errors and the amount of revenues lost due to the cancellation of contracts by those dissatisfied because of billing problems. The total cost to the company was estimated to be almost $200,000 during a six-month test period.

A team with representatives from the different departments that participated in the billing process was formed to improve billing performance. The team followed a multistep problem-solving process. First, the problem was identified and analyzed. During this stage, team members identified all those who might have an impact on billing errors and the likely causes of those errors. Next, possible solutions were considered. Here the focus was on ways to educate personnel about correct billing input and procedures. In the solution planning stage, the team chose to create a cartoon character, Captain Xero, to attract attention to the improvement program and to convey the program's message. Cartoons would be published weekly to educate personnel about billing. Finally, the team implemented the program and evaluated its results.

The focus on improving billing accuracy paid off handsomely. During a one-year period, billing errors were reduced 52 percent as the billing error rate fell from 3.54 percent to 1.71 percent. Surveys revealed that customer satisfaction with billing accuracy also improved significantly. The estimated reduction in costs associated with billing errors exceeded $100,000 during the second six-month period after the program was implemented.

Source: Adapted from David M. Beuhlmann and Donald Stover, "How Xerox Solves Quality Problems," *Management Accounting*, September 1993, pp. 33–36.

(S T O P & T H I N K)

What do you think researchers mean when they say that current performance evaluation methods don't give enough consideration to intangible capabilities and focus too much on financial returns?

develop the most appropriate performance measures and provide the necessary encouragement and motivation for employees to achieve the organization's objectives will be the most successful.

TO SUMMARIZE

In addition to cost considerations, nonmonetary measures should be used in evaluating performance. To be effective, these criteria must be well defined, objective, and measurable. New approaches to performance evaluation include quality and time considerations. The new approaches are required because all aspects of a company's performance need to be monitored. In the final analysis, those organizations that can deliver the highest quality products to their customers at the lowest prices and in the shortest amount of time will be most successful. Significant challenges exist in implementing new performance evaluation approaches.

REVIEW OF LEARNING OBJECTIVES

1 **Explain why performance evaluation is such an important activity in organizations.** Today information about how efficiently and effectively an organization is operating is easily accessible worldwide. For a company to survive in this information age, it must deliver the highest quality products to its customers at the least possible price in the shortest amount of time. The only way an organization can continue to improve on these dimensions is to assess its performance and identify areas for improvement. This need for continuous improvement makes performance evaluation more important than ever before.

2 **Describe the process of strategic planning in organizations.** Strategic planning is the systematic and formalized effort of a company to establish basic company purposes, policies, and strategies and to develop detailed plans to achieve these objectives and purposes. Strategic planning usually involves establishing a mission statement and then specifying goals, strategies, and activities that flow from the mission statement. The strategic plan also identifies the performance measurement criteria that will be used to determine if the company is accomplishing its activities and, hence, its mission. Strategic planning is future oriented, and includes examining the competition's strengths and weaknesses, market opportunities, and the company's own distinctive capabilities.

3 **Identify different types of organizational units in which performance evaluation occurs.** Most companies are divided into segments with responsibilities assigned to segment managers. These segments may be defined in terms of product line, geographic area, or function, for example. In a centralized organization, top management makes most of the important operating decisions; in a decentralized organization, decision-making authority is delegated to lower-level managers as well. The current trend is toward decentralization because it usually results in better, more informed decisions.

With responsibility accounting, managers are held accountable for the costs, assets, or revenues over which they have control. The three types of responsibility centers are cost, profit, and investment. Cost centers are usually found at relatively low levels in the organization, and the managers are held accountable for the costs they incur. Profit and investment centers are found at higher levels, and the managers are held accountable for the profits or the return on investments in assets they generate.

4 **Explain how performance is evaluated in cost centers.** Performance is evaluated in cost centers using standard costs. A standard cost system involves setting standard (predetermined) costs that serve as a benchmark for judging what actual costs should be. Standard costs are usually expressed as the per-unit cost of materials, labor, and manufacturing overhead and are used by managers for planning, implementing, and controlling decisions. Standard costs are developed on the basis of careful analysis using the experience of many types of staff, including engineers, supervisors, accountants, purchasing agents, and others. Standard costs have a quantity component and a price

component. A comparison of actual and standard costs usually results in two variances: a price (rate) variance and a quantity (usage) variance. Significant variances alert management to specific problem areas that require corrective action. The strategy of focusing on significant variances, called management by exception, is essential to the control function. A standard cost system is designed to accumulate actual costs, to compare actual and standard costs to identify variances, and to report operating results (including variances) to management for review and for corrective action when significant variances occur. Extensive use of standard costing systems is found in manufacturing firms. A complete standard cost system will include standards for materials, labor, and manufacturing overhead. Materials variances are usually called price variances and quantity variances. The materials price variance reflects the extent to which the actual price varies from the standard price for the actual quantity of materials purchased or used. The materials quantity variance measures the extent to which the quantity of materials used varies from the standard quantity allowed for the achieved level of production. Labor variances are called rate variances and efficiency variances. The labor rate variance is the difference between the actual and the standard labor rates multiplied by the actual hours worked. The labor efficiency variance is the difference between actual and standard hours multiplied by the standard wage rate.

5 **Explain how performance is evaluated in profit centers.** Profit center managers are responsible for revenues as well as costs. The best measure of performance in a profit center is a segment-margin income statement, which distinguishes between indirect and direct costs and reports a segment margin that is controllable by segment managers. Segment-margin income statements also divide direct segment costs into their variable and fixed components in order to compute the segment's contribution margin. Nonmonetary factors often must also be considered in assessing the performance of a profit center.

6 **Explain how performance is evaluated in investment centers.** Investment centers are usually found at higher levels in an organization than profit centers. The managers of investment centers are responsible for costs, revenues, and assets. Commonly used measures of investment center performance are return on investment (ROI) and residual income. ROI is calculated by dividing net income by total assets. An investment center can improve its ROI by (1) decreasing its costs to increase its operating performance ratio, (2) decreasing its assets to increase its asset turnover ratio, or (3) increasing revenue with a corresponding increase in net income. Residual income is the amount of net income an investment center is able to earn above a certain minimum rate of return on assets. The problem with both ROI and residual income is that they tend to encourage managers to make decisions that increase short-run profits but may diminish profits in the long run.

7 **Explain why it is important for a company to have quality and time standards as well as financial standards.** Successful companies deliver the highest quality goods to their customers at the lowest possible prices and in the least amount of time. These three criteria of quality, cost, and speed must be measured so that they can be continuously improved. All aspects of company performance must be evaluated, not just quantitative cost measures.

KEY TERMS AND CONCEPTS

REVIEW PROBLEM

Material and Labor Variances

The standard cost sheet for Kendra Box Company shows the following unit costs for direct materials and direct labor for each box made:

Direct materials (4 board feet of lumber @ $2)	$ 8
Direct labor (2 standard hours @ $6)	12
Total standard cost per unit (excluding overhead)	$20

During the month of October, 83,000 feet of lumber were used to produce 20,000 boxes, and the following actual costs were incurred:

Lumber purchased (100,000 board feet @ $2.20)	$220,000
Direct labor (39,600 hours @ $6.05)	$239,580

Required: Compute the materials and labor variances.

Solution

Materials Variances

The price variance is computed when the lumber is purchased, and the quantity variance is computed when the lumber is used.

Materials price variance:	
Purchase price per board foot for 100,000 feet	$ 2.20
Standard price per board foot	(2.00)
Difference	$ 0.20 U
Feet of lumber purchased	× 100,000
Total price variance	$ 20,000 U
Materials quantity variance:	
Actual lumber used	83,000 feet
Standard lumber required (20,000 boxes × 4 feet)	(80,000) feet
Difference	3,000 feet U
Standard cost per board foot	×$2.00
Total quantity variance	$ 6,000 U

Labor Variances

The labor rate and labor efficiency variances are both based on direct labor hours used; thus, they are computed at the same point in time.

Total direct labor variance:	
Actual direct labor cost (39,600 hours at $6.05)	$239,580
Standard direct labor cost (20,000 boxes × 2 hours = 40,000 hours × $6.00)	240,000
Total direct labor variance	$ 420 F
Labor rate variance:	
Actual rate	$ 6.05
Standard rate	(6.00)
Difference	$ 0.05 U
Actual hours	× 39,600
Total labor rate variance	$ 1,980 U
Labor efficiency variance:	
Actual direct labor hours	39,600
Standard direct labor hours	40,000
Difference	400 F
Standard direct labor rate	× $6.00
Total labor efficiency variance	$ 2,400 F

DISCUSSION QUESTIONS

1. Why is performance evaluation important to a business, especially in today's economy?
2. What is usually the first step in formulating a strategic plan?
3. Why is it important for specific goals and performance standards to be related to a company's overall strategic plan?
4. Why is it practically impossible for a firm to be completely centralized, that is, to have top management making all operating decisions?
5. Why is a system of responsibility accounting necessary in most businesses?
6. What are some important behavioral factors that must be considered when responsibilities are assigned to managers?
7. Why are most performance reports called exception reports?
8. What is the difference between a cost center and a profit center? Between a profit center and an investment center?
9. What is a standard cost?
10. What is the purpose of a standard cost system?
11. Who is responsible for the development of the standards to be used in a standard cost system?
12. What is a variance from standard?
13. What is the relationship of a standard cost system to the principle of management by exception?
14. What are the steps in establishing and operating a standard cost system?
15. What purpose is served by dividing the total direct materials variance into a price and a quantity variance, and dividing the total direct labor variance into a rate and an efficiency variance?
16. Who is usually responsible for each of the following variances?
    a. Direct materials price variance
    b. Direct materials quantity variance
    c. Direct labor rate variance
    d. Direct labor efficiency variance
17. What are the major advantages and disadvantages of a standard cost system?
18. If a profit center has a net loss, does that mean it is not making a contribution to the company as a whole?
19. What is the major disadvantage of using ROI to evaluate the performance of investment centers?
20. What is the major advantage of using residual income to evaluate the performance of investment centers?
21. Why is it important for a business to incorporate quality and time standards into its performance evaluation system?

DISCUSSION CASES

CASE 12-1 CONTINUOUS IMPROVEMENT NEEDED

One evening after a strenuous day at the office, Janis Walker, president of Western Mills, Inc., a leading textile manufacturing firm, was out jogging to help relieve the tensions of that day's work. While jogging, she focused her thinking on the firm's commercial carpeting division. The major customers of the division are companies that are building new office buildings, hotels, and motels and need quality carpet in their buildings. The carpet division is doing quite well, but nevertheless, Walker has a nagging feeling that the division could be doing better. She decided to discuss the performance of the division with the division manager. When she arrived home after jogging, Walker called the division manager and arranged a meeting for the next day.

At the meeting, Walker asked the division manager how long it took to deliver an order to the building site after production started. The manager's answer was 17 days. Walker then asked what the industry average was for delivery. The answer was 15 days. Walker wanted to know why Western Mills took longer than competitors to meet order requirements. The manager answered that their product was of a higher quality, so customers were willing to wait longer for the order to be filled. With this information in hand and without hesitation, Walker said, "I will give you six months to reduce the delivery time to 10 days! You study the problem and tell me what resources you need to meet this 10-day delivery goal. I want a report from you as soon as possible."

1. Assuming that the division already has a standard cost system, what were the limitations of that system that resulted in two more days of delivery time than its competitors?
2. Assuming this company has a standard cost system, what changes is the division manager likely to make in order to meet the president's 10-day delivery mandate?

CASE 12-2

USING SEGMENT DATA TO MAKE KEY DECISIONS

Sure-Check Company, a calculator manufacturer, is considering dropping one of its calculator product lines because of consistent losses from this model over the past three years. The recent poor performance of this product (known as model A) is shown here (in thousands).

	1998	1999	2000
Revenue (average price $100 per unit)	$14,600	$14,400	$14,200
Variable costs:			
Direct materials cost ($40 per unit)	$ 5,840	$ 5,760	$ 5,680
Direct labor cost ($20 per unit)	2,920	2,880	2,840
Variable manufacturing overhead costs ($15 per unit)	2,190	2,160	2,130
Selling expenses (10% of sales)	1,460	1,440	1,420
Total variable costs	$12,410	$12,240	$12,070
Contribution margin	$ 2,190	$ 2,160	$ 2,130
Less fixed costs controllable by segment managers	2,022	1,997	1,972
Segment margin	$ 168	$ 163	$ 158
Less company indirect fixed costs	438	432	426
Operating loss	$ (270)	$ (269)	$ (268)

Revenue and fixed costs (controllable by segment managers) are expected to decrease again in 2001 by $200,000 and $25,000, respectively, whereas direct materials and direct labor are expected to increase by 5 percent unless the production department purchases a new attachment with a 2-year life for $150,000. This new attachment would replace an attachment purchased only two years ago for $200,000 with, at that time, an expected 4-year life. If the new attachment is purchased, direct materials and direct labor will not increase in 2001.

1. Assuming that the new attachment is not purchased, should Sure-Check Company continue to manufacture and sell the model A calculator? Explain.
2. Should the new attachment be purchased? Explain.
3. How, if at all, would the production capacity made available by discontinuing model A affect your decision regarding the purchase of the attachment?
4. What qualitative factors could affect your responses to (1) and (2)?

CASE 12-3

WHAT ARE MY COSTS ANYWAY?

You have recently been promoted as the manager of the camera division of a large corporation. Your most profitable product is an instant camera that takes pictures and then develops them immediately. Historically, the pictures taken by the camera were of a poor quality, but due to large investments in research and new breakthroughs in technology, the instantly developed pictures are of increasingly higher quality. You have just received your segment financial statements for the period which report the following:

Revenue	$81,000,000
Cost of products sold	40,000,000
Gross margin	$41,000,000

On the basis of this performance you are due to receive a $3,000,000 bonus. The top executives of the company are ecstatic about your performance because you have increased quality, reduced defects, and dramatically increased the productivity of your segment. However, having studied management accounting, you know that the manufacturing costs are not the only ones that add value to your products. In fact, in your heart, you believe that were it not for research and development costs, aggressive marketing, and good customer service subsequent to sales, your segment would not be nearly so profitable. Yet, these costs are tracked in other departments and are not your responsibility.

As a manager who is benefiting from traditional performance evaluation methods, you wonder whether you should inform management that it is actually giving you a bonus that is too high. Apparently, you are the only one in your company that is aware that these other value-adding costs should be included in your performance evaluation. What should you do? Do you let well enough alone, or should you go to management and let them know that you are probably being overpaid?

EXERCISES

EXERCISE 12-1
Responsibility Accounting Reports

Lorlily Company is an agricultural supply firm. The management of the company is decentralized, with division managers heading the two operating divisions: Machinery and Seed/Fertilizer. Within each division, the sales are split between the two states of Indiana and Illinois.

The following data are applicable to revenue in 2000:

	Budget	Actual
Machinery—Indiana	$800,000	$750,000
Seed/Fertilizer—Illinois	500,000	580,000
Seed/Fertilizer—Indiana	400,000	530,000
Machinery—Illinois	350,000	250,000

1. Prepare a responsibility accounting report for the head of the Machinery division. For each of the two geographic areas (Indiana and Illinois), show whether the variance between budgeted and actual machinery revenue is favorable or unfavorable.
2. Prepare a responsibility accounting report for the head of the entire company. The company head wants to see only the overall results for each of the two operating divisions (Machinery and Seed/Fertilizer); a detailed breakdown by geographic area is not requested.

EXERCISE 12-2
Materials Price Variance

Hogan Manufacturing Company has just adopted a standard cost system. You have been asked to analyze the materials purchases and usage for the month of August to determine the materials price variance to be recorded at the end of the month. During August, 5,000 gallons of a chemical were purchased at $3.20 per gallon. Only

4,200 gallons were put into production. The standard price per gallon is $3.15. Compute the following variances:

1. The materials price variance if the chemical is carried in inventory at standard price.
2. The materials price variance if the chemical is carried in inventory at actual price and is charged to Work-in-Process Inventory at the standard price.

EXERCISE 12-3
Materials Price and Quantity Variances—Journal Entries

Genesis Enterprises produces one product—MX4. The following information relating to raw materials is available for the month of March:

Beginning direct materials inventory	1,500 pounds @ $3.10 per unit
Purchases made during the month	11,000 pounds @ $3.10 per unit
Direct materials placed in production	11,750 pounds

The standard materials usage for one unit of MX4 is 2 pounds with a standard price per pound of $3.00. Genesis produced 6,000 units of Product MX4 during the month.

1. Compute the materials price and quantity variances for Genesis assuming the materials price variance is computed at the time of purchase.
2. Provide the journal entries required to record:
   a. The purchase of direct materials and the materials price variance.
   b. Placing the direct materials in production and the materials quantity variance.

EXERCISE 12-4
Direct Materials Purchased and Used

Mary Clarke is concerned about her performance as a recently employed purchasing agent. The accounting department has provided her with the following data for the month of August:

Units produced	2,000
Materials used.	1,078 tons
Materials purchased	1,400 tons at $43 per ton

The standard materials usage set by management for one unit of product is half a ton of materials per unit, at $45 per ton. Her performance report shows the following variances:

Used (1,078 tons − 1,000 tons standard) × $45 per ton	$3,510 U
Purchased ($45 per ton standard − $43 per ton actual) × 1,400 tons	2,800 F
	$ 710 U

If you were Mary Clarke, how would you explain this report, which indicates a $710 unfavorable variance?

EXERCISE 12-5
Analyzing Materials Cost

Mr. Rogers, the production manager, has received a report showing a $16,500 unfavorable total materials variance. He knows that production used 10,000 pounds less than the budgeted amount for direct materials. Mr. Rogers also knows that the standard price for direct materials was determined to be 80 cents per pound.

What was the actual cost of direct materials used during the period if the budgeted amount was estimated to be 500,000 pounds?

EXERCISE 12-6
Materials Price and Quantity Variances

John Clarke, production manager, has just received a report stating that the total materials variance for last month was $3,000 unfavorable. However, he is not certain whether the production foremen are overdrawing from inventory or the purchasing department has been unable to acquire materials at reasonable prices. The information he needs is contained in the following report:

Standard production	150,000 units
Actual production.	146,000 units
Standard materials per unit	2 pounds
Materials used in March.	300,000 pounds
Standard price for materials.	$1.50 per pound
Actual price for materials	$1.47 per pound

1. Compute the materials price and quantity variances for the month.
2. **Interpretive Question:** What was the cause of the unfavorable variance, and what recommendation would you make to Mr. Clarke?

EXERCISE 12-7
Materials Price and Quantity Variances—Journal Entries

Starship Enterprises produces and sells calibrators. The company began the period with the following inventory of raw material:

200 units at $5.50 per unit (the materials price variance is taken at the time of purchase)

A standard of four units of material for each calibrator produced has been established. During the period, Starship purchased an additional 1,500 units of material at a total cost of $8,220. The dollar amount of materials transferred to Work-in-Process Inventory during the period was $8,800. At the end of the period, Starship had an ending materials inventory of 50 units.

1. Provide the journal entry required to record the materials price variance.
2. Provide the journal entry required to record the materials quantity variance.

EXERCISE 12-8
Labor Rate and Efficiency Variances

To produce one unit of Product OU812 requires 4 hours of labor at a standard cost per hour of $8.50. During the month of September, 15,000 units were produced. Actual hours and costs for the month are as follows:

Actual direct labor hours	58,800
Actual direct labor costs	$498,000

1. Compute the actual cost per hour of direct labor for the month of September.
2. Compute the labor rate variance.
3. Compute the labor efficiency variance.

EXERCISE 12-9
Responsibility for Labor Costs

Raymond Stone, a recent business school graduate, has taken a job with Farben Corporation as production manager. His job is to see that production is efficient. After his first month, he is given this memo.

Performance Report	
Ray Stone:	$8,000 Unfavorable

Given the following data, what justification would you give if you were in his position, keeping in mind that Stone is not responsible for hiring, firing, and wage rates?

Units produced	750 units
Direct labor used	7,600 hours at $5.00
Standard direct labor hours per unit	10 hours at $4.00

EXERCISE 12-10
Responsibility for Labor Rates

In Exercise 12-9, what is theoretically wrong with the conclusion that Ray Stone is not responsible for labor rates?

EXERCISE 12-11
Labor Variances

During the year, Thompson Plastics was in negotiation with the local union over wages. A settlement was finally reached, and the average wage per hour was increased to $3.28. Production fell to 145,000 units, and 220,000 hours were incurred. Standard production has been set at 150,000 units; 1.5 hours of labor were expected to produce one unit at a standard cost of $4.875 per unit. Actual labor cost for the period was $721,600.

1. Calculate the labor variances at Thompson Plastics.
2. Prepare the journal entry to enter labor costs in Work-in-Process Inventory, and set up the spending and efficiency variances for labor.
3. **Interpretive Question:** Are these variances significant in the light of the new wage agreement?

EXERCISE 12-12
Employee Morale and Production Efficiency

Crest Fabrics is a nonunion textile firm. Employee morale and production efficiency have dropped in the last few weeks, causing management some concern. Further, quality control problems have resulted in a 10 percent increase in rejects in the last two weeks. The following information may help management identify the causes of current problems:

Employee Production Efficiency Report (in percentages)

Employee	Wk. 14	Wk. 15	Wk. 16	Wk. 17	Wk. 18	Wk. 19	Wk. 20
Baker	96	100	86	93	91	89	85
Johnson	101	97	89	90	93	91	87
Becker	105	109	93	96	95	92	90
Howard	99	98	88	93	97	94	88
Kettle	92	93	81	85	90	91	90

Additional information:

a. Standards for measuring worker efficiency were raised at the start of week 16.
b. Crest Fabrics changed its source of supply of materials in week 15.

1. From the production efficiency report, can you identify trends in the efficiency of individual workers? Which ones might have low morale?
2. **Interpretive Question:** What clues to the causes of the diminishing efficiency and quality can you draw from the information given?

EXERCISE 12-13
Labor Variances

Compute the missing amounts.

Total labor variance	$ 47,500 U
Labor efficiency variance	42,000 U
Actual labor hours incurred	110,000
Standard labor hours allowed	(a)
Units produced	50,000
Standard hours allowed per unit	2
Total actual labor costs	$467,500
Actual labor cost per hour	(b)
Actual labor cost per unit	(c)
Labor rate variance	(d)
Standard labor cost per hour	(e)
Standard labor cost per unit	(f)

EXERCISE 12-14
Segment-Margin Income Statements

Professional Management, Inc., is a company that sponsors seminars for executives. It has two profit centers, or divisions: a time-management group and a money-management group. Financial information for the two divisions for the year just ended follows:

	Time Management	Money Management
Revenue	$842,000	$965,000
Mailing costs	48,000	102,000
Printing costs	146,000	98,000
Hotel rental costs	425,000	501,000
Travel expenses	72,000	60,000
Advertising costs	108,000	106,000

Of these costs, printing and advertising are direct fixed costs, whereas mailing, hotel rental, and travel are variable costs. Using this information, prepare segment-margin income statements for the two divisions.

EXERCISE 12-15
Evaluating Performance with Segment and Contribution Margins

Damond Corporation's three profit centers had the following operating data during 2000:

	North	East	West
Revenue (at $10 per unit)	$100,000	$150,000	$200,000
Fixed costs:			
Costs unique to the division	30,000	61,000	70,000
Costs allocated by corporate headquarters	20,000	30,000	40,000
Variable costs per unit	6	6	4

Damond's management is concerned because the company is losing money. They ask you to:

1. Calculate each profit center's contribution and segment margins and overall company profits.
2. Determine, on the basis of these calculations, which center(s), if any, should be discontinued. (Assume that the 2000 performance is indicative of all future years. Ignore all nonfinancial factors.)

EXERCISE 12-16
Measuring Performance Using Segment and Contribution Margins

El Pico Company has two divisions: Maya and Aztec. During 2000, they had the following operating data:

	Maya Division	Aztec Division
Revenue	$100,000	$120,000
Fixed costs:		
Costs unique to the division	50,000	45,000
Costs allocated by corporate headquarters	11,000	10,000
Variable costs per unit	4	4
Unit sales price of division's product	10	8

1. Compute each division's contribution and segment margins, and the contribution each makes to overall company profits.
2. **Interpretive Question:** Based on only the financial information given, should either division be discontinued? Why?

EXERCISE 12-17
Return on Investment

Compute the missing data, items (a) through (i), in the following table:

	Division X	Division Y	Division Z
Revenue	$600,000	$500,000	$ (g)
Net income	30,000	25,000	(h)
Total assets	(a)	100,000	200,000
Operating performance ratio	(b)	(d)	10%
Asset turnover ratio	(c)	(e)	4 times
ROI	12%	(f)	(i)

EXERCISE 12-18
Return on Investment

During 2000, the North and South divisions of Mayberry Company reported the following:

	North Division	South Division
ROI	18%	20%
Operating performance ratio	6%	5%
Revenue	$60,000	$80,000
Total assets	20,000	20,000

1. What was each division's asset turnover ratio in 2000?
2. What operating performance ratio would each division need in order to generate an ROI of 25 percent?

EXERCISE 12-19
Measuring Performance: Residual Income and ROI

McCormick Corporation measures the performance of its divisions by using the residual income approach, with a minimum accepted rate of return of 16 percent. In 2000, the printing division, which has total assets of $250,000, generated a net income of $55,000, or 8 percent of sales. The operating results are expected to be the same in 2001. In early 2001, the printing division receives a proposal for a $50,000 investment that would generate an additional $10,000 of income per year.

1. Should the manager of the printing division make the investment?
2. Would your answer to (1) be different if McCormick Corporation used the ROI approach to evaluate the performance of its various divisions? Why or why not?

EXERCISE 12-20
Measuring Performance: Residual Income and ROI

An investment center of Southwick Corporation made three investment proposals. Details of the proposals follow.

	Proposals		
	1	2	3
Required investment	$80,000	$50,000	$65,000
Annual return	13,000	9,000	9,500

Southwick Corporation uses the residual income method to evaluate all investment proposals. Its minimum rate of return is 15 percent.

1. As president of Southwick Corporation, which of the investments, if any, would you make? Why?
2. Assuming that Southwick Corporation uses the ROI approach to evaluate investment proposals, which investments, if any, would you make? (Southwick Corporation's current return on assets is 20 percent.)

PROBLEMS

PROBLEM 12-1
Responsibility Accounting Reports

Ryhan Company is a multinational computer services firm. The management of the company is decentralized, with division managers heading the following three divisions: Europe, Asia, and the Americas. Within each division, the three sources of revenue are software sales, service contracts, and consulting fees.

The following data are applicable to revenue in 2000:

	Budget	Actual
Europe—software sales	$200,000	$230,000
Asia—software sales	200,000	130,000
Americas—software sales	350,000	420,000
Europe—service contracts	120,000	90,000
Asia—service contracts	70,000	80,000
Americas—service contracts	250,000	190,000
Europe—consulting fees	40,000	90,000
Asia—consulting fees	50,000	35,000
Americas—consulting fees	100,000	60,000

Required:

1. Prepare a responsibility accounting report for the head of the Europe division. For each of the three revenue sources (software sales, service contracts, and consulting fees), show whether the variance between budget and actual is favorable or unfavorable.

2. Prepare a responsibility accounting report for the head of the entire company. The company head wants to see only the overall results for each of the three geographic divisions (budget vs. actual); a detailed breakdown by revenue source is not requested.

PROBLEM 12-2
Materials and Labor Variances

The standard cost data for Madison Machinery Company show the following costs for producing one of its machines:

Direct materials	400 pounds at $8 = $3,200
Direct labor	150 hours at $15 = $2,250

During April, four machines were built, with actual total costs as follows:

Materials purchased	2,000 pounds at $8.20 = $16,400
Materials used	1,700 pounds
Direct labor incurred	625 hours at $14.80 = $9,250

Required:

1. Compute the following variances:
   a. Materials price variance (inventory is carried at standard cost)
   b. Materials quantity variance
   c. Labor rate variance
   d. Labor efficiency variance
2. Record the standard materials and labor costs in Work-in-Process Inventory, and enter the variances in appropriate journal entries.

PROBLEM 12-3
Materials and Labor Variances

Gemini Incorporated provides the following standard cost data for one of its products:

Direct materials	5 pounds at $4.25 per pound
Direct labor	2 hours at $6.00 per hour

During the month of August, the following actual cost data was accumulated:

Materials purchased	16,000 pounds at $4.15 per pound
Materials used	14,500 pounds
Direct labor incurred	6,450 hours at a total cost of $38,571
Units produced	3,150 units

Required: Compute the following variances:

1. Materials price variance (this variance is computed at the time of purchase)
2. Materials quantity variance
3. Labor rate variance
4. Labor efficiency variance

PROBLEM 12-4
Materials and Labor Variances

Actual materials	2,000 tons
Actual hours used	1,500 hours
Standard materials for output (tons)	(a)
Standard hours for output	(b)
Actual cost per ton of material	(c)
Standard cost per ton of material	$ 4
Actual cost per direct labor hour	$ 4
Standard cost per direct labor hour	(d)
Total direct labor variance	$1,625 U
Total direct materials variance	$ 400 F
Direct materials price variance	(e)
Direct materials quantity variance	$ 0
Direct labor rate variance	$ 750 U
Direct labor efficiency variance	(f)

Required: Compute the missing amounts.

PROBLEM 12-5
Materials and Labor Variances

Sports Manufacturing Inc. produces and sells footballs. The standard cost for materials and labor for one regulation-size football is as follows:

Direct materials	2 feet of leather at $5.50 per foot
Direct labor	1/2 hour at $9.00 per hour

During the period, Sports Manufacturing recorded a materials price variance of $100 U and a materials quantity variance of $380 F. In addition, the company recorded a labor rate variance and a labor efficiency variance of $1,200 U and $450 U, respectively. Seven thousand footballs were produced during the period and the materials inventory did not change during the period.

Required:

1. Compute the actual costs for materials and labor during the period.
2. Provide the journal entries to record the materials price and quantity variances. (*Hint:* The amount of materials purchased and used are the same.)
3. Provide the journal entries to record the labor rate and efficiency variances.

PROBLEM 12-6
Materials and Labor Variances

The following information was taken from the records of Liberty Manufacturing Company for the month of July:

Materials (actual):

Purchases of material A:	1,300 pounds × $5.25
Purchases of material B:	750 pounds × $2.50
Used 900 pounds of material A	
Used 525 pounds of material B	

Direct labor (actual):

Manufacturing:	1,050 hours × $8.90
Assembly:	450 hours × $4.50

Standard cost per unit:

Material A: 2 pounds × $5.20 per pound	$10.40
Material B: 1 pound × $2.60 per pound	2.60
Direct labor—manufacturing: 2 hours × $8.50	17.00
Direct labor—assembly: 1 hour × $4.60	4.60
Standard cost per unit	$34.60

Units produced: 500

Required:

1. Calculate the materials price and quantity variances, assuming that the materials price variance is recognized at the time of purchase.
2. Calculate the labor rate and labor efficiency variances.
3. **Interpretive Question:** What is the advantage, if any, of calculating the materials price variance at the time of purchase rather than at the time of use?

PROBLEM 12-7
Materials and Labor Variance Analysis

Cooke Manufacturing Company produces high-quality men's pajamas for several large retail stores. The standard cost card for each dozen pairs of pajamas is as follows:

Direct materials, 30 yards at $0.80	$24.00
Direct labor, 4 hours at $5.00	20.00
Manufacturing overhead:	
Variable cost: 4 direct labor hours at $2.00	8.00
Fixed cost: 30% of direct labor cost	6.00
Total product cost per dozen pairs	$58.00

During the month of September, the company filled three orders of pajamas at the following costs:

Order	Number of Dozens	Yards Used	Labor Hours
8	400	12,200	1,500
9	900	26,750	3,750
10	500	15,450	2,140
	1,800	54,400	7,390

The following additional information involving materials and labor was supplied by the accounting department:

a. Purchases of materials during the month amounted to 60,000 yards at $0.82 per yard.
b. Total direct labor cost for the month was $37,689.

Required:

1. Compute the materials price variance for September. (Materials are carried in Direct Materials Inventory at standard.)
2. Compute the materials quantity variance for September.
3. Compute the labor rate and labor efficiency variances for September.

PROBLEM 12-8
Determining How Variances Are Computed

HIC Company uses a standard cost system in its accounting for the manufacturing costs of its only product. The standard cost information for materials and labor is as follows:

Direct materials: 3 pounds at $4	$12
Direct labor: 1 hour at $6	6

During April of its first year of operation, the company completed 4,400 units and had the following materials and labor variances:

Materials price variance	$ 700 F
Materials quantity variance	3,200 U
Labor rate variance	900 U
Labor efficiency variance	600 U

There was no Work-in-Process Inventory at the beginning or end of April.

Required: Compute the following amounts:

1. The amount of materials and labor debited to Work-in-Process Inventory during April.
2. The pounds of materials used in production.
3. The actual hours of labor used in production.
4. The actual labor rate per hour.

PROBLEM 12-9
Evaluation of Profit Centers—Segment Margin

Della Brown is the manager of one of the stores in the nationwide EatRite supermarket chain. The following information has been gathered about the performance of Della's store in the most recent quarter:

Operating Departments	Revenue	Contribution-Margin Ratio
Groceries	$600,000	20%
Fresh produce	200,000	40%
Dry goods	500,000	35%
Fixed costs controllable by:		
Manager of grocery department	$ 50,000	
Manager of fresh produce department	70,000	
Manager of dry goods department	80,000	
Store manager	100,000	
Corporate headquarters	100,000	
Total	$400,000	

Required: Prepare a segment-margin income statement for corporate headquarters' use in evaluating the store manager, Della Brown, and which Della can use to evaluate the managers of the three departments within the store.

PROBLEM 12-10
Evaluation of Profit Centers—Segment Margin

Derrald Pearl Company has two divisions, Computer Consulting and Construction. During the most recent year, the two divisions had the following operating data:

	Computer Consulting	Construction
Revenue	$600,000	$250,000
Contribution-margin percentage	45%	15%
Fixed costs controllable by division managers	$200,000	$ 30,000
Fixed costs allocated by corporate headquarters	$100,000	$100,000

Required:

1. Prepare a segment-margin income statement for Derrald Pearl Company. Include three columns—one for the company total and one for each of the two divisions.
2. Based on the segment-margin income statement prepared in (1), what would happen to overall company profits if the Construction Division were to be discontinued?
3. Should either of the divisions be discontinued? Explain.

PROBLEM 12-11
ROI and Contribution-Margin Analysis

Macro Data Corporation's three divisions had the following operating data during 2000:

	Fax Machine	Calculator	Computer
Revenue	$100,000	$150,000	$200,000
Variable costs	50,000	90,000	135,000
Fixed costs	45,000	56,000	53,000
Total assets	50,000	38,000	120,000

Required:

1. Compute the contribution margin for each division.
2. Compute the segment margin for each division.
3. Compute the ROI for each division.
4. Which division had the highest operating performance ratio?
5. **Interpretive Question:** Which division had the best performance in 2000? Why?

PROBLEM 12-12
ROI

Marcos Trade Corporation has two divisions: the Pacific division and the Atlantic division. Following are their operating data for 2000:

	Pacific Division	Atlantic Division
Revenue	$100,000	$100,000
Net income	8,000	7,000
Total assets	50,000	40,000
Stockholders' equity	24,000	16,000
Long-term debt	23,000	20,000

Required:

1. Calculate the ROI for each division.
2. **Interpretive Question:** On the basis of this return, which division appears to have the better performance? Why?

PROBLEM 12-13
ROI

The following information for 2000 applies to the two sales divisions of Ward Enterprises:

	Division A	Division B
Total inventory	$33,333	$37,500
Operating performance ratio	12%	16%
Net income	$12,000	$10,000

Required:

1. Calculate each division's revenue.
2. Calculate each division's asset turnover ratio assuming that controllable assets include inventory only.
3. **Interpretive Question:** Which division had the better performance for the period? Why?

PROBLEM 12-14
ROI and Residual Income

Pacific Corporation has a number of autonomous divisions. Its real estate division has recently reviewed a number of investment proposals.

a. A new office building would cost $450,000 and would generate yearly net income of $80,000.
b. A computer system would cost $350,000 and would reduce bookkeeping and clerical costs by $50,000 annually.
c. A new apartment house would cost $900,000 and would generate yearly net income of $150,000.

The real estate division currently has total assets of $1,800,000 and net income of $350,000.

Required:

1. Assuming that the performance of the manager of the real estate division is evaluated on the basis of the division's ROI, evaluate each of the independent proposals, and determine whether it should be accepted or rejected.
2. Assuming that the manager's performance is evaluated on a residual income basis, determine whether each of the proposals should be accepted or rejected. (The division's minimum accepted rate of return is 15 percent.)

PROBLEM 12-15
ROI and Residual Income

Albertson Furniture Company is a retailer of home furnishings. It currently has stores in three cities—San Francisco, Los Angeles, and Phoenix. Operating data for the three stores in 2000 were as follows:

	San Francisco	Los Angeles	Phoenix
Revenue	$1,500,000	$1,900,000	$1,800,000
Variable costs	900,000	1,200,000	1,200,000
Fixed costs	300,000	350,000	250,000
Total assets	1,800,000	2,500,000	1,300,000

Required:

1. Compute the segment margin for each store.
2. Compute the operating performance ratio for each store.
3. Compute the asset turnover for each store.
4. Compute the ROI for each store.
5. Compute the residual income for each store. (The minimum rates of return for the stores are San Francisco, 15 percent; Los Angeles, 13 percent; and Phoenix, 18 percent.)

PROBLEM 12-16
ROI and Residual Income

	Division W	Division X	Division Y	Division Z
Revenue	$100,000	$300,000	$ (i)	$850,000
Net income	$ (a)	$ 90,000	$ (j)	$ (m)
Total assets	$ 85,000	$ (e)	$550,000	$ (n)
Operating performance ratio	15%	(f)	6%	(o)
Asset turnover ratio	(b)	0.75 times	(k)	4.0 times
ROI	(c)	(g)	(l)	21%
Minimum accepted rate of return	13%	(h)	15%	12%
Residual income	$ (d)	$ 12,000	$ 17,500	$ (p)

Required: Compute the missing data, labeled (a) through (p).

PROBLEM 12-17
Measuring Performance: Residual Income and ROI

The gaming division of Nevada Corporation had income of $550,000 and total assets of $3,000,000 in 2000. The figures are expected to be similar in 2001. The manager of the gaming division has an opportunity to purchase some new gambling machines for $250,000. He concludes that the new machines would increase annual net income by $44,000.

Required:

1. Calculate the current ROI and the expected return on the proposed investment.
2. Calculate the gaming division's current residual income and the expected residual income on the proposed investment. (Assume that the division's minimum accepted rate of return is 17 percent.)
3. Should the new machines be purchased:
   a. If the division uses the ROI method?
   b. If the division uses the residual income method?

PROBLEM 12-18
ROI and Residual Income

The manager of the manufacturing division of Minolta Company is evaluated on a residual income basis. He is in the process of evaluating three investment proposals.

a. Pay $500,000 for a new machine that will increase production substantially. This will result in an increased income of $80,000 annually.
b. Pay $350,000 for a new machine that will reduce labor costs by $70,000 annually.
c. Pay $800,000 for a new machine that will increase annual net income by $115,000.

The manufacturing division currently has total assets of $1,200,000 and net income of $200,000. Its minimum accepted rate of return is 15 percent.

Required:

1. Evaluate the three investment proposals independently, and determine which should be accepted.
2. Assuming that the division manager is evaluated on the basis of the division's ROI, determine whether each of the proposals should be accepted or rejected.

Accounting is more than just doing textbook problems. These Competency Enhancement Opportunities provide practice in critical thinking, oral and written communication, research, teamwork, and consideration of ethical issues.

ANALYZING REAL COMPANY INFORMATION

• Analyzing 12–1 (Microsoft)

In the Annual Report for **Microsoft** (Appendix A), you will find in the Notes to Financial Statements, in a section titled "Geographic Information," data on U.S. operations, European operations, and Other International operations. This information is also provided here.

(amounts in millions)	1995	1996	1997
Revenue			
United States	$4,495	$6,739	$ 8,877
European	1,607	2,215	2,770
Other International	821	1,267	1,757
Income			
United States	$1,414	$2,137	$ 3,733
European	444	649	1,013
Other International	163	297	469
Assets			
United States	$5,862	$8,193	$11,630
European	1,806	2,280	3,395
Other International	689	1,042	705

1. Consider all the information provided for these three business segments of Microsoft. How do you think Microsoft primarily evaluates these segments—as cost centers, as profit centers, or as investment centers?
2. Regardless of your answer to question (1), compute the following data for each of the three segments:

- Segment-margin ratio—segment income divided by segment revenue
- Asset turnover
- ROI
- Residual income (assume that Microsoft's specified minimum rate of return is 20%)

• Analyzing 12-2 (Petersen Pottery)

Just outside Elkins, West Virginia, Clive Petersen has been making ceramic bathroom fixtures (sinks, toilets, and bathtubs) since 1960. Petersen fixtures had become known over the years for their distinctive customer features, their high quality, and their long life. **Petersen Pottery** started out as a two-man operation. By 1980 it had grown to 20 master potters. At this point, Clive Petersen felt that he had expanded to a point that he needed to instigate a formal accounting control system. The insistence of his banker that he get a "real" management accounting system in place was also compelling. As a result, Petersen hired a formally trained management accountant who began working with his most experienced master potters to design cost standards. After some research, Petersen's accountant arrived at the following cost standards for a toilet (note that variable manufacturing overhead is allocated based on direct labor hours):

Direct materials:		
Raw clay	25 lb × $0.95 per lb =	$23.75
Glazing mix	5 lb × $0.75 per lb =	3.75
Direct labor:		
Molding	1.0 hr × $15.00 per hour =	15.00
Glazing	0.5 hr × $15.00 per hour =	7.50
Variable manufacturing overhead	1.5 hr × $3.00 per hour =	4.50
Total per fixture		$54.50

After six months of operations, Petersen was disturbed over the lack of attention paid to the standards by his potters. He felt that the potters were just too set in their ways to pay any attention to the new system. Many of the potters told Petersen that the new system was "confusing" and didn't help them in their work. In reviewing the June production results, the following actual costs were noted in connection with manufacturing 1,145 toilets:

Materials used:	
Raw clay	28,900 lb @ $0.92 per lb
Glazing mix	5,900 lb @ $0.78 per lb
Direct labor:	
Molding	1,200 hr @ $15.25 per hour (average)
Glazing	600 hr @ $15.00 per hour (average)
Actual variable manufacturing overhead	$5,120

1. Compute all cost variances for the month of June.
2. What suggestions do you have for Mr. Petersen regarding his new standard cost system?

Source: Adapted from J.K. Shank, "Petersen Pottery" case, *Cases in Cost Management: A Strategic Emphasis,* South-Western, 1996.

INTERNATIONAL CASE

• Management accounting in Japan

Japan is always a good place for useful insight on innovative management accounting practice and technique. From early on, the Japanese recognized that the most efficient way to keep costs down was to *design* them out of their products, not to reduce them after the products entered production. This realization reflects a fundamental reality of cost management in Japan; the majority of a product's costs (as much as 90 to 95 percent according to some experts) are "designed in." Consequently, effective cost control programs in a Japanese business will typically focus heavily on the design process for a particular product. This is done primarily through target costing and value engineering (VE). Target costing is used to determine what the market is willing to pay for a product, then VE is used to design the product in order to achieve a prespecified targeted level of costs.

What do you think is the effect of target costing and VE on the use of variances? Specifically, will materials usage variances and labor efficiency variances be more or less important to a firm that strictly uses target costing and VE versus a traditional firm that is more focused on controlling daily production processes?

ETHICS CASE

• Cool Air, Inc.

Jack Lear, an internal auditor for Cool Air, Inc., met with Paul Marsh, the manager of the cost accounting department, to discuss a concern about a possible "glitch" in the standard cost system. Jack explained that he had been reviewing the employee time cards in the company division where air-conditioning units and refrigerators were assembled. The time cards reflected how much employee time was devoted to the assembly of air-conditioning units and how much time applied to refrigerators. Jack's concern was that the hours actually charged for each of these operations always seemed to be right on target with the standard labor times for each air-conditioning unit and each refrigerator unit assembled; yet Jack had been told a number of times by employees in the assembly department that the standard hours for assembling air-conditioning units were too low. The employees felt that they could not meet these standards without "fudging" their time cards or sacrificing some quality work in the assembly process. Since company policy emphasized product quality, Jack suspected that time sheets were being modified by shifting hours worked on air-conditioning units to the time sheets for assembling refrigerators.

Paul Marsh, the cost manager, thought for a minute about what Jack was telling him and then made an interesting observation. He said that he had been concerned about the fact that the company's prices for its air-conditioning units were generally lower than its competitors' prices for the same size and quality of units, whereas its prices for refrigerators were generally higher than those of its competitors. He wondered if the company's pricing structure, which was tied to its standard costs, was out of line with competition. This position was reinforced when Paul and Jack looked at the company's sales of each of these products. Over the past year or so, the company had gained market share in air-conditioner sales and had lost market share in refrigerators! Based on this information, Paul asked Jack to do some "detective" work on the time cards in the assembly division and report back his findings.

A few days later, Jack reported that he had found convincing evidence that the foremen in the assembly division had been in collusion to "doctor" employee time sheets in order to more closely meet the time standards for both air-conditioner and refrigerator assembly.

1. Who are the stakeholders affected by the "doctoring" of time sheets?
2. What are the ethical issues in this situation?
3. What should Paul do?

WRITING ASSIGNMENT

• Qualitative variance analysis

With the push for continuous improvement, stable standards may become a thing of the past. As companies strive for and achieve zero defects and no waste, variances quantifiable in terms of dollars become more and more difficult to obtain. Firms are now turning their attention to qualitative measures to determine variances from a standard. Examples include the number of customer complaints, number of machine setups, etc. In a one- to two-page paper, identify three standards that might be used in a manufacturing environment and three standards that might be used in a service environment that cannot be readily quantifiable in dollars. Discuss how each of those standards would be measured, as well as how variances from those standards would be measured.

THE DEBATE

• When might a favorable variance turn "bad?"

Consider the labor efficiency variance. As you now understand after working through this chapter, a labor efficiency variance occurs when the hours actually used are more or less than the standard hours allowed based on actual production output. Assume that a team of internal auditors was able to complete a particular auditing project in one of the company's divisions in fewer hours than originally expected. Does this team have a favorable labor efficiency variance? More importantly, assuming there is a favorable labor efficiency variance, is this a good or a bad thing?

Divide your group into two teams and prepare a two-minute defense of your team's assigned position.

- One team represents "Favorable labor efficiency variance—GOOD!" Answer the following in your discussion. (1) Is measuring the difference between auditing hours *originally* budgeted and the actual hours used the proper way to measure a labor efficiency variance? (2) Your team should take the position that favorable labor efficiencies are a *good* result in this operation. What positive aspects concerning the audit team's work are indicated by a favorable labor efficiency variance?
- The other team represents "Favorable labor efficiency variance—BAD!" Answer the following in your discussion. (1) Respond to Team #1's report on whether or not measuring the difference between auditing hours *originally* budgeted and the actual hours used is the proper way to measure a labor efficiency variance. If you disagree,

provide a correct response. (2) Your team should take the position that favorable labor efficiencies may *not* be a good result in this operation. What negative aspects concerning the audit team's work could be indicated by a favorable labor efficiency variance?

INTERNET SEARCH

• Caterpillar

Caterpillar's Web address is www.caterpillar.com. Sometimes Web addresses change, so if this Caterpillar address doesn't work, access the Web site for this textbook (stice.swcollege.com) for an updated link to Caterpillar.

Once you have gained access to Caterpillar's Web site, answer the following questions.

1. Who founded Caterpillar? When did Caterpillar form its joint venture with **Mitsubishi**?
2. Are Caterpillar's sales growing faster inside or outside the United States?
3. A key business indicator for Caterpillar is the quantity of inventory held by dealers. Excess inventory is a sign of a slump in sales. What does Caterpillar say about inventory levels in its most recent financial statement release?
4. How has Caterpillar structured its Parts & Services network to ensure that customers get the quality service they need when they need it?

CHAPTER

OPERATING BUDGETS 13

LEARNING OBJECTIVES

After studying this chapter, you should be able to:

1. *Describe different types of budgeting and identify the purposes of budgeting.*
2. *Describe the budgeting process and its behavioral implications.*
3. *Explain the master budget and its components for manufacturing firms, merchandising firms, and service firms.*
4. *Prepare pro-forma financial statements.*
5. *Distinguish between static and flexible budgets.*

SETTING THE STAGE

Every organization needs to budget. Budgets help allocate resources effectively so that the mission of the organization can be accomplished. Consider how budgeting can resolve problems at your university, for example. The administration probably wants to hold down spending and keep tuition competitive and affordable. At the same time, however, the department chairs and deans probably want to spend more money to enhance the education of the students.

Shouldn't the arts and humanities departments get more money this year to help emphasize the importance of a liberal arts education? Already, salaries of faculty in those areas are near poverty levels. What about the business school? Shouldn't business and accounting receive more operating funds because their classes have the highest demand and are the largest of any on campus? Wait a minute, shouldn't more money be put into program diversity to help make students more aware of the differences between cultures, races, and sexes for greater understanding? How about the building and grounds—the roofs need replacing and the sidewalks are cracking. Don't we need to make repairs? What's more, how can we have a winning basketball team without a new basketball arena?

The poor administration. How would you like to be responsible for resolving these questions and allocating limited funds among them? Each department within the university has its own sense of mission, priorities, goals, objectives, and agendas. All departmental priorities may not be consistent with university goals. However, it may be difficult to prioritize the proposed funding requests because there may be no clear, agreed-upon criteria in which to compare the benefits of one department's request over another. The difficulty in measuring benefits for each program makes it even more challenging. The budgeting process that we will discuss in this chapter can help the university resolve these conflicting objectives and facilitate order in the spending of the university. Without budgeting, no matter how difficult, the university will never be able to accomplish its objectives.

Source: James C. Horsch, "Redesigning the Resource Allocation Process," *Management Accounting,* July 1995, pp. 55–59.

budget A quantitative expression of a plan of action that shows how a firm or an organization will acquire and use resources over some specified period of time.

*A **budget** is a quantitative expression of a plan of action that shows how a firm or an organization (such as the university in the opening scenario) will acquire and use its resources over a specified period of time. Implicit in most budgets is management's expectation of earning sufficient profit to provide a reasonable return on investment. The budget identifies and allocates resources necessary to effectively and efficiently carry out the mission of the organization. While budgeting may sound to you like an unappealing activity (maybe you have tried budgeting your personal expenditures before), successful budgeting is absolutely critical to the success of a business. In this chapter, we will briefly touch on personal budgeting and then cover budgeting for manufacturing, merchandising, and service firms.*

1 *Describe different types of budgeting and identify the purposes of budgeting.*

TYPES AND PURPOSES OF BUDGETING

capital budget A systematic plan for long-term investments in operating assets.

Because budgeting is designed to help an organization accomplish its mission, the budgeting process begins with the company's strategic plan. Based on the strategic plan, the organization prepares **capital budgets** and budgets for operations. Failure to carefully perform strategic planning, capital budgeting, or budgeting for operations can have adverse consequences on organizations, even to the point of causing bankruptcy. The list of companies that have failed in recent years as a result of poor planning and execution is getting longer each day. Casualties of poor planning include such common names as **Eastern Airlines**; **Manville Corporation**; **Barings Brothers**, a 200-year-old British bank; **Atari Computers**; **Circle K**; and Orange County in California. In Chapter 12, we discussed strategic planning. In Chapter 15, we will discuss the capital budgeting elements of planning. In this chapter, our focus is on budgeting for operations.

operating (master) budget A network of many separate schedules and budgets that together constitute the overall operating and financing plan for the coming period.

The **operating (master) budget** is the most detailed and most heavily used budget an organization has. As the name implies, this budget details the immediate goals for revenues, production, expenses, and cash for the next period. Before we can examine the operating budget in detail, we need to identify its purposes, describe its evolution, and discuss the major issues involved in budget preparation. This will give us a framework for preparing an operating budget.

Purposes of Budgeting

The overall purpose of an operating budget is to quantify a general plan so that performance in relation to a goal can be carefully monitored. Thus, budgeting has a twofold purpose. The first purpose is to allow individuals or companies to develop a plan to meet a specified goal. The second purpose is to allow ongoing comparison between actual results and the plan in order to control operations or activities. To illustrate, let us assume that Dick Cotton earns $3,000 a month and has prepared a budget of his income and expenses.

disposable income Income left after withholding and fixed expenses have been subtracted from gross salary; the amount left to cover variable expenditures.

The budget in Exhibit 13-1 contains an important warning that spending is exceeding earnings. The commitment of $1,300 to fixed expenses leaves only $700 to cover all the necessary expenditures for utilities, food, clothing, and such. Since Dick cannot cover these expenditures using his **disposable income** of $700 a month, he must revise his plans; perhaps he could ask for a raise, get a second job or a new job that pays more, obtain a loan, or decrease his spending. This simple illustration shows that budgeting is extremely important. Unless Dick takes corrective action, he will soon join the growing number of individuals declaring bankruptcy.

FYI

A study conducted several years ago revealed that only 4 of every 100 employees who join the work force at age 25 have sufficient funds to retire at age 65. The other 96 must either keep working or depend on someone else for help.

In addition, someday Dick will want to retire. Currently, Dick's budget does not provide for any savings or investments. With all the planning tools available today, such as tax-sheltered retirement plans, investments, annuities, and so forth, an individual who plans and budgets well can pre-

EXHIBIT 13-1

Monthly Budget for Dick Cotton

Gross salary		$3,000
Withholdings:		
Federal income taxes	$500	
State income taxes	150	
FICA taxes	210	
Other withholdings	140	(1,000)
Net take-home pay		$2,000
Fixed expenses:		
House mortgage expense	$750	
Car payment expense	350	
Insurance expense	200	(1,300)
Disposable income		$ 700
Utilities expense	$200	
Food expense	400	
Clothing expense	100	
Entertainment expense	100	
Miscellaneous expenses	200	(1,000)
Net surplus (deficit)		$ (300)

pare adequately for the future. Unfortunately, at his present rate, Dick will not be one of these individuals.

Indeed, the penalty for not budgeting is severe. Individuals who budget successfully have found that they can spend just as much if they budget as they can if they don't. The only difference is that those who budget spend money how, where, and when they want to.

BUSINESS ENVIRONMENT ESSAY

Budgeting Woes The budgeting process can be frustrating if the prepared budgets are not realistic. For example, if a married couple determines it will spend only $100 per month on food when in reality it will cost at least $400 per month for food, communication and other problems will usually occur. The following list highlights some warning signs that the budgeting process needs revamping:

1. Frustration among decision makers who must comply with the budget.
2. Lack of agreement on amounts budgeted.
3. Difficulty in prioritizing expenditures or agreeing on the allocation of funds.
4. Confusion about who is accountable for funding decisions.
5. Budgeting is not integrated across various segments of the firm.
6. The "squeaky wheel gets the grease" rule is used to allocate resources.
7. The budgeting process requires more effort than it is worth.
8. Managers are held responsible for budgets that include elements over which they have no control.
9. Long-term budgeting and strategic planning are absent.
10. The budgeting process is "political."

Source: Adapted from James C. Horsch, "Redesigning the Resource Allocation Process," *Management Accounting,* July 1995, pp. 55–59.

The previous example was of a personal budget. The same advantages for budgeting on a personal level exist for organizations. Specifically, there are seven major reasons why budgeting is important to an organization's success.

1. *Planning and setting objectives.* The preparation of a budget forces managers to consider explicitly where the firm is going and how it is going to get there. It forces managers to quantify objectives for the organization and the means of achieving those objectives. The Business Environment Essay on page 607 illustrates how one company, **Penn Fuel Gas, Inc.**, realized the planning benefits of budgeting. By budgeting, an organization, such as the university described in the opening scenario, will be better prepared to decide where its scarce resources will be spent.
2. *Communication.* Budgets improve communication between the various management levels of a business, helping managers plan activities that enhance the smooth functioning of the enterprise. In general, budgets relay top management's expectations and show each segment how it fits into the overall plan. Budgets establish a benchmark to which actual performance will be compared. In both families and business organizations, it is usually not the lack of money that causes problems but the lack of communication about money. Couples and organizations that budget adequately find that their budgets are a great communication tool. For example, once the budget is established for the university in the opening scenario, the budget communicates to various departments and groups how university money will be spent.
3. *Coordination.* Budgets help management coordinate activities of business segments. By coordinating and integrating the goals of each segment, management ensures that its efforts to meet the overall objectives of the firm will be realized. In addition, budgeting helps to identify potential bottlenecks and allows management to develop plans to alleviate them. For example, the budgeting process may identify a resource, critical to the production process, as being in short supply. Management can then take action to address this shortage. Budgets help guarantee that the combined expenditures of the various segments do not exceed the total budgeted expenditures for the organization.
4. *Authorization.* Once budgets are approved by top management, they provide authorization for investing, spending, ordering, producing, and borrowing by lower-level managers and employees. At most major companies, **IBM**, for example, the budget becomes the law. If something is budgeted, it can be purchased. If not budgeted, the purchase cannot be made. This is one area where many personal budgets fail. For many individuals, budgets are used as a guide instead of as authorization to spend; as a result, personal budgets are often "exceeded."
5. *Motivation.* Budgets help motivate people. By providing a clear set of quantified objectives, budgets guide people to perform the activities that need to be accomplished. The motivational aspect of budgets can be quite strong. Care must be exercised in budgeting to ensure that budgets do not create a "success at any cost" attitude.
6. *Conflict resolution.* In most organizations, everyone usually wants additional resources. Budgeting forces up-front planning, which helps resolve conflicts over how limited resources will be allocated among an organization's various parts. (Remember the conflicting objectives of the university in the opening scenario?) Consider, for example, a family that will have $1,000 of disposable income next year. How shall they spend the money? Suppose the wife wants to spend $500 on clothes for the children because they are quickly outgrowing their wardrobes. In addition, assume she would like to spend the other $500 on piano lessons for the children. On the other hand, the husband would like to spend $500 to replace the garage door, which is falling down, and another $500 to fix the transmission on the car (it's starting to slip). A budget, prepared by the husband and wife together, could help them resolve these conflicting priorities.

7. *Performance measurement (evaluation).* Budgets provide quantitative measures of expectations and objectives. These objectives later serve as benchmarks against which the performance of managers and others in a firm can be evaluated. Employees and managers who meet or exceed budgets are often rewarded. When productivity is inadequate, as measured against budgeted performance, employees may be penalized or even terminated.

FYI

While budgeting is very helpful for decision making, organizations are often required to prepare detailed budgets before bankers will loan money or before a company can issue stock or debt for sale to the public. When companies declare bankruptcy and are taken over by court-ordered trustees, one of the first steps of the trustee is to prepare detailed budgets. These budgets help to determine whether the company should cease operations, or whether the trustee should ask the court to give the company time to work through its financial problems so it can fully or partially pay its debts.

The Evolution of Budgeting Within a Firm

Many small organizations don't recognize the value of budgeting. In fact, the typical small business usually evolves through three stages of development, with formal budgeting being the last. The first stage is represented by the new, small business (usually a proprietorship or partnership) in which there is no budgeting and very little record keeping; the owners do not understand the importance of budgets and financial records. When they open for business, owners often have no specific plans or goals beyond the general notion, for example, of running a restaurant or constructing houses. These owners evaluate their performance by counting the money in their pockets. In their minds, if they have cash to spend, they are successful.

The second stage of development is to measure revenues and expenses for past periods and to assess past profits. Even the "seat-of-the-pants" businesses soon develop a need for some record keeping. One of the main incentives for keeping good records is the need to comply with the regulations of the Internal Revenue Service. Some companies start to keep records because they have other needs (to obtain a bank loan, for example) that force them to measure how well they have performed. Yet, at this stage, there is very little budgeting. A business is still viewed as "successful" if the owners have cash to spend. This quantitative measure of historical performance usually satisfies the IRS, and even many banks, but it does not provide much help in the areas of planning, communication, coordination, authorization, motivation, conflict resolution, and performance evaluation.

BUSINESS ENVIRONMENT ESSAY

Budgeting: A Team Effort In 1995, **Penn Fuel Gas, Inc. (PFG)** initiated its first annual and long-range budgeting process. PFG is a public utility holding company with revenues of $125 million and 550 employees. In addition to selling natural gas, the company provides natural gas storage and transportation services and has a propane business. The motivation for budgeting came jointly from PFG's bankers, its board of directors, and its management.

Penn Fuel Gas used a consultant to set up its first budget and then hired a full-time, experienced professional to handle its budgeting. Budgeting for natural gas and propane operations is difficult because much of the demand for these products is dependent on Mother Nature. Penn Fuel experienced two abnormal winters in its first two years of budgeting. In 1994, Pennsylvania had its coldest, iciest winter in history. In 1995, it had one of its warmest winters.

By 1997, budgeting had improved communication throughout Penn Fuel Gas and had improved teamwork toward a common goal. It had helped the board of directors to better represent shareholders and had provided support to management on major decisions. PFG expects even better planning in the future to result in operational improvements, improved management of resources, better cost control, earnings growth, and improved responsibility; all resulting from managers' active participation in the planning process.

Source: Robert N. West and Amy M. Snyder, "How to Set Up a Budgeting and Planning System," *Management Accounting,* January 1997, pp. 20–26.

get connected
http://www.swcollege.com
net work

The best-known budget in the United States is the budget of the federal government. The Congressional Budget Office offers a monthly update on the level of government receipts and outlays relative to budgeted levels.

Go to the CBO's Web site to get a budget review for the most recent month.

cbo.gov

Because such measures of historical performance do not provide many of the most important benefits of a formal plan, most firms soon begin to budget. Thus, budgets usually evolve because firms grow tired of fighting one crisis after another (such as cash shortages) and of coping with the inefficiencies that result from a lack of planning. Typically, a firm develops its first budget by forecasting expected revenues or sales, then budgeting production costs and other expenses, and finally projecting net income and cash flows. These estimated expenses, profitability, and cash levels are the plans on which work schedules are based and against which performance is evaluated.

In recent years, the budgeting process has become very sophisticated. Now many companies have full-time computer hookups that tie sales orders to suppliers and sales to inventory. The time horizon for budgeting has decreased so that many elements of the budget are performed on a weekly, daily, or even hourly basis. Quality and productivity gains have decreased the time needed to produce products, and so lengthy production budgets, for example, are no longer needed in some companies. In many successful organizations, budgets are tools used in the quest for continuous improvement in quality and performance.

(STOP & THINK)

In this chapter, the emphasis is on budgeting costs and revenues, only one of the three elements management is interested in managing. Do you think management performs any budgeting related to quality or delivery time of products or services to customers?

TO SUMMARIZE

Budgeting in most organizations is based on that organization's strategic plan. Using the strategic plan to guide decisions, organizations perform two types of budgeting: capital budgeting and operations budgeting. The operating budget has several purposes: (1) assist in planning and setting objectives, (2) facilitate communication, (3) coordinate activities, (4) authorize expenditures and actions, (5) motivate employees, (6) assist in resolving conflicts, and (7) provide a vehicle for performance measurement. Most organizations do not develop a formal budgeting process in the beginning. Rather, budgeting usually evolves as needs for budget information become more critical.

Describe the budgeting process and its behavioral implications.

budget committee A management group responsible for establishing budgeting policy and for coordinating the preparation of budgets.

THE BUDGETING PROCESS

Budgeting is such an important activity that the top executives of most companies coordinate and participate in the process. Large firms usually establish a **budget committee**, which includes among its members the vice presidents for sales, production, purchasing, and finance and the controller or chief financial officer. These executives coordinate the preparation of a detailed budget in their areas of responsibility, and then together oversee the preparation of a comprehensive budget for the firm. Two important issues faced by executives in the budgeting process are:

1. Behavioral considerations, and
2. Delegation of responsibility for preparing the budget—the top-down versus bottom-up issue.

Behavioral Considerations

Research has shown that several behavioral factors determine how successful the budgeting process will be. First, the process must have the support of top management. Without a clear indication from top management that the budgeting process is important to the organization, managers will not be motivated to devote the time necessary to formulate an effective and efficient budget.

Second, all managers, and as many employees as possible, should participate in the budgeting process. Managers will be more motivated to achieve budget goals that they understand and help design. For this process to work, managers must feel that their opinions are respected and given full consideration. In addition, this communication and participation process must remain open throughout the year. If internal or external circumstances change, all parties must meet to discuss the necessary budget adjustments. The most efficient and effective companies are those that involve employees in the decision-making process.

Third, deviations from the budget must be addressed by managers in a positive and constructive manner. Identifying deviations from the plan is simply a way to focus management's attention on the areas needing improvement. Unfortunately, some managers treat these deviations as an opportunity to find fault and assign blame to lower-level managers. The result is usually a loss of motivation, accompanied by such dysfunctional behavior as interdepartmental bickering, defensive attitudes, and attempts to "build slack" into the budget. ("Building slack" is the process of inflating a department's budget request so that the department manager can more easily achieve the budget.) Obviously, all these behaviors waste an organization's resources and do not contribute to solving its problems. A more useful reaction to deviations is to focus on the action to be taken. As one CEO stated, "I never made a dime for the company by assessing blame or firing a manager. If I can provide help to a manager to solve a problem though, we can see the benefit." In administering the budget process, it is extremely important that top management not use the budget as a "club" or "whipping stick." To illustrate the negative effects of using budgets inappropriately, consider what happened at ABC Company, as described in the Business Environment Essay on page 610.

Who Prepares the Budget: Top-Down Versus Bottom-Up

A firm-wide operating budget could be prepared by top management, apportioned to the major segments of the firm, and then distributed to each lower-level segment manager. This is the top-down approach. Its proponents argue that only top management knows the strategic direction of the firm and is aware of all the external factors influencing its operations. Further, since top management involves only a few people who have risen to positions where they should no longer have special interests to protect, they are in the best position to efficiently coordinate the competing needs of the segments.

The alternative approach is bottom-up, whereby each division manager prepares a budget request for his or her segment. These requests are combined and reviewed as they move up the organization hierarchy, with adjustments being made to coordinate the needs and goals of individual units. Proponents of this approach contend that segment managers have the best information on the products or services they provide, the customers they serve, or the technology that is emerging; they are therefore in the best position to identify segment needs and to weigh alternative courses of action. More importantly, as mentioned earlier, managers who have a role in setting segment goals are more motivated to achieve these goals. It is also good training for managers to develop their planning skills in preparation for promotions to positions of greater authority. Naturally, it also benefits the organization to have managers proficient in planning.

Because these are both legitimate approaches, most organizations use some combination of the two. Top management knows the strategic direction of the firm and the important external factors that affect it, so they prepare a set of planning guidelines that are communicated to lower-level managers. These guidelines would include such things as a forecast of key economic variables and their potential impact on the firm, plans for introducing and advertising new products, and some

BUSINESS ENVIRONMENT ESSAY

Losing Focus on Budgeting Goals

ABC was a sleepy little firm, barely making a profit, when it got a new chief executive officer (CEO). He said, "I'm going to make this a go-go company. And pretty soon, instead of a price-earnings ratio [stock price divided by earnings per share] per share of 10:1, it's going to be 40:1. We're all going to get rich." In trying to make the company more profitable, he hired a group of high-powered executives, and the company as a whole, not just the CEO, adopted a new budgeting policy. Essentially, the CEO and division managers decided together on next year's earnings budgets for their respective divisions, and the managers were responsible for meeting these goals. Implied in the budgets was the idea that the budget represented a fair goal. However, as it turned out, the CEO leaned on managers at the start of the year. To one manager, for example, he said, "Look, this company is going to have an earnings per share of $1.90 next year. Your division's share of that is $0.42." As the year progressed, periodic meetings were held with the manager. If the division was not on target to earn $0.42 a share, the manager would be told by the CEO, "If you can't find a way to make your budget, we'll hire someone else who can."

One of the ways division managers met their budgets was to recognize sales before they occurred. "Who cares when you close the books at the end of the period? A sale is a sale, right? Does it really matter whether we reach a little into next week and take some of the sales we ship next week and include them with this week's sales? After all, the sales were all made in the same month." Soon, one week stretched into two weeks, then three, until eventually it wasn't too hard for managers to rationalize, "We know that a customer is going to buy our product eventually; let's record it as a sale now." Consequently, the company's managers were driven by their budgets rather than using budgets as goals, until finally they were so far beyond reality that the company was committing massive fraud, eventually causing it to collapse.

Source: Adapted from Robert J. Sack, "Ethical Issues in the Practice of Accounting." In W. Steve Albrecht, ed., *Ethical Issues in the Practice of Accounting* (Cincinnati: South-Western Publishing Co., 1992), pp. 24–25.

broad sales targets and resource allocations. With these guidelines in mind, lower-level managers prepare their individual budgets. Though these budgets are always reviewed to be sure they are consistent with the objectives of other segments and of the company as a whole, from a behavioral point of view, any changes to a manager's budget should be made with great care. This is not to suggest that changes should not be made, only that reasons for those changes should be substantial and should be discussed with the managers involved.

The blending of these two approaches will vary among organizations. A smaller organization with few management levels will rely more on the top-down approach than a larger organization. Top management in smaller organizations tend to be more knowledgeable about and more involved in the operating details.

TO SUMMARIZE

The behavioral factors that contribute to the success of the budgeting process include the support of top management, the participation of all managers in the budgeting process, and the need to address deviations from the budget in a positive and constructive manner. When top management prepares the entire budget, it is referred to as the top-down approach. When each segment manager makes budget requests, it is called bottom-up budgeting. Most firms use a combination of the two approaches.

3 *Explain the master budget and its components for manufacturing firms, merchandising firms, and service firms.*

THE MASTER BUDGET

The operating budget is called the *master budget*; it is an integrated group of detailed budgets that together constitute the overall operating and financing plans for a specific time period. The master budget in a manufacturing firm begins with a forecast of sales; it is followed by detailed budgets for the production, selling, administrative, and financial activities; and it culminates in a set of pro-forma (or budgeted) financial statements. The flow of the preparation of the individual budgets within this master network is shown in Exhibit 13-2. (Notice that the final items are the budgeted or "pro-forma" financial statements.) Review this exhibit carefully because we will follow these schedules in sequence in the next sections of this chapter.

To help explain these steps, we will illustrate budgeting for three different kinds of companies. First, we will illustrate the budgeting process in a manufacturing firm using an integrated example of budgets for the Sunbird Boat Company, a manufacturer of small fishing boats. Second, we will illustrate budgeting in merchandising firms (retail and wholesale) for Wind River Boats, a company that buys its boats for resale from other manufacturers rather than making the boats itself. Third, we will illustrate budgeting in service firms by illustrating the budgeting process for a small motel, the Boulder View Inn. You will see similarities in the budgeting process for all three types of businesses. Basically, the budgeting process involves budgeting (or forecasting) revenues and cash that will be generated by those revenues and budgeting costs that will be incurred and cash that will be expended. Budgeters—

EXHIBIT 13-2

The Master Budget for a Manufacturing Firm

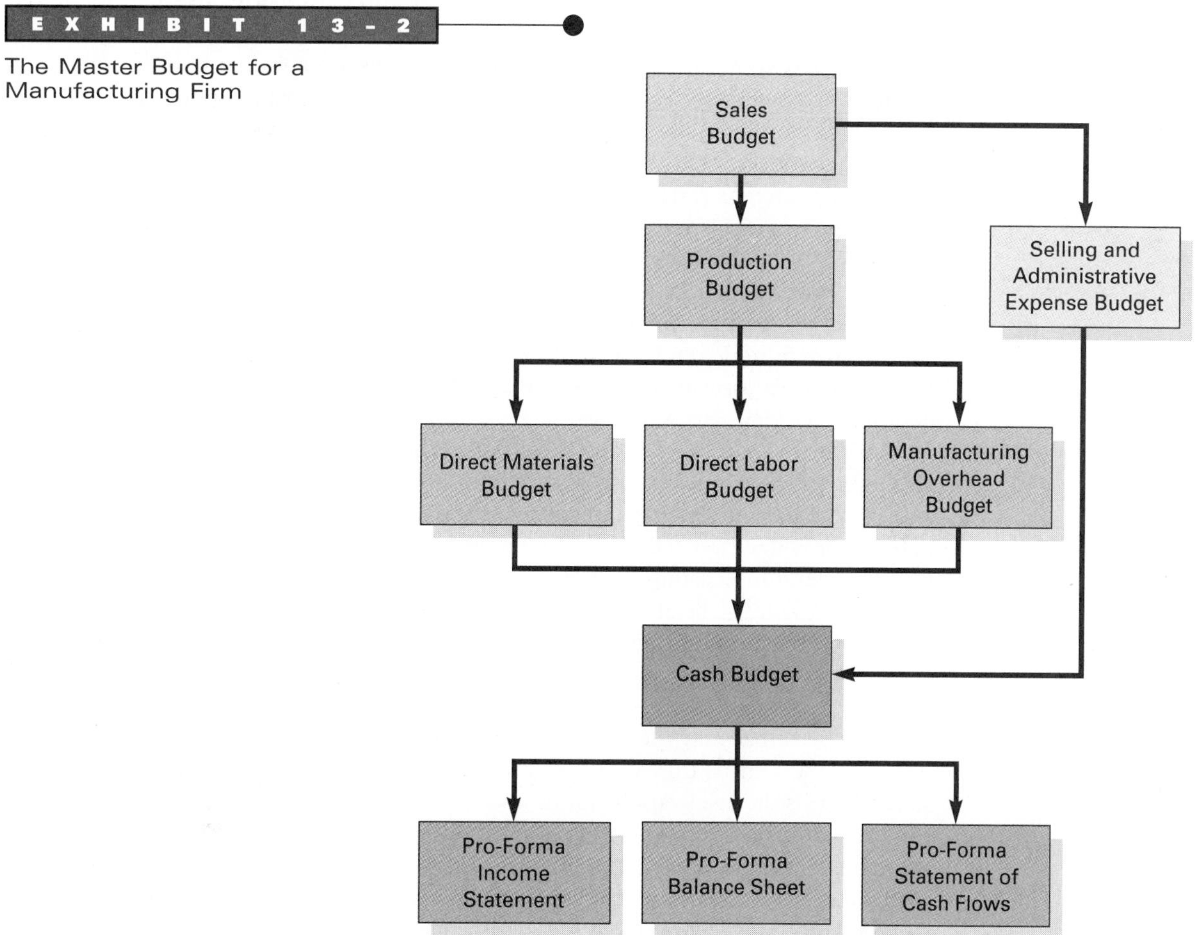

whether individuals, companies, or other entities—are always interested in how much revenues (inflows) and expenditures (outflows) they will have during each budgeted period and how much cash and assets they will have at the end of each budgeted period. The budgeting discussions that follow may seem mechanical, but you should keep in mind that this formalized budgeting activity forces management to make many important decisions that guide a company toward its goals. For example, decisions regarding production scheduling, pricing, borrowing, investing, and research and development need to be made before the budget can be completed.

In most companies today, the actual preparation of the master budget is usually done on computerized spreadsheets and other software packages. Although automation takes care of much of the drudgery or tedious work, it is important that you understand the budgeting process and what is being done by the computer.

Another factor you should recognize is that many of the recent developments in management accounting, such as ABC and JIT inventory systems, have a significant impact on the budgeting process. As we discuss the various elements of the master budget, we will explain how budgeting is affected by these developments.

Budgeting for Operations in a Manufacturing Firm

Our first illustration of the budgeting process is for Sunbird Boat Company, a manufacturing company that makes fishing boats. The boats are made of fiberglass and wood and come in 15-foot and 18-foot sizes. In explaining the budgeting for Sunbird Boat Company, we will begin with the sales budget and then discuss each budget identified in Exhibit 13-2.

Sales Budget

sales budget A schedule of projected sales over the budget period.

The first step in developing a master budget is to prepare a **sales budget**. As shown in Exhibit 13-2, all the other budgets are developed from this budget. Projecting accurate sales is very difficult, however, because sales are a function of both external variables (customer tastes and economic conditions, for example) and internal variables (such as price, sales effort, and advertising expenditures). In fact, in preparing a sales budget, internal variables (such as how much production capacity do we have?) and external variables must first be analyzed separately.

Analysis of external variables is accomplished through sales-forecasting techniques. These techniques may be as simple as having the sales staff ask major customers to reveal their buying plans for the next year, or as sophisticated as statistical market research techniques. Some firms use quantitative forecasting models: from simple growth rate trends derived from the past year's sales (e.g. regression analysis) to complex forecasting models that attempt to measure the influence of many economic and industry variables.

Data on which to base sales forecasts is abundant. For example, economic data about the United States and many other countries are available from private vendors and from trade associations and sector specialists. Data about regions, cities, or markets are provided by vendors and trade groups, as well as by university business departments and forecasting centers.

Demographic data such as population projections, household spending patterns, and lifestyles (nationally and locally—down to city blocks) are available from vendors. These vendors use various statistical methods to project data from the national 10-year census data to the current year. They use other data sources in their updating processes that may include the Current Population Survey (CPS) conducted annually by the Census Bureau, payroll taxes, home sales, apartment occupancy rates, state driver's licenses applications, school enrollments, and births and deaths. Government data often report economic conditions with some delay. The Consumer Price Index (CPI), a measure of inflation, is reported monthly at the national and regional levels with specific cities reported either monthly or semiannually. The CPI is a good indicator of a business's ability to pass along cost increases to its customers.

The Producer Price Index (PPI), another measure of inflation, reports changes in business costs and is subject to larger fluctuations than the CPI. The Gross Domestic Product (GDP) Implicit Price Deflator measures inflation in the consumer and business sectors simultaneously.

Consumer spending patterns by region and income level are reported from the annual Consumer Expenditure Survey, conducted by the Census Bureau since 1980. Because consumer spending represents more than 65 percent of GDP, an understanding of how households allocate their expenditures can be very helpful in business planning. For example, if your business expects to sell home entertainment systems to middle-income consumers, it is helpful to know whether they are changing the share of income they spend on in-home entertainment. Production, capacity utilization, and shipment data by sector are estimated in the course of developing GDP estimates. This information also is valuable in forecasting the availability and cost of materials.

Business environment data include the regulatory climate and change in regulations, product liability issues, competitive structure, technological changes, foreign markets, trends in consumer attitudes and behavior, and demographic trends. Government regulatory information is available on the Internet (for a price), and is available through many agency publications and reference sources such as the Commerce Clearing House. Business trends are tracked and reported by trade associations and magazines, as well as by consultants who specialize in various types of businesses.[1]

In analyzing the influence of internal variables, sales budgeting is viewed as an active process (what factors can we change to meet our sales targets?), not as a passive process (let us predict what customers will buy from us). Cost-volume-profit analysis (the subject of Chapter 11) is frequently used for analyzing the influence of internal variables.

Firms generally do not rely on a single approach to sales budgeting. Instead, they will develop several tentative sales budgets, using different combinations of various forecasting and budgeting techniques. These budgets will be reconciled through discussions between the planning and marketing staffs and top management, and a final sales budget will be agreed upon. As mentioned earlier, recent developments in management accounting have focused on quality and continuous improvement. The result has been that many organizations have significantly reduced delivery times using Just-in-Time (JIT) Inventory, Electronic Data Interchange (EDI), and other techniques. **Motorola Corporation**, for example, reduced the time needed from taking orders to delivery from 4 weeks to 6 hours. The effect of shorter lead times for production has significantly reduced the time horizons of sales and other budgets. Also, instead of the sales budget being fixed for an entire year (or period), there is flexibility to continuously revise the sales and other budgets. With full-time computer hookups to suppliers and customers and with automated budget preparation tools, the sales budget, as well as the entire budget process, is now much more dynamic than ever before. With shorter lead times, management can more quickly adapt to increases, decreases, and other trends in revising budgets.

For purposes of this illustration, we will not go into the details about the development of data for the sales budget. Rather, assume that Sunbird Boat Company has projected the year 2000 sales to be 100 15-foot boats and 120 18-foot boats. The anticipated sales prices are $7,000 for a 15-foot boat and $9,000 for an 18-foot boat.

Most organizations divide their yearly sales budget into monthly, weekly, or even daily budgets in order to plan production schedules and cash flows more precisely. Since this involves too much detail for our illustration, we will assume that Sunbird Boat Company projects its boat sales on a quarterly basis, as shown in Schedule 1.

1. Dianne Wilner Green, "Using Economic Data in Your Strategic Plan," *Management Accounting,* January 1997, p. 32.

Schedule 1
Sales Budget—2000

	Quarter				
	1	2	3	4	Total
15-foot boats:					
Selling price per unit	$ 7,000	$ 7,000	$ 7,000	$ 7,000	$ 7,000
Expected sales (units)	× 24	× 28	× 30	× 18	× 100
Expected revenues	$168,000	$196,000	$210,000	$126,000	$ 700,000
18-foot boats:					
Selling price per unit	$ 9,000	$ 9,000	$ 9,000	$ 9,000	$ 9,000
Expected sales (units)	× 28	× 32	× 36	× 24	× 120
Expected revenues	$252,000	$288,000	$324,000	$216,000	$1,080,000
Total expected revenues	$420,000	$484,000	$534,000	$342,000	$1,780,000

Production Budget

production budget A schedule of production requirements for the budget period.

The second detailed budget covers production, the number of units to be produced during the period. Factors to be considered in preparing this **production budget** are projected sales for the period, the desired amount of ending inventory, and the amount of time needed to obtain materials and then to make a unit of product.

Ending inventory is an important figure because management wants enough units on hand to meet customer demands, but not so many that unnecessary costs will be incurred because of excessive inventory. Usually, the desired ending inventory for any period is expressed as a percentage of the following period's expected sales volume. Sunbird Boat Company has determined that its desired ending inventory for each quarter should be approximately 80 percent of projected sales for the next quarter. The fourth quarter's ending inventory is 20 of the 15-foot boats and 22 of the 18-foot boats, which is 80 percent of the next quarter's (1st quarter of 2001) expected sales.

The production budget (Schedule 2) supplies information needed for all manufacturing cost budgets. Only after production quantities are known can management determine the amount of direct materials, direct labor, and manufacturing overhead needed during the period.

Although we are using quarterly production budgets in our example, the production budget has probably been most affected by recent developments in product costing and inventories. JIT inventory is a "pull-through" rather than a "push" system. This means that raw materials arrive just in time for production and that finished goods arrive just in time for sale. With short production times, the sales order pulls production and procurement. In organizations where JIT inventory systems work well, there is less need for a production budget with desirable levels of ending inventory. Indeed, the optimum level of inventory in these organizations is zero. Most companies, however, do not have perfect JIT inventory systems; even those few companies that do often keep a minimal level of inventory on hand for unexpected or "walk-in" sales.

direct materials budget A schedule of direct materials to be used during the budget period and direct materials to be purchased during that period.

Direct Materials Budget

The next detailed budget to be prepared is the **direct materials budget** (Schedule 3). Based on the engineering department's estimates of the materials required for each type of boat, this budget helps management schedule purchases from suppliers.

Schedule 2
Production Budget—2000

	Quarter 1	2	3	4	Total
15-foot boats:					
Expected sales (Schedule 1)	24	28	30	18	100
Add desired ending inventory of finished boats	22	24	15	20	20
Total number of boats needed	46	52	45	38	120
Less beginning inventory of finished boats	18*	22**	24	15	18
Total number of boats to be produced	28	30	21	23	102
18-foot boats:					
Expected sales (Schedule 1)	28	32	36	24	120
Add desired ending inventory of finished boats	25	29	20	22	22
Total number of boats needed	53	61	56	46	142
Less beginning inventory of finished boats	26*	25	29	20	26
Total number of boats to be produced	27	36	27	26	116

*These numbers represent ending inventory in 1999; the 1999 ending inventory cost $150,000.
**Differences in this table are due to rounding.

Sunbird's engineers estimate that the amounts of wood and fiberglass needed per boat are as follows:

	15-Foot Boat	18-Foot Boat
Direct materials requirements:		
Wood	70 board feet	100 board feet
Fiberglass	50 square feet	65 square feet

Based on these requirements for materials, the direct materials budget for Sunbird Boat Company for 2000 is shown in Schedule 3. The usage requirements are based not only on expected quarterly sales, but also on desired quarterly boat ending inventories. The materials purchase requirements are, in turn, based on the quarterly production requirements and the amount of raw materials inventory desired at the end of each quarter. Because raw materials can be obtained fairly soon after an order is placed, Sunbird has decided to maintain a supply of about 30 percent of the next quarter's production requirements for wood and fiberglass.

Like the production budget, the direct materials budget depends on the desired level of ending inventory. If management does not maintain sufficient materials inventory levels, costly work stoppages can occur; if inventories are excessive, inventory investment and storage costs may be unduly high.

As with the production budget, JIT inventory systems have decreased the time horizon, the amount of inventory needed, and in some cases, even the need for the direct materials budget. When materials can be secured immediately on demand, the need for direct materials budgets is decreased. As stated before, however, relatively few companies have perfect JIT inventory systems.

Schedule 3
Direct Materials Budget—2000

	Quarter 1	2	3	4	Total	Unit Cost of Materials[1]	Cost of Materials Sold
Direct materials usage per quarter:							
Wood (board feet):[2]							
15-foot boats (70 board feet per boat)	1,960	2,100	1,470	1,610	7,140		
18-foot boats (100 board feet per boat)	2,700	3,600	2,700	2,600	11,600		
Total board feet	4,660	5,700	4,170	4,210	18,740	$10.00/bd ft	$187,400
Fiberglass (square feet):[3]							
15-foot boats (50 square feet per boat)	1,400	1,500	1,050	1,150	5,100		
18-foot boats (65 square feet per boat)	1,755	2,340	1,755	1,690	7,540		
Total square feet.	3,155	3,840	2,805	2,840	12,640	$ 5.00/sq ft	63,200
							$250,600
Direct materials purchase requirements:							
Wood (board feet):							
Desired direct materials ending inventory	1,710	1,251	1,263	1,200[4]	1,200		
Direct materials needed for production	4,660	5,700	4,170	4,210	18,740		
Total direct materials needed	6,370	6,951	5,433	5,410	19,940		
Less beginning direct materials inventory	(1,396[5])	(1,710)	(1,251)	(1,263)	(1,396)		
Direct materials to be purchased. . . .	4,974	5,241	4,182	4,147	18,544		
Unit cost	×$10.00	×$10.00	×$10.00	×$10.00	×$10.00		
Cost of wood purchases	$49,740	$52,410	$41,820	$41,470	$185,440		
Fiberglass (square feet):							
Desired direct materials ending inventory	1,152	842	852	1,050[5]	1,050		
Direct materials needed for production	3,155	3,840	2,805	2,840	12,640		
Total direct materials needed	4,307	4,682	3,657	3,890	13,690		
Less beginning direct materials inventory	(947[5])	(1,152)	(842)	(852)	(947)		
Direct materials to be purchased. . . .	3,360	3,530	2,815	3,038	12,743		
Unit cost	× $5.00	× $5.00	× $5.00	× $5.00	× $5.00		
Cost of fiberglass purchases	$16,800	$17,650	$14,075	$15,190	$ 63,715		
Total direct materials cost.	$66,540	$70,060	$55,895	$56,660	$249,155		

[1]Supplier price quotations.
[2]Budgeted production in Schedule 2 multiplied by 70 and 100 board feet, respectively.
[3]Budgeted production in Schedule 2 multiplied by 50 and 65 square feet, respectively.
[4]Expected direct materials usage for the 1st quarter of 2001 is 4,000 board feet of wood and 3,500 square feet of fiberglass.
[5]Ending direct materials figure from 1999.

Direct Labor Budget

direct labor budget A schedule of direct labor requirements for the budget period.

The fourth detailed budget is the **direct labor budget** (Schedule 4). The direct labor budget for Sunbird Boat Company is based on an hourly rate of $15 per hour for production workers and the following estimated number of labor hours for each type of boat: 80 hours for 15-foot boats and 100 hours for 18-foot boats.

Schedule 4
Direct Labor Budget—2000

	Quarter 1	2	3	4	Total
15-foot boats:					
Production units	28	30	21	23	102
Direct labor hours per unit	× 80	× 80	× 80	× 80	× 80
Total direct labor hours per quarter	2,240	2,400	1,680	1,840	8,160
Rate per direct labor hour	× $15	× $15	× $15	× $15	× $15
Direct labor cost	$33,600	$36,000	$25,200	$27,600	$122,400
18-foot boats:					
Production units	27	36	27	26	116
Direct labor hours per unit	× 100	× 100	× 100	× 100	× 100
Total direct labor hours per quarter	2,700	3,600	2,700	2,600	11,600
Rate per direct labor hour	× $15	× $15	× $15	× $15	× $15
Direct labor cost	$40,500	$54,000	$40,500	$39,000	$174,000
Total direct labor cost	$74,100	$90,000	$65,700	$66,600	$296,400

Because labor is costly, the direct labor budget is often revised on a monthly or even weekly basis. Management must plan so that sufficient (but not excessive) labor is always available.[2] Otherwise, the company is likely to suffer the high cost of frequent hirings, firings, layoffs, and overtime work. Probably even more important than the high cost of employee turnover, however, is the feeling of demoralization among employees that such events can cause. If employees lack security, they usually behave in ways that maximize their own personal short-run benefits (e.g., they may slow down production, thus creating the need for overtime work).

The recent trend in many companies has been to keep a relatively small full-time staff and hire an increasing number of part-time employees. Companies have found that part-time employees offer the advantages of not having to pay retirement and other benefits and are much easier to hire and terminate. Banks, for example, have replaced many of their full-time tellers with part-time employees. As a result of a smaller full-time work force, companies that provide temporary workers are increasing in both size and number. From management's perspective, both part-time and temporary workers increase work-force flexibility and make direct labor budgeting easier. Unfortunately, these same trends probably mean less stable and secure careers for more and more workers.

2. Just how variable labor costs are has caused significant controversy in the management accounting literature. Some researchers argue that employees cannot easily be hired or terminated and, therefore, labor should be a fixed cost. Other researchers argue that labor can be easily hired and terminated—just read business newspapers where announcements of employee layoffs are printed every day. One thing is certain, though, and that is management strives to be able to control labor costs.

manufacturing overhead budget A schedule of production costs other than those for direct labor and direct materials.

Manufacturing Overhead Budget

The **manufacturing overhead budget** (Schedule 5) includes all production costs other than those for direct materials and direct labor. As noted in earlier chapters, manufacturing overhead is now a major element of total manufacturing costs in many organizations. As manufacturing overhead increases in size and complexity, it becomes much more important to use ABC and appropriate cost drivers.

In preparing this budget, Sunbird's accounting department first estimates the annual variable and fixed manufacturing overhead costs, as shown in the first column of Schedule 5. Total fixed costs are simply allocated evenly among the four quarters. The total variable cost of each item is allocated among the four quarters on the basis of some appropriate activity or cost driver. To keep the example simple, we will use direct labor hours to allocate manufacturing overhead to boats.[3] Schedule 4 showed that 19,760 direct labor hours (8,160 + 11,600) are projected for the year 2000. By dividing 19,760 projected hours into the total estimated cost of each item of variable manufacturing overhead, we get the variable manufacturing overhead rate per hour for that item. This rate is then multiplied by the number of direct labor hours estimated for each quarter (also from Schedule 4) to figure that item's budgeted variable manufacturing overhead cost for that quarter.

Schedule 5
Manufacturing Overhead Budget—2000

	Total Estimated Annual Manufacturing Overhead Costs	Manufactured Overhead Costs Assigned to Each Quarter			
		1	2	3	4
Variable costs:					
Indirect materials costs ($1.50 rate)	$ 29,640	$ 7,410	$ 9,000	$ 6,570	$ 6,660
Indirect labor costs ($3.50 rate)	69,160	17,290	21,000	15,330	15,540
Other payroll costs ($2.00 rate)	39,520	9,880	12,000	8,760	8,880
Utilities expense ($1.00 rate)	19,760	4,940	6,000	4,380	4,440
Total variable costs	$158,080	$39,520	$48,000	$35,040	$35,520
Fixed costs:					
Property taxes expense	$ 7,000	$ 1,750	$ 1,750	$ 1,750	$ 1,750
Insurance expense	6,000	1,500	1,500	1,500	1,500
Depreciation expense—plant	20,000	5,000	5,000	5,000	5,000
Supervisors' salaries	85,560	21,390	21,390	21,390	21,390
Total fixed costs	$118,560	$29,640	$29,640	$29,640	$29,640
Total manufacturing overhead	$276,640	$69,160	$77,640	$64,680	$65,160

To illustrate, estimated total indirect materials costs are $29,640. Dividing that number by 19,760 direct labor hours, yields a rate of $1.50 per hour. Multiplying the $1.50 rate by 4,940 direct labor hours (2,240 for 15-foot boats and 2,700 for 18-foot boats), produces $7,410 to be assigned to the first quarter as the budgeted cost of indirect materials. With 6,000 direct labor hours in the second quarter, the cost for that quarter is $9,000. The calculation is the same for the remaining quarters, as well as for other variable overhead items.

3. Remember, however, that direct labor hours is often not the relevant basis to allocate overhead in practice. We use direct labor hours here because using various cost drivers would unnecessarily complicate our examples.

The manufacturing overhead budget serves two important purposes. First, when compared with actual manufacturing overhead costs, the data on this budget provide management with a basis for controlling costs and evaluating the performance of the managers responsible for those costs. Second, it is used in product costing. As you will recall from Chapter 10, the manufacturing overhead costs that flow through Work-in-Process Inventory to Finished Goods Inventory (and eventually to Cost of Goods Sold) are applied costs, based on one or more predetermined overhead rates. In our example, this rate is calculated by dividing estimated annual direct labor hours into estimated annual manufacturing overhead ($276,640 ÷ 19,760 = $14).

When ABC is used, accurate measures of costs, identification of activities, and appropriate selection of cost drivers are important. Properly budgeting and assigning overhead costs to products is often difficult and is an area where exciting advances are being made.

Now that we have discussed direct materials, direct labor, and manufacturing overhead (the three elements of a product's cost), we can compute the cost of making the 15-foot and 18-foot boats. Using information from the previous sections, the manufacturing costs are calculated as follows (Schedule 6):

Schedule 6
Boat Manufacturing Costs—2000

	15-Foot Boat	18-Foot Boat
Wood (Schedule 3):		
70 board feet × $10 per board foot	$ 700	
100 board feet × $10 per board foot		$1,000
Fiberglass (Schedule 3):		
50 square feet × $5 per square foot	250	
65 square feet × $5 per square foot		325
Direct labor (Schedule 4):		
80 hours × $15 per hour	1,200	
100 hours × $15 per hour		1,500
Manufacturing overhead (Schedule 5):		
80 hours × $14 per hour	1,120	
100 hours × $14 per hour		1,400
Total cost per boat	$3,270	$4,225

Selling and Administrative Expense Budget

selling and administrative expense budget A schedule of all nonproduction spending expected to occur during the budget period.

The **selling and administrative expense budget** (Schedule 7) includes planned expenditures for all areas other than production. The costs of supplies used by the office staff, the salaries of the sales manager and company president, and the depreciation of office buildings all belong in this category. Because this budget covers several areas, it is usually quite large and may be supported by individual budgets for specific departments within the selling and administrative functions.

The selling and administrative expense budget for Sunbird is prepared in a manner similar to the manufacturing overhead budget. Total selling and administrative expenses are estimated for the year, with each expense then being distributed among the four quarters. As shown in Schedule 7, fixed expenses are assigned equally to each quarter, whereas variable expenses are allocated according to the number of boats to be sold. Variable delivery expenses, for example, are allocated to quarters

Schedule 7
Selling and Administrative Expense Budget—2000

	Estimated Annual Costs	Quarter 1	2	3	4
Variable expenses:					
Delivery expenses ($227.27 rate)	$ 50,000	$ 11,818	$ 13,636	$ 15,000	$ 9,546
Sales commissions ($727.27 rate)	160,000	37,818	43,636	48,000	30,546
Total variable expenses	$210,000	$ 49,636	$ 57,272	$ 63,000	$ 40,092
Fixed expenses:					
Executives' salaries	$220,000	$ 55,000	$ 55,000	$ 55,000	$ 55,000
Depreciation expense	40,000	10,000	10,000	10,000	10,000
Advertising expense	80,000	20,000	20,000	20,000	20,000
Miscellaneous expenses	10,000	2,500	2,500	2,500	2,500
Total fixed expenses	$350,000	$ 87,500	$ 87,500	$ 87,500	$ 87,500
Total selling and administrative expenses	$560,000	$137,136	$144,772	$150,500	$127,592

CAUTION

Remember that the budgets being discussed in this chapter are for only one level of expected sales. If the level of sales changes, the variable cost and expense amounts budgeted will change also. This means that all the direct materials and direct labor budgets will change, as will some of the manufacturing overhead and selling and administrative expense budgets.

by first determining the delivery expense rate ($50,000 estimated delivery expenses ÷ 220 boats expected to be sold during the year [from Schedule 1] = $227.27 per boat [rounded]). This rate is multiplied by the number of boats sold in a quarter to determine the delivery expenses allocated to that quarter. Since Sunbird expects to sell 52 boats in the first quarter at a rate of $227.27 per boat, the amount of delivery expense budgeted for that quarter would be $11,818 ($227.27 × 52 boats = $11,818 [rounded]). Sales commissions would be allocated to each quarter in the same way.

Cash Budget

cash budget A schedule of expected cash receipts and disbursements during the budget period.

The **cash budget**, which shows expected cash receipts and disbursements during a period, summarizes much of the information discussed thus far. A detailed cash budget will point out when a company has excess cash to invest and when it has to borrow funds. This allows a firm to earn maximum interest on excess funds and to avoid the costs of unnecessary borrowing. Most firms prepare a month-by-month, or even week-by-week, cash budget. Because of space limitations, however, we will continue to show Sunbird's budget on a quarterly basis.

Typically, a cash budget is divided into four sections:

1. Cash receipts
2. Cash disbursements
3. Cash excess or deficiency
4. Financing

The cash receipts section summarizes all cash expected to flow into the business during the budget period. Because companies generally extend credit to their customers, most of their sales are originally recorded as accounts receivable. The collection of accounts receivable is thus a major source of cash, and its timing is an important consideration in preparing a cash budget.

To illustrate how the collection of accounts receivable is budgeted, we will assume that all sales are on credit; that Sunbird's sales during the last quarter of 1999 were $280,000, and that expected sales for each quarter of 2000 (Schedule 1) are $420,000, $484,000, $534,000, and $342,000, respectively. On the basis of experience, Sunbird's

BUSINESS ENVIRONMENT ESSAY

Budgeting at Atlantic Dry Dock
Atlantic Marine Holding Company of Jacksonville, Florida, builds the ocean-going vessels that are used to pick up U.S. space shuttle booster rockets after they are parachuted into the Atlantic Ocean. One of Atlantic Marine's subsidiaries, **Atlantic Dry Dock**, contracts each year to perform millions of dollars of ship repairs and conversions. The process of estimating costs and submitting bids on jobs is critical to the company's success. If a bid is accepted, the estimate also becomes the budget for the job.

To prepare a bid, the estimator begins with an analysis of the job specifications, which are usually supplied by the customer. For complex operations, the job specifications may consist of several hundred pages. The requirements are broken down into smaller operations. Then, the estimator identifies the materials and labor tasks that will be required to complete each operation. For example, the estimator accesses the company's database to determine materials costs. The price of a certain material can be estimated by looking at recent purchases of the item, by searching previous job cost requirement lists, or by examining vendor lists. Once the quantity and price of materials have been estimated for each operation, these data are entered into a spreadsheet that is formatted with a template, developed in house, for estimating. The spreadsheet combines data for all operations involved in a particular job and provides management the information needed for bidding.

Ship repairs and maintenance is a fiercely competitive business. Atlantic Dry Dock's success depends on its ability to accurately project and budget costs, and then to work within those budgets.

Source: Adapted from Thomas L. Barton and Frederick M. Cole, "Atlantic Dry Dock's Unique Cost Estimation System," *Management Accounting,* October 1994, pp. 32–39.

accountants estimate that 80 percent of credit sales are collected during the quarter of sale and the remaining 20 percent are collected in the next quarter. Expected quarterly collections for the year 2000 would therefore be:

Collection of Accounts Receivable—2000

Sales Quarter	Sales Revenue	Collection Quarter 1	2	3	4	2000 Total
1999:						
Fourth.	$ 280,000	$ 56,000 (20%)				$ 56,000
2000:						
First	420,000	336,000 (80%)	$ 84,000 (20%)			420,000
Second.	484,000		387,200 (80%)	$ 96,800 (20%)		484,000
Third	534,000			427,200 (80%)	$106,800 (20%)	534,000
Fourth.	342,000				273,600 (80%)	273,600
Total	$2,060,000	$392,000	$471,200	$524,000	$380,400	$1,767,600

This analysis shows that total collections during 2000 are budgeted to be $1,767,600. In this example, we have assumed that all proceeds from credit sales are eventually collected. Usually, however, there are some customers who never pay, and these uncollectible accounts must be considered when analyzing estimated cash collections from accounts receivable. You should recognize that economic factors play a significant role in the timing of collections of accounts receivable. During recessionary periods, customers often drag out their payments much longer than in prosperous times.

The cash disbursements section of Schedule 8 summarizes all expected cash outlays by a firm during the budget period. These include payments of accounts payable, payroll, other costs and expenses, capital improvements, and dividends. Note that to compute cash disbursements for "other costs and expenses," depreciation and other noncash items must not be included.

The section related to cash excess or deficiency merely reports the difference between budgeted cash receipts and disbursements. With a prospective excess of cash, management should look for the most attractive short-term investments. A deficiency obviously means that additional short-term funds will be needed.

The financing section analyzes the timing and amounts of all projected borrowings and repayments during the period. It also estimates the amount of interest to be paid on borrowed funds. By accurately projecting these amounts and events, firms can give banks and other lending institutions advance notice of their needs. Banks appreciate, and sometimes insist, that companies plan their cash needs in advance. Because money has a time value, management always walks a tightrope between having too much or too little cash on hand.

Exhibit 13-3 shows how a typical company's cash balance and requirements fluctuate constantly. Most of this fluctuation is due to the varying amounts of raw materials and finished goods that are needed in the different seasons of the year. A prosperous firm could, if it desired, maintain enough cash on hand so that short-term borrowing would never be necessary, but such a policy might not be cost-beneficial. Long-term investments in productive assets usually earn considerably more than short-term cash investments; firms are generally better off maintaining lower cash balances, keeping as much capital as possible "at work" in the company's productive assets, and borrowing from time to time for short periods. For this reason, most companies obtain a line of credit from banks. A **line of credit** is a prearranged agreement whereby an organization or individual can borrow money on demand, up to a specific amount at specific rates.

line of credit An arrangement whereby a bank agrees to loan an amount of money (up to a certain limit) on demand for short periods of time, usually less than a year.

Schedule 8 gives the quarterly cash budget for Sunbird Boat Company for 2000. This cash budget assumes that when the company's cash balance at the end of a quarter is less than the desired minimum balance, cash is borrowed (in multiples of $10,000) and repaid at the end of a subsequent period when funds are available. It also assumes that loans are repaid on a first-in, first-out basis and that interest is paid only when the principal is repaid. Of the $120,000 budgeted to be repaid in the third quarter, $50,000 has been outstanding for two quarters (1/2 year), and $70,000 has been outstanding for one quarter (1/4 year). Furthermore, note that the entries in the Total column do not always equal the sum of the four quarters; the beginning cash balance and the minimum cash balance desired are the same for the year as they are for the first quarter.

EXHIBIT 13-3

A Typical Relationship Between Cash Balance and Cash Needs

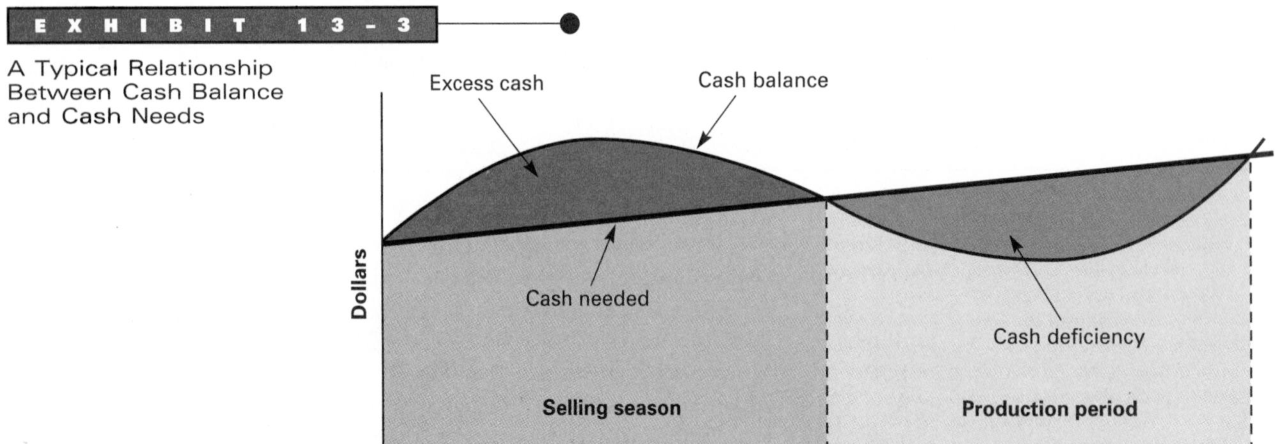

Schedule 8
Cash Budget—2000

	Quarter 1	Quarter 2	Quarter 3	Quarter 4	Total
Cash balance, beginning	$135,000[1]	$149,050	$ 142,780	$220,755	$ 135,000
Add collections from customers	392,000	471,200	524,000	380,400	1,767,600
(1) Total cash available before disbursement and financing	$527,000	$620,250	$ 666,780	$601,155	$1,902,600
Less disbursements for:					
Direct materials (Schedule 3)	$ 66,540	$ 70,060	$ 55,895	$ 56,660	$ 249,155
Direct labor (Schedule 4)	74,100	90,000	65,700	66,600	296,400
Manufacturing overhead (Schedule 5)[2]	64,160	72,640	59,680	60,160	256,640
Income tax expense	96,000[3]				96,000
Equipment purchase		150,000[4]			150,000
Selling and administrative expenses (Schedule 7)	127,150	134,770	140,500	117,580	520,000
Dividends		30,000[5]			30,000
(2) Total disbursements	$427,950	$547,470	$ 321,775	$301,000	$1,598,195
Minimum cash balance desired	140,000	140,000	140,000	140,000	140,000[6]
Total cash needed	$567,950	$687,470	$ 461,775	$441,000	$1,738,195
Excess (or deficiency) of cash available before financing	$ (40,950)	$(67,220)	$ 205,005	$160,155	$ 164,405
Financing:					
Borrowings	$ 50,000	$ 70,000			$ 120,000
Repayments			$(120,000)		(120,000)
Interest (at 10%)			(4,250)		(4,250)[7]
(3) Total effect of financing	$ 50,000	$ 70,000	$(124,250)		$(4,250)
(4) Ending cash balance [(1) − (2) + (3)]	$149,050	$142,780	$ 220,755	$300,155	$ 300,155

[1]Estimated 12/31/99 balance.
[2]Does not include depreciation expense.
[3]Income taxes owed at 12/31/99 are assumed to be $96,000.
[4]Equipment costing $150,000 is assumed to be purchased for cash during the second quarter.
[5]The company pays dividends of $30,000 during the second quarter of each year.
[6]Not a total of the four quarters—management's policy or plan.
[7]Computed as follows:

$50,000 × 0.10 × 1/2 = $2,500
$70,000 × 0.10 × 1/4 = 1,750
$4,250

CAUTION

When preparing a cash budget, be careful not to include expenditures that do not require cash (e.g., depreciation expense from the manufacturing overhead and selling and administrative expense budgets).

With the cash budget, the company is now able to make planning decisions regarding financing. For example, Sunbird is now aware that although the cash balance will be sufficient at the end of the year, there will probably be a cash shortage in the first and second quarters of 2000. With this knowledge, the company can take steps to deal with the situation. One solution would be to negotiate with a bank to obtain a loan. The company might also obtain money by attempting to get customers to pay sooner, trying to negotiate with creditors for a longer repayment period, or simply reducing the desired ending cash balance (currently at $140,000). The point is, with a knowledge of the coming cash shortfall, Sunbird is able to formulate a method of dealing with the problem now, rather than waiting until they actually find themselves short of cash.

TO SUMMARIZE

The master budget consists of detailed budgets for sales, production, selling and administrative expenses, and financing activities. Both the sales forecasting process and the development of the master budget may need to be repeated until the results are consistent with the company's strategic plan. The detailed budgets that make up the master budget are prepared in a logical sequence, as shown in Exhibit 13-2. The budgets related to sales, production, and other expenses allow the company to prepare a detailed cash budget. The cash budget shows expected cash receipts and disbursements; it also signals when the company can expect a cash shortage requiring outside financing, or a cash overage, which should be temporarily invested in income-producing assets.

Budgeting for Operations in a Merchandising Firm

The approach illustrated thus far in the chapter is the budgeting process used by most manufacturing companies. Many organizations, however, do not manufacture products; they either purchase products to resell or are organizations that sell services instead of "products."

As discussed previously in this text, organizations that purchase the products they resell are often referred to as merchandising companies; these include retailers that sell directly to consumers and wholesale distributors that buy products from manufacturers or other suppliers and sell to retailers. Well-known retail companies include Wal-Mart, Sears, and Kmart. While retail companies like Wal-Mart would buy many of the products they sell directly from manufacturers (e.g., Coca-Cola, Nabisco, Wrigleys, etc.), they would also buy from wholesalers who either buy from domestic manufacturers or import their products from other countries.

Because merchandising companies buy products (rather than make them), their budgeting process is less complicated than the budgeting done by manufacturing companies. For example, if Sunbird Boat Company were a merchandising firm rather than a manufacturing firm, the company would prepare a purchases budget rather than a production budget. The result of the purchases budget would be the number of units to be purchased rather than the number of units to be produced. The format of the purchases budget would be similar to the production budget, combining expected sales and desired ending inventory to arrive at needs for the period. Inventory on hand at the start of the period would then be subtracted to arrive at the amount to be purchased during the period.

Exhibit 13-4 compares the master budgeting process for a merchandising firm with that for manufacturing firms (from Exhibit 13-2).

Looking at Exhibit 13-4, you can see that in merchandising companies, one purchases budget replaces four budgets (production budget, direct materials budget, direct labor budget, and manufacturing overhead budget) used by manufacturing firms.

Because the sales budget, the selling and administrative expense budget, and the cash budget are similar to those prepared for manufacturing firms, we will not discuss them again. To illustrate budgeting in a merchandising company, we will assume that Wind River Boat Company is a retail company that buys boats from manufacturers and sells them to consumers.

Purchases Budget

purchases budget A schedule of projected purchases over the budget period.

Assuming the same level of sales as we did for Sunbird, the **purchases budget** for Wind River Boat Company is shown in Schedule 9.

You can see from Schedule 9 that Wind River Boat Company pays its suppliers $4,000 each for 15-foot boats and $5,000 each for 18-foot boats. (If you compare these costs with the total manufacturing cost for Sunbird Boat Company, you will

EXHIBIT 13-4 A Comparison of the Master Budgets for a Merchandising and a Manufacturing Firm

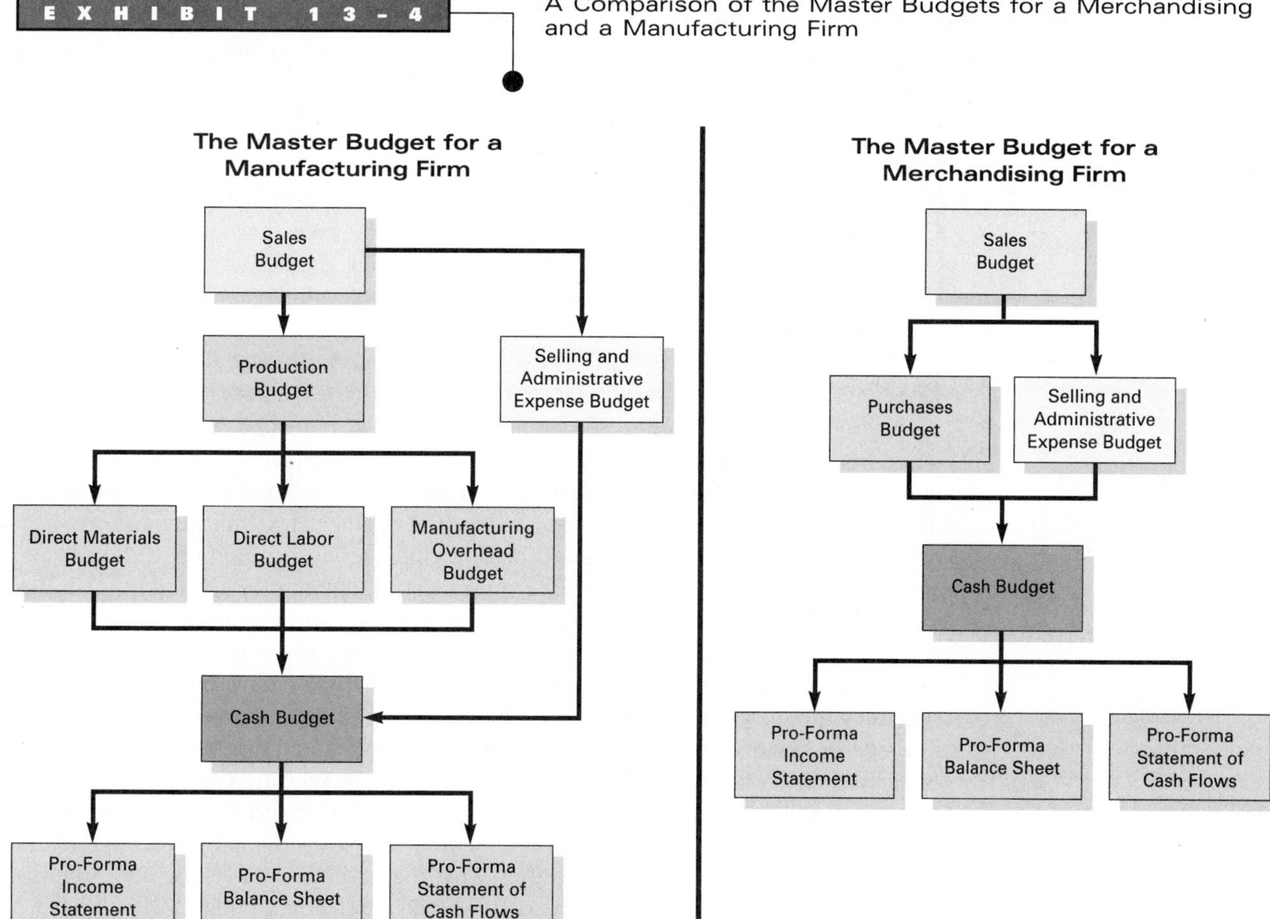

see that they are higher. This is because manufacturing companies also need to make a profit.) In Schedule 9, we have assumed the same beginning and ending inventory numbers we used in Schedule 2 for Sunbird, the manufacturing company. Total purchases in this schedule replaces the direct materials, direct labor, and manufacturing overhead lines in the cash budget for a manufacturing firm.

Schedule 9
Purchases Budget—2000

	Quarter 1		Quarter 2		Quarter 3		Quarter 4		Total	
	15 ft.	18 ft.	15 ft.	18 ft.	15 ft.	18 ft.	15 ft.	18 ft.	15 ft.	18 ft.
Expected sales	24	28	28	32	30	36	18	24	100	120
Desired ending inventory	22	25	24	29	15	20	20	22	20	22
Boats needed	46	53	52	61	45	56	38	46	120	142
Less beginning inventory	(18)	(26)	(22)	(25)	(24)	(29)	(15)	(20)	(18)	(26)
Boats to be purchased	28	27	30	36	21	27	23	26	102	116
Cost per boat	× $4,000	× $5,000	× $4,000	× $5,000	×$4,000	× $5,000	×$4,000	× $5,000	× $4,000	× $5,000
Total purchases	$112,000	$135,000	$120,000	$180,000	$84,000	$135,000	$92,000	$130,000	$408,000	$580,000

TO SUMMARIZE

The budgeting process for merchandising organizations (retail and wholesale companies) is similar, but easier, than that for manufacturing firms. The major difference is that a merchandising firm's purchases budget replaces four of a manufacturing firm's budgets—the production, direct materials, direct labor, and manufacturing overhead budgets. On the cash budget for a merchandising company, total purchases would replace cash expended for direct materials, direct labor, and manufacturing overhead. Otherwise, the entire master budgeting process is the same.

Budgeting for Operations in a Service Firm

Each year a larger and larger percentage of businesses in the United States are service entities. Service entities are different from manufacturing and merchandising companies in that they provide services to customers instead of products. Examples of service organizations are law, accounting, and engineering firms; doctors and dentists; hotels and motels; hunting and fishing guide services; automotive, home, and appliance repair services; and Internet providers. Budgeting for service firms is similar to budgeting for manufacturing firms. As was the case with both manufacturing and merchandising companies, the budgeting process for service firms begins with a sales budget. (For a service firm, this is usually called a revenue budget.) Expected revenues then drive the production budget, which is the number of billable hours in a CPA or law firm, the number of rooms to rent in a hotel, or the number of hours of service for an Internet provider. The production budget drives the separate budgets for supplies, wages and salaries, and overhead. These three budgets are similar to the direct materials, direct labor, and manufacturing overhead budgets in a manufacturing firm. These budgets, together with the revenue and selling and administrative expense budgets, provide the data needed for the cash budget. Once the cash budget is completed, pro-forma financial statements can be prepared. Exhibit 13-5 contrasts the budgeting process for manufacturing and service firms.

Revenue Budget

It is difficult to use either the Sunbird or Wind River examples discussed thus far to illustrate budgeting in service firms; both companies sold products—fishing boats. Therefore, to illustrate the budgeting process in service firms, we will use the example of a small motel that has 12 rooms to rent each night, the Boulder View Inn. The Boulder View Inn is located adjacent to a national park in Southern Utah and its business is highly seasonal, with April through December being busy (peak period) and January through March being very slow. The Boulder View Inn rents

BUSINESS ENVIRONMENT ESSAY

World's Largest Retailers In many industrialized countries, the growth rate for retail sales is barely keeping pace with the population growth rate. As a result, retailers are expanding into foreign markets to increase sales. Have you ever wondered which company was the largest retailer in the world? A recent report, *Global Powers of Retailing,* by **Deloitte & Touche** in association with *STORES* magazine, identified the top 200 global retailers. With total 1996 sales of almost $105 billion, Wal-Mart is the world's largest retailer. In addition to the United States, Wal-Mart operates stores in Argentina, Brazil, Canada, China, Indonesia, and Mexico. Thirty-nine percent of the top 200 retailers are U.S. companies, 14 percent are Japanese, and 10 percent are British. Four of the ten largest retailers are German companies. Here are the top ten global retailers.

Top Ten Global Retailers

Rank	Company	Country	Type of Store	1996 Sales (millions of U.S. dollars)*
1	Wal-Mart	United States	Discount, Warehouse	$104,859
2	Sears, Roebuck	United States	Department, Specialty	38,236
3	Rewe Zentrale	Germany	Supermarket	37,442
4	Metro	Germany	Department, Specialty, Supermarket	36,578
5	Tengelmann	Germany	Drug, Specialty, Supermarket	33,688
6	Aldi	Germany	Supermarket	32,000
7	Kmart	United States	Discount	31,437
8	Carrefour	France	Discount, Hypermarket	30,277
9	Ito-Yokado	Japan	Department, Discount, Specialty, Supermarket	27,752
10	Leclerc	France	Do-It-Yourself, Drug, Hypermarket, Specialty	26,466

*Currency converted using average 1996 exchange rates.
Sales figures are from various sources.

Source: *Deloitte & Touche Review,* Deloitte & Touche, LLC, Wilton, Connecticut, February 16, 1998, p. 4.

EXHIBIT 13-5

A Comparison of the Master Budgets for a Service and a Manufacturing Firm

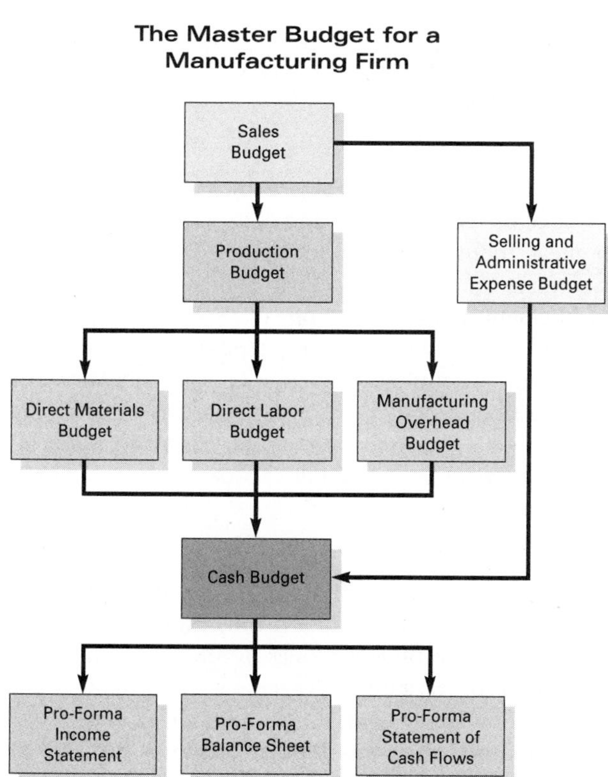

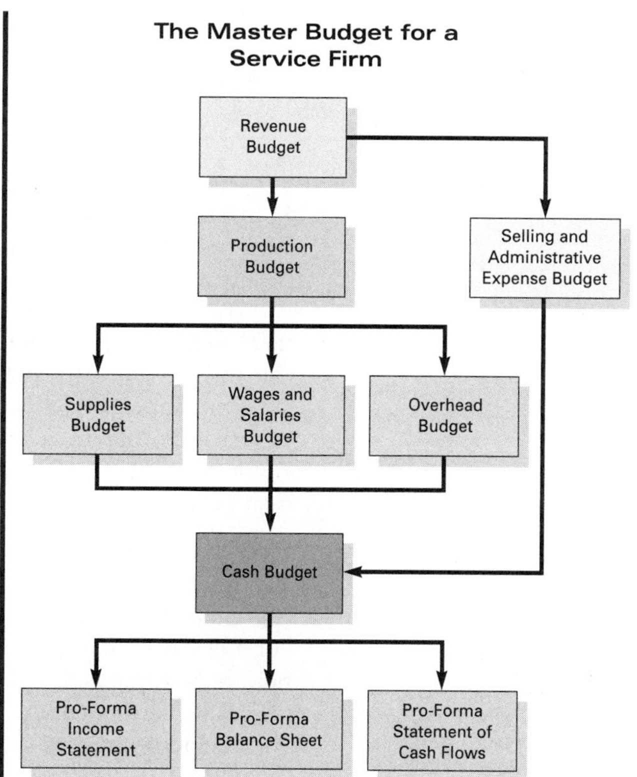

its rooms for an average rate of $55 per night during the peak period and $35 per night during the slow period. Guests who stay at the hotel either pay cash or use credit cards, such as Visa, Mastercard, American Express, or Discover. The motel has a direct link with its bank that immediately deposits credit card receipts in Boulder View Inn's bank account after charging a 4–5 percent discount fee, which covers the bank's costs as well as fees charged by the credit card companies. Historically, the Boulder View Inn has found that since most customers use credit cards to pay for their rooms, it pays an average of $2 per room per night to the credit card companies to cover the discount fee. After the discount fee, the net amount of revenues per room per night is $53 during peak periods and $33 during slow periods. Based on past experience, occupancy rates for the coming year are expected to be as follows:

January–March	25%
April–June	90%
July–September	80%
October–December	60%

revenue budget A service entity's budget that identifies how much revenue (and often cash) will be generated during a period.

Using these data, the **revenue budget** for the Boulder View Inn would be as shown in Schedule 10.

Schedule 10
Revenue Budget—2000

	January–March	April–June	July–September	October–December	Total
Gross revenue per room	$ 35	$ 55	$ 55	$ 55	
Number of days in quarter	× 90	× 91	× 92	× 92	
Total quarterly revenue per room	$ 3,150	$ 5,005	$ 5,060	$ 5,060	
Number of rooms to rent	× 12	× 12	× 12	× 12	
Possible revenues (at 100% occupancy)	$37,800	$60,060	$60,720	$60,720	
Occupancy rate	× 25%	× 90%	× 80%	× 60%	
Budgeted gross revenues	$ 9,450	$54,054	$48,576	$36,432	$148,512

This budget shows that the Boulder View Inn will generate gross revenues of $148,512 during the next year. Since the Boulder View Inn collects cash or its equivalent (credit cards) from each guest, there is no need to prepare a collection of accounts receivable budget as was done for the Sunbird Boat Company.

The revenue budget would be similar for other types of service firms, except that instead of a per room revenue, the revenue would be based on per patient visit (for doctors and dentists), per service performed (for engineers, accountants and lawyers), or per subscription (for Internet providers). Service companies that do not collect cash, but rather bill clients on a periodic basis (such as lawyers and accountants), would also prepare cash collection schedules to determine when the cash generated from revenues would be collected.

Production Budget

The production budget for a service firm determines the total amount of services (the number of units of service) that will be used to earn the revenues budgeted. For a law firm, for example, the production budget would be the total number of billable hours at each billing rate used to generate the revenues. For a hunting and fishing guide service, the production budget would be the number of guide days. For Boulder View Inn, the production budget is the number of rooms that will be rented each quarter, as shown in Schedule 11.

Schedule 11
Production Budget—2000

	January–March	April–June	July–September	October–December	Total
Gross revenues	$9,450	$54,054	$48,576	$36,432	$148,512
Room rental rate	÷ $35	÷ $55	÷ $55	÷ $55	
Rooms rented (rounded)	270	983	883	662	2,798

This production budget is necessary in order to determine the supplies, wages and salaries, and overhead budgets. You can see from this production budget that 2,798 rooms are expected to be rented next year.

Supplies Budget

supplies budget The budget, prepared by service entities, that identifies projected supplies expenses over the budget period.

Most service businesses need supplies to operate their business. For a restaurant, supplies would include the food used in preparing meals, napkins, after-dinner mints, and toothpicks. For a medical doctor, supplies might include needles, tape, bandages, and thread for stitching cuts. For Boulder View Inn, supplies include soap and shampoo for the guest rooms, as well as donuts, cereal, juice, and coffee for the continental breakfast. The **supplies budget** for the Boulder View Inn is shown in Schedule 12.

Schedule 12
Supplies Budget—2000

Supplies Needed per Room	January–March	April–June	July–September	October–December	Total
Soap	$ 0.40	$ 0.40	$ 0.40	$ 0.40	$ 0.40
Shampoo	0.60	0.60	0.60	0.60	0.60
Coffee	0.30	0.30	0.30	0.30	0.30
Juice	0.60	0.60	0.60	0.60	0.60
Cereal	0.40	0.40	0.40	0.40	0.40
Donuts	0.70	0.70	0.70	0.70	0.70
Total supplies per room	$ 3.00	$ 3.00	$ 3.00	$ 3.00	$ 3.00
Rooms rented	× 270	× 983	× 883	× 662	× 2,798
Total supplies cost	$810.00	$2,949.00	$2,649.00	$1,986.00	$8,394.00

Wages and Salaries Budget

wages and salaries budget The budget, prepared by service entities, that identifies projected labor costs involved directly in providing the service over the budget period.

The **wages and salaries budget** is reserved for labor costs involved directly in providing the service (similar to direct labor in a manufacturing firm). Administrative labor costs are not included in this budget; they are part of the selling and administrative expense budget. For a law firm, the wages and salaries budget would include salaries of lawyers (but not of paralegals), photocopy personnel, or computer specialists. For the Boulder View Inn, the only labor cost included in this budget is the $3 per room that is paid for cleaning the rooms. Schedule 13 is the wages and salaries budget for Boulder View Inn.

Schedule 13
Wages and Salaries Budget—2000

	January–March	April–June	July–September	October–December	Total
Rooms rented	270	983	883	662	2,798
Cleaning fee	× $3	× $3	× $3	× $3	× $3
Total wages and salaries	$810	$2,949	$2,649	$1,986	$8,394

Overhead Budget

service overhead budget The budget, prepared by service entities, that identifies projected costs associated with providing the service.

As was the case with manufacturing firms, the **service overhead budget** includes all the costs associated with providing the product, or service in this case. The overhead budget does not include selling and administrative costs not directly associated with providing the service. For the Boulder View Inn, overhead includes utilities, depreciation, TV and telephone service, and miscellaneous expenses. Schedule 14 is the overhead budget for the Boulder View Inn.

The depreciation is calculated by dividing the motel cost of $300,000 by its 30-year life to arrive at $10,000 per year. The utilities include heat, lights, sewer, and garbage removal. Because the Boulder View Inn expects to rent 2,798 rooms during the year, the overhead assigned to each room rented is $9.29 ($26,000 ÷ 2,798 rooms).

Schedule 14
Overhead Budget—2000

	January–March	April–June	July–September	October–December	Total
Utilities	$2,000	$2,000	$2,000	$2,000	$ 8,000
Depreciation expense	2,500	2,500	2,500	2,500	10,000
TV and telephone	800	800	800	800	3,200
Miscellaneous expense	1,200	1,200	1,200	1,200	4,800
Total overhead	$6,500	$6,500	$6,500	$6,500	$26,000

Based on the three production-related budgets (supplies, wages and salaries, and overhead), we know it costs the Boulder View Inn approximately $15.29 to provide the services needed to rent one room for one night. The calculation of this cost is shown in Schedule 15.

Schedule 15
Per Room Rental Cost—2000

Supplies cost	$ 3.00 per room
Wages and salaries cost	3.00 per room
Overhead	9.29 per room
Total cost to provide motel rooms	$15.29 per room

Selling and Administrative Expense Budget

As was the case for Sunbird Boat Company, the selling and administrative expense budget includes planned expenditures for all selling and administrative expenses. As in manufacturing companies, the selling and administrative expense budget for a service firm can be quite large, and it is sometimes supported by individual budgets for specific elements included in this budget. The selling and administrative expense budget for the Boulder View Inn would be as shown in Schedule 16.

Schedule 16
Selling and Administrative Expense Budget—2000

	Quarter				Estimated
	1	2	3	4	Annual Cost
Credit card fees*	$ 540	$1,966	$1,766	$1,324	$ 5,596
Manager's salary	5,000	5,000	5,000	5,000	20,000
Advertising expense	1,000	1,000	1,000	1,000	4,000
Total selling and administrative expenses	$6,540	$7,966	$7,766	$7,324	$29,596

*At $2 per room.

This selling and administration expense budget shows that the Boulder View Inn's total selling and administrative expense for the year is $29,596. The selling and administrative expenses include credit card charges, the manager's salary, and advertising expense, which includes yellow page directory advertisement and Internet listings.

Cash Budget

The cash budget, which shows expected cash receipts and disbursements during a period, summarizes information contained in both the revenue and the selling and administrative expense budgets. For the Boulder View Inn, and for most service organizations, once the individual budgets are prepared, preparing the cash budget is quite simple. As is the case with all cash budgets, the Boulder View Inn's cash budget allows the motel to determine when it will have excess cash and when it will have to borrow cash. The cash budget for the Boulder View Inn is shown in Schedule 17.

Schedule 17
Cash Budget—2000

	January–March	April–June	July–September	October–December	Total
Cash receipts	$ 9,450	$54,054	$48,576	$36,432	$148,512
Cash outflows:					
Supplies	$ (810)	$ (2,949)	$ (2,649)	$ (1,986)	$ (8,394)
Wages and salaries	(810)	(2,949)	(2,649)	(1,986)	(8,394)
Overhead*	(4,000)	(4,000)	(4,000)	(4,000)	(16,000)
Selling and administrative expenses	(6,540)	(7,966)	(7,766)	(7,324)	(29,596)
Total cash expenditures	$12,160	$17,864	$17,064	$15,296	$ 62,384
Net cash inflow (outflow)	$ (2,710)	$36,190	$31,512	$21,136	$ 86,128

*Depreciation Expense is not included because it is not a cash expenditure.

This cash budget makes several assumptions. First, the Boulder View Inn is a partnership, so there is no income tax. Instead, as in all partnerships, the income is allocated among the partners and claimed as income on their personal tax returns. Many service organizations are partnerships, so this assumption is not unusual (many are also corporations). Second, it is assumed that all expenditures are paid for in the quarter incurred. If the Boulder View Inn paid for some of its expenses in the quarters following their incurrence, a cash payments schedule would need to be prepared.

This cash budget shows that the Boulder View Inn generates excess cash in quarters two, three, and four, but has a net cash outflow of $2,710 in the first quarter. The Boulder View Inn can solve its cash flow shortage in the first quarter either by keeping enough cash in its bank account to cover the shortage, or by borrowing money in the first quarter and repaying it in the second quarter.

TO SUMMARIZE

The master budget for a service company is similar to budgeting in a manufacturing company. As a result, in addition to the pro-forma financial statements, seven budgets are prepared: the revenue budget, the production budget, the supplies budget, the wages and salaries budget, the overhead budget, the selling and administrative expense budget, and the cash budget. The revenue budget is usually based on whatever the service performed is (e.g., per room, per service performed, per patient, or per subscription basis). The production budget identifies the number of units of the service that will be performed so that supplies, wages and salaries, and overhead budgets can be prepared. The selling and administrative expense budget includes all costs not directly related to providing the service. The cash budget is net revenues received less cash spent for supplies, wages, overhead (not including depreciation expense), and selling and administrative expenses. As was the case with manufacturing and merchandising companies, the budgeting process allows a service company to determine when it will have excess cash and when it will experience cash shortages.

4 *Prepare pro-forma financial statements.*

PRO-FORMA FINANCIAL STATEMENTS

The budgeting process discussed to this point allows management to plan various activities within the firm, such as purchasing and borrowing. Armed with these budgets, management is now prepared to monitor the firm's performance and compare actual results to budgeted results. If corrective action is needed, management can identify deviations from the budget early and take the appropriate steps to remedy problems. In addition to preparing the detailed budgets, management can combine the various budgets to arrive at pro-forma, or budgeted, financial statements. In this section, we use the budgets from the Sunbird Boat Company to prepare a pro-forma income statement, balance sheet, and statement of cash flows.

The pro-forma income statement (often called a budgeted income statement) projects income for the coming period and, therefore, is valuable to management in making key decisions. Such questions as how high a dividend to pay, whether or not to invest in a new plant, and how strenuously to bargain with unions are usually decided on the basis of projected and actual profits. Because budgeting for manufacturing firms is the most complicated, we will illustrate pro-forma financial statements using the Sunbird Boat Company example illustrated earlier in the chapter. Sunbird's pro-forma income statement is shown in Schedule 18.

Schedule 18
Pro-Forma Income Statement
For the Year Ended December 31, 2000

Sales revenue (Schedule 1)			$1,780,000
Cost of goods sold:			
Beginning finished goods inventory (Schedule 2)		$150,000	
Manufacturing costs:			
Direct materials used (Schedule 3)	$250,600		
Direct labor (Schedule 4)	296,400		
Manufacturing overhead (Schedule 5)	276,640	823,640	
Total cost of goods available for sale		$973,640	
Less ending finished goods inventory*		(158,350)	
Cost of goods sold			(815,290)
Gross margin			$ 964,710
Selling and administrative expenses (Schedule 7)			(560,000)
Operating income			$ 404,710
Interest expense (Schedule 8)			(4,250)
Income before taxes			$ 400,460
Income taxes (approximate 27% rate)			(108,124)
Net income			$ 292,336

*Calculation of ending Finished Goods Inventory. (Schedule 2 states that the desired ending inventory is 20 15-foot boats and 22 18-foot boats.)
Per schedule: Cost of 15-foot boat: $3,270 × 20 boats = $65,400
Cost of 18-foot boat: $4,225 × 22 boats = $92,950
Total cost: $65,400 + $92,950 = $158,350

The final two items to be projected are the balance sheet and the statement of cash flows. These statements are presented in Schedules 19 and 20.

Schedule 19
Pro-Forma Balance Sheet
December 31, 2000

Assets

Current assets:		
Cash (Schedule 8)	$ 300,155	
Accounts receivable[1]	68,400	
Direct materials[2]	17,250	
Finished goods (Schedule 18)	158,350	$ 544,155
Long-term operating assets:		
Land (assumed)	$ 234,305	
Building and equipment[3]	1,650,000	
Less accumulated depreciation[4]	(180,000)	1,704,305
Total assets		$2,248,460

(continued)

Liabilities and Stockholders' Equity

Current liabilities:		
Accounts payable[5]	$ 90,000	
Income taxes payable[6]	108,124	$ 198,124
Stockholders' equity:		
Common stock, $5 par, 20,000 shares outstanding (assumed)	$1,000,000	
Paid-in capital in excess of par, common stock (assumed)	250,000	
Retained earnings[7]	800,336	2,050,336
Total liabilities and stockholders' equity		$2,248,460

[1]Accounts receivable:
beginning balance + sales (Schedule 1) − collections (Schedule 8) = ending balance
(assumed) $56,000 + $1,780,000 − $1,767,600 = $68,400

[2]Direct materials:
Wood $12,000 (1,200 × $10 per board foot) + fiberglass $5,250 (1,050 × $5) = $17,250

[3]Building and equipment:
beginning balance + equipment purchase (Schedule 8) = ending balance
(assumed) $1,500,000 + $150,000 = $1,650,000

[4]Accumulated depreciation:
beginning balance + plant overhead (Schedule 5) + selling and administrative expenses (Schedule 7) = ending balance
(assumed) $120,000 + $20,000 + $40,000 = $180,000

[5]Accounts payable:
beginning balance + direct materials purchased (Schedule 3) + direct labor (Schedule 4) + manufacturing overhead (less depreciation) (Schedule 5)
(assumed) $90,000 + $249,155 + $296,400 + $256,640 ($276,640 − $20,000)
+ selling and administrative expenses (less depreciation) (Schedule 7) + income tax expense (Schedule 8) + dividends (Schedule 8) + equipment (Schedule 8) − amount paid for cash payments (Schedule 8) = ending balance
+ $520,000 ($560,000 − $40,000) + $96,000 + $30,000 + $150,000 − $1,598,195 = $90,000

[6]Income taxes payable:
beginning balance + estimated taxes − payment = ending balance
(assumed) $96,000 + $108,124 − $96,000 = $108,124

[7]Retained earnings:
beginning balance + net income − dividends = ending balance
(assumed) $538,000 + $292,336 − $30,000 = $800,336

Schedule 20
Pro-Forma Statement of Cash Flows
For the Year Ended December 31, 2000

Cash flows from operating activities:		
Net income (Schedule 18)		$292,336
Add (subtract) adjustments:		
Depreciation (Schedules 5 and 7)	$ 60,000	
Decrease in direct materials*	1,445	
Increase in finished goods*	(8,350)	
Increase in accounts receivable*	(12,400)	
Increase in income taxes payable*	12,124	
		52,819
Net cash provided by operating activities		$345,155
Cash flows from investing activities:		
Purchase of equipment (Schedule 8)	$(150,000)	
Net cash used in investing activities		(150,000)
Cash flows from financing activities:		
Cash obtained from borrowing (Schedule 8)	$ 120,000	
Repayment of borrowed funds (Schedule 8)	(120,000)	
Payment of dividends (Schedule 8)	(30,000)	
Net cash used in financing activities		(30,000)
Net increase in cash		$165,155

*1999 year-end balances are assumed to be $18,695 for direct materials, $150,000 for finished goods, $56,000 for accounts receivable, and $96,000 for income taxes payable.

(S T O P & T H I N K)

How would the three financial statements be different if we assumed Sunbird was a merchandising company instead of a manufacturing company?

The master budget is now complete. It is ready for use to communicate information, coordinate and authorize activities, motivate employees, and measure performance. The decisions to be made on the basis of this budget depend on the answers to such questions as:

1. Is the net income of approximately $292,336 adequate? If not, how can it be increased?
2. How does the expected financial position at the end of the year fit with long-range objectives and goals?
3. Is the projected increase in cash sufficient to meet the firm's goals?
4. Are there sufficient liquid assets to purchase needed assets?
5. How should management be rewarded if these budgets are met?
6. Who should be responsible for meeting the goals set for sales, production, and costs?

These are only a few of the questions that management needs to answer. However, they should give you a sense of the master budget's usefulness. In fact, it is hard to imagine how a company could be profitable in the long run without such planning.

TO SUMMARIZE

Following the preparation of the cash budget, which provides an indication of the financing activities of the business, pro-forma financial statements can be prepared. The pro-forma income statement, balance sheet, and statement of cash flows follow directly from the components of the master budget. The pro-forma balance sheet also relies heavily on beginning account balances. Once these pro-forma financial statements have been prepared, management can then determine if budgeted sales and production levels will allow the company to achieve its strategic goals. These pro-forma financial statements serve as a basis for key management decisions.

Distinguish between static and flexible budgets.

static budget A quantified plan that projects revenues and costs for only one level of activity.

flexible budget A quantified plan that projects revenues and costs for varying levels of activity.

STATIC VERSUS FLEXIBLE BUDGETING

The budgets discussed thus far were **static budgets**; that is, they were geared to only one level of activity. Actual results were compared to budgeted costs at the budgeted activity level. Although such budgets help in planning, they are not very useful for controlling costs and measuring performance because the actual level of activity may have differed significantly from the planned level.

A **flexible budget** is much more useful for control and performance evaluation because it is not confined to one level of activity. Flexible budgets are dynamic; that is, they can be tailored to any level of activity within the relevant range. Using flexible budgeting, a manager can look at the actual level of activity attained and then determine what costs should have been at that level.

Weaknesses in Static Budgeting

To illustrate why a static budget is inadequate for controlling operations, we will use an example for Kemper Manufacturing Company and assume only variable costs. We use this different example so as not to complicate the Sunbird Boat Company example used throughout the chapter. Here we are interested only in illustrating the concept of flexible budgets.

BUSINESS ENVIRONMENT ESSAY

Budgeting at Theme Parks Although the rides are idle at many theme parks during the winter, theme park accountants are not without work. When the gates close for the last time each fall, accountants at Six Flags Great America in Illinois use the off-period to prepare the annual operating budget for the coming season.

The process begins with the development of the park's anticipated attendance levels and the daily operating schedule. Attendance levels from the preceding season are used to make projections for the next year. Attendance is computed by summing the number of tickets sold at the entrance, the number of presold tickets redeemed, and the number of season pass admissions. In addition, turnstiles are used at entrances and exits to count admissions and the number of guests riding each ride. Turnstile meters are "read" on an hourly basis to enable management to monitor varying attendance throughout the day. This information is used to anticipate and budget staffing needs.

Based on past performance and other information (such as planned improvements), revenues and expenses are projected for each area of the park. For example, gift shops, food outlets, moveable carts, and support areas are budgeted individually. The master budget, then, is a consolidation of the several hundred budgets of individual activity centers.

Theme parks are an established cultural phenomenon in America. Those parks that budget and then execute their budgets most effectively are the most financially successful.

Source: Adapted from Kevin A. Roth, "Theme Park Accounting: What Do We Really Do All Winter?" *Management Accounting,* February 1994, pp. 48–51.

Using information from various sources, Kemper developed the following budgeted per-unit manufacturing costs for its product:

Direct materials	$0.90
Direct labor	0.74
Manufacturing overhead	1.36
Total	$3.00

Extending these per-unit costs to establish a total budgeted amount for the month of August, the company might prepare a static budget as follows:

Kemper Manufacturing Company
Budgeted Manufacturing Costs
For the Month of August 2000

Budgeted production (units)	4,000
Budgeted manufacturing costs:	
Direct materials ($0.90 × 4,000)	$ 3,600
Direct labor ($0.74 × 4,000)	2,960
Manufacturing overhead ($1.36 × 4,000)	5,440
Total manufacturing costs	$12,000

Now, let's assume that Kemper produced only 3,800 units in August and that actual costs incurred were $3,370 for direct materials, $2,900 for direct labor, and $5,400 for manufacturing overhead. Comparing actual results with the static budget information, the performance report for the month would be as follows:

Kemper Manufacturing Company
Static Budget Performance Report
For the Month of August 2000

	Actual	Budgeted	Difference
Production (units)	3,800	4,000	(200)
Manufacturing costs:			
Direct materials	$ 3,370	$ 3,600	$(230)
Direct labor	2,900	2,960	(60)
Manufacturing overhead	5,400	5,440	(40)
Total actual and budgeted manufacturing costs	$11,670	$12,000	$(330)

Obviously, something is wrong with this performance report. Producing fewer units than budgeted (3,800 actual units versus 4,000 budgeted units) has led to actual costs that are $330 less than budgeted costs. Should management be rewarded for keeping costs down or penalized for producing fewer units than budgeted? The deficiencies of this static budget performance report can be explained as follows: A production manager is responsible for controlling two things—production (output) and costs; that is, he or she must try to meet budgeted production volume and control costs in the process. To measure a manager's performance, the production and cost control functions must be separated. It makes no sense to note that the actual cost of producing 3,800 units is less than the budgeted cost of producing 4,000 units. It obviously should be. The manager in our example clearly has not met budgeted production volume, but to determine whether he or she has controlled costs adequately, we must be able to compare actual costs to budgeted costs at the same number of units of production.

Using the Flexible Budget

Instead of providing budgeted costs for only one level of activity, the flexible budget covers a range of activity levels so that managers can easily determine what costs should have been at the actual activity level. Because it is possible to prepare budgeted costs at every possible activity level, per-unit costs that can be applied to any activity level within the relevant range are developed. The actual steps in preparing a flexible budget are:

1. Determine a relevant range over which production is expected to vary during the coming period.
2. Analyze the projected manufacturing costs for the coming period.
3. Using the per-unit costs for each element, prepare a budget showing what costs are expected to be incurred at several points within the relevant range.

To illustrate the preparation of a flexible budget, let us assume that Kemper's relevant range of activity per month is between 3,600 and 4,200 units. As noted earlier, the per-unit costs are:

Direct materials	$0.90
Direct labor	0.74
Manufacturing overhead	1.36
Total	$3.00

These per-unit costs can now be used to prepare a flexible budget showing expected costs for several levels of production.

Kemper Manufacturing Company
Manufacturing Cost Flexible Budget
For the Month of August 2000

	Manufacturing Costs per Unit	Range of Production (units)			
		3,600	3,800	4,000	4,200
Direct materials	$0.90	$ 3,240	$ 3,420	$ 3,600	$ 3,780
Direct labor	0.74	2,664	2,812	2,960	3,108
Manufacturing overhead	1.36	4,896	5,168	5,440	5,712
Total	$3.00	$10,800	$11,400	$12,000	$12,600

With the flexible budget prepared, Kemper can compare actual amounts against budgeted amounts for the production level attained. In this case, 3,800 units were actually produced, so the actual costs for the period can be compared with the budget for 3,800 units. If actual production had been 3,700 units, a number not included in the budget, Kemper could simply multiply the per-unit cost of each item (direct materials, direct labor, and manufacturing overhead) by the actual activity level in order to judge performance. The performance report based on flexible budgeting for the 3,800 units actually produced now makes much more sense.

Kemper Manufacturing Company
Flexible Budget Performance Report
For the Month of August 2000

Actual production (units)	3,800
Budgeted production (units)	4,000
Difference	(200)

	Cost per Unit	Actual Costs Incurred at 3,800 Units	Budgeted Costs for 3,800 Units	Difference
Direct materials	$0.90	$ 3,370	$ 3,420	$ (50)
Direct labor	0.74	2,900	2,812	88
Manufacturing overhead	1.36	5,400	5,168	232
Total costs	$3.00	$11,670	$11,400	$270

Notice that the actual costs for both direct labor and manufacturing overhead exceeded budgeted costs for the actual level of activity. We are now comparing apples with apples, or actual costs of producing 3,800 units with budgeted costs of producing 3,800 units. Using the same activity level has revealed that total manufacturing costs exceeded budget by $270 during the month and that the most significant difference was in the cost of manufacturing overhead.

Flexible budgets provide management with useful information for investigating problem areas. This flexible budget performance report shows that not only was planned production not achieved but also that the costs incurred exceeded those budgeted at the attained level of activity. Apparently, the manager is having problems with both production and cost control. Having meaningful cost comparisons is very useful for evaluating performance and overcoming breakdowns in cost control.

TO SUMMARIZE

The master budget described in this chapter was a static budget. A static budget is a budget that is prepared for only one level of activity. Static budgets are useful for planning purposes, but flexible budgets are much more useful for control and performance evaluation. A flexible budget is a budget prepared over a range of activity. Flexible budgets allow budgeted and actual costs to be compared at the same level of activity, thereby revealing cost and production effectiveness.

REVIEW OF LEARNING OBJECTIVES

1 **Describe different types of budgeting and identify the purposes of budgeting.** A budget is a quantitative expression of a plan of action. The budget identifies and allocates resources necessary to carry out the mission of the organization. Based on the strategic plan, the organization prepares a capital budget and a budget for operations. The operating budget provides quantitative estimates of sales and expected costs for each activity to be performed during a specified period of time (usually one year). The budgeting process has several purposes. Budgeting encourages planning, enhances communications, helps management at all levels coordinate activities, provides authorization for actions (investing, spending, borrowing, producing), helps motivate employees to perform, assists in reducing conflicts, and provides quantitative measures of expectations and objectives.

2 **Describe the budgeting process and its behavioral implications.** Most organizations establish a budget committee comprised of several vice presidents that coordinate the preparation of detailed budgets in their areas of responsibility and oversee the preparation of the overall budget. There are significant behavioral ramifications to consider in preparing an operating budget. For the process to be successful, top management must give its full support, all members of management must actively participate in the process, and deviations from the budget must be addressed in a constructive manner. If only the top management is involved in budget preparation, it is referred to as top-down budgeting. When each segment manager prepares a budget for that segment's operations, it is called bottom-up budgeting. Most budgeting processes incorporate both approaches to some degree.

3 **Explain the master budget and its components for manufacturing firms, merchandising firms, and service firms.** The operating budget, also called a master budget, is an integrated group of detailed budgets that together provide overall operating and financing plans for a specific time period. The master budget for a manufacturing firm starts with a sales forecast, which serves as the basis for the sales budget. The sales budget is followed in sequence with detailed budgets for production, direct materials usage and purchases, direct labor, manufacturing overhead, selling and administrative expenses, and cash. These detailed budgets are usually prepared on a monthly or quarterly basis. For operations budgeting in merchandising companies, a purchases budget replaces the production, direct materials, direct labor, and manufacturing overhead budgets used in manufacturing companies. Operations budgeting in service firms includes preparing revenue, production, selling and administrative expense, and cash budgets. Together these budgets provide management with a master plan of action for the coming year.

4 **Prepare pro-forma financial statements.** Once a cash budget is prepared to project the firm's ending cash balances and borrowing and investing activities, pro-forma financial statements can be prepared. The pro-forma balance sheet relies heavily on the balances at the beginning of the period, along with components of the master budget. The pro-forma income statement and statement of cash flows are prepared primarily from the detailed budgets included in the master budget. With these pro-forma financial statements, management is able to determine if budgeted results are consistent with the firm's master plan.

5 **Distinguish between static and flexible budgets.** Static budgets project expected results at only one activity level. When the actual production level differs significantly from the budgeted level, it is difficult to know what costs should have been for the actual production level. Flexible budgets estimate costs for various activity levels and allow actual costs to be compared to budgeted costs for the actual production level. Flexible budgets allow management to focus on both the production and cost control elements of budgeting.

KEY TERMS AND CONCEPTS

REVIEW PROBLEM

Budgeting in a Manufacturing Firm

The following information is available for the Call Company:

Expected sales (units):	
June	840
July	980
August	1,400
Selling price per unit	$15
Accounts receivable balance, June 1	$6,300
Desired finished goods inventory, August 31 (units)	250
Beginning finished goods inventory, June 1 (units)	270
Direct materials needed per unit	11 feet
Desired direct materials inventory, August 31	2,800 feet
Beginning direct materials inventory, June 1	2,700 feet
Total direct labor time per finished unit	3 hours
Direct materials cost per foot	$0.60
Direct labor cost per hour	$8

Additional information:

a. Seventy-five percent of a month's sales is collected by the month's end; the remaining 25 percent is collected in the following month.
b. The desired ending finished goods inventory every month is 25 percent of the next month's sales.
c. The desired ending direct materials inventory every month is 20 percent of the next month's production needs.

Required:

1. Prepare sales budgets for June, July, and August (in dollars).
2. Prepare cash collection budgets for June, July, and August (in dollars).
3. Prepare production budgets for June, July, and August (in units).
4. Prepare direct materials budgets for June, July, and August (in dollars).
5. Prepare direct labor budgets for June, July, and August (in dollars).

Solution

1. Sales Budgets

	June	July	August
Expected sales (units)	840	980	1,400
Selling price per unit	× $15	× $15	× $15
Expected revenues	$12,600	$14,700	$21,000

2. Cash Collection Budgets

	June	July	August
From accounts receivable	$ 6,300		
From June's sales (75%/25%)	9,450	$ 3,150	
From July's sales (75%/25%)		11,025	$ 3,675
From August's sales (75%/25%)			15,750
Total	$15,750	$14,175	$19,425

3. Production Budgets

	June	July	August
Expected sales (units)	840	980	1,400
Add desired ending inventory (25% of next month's sales)	245	350	250*
Total needed	1,085	1,330	1,650
Less beginning inventory	(270)*	(245)	(350)
Budgeted production (units)	815	1,085	1,300

*Given

4. Direct Materials Budgets

	June	July	August
Units to be produced	815	1,085	1,300
Direct materials needed per unit	× 11 feet	× 11 feet	× 11 feet
Total production needs	8,965 feet	11,935 feet	14,300 feet
Desired ending direct materials inventory (20% of next month's production needs)	2,387	2,860	2,800*
Total feet needed	11,352	14,795	17,100
Less beginning inventory	(2,700)*	(2,387)	(2,860)
Direct materials to be purchased	8,652	12,408	14,240
Cost per foot	× $0.60	× $0.60	× $0.60
Total direct materials cost (rounded)	$ 5,191	$ 7,445	$ 8,544

*Given

5. Direct Labor Budgets

	June	July	August
Units to be produced	815	1,085	1,300
Direct labor hours per unit (given)	× 3	× 3	× 3
Total hours needed	2,445	3,255	3,900
Cost per hour	× $8	× $8	× $8
Direct labor cost	$19,560	$26,040	$31,200

DISCUSSION QUESTIONS

1. How are strategic planning, capital budgeting, and operations budgeting different?
2. What are the advantages of budgeting?
3. How does management use the operating budget?
4. What are the typical stages in the evolution of budgeting and recordkeeping in a firm?
5. Describe the advantages of the top-down approach and the bottom-up approach to budgeting.
6. Why are budgets usually prepared for one year?
7. Why does the accuracy of the entire master budget depend on a reliable sales forecast?
8. Identify the sequence of schedules used in preparing a master budget for a manufacturing firm.
9. Describe the four sections of a cash budget.
10. How is the budgeting process for a merchandising firm different from the budgeting process for a manufacturing firm?
11. How is the budgeting process for a service firm similar to the budgeting process for a manufacturing firm? What are any differences?
12. How does a cash budget differ from a pro-forma income statement?
13. How are flexible budgets useful in controlling costs?

DISCUSSION CASES

CASE 13-1

WEST MOUNTAIN CANNING COMPANY

West Mountain Canning Company produces several food items, including certain tomato-based products. For about nine months during the year, the company is able to purchase tomatoes from various parts of the country. The tomatoes are then processed and canned for sale in grocery stores.

The processing department employs three highly skilled workers, who are paid an average of $15 per hour. Between January and March, tomatoes are not available, and the processing and canning departments are shut down. Rather than lay off these three specialists, who have excellent alternative job opportunities, the company transfers them to the shipping department, at the same $15 pay rate. The shipping department manager is not happy, however, because his five regular employees are paid only $9 per hour. This unhappiness became particularly acute when he was told he was $9,000 over budget for wages during the January-to-March quarter (budget was $36,000; actual was $45,000). Note that the actual amount includes 1,500 hours (3 employees × 500 hours) at $15 per hour and that 2,000 hours by each employee are worked in a year.

The shipping department manager felt that he was being unduly penalized for two reasons: (1) $15 is too much to pay even a good shipping clerk, and (2) the three skilled workers do not work as hard as his regular employees because they know they are needed for tomato processing and will not be fired. He has suggested to his boss, therefore, that the wages in excess of the $9 he normally pays should be assigned elsewhere, or he should be allowed to hire his own temporary employees during this busy period.

Answer the following questions.

1. Does the shipping department manager have a legitimate complaint? Explain.
2. Explain how management arrived at the budgeted figure for shipping wages.
3. How might the quarterly figures be reported to satisfy the shipping department manager?
4. How would you recommend that the problem be solved?

CASE 13-2

TIP TOP COMPANY

Tip Top Company recently hired a new hot-shot CEO. Traditionally, the budgeting process at Tip Top has been pretty relaxed, with the Executive Vice-President of Sales providing "best-guess" sales projections and the controller providing "ball-park" cost estimates. Although the budget has been due each year 30 days prior to the new fiscal year, it generally is not finalized until two or three months into the new fiscal year. One of the first actions of the new CEO is to institute a formalized top-down budgeting process, complete with fairly sophisticated sales projections and cost data based on benchmark statistics from industry competitors.

Discuss the issues involved in the new budgeting process for Tip Top Company.

EXERCISES

EXERCISE 13-1
Personal Budgeting

Jennifer Swartz works as an interior decorator for Modern Fashion Corporation. Her annual salary is $36,500. Of that amount, 20 percent is withheld for federal income taxes, 7.15 percent for state taxes, 7.5 percent for FICA taxes, and 2 percent as a contribution to the United Way. Another 5 percent is deposited directly into a company credit union for savings. Jennifer has four monthly payments: $225 for her car, $80 for furniture, $410 for rent, and $100 to repay college loans. Jennifer's other monthly expenses will be approximately:

Food expense	$250
Clothing expense	100
Entertainment expense	125
Utilities expense	80
Insurance expense	30
Gas and maintenance expenses on car	180
Miscellaneous expenses	200
Total	$965

Prepare both a monthly budget and an annual budget for Jennifer that identifies gross salary, net take-home pay, net disposable income, and net surplus or deficit.

EXERCISE 13-2
Personal Budgeting

Trent Jones, a recent college graduate, has been hired by Midwest Corporation at a salary of $36,000 per year. In anticipation of his salary, Trent purchased a $14,000 automobile and will pay for it at a rate of $350 per month, including interest, for four years. He also rented a townhouse for $475 a month and bought some furniture on account for $230 a month. In addition, Trent figures that his other monthly expenses will be:

Food expense	$200
Clothing expense	100
Entertainment expense	175
Insurance expense	100
Gas and other car expenses	170
Utilities expense	100

1. On the assumption that Trent also pays income and FICA taxes of 20 and 7.50 percent, respectively, prepare his monthly budget.
2. Trent plans to get married soon and have a family, so he intends to save enough money for a down payment on a house. If a $15,000 down payment is needed, how long will it take him to save the needed amount? (Ignore interest on savings, and assume that Trent does not have any savings at the present time.)

EXERCISE 13-3
Production Budgeting

Daytona Electric makes and sells two kinds of portable radios—an AM-FM radio with CD player and an AM-FM radio. The sales forecasts for these radios for the next four quarters are as follows:

	AM-FM with CD Player	AM-FM Radio
1st quarter	170	130
2nd quarter	178	139
3rd quarter	166	127
4th quarter	190	145
Totals	704	541

At December 31, Daytona has 140 AM-FM radios with CD players and 120 AM-FM radios in stock. Experience has shown that Daytona must maintain an inventory equal to two-thirds of the next quarter's sales.

How many radios of each type must be produced during each of the first three quarters to meet sales and inventory demands?

EXERCISE 13-4
Production Budgeting

James Seigel is the CEO of Seigel Monitor Company, a manufacturer of computer monitors. Seigel manufactures three types of computer monitors: SVGA, VGA, and EGA. The sales projections (in units) for 2000 and the first quarter of 2001 are:

	SVGA	VGA	EGA
1st quarter, 2000	3,000	5,000	2,000
2nd quarter, 2000	2,500	4,750	2,150
3rd quarter, 2000	2,850	4,900	1,800
4th quarter, 2000	3,200	4,876	2,150
1st quarter, 2001	2,900	5,100	2,200

Beginning inventory for SVGA, VGA, and EGA are 1,350, 1,500, and 1,275, respectively. Seigel requires that 1/2 of the next quarters' sales are maintained in inventory.

How many monitors must be manufactured for each quarter of 2000 to meet sales and inventory demand?

EXERCISE 13-5
Direct Materials Budgeting

Shaver Bicycle Shop assembles and sells tricycles and bicycles. The frames are purchased from one supplier and the wheels from another. The following materials are required:

Bicycles	Tricycles
One 22-inch frame, $35	One 12-inch frame, $15
Two 22-inch wheels, $10 each	Two 4-inch wheels, $10 each
	One 12-inch wheel, $7.50

Management anticipates that 150 bicycles and 160 tricycles will be assembled during the first quarter of 2000. On December 31, 1999, the following assembly parts are on hand:

22-inch frames	12
22-inch wheels	20
12-inch frames	8
4-inch wheels	24
12-inch wheels	10

Management also decides that, beginning in January, the inventory of parts on hand at the end of each month should be sufficient to make 10 bicycles and 10 tricycles.

Prepare a direct materials usage and purchases budget for the first quarter of 2000.

EXERCISE 13-6
Direct Materials Budgeting

Shanahan Corporation produces three types of videocassettes: VHS, S-VHS, and 8 millimeter. Shanahan purchases tape for the videocassettes from a firm in Mexico and purchases the cases from another supplier in Brazil. The following materials are required for production.

	VHS	S-VHS	8 MM
Tape	$1.75	$2.30	$3.05
Cases	2.50	2.50	2.00

Beginning inventory for Shanahan Corporation is 5,000, 7,000, and 3,500 tapes for VHS, S-VHS, and 8 MM, respectively. Management wants to have 5,000 VHS and 8 MM tapes and 2,500 S-VHS tapes in ending inventory. Projected sales for the first half of 2000 are 40,000 VHS tapes, 14,000 S-VHS tapes, and 21,000 8 MM tapes.

Prepare a direct materials budget for the first half of 2000.

EXERCISE 13-7
Direct Labor Budgeting

Super Good Chocolate Company makes and sells two kinds of candy: chocolate peanut bars and caramel bars. The production budget for the next three months for each of the bars is as follows:

	Boxes of Chocolate Peanut Bars	Boxes of Caramel Bars
January	640	700
February	870	450
March	920	630

From experience, Super Good's management knows that it takes approximately 20 minutes to make a box of chocolate peanut bars and 30 minutes to make a box of caramel bars. Super Good pays its direct labor employees $8 per hour.

Prepare a direct labor budget for each of the two products in both hours and costs for January, February, and March.

EXERCISE 13-8
Direct Labor Budgeting

Sanford Shoe Company makes three shoe styles: loafers, work boots, and tennis shoes. The production budget for the next three months for each type of shoe is:

	Loafers	Work Boots	Tennis Shoes
January	2,900	5,400	3,160
February	3,100	6,000	5,400
March	2,750	6,600	4,300

From experience, Sanford's management knows that it takes 15 minutes of direct labor to make a pair of loafers, 20 minutes to make a pair of work boots, and 12 minutes to make a pair of tennis shoes. At Sanford, direct labor employees are paid $5 per hour.

Prepare a direct labor budget in both hours and costs for each of the three months.

EXERCISE 13-9
Computation of Unit Costs

High Lift Garage Door Company makes two types of garage doors: aluminum and wood. During the past several years, management has kept accurate records of costs and resource requirements and has determined that the following is needed to make the garage doors:

Wood Door	Production Requirements	Unit Cost
Wood	200 board feet	$1.70
Paint	2 gallons	7.50
Direct labor	6 hours	9.00
Manufacturing overhead	6 hours	5.50
Aluminum Door		
Aluminum	40 pounds	$3.50
Paint	1½ gallons	7.50
Direct labor	12 hours	9.00
Manufacturing overhead	12 hours	5.50

Compute the total unit costs of both the wood and aluminum garage doors.

EXERCISE 13-10
Cash Budgeting—Hospital

The management of West Valley Memorial Hospital needs to prepare a cash budget for July 2000. The following information is available:

a. The cash balance on July 1, 2000, is $236,000.
b. Actual services performed during May and June and projected services for July are:

	May	June	July
Cash services (bills paid by individuals as they leave the hospital)	$110,000	$ 90,000	$120,000
Credit services (bills paid by insurance companies and Medicare)	900,000	1,000,000	875,000

Credit sales are collected over a 2-month period, with 60 percent collected during the month the service is performed and 40 percent in the following month.
c. Hospital personnel plan to purchase $80,000 of supplies during July on account. Accounts payable are usually paid one-half in the month of purchase and one-half in the following month. The Accounts Payable balance on July 1, 2000, is $35,000.
d. Salaries and wages paid during July will be approximately $600,000. (Ignore income and other tax withholdings.)
e. Depreciation on the hospital and equipment for July will be $100,000.
f. A short-term bank loan of $80,000 (including interest) will be repaid in July.
g. All other cash expenses for July will total $56,000.

Prepare the hospital's July cash budget.

EXERCISE 13-11
Cash Budgeting

Medical Supplies, Inc., purchases first-aid items from large wholesalers. Medical Supplies then assembles and sells first-aid kits to businesses and contracts to maintain the first-aid kits. You have been asked to prepare a cash budget for January. The following information is provided:

a. Cash in bank on January 1 is $33,000.
b. Actual sales for October, November, December, and projected sales for January are as follows:

	October	November	December	January
Cash	12,000	11,500	8,200	12,500
Credit.	31,000	29,400	32,000	28,000

Payments on credit sales are received 50 percent in month of sale, 31 percent in the month following sale, and 15 percent and 4 percent in the second and third months, respectively, following the sale.
c. Total administrative and selling expenses (all cash) are $25,000.
d. Purchases are always paid 30 days after delivery. Purchases for October, November, and December were $28,000, $39,000, and $29,500, respectively.
e. Cash dividends of $22,000 are paid.
f. Any cash excess is used to purchase 30-day government securities, and any cash deficiency is compensated by short-term borrowing.
g. Management desires a minimum balance of $9,000 in the bank.

Prepare a cash budget for the month of January.

EXERCISE 13-12
Cash Budgeting (Merchandising Company)

Whitlock, Inc., buys hardware parts from various manufacturers and sells them to retail stores. Management is presently trying to prepare a cash budget for August and has the following information available:

a. The cash balance on August 1 is $25,000.
b. Actual sales for June and July and projected sales for August are as follows:

	June	July	August
Cash sales	$ 30,000	$ 45,000	$ 50,000
Credit sales	100,000	120,000	130,000

Credit sales are collected 63 percent during the month of sale, 26 percent during the month following the sale, and 11 percent during the second month following the sale.

c. Whitlock's actual purchases for June and July and its projected purchases for August are as follows:

	June	July	August
Cash purchases	$10,000	$20,000	$25,000
Credit purchases	40,000	50,000	60,000

All accounts payable are paid in the month following the purchase.

d. Total administrative and selling expenses (including $14,000 depreciation) for August are expected to be $105,000.

e. Whitlock expects to pay a $26,000 dividend to stockholders and to purchase, for cash, a $25,000 piece of land during August.

f. Cash on hand should never drop below $25,000.

1. Prepare Whitlock's August cash budget, assuming that the company borrows any amounts needed to meet its minimum desired balance.
2. **Interpretive Question:** What types of expenses other than depreciation would be excluded from a cash budget?

EXERCISE 13-13
Budgeting for a Service Company

Dr. Dawn Gifford is a new dentist specializing in treating children under the age of 18. Dr. Gifford has two primary sources of revenues: (1) fees from regular dental work (check-ups, cleanings, fillings, etc.), and (2) fees from specialized dental reconstructive surgery. Last year, Gifford earned an average of $75 per patient visit from regular customers and $800 per surgery. The following operating expenses were incurred last year in running the office:

Variable operating expenses:	
Dental supplies (per patient)	$ 10
Hospital surgery room rental (per surgery)	200
Annual fixed operating expenses:	
Office manager's salary	$18,000
Dental hygienist's salary	26,000
Utilities	3,600
Rental of office space	12,000
Depreciation expense on office equipment*	20,000
Liability insurance	48,000
Other expenses	9,600

*Total equipment cost, $200,000; depreciated over 10 years on a straight-line basis.

Last year Dr. Gifford treated an average of 200 patients per month and performed an average of 8 surgeries per month. She expects to increase the number of patients serviced by 10 percent this coming year and increase the number of surgeries by two per month. She also expects the average patient fee to be $80 and the average surgical fee to be $850. Gifford expects the variable expenses to remain constant this year, but is expecting to raise the manager's salary by 5 percent and the hygienist's by 15 percent. She thinks the other expenses will stay about the same.

Based on these data (and ignoring payroll and income taxes):

1. What was the operating profit (loss) for last year?
2. Prepare a revenue budget, operating expense budget, and cash budget for this coming year.

EXERCISE 13-14
Pro-Forma Income Statement

Gold Manufacturing Inc. is a manufacturer of electric pencil sharpeners. The following is information regarding Gold Manufacturing for the fiscal year-end, May 31, 2000:

Beginning finished goods inventory	$ 55,000
Ending finished goods inventory	42,000
Interest expense	28,000
Selling and administrative expenses	72,000
Sales revenue	425,000
Direct materials used	52,000
Direct labor	63,000
Manufacturing overhead	32,000

Assume a tax rate of 33 percent. Prepare a pro-forma income statement for the year ended May 31, 2000, for Gold Manufacturing Inc.

EXERCISE 13-15
Pro-Forma Income Statement

Silver Company has asked you to prepare a pro-forma income statement for the coming year. The following information is available:

Expected sales revenue	$1,240,000
Manufacturing costs:	
Variable cost of goods sold	625,000
Fixed overhead	125,000
Selling expenses:	
Variable expenses	140,000
Fixed expenses	45,000
Administrative expenses:	
Variable expenses	45,000
Fixed expenses	160,000
Other:	
Interest expense	28,000
Income tax rate	35%

Prepare a pro-forma contribution margin income statement for Silver Company.

EXERCISE 13-16
Pro-Forma Statement of Cash Flows

The accountants at Bryant Hardware Company are currently preparing the pro-forma statement of cash flows for August. In getting ready to prepare the statement, they have the following information available:

Dividends to be paid in August	$ 7,500
Bonds to be issued in August	44,000
Equipment to be sold in August	27,000
Repayment of short-term loans in August	24,000
Depreciation expense during August	6,000
Expected August net income	15,000

(continued)

Expected changes in current assets and liabilities during August:	
Accounts receivable increase	$3,500
Accounts payable decrease	2,750
Increase in inventory	4,200
Decrease in income taxes payable	8,400

Prepare Bryant's pro-forma statement of cash flows.

EXERCISE 13-17
Pro-Forma Income Statement and Balance Sheet (Service Industry)

Horrock's Inc. is a small engineering corporation that surveys land for development. The company has grown rapidly over the past few years, and management has to decide whether new engineers should be hired and new offices opened. To assess future growth, the company's accountant has gathered budgeted information for the coming year, 2000.

Ending common stock balance	$ 48,000
Beginning retained earnings balance	34,000
Ending accounts payable balance	6,000
Ending equipment balance	159,000
Ending accumulated depreciation balance	24,000
Ending accounts receivable balance	19,500
Ending cash balance	18,000
Interest expense	3,000
Salary expense	105,000
Other expenses (including depreciation)	37,500
Service revenue	300,000
Income tax rate	33%

Income taxes due on the coming year's net income will be paid during 2001. Dividends of $70,000 are to be declared and paid during 2000.

1. Prepare a pro-forma income statement and balance sheet for 2000 from which the company president can make expansion decisions.
2. **Interpretive Question:** On the basis of this information, is the company very profitable? How should this level of profits affect its expansion plans?

EXERCISE 13-18
Static Versus Flexible Budgeting—Performance Reports (Service Firm)

Flannery Muffler Shop has budgeted to repair 10,000 mufflers during 2000. Each repair job takes 1½ hours, and employees are paid $12 per hour. During 2000, Flannery actually repaired 9,425 mufflers, and the salary expense amounted to $179,000.

1. Assuming a static budget, use the information to prepare a performance report for Flannery Muffler Shop for 2000.
2. Assuming a flexible budget, use the information to prepare a performance report for Flannery Muffler Shop for 2000.
3. **Interpretive Question:** The manager of the muffler shop believes he deserves a bonus because the actual salary expense ($179,000) was less than budgeted. Do you agree? Explain.

EXERCISE 13-19
Flexible Budgets (Service Firm)

Outdoors Unlimited operates a fishing lodge in northern Canada. The following cost information has been developed by the company's accountant:

Fixed costs:	
Salaries	$68,000
Mortgage payments	24,000
Taxes	4,000
Other	3,000
Variable costs (per guest):	
Fishing tackle	$20
Food	80
Other	16

1. In planning for its 2000 summer season, Outdoors Unlimited does not know exactly how many guests to expect and, hence, how much to charge per guest. Prepare a flexible budget showing expected total costs at 200, 300, 400, and 500 guests.
2. Assume that Outdoors Unlimited conservatively estimates 300 guests for the year. If it wants to earn profits of $100,000 for the 300 guests, how much should it charge per guest?

PROBLEMS

PROBLEM 13-1
Personal Budgeting

Ben Fleming has just received a job offer of $35,000 salary per year plus overtime pay, which will amount to 10% of his salary. The following is Ben's estimates of his living costs.

Federal, state, and FICA taxes amount to	35% of income
Rent	$550/month
Utilities	$90/month
Car payment	$210/month
Gas and maintenance—automobile	$130/month
Insurance	$75/month
Food	$240/month
Entertainment	$170/month
IRA	$1,500/year
Other savings	4% of net take-home pay
Clothing	$80/month

Required:

1. Prepare a budget for the year. Assume Ben starts his job on January 1.
2. Is Ben's offer sufficient to meet his projected expenses?
3. It has always been a dream of Ben's to go on a big-game hunt in Africa. The cost of the hunt will be $5,000. How long will it take Ben to save for the trip?

PROBLEM 13-2
Personal Budgeting

Carol Baum is an advertising specialist for Success Advertising, Inc. Her annual salary is $37,500, of which 20 percent is withheld for federal income taxes, 7 percent for state income taxes, 7.50 percent for FICA taxes, and 5 percent for a tax-sheltered annuity. She estimates that her monthly expenses are approximately as follows:

Rent	$ 475
Food	240
Automobile payment	250
Automobile gasoline and maintenance	120
Utilities	70
Clothing	100
Entertainment	150
Miscellaneous	130
Total monthly expenses	$1,535

Required:

1. Prepare Carol's monthly budget, assuming that the car payments will continue for about three years.
2. Assume that Carol would like to accumulate savings of $12,000 in order to take an extended leave from her job. This will allow her to travel and take courses as a way of generating some fresh ideas she can use in creating new approaches to advertising. How long will it take her to save the needed amount? (Ignore interest earnings, and assume that she has no savings at the present time.)
3. **Interpretive Question:** If Carol asked you for advice on how she might reduce her expenses, what would you suggest?

PROBLEM 13-3
Production Budgeting

Rockville Cabinet Company makes and sells two products: 2-drawer and 4-drawer cabinets. The sales forecasts for these cabinets for the next four quarters are as follows:

	2-Drawer Cabinets	4-Drawer Cabinets
1st quarter	30	30
2nd quarter	50	60
3rd quarter	90	76
4th quarter	96	48
Total	266	214

On January 1, Rockville has a stock of 40 completed 2-drawer cabinets and 30 4-drawer cabinets. Experience indicates that Rockville must maintain an inventory equal to one-half of the next quarter's sales.

Required:

1. How many 2-drawer and 4-drawer cabinets must be produced during each of the first three quarters to meet sales and inventory demands?
2. **Interpretive Question:** Assume Rockville is a wholesale merchandising company instead of a manufacturing company. How would the budget information provided in (1) change?

PROBLEM 13-4
Production and Direct Materials Budget

Chandler Manufacturing Company makes two products: widgets and gidgets. The following information is available on May 1:

a. Direct materials needed to make a widget: six units of X, three units of Y. Direct materials needed to make a gidget: two units of X, six units of Y.
b. Number of units available at beginning of May:

Direct material X	72 units
Direct material Y	43 units
Finished widgets	12
Finished gidgets	15

c. Expected sales during May:

Widgets	100
Gidgets	95

d. Desired levels of ending inventory:

Direct material X	70 units
Direct material Y	35 units
Widgets	11
Gidgets	13

e. Cost of direct materials:

Direct material X	$3 per unit
Direct material Y	$2 per unit

Required:

Prepare a production budget and a direct materials usage and purchases budget for Chandler Company for the month of May.

PROBLEM 13-5
Computation of Unit Costs

Jersey Candy Company makes and sells two kinds of candy bars: chocolate almond and coconut. During the past several years, the company has kept accurate records of costs and resource requirements and has determined that the following are needed to make the candy bars:

One Box of 24 Chocolate Almond Bars	Cost
Chocolate (1½ pounds)	$3.00/pound
Almonds (1 pound)	$5.00/pound
Sugar (2 pounds)	$0.50/pound
Direct labor (20 minutes)	$9.00/hour
Manufacturing overhead (20 minutes)	$7.00/direct labor hour

One Box of 24 Coconut Bars	Cost
Chocolate (1 pound)	$3.00/pound
Coconut (1¼ pounds)	$2.00/pound
Sugar (1¾ pounds)	$0.50/pound
Direct labor (30 minutes)	$9.00/hour
Manufacturing overhead (30 minutes)	$7.00/direct labor hour

Required:

1. Compute the unit cost of making a box of each type of candy bar.
2. If management wants to mark up each box of candy 30 percent to cover other costs and earn a profit, how much should be charged for a box of each type of candy bar?

PROBLEM 13-6

Unifying Concepts: Production and Direct Materials Budgets and Cost of Goods Sold Computations

San Antonio Furniture Company makes two products: bookshelves and rocking chairs. The following information is available for September:

a. Production requirements:

	Bookshelves	Rocking Chairs
Materials needed:		
Wood	100 board feet at $0.90/ft	90 board feet at $0.90/ft
Stain	2 gallons at $9/gallon	3 gallons at $9/gallon
Bolts, nuts, etc.	1 dozen at $1.50/dozen	1½ dozen at $1.50/dozen
Direct labor	12 hours at $8.50/hour	10 hours at $8.50/hour
Variable manufacturing overhead	12 hours at $4/ direct labor hour	10 hours at $4/ direct labor hour
Fixed manufacturing overhead	$16 per unit	$15 per unit

b. Levels of inventories:

	Actual Beginning Inventory	Desired Ending Inventory
Wood	1,100 board feet	1,000 board feet
Stain	11 gallons	12 gallons
Bolts, nuts, etc.	15 dozen	9 dozen
Finished bookshelves	3	5
Finished rocking chairs	6	7

c. Total actual resources used in production during September:

Direct materials	$4,259
Direct labor	3,850
Variable manufacturing overhead	1,500
Fixed manufacturing overhead	700

Required:

1. Prepare the production budget, assuming that the company expects to sell 40 bookshelves and 50 rocking chairs in September.
2. Based on the production budget and the desired ending inventory level, prepare the direct materials usage and purchases budget for September.
3. If the company actually sold the number of bookshelves and rocking chairs projected, how much would the cost of goods sold be for September?

PROBLEM 13-7

Unifying Concepts: Sales, Cash Collections, Production, Direct Materials, and Direct Labor Budgets

The following information is available for Raleigh Company:

Expected sales volume:	
April	1,600 units
May	1,500 units
June	1,750 units
Selling price per unit	$12
Accounts receivable balance, April 1	$6,000
Desired finished goods inventory, June 30	200 units
Beginning finished goods inventory, April 1	210 units
Direct materials needed per unit	5 pounds
Desired direct materials inventory, June 30	550 pounds
Beginning direct materials inventory, April 1	420 pounds
Total direct labor time per finished product	2 hours
Direct materials cost per pound	$0.50
Direct labor cost per hour	$8

Additional information:

a. Seventy percent of a month's sales is collected by month-end; the remaining 30 percent is collected in the following month.
b. The desired finished goods inventory every month is 20 percent of the next month's sales.
c. The desired direct materials inventory every month is 10 percent of the next month's production needs.

Required:

1. Prepare sales budgets for April, May, and June (in dollars).
2. Prepare cash collection budgets for April, May, and June (in dollars). Assume that all sales are on credit.
3. Prepare production budgets for April, May, and June (in units).
4. Prepare direct materials usage and purchases budgets for April, May, and June (in dollars).
5. Prepare direct labor budgets for April, May, and June (in dollars).

PROBLEM 13-8

Unifying Concepts: Sales, Cash Collections, and Purchases Budgets

The following information is available for Durham Company, a merchandising retail company:

Expected sales volume:	
April	3,200 units
May	3,000 units
June	3,500 units
Selling price per unit	$25
Accounts receivable balance, April 1	$12,000
Desired ending inventory, June 30	650 units
Beginning inventory, April 1	420 units

Additional information:

a. Seventy percent of a month's sales is collected by month-end; the remaining 30 percent is collected in the following month.
b. The desired inventory every month is 20 percent of the next month's sales.

Required:

1. Prepare sales budgets for April, May, and June (in dollars).
2. Prepare cash collection budgets for April, May, and June (in dollars). Assume that all sales are on credit.
3. Prepare purchases budgets for April, May, and June (in units).

PROBLEM 13-9
Cash Budgeting (Manufacturing Company)

Hare Manufacturing Company makes wax for automobiles. As part of overall planning, a cash budget is prepared quarterly each year. You have been asked to assist in preparing the cash budget for the fourth quarter of the company's fiscal year. The following information is available:

a. Sales:

Third quarter (actual)	$180,000
Fourth quarter (expected)	175,000

All sales are made on account, with 70 percent collected in the quarter in which the sales are made and 30 percent collected during the following quarter.

b. Materials purchases are scheduled as follows:

Third quarter (actual)	$90,000
Fourth quarter (expected)	80,000

Materials are purchased on account and paid for at the rate of 80 percent in the quarter of purchase and 20 percent in the following quarter.

c. Direct labor and manufacturing overhead costs (including $6,000 of depreciation) are expected to be $45,000 and $21,000, respectively, during the fourth quarter.
d. Selling and administrative expenses are expected to total $27,000 during the fourth quarter, including $2,000 of depreciation.
e. Plans have been made to purchase, for cash, $15,000 of equipment during the fourth quarter.
f. The cash balance at the beginning of the quarter is $16,000. The company can borrow money in $1,000 multiples at 12 percent interest from a local bank. The bank assesses interest for a full quarter, both for the quarter in which the money is borrowed and for the quarter in which it is repaid. All interest is paid at the time of note repayment. Hare ran short of cash during the third quarter and had to borrow $8,000 from the bank. Hare wishes to maintain a minimum cash balance of $16,000.

Required:

Prepare a schedule showing the cash budget and financing needs of Hare Manufacturing Company for the fourth quarter.

PROBLEM 13-10
Cash Budgeting (Merchandising Company)

Keven Johnson, owner of Meyers Department Store, is negotiating a $50,000, 15 percent, 4-month loan from the Lee County National Bank, effective October 1, 2000. The bank loan officer has requested that Meyers prepare a cash budget for each of the next four months as evidence of its ability to repay the loan. The following information is available as of September 30, 2000:

Cash on hand	$ 4,500
Accounts receivable.	48,750
Inventory.	32,000
Accounts payable	72,250

a. The accounts payable are for September merchandise purchases and operating expenses and will all be paid in October. Sales forecasts for the next few months are October, $110,000; November, $150,000; December, $200,000; January, $100,000; February, $70,000.

b. Collections on sales are usually made at the rate of 20 percent during the month of the sale, 60 percent during the month following the sale, and 16 percent during the second month after the sale. Four percent of accounts receivable are written off as uncollectible. Of the $48,750 of accounts receivable at September 30, $32,500 will be collected in October, and $16,250 will be collected in November. Cost of goods sold is 60 percent of sales, with all purchases paid for in the month following purchase. Ending inventory should always equal the cost of the goods that will be sold during the next month. Operating expenses are $12,000 a month plus 5 percent of sales, all paid in the month following their incurrence.

Required: Prepare a cash budget showing receipts and disbursements for October, November, December, and January. Also prepare supporting schedules for cash collections, purchases, and operating expenses. Assume that the loan plus interest will be paid on January 31.

PROBLEM 13-11
Cash Budgeting

Athlete World is a sporting goods store. The data for use in preparing its forecast of cash needs for June are:

a. Current assets (May 31):

Cash	$22,000
Inventory	17,500
Accounts receivable	29,400
Property, plant, and equipment	90,000
Accounts payable (merchandise purchases only)	13,100
Recent and estimated future sales:	
May	49,000
June	57,000
July	52,000

b. Sales are made 60 percent on credit and 40 percent for cash. All credit sales are collected in the month following the sale.

c. Athlete World's June expenses are estimated to be:

Salaries and wages expense	20% of sales
Rent expense	4% of sales
All other cash expenses	6% of sales
Depreciation expense	$600
Gross margin	40% of sales

d. Athlete World buys all its inventory from companies on the West Coast and wants to maintain an inventory level equal to one-half the next month's sales. Payments for merchandise are made 50 percent during the month of purchase and 50 percent in the next month.

e. Other cash expenditures planned for June are:
1. The purchase of $8,000 of furniture.
2. The payment of $5,000 of dividends.

f. Athlete World desires to maintain a minimum cash balance of $10,000. The store has an arrangement with a local bank whereby it can borrow money in multiples of $1,000. Interest is charged on all loans at an annual rate of 10 percent and is assessed for a full quarter both in the quarter in which the money is borrowed and in the quarter in which the money is repaid. Interest is paid when the loan is repaid.

Required: Prepare Athlete World's cash budget for June.

PROBLEM 13-12
Budgeting for a Service Company

Riverside Country Club has approximately 500 members. Each member has paid a $10,000 initiation fee and pays $100 a month in dues to remain an active member of the club. The club offers golf, tennis, and food and beverage services. The club is essentially run on a cash basis. Operating data for 1999 are shown below.

Riverside Country Club
Operating Data
For the Year 1999

Revenues:		
Dues[1]	$742,000	
Guest fees[2]	6,500	
Golf revenues	455,000	
Tennis revenues	145,000	
Food and beverage	325,000	
Miscellaneous	2,500	$1,676,000
Expenses:		
Golf course	$395,000	
Tennis courts	170,000	
Food and bar	272,000	
Administration and maintenance[3]	515,000	
Interest on debt[4]	50,000	
Miscellaneous	27,000	(1,429,000)
Net operating profit		$ 247,000

[1]Dues (410 × $1,200 = $492,000; 25 new members × $10,000 = $250,000)
[2]Guest fees (130 × $50 = $6,500)
[3]Maintenance includes $125,000 depreciation on facilities
[4]Interest ($500,000 × 0.10 × 1 year)

Assume the following additional facts for the year 2000:

a. There are 425 members paying dues, as well as 10 additional new members.
b. Guest fees are 110 percent of 1999.
c. Golf revenues are 125 percent of 1999.
d. Tennis revenues are 90 percent of 1999 (due to courts being closed for one month).
e. Food and beverage revenues are the same as 1999.
f. Operating expenses (golf, tennis, and food and beverage) are up five percent.
g. Administration and maintenance will increase $40,000 due to expected repairs.
h. Principal payment of $50,000 during 2000 will reduce interest expense by 10 percent for 2000.
i. Miscellaneous revenues will stay the same; miscellaneous expenses are expected to be $25,000.

Required:

1. Prepare an annual budget for Riverside for the year 2000.
2. What is the expected cash flow for Riverside for the year 2000?
3. **Interpretive Question:** Is Riverside in better shape financially in 2000 as compared to 1999? What areas of concern do you see?

PROBLEM 13-13
Unifying Concepts: The Pro-Forma Income Statement, Balance Sheet, and Statement of Cash Flows

Alex Corporation makes trailers for trucks. During the past few days, the company's accountants have been preparing the master budget for 2000. To date, they have gathered the following projected data:

For the Year Ended December 31, 2000:	
Sales revenue	$10,127,200
Variable selling expenses	448,000
Variable administrative expenses	672,000
Interest expense	67,200
Cost of goods sold (variable costs only)	5,600,000
Fixed manufacturing expenses	784,000
Fixed administrative expenses	492,000
Fixed selling expenses	336,000

(continued)

Account Balances at December 31, 2000:

Cash	$448,000
Accounts receivable	168,000
Land	417,200
Buildings	504,000
Equipment	358,400
Accumulated depreciation—equipment	89,600
Accumulated depreciation—buildings	80,000
Direct materials inventory	106,400
Finished goods inventory	117,600
Accounts payable	45,240
Common stock	700,000
Retained earnings	?
Paid-in capital in excess of par	40,000
Income taxes payable	200,000

Other Information:

Dividends to be declared and paid during 2000	$600,000
Income tax rate	33%

In addition, last year's balance sheet was as follows:

Alex Corporation
Balance Sheet
December 31, 1999

Assets		
Cash		$ 189,600
Accounts receivable		45,400
Direct materials inventory		90,000
Finished goods inventory		123,200
Land		336,000
Buildings	$448,000	
Less accumulated depreciation	(50,000)	398,000
Equipment	$324,800	
Less accumulated depreciation	(60,000)	264,800
Total assets		$1,447,000
Liabilities and Stockholders' Equity		
Liabilities:		
Accounts payable	$ 75,000	
Income taxes payable	225,000	
Total liabilities		$ 300,000
Stockholders' Equity:		
Common stock	$700,000	
Paid-in capital in excess of par, common stock	40,000	
Retained earnings	407,000	
Total stockholders' equity		1,147,000
Total liabilities and stockholders' equity		$1,447,000

Required:

1. Prepare a pro-forma income statement for 2000 (contribution margin approach).
2. Prepare a pro-forma balance sheet as of December 31, 2000.
3. Prepare a pro-forma statement of cash flows for 2000.

PROBLEM 13-14
Pro-Forma Income Statement and Balance Sheet

Style Right Company makes hair dryers. During the past few days, its accountants have been preparing the master budget for the coming year, 2000. To date, they have gathered the following projected data:

Sales revenue (at $20 per unit)	$281,750
Variable selling expenses	17,250
Variable administrative expenses	40,250
Interest expense (not included in selling and administrative expenses)	1,725
Cost of goods sold (includes only variable costs)	103,500
Ending cash balance	30,475
Ending accounts receivable balance	47,150
Ending land balance	24,150
Ending buildings balance	71,300
Ending equipment balance	24,150
Ending accumulated depreciation—buildings balance	47,150
Ending accumulated depreciation—equipment balance	9,200
Ending direct materials inventory balance	16,100
Ending finished goods inventory balance	25,300
Ending accounts payable balance	6,900
Ending common stock balance	32,200
Retained earnings balance, January 1	64,050
Balance in paid-in capital in excess of par account	23,000
Fixed selling expenses	23,000
Fixed administrative expenses	28,750
Fixed manufacturing overhead	11,150
Income tax rate	35%

Required:

1. Prepare a pro-forma income statement (contribution margin approach) and balance sheet for the coming year. Any income taxes owed on the coming year's net income will be paid the following year.
2. By approximately how much would Style Right's profits increase if another 3,000 units were produced and sold for $20 each?

PROBLEM 13-15
Pro-Forma Statement of Cash Flows

The accountants at Toledo Department Store are preparing the pro-forma statement of cash flows for 2000. The following information is available:

Expected net income	$70,000
Dividends to be paid	22,000
Equipment to be purchased	34,000
Expected short-term borrowing	8,000
Expected long-term borrowing	24,000
Expected depreciation expense for 2000	15,000
Expected issuance of common stock	80,000
Expected purchase of a new plant	71,000
Expected changes in current assets and liabilities during 2000:	
Increase in accounts receivable	$ 900
Increase in accounts payable	1,000
Increase in inventory	1,000
Decrease in income taxes payable	1,800

Required: Prepare the pro-forma statement of cash flows for Toledo Department Store.

PROBLEM 13-16
Static Versus Flexible Budgeting (Service Firm)

Wasatch Medical Clinic has three doctors on staff. The clinic's budget for 2000 is as follows:

Wasatch Medical Clinic
Budget for the Year Ended December 31, 2000

Expected number of patient visits		26,000
Average charge per patient		× $25
Total revenues		$650,000
Budgeted costs:		
Variable costs:		
Supplies for each patient ($2 × 26,000)		$ 52,000
Fixed costs:		
Utilities	$ 2,400	
Rent	9,600	
Nurses' salaries	90,000	
Malpractice insurance	150,000	
Equipment leases	25,000	
Other	30,000	
Total fixed costs		307,000
Total budgeted costs		$359,000
Expected net income		$291,000
Number of doctors on staff		÷ 3
Expected income per doctor		$ 97,000

Required:

1. Is this a static or flexible budget?
2. Prepare a flexible budget showing expected income per doctor at 22,000, 26,000, 30,000, and 34,000 total patient visits.
3. **Interpretive Question:** Why does the expected income per doctor increase so dramatically as the number of patient visits increases?

PROBLEM 13-17
Static Versus Flexible Budgeting (Service Firm)

Peterson Management, Inc., is a small firm that sponsors time-management seminars in hotels throughout the country. It sponsors 20 two-day seminars during the year for a tuition fee of $200 per student. The following is a budget for a single seminar:

Peterson Management, Inc.
Budget Per Seminar

Expected enrollment	40
Tuition per person	×$200
Revenue per seminar	$8,000
Variable costs:	
Books and handouts ($10 per person)	$ 400
Catering ($25 per person)	1,000
Fixed costs:	
Airfare	425
Hotel rental fee	600
Advertising	1,000
Other	300
Total costs	$3,725
Expected net income	$4,275

Required:

1. Bruce Peterson, owner of the company and the speaker at the seminars, would be pleased with an income of $4,275 per seminar. With 20 seminars per year, the company's annual income would be $85,500. He is concerned, however, that every seminar may not have 40 participants. Prepare a flexible budget, showing what annual net income would be if 10, 20, 40, or 50 people enrolled in each seminar.
2. What is the break-even point per seminar in number of participants?

Analyzing Real Company Information

International Case

Ethics Case

Writing Assignment

The Debate

Internet Search

Accounting is more than just doing textbook problems. These Competency Enhancement Opportunities provide practice in critical thinking, oral and written communication, research, teamwork, and consideration of ethical issues.

ANALYZING REAL COMPANY INFORMATION

• Analyzing 13-1 (Microsoft)

Auditors are extremely reluctant to publish any projections of future financial performance for the companies they are auditing. Deloitte & Touche LLP obviously has made no such predictions in its audit of Microsoft's 1997 financial performance (the annual report in Appendix A). However, the Management's Discussion of the Income Statement results, in the section titled "Outlook: Issues and Uncertainties," provide some hints about what executives may expect to affect future revenues. Elsewhere in the management discussion are insights useful in predicting future operating expenses, interest income, and income taxes. These discussions can be extremely useful to investors who are trying to understand what Microsoft plans to do in 1998. Essentially, these investors need to put together their own pro-forma financial statements on Microsoft for use in planning, controlling, and evaluating their investment decisions in this company.

Consider the 1997 income statement below and use the information provided in Microsoft's Management Discussion of "Outlook: Issues and Uncertainties" to prepare your own pro-forma 1998 income statement for Microsoft. Be sure to read and consider each item in the management discussion relating to Microsoft's income statement in the annual report in Appendix A. You may also want to consider the 1995 and 1996 revenue and cost trends from the income statement published in this same annual report. For each line item (i.e., for each revenue and cost category), briefly defend the budget number you chose to use.

	1997
Revenue	$11,358
Operating expenses:	
Cost of revenue	$ 1,085
Research and development	1,925
Sales and marketing	2,856
General and administrative	362
Total operating expenses	$ 6,228
Operating income	$ 5,130
Interest income	443
Other expenses	(259)
Income before income taxes	$ 5,314
Provision for income taxes	1,860
Net income	$ 3,454

• Analyzing 13–2 (Participative Living, Inc.)

Participative Living, Inc. (a fictitious name) is an actual charitable organization in a medium-size community in Canada. It was organized by parents of disabled adults to provide accommodation and training for severely disabled adults in the community. With the help of the Ministry of Community and Social Services, the parents eventually organized six different homes, each with two to four residents. In addition to the six homes, Participative Living also had an employment and education program that provided training and assistance for residents seeking employment or educational opportunities. Overall, the organization had eight divisions composed of six homes, the employment and education program, and an administrative program. A supervisor who reports to the Participative Living executive team staffs each division. The executive team, in turn, reports to a volunteer board of directors composed of 12 people from the community.

Participative Living is a not-for-profit organization. Hence, while surpluses and deficits are occasionally expected, each division is expected to break even each operating period. Seven of the eight divisions are established as break-even operations, with responsibility for both revenues and expenses. The main revenue source is the Ontario government, through the Ministry of Community and Social Services, which provides all funding necessary to support each home as well as the employment and education program. All costs of Participative Living's Administrative division in excess of any donations from the community are allocated to its other seven divisions. The Ministry follows a procedure of disbursing operating funds for all social service agencies under its direction based on annual operating budgets submitted to the Ministry. Generally, the Ministry is not concerned about whether or not an individual budget item was overspent as long as the overall spending is within the approved budget. As a result, it became a common practice among agencies to transfer expenses from one budget line to another and, in the case of Participative Living, to transfer expenses from one division to another depending on which division had excess budgeted funds. As with most government organizations, the administrative process of reviewing and approving a new home for Participative Living is often quite slow at the Ministry. As long as the Ministry is holding up the establishment of a proposed new home, it provides significant interest payments to Participative Living. The Ministry was making large interest payments during the first few months of Participative Living's 1992 fiscal year (which ended on March 31, 1992) while the organization waited for government approval and funding of the sixth group home.

In November 1991, Mr. Brad Dunford, the Executive Director of Participative Living, Inc., was reviewing the financial statements for the first seven months of the 1992 fiscal year. He was puzzled about how the agency could suddenly be $50,000 over budget in salaries and benefits when just last month the statements indicated that spending was slightly under budget.

1. As you review operating results for the last seven months at Participative Living, Inc., what problems do you foresee?
2. Consider the style of management and management accounting for this not-for-profit organization, as well as its relationship with the Ministry of Community and Social Services. What aspects of the way business is conducted here do you think has led to the current situation?

Participative Living, Inc.
Operating Results
For the Seven Months Ended October 31, 1991

YTD	Admin. Costs	Admin. Budget	Employ. and Edu. Costs	Employ. and Edu. Budget	Group Homes Costs	Group Homes Budget	Total Actual	Total Budget*	% of Budget
Revenues:									
Ministry**	$ —	$ —	$206,315	$297,675	$521,841	$476,714	$728,156	$774,389	94.0%
Interest	20,943	—	—	—	—	—	20,943	—	0%
Donations	1,567	—	—	—	—	—	1,567	—	0%
Total revenues	$ 22,510	$ —	$206,315	$297,675	$521,841	$476,714	$750,666	$774,389	96.9%
Expenses:									
Salaries	$ 59,029	$ 61,754	$141,034	$197,386	$434,014	$327,789	$634,077	$586,929	108.0%
Occupancy costs	10,392	12,264	39	2,205	61,598	68,761	72,029	83,230	86.5%
Services, supplies, and fo	4,375	7,000	3,643	14,147	16,812	35,301	24,830	56,448	44.0%
Personal needs	—	—	3,077	—	35	26,327	3,112	26,327	11.8%
New furnishing and equip	5	350	60	2,765	6,548	19,236	6,613	22,351	29.6%
Other expenses	1,176	4,669	197	7,707	15,681	7,868	17,054	20,244	84.2%
Travel and training	436	875	1,972	8,792	1,992	4,900	4,400	14,567	30.2%
Specific reimbursements	—	—	—	—	(32,119)	(35,707)	(32,119)	(35,707)	90.0%
Allocated admin. costs	(75,417)	(86,912)	56,293	64,673	19,123	22,239	(1)	—	0.0%
Total expenses	$ (4)	$ —	$206,315	$297,675	$523,684	$476,714	$729,995	$774,389	94.3%
Net surplus (deficit)	$ 22,514	$ —	$ —	$ —	$ (1,843)	$ —	$ 20,671	$ —	N/A

*Budget columns represent 7/12 s of the total annual budget (e.g., Participative Living is now seven months into its fiscal year).
**Ministry revenues are based actual payments made by the Ministry. Total payments limited to maximum of total annual budget approved.

Source: Adapted from M. Heisz Participative Living, Inc.," *Journal of Accounting Case Research* 2(3), 1995, pp. 87–91. Permission to use has been granted by Captus Press, Inc. and the Accou ing Education Resource Centre of The University of Lethbridge. [Journal Subscription: Captus Press Inc., York University Campus, 4700 Keele Street, North York, ario, M3J1P3, by calling (416) 736-5537, or by fax at (416) 736-5793, Email: info@captus.com, Internet: http://www.captus.com]

INTERNATIONAL CASE

• It's not easy being an accountant in Poland.

The late 1980s and early 1990s have been a very significant time for Eastern Europe. Several national boundaries and political ideologies, as well as the names of a few countries, have changed during this time period. Poland, like its neighbors, experienced tremendous upheaval in its political and economic climate during this time. In 1989, Poland changed to a non-Communist government and a free market economy. Since the end of World War II in 1945, Poland had been a centrally planned economy with government-enforced economic rules based on Marxism-Leninism. A Polish accountant's career life during the 1945–1989 period was not very exciting. Most university-trained accountants worked in a state-owned enterprise, earning a reasonable salary. The work was not complicated, generally entailing only basic bookkeeping. Performing the accounting work essentially required simple mathematical operations. In addition, the nature of Poland's history since the fifteenth century had generally created disdain for business and profiteering in general. These traditions, coupled with the social environment engendered by a Marxist government, resulted in a serious lack of respect (sometimes bordering on distrust) for accountants, economists, and business managers from 1945–1989.

The failure of the Communist system in 1989 was the beginning of a new career stage for most accountants in Poland. The accounting profession suddenly became prestigious. It also became very challenging. Past accounting knowledge and skills were simply inadequate for the present economic situation, particularly for accountants moving out of state-owned enterprises and into the private sector. Business terminology, performance measures, and goals were changed. Before 1989, the Communist regime promoted a view that everything a "capitalist" did was wrong and everything a Communist did was right. After the change in the political system, a lot of people began to see things in an opposite way; they expected that life in a capitalist country would be completely just and everyone would be employed with plenty of money. Obviously, life in a capitalist country is not perfect. There are problems, including injustice and unemployment. Complicating this reality, many people also carried over into the 1990s some of the prevailing pre-1989 attitudes that accountants and for-profit businesses were not trustworthy. Today Poland is progressing well. However, the accounting profession continues to have a number of challenges as transitions in attitudes and business processes are completed.

Source: Adapted from P. Stec, "Mr. Kowalski: A Man Against All Odds," *Journal of Accounting Case Research* 2(3), 1995, pp. 52–54. Permission to use has been granted by Captus Press, Inc. and the Accounting Education Resource Centre of The University of Lethbridge. [Journal Subscription: Captus Press Inc., York University Campus, 4700 Keele Street, North York, Ontario, M3J1P3, by calling (416) 736-5537, or by fax at (416) 736-5793, Email: info@captus.com, Internet: http://www.captus.com]

Assume that you have just been transferred by your U.S.-based company to an accounting or management position in the company's Poland division. Your assignment is to implement, within a large-scale manufacturing plant, a traditional budgeting system (similar to the budget systems described in this chapter). Based on your understanding of the history and attitudes in Poland, what specific challenges would you expect to encounter in this new assignment? Do you have any ideas on how to handle these challenges?

ETHICS CASE

• Skipper Enterprises

You are the management accountant for Skipper Enterprises, a manufacturer of screen doors. Recently, one of the commissioned salespersons (your close personal friend) confided in you that a problem with the budgets is hurting the company's profitability. Essentially, this is what he told you:

Salespersons are paid a straight commission of $15 for every screen door they sell. If each meets the budgeted sales of 3,000 screen doors per year, each salesperson is paid an annual bonus of $5,000. Your friend stated that it is actually quite easy to reach budgeted sales of 3,000 doors by October or early November. Because there is no financial incentive to sell additional doors once the 3,000 sales level is met and the $5,000 bonus is earned, salespersons only "line up" sales for next year during the last couple of months of each year. In other words, instead of selling additional doors during November and December, they commit customers to buy during January of next year. This way, the doors count as next year's sales, making it so the commissioned salespersons are well on the way to meeting the sales budget for next year.

You realize the current bonus plan is causing two problems. First, valuable sales are being deferred each year because there is less incentive to sell near the end of the year. Second, customers are not being served as well as they should be in that it can take as long as two months for customers to get their desired doors.

You don't know what to do with your new information.

1. Should you inform management that the sales plan is hurting company profits, or should you keep the information confidential as your friend requested?
2. If it becomes known that you had this information and didn't come forward, it could cost you your job. On the other hand, you hate to lose a good friend. What should you do?

WRITING ASSIGNMENT

• Preparing a personal budget

Most people have the ability to spend more than they make. As a student, you probably fit in that category. This writing assignment requires you to prepare a personal budget for a one-month period. Forecast your income and expenses to determine what your cash position will be at the end of the month. If you forecast a cash shortage, what actions can you take to address the problem (e.g., increase income, reduce expenses, borrow money, etc.)? If you forecast a cash surplus, what options do you have with the surplus?

THE DEBATE

• The hatchet has arrived!

Assume that your local hospital has just hired a new COO (Chief Operating Officer). Everyone in the hospital understands that the new COO was essentially hired to save the hospital. During the last five years, cost overruns have created tremendous spending deficits in the organization. The hospital is clearly headed for insolvency within three to five years if something isn't done. The new COO has a reputation as a focused manager, able to make difficult decisions. She doesn't waste any time proving her reputation in the new job. At the first meeting with the chief medical staff and administrators, the COO rolls out the new budget goals with the following statement:

> Everyone here knows that this hospital is in serious financial trouble, and it's not hard to understand why. After carefully reviewing cost reports for the last several years, it's obvious that there has been very little discipline in controlling costs. There are no improvement goals for cost savings, and no one is required to take responsibility when cost overruns occur. Looking

at next quarter's operating budget doesn't give me much hope for improvement in this mess. Well, folks, that party is over! It's time to get to work saving this hospital. We will reconvene in one week; I expect each department head to provide a new departmental operating budget that demonstrates a reduction in costs that is equal to five percent of department revenues. Thereafter, until we turn this situation around, each new quarterly budget will reflect an *additional* decrease in operating costs equal to two percent of department revenues. Any questions?

There were no questions. Everyone filed out of the meeting in shocked silence. Five percent of revenues is a big number!

Divide your group into two teams and prepare a two-minute defense of your team's assigned position.

- One team represents "Support the COO!" A difficult situation requires a tough response. Defend the COO's new budget proposal. What should be the positive results in the hospital if the COO's budget instructions are fully implemented?
- The other team represents "Out with the new budget proposal!" Overreacting to a difficult situation only worsens the problem. Criticize the COO's new budget proposal. What could be the negative results in the hospital if the COO's budget instructions are fully implemented?

INTERNET SEARCH

• Using the Internet to budget personal finances

There are a number of terrific tools on the Internet that can be very useful to you in managing your finances. For one example, go to www.financenter.com. Sometimes Web addresses change, so if this address does not work, access the Web site for this textbook (stice.swcollege.com) for an updated link. Once there, select the "Budgeting" link, then select "How much am I spending?" from the SmartCalcs™ menu. You will see here that FinanCenter provides a form on which you can enter your current income and budgeted expenditures, as well as your desired expenditures.

1. Complete the information on the input form, then hit the "Calculate" button. You should now learn whether or not your income is sufficient to handle your expenditures (actually, you probably already knew the answer to this question). Print out your budget.
2. Now go back to the input form and change the numbers in order to assess what might need to change in your future personal "operations." Put together a realistic budget. Try to create a little "extra" that can be used for investment. Note how the difference affects your long-term savings. When you're satisfied, print out your new budget.
3. Now that you have a better understanding of your cash budget, work through FinanCenter's tools to identify and answer another important personal finance and budgeting question for yourself. Go back to the SmartCalcs™ page and select an additional budgeting function to perform. When completed, list two important insights you learned about your personal budgeting process.

CHAPTER 14 NONROUTINE DECISIONS AND RELEVANT INFORMATION

SETTING THE STAGE

Hardly a day goes by without a major company announcing layoffs or the sale of some business unit. In late 1997, for example, General Motors announced that it would cut at least 42,000 U.S. jobs in the next five years as it streamlines key factories and unloads key business segments. That is 20 percent fewer workers than it had in 1997 and 45 percent fewer than in 1990. In total, General Motors has gone from 310,000 workers in 1990 to 222,000 in 1997, with plans to be at 180,000 employees in 2003. GM announced that it will sell or close all 15 of its Delphi parts plants and buy the parts from outsiders. It also announced that it will sell Hughes Tool, a major segment of the company.

Why is GM selling these units and laying off employees? These changes are all a result of a worldwide efficiency study to determine which plants to keep, modernize, or close. The efficiency study was conducted because GM's U.S. assembly plants are 43 percent less productive than industry leaders Nissan and Toyota.

Exhibit 14–1 shows GM's total global sales and income per vehicle, compared to Toyota and Ford. Not only is Toyota more profitable than GM, but GM acknowledges that Toyota is the benchmark in manufacturing and product development. A professor at MIT's Sloan School who has studied and written extensively about the automobile industry says, "I don't know of a company that better combines superior skills in all critical areas: manufacturing, engineering, and marketing, than Toyota. If they wanted to blow GM away, they could."

GM realizes that even with its efficiency moves, it is chasing a moving target. GM is convinced that to compete, it must sell some of its business units and buy parts from outsiders. While Toyota produces just 30 percent of the parts that go into its cars, GM makes 65 percent of its own parts. But, can GM be as efficient as Toyota even if it buys more parts from outsiders? Toyota works hard to make its suppliers an integral part of the company, while GM still seems to treat suppliers as independent companies. For example, Toyota's independent suppliers are an average of only 59 miles away from the assembly plants to which they make eight daily deliveries. GM's suppliers, on the other hand, are an average of 427 miles away from the plants they serve and make fewer than two daily deliveries. As a result, Toyota and its sup-

LEARNING OBJECTIVES

After studying this chapter, you should be able to:

1. *Explain the difference between routine and nonroutine decisions.*
2. *Understand the concept of differential costs and revenues, and be able to identify those costs and revenues that are relevant to making nonroutine decisions.*
3. *Identify several examples of nonroutine decisions and be able to analyze and select the best alternative for each example.*

pliers maintain inventories that are one-fourth of GM's, when measured as a percentage of sales. One automobile analyst commented, "If GM were as efficient as Toyota, it would save about $500 million annually."[1]

1. Alex Taylor III, "How Toyota Defies Gravity," *Fortune,* December 8, 1997, pp. 100–110; Micheline Maynard, "GM Plans to Unload Plants, 42,000 Jobs," *USA Today,* November 17, 1997, p. B1; and "GM Plans Sweeping Cuts in Jobs, Plants," *USA Today,* November 12, 1997, p. B1.

EXHIBIT 14-1

Global Sales and Income per Vehicle for GM, Ford, and Toyota

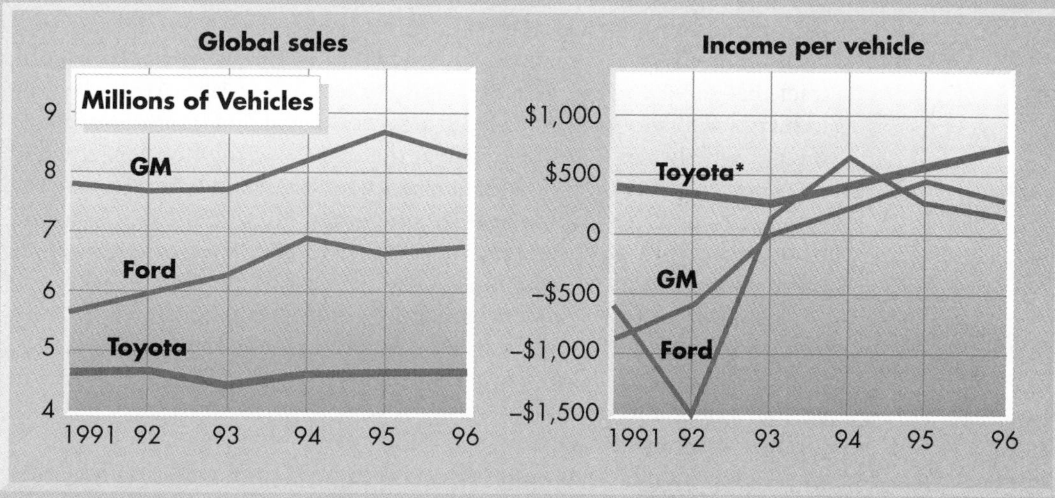

*Data from Harbour & Associates, based on total net income.

This scenario identifies some of the ways GM is working to catch up with the more efficient automobile manufacturers such as Toyota. Some of the decisions GM is making, such as employee layoffs, are routine decisions that are made every day (though generally not made in such large numbers as discussed in the opening scenario). Other decisions, such as selling its Delphi Automotive Systems and Hughes Tool companies, closing plants, and buying parts from outside suppliers, are important nonroutine decisions that are not made on a daily basis.

1 *Explain the difference between routine and nonroutine decisions.*

ROUTINE AND NONROUTINE DECISIONS

In Chapter 9, we talked about two basic types of planning; long-term and short-term. Short-term planning was then divided into short-term operating decisions and short-term nonroutine decisions. Long-term planning was divided into strategic planning and capital budgeting. Up to this point in the text, our discussions of short-term operating decisions have focused on accounting concepts and procedures that are designed to help management make decisions about routine operations of the firm. We have focused on ways to continuously improve the quality, speed, and profitability of operations. In Chapter 12, we explained the use of standards and benchmarking to identify performance problems and alert management to the potential need for corrective actions. In Chapter 13, we explained how to prepare an operating budget. Decisions that involve ongoing operations to make the process more efficient are typically made daily, weekly, or monthly and do not involve fundamental changes in operations. Most organizations, including manufacturers, merchandisers, and service firms, make these types of **routine decisions** regularly.

routine decisions
Decisions that involve the routine or daily operations of a firm; planning, controlling, and evaluating decisions that are made on a regular and repetitive basis.

nonroutine decisions Decisions made less frequently and that usually have a more significant strategic impact on operations than routine decisions.

In contrast to short-term operating decisions, short-term **nonroutine decisions** are made less frequently, yet have a more significant impact on the basic operating process than do the corrective actions related to routine decisions. Nonroutine decisions can affect the profitability, quality, or timeliness of products of an organization for several periods and so must be considered very carefully. In a manufacturing company, for example, nonroutine decisions might involve whether to accept a special order; whether to make or buy manufacturing components; whether to build or sell plants; and how to best use limited raw materials in the manufacturing process. In a merchandising company, nonroutine decisions could include how to use limited store shelves and whether to open a new store. In a service company, nonroutine decisions might involve whether to hire a particular specialist or contract that service to another firm; how to use scarce labor resources; and whether to merge with another company. In a governmental unit, nonroutine decisions might involve whether to collect garbage at the curb or at the house site; whether to hire an in-house lawyer or contract out all legal services; and whether to develop a water system or buy water from a nearby community. Nonroutine decisions that might be made in all types of businesses are whether to exit or enter a market and whether to buy or sell business segments.

Nonroutine decisions are generally considered short-term because once the decision is made, they are usually effected immediately. They are unlike capital budgeting decisions that involve the acquisition of assets, affect organizations for several years, and cannot be easily reversed. We will discuss these capital budgeting decisions in Chapter 15.

To illustrate how nonroutine decisions help companies improve their competitive position, see the Business Environment Essay on page 669. Especially note the types of actions taken by **Bumper Works** to improve product quality, cut production time, acquire new equipment, reduce inventory, and increase worker participation. All these actions involved changes in the fundamental operating process that Bumper Works had been using. The nonroutine decisions made by Bumper Works enabled the company to continue to be successful in a very competitive market.

Nonroutine Decisions Are Routine

Making nonroutine decisions involves the same sequence of decision-making steps that was discussed earlier: (1) define the problem, (2) identify the alternative solutions, (3) gather information about each alternative, and (4) choose and implement the best one. What stimulates management to begin this decision-making process? Often it is nothing more than an idea that occurs to a manager as he or she goes through the process of planning, implementing, controlling, and evaluating. In preparing a production budget, for example, management might notice that costs have increased gradually over the last few years. This may stimulate thoughts about purchasing new equipment to reduce production costs. Similarly, a discussion with a supplier might result in an opportunity to add a new product, which requires that production of another item be cut back (because of limited capacity). Further, in reading performance reports, a manager may see a way to stimulate lagging sales.

As noted many times in this book, businesses are changing faster today than ever before. The result of this rapid change is that many decisions that have traditionally been thought of as nonroutine are now made routinely. Instead of making a decision to exit or enter a market every few years, for example, these types of decisions might be made several times a year. While many types of nonroutine decisions could be covered in this chapter, we will focus on four types: (1) decisions involving special orders (either buying or selling), (2) decisions involving markets (either exiting or entering), (3) decisions involving scarce resources, and (4) decisions involving at what stage to sell products.

TO SUMMARIZE

Decisions that involve ongoing operations that are made daily, weekly, or monthly are called routine decisions. Decisions that are made less frequently, such as the types of products to offer and whether to expand, are nonroutine decisions. Because of rapid changes taking place in business today, decisions that traditionally have been considered to be nonroutine are now made quite routinely.

BUSINESS ENVIRONMENT ESSAY

A Better Bumper Factory Shahid Khan is the founder and owner of **Bumper Works** in Danville, Illinois. Bumper Works designs and manufactures bumpers for lightweight pickup trucks for Japanese auto makers, including **Toyota Motor Corp.**, whose standards are very exacting. "There was nothing Toyota could teach us," says Khan, "about engineering low-cost bumpers." But on how to run a bumper factory, Khan is more humble. "We had benchmarked ourselves against American industry," he says. "I don't think we knew how bad we were."

Toyota, a world leader in factory efficiency, did know. But rather than take its business elsewhere, Toyota dispatched a team of manufacturing experts to the bumper plant to conduct a crash course in the Toyota system. Productivity at Bumper Works rose 60 percent from the previous year, and the number of defects was reduced by 80 percent.

Khan made sales calls to Toyota for five years before landing his first contract with the company in 1985. Then, in 1987, Khan and two other bumper makers were told by Toyota to design new bumpers considerably more durable than the Big Three (**GM**, **Chrysler**, and **Ford**) specifications required. Such demands from Japanese companies are common. "We were the only company that could demonstrate we could do that," Khan says. As a result, in 1988, his firm became the sole supplier of bumpers to U.S. facilities where Toyota attaches rear bumpers and other accessories to trucks made in Japan.

In 1989, Toyota made additional demands. Toyota wanted annual price reductions despite rising costs for materials and labor. It also wanted better bumpers and more punctual deliveries. Toyota wanted to help Khan meet these demands. However, little could be done until Bumper Works cut the time it took to change dies in the metal-stamping presses to less than 22 minutes (present change time was 90 minutes or more). Only then would Bumper Works be flexible enough to make 20 different bumper models each day. Bumper Works could not afford new presses with quick-change features, so, with Toyota's help, Khan's workers improvised. They welded homemade metal tabs to their nine-ton dies to facilitate lining up the dies on pins attached to the presses. Workers also videotaped die-change procedures and produced an instruction manual—a Bumper Works first. "We had no organization," recalls the die coordinator. "There were a lot of simple things we didn't think about until the Toyota team came in."

By July 1990, Bumper Works achieved the die-change objective. Toyota then dispatched two more consultants from Japan to lead what Khan calls "boot camp." In about two weeks of 16-hour days, the plant was turned upside down. Virtually every piece of equipment, except the massive metal presses, was moved. Employees had to relearn their jobs. Toyota's goal was for a piece of raw steel to come in one end of the building and go out the other end on the same day as a finished bumper. The employees now schedule their own work rather than wait for a supervisor's direction. When a batch of Toyota bumpers is shipped, a card is returned to the press operators and they press out more. Bumper quality improved significantly, and costs came down.

Source: Adapted from "Japanese Auto Makers Help U.S. Suppliers to Become More Efficient," *The Wall Street Journal*, September 9, 1991.

2 *Understand the concept of differential costs and revenues, and be able to identify those costs and revenues that are relevant to making nonroutine decisions.*

differential costs
Future costs that change as a result of a decision.

DIFFERENTIAL COSTS AND REVENUES

Before making various nonroutine decisions, a framework is necessary with which to make these decisions. This means that the costs and revenues that are different for, and hence relevant to, each alternative course of action must be identified. Analysis of these **differential costs** and revenues is the key to both long- and short-term, nonroutine decisions. As discussed in Chapter 9, the differential costs of a decision are the future costs that change as a result of that decision. For example, though GM estimates a cost of nearly $4 billion to close plants and lay off employees, it expects to save hundreds of millions of dollars in all future years because of being more efficient. The term *differential* is also commonly applied to future revenues that will be affected by these decisions.

To illustrate, assume that you own the Speedy Print Shop. A customer wants you to print 500 copies of a one-page flyer immediately. To price the job, you need to know what it will cost. Exhibit 14-2 includes both an incorrect and a correct analysis of the available cost data. The left column (the incorrect analysis) includes all costs; the right column (the correct analysis) includes only the differential costs. We will explain each cost and how we determined whether it was relevant to the pricing decision.

1. *Paper.* The cost of the paper for the printing job is differential because it is a future expenditure that must be made as a result of the decision to accept the order. In a sense, therefore, it is a cost that changes as a result of the decision. If we do not accept the order, we do not need to purchase the paper. Note also that paper is a variable cost—its total cost increases proportionately to the size of the order.
2. *Printing labor.* Accepting the order will require a future expenditure for additional labor to operate the press. This again obviously represents a change from the existing situation—without the order, we would not incur the cost of labor. Also, this example illustrates another important point about measuring future costs. Since this rush order will have to be printed during overtime hours, the appropriate labor rate is time and a half. (Given a normal hourly rate of $16, the labor rate for this job would be $24.) It is easy to overlook this and assume that the normal labor cost per hour ($16) applies. The differential cost of $24 per hour that will be incurred as a result of the decision, however, is the appropriate cost to use. Like paper, printing labor is a variable cost that increases in total proportionately to the size of the order.

EXHIBIT 14-2

Speedy Print Shop Rush Order Analysis

	Incorrect Analysis (all costs)	Correct Analysis (differential costs)
Variable costs:		
Paper (500 at 10¢)	$ 50	$ 50
Printing labor (5 hours at $16; 5 hours at $24)	80	120
Fixed costs:		
Printing plates	100	100
Printing press depreciation (5 hours at $10)	50	
Manager's salary (5 hours at $20)	100	
Totals	$380	$270

t connected
://www.swcollege.com
net work

The activities of the Speedy Print Shop in this illustration mirror the real-life business of Kinko's. The first Kinko's store was opened in September 1970 near the campus of the University of California at Santa Barbara. The store occupied 100 square feet and had one copy machine. Kinko's now has over 850 locations worldwide. Through its Corporate Document Solutions (CDS) Division, Kinko's offers "targeted products and services" to help customers with special orders.

Access Kinko's Web site and locate one case history describing how Kinko's CDS Division was able to help a customer with a special order.

kinkos.com

3. *Printing plates.* New printing plates must be prepared for this order, so it is a future expenditure that changes as a result of the decision to accept the order. The important point here is that printing plates are a fixed cost (you can print as many copies as you want from the same set of plates), but the cost is still differential because it is an additional expenditure for this order. A common but incorrect assumption sometimes made is that only variable costs are relevant (that fixed costs do not have to be taken into account). This is not the case. All future costs that change as a result of accepting the order, whether fixed or variable, are differential.
4. *Printing press depreciation.* This cannot be a differential cost because it is not a future cost (depreciation is an allocation of a past cost), and it does not change as a result of the decision to accept the order. (Assuming a time-based depreciation method, the press depreciates over time, whether or not it is used.) Costs such as depreciation, which are past costs and do not change, are referred to as **sunk costs**. No decision can change past, or sunk, costs; they are never relevant to a decision.
5. *Manager's salary.* Although the manager's salary is a future cost (we will be paying for future services), it will be paid whether or not the order is accepted. Consequently, the manager's salary is not a differential cost; it does not change as a result of the decision to accept this order.

sunk costs Costs, such as depreciation, that are past costs and do not change as the result of a future decision.

The differential costs for this rush order total $270. This means that in pricing the job, Speedy Print Shop will be losing money unless it charges at least this much. Similarly, if Speedy Print Shop declines the job at an offered price of $300 because that price is less than the incorrectly calculated differential cost of $380, the company will experience an opportunity cost (loss) of $30.

To further illustrate the role of differential and sunk costs in making a nonroutine decision, we assume that Dixon Wholesale Company is thinking of purchasing a delivery truck with an estimated useful life of five years. Following are the costs of acquiring and operating a truck:

Original cost		$10,000
Variable costs per mile:		
Gasoline and oil	$ 0.25	
Repairs and maintenance	0.03	
Tires	0.02	
Total variable costs per mile		$ 0.30
Fixed costs per year:		
Insurance	$ 500	
Licenses	110	
Depreciation expense ($10,000 ÷ 5 years)	2,000	
Total fixed costs per year		$ 2,610

These variable and fixed operating costs are incurred each year the truck is used. However, they are not all differential costs; they are not all relevant to every decision made about the truck. For the following decisions, we identify the differential costs, the sunk costs, and the reason for the classifications.

Decision 1

Should the truck be purchased? Whether to purchase the truck is really a capital budgeting decision, a topic we will discuss in Chapter 15. But the decision is based on differential (future) costs to be incurred if the truck is purchased.

Differential costs: All variable costs (30 cents per mile driven); all fixed costs except depreciation, (which is already included in the purchase cost); and the purchase cost ($10,000).

Sunk costs: None.

Comment: All costs except depreciation are differential costs because the truck has not yet been purchased; all costs can be avoided by an alternative decision.

Decision 2

Let's now jump forward in time two years. The truck has now been owned and used for two years, but it has not been licensed or insured for the current (third) year. Should it be licensed and insured, or should some other means of transportation be used?

Differential costs: All variable costs (30 cents per mile driven) and some fixed costs (insurance, $500; licenses, $110).

Sunk costs: Remaining book value of the truck ($6,000 at the beginning of the year).

Comment: As soon as the truck is purchased, its cost becomes a sunk cost. During its estimated life, its remaining book value is a sunk cost if we assume, for simplicity, that the truck has no resale value. The company must absorb the cost of the truck either by using the truck (and depreciating its cost each year) or by writing off the entire cost. All costs except depreciation and the remaining book value are, therefore, differential costs.

Decision 3

The truck has been owned and used for two years and has been licensed and insured for the current (third) year. Should the truck be used for transporting inventory this year? Should other means be arranged?

Differential costs: All variable costs (30 cents per mile driven) and no fixed costs.

Sunk costs: Insurance ($500); licenses ($110); remaining book value ($6,000 at the beginning of the year).

Comment: If insurance and license fees are not refundable, these are sunk costs, as is the remaining book value.

Analysis of the costs that are relevant in making these three decisions should help you understand how differential costs are determined. As you can see, variable costs are *usually* differential; fixed costs are *sometimes* differential; and past costs are *never* differential.

Total Costs Versus Differential Costs

In making nonroutine decisions, managers usually prefer to use the differential cost approach; that is, they disregard sunk costs and other costs that are the same for each alternative being considered. This approach highlights costs that make a difference, takes less time, and reduces the chance of error in the calculation (fewer numbers reduce the chances for mistakes). In some cases, however, a manager may want to review the **total cost**, fearing that some relevant costs may otherwise be overlooked.

total cost The total variable and fixed costs incurred in making a product or providing a service.

To illustrate this total-cost approach, we will assume that Dixon Wholesale Company has another decision to make about its truck.

Decision 4

The truck has been owned for four years, but it has not yet been licensed or insured for the current (fifth) year. Should the truck be used for the last year of its economic life, or should it be traded for a new truck that will be driven five years?

Pertinent information is presented in the following table:

	Old Truck	New Truck
Original cost	$10,000	$12,500
Current book value	2,000	
Current resale value	1,700	
Resale value at end of year	0	10,000
Variable operating costs	$0.30 per mile	$0.27 per mile
Annual fixed costs:		
Insurance	$ 500	$ 550
Licenses	110	110
Depreciation expense	2,000	2,500
Estimated mileage per year	50,000 miles	50,000 miles

On the basis of this information, the total cost of operating the old truck and the total cost of operating a new truck are shown in Exhibit 14-3.

Note that the total cost of operating the old truck includes the yearly $2,000 depreciation expense. If the new truck is bought, the $2,000 book value of the old truck must still be written off. Thus, the $2,000 is a sunk cost and is the same under both alternatives, so it is not relevant to the decision at hand. The current resale value of the old truck, however, is a reduction in cost that will occur only if the new truck is purchased.

EXHIBIT 14-3 Total-Cost Analysis for the Current Year: Keeping the Old Truck Versus Selling It and Buying a New Truck*

Total Costs	Old Truck	Difference	New Truck
Variable costs:			
$0.30 × 50,000 miles	$15,000		
$0.27 × 50,000 miles			$13,500
Fixed costs:			
Insurance	500		550
Licenses	110		110
Depreciation expense	2,000		2,500
Book value of old truck to be written off			2,000
Resale value of old truck	0		(1,700)
Total cost	$17,610		$16,960
Difference		$650	

*Be aware that in order to emphasize the total-cost and differential-cost approaches, this analysis ignores the time value of money and related income tax effects, which will be discussed in Chapter 15.

Two observations should be made about the total-cost approach to analyzing alternatives. First, it highlights the more attractive alternative in terms of cost only. In our example, the data appear to favor buying a new truck. However, this requires an investment of additional funds, which forces consideration of other factors. Since these factors are covered in Chapter 15, we have tried to keep our example simple by assuming a fair market value of $10,000 for the new truck at the end of one year. This means that the new truck's annual depreciation expense of $2,500 is equal to the difference between its original cost and its resale value after one year. Had the drop in value been greater than the depreciation expense, the excess would have been an additional cost of using the new truck during its first year.

Second, the total-cost approach is time consuming because it involves differential costs as well as costs that are the same for all alternatives under consideration. With the differential-cost approach, only costs that are different need to be accumulated and analyzed. Thus, the costs of licensing both trucks and the $2,000 book value of the old truck to be depreciated or written off would not be considered. Exhibit 14–4 provides a list of the differential costs taken from Exhibit 14–3.

Although the differential-cost approach accumulates comparative costs and revenues that are different from those of the total-cost approach, it does not alter the relative attractiveness of the alternatives. Both the total and the differential analyses show a savings of $650 if the new truck is purchased. Thus, the acquisition of the new truck should bring future benefits to the company.

It should be noted that in both the total analysis and the differential analysis, the resale value of the old truck was treated as a negative cost. Instead, it could have been treated as a differential revenue from which the differential costs had been subtracted. It should also be noted that since both methods of analysis provide the same answer, it is likely that a firm will use the differential analysis method to save time in the collection of data and in the analysis. The only time the total-cost revenue method might be used is if there was considerable uncertainty about whether all differential costs and revenues had been accounted for in the differential cost approach.

Qualitative Considerations

As has been the case with all management accounting decisions discussed in this book, the effect of nonroutine decisions on the time and quality with which products or services can be delivered must be considered. In deciding whether to accept the rush print job, for example, Speedy Print Shop must consider the possibility that while accepting the job might lead to additional business, it could affect the quality of printing services to other customers. Likewise, if accepting the rush print job will

EXHIBIT 14-4 Differential Cost and Revenue Analysis for the Current Year: Operating the Old Truck Versus Selling It and Buying a New Truck

Differential Costs and Revenues	Old Truck	New Truck	Difference
Variable costs	$15,000	$13,500	$ 1,500
Insurance	500	550	(50)
Depreciation expense		2,500	(2,500)
Resale value of old truck	0	(1,700)	1,700
Total differential costs and revenues	$15,500	$14,850	$ 650

slow down service to other customers, no matter how financially attractive, accepting the job may not be a good decision.

In making a final decision, the cost and qualitative factors may lead you to the same conclusion. If they do not, you must decide what to do to enhance your company's overall profitability in the future. You might decide, for example, to accept the rush print job for an amount near or even below your differential cost to ensure that you get the order.

TO SUMMARIZE

Differential costs are the future costs that change as a result of a decision. Differential costs and revenues are those costs and revenues that are relevant to decisions. Sunk costs are never relevant because they are past costs that cannot be changed. Care must be exercised when estimating future costs because past cost relationships may not continue into the future. Some future costs may not be differential because they do not change as a result of a decision. Both variable and fixed costs may be differential.

There are two approaches to analyzing alternatives: total cost and differential cost. With the total-cost approach, all costs (including sunk costs) are accumulated. The differential-cost approach excludes sunk costs and all common costs, dealing only with costs that are different for the alternatives being considered. Once the quantitative analysis has been completed, qualitative factors must be considered.

3 *Identify several examples of nonroutine decisions and be able to analyze and select the best alternative for each example.*

EXAMPLES OF SHORT-TERM, NONROUTINE DECISIONS

The concept of differential costs applies to all nonroutine decisions covered in this and the next chapter. In the remainder of this chapter, we will apply differential costing to several examples of short-term, nonroutine decisions. First, we will consider the issue of special orders. A **special order** is an order that may be priced below the normal price in order to utilize excess capacity, thus contributing to company profits. We will look at special orders from both the perspective of the buyer and the seller. Second, we will look at the decisions of exiting or entering a market (dropping or adding plants, segments, product lines, geographic territories, etc.). Third, we will look at the use of scarce resources, such as limited raw materials in a manufacturing firm, limited shelf space in a merchandising company, and limited expertise or labor in a service firm. Fourth, we will look at the manufacture of products and at what stage to sell them. Finally, we will consider the issues of pricing regular products and services.

special order An order that may be priced below the normal selling price in order to utilize excess capacity and thereby contribute to company profits.

(STOP & THINK)

In addition to the specific examples of nonroutine decisions covered in this chapter, identify two other types of nonroutine decisions that organizations make.

Special Orders

In the opening scenario, we stated that Toyota makes only 30 percent of its automobile parts internally, while GM makes 65 percent internally. The decision to outsource the making of parts or services is the first type of nonroutine decision we cover in this chapter. These types of special order decisions can involve long-term purchase and sales arrangements (as is the case with Toyota) or only one-time orders (like the Speedy Print Shop example). In either case, both the buyer (Toyota in the opening scenario) and the seller (the parts manufacturer) have decisions to make. These decisions can be outlined in the following diagram.

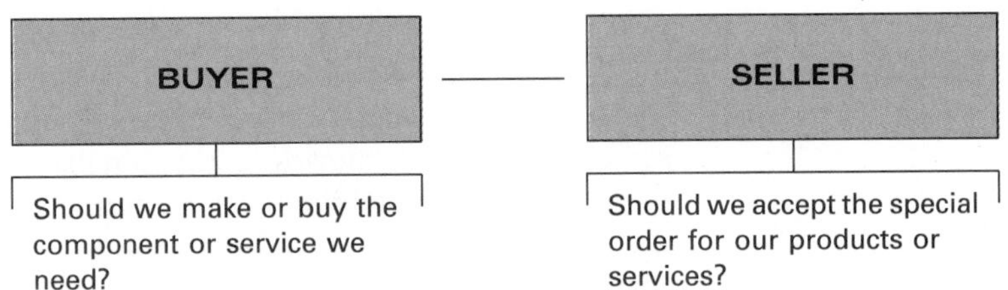

As shown in the diagram above, special orders can involve products or services. For example, in manufacturing companies, the special order might involve buying parts on a one-time basis from other companies because of a sudden surge in demand; or it could involve a company outsourcing or purchasing its internal audit services from a CPA firm. When parts are involved, both companies are manufacturing firms. When a service (such as internal auditing) is involved, the buyer may be a manufacturing, merchandising, or service company, but the provider is always a service company.

We will first look at special order decisions from the perspective of the buyer. Then, we will look at special order decisions from the perspective of the seller. In both cases, we will examine buying and selling products and services.

Special Orders—The Buyer's Decision

In Chapter 10, we included a Business Environment Essay describing the virtual bakery owned by Franco Harris, a former running back for the **Pittsburgh Steelers**. Harris's profitable bakery had made the decision to purchase almost all products and services from other companies. Other organizations make or provide most of their products and services internally. In the following section, we describe the factors companies must consider when deciding whether to make or to buy products and services.

Making or Buying Manufactured Parts Companies, such as **GM** and **Toyota**, must decide which products and services they will produce and offer internally and which ones they will outsource or buy from outsiders. With respect to manufactured products, if a product consists of a number of parts, management must decide for each component whether to produce it or purchase it from an outside supplier. Over time, and based on a consideration of the relevant quantitative and qualitative factors, management develops a long-term policy regarding the use of its facilities to produce components for its products.

The fact that a long-term policy has been established does not mean that the issue is permanently closed. In fact, management is always reconsidering its decisions and looking for new ways to save money, improve quality, or speed up manufacturing and delivery processes. If a firm has idle facilities, for example, management may wish to find a use for those facilities. One possibility is to manufacture components that are normally purchased. Whether this decision is wise depends not only on cost considerations but also on a number of qualitative factors, such as the likely effect on the regular source of supply; the company's ability to produce a high-quality component; speed of delivery; and management's interest in keeping workers on the payroll. Thus, even though a firm has a long-term policy of purchasing some components and producing others, certain situations may require decisions that alter that policy.

Assuming that the qualitative factors favor the use of idle facilities in producing the part, what costs are relevant to a make-or-buy decision? In general, the purchase cost and all other costs that can be avoided if the part is manufactured are differential costs. Any cost that will be incurred regardless of whether the part is purchased or manufactured is not a differential cost and is irrelevant.

To illustrate how the differential costs in such a decision are identified, we assume that Ritter Manufacturing Company has excess capacity that could be used in producing wheel bearings. The accounting department has compiled the following projected total-cost figures for producing the bearings:

	Cost per Unit	Costs for 1,000 Units
Direct materials	$ 3.00	$ 3,000
Direct labor	8.00	8,000
Variable manufacturing overhead	4.00	4,000
Fixed manufacturing overhead, direct	2.50	2,500
Fixed manufacturing overhead, indirect	5.00	5,000*
Total costs	$22.50	$22,500

*Total indirect fixed costs are the same under both alternatives.

The company has been buying this bearing from a regular supplier in 1,000-unit quantities at a price of $19 per unit. Should Ritter continue to buy or start making the bearings? To answer this question, management must identify the differential costs of each alternative, taking into account any additional resources that may be needed, as well as alternative uses for the currently idle facilities. Two possible situations are presented here.

Situation 1

The currently idle facilities have no alternative uses. If the idle facilities do not have any practical alternative use, the opportunity cost is zero. With no opportunity cost, the differential costs would be the costs strictly associated with manufacturing (direct labor, direct materials, and so on).

The costs of the two alternatives can be presented on a total-cost or a differential-cost basis, as shown in Exhibit 14-5. Although each analysis produces different total costs, both demonstrate that the firm would save $1,500 per 1,000 units ($1.50 per unit) by making the component rather than buying it. The company's final decision

EXHIBIT 14-5 Analyses of the Costs of Using Idle Facilities (Situation 1)

	Total-Cost Analysis (per 1,000 Units)		Differential-Cost Analysis (per 1,000 Units)	
	Buy	Make	Buy	Make
Purchase cost	$19,000		$19,000	
Direct materials		$ 3,000		$ 3,000
Direct labor		8,000		8,000
Variable manufacturing overhead		4,000		4,000
Fixed manufacturing overhead:				
Direct		2,500		2,500
Indirect	5,000	5,000		
Total cost	$24,000	$22,500	$19,000	$17,500
Difference	$1,500		$1,500	

would depend, of course, on whether there were negative qualitative factors that would, in the opinion of management, more than offset the $1.50 unit-cost advantage of making the part.

Situation 2

The idle facilities can be rented for $4,000 if they are not used to manufacture bearings. Management estimates that, if the facilities are used for manufacturing, 1,000 wheel bearings could be manufactured during this time.

In this case, the opportunity cost of producing the bearings is $4,000, or an average cost of $4 per unit ($4,000 ÷ 1,000 units). This opportunity cost is an important consideration in the firm's decision whether to buy or make the part, as shown in Exhibit 14-6. When the opportunity cost is considered, the cost of producing the part is $2,500 more than the cost of buying it. Unless there are quality, time, or other qualitative factors that override this cost, Ritter should buy the bearing and rent the idle facilities. Remember, the essence of the make-or-buy problem is management's desire to achieve the best utilization of existing facilities in the short term.

Because opportunity costs do not represent actual transactions, they are not recorded in the accounts. Yet, they are always significant in the decision-making process since each situation has at least two alternatives. Thus, opportunity costs provide a good illustration of why a manager cannot rely solely on the data collected for external financial reports.

Purchasing Services or Providing Them Internally In recent years, companies have not only outsourced product parts, but more and more they are outsourcing services such as cafeteria service, internal auditing, garbage removal, payroll accounting, legal services, and even basic accounting. In deciding whether or not to acquire services or provide them internally, companies go through the same kind of analysis as if they were buying products. That is, they consider the differential costs of each alternative, as well as qualitative factors, such as the quality of the service; whether space exists to house the service; whether services can be delivered on a timely basis; and management's interest in keeping workers on the payroll. Assuming

EXHIBIT 14-6 The Effect of an Opportunity Cost on Analyses (Situation 2)

	Total-Cost Analysis (per 1,000 Units)			Differential-Cost Analysis (per 1,000 Units)		
	Buy		Make	Buy		Make
Purchase cost	$19,000			$19,000		
Direct materials			$ 3,000			$ 3,000
Direct labor			8,000			8,000
Variable manufacturing overhead			4,000			4,000
Fixed manufacturing overhead:						
Direct			2,500			2,500
Indirect	5,000		5,000			
Opportunity cost, rental			4,000			4,000
Total cost	$24,000		$26,500	$19,000		$21,500
Difference		$2,500			$2,500	

management believes it can acquire high quality services both within and outside the company, what costs are relevant to the purchase-or-provide decisions? Costs that will be incurred regardless of whether the service is purchased or provided internally are not differential costs and are irrelevant to the decision.

To illustrate how the differential costs are identified, we assume that Ritter Manufacturing Company is considering outsourcing its internal audit function. The following annual cost information relating to internal auditing is available.

Costs of Internal Auditing Department

Salaries of internal audit employees	$1,200,000
Travel costs	1,400,000
Training costs	100,000
Depreciation on internal audit offices	50,000
Utilities for internal audit offices	40,000
Computers, software, and supplies	150,000
Other variable costs	75,000
Total costs of internal audit	$3,015,000

FYI

In recent years, major CPA firms have become professional service firms and are offering all kinds of new services. In fact, in non-U.S. countries where accountants can practice law, three of the world's largest law firms are "Big 5" CPA firms. One of the fasting growing services being offered by CPA firms is internal audit services for major corporations, such as the example in this chapter.

A CPA firm has offered to perform the internal audit services for $3,100,000 per year. You have determined that if internal audit services were contracted out to the CPA firm, the space currently used by the internal auditors could be used by the purchasing department, which is currently occupying rented space in a nearby city. The rent paid for offices used by the purchasing department is $10,000 per month.

Should Ritter continue to have its own internal audit department, or should it outsource its internal audit function to the CPA firm? From a strictly financial point of view, Ritter should not outsource, as shown below.

Cost of outsourcing:		
CPA firm cost		$3,100,000
Rent saved by relocating purchasing department ($10,000 per month × 12 months)		(120,000)
Net cost of outsourcing		$2,980,000
Cost of maintaining internal audit department:		
Total cost of internal audit department		$3,015,000
Less: nondifferential costs (incurred under either alternative)		
Depreciation expense	$50,000	
Utilities	40,000	
Total nondifferential costs		(90,000)
Differential cost of maintaining internal audit department		$2,925,000
Excess cost incurred by outsourcing internal auditing		$ 55,000

CAUTION

Be careful to consider all differential costs and revenues in making nonroutine decisions and to exclude the nondifferential costs. For example, in this internal audit example, if depreciation and utilities (which will be incurred whether or not internal audit services are outsourced) are not considered, an incorrect decision will be made.

Of course, the one-year cost analysis is really an incomplete analysis. In making the decisions, management must decide what the future costs of each alternative will be. If, for example, management can lock into a 5-year commitment of $3,100,000 annually and it believes costs of keeping the internal audit department will rise $100,000 per year, from a cost perspective, the company may want to outsource even though the cost is higher in the current year.

In addition to costs, management must consider many other factors. For example, will the same or higher quality audit services be provided by the outside CPA firm as is being provided by the internal auditors?

Having good internal audit services is important because the auditors can help ensure efficiency and effectiveness of operations, assure that controls are implemented and followed, and even prevent and detect fraud and other problems. Quality of services is very important in an area like internal auditing, where it is difficult for management to judge whether they are getting value for their money. Other factors management would want to consider are: (1) Will the CPA firm be able to provide the services in the long run? (2) Can the company use the displaced internal audit employees in other positions, or is the company willing to lay off employees? (3) Will outsourcing the internal audit service affect the cost of other services received by the company (for example, will outsourcing internal audit services reduce the cost of the external audit or the cost of cafeteria or other services)? (4) If internal audit was used as a management trainee development area (as it is in many companies), are there other efficient and effective ways to train future managers?

Special Orders—The Seller's Decision

If sellers can sell their services profitably at market prices, the decision is an easy one—provide the service. After all, that is the purpose of being in business. Where the difficulty comes is in deciding whether to reduce the normal price of a product or service in order to obtain a special order. Typical situations involving a possible price reduction when idle capacity exists are:

1. A manufacturer sells products under its own brand name, as well as to retail chain stores for sale under the chain's brand name.
2. A firm, such as a building contractor or an equipment manufacturer, sells its products or services in a competitive bidding situation.
3. A firm sells a product under distress conditions, for instance, when there has been a sharp decline in demand for its products because of a new product offered by a competitor.
4. A product has a significant sales potential with a foreign distributor, whose market demands lower prices than those in the United States.
5. A provider of a service has extra capacity and has the opportunity to sign a large contract, at a lower than normal price, that would consume the excess capacity.

In each of these situations, we assume that a firm has available capacity that can be utilized to fill the special order. The relevant costs for this decision are the additional, or incremental, costs necessary to produce and deliver the special order. Management must therefore know the incremental costs. This information will indicate the lowest price at which the special order will begin to contribute to the firm's profits.

To illustrate, we will assume that Kent Electronics, which usually sells hand calculators for $19, receives an order from a large department store chain for 10,000 calculators at a price of $13 each. The requested calculators are to be sold under the store's brand name. Kent currently has excess capacity that could be used in producing enough calculators to fill the order. Should the company accept the order?

The answer to this question does not, of course, depend on cost and price factors alone. An obvious consideration, for example, would be whether the order would result in a significant loss of sales of the company's own brand of calculators. Let's assume that this is not a problem.

If the accounting department presents the data on a total-cost basis, the manager might erroneously reject the order. It appears from the following that the firm would have a loss if the special order were accepted:

Special Order for Calculators—Total-Cost Approach		
Sales price		$ 13
Manufacturing costs:		
Direct materials	$3	
Direct labor	4	
Manufacturing overhead	9	
Total manufacturing costs		16
Loss per unit		$ (3)
Number of units in order		× 10,000
Expected loss exclusive of selling and administrative expenses		$(30,000)

It is not unusual for managers to base decisions on total-cost information because the data are readily available, having been collected in order to prepare financial statements and income tax returns. Unfortunately, such information may lead management to the wrong conclusion—in this case, to reject the order.

The only differential costs, however, are those future costs that change if the order is accepted. These include the variable product costs as well as the direct fixed costs. Fixed costs that are incurred regardless of whether the order is accepted should not be considered. The following analysis, prepared on a differential-cost basis, shows that Kent Electronics should accept the order.

Special Order for Calculators—Differential-Cost Approach		
Sales price		$ 13
Variable and differential fixed costs:		
Direct materials	$3	
Direct labor	4	
Variable manufacturing overhead costs	2	
Differential fixed overhead costs	1	
Variable selling and administrative expenses	1	
Total variable and differential fixed costs		11
Remaining margin to cover fixed costs and provide a profit		$ 2
Number of units in order		×10,000
Expected contribution to fixed costs and profit		$ 20,000

These data assume that additional fixed costs of $1 per unit will be incurred if the order is accepted. If no additional fixed costs would be incurred, the margin would be increased to $3. The analysis clearly suggests that, from a financial point of view, management should accept the order. This approach identifies not only the differential costs but also a price floor (the total variable and differential fixed costs of $11) below which management should probably not accept an order. As long as the price exceeds total variable and differential fixed costs, the firm will increase its profits by accepting the order. This analysis assumes that the company has no better alternative uses for its excess capacity and that special sales by the chain will have no adverse effect on Kent's normal sales. However, what if regular customers hear about this special order and insist on lower prices, thus disrupting the normal pricing structure? Or, what if filling the special order will have an adverse effect on the quality of current products or the speed with which products can be offered to regular customers? These and other qualitative factors must also be considered.

A manager must also consider whether acceptance of such an order would be a violation of the Robinson-Patman Act. This legislation, enacted in 1936, prohibits firms from quoting different prices to competing customers for the same goods unless differences in price can be attributed to differences in cost. In the case of Kent Electronics, the sale is probably legal because the calculators are to be sold under the store's brand name, and the department store will assume all advertising costs.

The differential-cost approach to pricing can also be used in explaining why theater tickets are less expensive for matinees than for evening performances, why airline economy fares are less expensive than business-class fares, and why it is cheaper to make telephone calls at night and on weekends than on weekdays. If there is excess capacity that can be used to provide a service or make a product that will generate more revenue than the variable cost of providing the service or making the product, the firm will increase its profits by the amount of the margin remaining after deducting differential costs.

A few words of caution are in order when making these types of decisions. First, in some situations, there may also be some additional fixed costs that are relevant to the pricing decision. Second, a company must not accept too many orders that barely cover variable costs, or it will not be able to cover all its fixed costs. Third, using all extra capacity to fill a special order at a lower-than-normal price may prohibit a company from being able to accept additional work at higher prices in the future. Fourth, accepting a special order may force a company to cut corners with normal customers, resulting in lower-quality products or services to those customers or decreasing the speed at which other customers could be served.

TO SUMMARIZE

In choosing whether to make or buy a component or service, management must compare the differential costs of making the part or providing the service (including the opportunity costs of alternative uses of the facilities) with the cost of purchasing (outsourcing) the part or service. Qualitative factors must also be considered, since they may be significant enough to reverse a decision based only on quantitative considerations. In deciding whether to accept special orders, the differential-cost approach is appropriate. Using this approach, only variable costs and differential fixed costs are considered.

Exiting or Entering a Market

The decision of whether to exit or enter a market is a nonroutine decision, although companies seem to be buying and selling businesses quite often these days. We will first consider the decision of whether to exit a market and then whether to enter a market.

Exiting a Market

When a segment (product or line of products) is losing money, management must decide whether to drop it. Such decisions are particularly difficult because the differential costs are not easy to identify, and this can lead to analyses based on invalid assumptions, as the following example demonstrates.

To illustrate, we will assume that Augusta Retail Company is thinking of closing one of its stores. The question of the store's value arose because of the July financial results for the company's three stores (amounts are in thousands):

	Store 1	Store 2	Store 3	Total
Sales revenue	$250,000	$90,000	$60,000	$400,000
Cost of goods sold	170,000	40,000	30,000	240,000
Gross margin	$ 80,000	$50,000	$30,000	$160,000
Operating expenses	55,000	30,000	35,000	120,000
Net income (or loss)	$ 25,000	$20,000	$ (5,000)	$ 40,000

If Store 3 is closed, it would seem reasonable to assume that Augusta Retail Company's profits will increase by $5 million, as shown here.

	Store 1	Store 2	Total
Sales revenue	$250,000	$90,000	$340,000
Cost of goods sold	170,000	40,000	210,000
Gross margin	$ 80,000	$50,000	$130,000
Operating expenses	55,000	30,000	85,000
Net income	$ 25,000	$20,000	$ 45,000

This analysis is based on three assumptions:

1. That all costs shown are differential and therefore relevant to the decision. In other words, there are no joint costs (costs that are common to two or more stores).
2. That the sales of the other stores will not be affected by dropping Store 3.
3. That no qualitative factors have a bearing on the decision.

Before closing Store 3, the company's general manager should check the validity of these assumptions. For simplicity, suppose that the second and third assumptions are valid, and that only the first assumption needs verification. First, the accounting department must separate the total costs of each store into variable costs, direct fixed costs, and indirect (or unavoidable) fixed costs. With this new information, the accounting department might prepare the following modified report for July (amounts are in thousands).

	Store 1	Store 2	Store 3	Total
Sales revenue	$250,000	$90,000	$60,000	$400,000
Variable costs	190,000	50,000	40,000	280,000
Contribution margin	$ 60,000	$40,000	$20,000	$120,000
Direct fixed costs	20,000	15,000	18,000	53,000
Segment margin	$ 40,000	$25,000	$ 2,000	$ 67,000
Indirect fixed costs (not allocated)				27,000
Net income				$ 40,000

The manager can use this modified report to determine whether Store 3 made a positive contribution toward covering the indirect (unavoidable) fixed costs. In looking at this modified report, the manager would immediately see that the segment margin for Store 3 is a positive $2 million. This means that Store 3 is contributing $2 million to the company's overall profit. Thus, if Store 3 is dropped, profits will decrease by $2 million unless another store with greater profit potential is added or Store 3 can be sold to another company. To illustrate the potential decline in profits if Store 3 is dropped, the manager might ask the accounting department to prepare a report to indicate what the company's July financial results would show without Store 3. This pro-forma report would show the following information (amounts are in thousands):

	Store 1	Store 2	Total
Sales revenue	$250,000	$90,000	$340,000
Variable costs	190,000	50,000	240,000
Contribution margin	$ 60,000	$40,000	$100,000
Direct fixed costs	20,000	15,000	35,000
Segment margin	$ 40,000	$25,000	$ 65,000
Indirect fixed costs (not allocated)			27,000
Net income			$ 38,000

Although the original report suggested that profits would increase by $5 million if Store 3 were dropped, total profits would actually decrease by $2 million ($40 million − $38 million). The reason is that Store 3 is generating revenues that are $2 million greater than differential costs (variable costs and avoidable fixed costs). This analysis suggests that Store 3 should not be dropped, unless it can be replaced by another store or business that will contribute more than $2 million to cover unavoidable indirect fixed costs. (Obviously, we have not considered any sales price Augusta could receive from selling Store 3. Any money received from selling Store 3 would need to be deducted from the $2 million annual contribution Store 3 is making toward covering indirect costs.)

Entering a Market

The considerations involved in deciding whether to enter a market are quite similar to those when deciding whether or not to exit a market. From a financial perspective, if adding a product line (segment) will contribute to the income of a firm, it is generally a good decision. The contribution can come in several forms. First, entering a new market can reduce the current cost of doing business. For example, assume that Augusta is considering purchasing a wholesale distribution company that will allow the company to buy directly from manufacturers, rather than from other wholesalers, when acquiring merchandise for its stores. Even if the new wholesale company is not profitable on its own, if it could reduce Augusta's costs enough so that overall profits are higher, the decision to buy might be a good one. Buying a new company or entering a new market could increase overall company profits by having the new segment cover some of the indirect fixed costs now being borne entirely by existing businesses. From a financial perspective, the important point to consider is whether total profits will be higher or lower after the purchase.

In addition to the financial considerations, organizations consider the effects on quality and time to deliver products to customers when deciding whether to enter a market. For example, suppose there is a small company that has superior quality products, manufacturing knowledge, or other attributes that could enhance the quality of the organization's products. Would it be wise to buy this smaller company even if the purchase didn't increase overall short-term profits? Probably so. Or, what if a company occupies a strategic location for serving an organization's customers and buying the company would allow the organization to more quickly deliver its products to customers? Would buying the strategically located company be a good decision even if short-term overall profits aren't increased? Again, probably so. Both purchases would allow the organization to serve its customers better by increasing quality and decreasing delivery time. Hopefully, the result of both purchases would be a larger market share and higher profits in the long run. Unfortunately, it is hard to quantify by how much quality and/or delivery time must improve before a pur-

BUSINESS ENVIRONMENT ESSAY

Toyota—The Learning Curve Deciding when to add a product line or to enter a new market is one of the toughest decisions a company has to make. Take the automobile industry, for example. Every auto company has made mistakes and produced new models that didn't sell. Probably the most famous of these failed cars was the Edsel, which hardly sold at all. However, one car company has a unique ability to learn from its mistakes. Certainly, Toyota has had failures. The process of learning from failures has become an essential part of Toyota's culture, so much so that anecdotes about failures are a big part of the company's heritage. Product blunders are particularly embarrassing, but Toyota usually chooses to recalibrate, reload, and fire again—often with amazing accuracy, as the following examples from the U.S. market demonstrate.

In 1997, Toyota decided to enter the van market and produced the Previa LE. An engineering tour de force, it was powered by a small engine under the floor. Prospective buyers found it sluggish and too expensive at $30,000. In 1998, however, Toyota produced the Sienna XLE, a van that looks very similar to the Previa LE. While it won't win prizes for ingenuity, this van (made in the United States) has a bigger engine, conventional technology, and a $22,000 price tag—it's already selling well!

Also in 1997, Toyota entered the luxury sports car market with its Lexus GS 300. This sports sedan had a tiny trunk, wimpy acceleration (0 to 60 mph in 8.3 seconds), a lackluster V-6 engine, and a stiff price: $44,800. Like the Previa LE, it didn't sell. Again, Toyota rebounded and in 1998 produced the Lexus GS 400. A pavement ripper, this car sports a V-8 engine, accelerates to 60 mph in 6.0 seconds, holds several golf bags, and costs little more than the old one. Again, it is selling well.

A final example is the 1997 T100. This pickup was undersized, underpowered, and overpriced, as compared to its Detroit competition. Built in Japan, some models cost $25,000. While it didn't sell, in 1998 Toyota produced a new model T100. This truck will attack the Big Three head-on. It has a bigger engine and cab and, since it will be built in Indiana, no 25 percent import duty.

Source: "The Learning Curve," *Fortune,* December 8, 1997, p. 104.

chase is a good one. Because quality and time decisions are subjective, we will focus on the short-term financial considerations in deciding whether to enter a market. You should realize, however, that quality and time considerations are very important, and in considering some purchases, may be the overriding factors that outweigh short-term financial considerations.

To illustrate entering a new market, assume that Augusta Retail Company now has only two stores. Further, assume that it is considering purchasing the wholesale company just discussed. The following data are available for Augusta Retail Company, prior to making the purchase (amounts are in thousands):

	Store 1	Store 2	Total
Sales revenue	$250,000	$90,000	$340,000
Cost of goods sold	170,000	40,000	210,000
Other variable costs	20,000	10,000	30,000
Contribution margin	$ 60,000	$40,000	$100,000
Direct fixed costs	20,000	15,000	35,000
Segment margin	$ 40,000	$25,000	$ 65,000
Indirect fixed costs (not allocated)			27,000
Net income			$ 38,000

As these data show, Augusta currently makes a net income of $38,000,000. Now, assume that Augusta can purchase a wholesale company that will allow Augusta to buy directly from manufacturers, thus decreasing its cost of goods sold by 30 percent. However, the wholesale company is currently losing $10,000,000 per year. Should Augusta buy the wholesale company? The following analysis shows that, from a financial perspective, buying the wholesale company would be a good decision (again, amounts are in thousands).

Effect on Current Stores

	Store 1		Store 2		Total (before and after purchase)			Total (including wholesale company)
	Before	After	Before	After	Before	After	Wholesale Company	
Sales revenue	$250,000	$250,000	$90,000	$90,000	$340,000	$340,000	$110,000	$450,000
Cost of goods sold	170,000	119,000[1]	40,000	28,000[2]	210,000	147,000	70,000	217,000
Other variable costs	20,000	20,000	10,000	10,000	30,000	30,000	15,000	45,000
Contribution margin	$ 60,000	$111,000	$40,000	$52,000	$100,000	$163,000	$ 25,000	$188,000
Direct fixed costs	20,000	20,000	15,000	15,000	35,000	35,000	35,000	70,000
Segment margin	$ 40,000	$ 91,000	$25,000	$37,000	$ 65,000	$128,000	$ (10,000)	$118,000
Indirect fixed costs (not allocated)					27,000	27,000	—	27,000
Net income					$ 38,000	$101,000	$ (10,000)	$ 91,000

[1]$170,000 − (0.3 × $170,000) = $119,000
[2]$40,000 − (0.3 × $40,000) = $28,000

This analysis shows that even though the wholesale company is losing $10,000,000 per year, purchasing the wholesale company will increase overall company profits by $53,000,000 ($91,000,000 − $38,000,000). Of course, this elaborate analysis really wasn't necessary since many costs (other variable costs, direct fixed costs, and indirect fixed costs) stayed the same. In fact, the only differential costs were the decrease in cost of goods sold (facilitated by being able to buy directly from manufacturers instead of wholesalers) and the $10,000,000 loss the wholesale company incurs. Focusing only on the differential costs, you can see that the net income of the company would be increased by $53,000,000 by buying the wholesale company (numbers are in thousands).

FYI

Pick up practically any business newspaper or periodical and you'll read about companies exiting or entering markets. For example, the front page of the December 16, 1997, *Wall Street Journal* carried stories about **U.S. Bancorp** (bank) acquiring **Piper Jaffray** (investment banker); **Northwest Airlines** attempting to acquire 14 percent of **Continental Airlines**; **Bethlehem Steel** buying **LuKens** (another steel maker); and **Liz Claiborne** (clothing and fragrance maker) buying and signing exclusive agreements to market **Donna Karan** jeans and active wear.

Differential Costs of Deciding to Enter a Market

Decrease in cost of goods sold of Store 1	$51,000
Decrease in cost of goods sold of Store 2	12,000
Loss incurred by wholesaler	(10,000)
Increase in income from buying wholesaler	$53,000

This analysis suggests that, from a financial perspective, the wholesale company should be purchased. The decreases in cost of goods sold that will result in Store 1 and Store 2 more than compensate for the losses currently being incurred by the wholesaler.

TO SUMMARIZE

In deciding whether to exit or enter a market, the effect on profits, quality, and speed of delivery should be considered. When focusing on the financial aspects of exiting or entering a market, only the differential costs and revenues need be considered. A product or line of products should not be dropped unless it does not make a contribution toward covering indirect fixed costs. An alternative product or line of products can be added that will contribute more toward covering unavoidable indirect fixed costs. A segment should be added if it increases overall company profits. The increase in overall company profits can come from reduced costs in existing segments or from the profitable margin of the acquired segment.

Selecting the Best Use of a Scarce Resource

Organizations are often faced with the decision of how to best use scarce resources. In a manufacturing company, the scarce resource might be limited raw materials or limited production capacity. For a retail merchandising firm, such as **Wal-Mart**, the scarce resource might be limited shelf space. For a service firm, the scarce resource might be limited expertise. We will illustrate the concept of scarce resources using limited shelf space for a retail merchandising firm.

When a retail merchandising firm sells more than one product and store shelves are inadequate to display all products equally, management has to decide to which products the store should allocate shelf space and how much space should be allocated to each product. With limited shelf space, stocking one product means that another product can't be stocked or will have to be stocked on a more limited basis. In deciding which products to stock, management needs to know which products and how much of each product to stock in order to maximize net income. A retail store will normally maximize net income by stocking those products that contribute the most toward covering fixed costs and providing profit in relation to the "critical resource factor," in this case, shelf space. The **critical resource factor** refers to the resource that limits operating capacity according to the availability of that resource. For example, in a manufacturing company, if machine hours are the most critical resource, a company should concentrate on the product for which revenues exceed variable costs by the highest margin per machine hour. Other critical resources in manufacturing companies might include labor hours, floor space, or special raw materials. Since shelf space is the critical resource factor for our retail store example, from a financial point of view, management should stock those products for which revenues exceed variable costs by the highest margin per square foot of shelf space.

critical resource factor The resource that limits operating capacity by its availability.

To illustrate, we assume that Bolten Retail Company stocks potato chips and cookies. Let's further assume that its capacity, at least in the short term, is limited by the availability of only 20 square feet of shelf space for these two products. The revenue and cost data for one package each of potato chips and cookies are:

	Potato Chips	Cookies
Selling price	$3.10	$3.50
Variable costs	2.48	3.15
Contribution margin per unit	$0.62	$0.35
Percentage contribution margin (contribution margin ÷ selling price)	20%	10%

On the basis of this limited information, it would appear that potato chips are more profitable than cookies. The sale of one bag of potato chips will contribute $0.62 toward fixed costs, whereas the sale of one package of cookies will contribute only $0.35.

Before Bolten can decide whether or not to emphasize potato chips, however, management must consider the extent to which each product uses the critical resource, limited shelf space. If a bag of potato chips takes up twice as much space as a package of cookies (two bags of potato chips occupy one square foot of shelf space, while four packages of cookies can occupy the same one square foot of shelf space), the sale of cookies will make a greater total contribution to profits than the sale of potato chips, as shown by the following calculations:[2]

	Potato Chips	Cookies
Contribution margin per unit	$0.62	$0.35
Packages per square foot	× 2	× 4
Contribution margin per square foot of shelf space	$1.24	$1.40

(S T O P & T H I N K)

Why do you think that most grocery stores allocate more space to breakfast cereals than to most other products?

Even though potato chips have a higher contribution margin per unit of product ($0.62 versus $0.35), cookies have a higher contribution margin per square foot of shelf space ($1.40 versus $1.24), which is the critical resource. The management of Bolten Retail Company should stock cookies rather than potato chips, assuming that the company's only critical resource is shelf space.

However, if the demand for cookies is limited and Bolten never has potato chips for sale, will customers start shopping at other stores? In that case, Bolten should stock as many cookies as it can sell and use the balance of the critical resource for stocking potato chips. To illustrate, we assume that the market demand for cookies is 1,800 packages per month or an average of 60 per day. Since it takes only 15 square feet of shelf space (60 packages ÷ 4 packages per square foot) to store one day's worth of cookies, 5 square feet of shelf space is available to stock potato chips. This means that 10 bags of potato chips can be stocked. Assuming all 10 bags are sold during each day, the combined sales of cookies and potato chips will contribute $27.20 to cover fixed costs and provide a profit, as shown below.

	Daily Contribution Margin
Packages sold:	
Potato chips (10 bags × $0.62 per bag)	$ 6.20
Cookies (60 packages × $0.35 per package)	21.00
Total	$27.20

This analysis shows that from a financial perspective, the best use of the 20 square feet of shelf space is to use 15 square feet for cookies and 5 square feet for potato chips. Because demand for cookies is limited, only a $21 daily contribution margin can be earned by selling cookies. The other 5 feet of shelf space should be

2. We are assuming that the company can sell all the potato chips and cookies it stocks. If it can't, or if one product sells faster than the other, rate of turnover must be considered.

CAUTION

It is essential to carefully and accurately identify the scarce resource and the quantity of the scarce resource consumed by each product. For example, in the store shelf space decision, if you don't carefully calculate the amount of space needed for cookies and potato chips, and instead only look at the contribution margin per unit, an incorrect decision will be made. It is only when you consider the contribution margin per square foot of shelf space that the correct decision is made.

used to stock potato chips. Obviously, nonfinancial factors, such as customer satisfaction, would also have to be considered in making the final decision of how much of each product to stock.

The foregoing analysis dealt with only two constraints: store shelf space and product demand. If a firm is further limited by other factors (such as the ability to buy certain amounts of particular products), management generally has to use the quantitative technique of linear programming to help decide how many of each product to produce and/or sell. You can learn about this technique in advanced accounting or business management courses. Regardless of the number of constraints, though, the essence of the decision is to achieve the best short-term utilization of available resources.

TO SUMMARIZE

In deciding how to make the best use of critical resource factors, management should choose the item that provides the greatest contribution margin per unit of the most critical resource.

Deciding at What Stage to Sell a Product

joint manufacturing process Using a single material input to produce more than one product.

In some companies, all the products evolve out of a **joint manufacturing process**, meaning that one material input is used to produce more than one product. Gasoline, oil, and kerosene, for example, are all produced from refining crude oil; various cuts of beef are provided from butchering a steer; and different qualities and types of lumber are available from processing timber. In all these cases, the products are produced simultaneously and are not individually identifiable until the split-off point in the process. When this is the case, management must decide whether a particular product from the joint manufacturing process should be sold as is, or processed further at additional cost, with the expectation of obtaining a higher price.

In choosing the best time to stop processing a product, management basically compares the additional costs that would be incurred from further processing with the additional revenues. If the revenues are greater than the costs, net income is increased, and additional processing is worthwhile (unless qualitative factors dictate otherwise). If the revenues are less than the costs, the product should probably be sold without further processing. The costs that a firm incurs before the point at which the different products are separated for further processing or immediate sale are called **joint product costs**. These costs are incurred whether the separate products are sold at the point of separation or after further processing. Thus, they are not relevant to a choice between the two alternatives.

joint product costs All costs incurred before various products are separated for further processing or immediate sale.

To illustrate the decision-making process related to further processing, we will assume that Armaco Oil Company derives two products, jet fuel and reformate, from crude oil. Although crude oil cannot be sold independently, both jet fuel and reformate can be, either at the point of separation or after further processing. Further processing jet fuel results in a petrochemical product called xylene, while further processing of reformate results in a petrochemical called tolulene. The cost of refining 375,000 gallons of crude oil up to the point of separation is $300,000. Crude oil is then separated into 200,000 gallons of jet fuel and 150,000 gallons of reformate. The remaining 25,000 gallons are lost in the process of refining. The selling prices of jet fuel and reformate at the point of separation, the costs of processing further, and the selling prices after this further processing are estimated by the accounting department to be:[3]

	Gallons	Net Selling Price per Gallon at Separation	Additional Processing Costs	Net Selling Price of Xylene and Tolulene per Gallon After Processing
Jet fuel	200,000	$1.20	$80,000	$1.70 (Xylene)
Reformate	150,000	1.00	90,000	1.50 (Tolulene)

To help management decide whether to sell jet fuel or reformate at the point of separation or to process them further, the following analysis might be prepared.

Product: Jet Fuel/Xylene	
Sales revenue after further processing (200,000 gallons at $1.70)	$340,000
Sales revenue at point of separation (200,000 gallons at $1.20)	240,000
Additional revenue from further processing	$100,000
Additional processing costs	80,000
Additional profit from further processing	$ 20,000

Product: Reformate/Tolulene	
Sales revenue after further processing (150,000 gallons at $1.50)	$225,000
Sales revenue at point of separation (150,000 gallons at $1.00)	150,000
Additional revenue from further processing	$ 75,000
Additional processing costs	90,000
Additional loss from further processing	$ (15,000)

This analysis shows that further processing of jet fuel into xylene will contribute an additional $20,000 to net income, because the additional revenues generated exceed the additional processing costs by $20,000. On the other hand, further processing of reformate into tolulene will reduce net income by $15,000, because the additional processing costs are greater than the additional revenues by that amount. Therefore, reformate should be sold at the point of separation.

A total cost approach to analyzing this decision is shown in Exhibit 14-7. Selling both products after further processing increases net income by $5,000, but the best choice is to sell reformate at the point of separation and to process jet fuel into xylene before it is sold. The worst choice is to sell jet fuel at the point of separation and further process reformate, resulting in only $75,000 of profit. Note that the joint processing costs were not considered in the earlier analysis of the individual products since they are not differential costs but are the same for each alternative. In the later analysis of the alternative treatments of jet fuel and reformate, however, the joint costs are included simply to illustrate the total-cost approach. But they are not really necessary since the difference in net income is the same whether or not the $300,000 of joint costs are included.

In deciding whether to sell products at the point of separation or after further processing, management must also consider qualitative factors. For example, management will need to consider quality and time issues, as well as the hiring or firing of employees and customers' demands for particular products.

3. This analysis assumes that there is no loss from refining jet fuel into Xylene or reformate into Tolulene.

EXHIBIT 14-7 A Comparison of Alternatives: Selling at Point of Separation or After Further Processing

	Sell Both Products at Separation	Sell Both Products After Further Processing	Sell Reformate at Separation and Process Jet Fuel Further	Sell Jet Fuel at Separation and Process Reformate Further
Sales revenue:				
Jet Fuel/Xylene	$240,000	$340,000	$340,000	$240,000
Reformate/Toluene	150,000	225,000	150,000	225,000
Total sales revenue	$390,000	$565,000	$490,000	$465,000
Joint product costs	$300,000	$300,000	$300,000	$300,000
Further processing costs	0	170,000	80,000	90,000
Total costs	$300,000	$470,000	$380,000	$390,000
Net income	$ 90,000	$ 95,000	$110,000	$ 75,000

TO SUMMARIZE

In situations involving products derived from a joint process, joint costs prior to the point of separation are not differential costs; these costs can be ignored in deciding whether products should be sold at the point of separation or after further processing. Only the differential revenues and costs after the point of separation are relevant to the decision.

Setting Selling Prices

Some people argue that a discussion of setting prices in a book such as this is a waste of time because the market sets the price and there is nothing management can do to affect prices. Others argue that, especially in some markets, management does set prices, or at least influence prices. In this section, we assume that management can influence prices and discuss those factors management should consider.

Pricing a product is partly a matter of guesswork, because managers rarely know with any precision how price affects demand (e.g., how many more units could be sold if the price were to be lowered by a certain amount). In addition, other factors, such as advertising and packaging, affect the sale of a product.

The pricing process is further complicated by the fact that there are several broad categories of pricing decisions and the same cost information is not appropriate to all of them. Earlier, we considered the pricing of special orders. In this section, we cover the pricing of normal products. Other pricing categories, including the pricing of new products, are covered in advanced accounting and marketing texts.

Normal Pricing of Products

In deciding whether or not to accept special orders, we stated that the price must be high enough to cover variable and incremental fixed costs. The price normally charged for a product or service, however, must be high enough to cover all costs (including production, selling, and administrative costs) and still provide a reasonable return on the owners' investments. Therefore, all costs (variable, as well as a fair share of fixed costs) are relevant to the pricing decision. In some cases, however, the final price may be set somewhat above or below the price suggested by total cost plus a reasonable return. This occurs when pricing decisions are based primarily on supply and demand, competition, and other market factors. For example, textbook prices are strictly competitive. Whether it costs $250,000 or $500,000 to produce a textbook, its price has to be close to that of the nearest competitors.

In supplying cost data to aid management in normal pricing decisions, accountants may use a functional approach, summarizing costs by function (manufacturing, selling, or administrative) or use a contribution approach, classifying costs by behavior (fixed or variable). To illustrate the two approaches, we assume that Kent Electronics (from the calculator example earlier in the chapter) is pricing a desk calculator. The relevant costs for each approach are as follows:

Functional Cost Approach	
Direct materials	$ 6
Direct labor	8
Manufacturing overhead (200% × direct labor cost)	16
Total manufacturing cost	$30
Markup to cover selling and administrative expenses and provide a reasonable return on investment (0.40 × selling price)	20
Estimated normal selling price	$50

Contribution Approach	
Direct materials	$ 6
Direct labor	8
Variable manufacturing overhead	7
Variable selling and administrative overhead expenses	4
Total variable costs	$25
Markup to cover fixed costs and provide a reasonable return on investment (0.50 × selling price)	25
Estimated normal selling price	$50

The markups calculated here are based on the selling price, since marketing people generally use this approach. How do we calculate the markup as a percentage of the selling price before that price is known? If the markup is to be 40 percent of the selling price, as in our first example, the total manufacturing cost must be 60 percent of the selling price. So we simply divide the manufacturing cost by 60 percent to get the selling price ($30 ÷ 0.60 = $50). Then, the selling price minus the manufacturing cost is the markup ($50 − $30 = $20).

If a functional cost approach is used, the markup must be large enough to cover all selling and administrative costs and provide a reasonable return on investment. If a contribution approach is used, the markup must be large enough to cover all fixed costs and generate a reasonable return on investment.

TO SUMMARIZE

For normal pricing of products, management should consider all costs, not just differential costs (as was the case with pricing special orders). The markups applied must be high enough to cover all costs and expenses and provide a reasonable return on investment.

REVIEW OF LEARNING OBJECTIVES

1 **Explain the difference between routine and nonroutine decisions.** Routine decisions are decisions designed to improve the efficiency and cost-effectiveness of existing operations related to products and operating processes. Such decisions usually are in the form of corrective actions regarding machinery efficiency, reduction of waste, efficient task performance, and overcoming bottlenecks. This type of decision is made regularly, often daily, weekly, or monthly. Nonroutine decisions are more likely to be strategic in that they deal with changes in the product or the processes. These nonroutine decisions might be related to the type or quality of the company's products, fundamental changes in the production process, changing suppliers or types of raw materials, or changing the product distribution system. The concepts of routine and nonroutine decisions are also applicable to merchandising and service companies.

2 **Understand the concept of differential costs and revenues, and be able to identify those costs and revenues that are relevant to making nonroutine decisions.** Making nonroutine decisions involves a consideration of differential costs and revenues. These are future costs and revenues that will change as a result of the decision and therefore are the relevant costs in determining whether the decision to change should be made. Differential costs may be variable, fixed, or both. Past costs that do not change as a result of a decision are not relevant to the decision and are called sunk costs.

3 **Identify several examples of nonroutine decisions, and be able to analyze and select the best alternative for each example.** Short-term, nonroutine decisions include (1) special orders (including whether to make or buy a component or service and whether to accept special orders), (2) whether to exit or enter a market, (3) selecting the best utilization of a critical resource, (4) whether to process a product further or sell it as is, and (5) setting normal selling prices. In choosing whether to make or buy a component or service, management must compare the differential costs of making the part or providing the service (including the opportunity cost of alternative uses of the facilities or labor) with the cost of purchasing the part or service. In deciding whether or not to accept a special order in situations where there is excess capacity, the price should be high enough to provide a positive contribution toward covering normal fixed costs and increasing profit. A product or product line should not be dropped or a market exited unless that unit does not make a positive contribution toward covering indirect fixed costs. An alternative product or line of products can be added that will contribute more toward covering unavoidable indirect costs. A market should be entered only if it contributes to the overall profitability of the firm. In deciding how to use a scarce resource, management should choose the item that provides the greatest contribution margin per unit of the most critical resource. A product should be processed further if the additional revenues from further processing will exceed the additional costs of further processing. For normal pricing, management should consider all costs, not just differential costs.

KEY TERMS AND CONCEPTS

critical resource factor 687
differential costs 670
joint manufacturing process 689
joint product costs 689
nonroutine decisions 668
routine decisions 667
special order 675
sunk costs 671
total cost 672

REVIEW PROBLEM

A Short-Term, Nonroutine Decision: Whether to Make or Buy a Part

Schill Manufacturing Company makes lawn mowers. It has been buying a component from a regular supplier for $11.50 per unit. Since Schill recently has been operating at less than full capacity, the president is considering whether to make the part rather than purchase it. The estimated total cost of making the part under the company's costing system is $14.40, computed as follows:

Direct materials	$ 3.20
Direct labor	5.60
Manufacturing overhead (100% of direct labor cost)	5.60
Estimated total cost to make	$14.40

Variable manufacturing overhead costs are estimated to be 40 percent of direct labor cost. Fixed manufacturing costs which are not differential are 60% of direct labor costs.

Required: Decide whether Schill should make or buy the component.

Solution

Differential-Cost Analysis

	Cost to Make	Cost to Buy
Purchase price		$11.50
Direct materials	$ 3.20	
Direct labor	5.60	
Variable manufacturing overhead (40% of direct labor cost)	2.24	
Differential cost to make the part	$11.04	
Differential cost to buy the part		$11.50
Cost savings by making the part	$ 0.46	

Total-Cost Analysis

	Cost to Make	Cost to Buy
Purchase price		$11.50
Direct materials	$ 3.20	
Direct labor	5.60	
Variable manufacturing overhead (40% of direct labor cost)	2.24	
Fixed manufacturing overhead	3.36	3.36
Total cost to make	$14.40	
Total cost to buy		$14.86
Cost savings by making the part	$ 0.46	

Calculations:
$5.60 × 0.40 = $2.24 variable manufacturing overhead
$5.60 × 0.60 = $3.36 fixed manufacturing overhead

Unless qualitative factors override the cost estimate, Schill should make the part rather than purchase it. The decision will be the same whether the calculation is based on differential costs only or on total costs. Note that the fixed manufacturing overhead cost applies to both making and buying the part under the total-cost analysis, since these costs will be incurred whichever alternative is selected.

DISCUSSION QUESTIONS

1. Distinguish between routine and nonroutine decisions.
2. Many accounting systems are designed to collect financial information for the purpose of preparing financial statements. What problem does this create for an accountant who is asked to compile relevant data for use by managers to make short-term nonroutine decisions? Explain.

3. What is a differential cost? Give an example of how differential costs are used by managers making short-term nonroutine decisions.
4. Distinguish between variable costs and differential costs. Why is the distinction important?
5. Can a fixed cost be relevant to a decision? Explain.
6. What is a sunk cost? Why are sunk costs irrelevant in short-term nonroutine decision making?
7. In deciding whether to replace an old asset with a new one, which of the following are differential revenues and costs?
   a. Cost of the new equipment
   b. Resale value of the old equipment
   c. Resale value of the new equipment
   d. Book value of the old equipment
   e. Operating costs of the new equipment
8. Distinguish between the total-cost approach and the differential-cost approach to analyzing data for short-term nonroutine decisions.
9. What is the major limitation in using the total-cost approach to analyze data for short-term nonroutine decisions?
10. Why must business decisions be based on qualitative as well as quantitative information? Explain.
11. Explain what costs are generally relevant to make-or-buy decisions.
12. Explain why opportunity costs are not included in the accounting records.
13. What is the significance of idle capacity in determining the price of a special order?
14. If total manufacturing costs, including fixed manufacturing overhead, are larger than the price offered by a purchaser for a special order, the order should not be accepted because the profits of the company will be adversely affected. Do you agree? Explain. (Ignore qualitative factors.)
15. In deciding whether to exit or enter a market, what factors should be considered?
16. When should a segment (product, product line, division, etc.) be dropped? When should a segment be added?
17. Why is the contribution margin per unit of a critical resource more important than the contribution margin per unit of product in deciding which products to produce and sell?
18. What determines whether a product should be sold at the point of separation from a joint process or after further processing? (Assume that a decision is to be based solely on quantitative information.)

DISCUSSION CASES

CASE 14-1 BUYING FROM INSIDE OR OUTSIDE THE COMPANY

E & B Company has two divisions, processing and finishing. The Finishing Division has been purchasing certain products from the Processing Division at a price of $80 per unit. (A unit consists of 100 yards of material.) The Processing Division has announced that, starting with next month's operations, it will raise its price to $100 per unit. As the manager of the Finishing Division, you object to this price and have indicated that you are planning to purchase these units of material from outside suppliers at a price of $85 per unit. You have asked the accounting department to furnish cost data to help you understand why the Processing Division's price has to be raised to $100 per unit. Following is the information supplied about the Processing Division's operations:

Units produced for Finishing Division	2,000
Variable production costs per unit	$60
Indirect fixed costs allocated to the Processing Division	$50,000
Normal profit per unit in Processing Division	$15

If the Finishing Division buys from outside suppliers, the facilities used by the Processing Division to manufacture these units for the Finishing Division will remain idle.

Answer the following questions:

1. If the Processing Division is successful in imposing the $100 price and the Finishing Division elects to buy from outside suppliers, what impact does this action have on the overall profit of E & B Company?
2. Explain why the variable production costs, the fixed costs, and the normal profit are, or are not, each relevant to this decision. (You are not being asked to discuss whether the $100 price is an appropriate price or whether the division managers should be allowed to maintain an autonomous posture in this decision.)
3. What additional factors should E & B Company's top management consider in resolving this matter?

CASE 14-2

SUNK COSTS

Sam Love owns and manages a small but growing service business. In fact, this year has been so good that Sam is moving his office to a larger, more centrally located site. In an effort to save on moving costs, Sam employs his brother Dan (who owns a large truck) to haul his office furniture and equipment. Unfortunately, Dan doesn't properly secure the rear door of the truck and one of Sam's two copy machines winds up in a million pieces in the middle of the highway. As the two brothers survey the damage, Sam's office manager approaches and says, "Well, look on the bright side, the machine was half depreciated."

Should Sam take comfort from this statement? Explain your answer.

EXERCISES

EXERCISE 14-1
Classifying Decisions

For each of the following situations, indicate whether the decision appears to be a routine operating decision; a short-term, nonroutine decision; or a long-term investment decision.

1. Able Corporation is deciding whether to make a part for a new product or to buy the part from another company.
2. Baker Company produces three products. The production manager needs to prepare a weekly schedule in order to determine how much of each product to manufacture on each machine.
3. Carter Corporation is considering investing in a new production plant in Mexico.
4. Diamond Company is considering discontinuing production of marked playing cards.
5. The inventory manager of Echo Company is determining how much raw material to order next month.
6. Franklin Inc. has received a special order for 10,000 units of its best-selling product, but the selling price for the order is less than the normal selling price.
7. The City Council of Granada is trying to decide whether to continue collecting garbage in the city or to contract the collection to a private company.

EXERCISE 14-2
Relevant Costs

Quick Serve Company provides janitorial services for office buildings. Last year the firm acquired a cleaning machine for $100,000. The firm expected to use the machine for five years. However, this year a new, more efficient machine has been introduced on the market. The accountant for Quick Serve has determined that the annual total operating costs for the old machine are $240,000. The annual operating costs for the new machine would be $200,000, and the purchase price is $130,000. The president of Quick Serve feels that the company should not buy the new machine. He points out that the operating costs of $200,000 and the purchase price of $130,000 for the new machine, plus the original cost of the old machine of $100,000, are greater than the operating costs of the old machine.

1. Do you agree with the president?
2. What type of cost is the $100,000 purchase price of the old machine?

EXERCISE 14-3
Qualitative Factors

Sturdy Chair Company manufactures wooden chairs. In producing the chairs, a great deal of scrap wood is created. The company presently uses the wood as fuel in a factory furnace. However, it has the opportunity to send the scrap wood to a subcontractor, who would turn it into pressed board to be used to produce small end tables as a new product of Sturdy Chair.

Identify any qualitative factors that Sturdy Chair Company might want to consider in deciding how to use the scrap wood.

EXERCISE 14-4
Special-Order Pricing

You are the controller for Comfort Shoe Company. The company has excess shoes, which it has not been able to market through its own distribution outlets. The president is negotiating with a large department store chain to sell Comfort shoes in order to utilize the excess capacity. He has asked you to estimate the minimum selling price below which Comfort should not accept an order from the retail chain. Cost information per pair of shoes is:

Direct materials	$8
Direct labor	5
Manufacturing overhead:	
Variable	3
Fixed	2
Selling and administrative expenses:	
Variable	1
Fixed	3

The fixed costs are the same whether or not the order is accepted.

1. What is the minimum selling price the company should accept based solely on cost information (not considering qualitative factors)?
2. Assume that the president agrees to sell 20,000 pairs at a price of $19 per pair. What would be the expected increase in profit?

EXERCISE 14-5
Make-or-Buy Decisions

Tiny Toy Company needs 40,000 miniature engines to complete its toy fire trucks. If Tiny Toy Company buys rather than makes the part, some of the facilities still cannot be used in another manufacturing activity. Twenty-five percent of the fixed manufacturing overhead costs are indirect and will still be incurred regardless of which decision is made. The following costs of making and buying the part are:

Cost to make the part:	
Direct materials	$ 5.00
Direct labor	10.00
Variable manufacturing overhead	7.00
Fixed manufacturing overhead	8.00
	$30.00
Cost to buy the part from another company	$28.80

Identify the differential costs of making the part as a basis for deciding whether to make or buy it.

EXERCISE 14-6
Make-or-Buy Decisions

Miller Manufacturing builds and markets personal computers for home and small business use. The company has been approached by an outside supplier offering to provide completed monitors to the company for $65 each. The company's marketing director negotiated the deal personally and is thrilled about how much cheaper it will be to purchase the monitors from outside. Producing the cost data outlined below, the manager proudly proclaims, "Look, a $9 per unit savings!"

	Per Unit	15,000 Units per Year
Direct materials	$28	$ 420,000
Direct labor	10	150,000
Variable manufacturing overhead	3	45,000
Fixed manufacturing overhead, direct	6	90,000
Fixed manufacturing overhead, indirect	27	405,000
Total cost	$74	$1,110,000

1. Assuming zero opportunity costs, should the company accept the outside offer?
2. If the display units are purchased from outside, Miller can produce an alternative product that will contribute $250,000 per year toward covering indirect fixed overhead. Will this affect your decision in item (1) above?

EXERCISE 14-7
Make-or-Buy Decisions

Alta Company has been manufacturing 8,000 units of part X for its products. The unit cost for the part is as follows:

Direct materials	$ 3
Direct labor	8
Variable manufacturing overhead	4
Fixed manufacturing overhead	6
Total	$21

A supplier has offered to sell 8,000 units of part X to Alta for $18 each. If the part is purchased, Alta can use its facilities to manufacture another product, which would generate a contribution margin of $4,000. Seventy-five percent of the fixed manufacturing overhead costs are indirect and will still be incurred even if the part is purchased.

Compute the net differential cost in deciding whether to make or buy the part.

EXERCISE 14-8
Purchasing Services from Outside

Dr. Anderson, a local dentist, is considering reducing his office staff and outsourcing the management of his accounts receivable. Currently, he has an office manager and two part-time workers on his staff. It takes one part-time employee almost 100 percent of her time to send out billing notices and follow up on collections. Even then, Dr. Anderson is able to collect on only about 80 percent of the receivables. A collection agency wants Dr. Anderson's business. It will handle all billing and collection details for a monthly fee of $1,500. The agency believes it can deliver a 90 percent collection of receivables. Another firm, We Collect, Inc., has approached Anderson with a proposal that would shift all accounts receivable risk to We Collect, Inc. Anderson would receive 85 percent of all receivables automatically. Additional information follows.

Anderson's average yearly accounts receivable	$400,000
Anderson's average annual bad debt expense	80,000
Part-time accounts receivable employee salary	12,000

Which of the following alternatives should Anderson pursue concerning his accounts receivable?

1. Maintain status quo (part-time employee handling accounts receivable).
2. Outsource to collection agency.
3. Outsource to We Collect, Inc.

EXERCISE 14-9
Discontinuing a Product Line

Swanton Company presently sells three products: desk calendars, pen sets, and paper-clip holders. The company is thinking of discontinuing the production and sales of paper-clip holders. However, because many customers buy the products as a set, Swanton estimates that the sales of the other two products will decrease by 20 percent if the paper-clip holders are discontinued.

Current data on each of the three products are provided below.

	Desk Calendars	Pen Sets	Paper-Clip Holders	Total
Units	40,000	20,000	12,000	
Sales revenue	$280,000	$240,000	$24,000	$544,000
Variable costs	160,000	160,000	26,000	346,000
Direct fixed costs	40,000	20,000	5,000	65,000
Indirect fixed costs	30,000	40,000	6,000	76,000

1. What is the segment margin of the paper-clip holders?
2. **Interpretive Question:** Would you recommend dropping the paper-clip holder product line? Why or why not?

EXERCISE 14-10
Adding a New Product

Lipston Corporation is thinking about adding a new product line. Marketing surveys indicate that sales of the new product would be 200,000 units. Each unit sells for $4. Direct variable costs would be $2.80 per unit, direct fixed costs would be $120,000, and $90,000 represents the company's indirect fixed costs. The company does not expect the new product to affect the sales of its other products.

Should Lipston add the new product? Why or why not?

EXERCISE 14-11
Contribution Margin per Unit of a Critical Resource

Santana Sports Company produces two products, soccer balls and volleyballs. Both products are extremely popular, and the company can sell as many of either ball as it can produce. Santana Sports, however, can produce only a limited number of balls because only 12,000 direct labor hours are available due to the isolated location of the community. It takes two hours of direct labor to produce a soccer ball and one-and-one-half hours to produce a volleyball. The selling price of a soccer ball is $34, and the variable costs are $20. The selling price of a volleyball is $26, with variable costs of $14.

Which product should Santana Sports Company produce if its direct labor hours are limited?

EXERCISE 14-12
Critical Resource Constraints

Whiz Kids manufactures two computer games. Far Out is a quiz game about astronomy, and Dynamite is a mystery game. The company has a limited supply of skilled labor and also has been able to obtain only a limited number of "chips," a necessary part in the production process.

Information on each product is as follows:

	Far Out	Dynamite
Contribution margin per unit	$4	$3
Units produced per hour	2	3
Units produced per 100 chips	80	60

Anticipated sales exceed capacity for both products.
Total labor hours available: 9,000 hours
Total chips available: 30,000 chips

1. Identify the critical resource restraint under which Whiz Kids must operate.
2. Which product should be produced?

EXERCISE 14-13
Joint Costs and Further Processing

Pure Paint Company has been known for years for its two excellent interior wall paints: Nice & Smooth and Rich & Thick. The company has discovered that by processing Rich & Thick further it could produce a slightly different paint.

Nice & Smooth and Rich & Thick are produced jointly at a cost of $160,000, which is allocated equally between them. If Rich & Thick were processed further, its selling price would increase by $2.25 per unit, and the additional cost per unit would be $1.80.

1. On the basis of the information given (and disregarding qualitative factors), should the company process Rich & Thick further? Do you have enough information to make a recommendation? Explain.
2. **Interpretive Question:** Is the joint cost of $160,000 relevant to this discussion? Why or why not?

EXERCISE 14-14
Sell Now or Process Further

Colorado Company uses a joint process to manufacture products R, S, and T. Each product can be sold at the point of separation, or it can be processed further. All additional processing costs are directly traceable to each product that is processed further. Joint production costs for the year are $140,000 and are allocated to products R, S, and T on the basis of their sales values at the point of separation. The pertinent data accumulated by the accounting department for these products are:

				Sales Value and Additional Costs of Processing Further	
Product	Units	Sales Value at Separation	Allocation of Joint Costs	Sales Value	Additional Costs
R	18,000	$150,000	$70,000	$190,000	$24,000
S	20,000	120,000	56,000	150,000	40,000
T	10,000	30,000	14,000	60,000	25,000

1. Which products should Colorado Company process further (after separation) in order to maximize its profits? Show computations.
2. Explain why you did or did not use the allocated joint costs in deciding which of the products to process further.

EXERCISE 14-15
Pricing Regular Products

Medical Care Inc. is considering what price to charge for Sparkle, a toothpaste that is sold in their leased store at a hospital. The accountant has been asked to prepare an estimated normal selling price based on the costs that Medical Care incurs in making the product in a factory it operates. Costs of producing one tube of Sparkle are 20 cents for direct materials, 10 cents for direct labor, 20 cents for variable manufacturing overhead, and 10 cents for variable selling and administrative costs. Total direct fixed costs are $10,000. The company estimates that a markup of 40 percent of the selling price is necessary to cover the fixed costs and provide a reasonable return on investment.

1. Calculate the estimated normal selling price.
2. Would you recommend that the company obtain any other information before establishing a sales price?

PROBLEMS

PROBLEM 14-1
Special-Order Pricing

Midwest Company manufactures portable radios. Shop Smart, a large retail merchandiser, wants to buy 200,000 radios from Midwest Company for $12 each. The radio would carry Shop Smart's name and would be sold in its stores.

Midwest Company normally sells 420,000 radios a year at $16 each; its production capacity is 540,000 units a year. Cost information for the radios is as follows:

Production costs:	
Variable production costs	$7
Fixed manufacturing overhead ($2,100,000 ÷ 420,000 units)	5
Selling and administrative expenses:	
Variable	1
Fixed ($420,000 ÷ 420,000 units)	1

The $1 variable selling and administrative expenses would not be applicable to the radios ordered by Shop Smart since that is a single large order. Shop Smart has indicated that the company is not interested in signing a contract for less than 200,000 radios. Total fixed costs will not change regardless of whether the Shop Smart order is accepted.

Required:

1. Identify any opportunity costs that Midwest Company should consider when making the decision.
2. Determine whether Midwest Company should accept Shop Smart's offer.
3. **Interpretive Question:** What qualitative factors might be relevant to this decision?

PROBLEM 14-2
Make-or-Buy Decisions

Logan Company manufactures several toy products. One is a large plastic truck, which requires a plastic truck body, two metal axles, and four rubber wheels. Logan presently manufactures and assembles all the parts.

Another toy company has offered to sell the parts to Logan at $1.70 per truck if 20,000 or more parts are purchased each year, and at $2 per truck if less than 20,000 parts are purchased. Logan is considering this offer. The space used in producing the parts could be used for a new toy, which is scheduled to begin production next year. If Logan continues to produce the parts for the plastic truck, the company will have to lease space from another company in an adjacent building to produce the new toy. The rent would be $8,000 per year.

Other information related to the truck is:

	Produce Parts	Assemble Truck	Total
Direct materials	$1.10	$0.20	$1.30
Direct labor	0.30	0.20	0.50
Variable manufacturing overhead	0.20	0.15	0.35
Fixed manufacturing overhead	0.20	0.40	0.60
Total manufacturing costs	$1.80	$0.95	$2.75

The marketing department has estimated that sales for the plastic truck will be approximately 16,000 units per year for the next three years. The fixed manufacturing overhead is indirect and will still be incurred regardless of which decision is made.

Required:

1. Describe Logan Company's two alternatives for this decision.
2. What costs are relevant to the decision?
3. Which alternative should Logan Company select?
4. What would be the best decision had Logan not planned to produce the new toy?
5. **Interpretive Question:** What are some of the qualitative factors that Logan Company might consider in making the decision?

PROBLEM 14-3
Choosing Between Two Machines

Tasty Burger is thinking of making the hamburger rolls for its chain of fast food restaurants. Two machines, A and B, are being considered for purchase. The company now purchases the rolls from an outside supplier for 12 cents each. The cost information for producing the rolls would be:

	Machine A	Machine B
Variable costs per roll	$0.08	$0.07
Annual fixed costs	$1,750	$2,500
Initial cost of machine	$5,000	$12,000
Salvage value at end of five years	$0	$4,000
Estimated life of machine	5 years	5 years

Required:

1. At a sales volume of 300,000 rolls per year, which of these alternatives is better —buying the rolls, using machine A, or using machine B? (Ignore the time value of money, and assume straight-line depreciation.)
2. At what level of production would you be indifferent to machine A and machine B? Which machine is preferable if production exceeds this volume?

PROBLEM 14-4
Purchasing Services from Outside

Northeast Reinsurance Company is growing rapidly. As it has grown, it has added legal staff to provide for its legal services. One of the principals of the company is an attorney who has provided oversight over the growing legal department. However, she is now too busy to continue this "legal counsel" role. She suggests that the senior company attorney become an officer of the company and be given the title "legal counsel and secretary." Another of the principals is good friends with an attorney of a prestigious regional law firm. That law firm has offered to provide Northeast with legal services for an annual retainer of $500,000 plus an average billing rate of $100 an hour for all work done over 5,000 hours per year. It is expected that legal work, whether done inside or outside the company, will require about 6,000 hours this coming year and will probably increase by 10 percent a year thereafter. The current company legal staff may be able to handle the work load for two years before it will have to hire another attorney (at an expected salary and benefit package of $100,000). Other variable costs are expected to increase by 5 percent a year.

Additional information follows:

	Current Costs of Internal Legal Department
Salaries and benefits of legal staff	$350,000
Travel costs	80,000
Required continuing education costs	10,000
Legal support costs (library, computers, software, supplies, etc.)	100,000
Other variable costs	25,000
Allocated office overhead (depreciation, utilities, etc.)	40,000
Total costs of legal department	$605,000

Required:

1. What are the relevant costs for Northeast to consider in making this decision?
2. From a financial standpoint, should Northeast continue to use its own legal department for legal services or outsource this function to the regional law firm?
3. What other factors might Northeast consider in making this decision?

PROBLEM 14-5
Unifying Concepts: Make-or-Buy Decisions (Differential Costs, Sunk Costs, Opportunity Costs)

Snow Corporation manufactures freezers for residential use. The company is planning to produce a new freezer suitable for apartments. These smaller freezers require a component that Snow Corporation can either make or buy from a subcontractor. The subcontractor will sell the part for $46. The costs for making 12,000 units of the part are as follows:

Direct materials	$20 per unit
Direct labor	$15 per unit
Variable manufacturing overhead	$10 per unit
Fixed manufacturing overhead	$40,000*

*The $40,000 fixed manufacturing overhead includes $24,000 of indirect fixed costs allocated to the part and $16,000 for a production manager.

If the part is produced, Snow Corporation will use an idle machine it already owns. If the part is bought, the company plans to rent the machine and the factory space to another company for $8,000 and $14,000 a year, respectively.

Snow expects that, if the part is produced, the company will be able to schedule production so that no warehouse space will be needed. However, if the part is bought, Snow will need to use warehouse space, for which it will have to pay $2,000 a year in rent.

Required:

1. Identify any opportunity costs relevant to the decision to make or buy the component.
2. Determine the differential costs of making the product.
3. Determine the differential costs of buying the product.
4. **Interpretive Question:** Would you recommend that Snow make or buy the component? Why?

PROBLEM 14-6
Dropping a Product Line

Mountain Land Inc. manufactures skis, ski boots, and ski poles for downhill skiing. The company is thinking of dropping ski poles as a product line. The following report was prepared by the accounting department:

	Skis	Ski Boots	Ski Poles	Total
Sales revenues	$480,000	$210,000	$50,000	$740,000
Variable costs	(370,000)	(140,000)	(24,000)	(534,000)
Contribution margin	$110,000	$ 70,000	$26,000	$206,000
Direct fixed costs	(40,000)	(20,000)	(27,000)	(87,000)
Segment margin	$ 70,000	$ 50,000	$ (1,000)	$119,000
Indirect fixed costs	(35,000)	(20,000)	(5,000)	(60,000)
Net income	$ 35,000	$ 30,000	$ (6,000)	$ 59,000

Required:

1. Should the ski pole line be dropped? Why or why not?
2. **Interpretive Question:** What qualitative factors should be considered in deciding whether to drop the ski pole line?

PROBLEM 14-7
Adding and Dropping Product Lines

Hansig Manufacturing Company has been producing three products: A, B, and C. Now that the plant has been shifted to an assembly-line operation, a fourth product, D, has been added. Each product has its own assembly-line operation, producing 10,000 units. Total indirect fixed costs of $23,000 are divided proportionately, based on the space allocated to each assembly line. Other pertinent information is given below.

	A	B	C	D
Selling price per unit	$3.00	$2.50	$2.70	$1.50
Variable cost per unit	$2.00	$1.80	$1.80	$1.30
Number of square feet	800	600	500	400

Required:

1. Prepare a schedule that shows net income for each product line.
2. Would total company income increase if product D were dropped? Why or why not?
3. **Interpretive Question:** If you could double the production of A, B, or C in place of having D, which would you choose? Why?

PROBLEM 14-8
Shutting Down or Continuing Operations

End Trail Campground is open year-round. However, 80 percent of its revenues are generated from May through October. Since only 20 percent of the revenues are generated from November to April, the campground is considering closing during those months. The yearly revenues and cost information expected by End Trail for next year if the campground does not close are:

Camping fees	$1,800,000
Variable costs	990,000
Fixed costs ($40,000 per month)	480,000

The cost to close the campground at the end of October would be $20,000, and the cost to reopen in May would be $50,000. If the campground is closed, the total fixed costs are only $25,000 per month, rather than the $40,000 per month when the campground is open.

Required: Determine whether End Trail Campground should close from November to April or remain open for the entire year.

PROBLEM 14-9

Determining Production with a Critical Resource Limitation

Clarity Corporation produces three sizes of television sets: 10-inch screen, 19-inch screen, and 24-inch screen. The revenues and costs per unit for each size are as follows:

	Screen Size		
	10-inch	19-inch	24-inch
Selling price	$195	$325	$450
Variable costs:			
Direct materials	$ 55	$100	$126
Direct labor	80	120	180
Variable manufacturing overhead	40	60	90
Total variable costs	$175	$280	$396
Contribution margin	$ 20	$ 45	$ 54
Units ordered for next week	200	150	75

The company has a constraint on the amount of skilled labor available to produce television sets. Direct labor employees are paid $8 per hour. The total amount of labor time available for next week's production is 2,700 hours.

Required: Given the units ordered for next week, which size or sizes of television sets should be produced and sold to maximize the company's profit?

PROBLEM 14-10

Determining Production with a Critical Resource Limitation

A company is examining two of its products, X-121 and Y-707. The following information is being reviewed:

	X-121	Y-707
Unit selling price	$28.50	$21.00
Materials required per unit	$3.00	$1.50
Direct labor required per unit	$2.50	$1.25
Variable manufacturing overhead per unit	$0.50	$1.00
Production time per unit (in hours)	1.5	1

Required:

1. Which item should the company manufacture if there is no constraint on hours of production?
2. If full production capacity is 1,500 hours, and if the company can sell all the units it makes, which item should it manufacture? Why?

PROBLEM 14-11
Contribution Margin per Unit of a Critical Resource

Dresser Inc. manufactures three super-sports-hero dolls: Super Dunk, Pete Tulip, and Zonk. Production, however, is limited by the skilled labor necessary to produce these unique dolls. Data on each of the dolls are as follows:

	Super Dunk	Pete Tulip	Zonk
Contribution margin per doll	$6	$4	$5
Dolls produced per hour	20	28	25
Expected total market volume (units)	20,000	9,000	100,000

Total skilled labor hours available: 4,500 hours.

Required: Assuming that there are no relevant qualitative factors, how many dolls of each type should be produced by Dresser?

PROBLEM 14-12
Unifying Concepts: Production and Advertising

Cole Company manufactures only two products—a battery charger and a testing machine for automobile engines. An average of 30,000 chargers and 50,000 testers are sold each year. This year, the company can afford only $60,000 for advertising the products, which is just enough to advertise one product effectively. The marketing manager expects that the sales of chargers will increase by 20 percent if they are advertised and that the sales of testers will increase by 10 percent if they are advertised.

The following information about the two products has been provided by the accountant:

	Charger	Tester
Selling price per unit	$70	$90
Variable cost per unit	$30	$40
Fixed cost per unit	$30	$40
Production time per unit (in hours)	2	4

Required:

1. If Cole had an unlimited number of labor hours, would you recommend that it advertise either of its products? If yes, which one and why?
2. Assume that Cole has a capacity of 260,000 labor hours. Would you still advertise? If so, which product would you advertise?

PROBLEM 14-13
Processing Past the Point of Separation

Style Company manufactures three items, S1, S2, and S3, which are used in the production of fabrics. Each item can be sold at the point that all three are separated from the joint production process, or they can be processed further. Presently, S1 and S2 are processed past the point of separation. The joint cost of producing the three items to the point of separation is $450,000. The costs past the point of separation are variable and can be traced to each product. The $450,000 joint costs are allocated to each product equally.

The following information is available:

	Number of Units Produced	Selling Price per Unit at Point of Separation	Additional Processing Costs	Selling Price per Unit After Processing
S1	100,000	$10	$120,000	$12
S2	40,000	9	90,000	11
S3	60,000	11	?	13

Required:

1. Should S1 and S2 be processed after the separation point?
2. What maximum additional processing costs could be incurred to process S3 further and still leave a profit?

PROBLEM 14-14
Normal Selling Price

TeleCom Products manufactures desktop and wall-mounted telephone units. The company is seeking to come up with a reasonable price for its desktop slimline model. Production costs for each unit follow:

Direct materials	$3.50 per unit
Direct labor	0.5 hour per unit
Direct labor rate	$6 per hour
Variable manufacturing overhead	$4 per labor hour
Variable selling and administrative costs	$1 per unit
Fixed overhead (direct)	$1.50 per unit
Markup of selling price to cover indirect overhead and expected profit	40%

Required: Calculate the estimated normal selling price.

Analyzing Real Company Information

International Case

Ethics Case

Writing Assignment

The Debate

Internet Search

Accounting is more than just doing textbook problems. These Competency Enhancement Opportunities provide practice in critical thinking, oral and written communication, research, teamwork, and consideration of ethical issues.

ANALYZING REAL COMPANY INFORMATION

• Analyzing 14–1 (Microsoft)

Go to the annual report for **Microsoft** provided in Appendix A at the back of this textbook. Read through the report to determine how many segments of business exist within Microsoft. What approach does Microsoft appear to use in identifying operating segments within the company at large?

• Analyzing 14–2 (Main Line Pictures, Inc. vs. Kim Basinger)

Hollywood produces a lot of entertainment, including accounting entertainment! In early 1993, the Superior Court of the State of California (Los Angeles County) heard a litigation suit filed by **Main Line Pictures, Inc.**, against the actress Kim Basinger for breach of contract. At question was Basinger's decision to withdraw from a film project after making a verbal commitment to appear in it. The film, released in September 1993, was "Boxing Helena." Didn't see it? That's the point of Main Line's lawsuit; a lot of people didn't see "Boxing Helena," since the actress they used to replace Basinger (Sherilyn Fenn) did not have nearly the same box office appeal.

Main Line claimed damages due to an incremental difference in revenues and costs, which led to actual profits being less than expected, all due to not having Basinger in the film. An expert economist and an expert in film finance were called to testify regarding the appropriate size of the incremental revenue and cost differences. Hence, the case essentially became an accounting argument.

COMPETENCY ENHANCEMENT OPPORTUNITIES

Main Line's lawyers argued that their client lost between $5.1 million and $9.7 million as a result of Basinger's withdrawal. The $5.1 million loss calculation is shown below (all amounts are in millions).

Minimum Damages, Plaintiff

	With Basinger	Without Basinger	Difference
Foreign presales	$ 7.60	$ 2.70	$4.90
Domestic presales	3.00		3.00
Total revenue	$10.60	$ 2.70	$7.90
Production costs	(7.60)	(4.80)	(2.80)
Profit (loss)	$ 3.00	$(2.10)	$5.10

In order to understand the numbers above, there are a couple of things you need to know about revenues and costs in the movie business and this film in particular.

- It is extremely difficult to predict what a film will actually earn when released. There are *plenty* of examples of big budget films that did poorly at the box office, as well as inexpensive, independent films that have done very well. Hence, presale revenue (guaranteed minimum payments by a film distributor to the film producer) is the only sure revenue the producer can bank on when budgeting costs of making the film. If the film does well, then the distributor and producer share in the profits.
- After Basinger dropped from the film, one of Main Line's partners loaned $1.7 million to the project, to be repaid out of domestic revenues.
- Often the producer will contract to share profits from presales, as well as incremental profits, with key actors. Basinger was to be paid a guaranteed $1 million to star in the film. However, she, her proposed co-star Ed Harris, and writer/director Jennifer Lynch were to be paid a total of 20.5 percent of the producer's net profits. On the other hand, Sherilyn Fenn and her co-star, Julian Sands, each received only a $100,000 guaranteed salary.
- After Basinger dropped from the film project, the producer made some changes to scale back production costs by $1.9 million.
- Often there are many investing partners in a movie project. Main Line had a partnership with Philippe Caland, who was, essentially, to receive 50 percent of net profits (after participation payments to the actors and writer), up to a maximum of $2 million.
- After withdrawing from "Boxing Helena," Basinger received $3 million from a separate producer to star in "Final Analysis."

Do you agree with the numbers presented above by the plaintiff? Consider all the information provided above and adjust the incremental profit analysis if needed. Be sure to defend your decision to use or not use each piece of information provided.

Source: Adapted from T. L. Barton, W. G. Shenkir, and B. C. Marinas, "Main Line vs. Basinger: A Case in Relevant Costs and Incremental Analysis," *Issues in Accounting Education,* Spring 1996, pp. 163–174.

INTERNATIONAL CASE

• Ameripill Company

Located in Bartow, Alabama, the Pharmaceutical Division of **Ameripill Company** ranks among the top fifteen drug companies in the world. The European Unit of the Pharmaceutical Division is divided into three markets: United Kingdom (U.K.), Germany, and France. Actual and budgeted operating reports for 1992 and 1993 are presented below for these three markets.

	United Kingdom		Germany		France	
	1993 Budget	1992 Actual	1993 Budget	1992 Actual	1993 Budget	1992 Actual
Sales	$49,960	$48,080	$156,840	$137,440	$108,720	$102,560
Cost of sales	(21,982)	(21,155)	(65,872)	(57,995)	(53,414)	(50,254)
Direct expenses	(14,658)	(14,512)	(50,286)	(46,603)	(31,529)	(29,742)
Other income/expenses	(1,499)	(1,155)	(300)	(210)	(946)	(1,026)
Responsibility earnings	$11,821	$11,258	$ 40,382	$ 32,632	$ 22,831	$ 21,538
Interest income/expense*	(358)	(241)	(1,312)	(939)	(1,033)	(1,047)
Exchange gain/loss**	(142)	(338)	(150)	(210)	(272)	(286)
Division charges***	(1,629)	(1,640)	(4,700)	(4,123)	(3,262)	(3,077)
Earnings before taxes	$ 9,692	$ 9,039	$ 34,220	$ 27,360	$ 18,264	$ 17,128
Segment assets	$84,500	$88,860	$ 73,760	$ 72,900	$ 74,220	$ 73,460
Earnings before taxes	19.4%	18.8%	21.8%	19.9%	16.8%	16.7%
Return on assets	11.5%	10.2%	46.4%	37.5%	24.6%	23.3%

*Based on locally incurred debt.
**Based on the average 1992 exchange rate with the United States.
***Fixed charge negotiated annually between the Bartow Division and the market subsidiary.

1. Analyze these reports carefully. Assuming that Ameripill requires a minimum ROA of 12 percent, should the company consider dropping the U.K. market?
2. Ameripill currently has a problem with one of the drugs sold in France. In the French market, Saincoeur is a highly successful treatment for heart-attack victims. (It is also sold under other names in all of Ameripill's markets.) Because of regulatory pressure in France, Saincoeur is being sold at a much lower price in France than in Germany or the U.K. Despite the price ceiling, Saincoeur is a profitable product

(barely) in France. However, word of the lower price is creating a lot of pressure in the neighboring markets to reduce the prices to a level similar to the French market. Saincoeur is a very profitable product in both Germany and the U.K. How do these facts affect your previous decision regarding the U.K. market in (1)?

Source: Adapted from S. F. Haka, B. A. Lamberton, and H. M. Sollenberger, "International Subsidiary Performance Evaluation: The Case of the Ameripill Company," *Issues in Accounting Education,* Spring 1994, pp. 168–190.

ETHICS CASE

• Play World Inc.

Roger Smith, the controller of Play World Inc., a toy company, has just completed an analysis of a make-or-buy decision with respect to a particular part for one of the new toys the company is planning to manufacture. The result of the analysis clearly shows that the company should buy the part from one of the three available suppliers (based on written price quotations received from those suppliers within the past few weeks). Based on this analysis, Smith and the division manager, Kate Pfirman, agreed to proceed with placing an order. They issued instructions to the purchasing department indicating that the order should be placed for a price not higher than $3.40 per part. A few days later, Smith received a phone call from the purchasing department indicating that all three suppliers had raised their price to $4.00 per unit. It was a normal business practice to raise prices after written quotations had been issued.

It was immediately clear to Smith that it would be disadvantageous to his company to buy the part at the higher price. He discussed the new information with Pfirman, and they agreed to proceed with manufacturing plans to make the part internally. Smith thought it was rather strange that all three suppliers had raised their price to the same amount, but felt there was nothing he could do about it.

A few days later, Smith's secretary, Lynn Berry, asked if she could have a private conversation with him. Berry was obviously upset, so Smith asked her to come into his office and shut the door. Berry told him she was good friends with the secretary for the president of one of the suppliers from which Play World had planned to buy the part for the new toy. Berry's friend had casually mentioned that her boss had been on the phone with the other suppliers and they had agreed to raise the price for certain parts they were manufacturing to specified dollar amounts. Berry said she was reluctant to tell Smith because she didn't want her friend to get in trouble for revealing confidential information outside her company. This information was the missing piece for Smith that explained why the price for the part had been raised to $4.00 by all three companies. Smith thanked Berry for the information and told her not to worry; he would keep the information to himself but would give some thought to what he would eventually do with what she had told him.

1. Who are the parties that are affected by this bid-rigging scheme?
2. What should Smith do with the information he received from Berry (keep in mind his responsibilities to the accounting profession, to his company, and to Berry)?

WRITING ASSIGNMENT

• Airline ticket prices

If you have ever shopped for airline tickets, you are aware of the tremendous diversity in ticket prices for the same flight, even for those who sit in the same classification (first-class, coach, etc.) Much of the difference is based on two factors: (1) when you bought your ticket and (2) whether or not you plan to stay over a Saturday night.

Write a one- to two-page paper describing why airline companies have so many different ticket prices. Also, why do you think it is important to the airline that clients fly back from their business trips on Sunday instead of Saturday?

THE DEBATE

• Total costs vs. differential costs

As discussed in this chapter, a management accountant can select whether to present information using total costs or differential (e.g., incremental) costs. Divide your group into two teams. Each group will defend cost analysis for relevant decision-making using either total costs or differential costs.

- One team represents "Total Costs." Present the advantages of using total costs for decision making. What are the disadvantages of using differential costs?
- The other team represents "Differential Costs." Present the advantages of using differential costs for decision making. What are the disadvantages of using total costs?

INTERNET SEARCH

• The Outsourcing Institute and RalCorp's experience

The "make-or-buy" decision is really an outsourcing decision. Outsourcing has become a tremendous business in the service industry in the last five to ten years. The Outsourcing Institute is a network and forum for business executives interested in the strategic use of outside resources. It has a dedicated Web site at www.outsourcing.com. (Sometimes Web addresses change, so if this address does not work, access the Web site for this textbook [stice.swcollege.com] for an updated link.) Go to this site and select the "Getting Started with Outsourcing" link.

1. Select the "Top Ten Reasons to Outsource" link and read about the potential benefits for outsourcing a particular process. List the top ten reasons for outsourcing.
2. Return to the home page and select the provided link to the *Business Week* reprint of "Outsourcing: The New Midas Touch" (Dec. 15, 1997). Go to the link describing "Case Studies" in this article and read about the **RalCorp Company**. Identify which of the institute's top ten reasons for outsourcing are described as benefits that RalCorp has realized by "buying" its information technology (IT) from **Cap Gemini** rather than "making" its own IT.

CHAPTER

15

STRATEGIC AND CAPITAL INVESTMENT DECISIONS

LEARNING OBJECTIVES

After studying this chapter, you should be able to:

1. *Understand the importance of capital budgeting and the concepts underlying strategic and capital investment decisions.*
2. *Describe and use two nondiscounted capital budgeting techniques: the payback method and the unadjusted rate of return method.*
3. *Describe and use two discounted capital budgeting techniques: the net present value method and the internal rate of return method.*
4. *Explain how to use capital budgeting techniques in ranking capital investment projects.*
5. *Understand the need for evaluating qualitative factors in strategic and capital investment decisions.*

SETTING THE STAGE

Federal Express Corporation (FedEx) is the largest air-freight company in the world. Every day FedEx moves millions of pounds of freight around the world, delivering the freight from one city to another, most of it over-night. For FedEx and other firms in the air-freight industry, their most important investment is the airplanes that haul the freight. Indeed, making good airplane purchase decisions is critical to the success of FedEx and its competitors. Though FedEx is profitable and expanding, questions have been raised recently about whether or not the company has made the right kind of airplane investment decisions. In early 1998, the Federal Aviation Administration (FAA) began public hearings to question the structural safety of scores of FedEx's aircraft. Presently, FedEx has 120 **Boeing** 727 freighter aircraft, more than half the industry total. The FAA is contending that the maximum allowed weight limit of these 727s should be cut in half, which would significantly increase the costs of using these planes and reduce FedEx's profitability.

For years, the air-freight industry has relied heavily on the practice of converting retired passenger planes into cargo freighters. The safety questions raised by the FAA involve how cargo doors were installed and other structural changes made when the aircraft were modified. Safety concerns range from the stability of cargo doors to the ability of aircraft to survive a strong downward gust. FAA research has shown that under combinations of certain extreme conditions, the floor beams of 727s might fail, causing the aircraft to suddenly break apart in a massive midair convulsion.

FedEx counters that the probability of the combination of conditions that would cause such an accident is highly remote. The FAA says it doesn't want to wait until after an accident has occurred to raise safety issues about the 727s. The FAA maintains that we cannot afford to lose even one plane before the problem is fixed.

While FedEx is fighting the FAA claims and allegations, the company must be wondering if it made the right kind of investment decision by purchasing and converting the 727s. If the FAA is successful in reducing the weight limits on 727s, FedEx may wish it would have purchased different airplanes or at least had the Boeing Corporation do the conversions. Those planes converted by Boeing are not being questioned by the FAA. At a minimum, the questions being raised about the safety of FedEx's operations represent a public relations nightmare for FedEx.

Source: Douglas A. Blackmon, "FedEx Faults Claims by FAA Over Aircraft" *The Wall Street Journal,* Wednesday, February 18, 1998, p. A3.

capital budgeting Systematic planning for long-term investments in operating assets.

How do FedEx and other companies decide which types of equipment to buy and what other capital investments to make? In this chapter, we examine that part of planning called ***capital budgeting****, the systematic planning for long-term investments in operating assets (primarily property, plant, equipment, intangible assets, and natural resources). Capital budgeting generally does not include investments in stocks and bonds, although these assets are also sometimes referred to as long-term investments.*

Capital budgeting differs from the types of planning already discussed in that it is more permanent and less retractable. A decision to increase inventory levels, for example, can be reversed within a relatively short time by cutting back on future purchases or by lowering prices to increase sales. Even a nonroutine decision to purchase, rather than make or deliver internally, a component or service can generally be changed without too much disruption to operations. On the other hand, a capital investment decision to purchase 120 Model 727 freight aircraft at several million dollars each requires a long-term commitment of resources, a commitment that will probably be difficult and very expensive to change at a later date.

Like the pricing and relevant cost decisions discussed in Chapter 14, capital budgeting requires differential cost analysis. Because capital budgeting involves a long time period, the time value of money must also be considered. In addition, profitability measures may be used to rank alternative projects. But before we begin to explain how capital budgeting provides management with information for evaluating long-term investments in operating assets, we must introduce some basic concepts.

1 *Understand the importance of capital budgeting and the concepts underlying strategic and capital investment decisions.*

CONCEPTUAL BASIS OF CAPITAL BUDGETING

capital The total amount of money or other resources owned or used to acquire future income or benefits.

Just as businesses are operated to make a profit, investments in property, plant, equipment, and other long-term assets are made to earn a profit for a company. In fact, if an investment will not be profitable, it shouldn't be made. An organization would be better off leaving its money in a bank savings account than investing in unprofitable assets. The major questions with capital budgeting, though, are how do you determine whether an investment will be profitable and at what level of profitability does the investment make sense? To answer these questions, some basic knowledge about capital budgeting is necessary.

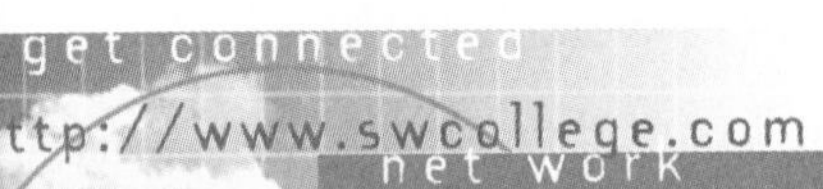

Each year the Federal Government spends billions of dollars on capital budgeting projects. Go to the Web site below and determine what percentage of the federal government's 1998 capital budgeting projects relate to defense spending.

Did the percentage of capital budgeting expenditures related to defense increase or decrease from 1996 and 1997?

http://www.fas.org/man/docs/fy98/analytical/099-141.htm

The term **capital** may be defined broadly as any form of material wealth. As used in business, it is more specifically defined as the total amount of money or other resources owned or used by an individual or a company to acquire future income or benefits.

Thus, capital is something to be invested with the expectation that it will be recovered along with a profit, and capital budgeting is the planning for that investment. From a quantitative viewpoint, the success of an investment depends on the amount of net future cash inflows (or future cash savings) in relation to the cost (current cash outlays) of the investment. Ignoring the time value of money for the moment, if a company invests \$10,000 and receives only \$10,000 in the future, there has been only a return of the investment but no profit. However, if \$15,000 is received in the future, there is not only a return of the original investment but also an additional return, or profit, of $5,000. Other things being equal, investors seek to receive the greatest future benefits for the least investment cost.

Capital Investment Decisions and Profitability

Three aspects of capital investment decisions are critical to long-run profitability:

1. Decisions to invest in assets such as land, buildings, and equipment usually require large outlays of capital. Unless a reasonable return is received on such significant investments, the overall profitability of a firm will suffer.
2. Long-term investments, by definition, extend over several years. Thus, poor capital budgeting, resulting in bad investment decisions, is likely to have an adverse effect on earnings over a long period.
3. Long-term investments in land, buildings, and specialized equipment are much less liquid than other investments. Investments in stocks and bonds, for example, can usually be terminated by sale through regularly established markets at almost any time; operating assets may not be so readily disposed of.

These three factors—large outlays, long-term impact on earnings, and lack of liquidity—are evident in the FedEx opening scenario.

Uses of Capital Budgeting: Screening and Ranking

Clearly, all long-term investment decisions are important. The larger the investment, however, the more critical is the need to budget for that expenditure. And the longer the time period, the more difficult it is to assess future outcomes and to plan accordingly. Following are some typical business situations that lend themselves to analysis with capital budgeting techniques:

1. A machine breaks down. Should the manager have the machine repaired or replaced?
2. If it is decided to replace the machine, should machine A, B, or C be purchased?
3. Should a company add to its manufacturing facility or build a new, larger factory?
4. Should a new warehouse or office building be constructed?
5. Should Company A purchase Company B and, if so, on what terms?

Situations such as these require careful consideration of all factors, qualitative as well as quantitative, and it is just as important for nonprofit organizations to make sound strategic and capital investment decisions as for-profit organizations. Thus, the concepts and techniques discussed in this chapter are applicable to all types of organizations—companies, governmental agencies, school districts, hospitals, city governments, and so forth. (See the Business Environment Essay about government capital budgeting on page 714.)

Capital budgeting analysis can help by answering two basic questions. First, does the investment make sense? That is, does it meet a minimum standard of financial acceptability? This is the **screening** function of capital budgeting. Second, is an investment the best among available acceptable alternatives? We determine this by **ranking** the alternatives. Before we discuss the screening and ranking of investment alternatives, we will briefly review the time value of money concept.

screening Determining whether a capital investment meets a minimum standard of financial acceptability.

ranking The ordering of acceptable investment alternatives from most to least desirable.

The Time Value of Money

Like other commodities, money has value because it is a scarce resource. Therefore, a payment is generally required for its use. This payment is called **interest** or, when deducted or paid in advance, discount. Because the time value of money is widely recognized, few people would consider hiding money under a mattress or otherwise keeping large amounts of idle cash; they realize that there is a significant opportunity cost in doing so. Money left idle will not earn interest, nor will it earn the potentially higher returns that can be obtained from investments in corporate stocks and bonds or real estate, for example.

interest The payment (cost) for the use of money.

BUSINESS ENVIRONMENT ESSAY

Capital Budgeting and the Federal Government The federal government's system of accounting has been criticized for its emphasis on current cash flows and its lack of attention to capital budgeting. The following excerpts point out the dangers of planning only for the current period and show how capital budgeting, coupled with reformed accounting practices, can benefit even the federal government.

> Rep. Joseph J. DioGuardi is an accountant. After a career spent poring over the books of private corporations, he won a seat in Congress and began studying the books of the federal government.
>
> "I'm appalled at the way we account for government spending around here," he says, his voice rising with indignation. "We're using a Mickey Mouse, cash-basis accounting system."
>
> Bad accounting methods, critics say, can produce bad government policy. Because Washington focuses primarily on the cash it spends and gets each year—and the difference, or deficit, between them—its drive to cut immediate outlays can lead to actions that turn out to be "penny-wise and pound-foolish." For example, the federal government often leases buildings to avoid the big cash outlay of a purchase even though leasing costs more in the long run.
>
> "Basically, the government is like someone who uses only a checkbook," says a top partner in **Arthur Andersen & Co.**, a Big 5 accounting firm. "That's not a complete picture of its financial affairs. It doesn't reflect assets, liabilities, or commitments in the future. How can you run a trillion-dollar business without knowing what its financial position is?"
>
> By paying more attention to a capital budget, the government would be less likely to adopt costly extended military purchases, to delay investments that might save money in the long run, or to sell capital assets to reduce operating deficits.
>
> "We equate a dollar going into salaries with a dollar going into a building that will last 15 years," the General Accounting Office's (GAO) Mr. Wolf says. "That idea has been rejected by nearly everyone else." A capital budget would help policy makers make such distinctions, he adds.

A resolution submitted to the federal government in 1989 by the California Society of CPAs paints a stark picture of the state of accounting in the federal government. The Society recommended the following:

- Appointment of a Chief Financial Officer for the entire federal government, as well as CFOs for each agency.
- Preparation of meaningful and useful financial statements and operating reports for the federal government.
- Adoption of an annual federal audit for presentation to the President, Congress, and the American people.

The federal government's own Securities and Exchange Commission would certainly take a dim view of any public company that did not have such basic accounting and organizational structures in place. Yet, as of late 1998, the federal government itself has done little toward adopting any such structures. The old cash-basis budgeting system remains in place, and meaningful reforms such as capital budgeting are still slow in coming.

Sources: Adapted from Alan Murray, "Government's System of Accounting Comes Under Rising Criticism," *The Wall Street Journal*, February 3, 1986, p. 1, col. 6; "California CPAs Call for Stronger Federal Financial Accounting Methods," *Business Wire, Inc.*, February 7, 1989.

Since money has value over time, the timing of expected cash flows is important in investment decisions. This is the essence of capital budgeting—comparing the cost of an investment with the expected future net cash inflows to decide whether, given the risks and available alternatives, the project should be undertaken. An investment made today will not generate cash inflows until the future, either periodically over a number of years or in a lump sum several years hence. Thus, for the comparison of cash flows to be accurate, all amounts should be stated at their value at one point in time, generally the present; this means that all future cash flows should be discounted to their present values.

Remember also that when prices are rising, the purchasing power of the dollar declines with time. Consequently, the inflation rate must also be taken into account in determining the rate at which future amounts should be discounted. We will return later to the problem of selecting a discount rate for making capital investment decisions.

In the remainder of this chapter and in the end-of-chapter exercises and problems, we will assume that you understand the concepts of present value and the underlying notion of the time value of money. If you do not, or if you want to refresh your memory, you might want to review the appendix to this chapter.

Discounting Cash Flows

Because of the time value of money, a difference in the timing of cash flows can make one investment more attractive than another, even if both involve the same total amount of money. To illustrate, we assume that project A will produce $100,000 at the end of one year and that project B will return $50,000 at the end of each year for two years. Both projects will generate a total of $100,000. However, by using present value tables (shown in the chapter appendix) and assuming a discount (interest) rate of 10 percent per year, you will see that the discounted cash flows from project A are $90,910 and from project B are $86,775. If all other factors—that is, any qualitative considerations—are the same, an investor would be $4,135 (in today's dollars) better off by investing in project A.

Project A

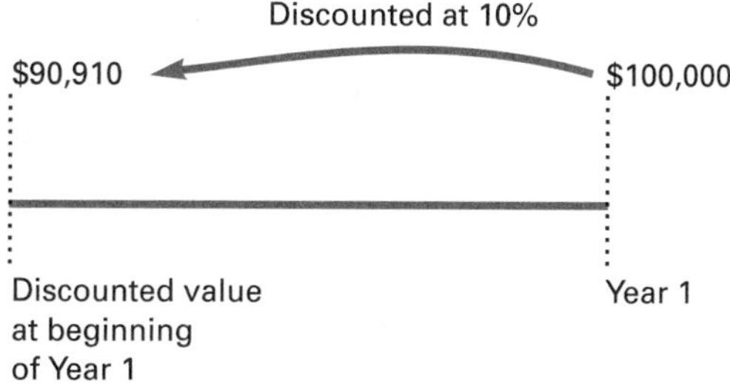

Project B

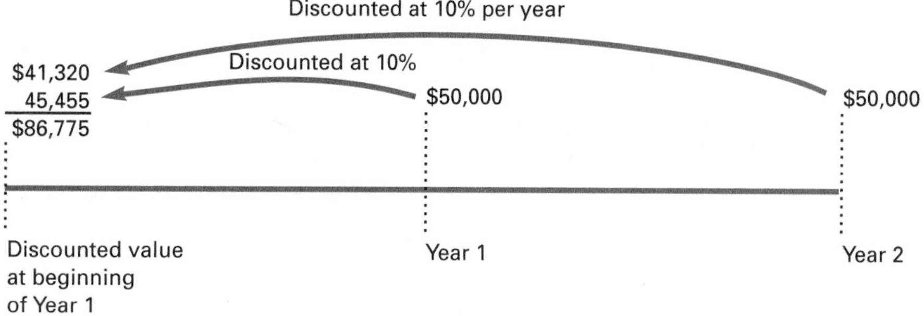

As this analysis shows, discounted cash flows reflect the time value of money and should be considered in capital budgeting. The determination of net income in accordance with GAAP is based, as you know, on accrual concepts that recognize income when it is earned, not when cash is actually received. Thus, accounting net income ignores the time value of money. For short-term investments, this approach does not significantly affect the results. Ignoring the time value of money can be misleading, however, for long-term investments.

To be able to compare cash outflows and inflows, you need a solid understanding of the discounting of cash flows. In the following paragraphs, we provide some definitions and examples.

Cash Outflows

cash outflows The initial cost and other expected outlays associated with an investment.

Cash outflows include the initial cost of an investment plus any other expected future cash outlays associated with the investment. For example, suppose that a company purchases a drill press for $8,000 cash less a trade-in allowance of $500 for its old press. With maintenance expenses of $400 at the end of each year for the 5-year life of the press, and assuming a 12 percent discount rate, the present value of the cash outflows for the investment is:

	Time Period	Cash Outflows	Present Value Factor	Present Value of Cash Outflows
Initial cash outlay	Today	$7,500	1.0000	$7,500
Future cash outlays	Years 1–5	400	3.6048*	1,442
Total present value of cash outflows				$8,942

*From Table II, 5 years at 12 percent.

The $7,500 is invested immediately, so it is already stated at its present value. The $400 series of equal payments (an annuity) is to be extended over five years, so it must be discounted to its present value equivalent.

Maintenance expense is only one category of future cash outflows. Another is manufacturing overhead costs, such as heat, electricity, and rent, that may be incurred as a consequence of an investment. In addition, income taxes are expenses that must be considered in almost all capital budgeting decisions made by businesses. For simplicity, income taxes are ignored in this chapter. In brief, all current or expected cash outlays (expressed in terms of present values) should be considered as cash outflows in evaluating investments.

Note that some expenses, although deducted from revenues in arriving at accounting net income, do not involve actual cash disbursements and so should not be considered outflows in capital budgeting. It would obviously be wrong, for example, to include depreciation expense as an outflow, since no cash flow is directly involved.

Cash Inflows

cash inflows Any current or expected revenues or savings directly associated with an investment.

Cash inflows include all current and expected future revenues or savings directly associated with an investment. For example, rent receipts, installment payments, and other revenues represent cash inflows. Returning to our earlier example, we now assume that the drill press is expected to generate annual revenues of $2,500 for five years, after which it can be sold as scrap for $750. The present value of the cash inflows for the investment is:

	Time Period	Cash Inflows	Present Value Factor	Present Value of Cash Inflows
Revenues	Years 1–5	$2,500	3.6048*	$9,012
Salvage value.	Year 5	750	0.5674**	426
Total present value of cash inflows				$9,438

*From Table II, 5 years at 12 percent.
**From Table I, 5 years at 12 percent.

CAUTION

In the examples used in this chapter, we provide the amounts of the future cash flows that are discounted. With real capital budgeting decisions, however, it is often very difficult to determine what the amounts of future cash inflows and outflows will be. With capital budgeting, we are dealing with future outcomes that are often difficult to project. It is this uncertainty about the future that makes capital budgeting so complex in the real world.

These revenues may be shown "net"—that is, reduced by any direct expenses, such as those for maintenance or materials and supplies. Thus, the net annual cash inflows from the drill press would be $2,100 per year ($2,500 − $400 maintenance expense).

Less obvious cash inflows are represented by the present value of the savings to be derived from an investment that reduces costs. In brief, the present value of all cash that is likely to be received or saved as a result of an investment should be included as cash inflows.

TO SUMMARIZE

Certain long-term investment decisions require significant capital outlays. Proper planning for these decisions is critical to long-run profitability. Capital budgeting techniques are designed to help in analyzing the quantitative factors relating to these decisions. Essentially, capital budgeting involves a comparison of the current and expected cash outflows and inflows in order to decide whether, given the risks and available alternatives, an investment should be made. To make comparisons more meaningful, all future cash flows should be discounted to the present.

2 *Describe and use two nondiscounted capital budgeting techniques: the payback method and the unadjusted rate of return method.*

NONDISCOUNTED CAPITAL BUDGETING TECHNIQUES

The four most commonly used capital budgeting techniques are (1) the payback method, (2) the unadjusted rate of return method, (3) the net present value method, and (4) the internal rate of return method. We will discuss the first two methods in this section and the latter two in the next section.

We have chosen the sequence of our discussion to parallel the pattern of most companies as they grow larger and become more sophisticated in the way that they make investment decisions. That is, companies generally first use the payback method or the unadjusted rate of return method because these techniques are relatively simple. Both of these techniques have a serious weakness, however, in that they ignore the time value of money. As a result, most companies eventually turn to either the net present value method or the internal rate of return method, both of which are more theoretically correct approaches to capital budgeting. The last two techniques are referred to as **discounted cash flow methods** because they use a discount rate in comparing the cash flows of investments.

discounted cash flow methods Capital budgeting techniques that take into account the time value of money by comparing discounted cash flows.

payback method A capital budgeting technique that determines the amount of time it takes the net cash inflows of an investment to repay the investment cost.

Payback Method

The **payback method** is widely used in business because it is simple to apply and it provides a preliminary screening of investment opportunities. It can also be used as a crude measure of a project's risk. Basically, this method is used to determine the length of time it will take the net cash inflows of an investment to equal the cash outlay. The payback period may be a particularly important consideration for companies in a tight credit position. Assuming that the payback period is to be computed in years (any time frame can be applied) and that equal cash flows are generated for each period, the formula for a project's payback period is:

$$\frac{\text{Investment cost}}{\text{Annual net cash inflows}} = \text{Payback period}$$

To illustrate the payback method, we will consider Kristi Felt's decision to purchase a personal computer, printer, and software for typing and printing essays and term papers for other students. A reasonably good PC, printer, and appropriate software will cost Kristi a total of $1,500. She can borrow the $1,500 from her father, who requires no interest but needs to be repaid at the end of 18 months. Kristi expects to make $100 per month after paying for supplies and other related expenses. The payback period (in months) may be computed as follows:

$$\frac{\$1,500}{\$100} = 15 \text{ months}$$

Since Kristi would generate sufficient cash to recover the investment in 15 months, she could repay her father within the agreed period of time (assuming she spends none of the money).

This is one of the strengths of the payback method: It can be used to determine whether an investment fits within an acceptable period for the use of funds. For example, a company's cash position may lead it to establish a rule of thumb that no investment with a payback period exceeding three years will be accepted. In such a situation, a manager may be obliged to select an investment alternative with a slightly lower rate of return but a shorter payback period.

The payback method has several weaknesses, however. One is that it measures the time needed to recover the initial outlay but does not consider the investment's profitability. Investments obviously are made in order to earn an acceptable return, not just to recover their costs. In our example, Kristi is not solely interested in recovering the $1,500 in the shortest time possible. Her purpose in buying the equipment is to earn some extra money. Assuming that the equipment will last for more than 15 months, Kristi not only will recover her initial investment, but will also generate subsequent earnings (at least $100 per month). Although the payback method may provide some clues about the advisability of investments, it does not directly measure profitability.

To clarify this last point and show why the payback method must be used with care, consider a manager's decision to purchase one of two machines. Machine A costs $5,500 and is expected to generate $1,000 of net cash inflows annually. Machine B costs $3,500 and will produce $800 of net cash inflows annually. The payback period for machine A is 5.5 years ($5,500 ÷ $1,000); for machine B, the payback period is 4.4 years ($3,500 ÷ $800). Other things being equal, the payback method would indicate that the manager should purchase machine B because it would result in a shorter payback period. That is, its original cost would be recovered in a shorter time. However, if machine B were expected to last less than 4.4 years, such an investment would be unwise. The machine would not last long enough to recover its original cost, let alone generate any earnings.

Now suppose that both machines were estimated to have a 7-year life. Which machine would be the better investment? What if the estimated lifetimes of both machines were more than ten years? To answer these questions, we would have to use one of the discounted cash flow methods (to be discussed later) in conjunction with the payback period.

This example highlights the other major weakness of the payback method; it does not take into account the time value of money. As a result, incorrect investment decisions may result unless the payback period is relatively short.

Unadjusted Rate of Return Method

unadjusted rate of return method A capital budgeting technique in which a rate of return is calculated by dividing the increase in the average annual net income a project will generate by the initial investment cost.

Another commonly used capital budgeting technique is the **unadjusted rate of return method**. Also referred to as the simple rate of return method or the accounting rate of return method, it is computed as follows:

$$\frac{\text{Increase in future average annual net income}}{\text{Initial investment cost}} = \text{Unadjusted rate of return}$$

To illustrate the unadjusted rate of return method, consider the following situation. Seal Right Company manufactures cans for fruits, vegetables, and other farm produce. Management wants to add a new, larger can size to the product line in order to take advantage of a potential demand for food storage items in the western states. This new can is expected to increase the company's annual net income by an average of $30,000 a year for ten years. The additional machinery needed to manufacture the can will cost $215,000. The expected return on the investment is $30,000 ÷ $215,000 = 14% (rounded).

Unlike the payback method, the unadjusted rate of return method attempts to measure the profitability of an investment. A company compares the unadjusted rate of return with a preselected rate that it considers acceptable. Management invests only in projects with rates of return that are equal to or greater than the established standard. Thus, if Seal Right's standard acceptance rate is less than or equal to 14 percent, the project would be acceptable.

The main weakness of the unadjusted rate of return method is that, like the payback method, it does not consider the time value of money. The computation uses average future net income rather than expected future earnings discounted to the present. A second problem is that this method counts the initial investment cost twice. This occurs because depreciation is a component in the computation of the average net income added by a project.

The problem of double counting can be eliminated by using refined models of the unadjusted rate of return method. The more serious problem—the omission of the time value of money—cannot be corrected. And since this omission can produce misleading results and incorrect long-term investment decisions, the unadjusted rate of return method must be used with extreme care.

FYI

While the payback and unadjusted rate of return methods do not consider the time value of money, they are widely used in practice because they involve simple computations and are so easy to use. In fact, smaller, unsophisticated companies rarely use the more complex discounted methods.

TO SUMMARIZE

The payback method measures the time required to recover the initial cost of an investment from future net cash inflows (investment cost divided by annual net cash inflows). It may be useful as a preliminary screen of investment projects. The unadjusted rate of return method provides a measure of the profitability of an investment (increases in future average annual net income divided by the cost of the investment). If the resulting return is greater than the company's minimum standard of acceptability, the project is acceptable quantitatively. Because the payback and the unadjusted rate of return methods do not consider the time value of money, they should be used only in conjunction with one of the discounted cash flow methods.

3 *Describe and use two discounted capital budgeting techniques: the net present value method and the internal rate of return method.*

DISCOUNTED CAPITAL BUDGETING TECHNIQUES

Two widely used capital budgeting techniques recognize the time value of money—the net present value method and the internal rate of return method. Both methods apply discounted cash flow principles in determining the acceptability of an investment. The net present value method uses a standard discount rate to restate all cash flows in terms of present values and then makes comparisons. The internal rate of return method calculates the investment's "true" discounted rate of return and compares it with the firm's "hurdle" rate. Thus, an appropriate discount rate is extremely important in capital budgeting. Before explaining each of the two methods, we first discuss how to select an appropriate discount rate.

Selecting a Discount Rate

cost of capital The average cost of a firm's debt and equity capital; equals the rate of return that a company must earn in order to satisfy the demands of its owners and creditors.

The most theoretically correct discount rate is a rate equal to a business entity's cost of capital. The **cost of capital** is basically an average cost of a firm's debt (primarily bank loans and bonds) and its equity (primarily common and preferred stock and retained earnings). These costs are measured in terms of interest payments, bond amortizations, dividend payments, and the opportunity cost of retained earnings. In essence, then, the cost of capital is the rate a company must earn in order to satisfy its owners and creditors.

The computation of the cost of capital is complex and beyond the scope of this book. However, the following example should help you understand the concept. Assume that 30 percent of a company's total capital is debt, 20 percent is equity from the issuance of stock, and 50 percent is equity from retained earnings. Upon analysis, the company has determined that the cost of its debt capital is 10 percent, and the cost of its equity capital is 16 percent from stock and 22 percent from retained earnings. The firm's cost of capital would be determined as follows:

Type	Cost of Capital	×	Weight	=	Average Cost of Capital
Debt (bonds)	10%	×	30%	=	3.0%
Equity (stocks)	16%	×	20%	=	3.2%
Equity (retained earnings)	22%	×	50%	=	11.0%
Total cost of capital			100%		17.2%

(STOP & THINK)

Assume you were trying to decide whether to purchase or lease an automobile and you wanted to use the net present value method to determine which alternative to choose. What factors would you consider in determining the rate at which to discount the future cash outflows (i.e., what factors would determine your personal cost of capital)?

The weighting procedure may seem fairly simple. As you will learn in more advanced courses, however, it is not always easy to calculate the costs of the different types of capital. This is because the necessary information is often not readily available or absolutely verifiable. For example, debt costs must be adjusted to an after-tax basis, and equity costs include some subjective elements, such as the opportunity cost of retained earnings. Although you now have a general understanding of the cost of capital, you will need further study to use this concept.

Nonprofit organizations may have difficulties determining an appropriate discount rate for use in analyzing data. Nonprofit organizations usually have no shareholders or other equity interests to factor into the cost of capital consideration. Accordingly, some nonprofit organizations use the market rate of interest for special bond issues (for example, a school bond issue or a city library bond issue). Others use an opportunity cost rate (for example, the market interest that could be earned on secure investments as opposed to being spent on a capital project). Another alternative for nonprofit organizations is to use rates determined by government restrictions or set by boards of directors.

Care must be exercised that discount rates are not set too low, resulting in unwise investment decisions. As a general rule, it would seem wise for nonprofit organizations to use discount rates that are comparable to the average rate of return on similar private sector investments. By following this guideline, even though not having a profit motive, nonprofit organizations would be more likely to invest only in those projects that have a sound financial basis, thus benefiting the constituencies of the nonprofit organization.

Net Present Value Method

net present value method A capital budgeting technique that uses discounted cash flows to compare the present values of an investment's expected cash inflows and outflows.

The **net present value method** compares all expected cash inflows associated with an investment with the current and future cash outflows. All cash flows are discounted to their present values, giving recognition to the time value of money. For this reason, the net present value method is superior to both the payback method and the unadjusted rate of return method.

In general, the net present value method involves the following three steps:

1. Using a predetermined interest rate or discount factor, compute the present values of all the expected cash inflows and outflows of an investment. (Note that most present value tables assume end-of-year inflows and outflows.)
2. Subtract the total present value of the cash outflows from the total present value of the cash inflows. The difference is the investment's net present value.
3. If the net present value of the investment is positive, or at least zero, the project is acceptable from a financial standpoint.

The following case illustrates the net present value method. The fleet manager of MBK Company is thinking of replacing an old truck before it begins to need major repairs. Because the company has limited funds and cannot spend more than $18,000, the manager is considering a small, fuel-efficient pickup truck that is presently selling for that amount. The truck would save the company $5,625 a year in gas and other expenses. The truck's estimated useful life is four years, and the expected salvage value is $1,800. The company uses a 10 percent discount rate. What is this investment's net present value? Should the truck be purchased?

Step 1 of the net present value method is to use the predetermined discount rate to state all cash flows at their present values (rounded to the nearest dollar in this example).

Cash inflows:

Annual cash savings	×	Discount factor	=	Present value
$5,625	×	3.1699*	=	$17,831
Salvage value	×	Discount factor	=	Present value
$1,800	×	0.6830**	=	$1,229

Cash outflows:

Initial cost	×	Discount factor	=	Present value
$18,000	×	1.0000	=	$18,000

*From Table II, 4 years at 10 percent.
**From Table I, 4 years at 10 percent.

net present value The difference between the present values of an investment's expected cash inflows and outflows.

Step 2 is to compute the **net present value**, that is, the difference between the present value of cash inflows and outflows.

Present value of inflows:	
Cash savings	$17,831
Salvage value	1,229
Total	$19,060
Less present value of outflows:	
Cost of truck	18,000
Net present value	$ 1,060

The analysis in Step 2 shows that investing in the truck would produce a positive net present value. In other words, there would be a savings if the expected cash inflows and outflows were discounted at the 10 percent rate required by the company. Thus, from a quantitative standpoint, it seems that the truck should be purchased. Exhibit 15-1 illustrates the process just described.

Before the company decides whether to purchase the truck, however, management must consider other factors. For example, a policy of support for U.S. car manufacturers or a lack of certain safety features on the pickup might dictate a particular course of action. Qualitative factors are discussed in greater detail later in the chapter.

Least-Cost Decisions

The net present value method generally assumes that an investment must be justified by cash savings or increased revenues. Sometimes, however, funds must be used to purchase assets regardless of whether they can be justified financially. Such situations arise, for example, when (1) government regulations require a firm to purchase safety or pollution-control equipment, (2) personnel contracts stipulate the establishment of retirement funds, or (3) a company is required to invest in cafeteria or recreational facilities, either to comply with a labor union contract or because management is persuaded that morale considerations warrant it.

EXHIBIT 15-1 Computing Net Present Value

	Present Time	Year 1	Year 2	Year 3	Year 4
Cost	$18,000				
Savings		$5,625	$5,625	$5,625	$5,625
Salvage value					1,800

	Time Period	Cash Flows	Present Value Factor	Present Value of Cash Flows
Present value of cash inflows:				
Savings	Years 1–4	$ 5,625	3.1699*	$17,831
Salvage value	Year 4	1,800	0.6830**	1,229
				$19,060
Present value of cash outflows:				
Cost.	Today	(18,000)	1.0000	18,000
Net present value				$ 1,060

*From Table II, 4 years at 10 percent.
**From Table I, 4 years at 10 percent.

BUSINESS ENVIRONMENT ESSAY

Investing for a Cleaner World Businesses have traditionally used capital budgeting to guide them on making wise investments in property, plant, and equipment that will earn a return. However, in recent years, investments in environmental cleanup activities have become extremely common. Companies today face a climate with increasingly significant environmental concerns. Environmental costs have soared, in some cases to billion of dollars each year. Fines and penalties for violation of environmental regulations are substantial. And, due to new sentencing guidelines, strict liability for environmental losses has been imposed on directors and officers of companies. There is currently a myriad of environmental laws forcing companies to spend huge amounts of money to comply with these laws and to clean up environmental damage. Some of the most costly laws are The Clean Air Act, The Clean Water Act, The Resource Conservation and Recovery Act of 1976, the Comprehensive Environmental Response, the Compensation and Liability Act of 1980 (known as Superfund), and The Superfund Amendments Reauthorization Act of 1986 (SARA). The impact of these laws on capital investment decisions can be substantial. For example, under SARA, purchasers in real property are usually financially liable for environmental cleanup costs even if the property was contaminated before it was purchased.

Environmental concerns impact several stages of the capital budgeting decision. First, capital budgeting decision makers must expand traditional company boundaries to consider all entities affected by environmental degradation. Even though a project may be profitable from the firm's perspective, if it pollutes the environment, cleanup liability may make the investment a real loser. Second, environmental laws, current conditions, and trends can significantly affect the feasibility of an investment. Third, in deciding whether an investment is profitable, environmental costs and benefits, as well as environmental risk, must be considered. Finally, once an investment in a capital asset is made, attention must be given to environmental events such as accidents or increased regulation, which might affect the continued viability of the investment.

Source: Devaun Kite, "Capital Budgeting: Integrating Environmental Impact," *Journal of Cost Management,* Summer 1995, Vol. 9, No. 2, pp. 11–14.

least-cost decision A decision to undertake the project with the smallest negative net present value.

Such situations may seem to be beyond help from capital budgeting. However, the net present value method may assist managers in making a **least-cost decision**—a decision that satisfies certain requirements at the lowest possible cost to the firm. The two major differences between least-cost decisions and all other capital budgeting decisions are:

1. Least-cost decisions are limited to alternatives that fulfill certain imposed requirements.
2. None of the alternatives may produce a positive net present value.

To illustrate, we will assume that New England Steel Company has been told by the Environmental Protection Agency to install a pollution-control device. One alternative would cost $1,000,000 immediately but would not add to operating costs. It would last for 10 years. A second alternative is a device that costs $200,000 immediately but would add $125,000 to annual operating costs. Like the first device, it would last 10 years. Which device should be purchased? The firm uses a 12 percent discount rate.

The first alternative involves no future cash inflows or outflows. Its outlay cost in net present value terms is its initial cash outlay of $1,000,000. The second alternative has an initial cost of $200,000 plus future cash outflows of $125,000 per year for the next 10 years. Therefore, its outlay cost in net present value terms would be:

Annual cash outflows	×	Discount factor	=	Present value
$125,000	×	5.6502*	=	$706,275
Initial cost				200,000
Outlay cost at net present value.				$906,275

*From Table II, 10 years at 12 percent.

(STOP & THINK)

Over your lifetime, you will make many personal, long-term investments such as buying automobiles and buying a home. Are the capital budgeting techniques we have discussed in this chapter relevant to these personal decisions? Since you probably won't be earning a return on your automobile and home investments, what type of capital budgeting decisions are these?

If the company had a choice between installing and not installing, neither alternative would be acceptable because both net present values are negative. However, one of the alternatives must be accepted. Since a cost of $906,275 is less than a cost of $1,000,000, the second alternative should be chosen to minimize costs.

Internal Rate of Return Method

internal rate of return method A capital budgeting technique that uses discounted cash flows to find the "true" discount rate of an investment; this true rate produces a net present value of zero.

The **internal rate of return method**, also known as the time-adjusted rate of return method or the discounted rate of return method, is similar to the net present value approach in that it emphasizes the profitability of investments and takes into account the time value of money. As a discounted cash flow method, it is superior to either the payback method or the unadjusted rate of return method. Because the calculation involves discounting by "trial and error" when uneven cash flows exist, some accountants consider the internal rate of return method more tedious than the net present value method. Some managers, however, prefer to analyze investment alternatives in terms of comparative rates of return rather than net present values.

internal rate of return The "true" discount rate that will produce a net present value of zero when applied to the cash flows of investment inventory goods held for resale.

The **internal rate of return** is defined as the "true" discount rate that an investment yields. Stated differently, the internal rate of return is the discount rate that yields a net present value of zero when applied to the cash flows of an investment—both inflows and outflows.

Like the net present value approach, the internal rate of return method involves three steps.

1. Calculate the present value factor by dividing the investment cost by the annual net cash inflows.
2. Using applicable present value tables and the life of the investment, find the present value factor closest to the number derived in step 1.
3. Using interpolation, if necessary, find the exact internal rate of return represented by the present value factor in step 1.

To help you understand this concept, we will again refer to MBK Company's plan to purchase a new truck. For the purpose of this explanation, however, we will ignore the truck's salvage value; later, we will show how to incorporate salvage value into the calculation. The calculations for the MBK example are as follows:

1. Calculate the present value factor with the following formula:

$$\frac{\text{Investment cost}}{\text{Annual net cash inflows}} = \text{Present value factor}$$

$$\frac{\$18{,}000}{\$5{,}625} = 3.2000$$

(Note that this is also the formula for calculating the payback period.)

2. In Present Value Table II, find the applicable row for the life of the investment. By moving across the table, you can find the present value factor closest to the

number derived in step 1. In our example, the investment's life is known to be 4 years, so find row 4 and move across the row until you come to the factor 3.2397. This is the factor for 9 percent. The next factor, 3.1699, represents 10 percent. Since the factor is between these two numbers, the truck purchase yields between a 9 and 10 percent return.

interpolation A method of determining the internal rate of return when the factor for that rate lies between the factors given in the present value table.

3. If necessary, use **interpolation** to find the exact internal rate of return. Interpolation is most easily visualized by setting up a table as follows[1]:

		Present Value Factors	
	Rate of Return (Discount Rate)	High and True Factors	High and Low Factors
High factor*	9%	3.2397	3.2397
True factor		3.2000	
Low factor	10%		3.1699
Differences	1%	0.0397	0.0698

*Note that the high factor is associated with the low rate and that the low factor is associated with the high rate.

The number 0.0397 is the difference between the high factor and the true factor determined in step 1. The number 0.0698 is the difference between the high factor and the low factor. One percent is the difference between the discount rates for the high and the low factors. To find the exact rate of return in this example, you would make the following calculation:

$$\text{Internal rate of return} = 0.09 + \left(0.01 \times \frac{0.0397}{0.0698}\right) = 0.0957 \text{ or } 9.6 \text{ percent (rounded)}$$

CAUTION

Although the internal rate of return and net present value capital budgeting methods provide answers that appear to be very precise, they should be used with caution. There are many assumptions made when using these methods. Some of these assumptions are (1) that the discount rate (cost of capital) is accurate and (2) that the future cash flows, useful lives of the assets, and salvage values are known. It is often easy in accounting to assume that precise calculations are accurate without giving due consideration to the assumptions underlying the calculations.

What we are doing is adding the proportion 0.0397 ÷ 0.0698 of the 1 percent difference to the low rate to get the true rate. The result, 9.6 percent, means that if the annual savings of $5,625 were discounted at 9.6 percent, the net present value of the investment would be zero. (Note that there may be slight differences due to rounding.)

The purpose of interpolation is to determine the "true" rate of interest indicated by the present value factor. Although the factor's true rate of interest is fairly easy to estimate, interpolation produces a more precise rate. Of course, if you have access to an annuity table with factors for numerous interest rates, or to a calculator or computer to make these computations directly, interpolation may not be necessary.

Using the Internal Rate of Return

To determine the value of an investment, management must compare the project's internal rate of return with the company's usual discount rate, often called the **hurdle rate**, or the rate that must be cleared for a project to be acceptable. If the internal rate is higher than or equal to the company's hurdle rate, the project is acceptable. If the internal rate is lower than the hurdle rate, the project is usually rejected. As with any of the capital budgeting techniques, even if the investment is acceptable from an internal rate of return standpoint, qualitative factors must still be considered before a final decision can be made.

hurdle rate The minimum rate of return that an investment must provide in order to be acceptable.

1. While we use interpolation in this simple example, true internal rates of return are computed quite easily using computer simulation programs.

The Problem of Uneven Cash Flows

In the truck example, annual cash flows were the same because salvage value was ignored. However, when salvage value is considered, the investment will have uneven cash flows. When this occurs, an annuity table cannot be used. Each cash flow has to be discounted back at an assumed discount rate until the net present value of all the cash flows discounted at this rate approximates zero. The rate that results after a trial-and-error process or a computer simulation is the internal rate of return. A simplified example of this method is shown on page 729. Although this can be a tedious procedure, it is facilitated by using computers or calculators.

Approximating the Internal Rate of Return

payback reciprocal method A capital budgeting technique in which the reciprocal of the payback period is used in computing an investment's approximate internal rate of return.

When an investment has (1) a useful life that is at least twice as long as the payback period and (2) relatively uniform annual cash inflows over its life, the reciprocal of the payback method provides an approximation of the internal rate of return. The **payback reciprocal method** has the advantage of being a simple procedure that does not require the use of present values. It has the disadvantage of producing a figure that only approximates the true internal rate of return. The payback reciprocal is computed as follows:

$$\frac{\text{Annual net cash inflows}}{\text{Investment cost}} = \text{Payback reciprocal}$$

To illustrate the payback reciprocal method, we will assume that MBK Company has decided to purchase a new carpet-cleaning machine. The machine costs $8,384 and will last for 10 years. Management expects the machine to save the company $2,000 a year over its useful life. The first step is to compute the payback period.

$$\frac{\$8,384}{\$2,000} = 4.192 \text{ years}$$

Since the machine's useful life is more than twice the payback period and the annual cash inflows are uniform over the life of the investment, the payback reciprocal method may be used to approximate the internal rate of return.

$$\frac{\$2,000}{\$8,384} = 23.9 \text{ percent}$$

If you examine the 10-year row in Table II, you will see that the factor 4.1925, which is the present value factor for this investment as well as the payback period, appears in the 20 percent column. Therefore, the true internal rate of return for the project is 20 percent. As the example illustrates, the payback reciprocal only approximates the internal rate of return. In this case, there is an error of almost 4 percent. As long as management recognizes the limitations of this method, the payback reciprocal method can save considerable time in screening investment alternatives. However, the payback reciprocal method should not be considered a substitute for the more accurate internal rate of return method.

TO SUMMARIZE

The net present value method is a capital budgeting technique that takes into consideration the time value of money by discounting future cash flows to their present values. By comparing the discounted net cash inflows and outflows, this method derives a net present value figure. If the net present value is zero or positive, the project is acceptable from a quantitative standpoint. The discount rate used is the minimum rate of interest that a company will accept. The net present value method also may be used in making least-cost decisions. The internal rate of return is a capital budgeting technique that utilizes discounted cash flows. It derives the "true" rate of return for an investment by comparing the cost of the project with the amounts to be returned. This produces a present value factor that is associated with the internal rate of return for the project. Often, the rate must be derived by interpolation and, if uneven cash flows are involved, by trial and error or computer simulation. Under some circumstances, the payback reciprocal method can be used to approximate the internal rate of return on an investment.

COMPARATIVE EXAMPLE OF CAPITAL BUDGETING TECHNIQUES

To solidify your understanding of the capital budgeting techniques introduced thus far in this chapter, we present the example of Will's Pit Stop, a small service station that sells gasoline on a self-service basis as its only source of revenue. Since one wall of the enclosed station area is vacant, the manager has decided to install one or two food vending machines. A sales representative has suggested that a freezer for ice cream and other dairy items would do well. The freezer would cost $42,045. It has an estimated useful life of 10 years, with an expected salvage value of $4,000. The sales representative is confident that the freezer will generate revenues of $15,000 a year on goods that cost $7,600. The freezer will need $8,000 of servicing during

BUSINESS ENVIRONMENT ESSAY

McDonald's Probably the most successful fast food restaurant of all time is **McDonald's**. However, as of early 1997, things weren't going so well for McDonald's. Jokes about McDonald's food were rampant. Ronald McDonald had become a symbol for botched marketing schemes. McDonald's sales were off target. McDonald's image was off kilter. And, McDonald's solutions to problems were off the mark.

By 1997 McDonald's had realized that it needed to take drastic action to correct these problems and lift the company back above its competitors. So what was McDonald's solution? In 1997 and 1998, it started investing $500 million in a new cooking and food delivery system that should allow the company to serve hot food to every customer, made to order, faster than ever before. For the first time in decades, McDonald's planned to serve hotter, fresher food, in less than three-and-a-half minutes per customer.

The new ad campaign is to be called "made for you." At the time this book went to press, whether or not the new approach would work remained to be seen. In two test stores, sales were up 20 percent, even without advertising. One thing was certain, however. Investing $500 million in new equipment and technology was a lot more risky than McDonald's earlier attempted solutions to resurrect its image. These involved offering new products such as the Arch Deluxe and McRib Sandwich. By early 1998, McDonald's was convinced that the investment would result in increased sales, higher profits, and an improved reputation. Franchise owners, who were being asked to pay $300 million of the $500 million total cost, weren't so sure. To some of them, the charge seemed like an awfully big and risky capital investment gamble. Only time will tell if the $500 million was well spent.

Source: Bruce Horovitz, "Fast-Food Giant's New Plan: Hot, Juicy, Made to Order," *USA Today*, February 20, 1998, p. B1.

its fifth year of operation. The increase in Will's average yearly net income if the freezer is purchased is estimated to be $3,500. Note that the difference between annual net cash inflows of $7,400 ($15,000 − $7,600) and the estimated average net income of $3,500 is due to noncash expenses, such as depreciation, which are deducted on the income statement.

The manager of the station has come to you for advice, indicating that the firm's hurdle rate is 12 percent—Will's estimated cost of capital. Compute the payback period, the unadjusted rate of return, the net present value, and the internal rate of return of the project. Then give your recommendations. Note that companies generally do not analyze an investment with all these techniques. They are all used here for illustrative purposes.

1. *Payback period:*

$$\frac{\$50{,}045 \text{ (investment cost)*}}{\$7{,}400 \text{ (annual net cash inflows)}} = 6.76 \text{ years}$$

*$42,045 initial investment + $8,000 servicing cost after 5 years.

Note that the salvage value is not considered here because it is received in the tenth year.

2. *Unadjusted rate of return:*

$$\frac{\$3{,}500 \text{ (increase in future average annual net income)}}{\$42{,}045 \text{ (initial investment cost)}} = 8.3 \text{ percent}$$

3. *Net present value:*

	Time Period	Cash Flows	Present Value Factor	Present Value of Cash Flows
Present value of cash inflows:				
Net revenues				
($15,000 − $7,600)	Years 1–10	$ 7,400	5.6502*	$41,811
Salvage value	Year 10	4,000	0.3220**	1,288
Total cash inflows				$43,099
Present value of cash outflows:				
Initial cost	Today	$42,045	1.0000	$42,045
Servicing cost	Year 5	8,000	0.5674***	4,539
Total cash outflows				$46,584
Net present value				$ (3,485)

*From Table II, 10 years at 12 percent.
**From Table I, 10 years at 12 percent.
***From Table I, 5 years at 12 percent.

4. *Internal rate of return:*

Since the cash flows are uneven due to the servicing cost and the salvage value, a trial-and-error process is required in computing the internal rate of return. From the net present value method, we can see that the 12 percent rate is too high. A 10 percent rate is selected for trial, and the net present value at that rate is calculated.

	Time Period	Cash Flows	Present Value Factor	Present Value of Cash Flows
Present value of cash inflows:				
Net revenues				
($15,000 − $7,600)	Years 1–10	$ 7,400	6.1446*	$45,470
Salvage value	Year 10	4,000	0.3855**	1,542
Total cash inflows				$47,012
Present value of cash outflows:				
Initial cost	Today	$42,045	1.0000	$42,045
Servicing cost	Year 5	8,000	0.6209***	4,967
Total cash outflows				$47,012
Net present value				$ 0

*From Table II, 10 years at 10 percent.
**From Table I, 10 years at 10 percent.
***From Table I, 5 years at 10 percent.

At 10 percent, the net present value is zero. Therefore, 10 percent is the internal rate of return.

On the basis of the foregoing information, you should recommend rejection. The payback period is well within the life of the investment; however, it is not short enough to warrant any special consideration. The unadjusted rate of return is only 8.3 percent, and the internal, or adjusted, rate of return of 10 percent is well under Will's hurdle rate, which means that the project's net present value is negative. Therefore, on the basis of the quantitative results, the manager should look for an opportunity that is more attractive financially. However, if the 10 percent rate is close enough to the 12 percent hurdle rate, perhaps qualitative factors, such as the probability that the additional customers attracted by the freezer items will also buy gas, might make the project acceptable.

4 *Explain how to use capital budgeting techniques in ranking capital investment projects.*

CAPITAL RATIONING

Thus far, we have dealt exclusively with the screening function of capital budgeting —that is, determining whether an investment meets a minimum standard of acceptability. In many cases, however, a company has not one but several investment opportunities, all of which offer returns in excess of the company's hurdle rate. Since a company's resources are limited, some projects should be given priority. The ranking function of capital budgeting enables management to select the most profitable investments first. Projects should not be ranked, however, until the screening process is completed.

Another factor to consider in ranking projects is whether particular projects are compatible, complementary, or mutually exclusive. We assume mutually exclusive projects in this section on ranking, that is, that each project is independent and adds neither an advantage nor a disadvantage to other projects. Certainly, there are situations where the acceptance of one project adds value, directly or indirectly, to another project and might therefore alter a ranking consideration. These factors, like the qualitative factors that we discussed earlier, may significantly influence the strategy involved in a capital investment decision.

The objective of ranking is to help a company use limited resources to the best advantage by investing only in the projects that offer the highest return. The

capital rationing Allocating limited resources among ranked acceptable investments.

process of allocating limited resources based on the ranking of projects is called **capital rationing**. Either the internal rate of return method or the net present value method may be used in ranking investments.

Ranking by the Internal Rate of Return Method

If the internal rate of return method is used, investments that pass the screening test are ranked in the order of their internal rate of return, from highest to lowest. This method is simple, requires no additional computations, and is widely used.

To illustrate the process, we will assume the following situation. Sundance Enterprises is considering six capital investment projects. Management requires a minimum return of 15 percent on its investments. The six projects are first screened, then ranked by their internal rates of return, as shown below.

Project	Expected Rate of Return	Screening Decision	Ranking Decision
A	10%	Reject	—
B	18	Accept	3
C	12	Reject	—
D	22	Accept	1
E	20	Accept	2
F	16	Accept	4

From a quantitative standpoint, Sundance should invest in all four of the projects that passed the screening test. If resources are limited, however, capital must be rationed. In this situation, the ranking process indicates that limited resources would be allocated to project D first, then to projects E, B, and F, respectively. This conclusion ignores the additional complications of the investments having different lives. It also does not consider differences in the size of the initial investment.

Ranking by the Net Present Value Method

If the net present value method is used for ranking investments, additional computations are necessary because the net present value of one investment usually cannot be directly compared with that of another. Only projects that require the same amount of investment are comparable. For example, you cannot readily compare an investment of $10,000 that produces a $2,000 net present value (project A) with a $20,000 investment that also results in a $2,000 net present value (project B), although project A certainly seems more desirable. To rank such projects, we need to compute a **profitability index**.

profitability index The present value of net cash inflows divided by the cost of an investment.

$$\frac{\text{Present value of net cash inflows}}{\text{Investment cost}} = \text{Profitability index}$$

Projects can then be ranked from highest to lowest in terms of their respective profitability indexes. The project with the highest profitability index should obviously be undertaken first; other projects will be undertaken according to the amount of resources available for investment.

To illustrate the ranking of projects using the net present value method, we will use the example in the preceding paragraph. The amount of the investment and its net present value are added to arrive at the present value of net cash inflows. Then, present value is divided by the investment cost to calculate a profitability index and respective ranking.

	Project A	Project B
Present value of net cash inflows	$12,000 (a)	$22,000 (a)
Investment cost	10,000 (b)	20,000 (b)
Net present value	$ 2,000	$ 2,000
Profitability index (a ÷ b)	1.20	1.10
Rank	1	2

Note that the profitability index must be 1.0 or greater for a project to be acceptable; this means that the net present value is at least zero.

Exhibit 15-2 summarizes the rules for making screening and ranking decisions using the net present value (with a profitability index) and the internal rate of return methods. Note that each technique leads management to the same screening decision. However, the methods may produce different rankings. In selecting between the two for the purposes of ranking, the profitability index is preferred because it considers directly the amount invested in each project, which results in the selection of the most profitable alternative.

EXHIBIT 15-2

Capital Budgeting Decision Rules

Selected Capital Budgeting Techniques	Decision Rules: Screening	Decision Rules: Ranking
Net present value method (NPV) using the profitability index (PI)	If PI > 1, invest PI = 1, indifferent PI < 1, don't invest	For two projects, a and b; If $PI_a > PI_b$, pick a, etc.
Internal rate of return (IRR)	If IRR > CC*, invest IRR = CC, indifferent IRR < CC, don't invest	For two projects, a and b; If $IRR_a > IRR_b$, pick a, etc.

*CC = cost of capital, or hurdle rate.

TO SUMMARIZE

The screening function determines if projects are acceptable; the ranking function enables management to select the most profitable investment first and thus use limited resources to the best advantage. Ranking may be accomplished by the internal rate of return or by the net present value method.

5 *Understand the need for evaluating qualitative factors in strategic and capital investment decisions.*

QUALITATIVE FACTORS IN STRATEGIC AND CAPITAL INVESTMENT DECISIONS

In explaining the fundamental concepts of capital budgeting, we have focused on the financial (quantitative) aspects of analyzing investment alternatives. However, a discussion of capital budgeting is incomplete without mentioning factors that cannot

FYI

In today's world economy, most companies have to be competitive on a cost basis. What makes good companies even better is their attention to quality and time (speed of delivery of products and services) considerations—the same factors that are important in capital investment decisions.

be reduced to numbers. These qualitative factors are often of overriding importance in strategic and capital investment decisions. Here, we consider three types of qualitative factors: (1) an investment's effect on the *quality* of products and services offered, (2) an investment's effect on the *time* with which products and services can be produced and delivered to customers, and (3) other qualitative factors. Thus far in the chapter, we have made the determination of whether a capital investment decision is a good one solely on the basis of its financial return, computed using one of four methods. If the financial return were positive, our conclusion was to invest; if the financial return were negative, we recommended that the project not be undertaken. However, throughout the management accounting chapters of this book, we have focused on three aspects of decision making: cost, quality, and time.

Quality and time considerations can sometimes dictate that a capital investment should be made even if the financial returns don't justify the expenditure. For example, if buying a new machine will help the company produce higher quality products or deliver those products to its customers faster, the machine may be a good investment. Companies know that their competitors are doing everything possible to speed up delivery and increase quality. Thus, even if a company has a cost of capital of 12 percent, and an investment will return only 8 percent, if buying a machine will allow the company to deliver products or services faster than competitors, the purchase may be a good one. Likewise, if buying a machine will mean fewer defects, higher quality, and more satisfied customers, the purchase may be a good one. Companies must always be continuously improving in order to keep up with or surpass their competition. Unfortunately, capital investments often are long-term decisions that make continuous improvement difficult. Thus, even if a company has not completely recovered its investment in a capital project, recognizing that competitors have better or more efficient equipment may motivate a company to abandon an investment (a machine that works fine, for example) and make a costlier new investment that will allow the company to remain competitive. The impact of quality and time on capital budgeting decisions cannot be underestimated. In fact, because of the need to continuously improve, companies are always looking for shorter and shorter capital investment opportunities so that they are more flexible, such as leasing or renting equipment and other operating assets where possible.

In addition to quality and time, there are a number of other qualitative factors that must be considered when making capital budgeting decisions. Consider, for example, consumer safety. In one lawsuit, a major U.S. automobile manufacturer was cited for producing cars that were not as safe as they should have been. The company was essentially accused of comparing the present value of the legal and other costs that might result from the unsafe condition of the cars with the cash savings from manufacturing the cars more cheaply and of choosing the less expensive route. The question was then posed: What is the value of a life? This situation provides a dramatic illustration of the need to include qualitative factors in capital investment decisions.

Other qualitative factors include such matters as (1) government regulations, (2) pollution control and environmental protection, (3) worker safety, (4) company image and prestige, (5) preferences of owners and management, and (6) the general welfare of the community in which the company operates. The accompanying Business Environment Essay (on page 733) provides a specific example of one company that combined strategic objectives with humanitarian motives in making a major capital investment decision. Many more examples could be mentioned, but the point is that numbers alone do not control the investment decisions of a good manager. Quality, time, and other qualitative, as well as quantitative, factors should all be considered in reaching long-term investment decisions.

TO SUMMARIZE

In making capital budgeting decisions, the effects of a decision on the quality of and the time with which products can be delivered to customers must be considered. In addition, other qualitative factors such as litigation effects, government regulations, environmental impact, worker safety, company image, preferences of owners, and welfare of community must also be considered.

BUSINESS ENVIRONMENT ESSAY

Ethics in Capital Investment Decisions In 1990, after making substantial investments in two plants in Thailand and one in China, Huntsman Chemical Corporation (HCC) abruptly sold out its business interests when unethical practices were encountered. After winning a major bid in competition with worldwide firms, HCC was virtually guaranteed a significant profit on a $40 million investment. It became clear, however, that business practices involving bribes, payoffs, inflated invoices, and the like were going to be a part of the deal. As soon as Jon Huntsman, founder, chairman, and CEO of HCC, became aware of these unethical practices, he called his managers home and refused to participate further in the projects. HCC sold all its interests and walked away from the deal. When asked about this situation, Mr. Huntsman was quoted as saying, "We simply refuse to carry out negotiations based on factors other than competitiveness, quality, and productivity."

Although the quantitative factors led HCC to become involved in a major capital investment project, other factors caused the company to withdraw. As noted in the text, qualitative factors often override purely quantitative results.

Source: Adapted from "The Heart of the Deal," *Wharton Alumni Magazine* (Summer 1991), pp. 8–14.

APPENDIX

The Time Value of Money

Present Value and Future Value Concepts

The concepts of present value and future value are used to measure the effect of time on the value of money. To illustrate, if you are to receive $100 one year from today, is it worth $100 today? Obviously not, because if you had the $100 today you could either use it now or invest it and earn interest. If the $100 isn't to be received for one year, those options are not available. The present value of $1 is the value today of $1 to be received or paid in the future, given a specified interest rate. To determine the value today of money to be received or paid in the future, we must "discount" the future amount (reduce the amount to its present value) by an appropriate interest rate. For example, if money can earn 10 percent per year, $100 to be received one year from now is approximately equal to $90.91 received today.

Putting it another way, if $90.91 is invested today in an account that earns 10 percent interest for one year, the interest earned will be $9.09 ($90.91 × 10% × 1 year = $9.09). The sum of the $90.91 principal plus $9.09 interest would equal $100 at the end of one year. Thus, the present value of $100 to be received (or paid) in one year with 10 percent interest is $90.91. This present value relationship can be diagramed as follows:

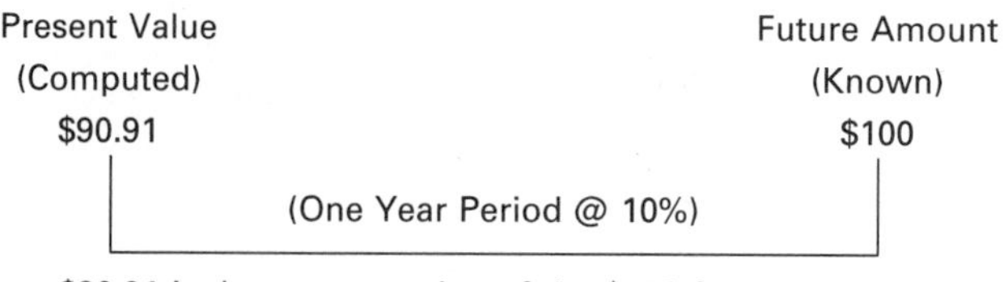

$90.91 is the present value of the $100 future amount.

The relationships in this diagram can be described in two ways. We have just looked at the relationship by recognizing that the $90.91 is the present value of $100 to be received one year from now when interest is 10 percent. In this example, the $100 to be received one year from now is known, and the present value of $90.91 must be computed. We are computing a present value amount from a known future value amount.

Another way to look at the relationship is on a future value basis. Future values apply when the amount today ($90.91) is known, and the future amount must be calculated. Future values are exactly the opposite of present values. Thinking in terms of future values, $100 is the future amount we can expect to receive in one year, given a present known amount of $90.91 when the interest rate is 10 percent. We can diagram this relationship as follows:

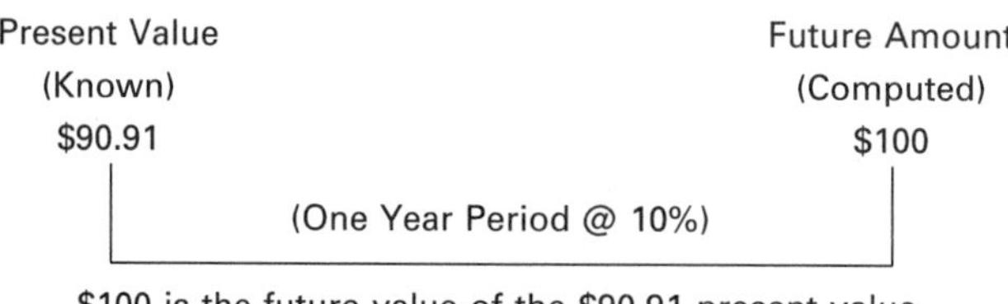

$100 is the future value of the $90.91 present value.

Present and future values can be calculated using formulas. However, if more than one period is involved, the calculations become rather complicated. Therefore, it is more convenient to use either a present value table or a calculator that gives the present value of $1 for various numbers of periods and interest rates (see Table I, page 737) or a future value table that gives the future value of $1 for various numbers of periods and interest rates (see Table III, page 739). We will illustrate the use of both a present value table and a future value table.

Present Value Table

To use a present value table, you simply locate the appropriate number of periods in the leftmost column and the interest rate in the row at the top of the table. The intersection of the row and column is the factor representing the present value of $1 for the number of periods and the relevant interest rate. To find the present value of an amount other than $1, multiply the factor in the table by that amount.

To illustrate the use of a present value table (Table I) to find the present value of a known future amount, assume that $10,000 is to be paid four years from today when the interest rate is 10 percent. What is the present value of the $10,000 payment?

Amount of payment	$10,000
Present value factor of $1 to be paid in 4 periods at 10% interest (from Table I)	× 0.6830
Present value of payment	$ 6,830

This present value amount, $6,830, is the amount that could be paid today to satisfy the obligation that is due four years from now. As indicated, this procedure is sometimes referred to as "discounting." Thus, we say that $10,000 discounted for four years at 10 percent is $6,830. Stated another way, if $6,830 is invested today in an account that pays 10 percent interest, in four years the balance in that account would be $10,000.

Future Value Table

To find the future value of an amount that is known today, you use a future value table. When using a future value table, you simply locate the appropriate number of periods in the leftmost column and the interest rate in the row at the top of the table. The intersection of the row and column is the factor representing the future value of $1 for the number of periods and the relevant interest rate. To find the future value of an amount other than $1, multiply the factor in the table by that amount.

To illustrate the use of a future value table (Table III), we will use the same information that was presented before, except that we will now assume that the present value of $6,830 is known, not the future amount of $10,000. Assume that we have a savings account with a current balance of $6,830 that earns interest of 10%. What will be the balance in that account in four years?

Present value in savings account.................	$ 6,830
Future value factor of $1 in 4 periods	
at 10% interest (from Table III).................	× 1.4641
Future value	$10,000*

*Rounded

When computing future values, we often use the term *compounding* to mean the frequency with which interest is added to the principal. Thus, we say that interest of 10 percent has been compounded once a year (annually) to arrive at a future value at the end of four years of $10,000. If the interest is added more or less frequently than once a year, the future amount will be different.

The preceding example assumed an annual compounding period for interest. If the 10 percent interest had been compounded semiannually (twice a year) for four years, the calculation would have involved using a 5% (one-half of the 10%) rate for 8 periods (4 years × 2 periods per year) instead of 10% for 4 periods. To illustrate, what is the present value of $10,000 to be paid in four years if interest of 10% is compounded semiannually?

Amount of payment	$10,000
Present value factor of $1 to be paid in 8 periods	
at 5% interest (from Table I)....................	× 0.6768
Present value of payment	$ 6,768

Thus, the present value of $10,000 to be paid in four years is $6,768 if interest is compounded semiannually. Likewise, if semiannual compounding is used to determine the future value of $6,768 in four years at 10 percent compounded semiannually, the result is as follows:

Present value in savings account................	$ 6,768
Future value factor of $1 in 8 periods	
at 5% interest (from Table III)..................	× 1.4775
Future value	$10,000*

*Rounded

Note that the present value ($6,768) is lower with semiannual compounding than with annual compounding ($6,830). The more frequently that interest is compounded, the greater the total amount of interest deducted (in computing present values) or added (in computing future values).

Since interest may also be compounded quarterly, monthly, daily, or for some other period, you should learn the relationship of interest to the compounding period. Semiannual interest means that you double the interest periods and halve the annual interest rate; with quarterly interest you quadruple the periods and take one-fourth of the annual interest rate. The formula for interest rate is:

$$\frac{\text{Yearly interest rate}}{\text{Compounding periods per year}} = \text{Interest rate per compounding period}$$

The number of interest periods is simply the number of periods per year times the number of years. That formula is:

$$\text{Compounding periods per year} \times \text{Number of years} = \text{Number of interest periods}$$

The Present Value of an Annuity

In discussing present values and future values, we have assumed only a single present value or future value with one of the amounts known and the other to be computed. With liabilities, we generally know the future amount that must be paid and would like to compute the present value of that future payment.

Many long-term liabilities involve a series of payments rather than one lump-sum payment. For example, a company might purchase equipment under an installment agreement requiring payments of $5,000 each year for five years. Determining the value today (present value) of a series of equally spaced, equal amount payments (called annuities) is more complicated than determining the present value of a single future payment. If you were to try to calculate the present value of an annuity by hand, you would have to discount the first payment for one period, the second payment for two periods, and so on, and then add all the present values together. Because such calculations are time-consuming, a table is generally used (see Table II, page 738). The factors in the table are the sums of the individual present values of all future payments. Based on the present value of an annuity of $1, the table provides factors for various interest rates and payments.

To illustrate the use of a present value of an annuity table (Table II), we will assume that $10,000 is to be paid at the end of each of the next 10 years. If the interest rate is 12% compounded annually, Table II shows a present value factor of 5.6502. This factor means that the present value of $1 paid each year for 10 years discounted at 12 percent is approximately $5.65. Applying this factor to payments of $10,000 results in the following:

Amount of the annual payment.	$10,000
Present value factor of an annuity of $1 discounted for 10 payments at 12%	× 5.6502
Present value	$56,502

This amount, $56,502, is the amount (present value) that could be paid today to satisfy the obligation if interest is 12%.

TABLE I The Present Value of $1 Due in *n* Periods*

Period	1%	2%	3%	4%	5%	6%	7%	8%	9%	10%	12%	14%	15%	16%	18%	20%
1	.9901	.9804	.9709	.9615	.9524	.9434	.9346	.9259	.9174	.9091	.8929	.8772	.8696	.8621	.8475	.8333
2	.9803	.9612	.9426	.9246	.9070	.8900	.8734	.8573	.8417	.8264	.7972	.7695	.7561	.7432	.7182	.6944
3	.9706	.9423	.9151	.8890	.8638	.8396	.8163	.7938	.7722	.7513	.7118	.6750	.6575	.6407	.6086	.5787
4	.9610	.9238	.8885	.8548	.8227	.7921	.7629	.7350	.7084	.6830	.6355	.5921	.5718	.5523	.5158	.4823
5	.9515	.9057	.8626	.8219	.7835	.7473	.7130	.6806	.6499	.6209	.5674	.5194	.4972	.4761	.4371	.4019
6	.9420	.8880	.8375	.7903	.7462	.7050	.6663	.6302	.5963	.5645	.5066	.4556	.4323	.4104	.3704	.3349
7	.9327	.8706	.8131	.7599	.7107	.6651	.6227	.5835	.5470	.5132	.4523	.3996	.3759	.3538	.3139	.2791
8	.9235	.8535	.7894	.7307	.6768	.6274	.5820	.5403	.5019	.4665	.4039	.3506	.3269	.3050	.2660	.2326
9	.9143	.8368	.7664	.7026	.6446	.5919	.5439	.5002	.4604	.4241	.3606	.3075	.2843	.2630	.2255	.1938
10	.9053	.8203	.7441	.6756	.6139	.5584	.5083	.4632	.4224	.3855	.3220	.2697	.2472	.2267	.1911	.1615
11	.8963	.8043	.7224	.6496	.5847	.5268	.4751	.4289	.3875	.3503	.2875	.2366	.2149	.1954	.1619	.1346
12	.8874	.7885	.7014	.6246	.5568	.4970	.4440	.3971	.3555	.3186	.2567	.2076	.1869	.1685	.1372	.1122
13	.8787	.7730	.6810	.6006	.5303	.4688	.4150	.3677	.3262	.2897	.2292	.1821	.1625	.1452	.1163	.0935
14	.8700	.7579	.6611	.5775	.5051	.4423	.3878	.3405	.2992	.2633	.2046	.1597	.1413	.1252	.0985	.0779
15	.8613	.7430	.6419	.5553	.4810	.4173	.3624	.3152	.2745	.2394	.1827	.1401	.1229	.1079	.0835	.0649
16	.8528	.7284	.6232	.5339	.4581	.3936	.3387	.2919	.2519	.2176	.1631	.1229	.1069	.0930	.0708	.0541
17	.8444	.7142	.6050	.5134	.4363	.3714	.3166	.2703	.2311	.1978	.1456	.1078	.0929	.0802	.0600	.0451
18	.8360	.7002	.5874	.4936	.4155	.3503	.2959	.2502	.2120	.1799	.1300	.0946	.0808	.0691	.0508	.0376
19	.8277	.6864	.5703	.4746	.3957	.3305	.2765	.2317	.1945	.1635	.1161	.0829	.0703	.0596	.0431	.0313
20	.8195	.6730	.5537	.4564	.3769	.3118	.2584	.2145	.1784	.1486	.1037	.0728	.0611	.0514	.0365	.0261
25	.7798	.6095	.4476	.3751	.2953	.2330	.1842	.1460	.1160	.0923	.0588	.0378	.0304	.0245	.0160	.0105
30	.7419	.5521	.4120	.3083	.2314	.1741	.1314	.0994	.0754	.0573	.0334	.0196	.0151	.0116	.0070	.0042
40	.6717	.4529	.3066	.2083	.1420	.0972	.0668	.0460	.0318	.0221	.0107	.0053	.0037	.0026	.0013	.0007
50	.6080	.3715	.2281	.1407	.0872	.0543	.0339	.0213	.0134	.0085	.0035	.0014	.0009	.0006	.0003	.0001
60	.5504	.3048	.1697	.0951	.0535	.0303	.0173	.0099	.0057	.0033	.0011	.0004	.0002	.0001	†	†

*The formula used to derive the values in this table was $PV = F \frac{1}{(1 + i)^n}$ where PV = present value, F = future amount to be discounted, i = interest rate, and n = number of periods.

†The value of 0 to four decimal places.

TABLE II

The Present Value of an Annuity of $1 per Number of Payments*

Number of Payments	1%	2%	3%	4%	5%	6%	7%	8%	9%	10%	12%	14%	15%	16%	18%	20%
1	0.9901	0.9804	0.9709	0.9615	0.9524	0.9434	0.9346	0.9259	0.9174	0.9091	0.8929	0.8772	0.8596	0.8621	0.8475	0.8333
2	1.9704	1.9416	1.9135	1.8861	1.8594	1.8334	1.8080	1.7833	1.7591	1.7355	1.6901	1.6467	1.6257	1.6052	1.5656	1.5278
3	2.9410	2.8839	2.8286	2.7751	2.7232	2.6730	2.6243	2.5771	2.5313	2.4869	2.4018	2.3216	2.2832	2.2459	2.1743	2.1065
4	3.9820	3.8077	3.7171	3.6299	3.5460	3.4651	3.3872	3.3121	3.2397	3.1699	3.0373	2.9137	2.8550	2.7982	2.6901	2.5887
5	4.8884	4.7135	4.5797	4.4518	4.3295	4.2124	4.1002	3.9927	3.8897	3.7908	3.6048	3.4331	3.3522	3.2743	3.1272	2.9906
6	5.7985	5.6014	5.4172	5.2421	5.0757	4.9173	4.7665	4.6229	4.4859	4.3553	4.1114	3.8887	3.7845	3.6847	3.4976	3.3255
7	6.7282	6.4720	6.2303	6.0021	5.7864	5.5824	5.3893	5.2064	5.0330	4.8684	4.5638	4.2883	4.1604	4.0386	3.8115	3.6046
8	7.6517	7.3255	7.0197	6.7327	6.4632	6.2098	5.9713	5.7466	5.5348	5.3349	4.9676	4.6389	4.4873	4.3436	4.0776	3.8372
9	8.5660	8.1622	7.7861	7.4353	7.1078	6.8017	6.5152	6.2469	5.9952	5.7590	5.3282	4.9464	4.7716	4.6065	4.3030	4.0310
10	9.4713	8.9826	8.5302	8.1109	7.7217	7.3601	7.0236	6.7101	6.4177	6.1446	5.6502	5.2161	5.0188	4.8332	4.4941	4.1925
11	10.3676	9.7868	9.2526	8.7605	8.3064	7.8869	7.4987	7.1390	6.8052	6.4951	5.9377	5.4527	5.2337	5.0286	4.6560	4.3271
12	11.2551	10.5733	9.9540	9.3851	8.8633	8.3838	7.9427	7.5361	7.1607	6.8137	6.1944	5.6603	5.4206	5.1971	4.7932	4.4392
13	12.1337	11.3484	10.6350	9.9856	9.3936	8.8527	8.3577	7.9038	7.4869	7.1034	6.4235	5.8424	5.5831	5.3423	4.9095	4.5327
14	13.0037	12.1062	11.2961	10.5631	9.8986	9.2950	8.7455	8.2442	7.7862	7.3667	6.6282	6.0021	5.7245	5.4675	5.0081	4.6106
15	13.8651	12.8493	11.9379	11.1184	10.3797	9.7122	9.1079	8.5595	8.0607	7.6061	6.8109	6.1422	5.8474	5.5755	5.0916	4.6755
16	14.7179	13.5777	12.5611	11.6523	10.8378	10.1059	9.4466	8.8514	8.3126	7.8237	6.9740	6.2651	5.9542	5.6685	5.1624	4.7296
17	15.5623	14.2919	13.1661	12.1657	11.2741	10.4773	9.7632	9.1216	8.5436	8.0216	7.1196	6.3729	6.0472	5.7487	5.2223	4.7746
18	16.3983	14.9920	13.7535	12.6593	11.6896	10.8276	10.0591	9.3719	8.7556	8.2014	7.2497	6.4674	6.1280	5.8178	5.2732	4.8122
19	17.2260	15.6785	14.3238	13.1339	12.0853	11.1581	10.3356	9.6036	8.9501	8.3649	7.3658	6.5504	6.1982	5.8775	5.3162	4.8435
20	18.0456	16.3514	14.8775	13.5903	12.4622	11.4699	10.5940	9.8181	9.1285	8.5136	7.4694	6.6231	6.2593	5.9288	5.3527	4.8696
25	22.0232	19.5235	17.4131	15.6221	14.0939	12.7834	11.6536	10.6748	9.8226	9.0770	7.8431	6.8729	6.4641	6.0971	5.4669	4.9476
30	25.8077	22.3965	19.6004	17.2920	15.3725	13.7648	12.4090	11.2578	10.2737	9.4269	8.0552	7.0027	6.5660	6.1772	5.5168	4.9789
40	32.8347	27.3555	23.1148	19.7928	17.1591	15.0463	13.3317	11.9246	10.7574	9.7791	8.2438	7.1050	6.6418	6.2335	5.5482	4.9966
50	39.1961	31.4236	25.7298	21.4822	18.2559	15.7619	13.8007	12.2335	10.9617	9.9148	8.3045	7.1327	6.6605	6.2463	5.5641	4.9995
60	44.9550	34.7609	27.6756	22.6235	18.9293	16.1614	14.0392	12.3766	11.0480	9.9672	8.3240	7.1401	6.6651	6.2482	5.5553	4.9999

*The formula used to derive the values in this table was $PV = F\left(\frac{1 - \frac{1}{(1+i)^n}}{i}\right)$ where PV = present value, F = periodic payment to be discounted, i = interest rate, and n = number of payments.

TABLE III Amount of $1 Due in *n* Periods

Period	1%	2%	3%	4%	5%	6%	7%	8%	9%	10%	12%	14%	15%	16%	18%	20%
1	1.0100	1.0200	1.0300	1.0400	1.0500	1.0600	1.0700	1.0800	1.0900	1.1000	1.1200	1.1400	1.1500	1.1600	1.1800	1.2000
2	1.0201	1.0404	1.0609	1.0816	1.1025	1.1236	1.1449	1.1664	1.1881	1.2100	1.2544	1.2996	1.3225	1.3456	1.3924	1.4400
3	1.0303	1.0612	1.0927	1.1249	1.1576	1.1910	1.2250	1.2597	1.2950	1.3310	1.4049	1.4815	1.5209	1.5609	1.6430	1.7280
4	1.0406	1.0824	1.1255	1.1699	1.2155	1.2625	1.3108	1.3605	1.4116	1.4641	1.5735	1.6890	1.7490	1.8106	1.9388	2.0736
5	1.0510	1.1041	1.1593	1.2167	1.2763	1.3382	1.4026	1.4693	1.5386	1.6105	1.7623	1.9254	2.0114	2.1003	2.2878	2.4883
6	1.0615	1.1262	1.1941	1.2653	1.3401	1.4185	1.5007	1.5869	1.6771	1.7716	1.9738	2.1950	2.3131	2.4364	2.6996	2.9860
7	1.0721	1.1487	1.2299	1.3159	1.4071	1.5036	1.6058	1.7138	1.8280	1.9487	2.2107	2.5023	2.6600	2.8262	3.1855	3.5832
8	1.0829	1.1717	1.2668	1.3686	1.4775	1.5938	1.7182	1.8509	1.9926	2.1436	2.4760	2.8526	3.0590	3.2784	3.7589	4.2998
9	1.0937	1.1951	1.3048	1.4233	1.5513	1.6895	1.8385	1.9990	2.1719	2.3579	2.7731	3.2519	3.5179	3.8030	4.4355	5.1598
10	1.1046	1.2190	1.3439	1.4802	1.6289	1.7908	1.9672	2.1589	2.3674	2.5937	3.1058	3.7072	4.0456	4.4114	5.2338	6.1917
11	1.1157	1.2434	1.3842	1.5395	1.7103	1.8983	2.1049	2.3316	2.5804	2.8531	3.4785	4.2262	4.6524	5.1173	6.1759	7.4031
12	1.1268	1.2682	1.4258	1.6010	1.7959	2.0122	2.2522	2.5182	2.8127	3.1384	3.8960	4.8179	5.3502	5.9360	7.2876	8.9161
13	1.1381	1.2936	1.4685	1.6651	1.8856	2.1329	2.4098	2.7196	3.0658	3.4523	4.3635	5.4924	6.1528	6.8858	8.5994	10.699
14	1.1495	1.3195	1.5126	1.7317	1.9799	2.2609	2.5785	2.9372	3.3417	3.7975	4.8871	6.2613	7.0757	7.9875	10.147	12.839
15	1.1610	1.3459	1.5580	1.8009	2.0789	2.3966	2.7590	3.1722	3.6425	4.1772	5.4736	7.1379	8.1371	9.2655	11.973	15.407
16	1.1726	1.3728	1.6047	1.8730	2.1829	2.5404	2.9522	3.4259	3.9703	4.5950	6.1304	8.1372	9.3576	10.748	14.129	18.488
17	1.1843	1.4002	1.6528	1.9479	2.2920	2.6928	3.1588	3.7000	4.3276	5.0545	6.8660	9.2765	10.761	12.467	16.672	22.186
18	1.1961	1.4282	1.7024	2.0258	2.4066	2.8543	3.3799	3.9960	4.7171	5.5599	7.6900	10.575	12.375	14.462	19.673	26.623
19	1.2081	1.4568	1.7535	2.1068	2.5270	3.0256	3.6165	4.3157	5.1417	6.1159	8.6128	12.055	14.231	16.776	23.214	31.948
20	1.2202	1.4859	1.8061	2.1911	2.6533	3.2071	3.8697	4.6610	5.6044	6.7275	9.6463	13.743	16.366	19.460	27.393	38.337
30	1.3478	1.8114	2.4273	3.2434	4.3219	5.7435	7.6123	10.062	13.267	17.449	29.959	50.950	66.211	85.849	143.37	237.37
40	1.4889	2.2080	3.2620	4.8010	7.0400	10.285	14.974	21.724	31.409	45.259	93.050	188.88	267.86	378.72	750.37	1469.7
50	1.6446	2.6916	4.3839	7.1067	11.467	18.420	29.457	46.901	74.357	117.39	289.00	700.23	1083.6	1670.7	3927.3	9100.4
60	1.8167	3.2810	5.8916	10.519	18.679	32.987	57.946	101.25	176.03	304.48	897.59	2595.9	4383.9	7370.1	20555.	56347.

TABLE IV Amount of an Annuity of $1 per Number of Payments

Number of Payments	1%	2%	3%	4%	5%	6%	7%	8%	9%	10%	12%	14%	15%	16%	18%	20%
1	1.0000	1.0000	1.0000	1.0000	1.0000	1.0000	1.0000	1.0000	1.0000	1.0000	1.0000	1.0000	1.0000	1.0000	1.0000	1.0000
2	2.0100	2.0200	2.0300	2.0400	2.0500	2.0600	2.0700	2.0800	2.0900	2.1000	2.1200	2.1400	2.1500	2.1600	2.1800	2.2000
3	3.0301	3.0604	3.0909	3.1216	3.1525	3.1836	3.2149	3.2464	3.2781	3.3100	3.3744	3.4396	3.4725	3.5056	3.5724	3.6400
4	4.0604	4.1216	4.1836	4.2465	4.3101	4.3746	4.4399	4.5061	4.5731	4.6410	4.7793	4.9211	4.9934	5.0665	5.2154	5.3680
5	5.1010	5.2040	5.3091	5.4163	5.5256	5.6371	5.7507	5.8666	5.9847	6.1051	6.3528	6.6101	6.7424	6.8771	7.1542	7.4416
6	6.1520	6.3081	6.4684	6.6330	6.8019	6.9753	7.1533	7.3359	7.5233	7.7156	8.1152	8.5355	8.7537	8.9775	9.4420	9.9299
7	7.2135	7.4343	7.6625	7.8983	8.1420	8.3938	8.6540	8.9228	9.2004	9.4872	10.8090	10.7305	11.0668	11.4139	12.1415	12.9159
8	8.2857	8.5830	8.8923	9.2142	9.5491	9.8975	10.2598	10.6366	11.0285	11.4359	12.2997	13.2328	13.7268	14.2401	15.3270	16.4991
9	9.3685	9.7546	10.1591	10.5828	11.0266	11.4913	11.9780	12.4876	13.0210	13.5795	14.7757	16.0853	16.7858	17.5185	19.0859	20.7989
10	10.4622	10.9497	11.4639	12.0061	12.5779	13.1808	13.8164	14.4866	15.1929	15.9374	17.5487	19.3373	20.3037	21.3215	23.5213	25.9587
11	11.5668	12.1687	12.8078	13.4864	14.2068	14.9716	15.7836	16.6455	17.5603	18.5312	20.6546	23.0445	24.3493	25.7329	28.7551	32.1504
12	12.6825	13.4121	14.1920	15.0258	15.9171	16.8699	17.8885	18.9771	20.1407	21.2843	24.1331	27.2707	29.0017	30.8502	34.9311	39.5805
13	13.8093	14.6803	15.6178	16.6268	17.7130	18.8821	20.1406	21.4953	22.9534	24.5227	28.0291	32.0887	34.3519	36.7862	42.2187	48.4966
14	14.9474	15.9739	17.0863	18.2919	19.5986	21.0151	22.5505	24.2149	26.0192	27.9750	32.3926	37.5811	40.5047	43.6720	50.8180	59.1959
15	16.0969	17.2934	18.5989	20.0236	21.5786	23.2760	25.1290	27.1521	29.3609	31.7725	37.2797	43.8424	47.5804	51.6595	60.9653	72.0351
16	17.2579	18.6393	20.1569	21.8248	23.6575	25.6725	27.8881	30.3243	33.0034	35.9497	42.7535	50.9804	55.7178	60.9250	72.9390	87.4421
17	18.4304	20.0121	21.7616	23.6975	25.8404	28.2129	30.8402	33.7502	36.9737	40.5447	48.8837	59.1176	65.0751	71.6730	87.0680	105.9306
18	19.6147	21.4123	23.4144	25.6454	28.1324	30.9057	33.9990	37.4502	41.3013	45.5992	55.7497	68.3941	75.8364	84.1407	103.7403	128.1167
19	20.8190	22.8406	25.1169	27.6712	30.5390	33.7600	37.3790	41.4463	46.0185	51.1591	63.4397	78.9692	88.2118	98.6032	123.4135	154.7400
20	22.0190	24.2974	26.8704	29.7781	33.0660	36.7856	40.9955	45.7620	51.1601	57.2750	72.0524	91.0249	102.4436	115.3797	146.6280	186.6880
30	34.7849	40.5681	47.5754	56.0849	66.4388	79.0582	94.4608	113.2832	136.3075	164.4940	241.3327	356.7868	434.7451	530.3117	790.9480	1181.8816
40	48.8864	60.4020	75.4013	95.0255	120.7998	154.7620	199.6351	259.0565	337.8824	442.5926	767.0914	1342.0251	1779.0903	2360.7572	4163.2130	7343.8578
50	64.4632	84.5794	112.7969	152.6671	209.3480	290.3359	406.5289	573.7702	815.0836	1163.9085	2400.0182	4994.5213	7217.7163	10435.6488	21813.0937	45497.1908
60	81.6697	114.0515	163.0534	237.9907	353.5837	533.1282	813.5204	1253.2133	1944.7921	3034.8164	7471.6411	18535.1333	29219.9916	46057.5085	114189.6665	281732.5718

REVIEW OF LEARNING OBJECTIVES

1 Understand the importance of capital budgeting and the concepts underlying strategic and capital investment decisions. Strategic planning, especially as related to capital investment decisions, is critical to the success of organizations. The systematic planning for long-term investments in operating assets is known as capital budgeting. Long-term investments are usually large and represent commitments that are difficult to change, so capital budgeting is crucial to the long-run profitability of a company.

2 Describe and use two nondiscounted capital budgeting techniques: the payback method and the unadjusted rate of return method. Several capital budgeting techniques have been developed to assist in the decision-making process. The payback and unadjusted rate of return methods are commonly used in business because they are simple to apply. However, they generally should be used together with the discounted cash flow methods—net present value and internal rate of return—which are theoretically more correct because they consider the time value of money.

3 Describe and use two discounted capital budgeting techniques: the net present value method and the internal rate of return method. The net present value method uses a predetermined discount rate to state all the cash flows of an investment in present value terms. This rate is a company's cost of capital. The discounted cash inflows and outflows are then compared, and if the result is positive, or at least zero, the project is acceptable from a quantitative standpoint.

The internal rate of return method determines the "true" rate of return on an investment. This is the discount rate at which a project would have a net present value of zero. The internal rate is compared with the company's hurdle rate. If the internal rate is higher than or equal to the hurdle rate, the project is acceptable from a quantitative standpoint.

4 Explain how to use capital budgeting techniques in ranking capital investment projects. Capital budgeting deals with both the screening and the ranking of projects. Investments must first be screened to determine which are acceptable. They must then be ranked to ensure that a company's limited funds are invested in the projects that will earn the greatest rate of return and otherwise accomplish the company's overall objectives.

5 Understand the need for evaluating qualitative factors in strategic and capital investment decisions. Qualitative factors—such as the effect of an investment on quality and time, consumer and worker safety, and environmental and civic responsibility—are important considerations in capital investment decisions and may override the conclusions suggested by quantitative data.

KEY TERMS AND CONCEPTS

capital 712
capital budgeting 712
capital rationing 730
cash inflows 716
cash outflows 716
cost of capital 720
discounted cash flow methods 717
hurdle rate 725
interest 713
internal rate of return 724
internal rate of return method 724
interpolation 725
least-cost decision 723
net present value 721
net present value method 721
payback method 717
payback reciprocal method 726
profitability index 730
ranking 713
screening 713
unadjusted rate of return method 719

REVIEW PROBLEM

Capital Budgeting

High Flying Company has an opportunity to make an investment that will yield $1,000 net cash inflow per year for the next 10 years. The investment will cost $6,000 and will have no salvage value. After cost reductions and depreciation related to the new investment, the future average annual net income will increase $800.

Required: Compute the following:

1. The payback period.
2. The unadjusted rate of return.
3. The net present value. (Use a 10 percent discount rate.)
4. The internal rate of return. (The hurdle rate is 10 percent.)

Solution

1. The Payback Period

To compute the payback period, divide the investment cost by the annual net cash inflows.

$$\frac{\text{Investment cost}}{\text{Annual net cash inflows}} = \frac{\$6{,}000}{\$1{,}000} = 6 \text{ years}$$

2. The Unadjusted Rate of Return

To compute the unadjusted rate of return, divide the increase in future average annual net income by the initial investment cost.

$$\frac{\text{Increase in future average annual net income}}{\text{Initial investment cost}} = \frac{\$800}{\$6{,}000} = 13.3 \text{ percent}$$

3. The Net Present Value

To compute the net present value, first state in present value terms all expected cash outflows and inflows.

Present value of 10 annual payments of $1,000 discounted at 10 percent	=	$6,145
Present value of payment of $6,000 now	=	6,000
Net present value of project (present value of cash inflows minus present value of cash outflow)	=	$ 145

Since this investment's net present value is greater than zero, it is acceptable from a quantitative standpoint.

4. The Internal Rate of Return

To compute the internal rate of return, first compute the present value factor, as follows:

$$\frac{\text{Investment cost}}{\text{Annual net cash inflows}} = \frac{\$6{,}000}{\$1{,}000} = 6.000$$

Next, use this present value factor to find the investment's internal rate of return in a present value table. Using Table II, find the row for 10 years, the life of the investment. Move across the row until you find the present value factor closest to 6,000, which is 6.1446. This is the factor for 10 percent. Since 6.0000 is between 6.1446 and 5.6502, the investment's internal rate of return is between 10 and 12 percent. Next, use interpolation to find a more exact internal rate of return.

	Rate of Return	Present Value Factors	
High factor	10%	6.1446	6.1446
True factor		6.0000	
Low factor.	12%		5.6502
Differences	2%	0.1446	0.4944

The number 0.1446 is the difference between the high factor and the true factor. The number 0.4944 is the difference between the high factor and the low factor. The difference between the high rate and the low rate is 2 percent. The proportion 0.1446 ÷ 0.4944 of this 2 percent difference must be added to the low rate to give the true internal rate of return.

$$\text{True internal rate of return} = 0.10 + \left(\frac{0.1446}{0.4944} \times 0.02\right) = 10.58 \text{ percent}$$

Next, this internal rate of return is compared with the hurdle rate. Since it is greater, the investment is acceptable quantitatively. Note that this is the same decision reached by calculating the net present value.

DISCUSSION QUESTIONS

1. Define capital budgeting. Give two examples of long-term investment decisions that require capital budgeting.
2. Why do long-term capital investment decisions often have a significant effect on a company's profitability?
3. Distinguish between the screening and ranking functions of capital budgeting.
4. Why is the time value of money so important in capital budgeting decisions?
5. If the time value of money is so important, why isn't the timing of cash flows emphasized in the accounting cycle?
6. How is depreciation expense treated when the discounted cash flow methods are used? Why?
7. How are cost savings and increased revenues related in capital budgeting?
8. Identify four capital budgeting methods, and explain why some are considered better than others.
9. Why is the payback method inferior to the discounted cash flow methods? When is the payback method helpful?
10. What is the major weakness of the unadjusted rate of return method?
11. Does a net present value of zero indicate that a project should be rejected? Explain.
12. As the desired rate of return increases, does the net present value of a project increase? Explain.
13. Under what circumstances might a project with a negative net present value be accepted?
14. What discount rate yields a net present value of zero? How is it determined?
15. What is a company's hurdle rate? How is it used?
16. What rate does the payback reciprocal approximate, and how can this information be useful?
17. Of what value is a profitability index in capital budgeting?
18. How do quality and time considerations affect capital budgeting decisions?
19. Identify several qualitative factors, other than quality and time consideration, that may affect strategic and capital investment decisions. Why are qualitative factors important?

DISCUSSION CASES

CASE 15-1

SHOULD WE PURCHASE THAT NEW COPIER?

Campus Print Shop is thinking of purchasing a new, modern copier that automatically collates pages. The machine would cost $22,000 cash. A service contract on the machine, considered a must because of its complexity, would be an additional $200 per month. The machine is expected to last eight years and have a resale value of $4,000. By purchasing the new machine, Campus would save $450 per month in labor costs and $100 per month in materials costs due to increased efficiency. Other operating costs are expected to remain the same. The old copier would be sold for its scrap value of $1,000. Campus requires a return of 14 percent on its capital investments.

1. As a consultant to Campus, compute:
   a. The payback period.
   b. The unadjusted rate of return.
   c. The net present value.
   d. The internal rate of return.
2. On the basis of these computations and any qualitative considerations, would you recommend that Campus purchase the new copier?

CASE 15-2 COST AND QUALITATIVE FACTORS IN CAPITAL INVESTMENT DECISIONS

Yoshika Landscaping is contemplating purchasing a new ditchdigging machine that promises savings of $5,600 per year for 10 years. The machine costs $21,970, and no salvage value is expected. The company's cost of capital is 12 percent. You have been asked to advise Yoshika relative to this capital investment decision. As part of your analysis, compute:

1. The payback period.
2. The unadjusted rate of return.
3. The net present value.
4. The payback reciprocal.
5. The internal rate of return.

What factors besides your quantitative analysis should be considered in making this decision?

EXERCISES

Note: Unless otherwise indicated, the exercises and problems assume that all payments are made or received at the end of the year.

EXERCISE 15-1 Present Values

Consider each part independently.

1. Super-Fix Company would like to move its auto repair shop to a downtown location in order to attract more customers. What is the maximum Super-Fix should pay to purchase a building at the new location, assuming that the company needs to earn 12 percent? The new building will last 40 years. Super-Fix estimates that moving to the new location will result in a $10,000 increase in annual income.
2. If Audrey Ostler buys a new small automobile that costs $14,000 and provides annual gasoline savings of $1,200, how long must she own the car before the savings justify its cost? Assume an 8 percent cost of capital.

EXERCISE 15-2 Time Value on Money

Your late, rich uncle left you $250,000. The executor of the estate has asked if you would rather receive the full amount now or $30,000 a year for the next 40 years.

Which of these options would you take, assuming that your desired rate of return is:

1. 10 percent?
2. 12 percent?

EXERCISE 15-3
Payback Method

The manager of Simple Company must choose between two investments. Project A costs $50,000 and promises cash savings of $10,000 a year over a useful life of 10 years. Project B costs $60,000, and the estimated cash savings are $11,000 per year over a useful life of 11 years. Using the payback method, determine which project the manager should choose.

EXERCISE 15-4
Unadjusted Rate of Return Method

Um Good, Inc., a candy maker, is thinking of purchasing a new machine. A marketing firm has estimated that the new machine could increase revenues by $30,000 a year for the next 5 years. The expenses directly relating to the machine total $60,000 ($12,000 × 5 years). The initial purchase cost would be $80,000. What is the unadjusted rate of return?

EXERCISE 15-5
Net Present Value Method

The Carroll Broom Company is thinking of purchasing a new automatic straw-binding machine. The company president, Joan Carroll, has determined that such a machine would save the company $10,000 per year in labor costs. The machine would cost $46,500 and would have a useful life of 10 years and a scrap value of $500. The machine would require servicing after 5 years at a cost of $1,000. Carroll uses a discount rate of 16 percent. Compute the net present value. From a quantitative standpoint, should the machine be purchased?

EXERCISE 15-6
Least-Cost Decision

The local fire department has determined the Sleep-Eazy Mattress Company is not in full compliance with local fire regulations. To comply, Sleep-Eazy has two alternatives: It may install an automatic sprinkler system, or it may hire a fire safety expert to make weekly fire safety checks. The automatic sprinkler system will cost $125,000, including installation charges, and will last for 10 years. It will have no salvage value. The entire system is virtually maintenance-free. The fire safety expert's fee is $14,000 per year. The cost of capital is 10 percent. Which alternative should Sleep-Eazy Mattress Company choose? Why?

EXERCISE 15-7
Internal Rate of Return

Juan Gonzales, the president of Nogalis Corporation, is trying to decide whether he should buy a new machine that will improve production efficiency. The machine will increase cash inflows $5,000 a year for 5 years. It will cost $18,000, and there will be no salvage value. What is the internal rate of return?

EXERCISE 15-8
Cost of Capital

Daphney Corporation has 20,000 shares of $10 par value common stock outstanding. Stockholders expect to receive annual dividends of $2 per share. In addition, the corporation has issued $100,000 of 10 percent bonds. The corporation has also accumulated $25,000 in earnings that have been retained in the company. If this cash were deposited in money market certificates, it would earn 12 percent interest. Using the weighting procedure discussed in the chapter, calculate Daphney Corporation's cost of capital. (Ignore taxes in calculating the cost of debt.)

EXERCISE 15-9
Screening Function

Your company's cost of capital was determined to be 12 percent. Several investment alternatives are being considered, and the discounted cash flows have given the following results:

Net present value:

1. A new machine was analyzed, and a net present value of zero resulted.
2. A new product line was analyzed, and a negative net present value of $60 resulted.
3. An investment was being considered. The analysis yielded a net present value of $250.

Internal rate of return:

1. A plant expansion project promised a yield of 12 percent.
2. An investment in additional transport trucks would yield an internal rate of return of 10 percent.

3. The addition of another assembly line would add cash flows that would give an internal rate of return of 16 percent.

Determine which projects should be accepted as investment opportunities and which should be rejected.

EXERCISE 15-10
Ranking Projects

Using net present value (NPV) analysis, a manager can select those projects that will maximize the present value of future cash flows. NPV analysis is a powerful tool; however, surveys of current practice indicate that the internal rate of return (IRR) method enjoys considerable popularity among decision makers. What would account for IRR's appeal? What are the drawbacks to using only the IRR method to rank projects?

EXERCISE 15-11
Profitability Index

California Company is trying to determine the relative profitability of two alternative investments. Investment A requires an initial cash outlay of $10,000 and has a net present value of $500. Investment B requires an initial cash outlay of $2,000 and has a net present value of $150. Compute the profitability index of each investment. Which alternative is more profitable?

EXERCISE 15-12
Quality and Time Factors

Tucker Yard Service Company is contemplating purchasing a new riding lawnmower for its business. One particular model has special features that enhance the cutting and the collecting of the mowed grass, but that mower is quite expensive. Another model is more basic and costs $1,000 less. The payback period on the more expensive model is estimated to be 3.5 years and on the less expensive model, 2.5 years. The "bumper-to-bumper" warranties are two years and one year, respectively. From these limited data, what factors should Tucker consider in making this decision?

EXERCISE 15-13
Qualitative Considerations

The Upscale Department Store has been plagued with shoplifting. The president, Hector Conrad, has suggested that the store hire a security force to "frisk" all customers as they leave the store. It is estimated that annual shoplifting losses are $100,000. Expenses associated with the security force are estimated to be $50,000 annually. Before Mr. Conrad makes his final decision, what other factors might he consider?

PROBLEMS

PROBLEM 15-1
Net Present Value Method

A fast-food establishment is thinking of buying a new cooking grill and refrigeration unit. The cost of these new machines is $12,500 and $9,000, respectively. The installation costs of the new equipment will run about $800. It is estimated that 10 percent more customers can be served with the new equipment, which would mean an additional annual net cash flow of approximately $4,500. The salvage value of the old grill and refrigeration unit is estimated to be $1,000.

The firm's cost of capital is 12 percent. The equipment should last 10 years, at a minimum.

Required: Using the net present value method, should the company purchase the new equipment? (Ignore income tax effects.)

PROBLEM 15-2
Net Present Value Method—Uneven Cash Flows

Southside Junk Yard needs to buy a car smasher. The machine would add the following revenues to the business over the next three years:

Year 1 Cash savings = $30,000
Year 2 Cash savings plus additional scrap sales = $40,000
Year 3 Cash savings plus additional scrap sales = $55,000

The initial cost of the machine is $100,000. At the end of three years, its salvage value is estimated at $20,000. The firm has a cost of capital of 12 percent.

Required: Using the net present value method, determine whether the company should purchase the machine. (Ignore income tax effects.)

PROBLEM 15-3
Internal Rate of Return

You have been offered the opportunity to purchase a franchise of Sunshine Juice Stores. You will have to pay $155,625 for the initial investment in the store and its equipment, plus $30,000 per year for the lease payments and the franchise fee. The franchise contract obligates you for 10 years. Operating costs for each year will be $125,000, and the expected revenue is $180,000 a year. Your hurdle rate is 10 percent. Ignore income taxes.

Required:

1. Does this investment yield a satisfactory rate of return?
2. What qualitative factors might be considered?

PROBLEM 15-4
Internal Rate of Return and Hurdle Rate

Nina Roberts has the opportunity to invest in a timber forest. She would have to invest $100,000. Revenues of $20,000 per year are projected for 20 years. However, these revenues will not begin coming in for five years because the timber must be seasoned before cutting and selling can begin. Ms. Roberts' hurdle rate is 10 percent. Ignore income taxes.

Required:

1. Calculate the internal rate of return, and determine whether or not Ms. Roberts should make the investment.
2. If Ms. Roberts has to borrow the $100,000 necessary for the investment from her bank at 12 percent interest, should she make the investment?
3. **Interpretive Question:** Why is it important for Ms. Roberts to determine her cost of capital before making this investment decision?

PROBLEM 15-5
Payback, Net Present Value, and Internal Rate of Return Methods

Nucore Company is thinking of purchasing a new candy-wrapping machine at a cost of $370,000. The machine should save the company approximately $70,000 in operating costs per year over its estimated useful life of 10 years. The salvage value at the end of 10 years is expected to be $15,000. (Ignore income tax effects.)

Required:

1. What is the machine's payback period?
2. Compute the net present value of the machine if the cost of capital is 12 percent.
3. What is the expected internal rate of return for this machine?

PROBLEM 15-6
Using the Payback Reciprocal Method to Approximate the Internal Rate of Return

The manager of Soft & Creamy Ice Cream is thinking of buying a new soft ice cream machine. The machine will cost $13,500 and will last 10 years. Soft ice cream sales are expected to generate $3,000 in income per year.

Required:

1. Using the payback reciprocal method, approximate the internal rate of return.
2. What is the "true" internal rate of return from Table II?

PROBLEM 15-7
Payback Reciprocal Method

Brad Miller is considering investing in a coin-operated laundromat. He can buy a small laundromat for $30,000. Expected net revenues after expenses for maintenance and cleaning are $7,500 per year for the next 10 years. At the end of 10 years, the machines will have a total scrap value of $500.

Required:

1. Use the payback reciprocal method to estimate the internal rate of return.
2. **Interpretive Question:** Under what circumstances would you recommend using the payback reciprocal method?

PROBLEM 15-8
Choosing Among Alternatives

Tom Thurlow wants to buy a boat but is short of cash. Two alternatives are available: Tom can accept $2,000 per year from his brother for partial ownership in the boat, or he can earn money by renting the boat to others. Rental income would be $2,500 per year. Under either alternative, the boat will last eight years. If Tom rents the boat out, he will have to pay $3,000 to overhaul the engine at the end of the fourth year.

Required:

Which alternative should Tom select, assuming that the cost of capital is 12 percent and that only quantitative considerations are involved?

PROBLEM 15-9
Lease-or-Buy Decision

A small sales company is committed to supplying three sales representatives with new cars. The company has two alternatives. It can either buy the three cars and sell them after two years, or it can lease the cars for two years. The company uses a 16 percent discount rate. The information for each alternative is as follows:

Alternative 1: Buy

Cost	$36,000
Annual service costs	3,000
Anticipated repairs during the 1st year	700
Anticipated repairs during the 2nd year	1,500
Salvage value at the end of 2 years	10,000

Alternative 2: Lease

To lease the cars, the company would simply pay $20,000 a year for the two years.

Required: Assuming the lease is paid at the end of each year, determine the better alternative.

PROBLEM 15-10
Rent-or-Purchase Decision

As one aspect of its business, New Lawn Company currently rents a ditchdigging machine for an average of $48 per job. A used machine is available for $995 but would cost $498 to repair. The machine, if purchased, would cost $800 a year to maintain and in two years would need a new chain costing $394. The used digger has a useful life of four years with no salvage value.

Required: If the company averages 30 jobs a year and has a cost of capital of 10 percent, which alternative is more profitable?

PROBLEM 15-11
Sell-or-Rent Decision

Clarence Gleason has inherited an apartment complex. He is now faced with the decision of whether to sell or to rent the property. A real estate advisor believes that Clarence should rent the property, because he could receive $65,000 per year for 10 years and then could sell the property for $400,000. A development company has offered Clarence $300,000 down and promises to pay $50,000 per year for the next 15 years. The land has a remaining mortgage of $130,000. If Clarence sells the complex, he will have to pay that sum now. If he rents the property, he will have to pay $20,000 per year for 10 years. The cost of capital is 16 percent.

Required:

1. Calculate the net present value of each alternative.
2. **Interpretive Question:** Discuss the qualitative factors that might affect the decision to sell or rent.

PROBLEM 15-12
Unifying Concepts: Net Present Value and Internal Rate of Return Methods

Julie Kowalis, an investment analyst, wants to know if her investments during the past four years have earned at least a 12 percent return. Four years ago, she had the following investments:

a. She purchased a small building for $50,000 and rented space in it. She received rental income of $8,000 for each of the four years and then sold the building this year for $55,000.
b. She purchased a small refreshment stand near the city park for $25,000. Annual income from the stand was $5,000 for each of the four years. She sold the stand for $20,000 this year.
c. She purchased an antique car for $5,000 four years ago. She sold it this year to a collector for $7,000.

Required:

1. Using the net present value method, determine whether or not each investment earned at least 12 percent.
2. Did the investments as a whole earn at least 12 percent? Explain.

PROBLEM 15-13
Net Present Value Used to Rank Alternatives

Taglioni's Pizza Company has to choose a new delivery car from among three alternatives. Assume that gasoline costs $1.30 per gallon and that the firm's cost of capital is 12 percent. The car will be driven 12,000 miles per year.

	Car 1	Car 2	Car 3
Cost	$12,000	$4,000	$8,000
Mileage per gallon	40	8	12
Useful life	5 years	5 years	5 years
Salvage value	$2,000	$500	$1,000

Required:

1. Which car should the company purchase?
2. How would your answer change if the price of gasoline increased to $2 per gallon?

PROBLEM 15-14
Screening and Ranking Alternatives

Sunshine Corporation is considering several long-term investments. Management wants to accept the two best projects, given the following data:

	Project				
	A	B	C	D	E
Present value of net cash inflows	$24,000	$44,000	$15,000	$30,000	$50,000
Investment cost	20,000	40,000	16,000	24,000	41,000

Required:

1. Determine the net present value and the profitability index for each project.
2. Which projects are acceptable using the profitability index as a screening tool?
3. What would be the ranking of the acceptable projects according to the profitability indexes?
4. **Interpretive Question:** What additional information would be needed to screen and rank the projects using the internal rate of return method? What are the decision rules using the IRR method for screening and ranking capital budgeting projects?

PROBLEM 15-15
Unifying Concepts: Comparing the Internal Rate of Return and the Net Present Value Methods

Get Rich Corporation has to choose between two investment opportunities. Investment A requires an immediate cash outlay of $100,000 and provides after-tax income of $20,000 per year for 10 years. Investment B requires an immediate cash outlay of $1,000 and generates after-tax income of $350 per year for 5 years.

Required:

1. Using a cost of capital of 12 percent, calculate the net present value of each investment, and determine which one Get Rich should select.
2. Calculate the internal rate of return of each investment. On the basis of this method, which investment should Get Rich select?
3. **Interpretive Question:** How do you account for the difference in rankings? Under the circumstances, which method would you rely on for your decision?

PROBLEM 15-16
Unifying Concepts: Payback, Internal Rate of Return, and Payback Reciprocal Methods

The management of Kitchen Shop is thinking of buying a new drill press to aid in adapting parts for different machines. The press is expected to save Kitchen Shop $8,000 per year in costs. However, Kitchen Shop has an old punch machine that isn't worth anything on the market and that will probably last indefinitely. The new press will last 12 years and will cost $41,595. (Ignore income tax effects.)

Required:

1. Compute the payback period of the new machine.
2. Compute the internal rate of return.
3. Compute the payback reciprocal and determine if it is close to the internal rate of return.
4. **Interpretive Question:** What uncertainties are involved in this decision? Discuss how they might be dealt with.
5. **Interpretive Question:** Explain the relationship between the payback reciprocal and the internal rate of return.

PROBLEM 15-17
Unifying Concepts: Capital Rationing Using the Payback and Net Present Value Methods

Dino Corporation is trying to decide which of five investment opportunities it should undertake. The company's cost of capital is 16 percent. Owing to a cash shortage, the company has a policy that it will not undertake any investment unless it has a payback period of less than three years. The company is unwilling to undertake more than two investment projects. The following data apply to the alternatives:

Investment	Initial Cost	Expected Returns
A	$100,000	$30,000 per year for 5 years
B	50,000	25,000 per year for 6 years
C	30,000	8,000 per year for 10 years
D	20,000	7,000 per year for 6 years
E	10,000	3,500 per year for 3 years

Required:

1. Using the payback method, screen out any investment project that fails to meet the company's payback period requirement.
2. Using the net present value method, determine which of the remaining projects the company should undertake, keeping in mind the capital rationing constraint.
3. **Interpretive Question:** What advantages do you see in using the payback method together with other capital budgeting methods?

Analyzing Real Company Information

International Case

Ethics Case

Writing Assignment

The Debate

Internet Search

Accounting is more than just doing textbook problems. These Competency Enhancement Opportunities provide practice in critical thinking, oral and written communication, research, teamwork, and consideration of ethical issues.

ANALYZING REAL COMPANY INFORMATION

• Analyzing 15-1 (Microsoft)

The 1997 annual report for **Microsoft** is included in Appendix A. The section of the annual report relating to management's discussion and analysis provides detail as to factors that might affect Microsoft's future and, as a result, the company's long-term decisions. Review the financial statements and the "Management Discussion and Analysis" section and answer the following questions:

1. Microsoft has no long-term debt. Does that mean its cost of capital is zero? Explain.
2. Microsoft specifically states that the company "does not provide forecasts of future financial performance." If that is the case, how can they make any capital budgeting decisions?
3. Microsoft lists 20 factors under the heading "Outlook: Issues and Uncertainties." How would factors such as price, saturation, and integrated suites affect the company's capital budgeting process? What specific inputs into the capital budgeting models would be affected by these factors?

• Analyzing 15-2 (The Boeing Company)

As you probably know, **Boeing** builds airplanes. While most famous for the big 747, Boeing is continually developing newer models. Over the past several years, Boeing has been developing the 737 and 777 families of airplanes. In 1996, Boeing formed a joint venture with **General Electric** to develop planes that can fly over 6,000 miles without refueling.

1. What factors must Boeing consider when making the decision to produce a new family of airplanes like the 777? What would be the expected inflows, and what would be the expected cash outflows? Categorize the outflows into two types: one-time outflows and annual outflows.
2. The costs of developing a new family of airplanes are enormous. Why would Boeing agree to incur these costs when it is able to continue producing older model planes like the 747 and the 767? Frame this discussion in terms of a capital budgeting decision. That is, evaluate the opportunities in terms of cash inflows and cash outflows.

INTERNATIONAL CASE

• Toyota Motor Corporation

Toyota discloses the following information relating to its long-term debt in its 1997 annual report:

- $5\frac{5}{8}$% U. S. dollar bonds
- $6\frac{7}{8}$% U. S. dollar bonds
- 1.2% convertible debentures
- 1.7% convertible debentures

Ford Motor Company also provides information relating to its debt in the notes to its annual report. That information is given below.

- Secured indebtedness, 8.5%
- Unsecured senior indebtedness—notes and bank debt, 6.7%
- Unsecured senior indebtedness—debentures, 5.6%
- Unsecured subordinated indebtedness—notes, 8.8%
- Unsecured subordinated indebtedness—debentures, 7.3%

1. Assume that each company's debt is distributed equally across the various categories. Compute an average cost interest rate for each company.
2. If your answer from (1) represented each firm's cost of capital, what would it tell you about the kinds of projects that Toyota can undertake as compared to Ford?

ETHICS CASE

• Wheeler, Nevada

The city council of Wheeler, Nevada, is faced with an important decision: whether or not to rezone a parcel of property and allow ChemStor Inc. to purchase the land and build a chemical waste storage facility on the property. Several factors enter into the decision.

a. The property is currently zoned for agricultural use and is surrounded by ranching operations in a rural community.
b. Several ranchers have joined together and offered to buy the property from the city over a 40-year period. In return for an agreed-upon interest rate of one point below prime, they will donate 20 acres of the land for a city park.
c. ChemStor has offered to pay cash for the land. Company management also points out that the facility will create about 25 new jobs for local residents and generate close to $100,000 a year in increased property taxes for the city.
d. ChemStor, a New Jersey-based company, learned of this property from its controller, who is a brother-in-law to one of the Wheeler City council members. ChemStor has offered a "finder's fee" for locating a waste storage site. The finder's fee would be split between the controller and the brother-in-law.

Identify the ethical and other issues involved in this capital investment decision.

WRITING ASSIGNMENT

• Lease versus buy

You are fresh out of college, have your first real job, and you just received your first big paycheck. You decide you need some wheels. Off you go to the car dealer. You carefully review the various makes and models of cars, determine the price range you can afford, and select "YOUR FIRST CAR." You thought that was the hard part. Now you need to decide on financing. The salesperson says you can either borrow money to purchase the vehicle or you can lease the car.

What factors should you consider in making this capital budgeting decision? Identify those factors that should enter into the lease-versus-buy decision. Prepare a short memo discussing the pros and cons of leasing versus buying and identifying the cash inflows and outflows associated with each option.

THE DEBATE

• The time value of money

The text discusses two general types of capital budgeting techniques: nondiscounted and discounted. The nondiscounted methods involve comparing the outflows of cash to the inflows. These methods do not take into account the time value of money. The discounted capital budgeting techniques factor into the evaluation the time value of money.

Divide your group into two teams.

- Team 1 is to take the position that the nondiscounted methods provide the best means of evaluating capital budgeting alternatives. Prepare a short presentation that identifies the advantages of using the nondiscounted methods and discusses the disadvantages of the discounted capital budgeting techniques.

- Team 2 is to take the position that the discounted methods are preferred. Prepare a short presentation in support of the various methods that incorporate into their analysis the time value of money.

INTERNET SEARCH

Federal Express

We began this chapter with a look at Federal Express. Let's continue our examination of this company using its Internet site. Access Federal Express's site at www.federalexpress.com. Sometimes Web addresses change, so if this address doesn't work, access the Web site for this book at stice.college.com for an updated link to Federal Express.

Once you have gained access to the company's Web site, answer the following questions:

1. Federal Express allows customers to track a package as it moves around the world. What information do you need to track a package?
2. How many aircraft does Federal Express have in its worldwide fleet?
3. Access Federal Express's notes to its financial statements to determine what percentage of its capital equipment is leased and what percentage has been purchased. What factors would the company have considered when determining whether to lease or buy its aircraft and equipment?

APPENDIX A

MICROSOFT CORPORATION
1997 ANNUAL REPORT

msft

financial highlights

(in millions, except earnings per share)

year ended june 30	1993	1994	1995	1996	1997
Revenue	$3,753	$4,649	$5,937	$ 8,671	$11,358
Net income	953	1,146	1,453	2,195	3,454
Earnings per share[1]	0.79	0.94	1.16	1.71	2.63
Return on revenue	25.4%	24.7%	24.5%	25.3%	30.4%
Cash and short-term investments	$2,290	$3,614	$4,750	$ 6,940	$ 8,966
Total assets	3,805	5,363	7,210	10,093	14,387
Stockholders' equity	3,242	4,450	5,333	6,908	10,777

[1] earnings per share have been restated to reflect a two-for-one stock split in December 1996

to our shareholders

1997 was an outstanding year. Our customers were asking for Microsoft to build products that allowed them to get business benefit out of the Internet, and we delivered. Across the board, with productivity applications, tools, desktop systems, and server products, we are gaining significant momentum. Like any time in our 23-year history we have great opportunities but face a number of threats.

Our top priority in fiscal 1998 is simplicity: reducing the total cost of ownership, and reducing complexity. We will need to keep this focus even as we roll out numerous products, and while competitors are battling with us on many fronts.

As we chart our path going forward, we are focused on four key areas:

Windows on the desktop. A few years ago, we developed the concept of "Windows Everywhere," an architecture that allows customers to have a family of operating systems and a set of compatible applications spanning a family of devices from the very small to the very large. We've had great success moving computing desktops to 32-bit systems — Microsoft® Windows® 95 and Windows NT® Workstation — as well as introducing Windows CE, a new version of the Windows operating system initially focused on handheld devices for mobile professionals. Microsoft Internet Explorer 4.0 will be another major step on our way to marrying the PC and the Internet. A core strength of Windows is its collection of development tools, allowing developers to tap into the richness of our platform and get great performance from their applications.

Productivity applications. Microsoft Office 97 was a major release, setting a new bar for features, functionality and integration. We put years of R&D into it and incorporated some of the discoveries coming out of our Research Division. Office 97 features natural language systems and sophisticated grammar checking. But that is just a start. Our goal is to allow people to get their work done in the easiest way possible, without thinking about the tools they're using.

Enterprise solutions. Windows NT Server and the Microsoft BackOffice® family line of server applications are growing at a phenomenal rate. As computer chips have become faster and faster, we have been able to deliver performance to customers previously accomplished only by mainframes. And beyond performance, we are now focused on simplicity and manageability. But there is still a lot more we intend to do to make high-end computing easier and less costly.

Interactive media and services. Our Interactive Media Group (IMG) has three areas of concentration: packaged software, hardware, and online services. All are about enhancing the consumer experience around the PC and Web lifestyle. Our packaged software efforts are focused on delivering great titles in the games, learning, personal finance and mapping categories. For hardware, our goal is to enhance the software experience.

In online services, the focus is on producing an exciting combination of software and content that will help customers tap the power of the Internet to lead more informed, more fun and more productive lives. Increasingly, you'll see us emphasizing products and services where excellence in software makes the difference. Some of the investments we are making in this new area will pay off — others won't. We still have a lot of learning to do. Just like everyone else on the Web, we don't know what the mix of revenue will be — subscription, advertising, or promotions.

Digital Nervous System

I use the phrase "digital nervous system" to mean the electronic system that companies use to solve business and customer problems. A great digital nervous system starts with a powerful operating system and network, but if any business is to automate, it also has to have a great database system and messaging system. Microsoft has, over the years, invested heavily in the technical development of Microsoft SQL Server™ and Microsoft Exchange, as well as other components of Microsoft BackOffice, hiring the best people and building products with great performance and interoperability.

This year we are also going to invest heavily in the technical and marketing support of software developers and solution providers in vertical markets. We want to ensure that virtually any customer will be able to find their specific business application on a high-performance Windows-based system. You're also going to see broader coverage of corporate accounts worldwide. These are major investments in a time of moderate sales growth.

On May 20, we met with customers on Scalability Day, an important milestone because we demonstrated that any company, of any size, can run its business on our software, using solutions built on top of PC hardware. Hardware manufacturers have been busy producing world-class machines for a fraction of the price of mainframes. I am very optimistic that customers in the enterprise space will recognize, as they have on the desktop, that increasing performance, rising quality and falling prices make personal computer servers the best choice.

Simplicity

In fiscal 1998, we expect to spend nearly $2.6 billion on research and development, broadly defined. It's very exciting for me to see Microsoft bringing in world-class experts to work on areas like networking, security, graphics and linguistics.

Our industry makes incredible productivity devices that are impacting people around the world. But the complexity of technology has prevented users and system administrators from getting maximum value from their investments. Across the board, in applications, tools, desktop and server systems and interactive content, we have to make things simpler for users and system administrators. The three broad areas are Total Cost of Ownership (TCO) and manageability, reducing complexity, and new, simpler devices on the low-end.

Total Cost of Ownership. Addressing TCO is important for companies of all sizes. And the issue is not just reducing costs — it's about increasing usability and functionality without increasing complexity. Our Zero Administration Initiative is the focus here.

We believe every knowledge worker should have a personal computer. We believe employees are more than cogs in a machine. We believe businesses succeed because of the intelligence and creativity of their employees. We believe that in order for a business to stay competitive in this fast-paced world, it needs a digital approach. But to allow our customers to reap the true rewards of building a digital nervous system, we need to help them get off the treadmill of having to dedicate so many of their resources just to keep systems up and running.

Windows NT Server 5.0 is a major breakthrough in addressing TCO issues. It will allow an organization to easily control user configurations, to intelligently mirror the client machine's state on the server, and to allow users to roam from machine to machine. We also will enable mobile users to get the full benefit of their machines while traveling and have the ability to fully synchronize with the server when they return, so their local data and system state are protected. We will combine the power and flexibility of the PC with the benefits of central management.

Reducing complexity. Though we firmly believe in the power of the personal computer, it's not always true that one size fits all. Some customers have older PC hardware that for various reasons they are not ready to upgrade. Some need a simpler, standard configuration for many workers. Some customers have existing investments in terminals.

We have worked with other companies to introduce the NetPC and Windows-based terminals. The NetPC is a simpler, easily managed PC configuration for corporate desktops that PC manufacturers are beginning to roll out now. The technology behind Windows-based terminals helps customers by extending the life of older, less-powerful PCs by running a limited number of newer applications off a server, and opens a new customer segment to us.

New devices. "Windows Everywhere" means we're scaling down as well as up. Our Windows CE operating system is initially focused on handheld devices. Users will range from retail clerks monitoring inventory to healthcare workers charting patients to utility workers installing electrical lines.

Windows CE will also be suitable for still smaller "wallet" PCs, wireless-communication devices such as digital information pagers and cellular smart phones, next-generation entertainment and multimedia consoles, including game machines and smarter DVD players and purpose-built Internet access devices such as WebTVs, digital set-top boxes for cable and satellite systems and Internet "Web phones."

Connected PCs, Connected TVs

We've long held the belief that the PC was moving from the stand-alone PC to the connected PC. Today, this is well under way. PC networks are broadly prevalent in business, and the Internet is creating a worldwide web of PCs. Windows NT 5.0 and Windows 98 will do more to make PCs connected. Our vision has now evolved to the "Connected PC and the Connected TV" — the idea of integrating the intelligence and interactivity of PCs with the video and sound of TV. This will accelerate as TV moves to a digital format. Making this vision a reality is reliant on the physical infrastructure — the high-speed connections — that will join these devices. Earlier this year, we invested in Comcast, the U.S.'s fourth-largest cable company, primarily to spur the cable and phone industries to build two-way, high-speed networks. We acquired WebTV to hasten the day when TVs and PCs use Windows technologies, providing complementary sources of information and entertainment in the home. Windows CE, a compatible subset of our Windows family, makes it a lot easier for consumer electronics manufacturers to do things such as a customized guide to television shows or applications to let you view Web pages and see simple electronic mail on your TV, control home heating and lighting systems or even let you connect up a digital camera and post or e-mail photos using the Internet.

These developments, and our work in IMG, will help make the "Web lifestyle" a reality. This is a lifestyle in which people take advantage of the Internet to lead more informed and productive lives, and have more fun. With a Web lifestyle, people will naturally turn to the Internet first to get information, manage their finances, make better purchase and travel decisions and communicate with friends and others with whom they have common interests.

Our business is one of risks and challenges and great potential rewards. I appreciate the continuing trust and support of our shareholders in the long-term vision and potential of this company. I am confident that through the dedication and hard work of our employees, we can deliver the products and services that will mean success for both Microsoft and our customers.

William H. Gates

William H. Gates

income statements

(In millions, except earnings per share)

year ended june 30	1995	1996	1997
Revenue	$5,937	$8,671	$11,358
Operating expenses:			
Cost of revenue	877	1,188	1,085
Research and development	860	1,432	1,925
Sales and marketing	1,895	2,657	2,856
General and administrative	267	316	362
Total operating expenses	3,899	5,593	6,228
Operating income	2,038	3,078	5,130
Interest income	191	320	443
Other expenses	(62)	(19)	(259)
Income before income taxes	2,167	3,379	5,314
Provision for income taxes	714	1,184	1,860
Net income	1,453	2,195	3,454
Preferred stock dividends	–	–	15
Net income available for common shareholders	$1,453	$2,195	$ 3,439
Earnings per share[1]	$ 1.16	$ 1.71	$ 2.63
Weighted average shares outstanding[1]	1,254	1,281	1,312

see accompanying notes

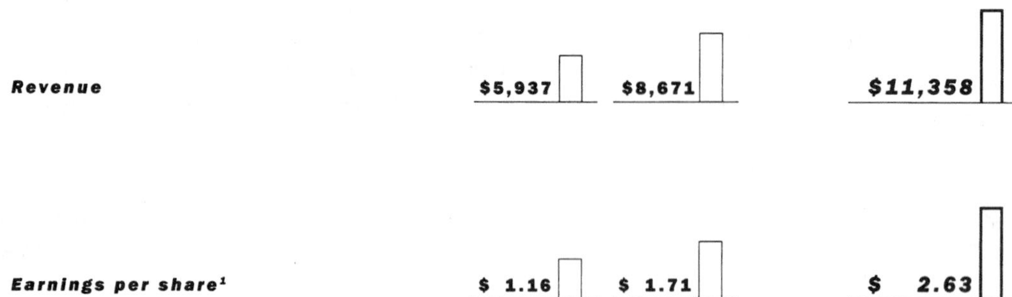

[1] share and per share amounts have been restated to reflect a two-for-one stock split in December 1996

msft

cash flows statements

(In millions)

year ended June 30	1995	1996	1997
Cash flows from operations			
Net income	$ 1,453	$ 2,195	$ 3,454
Depreciation and amortization	269	480	557
Unearned revenue	69	983	1,601
Recognition of unearned revenue from prior periods	(54)	(477)	(743)
Other current liabilities	404	584	321
Accounts receivable	(91)	(71)	(336)
Other current assets	(60)	25	(165)
Net cash from operations	1,990	3,719	4,689
Cash flows used for financing			
Common stock issued	332	504	744
Common stock repurchased	(698)	(1,385)	(3,101)
Put warrant proceeds	49	124	95
Preferred stock issued	–	–	980
Preferred stock dividends	–	–	(15)
Stock option income tax benefits	179	352	796
Net cash used for financing	(138)	(405)	(501)
Cash flows used for investments			
Additions to property, plant, and equipment	(495)	(494)	(499)
Equity investments and other	(230)	(625)	(1,669)
Short-term investments	(651)	(1,551)	(921)
Net cash used for investments	(1,376)	(2,670)	(3,089)
Net change in cash and equivalents	476	644	1,099
Effect of exchange rates on cash and equivalents	9	(5)	6
Cash and equivalents, beginning of year	1,477	1,962	2,601
Cash and equivalents, end of year	1,962	2,601	3,706
Short-term investments	2,788	4,339	5,260
Cash and short-term investments	$ 4,750	$ 6,940	$ 8,966

see accompanying notes

Cash flows from operations	$1,990	$3,719	$4,689

msft

management's discussion and analysis

Results of Operations for 1995, 1996, and 1997

Microsoft develops, manufactures, licenses, sells, and supports a wide range of software products, including scalable operating systems for information appliances, personal computers (PCs), and servers; server applications for client/server environments; business and consumer productivity applications; software development tools; and Internet and intranet software and technologies. The Company has recently expanded its interactive content efforts, including entertainment and information software programs, MSN, The Microsoft Network online service, Internet-based services, and alliances with companies involved with other forms of digital interactivity. Microsoft also sells personal computer input devices and books, and researches and develops advanced technologies for future software products.

Revenue

The Company's revenue grew 46% in the fiscal year ended June 30, 1996 and 31% in fiscal 1997. Revenue growth was particularly strong in 1996 due to the retail introduction of the Microsoft Windows 95 operating system. Software license volume increases have been the principal factor in Microsoft's revenue growth. The average selling price per license has decreased, primarily because of general shifts in the sales mix from retail packaged products to licensing programs, from new products to product upgrades, and from stand-alone desktop applications to integrated product suites. Average revenue per license from original equipment manufacturer (OEM) licenses and corporate and organization license programs, such as Microsoft Select, is lower than average revenue per license from retail versions. Likewise, product upgrades have lower prices than new products. Also, prices of integrated suites, such as Microsoft Office, are less than the sum of the prices for the individual programs included in these suites when such programs are licensed separately. During 1996 and 1997, an increased percentage of products and programs became subject to ratable revenue recognition, such as Windows operating systems, Office 97, maintenance, and other subscription models. (See accompanying notes.)

Product groups Microsoft has a Platforms Product Group and an Applications and Content Product Group.

Platforms Product Group revenue was $2.36 billion, $4.11 billion, and $5.97 billion in 1995, 1996, and 1997. Platform revenue is primarily from licenses of PC operating systems, business systems with client/server architectures, and software development tools.

The Company's principal desktop platform products in 1996 and 1997 were its 32-bit operating systems, Microsoft Windows 95 and Microsoft Windows NT Workstation. Released in August 1995, Windows 95 was a successor to MS-DOS® and Microsoft Windows 3.x operating systems. Windows NT Workstation version 4.0 was released in fiscal 1997. Desktop operating systems increasingly contributed to revenue as shipments of new PCs preinstalled with such systems increased rapidly during the three-year period. Additionally, increased penetration of higher value 32-bit operating systems led to growth in 1996 and 1997. In 1996, retail license sales of Windows 95 were a major factor in the Platforms revenue increase, reflecting the typical sales pattern for major operating system upgrades. Also in 1996, a portion of Windows operating system revenue became subject to ratable recognition.

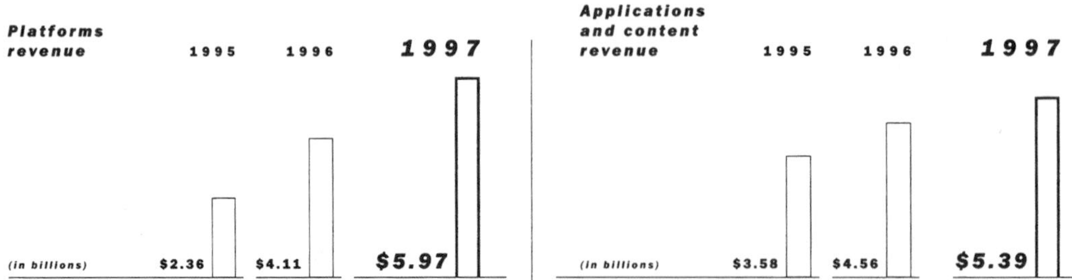

msft

management's discussion continued

Business systems products offer an enterprise-wide distributed client/server environment based on the Microsoft Windows NT Server operating system and the server applications in the Microsoft BackOffice family of products. Revenue from these products increased strongly in 1995, 1996, and 1997 due to greater corporate demand, particularly for intranet solutions.

Revenue from developer products increased steadily in all three years, as more independent software vendors, corporate developers, and solutions developers licensed tools such as the Microsoft Visual Basic® programming system to develop software for Windows 95 and Windows NT operating systems and the Internet.

Applications and Content Product Group revenue was $3.58 billion, $4.56 billion, and $5.39 billion in 1995, 1996, and 1997. Applications and Content revenue includes primarily licenses of desktop and consumer productivity applications, interactive media programs, and PC input devices. Microsoft Office for Windows 95 was released in fiscal 1996 and Microsoft Office 97 was released in fiscal 1997. Applications and Content revenue grew 27% in 1996 and 18% in 1997. The lower growth rate in 1997 was due to the expected impact of saturation of desktop applications, the continued shift in mix toward corporate licenses from packaged products, and the ratable revenue recognition model for Office 97.

Absolute increases in desktop applications revenue during the three-year period were led by Microsoft Office. The primary programs in Microsoft Office are Microsoft Word word processor, Microsoft Excel spreadsheet, and Microsoft PowerPoint® presentation graphics program. Various versions of Office, which are available for the 32-bit version of Windows, the 16-bit version of Windows, and Macintosh® operating systems, also include Microsoft Access database management program, Microsoft Outlook™ desktop information manager, or other programs. Revenue from stand-alone versions of Microsoft Excel, Microsoft Word, and Microsoft PowerPoint continued to decrease as the sales mix shifted to integrated product suites. Microsoft Project scheduling and project management program revenue increased during the three-year period.

Microsoft offers a broad range of interactive media products, which also showed moderate growth. Products include CD-ROM multimedia reference titles and programs for home and small office productivity, children's creativity, and entertainment. In addition to The Microsoft Network, recently introduced online Internet services include travel information and reservations, local event information, and new-car buying.

The Company also markets input devices. Mouse and gaming device sales increased while keyboard revenue was steady during the three-year period.

Sales channels The Company distributes its products primarily through OEM licenses, corporate and organizational licenses, and retail packaged products. OEM channel revenue represents license fees from original equipment manufacturers. Microsoft has three major geographic sales and marketing organizations: the United States and Canada, Europe, and elsewhere in the world (Other International). Sales of corporate and organization licenses and packaged products in these channels are primarily to distributors and resellers.

OEM channel revenue was $1.65 billion in 1995, $2.50 billion in 1996, and $3.48 billion in 1997. The primary source of OEM revenue is the licensing of desktop operating systems, and OEM revenue is highly dependent on PC shipment volume.

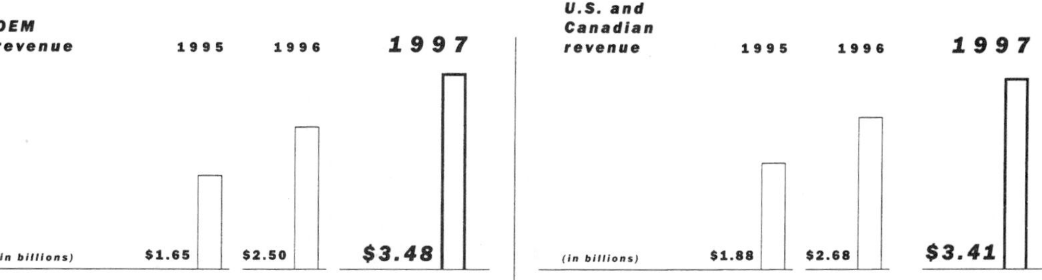

management's discussion continued

Licensing programs continued to grow in popularity across all geographic areas during the three-year period. Packaged product volume increased in 1996 due to the release of retail upgrade versions of Windows 95. U.S. and Canadian channel revenue was $1.88 billion, $2.68 billion, and $3.41 billion in 1995, 1996, and 1997. Revenue in Europe was $1.49 billion, $2.02 billion, and $2.54 billion in 1995, 1996, and 1997. Growth rates have been lower in Europe than in other geographic areas due to general economic slowness, higher existing market shares, and a more dramatic shift to licensing programs. Other International channel revenue was $924 million in 1995, $1.47 billion in 1996, and $1.93 billion in 1997. Growth rates were higher in the Other International channel due to customers accepting newly localized products, particularly in Japan, and penetration in emerging markets.

The Company's operating results are affected by foreign exchange rates. Approximately 37%, 34%, and 32% of the Company's revenue was collected in foreign currencies during 1995, 1996, and 1997. Since a portion of local currency revenue is hedged and much of the Company's international manufacturing costs and operating expenses are also incurred in local currencies, the impact of exchange rates is partially mitigated.

Operating expenses

Cost of revenue As a percentage of revenue, cost of revenue was 14.8% in 1995, 13.7% in 1996, and 9.6% in 1997. The decrease was due to the shifts in mix to CD-ROMs (which carry lower cost of goods than disks), licenses to OEMs and corporations, and higher-margin Windows NT Server and other BackOffice server products.

Research and development Microsoft invested heavily in the future by funding research and development (R&D). Expense increases of 67% in 1996 and 34% in 1997 resulted primarily from development staff headcount growth and higher levels of third-party development costs in many areas, including continued development efforts for Windows desktop operating systems, Office, BackOffice, and Internet and intranet technologies. R&D costs also increased for development tools, consumer systems, and interactive media initiatives such as MSN and other online services.

Sales and marketing The increase in the absolute dollar amount of sales and marketing expenses in the three-year period was due primarily to expanded product-specific marketing programs, particularly for Windows 95 during 1996. Sales and marketing costs as a percentage of revenue decreased, particularly in 1997, reflecting moderate headcount growth. Also in 1997, Microsoft brand advertising and product support expenses declined.

General and administrative Increases in general and administrative expenses were primarily attributable to growth in the number of people and computer systems necessary to support overall increases in the scope of the Company's operations.

Nonoperating items and income taxes

Interest income increased primarily as a result of a larger investment portfolio generated by cash from operations. Other expenses increased due to recognition of Microsoft's share of joint venture activities, including DreamWorks Interactive and the MSNBC entities. During 1995, Microsoft paid a $46 million

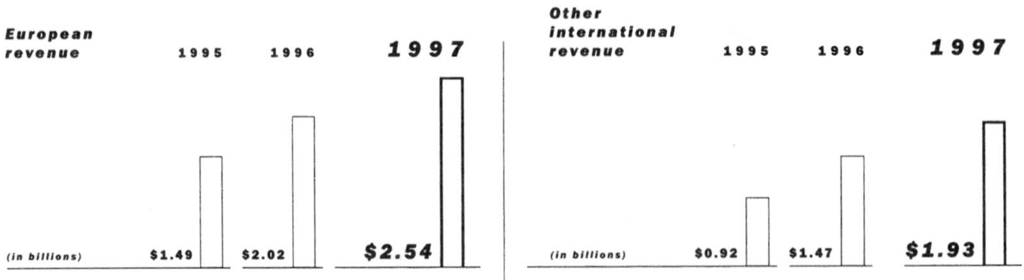

msft

management's discussion continued

breakup fee to Intuit Inc. in connection with the termination of a planned merger. The effective income tax rate was 33% in 1995 and 35% in 1996 and 1997.

Net income

Net income as a percent of revenue increased in 1996 and 1997 due to the lower relative cost of revenue, sales and marketing expenses, and general and administrative expenses, partially offset by investments in research and development and joint ventures.

Financial Condition

Microsoft's cash and short-term investment portfolio totaled $8.97 billion at June 30, 1997. The portfolio is diversified among security types, industries, and individual issuers. Microsoft's investments are generally liquid and investment grade. The portfolio is invested predominantly in U.S. dollar denominated securities, but also includes foreign currency positions in anticipation of continued international expansion. The portfolio is primarily invested in short-term securities to minimize interest rate risk and facilitate rapid deployment in the event of immediate cash needs.

During 1996, Microsoft and National Broadcasting Company (NBC) established two joint ventures: a 24-hour cable news and information channel and an interactive online news service. Microsoft agreed to pay $220 million over a five-year period for its interest in the cable venture and to pay one-half of operational funding of both joint ventures for a multiyear period.

During 1997, Microsoft invested $1.0 billion in Comcast Corporation, a cable television and diversified telecommunications company. Comcast Special Class A common stock of $500 million and convertible preferred stock of $500 million are included in equity investments on the balance sheet.

Microsoft has no material long-term debt and has $70 million of standby multicurrency lines of credit to support foreign currency hedging and cash management. Stockholders' equity at June 30, 1997 was $10.78 billion.

Microsoft will continue to invest in sales, marketing, and product support infrastructure. Additionally, research and development activities will include investments in existing and advanced areas of technology, including using cash to acquire technology and to fund ventures and other strategic opportunities. Additions to property and equipment will continue, including new facilities and computer systems for research and development, sales and marketing, support, and administrative staff. Commitments for constructing new buildings were $300 million on June 30, 1997.

Cash will also be used to repurchase common stock to provide shares for employee stock option and purchase plans. Despite recent increases in stock repurchases, the buyback program has not kept pace with employee stock option grants or exercises. Beginning in fiscal 1990, Microsoft has repurchased 154 million common shares for $6.2 billion while 363 million shares were issued under the Company's employee stock option and purchase plans. The market value of all outstanding stock options was $30.2 billion as of June 30, 1997. Microsoft enhances its repurchase program by selling put warrants. During December 1996, Microsoft issued 12.5 million shares of 2.75% convertible preferred stock. Net proceeds of $980 million were used to repurchase common shares.

Management believes existing cash and short-term investments together with funds generated from operations will be sufficient to meet operating requirements for the next 12 months. Microsoft's cash and short-term investments are available for strategic investments, mergers and acquisitions, other potential large-scale cash needs that may arise, and to fund an increased stock buyback program over historical levels to reduce the dilutive impact of the Company's employee stock option and purchase programs.

Microsoft has not paid cash dividends on its common stock. The preferred stock pays $2.196 per annum per share.

management's discussion continued

Outlook: Issues and Uncertainties

Microsoft does not provide forecasts of future financial performance. While Microsoft management is optimistic about the Company's long-term prospects, the following issues and uncertainties, among others, should be considered in evaluating its growth outlook.

Rapid technological change and competition **Rapid change, uncertainty due to new and emerging technologies, and fierce competition characterize the PC software industry. The pace of change has recently accelerated due to the Internet and new programming languages, such as Java™.**

Future initiatives **The Company is expanding its efforts to provide and support mission-critical systems to large enterprises. Scalability of BackOffice server and application products, manageability of Windows- and Office-based systems, and Internet and intranet integration are also major focus areas. Additionally, Microsoft is committed to providing technologies, operating systems, and interactive content for the future convergence of PCs, televisions, and the Internet. Future revenue from these initiatives may not duplicate historical revenue growth rates.**

PC growth rates **The underlying PC unit growth rate, which may decrease in the future, directly impacts software revenue growth.**

Product ship schedules **Shipments of new versions of major products such as Windows 95 have generally had positive impacts on revenue growth rates. The Company does not currently expect that individual products to be released in 1998 will repeat the financial performance of Windows 95. Also, delays in new-product releases can cause operational inefficiencies that impact manufacturing and distribution logistics, independent software vendor (ISV) and OEM relationships, and telephone support staffing.**

Customer acceptance **While the Company performs extensive usability and beta testing of new products, user acceptance and corporate penetration rates ultimately dictate the success of development and marketing efforts.**

Prices **Future product prices may decrease from historical levels, depending on competitive market and cost factors. European and Far Eastern software prices vary by country and are generally higher than in the United States to cover localization costs and higher costs of distribution. Increased global license agreements, European monetary unification, or other factors could erode such price uplifts in the future.**

Earnings process **An increasingly higher percentage of the Company's revenue is subject to ratable recognition. Subsequent product support and delivery of unspecified enhancements require the applicable portion of revenue for certain products to be recognized over the product's life cycle. This policy may be required for future products, depending on specific license terms and conditions. Also, maintenance and other subscription programs may continue to increase in popularity, particularly with corporations and other large organizations.**

Saturation **Product upgrades, which enable users to upgrade from earlier versions of the Company's products or from competitors' products, have lower prices and margins than new products. As the desktop applications market has become saturated, the sales mix has shifted from standard products to upgrade products. This trend is likely to continue.**

Corporate licenses **Average revenue per unit from corporate and organization license programs is lower than average revenue per unit from retail versions shipped through the finished goods channels. Unit sales under licensing programs may continue to increase.**

Channel mix **Average revenue per license is lower from OEM licenses than from retail versions, reflecting the relatively lower direct costs of operations in the OEM channel. An increasingly higher percentage of revenue was achieved through the OEM channel during 1996 and 1997.**

msft

management's discussion continued

Integrated suites The price of integrated suites, such as Microsoft Office, is less than the sum of the prices for the individual programs included in these suites when such programs are licensed separately. Revenue from integrated suites may continue to increase as a percentage of total revenue.

Cost of revenue Although cost of revenue as a percentage of revenue decreased in 1996 and 1997, it varies with channel mix and product mix within channels. The trend of declining cost of revenue as a percentage of revenue is unlikely to continue in 1998.

Pay and participation model Microsoft employees currently receive salaries, incentive bonuses, other fringe benefits, and stock options. New government regulations, poor stock price performance, or other factors could diminish the value of the option program and force the Company into more of a cash compensation model. Had the Company paid employees in cash the grant date Black-Scholes value of options vested in 1995, 1996, and 1997, the pretax expense would have been approximately $310 million, $450 million, and $620 million.

Long-term research and development investment cycle Developing and localizing software is expensive and the investment in product development often involves a long payback cycle. The Company plans to continue significant investments in software research and development and related product opportunities from which significant revenue is not anticipated for a number of years. Management expects total spending for research and development in 1998 to increase over spending in 1997.

Sales and marketing and support investments The Company's plans for 1998 include accelerated investments in its sales and marketing and support groups.

Foreign exchange A large percentage of the Company's sales, costs of manufacturing, and marketing is transacted in local currencies. As a result, the Company's international results of operations are subject to foreign exchange rate fluctuations.

Interest rate sensitivity The Company's cash and short-term investment portfolio is subject to interest rate risk. An abrupt increase in interest rates would decrease the market value of the Company's fixed income securities. For example, a 200 basis point increase in short-term treasury security yields would reduce the carrying value of the portfolio at June 30, 1997 by $200 million.

Intellectual property rights Microsoft diligently defends its intellectual property rights, but unlicensed copying of software represents a loss of revenue to the Company. While this adversely affects U.S. revenue, revenue loss is even more significant outside of the United States, particularly in countries where laws are less protective of intellectual property rights. Throughout the world, Microsoft actively educates consumers on the benefits of licensing genuine products and educates lawmakers on the advantages of a business climate where intellectual property rights are protected. However, continued efforts may not affect revenue positively.

Future growth rate The revenue growth rate in 1998 may not approach the level attained in 1997, particularly when compared to the second half of 1997. As discussed above, operating expenses are expected to increase in 1998. Because of the fixed nature of a significant portion of such expenses, coupled with the possibility of slower revenue growth, operating margins in 1998 may decrease from those in 1997.

Litigation Litigation regarding intellectual property rights, patents, and copyrights occurs in the PC software industry. In addition, there are government regulation and investigation risks along with other general corporate legal risks.

msft

balance sheets

(In millions)

June 30	1996	1997
Assets		
Current assets:		
Cash and short-term investments	$ 6,940	$ 8,966
Accounts receivable	639	980
Other	260	427
Total current assets	7,839	10,373
Property, plant, and equipment	1,326	1,465
Equity investments	675	2,346
Other assets	253	203
Total assets	$10,093	$14,387
Liabilities and stockholders' equity		
Current liabilities:		
Accounts payable	$ 808	$ 721
Accrued compensation	202	336
Income taxes payable	484	466
Unearned revenue	560	1,418
Other	371	669
Total current liabilities	2,425	3,610
Minority interest	125	–
Put warrants	635	–
Commitments and contingencies		
Stockholders' equity:		
Convertible preferred stock – shares authorized 0 and 100; shares issued and outstanding 0 and 13	–	980
Common stock and paid-in capital – shares authorized 4,000; shares issued and outstanding 1,194 and 1,204	2,924	4,509
Retained earnings	3,984	5,288
Total stockholders' equity	6,908	10,777
Total liabilities and stockholders' equity	$10,093	$14,387

see accompanying notes

msft

stockholders' equity statements

(In millions)

year ended June 30	1995	1996	1997
Convertible preferred stock			
Convertible preferred stock issued	–	–	$ 980
Balance, end of year	–	–	980
Common stock and paid-in capital			
Balance, beginning of year	$1,500	$ 2,005	2,924
Common stock issued	332	504	744
Common stock repurchased	(30)	(41)	(91)
Proceeds from sale of put warrants	49	124	95
Reclassification of put warrant obligation	(25)	(20)	45
Stock option income tax benefits	179	352	792
Balance, end of year	2,005	2,924	4,509
Retained earnings			
Balance, beginning of year	2,950	3,328	3,984
Net income	1,453	2,195	3,454
Preferred stock dividends	–	–	(15)
Common stock repurchased	(668)	(1,344)	(3,010)
Reclassification of put warrant obligation	(380)	(210)	590
Net unrealized investment gains and other	(27)	15	285
Balance, end of year	3,328	3,984	5,288
Total stockholders' equity	$5,333	$ 6,908	$10,777

see accompanying notes

Stockholders' equity $5,333 $6,908

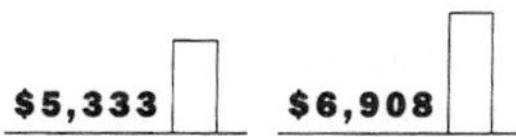

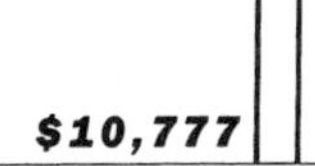

notes to financial statements

Significant accounting policies

Accounting principles The financial statements are prepared on a basis consistent with U.S. generally accepted accounting principles and International Accounting Standards formulated by the International Accounting Standards Committee (IASC).

Principles of consolidation The financial statements include the accounts of Microsoft and its subsidiaries. Significant intercompany transactions and balances have been eliminated. Investments in 50% owned joint ventures are accounted for using the equity method; the Company's share of joint ventures' activities is reflected in other expenses.

Estimates and assumptions Preparing financial statements requires management to make estimates and assumptions that affect the reported amounts of assets, liabilities, revenue, and expenses. Examples include provisions for returns and bad debts and the length of product life cycles and buildings' lives. Actual results may differ from these estimates.

Foreign currencies Assets and liabilities recorded in foreign currencies are translated at the exchange rate on the balance sheet date. Translation adjustments resulting from this process are charged or credited to equity. Revenue, costs, and expenses are translated at average rates of exchange prevailing during the year. Gains and losses on foreign currency transactions are included in other expenses.

Revenue recognition Revenue is recognized when earned. Revenue from products licensed to original equipment manufacturers is recorded when OEMs ship licensed products while revenue from corporate and organization license programs is recorded when the user installs the product. Revenue from packaged product sales to distributors and resellers is recorded when related products are shipped. Maintenance and subscription revenue is recognized ratably over the contract period. Revenue attributable to significant support (technical support and unspecified enhancements such as service packs and Internet browser updates) is based on the price charged or derived value of the undelivered elements and is recognized ratably on a straight-line basis over the product's life cycle. Costs related to insignificant obligations, which include telephone support for certain products, are accrued. Provisions are recorded for returns and bad debts.

Research and development Research and development costs are expensed as incurred. The current U.S. accounting rule, Statement of Financial Accounting Standards (SFAS) 86, *Accounting for the Costs of Computer Software to Be Sold, Leased, or Otherwise Marketed*, does not materially affect the Company.

Telephone support Telephone support costs are included in sales and marketing.

Income taxes Income tax expense includes U.S. and international income taxes, plus an accrual for U.S. taxes on undistributed earnings of international subsidiaries. Certain items of income and expense are not reported in tax returns and financial statements in the same year. The tax effect of this difference is reported as deferred income taxes. Tax credits are accounted for as a reduction of tax expense in the year in which the credits reduce taxes payable.

Earnings per share Earnings per share is computed on the basis of the weighted average number of common shares outstanding plus the effect of outstanding stock options using the "treasury stock" method and preferred shares using the "if-converted" method. Beginning in the second quarter of 1998, Microsoft will be required to report earnings per outstanding common share in addition to diluted earnings per share. Earnings per common share computed under the new pronouncement would have been $1.25, $1.85, and $2.87 while reported diluted earnings per share were $1.16, $1.71, and $2.63 in 1995, 1996, and 1997.

Stock split In December 1996, outstanding shares of common stock were split two-for-one. All share and per share amounts have been restated.

Financial instruments The Company considers all liquid interest-earning investments with a maturity of three months or less at the date of purchase to be cash equivalents. Short-term investments generally mature between three months and five years from the purchase date. All cash and short-term investments are classified as available for sale and are recorded at market. Cost approximates market for all classifications of cash and short-term investments; realized and unrealized gains and losses were not material.

msft

notes continued

Publicly tradeable equity securities are recorded at market; unrealized gains and losses are reflected in stockholders' equity.

Property, plant, and equipment Property, plant, and equipment is stated at cost and depreciated using the straight-line method over the shorter of the estimated life of the asset or the lease term, ranging from one to 30 years.

Reclassifications Certain reclassifications have been made for consistent presentation.

Unearned revenue

In fiscal 1996, Microsoft committed to integrating its Internet technologies, such as the Company's Internet browser, Microsoft Internet Explorer, into existing products at no additional cost to its customers. Given this strategy and other support commitments such as telephone support, Internet-based technical support, and unspecified product enhancements, Microsoft recognizes approximately 20% of Windows operating systems revenue over the product life cycles, currently estimated at two years. The unearned portion of revenue from Windows operating systems was $425 million and $860 million at June 30, 1996 and 1997.

Since Office 97 is also tightly integrated with the rapidly evolving Internet, and subsequent delivery of new Internet technologies, enhancements, and other support is likely to be more than minimal, a ratable revenue recognition policy became effective for Office 97 licenses beginning in 1997. Approximately 20% of Office 97 revenue is recognized ratably over the estimated 18-month product life cycle. Unearned revenue associated with Office 97 totaled $300 million at June 30, 1997.

Unearned revenue also includes maintenance and other subscription contracts, including custom corporate license agreements.

Financial risks

The Company's investment portfolio is diversified and consists primarily of short-term investment grade securities. At June 30, 1996 and 1997, approximately 38% and 31% of accounts receivable represented amounts due from 10 channel purchasers. One customer accounted for approximately 12%, 13%, and 12% of revenue while another customer accounted for approximately 12%, 8%, and 5% of revenue in 1995, 1996, and 1997.

Finished goods sales to international customers in Europe, Japan, and Australia are primarily billed in local currencies. Payment cycles are relatively short, generally less than 90 days. European manufacturing costs and international selling, distribution, and support costs are generally disbursed in local currencies. Local currency cash balances in excess of short-term operating needs are generally converted into U.S. dollar cash and short-term investments on receipt. Therefore, foreign exchange rate fluctuations generally do not create a risk of material balance sheet gains or losses. As a result, Microsoft's hedging activities for balance sheet exposures have been minimal.

At June 30, 1997, the Company had contracts to deliver $500 million in a foreign currency, expiring July 1998, which hedge foreign exchange rate risk related to a foreign currency denominated investment.

Foreign exchange rates affect the translated results of operations of the Company's foreign subsidiaries. The Company hedges a percentage of planned international revenue with purchased options. The notional amount of the options outstanding at June 30, 1997 was $2.1 billion. At June 30, 1997, the fair value and premiums paid for the options were not material.

notes continued

(In millions)

Cash and short-term investments

June 30	1996	1997
Cash and equivalents:		
Cash	$ 64	$ 246
Commercial paper	1,664	1,660
Money market preferreds	105	946
Certificates of deposit	768	854
Cash and equivalents	2,601	3,706
Short-term investments:		
Municipal securities	1,357	571
Corporate notes and bonds	1,125	1,907
U.S. Treasury securities	1,591	1,513
Certificates of deposit	266	1,269
Short-term investments	4,339	5,260
Cash and short-term investments	$6,940	$8,966

Property, plant, and equipment

June 30	1996	1997
Land	$ 183	$ 183
Buildings	787	1,027
Computer equipment	885	1,064
Other	491	503
Property, plant, and equipment – at cost	2,346	2,777
Accumulated depreciation	(1,020)	(1,312)
Property, plant, and equipment – net	$ 1,326	$ 1,465

During 1996 and 1997, depreciation expense, of which the majority related to computer equipment, was $363 million and $353 million; disposals were immaterial.

msft

notes continued

(in millions)

Income taxes

The provision for income taxes consisted of:

year ended June 30	1995	1996	1997
Current taxes:			
U.S. and state	$518	$1,139	$1,710
International	151	285	412
Current taxes	669	1,424	2,122
Deferred taxes	45	(240)	(262)
Provision for income taxes	$714	$1,184	$1,860

U.S. and international components of income before income taxes were:

year ended June 30	1995	1996	1997
U.S.	$1,549	$2,356	$3,775
International	618	1,023	1,539
Income before income taxes	$2,167	$3,379	$5,314

Income taxes payable were:

June 30	1996	1997
Deferred income tax assets:		
Revenue items	$ 193	$ 474
Expense items	322	505
Deferred income tax assets	515	979
Deferred income tax liabilities:		
International earnings	(261)	(465)
Other	(6)	(4)
Deferred income tax liabilities	(267)	(469)
Current income tax liabilities	(732)	(976)
Income taxes payable	$(484)	$(466)

Income taxes have been settled with the Internal Revenue Service for all years through 1989. The IRS has assessed taxes for 1990 and 1991 that the Company is contesting in Tax Court. The IRS is examining the Company's U.S. income tax returns for 1992 through 1994. Management believes any related adjustments that might be required will not be material to the financial statements. Income taxes paid were $430 million, $758 million, and $1.1 billion in 1995, 1996, and 1997.

notes continued

(In millions)

Convertible preferred stock

During December 1996, Microsoft issued 12.5 million shares of 2.75% convertible exchangeable principal-protected preferred stock. Dividends are payable quarterly in arrears. Preferred shareholders have preference over common stockholders in dividends and liquidation rights. In December 1999, each preferred share is convertible into common shares or an equivalent amount of cash determined by a formula that provides a floor price of $79.875 and a cap of $102.24 per preferred share. Net proceeds of $980 million were used to repurchase common shares.

Common stock

Shares of common stock outstanding were as follows:

year ended June 30	1995	1996	1997
Balance, beginning of year	1,162	1,176	1,194
Issued	38	44	47
Repurchased	(24)	(26)	(37)
Balance, end of year	1,176	1,194	1,204

The Company repurchases its common stock in the open market to provide shares for issuing to employees under stock option and stock purchase plans. The Company's Board of Directors authorized continuation of this program in 1998.

Put warrants

To enhance its stock repurchase program, the Company sells put warrants to independent third parties. These put warrants entitle the holders to sell shares of Microsoft common stock to the Company on certain dates at specified prices. On June 30, 1996 and 1997, 13.0 million and 3.0 million warrants were outstanding. Outstanding put warrants at June 30, 1997 expire in September 1997 and have strike prices of $105 per share. At June 30, 1996, the outstanding put warrants were settleable in cash at Microsoft's option thus resulting in a reclassification of the maximum potential repurchase obligation of $635 million from stockholders' equity to put warrants. The outstanding put warrants at June 30, 1997 permitted a net-share settlement at the Company's option and did not result in a put warrant liability on the balance sheet.

Employee stock and savings plans

Employee stock purchase plan The Company has an employee stock purchase plan for all eligible employees. Under the plan, shares of the Company's common stock may be purchased at six-month intervals at 85% of the lower of the fair market value on the first or the last day of each six-month period. Employees may purchase shares having a value not exceeding 10% of their gross compensation during an offering period. During 1995, 1996, and 1997, employees purchased 2.1 million, 1.8 million, and 1.4 million shares at average prices of $23.38, $37.72, and $59.64 per share. At June 30, 1997, 19.4 million shares were reserved for future issuance.

Savings plan The Company has a savings plan, which qualifies under Section 401(k) of the Internal Revenue Code. Participating employees may defer up to 15% of pretax salary, but not more than statutory limits. The Company contributes fifty cents for each dollar a participant contributes, with a maximum contribution of 3% of a participant's earnings. Matching contributions were $12 million, $15 million, and $28 million in 1995, 1996, and 1997.

msft

notes continued

(In millions, except per share amounts)

Stock option plans The Company has stock option plans for directors, officers, and all employees, which provide for nonqualified and incentive stock options. The option exercise price is the fair market value at the date of grant. Options granted prior to 1995 generally vest over four and one-half years and expire 10 years from the date of grant. Options granted during and after 1995 generally vest over four and one-half years and expire seven years from the date of grant, while certain options vest over seven and one-half years and expire after 10 years. At June 30, 1997, options for 113 million shares were vested and 290 million shares were available for future grants under the plans.

Stock options outstanding were as follows:

		Price per Share			
	Shares	Range			Weighted Average
Balance, June 30, 1994	228	$ 0.16	–	$ 25.07	$ 11.65
Granted	44	23.88	–	41.57	25.25
Exercised	(35)	0.16	–	23.88	7.91
Canceled	(9)	2.56	–	37.50	17.70
Balance, June 30, 1995	228	0.77	–	41.57	14.56
Granted	57	40.10	–	58.94	44.99
Exercised	(40)	0.77	–	45.25	10.75
Canceled	(7)	2.59	–	55.44	27.85
Balance, June 30, 1996	238	1.10	–	58.94	22.07
Granted	55	55.31	–	119.19	58.29
Exercised	(45)	1.10	–	58.94	13.27
Canceled	(9)	17.00	–	97.13	38.83
Balance, June 30, 1997	239	2.24	–	119.19	31.43

For various price ranges, weighted average characteristics of outstanding stock options at June 30, 1997 were as follows:

Range of exercise prices			Outstanding options			Exercisable options	
			Shares	Remaining life (years)	Weighted average price	Shares	Weighted average price
$ 2.24	–	$ 17.00	65	3.5	$ 9.64	64	$ 9.63
17.01	–	24.00	65	5.4	20.81	39	20.10
24.01	–	55.00	56	5.8	43.13	10	41.02
55.01	–	119.19	53	6.6	58.47	–	–

The Company follows APB Opinion 25, *Accounting for Stock Issued to Employees*, to account for stock option and employee stock purchase plans. No compensation cost is recognized because the option exercise price is equal to the market price of the underlying stock on the date of grant. Had compensation cost for these plans been determined based on the Black-Scholes value at the grant dates for awards as prescribed by SFAS Statement 123, *Accounting for Stock-Based Compensation*, pro forma net income and earnings per share would have been:

year ended June 30	1995	1996	*1997*
Pro forma net income	$1,243	$1,902	*$3,053*
Pro forma earnings per share	$ 0.99	$ 1.48	*$ 2.32*

notes continued

(In millions)

The pro forma disclosures above include the amortization of the fair value of all options vested during 1995, 1996, and 1997. If only options granted during 1996 and 1997 were valued, as prescribed by SFAS 123, pro forma net income would have been $2,073 million and $3,179 million, and earnings per share would have been $1.62 and $2.42 for 1996 and 1997.

The weighted average Black-Scholes value of options granted under the stock option plans during 1995, 1996, and 1997 was $10.46, $17.72, and $23.43. Value was estimated using an expected life of five years, no dividends, volatility of .30, and risk-free interest rates of 7.0%, 6.0%, and 6.5% in 1995, 1996, and 1997.

MSN, The Microsoft Network

During October 1996, Microsoft and a subsidiary of Tele-Communications, Inc. (TCI) terminated a partnership under which TCI owned a 20% minority interest in The Microsoft Network, LLC, owner of the business assets of MSN, an online service. Due to the evolving nature of the online industry and the move by MSN to a Web-based offering, the original direction of the partnership changed and both Microsoft and TCI agreed to terminate this partnership focused exclusively on MSN. In return for approximately $125 million of TCI securities, Microsoft became the sole owner of MSN and the minority interest on the accompanying balance sheet was eliminated. There was no other material financial impact of the dissolution.

Acquisition

On August 1, 1997, the Company acquired WebTV Networks, Inc. (WebTV), an online service that enables consumers to experience the Internet through their televisions via set-top terminals based on proprietary technologies. A director of the Company owned 10% of WebTV. Microsoft paid $425 million in stock and cash for WebTV. The Company expects to record an in-process R&D write-off of $300 million in the first quarter of 1998.

Commitments and contingencies

The Company has operating leases for most U.S. and international sales and support offices and certain equipment. Rental expense for operating leases was $86 million, $92 million, and $92 million in 1995, 1996, and 1997. Future minimum rental commitments under noncancelable leases, in millions of dollars, are: 1998, $67; 1999, $54; 2000, $43; 2001, $30; 2002, $12; and thereafter, $16.

In connection with the Company's communications infrastructure and the operation of MSN, Microsoft has certain communication usage commitments. Future related minimum commitments, in millions of dollars, are: 1998, $133; 1999, $119; 2000, $92; and 2001, $20. Also, Microsoft has committed to certain volumes of outsourced telephone support and manufacturing of packaged product and has committed $300 million for constructing new buildings.

During 1996, Microsoft and National Broadcasting Company (NBC) established two MSNBC joint ventures: a 24-hour cable news and information channel and an interactive online news service. Microsoft agreed to pay $220 million over a five-year period for its interest in the cable venture, to pay one-half of operational funding of both joint ventures for a multiyear period, and to guarantee a portion of MSNBC debt.

In an ongoing investigation, the Antitrust Division of the U.S. Department of Justice requested information from Microsoft concerning various issues. Microsoft is also subject to various legal proceedings and claims that arise in the ordinary course of business. Management currently believes that resolving these matters will not have a material adverse impact on the Company's financial position or its results of operations.

msft

notes continued

(in millions)

Geographic information

year ended june 30	1995	1996	1997
Revenue			
U.S. operations	$ 4,495	$ 6,739	$ 8,877
European operations	1,607	2,215	2,770
Other international operations	821	1,267	1,757
Eliminations	(986)	(1,550)	(2,046)
Total revenue	$ 5,937	$ 8,671	$11,358
Operating income			
U.S. operations	$ 1,414	$ 2,137	$ 3,733
European operations	444	649	1,013
Other international operations	163	297	469
Eliminations	17	(5)	(85)
Total operating income	$ 2,038	$ 3,078	$ 5,130
Identifiable assets			
U.S. operations	$ 5,862	$ 8,193	$11,630
European operations	1,806	2,280	3,395
Other international operations	689	1,042	705
Eliminations	(1,147)	(1,422)	(1,343)
Total identifiable assets	$ 7,210	$10,093	$14,387

Intercompany sales between geographic areas are accounted for at prices representative of unaffiliated party transactions. "U.S. operations" include shipments to customers in the United States, licensing to OEMs, and exports of finished goods directly to international customers, primarily in Asia, South America, and Canada. Exports and international OEM transactions are primarily in U.S. dollars and totaled $1.3 billion, $2.1 billion, and $2.5 billion in 1995, 1996, and 1997.

"Other international operations" primarily include subsidiaries in Japan, Canada, Australia, and Brazil. International revenue, which includes European operations, other international operations, exports, and OEM distribution, was 55%, 56%, and 56% of total revenue in 1995, 1996, and 1997. Most international identifiable assets are U.S. dollar denominated investment securities.

notes continued

(in millions, except per share amounts)

Quarterly information (unaudited)

	quarter ended				
	sept. 30	dec. 31	mar. 31	june 30	year
1995					
Revenue	$ 1,247	$ 1,482	$ 1,587	$ 1,621	$ 5,937
Operating income	437	520	549	532	2,038
Net income	316	373	396	368	1,453
Earnings per share	0.25	0.30	0.32	0.29	1.16
Common stock price per share:					
High	29.63	32.56	37.06	46.19	46.19
Low	23.44	26.94	29.13	34.38	23.44
1996					
Revenue	$ 2,016	$ 2,195	$ 2,205	$ 2,255	$ 8,671
Operating income	708	786	774	810	3,078
Net income	499	575	562	559	2,195
Earnings per share	0.39	0.45	0.44	0.43	1.71
Common stock price per share:					
High	54.63	51.69	53.53	62.94	62.94
Low	42.50	40.19	39.94	49.81	39.94
1997					
Revenue	$2,295	$2,680	$ 3,208	$ 3,175	$11,358
Operating income	902	1,081	1,568	1,579	5,130
Net income	614	741	1,042	1,057	3,454
Earnings per share	0.47	0.57	0.79	0.80	2.63
Common stock price per share:					
High	69.31	86.13	103.50	134.94	134.94
Low	53.75	65.44	80.75	89.75	53.75

The Company's common stock is traded on The Nasdaq Stock Market under the symbol MSFT. On July 31, 1997, there were 53,390 holders of record of the Company's common stock. The Company has not paid cash dividends on its common stock.

msft

subsidiaries

Microsoft Corporation
One Microsoft Way
Redmond, WA
98052-6399

Microsoft FSC Corp.
(U.S. VIRGIN ISLANDS)

Microsoft Investments, Inc.
(NEVADA)

Microsoft Licensing, Inc.
(NEVADA)

Microsoft Manufacturing B.V.
(THE NETHERLANDS)

Microsoft Puerto Rico, Inc.
(Manufacturing)
(DELAWARE)

Microsoft Research Limited
(UNITED KINGDOM)

The Microsoft Network L.L.C.
(DELAWARE)

GraceMac Corporation
(NEVADA)

Vermeer Technologies, Inc.
(DELAWARE)

Microsoft de Argentina S.A.

Microsoft Pty. Limited
(AUSTRALIA)

Microsoft Gesellschaft m.b.H.
(AUSTRIA)

Microsoft N.V.
(BELGIUM)

Microsoft Informatica Limitada
(BRAZIL)

Microsoft Canada Co.

SOFTIMAGE, Inc.
(CANADA)

Microsoft Chile S.A.

Microsoft Colombia Inc.
(DELAWARE)

Microsoft de Centroamérica S.A.
(COSTA RICA)

Microsoft Hrvatska d.o.o.
(CROATIA)

Microsoft s.r.o.
(CZECH REPUBLIC)

Microsoft Danmark ApS
(DENMARK)

Microsoft Del Ecuador S.A.

Microsoft Corporation
(Representative Office)
(EGYPT)

Microsoft Oy
(FINLAND)

Microsoft France S.A.R.L.

Microsoft G.m.b.H.
(GERMANY)

SOFTIMAGE G.m.b.H.
(GERMANY)

Microsoft Hellas S.A.
(GREECE)

Microsoft de Guatemala, S.A.

Microsoft Hong Kong Limited

Microsoft Hungary Kft.

Microsoft Corporation (India) Private Limited

PT. Microsoft Indonesia

Microsoft Israel Ltd.

Microsoft S.p.A.
(ITALY)

Microsoft Côte d'Ivoire
(IVORY COAST)

Microsoft Company, Limited
(JAPAN)

East Africa Software Limited
(KENYA)

Microsoft CH
(KOREA)

Microsoft (Malaysia) Sdn. Bhd.

Microsoft México, S.A. de C.V.

Microsoft Maroc S.A.R.L.
(MOROCCO)

Microsoft B.V.
(THE NETHERLANDS)

Microsoft International B.V.
(THE NETHERLANDS)

Microsoft New Zealand Limited

Microsoft Norge AS
(NORWAY)

Microsoft de Panama, S.A.

Microsoft (China) Company Limited
(THE PEOPLE'S REPUBLIC OF CHINA)

Microsoft Peru, S.A.

Microsoft Philippines, Inc.

Microsoft sp. z.o.o.
(POLAND)

MSFT-Software Para Microcomputadores, LDA
(PORTUGAL)

Microsoft Caribbean, Inc.
(PUERTO RICO)
(DELAWARE)

Microsoft Romania SRL

Microsoft ZAO
(RUSSIA)

Microsoft Singapore Pte Ltd

Microsoft Slovakia s.r.o.

Microsoft d.o.o., Ljubljana
(SLOVENIA)

Microsoft (S.A.) (Proprietary) Limited
(SOUTH AFRICA)

Microsoft Iberica S.R.L.
(SPAIN)

Microsoft Aktiebolag
(SWEDEN)

Microsoft AG
(SWITZERLAND)

Microsoft Taiwan Corporation

Microsoft (Thailand) Limited

Microsoft Bilgisayar Yazilim Hizmetleri Limited Sirketi
(TURKEY)

Microsoft Corporation
(UNITED ARAB EMIRATES)

Microsoft Limited
(UNITED KINGDOM)

SOFTIMAGE U.K. Limited

Microsoft Uruguay S.A.

Corporation MS 90 de Venezuela S.A.

The Resident Representative Office of MICROSOFT Corporation in Hanoi
(VIETNAM)

DreamWorks Interactive L.L.C.
(WASHINGTON, 50% owned)

MSBET L.L.C.
(DELAWARE, 50% owned)

MSFDC, L.L.C.
(DELAWARE, 50% owned)

MSNBC Cable, L.L.C.
(DELAWARE, 50% owned)

MSNBC Interactive News, L.L.C.
(DELAWARE, 50% owned)

msft

reports of management and independent auditors

Management is responsible for preparing the Company's financial statements and related information that appears in this annual report. Management believes that the financial statements fairly reflect the form and substance of transactions and reasonably present the Company's financial condition and results of operations in conformity with accounting principles generally accepted in the United States and International Accounting Standards. Management has included in the Company's financial statements amounts that are based on estimates and judgments, which it believes are reasonable under the circumstances.

The Company maintains a system of internal accounting policies, procedures, and controls intended to provide reasonable assurance, at appropriate cost, that transactions are executed in accordance with Company authorization and are properly recorded and reported in the financial statements, and that assets are adequately safeguarded.

Deloitte & Touche LLP audits the Company's financial statements in accordance with generally accepted auditing standards and provides an objective, independent review of the Company's internal controls and the fairness of its reported financial condition and results of operations.

The Microsoft Board of Directors has an Audit Committee composed of nonmanagement Directors. The Committee meets with financial management, internal auditors, and the independent auditors to review internal accounting controls and accounting, auditing, and financial reporting matters.

Gregory B. Maffei
Vice President, Finance;
Chief Financial Officer

To the Board of Directors and Stockholders of Microsoft Corporation:

We have audited the accompanying balance sheets of Microsoft Corporation and subsidiaries as of June 30, 1996 and 1997, and the related statements of income, cash flows, and stockholders' equity for each of the three years ended June 30, 1997, appearing on pages 24, 25, 32, 33, and 34 through 43. These financial statements are the responsibility of the Company's management. Our responsibility is to express an opinion on these financial statements based on our audits.

We conducted our audits in accordance with generally accepted auditing standards. Those standards require that we plan and perform the audit to obtain reasonable assurance about whether the financial statements are free of material misstatement. An audit includes examining, on a test basis, evidence supporting the amounts and disclosures in the financial statements. An audit also includes assessing the accounting principles used and significant estimates made by management, as well as evaluating the overall financial statement presentation. We believe that our audits provide a reasonable basis for our opinion.

In our opinion, such financial statements present fairly, in all material respects, the financial position of Microsoft Corporation and subsidiaries as of June 30, 1996 and 1997, and the results of their operations and their cash flows for each of the three years ended June 30, 1997 in conformity with accounting principles generally accepted in the United States and International Accounting Standards.

Deloitte & Touche LLP
Seattle, Washington
July 17, 1997
(August 1, 1997 as to Acquisition Note)

msft

directors and officers

Directors

William H. Gates
Chairman of the Board;
Chief Executive Officer,
Microsoft Corporation

Paul G. Allen
Founder, Asymetrix Corp.;
Owner, Starwave Corp.;
Interval Research Corp.;
Vulcan Ventures Inc.

Jill E. Barad
President and
Chief Executive Officer,
Mattel, Inc.

Richard A. Hackborn
Executive
Vice President,
Hewlett-Packard
Company (retired)

David F. Marquardt
General Partner,
Technology Venture
Investors and
August Capital

Robert D. O'Brien
Through November 14, 1997
Chairman of the Board,
PACCAR, Inc. (retired)

Wm. G. Reed, Jr.
Chairman, Simpson
Investment Company

Jon A. Shirley
President and
Chief Operating Officer,
Microsoft Corporation
(retired)

Officers

William H. Gates
Chairman of the Board;
Chief Executive Officer

Steven A. Ballmer
Executive Vice President,
Sales and Support

Robert J. Herbold
Executive Vice President;
Chief Operating Officer

Frank M. (Pete) Higgins
Group Vice President,
Interactive Media

Paul A. Maritz
Group Vice President,
Platforms and
Applications

Nathan P. Myhrvold
Group Vice President,
Chief Technology Officer

Jeffrey S. Raikes
Group Vice President,
Sales and Marketing

James E. Allchin
Senior Vice President,
Personal and Business
Systems Group

Joachim Kempin
Senior Vice President,
OEM Sales

Michel Lacombe
Senior Vice President,
Microsoft;
President,
Microsoft Europe

Craig Mundie
Senior Vice President,
Consumer Platforms

William H. Neukom
Senior Vice President,
Law and Corporate
Affairs; Secretary

Brad A. Silverberg
Senior Vice President,
Applications and
Internet Client Group

Bernard P. Vergnes
Senior Vice President,
Microsoft;
Chairman,
Microsoft Europe

Orlando Ayala Lozano
Vice President,
Intercontinental Region

Robert J. Bach
Vice President,
Learning and
Entertainment

Michael W. Brown
Vice President,
Finance;
(Chief Financial Officer,
retired)

Brad Chase
Vice President,
Developer Relations
and Marketing, Internet
Client and Collaboration

Frank M. Clegg
Vice President,
Central United States
and Canada Region

David Cole
Vice President,
Internet Client and
Collaboration

John G. Connors
Vice President,
Information Technology;
Chief Information Officer

Jon DeVaan
Vice President,
Desktop Applications

Richard R. Devenuti
Vice President,
Operations

Moshe T. Dunie
Vice President,
Windows Operating
Systems

Richard Fade
Vice President,
Desktop Applications

Dianne L. Gregg
Vice President,
Eastern United States
Region

Paul Gross
Vice President,
Developer Tools

Sam Jadallah
Vice President,
Organization
Customer Unit

Laura Jennings
Vice President,
The Microsoft Network

John Lauer
Vice President,
Far East Region

John Leftwich
Vice President,
Europe Marketing

Lewis Levin
Vice President,
Desktop Finance

John Ludwig
Vice President,
Internet Client
and Collaboration

Gregory B. Maffei
Vice President,
Finance;
Chief Financial Officer

Robert L. McDowell
Vice President,
Enterprise Business
Relationships

Bob Muglia
Vice President,
Server Applications

Mike Murray
Vice President,
Human Resources
and Administration

Cameron Myhrvold
Vice President,
Internet Customer Unit

John F. Neilson
Vice President,
Interactive Service Media

Peter Neupert
Vice President,
News, Sports,
and Commentary

Chris Peters
Vice President,
Web Authoring

Rick Rashid
Vice President,
Research

Jon Reingold
Vice President,
Office Marketing

Darryl E. Rubin
Vice President,
Advanced Architecture

Stephen A. Schiro
Vice President,
End-User Customer Unit

Charles Stevens
Vice President,
Application Developers
Customer Unit

Rick Thompson
Vice President,
Hardware

Richard Tong
Vice President,
Marketing, Desktop
and Business Systems

David Vaskevitch
Vice President,
Database and
Transactions

Joe Vetter
Vice President,
Western United States
Region

Deborah N. Willingham
Vice President,
Enterprise
Customer Unit

msft

shareholder services

http://www.microsoft.com/msft/

As a Microsoft shareholder, you're invited to contact us for a variety of shareholder services or to request more information about Microsoft. Here are some suggestions on how to reach us:

Account questions

Our transfer agent can help you with a variety of shareholder-related services, including:

- **Change of address**
- **Lost stock certificates**
- **Transfer of stock to another person**
- **Additional administrative services**

You can call our transfer agent toll-free at (800) 285-7772.

You can also write them at:

ChaseMellon
Shareholder Services
P.O. Box 3315
South Hackensack, NJ
07606-1915

Or you can e-mail our transfer agent at: msft@chasemellon.com

Shareholders of record who receive more than one copy of this annual report can contact our transfer agent and arrange to have their accounts consolidated. Shareholders who own Microsoft stock through a brokerage can contact their broker to request consolidation of their accounts.

Investor relations

You can contact Microsoft's Investor Relations group any time to order financial documents such as this annual report and the Form 10-K. Call us toll-free at (800) 285-7772. (Outside the United States, call (425) 936-4400.) Or send a fax to (425) 936-8000. We can be contacted during West Coast business hours to answer investment-oriented questions about Microsoft. In addition, you can write us at:

Investor Relations Department
Microsoft Corporation
One Microsoft Way
Redmond, Washington
98052-6399

Or better yet, send us an e-mail at msft@microsoft.com

Annual meeting

Microsoft shareholders are invited to attend our annual meeting, which will be held on Friday, November 14, 1997 from 8 to 9 A.M. at the Washington State Convention and Trade Center, 800 Convention Place, Seattle, Washington.

Get financial information online

Anyone with access to the Internet can view an electronic copy of this annual report along with a wide variety of other financial materials at http://www.microsoft.com/msft/

About the cover

We are dedicated to making the Microsoft brand one of the most recognized in the world. Our brand is defined in part by the use of four colors that represent the diverse and dynamic nature of the company. Our 1997 Annual Report covers use these colors in four different configurations in recognition of that strategy.

Recycled paper

GLOSSARY

A

Account. An accounting record in which the results of transactions are accumulated; shows increases, decreases, and a balance.

Accounting. A system for providing quantitative, financial information about economic entities that is useful for making sound economic decisions, Accounting is often called the "language of business" because it provides the means of recording and communicating business activities and the results of those activities.

Accounting cycle. The procedures for analyzing, recording, classifying, summarizing, and reporting the transactions of a business.

Accounting equation. An algebraic equation that expresses the relationship between assets (resources), liabilities (obligations), and owners' equity (net assets, or the residual interest in a business after all liabilities have been met): assets = liabilities + owners' equity.

Accounting model. The basic accounting assumptions, concepts, principles, and procedures that determine the manner of recording, measuring, and reporting a company's transactions.

Accounting system. The procedures and processes used by a business to analyze transactions, handle routine bookkeeping tasks, and structure information so it can be used to evaluate the performance and health of the business.

Accounts receivable. A current asset representing money due for services performed or merchandise sold on credit.

Accounts receivable turnover. A measure used to indicate how fast a company collects its receivables; computed by dividing sales by average accounts receivable.

Accrual-basis accounting. A system of accounting in which revenues and expenses are recorded as they are earned and incurred, not necessarily when cash is received or paid.

Acid-test (quick) ratio. A measure of a firm's ability to meet current liabilities; more restrictive than the current ratio, it is computed by dividing net quick assets (all current assets, except inventories and prepaid expenses) by current liabilities.

Adjusting entries. Entries required at the end of each accounting period to recognize, on an accrual basis, revenues and expenses for the period and to report proper amounts for asset, liability, and owners' equity accounts.

Aging accounts receivable. The process of categorizing each account receivable by the number of days it has been outstanding.

Allowance for bad debts. A contra account, deducted from accounts receivable, that shows the estimated losses from uncollectible accounts.

Allowance method. The recording of estimated losses due to uncollectible accounts as expenses during the period in which the sales occurred.

American Institute of Certified Public Accountants (AICPA). The national organization of CPAs in the United States.

Amortization. The process of cost allocation that assigns the original cost of an intangible asset to the periods benefited.

Annual report. A document that summarizes the results of operations and financial status of a company for the past year and outlines plans for the future.

Annuity. A series of equal amounts to be received or paid at the end of equal time intervals.

Arm's-length transactions. Business dealings between independent and rational parties who are looking out for their own interests.

Articulation. The interrelationships among the financial statements.

Asset turnover. A measure of company efficiency, computed by dividing sales by total assets.

Asset turnover ratio. An overall measure of how effectively assets are used during a period; computed by dividing revenue by total assets.

Assets. Economic resources that are owned or controlled by a company.

Audit report. A report issued by an independent CPA that expresses an opinion about whether the financial statements present fairly a company's financial position, operating results, and cash flows in accordance with generally accepted accounting principles.

Available-for-sale securities. Debt and equity securities not classified as trading, held-to-maturity, or equity method securities.

Average collection period. A measure of the average number of days it takes to collect a credit sale; computed by dividing 365 days by the accounts receivable turnover.

Average cost. An inventory cost flow assumption whereby cost of goods sold and the cost of ending inventory are determined by using an average cost of all merchandise available for sale during the period.

B

Bad debt. An uncollectible account receivable.

Bad debt expense. An account that represents the portion of the current period's credit sales that are estimated to be uncollectible.

Balance sheet (statement of financial position). The financial statement that reports a company's assets, liabilities, and owners' equity at a particular date.

Basket purchase. The purchase of two or more assets acquired together at a single price.

Board of directors. Individuals elected by the stockholders to govern a corporation.

Bond. A contract between a borrower and a lender in which the borrower promises to pay a specified rate of interest for each period the bond is outstanding and repay the principal at the maturity date.

Bond discount. The difference between the face value and the sales price when bonds are sold below their face value.

Bond indenture. A contract between a bond issuer and a bond purchaser that specifies the terms of a bond.

Bond maturity date. The date at which a bond principal or face amount becomes payable.

Bond premium. The difference between the face value and the sales price when bonds are sold above their face value.

Book value. The value of a company as measured by the amount of owners' equity; that is, assets less liabilities.

Bookkeeping. The preservation of a systematic, quantitative record of an activity.

Break-even point. The amount of sales of the number of units sold at which total costs equal total revenues; the point at which there is no profit or loss.

Budget. A quantitative expression of a plan of action that shows how a firm or an organization will acquire and use resources over some specified period of time.

Budget committee. A management group responsible for establishing budgeting policy and for coordinating the preparation of budgets.

Business. An organization operated with the objective of making a profit from the sale of goods or services.

Business documents. Records of transactions used as the basis for recording accounting entries; includes invoices, check stubs, receipts, and similar business papers.

C

Callable bonds. Bonds for which the issuer reserves the right to pay the obligation before its maturity date.

Capital. The total amount of money or other resources owned or used to acquire future income or benefits.

Capital budget. Systematic plan for long-term investments in operating assets.

Capital budgeting. Systematic planning for long-term investments in operating assets.

Capital rationing. Allocating limited resources among ranked acceptable investments.

Capital stock. The portion of a corporation's owners' equity contributed by owners in exchange for shares of stock.

Capital structure. The relationship between the quantities of debt and equity a company has used for financing.

Cash. Coins, currency, money orders, checks, and funds on deposit with financial institutions; the most liquid of assets.

Cash budget. A schedule of expected cash receipts and disbursements during the budget period.

Cash dividend. A cash distribution of earnings to stockholders.

Cash equivalents. Short-term, highly liquid investments that can be converted easily into cash.

Cash inflows. Any current or expected revenues or savings directly associated with an investment.

Cash outflows. The initial cost and other expected outlays associated with an investment.

Centralized company. An organization in which top management makes most of the major decisions for the entire company rather than delegating them to managers at lower levels.

Certified management accountant (CMA). A person who has been certified by the Institute of Management Accountants after having passed a qualifying examination similar in rigor to the CPA exam.

Certified public accountant (CPA). A special designation given to an accountant who has passed a national uniform examination and has met other certifying requirements.

Chart of accounts. A systematic listing of all accounts used by a company.

Classified balance sheet. A balance sheet in which assets and liabilities are subdivided into current and long-term categories.

Closing entries. Entries that reduce all nominal, or temporary, accounts to a zero balance at the end of each accounting period, transferring their preclosing balances to a permanent balance sheet account.

Common stock. The most frequently issued class of stock; usually it provides a voting right but is secondary to preferred stock in dividend and liquidation rights.

Comparative financial statements. Financial statements in which data for two or more years are shown together.

Compound journal entry. A journal entry that involves more than one debit or more than one credit or both.

Compounding period. The period of time for which interest is computed.

Consolidated financial statements. Statements that report the combined operating results, financial position, and cash flows of two or more legally separate but affiliated companies as if they were one economic entity.

Contra account. An account that is offset or deducted from another account.

Contributed capital. The portion of owners' equity contributed by investors (the owners) in exchange for shares of stock.

Contribution margin. The difference between total sales and variable costs; it is the portion of sales revenue available to cover fixed costs and provide a profit.

Contribution-margin ratio. The percentage of net sales revenue left after variable costs are deducted; the contribution margin divided by net sales revenue.

Controlling. Implementing management plans and identifying how plans compare with actual performance.

Convertible bonds. Bonds that can be traded for, or converted to, other securities after a specified period of time.

Convertible preferred stock. Preferred stock that can be converted to common stock at a specified conversion rate.

Corporation. A legal entity chartered by a state; ownership is represented by transferable shares of stock.

Cost. Cash or cash-equivalent value sacrificed for goods and services that are expected to provide benefits to an organization.

Cost behavior. The way in which a cost is affected by changes in activity levels.

Cost center. An organizational unit in which a manager has control over and is held accountable for costs.

Cost driver. Base used to allocate costs of activities consumed in manufacturing to the products using those activities.

Cost of capital. The average cost of a firm's debt and equity capital; equals the rate of return that a company must earn in order to satisfy the demands of its owners and creditors.

Cost of goods available for sale. The cost of all merchandise available for sale during the period; equal to the sum of beginning inventory and net purchases.

Cost of goods manufactured schedule. A schedule supporting the income statement; summarizes the total cost of goods manufactured during a period, including direct materials, direct labor, and manufacturing overhead

Cost of goods sold. The expenses incurred to purchase or manufacture the merchandise sold during a period.

Cost principle. The idea that transactions are recorded at their historical costs or exchange prices at the transaction date.

Cost-volume-profit (CVP) analysis. Techniques for determining how changes in revenues, costs, and level of activity affect the profitability of an organization.

Coupon bonds. Unregistered bonds for which owners receive periodic interest payments by clipping a coupon from the bond and sending it to the issuer as evidence of ownership.

Credit. An entry on the right side of a t-account.

Critical resource factor. The resource that limits operating capacity by its availability.

Cumulative-dividend preference. The right of preferred stockholders to receive current dividends plus all dividends in arrears before common stockholders receive any dividends.

Current assets. Cash and other assets that can be easily converted to cash within a year.

Current (working capital) ratio. A measure of the liquidity of a business; equal to current assets divided by current liabilities.

Current-dividend preference. The right of preferred stockholders to receive current dividends before common stockholders receive dividends.

Curvilinear costs. Variable costs that do not vary in direct proportion to changes in activity level but at decreasing or increasing rates due to economies of scale, productivity changes, and so on.

D

Date of record. The date selected by a corporation's board of directors on which the stockholders of record are identified as those who will receive dividends.

Debentures (unsecured bonds). Bonds for which no collateral has been pledged.

Debit. An entry on the left side of a t-account.

Debt ratio. A measure of leverage, computed by dividing total liabilities by total assets.

Debt securities. Financial instruments issued by a company that carry with them a promise of interest payments and the repayment of principal.

Debt-equity ratio. The number of dollars of borrowed funds for every dollar invested by owners; computed as total liabilities divided by total equity.

Decentralized company. An organization in which managers at all levels have the authority to make decisions concerning the operations for which they are responsible.

Declaration date. The date on which a corporation's board of directors formally decides to pay a dividend to stockholders.

Depletion. The process of cost allocation that assigns the original cost of a natural resource to the periods benefited.

Depreciation. The process of cost allocation that assigns the original cost of plant and equipment to the periods benefited.

Differential costs. Future costs that change as a result of a decision; also called incremental or relevant costs.

Direct costs. Costs that are specifically traceable to a unit of business or segment being analyzed.

Direct labor. Wages that are paid to those who physically work on the direct materials to transform them into a finished product and are traceable to specific products.

Direct labor budget. A schedule of direct labor requirements for the budget period.

Direct materials. Materials that become part of the product and are traceable to it.

Direct materials budget. A schedule of direct materials to be used during the budget period and direct materials to be purchased during that period.

Direct method. A method of reporting net cash flow from operations that shows the major classes of cash receipts and payments for a period of time.

Direct write-off method. The recording of actual losses from uncollectible accounts as expenses during the period in which accounts receivable are determined to be uncollectible.

Discounted cash flow methods. Capital budgeting techniques that take into account the time value of money by comparing discounted cash flows.

Disposable income. Income left after withholding and fixed expenses have been subtracted from gross salary; the amount left to cover variable expenditures.

Dividend payment date. The date on which a corporation pays dividends to its stockholders.

Dividend payout ratio. A measure of the percentage of earnings paid out in dividends; computed by dividing cash dividends by net income.

Dividends. Distributions to the owners (stockholders) of a corporation.

Dividends in arrears. Missed dividends for past years that preferred stockholders have a right to receive under the cumulative-dividend preference if and when dividends are declared.

Double-entry accounting. A system of recording transactions in a way that maintains the equality of the accounting equation.

E

Earnings per share (EPS). The amount of net income (earnings) related to each share of stock; computed by dividing net income by the number of shares of stock outstanding during the period.

Entity. An organizational unit (a person, partnership, or corporation) for which accounting records are kept and about which accounting reports are prepared.

Equity method. Method used to account for an investment in the stock of another company when significant influence can be imposed (presumed to exist when 20 to 50 percent of the outstanding voting stock is owned).

Equity securities (stock). Shares of ownership in a corporation that can change significantly in value and that provide for a return to investors in the form of dividends.

Evaluating. Analyzing results, rewarding performance, and identifying problems.

Exception report. A report that highlights variances from, or exceptions to, the budget.

Expenses. Costs incurred in the normal course of business to generate revenues.

Extraordinary items. Nonoperating gains and losses that are unusual in nature, infrequent in occurrence, and material in amount.

F

FIFO (first in, first out). An inventory cost flow whereby the first goods purchased are assumed to be the first goods sold so that the ending inventory consists of the most recently purchased goods.

Financial accounting. The area of accounting concerned with reporting financial information to interested external parties.

Financial Accounting Standards Board (FASB). The private organization responsible for establishing the standards for financial accounting and reporting in the United States.

Financial ratios. Ratios that show relationships between financial statement amounts.

Financial statement analysis. Examining both the relationships among financial statement amounts and the trends in those numbers over time.

Financial statements. Reports such as the balance sheet, income statement, and statement of cash flows, which summarize the financial status and results of operations of a business entity.

Financing activities. Transactions and events whereby resources are obtained from, or repaid to, owners (equity financing) and creditors (debt financing).

Finished goods. Manufactured products ready for sale.

Finished goods inventory. Inventory that has completed the production process and is ready for sale to customers.

Fiscal year. An entity's reporting year, covering a 12-month accounting period.

Fixed costs. Costs that remain constant in total, regardless of activity level, at least over a certain range of activity.

Flexible budget. A quantified plan that projects revenues and costs for varying levels of activity.

Franchise. An entity that has been licensed to sell the product of a manufacturer or to offer a particular service in a given area.

G

Gains (losses). Money made or lost on activities outside the normal operation of a company.

Generally accepted accounting principles (GAAP). Authoritative guidelines that define accounting practice at a particular time.

Goal congruence. The selection of goals for responsibility centers that are consistent, or congruent, with those of the company as a whole.

Going concern assumption. The idea that an accounting entity will have a continuing existence for the foreseeable future.

Goodwill. An intangible asset that exists when a business is valued at more than the fair market value of its net assets, usually due to strategic location, reputation, good customer relations, or similar factors; equal to the excess of the purchase price over the fair market value of the net assets purchased.

Gross profit (gross margin). The excess of net sales revenue over the cost of goods sold.

Gross sales. Total recorded sales before deducting any sales discounts or sales returns and allowances.

H

Held-to-maturity securities. Debt securities purchased by an investor with the intent of holding the securities until they mature.

High-low method. A method of segregating the fixed and variable components of a mixed cost by analyzing the costs at the high and the low activity levels within a relevant range.

Historical cost. The dollar amount originally exchanged in an arm's-length transaction; an amount assumed to reflect the fair market value of an item at the transaction date.

Holding costs. The financial opportunity costs that result from investing money in an asset such as inventory. Whatever income the money could generate in an alternative investment is the holding cost of the current investment.

Hurdle rate. The minimum rate of return that an investment must provide in order to be acceptable.

I

Income statement (statement of earnings). The financial statement that reports the amount of net income earned by a company during a period.

Income taxes payable. The amount expected to be paid to the federal and state governments based on the income before taxes reported on the income statement.

Indirect costs. Costs normally incurred for the benefit of several segments within the organization. Indirect costs are sometimes called common costs.

Indirect method. A method of reporting net cash flow from operations that involves converting accrual-basis net income to a cash basis.

Institute of Management Accountants (IMA). The organization in the United States most concerned with the management accounting function; publishes *Management Accounting* and administers the CMA exam.

Intangible assets. Long-lived assets without physical substance that are used in business, such as licenses, patents, franchises, and goodwill.

Interest. The payment (cost) for the use of money.

Internal rate of return. The "true" discount rate that will produce a net present value of zero when applied to the cash flows of investment inventory goods held for resale.

Internal rate of return method. A capital budgeting technique that uses discounted cash flows to find the "true" discount rate of an investment; this true rate produces a net present value of zero.

Internal Revenue Service (IRS). A government agency that prescribes the rules and regulates the collection of tax revenues in the United States.

International Accounting Standards Committee (IASC). The committee formed in 1973 to develop worldwide accounting standards.

Interpolation. A method of determining the internal rate of return when the factor for that rate lies between the factors given in the present value table.

Inventory. Goods held for resale.

Inventory shrinkage. The amount of inventory that is lost, stolen, or spoiled during a period; determined by comparing perpetual inventory records to the physical count of inventory.

Inventory turnover. A measure of the efficiency with which inventory is managed; computed by dividing cost of goods sold by average inventory for a period.

Investing activities. Transactions and events that involve the purchase and sale of securities (excluding cash equivalents), property, plant, equipment, and other assets not generally held for resale, and the making and collecting of loans.

Investment center. An organizational unit in which a manager has responsibility for costs, revenues, and assets.

J

Job cost sheet. A document prepared for each manufacturing job that is job order costed; it contains a summary of direct materials, direct labor, and overhead costs.

Job order costing. A method of product costing whereby each job, product, or batch of products is costed separately.

Joint manufacturing process. Using a single material input to produce more than one product.

Joint product costs. All costs incurred before various products are separated for further processing or immediate sale.

Journal. An accounting record in which transactions are first entered; provides a chronological record of all business activities.

Journal entry. A recording of a transaction where debits equal credits; usually includes a date and an explanation of the transaction.

Journalizing. Recording transactions in a journal.

Junk bonds. Bonds issued by companies in weak financial condition with large amounts of debt already outstanding; these bonds yield high rates of return because of high risk.

L

Labor efficiency variance. The extent to which the actual labor used varies from the standard quantity; computed by multiplying the difference between the actual quantity and the standard quantity of labor by the standard rate.

Labor rate variance. The extent to which the actual labor rate varies from the standard rate for the quantity of labor used; computed by multiplying the difference between the actual rate and the standard rate by the quantity of labor used.

Lead time. Generally, the time interval between initiating a request and finally fulfilling the request.

Least cost decision. A decision to undertake the project with the smallest negative net present value.

Ledger. A book of accounts in which data from transactions recorded in journals are posted and thereby summarized.

Liabilities. Obligations to pay cash, transfer other assets, or provide services to someone else.

License. The right to perform certain activities, generally granted by a governmental agency.

LIFO (last in, first out). An inventory cost flow whereby the last goods purchased are assumed to be the first goods sold so that the ending inventory consists of the first goods purchased.

Limited liability. The legal protection given stockholders whereby they are responsible for the debts and obligations of a corporation only to the extent of their capital contributions.

Line of credit. An arrangement whereby a bank agrees to loan an amount of money (up to a certain limit) on demand for short periods of time, usually less than a year.

Liquidity. A company's ability to meet current obligations with cash or other assets that can be quickly converted to cash.

Long-term assets. Assets that a company needs in order to operate its business over an extended period of time.

Long-term liabilities. Debts or other obligations that will not be paid within one year.

Long-term operating assets. Assets expected to be held and used over the course of several years to facilitate operating activities.

Losses. Costs that provide no benefit to an organization.

M

Management accounting. The area of accounting concerned with providing internal financial reports to assist management in making decisions.

Management by exception. The strategy of focusing attention on significant deviations from standard.

Manufacturing organizations. Organizations that focus on using labor and/or machinery to convert raw materials into marketable products.

Manufacturing overhead. All costs incurred in the manufacturing process other than direct materials and direct labor.

Manufacturing overhead budget. A schedule of production costs other than those for direct labor and direct materials.

Manufacturing overhead rate. The rate at which manufacturing overhead is assigned to products; estimated manufacturing overhead for the period divided by the number of units of the activity base being used.

Market Adjustment—Trading Securities. An account used to track the difference between the historical cost and the market value of a company's portfolio of trading securities.

Market rate (effective rate or yield rate) of interest. The actual interest rate earned or paid on a bond investment.

Market value. The value of a company as measured by the number of shares of stock outstanding multiplied by the current market price of the stock; the current value of a business.

Matching principle. The concept that all costs and expenses incurred in generating revenues must be recognized in the same reporting period as the related revenues.

Materials price variance. The extent to which the actual price varies from the standard price for the quantity of materials purchased or used; computed by multiplying the difference between the actual and standard prices by the quantity purchased or used.

Materials quantity variance. The extent to which the actual quantity of materials varies from the standard quantity; computed by multiplying the difference between the actual quantity and the standard quantity of materials used by the standard price.

Merchandising organizations. Organizations that focus on procuring tangible products, then distributing them to customers. These customers may include individuals or other business organizations such as manufacturing organizations.

Mixed costs. Costs that contain both variable and fixed cost components.

Monetary measurement. The idea that money, as the common medium of exchange, is the accounting unit of measurement, and that only economic activities measurable in monetary terms are included in the accounting model.

Mortgage amortization schedule. A schedule that shows the breakdown between interest and principal for each payment over the life of a mortgage.

Mortgage payable. A written promise to pay a stated amount of money at one or more specified future dates; a mortgage is secured by the pledging of certain assets, usually real estate, as collateral.

N

Natural resources. Assets that are physically consumed or waste away, such as oil, minerals, gravel, and timber.

Net assets. The owner's equity of a business; equal to total assets minus total liabilities.

Net income (net loss). An overall measure of the performance of a company; equal to revenues minus expenses for the period.

Net operating profit. The difference between normal business sales and normal business expenses.

Net present value. The difference between the present values of an investment's expected cash inflows and outflows.

Net present value method. A capital budgeting technique that uses discounted cash flows to compare the present values of an investment's expected cash inflows and outflows.

Net purchases. The net cost of inventory purchased during a period, after adding the cost of freight in and subtracting returns and discounts.

Net realizable value of accounts receivable. The net amount that would be received if all receivables considered collectible were collected; equal to total accounts receivable less the allowance for bad debts.

Net sales. Gross sales less sales discounts and sales returns and allowances.

Nominal accounts. Accounts that are closed to a zero balance at the end of each accounting period; temporary accounts generally appearing on the income statement.

Noncash items. Items included in the determination of net income on an accrual basis that do not affect cash; examples are depreciation and amortization.

Noncash transactions. Investing and financing activities that do not affect cash; if significant, they are disclosed below the statement of cash flows or in the notes to the financial statements.

Nonprofit organization. An entity without a profit objective, oriented toward providing services efficiently and effectively.

Nonroutine decisions. Decisions made less frequently and that usually have a more significant strategic impact on operations than routine decisions.

Notes to the financial statements. Explanatory information considered an integral part of the financial statements.

Number of days' sales in accounts payable. The average number of days from the purchase of inventory from suppliers until payment is made.

Number of days' sales in inventory. An alternative measure of how well inventory is being managed; computed by dividing 365 days by the inventory turnover ratio.

O

Operating activities. Transactions and events that involve selling products or services and incurring the necessary expenses associated with the primary activities of the business.

Operating (master) budget. A network of many separate schedules and budgets that together constitute the overall operating and financing plan for the coming period.

Opportunity costs. The benefits lost or forfeited as a result of selecting one alternative course of action over another.

Other revenues and expenses. Items incurred or earned from activities that are outside, or peripheral to, the normal operations of a firm.

Out-of-pocket costs. Costs that require an outlay of cash or other resources.

Overapplied manufacturing overhead. The excess of applied manufacturing overhead (based on a predetermined application rate) over the actual manufacturing overhead costs for a period.

Owners' equity. The ownership interest in the net assets of an entity; equals total assets minus total liabilities.

P

Par value. Nominal value assigned to and printed on the face of each share of a corporation's stock.

Partnership. An association of two or more individuals or organizations to carry on economic activity.

Patent. An exclusive right granted for 17 years by the federal government to manufacture and sell an invention.

Payback method. A capital budgeting technique that determines the amount of time it takes the net cash inflows of an investment to repay the investment cost.

Payback reciprocal method. A capital budgeting technique in which the reciprocal of the payback period is used in computing an investment's approximate internal rate of return.

Pension. An agreement between an employer and employees that provides for benefits upon retirement.

Period costs. Costs not directly related to a product, service, or asset that are charged as expenses to the income statement in the period in which they are incurred.

Periodic inventory system. A system of accounting for inventory in which cost of goods sold is determined and inventory is adjusted at the end of the accounting period, not when merchandise is purchased or sold.

Perpetual inventory system. A system of accounting for inventory in which detailed records of the number of units and the cost of each purchase and sales transactions are prepared throughout the accounting period.

Per-unit contribution margin. The excess of the sales price of one unit over its variable costs.

Planning. Outlining the activities that need to be performed for an organization to achieve its objectives.

Post-closing trial balance. A listing of all real account balances after the closing process has been completed; provides a means of testing whether total debits equal total credits for all real accounts prior to beginning a new accounting cycle.

Postemployment benefits. Benefits paid to employees who have been laid off or terminated.

Posting. The process of transferring amounts from the journal to the ledger.

Predetermined overhead rate. A rate at which estimated manufacturing overhead costs are assigned to products throughout the year; equals total estimated manufacturing overhead costs divided by a suitable allocation base, such as number of units produced, direct labor hours, direct materials used, or direct labor costs.

Preferred stock. A class of stock that usually provides dividend and liquidation preferences over common stock.

Present value of $1. The value today of $1 to be received or paid at some future date given a specified interest rate.

Present value of an annuity. The value today of a series of equally spaced, equal-amount payments to be made or received in the future given a specified interest rate.

Price-earnings (P/E) ratio. A measure of growth potential, earnings stability, and management capabilities; computed by dividing market price per share by earnings per share.

Primary financial statements. The balance sheet, income statement, and statement of cash flows, used by external groups to assess a company's economic standing.

Principal (face value or maturity value). The amount that will be paid on a bond at the maturity date.

Process costing. A method of product costing whereby costs are accumulated by process or work centers and averaged over all products manufactured in those centers.

Product costs. Costs associated with products or services offered.

Production budget. A schedule of production requirements for the budget period.

Profit center. An organizational unit in which a manager has responsibility for both costs and revenues.

Profit graph. A graph that shows how profits vary with changes in volume.

Profit margin (operating performance) ratio. An overall measure of the efficiency of operations during a period; computed by dividing net income by revenue.

Profitability index. The present value of net cash inflows divided by the cost of an investment.

Property, plant, and equipment. Tangible, long-lived assets acquired for use in business operations; includes land, buildings, machinery, equipment, and furniture.

Proprietorship. A business owned by one person.

Prospectus. Report provided to potential investors that presents a company's financial statements and explains its business plan, sources of financing, and significant risks.

Purchases budget. A schedule of projected purchases over the budget period.

R

Ranking. The ordering of acceptable investment alternatives from most to least desirable.

Raw materials. Materials purchased for use in manufacturing products.

Raw materials inventory. The inventory or raw (or direct) materials that have not yet begun the production process.

Real accounts. Accounts that are not closed to a zero balance at the end of each accounting period; permanent accounts appearing on the balance sheet.

Realized gains and losses. Gains and losses resulting from the sale of securities in an arm's-length transaction.

Receivables. Claims for money, goods, or services.

Registered bonds. Bonds for which the names and addresses of the bondholders are kept on file by the issuing company.

Regression line. On a scattergraph, the straight line that most closely expresses the relationship between the variables.

Relevant range. The range of operating level, or volume of activity, over which the relationship between total costs (variable plus fixed) and activity level is approximately linear.

Residual income. The amount of net income earned above a specified minimum rate of return on assets; used to evaluate investment centers.

Responsibility accounting. A system of evaluating performance; managers are held accountable for the costs, revenues, assets, or other elements over which they have control.

Responsibility center. An organizational unit in which a manager has control over and is held accountable for performance.

Retailers. Second-tier merchants who typically purchase products from wholesalers to distribute to end customers. Many large retailers, however, will often pass by wholesalers to purchase product directly from original manufacturers.

Retained earnings. The portion of a corporation's owners' equity that has been earned from profitable operations and not distributed to stockholders.

Return on equity. A measure of the amount of profit earned per dollar of investment, computed by dividing net income by owners' equity.

Return on investment (ROI). A measure of operating performance and efficiency in utilizing assets; computed in its simplest form by dividing net income by average total assets.

Return on sales. A measure of the amount of profit earned per dollar of sales, computed by dividing net income by sales.

Return on sales revenue. A measure of operating performance; computed by dividing net income by total sales revenue.

Revenue. Increase in a company's resources from the sale of goods or services.

Revenue budget. A service entity's budget that identifies how much revenue (and often cash) will be generated during a period.

Revenue recognition. The process of recording revenue in the accounting records; occurs after (1) the work has been substantially completed and (2) cash collection is reasonably assured.

Revenue recognition principle. The idea that revenues should be recorded when (1) the earnings process has been substantially completed and (2) cash has either been collected or collectibility is reasonably assured.

Routine decisions. Decisions that involve the routine or daily operations of a firm; planning, controlling, and evaluating decisions that are made on a regular and repetitive basis.

S

Sales budget. A schedule of projected sales over the budget period.

Sales discount. A reduction in the selling price that is allowed if payment is received within a specified period.

Sales mix. The relative proportion of total units sold (or total sales dollars) that is represented by each of a company's products.

Sales returns and allowances. A contra-revenue account in which the return of, or allowance for reduction in the price of, merchandise previously sold is recorded.

Sales tax payable. Money collected from customers for sales taxes that must be remitted to local governments and other taxing authorities.

Salvage value. The amount expected to be received when an asset is sold at the end of its useful life.

Scattergraph (visual-fit) method. A method of segregating the fixed and variable components of a mixed cost by plotting on a graph total costs at several activity levels and drawing a regression line through the points.

Screening. Determining whether a capital investment meets a minimum standard of financial acceptability.

Secured bonds. Bonds for which assets have been pledged in order to guarantee repayment.

Securities and Exchange Commission (SEC). The government body responsible for regulating the financial reporting practices of most publicly owned corporations in connection with the buying and selling of stocks and bonds.

Segment. Parts of an organization requiring separate reports for evaluation by management.

Segment margin. The difference between segment revenue and direct segment costs; a measure of the segment's contribution to cover indirect fixed costs and provide profits.

Segment-margin income statement. An income statement that identifies costs directly chargeable to a segment and further divides them into variable and fixed cost behavior patterns.

Segment-margin ratio. The segment margin divided by the segment's net sales revenue; a measure of the efficiency of the segment's operating performance, and therefore of its profitability.

Selling and administrative expense budget. A schedule of all nonproduction spending expected to occur during the budget period.

Separate entity concept. The idea that the activities of an entity are to be separated from those of the individual owners.

Serial bonds. Bonds that mature in a series of installments at specified future dates.

Service organizations. Organizations that focus on delivery of marketable services, such as legal advice or education, to individuals or other organizations.

Service overhead budget. The budget, prepared by service entities, that identifies projected costs associated with providing the service.

Short-run nonroutine decisions. Managerial decisions that require more extensive analysis than short-run operating decisions but less than long-run asset purchase decisions.

Short-run operating decisions. Managerial decisions about current operations and those of the immediate future characterized by their regularity and frequency.

Social security (FICA) taxes. Federal insurance contributions act taxes imposed on employee and employer; used mainly to provide retirement benefits.

Special order. An order that may be priced below the normal selling price in order to utilize excess capacity and thereby contribute to company profits.

Specific identification. A method of valuing inventory and determining cost of goods sold whereby the actual costs of specific inventory items are assigned to them.

Standard cost card. An itemization of the components of the standard cost of a product.

Standard cost system. A cost-accumulation system in which standard costs are used as product costs instead of actual costs.

Standard costing. The method of comparing standard costs to actual costs and computing variances; commonly used in cost centers to provide objective information about costs.

Stated rate of interest. The rate of interest printed on the bond.

Statement of cash flows. The financial statement that shows an entity's cash inflows (receipts) and outflows (payments) during a period of time.

Statement of retained earnings. A report that shows the changes in retained earnings during a period of time.

Static budget. A quantified plan that projects revenues and costs for only one level of activity.

Stepped costs. Costs that change in total in a stair-step fashion (in large amounts) with changes in volume of activity.

Stock options. Rights given to employees to purchase shares of stock of a company at a predetermined price.

Stockholders. Individuals or organizations that own a portion (shares of stock) of a corporation.

Stockholders' equity. The owners' equity section of a corporate balance sheet.

Straight-line depreciation method. The depreciation method in which the cost of an asset is allocated equally over the periods of an asset's estimated useful life.

Strategic planning. Broad, long-range planning, usually conducted by top management.

Sunk costs. Costs, such as depreciation, that are past costs and do not change as the result of a future decision.

Supplies budget. The budget, prepared by service entities, that identifies projected supplies expenses over the budget period.

T

T-account. A simplified depiction of an account in the form of a letter T.

Target income. A profit level desired by management.

Term bonds. Bonds that mature in one lump sum at a specified future date.

Time period (or periodicity) concept. The idea that the life of a business is divided into distinct and relatively short time periods so that accounting information can be timely.

Time value of money. The concept that a dollar received now is worth more than a dollar received far in the future.

Total cost. The total variable and fixed costs incurred in making a product or providing a service.

Trading securities. Debt and equity securities purchased with the intent of selling them should the need for cash arise or to realize short-term gains.

Transactions. Exchange of goods or services between entities (whether individuals, businesses, or other organizations), as well as other events having an economic impact on a business.

Treasury stock. Issued stock that has subsequently been reacquired by the corporation.

Trial balance. A listing of all account balances; provides a means of testing whether total debits equal total credits for all accounts.

U

Unadjusted rate of return method. A capital budgeting technique in which a rate of return is calculated by dividing the increase in the average annual net income a project will generate by the initial investment cost.

Underapplied manufacturing overhead. The excess of actual manufacturing overhead costs over the applied overhead costs for a period.

Units-of-production method. The depreciation method in which the cost of an asset is allocated to each period on the basis of the productive output or use of the asset during the period.

Unrealized gains and losses. Gains and losses resulting from changes in the value of securities that are still being held.

V

Variable cost rate. The change in cost divided by the change in activity; the slope of the regression line.

Variable costs. Costs that change in total in direct proportion to changes in activity level.

Variance. Any deviation from standard.

W

Wages and salaries budget. The budget, prepared by service entities, that identifies projected labor costs involved directly in providing the service over the budget period.

Wholesalers. Top-tier merchants who typically deal directly with the original manufacturers to distribute products to retailers.

Work in process. Partially completed units in production.

Work-in-process inventory. Inventory that is partly completed in the production process, yet not ready for sale to customers.

Z

Zero-interest bonds. Bonds issued with no promise of interest payments; only a lump sum payment will be made.

APPENDIX C

CHECK FIGURES

Note: Check figures are provided for even-numbered exercises and problems, where applicable.

CHAPTER 1

Not Applicable

CHAPTER 2

Exercises

2-2 (c) Owners' equity = $30,000
2-4 Revenues = $47,500
2-6 12/31/00 Owners' equity = $249,000
2-8 Income Taxes = $34,440
2-10 (1) Net income = $380,000
2-12 EPS = $9.07
2-14 N/A
2-16 Debt ratio = 0.6483
2-18 N/A
2-20 N/A

Problems

2-2 (1) Total assets = $17,525
2-4 (1) Net income for 2000 = $21,000
2-6 (5) Net Income = $107,250
2-8 Net increase in cash = $30,000
2-10 (2) ROE = 8.73%
2-12 PE ratio = 13.81
2-14 (3) Total revenue = $65,800

CHAPTER 3

Exercises

3-2 N/A
3-4 (2) OE—R
3-6 (3) Debit to Inventory = $8,000
3-8 Cash balance = $176,500
3-10 Retained Earnings = $27,000 credit
3-12 (4) Adjusting entry, credit to Consulting Fees Revenue = $350
3-14 N/A
3-16 (2) Retained Earnings = $35,500 credit

Problems

3-2 (2) Cash balance = $96,700
3-4 (2) Cost of goods sold balance = $50,000
3-6 (3) Net loss = ($300)
3-8 (4) EPS = $1.84
3-10 N/A

CHAPTER 4

Exercises

4-2 N/A
4-4 N/A
4-6 6/21 Debit to Cash = $3,800
4-8 (1b) Debit to Bad Debt Expense = $890,000
4-10 Debit to Bad Debt Expense = $33,700
4-12 2000 Debit to Bad Debt Expense = $60,000
4-14 N/A
4-16 Jan. 2001 Debit to Estimated Liability for Service = $675

Problems

4-2 (1) Estimated bad debts = $264,800
4-4 (3b) Debit to Bad Debt Expense = $7,500
4-6 (4) Debit to Bad Debt Expense = $546

CHAPTER 5

Exercises

5-2 Ending inventory = $14,010
5-4 June 30, debit to Cash = $39,200
5-6 Net purchases = $263,880
5-8 (2) Cost of goods sold = $104,340
5-10 (1) Net purchases = $4,800
5-12 FIFO Total cost = $6,450
5-14 (2) Debit to Payroll Tax Expense = $10,322
5-16 (1) Credit to Cash = $7,600
5-18 Earnings per share = $2.73
5-20 12/31/2000 Income before income taxes = $10,000
5-22 (2) Current ratio 1999 = 1.00

Problems

5-2 (3) Cost of goods sold = $262,500
5-4 (b) LIFO Gross margin = $9,560
5-6 (1) Debit to Salaries Expense = $14,200

5-8 (6) 1998 Gross margin = $10,000
5-10 (1) Net income Dec. 31, 2000 = $20,534
5-12 (3) 2000 A/R turnover = 16.97

CHAPTER 6

Exercises

6-2 (4) $20,001
6-4 6/30/2000 Credit to Cash = $1,250
6-6 (2) Credit to Cash = $10,500
6-8 Interest payments = $2,240
6-10 (d) Debit to Cash = $125,000
6-12 (e) Debit to Cash = $20,800
6-14 (e) Credit to Dividends Payable = $79,800
6-16 (3) $1.69 per share
6-18 (2) Total dividends paid = $172,485
6-20 Total contributed capital = $975,000

Problems

6-2 (2) (a) $32,210
6-4 (1) Credit to Mortgage Payable = $200,000
6-6 August 31 Bonds interest payments = $13,900
6-8 Total current liabilities = $311,300
6-10 (2) Total contributed capital = $1,802,200
6-12 (2) Total stockholders' equity = $398,175
6-14 (2) Net income = $30,750
6-16 (1d) Credit to Treasury Stock = $6,000

CHAPTER 7

Exercises

7-2 (1) Total cost = $83,000
7-4 Debit to Building = $262,500
7-6 (1) Depreciable amount = $30,000
7-8 (1) Credit to Gain on Sale of Machine = $5,000
7-10 (3) Credit to Franchise = $25,000
7-12 2/20/2000 Credit to Investment in Trading Securities Stock = $3,825
7-14 Debit to Market Adjustment—Trading Securities = $250
7-16 Credit to Realized Gain on Sale of Securities = $800

Problems

7-2 N/A
7-4 (3) Depreciation = $50,400
7-6 (2) Depreciation of building = $3,333
7-8 (1a) Debit to Truck = $6,100
7-10 (2) Credit to Goodwill = $750
7-12 8/31 Debit to Realized Loss on Sale of Trading Securities = $28,000
7-14 (3) Debit to Realized Loss on Sale of Available-for-Sale Securities = $8,000

CHAPTER 8

Exercises

8-2 N/A
8-4 (1) (d) Credit to Interest Revenue = $1,500
8-6 (1) Cash collected from customers = $223,000
8-8 Net cash flows provided by operations = $21,700
8-10 Net cash flows provided by operating activities = $161,600
8-12 Net cash flows provided by operating activities = $243,000
8-14 Net cash flows provided by operating activities = $116,000
8-16 Net cash flows used in investing activities = ($60,000)
8-18 N/A

Problems

8-2 (2) Net increase in cash = $22,300
8-4 (1) Net cash flows provided by operating activities = $13,000
8-6 (1) Net cash flows from operations = $15,490
8-8 Net income = $95,000
8-10 (1) Net cash flows from operations = $580
8-12 (1) Cash paid for taxes = $8,400

CHAPTER 9

Not Applicable

CHAPTER 10

Exercises

10-2 (1) Predetermined manufacturing overhead rate = $5
10-4 (1) (b) 1999 Predetermined overhead rate = 26%
10-6 N/A
10-8 (3) Applied manufacturing overhead = $66,500
10-10 (3) Cost per unit = $194
10-12 (1) Overhead rate = $81.82 per direct labor hour
10-14 (1) (c) 2000 = $2.01 per mile
10-16 (1) Kelly's asset turnover = 1.46

Problems

10-2 (1) (g) Credit to Manufacturing Overhead = $400
10-4 (3) Work-in-process inventory, beg. bal. = $19,000
10-6 (1) (d) Average unit cost for A = $3.29
10-8 (2) Cost of goods manufactured = $1,138,050
10-10 (3) Cost of goods sold = $746,000
10-12 (2) Overhead = $2,872.70
10-14 (1e) Debit to Work-in-Process Services = $9,000

CHAPTER 11

Exercises

11-2 (3) $500 per unit
11-4 (3) $30.25
11-6 (2) Total cost = $60,000
11-8 (1) Income = $17
11-10 (4) Additional fixed costs = $100,000
11-12 (1) (c) 25,000 units
11-14 (4) Loss of approximately $7,500
11-16 N/A
11-18 (7) Income = $141,750
11-20 (1) Product X contribution margin = $4

Problems

11-2 (1) (a) Variable cost = $4 per unit
11-4 (1) Contribution margin = $110,000
11-6 (1) Loss = $(18,400)
11-8 (3) (b) $4,500,000
11-10 (1) Y = 900 bags
11-12 (7) Income = $850,000
11-14 (4) Profit = $56,250
11-16 (1) Total variable costs = $195,000

CHAPTER 12

Exercises

12-2 (1) Price variance = $250U
12-4 N/A
12-6 (1) Price variance = $9,000F
12-8 (3) Efficiency variance = $10,200F
12-10 N/A
12-12 N/A
12-14 Time Management Group net income by segment = $43,000
12-16 (1) Maya Division segment margin = $10,000
12-18 (1) South Division asset turnover ratio = 4.0
12-20 (1) Proposal 1 residual income = $1,000

Problems

12-2 (1) (b) Quantity variance = $800U
12-4 (d) Standard cost per direct labor hour = $3.50 per hour
12-6 (2) Manufacturing rate variance = $420U
12-8 (4) Actual labor rate per hour = $6.20
12-10 (1) Computer Consulting division margin = $70,000
12-12 (1) Atlantic Division ROI = 17.5%
12-14 (1) (a) ROI without investment = 19.4%
12-16 (d) Residual income = $3,950
12-18 (1) (a) Total residual income = $25,000

CHAPTER 13

Exercises

13-2 (1) Net income = $275
13-4 Quarter 4 EGA units to be produced = 2,175
13-6 VHS total direct materials cost = $170,000
13-8 March total direct labor cost = $18,740
13-10 Projected cash balance July 31, 2000 = $470,000
13-12 Deficiency of cash = $(42,900)
13-14 Income before taxes = $165,000
13-16 Net increase in cash = $41,650
13-18 (1) Budgeted salary expense = $180,000

Problems

13-2 (2) 34 months
13-4 Total cost of material used = $4,050
13-6 (2) Direct materials costs, bolts = $168.75
13-8 (3) June budgeted purchases (units) = 3,450
13-10 January excess cash = $45,100
13-12 (1) Net operating profit = $140,050
13-14 (2) Additional net income = $16,714
13-16 Expected income per doctor at 34,000 visits = $158,333

CHAPTER 14

Exercises

14-2 (1) New machine total relevant costs = $930,000
14-4 (2) Expected increase in profit if order is accepted = $40,000
14-6 Total Cost Buy = $1,380,000
14-8 Alternative 2 net expected benefit = $342,000
14-10 Variable costs = ($560,000)
14-12 (2) Dynamite Labor = 27,000 units
14-14 (1) "R" profit from further processing = $16,000

Problems

- 14-2 (2) Total cost per unit to make = $2.10
- 14-4 (2) Alternative 1 differential costs = $565,000
- 14-6 (1) Skis and ski boots net income = $60,000
- 14-8 Net cost of closing = $(142,000)
- 14-10 (1) Y-707 contribution margin = $17.25
- 14-12 (2) Charger lost contribution = $(150,000)
- 14-14 Estimated normal selling price = $18.33

CHAPTER 15

Exercises

- 15-2 (2) Present value = $247,314
- 15-4 Unadjusted rate of return = 22.5%
- 15-6 Alternative 2 net present value = ($86,024)
- 15-8 Average cost of capital = 16.4%
- 15-10 N/A
- 15-12 N/A

Problems

- 15-2 Net present value = $12,060
- 15-4 (1) IRR = 10.55%
- 15-6 (2) Internal rate on return = 4.5 factor
- 15-8 Alternative 2 = $10,512
- 15-10 Present value over 4 years, cost of renting = $4,565
- 15-12 (2) $11,597
- 15-14 (1) Project C profitability index = 0.94
- 15-16 (1) Payback period = 5.2 years

INDEXES

SUBJECT INDEX

A

D

J

L

M

N

O

P

T

U

V

W

Y

Z

INDEXES

REAL WORLD COMPANY INDEX

A

B

C

D

E

F

G

H

I

J

K

INDEXES

INTERNET INDEX